Medieval Mythography

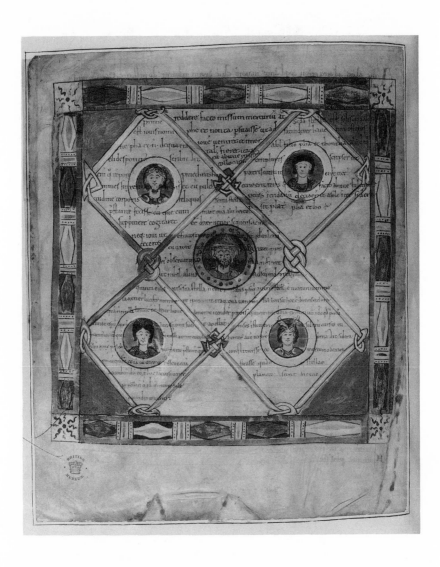

Medieval Mythography

FROM ROMAN NORTH AFRICA
TO THE SCHOOL OF CHARTRES,
A.D. 433–1177

JANE CHANCE

UNIVERSITY PRESS OF FLORIDA

GAINESVILLE / TALLAHASSEE / TAMPA / BOCA RATON

PENSACOLA / ORLANDO / MIAMI / JACKSONVILLE

99 98 97 96 95 6 5 4 3 2 1

Chance, Jane, 1945–
    Medieval mythography: from Roman North Africa to the School
of Chartres, A.D. 433–1177 / Jane Chance.
        p.   cm.
    Includes bibliographical references (p.) and index.
    ISBN 0-8130-1256-2 (alk. paper)
    1. Latin literature—Criticism and interpretation—History.
2. Civilization, Medieval—Classical influences.   3. Literature,
Medieval—Roman influences.   4. Mythology, Classical, in
literature.   5. Criticism, Medieval—History.   6. Mythology—
Historiography.   7. École de Chartres.   I. Title.
PA6029.R4C48   1994
870.9'002—dc20   93-42805

Frontispiece: Heads of the Planets (Jupiter, Sol or Saturn, Mars,
Venus, Mercury). From Cicero, *Aratea.* MS. Cotton Tiberius B. V.
Part 1, fol. 44v. (991–1016, English). By permission of
the British Library, London.

Publication of this book was made possible in part by a grant from
the John Simon Guggenheim Memorial Foundation.

The University Press of Florida is the scholarly publishing agency
for the State University System of Florida, comprised of Florida
A & M University, Florida Atlantic University, Florida
International University, Florida State University, University of
Central Florida, University of Florida, University of North Florida,
University of South Florida, and University of West Florida.

University Press of Florida
15 Northwest 15th Street
Gainesville, FL 32611

For my family,
especially my father, stepmother,
Aunt Thelma, Aunt Bobbye, Aunt Vi, and Uncle Steve;
and, most of all,
in memory of my mother and grandparents:
in tribute to the pioneer and immigrant qualities
of determination, independence, enterprise, and courage,
and to the Quaker belief
in peace and freedom.

CONTENTS

ILLUSTRATIONS

The development of the literary description of the gods in the Middle Ages did not match exactly the history of the iconological or iconographical treatment of the gods in manuscript illuminations. As Jean Seznec and Erwin Panofsky have frequently observed, the posterity of an image exists separately and may be propelled by its own life. Exhaustive studies of the astrological and mythological illuminations, most significantly by Fritz Saxl under the auspices of the Warburg Institute, have revealed a paucity of illustrations of the gods before the twelfth century, at least relative to the enormous collection of materials from the fourteenth and fifteenth centuries. Up to the twelfth century the planetary and constellatory equivalents of the gods illustrated primarily astronomical, herbal, and bestiary texts. Thereafter, stories of the gods in a variety of texts about history and mythography were matched with appropriate depictions. But there were also time lags in the correspondences between literary texts and iconic depictions. Christine de Pizan's stunning and elaborate illustrations for her early fifteenth-century *Epistre Othea,* for example, incorporate detail from important mythographic commentaries dating from the twelfth century, most probably drawn from the collection of Chartrian manuscripts available in the royal library in her own time. In tracing the history of a myth, more important than the date of any manuscript illumination is the idea incarnated in its imagery.

Illustrations up to the twelfth century very often reflect the influence of the written text of the bestiary or the astronomicon (often that of Hyginus or Cicero), or else legitimate a classical or late antique author (Boethius, for example) or signify his importance for the Middle Ages (Bernard Silvestris) or the importance for a literary text of a particular figure (Pallas Athena), especially in place of the *accessus.* Because of this, the illustrations frequently will have no direct bearing on a mythological passage in a commentary and are used herein to suggest parallels that exist in two different traditions, written and visual. Because the fullest and most interesting illustrations come from the fourteenth and fifteenth centuries, but with possible influence from the commentaries, say, of the twelfth century, they are used here as illustrations of significant but much older ideas (*Somnium Scipionis,* Oedipus, Hercules and Theseus, etc.).

Frontispiece: Heads of the Planets (Jupiter, Sol or Saturn, Mars, Venus, Mercury). From Cicero, *Aratea.*

TABLES

ACKNOWLEDGMENTS

The scholarly forebears of this study include monumental works on classical allegoresis and the mythographers of late antiquity, chiefly Macrobius and Servius, and on the process of mythography in relation to the Renaissance and to art history as well as to patristic exegesis, by Pépin, de Lubac, Curtius, Panofsky, Seznec, D. C. Allen, Robertson, Bush, and Tuve. They also include more recent studies of medieval renaissances and literary theory and philosophy by Smalley, Judson Boyce Allen, Minnis, Stock, Wetherbee, and Dronke. Finally, this volume in its approach and conclusions is indebted to those studies of the commentary traditions of Virgil, Ovid, and the other poets by scholars such as Jeauneau, Courcelle, Comparetti, Hexter, Baswell, Westra, Gibson, and many others.

It will be clear to the reader, I hope, that this study does not pretend to be exhaustive. Hundreds of manuscripts in European libraries remain at present unedited, incorrectly identified, or miscatalogued, and in them, presumably, are glosses and comments that would vary the material presented in this volume. Their editing would no doubt alter what I said. But I believe that the outlines of this study will hold true, despite minor variations in, say, the Remigian commentary on Martianus Capella which dominated the ninth to the twelfth century.

The research, writing, and publication of this volume were fostered by various institutions, foundations, and libraries as well as by many individuals, to whom I would like to express my gratitude. The National Endowment for the Humanities Foundation provided a Fellowship for Independent Study and Research during 1977–78, during which the bulk of the research for this book was completed in London. I am also grateful to University College of the University of London for the Honorary Research Fellowship in English for 1977–78 that gave me access to the University of London Senate Library and the University College Library. In many ways that cannot be tallied I am also indebted to the John Simon Guggenheim Memorial Foundation for its Fellowship during 1980–81 that allowed me to complete the writing of a partial first draft of the first half of the book in Rome and Venice, and for the publication subvention to aid in producing this volume. In addition, Rice University's research grants—for a month of summer salary in 1978, for a sabbatical semester in 1980–81, for travel and for clerical expenses incurred in putting part of the manuscript on computer disk in 1984–85, for travel funds and for a Mellon grant in 1988–89, for research assistance and travel expenses in producing the final manuscript in the summer of 1992—furthered the completion of this study; the Dean of Humanities also paid for indexing this volume.

Other academic experiences immeasurably influenced the writing of this book; to the organizations that made them possible I am also deeply grateful. The National Endowment for the Humanities Summer Seminar for College Teachers on "Chaucer and Mythography" in the summer of 1985 provided a necessary audience and the perspective for pulling together and shaping the book into a series of twelve two-hour lectures. When I returned to the study after a hiatus, the Rockefeller Foundation awarded a month's luxurious residency at its Villa Serbelloni at Bellagio on Lake Como, Italy, in July 1988, which enabled me to pull together my ideas for the latter half of the study, dealing with the late Middle Ages, so that I could continue my work at the Institute for Advanced Study at Princeton during 1988–89 at the School of Historical Studies.

Various libraries graciously permitted me to use their archives and to request microfilms and photocopies of needed materials and photographs of manuscript illuminations. For their generosity I would like to thank Rice University's Fondren Library, the British Library, Oxford's Bodleian and Duke Humphries Libraries, the Cambridge University Library, the University College Library and the Senate Library of the University Library of London, the York University library, the Biblioteca Apostolica Vaticana, the Library of the American Academy of Rome and the Istituto Storico Italiano per il Medio Evo, also of Rome, the Biblioteca Nazionale Marciana of Venice, the Biblioteca Centrale Nazionale and the Biblioteca Medicea Laurenziana of Florence, the Bibliothèque Nationale and the Bibliothèque Mazarine of Paris, the Staatsbibliothek Preussischer Kulturbesitz of Berlin, and Harvard's Widener Library. The Hill Monastic Library in Collegeville, Minnesota, generously permitted me to use its archives in researching the volume. I am grateful also to Princeton University's Firestone Library and the Library of Historical Studies and Social Sciences at the Institute for Advanced Study for their many kindnesses during my stay at the Institute in 1988–89.

Many individuals generously contributed in various ways to the research and writing of this book. Colleagues and mentors who provided invaluable encouragment and support include the late Richard Hamilton Green, George Economou, Jackson J. Campbell, Joseph B. Trahern, Jr., Charles Muscatine, and the late Bernard F. Huppé. The late Richard W. Hunt, former director of the Bodleian, provided information about mythographic publications and specific manuscripts; Diane K. Bolton of the Institute of Historical Research of the University of London helped with Remigius and Boethius glosses of the tenth and eleventh centuries, offprints of her articles, and other bibliographic information; the late Professor Judson Boyce Allen of the University of Florida gave me information concerning late Ovid commentaries and access to his unpublished transcription of Alexander Neckam on Martianus. Thanks are also extended to Dr. Haijo J. Westra of the University of Calgary for information about Bernard's commentary on Martianus, the Berlin Martianus, and the Florentine commentary; to Fabio Troncarelli, for information relating to MS. Vat. lat. 3363 on Boethius and a copy of his book; and to Professor Richard Johnson of the Australian National University for information concerning Martianus Capella. Professors Petrus Tax and Joseph Wittig of the Department of Germanic Languages at the University of North Carolina very kindly loaned me transcriptions of their St. Gall and Remigian glosses on Boethius prior to publication. Professor Traugott Lawler of Yale and Mrs. Eleanor Silk made available glosses from the late Professor Edmund Silk's edition of Nicholas Trivet on Boethius. Readers of this manuscript at various stages, among them Winthrop Wetherbee, Stephen Russell, and Margaret Ehrhart, indicated changes that needed to be made; what mistakes remain, of course, are my own.

In addition, friends, colleagues, and students offered countless aids. William D. Reynolds of Hope College read a paper on my behalf at a conference when I was in England. Professor Paul O. Kristeller made thorough and invaluable comments on early portions of the manuscript. Dr. Arthur Field also provided helpful information concerning Landino's *Aeneid* commentaries; Theodore Steinberg, William Reynolds, Lois Roney, and Laura Hodges all read versions of the introduction and long sections of what were originally large Boethius and Virgil chapters. I am especially grateful to the participants in my 1985 NEH Summer Seminar for College Teachers for their enthusiastic support and helpful comments—especially Sister Rosemarie Julie Gavin, Deborah Rubin, Judith Kellogg, Charles Moore, and Jeanne Nightingale. Julia Bolton Holloway insisted that I first write a book on Chaucer's mythography before writing this book—an idea (once implemented) that helped to define in a practical way the fourteenth-century uses of mythography. I am also very happy to have spent several wonderful dinners with Estelle James and Joel Williamson discussing fruitful possibilities for organizing the volume during my stay at the

Rockefeller Foundation's Villa Serbelloni in Bellagio on Lake Como in northern Italy, July 7–August 4, 1988. Finally, the Institute for Advanced Study at Princeton has earned my eternal thanks for the year granted me in 1988–89 to finish the volume and to engage in dialogue with the many professors there, among them Vittore Branca, Irving Lavin, Michael Richter, John Fleming, Peter Schmidt, Anna Kartsonis, and Deborah Pincus, who offered so generously new perspectives, bibliographic suggestions, and ideas for shaping my material. Enlightening conversations with Chris Baswell about *Aeneid* commentaries and the mythographic tradition helped spur the writing of this book in the fall of 1988. Readers for the University Press of Florida offered constructive ideas for improving the volume; I appreciate their thoughtful suggestions and hope that the completed book measures up. During the time in which I revised this volume, current and former graduate students Edie Hoffman, Padmaja Challakere, and Dr. Faye Walker-Pelkey challenged my ideas in stimulating ways. Last but by no means least, Judy Shoaf 's careful copyediting of the manuscript strengthened the argument and made the study more accessible and useful to the reader. To her I am especially grateful for all manner of suggestions and ideas, as I am to Michael Senecal, who oversaw production of the book.

As the study progressed, various student graduate and undergraduate assistants, among them Valerie Luessenhop, Dr. Elizabeth Alkaood, Dr. Laura Hodges, Dr. Madeline Fleming, Ted Reed, Larry Kraemer, Padmaja Challakere, Karen Palermo, Holly Pinchevsky, and Dejan Kuzmanovic, helped compile a working bibliography and manuscript listings, collect texts, check references, and read proofs. The participants in my spring 1988 graduate seminar in feminist mythography, particularly Ann Bradley and Laura McRae, contributed in various ways to the advancement of this project. Undergraduates and graduates from my own department and others aided in the retyping, including Cindy Pfeiffer, Thelma Zavala, Kristine Hain, Robert Barber, and Jenny Hyan. Marcia Carey at the Institute for Advanced Study's Historical and Social Sciences Library verified documentation for some citations and located missing references. To all of these individuals and the institutions that support them I am grateful.

Dr. Helen Eaker of the Classics Department at Rice University checked and revised Latin and Greek translations and transcriptions, my own and others', throughout this volume and in many cases supplied her own, for which I owe her an incalculable debt, given the difficulty of some of the passages; of course, whatever translation errors that remain are my own. Dr. Eaker has also, where appropriate, silently changed errors in transcriptions from published editions. Professor Joseph Wilson of the German department at Rice either translated the Old High German in the Notker chapter or rechecked my own translations; I am grateful to him for lending his expertise to this project.

Portions of this study have been delivered as conference papers, beginning in order of delivery with "The Epic Origins of Medieval Mythography," Thirteenth Annual Conference on Medieval Studies, Western Michigan University, Kalamazoo, Michigan, May 5, 1978; "Revising Macrobius on Fiction: The 'Fabulous Cosmogony' of William of Conches," Session on Mythography and Literature, Fifth Citadel Conference on Literature: The Poetry, Drama, and Prose of the Renaissance and Middle Ages, The Citadel, Charleston, South Carolina, March 15–16, 1985; "The Virgilization of 'Ovid' and Boethius: Mythographic Exegesis in the Early Middle Ages," Medieval Seminar, School of Historical Studies, Institute for Advanced Study, Princeton, New Jersey, October 26, 1988; and "Originality and Marginality: Pallas Athena, Goddess of Wisdom, and Christine de Pizan," English Department, Purdue University, West Lafayette, Indiana, November 15, 1989.

Portions of this study have been previously published in other forms, and permission to reprint has been obtained for all, including "The Origins and Development of Medieval Mythography: From Homer to Dante," in *Mapping the Cosmos,* edited by Jane Chance and R. O. Wells, Jr. (Houston: Rice University Press, 1985), 35–64; portions of "Allegory and Structure in *Pearl:* The Four Senses of the *Ars Praedicandi* and Homiletic Poetry of the Fourteenth Century," in *Text and Matter: New Critical Perspectives of the Pearl-Poet,* edited by Robert J. Blanch, Miriam Youngerman Miller, and Julian N. Wasserman (Troy, N.Y.: Whitston Press, 1991); portions of the introduction to *Christine de Pizan, Letter of Othea to Hector, Translated, with Introduction, Notes, and Interpretative Essay,* Focus Library of Medieval Women (Newburyport, Mass.: Focus Press, 1990); and portions of the "Introduction. The Medieval 'Apology for Poetry': Fabulous Narrative and Stories of the Gods," in *The Mythographic Art: Classical Fable and the Rise of the Vernacular in Early France and England,* edited by Jane Chance (Gainesville: University of Florida Press, 1990).

ABBREVIATIONS

AND CITATION EDITIONS

The following is a list of short titles and abbreviations used in the parenthetical references to the main works discussed in the text and in the notes at the end of this book. Where it seemed useful, I have used the set of numbers with the widest possible range of referents: to the myth number rather than the page number in a myth collection, to the book and line number of a classical text or of a commentary on a classical text. Thus not only Virgil's *Aeneid* but several of the commentaries on it are indexed by book and line numbers; thus the paragraph numbers of Martianus Capella's *De nuptiis* can be used by the reader whether Dick's or Willis's edition is in hand, or Stahl's translation (though in this case the commentaries follow a different system of numbering).

Where available, Loeb Classics have been cited. References to book, chapter, and line numbers of a primary text will appear by author and/or short title in decimal form, e.g., *Aen.* 1.10.11; references to multivolume primary works with page or column numbers cited will appear in colonic form, e.g., *PL* 150:36. Titles in Greek are either transliterated into Roman alphabet or translated into Latin. All translations, unless otherwise indicated, are original. Further bibliographic information on the editions and translations mentioned here appears in the bibliography.

AHDLMA	*Archives d'histoire doctrinale et littéraire du moyen âge*
AJP	*American Journal of Philology*
Alexander Neckam, *Nat. rerum*	Alexander Neckam, *De naturis rerum.* Ed. Wright. Cited by page number. My translations.
AM	*Annuale mediaevale*
AR	*Archivum romanicum*
ASNSL	*Archiv für das Studium der Neuern Sprachen und Literaturen*
Augustine, *Civ. Dei*	Augustine, *De civitate Dei.* 6 vols. Ed. and trans. Green. Cited by book and chapter.

Barb. Raia	Anonymous Barberinus Commentary on Martianus Capella from MS. Barb. lat. 10. Ed. Anne Rose Raia, "Barberini Manuscripts 57–66 and 121–130." Cited by page number. My translations.
Bernard, *In Theod.*	Bernard of Utrecht, *Commentum in Theoduli.* Ed. Huygens. My translations. The accessus is quoted from Jacobs's edition (cited in the notes). Cited by book and paragraph number. The book and paragraph numbers are the same in both editions.
Bern. Sil., *In Mart.*	*Commentary on Martianus Capella's* De nuptiis Philologiae et Mercurii *Attributed to Bernardus Silvestris.* Ed. Westra. My translations. Cited by page and line number of Dick's edition of Martianus.
Bern. Sil., *Sup. En.*	*Commentary on the First Six Books of Vergil's* Aeneid *by Bernardus Silvestris.* Ed. Jones and Jones, trans. Schreiber and Maresca. Cited by book and line number of the *Aeneid* in the edition, by page number in the translation.
B.L.	British Library
B.N.	Bibliothèque Nationale
Bode	Mythographi Vaticani. *Scriptores rerum mythicarum Latini tres Romae nuper reperti.* Ed. Bode. 2 vols. Repr. 1 vol.
Bodl.	Bodleian Library
Boethius, *Consolatio*	Boethius, *De consolatione Philosophiae.* In *Tractates, De consolatione Philosophiae.* Ed. and trans. Stewart, Rand, Tester. Loeb Classics. Cited by book, prose or poem (metrum), and line number.
C&M	*Classica et mediavalia*
CCSL, CCCM	*Corpus christianorum,* series Latina, or *continuato medievalis*

Cicero, *Nat. deorum*	Cicero, *De natura deorum.* In *De natura deorum, Academica.* Ed. and trans. Rackham. Loeb Classics. Cited by book and chapter number.
CJ	*Classical Journal*
CP	*Classical Philology*
CQ	*Classical Quarterly*
CR	*Classical Review*
CSEL	Corpus scriptorum ecclesiasticorum Latinorum
CTC	*Catalogus translationum et commentarium*
DA	*Dissertation Abstracts*
DAEM	*Deutsches Archiv für Erforschung des Mittelalters*
DAI	*Dissertation Abstracts International*
Dante, *Inf., Purg., Par.*	Dante, *Divine Comedy: Inferno, Purgatorio, and Paradiso,* respectively. Ed. and trans. Singleton. Cited by canto and line number.
Dunchad, *In Mart.*	Martin of Laon, *Glossae in Martianum.* Ed. Lutz. Cited by section and paragraph (derived by Lutz from page and line numbers in Dick's edition of *De nuptiis*). My translations.
Ecl. Theod.	*Ecloga Theoduli.* Ed. Osternacher. Trans. Thomson in *Ten Latin School Texts.* Ed. Thomson and Peraud. Cited by line number.
EETS	Early English Text Society
EHR	*English Historical Review*
ES	*English Studies*
Fulgentius, *Cont. Virg.*	Fulgentius, *Expositio continentiae Virgilianae.* In Fulgentius, *Opera.* Ed. Helm. Trans. Whitbread in *Fulgentius the Mythographer.* Helm cited by page, Whitbread by paragraph.
Fulgentius, *Mit.*	Fulgentius, *Mitologiae.* In *Opera,* as above. Cited by book and fable number in the translation, page number in the edition.

Fulgentius, *Sup. Theb.*

Fulgentius, *Super Thebaiden.* In *Opera,* as above. Cited by page number in both edition and translation.

HLF

Histoire littéraire de la France

HSCP

Harvard Studies in Classical Philology

Hyginus, *Astronomica*

Hyginus, *Astronomica.* Ed. Bunte. Trans. Grant. In *The Myths of Hyginus.* Cited by fable number.

Hyginus, *Fab.*

Hyginus, *Fabulae.* Ed. Rose. Trans. as above. Cited by fable number.

Isidore, *Etym.*

Isidore of Seville, *Etymologiarum libri XX.* Ed. Lindsay. 2 vols; my translations. Cited by book, chapter, and item number.

JCP

Jahrbücher für classische Philologie

JEGP

Journal of English and Germanic Philology

JHI

Journal of the History of Ideas

John of Salisbury

Policraticus. Ed. Webb. 2 vols. Cited by book and chapter; trans. in part by Pike, cited by page number.

John Scot, *In Mart.*

John Scot of Ireland, *Annotationes in Marcianum.* Ed. Lutz; my translations. Cited by section and paragraph (derived by Lutz from page and line numbers of Dick's edition of *De nuptiis*).

JRS

Journal of Roman Studies

JWCI

Journal of the Warburg and Courtauld Institutes

Juvenal, *Satires*

Saturae. In *Juvenal and Persius.* Ed. and trans. Ramsay. Loeb Classics. Cited by satire and line number.

Kulcsár

Peter Kulcsár, ed. *Mythographi Vaticani I et II.*

Lactantius, *Achilleid, Thebaid.*

In *Commentarii in Statii Thebaida et commentarius in Achilleida.* Ed. Jahnke. Vol. 3 of *P. Papinius Statius.* Cited by book and line of Statius and page number. My translations.

Lactantius, *Narrationes*

Narrationes fabularum Ovidianarum. Ed.

	Magnus. In *P. Ovidii Nasonis Metamorphoseon libri XV et Lactantii Placidi qui dicitur Narrationes fabularum Ovidianarum.* Cited by book and line number of *Metamorphoses* and page number. My translations.
M&H	*Mediaevalia et humanistica*
Macrobius, *Sat.*	Macrobius, *Saturnalia.* In *Macrobius.* 2 vols. Ed. Willis. Trans. Davies. Cited by book and chapter.
Macrobius, *Somn. Scip.*	Macrobius, *Commentarii in Somnium Scipionis.* In *Macrobius.* 2 vols. Ed. Willis. *Commentary on the Dream of Scipio,* trans. Stahl. Cited by book and chapter.
MAE	*Medium aevum*
Manitius, *Geschichte*	Max Manitius, *Geschichte der lateinischen Literatur des Mittelalters. Handbuch der klassischen Altertums-Wissenschaft.* Vol. 9, part 2. 3 vols.
Martianus, *De nuptiis*	Martianus Capella, *De nuptiis Philologiae et Mercurii.* In *Martianus Capella.* Ed. Willis. Trans. Stahl, Johnson, and Burge, *Martianus Capella and the Seven Liberal Arts.* Vol. 2. Cited by paragraph (paragraphs are numbered continuously through the book, identically in Dick's edition as well as in those used for citation).
MGH	Monumenta Germaniae historica
MJ	*Mittelateinisches Jahrbuch*
MLN	*Modern Language Notes*
MLQ	*Modern Language Quarterly*
MLR	*Modern Language Review*
MLS	*Modern Language Studies*
MP	*Modern Philology*
MRS	*Medieval and Renaissance Studies*
MS	*Mediaeval Studies*
Mythogr. I	First Vatican mythographer. See Kulcsár. Cited by fable number.

Mythogr. II	Second Vatican mythographer. See Kulcsár. Cited by fable number.
Mythogr. III	Third Vatican mythographer. See Bode.
NA	*Neues Archiv der Gesellschaft für altere deutsche Geschichtkunde*
Notker	Notker Labeo, translation of and commentary on *De nuptiis Philologiae et Mercurii.* Ed. Schulte. In *Das Verhaltnis von Notkers Nuptiae Philologiae,* etc. Translations from Old High German generally provided by Joseph Wilson (who provided the same service for Notker's Boethius glosses); Latin translations mine. Cited by page number.
Ovid, *Metamorphoses*	In *Ovid in Six Volumes.* Ed. and trans. Miller. Loeb Classics. 2 vols. Cited by book and line number.
Paulys-Wissowa	Georg Wissowa and Wilhelm Kroll, *Paulys Real-Encyclopädie der classischen Altertumswissenschaft*
PG	*Patrologia cursus completus: Series Graeca.*
PL	*Patrologia cursus completus: Series Latina.* Ed. Migne. Cited by volume and column.
PQ	*Philological Quarterly*
Raby, *Secular Latin Poetry*	F.J.E. Raby, *A History of Secular Latin Poetry in the Middle Ages.* 2 vols.
REL	*Revue des études latines*
Remi., *In Mart.*	Remigius of Auxerre, *Commentum in Martianum Capellam.* Ed. Lutz. 2 vols. Cited by section and paragraph number (derived from Lutz from page and line number of Dick's edition of *De nuptiis*). My translations.
RES	*Review of English Studies*
RF	*Romanische Forschungen*
RJ	*Romanistiches Jahrbuch*
RMP	*Rheinisches Museum für Philologie*

Schol., *Ad Buc.*	Berne scholia (Adanan the Scot?), gloss on Virgil's *Eclogues*. In *Scholia Bernensia ad Vergilii Bucolica atque Georgica*. Ed. Hagen. Cited by eclogue and line number. My translations.
Schol., *Ad Georg.*	Berne scholia, gloss on Virgil's *Georgics*. Same as above. Cited by book and line number. My translations.
Servius, *In Aen.*	Servius, *Commentarius in Aeneidos*. In *Servii Grammatici qui feruntur in Vergilii carmina commentarii*. Ed. Thilo and Hagen. Vols. 1–2. Cited by book and line number; my translations.
Servius, *In Buc.*	Servius, *Commentarius in Bucolicon*. Ed. Thilo and Hagen, same title as preceding, vol. 3. Cited by book and line number; my translations.
Servius, *In Georg.*	Servius, *Commentarius in Georgicon*. Ed. Thilo and Hagen, same title and vol. as the preceding; cited by book and line number; my translations.
SM	*Studi medievali*
SP	*Studies in Philology*
Statius, *Achilleid*	*Statius*. Ed. and trans. Mozley. Vol. 2. Loeb Classics. Cited by book and line number.
Statius, *Thebaid*	*Statius*. Vols 1–2, as indicated above.
TAPA	*Transactions and Proceedings of the American Philological Association*
Theodulf, "De libris"	Theodulf of Orleans: "De libris quod legere solebam," "The Books I Used to Read" (*Carmina* 45). In *Poetry of the Carolingian Renaissance*. Ed and trans. Peter Godman. Cited by line number.
Vat.	Vatican Library
Virgil, *Aeneid*	In *Virgil*. Ed. and trans. Fairclough. 2 vols. Loeb Classics. Cited by book and line number.

Virgil, *Eclogues*   In *Virgil*. Ed. and trans. Fairclough. Vol.
                                        1. Cited by book and line number.

Virgil, *Georgics*   As above, vol. 1. Cited by eclogue and
                                        line number.

William, *In Iuvenalem*   William of Conches, *Glosae in Iuvenalem*.
                                        Ed. Wilson. Cited by satire, line, and
                                        page number.

CHRONOLOGY
OF MEDIEVAL MYTHOGRAPHERS
AND COMMENTARY AUTHORS

The nature of the records for most of the Middle Ages and critical scholarship are such that it is impossible to name or date most of the works studied in this volume. All but the firmest attributions have been disputed and even the most distant terminus post quem may be challenged by a determined sceptic. "Remigius of Auxerre," therefore, can be shorthand for a group of works including, on the one hand, the second Vatican mythography—which may well have been written a century before the historical Remigius's birth, or, as I speculate, by a woman—and, on the other, the revisers of a Martianus commentary working in the generation after the historical Remigius's death.

While I have recorded many of these disputes in my chapters and notes, I am listing here the names and dates that will serve as a guide to the development of mythographic themes. In general, I prefer to speak of a work as belonging to a known author and to establish a chronologically probable relationship of influence (this is not always possible, of course). Thus, I will refer to the "Florentine Commentary" on Martianus Capella as a work of William of Conches, though it is almost certainly a set of notes by one of his students, and I will assume that its contents could have influenced Bernard Silvestris's *Aeneid* commentary, even though the attribution of that commentary has in its turn been questioned, and Bernard may never have seen the "Florentine" work himself.

What can usefully be assumed, in fact, is that each period's writers came to the classics of Rome and the late Empire through the commentaries and mythographies of the preceding period: Theodulf of Orleans read Ovid using Isidore and Fulgentius; William read Martianus through the Carolingian commentators. Each new set of ideas and attitudes overspread what had gone before and defined the way the next generation or school would approach the great myths. The giants on whose shoulders the pygmies stand, to use Bernard of Chartres's famous image, were not the *auctores* or classics themselves, but the great commentaries on them.

The absence of firm attributions opens up the possibility that some of the works listed here may have been written by women. The marginal and dangerous nature of classical myth may have attracted women taught to think of themselves as marginal and dangerous; the variety of roles played by goddesses, heroes, and sorcerers might provide new insights into patriarchalized biblical, contemporary, and imagined worlds. We know that this was true for Christine de Pizan, writing around the year 1400, and something of the sort applies to Hrotsvit of Gandersheim, the tenth-century German nun who wrote Terentian comedies; I have taken the liberty, in chapters 8 and 9, of speculating on how one would read two medieval works if Hrotsvit or someone like her had written them.

FOURTH THROUGH SEVENTH CENTURIES

Italian

Verona scholia on Virgil (late 3d c.)

Junilius Philargyrius (4th c.), commentary on Virgil's *Eclogues* and *Georgics* (frag.)

Charisius (365), *Ars grammatica*

Servius (ca. 389), *Commentarii in Vergilii carmina*

Boethius (b. ca. 480–524), *De consolatione Philosophiae*

North African

Nonius Marcellus (ca. 373), *De compendiosa doctrina*

Ambrosius Theodosius Macrobius (ca. 360–ca. 435), *Saturnalia; Commentarius in Somnium Scipionis*

Martianus Capella (fl. 410–439), *De nuptiis Philologiae et Mercurii*

Fulgentius Planciades (468–533), *Mitologiae; Expositio continentiae Virgilii; Super Thebaiden*

Lactantius Placidus (6th c.), *Commentarii in Thebaida; Commentarius in Achilleida; Narrationes fabularum Ovidianarum* (?)

Iberian

Isidore of Seville (ca. 560–636), *Etymologiae* (8.11.1–104, "De diis gentium")

EIGHTH AND NINTH CENTURIES:
CAROLINGIAN RENAISSANCE

Irish

First Vatican mythographer (late 7th–8th c.)

Adanan (Adamnan) the Scot? (ca. 624–704), Berne scholia on the *Eclogues* and *Georgics*

Anonymous Galliensis (Anonymous of St. Gall), commentary on Boethius

Anonymous Cambridge commentator, commentary on Martianus

John Scot Eriugena (fl. 846–877), *Annotationes in Marcianum*

"Dunchad" (Martin of Laon, 819–875), *Glossae in Martianum*

French

Second Vatican mythographer (ca. 9th–10th c.)

Remigius of Auxerre (ca. 841–ca. 908), *Commentum in Martianum Capellam; Expositio in libro Boetii* De consolatione Philosophiae

Spanish

Theodulf, Bishop of Orleans (ca. 760–821), "De libris quos legere solebam et qualiter fabulae poetarum a philosophus mystice pertractentur"

German

Hraban Maur (ca. 780–856), "De diis gentium" (of Isidore) in *De universo*

Italian

Paul the Deacon (ca. 720–ca. 799), epitome of Festus's excerpts from Verrius Flaccus's *De verborum significatu* (10 B.C.)

TENTH AND ELEVENTH CENTURIES: POST-CAROLINGIAN
PERIOD

Italian

Rather of Verona (ca. 887–974), glosses on Martianus

Stephen and Gunzo of Novara, glosses on Martianus

Liutprand of Cremona (ca. 920–972), glosses on Martianus

Eugenius Vulgarius (d. ca. 928), glosses on Martianus

Glossator of *Gesta Berengarii* (10th c.)

Papias the Lombard (ca. 1050), *Vocabularium* or *Elementarium,* from the anonymous *Liber glossarum* (690–750)

Belgian

Anonymous Bruxellensis (early 10th c.), commentary on Boethius

German

Hrotsvit of Gandersheim (ca. 932–ca. 1000), dramas, legends, epics
Ecloga Theoduli (ca. 10th c.)
Notker Labeo (d. ca. 1022), commentaries on Martianus and Boethius
Manegold of Lautenbach (1086–94), commentary on Ovid

Swabian

Bernard of Utrecht (11th c.), commentary on *Ecloga Theoduli*

French

Bovo II of Corvey (10th–11th c.?), commentary on 9th Poem, 3d Book of Boethius
Baudri of Bourgueil (1046–1130), Poem 216: fragment of a moralized mythology

TWELFTH AND THIRTEENTH CENTURIES

French

Anonymous commentaries on Ovid's *Fasti* (e.g., *Glosule super librum Fastorum*)
William of Conches (1080–1154/60), *Glosulae super Boethium; Super commentarium Macrobii in Somnium Scipionis;* commentaries on Martianus Capella and Plato's *Timaeus*
Bernard Silvestris (1085–1178), *Commentum super sex libros Eneidos Virgilii;* commentary on Martianus
Arnulf of Orleans (fl. 1175), *Glosule super Lucanum; Allegoriae super Ovidii Metamorphoses;* commentary on Ovid's *Fasti*

English

Osbern of Gloucester (12th c.), *Derivationes*
Pseudo-John Scot (Anonymous of Erfurt), commentary on Boethius
Ralph of Beauvais (fl. 1170s), *Liber Titani;* commentary on Lucan

Digby Mythographer (ca. 1180), *De natura deorum*

John of Salisbury (1115/20–1180), *Policraticus*

Alberic of London (third Vatican mythographer), *De diis gentium et illorum allegoriis,* or *Allegoriae poeticae*

Alexander Neckam (1157–1217), *Super Marcianum de nupciis Mercurii et Philologiae; De rerum naturis*

John of Garland (1180–1252), *Integumenta Ovidii*

Italian

Anonymous Barberinus (late 12th c.), commentary on Martianus, books 1 and 2

Huguccio of Pisa (1200), *Magnae derivationes*

Giovanni Balbi of Genoa (1286), *Catholicon*

FOURTEENTH AND FIFTEENTH CENTURIES:
ENGLAND, FRANCE, SPAIN

English

Nicholas Trivet (fl. 1314), *Exposicio super librum Boecii Consolatione;* commentary on St. Augustine's *De civitate Dei* (books 11–23); commentary on Seneca's *Tragedies*

Thomas Waleys (fl. 1326–33), commentary on *De civitate Dei,* 1–10

John Ridewall (fl. 1331–40), *Fulgentius metaforalis;* commentary on *De civitae Dei,* 1–3, 6–7

Robert Holkot (ca. 1290–1349), *In librum Sapientiae; In librum duodecim prophetas; In librum Ecclesiastici; Moralitates*

Thomas Hopeman (fl. 1344–45), commentary on Hebrews

Anonymous, *De deorum imaginibus libellus* (before 1380)

Thomas Walsingham (d. 1422?), *Archana deorum*

French

Pierre Bersuire (fl. 1342), *Ovidus moralizatus*

Ovide moralisé (verse; 14th c.)

Colard Mansion's edition of the *Ovide moralisé* (independent French prose version plus French prose translation of early version of Bersuire)

Christine de Pizan (ca. 1365–ca. 1430), *L'Epistre Othea a Hector; Le Livre de la Cité des Dames*

Tholomaeus de Asinariis (14th c.), commentary on Boethius

William of Aragon (14th c.), commentary on Boethius
False Thomas Aquinas, commentary on Boethius
Pierre d'Ailly (1372), commentary on Boethius
Regnier of St. Tron (1381), commentary on Boethius
Dionysius the Carthusian (Denis the Carthusian of Leewis) (1403–71),
    commentary on Boethius
Arnoul Greban (15th c.), commentary on Boethius
    Josse Bade d'Assche (end 15th c.), commentary on Boethius

Spanish

Guillermus de Cortumelia (14th c.), commentary on Boethius

FOURTEENTH AND FIFTEENTH CENTURIES: ITALY

Dante, *Commedia* (begun 1307)
Ottimo commentary on Dante's *Commedia* (1300–10) (? by Andrea Lancia)
Anonymous Selmi (1321–37), *Chiose . . . alla prima cantica della divina Commedia*
Graziolo de Bambaglioli (1324), *Il commento Dantesco*
Jacopo Alighieri (1322–24?), *Chiose alla cantica dell'Inferno; Chiose di Dante: Purgatorio*
Jacopo della Lana (before 1328?), *Commento* on Dante
Petrarch (1304–74), *Africa*, 3.136–264
Giovanni del Virgilio (fl. 1332–33), *Allegorie librorum Ovidii Metamorphoseos*
Pietro Alighieri (1340–41), *Super Dantis ipsius genitoris Comoediam commentarium*
Fra' Guido da Pisa (1343–50), *Expositiones et glose super Comediam Dantis; Dichiarazione poetica dell' Inferno Dantesco*
Giovanni Bonsignore (ca. 1370), *P. Ovidio Methamorphoseos vulgare*
Giovanni Boccaccio (fl. 1313–75), *Genealogie deorum gentilium libri; Esposizioni sopra la Comedia di Dante (Inferno 1–17)*
The False Boccaccio (Roveta) (14th c.), *Chiose sopra Dante*
Benvenuto Rambaldi da Imola (b. 1336–40), *Commentum super Dantis Comoediam; Expositiones super Pharsalia Lucani* (1386)
Coluccio Salutati (1331–1406), *De laboribus Herculis*
Pietro da Muglio (1385), Dante commentary
Giovanni Travesio (late 14th c.), Dante commentary
Francesco Bartola da Buti of Pisa (ca. 1395), *Commento sopra la divina Comedia*

The Anonymous Florentine (late 14th c.), *Commento alla divina Commedia*
Giovanni da Serravalle (1416–17), Dante commentary
Stefano Talice da Ricaldone (ca. 1474), Dante commentary
Giuniforto delli Bargigi (ca. 1440), Dante commentary (*Inferno* 1–24)
Cristoforo Landino (1481), *Expositione* (Dante); *Disputationes Camaldulenses*,
    commentary on Virgil

"Until recent times, myth crouched at the gates of Paradise without hope of admittance."

DON CAMERON ALLEN
Mysteriously Meant: The Rediscovery of Pagan Symbolism and Allegorical Interpretation in the Renaissance

"Othea selon grec peut estre pris pour sagece de femme, et comme les ancians, non ayans ancore lumiere de vraye foy, adourassent plusiers dieux, soubz la quelle loy soient passees les plus haultes seignouries qui au monde ayent esté, comme le royaume d'Assire, de Perse, les Gregois, les Troyans, Alixandre, les Rommains et mains autres et mesmement tous les plus grans philosophes, comme Dieux n'eust ancore ouverte la porte sa misericorde. A present nous crestiens, par la grace de Dieu enluminez de vraye foy, povons ramener a moralite les oppinions des ancians, et sur ce maintes belles allegories pevent estre faites."

[Othea in Greek can be taken for the wisdom of woman, and as the ancients, not yet possessing the light of true faith, idolized several gods, under whose law passed the noblest lordships which have existed in the world, such as the kingdom of Assyria, of Persia, the Greeks, the Trojans, Alexander, the Romans, and many others and even the greatest philosophers, as God had not yet opened the door of his mercy. At the same time, we Christians, by the grace of God enlightened with true faith, are able to restore to mortality the opinions of the ancients, and on these, many excellent allegories can be made.]

CHRISTINE DE PIZAN
L'Epistre Othea la deesse que elle envoya a Hector quand il estoit en l'aage de quinze ans

Introduction

MYTHOGRAPHY:

MARGIN AS TEXT, TEXT AS IMAGE

Always already a cultural sign, the body sets limits to the imaginary meanings that it occasions, but is never free of an imaginary construction. The fantasized body can never be understood in relation to the body as real; it can only be understood in relation to another culturally instituted fantasy, one which claims the place of the "literal" and the "real." The limits to the "real" are produced within the naturalized heterosexualization of bodies in which physical facts serve as causes and desires reflect the inexorable effects of that physicality.

JUDITH BUTLER,
Gender Trouble: Feminism and the Subversion of Identity

Mythography and its allegorical methods, growing up in the classical and medieval schools where study of philosophy, or of the liberal arts leading to philosophy, flourished, existed by definition as a marginal and intertextual process. That is, it presupposed an original or poetic ("lying") text and it flourished as a separate text in the margins of the page, as a secondary and explanatory project. Our modern idea of literary criticism has its roots in medieval mythography as a hermeneutic employed by the Church in an attempt to educate its priests and monks in the universal language so that they might assimilate the knowledge of the greatest works of classical antiquity—not the mother tongue, the vernacular, but the tongue of Empire, of the fatherland, Latin. Written by grammarians, scholars, and philosophers, medieval mythography developed as a means of elucidation and translation, specifically of *translatio studii,* the translation from the Greek and Roman to vernacular cultures.

The authority for the determination of figurative meaning in classical antiquity and the Middle Ages derived from ancient Greek Stoic rationalization of the epics of Homer and has been termed "mythography," meaning the moralization and allegorization of classical mythology. "Mythography" differs from "mythology" chiefly in its form: "mythology" is a unified system of myth, often in narrative form, whereas "mythography" is an explanation and rationalization of one or more myths, often in didactic form. For Homer, the earliest known user of myth in the Graeco-Roman world, *muthos* or *mythos* signified either speech or else unspoken words and thoughts as contrasted with deeds, although the word could also signify true or false story, rumor.[1]

A definition of *mythos* possibly clearer to the modern reader is the later Aristotelian definition as "plot," interpreted anthropologically by Northrop Frye as "verbal imitation of ritual."[2] Mythography, in contrast, is the interpretation of myth—what the ancient philosophers termed its *hyponoia,* or "undermeaning." As exegesis it employs the tool of allegorical interpretation, which belongs more to the ancient exegete—whether philosopher or grammarian—than to the poet, although Roger Hinks has noted that "allegory stands, as it were, midway between poetry and prose: in its creative aspect it is the poetic rendering of a prosaic idea; in its interpretative aspect it is the prosaic rendering of a poetic image. Like the daemonic faculty in the words of Diotima, it reveals the ways of man to the gods and the ways of the gods to man."[3]

This tradition of developing fiction and fictionalizing depended upon the use of fables of the gods and heroes drawn initially from the Greeks and Romans and from Near Eastern cultures. The fables served as common denominators in the use of systematized and coherent metaphor—in the sustained fabulous narrative that would require allegorical interpretation by the philosopher for understanding during the Middle Ages. By rationalizing pagan gods through various historical, moral, physical, and allegorical means, medieval scholars also disseminated what came to be a theory of medieval fable and fabulizing. As in classical antiquity, such rationalizing of the gods was bolstered by the philosophers—the Neo-Stoics, especially in the Carolingian period, the Neoplatonists in the twelfth century, the Neo-Aristotelians (the Nominalists) in the fourteenth and fifteenth centuries. What is novel about this minihistory of classical mythography in the Middle Ages is its constant and concomitant Christianization—the commentators were Neo-Stoic Christians, Neoplatonist Christians, Neo-Aristotelian Christians.

The major focus of the mythographic commentators in the Middle Ages was the sixth book of the *Aeneid,* in which Aeneas descends into the underworld and encounters the shades of his father Anchises, his abandoned lover Dido, and a host of other mythological figures and beings. This marvelous descent into hell came to be linked with other descents into hell made by Boethius's heroes Orpheus and Hercules and by Martianus Capella's god Mercury and personification Philology, who descend and ascend through the cosmos. This descent was also used as a paradigm for the interpretation of myth in terms of ethics, cosmography, and poesis.

How the Middle Ages received and reconstructed the classical heroes Aeneas, Perseus, Orpheus, Ulysses, Hercules, Theseus, and Oedipus and the gods Mercury, Pluto, Proserpina, Ceres, Juno, Pallas Athena and others, why they were associated with an underworld, why scholars and poets enabled the pagan gods to function in their commentaries and their poems, what they came to signify, will be the subject of this book. The steps in the process are clear: the pagan gods, in the view of St. Augustine, are devils, demons. But also in the view of St. Augustine, after death noble pagan humans are called "heroes." Within the underworld, then, lived these demons, devils, and heroes, conceived in ancient belief as rational beings, as powers of the air in the sublunary realm. Gradually the demonized gods came to be understood (through Stoic and Neoplatonic readings) as belonging to the underworld of earth itself, the massive and female center of material corruption called Nature (as opposed to the aetherial and masculine heavens). "Gods" ultimately became personifications in some cases, and "heroes" became weak individuals who required divine assistance in their epic quests in late medieval "epics" such as Dante's *Commedia*.

A different, valorizing, approach to the gods was facilitated by scholastics, in particular the Carolingians, because of their interest in education and therefore wisdom displayed within an heroic mythological context. The hero as demigod, when ideally constructed, should dominate the underworld, whether the underworld is hell itself or is figuratively understood as carnality, the mutable earth and its monstrosities. The basis for such an understanding of epic can be found in the earlier work of Fulgentius. In his commentary on the *Aeneid,* Fulgentius understands the epic hero Aeneas as representing the human ideal of arms and the man, that "manliness of body" (*virtus corporis*) and "wisdom of mind" (*sapientia ingenii*) perfected in the *fortitudo* and *sapientia* of Christ (*Cont. Virg.,* 7); he accordingly interprets the *Aeneid* as an allegory of the ideal human's development from birth to maturity. Fulgentius wrote commentaries on the epics of Statius, Virgil, and Ovid, and his setting in the *Mitologiae* is indebted to Martianus Capella.[4] By extension, the ideal epic hero of Martianus might be identified as a combination of the two chief figures of his *De nuptiis Philologiae et Mercurii,* the god Mercury, who represents eloquence, and the mortal Philology, who represents knowledge; their wedding symbolizes the human ideal of earthly knowledge conjoined to divine eloquence. Examined using the same Fulgentian definition, the ideal epic hero of Boethius's *De consolatione Philosophiae* can also be seen as fragmented into separate figures, represented by Philosophy (or *ratio*) and the narrator Boethius (the willful and irrational, earthbound "body").

The Carolingian interest in classical wise heroes—in Prometheus as prudent and in the cycle of creation in which such classical figures appear as if impelled by a knowing Shaper—was introduced in the first Vatican mythography. Orpheus, Ulysses, and Hercules, in the various glosses on Boethius, all try to master the dark Neoplatonic underworld of the flesh in order to reach the light of "sovereign day"—and of God. In the Martianus glosses, Pallas Athena, the armed virgin goddess of wisdom, portrays a monastic ideal, an androgynous figure who in her ontology transcends the singular issue of gender. This issue, which surfaces consciously in mythography for the first time in the Carolingian commentaries on Martianus, elevates to greater prominence the Stoic physical rationalization of the gods; it also fleshes out the female deities previously depicted in somewhat marginal roles.

The tradition finally produces the epic hero of Dante's *Commedia,* the character Dante, in combination with the guide Virgil (in the *Inferno* and *Purgatorio*) and Beatrice (in the *Paradiso*): as Everyman, Dante learns from his initial guide Virgil, who signifies, according to Dante's son Pietro Alighieri, "ratio," or "philosophia rationalis," and from his later guide Beatrice, "theologia," with his vision of her signifying "studio theologica."[5] Behind these allegorical projections of the human ideal looms Christ, whose superhuman love for humankind is suggested by the Good Friday setting and thirty-three cantos of each *cantica,* or book (thirty-four in the *Inferno,* although the first serves as an introduction to the whole of the *Commedia*). Thirty-three was of course Christ's age at his death, and one hundred—for the total number of cantos—was considered a perfect number in the Middle Ages.

Within and during these different periods when interest in classical texts resulted in reinterpretations of the antique, the common purpose of medieval mythography involved the repressed transmission of human sexuality, essentialized as female and textualized, embodied as text. Because of this scholastic context and because of its allegorical methodology, mythography served the purposes of patriarchy within the Church. Within this phallogocentric point of view, allegory has been identified by medieval scholar Howard Bloch as an antifeminist form of discourse.[6]

Yet even in these terms mythography, if not allegory, as *translatio studii* would have occupied a role as institutionally subversive, empowering authority regarded as marginal, whether pagan or feminine, and therefore in the context of postmodern discourse to be designated as female in its difference, its "otherness." Such difference can be readily detected in the use of allegory, defined as "other speaking," *alienus.* A requisite usually for mythography and scriptural reading, allegory and its three "mystical" levels of meaning are discussed by Dante as a group in the "Letter to Can Grande" because, he explains, "allegory" comes from the Greek *alleon* (*sic,* probably in fact from *allelon* or *allon*), which in Latin is *alienus,* "strange," or *diversus,* "different,"[7] that is, different from the literal or historical sense and therefore figurative, "polysemous."

In a recent discussion by Gregory L. Ulmer, allegory similarly constitutes a nonrealistic or representational mode. So Derrida, Ulmer notes, deconstructs the philosophy of mimesis: " 'Mimesis,' which Derrida labels 'mimetologism,' refers to that capture of representation by the metaphysics of 'logocentrism,' the era extending from Plato to Freud (and beyond) in which writing (all manner of inscription) is reduced to a secondary status as 'vehicle,' in which the signified or referent is always *prior* to the material sign, the purely intelligible prior to the merely sensible."[8] Grammatology is the answer—the sign, both signifier and signified, coupled with the gram, or *différance,* is a trace interwoven into a textile, or text. "The tendency of Western philosophy," says Ulmer, "throughout its history ('logocentrism') to try to pin down and fix a specific signified to a given signifier violates, according to grammatology, the nature of language, which functions not in terms of matched *pairs* (signifier/signifieds) but of *couplers* or *couplings*—'a person or thing that couples or links together.' "[9]

This coupled textuality might well describe the polysemy associated by Dante with medieval allegory. The new "representation," according to Ulmer, shifts from the conceptual concision of commentary and explanation to the specificity and density of example. The montage of fragments and examples associated with "invagination" is explicitly nonlogocentric (or nonphallogocentric). The boundary or parameter of marking a set, because it fixes difference from other, invaginates by means of "matting or mounting the example." Allegory, as a "surplus value" of writing, becomes a form of repetition, mimicry, different from allegoresis. Finally, Ulmer suggests, "narrative allegory favors the material of the signifier over the meanings of the signifieds."[10]

The history of the mythographic tradition, then, might be described as the history of montage, of examples mounted in a frame whose boundaries of difference continually re-form. In other words, mythography is the history of the invagination of mythological premise and image—of text as image, of text *as* margin.

The embodying of the text serves to feminize the essentially patriarchal and misogynistic exegetical traditions of the Church—producing what might be termed "the hegemony of Juno" in the Middle Ages. For example, the classical figure of Eridanus that appears in a mid-ninth-century Carolingian manuscript (fig. 1) can be said to embody a text as image, or, more accurately in this case, a text situated within the body of an image—*embodied text*. The figure appropriately fixes the image of medieval mythography: a visual description in words, which in its writing of the body—*écriture*—speaks woman, *parle femme*.

If the purpose of medieval mythography was to recover or recuperate a lost image through text—the text embodying or envisioning or visualizing the god or hero—as a process of writing down the meaning of the story, then this recovery absorbs iconography, the illustration or script of the being. The process is repetitive, mimetic, full of cultural noise. So "Eridanus" depicts the figure Eridanus (Fluvius, Currus), the river god, with his jug, initially as a man (in later depictions he will appear as female). This image already makes him concrete—a river is not a man. But he is depicted as a man recumbent, with a sheaf of grain and a fallen jug—the river's flowing results in grain. In the manuscript, the river is not only anthropomorphized (= a man), iconographized (water jug and sheaf, illustrative of its purpose) but it is also named, in the text that it embodies, "Eridanus."

"Eridanus," according to Hyginus's first-century A.D. *Astronomica*, refers either to the Nile River or to the Ocean, both specific bodies of water in a specific, non–Western European geographical area.[11] In Virgil's *Aeneid*, "Eridanus" is identified as the Italian Po River, but also as part of the Elysian Fields; near its source, the Po apparently has an underground portion nearly two miles in length that allows it to be construed by the commentators as a river with underworld connections. Because Eridanus is also a constellation, it signifies and links the heavenly or otherworldly with the earthly. As a river, Po or Nile, its significations bridge Western Europe and North Africa. Mythologically, in genealogies of the gods Eridanus is

1. Eridanus. MS. Harley 647, fol. 10v (mid-9th c.). By permission of the British Library, London.

sometimes called Oceanus, to refer to the husband of Thetis and grandfather of Saturn. In this Carolingian manuscript, Eridanus is embodied text, a humanized text, a natural object, or its idea, transformed into a man (name, icon, figure) who is shaped out of words on the page. Even his spilling jug and quill-like sheaf might incarnate the process of embodying text—the transmission of idea, or image, through writing on a surface.

I take this figure to symbolize mythography—text as image, the margins of a manuscript made into text borrowed from other texts, that is, intertextualized. The way the figure is constructed reverses the iconographic process in which text describes the image or idea (substance) of a thing. For the figure can do what no icon can do—exist, simultaneously, on several levels of meaning, just as Eridanus is:

An Image

1. a literal, inscribed image on the page
2. an image of a man recumbent with jug and sheaf
3. an image of a man pouring, nude or clothed
4. an image, later on, of a woman pouring, and

A Man

5. a being known as Oceanus, husband of Thetis and grandfather of Saturn
6. a man or woman personifying a river
7. a force, personified
8. the writer or scribe or poet-priest, and

A River

9. a literal, natural river
10. the idea of a river, that is, a generative force
11. Eridanus (Fluvius, Currus)—a proper name
12. a specific river—the Nile River, Ocean (N. Africa = Egypt) or an alternate specific river—the Po River (Italy)
13. a heavenly river located in the Elysian fields or an underground/underworld river, and

A Constellation

14. a constellation depicting a river and therefore representing all of the above, and

A Text

15. a literary text, specifically Virgil's *Aeneid* 6.659, or Hyginus's *Astronomica* 2.32.

The complex *vox*, the *voces*, associated with this one figure sum up the

2. Constellations. MS. 210, fols. 119v–120r. Courtesy of Bayerische Staatsbibliothek, Munich.

philosophical problem of literary exegesis in antiquity and (given the influence of Virgil and Hyginus on the Middle Ages) the medieval period. In some medieval manuscripts of astrological treatises, chiefly Cicero's *Aratea,* the constellations stellify stories through their mostly star-connected animal figures, which are described both by illustrations and by the accompanying didactic text (see fig. 2).

In its embodiment of text, or text as image, mythography was associated even in the medieval Church primarily with Stoic philosophy. Stoic philosophy functioned to humanize, or feminize, the dissemination of mythography in the Middle Ages, not so much in terms of a corpus of Stoic writings translated into Latin (as was the case with Aristotle in the thirteenth century) as in a passive presence, especially in the realm of ethics. Even in the Hellenistic period covering five centuries, it was more important than the other great philosophies—Epicurean, Peripatetic, Platonic, Pythagorean. The humanism of this philosophy—and its permission for female equality, its "feminism"—depends upon its tenet that, in the words of Gerard Verbeke,

all human beings—free citizens and slaves, men and women, Greeks and barbarians—are fundamentally equal. . . . Even Aristotle admits

that some individuals are slaves by nature, and that women and
barbarians represent a lower level of humanity. . . . Quite in agreement with their own physical system, the Stoics reject such discrimi-
nation. The soul of each individual, whatever his rank in society, is a
particle of the divine Spirit.

Even though Neoplatonism as a philosophical approach dominated the
schools beginning in the third century, it was itself full of some Stoic
ideas—whereas Neoplatonism is spiritual, Stoicism is "a kind of materialistic pantheism," so that "even the immanent divine Spirit is corporeal," as
Gerard Verbeke writes.[12] Further, Stoicism influenced the construction of
early Christian ideas, in the Greek Christian writers Clement of Alexandria, Origen, Gregory of Nyssa, and Nemesius of Emesa, and the Latin
Christians Tertullian, Lactantius, St. Jerome, St. Ambrose, and St. Augustine.[13]

In its feminizing impulse Stoic mythography simultaneously acts as a
vehicle not for Jupiter, understood as God, the World Soul, aether, and
father of Apollo, Hercules, and others, but for his sister-consort, Juno.
Within what might be perceived as phallogocentric narrative allegory—
the journeys of Aeneas, the genealogy of the gods, the descent of the hero,
the adulteries, rapes, castrations of Jupiter (an image, in Derridean terms,
for critical action)—also appear the invaginated boundaries, or frames, for
each of these. Material spaces were associated with women, whether Dido
or Lavinia, the invisible mother linking one father to son, or with the
monstrous (female, pagan, infernal) underworld itself, that is, symbolic
invagination, identified variously as Proserpina, Ceres, Cybele, Berecynthia, Circe. Together these women introduce the mortal victims of Jupiter's desire and also the immortal consort and sister whom he insults and
ignores, Juno herself. Whereas most of the philosophical explanations of
the gods begin with Jupiter as the One God, Progenitor, World Soul, most
of the narrative allegories actually create a montage of females and are
other, different, from what has been located as patriarchal discourse in both
classical myth and medieval mythography.

According to Stoic philosophy, Jupiter (aether) and Juno (air) produce
all creation. In addition, Juno acts as a conflation, or montage, of all the
female deities, beginning with Saturn's consort Ops; she is the central
female principle, matter to his time, associated with the lower element (air,
that sublunary region between earth and moon) and negatively constructed
according to the Neoplatonic cosmos in which earth was the dense center.

Specific agents of the one deity include Diana the moon, Duana, Trivia, Lucina goddess of childbirth, Ceres, Proserpina, Ops, Rhea, Cybele, and Berecynthia. Because of the late antique North African and Eastern Magna Mater cult (associated with Isis and others), readings of the female crept into the already Stoicized mythographies by the North African Roman Macrobius, Martianus Capella, Fulgentius, and then in the late Roman provincial writings of the Iberian Isidore. In the ninth-century commentaries on Martianus, glosses on such deities carefully proceed to introduce into Western culture many more female figures and new gods; this was largely the work of Irish scholars still full of Celtic native beliefs who came to Charlemagne's court to help him in his platform of educational reform.

Given this Stoic concept, there is another mythographic means of interpreting classical female deities, especially Juno. Juno is everywhere apparent beneath the mythological text; understanding her role is necessary to unravel the complex textuality of mythography. The story of mythography is her story, and the story of her subversive presence in the authoritative discourse of the Church. As virgin mother she represents a pagan Virgin Mary. The virginity of Juno would be matched by that of Jupiter's female progeny Diana and also Minerva, but opposed to the full-blown cosmic sexuality of Venus and Ops-Rea-Ceres-Cybele. And why Jupiter raped mortal females (and why Juno was so hostile to those women and the heroes they bore) is in pagan terms the story of human history—in Christian terms, of Original Sin. For example, Jupiter slept with a daughter of Atlas and produced Mercury; he raped Europa, whose brother Cadmus in following her founded Thebes. Juno was as hostile to her stepson Hercules, child of Alcmene and Jupiter, as to Paris of Troy, who chose Venus over Juno and Minerva. Her only true son was Vulcan, who as an embryo was carried in her thigh and who in Stoic terms represents the fire of creativity. In another sense, other "sons" might be identified as the centaurs who were produced by the lust of Ixion for Juno, and whose line eventually produced Chiron, the Christlike centaur who sacrificed his immortality to save the first man, Prometheus—thief of fire from the gods—from hell's torments.

From life on earth as an underworld it is not far to fiction as an "underworld," and female—the former concept articulated by the twelfth-century Neoplatonists William of Conches and Bernard Silvestris. The philosopher's task is to emulate Aeneas and descend into the underworld to reveal truth; the poet's job is to create that successful underworld. Thus the Neoplatonism of the twelfth century is not so much the beginning of a new approach to poetry and fiction as it is the outgrowth and culmination of a process that had begun around the year 400 with Macrobius and continued with Fulgentius up into the sixth century.

Reading a pagan text, a seductive and entertaining fiction, was imagined by late medieval mythographers as a duplication of the heroic descent into an underworld. An archetype for the underworld, the name of "Demogorgon," the mythical progenitor from whom descend the other gods and heroes in Boccaccio's *Genealogia deorum,* implies that the reader of this mythographic encyclopedia, like Dante in the *Commedia,* will explore hell. Derived from Bernard of Utrecht's late-eleventh-century commentary on the *Ecloga Theoduli,* "Demogorgon," or Demorigon, the Demiurge, who shares rule of the subdivided underworld with Pluto, combines *daemon,* suggesting the infernal, with Gorgon, the terrible and fierce quality associated with Medusa and her sisters. Coluccio Salutati's fifteenth-century encyclopedia *De laboribus Herculis* in its first two books defends poetry as itself a kind of descent into the underworld of artifice or fable, with its third book detailing the labors of Salutati's ideal epic hero, Hercules, and its fourth and last book discussing various kinds of descents into hell.

Finally, there remains another way in which mythography occupied a feminized and feminizing role in the cultures of the Middle Ages. To us mythography might appear largely mimetic, unoriginal, and, like the manuscripts with which commentaries grew up, a matter of copying and recopying. A gloss on a Virgil myth in the fourth century (say, by Servius) might be used in a ninth-century scholium on another classical author, whose glossator might add to it other glosses on the same myth from different authors. One danger in recuperating the mythographic tradition is to assume that such commentators and scholars reworking the meanings of the classics were marginal in the modern sense of trivial or unimportant. True, a commentator such as Fulgentius might subscribe to the rhetorical modesty topos in terming himself a "homunculus," a humble interpreter of the greatest ancient poets, Homer and Virgil. And often an anonymous glossator would write in the physical margins of the great manuscripts of those works, or above the lines of the poem or text being studied.

"Marginality," of course, can refer to that which is marginal, not central, or part of authority. "Margin" as a noun is an economic term for the difference between cost and selling price; "marginal," in recent theories of social science, expresses the ontology of the situation of women, blacks, and other disempowered groups. In paleography it refers to the text outside the text—in the Middle Ages that which exists as commentary: contemporary prose, explanations of terms and ideas written frequently in the vernacular in the margin next to an important (meaning classical, poetic, ancient) text. Marginal and writing marginally in all of the above senses, Christine de Pizan, a woman poet and philosopher who lived from 1360 to about 1430, wrote what might be termed a commentary on Ovid's *Metamorphoses*. The question we might then ask, given the above, is in what sense a marginal writer—a scholarly commentator, or a woman like Christine writing a marginal text like the *Epistre Othea*—is "original" in the modern sense, and therefore important, worthy of study.

The greatest marginality, the largest hem between the authority of the classical period and its renewal in the sixteenth century, has been identified as the "mimetic" and "unoriginal" Middle Ages itself, which has been perceived as borrowing its culture from the Graeco-Romans. The lofty regard for antiquity and its giants in the twelfth century led the scholar Bernard of Chartres to envisage himself as a dwarf, a little man, sitting on the shoulders of giants. The ancients were read from the perspectives of the medieval commentators who sought to elucidate them in an age when "originality" was not spiritually authorized—an age of the dwarf, the margin, the unoriginal, the unauthoritative. For such reasons Petrarch, in a bold but mistaken attempt to bolster his and his nation's confidence, first described the Christian Middle Ages as the "Dark Ages," anterior to the light of the "new time" and its study of antiquity and the classics—the *rinascimento* of his own day. Such marginality could itself empower a new perspective, however, enabling the dwarf to "see more and further" than the Roman giants whose writings taught the dwarf so much.

Medievalists have begun to question, rightly, just how naively classicism was accepted in the Middle Ages and just how naively we continue today to construe classicism's medieval reception. The outlines of the reception of classicism in the Middle Ages were well documented earlier in this century, with the classical privileged over what might be essentialized as the "medieval."[14] Jean Seznec's tracing of the three traditions of mythological interpretation (natural or physical, moral, grammatical or philosophical) from medieval models to Renaissance art was intended to show "the debt of the Renaissance to the Middle Ages" and thereby demonstrate the continuity of the classical tradition of mythology. But he denigrated the textual tradition of medieval mythography from which Renaissance artists drew for their subjects as a "complex and often very corrupt tradition." Because the medieval period was "unable and unwilling to realize that classical *motifs* and classical *themes* structurally belonged together," the period "avoided preserving the union of these two. Once the Middle Ages had established their own standards of civilization and found their own methods of artistic expression, it became impossible to enjoy or even to understand any phenomenon which had no common denominator with the phenomena of the contemporary world."[15]

Like Seznec, Erwin Panofsky regarded the Middle Ages as flawed, ignorant, and most of all monolithic, a single cultural entity—the "medi-aeval mind," anthropomorphized as a misguided individual whose own "phenomenona of the contemporary world" were perceived by Panofsky, from the Renaissance vantage-point, as empty and unimportant.[16] For these scholars what was important was the recurrence of classical themes and motifs—as if the historical preservation of classical culture should have been uppermost in the medieval "mind."

Very recently, Lawrence Nees's revisionist critique of Panofsky reassesses the normally pejorative term *medieval* to identify patristic as well as classical sources crucial to its culture in an accurate reflection of the specific historical period in which the art or writing actually occurred.[17] No longer can we examine, say, Carolingian "classicism" (no matter how closely allied to antique representations) without understanding its polemical and political character, its alterity, its singularity—its medieval historicity. For that matter, naive acceptance of what has been termed "classical" (presumably Graeco-Roman) has been questioned by modern scholars: the way in which nineteenth-century classical scholars have constructed what they imagined to be the history of ancient culture in reality reflects their own prejudices for the Aryan over the Levantine, as Martin Bernal has shown with such stunning postmodern effect in *Black Athena*.[18] History itself has been conceived as textual, a fabric whose "competing discourses" result in "patterns of interference" termed by Laurie A. Finke "noise." Historical noise, within the constructed subject of Western history as consciously male, is information not in itself meaningful whose examination involves " 'a putting into discourse *woman*.' "[19] In the forthcoming book *Reading Dido: Gender, Textuality, and the Medieval Aeneid*, Marilynn Desmond argues that (male) Virgil readers throughout history have read the epic, and its fourth book, as an "epitome of patriarchal poetry" that marginalizes the role and power of the African queen Dido.[20] Understanding the politics of reading classical texts in the Middle Ages will also place sanctioned interpretations against an appropriate background of cultural alterity, or noise.

In relation to mythography, then, "marginality" and "originality" accrue new, varied, and specific hues of meaning. Because medieval Christian students of Latin grammar far removed from the Roman Empire increasingly needed assistance in deciphering references to pagan gods and goddesses, help was provided by masters and lecturers who had studied glosses (interlinear or marginal annotations of the text) or commentaries (longer expositions that could stand alone and that introduce lines from the text for elaborate explanation) on those school texts. The difference between the two forms of annotation was clarified by the twelfth-century Huguccio of Pisa: the commentary is an exposition which does not consider the particular conjunction of words but only their sense or meaning, for it is in itself a study of the various doctrines or thoughts collected together about one work. In contrast the gloss focuses on individual phrases or words: "It is an exposition on words or lines and their meanings, as the sense does not exist except through words, so that the gloss is an exposition of the sense the word or line contains."[21] Of course the two forms were not mutually exclusive. Huguccio's contemporary William of Conches distinguished between the gloss and commentary, but in his own work wished to combine the best from both types of analysis.

William of Conches also perceived the role of the commentator as more than marginal, trivial, or imitative in its shaping, clarifying, and unifying function, compelling us in this study of mythography to consider such "marginality" and "originality" from a more firmly medieval and historicized perspective. William declares,

> Although we do not doubt many have commented on Plato, many glossed, nevertheless because commentators, neither connecting nor expounding the letter of the text, alone serve the ideas, and glossators are found in truth superfluous on light trifles, in truth most obscure on the weighty matters, we, aroused by the entreaty of friends to whom we owe all noble things, propose to say something on the abovesaid, cutting off the superfluous of others, adding the overlooked, clarifying the obscure, *removing abusive things,* and imitating the things said well. (My emphasis)[22]

And in the twelfth-century handbook or commentaries, such glosses might be compiled with still other related glosses, and perhaps slightly changed to reflect some current scholastic or literary interest, until, in the fourteenth and fifteenth centuries, the collection of myths will have been organized into a unified entity with its own authority. Nevertheless, "marginality" and "originality" as issues germane to the study of the medieval mythographic tradition can help to elucidate the importance of mythographic "texts" and the (mainly) men who compiled and wrote them in innovative ways that reinterpreted the original myths and the classical texts in which they appeared.

To document the way in which mythography changed in the Middle Ages, I would like to demonstrate by means of examples drawn primarily from the most "innovative" mythographers the confluence of historical necessity, the power of literary convention, and the creation of new paradigms, to use Thomas Kuhn's term. By "innovation" I mean those changes in the conventions of literary interpretation instituted by grammarians and scholars who applied what they knew to new mythological texts or situations for which there were no paradigms, working, as has been demonstrated, at least by the philologists tracing the history of Old and Middle English, by analogy. Such changes occurred through multicultural shifts and affected the genres of mythography, the pagan hero and god, the underworld with which the demigod or deity was associated, to result in an assimiliation and transmogrification of pagan into Christian culture.

This first volume focuses primarily on the Carolingian mythographers. Their major resources derived from Macrobius and Fulgentius, two scholars working with Graeco-Roman materials in North Africa whose mythographic methods and materials were not only influenced but shaped by indigenous religious beliefs and practices, such as Egyptian heliocentricism and the Magna Mater cult. Moreover, the bringing together of scholars from York, Spain, Ireland, and St. Gall in Switzerland at Charlemagne's court would also allow innovative changes in mythographic paradigms because of cross-cultural intertextuality. As Thomas Kuhn notes, "Almost always the men [sic] who achieve these fundamental inventions of a new paradigm have either been very young or very new to the field whose paradigm they change."[23] These influential innovative mythographers perceived as new a culture different from their own. From Spain Theodulf brought with him to Orleans the old Roman education fossilized in Visigothic form and the encyclopedic knowledge of his countryman Isidore of Seville, based as that knowledge was on African sources like Martianus Capella. In Anglo-Saxon England, the desire of King Alfred of Wessex to translate Latin texts into the vernacular directed him to Boethius and the *Consolation of Philosophy,* with its mythological poems on the heroes of antiquity; the spread of King Alfred's scholars and scholarship to St. Gall in Switzerland and thence to Charlemagne's court through Remigius of Auxerre would provide another conduit for cross-cultural innovation. John Scot from Ireland, along with Remigius of Auxerre, would demonstrate the great learning of the Carthaginian Martianus Capella, whose mythological figures would receive such Neo-Stoic glossation and feminize the essentially masculine and misogynistic mythographic tradition. The first two Vatican mythographers—perhaps Adanan the Scot of York and either Remigius of Auxerre or possibly a woman ecclesiastic—would gather together in what they saw as cohesive collections the ancient myths, the former collection an attempt at a universal genealogy of the world, a history of the world from the first man, Prometheus; the latter a history from the Creation. Such a parallel concept of history would lead to the *Ecloga Theoduli,* yoking the history of Old Testament legend to the genealogy of the pagan gods—one of the most widely circulated school book texts in existence and a text used by Chaucer and other late medieval poets.

The mythographers in this study, original in the only way they knew how, painstakingly worked out a means of understanding texts alien to them—written in an alien tongue, by alien giants, from a time different and therefore strange. Such supremely wise authorities, greater than any living authority, had much to hide from small, base, simple men who spoke only the vernacular. From such a nexus modern literary criticism springs and with it the modern notion of fiction as secretive and complex, polysemous, psychologically full. Whatever the tiny grammatical point made by the grammarian, whatever the Stoic or Neoplatonist explanation offered by the philosopher and the scholar, the centuries of scholasticism in the Middle Ages insisted that a text required a gloss, an interpretation. Only in the Renaissance, which demanded a return to the original classical text, without the intermediary medieval commentary, did Protestantism and Reformation also flourish, when it was possible for all to read the Word without a priest—as long as the reader was literate and books were relatively cheap. For us today, who read Spenser's *Faerie Queene* or Joyce's *Ulysses* only with a written guide by a literary critic or within the formal structure of a classroom, the medieval concept of the text and its requiring lecture-commentary is one for which we have an affinity. And for those medieval grammarians and philosophers, John Updike's *Centaur* or Joyce's *Ulysses* would have been, at least in idea (except for the privileging of contemporary subject matter), a wholly familiar kind of fiction.

Chapter One

THE ALLEGORIZATION OF CLASSICAL MYTH IN THE LITERARY SCHOOL COMMENTARY

In all of its forms throughout its long history, including the earliest, allegoresis developed as a necessary alternative to historical interpretation, that is, restriction of meaning to the letter alone. In this conflict between the letter and the spirit, some scholars wished to demythologize mythology, to make it historical through euhemerist or typological readings. In contrast, its defenders argued that the apparent immorality or blasphemy of Greek and Roman myths used by the greatest classical poets, like that of the Old and New Testament, cloaked a more spiritual meaning than was apparent from the literal or historical level.

The two systems or approaches to the text developed in reaction to one another. Allegorical interpretation offered in defense of Homer and Hesiod (ca. 700 B.C.) appeared within a century after these texts' composition and continued in the allegorism of the Ionians, Sophists, and other pre-Socratic philosophers, the Stoics, the Neoplatonists, and the Jewish and Christian theologians of the Alexandrian School. Among the descendants of Homer's attackers were the rationalizing theorists—Euhemerus and his school and the early Greek and Latin Church Fathers, who often inadvertently preserved what they had been trying to attack.[1] Further, a multilevel method of allegorical exegesis was vital not only in the works of the Greek Alexandrians and the Church Fathers but also in those of the Benedictine and Carolingian commentators, the Victorines and the Dominicans, and in texts from the *Commedia* down to little-known sermon writers of the fourteenth century such as Robert of Basevorn and Master Robert Rypon, who subscribed to the methods of the *artes praedicandi*.[2] Finally, the mythographic methods first used by Homer's defenders reappeared in Christian guise in the Middle Ages in commentaries on classics used by scholars in the medieval schools and universities and then by poets creating their own classicized poems.

Homer and Dante supply appropriate poles in the continuum of any survey of the origins of mythographic allegoresis, especially given their depictions of Hades, or the underworld, because both use gods, heroes, and monsters supposedly engaged in immoral activity. The actual Greek text of Homer was, however, not known in the Middle Ages; the stories came down by hearsay and through the so-called *Ilias Latina* attributed to "Pindarus Thebanus" (still very tentatively identified as Baebius Italicus, perhaps of the first century A.D.). Note the garbled example provided by a thirteenth-century Oxford manuscript (fig. 3), where Homer himself is being given the flower moly (like nightshade, according to Pliny) by Mercury (Hermes in Homer), Roman (and Greek) messenger of the gods and god of eloquence, but Egyptian god of the underworld; in book 10 of the *Odyssey* Odysseus uses the magical powers of the herb to counter Circe's incantation. There is no good Latin translation of Homer before the mid-fourteenth century, when Leontius Pilatus's translation was widely copied until it was superseded by better translations in the fifteenth century.[3] Though Dante could not know Homer directly, Homer and Dante serve as the great chronological poles: Homer's poetry was responsible for initiating the practice of mythography in Greek antiquity, and Dante's poetry was responsible not so much for ending it—it continued for several centuries—as for using specifically medieval versions of mythography in a unified way no later poet would.

What this survey will reveal is that the ancient classical techniques advanced by the pre-Socratics, Platonists, and Stoic philosophers can be compared with the allegorical senses defined by Dante in the fourteenth century in his famous "Letter to Can Grande." The moral, etymological, and physical types of Greek allegorism at least vaguely resemble, respectively, Dante's moral or tropological, allegorical, and anagogical levels, as defined in his letter to his patron, Can Grande della Scala. Dante's moral or tropological level, which applies to the virtues or vices of the individual human, corresponds to the moral level of the Stoics. The Stoic moral level of meaning, which sees the gods as expressions of human faculties or vices and virtues, remains the same whether Greek or Christian. Dante's allegorical level refers either to the life of Christ (if a sacred text) or to an idea (if a classical myth); often an elaborate etymological explanation accompanies this form of allegoresis. This allegorical level, which reveals truths about Christ or Christ's life, can be seen in some way as similar to the Stoic etymological, which probes meaning through the origins and development of words—suggesting an absolute moral reality outside of the human.

3. Homer, Mercury, and the herb immolum. From an herbal. MS. Ashmole 1462, fol. 26v (12th c.). By permission of the Bodleian Library, University of Oxford.

Finally, Dante's anagogical level corresponds not to the physical or natural world but to a *super*natural world, referring to the life of the Church or the afterlife; it thus transforms the physical level of classical allegorical interpretation. But the physical meanings of the Stoics parallel Dante's anagogical in that both reveal truths about the cosmos; the difference is that the Stoics were interested in Hades and earth whereas the Christians, like Dante, were interested in the underworld and paradise. The remarkable parallels between ancient philosophical and medieval theological and scholastic practice cannot perhaps be explained only by direct influence. At any rate, however, the allegoresis of the Stoics and pre-Socratics in its rationalization of classical mythology did not die out in the Middle Ages, as another Dante text, a passage on allegory in *Convivio* 2.1, attests.

We will trace the origins of mythography back to Greece in its accompaniment of the development of Stoic and Platonic cosmography and ethics and forward into the fourfold or polysemous exegesis of the text by Christian scholars in the Middle Ages. We will also explore the reasons for the preservation of classical myth in the Middle Ages, including the rise of medieval schools and medieval universities and the need to read Latin by means of the authoritative texts of Virgil, Statius, Lucan, Ovid, and others. From them emerged traditions of school commentary that would affect the portrayal of the gods as characters in late medieval poetry and would develop as an early form of literary criticism in the Middle Ages.

I. STOIC COSMOGRAPHY AND ETHICS
IN READING HOMER'S SCANDALOUS GODS

In ancient Greek justifications of Homer there were basically three kinds of hidden meaning, or *hyponoia,* that licentious material could conceal—the natural or physical, the moral, and the grammatical.[4] The physical undermeaning referred to natural forces or phenomena, the moral undermeaning referred to human faculties or qualities, and the grammatical referred to the philosophical reality of a name. In the Greek period the physical meaning was initially the most discussed, followed by the other two, while in the Middle Ages all three were given equal weight from the earliest examples. But in the Middle Ages the grammatical and moral came to be conflated into a single sense, very important in the period up to and including the Carolingian period (the late eighth through the ninth century) though it was supplemented (even supplanted) by a fourth type of meaning, the Christian Neoplatonic, introduced between the twelfth and fourteenth centuries.

The earliest form of reading, the physical, was described by the pre-Socratic philosophers in the sixth century B.C. and passed to the Stoics, both groups wishing to defend Homer; it was then used as a method of biblical exegesis by Philo, Origen, St. Ambrose, and St. Augustine. The moral type was passed from the Platonists of the fifth and fourth centuries B.C. to the Neoplatonists of the early centuries A.D.—from Plato to the pseudo-Heraclitus to Porphyry, Iamblichus, Macrobius, and so into the Middle Ages. The grammatical, the third and latest form, closely related to the moral, came from the etymologizing Sophists and Stoics of the fourth century B.C. and passed into the Alexandrian school, especially to Origen and Porphyry, and then to St. Augustine, St. Jerome, and Isidore of Seville. Origen and Augustine used both the Stoic physical and the grammatical forms, and all of the methods together were used in the pseudo-Heraclitus of Pontus.

All these styles of reading stemmed from philosophic reactions to attacks on the morality of the gods of Homer and Hesiod. Homer, author of the epic poems *Iliad* and *Odyssey,* and Hesiod, author of the short epic treatise *Works and Days* and the cosmological poem explaining the origin of the gods, *Theogony,* were both criticized by early philosophers for their descriptions of the gods engaging in immoral behavior. Critics fantasized that both poets received appropriate punishments for their infractions in Hades: Pythagoras of Samos (582–500 B.C., the dates set by Diogenes Laertius), who supposedly descended to Hades, claimed that he had witnessed "the soul of Hesiod bound fast to a brazen pillar and gibbering, and the soul of Homer hung on a tree with serpents writhing about it, this being their punishment for what they had said about the gods."[5] Xenophanes sternly declared that both "Homer and Hesiod have attributed to the gods all things that are shameful and a reproach among humankind: theft, adultery, and mutual deception."[6] Heraclitus (540–470 B.C.) also lambasted both Homer ("Homer deserves to be flung out of the contests and given a beating") and, to a lesser extent, Hesiod ("Hesiod is the teacher of very many, he who did not understand day and night: for they are one").[7]

In the century and a half after Homer's poems were composed, pre-Socratic philosophers first offered specifically physical, or cosmographic, allegorical interpretations in defense of the poets' treatment of the bickering of Zeus (Jupiter) and Hera (Juno) and his violence toward his wife and her son Hephaestos (Vulcan). One of the earliest defenses, that the narrative veils secrets about the underworld, occurs in support of episodes in the first and fifteenth books of the *Iliad*. Near the end of book 1, Hera's son Hephaestos begs her to placate Zeus so that her consort will not batter her, reminding her that when Hephaestos took Hera's part one other time Zeus hurled him below the divine threshold to Lemnos, where he nearly died. At the beginning of book 15, as Zeus views the devastation of the Trojans and the felling of Hektor, Zeus angrily blames Hera for this situation and reminds her of his punishment for her antipathy toward her stepson Hêraklês, when Zeus bound her with golden chain or cord, weighted her feet with anvils, and hung her from the aether and clouds. Both passages were interpreted by early defenders of Homer as descriptions of cosmological justice. For example, Pherecydes of Syros in the seventh century or mid-sixth century B.C. in *Heptamychos* (*The Seven-Chambered Cosmos*) explains that an underworld for the punishment of the gods exists beneath our known world: "Below this part of the world is the Tartarean part; its guardians are the daughters of Boreas, the Harpies and the Storm-wind. Thither does Zeus banish any god who commits an act of lawlessness."[8] According to Origen's recitation of this myth in *Contra Celsum,* pride or arrogance is the specific act of lawlessness that results in this punishment. Later, Celsus would agree with this cosmological interpretation: he understood that Zeus is really God and Hera is Matter, that the earth beneath the "divine threshold" is in reality the underworld, and that Hephaestos was sent there as punishment for his arrogance.[9]

Theagenes of Rhegium (ca. 525 B.C.), the first defender of Homer to use allegory explicitly, provided natural and moral explanations of another passage criticized by early philosophers. These two explanations would develop into separate approaches later in the evolution of mythography. In a scholium on the *Iliad* cited by Porphyry in the *Theomachy,* on the partisan involvement of the gods in the Trojan War, he explains the battling of the gods as representative of physical conflict among the elements: just as there exists a natural conflict between contrary elements, hot versus cold, light versus heavy, so also water quenches fire, with fire expressed by Apollo, Helios, and Hephaestos, and water by Poseidon and Scamander (and the moon by Artemis and the air by Hera).[10] He also suggests such battling among the gods can be explained by moral oppositions. Athena or Phronesis (Wisdom) wars with Ares (Foolishness); Aphrodite (Desire) wars with Hermes (Logos, the Word, Reason).

The physical interpretations of Homer and Greek myths in general became more specific in the latter half of the fifth century B.C., especially in the hands of the Ionian and Sophist philosophers, and later, in the fourth century, with the Cynics. Several Ionians argued that Homer's purpose had been to propound virtue and justice (not to excuse whatever apparently immoral divine activities were portrayed).[11] Anaxagoras of Clazomenae (ca. 460 B.C.) views Zeus as mind and Athena as art or technical skill,[12] and the rays of the sun as the arrows of Apollo.[13] He says, "We give the name Iris to the reflection of the sun on the clouds. It is therefore the sign of a storm, for the water which flows round the cloud produces wind or forces out rain."[14] His pupil Metrodorus of Lampsacus (d. 464 B.C.), according to Tatian, claimed that neither the gods nor the heroes existed but they were introduced by the poet for artistic reasons, "referring all to physiology," so that Hera, Athena, and Zeus can be equated with "the parts of nature and dispositions of the elements."[15] Similarly, Metrodorus correlated the heroes of the *Iliad* with physical phenomena—Agamemnon with aether, Achilles with the sun, Helen with the earth, and Paris with the air—while he identified the gods as having cosmological influence on and correspondence to parts of the human body—Demeter to the liver, Dionysus to the spleen, and Apollo to the gall.[16] That such cosmographic explanations were common is clear from the comedies and memoirs of Epicharmus of Syracuse (ca. 550–460 B.C.): Jupiter is facetiously said to be "Air; who is wind and clouds, and afterwards rain, and from rain comes cold, and after that, wind and again air. Therefore these elements of which I tell you are Jupiter, because with them he helps all mortals, cities and animals."[17]

The Sophists stressed etymological interpretation of myth even as they explained the gods as aspects of the natural world. Prodicus of Ceos, in the latter half of the fifth century B.C., used etymology to explain how myths cloak truth: he declared that the ancients found that the sun, moon, rivers, springs, and all other things beneficial to humankind were gods because they served humankind, as was the case with the Nile for the Egyptians. Thus bread was understood as Demeter, wine as Dionysus, water as Poseidon, fire as Hephaestos.[18] Later, Democritus (ca. 420 B.C.), although not a Sophist, similarly equated Zeus with air, and noted that "Tritogeneia," literally "thrice-born," means that wisdom, or Athena, consists of three parts.[19]

In the fourth century Plato advanced etymological allegorism as a reflection of both moral and physical allegorism. In the *Cratylus*, he begins with Homer, as do so many of the philosophers. Plato argues that Homer correctly attributed names to particular things, as witnessed in the denotations of such names, for example, as "Xanthus" for the name of a river rather than "Scamander," and the connotations of such names, for example, of Agis as "leader," Polemarchus as "war lord," and Acesimbrotus as "healer of mortals." But Plato also argues that names reveal an innate moral reality in addition to etymological connotations. Thus the name "Agamemnon" ("admirable for remaining") mirrors his character as "one who would resolve to toil to the end and to endure, putting the finish upon his resolution by virtue. And proof of this is his long retention of the host at Troy and his endurance."[20] The discussion concludes, after additional examples are cited, with a display of how etymological allegorism can also support a physical interpretation of the gods: the names of the gods are representative (for the earliest Greeks, at least) of the sun, moon, earth, stars, and sky because the Greek word for "god" (*theos*) comes from the fact of their constant running (*thein*).

Such etymological and physical allegorism culminated in the practices of the Stoics, who in the fourth to third centuries B.C. created a system of allegorical details in support of Homer: they assumed that Homer wrote with an understanding of Stoic physical and moral dogma.[21] Zeno of Citium (340–265 B.C.), father of the Stoics, rationalized Homer's use of the gods by showing how all of them fit into an orderly natural schema wherein names signify natural forces.[22] The major gods represent the regions of the universe: Juno is air, Jupiter, the heavens, Neptune, the sea, Vulcan, fire;[23] aether is a god and a principle of reason;[24] the Titans are the elements of the universe, as determined by the etymology of their name.[25] Zeno's teachings were expanded and developed by his followers, his pupil Cleanthes of Assos (b. ca. 300 B.C.) and Cleanthes's pupil Chrysippus (ca. 280 B.C.), as well as others.[26]

Perhaps in reaction to the allegorical nature of much of Greek philosophy, the literal level developed its own school of adherents through a form of historical (nonallegorical) interpretation known as euhemerism, after its fourth-century B.C. founder Euhemerus, a Sicilian from Messina (fl. 316 B.C.). In his opposition to the allegorists Euhemerus rationalized the appearance of the gods as historical persons. While his rationalizations had been anticipated by a minor Stoic named Persaeus, who thought these gods had been men who had made discoveries in the arts and sciences improving our lives, Euhemerus did offer an important contribution to this school. In his *Sacred History,* on the basis of his travel records he inferred that the places sacred to the various gods and goddesses in fact were merely burial places of men and women. The importance of the work is reflected in its currency: it was later translated into Latin by Ennius.[27] In addition, both

Cicero and Plutarch referred to this interpretation of the gods, although they denied it as absurd.

Among the extant fragments of Euhemerus's work, treatments have survived for Jupiter as "the father both of gods and men" (and also, strangely, as the firmament);[28] for the Prometheus myth, which was attributed to Agroetas, Theophrastus, and Herodorus, in a scholium on Apollonius of Rhodes's *Argonautica;*[29] for the myth of Cerberus revealed as a poisonous snake and for the myth of Geryon revealed as a king, in the view of Hecataeus;[30] and for the serpent Pytho revealed as a cruel king known as the Dragon (according to Ephorus).[31]

Euhemerus's impact as a thinker is suggested by the fact that he had followers—chiefly Palaephatus, who thought myths were misunderstandings of ambiguous phraseology and accordingly wrote a rationalizing essay on the subject, but also Polybius and Diodorus—even though he and not his followers had the greatest influence on others.[32] Indeed, Euhemerus's method and his interpretations are preserved in the third book of Cicero's *De natura deorum,* in the euhemeristic interpretations offered by Cotta the pontifex, as we shall see. Beyond this classical continuation of Euhemerus's ideas voiced by Cicero's high priest, Euhemerus also had a profound effect on the early Church Fathers, many of whom cited his rationalizations of the gods as historical persons and passed them on to the Middle Ages, and on Isidore of Seville (A.D. 575–636) in the enormously influential *Etymologiae,* which promoted not only the idea that the gods as men had founded and ruled over various cities but also the idea that they had discovered various arts and trades (Aesculapius, medicine; Mercury, the mercantile trade; Prometheus, statue making).

In the century before and after Christ several Roman writers fully developed etymological, moral, and physical allegorism and also historical euhemerism, among them Cicero in *De natura deorum,* especially in the second book, and the pseudo-Heraclitus at the end of the first century A.D. in his *Allegoricae Homericae.* Both of these treatises were heavily influenced by the earlier Stoic philosophers: although Cicero is an Academic and not a Stoic, nevertheless he cites Stoic sources.

De natura deorum, whose title resembles those of works by Zenocrates and Chrysippus, is an imaginary dialogue or debate in three books, intended as an encyclopedia of cosmology and theology.[33] The dialogue is set in 77 or 76 B.C. at the home of Gaius Aurelius Cotta, a well-known pontifex or priest of the first quarter of the century and an adherent of the Academy who was also expert on Philo. The other debaters included Gaius Velleius (a typical Epicurean and a real person about whom nothing is now known), Quintus Lucilius Balbus (a typical Stoic), and Cicero himself (who in the year 77 or 76 would have been too young to participate actively in the debate, although he claimed to belong to the Academy). The three books are divided to reflect three different approaches to the gods, with the Epicurean Velleius in the first book relaying a history of the Greek philosophers, the Stoic Lucilius Balbus in the second book declaiming on the gods, and in the third the Academic Cotta denigrating them but in the process also disseminating bits of information about them. The Stoic defense of the gods in the second book, which was derived from Zeno, Cleanthes, and Chrysippus, provides a very clear exposition of physical allegorism, and the long genealogies of the gods in the third book (for example, for the three Jupiters, four Vulcans, etc., all with different parents) inadvertently affirm Euhemerus's position. In the first book, what information there is centers on the physical and cosmological explanations of the gods; in the second Cicero adds the etymological and moral explanations; but in the third primarily genealogical or historical explanations begin with the oldest gods like Aether and Day and move to the least important and most recent heroes like Aegisthus and Paris.

The Stoic defense of the gods in the second book is derived from the writings of Zeno, Cleanthes, and Chrysippus on the gods as natural forces, "physica ratio" (*Nat. deorum* 2.63), with the immoral interactions of the gods perceived as veiling cosmography. For example, the fable of the castration of Caelus by Saturn signifies that the highest heavenly aether, that seed-fire which generates all things, did not require the equivalent of human genitals to proceed in its generative work (2.64). But Cicero depends heavily on etymological allegorism to make his points. When Jupiter puts Saturn in chains in an attempt to restrain his course and bind him in the stars' network, Cicero understands that "iuvans pater" (helping father, our father and the father of the gods) is attempting to bind and restrain time (in that "Saturn" comes from "quod saturaretur annis" ["sated with years"], 2.64).

The comments on the gods by Cotta in the third book—literalistic, euhemeristic, and genealogical in nature—are anticipated by Balbus's comments in the Stoic second book on several heroes, such as Hercules, Castor and Pollux, Aesculapius, Liber and Libera, and Romulus, all of whom Balbus regards as men or women who have been deified for their great contributions to humankind ("quorum cum remanerent animi atque aeternitate fruerentur, rite di sunt habiti, cum et optimi essent et aeterni,"

2.62). Cotta, commenting on such beliefs in those heroes as gods in the third book, responds contemptuously that this Stoic philosophy is rubbish, superstitions which appeal to the ignorant (3.39). His premise and conclusion remain the same: those which they call gods are not "figuras deorum" but "rerum naturas," whatever men may believe and the Stoic philosophers conceive to rationalize them (3.63). While Cotta does not seem to understand Stoic philosophy at all, he does disseminate it. In his long diatribe intended to prove that these gods and heroes are natural things or beings and not divinities, Cotta discusses six different Hercules coming from six different regions with six different fathers: Hercules the son of Jupiter and Lysithoë; the Egyptian Hercules, son of the Nile; Hercules of the Digiti at Mount Ida; Hercules son of Jupiter and Asteria and father of the nymph Carthago; an Indian Hercules, Belus; and Hercules, son of Jupiter and Alcmene (3.42). He also discovers three Jupiters, and similarly multiple sons and daughters of Jupiter, including the sun god, Vulcan, Mercury, Aesculapius, Apollo, Diana, Dionysus, Venus, Minerva, and Cupid.

Similarly Stoic in their desire to embrace all natural and moral knowledge through the principles of etymological allegorism are the *Allegoriae Homericae* of pseudo-Heraclitus (of Pontus, at the time of Augustus) and the *Compendium theologiae Graecae* of Cornutus (at the time of Nero).[34] While both writers addressed themselves to Homer, with Cornutus presenting a list of etymologies of the names of the gods and their epithets to reveal Greek origins, for the more important pseudo-Heraclitus the myths of the gods and heroes had three types of signification that summarize the three mythographic strands—the historical, in the explanation of events (the tradition inherited from Euhemerus); the natural, in allegories of conflict between forces (the physical tradition inherited from the early Heraclitus and the pre-Socratics); and the moral, in various personal and psychological qualities (the tradition inherited from the etymologizing Stoics like Chrysippus).

These Roman scholars who preserved so well the methods of Greek Stoic allegorism met with varied receptions in the Middle Ages. Cicero played a more important role than did the pseudo-Heraclitus:[35] St. Augustine used *De natura deorum* in *De civitate Dei;* St. Gregory in the sixth century wanted to destroy and ban all works by Cicero, his indignation in proportional measure to Cicero's importance; Abelard admired him in the twelfth century; the Italian Renaissance found him especially significant. More important, many of the Stoic ideas in *De natura deorum* influenced Macrobius, Martianus Capella, and Fulgentius, and through them a variety of later medieval mythographers including the Vatican mythographers. Pseudo-Heraclitus affected the cast of Homeric scholia and other late Greek works which were not vitally important to the development of medieval mythography, such as the pseudo-Plutarchan *De vita et poesi Homeri,* the Stoic passages in Porphyry's *Homeric Questions,* and Eustathius's comments upon the Homeric poems.[36]

At this stage, the history of mythography was profoundly affected by the advent of Christianity, which caused a dissociation between mythographic methods and mythographic substance and subjects. This dissociation of form from matter resulted in two consequences important for our study. The first consequence, which affected mythographic methodology, was more far-reaching and more important. The various religious controversies of this period—between Christians and Jews and between Christians and pagans[37]—allowed apologists to adapt to Judaism or Christianity Stoic methods for rationalization of classical myths, thus preserving those methods of mythography for the Middle Ages. In the early centuries A.D., the Jewish and Christian scholars of the Greek Alexandrian School resuscitated early Hebrew exegesis in defense of the apparent immorality of the Old Testament. Thereafter, in the late second to the fourth centuries, the methods of allegoresis inherited from the pre-Socratic and Stoic philosophers were applied chiefly to scriptural materials, largely because the myths and their classical contexts were denigrated by the Christians as part of a move to discredit paganism. Euhemeristic methodology also was transmogrified into two late antique forms of interpretation markedly different from mythographic allegoresis and centering on the literal (or historical) sense—typology and etiology.

The second result of the Christian dissociation of form from content has to do with mythographic subject matter. The early Church Fathers who wrote in Latin, in their attacks on the pagan gods and the elaborate cosmic machinery often associated with them by the Stoics, often unwittingly preserved those earlier Greek mythographic interpretations which Euhemerus had attempted to strip away. The latter phenomenon is apparent especially in the writings of Tertullian (A.D. 145–220), Minucius Felix (ca. A.D. 210), Arnobius (fl. A.D. 300), Lactantius (ca. A.D. 306), and most influentially, St. Augustine (A.D. 354–430).

It is important, however, to qualify both of these statements of influence. Many of these writings, including those of the Alexandrian School, appeared in Greek, a language used because of the revival of Greek culture in the second century under the impact of imperial patronage and because of the Greek New Testament; this revival on the one hand brought back the stylistic effects of the early Greek sophists but on the other may have influenced the use of Greek for liturgical purposes as a universal language by the Western Church until the mid-third century.[38] Because of the limited duration of this revival of interest in Greek, some of the writers mentioned here did not directly affect the Middle Ages, or at least the development of medieval mythography. Whether they wrote in Greek or in Latin, writers like Justin Martyr, Minucius Felix, Tertullian, and Clement and Origen of Alexandria[39] were not much liked by the medieval West, and although the fourth-century Latin writer Lactantius was the earliest Christian author to have any vogue in the Middle Ages, he was not very influential; instead, it was Ambrose, Jerome, Augustine, and Hilary of Poitiers who commanded the respect of the Middle Ages.

II. CHRISTIAN READINGS OF SACRED AND PAGAN TEXTS

In relation to the first consequence of the advent of Christianity and its effect on the history of mythographic allegoresis, that is, the preservation of the early mythographic method, the continuing reliance upon figurative rather than literal interpretation of the Bible derived initially from the Alexandrian School of mysticism (as opposed to the literalistic School of Antioch). The important Philo Judaeus of Alexandria (20 B.C.–A.D. 50) held the same ideas about Jewish sacred literature that the Stoics held about Homeric literature[40] and even incorporated Stoic methods of exegesis employed in the defense and study of Homer in his interpretation of licentious or incestuous stories of the Old Testament: he viewed persons and things of the Old Testament as faculties of the soul, and tried to prove that Greek philosophical ideas, through the faculties of the soul, underlay the story of the Old Testament.[41]

Philo's followers Clement (A.D. 150–245) and Origen (A.D. 185?–254?) of Alexandria were Christian theologians who wrote in Greek and used and adapted Stoic methods for their treatment of the Old Testament. Clement, Origen's teacher and a founder of biblical criticism in debt to the philosophizing Jew Philo, introduced a rabbinical version of Greek interpretation into the Christian realm of *apologeticus* and *exegesis*. Plato to him was a great Christian before Christ, a "Moses Atticus"; but Clement also believed pagan writings rightly understood could yield Christian meanings and thus he divided all nonliteral meaning into ethical, theological, and physical levels, deriving from the Greeks his understanding of the veiling of first principles of things in enigmas, symbols, allegories.[42] Origen in his *Contra Celsum* battled the view of the Jewish Celsus that Christian doctrines were warped versions of Platonic idealism, or that the rites of the Christians derived from Stoic philosophy, Jewish tradition, Mithraic mysteries, the myths of Typhon, Osiris, and the Cabeiri, or even that the biography of Christ combined aspects of the myths of Hercules, Bacchus, Aesculapius, and Orpheus.[43] In one sense Origen then is *anti-euhemerist*—toward Christ as a divinity. Indeed, Origen brought multiple senses of Scripture to the Christian Church. Treating Philo as a Christian Father, Origen developed the simple contrast of the *sensus historicus* or *literalis* and the *sensus spiritualis* into a threefold schema of literal, moral, and spiritual senses.[44]

The Latin Church Fathers also distinguished levels of meaning in biblical texts in a way similar to that of the mythographers. Tertullian distinguished two levels of meaning, the literal and the figurative, but believed that the figurative could be correctly understood only by the Church.[45] St. Ambrose (d. 397) offered three only superficially novel senses—the somatic (literal, grammatical), psychic (moral), and pneumatic (allegorical, mystical) interpretation of Scripture; in contrast, St. Jerome (ca. 340–420) presented a scientific, objective, more historical method of exegesis.[46] Nevertheless, although he vowed never again to read Cicero or Virgil,[47] St. Jerome influenced the development of allegory in this period through his interest in etymology as an index of moral reality, a view markedly similar to the earlier Stoic views. He played on Hebrew words and names in the *Libri nominum Hebraicorum,* which influenced later philosophical treatments of words, such as those in Porphyry and St. Augustine, Isidore's *Etymologiae,* and later in the dictionaries of Osbern of Gloucester, Papias the Lombard, and Huguccio of Pisa.[48]

Of all the Church Fathers, St. Augustine was the most substantial contributor to the doctrinal development of the allegorical senses (and yet one of the most influential adversaries of paganism). In his *De doctrina Christiana* he encouraged clerical study of the branches of knowledge of the trivium so as to better understand the multiple meanings contained in the Word of God. His interest in allegory, chiefly visible in the second book of *De doctrina* and inherited in part from Origen's *sensus historicus* (literal level) and *sensus spiritualis* (moral and spiritual levels), led him to apply the old Stoic idea of physical, moral, and grammatical (or etymological) allegoresis to the Bible. Augustine objected to improper interpretations being applied to Christ in the New Testament, such as the anointing of his feet with nard in the manner of dissolute women, just as the early pre-Socratics objected to improper interpretations of the gods in Homer. St. Augustine drew upon Greek allegory in homiletic works like *Enarrationes in psalmos* and also used multiple explication in apologetics like *De utilitate credendi*.[49] He explains four different levels of meaning, as did Jerome, and, like Origen, distinguishes the literal from the figurative meanings, but Augustine takes care to warn in *De doctrina Christiana* that grammar and other *artes* be used to understand the sense of the literal level before the student moves on to the figurative levels of meaning. To read a text by the letter only, without understanding its figurative meaning, is to read it carnally, according to the Old Law, as if a work had a body (letter) and a soul (figure); "Littera occidit," he notes in glossing Second Corinthians 3:6.[50]

Other Church Fathers followed Augustine in differentiating the literal from the figurative sense, generally privileging the figurative sense as long as it was used for scriptural exegesis. Eucherius of Lyons (d. ca. 449–55) agrees with the distinction between two major senses, allegorical and spiritual versus literal, although he posits only three senses—literal, tropological, and anagogical.[51] Gregory the Great (d. 604) in *Moralia in Job,* intended to interpret the book of Job according to the literal, allegorical, and moral senses, but after the fourth book concentrated on the moral and allegorical (valued as highly here as in his homilies on the Gospels and the book of Ezekiel).[52] Last but not least, Isidore of Seville (d. 636) wrote on the allegories of scripture in a work entitled *Allegoriae quaedam sacrae scripturae* and also in one on the exegesis of scriptural texts, *Mysticorum expositiones sacramentorum seu quaestiones in Vetus Testamentum,* important for the propagation of allegorical exegesis of the Bible; thereafter every commentary on the Bible for three centuries showed Isidore's influence.[53]

Euhemerism in the hands of the Church Fathers did influence the development of two forms of interpretation different from the exegetical methods of the Stoic allegorists. Indeed, in late antiquity and the early Middle Ages, euhemerism as a method came to be preserved in the factual—or literal, historical—level of meaning, a source for what came to be known as biblical typology (in which the Old Testament prefigures persons mentioned in the New) and also for etiological interpretation (having to do with causes).

Both euhemerism and typology are literalistic systems of meaning. The euhemerist reader understands the Greek and Roman gods as historical persons; the typological reader understands Old Testament figures as types of Christ or the Virgin Mary. Such a system made reading the ancient poets an acceptable activity to Greek philosophers and reading the Old Testament an acceptable activity to Christian scholars and teachers. In this sense a kinship can be discerned between euhemerism, typological analysis, and mythography: for all their variety of methods and goals, they all defend reading the text.

Typology is, then, a biblical cousin to classical euhemerism, which also centers on *historia.* The Greek Christian theologians of the first two centuries A.D. adopted typological explanations of the pagan myths using a form of symbolism (rather than allegory) involving the literal or historical level of a narrative.[54] Justin Martyr, in his *Apologia pro Christianis,* at one point interpreted Hercules, Bacchus, Bellerophon, and Perseus positively, as types of Christ, with the strength of Hercules, for example, anticipating that of Christ. In another place Justin viewed them more negatively, as figures created by devils to block the progress of Christianity, so that, for instance, Perseus's immaculate origin would weaken belief in the Virgin Birth.[55] Theophilus saw the ancient myths of the Greeks as corresponding to biblical accounts, as in the floods of Deucalion and Clymenus which parallel the deluge of Noah.[56] Tatian viewed Moses as leader of the most ancient of nations who lived before the Trojan War.[57]

That these two groups of special pleaders, the Christian euhemerists and biblical typologists, both expatiated on the literal level of the text rather than on figurative levels becomes clearer when examining a definition of the different levels of meaning, including the etiological, offered by St. Augustine in *De utilitate credendi.* St. Augustine distinguishes between the literal—which includes the historical (from *historia,* the letter), the etiological (from *aetiologia,* consideration of causes), and the analogical (from *analogia,* typology, the study of a text in relation to the congruity of the Old and New Testaments)—and the allegorical (from *allegoria,* figurative interpretation), a distinction similar to that of Origen. Nevertheless, he subsumes the first three levels under *historia.*[58] For Augustine, "history" is God's history, the history of Creation: in *De Genesi ad litteram* 1.1 he describes the fourfold division in a sacred book as "things of eternity," "facts of history," "future events foretold," and "moral precepts."[59]

Etiology—where things come from—was of interest to euhemerists and the Christian apologists; analogy—comparing two different but in some way similar things, for example, the Old and New Testaments—was of interest to the Greek Alexandrians. Neither reading goes beyond the historical level of meaning; rather, they compare one text with a privileged text or with "reality." Greek gods etiologically may be seen as mortal kings; Old Testament heroes who seem virtuous can be paralleled with New Testament figures by analogy. Moses may be seen *by analogy* as a type of Christ, through the strength of his faith in God; he is then an anticipation or prefiguring of Christ. Though Augustine uses "mystical" (allegorical) interpretation in *De civitate Dei,* he elsewhere and more often uses a typological interpretation that expounds on concrete historical events in the Hebraic sense.[60]

The etiological sense was never very popular in post-Augustinian theory, perhaps because of its connection with the literal rather than the figurative sense of meaning: in the eighth century, Bede identifies "typical" with "allegorical," and in the thirteenth, St. Thomas Aquinas again notes, in the *Summa theologica,* that the three Augustinian topics—*historia* (the literal sense), *aetiologia* (etiology, having to do with causes), and *analogia* (the relationship of like things), are all subsumed under *historia.*[61] The typological sense, as defined by St. Augustine, later merged with the moral or tropological sense—so that Old Testament figures came to represent specific virtues—or else merged with the allegorical sense, so that Old Testament figures foreshadowed Christ and events in his life. By the fourteenth century this second merger had become predominant in discussions of the senses, but was often combined with the first merger as well so that Old Testament figures signified not only Christ but also various virtues and ideas.

As for the pagan myths themselves, the Latin apologists and Church Fathers utilized euhemerism to discredit paganism and the demigods in particular. The different levels of meaning were valid for biblical texts only, even though the study of pagan literature was permitted and pursued.[62] Tertullian, who believed that the figurative level could be correctly understood only by the Church, especially objected to pagan allegorical readings (for example, Vesta as fire; the Muses—Camenae—as water; the Great Mother as earth; Osiris as the rejuvenation of life in the natural cycle). Tertullian also denigrated Saturn, Jupiter, and their disciples as murderers and incestuous fornicators; he viewed Moses as a contemporary of Inachus living before Saturn and a thousand years before the Trojan War, or fifteen hundred years before Homer. Like the anti-Homeric philosophers and euhemerists before him, he condemned all poets as liars from whom no truth about the gods could be expected.[63]

For the Latin writers who believed in Christianity and who openly disparaged paganism, the euhemeristic (or historical) rationalization of the gods was an important tool. Minucius Felix (ca. 210) portrayed in his *Octavius* a dialogue among the Christian Octavius, the pagan Caecilius, and the arbiter Minucius, with the result that Christianity defeats Epicureanism. Arnobius (fl. 300), an African professor of rhetoric, after converting to Christianity wrote *Adversus nationes* as a pledge of fidelity to a mistrustful bishop. In the first two books he apologized for Christianity and in the last five attacked mythology as found in the poets and theater; in the best euhemeristic fashion he mocked moral and physical allegorization of myths and reduced the gods to men.[64] Lactantius (ca. 306), like Arnobius a convert, in contrast was not opposed to the Egyptian cults but rather regarded the pagan gods as literary souvenirs. He reintroduced two systems, one euhemeristic and historical (he actually quotes Euhemerus in describing the gods as conquerors, legislators, and so on), the other Stoic (that is, he views the gods as natural forces). As a pupil of Arnobius, Lactantius wrote a work entitled *Divinae institutiones* that was structured similarly to that of his teacher, in that three of its books attack paganism and four celebrate Christianity as the true religion—with much information about paganism perpetuated in those first three books. Like Arnobius he applauded euhemeristic justifications of the heroes and gods, as in the cases of Hercules and Saturn.[65]

The greatest figure to discredit paganism was the Church Father Augustine, whose *De civitate Dei* attacked paganism in a way similar to that of Tatian, Clement and Origen, Minucius Felix, Tertullian, Arnobius, and Lactantius, and who similarly advanced the euhemeristic interpretation of the gods as divinized men so popular with the other writers. St. Augustine's references to pagan deities in *De civitate Dei,* many drawn from Varro's lost *Antiquitates,* are mostly negative: throughout he objects to the variety and licentiousness of the gods and in mentioning pagan worship of them attempts to convince his reader of the superiority of Christianity.[66] Although Augustine greatly loved Virgil and felt that the truth about God or his Son might exist in heathen works, his view of the pagan gods was basically euhemeristic—for example, his view of Aesculapius and Mercury, for which he uses the third, euhemeristic, book of Cicero's *De natura deorum*—and references to the divinities outside *De civitate Dei* are few and incidental.[67]

After the close of the patristic era, the fourfold method of allegorical interpretation continued to be applied in Bible commentaries by theologians and eventually was assimilated into the *artes praedicandi* by preachers, whereas mythographic allegoresis continued in the Middle Ages, especially in the works of Neoplatonic philosophers and the commentaries on certain classics of the school grammarians. We shall examine these two developments separately, beginning with the fourfold method of allegoresis.

The conduit for the transmission of scriptural allegoresis from the Greek Alexandrians to the later Middle Ages was provided by the Latin Fathers and early commentators; thereafter, Benedictine and Carolingian commentators interested in glossing the four senses included Aldhelm, Bede, and Hraban Maur.[68] Among the later writers and commentators of the twelfth century were John of Salisbury,[69] Bonaventure,[70] and, one of the most important, Hugh of St. Victor, whose *Didascalicon* urged three readings of Scripture, the historical, allegorical, and tropological. Hugh also declared in *De scripturis et scriptoribus sacris* that *allegoria* comes from a relation between two concretes: "Est autem allegoria, cum per id quod ex littera significatum proponitur, aliud aliquid sive in praeterito sive in praesenti sive in futuro factum significatur" ["allegory exists, moreover, when that meaning which is set forth literally, *ex littera*, signifies something done either in the past, the present, or the future"]. After Scripture is studied historically, he goes on, then it can be studied allegorically and morally (tropologically).[71] He is followed by St. Thomas Aquinas and Dante in the thirteenth and fourteenth centuries, whom we have already mentioned,[72] and by Hugh of St. Cher. Hugh of St. Cher notes that "historia docet factum, tropologia quid faciendum, allegoria quid intellegendum, anagoge quid appetendum" ["history teaches what has been done, tropology what is to be done, allegory what is to be understood, analogy what is to be striven for"]; he also compares the four senses to the four coverings of the tabernacle, the four winds, the fourfold cherubim, and the four rivers of paradise.[73]

More important for the history of mythographic allegoresis, the purpose of scriptural allegoresis gradually changed in the Middle Ages as the power of the Church increased. From institutional apology and textual rationalization emerged the Augustinian focus on the spiritual training of the individual cleric, needed to propagate the Church teachings, and, later still, on the spiritual edification and enhancement of the Church's members. By the twelfth century, the fourfold method was regarded as an aid to the mystical *ascensus ad Deum;* by the fourteenth century, preachers intent on combatting heresy and the weakening of the Church used the method to adorn their sermons.

In the later Middle Ages, if not in ancient Greece, both interpretations of meaning, literal and figurative, were viewed as equally true, but true in different ways. St. Bonaventure in discussing the "fourth light," that which illuminates the mind for the understanding of truth, declares: "Although in its *literal* sense it is *one*, still, in its spiritual and *mystical* sense, it is *threefold*, for in all the books of Sacred Scripture, in addition to the *literal* meaning which the words outwardly express, there is understood a threefold *spiritual* meaning."[74] The four senses might overlap but there is no ambiguity or equivocation, according to St. Thomas: "These various readings do not set up ambiguity or any other kind of mixture of meanings, because, as we have explained, there are many, not because one term may signify many things, but because the things signified by the term can themselves be the signs of other things."[75] Most important, the literal meaning is one with, inhabited by, the figurative meaning: they are, like God and human in the Incarnation, one and the same. Dante declares in his "Letter to Can Grande," now citing Aristotle, " 'As a thing is with respect to being, so it is with respect to truth'; and the reason for this is that the truth concerning a thing, which consists in the truth as its subject, is the perfect image of the thing as it is."[76]

The seeds for this later usage appear even in the early Church Fathers. We have already discussed the well-known pedagogical passage from the *De doctrina Christiana* (3.5), which describes the Word of God as having an incarnational nature, both divine and human, in its figurative and literal meanings. Other Christian exegetes of the late empire similarly expatiated on the spiritual or figurative level of the text, as opposed to the literal, corporal level, as leading to understanding and then moral change. For John Cassian (ca. 360–435), allegorical methods of exegesis open up the deepest meaning of Scripture, beginning with *theoria*, or the three senses, tropological, allegorical, and anagogical, which terminate in the most profound understanding of divine and sacred truth. Thus, *theoria* or contemplation comes before purgation or *actualis*—correction of morals and elimination of vices.[77] Similarly, in the fifth century Eucherius of Lyons, in his preface to *Formulae spiritualis intellegentiae*, correlates the three figurative senses of allegory with the threefold "wisdom of the world"— physical, ethical, and logical or natural, moral, rational—concealed under a historical narrative, "quam gestorum narratione futurorum umbram praetulisse confirment" ["which {allegory} they confirm has given, by a narration of deeds, a foreshadowing of the future"]. Thus the moral sense "ueritatem nobis factorum ac fidem relationis inculcat" ["inculcates in us the truth of the deeds and reliability in the telling of them"], the allegorical sense "ad uitae emendationem mysticos intellectus refert" ["applies mystical knowledge to the improvement of life"], and "anagoge ad sacratiora caelestium figurarum secreta perducit" ["the anagogical uncovers the more sacred secrets of the celestial figures"].[78] According to this fourfold method, "heaven" might be understood literally as the sky, tropologically as heaven, anagogically as angels, and allegorically as baptism.[79]

By the Carolingian period, later in the Middle Ages, the three allegorical senses had multiplied into seven, in the *Enarrationes in libros regum* by Angelom of Luxeuil, all still meant to enhance faith, morals, and understanding. Angelom reveals that the original triple division was the origin of these *septem sigilli,* which include, in addition to *historialis,* the *allegorialis* (allegorical); a combination of these first two; the proper or topical in relation to any hint of Deity; *parabolaris* (one thing written in Scripture but something else meant—parable); prefigurations of the two comings of the Savior, of either the first or the second or both; and finally, the method (like *allegorialis* but differing in that it serves morals rather than faith) that has a "twofold preceptive quality, in that it both points to a definite moral to correct living, and also carries a figure of a larger life meant to be foreshown."[80]

If the figurative senses exercise human faculties in understanding, as distinct from the more corporal association of the literal sense, then St. Bonaventure's twelfth-century definition makes this distinction more specialized: he relates the allegorical sense to the understanding of divinity, the tropological to the spiritual life, and the anagogical to the interrelationship between the two. There exists a threefold *spiritual* meaning, which the appropriate guide should pursue, whether the doctor of divinity, the preacher, or the mystic,

> namely, the *allegorical,* by which we are taught what to believe concerning the Divinity and humanity; the *moral,* by which we are taught how to live; and the *anagogical,* by which we are taught how to to be united to God. Hence all Sacred Scripture teaches these three truths: namely, the eternal generation and Incarnation of Christ, the pattern of human life, and the union of the soul with God. The first regards *faith;* the second, *morals;* and the third, the *ultimate end of both.* The doctors should labor at the study of the first; the preachers, at the study of the second; the contemplatives, at the study of the third. The first is taught chiefly by Augustine; the second, by Gregory; the third, by Dionysius. Anselm follows Augustine; Bernard follows

Gregory; Richard (of Saint Victor) follows Dionysius. For Anselm excels in reasoning; Bernard in preaching; Richard, in contemplating; but Hugh (of Saint Victor) in all three.[81]

The sermon-writer Robert of Basevorn, in his *Forma praedicandi* of 1322, understands the types of meaning to reflect the gradual perfecting of human in his ascent to God. The purpose in using the various senses differs in each case, but follows Bonaventure's distinction: "Faith is built by allegory; morals are formed by tropology; the contemplatives are raised by anagoge." Robert's allegorical sense, like his tropological sense, focuses on the human microcosm: human spiritual history (here represented by Old Testament figures and thereby suggesting the older typological sense) concerns Christ: "An allegorical exposition occurs when one part is understood by another. For example, by the fact that David slew Goliath it is understood that Christ overcame the devil." Robert explains that not all allegories are about Christ—they can also concern the Church and her parts, whether Gentiles, Jews, Apostles, the blessed Virgin, or the saints. The tropological sense focuses on our human and individual moral life: "A moral exposition occurs when one deed that must be done by us is understood through another, as the fact that David conquered Goliath signifies that every believer ought to overcome the devil." Finally, the anagogical sense concerns the Church Triumphant and the relationship between earth and heaven: "An anagogical exposition is one in which by some deed on earth is understood another that must be done in heaven or in the Church triumphant. This is seen in many mysteries concerning the temple, by which is meant the triumphant Church as the Church militant is understood by the tabernacle. Anagoge is derived from *ana* and *goge,* the former meaning 'up' and the latter, 'leading,' as if *leading up.*"[82]

In the late Middle Ages, such an exegetical technique probably developed concomitantly with the use of the rhetorical arts of the preacher. The late medieval preacher, unlike his predecessors interested in the fourfold method, was instructed to implement his moral aim through the use of the multiple senses of scriptural interpretation. Indeed, even as early as the eleventh century, Guibert of Nogent, in *Liber quo ordine sermo fieri debeat,* forming his *Prooemium ad commentarios in Genesim* (a work to provide the preacher with sermon materials), tells the preacher to enhance his moral aim by means of any or all of the four senses of scriptural interpretation.[83]

While preaching was theoretically always significant, beginning with (presumably) the early defenders of the Old Testament, major preaching tracts early in the Middle Ages were relatively few, even with the tracts of the early Church Fathers so influencing later preachers (for example, the *De doctrina Christiana* of Augustine, finished after 426, and Gregory the Great's *Cura pastoralis,* 591). Even later, few were written—among them, Hraban Maur's *De institutione clericorum* (819), Guibert of Nogent's *Liber quo ordine sermo fieri debeat* (1084), and Alan of Lille's *De arte praedicatoria* (ca. 1199).[84] But by the fourteenth century, preaching was regarded as an imitation of the Highest Authority and was modeled apparently on the act of Creation as a kind of communication between God and human: Robert of Basevorn in 1322 declared that when God preached to Adam, He preached through Moses and some Prophets, through John the Baptist, and as Christ.[85] The purpose of contemporary homilists and poets was similar to that of the Church Fathers and early homilists, that is, to combat heresy at a time of weakening of the Church.[86]

Accordingly, "thematic preaching" developed in this third and most important phase of the evolution of preaching, beginning in the early thirteenth century. Such "thematic preaching," as exemplified by the tracts of Thomas of Salisbury, Richard of Thetford, Alexander of Ashby, and Robert of Basevorn, depended heavily on the rhetorical strategies related to *amplificatio.* Medieval structuring of the sermon rejected the rhetorical practice of *divisio,* rhetorical divisions, in favor of amplification and dilation, *dilatio* or *dilatatio.* According to late medieval tracts on the *ars praedicandi,* one means of amplifying a sermon was the use of the three allegorical senses. A late Dominican tractate indebted to St. Thomas Aquinas—a "more representative" manual than Guibert's, entitled "Tractatulus solemnis de arte et uero modo praedicandi"—lists nine ways to expand a sermon, the fourth of which is "multiplication of explanations,"[87] or a means of *dilatatio* in general. In addition, among the eight "modes of amplification"—*dilatio*—noted by one of the most prominent homilists of the early and middle thirteenth century, Richard of Thetford (fl. 1245), in an "extremely popular" *Ars dilatandi sermones,* lists as his seventh, "Exposing the theme through diverse modes, that is, literal, allegorical, tropological or moral, and anagogical senses."[88]

Similarly, in the fourteenth century Robert of Basevorn, in his *Forma praedicandi,* wrote on the "University-style" or thematic sermon associated with Paris and Oxford; he defined the various ornaments, with division as the fifth (applied, however, to the way a statement is divided into parts for amplifying) and amplification as the eighth ornament. Among the eight ways of amplifying a theme, the seventh is through the four levels of meaning. "The seventh way is to expound the theme in various ways: historically, allegorically, morally, anagogically. For example, *Jerusalem which is built as a city* may be taken historically about the Church on earth; allegorically about the Church militant; morally about any faithful soul; anagogically, about the Church triumphant."[89] In the 1080s, Guibert of Nogent had also interpreted Jerusalem in these four senses, that is, as a literal city; allegorically, Holy Church; tropologically, the faithful soul aspiring to a vision of eternal peace; anagogically, the life of the dwellers in Heaven who see God revealed in Zion.[90]

So it comes as no surprise that when, in the early fourteenth century in Italy, Dante wished to explain to his patron Can Grande the rationale for the *Commedia*, he pointed to the multiple allegorical levels operating in the following Psalm text (Vulgate 113:1–2; King James 114:1–2) based on the story in Exodus: "When Israel came forth from Egypt, the house of Jacob from a people of alien tongue, Juda became his sanctuary, Israel his domain." The Psalm verse can be interpreted as follows if the literal meaning is distinguished from the allegorical:

> Qui modus tractandi, ut melius pateat, potest considerari in his versibus: "In exitu Israel de Aegypto, domus Iacob de populo barbaro, facta est Iudaea sanctificatio eius, Israel potestas eius." Nam si ad literam solam inspiciamus, significatur nobis exitu filiorum Israel de Aegypto, tempore Moysis; si ad allegoriam, nobis significatur nostra redemptio facta per Christum; si ad moralem sensum, significatur nobis conversio animae de luctu et miseria peccati ad statum gratiae; si ad anagogicum, significatur exitus animae sanctae ab huius corruptionis servitute ad aeternae gloriae libertatem.

> [For if we consider the letter alone, the thing signified to us is the going out of the children of Israel from Egypt in the time of Moses; if the allegory, our redemption through Christ is signified; if the moral sense, the conversion of the soul from the sorrow and misery of sin to a state of grace is signified; if the anagogical, the passing of the sanctified soul from the bondage of the corruption of this world to the liberty of everlasting glory is signified.][91]

The fourfold method of allegoresis came to be used by late medieval poets as well as preachers to interpret literary texts with theological or sacred subjects, such as Dante's *Commedia*. For the Middle Ages, the similarity between secular and sacred texts derived from the texts' common use of multiple levels of meaning. Thus Dante wished Can Grande to understand that his *Commedia* on the literal level concerns the state of souls after death, whether in hell, purgatory, or paradise, but on the other three levels concerns the consequences of human free will—either just reward or punishment. That is, the third part of Dante's work, the *Paradiso,* presented to his patron along with this letter of explanation, has as its literal subject "status animarum post mortem simpliciter sumptus" ["the state of souls after death, pure and simple"]. Dante implies that this third part of the *Commedia* must be read with the promise of *anagoge* in mind:

> Si vero accipiatur opus allegorice, subiectum est homo prout merendo et demerendo per arbitrii libertatem iustitiae praemiandi et puniendi obnoxius est.

> [If, however, the work be regarded from the allegorical point of view, the subject is man according as by his merits or demerits in the exercise of his free will he is deserving of reward or punishment by justice.][92]

In what might be termed his accessus to the *Commedia,* Dante thus suggests that the understanding, morality, and faith of the soul may be advanced by means of the fourfold method—in effect an idea illustrated in the journey of his pilgrim persona through the three spiritual realms of the *Inferno, Purgatorio,* and *Paradiso* as an intellectual, moral, and theological education, an *ascensus ad Deum.*

Several critics in the past questioned Dante's seemingly heretical notion of applying biblical exegesis (explanation or annotation, interpretation) to his own poem, and indeed scholars have questioned the authenticity of Dante's letter itself.[93] But Dante's son Pietro Alighieri invoked the four levels of allegory in glossing his father's purpose in his commentary on the *Inferno,* Boccaccio also commented on the four levels in the last two books, *On Poetry,* of his *Genealogia gentilium deorum,* and it now seems clear that the levels were used by poets and preachers in England from the tenth through the fourteenth centuries. Certainly the tripartite structure of *Pearl* resembles that of the *Commedia*—*Pearl*'s setting, an arbor at harvest, leads to the underworld of the earthly paradise; the vineyard and the laborers suggest the *Purgatorio;* and the heavenly Jerusalem suggests the *Paradiso*—but in addition the structure depends on an allegorical system very like the one enunciated in Dante's "Letter to Can Grande." The allegorical structuring of *Pearl* is mirrored in other fourteenth-century poems, chiefly *Piers*

Plowman; poetic use of such a homiletic rhetorical device may explain the disjointed structure of other fourteenth-century non-homiletic poems such as Chaucer's *Book of the Duchess.*

But just as there exists a body of thirteenth- and fourteenth-century poetry with sacred subjects to which such allegorical exegesis applies, there also exists a body with more secular subjects, including mythological figures drawn from classical antiquity, to which a similar exegesis and narrative structure might apply, such as the *Roman de la Rose,* John Gower's *Confessio Amantis,* and many of the poems of Chaucer—as well as the heavily mythological cantos of Dante's own *Inferno.* Although the poetic examples mentioned above involve sacred subjects, Dante elsewhere uses secular, indeed classical figures to illustrate the third, allegorical, level: Orpheus who tames wild beasts with the music of his lyre signifies the wise human whose voice—his instrument—tames cruel hearts (*Convivio* 2.1). Dante thus distinguishes the poet's sense of allegory, with examples drawn from pagan fictions, from the theologian's, with examples drawn from the history of Christ and the Church.

Most probably there was some fourteenth-century connection between the arts of preaching and the late medieval vernacular didactic poem, and that one means of amplifying a theme—whether literally or more figuratively homiletic, whether in sermons or in homiletic poems—depended upon the multiple allegorical senses. In relation to a late vernacular poem like *Pearl,* for example, it seems very likely that these well-known and popular treatises of Christianity held far more sway over the poem than "the esoteric and far less accessible corpus of scriptural exegesis,"[94] and that vernacular treatises of the fourteenth century influenced the depiction of both the Pearl-Maiden and the penny, according to Robert Ackerman. So perhaps the *Pearl*-poet uses signs in his poem similar to the "riot" of figures—castle, ship, plow, etc.—used by the preacher.[95] Further, critics who have analyzed other poems by the *Pearl*-poet have noted his knowledge and use of the *ars praedicandi* in at least *Patience* and *Cleanness,* if not in *Pearl* and *Sir Gawain and the Green Knight.*[96]

The moral, physical, and etymological allegorism of the ancients was thus reproduced by medieval commentators and such mythography survived into the seventeenth century. One last type of allegorism was added and elaborated in the fourteenth century in particular: mythographers began to provide an ecclesiastical or Christian allegorism superficially very like that typological symbolism of the early Greek Alexandrian School that saw in classical myths aspects of events in the Old Testament or the

New—in Christ's nature or his life. The fourteenth-century voluminous *Ovide moralisé* detailed such correspondences, a practice continued by Pierre Bersuire in his much more influential *Ovidius moralizatus*. For example, Jupiter as that son of Saturn to whom the rule of heaven came by lot signifies God, the lord and master of heaven itself; Bersuire cites Isaiah 66:1, "Heaven is my throne," to tie the religious explanation firmly to the classical myth.[97] And yet he also supplies all of the other types of allegorism in his mythographic tract—often using the same examples provided by earlier mythographers reading the classics.

III. READING VIRGIL: THE COMMENTARY TRADITIONS IN THE MEDIEVAL SCHOOLS

The continuation and elaboration of the subject matter of classical mythography in the Middle Ages to a large extent depended upon and accompanied the preservation of certain classics used as schoolbooks. The works receiving annotation or commentary were selected carefully. Just as Greek mythography began with the composition of the mythological long poem, or epic, particularly Homeric epic, so it continued in some way to be associated with that genre in the late antique era, even though it also came to be applied to other literary forms. Of the classical writers to whom medieval commentators were especially attracted—Terence, Virgil, Seneca, Ovid, Lucan, Statius, and then in the period of late antiquity, Augustine, Macrobius, Calcidius, Martianus Capella, Boethius, and Fulgentius—the most important in parenting commentary traditions with mythographic significance were Virgil (70–19 B.C.), Ovid (43 B.C.–A.D. 17?), Lucan (39–65 A.D.), Statius (45–96 A.D.), Martianus Capella (ca. 410–439 A.D.), Boethius (ca. 480–534 A.D.), and, later in the Middle Ages, Fulgentius (ca. 439–533 A.D.). In addition, two other medieval works with commentary traditions were modeled on the classical eclogues and epics of Virgil—the ninth-century *Ecloga Theoduli* and the fourteenth-century *Commedia* of Dante. This latter work did not so much influence the Middle Ages as reflect in the many commentaries written upon it the late medieval interest in the commentary tradition. (For the fourteenth- and fifteenth-century Italian Dante commentaries, see the "Chronology of Medieval Mythographers and Commentary Authors" at the beginning of this volume.)

Of the classical works receiving special attention from medieval commentators, many are epic in form, a genre which itself derived from the

TABLE 1
MEDIEVAL COMMENTARY TRADITIONS

Virgil Glosses and Commentaries:
The *Aeneid* as an Allegory of Human Life

Servius and Macrobius (4th c.)
Fulgentius (also on *Thebaid*) and Remigius of Auxerre (6th–10th c.)
William of Conches on Macrobius, Bernard Silvestris, John of Salisbury, and
  Alexander Neckam (*De natura rerum*) (12th c.)
Dante and Petrarch (13th–14th c.)
Folchino Borfoni, Pomponio Leto, Zono de Magnalis, and Cristoforo Landino
  (15th c.)

Statius and Lucan Scholia:
The Greek and Theban Heroes Oedipus,
Theseus, Achilles, Hercules

Fulgentius and Lactantius Placidus on the *Thebaid* and the Scholia on the
  Achilleid (5th–10th c.)
Arnulf of Orleans and Tenth-Eleventh Century Lucan Scholia (10th–12th c.)
Lucan commentaries of Benvenuto Rambaldi da Imola, Folchino Borfoni,
  Pomponio Leto, Zono de Magnalis
  (14th–15th c.)

Glosses on the Encyclopedia of Martianus Capella:
The Wise and Eloquent Gods Apollo and Mercury and Their
Mythographic Ascent to Jupiter

The Greek Tradition: Cicero's *De natura deorum,* Macrobius's *Saturnalia,* and
  Martianus Capella (1st c. B.C.–5th c. A.D.)
Isidore, Paul the Deacon, and Hraban Maur (7th–9th c.)
Martin of Laon, the Anonymous Cambridge Commentator, and John Scot
  (9th c.)
Remigius of Auxerre (9th–10th c.)
Rather of Verona, Notker Labeo, and the Anonymous Barberinus
  (10th–12th c.)
The Florentine Commentary (William of Conches), Bernard Silvestris, and
  Alexander Neckam (12th c.)

Digby Mythographer, Arnulf of Orleans, and John of Garland on the
   Metamorphoses (12th–13th c.)
Giovanni del Virgilio, Guillelmus de Thiegiis (Paris 8010), Petrarch, and
   Giovanni Bonsignore, Comments on and Translations of the *Metamorphoses*
   (14th c.)
Pierre Bersuire and the *Ovide moralisé* (14th c.)

Glosses on Virgil's *Eclogues* and *Georgics, Ecloga Theoduli,*
and Augustine's *De civitate Dei:*
Christian Neo-euhemerism

Adanan the Scot, glosses on Virgil's *Eclogues* and *Georgics* (Berne Scholia, 7th–
   8th c.) and the *Ecloga Theoduli* (9th–10th c.)
Bernard of Utrecht and Alexander Neckam on the *Ecloga Theoduli* (12th c.)
Ecloga Theoduli Commentaries of "Steven Patrington," Odo of Picardy, and
   Anonymous Teutonicus (14th–15th c.)
Glosses on Virgil's *Eclogues* and *Georgics* by Benvenuto Rambaldi da Imola,
   Folchino Borfoni, Pomponio Leto, Zono de Magnalis (14th–15th c.)
Augustine Commentaries of Nicholas Trivet (*De civitate Dei,* books 1–22)
   (14th c.)
Augustine Commentaries of Thomas Waleys (*De civitate Dei,* books 1–10), John
   Ridewell (*De civitate Dei,* books 1–3, 6–10), and John Baconthorpe (*De
   civitate Dei,* books 1–5) (14th–15th c.)

Greek poems of Homer and was marked by the appearance of dactylic
hexameter in a long poetic narrative, or else were thought of as epic by
medieval commentators and poets. Virgil's *Aeneid* demonstrates Homeric
simplicity, unity, and consistency, whereas Lucan's *Pharsalia* and Statius's
Thebaid, in contrast, were criticized by their contemporaries as faulty.[98]
Ovid's *Metamorphoses* has recently been discussed and interpreted as an
epic,[99] and the later works—those of Martianus, Boethius, and Dante—can
be viewed as epic only in a more medieval and hence allegorical sense.

   That all these Latin works were widely influential in the Middle Ages,
however, both in themselves and as source books for mythographic commentaries, is clear from the attention paid to them by late poets like Dante
and Chaucer. Dante not only chose Virgil as a guide in the *Commedia,* but
he also included Statius as a central (and centrally positioned) character in
the *Purgatorio* (cantos 21 and 22) and Lucan, Homer, Horace, and Ovid
(along with Virgil) as the five best classical poets in the *Inferno* (canto 3).
Chaucer in the *House of Fame* (lines 1456–1512) positions various classical
poets on pillars, including the epic poets Statius, Homer, Virgil, Ovid,

Lucan, and Claudian, as well as writers on the Troy legend such as Dares, Dictys, "Lollius" (still unidentified), Guido delle Colonne, and Geoffrey of Monmouth. That Chaucer regarded the legend of Troy as epic material in the tradition of the great classical epics is perhaps also evident in his request that his "litel bok," *Troilus and Criseyde,* "kis the steppes where as thow seest pace / Virgile, Ovide, Omer, Lucan, and Stace."[100]

Virgil was one of the most important classical poets in the Middle Ages; some judge him to be the most important.[101] He achieved this position because of his authority in school instruction of rhetoric, grammar, and, at least in Macrobius's *Saturnalia,* the other *artes,* and also because of the Homeric allegorizing treatment to which his works were subjected, beginning most fully with Servius in the fourth century.[102] In addition, because of the sixth book of the *Aeneid* tracing Aeneas's descent into the underworld, he became so popular a figure in medieval legend that he was regarded as a necromancer.[103] But it is due to the pedagogical use of Virgil rather than the popular conception of him as a magician or poet that commentaries on Virgil in antiquity and the Middle Ages continued the practice of glossation of schoolbooks, which had formed part of the Greek exegetical and grammatical tradition.

In the first century A.D., Virgil was viewed as an authority in rhetorical instruction, second only to Homer. Other epic poets like Lucan, Valerius Flaccus, and Statius merely wrote heavily rhetorical oratorical verse.[104] Later, in the medieval schools, Virgil was regarded as an authority in the most significant art in the Middle Ages, grammar, a phenomenon which reflects the attenuation of the seven liberal arts into the narrowest possible confines and the vocation of most authors of the time as grammarians.[105] Thus, when St. Gregory of Tours in the sixth century declared that Andarchius had been instructed in the "works of Virgil, in the Codex Theodosianus, and in arithmetic," the bishop meant by Virgil "grammar."[106] Virgil's use in the medieval schools and his position as chief authority constituted the main difference between him and other grammatical authorities like Donatus and Priscian, or the compilers Charisius, Diomedes, and others.[107]

Why Virgil in particular should have found acceptance in Christian schools can be explained through the points of contact which he and his works shared with Christianity and through his general acceptance by the Church Fathers, many of whom studied him at a time when education remained essentially a classical experience. Most important, Virgil's fourth eclogue supposedly had prophesied the coming of Christ; in addition, the fourth-century Vulgate Bible was written in a Latin language thought to resemble that of the *Aeneid;* and Fulgentius's sixth-century allegories implied a Virgilian view of life as a pilgrimage identical to the Christian view.[108] Perhaps because of this prophecy, the *Eclogues* were more influential than the *Aeneid* up to the twelfth century,[109] when Bernard Silvestris and John of Salisbury continued the allegorization of the epic initiated by Fulgentius. But it was the esteem of the early Church Fathers who had cited Virgil profusely—Tertullian, Lactantius, Prudentius, the influential Jerome and Augustine—particularly in relation to the descent into the underworld in the *Aeneid,* that encouraged the reading of Virgil in later centuries.[110]

Although Jerome (born 340) knew many classical authors whom he quotes constantly—especially Virgil—nevertheless he criticized reading of the pagans. In the *Epistula ad Eustachium,* he fulminates, "What has Horace to do with the Psalter, or Virgil with the Gospel, or Cicero with the Apostle?"[111] He resolved this dilemma by citing Virgil as an authority only on literature, art, science, prosody, or mythology, and never on questions pertaining to Christian faith.[112] He did, however, establish a school in which grammar and rhetoric were taught and Virgil was used for his information on literary, cultural, and pagan religious matters.

Augustine, too, used Virgil as a literary model in *De civitate Dei,* wherein the poet is cited some seventy times in passages concerning Roman history, religion, and mythology, the magic arts, and the coming of Christ as heralded by the fourth *Eclogue.*[113] But Augustine also had changed his view of Virgil before he wrote *De civitate Dei,* that is, before the age of seventy-two: in the *Confessions* he reveals that in his youth he read, loved, and memorized much of the *Aeneid,* but that later he came to despise those days on which he had been moved by Dido.[114]

The second reason for Virgil's importance in the Middle Ages stems from the Homeric allegorization to which his works, particularly the *Aeneid,* were subjected. The first commentaries were not entirely or exclusively allegorical, but, because of the fourth-century philosophizing commentaries on the *Aeneid,* the *Aeneid*'s allegorically profound sixth book would come to dominate Virgil commentary of the later Middle Ages. Commentaries and scholia, most of them grammatical and not very interesting, had been written from the beginning to elucidate his poetry: often a master would compile a set from earlier authorities and then attribute the compilation to himself, or insert glosses from others while remaining anonymous, or add material to the original commentaries but ascribe it to the first author. Although the earliest scholia from the schools before the age of Trajan (A.D. 52–117) no longer exist, we know of them because of citations and allusions in other sources.[115] The earliest derive from the lectures of Caecilius Epirota in his school for young men. A Latin lexicon dependent on Virgil and surviving only in an abridged version was compiled by Verrius Flaccus in *De verborum significatu;* there was also a lost *Commentarius in Vergilium* by Hyginus, "scattered remarks" by Virgil's scholar-freedman, Iulius Modestus, and a lost commentary by Cornutus, banished in A.D. 68. Aemilius Asper authored commentaries on Virgil, Terence, and Sallust, notes from which have been preserved either in the Verona scholia or in Philargyrius and Servius, two later and very important commentators on Virgil.[116] M. Valerius Probus, a Syrian scholar, devoted himself to Terence, Lucretius, and Virgil, although he published little during his life; he influenced especially Aulus Gellius and others, leaving unpublished at his death various observations on antique works. Probus's notes have also been preserved in Servius and later writers, which suggests his preeminence among the early commentators on Virgil.[117] Many earlier scholars were used second-hand: Nonius Marcellus, a well-known fourth-century scholar, in his *De compendiosa doctrina* (whose grammatical books derive from Pliny and Probus) cites among others especially Verrius Flaccus as handled by intermediaries (for example, Caesellius Vindex and Suetonius). In the age of Trajan there were many such minor commentators, among them the grammarian Flavius Caper (who never wrote a full-fledged commentary but was cited by several sources used by Servius); Velius Longus, whose notes reappear in Macrobius's *Saturnalia* and the Verona scholia; Urbanus; and glossators Caesellius Vindex, Terentius Scaurus, and Sulpicius Apollinaris.[118]

The most important Virgil commentators in late antiquity, and the most interesting and influential in their figurative interpretations, were those of the fourth century, beginning with Aelius Donatus, whose commentary probably initiated the later scrutinization of the lines for hidden philosophical meaning. Donatus's mid-fourth-century commentary has been lost except for the life of Virgil, his dedicatory letter, and his introductory comments on bucolic poetry; we know about his comments only from Servius and references in other glosses. Donatus's *Vita* of Virgil was originally prefaced to a commentary on the *Eclogues* but was also used regularly in the schools, according to his pupil Jerome. Indeed, it was this *Vita,* repeated in Servius's *prooemium* to his own *Eclogues* commentary, which viewed Virgil's life allegorically, his works a simile for stages in psychological development.[119]

Of the remaining fourth-century commentators, other than Tiberius Claudius Donatus, whose surviving commentary from the late fourth century differs from others in that it is a lengthy prose paraphrase rhetorical rather than grammatical in focus, and Servius, whom we shall examine in detail, the most interesting and independent is Iunius Philargyrius, who wrote a fragmentary commentary on the *Eclogues* and an incomplete one on the *Georgics.* Philargyrius's explanations and glosses are simple, probably intended for someone whose Latin is unformed, perhaps school pupils. They are, however, Christian, unlike those of Donatus and Servius: in the interpretation of the fourth, "Messianic," eclogue, for example, the liberation of which Virgil speaks in line 14 is the liberation of man from sin; the blossoms on the child's cradle represent gifts from the Magi; and the snake and herbs the child will destroy symbolize the devil and pagan doctrines.[120]

Although Philargyrius was one of the two most influential Virgil commentators in the development of a commentary tradition in the Middle Ages, he cannot compare in importance with Servius, who came to be regarded as the standard Virgil critic. The so-called "Vulgate commentary" on Virgil is probably by Servius, and the additions, drawn from ninth- and tenth-century manuscripts and published with the "Vulgate commentary" by Pierre Daniel in 1600, subsequently called the *Scholia Danielis,* were probably from another, earlier commentary, possibly that of Donatus, although there is no final word concerning the controversy.[121] Servius's commentary was not only the most popular commentary on Virgil, and the only one complete, but also the only one used regularly in the medieval schools. Servius himself was a grammarian, writing for the grammar schools; grammar remained the dominant art of the trivium in the early Middle Ages.[122] While there were other influential grammarians (chiefly Aelius Donatus, whose commentary is lost, and Priscian, who cited Virgil some twelve hundred times in his various grammatical works),[123] only Servius actually wrote a full commentary which lasted. Servius's commentaries reveal an indebtedness to the more obscure, earlier commentaries, for example, that of Flavius Caper, but none at all to the commentary of Aelius Donatus; to those of Varro and Verrius Flaccus on grammar, philology, and especially antiquarian lore; and to that of Hyginus on mythology; however, he also cites many classical authors not actually used as sources—namely Sallust and Terence, after which come Cicero, Cato, Pliny, Plautus, Horace, Juvenal, Lucretius, Ovid, Lucan, Persius, Statius, Martial, and many more minor writers.[124]

Of the Roman epic poets other than Virgil, Statius, and Lucan also received some attention in the early Middle Ages. Statius had admitted modeling his epic upon that of Lucan, also criticized as an epic poet: both fail to include the epic machinery of the gods as characters while stressing the supernatural through witchcraft, which Statius, along with battle description and gory or pathetic deaths, would most admire and adopt.[125] Because of this omission, perhaps, coupled with the lack of clearly discernible unity, fewer medieval scholia and glosses exist on Statius than on any other epic writer except Lucan (fewer in number of commentators, but not necessarily in terms of numbers of glosses per commentator), although there exist three hundred copies of the *Thebaid;*[126] only thirty include glosses and marginalia, and of these only three form autonomous commentaries—those of Lactantius Placidus, Fulgentius, and Remigius of Auxerre.[127]

The other three important late classical and late medieval works, Martianus Capella's *De nuptiis Philologiae et Mercurii,* Boethius's *Consolatio Philosophiae,* and Dante's *Commedia,* transform elements of classical epic into uniquely medieval form. Martianus's *satura* or *prosimetrum,* a mixture of verse and prose which originated in the Menippean satire,[128] uses as its predominant verse form the dactylic meter of epic, invokes at the beginning the Muse of epic poetry, Calliope ("Calliope is glad to have you [Hymen] bless the beginning of her poem concerning the wedding of a god," *De nuptiis* 1), and borrows most heavily from the epics of Virgil, Lucan, and Ovid.[129] Boethius's *Consolatio* has been regarded as an imitation of Martianus's work, not inferior to Virgil in poetry and to Cicero in prose.[130] Dante's *Inferno* elaborates on the sixth book of the *Aeneid* by making Dante a type of Aeneas and Virgil a type of the Sybil.

A closer look at the influence of Martianus and Boethius on medieval letters will underscore their claims to Virgilian stature in the commentary tradition. The Carthaginian Martianus Capella's *De nuptiis Philologiae et Mercurii* exists in 243 manuscripts—it was almost as popular as Boethius's *Consolatio,* itself a school text. *De nuptiis* was also used as a textbook for its first two centuries, in North Africa, Italy, Gaul, and Spain; competing treatises on the *artes* included Boethius's handbooks on the subjects of the quadrivium, Priscian and Donatus's works on grammar, and Cassiodorus's and Isidore's introductions to the seven arts.[131] The impact of this work on the later medieval imagination has yet to be assessed, primarily because of the difficulty of its African Latin and the relatively recent date of an English translation.[132] And the few studies of this enormously influential work primarily focus on aspects that had very little impact on the later Middle Ages.[133]

De nuptiis influenced later medieval works in many ways, as William Stahl has indicated: "the fact remains that Martianus was one of the half-dozen most popular and influential writers of the Middle Ages."[134] The manuscripts in which it exists, it has been argued, even epitomize the intellectual history of the West.[135] As Professor Stahl and others have indicated, in addition to being used as a schoolbook author Martianus also affected the form of medieval allegory in prosimetrum—Boethius himself may have been inspired by him, as well as Fulgentius; Isidore borrowed from him throughout the Etymologiae. The ninth-century Irish émigrés who taught at Laon, Auxerre, Corbie, and Rheims, in northeastern France, were especially fond of him (although Martianus was never a popular author in Great Britain) and as a result spurred the writing of mythological material in another popular schoolbook, the Ecloga Theoduli, written most likely in Germany and used from the eleventh century on. Tenth-century Italian scholars took a particular interest in Martianus. Many of his allegorical figures shaped the graphic and plastic arts—manuscript miniatures of the ninth and tenth centuries and façades of cathedrals at Chartres, Laon, Auxerre, and Paris. This later medieval influence was strong in letters as well as in visual art—through the prosimetrum of the Anticlaudianus of Alan of Lille, Martianus influenced specific works, especially in the twelfth century, including Bernard Silvestris's Cosmographia, Adelard of Bath's De eodem et diverso, Thierry of Chartres's Eptateuchon.[136]

In the later Middle Ages the work declined in popularity, except for the frame (books 1 and 2) and the frequently excerpted book on astronomy (book 8).[137] Of course indebtedness to Martianus as a literary model (via Alan's Anticlaudianus) is evident in Dante's trip through the spheres (as well as Chaucer's in the House of Fame); in addition, there are other thematic and structural influences—for example, the parliament of gods to consider the granting of a human's petition (here, to grant divinity to a mortal—Philology—in order to make her worthy of her divine bridegroom Mercury) can be seen especially in Chaucer's Knight's Tale and in more comic fashion in the judging of January and May by Pluto and Proserpina in the Merchant's Tale.

Although the most important books of De nuptiis in the history of learning involved the quadrivium (here, books 6 to 9), both the setting (books 1 and 2) and the *trivium* books (books 3 to 5) affected the development of the program of the seven liberal arts. Much of Martianus's power derived from the many school glosses and commentaries on the work commencing in the eighth and ninth centuries,[138] at the time of Carolingian educational reforms which stimulated interest in the classics, and his influence was still felt in the schools in the first part of the twelfth century.

As for the *Consolatio Philosophiae*, despite an eclipse in scholastic interest in the work from the time of Boethius's death to a few centuries thereafter,[139] it was much cited, copied, translated into the vernacular, and imitated in the Middle Ages; its chief personifications of Philosophy and Fortune eventually developed distinctive iconographic traditions, especially in sculpture.[140] Over four hundred surviving manuscripts of the *Consolatio Philosophiae* attest to Boethius's popularity in the period dating from the ninth to the fifteenth century, some of the most beautiful manuscripts from the tenth and eleventh centuries, its lavish embellishment indicating that the prosimetrum[141] was preserved and treated almost like Holy Writ. A third of all of the Boethius commentaries written between the ninth and the fifteenth centuries came into being during the Carolingian period, a fifth came into being during the twelfth century, and half came into being during the fourteenth and fifteenth centuries.[142]

Like other glosses on classical epics, the Boethius commentaries grew out of the medieval schools. It has been argued that an early edition of Boethius was either owned or copied by Cassiodorus, whose ideas on education so influenced the Middle Ages, and that Boethius was well known in England in the sixth through the eighth centuries.[143] This idea is not improbable if, as Diane K. Bolton suggests,[144] the *Consolatio* was a frequently used schoolbook, an hypothesis bolstered by the fact that several manuscripts exist filled with the scholia of successive masters and their students. Boethius was probably one of the first texts to be studied in the schools, beginning with the Englishman Alcuin, who headed the episcopal school at York, regarded as one of the most important intellectual centers of the period.[145] After Alcuin, early ninth-century writers familiar with the *Consolatio* included Modoinus of Auxerre and Jonas of Orleans and in the mid-ninth century Walafrid Strabo, Sedulius Scottus, Gottschalk, and John Scot; and library catalogues of the period record copies of the *Consolatio* at St. Riquier, Nevers, Reichenau, Freising, St. Gall, Lorsch, and Murbach.[146] The most significant commentaries stemmed from the ninth century, apparently part of the Carolingian revival of the classics and education fostering the study of this work, and to a lesser extent from the Neoplatonic revival of the twelfth century. The reason for Boethius's importance stemmed from the Carolingian age's great interest, both on the continent and in England, in education and the *artes,* which mirrored Lady Philosophy's advocation of the pursuit of wisdom to the desolate Boethius.

The history of education, which relied on the classics, provides an important context for the history of mythography, or the allegorization of classical mythology; the high points of each are the same. Thus, in the Middle Ages the strongest revivals, or renaissances, of classical learning occurred during the eighth to the tenth centuries, that is, the periods of Benedictine and Carolingian reform in England and on the continent; during the twelfth century, in the school of Paris (formerly known as the school of Chartres); and during the fourteenth to the fifteenth centuries, especially in England and in the rise of Italian humanism. And within these renaissances of classical learning so important for medieval education and mythography, various classical authors with important mythological references were glossed and stressed in the schools—Virgil, Lucan, and Statius initially, in the late antique period, supplemented by Boethius, Martianus Capella, and Fulgentius, in particular, in the Carolingian period, and then all of these plus Ovid and mythographic handbooks in the twelfth and fourteenth centuries, followed by the addition of Seneca and Dante in Italy. Such revivals of learning traced their inspiration back to the classical schools, which regarded Greek Homer and Roman Virgil as having almost divine authority, especially as masters of grammar and rhetoric, and therefore as necessary for the study of the trivium.[147]

In the schools of the later Roman Empire, of course, young men destined for public life received an education bound up in part with "paganism," both because rhetoricians and philosophers in these schools were pagan[148] and because allegorical interpretation helped defend the established polytheistic religions. Indeed, in the year 362, with Julian the Apostate's creation of the Scholastic Law, Christians who taught Homer and Hesiod but who did not believe in their gods were compelled to give up teaching.[149] (Evidence also exists for the continuance of pagan rites involved in the cults of Ceres at Eleusis, Neptune at Ostia, Jupiter, Juno, and Isis at Rome;[150] and the Edict of Theodosius in the year A.D. 392 banning various pagan customs actually reveals their continuing practice.)[151] Thus, both pagan and Christian children read Homer and the poets in the fourth-century schools, such study having been granted an immunity by Julian from the threats of Church and parent.

It should come as no surprise that at this time Virgil was used widely in the schools and received much attention from commentators and lecturers, particularly from North Africa. African rhetoricians commenting on Virgil included Macrobius, Fulgentius, and Martianus Capella; the Spanish commentator Isidore of Seville also provided glosses in his *Etymologiae*. Of these, the chief proponent of Virgil was the North African scholar Macrobius. Like Donatus (whose commentaries are lost) and Servius, who commented on all of Virgil's works at the end of the fourth century, Macrobius "commented" on all aspects of Virgil's knowledge of the arts and related subjects in his *Saturnalia* in the early fifth century and glossed significant quotations from his works in his commentary on Cicero's *Somnium Scipionis*. Macrobius also shared with these other provincial scholars of Virgil an interest in etymological allegorism, the handbook and encyclopedia, and the seven liberal arts: Martianus's encyclopedic *De nuptiis* details the seven liberal arts in seven of its nine books—"perhaps the most widely used school book of the Middle Ages"[152]—and Isidore's friend posthumously organized the divisions of his encyclopedia *Etymologiae* roughly into divisions approximating the *artes*.

That these scholars of ancient classical works and culture were African or Spanish was no accident. In the late Roman Empire there was a close commercial and intellectual connection between Rome and its provinces in Africa, Spain, and Gaul, with the provinces eventually becoming more important than Italy (the Emperor Theodosius himself was from Spain).[153] Indeed, Roman civilization did not completely decline, but remained intact in the provinces, or assumed new forms. Whereas Roman civilization disappeared from Africa first, it lingered on in Spain, where the classical writers continued to be read;[154] with the Germanic invasions of the fifth century, Roman civilization was nearly destroyed, except perhaps in Vandal Africa and Italy, in the latter perhaps because of the humanistic interests of the uneducated Ostragoth king, Theodoric (493–526), under whom Boethius served.[155] The Ostragoth attracted to him not only Boethius but also Cassiodorus, who was appointed *magister officiorum,* chief of the chancellery, in 523, and who instituted various educational reforms—he brought students to Rome from the provinces, built Vivarium, a double monastery in Calabria with a vast library which attempted to synthesize traditional humanism with Christianity, and wrote the two-volume *Institutiones* outlining his system of education.

Although education had remained dual, with the secular adhering faithfully to pagan humanism and the clerical to religious asceticism,[156] the arrival of the Germanic Lombards in 568 and their gradual, incomplete, conquest of Italy in 572 brought to the northern part of the country the barbarism that had devastated the rest of Europe since the early fifth century and expunged secular education. Secular education, when it occurred at all, took place in the home in the Merovingian age of the seventh century, as evidenced in the example of Felix of Pavia educating his own nephew Flavian, who later became tutor to Paul the Deacon. Only religious education remained available, primarily to ensure an adequate supply of educated priests, either in the monasteries and their schools (with the influence of Celtic monasticism now being felt on the continent) or in episcopal schools (as occurred very early in Gaul).[157]

A more traditional form of classical education did continue in England and Ireland in the late sixth and seventh centuries because of the missionaries sent from Italy—the first, St. Augustine, sent by St. Gregory the Great in 597 and later named first Archbishop of Canterbury, and the second, his Greek successor, Theodore of Tarsus. Benedict Biscop stocked the famous monasteries Wearmouth and Jarrow in the north of England with books collected from six different trips to Rome.[158] In the early Irish schools study of the classics continued,[159] perhaps because their priests came from Britain, Gaul, and later, Spain. Only in Ireland, where Christian culture was not so burdened with classical associations and where the pre-Christian native culture had always been tolerated by the Church, could the schools synthesize Christianity and pagan antiquity. This synthesis came to Northern England and Scotland via the spread of Irish monasticism and art.[160]

Among these Irish teachers and missionaries sent to England and Scotland might have been the first Vatican mythographer,[161] possibly the same Adanan the Scot of the eighth century who glossed the *Eclogues* and *Georgics* of Virgil in an eccentric allegorical way through elaborate political parallels and who brought to Hibernian studies an interest in Greek and Roman myth, gathering loosely into one handbook all the myths he could obtain from Servius, Fulgentius, and Lactantius Placidus's commentary on Statius. The first Vatican mythographer is important as perhaps the first medieval scholar who, in his desire to collect and assimilate myth, can be termed "mythographer" rather than merely "commentator."

The Irish schools of the Merovingian period inspired renaissances both in the eighth-century Benedictine age of Northumbria and in the ninth- and tenth-century Carolingian age of France; these renaissances would lead to gloss and commentary on Martianus Capella and Boethius and to extensive use of Fulgentius, in particular. The classical tradition reemerged in a new medieval cultural synthesis of Lombard and British cultural elements exemplified by the meeting of the English Alcuin and the Lombard Paulus Diaconus (Paul the Deacon, ca. 720–97) at the court of Charlemagne.[162] Indeed, the spur of the Carolingian revival of classical humanism was the Irish and Northumbrian cleric: this scholar was involved in the creation by Charlemagne of the great court schools and in the creation by the *Scoti* (or the Irish, called so until the eleventh century)[163] of monastic schools and missions on the continent as well as in copying classical texts, writing commentaries, and book making. The Irish scholar sent to the continent helped revive the learning diminished by the Norse.[164] This Irish cleric's traces have been found in northern France, Burgundy, the territories of modern Switzerland and northern Italy, the Rhine Valley, Franconia, Bavaria, and the Salzburg area.[165] In addition to preserving the early Irish language[166] the cleric also preserved Latin and education in general: "There is a line from Ireland and Iona to Jarrow and York, and from there to the Court of Charles. Alcuin's school at Tours is the parent of the school at Fulda where Hraban carried on the same work. Different lines of descent are united at Reichenau and St. Gall, which are in relation with the newer school at Fulda on the one hand, and with the Irish on the other. Bede (Jarrow) taught Egbert (York), who taught Alcuin (Tours), who taught Hraban (Fulda), who taught Walafrid Strabo (Reichenau)."[167]

Of the activities of the Irish clerics mentioned here, the most significant for the history of mythography was the writing of commentaries. The *scoti* commented on both Martianus Capella and Boethius, probably because both were used as school authors. The earliest (and not very important) extant glosses derive from the ninth century and may have been lecture notes of teachers or their transcription by students. These early glosses on Martianus in Welsh exist in two Cambridge manuscripts (Corpus Christi MSS. 153 and 330); there is also an early commentary on Boethius (Vatican Library MS. Vat. lat. 3363) possibly by the Welsh Asser;[168] and there is a very old anonymous commentary on Boethius associated with the monastery at St. Gall (linked with St. Gall MS. 844 and Naples MS. IV.G.68, fols. 1v-92r; a longer version exists in St. Gall MS. 845, fols. 3–240, and Einsiedeln MS. 179)[169] with Old High German glosses that may have been written by one of the many Irish or Scot scholars in exile at St. Gall. These early glosses on Martianus were expanded by "Dunchad" (probably Martin of Laon) and by John Scot Eriugena, who then catalyzed the writing of the more famous and influential late-ninth-century commentary by Remigius of Auxerre on the continent.

In addition to these ninth-century commentators, influential mythographers themselves collected myths and moralized them. Of these, Remigius was the single most important figure: he can probably be identified as the second Vatican mythographer, an identification which makes sense, given the echoes of mythographic (chiefly Fulgentian) material from Remigius's Boethius and Martianus commentaries also found in the second Vatican mythographer. Also attributed to Remigius are commentaries on Terence, Priscian, and the *Aeneid*. Other mythographers of this period included the less prominent Spanish Theodulf, the bishop who taught at Orleans and wrote a poem with mythological elements, "De libris quos legere solebam," in imitation of Ovid's *Metamorphoses* and indebted to Isidore's *Etymologiae*; and the author of the very influential *Ecloga Theoduli* (possibly Gottschalk), who debated in this heavily mythographic work the superiority of biblical to classical stories.

In the tenth and eleventh centuries a lull occurred in the development of humanistic studies involving mythographers, although the Carolingian interest in certain of the classics, especially Martianus Capella and Boethius, continued, if in a literalistic and diminished way. Much of the mythographic work became derivative, minor, and performed by scholars in isolated geographical regions. Translations, grammatical glosses, and dictionaries predominated among the types of commentaries extant. In Italy in the eleventh century Papias the Lombard completed his dictionary indebted, in part, to the Carolingian commentaries on Martianus Capella with their plethora of references to obscure Roman gods. In Germany a similar interest was furthered by Notker Labeo, who translated into Old High German both Martianus's *De nuptiis* and Boethius's *Consolatio*, in the process transcribing many of Remigius's glosses.

The only new development in this rather sterile period of the tenth and eleventh centuries stemmed from the grammatical interest in Ovid, Lucan, and Statius: we have literalistic glosses on Ovid, supposedly notes from the eleventh-century lectures of the German Manegold of Lautenbach on the *Metamorphoses* (in Munich MS. Clm 4610, coming from Benediktbeuern), and also minor anonymous commentaries on Ovid's *Fasti*, in manuscripts now housed in England and Brussels; there are various tenth- and eleventh-century scholia on Lucan, mostly from Switzerland and France; and scholia on Statius's *Achilleid* were written.

Two relatively rich sources of mythographic material—and certainly reflecting the earliest explicit interest in either Fulgentius or the *Ecloga Theoduli*, which at this time came to be used as a school book—were the eleventh-century fragment by the French Baudri of Bourgueil of a moralized mythology taken verbatim from the *Mitologiae* of Fulgentius and the late-eleventh-century, very full commentary by Bernard of Utrecht on the *Ecloga*. This interest in Lucan, Ovid, Fulgentius, and the *Ecloga*—in addition to the elaboration of the earlier Carolingian interest in Boethius and Martianus and the interest in Virgil last expressed by the late antique commentators—began to grow in the twelfth century.

It was also in the twelfth century that the high-water mark in medieval commentary on Boethius, Martianus Capella, Virgil, and Ovid was reached via the intensified and intense interest in the classics found especially in France and England, where the focus of study began to shift from the rhetoric and grammar of times past to logic or dialectic and philosophy.[170] Boethius commentators looked for Neoplatonic parallels in the *Consolatio,* especially in the ninth meter of the third book, beginning "O qui perpetua"; the various mythic portions were treated similarly by the Erfurt Commentator and the very important Parisian philosopher William of Conches, the latter of whom also wrote explicitly Neoplatonic commentaries on the *Timaeus* and on Macrobius's commentary on the *Somnium Scipionis.* Martianus commentaries continued to be written, among them one by the Anonymous Barberinus (whose commentary essentially expands the earlier work of Remigius), the Florentine Commentary, a fragmentary commentary on the first book by Bernard Silvestris, and a long, less influential commentary by Alexander Neckam. These commentaries focused only on the first two (allegorical) books of *De nuptiis,* which introduce the remaining seven on the liberal arts. The Fulgentian view of the *Aeneid* as an allegory of human life was elaborated by Bernard Silvestris in his extensive commentary on the first six books (especially the sixth) and adopted by John of Salisbury in his various comments in the *Policraticus.*

Other interests from the tenth and eleventh centuries burgeoned in the twelfth century with the attention to the *integumentum* of classical myth as a (Neoplatonic) "cloak" for hidden truth (Neo-Stoic), mostly moral or cosmological. There were moralized commentaries on Lucan and Ovid (on both *Fasti* and the *Metamorphoses*) by the influential Arnulf of Orleans and Fulgentian handbooks by the English Digby mythographer and the extremely important third Vatican mythographer (who can be identified either as Alexander Neckam or Alberic of London and who wrote a well-organized allegorical version of the handbooks of the first two Vatican mythographers). The dictionary tradition begun by Papias continued, with many mythological references, in etymological works by Osbern of Gloucester and Huguccio of Pisa. There is also a commentary on the *Ecloga Theoduli* by Alexander Neckam, although it was never popular enough to drive out that of Bernard of Utrecht.

The reasons for this particular twelfth-century renaissance have been well documented. In the twelfth century, the French cathedral schools, especially in Chartres, Orleans, Rheims, and Laon, had continued the work of the Carolingian humanists, combining study of the best of the ancients and the Church Fathers; from the ninth to the eleventh century they had trained men for the Church by giving them a very rigorous education, unlike the monastery schools where standards had fallen and secular studies had been discouraged.[171] In the early twelfth century a change occurred: at the episcopal, or chapter, schools associated with cathedrals, like Chartres, where the bishop had always been the chief teacher, he became too busy (or powerful) and accordingly delegated his functions to an assistant who came to be known as the *Magister scholae*.[172] Thus, in France and Germany more than in Italy, the Latin classics were revived and the libraries expanded. The flurry of academic activity resulted in one quarter of the works in Migne's massive *Patrologia Latina* being written during this period.[173] Most twelfth-century libraries (as we can tell from their catalogues then and in later centuries)[174] included some classics, usually at least Boethius's translation of the logical works of Aristotle and those of Virgil as a school author; Greek books generally were rare.[175] Poets were read more than prose writers, except for textbook authors like Martianus and Boethius, although the range of authors read had shrunk from Carolingian times, partly because of the development of *florilegia* (collections of excerpts or quotations from various works). These anthologies came to be used in place of the entire texts, a phenomenon which probably originated in northern France.[176] The resurgence of interest in the classics, accompanied by the growth of the cathedral schools at the beginning of the twelfth century in certain locations, led to the development by the end of the century of the universities at Salerno, Bologna, Paris, Montpellier, and Oxford.[177]

In the thirteenth century the interest in the classical epic continued but, as in the watershed tenth and eleventh centuries, in a subdued fashion. Elementary education as always focused on the classics, although Ovid and Statius were not included among authors read,[178] but very few commentaries with mythographic significance were written at this time. There were several reasons for this: interest had shifted from literature to philosophy and science, an interest stimulated by the translations from Greek and Arabic and the recovery of some of Aristotle's works through Averroes;[179]

further, the writings of the twelfth-century masters drove out the classics in the thirteenth, even though these modern writers were themselves strongly indebted to the classics and the humanistic tradition.[180] Thus, only two relatively minor texts written in the thirteenth century contributed to the mythographic tradition—John of Garland's *Integumenta Ovidii* and Giovanni Balbi's dictionary, heavily indebted to his predecessors Papias, Osbern, and especially Huguccio. The one development of the period strongly influencing subsequent centuries was the spread of classical florilegia, supposedly responsible for encouraging the humanism that flowered in the sixteenth-century English Renaissance.[181]

The major interests of French and English mythographers of the fourteenth and fifteenth centuries centered on Ovid and Boethius, with the earlier interest in Virgil, Lucan, and Martianus almost dying out and being replaced by a new interest in Seneca, Augustine, and new mythographic techniques. Of these developments, the most important involved Ovid. Ovidian commentaries and handbooks became longer, more elaborate and even more heavily allegorical, especially the very important *Ovidius moralizatus* of Pierre Bersuire. This concept of "moralized Ovid" had evolved from the early epitome of the *Metamorphoses* in the *Narrationes* of Lactantius Placidus to the twelfth-century moralization of Ovid by Arnulf of Orleans and to the immense compendium of the *Ovide moralisé*, in verse, revised into prose and published by Colard Mansion in the fifteenth century. In England the major Ovidian and Fulgentian interests of mythographers were reflected in the *Fulgentius metaforalis* of John Ridewall; the *De deorum imaginibus libellus,* an anonymous and literalistic Latin handbook using Bersuire's early draft of the *Ovidius moralizatus* as a base; and the fifteenth-century *Archana deorum* of Thomas Walsingham, among others.

In addition, a plethora of Boethius commentaries introduced heavily Christianized or heavily Aristotelian glossation in their interpretations. The Boethius commentators ranged from William of Aragon, Tholomaeus de Asinariis, the False Thomas Aquinas, Pierre d'Ailly, and Regnier of St. Tron, to the fifteenth-century Dionysius Carthusianus (Denis the Carthusian, or Denis de Leewis) and Arnoul Greban and the sixteenth-century Josse Bade d'Assche in France, with Nicholas Trivet in the early fourteenth century in England and Guillermus de Cortumelia in Spain.

Of these the most important commentator, Nicholas Trivet, anticipated the Italian and French renaissances with his commentary on Seneca's tragedies and, apparently in tandem with Thomas Waleys, with a commentary on Augustine's *De civitate Dei*. There also appeared commentaries on Augustine by John Ridewall and John Baconthorpe. In the same period the *Ecloga Theoduli* received new attention from an English commentator known as "Stephen Patrington" who depended heavily on Alexander Neckam's earlier commentary in England, from Odo of Picardy in France, and in the fifteenth century from the Anonymous Teutonicus in Germany. New mythographic techniques developed too. Special exempla called "pictures" drawn from classical mythology and moralized, adorned the homiletic and patristic writings of fourteenth-century friars like Nicholas Trivet, Robert Holkot, and Thomas Hopeman.[182]

Also at this time in Italy, Ovidian commentaries and mythographic handbooks flourished, as well as Dante commentaries. Specific commentaries on the *Metamorphoses* included the allegorical commentary by Giovanni del Virgilio and the moralized translation by Giovanni Bonsignori. Mythographic encyclopedias designed to present complete and exhaustive material about the gods provided, in addition, defenses of poetry and theories of various types of poetry. These manuals, whose authors returned to classical sources for information rather than relying on medieval florilegia culled from those sources, included two very significant handbooks, the *Genealogie deorum gentilium libri* of Boccaccio and the *De laboribus Herculis* of Coluccio Salutati (d. 1406). It is possible that Salutati was influenced by Trivet's commentaries on Seneca's Hercules tragedies, or those of the fourteenth century on Boethius's poem on the Labors of Hercules (*Consolatio* 4m7). Certainly it is likely that he himself influenced the fifteenth-century Spanish work on Hercules by Henry of Aragon.

In addition to the Ovidian commentaries and Fulgentian handbooks, there also appeared primarily grammatical commentaries on Virgil and Lucan and various full-length commentaries on Dante. Among those glossing the *Aeneid* we find Petrarch, Benvenuto Rambaldi da Imola, Folchino Borfoni, Pomponio Leto, Zono de Magnalis, and Cristoforo Landino, all of whom except Landino also wrote commentaries on Lucan. Finally, various fourteenth- and fifteenth-century writers, often borrowing material from one another, commented on Dante. The most allegorical commentaries belong to Jacopo della Lana, Pietro Alighieri, Giovanni Boccaccio, and Benvenuto Rambaldi da Imola. The others, from the earliest to the latest, inform, describe, and explain rather than allegorize: the Ottimo commentary, the Anonymous Selmi, those of Graziolo de Bambaglioli, Jacopo Alighieri, Fra' Guido da Pisa, the so-called False

Boccaccio, Francesco da Buti, the Anonymous Florentine, and, in the fifteenth century, those of Giovanni da Serravalle, Guiniforte Barziza, Stefano Talice da Ricaldone, and Cristoforo Landino.

In this introduction to the backgrounds of medieval mythography, the method of allegorizing classical myths has been defined, first, by tracing the origins of the method back to the defense of Homer by ancient Greek philosophers. This early incarnation has revealed even then the pattern of conflict between letter and spirit, a pattern which in the Middle Ages culminated in the arts of the preacher and the fourteenth-century poet. Second, the reasons for the medieval preservation of rationalized classical mythology—the subject matter of classical mythography—have been explored in the classics used in the medieval schools and universities and then by the vernacular poets. From its inception to its final medieval presence mythography supports the figure as transcendent over the letter.

To turn from the origins of mythographic allegoresis, in classical philosophy, to its deployment in the medieval construction of an early literary criticism by means of an ethics and cosmography dependent upon pagan mythology, necessitates a closer look at two major scholars whose work grew out of a North African nexus and who were equally important in creating a Latin and vernacular literary tradition—Macrobius and Fulgentius. In both cases their focal point was Virgil.

Chapter Two

THE HELIOCENTRIC COSMOGONY
AND THE TEXTUAL UNDERWORLD:
MACROBIUS'S MULTICULTURAL
READING OF VIRGIL

Despite the Christian denigration of classical myth and the application of Greek methods of allegoresis to scriptural materials in the period from the second to the fourth century, in the same period the ancient methods and matter of mythography were advanced by provincial scholars who sought to keep alive the earlier Greek traditions.

Macrobius's multicultural background perhaps explains his pluralistic philosophical and theological scholarship on Virgil and Plato. In his *Saturnalia,* this North African provincial offers an Egyptian and heliocentric interpretation of Stoic doctrine: the one god manifested through many gods is the sun god Apollo. His two oldest Italian gods, Saturn and Janus, he identifies with concepts of primeval time. His interest in cosmology blossoms in his Neoplatonic, Stoic, and Neopythagorean commentary on the *Somnium Scipionis,* Cicero's *Dream of Scipio.* Both the *Somnium* commentary and the *Saturnalia* were influenced by Cicero, in form and theme, and by Servius, in their treatment of mythological references from Virgil. The commentary is riddled with quotations from and glosses on the Roman master Virgil, especially on the sixth book of the *Aeneid* and the hero's descent into the underworld. For the Middle Ages, the most important aspect of the *Aeneid* was the epical *descensus ad inferos* in the sixth book, in which Aeneas with the aid of the Sybil meets the spirit of his father (who reveals to him secrets about his own future), as well as the shades of Dido and other infernal inhabitants.

Macrobius contributed to the development of Virgilian exegesis and medieval mythography in specific ways: he advanced a Neoplatonic-Stoic allegoresis of the gods and he interpreted the underworld in the sixth book of the *Aeneid* both Neoplatonically and Stoically, that is, as an image for this world and as the physical *under*world. He would inspire later commentators to read the whole of the *Aeneid* in a similarly complex, moral way, chief among them Fulgentius in his exposition on the content of Virgil and Bernard Silvestris in his twelfth-century commentary on the first six books. In addition, Macrobius's Stoic and Neoplatonic approaches would influence William of Conches in the twelfth century, not only in his own commentary on Macrobius's *Somnium* commentary, but also in his commentary on the *Timaeus,* his glosses on Boethius's *Consolatio Philosophiae,* and his so-called Florentine Commentary on Martianus Capella.

Motivated by the desire to defend Virgil from his detractors, Macrobius resembles the early Greek Stoic defenders of Homer. So well known was Virgil by the late fourth century that Macrobius in the *Saturnalia* assumes his reader's familiarity with the text of Virgil and rationalizes Virgil's "errors" as problems in literary criticism.[1] While neither of Macrobius's major works can be described as a commentary on Virgil, nevertheless he cites and glosses Virgil in the *Saturnalia* (written as early as 395 or as late as 430) and, more diffusely, in his later *Commentarii in Somnium Scipionis* (written as early as 410 or as late as 430).[2] Primarily interested in the *Aeneid,* even though he occasionally cites examples from the *Eclogues* and *Georgics,* he includes in the *Saturnalia* perhaps an average of fifty references to each book of the *Aeneid,* most of these clustering in the third to the sixth books of the *Saturnalia,*[3] and in the commentary only twenty-two references total to all of Virgil's works, most of them referring to the sixth book of the *Aeneid.*

Rather interestingly, Macrobius's use of Virgil in the two works changed in the years (as many as fifteen) between the purported times they were written. In the earlier work, the defense of Virgil, which stems from Macrobius's desire to examine "literary problems," is based upon Virgil's knowledge of all the liberal arts, a knowledge assumed because of the Roman poet's understanding of the underworld as it was portrayed in the sixth book of the *Aeneid* and which accordingly directs Macrobius's mythography in the *Saturnalia.* In the later work, the *Somnium* commentary, Macrobius's reliance on specific mythological references from the sixth book of the *Aeneid,* probably influenced by Servius's own Stoic moralization, develops into a Neoplatonic and Stoic view of the earth as an underworld. Macrobius's Stoic philosophical view of a heliocentric universe governs the mythography in the *Saturnalia*—the gods there function as aspects of the sun, or the one god; this is not an exclusively Virgilian idea. Macrobius continues this interest in Stoic cosmology in the Neoplatonic and Neopythagorean commentary on the *Somnium Scipionis,* but the rest of that long treatise is not especially Virgilian or mythographic. The approach to Virgil in the *Saturnalia,* then, can be characterized as rationalizing, literary, structural; but it is allegorizing, philosophic, and specific in the commentary on the *Somnium.* These differences match those in the literary models provided by the Roman Cicero and the two works' respective Greek antecedents.

Cicero's Stoic influence is strong in both works. According to Macrobius in the *Saturnalia* (1.1.5), the form of this work reflects the common post-Augustan use of the dialogue, or else the genre of the banquet, based on Plato's *Symposium,*[4] but perhaps in its mythography the *Saturnalia* is most indebted to Cicero's *De natura deorum. De natura deorum* represents a model dialogue among exponents of different views of cosmology and philosophy, including the Stoic and euhemeristic. As for the second work, Cicero's *Somnium Scipionis,* a pastiche of the "Vision of Er" which ends Plato's *Republic,* is the base text for Macrobius's own long commentary.

Philosophically, the model for each Macrobian work guides the North African scholar's mythographic purpose in each, although both works are Stoic or Neoplatonic in approach.[5] That is, in the *Saturnalia* Macrobius sees all the gods discussed as Stoic manifestations of one god, the sun, an ancient Egyptian belief in part overlaid by Neoplatonic and Neopythagorean as well as Stoic ideas. Macrobius's sources in the *Saturnalia* include the Greek treatises of Porphyry the Neoplatonist and allegorist (ca. A.D. 233–301): *On the Sun, On the Styx, On the Return of the Soul,* the *Homeric Questions,* and the *Cave of the Nymphs,* this last work a mystical description of the universe that pretends to be a commentary on book thirteen of the *Odyssey.*[6] In the commentary, Macrobius's mythological Virgilian glosses stress the Stoic view of this world as a physical underworld. Again Macrobius is indebted to Porphyry in the commentary on the *Somnium Scipionis:* Porphyry in the *Cave of the Nymphs* views caves as symbols of the visible and invisible world; so, too, the gods are planets and the poet hides truth under poetic imagery, or so Macrobius argues in agreement with the earlier Stoic defenders of Homer (*Somn. Scip.* 2.10.11, on *Iliad* 1.423).[7]

Even though Macrobius's two works share a common interest in Virgil, a common literary model in Cicero, and a common Stoicism or Neoplatonism, they influenced the Middle Ages in diverse ways. The commentary on Cicero's *Dream* became enormously influential in the Middle Ages, not so much for its Virgil glosses as for its discussion of dreams and fabulous narrative, which affected the development of vernacular poetic in the later periods.[8] Macrobius's *Somnium* commentary fostered the development of a literary theory, based on dream narrative, that would later affect the composition of medieval poetic fiction. Macrobius commenting in the *Somnium* on Cicero's commentary on Plato was followed by various Neoplatonist commentators in the twelfth century, especially William of Conches, who wrote a commentary on this Macrobian work. The earlier work, the *Saturnalia,* remained too large and unwieldy to use as a school text[9] and was also little used in Virgil commentaries, much less in mythographic texts, perhaps because its myths derived from the Egyptians and Greeks rather than the Romans. While the *Saturnalia* was not generally known, its dialogue form influenced Fulgentius in choosing the genre of his commentary on Virgil's *Aeneid* and much of its Neoplatonism influenced Martianus.[10] In addition, Isidore certainly knew the work, Bede seems to have known it in *Disputatio hori et praetexti,* and John of Salisbury extracted portions of it, many of them different from the text we know, in the *Policraticus;* both Isidore and Bede compiled miscellanies very like the *Saturnalia,* itself modeled on the *Noctes atticae* of Gellius (from the first century A.D., when such collections became popular).[11] The allegorical frame—the fiction of Virgil's knowledge of the seven liberal arts—used to structure the work in seven books would appeal especially to another Virgil commentator and allegorizer, as we shall see in the next chapter—Fulgentius.

Especially in the *Somnium* commentary, Macrobius was also influenced in his mythography by the Neoplatonism and Stoicism of his near contemporary, Servius. Like Servius, Macrobius provided extravagant (if more extensive) allegorizations of the gods, in the "commentary" on Virgil known as the *Saturnalia,* and like Servius, he employed Neoplatonic and Stoic glosses on Virgil in his commentary on the *Somnium Scipionis.* Macrobius names the grammarian as one of the twelve chief characters in the *Saturnalia,* all of whom are supposedly based on historical persons, even though the real Servius (b. ca. A.D. 365–370) would have been very young at the time the *Saturnalia* ostensibly took place (384, but newer speculations set it after 430).[12]

Although Neoplatonist and Neopythagorean views have been attributed to him because he cites Plotinus,[13] Servius's contributions to mythography are also colored by Stoicism and euhemerism and reflect in his defense of Virgil the allegorical interpretations—physical and moral or grammatical—of which the early Greek commentators were fond. In addition to the transmission of rather conventional but allegorical or rationalistic mythological glosses from these philosophical systems, Servius's contributions were primarily two: the use of topical allegory in relating Virgil's work to stages and incidents in the poet's own life (an idea which will be examined more intensively in the next chapter of this study) and a cosmological (Neoplatonic and Neopythagorean) allegory of the underworld in the sixth book of the *Aeneid* that provides a frame for some of the mythological references in this same book and elsewhere reflecting especially moral or grammmatical allegorism.

This latter contribution is the most important for Macrobius, in the *Saturnalia* in particular (although Servius is not consistent in his treatment of the gods). Of the conventional mythological glosses found in the commentary on the *Aeneid,* the explanations of the gods and heroes as physical phenomena come from the Stoics, their rationalization as historical figures come from the euhemerists, and their moral significations, often based on Greek etymologies, come from the Stoics and Neoplatonists.[14] These types of mythographic comment would reappear in the *Saturnalia,* just as they had appeared in the important intermediary of Cicero's *De natura deorum.*

Given this Virgilian-Servian context, we can now turn to a more detailed discussion of Virgil references and literary cruxes in Macrobius's *Saturnalia.* In both the *Saturnalia* and the *Somnium* commentary we shall be interested in Macrobius's use of Virgil and the role played by Servius the Grammarian. The three-day December festival of the Saturnalia comes to symbolize the knowledge of the seven liberal arts displayed by Virgil—and therefore to symbolize the cultural movement from darkness to light.

I. HELIOCENTRIC STOICISM IN THE *SATURNALIA:* THE EGYPTIAN APOLLO

The stated purpose of the *Saturnalia,* as Macrobius reveals in the dedication to his son Eustachius (*Sat.* 1. *praef.* 1ff), is to transmit the Hellenic culture he has derived from his reading, even though much of his treatment of gods is colored by Egyptian and North African mythology and theology, which also affect his interpretation of Virgil. Macrobius was not himself Greek but probably a Roman provincial from Africa who could read Greek at sight. The *Saturnalia* opens, appropriately, on the evening of the Saturnalia, when some guests gather at the home of learned Vettius Agorius Praetextatus, an anti-Christian character based on the prefect of the city of Rome in A.D. 367 who had been honored for his knowledge of religion, philology, Greek and Latin poetry and prose; he explains most of the mythology in the dialogue. Most of the other characters are Greek-born or know Greek at least slightly, except for the nobleman Evangelus, who is hostile to Hellenism. Other aristocrats are present: Nicomachus Flavianus, Symmachus, and the Albini, Rufius and Caecina. There is a group of scholars—the host's friend Eustathius, a philosopher; the rhetorician Eusebius; and Servius the grammarian—as well as three self-invited guests, the Greek physician Disarius or Dysarius; the former boxer and supposed Cynic philosopher Horus (an Egyptian by birth); and the youth Avienus, who may be the fabulist Avianus or Avienus.

It is Evangelus whose cutting remark (*Sat.* 1.24.2) prompts the introduction of the work's main theme, Virgil's knowledge. The "debate" over Virgil's knowledge continues until the following day, when other guests arrive and there follow dinner and postprandial conversation, all in the course of seven (unfinished) books. The seven books treat of the main theme, Virgil as an authority on all branches of learning—the seven liberal arts, in effect: philosophy, astronomy, augural and pontifical law, rhetoric and oratory, and the use of earlier Greek and Latin writers.

The order of the books and the knowledge of Virgil discussed can be epitomized as follows: after the first day and the defense of Virgil against the attacks of Evangelus, on the second day Eustathius demonstrates Virgil's understanding of astrology and philosophy, Flavianus in a lost portion declaims on his knowledge of augury, and Praetextatus exposes his knowledge of pontifical and augural law (although only the first twelve chapters, on pontifical law, have survived), all in the third book. On the third day Symmachus apparently explains Virgil's knowledge of rhetoric (at the beginning and end of the fourth book, which have been lost); and in the fifth and sixth books, on this same day, literary matters are taken up, namely through Eusebius on Virgil's oratory (*Sat.* 5.1), Eustathius on Virgil's indebtedness to Homer (5.2–17) and on various passages (5.18–22), Furius on Virgil's indebtedness to Latin poets in entire verses (6.1–3), Caecina on Virgil's indebtedness in single words (6.4, 5), and Servius on other passages (6.6 to the end of the book). The seventh and last book contains non-Virgilian material—after-dinner conversation on philosophy's suitability to a social gathering, table etiquette, and the physiology of eating, drinking, clothes, science, and so on.

The range of Virgil's purported knowledge in the *Saturnalia* is impressively broad-ranging and profound, a topos that Macrobius may have gleaned from Servius in his commentary on book 6 of the *Aeneid.* During his descent Aeneas receives "knowledge" about the underworld not normally available to the living. On the basis of those secrets, the grammarian Servius introduces this sixth book in his own commentary by declaring, "Totus quidem Vergilius scientia plenus est, in qua hic liber possidet principatum, cuius ex Homero pars maior est. et dicuntur aliqua simpliciter, multa de historia, multa per altam scientiam philosophorum, theologorum, Aegyptiorum" ["all of Virgil, but especially this {sixth} book {of the *Aeneid*}, is full of knowledge, of which the greater part is from Homer and the rest from history and from the high knowledge of philosophers, those who discourse on the gods, and Egyptians"] (Servius, *In Aen.* 6, *praef.*). Servius, like his contemporary Macrobius, occupies the role of defender of Virgil, in echo of the Stoic philosophers who first defended Homer's use of mythology by means of moral allegoresis.

In Macrobius the mythological glosses deriving partly from the *Aeneid* and partly from other sources mostly appear in the first book (*Sat.* 1.7–23), and actually involve religious customs and practices rather than the features of mythology. While there are brief references to Roman religious practices in later books, especially the third and fourth,[15] these very long descriptions of the gods in the first book appear here and not elsewhere for a signal reason: the evening when most of the guests have gathered initiates the festivals of the Saturnalia and Sigillaria and hence it is appropriate that the host Praetextatus explains their mythological origin (*Sat.* 1.7.14–1.11) by defining the Saturnalia as a celebration of light, or knowledge, whose sum total in the seven liberal arts is reflected in the works of Virgil.

Macrobius's understanding of the Saturnalia as a festival of light (representing truth) is based on a euhemeristic explanation, perhaps to grant it historical validity, although this powerful, symbolic euhemeristic explanation is in fact preceded by two quite different but euhemeristic explanations of the feast's name.[16] The third and most powerful explanation of the origins of the Saturnalia (in *Sat.* 1.7.28) reveals that the Pelagians, when driven from their homes, were told by an oracle in Greek to settle a land sacred to Saturn, "erectisque Diti sacello et Saturno ara" ["having erected a temple to Dis and an altar to Saturn"].[17] And so they offered to Dis human heads and to Saturn men, until Hercules insisted they offer as their symbol the mask or effigy, instead of heads, and instead of blood, candles, because in Greek the word *phota* means not only *vir,* "man," but also *lumina,* "lights" (*Sat.* 1.7.31). As a consequence, during the Saturnalia wax tapers are sent around, although "alii cereos non ob aliud mitti putant, quam quod hoc principe ab incomi et tenebrosa vita quasi ad lucem et bonarum artium scientiam editi sumus" ["others think that the practice is derived simply from the fact that it was in the reign of Saturn that we made our way, as though to the light, from a rude and gloomy existence to a knowledge of the liberal arts"] (1.7.32).

The actual philosophical basis for the festival transcends the historical explanation of its origins. In Macrobius, Saturn, his wife Ops, and his daughter Venus represent the Stoic World Soul and its processes of generation and regeneration of all that exists through the seed-fire that animates the universe. This more physical allegorical interpretation of Saturn (and then Janus) begins with Saturn understood as Chronos or Time, an idea derived from Cicero's De natura deorum (2.64) and passed on through Servius. This idea is derived from that part of the myth in which Saturn castrates his father Caelum or Heaven and throws the genitals into the sea, whence Venus appears, her name Aphrodite coming from the foam out of which she sprang. The cutting off of Caelum's genitals signifies the demarcation between Chaos and the fixed measurements of Time (Saturn) determined by the revolutions of the Heavens (Caelum).[18] The original seed-fire was responsible for creating the world, of which the individual gods represent specific faculties and attributes:

> cumque semina rerum omnium post caelum gignendarum de caelo fluerent, et elementa universa quae mundo plenitudinem facerent ex illis seminibus fundarentur, ubi mundus omnibus suis partibus membrisque perfectus est, certo iam tempore finis factus est procedendi de caelo semina ad elementorum conceptionem, quippe quae iam plena fuerant procreata.

> [And since the seeds of all things which were to be created after the heavens flowed from the heavens and since all the elements which could comprise the complete universe drew their origin from those seeds, it followed that, when the universe had been provided with all its parts and members, then, at a fixed point in time, the process whereby seeds from the heavens caused the elements of the universe to be conceived came to an end, inasmuch as the creation of those elements had now been completed.] (Sat. 1.88)

Macrobius then shifts from the Stoic concept of the Generative Reason, or Logos spermatikos, to Stoic etymologizing: that Saturn's name derives from the Greek word for phallus, "quae membrum virile declarat, veluti Sathunnum: inde etiam satyros veluti sathunos, quod sint in libidinem proni, appellatos opinantur" ["as though to say 'Sathunnus'; and, since Satyrs are prone to lewdness, this name is thought to have the same derivation and to stand for 'Sathun' "] (*Sat.* 1.8.9).[19] It is appropriate that Saturn's sickle that fell on the island of Sicily was also said to be responsible for its fertility, although Macrobius also admits that the sickle symbolizes the (destructive) passing of time.

Complementing this process of celestial regeneration, the process of earthly regeneration (presumably nonhuman) in Macrobius is governed by the figure of Ops, Saturn's wife, whose joint-festival, the Opalia, is also celebrated in December (sixteen days before the "Kalends of January," *Sat.* 1.10.23). Saturn and Ops are worshipped together because it is at this time that the fruits for which they are responsible have been harvested. Saturn is identified as heavenly, and Ops as earthly, growth, both identifications based on etymologies of their names, "Saturn" from *satur,* or "growth from seed," as the gift of heaven, and "Ops" either from *ops,* "bounty," through which life is nurtured, or from *opus,* the work necessary to produce the fruits of the fields ("quos etiam non nullis caelum ac terram esse persuasum est Saturnumque a satu dictum cuius causa de caelo est, et terram Opem cuius ope humanae vitae alimenta quaeruntur, vel ab opere, per quod fructus frugesque nascuntur," 1.10.20).

Analogous to the macrocosmic regeneration, there exists a second, microcosmic, kind of generation, that which reproduces life already created by the original seed-fire, and this form of seed-power is represented by Saturn's daughter Venus, responsible for human intercourse: "animalium vero aeternam propagationem ad Venerem generandi facultas ex umore translata est, ut per coitum maris feminaeque cuncta deinceps gignerentur" (*Sat.* 1.8.8).

Macrobius's approach can be described as Stoic, derived in part from Cicero's *De natura deorum* in its second book and inspired in part by the grammarian Servius's commentary on the *Aeneid,* although neither Cicero's Balbus nor Servius systematizes his mythology as thoroughly as Macrobius. In Cicero's *De natura deorum,* after dividing the gods into two classes, gods of the universe and gods of the "little universe" of the human household (Roman religion, with Janus, Vesta, the Penates), Balbus explains all of them through Stoic means, that is, cosmologically, physically, morally, and etymologically, or architecturally and domestically. Among the gods discussed in the second book are Liber and Ceres, Saturn and Caelus, Jupiter and Juno, Neptune and Pluto, Pluto and Proserpina, Janus, Vesta, and the Penates, Apollo and Diana, and Venus, briefly; of these, he rationalizes immoral tales by means of physical explanations—about the castration of Caelus by his son Saturn, his devouring of his own children, his own capture by his son Jupiter, Jupiter's marriage to his sister Juno, and the rape of Proserpina (*Nat. deorum* 2.60–69).

The immoral tales in Cicero conceal a Stoic cosmological theory: the gods personify the four elements and the four regions of the universe (*Nat. deorum* 2.64–66). Saturn's castration of Caelus signifies that "the highest heavenly aether, that seed-fire which generates all things, was dissociated from the human genitals" and did not require them to proceed in its generative work: "Caelestem enim altissimam aetheriamque naturam, id est igneam, quae per sese omnia gigneret, vacare voluerunt ea parte corporis quae coniunctione alterius egeret ad procreandum." Saturn, in Greek Kronos or Chronos, or "spatium temporis," attempts to eat all of his children, who signify the passing years, devoured by age that is never sated (hence "Saturn" comes from "quod saturaretur annis," "sated with years"). When Jupiter (Jove) puts him in chains in an attempt to restrain his course and bind him in the stars' network, this "iuvans pater" or "helping father" (our father and the father of the gods, whose name "Jove" comes from *iuvare*) attempts to bind and restrain time. His wife Juno who is also his sister is actually the soft air between the sea and sky closely connected to the aether, or Jupiter; her name too is derived from *iuvare*. Saturn's two other sons are Neptune and Dis, or Pluto. Neptune governs the water (his name comes from *nare*, "to swim" with the first letters changed and a suffix added, just as "Portunis" the harbor god comes from *portus*, "harbor"); Dis or Dives rules the earth and is called "the rich," Pluto in Greek, "quia et recidunt omnia in terras et oriuntur a terris" ["because everything returns to the earth and is born from the earth"]. When Dis raped Proserpina, in Greek Persephone, or the seed of the corn, and she vanished from the earth, her mother Ceres who is bearer of the corn searched for her in a fable which accounts for the passing of the seasons. "Ceres," from Geres, *gero*, "to bear," is explained by Balbus: the first letter of her name is accidentally changed in the Greek form "Demeter," from *Ge Meter*, "Mother Earth," just as the name "Mavors" comes from *magna vertere*, "to overturn the great," and the name "Minerva" signifies "she who levels down" or "she who threatens."

The grammarian Servius in his commentary on the *Aeneid* also identifies many of the gods by means of Stoic explanations, as representing physical forces or phenomena, primarily because he believes Virgil was following a *physica ratio* in the creation of his poem, although he argues that the gods can choose to assume mortal bodies and thus gain anthropomorphic being if they wish to be seen by mortal eyes (*In Aen.* 7.416). These Stoic ideas stem from the Stoic portions of Cicero's *De natura deorum* as well as Cornutus's *Theologiae Graecae compendium,* the pseudo-Heraclitus's *Quaestiones Homericae,* and apparently the sixteenth book of Varro's lost *Libri divinarum rerum.*[20] Most of the physical interpretations occur in the first and eighth books, with slightly fewer in books 2, 3, 4, 6, and 7, and only one each in books 5, 10, and 12 (none in books 9 or 11). Among the thirty-one notes revealing physical allegorism, some listing more than one mythological figure, the conventional views reappear, of Juno as *aer,* "lower sky" (sister and wife of Jupiter, *aether,* "upper sky"); Neptune as the sea; Ceres as the earth that consumes dead bodies; Minerva as the highest part of the upper air; Vesta as earth, the container of fire; Vulcan as the fire that flies through the air (or Volicanus, from *volare*); Iris as the rainbow; Venus as sexual energy; and Cerberus, like Ceres, as the earth that consumes the dead.[21] There are fourteen other notes involving physical allegory but not concerning the gods.[22]

Servius also moralizes some of the gods by using rather conventional Stoic etymologies based on their functions, many of which are taken from the Stoic portions of Cicero's *De natura deorum.* Jove's and Juno's names both derive from *iuvando,* "helping" or "assisting" (*In Aen.* 1.4, 1.47); "Jupiter" comes from *iuvans pater,* "helping father" (*In Aen.* 4.638); and Juppiter, "quo constat omnia," is Zeus in Greek, "id est vita," or "life" (*In Aen.* 1.388). Venus is called Acidalia because she causes worries (*acidas* in Greek), or because of the fountain Acidalius in the city of Orchomenus, Boeotia, wherein the Graces wash themselves and which is sacred to her (*In Aen.* 1.720). "Liber" comes from "freeing" ("a libertate," *In Aen.* 4.638, and also *Georgics* 1.166, "ab eo, quod liberet, dictus") and "Mercury" from his vocation, because he governs traders, "quod mercibus praeest" (*In Aen.* 4.638).

Because Janus shared with Saturn the original rule of Italy and because their months January and December are contiguous, Macrobius in the *Saturnalia* also explains Janus as a type of cosmic principle in a discussion indebted to Cicero on the household gods. Cicero's Stoic interpretation of the Roman household gods, that is, Janus, Vesta, and the Penates, has explained their general name "Penates" from *penus,* a word used to describe "a store of human food of any kind," or *penitus,* meaning those who dwell within the recesses of the house, whence the gods are called occasionally "Penetrales" ("the dwellers within") by the poets (*Nat. deorum* 2.68); Vesta is included because we address our last prayers and sacrifices to her as guardian of the hearth who also guards our most private lives. Cicero's etymologies reappeared in the North African Martianus Capella as well as in Macrobius's *Saturnalia,* but thereafter met with little further interest. Cicero says that Janus as the god of household doorways derives his name from *ire,* "to go," so that *jani* are archways and *januae* are portals in secular buildings; he leads in every sacrifice because it is the beginning and end that are most important (2.68).

In Macrobius's more figurative interpretation in book 1 of the *Saturnalia* (1.9.9–16), Janus's two faces signify either knowledge of the past and future, or Apollo and Diana, Janus and Jana, because Apollo is worshiped by the Greeks as "God of the Door" and Diana is worshipped as keeper of the city's streets, or because in his role as Apollo the sun he controls the two heavenly gates which the sun opens at day and closes at night. Alternatively, in Macrobius, Janus is the universe itself, based on an etymological interpretation: "alii mundum id est caelum esse voluerunt Ianumque ab eundo dictum, quod mundus semper eat, dum in orbem volvitur et ex se initium faciens in se refertur" ["Others hold that Janus is the universe, that is to say, the heavens, and that the name is derived from *eundo,* since the universe is always in motion, wheeling in a circle and returning to itself at the point where it began"]. Janus was also thus viewed by the Phoenicians as a coiled serpent which swallows its own tail "as a visible image of the universe which feeds on itself and returns to itself again." Other Neoplatonic views of Janus describe him as the two-faced doorkeeper of heaven and hell (this from Gavius Bassus in his book on gods, cited in Macrobius, "quasi superum atque inferum ianitorem"), or even as the god of gods (according to the ancient songs of the Salii). Similarly, Marcus Messala referred to Janus as the "compass" of the heavens which joins the four regions of earth, air, water, and fire, a "vis caeli maxima," "great power of the heavens," that unites two opposing forces. The remainder of this section of the *Saturnalia* is devoted to the reasons for various names used to invoke Janus and to Roman religion; one interesting name, Consivius, comes from *conserendo,* "sowing," "id est a propagine generis humani, quae Iano auctore conseritur" ["that is to say, as the patron of the propagation of the human race, whose sowing and increase are of him"]. Vestiges of many of these ideas linking Janus to cosmic generation, the sun, and household stores reappear in an early twelfth-century English calendar illumination where Janus appears in a feasting scene for the month of January (see fig. 4).

One important aspect of Macrobius's Stoic cosmogony has no source in Cicero or Servius, or the approaches they represent. Praetextatus, as a pagan

4. Janus, for January, with cauldron; the occupation of January, feasting. Calendar. MS. Bodley 614, fol. 3r (1100–1150, English). By permission of the Bodleian Library, University of Oxford.

and lover of the antiquarian, in a long discourse attempts to relate all the Roman gods to one god, but instead of the Stoic choice of Jupiter (or Zeus) picks as the one god Apollo, source of all truth, playing the role of the Egyptian sun god. In Egyptian mythology from the beginning—as recorded in the fifth century B.C. by Herodotus, the Greek historian—the creator and demiurge was a sun god, "lord of Heliopolis" northeast of Cairo, beginning with Atum (ca. 2000 B.C.) and continuing with the Theban Amun in the New Kingdom (ca. 1000 B.C.); from the sun god descended the rulers of the throne of Egypt, including Osiris, beloved of Isis.[23] To construct this philosophical shift, the noble and learned Praetextatus relies on the opening question of Virgil's *Aeneid* (1.8) which asks concerning Juno, "quo numine laeso" ["What divine power had been offended"]. Praetextatus answers by means of a Neo-Stoic view of all gods as one god. Virgil's question "ostendit unius dei effectus varios pro variis censendos esse numinibus, ita diversae virtutes solis nomina dis dederunt. unde *en to pan* sapientum principes prodiderunt" ["shows that the various activities of a single deity are to be regarded as equivalent to as many

various divinities, so the diverse powers of the sun have given names to as
many gods. And this is the origin of the maxim proclaimed by the leading
philosophers: that the Whole is One"] (*Sat.* 1.17.4).

Praetextatus accordingly, after introducing Saturn as the founder in
whose honor the Saturnalia was celebrated in December, thereafter explains
the development of the (Roman) solar calendar. Saturn's wife Ops and the
god Janus are honored in the month of January; the other months are also
named after the gods, we learn in a discussion which includes Jupiter,
Pluto, Apollo (or Dionysus-Bacchus-Apollo), Liber Pater (Dionysus),
Mars (identified with Liber), Mercury, Adonis and Osiris-Apollo, Pan,
Echo and Saturn, and again Jupiter. In the exegesis which follows, even
though, as we have seen, the earliest Italian gods Saturn and Janus were
deployed as Stoic metaphors for the World and Time and the origins of the
world, these later gods and heroes—Liber Pater, Ceres, Mars, Mercury,
Aesculapius, Salus, Hercules, Sarapis and Isis, Adonis, Nemesis, and
Jupiter—manifest aspects of the Egyptian sun god, or Apollo. The Egyptian and Neo-Stoic cast to this approach has affinities with Christian
hierarchy, given Saturn the generative principle as the Father and Apollo
the sun as the Son of God.

Apollo is of course the god whom Praetextatus in the *Saturnalia*
(1.17.5–65) chiefly relates in various ways to the sun. Apollo stands for
that physical power of the sun which governs healing and prophecy (just as
Hermes or Mercury is the name of that power from which speech comes).
According to various authorities—among them Plato, Chrysippus, Speu-
sippus, Cleanthes, and Cornificius—Apollo is one and not many, *solus,*
because the sun possesses great brilliance and hurls forth rays, apparently
unlike any other heavenly body. Its rays have been likened to Apollo's bow
and arrows in that they overcome feverish men. Thus Apollo appears with
the Graces actually held in his right hand and the bow and arrows in his left
to show that he heals faster than he harms. Because the heat of the sun helps
men recover from disease, the god derives his name Apollo as if it were
Apello (so he drives away—*appellentem*—ills.) His many names reveal his
relationship with the sun: Loxias, Delius, Phoebus, Phanes, "the Ever-
begotten and Ever-begetting," Lycian Apollo, Lykos, "Father of the People," "God of Shepherds," Eleleus the Golden-haired, Smintheus or God of
the Silver Bow, Karneios, Killaios, Thymbraios or the Rainmaker, Phile-
sios, and Pythian, the latter from a word meaning "to make rotten"—as the
result of great heat—and not from the killing of the serpent Python, whom

the newborn Apollo battled and killed after the snake had attacked the cradle where he and his twin Diana were sleeping.

The act of killing the Python, as explained physically or naturally by Macrobius's Stoic glossator Praetextatus, signifies that at the creation of earth, after shapes began to form over the mass of the matter, the heats of the heavens allowed fiery seed to flow into earth and two stars were born, the sun and the moon, the sun higher and the moister moon lower, as if they were the "substance" of a father and mother. Their actual mother Latona was the earth, according to physicists, and Juno, who sent the Python and who had wanted to prevent the birth because of her jealousy of Latona, was the moist and heavy air which prevented the sun and moon from shining through the dense air. The serpent (here Macrobius follows the Stoic Antipater) in reality was a spiral of serpentine vapor infecting things with the corruption caused by heat and moisture, eventually burned away by the sun (Apollo).[24] In a related explanation, Apollo's other names include Janus, by which some Romans worship him because as a twin god he gives light to the moon and thus truly illumines both day and night (*Sat.* 1.17.64), and Delphian. As a bearded statue Apollo is also worshipped by the Assyrians in Hierapolis.

In Cicero's *De natura deorum* (2.68–69), the sun and moon play important cosmic roles, but without the Neoplatonic and Egyptian mythological significance accorded them by Macrobius. To the four regions of the earth made fabulous through the gods, Balbus adds the sun and the moon, and then household gods (mostly Italic in nature) associated with human life on earth. Apollo is the sun and Diana the moon, Apollo called Sol from *solus*, "alone," either because he alone of all the heavenly bodies is of such great size or because when he rises his brightness dims the other stars and he appears "alone." Diana the moon, or Luna, is the same as "Lucina" (from *lucere*, "to shine"). Among her epithets is that of "Omnivaga," or the Wandering One, because she is one of the seven "wandering" planets (*vagantibus*). Diana is from *dies*, "day," and is called so "quia noctu quasi diem efficeret," because she turns night into day through her light. Finally, she is summoned in childbirth because the embryo matures in seven to nine "moons" (*lunae*), "qui quia mensa spatia conficiunt menses nominantur," called months (*menses*) because they form measured (*mensa*) spaces or times. Cicero adds that "Venus" comes from *venire*, "to come," and means she who "comes" to all things.

So it is from Macrobius's Greek sources, especially Porphyry, rather than from Cicero's Stoic book in *De natura deorum,* that he gets his Neoplatonic and Egyptian regard for the sun (or Apollo) as a central cosmic force to which all the other gods relate. Jupiter (*Sat.* 1.15.14) is *auctor lucis,* "author of the light," and Diespiter is "Father of the Day." Mars is called the sun, as are Minerva and Jupiter (1.17.68–70). Liber Pater or Dionysus is identified with Apollo and the sun in a long chapter (1.18) based on Aristotle's *Inquiries into the Nature of the Divine* that centers on temples and statues, religion and ritual, rather than mythology. Liber Pater governs the soil and crops in his function, as the sun couples with the moon, Ceres (1.18.23).[25] However, Liber Pater is the same as Mars (hence Bacchus is called by that epithet used to describe Mars—"warlike"), and therefore is also the sun (1.19.1–6), just like Mercury, at least when he expresses the warlike activity of Mars—that is, when anger is inflamed by the fiery danger of the sun. Mercury is also equated with Apollo (1.19.7–8), his wings suggesting the swiftness of thought, in that he apparently rules over the mind just as the sun represents the mind of the universe; for this reason he is called Argiphontes because *argus* (Argos, whom he lulled to sleep) functions as the sky shining with many eyes—the stars—and because the sky is both bright and speedy in its movement.

    In addition to these gods appear other demigods and heroes analogous in function to Osiris as king and related to the sun by birth or function (*Sat.* 1.20). Aesculapius is associated with the sun as a healthful power aiding minds and bodies, and Salus, performing a similar function, is associated with the moon; both are identified with serpents, although only Aesculapius is linked with Apollo because of his skill in divination and augury. The Egyptian (Theban) Hercules resembles "solis potestas quae humano generi virtutem ad similitudinem praestat deorum" ["that power of the sun which gives to the human race a valor after the likeness of that of the gods"]. (While there has existed many a Hercules, this demigod of divine valor as the last slayed the Giants in defense of Heaven; these Giants represented men who refused to believe in the gods.) Hercules or Heracles, "Pride of the air," must be the sun because the light of the sun *is* the pride of the air. Sarapis also is the sun, just as the Egyptian sister of Osiris, Isis, is "terra vel natura rerum subiacens soli. hinc est quod continuatis uberibus corpus deae omne densetur, quia vel terrae vel rerum naturae altu nutritur universitas" ["the earth, or the world of nature, that lies beneath the sun; and so the whole body of the goddess is thickly covered with a series of breasts, because everything that exists draws its sustenance and nourishment from the earth or world of nature"].

In an adaptation of the myth of the descent into the underworld, Adonis too is revealed as the sun through the religious practices of the Assyrians (*Sat.* 1.21.1–12): the upper hemisphere is Venus, the lower, Proserpina, with six of the zodiacal signs located in the upper and six in the lower hemisphere; when the sun enters the lower sector, Venus mourns as if the sun had died and had passed into the power of Proserpina, or the antipodes. The sun (or Adonis) is reborn when it enters the upper six signs. In the myth of the killing of Adonis by the boar, the boar signifies winter. Similarly, the Mother of the Gods is earth and Attis is the sun—also like Isis and Osiris.

Other gods or beings associated with darkness, the underworld, or earth itself are similarly read as aspects of the sun (*Sat.* 1.22. 1–6). Nemesis constitutes the power of the sun, "ista natura est ut fulgentia obscuret et conspectui auferat, quaeque sunt in obscuro inluminet offeratque conspectui" ["whose nature it is to make dark the things that are bright and remove them from our sight and to give light to things that are in darkness and bring them before our eyes"], or else that "which we worship to keep us from pride." Pan can also be understood as the sun because he rules all material substance, elemental matter, according to the Arcadians. Thus his horns and long beard suggest the way the light of the sun lights up the sky above and below, and his goat's feet symbolize the way matter acts as the first principle of earth, in that the goat always moves upward as it feeds, just like the sun which sends its rays to earth from above. Echo as his sweetheart represents the harmony of the heavens. Finally, in chapter 23, in a curious Egyptian reversal of the usual Stoic role, even Roman Jupiter is treated as a power of the sun, the great leader of the other gods and spirits analogous to the sun as leader of the zodiacal signs and constellations—an idea derived from Plato on Zeus.

Euhemeristic explanations of the gods, one of the three approaches to mythology in Cicero and Servius, play little part in Macrobius's *Saturnalia.* Macrobius insists on Virgil's knowledge as the single guiding structural principle. In Cicero, the euhemeristic—and antimythological—historical explanations (in his third book only) do not influence Macrobius's euhemeristic histories of the Saturnalia; none of Cicero's genealogies centers on Saturn, first founder.[26] What few interpretations Macrobius offers may have come from Servius, who appears unfamiliar with Cicero's third book. In the euhemeristic glosses mostly found in the first, third, and sixth books of Servius's commentary on the *Aeneid,* in a total of about forty notes,[27] Servius cites Varro, Sallust, Hyginus, Septimius Serenus (a second-century poet), Eratosthenes, and Diodorus Siculus, although the commentator's methodology and approach are derived from the euhemerist Palaephatus and the euhemerizing historian Polybius.[28] Some of these glosses, like Macrobius's histories of the Saturnalia, are etymological and reveal the connection between an eponymous hero and a specific tribe or nation; but many such explanations are rejected by Servius as fabulous. He supplies instead a rationalization, as in the origin of the Myrmidons (*In Aen.* 2.7), the birth of Orion (1.535), Minotaurus (6.14), and the she-wolf that suckled Romulus and Remus (1.273).[29] Such euhemeristic explanations were useful in debunking all sorts of pagan myths and would appeal to the point of view of Servius's Christian readers in the Middle Ages.

As a theme for the *Saturnalia,* the passage from darkness to light dramatizes the revelation of Virgil's hidden knowledge in the *Aeneid* and, among other things, the *Saturnalia*'s understanding of Saturn's (formerly pagan) festival as having heliocentric cosmological and philosophical (Stoic) significance. Apollo the sun god, revealer of truth, symbolizes the intellectual light provided by the scholar reading his text(s). In this sense, the illustration provided for an eleventh-century manuscript of *Dionysius de cyclis cum aratis historicis* epitomizes the relationships (see fig. 5). Here two teachers, one at either side of the page, stand next to the sun or the moon, in order to understand (presumably) the figures of the constellations massed chaotically above them. From the vantage point of the philosopher or scholar "reading" the stars or the heavens, or else explaining what these "texts" signify to their students, the literary theory associated with the reading of Virgil in Macrobius's works merely extends the Neoplatonic symbolism to the "underworld" of *fabula* itself.

II. THE TEXTUAL AND STOIC UNDERWORLD IN THE COMMENTARY ON THE *SOMNIUM SCIPIONIS*

As noted previously in this chapter, the development of a literary theory based on earlier Greek methods that would later in the Middle Ages affect the composition of poetic fiction was chiefly fostered by Macrobius's commentary on the *Somnium Scipionis,* which was in turn Cicero's commentary on Plato, and by various Neoplatonist commentators in the twelfth century, especially William of Conches, who wrote a commentary on this Macrobian work.

In his commentary on Cicero's *Somnium Scipionis,* Macrobius combines

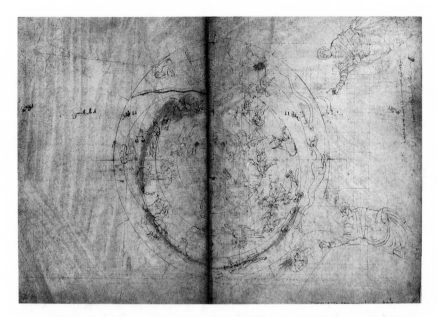

5. Two teachers, sun, moon, constellations. From *Dionysius de cyclis cum aratis historicis.* MS. Phillip. 1830, fols. 11v–12r (11th c.). Courtesy of Staatsbibliothek zu Berlin, Preussischer Kulturbesitz.

ideas from Cicero's partly lost *De re publica* (begun in 54 B.C. and published in 51 B.C.), this section of which was modeled on the closing episode in the tenth book of Plato's *Republic,* and from Plato's *Republic* itself. As he had in the *Saturnalia,* he drew on several Greek sources, especially the Neoplatonist Porphyry, who had written on Homer in his works *Homeric Questions* and *Cave of the Nymphs.*[30] But the most important Greek influence may have been the very idea of a dream apparition as modeled on the literary dream appearances described by Homer and Hesiod, and imitated by Cicero in his account of the dream of Scipio Africanus.

The concept of a visionary dream allowed for the intersection between the mortal and the immortal. Hesiod in the *Theogony* has a waking vision in which he sees the Muses on Mount Helicon and receives instruction from them. His waking vision was transformed into the topos of the relevatory dream, possibly by Callimachus in the now fragmentary and mostly lost *Aitia,* then by Ennius and Propertius; in Ennius's *Annales,* Homer's shade appears in a dream and instructs Ennius in Pythagorean metempsychosis, the topography of the underworld. In Cicero's *De re publica,* Scipio Africanus, as the dead grandfather of the interlocutor, appears within a dream to talk about the future and discourse on the soul, the cosmos, and the Other World (or Milky Way). This dream is the text for Macrobius's two-book commentary.

In Cicero's Greek model for the visionary dream, Plato's eschatalogical "Vision of Er," Er of Pamphylia dies in battle, but returns to life before the funeral to tell how he has traveled with other souls to a strange place where there exist two chasms, in the sky and earth. Here judges allow the just to take the right-hand side but the unjust must take the left-hand side leading downward. The souls proceed to Lachesis and in a lottery take a lot for the next round of mortal life. (To make the right choice one must be able to distinguish good from evil—some follow the habits of past life, as when Thersites became an ape.) Each soul is led to a chosen guardian angel for his protection and then to Clotho, who ratifies the choice, while Atropos spins it out. Finally, they pass to the river Lethe to drink and forget and then to be born again.

Cicero's *De re publica* ends with a mystical experience like that of the "Vision of Er," but more politically attuned to the needs of the Empire. In this Roman and patriotic work, those who have aided the commonwealth will have a blessed future; the discourse on the soul and the underworld (the Milky Way) is here delivered not by a stranger but by the interlocutor's dead grandfather, Scipio Africanus, who appears in a dream.

To construct what might be termed a vision of the underworld, conceived physically as earth, Macrobius in his commentary on Cicero's *Somnium* employs Stoic allegorical and mythological glosses from Virgil, all of which involve the underworld, the afterlife, or the supernal and cosmic regions. Most of these Virgil references either relate the gods to the underworld, Hades, or discuss life on earth as an underworld, or interpret Virgil cosmologically and physically. The Virgil glosses cluster in the Macrobian commentary's first book (a total of fifteen), with only seven in the second; of twenty-two references in both books of the commentary, fifteen concern the *Aeneid,* with only six on the *Georgics* and one on the *Eclogues.* Of the non-*Aeneid* references, which appear primarily in book 1, chapters 15 through 18, and sporadically in book 2, most concern cosmological and astronomical matters. The fifteen *Aeneid* glosses, found mostly in book 1, chapters 3 through 14, refer to mythological or cosmological matters, with a few exceptions,[31] and eleven of them focus on the sixth book and Aeneas's descent into the underworld. Unifying many of these glosses because it introduces the concept of human life as an underworld, the sixth book is also Macrobius's choice for the first reference in his Stoic (or Neo-Stoic) reading of Virgil.

Macrobius's initial reference to Virgil carefully segregates the present, mortal world from the world of the afterlife. Macrobius constructs an analogy between earth and sky and Hades and earth by glossing Virgil's concept of "insomnia": *Insomnia,* according to Virgil, constitute false dreams "sent by departed spirits to their sky" (from *Aeneid* 6.896). For Macrobius, Virgil "caelum hic vivorum regionem vocans quia sicut di nobis, ita nos defunctis superi habemur" ["used the word 'sky' with reference to our mortal realm because the earth bears the same relation to the regions of the dead as the heavens bear to the earth"] (*Somn. Scip.* 1.3.6).

For the individual to perceive the secrets of the afterlife is difficult during our mortal life because, according to Macrobius in a Stoic comment on Aeneas's vision of the gods destroying Troy in book 2 of the *Aeneid,* a cloud obfuscates the mortal vision of the soul, only partly lifted during sleep when the soul is disengaged from the body's physical functions (*Somn. Scip.* 1.3.19, on *Aeneid* 2.604–6). Similarly, the soul enslaved by the body hesitates to leave it at death, an idea bolstered by the last words of the *Aeneid,* "nisi cum gemitu fugit indignata sub umbras" ["with a moan it passes indignant to the Shades below"] (*Somn. Scip.* 1.9.4, on *Aeneid* 12.952).

This concept of a "vision below" complements Macrobius's Stoic view in the *Saturnalia* that all the gods above function as aspects of the sun, or the one god. In the commentary, however, his Neoplatonic interpretation of the Virgilian underworld is directed by his antecedents—the description of the afterlife in Plato's "Vision of Er" at the end of the ten books of the *Republic* and the *Somnium Scipionis* from Cicero's *De re publica.* Thus Macrobius declares about this *Somnium* that "ut animas bene de republica meritorum post corpora caelo reddi et illic frui beatitatis perpetuitate nos doceat" ["the purpose of the dream is to teach us that the souls of those who serve the state well are returned to the heavens after death and there enjoy everlasting blessedness"] (*Somn. Scip.* 1.4.1). Comparing Cicero's *Somnium* with Plato's "Vision," Macrobius acknowledges that both describe the afterlife and underworld but that it is a recently dead man who in Plato's "Vision" returns to life to utter one revelation, whereas in Cicero's book all is revealed by an ancestor to a living sleeper (1.1.2).

Macrobius accordingly explains that the human place in the afterlife (or underworld) is determined by individual strength in refusing the temptations of the body while on earth. First, according to the *Aeneid,* heroes are assigned to the underworld in a special "aethera largiorem" ["ample ether"] (*Aeneid* 6.640), wherein "nosse eos solem suum ac sua sidera profitetur" ["they know their own sun and stars of their own"] (*Somn. Scip.* 1.9.8). Second, whatever consumed men during mortal life, whether good or evil, will similarly consume them in the afterlife:

> . . . quae gratia currum
> armorumque fuit vivis, quae cura nitentis
> pascere equos, eadem sequitur tellure repostos.

[The selfsame pride in chariot and arms that was theirs in life, the selfsame care in keeping sleek steeds, attends them when hidden beneath the earth.] (*Aeneid* 6.653–55; cited *Somn. Scip.* 1.9.9)

Also mostly from the sixth book of the *Aeneid* Macrobius draws his Stoic description of the geography of the underworld and the mythological rivers or figures of Lethe, Phlegethon, Acheron, Cocytus, Styx, Prometheus, and Sisyphus. The context for the discussion derives from Cicero, however. Macrobius cites Cicero's Scipio Africanus as speaking of life on earth as a death in which men depart from their bodies as from a prison (*Somn. Scip.* 1.10.6). This pronouncement prompts Macrobius to clarify the moral significance of the geography of Hades, beginning with the rivers: the underworld is a figure for human vice.

> Oblivionis fluvium aliud non esse adserentes quam errorem animae obliviscentis maiestatem vitae prioris, qua antequam in corpus truderetur potita est, solamque esse in corpore vitam putantis; pari interpretatione Phlegethontem ardores irarum et cupiditatum putarunt, Acherontem quicquid fecisse dixisseve usque ad tristitiam humanae varietatis more nos paenitet, Cocytum quicquid homines in luctum lacrimasque compellit, Stygem quicquid inter se humanos animos in gurgitem mergit odiorum.

[The river Lethe was to them {philosophers} nothing more than the error committed by the soul in forgetting its former high estate before it was thrust into a body, and in thinking that its sole existence was in a body. Similarly, they thought that Phlegethon was merely the fires of our wraths and passions, that Acheron was the chagrin we experienced over having said or done something, even to the point of becoming melancholy, as is the way with human beings, that Cocytus was anything that moved us to lamentation or tears, and that Styx was anything that plunged human minds into the abyss of mutual hatred.] (*Somn. Scip.* 1.10.10–11)[32]

Constructing a concept of the underworld as morally delinquent, its inhabitants flawed and marred, Macrobius first alludes to the punishment of Tityus and the vulture which gnaws incessantly at his liver (*Aeneid* 6.598). He explains that this is

nihil aliud intellegi volentes quam tormenta conscientiae, obnoxia flagitio viscera interiora rimantis, et ipsa vitalia indefessa admissi sceleris admonitione laniantis, semperque curas, si requiescere forte temptaverint, excitantis tamquam fibris renascentibus inhaerendo, nec ulla sibi miseratione parcentis lege hac.

[nothing more than the pangs of conscience prying into our insides as though they were guilty of offense, and incessantly tearing at our vitals with the chastisement of a sense of guilt, and like the vulture clinging to the "liver that grows anew" {*Aeneid* 6.600}, always stirring up cares that are ready to subside, never relenting with a feeling of pity.] (*Somn. Scip.* 1.10.12)

There follow references to Tantalus and Sisiphus who are similarly punished in Virgil's Hades for their vices.

These two glosses concern those who "hang outstretched on spokes of wheels" (represented by Tantalus) and those who "roll a huge stone up a hill" (represented by Sisyphus). The first signifies someone who never thinks of the future, controls his actions with reason, or solves problems virtuously—this person is whirled around, as if on a wheel, by chance and accident, "casibus et fortuitis," because he depends too heavily on fortune. The second wastes his life in useless efforts, as if he rolls a stone up a hill, "atram silicem lapsuram semper et cadenti similem illorum capitibus imminere qui arduas potestates et infaustam ambiunt tyrannidem numquam sine timore victuri" ["the dark stone ever wavering and seeming ready to fall back on their heads, who strive for the arduous places of power and the accursed sovereignty of an autocrat, destined never to reach their goal without fear"] (*Somn. Scip.* 1.10.14–15). Finally, Macrobius repeats Virgil's phrase (*Aeneid* 6.743), "patimur manes," to suggest that "each of us suffers his own punishment," underscoring the idea that the body actually represents the underworld and mortal life is death for the soul (*Somn. Scip.* 1.10.17).

Again and again Macrobius in his Neoplatonism distinguishes between a material and spiritual realm while he singles out earth, the epitome of materialism, as a kind of Stoic underworld, in other, minor, references to the individual soul and the World Soul in the *Somnium* that illustrate their points by means of references to the *Aeneid*.[33] Some nonmythological, more astronomical and cosmological, Stoic Virgilian references explain planetary bodies and the structure of the universe, mostly in chapters 15 through 18 of book 1.[34] In addition there remain several non-Virgilian mythological references to Saturn and Caelus, Lethe, Bacchus and Orphic rites. Saturn and Caelus are mentioned as examples of base fabulous narrative that provides through plot "matters that are base and unworthy of divinities and are monstrosities of some sort" (*Somn. Scip.* 1.2.11). The river Lethe is interpreted as part of the underworld signified by the earth, the "drink of souls" or *potus animarum* found in the lower part of the material universe, which contrasts with the drink of the nectar of the gods found in the highest and purest part of the universe, in the heavenly realm (1.12.11).

Macrobius's concept of the underworld may also have been influenced by Servius's allegorical and Neoplatonic-Neopythagorean interpretations of book 6 of the *Aeneid,* which similarly inspired and directed the commentaries on the *Aeneid* of sixth-century Fulgentius and twelfth-century Bernard Silvestris, and later Dante's *Inferno,* itself a kind of greatly amplified "comment" on this particular Virgilian book. Human life interpreted as tainted, an underworld, would influence these later allegorizations of Aeneas as an ideal man whose masterful journey into the underworld is a figure for human life. In describing the punishments of the underworld, Macrobius, like Servius before him, shows the relation between human choices of good and evil and the afterlife.

Servius's greatest contribution to mythography in general and Virgil commentaries in particular was his Stoic—or physical—view of our earth as a literal underworld surrounded by the nine spheres (the seven planetary spheres plus the two "great circles" beyond) equivalent to the circuits of the Styx and thus inhabited by those who are lower (*inferos*), inferior and infernal. Servius is glossing Virgil's line, "Noctes atque dies patet atri ianua Ditis" ["night and day the door of gloomy Dis stands open"] (*Aeneid* 6.127). This important Stoic interpretation may explain why most of the mythological references in Servius, like most of the allegorical notes (the latter of which do not necessarily involve the gods), come from the sixth book of the *Aeneid*.[35] While there are eight major moral mythological glosses in book 6 of Servius on the *Aeneid*—on Proserpina, Tartarus, Cerberus, the Styx, Tityus, Tantalus, Elysium, and the *manes*—there are a few allegorized references in other books, for example, in book 1 on Achates as anxiety ("which is always the companion of things," *In Aen.* 1.312) and in book 8 on Minerva as Prudentia (8.438). Some of these are moral, reflecting Servius's frequently fanciful explanation of their Greek etymologies and derivations, probably a holdover from the Stoic tendency to etymologize. These derivations, often false, themselves later influenced medieval mythography as they were transmitted from one writer to another who knew no Greek but who thought that the appearance of Greek words in the works of Servius (and Donatus and Priscian) signified a knowledge of Greek.[36]

Virgil's Sibyl, in responding to Aeneas about the ease with which it is possible to descend to Avernus, also suggests the difficulty of the reascent into the upper air. Servius, who is concerned about the physical location of the underworld, notes that it is not in fact under the world but that it does exist and is not merely a poetic fiction:

> in media vero terra eos esse nec soliditas patitur, nec *kentron* terrae: quae si in medio mundi est, tanta eius esse profunditas non potest, ut medio sui habeat inferos, in quibus esse dicitur Tartarus, de quo legitur bis patet in praeceps tantum tenditque sub umbras, quantus ad aetherium caeli suspectus Olympum. ergo hanc terram in qua vivimus inferos esse voluerunt, quia est omnium circulorum infima, planetarum scilicet septem, Saturni, Iovis, Martis, Solis, Veneris, Mercurii, Lunae, et duorum magnorum. hinc est quod habemus et novies Styx interfusa coercet: nam novem circulis cingitur terra. ergo omnia quae de inferis finguntur, suis locis hic esse conprobabimus.

> [Indeed, neither the solidity nor the central point of the earth permits the underworld to be in the middle of the earth: if the earth is in the middle of the universe, its depth cannot be so great that it contains, in its own middle, the underworld, where Tartarus is said to be. For concerning Tartarus one reads, "Then Tartarus itself yawns sheer down, stretching into the gloom twice as far as is yon sky's upward view to heavenly Olympus" {*Aen.* 6.578}. Therefore they thought that this earth on which we live was the underworld, because it is the lowest of all the circles, that is, the seven planets, Saturn, Jupiter, Mars, the sun, Venus, Mercury, the moon, and the two great ones. Hence we have the statement, "Styx imprisons with his ninefold circles" {*Aen.* 6.439}: for the earth is girded by nine circles. Therefore one shall demonstrate that all the things which are invented about the underworld are here, in their own places.] (*In Aen.* 6.127)

Servius supplements this Stoic view of earth as a cosmic underworld (veiled by darkness because beneath the moon, the point at which bright aether begins)[37] with a Neopythagorean gloss on the golden bough of knowledge necessary to enter the underworld, as the letter Y, symbol of the individual human life. Its forked branches suggest a means for Aeneas to return to "upper air." These branches epitomize the forked paths of Aeneas in Hades in book 6, themselves resembling the afterlife choices in the "Vision of Er"—and said to emerge in human life at the time of adolescence. After Aeneas had entered Hades, he encountered a path which forked to the left, to Tartarus, place of the wicked, and to the right, to Elysium, place of the virtuous. According to Pythagoras, human life is divided like the letter Y, in that the early first years are uncertain and drawn neither to virtue nor to vice, but at adolescence human life divides, either to the left and to vice or to the right and to virtue. About the return of the soul from the underworld,

> novimus Pythagoram Samium vitam humanam divisisse in modum Y litterae, scilicet quod prima aetas incerta sit, quippe quae adhuc se nec vitiis nec virtutibus dedit: bivium autem Y litterae a iuventute incipere, quo tempore homines aut vitia, id est partem sinistram, aut virtutes, id est dexteram partem sequuntur.

> [We know that Pythagoras the Samian divided human life like the letter Y: that is, the first part of life is undetermined, being not yet given to either vices nor virtues; but the fork of the Y begins at adolescence, the time at which men pursue either vices, that is, the left part, or virtues, the right part.] (*In Aen.* 6.136)

The golden bough is said to be divided in imitation of the letter Y and concealed in the woods through which Aeneas must pass and which is filled with beasts, just as truth, virtue, and integrity are hidden in the confusion of this life and amidst the greater part of the vices:

> ergo per ramum virtutes dicit esse sectandas, qui est Y litterae imitatio: quem ideo in silvis dicit latere, quia re vera in huius vitae confusione et maiore parte vitiorum virtus et integritas latet. alii dicunt ideo ramo aureo inferos peti, quod divitiis facile mortales intereunt. Tiberianus aurum, quo pretio reserantur limina Ditis.

> [Therefore he says that virtues are to be pursued by means of the bough, which is an imitation of the letter Y: and he says the bough

lies hidden in the woods because indeed virtue and integrity lie hidden in the confusion of this life and in its greater portion of vices. Others say that the golden bough leads to the underworld because mortals are easily destroyed by riches. Tiberianus says, "For the price of gold, the doors of Dis are unlocked."] (*In Aen.* 6.136)

Rather interestingly, given Servius's concealment of the bough in the wood, Dante also presents a "dark wood of error" at the beginning of the *Inferno* from which he will emerge with the help of Virgil, who guides him through the underworld.

Servius glosses the two paths twice later, once from Pythagoras again (on *Aeneid* 6.295) and once on the symbol of the letter Y (on *Aeneid* 6.477). The latter passage concludes that in the letter Y are mixed virtues and vices, and that which leads to merits and penalties. For the inferior things restrain or imprison human life, defined as the soul while it exists in the body:

sed dixit quantum ad y pertinet litteram: in his enim quae dixit mixta sunt virtutibus vitia, in his autem quae dicturus est nocentum poenas a piorum segregat meritis. nam inferi, ut diximus supra, humanam continent vitam, hoc est animam in corpore constitutam.

[But he said, insofar as it concerns the letter Y: for in these things which he said, vices are mixed with virtues; but in these things which he is going to say, he separates the punishment of the guilty from the rewards of the pious. For the underworld, as we have said above, holds human life, that is, the souls existing in bodies.] (*In Aen.* 6.477)

Among the earthly flaws and sins, symbolized by the inhabitants of Hades in Servius (as they are in Macrobius), Tityus, son of Earth, is stretched over nine acres because he was guilty of lust (*In Aen.* 6.595–6) and the Weeping Fields stretch everywhere because lust dominates a great number (*In Aen.* 6.441). And when Charon says that Hercules chained Cerberus and dragged him from the underworld, Hercules is read as the hero who subdues earthly vices, or more particularly earth as the consumer of bodies (*In Aen.* 6.395). The underworld of human life in its viciousness leads to psychological pain and suffering; hence "Acheron" means "quasi sine gaudio" ["as if without joy"] (*In Aen.* 6.107), and "Tartarus" comes from the Greek for "a tremore frigoris" ["the shivering of cold"] (*In Aen.* 6.577). Servius's moral vision of the underworld and its two paths was indeed shaped, like Macrobius's, by Plato's "Vision of Er."

III. CODA: PHILOSOPHY AND FICTION

Combining his sources of Plato/Cicero and Virgil/Servius, Macrobius interweaves the Servian Neoplatonic-Stoic reading of book 6 of the *Aeneid* and its underworld with an analogously Stoic reading of narrative as drawn from Cicero in the *De natura deorum*. That is, he defines certain kinds of mythological narratives involving supernal beings and matters as morally appropriate for the philosopher and others, involving the ignoble and vicious, as immoral if interpreted literally but acceptable if expounded naturally or physically (that is, figuratively). In an influential analysis of the nature of fiction, Macrobius warns that not all fables may be suitable for the "sacred precincts" of philosophy, a warning that makes Philosophy a goddess and its practitioners priests in her temple:

> nec omnibus fabulis philosophia repugnat, nec omnibus adquiescit; et ut facile secerni possit quae ex his a se abdicet ac velut profana ab ipso vestibulo sacrae disputationis excludat, quae vero etiam saepe ac libenter admittat, divisionum gradibus explicandum est.

> [Philosophy does not discountenance all stories nor does it accept all, and in order to distinguish between what it rejects as unfit to enter its sacred precincts and what it frequently and gladly admits, the points of division must needs be clarified.] (*Somn. Scip.* 1.2.6)

Macrobius argues that the poet uses a fictitious *style* to communicate truth in the morally excellent "narratio fabulosa," the "fabulous narrative." This purpose sets it apart from fables without moral excellence, those that merely please the ear (such as comedies by Menander or love stories by Petronius and Apuleius) and even from fables equally moral but with fictitious plots and settings as well as styles, such as Aesop's fables, in which animals speak.

This "morally excellent" fable treating of truth in a fictitious style is used when "haec ipsa veritas per quaedam composita et ficta profertur" ["the argument is real but is presented in the form of a fable"] (*Somn. Scip.* 1.2.9). Fabulous narrative is used by (Stoic) philosophers to discuss the soul, the spirits of lower and upper air, and the gods more generally, at least as exemplified in the stories of Hesiod and Orpheus. More specifically, such a narrative is appropriate for "cerimoniarum sacra," that is, the performance of sacred rites, the stories of Hesiod and Orpheus "quae de deorum progenie actuve narrantur" ["that treat of the ancestry and deeds of the gods"], the mystic concepts of the Pythagoreans (*Somn. Scip.* 1.2.9), and discourses about the soul, or spirits of the lower or upper air (*Somn. Scip.* 1.2.13).

Fabulous narrative, however, is *not* appropriate for discourses on God, the Good, the First Cause, the Mind, Intellect, or Nous. Here Macrobius distinguishes between human and divine matters, or philosophy and theology. For fabulous narrative to be appropriate the philosopher constructing it must be "prudent": it is used when "sacrarum rerum notio sub pio figmentorum velamine honestis et tecta rebus et vestita nominibus enuntiatur" ["a decent and dignified conception of holy truths, with respectable events and characters, is presented beneath a modest veil of allegory"] (*Somn. Scip.* 1.2.11). When a philosopher is not prudent and openly reveals these *arcana,* holy truths or "secrets of Nature," as did Numenius when he interpreted the Eleusinian mysteries, not only does he debase and offend the gods but also he permits vulgar or immoral men to gaze on Nature "apertam nudamque" ["openly naked"] (*Somn. Scip.* 1.2.17–19).

Macrobius denigrates as unfit for fabulous narrative the use of immoral stories involving the gods (adultery, the castration of Caelus by Saturn) or involving monstrosities. That is, when this dictum is violated, according to Macrobius, it debases and offends the gods (*Somn. Scip.* 1.2.19)—the text becomes a kind of vicious underworld. The violation occurs in Macrobius's second type of fabulous narrative, "quod genus totum philosophi nescire malunt" ["which philosophers prefer to disregard altogether"]—a type describing immoral activities. Macrobius declares this type of fabulous narrative inappropriate when

> contextio narrationis per turpia et indigna numinibus ac monstro similia componitur ut di adulteri, Saturnus pudenda Caeli patris abscidens et ipse rursus a filio regni potito in vincla coniectus, quod genus totum philosophi nescire malunt.

> [the presentation of the plot involves matters that are base and unworthy of divinities and are monstrosities of some sort {as, for example, gods caught in adultery, Saturn cutting off the privy parts of his father Caelus and himself thrown into chains by his son and successor}.] (*Somn. Scip.* 1.2.11)

In Cicero's *De natura deorum* the Stoic character Balbus's discussion of the reasons for the use of the gods anticipates Macrobius's: in the second, Stoic, book, Balbus declares that the gods, both Greek and ancient Italic, assumed human form to provide *fabulae* for the *poetes* and superstitions and legends to human life, their "impias fabulas" a cover for "physica ratio" (*Nat. deorum* 2.63). Cicero rationalizes immoral tales, including the castration of Caelus by his son Saturn, Saturn's devouring of his own children, his own capture by his son Jupiter, Jupiter's marriage to his sister Juno, and the rape of Proserpina, because they hide natural principles. The embodying of the gods, their incarnation in often scandalous stories that conceal natural truths, triggers Macrobius's literary theory of fabulous narrative.

For with the help of Macrobius's (Stoic) philosopher, almost any immoral myth can be rationalized. One of Macrobius's most unusual Neo-Stoic readings of a literally offensive myth involves Bacchus, a demigod he interprets in the light of Orphic rites as representing material mind "born of a single parent" but "divided into separate parts" in sacred rites by angry Titans, only to arise, Osiris-like, we surmise (though with a logic that would appeal to Christian readers), "from his buried limbs safe and sound." This reveals that Nous, or Mind, "by offering its undivided substance to be divided, and again, by returning from its divided state to the indivisible, both fulfills its worldly functions and does not forsake its secret nature."[38] The cosmological interpretation of Bacchus would resurface, if not frequently, then in those later commentaries and collections with some Neoplatonic bias, such as that of William of Conches on Macrobius.

Because so many pagan fabulous narratives involve such base and impious matters, medieval philosophers and exegetes in following Macrobius's pronouncements would be able to develop highly complex moral and allegorical explanations. In the twelfth-century commentary on Macrobius by the Neoplatonist William of Conches, who has been credited with knowing Cicero's *De natura deorum* firsthand,[39] those specific immoral tales would be indeed rationalized according to the Stoic and Platonic principles of physical and moral allegorism as filtered through medieval Latin commentators. Thus in the hands of an adept mythographer even the most scandalous myths achieve propriety. For example, the castration of Saturn by Jupiter (Macrobius is mistaken to refer to the castration of Caelus by Saturn, says William): William explains that the testicles signify the fruits of the earth which are ripened by the warmth of the upper element, or Jupiter, and which, when cast into the sea (or figuratively into the human belly) give birth to Venus or sensual delight.[40] This example mingles physical and moral allegoresis. But long before William, another influential mythographer would adopt similarly Neoplatonist and Stoic readings of Virgil—the multicultural schoolmaster Fulgentius.

Chapter Three

THE VIRGILIAN HERO
IN NORTH AFRICA:
FULGENTIUS THE GRAMMARIAN
AND CALLIOPE, MUSE OF EPIC
POETRY

Borrowing from Servius's Neoplatonic gloss on the hero's descent in book 6 of Virgil's *Aeneid*, Fulgentius deploys the last fable of his *Mitologiae*, on Alpheus and Arethusa (from book 5 of Ovid's *Metamorphoses*), to exemplify the heroic integrity of truth in the lower world despite its contact with impurity and mendaciousness. The river Alpheus, or *veritas*, loves and pursues the nymph Arethusa, or *aequitas*, transformed into a fountain, just as the light loves *nobilitas*, excellence. Like the heroic Aeneas, the truthful Alpheus is not perverted by the monsters and criminals he meets: "Ergo quid amare poterat ueritas nisi aequitatem, quid lux nisi nobilitatem. Ideo et in mari ambulans non miscetur, quia lucida ueritas omni malorum morum salsidine circumdata pollui aliqua commixtione non nouit" ["For what can the truth love but equity, or the light, but excellence? And it {Alpheus} retains its freshness when passing through the sea because clear truth cannot by any mingling be polluted by the surrounding saltiness of evil ways"]. Alpheus moving through the middle of the sea always retains his freshness because he plunges into her hollow, suggesting that the lower world accordingly provides oblivion for souls contaminated by its immorality: "Ille in mediis undis ambulans non inmixtus in sinu eius inmergitur; unde et *aput inferos* obliuionem animarum trahere dicitur" ["When passing through the midst of the sea, it retains its freshness as it plunges into her hollow. Hence it is said that *in the lower world* it bears oblivion to the souls"] (my emphasis). Because of the light of truth, no doubt projected from supernal realms, as it descends into the *inferno,* or "in secreta conscientia," the memory of evil is forgotten: "Sed tamen in situ aequissimae potestatis omnis lux ueritatis delabitur; nam et descendens in infer-

num, id est in secreta conscientia, ueritatis lux malarum rerum semper
obliuionem inportat" ["Yet all the light of truth sinks into the hollow of
equitable power, for as it goes down *to the lower world,* that is into the
hidden knowledge of good and evil, the light of truth always entails the
forgetting of evil things"] (*Mit.* 3.12; Helm, p. 80; my emphasis).

This thematic link with Aeneas's descent into the underworld,[1] the
latter glossed explicitly in Fulgentius's *Expositio continentiae Virgilianae,*
implies that the *Mitologiae* itself, presided over by Calliope, is epic and
heroic and, more specifically, keyed to Virgil and late antique commentaries on the Roman poet. It is well known that Fulgentius contributed to
Virgil mythography by providing the first holistic, extended allegorization
of the meaning of the *Aeneid* as representative of the three stages of heroic
life, a treatment echoed first by Bernard Silvestris in the twelfth century
and then by Cristoforo Landino in the fifteenth. But as was the case with
his North African contemporary, Macrobius, Fulgentius also carries over
from his other, Neoplatonically flavored mythologies an interest in wisdom and the seven liberal arts—and so his allegorization of Virgil's chief
hero reflects an educational allegory, especially relating to the trivium and
grammar, in keeping with his own profession as a grammarian and with his
sources. This interest in education creeps into, imbues, the other uniquely
Fulgentian contribution to Virgil commentary—the *Expositio continentiae
Virgilianae,* a satiric dialogue between Fulgentius and Virgil which
functions dramatically as a frame for the glossation and illustrates the need
for literacy and education. Whatever myths appear in the *Continentia* are
stretched and shaped until they fit Fulgentius's overall allegorical schema.
The interpretation of Aeneas's journey as an epitome of heroic (literate) life
supports the argument that he also wrote the interpretation of the history
of Thebes, in the *Super Thebaiden,* as the journey of Theseus.

In sum, Fulgentius's highly original—and influential—mythographies
are thematically interwoven with each other and indebted to the allegorizing of other African and Roman scholars. In this chapter we shall argue
that Fulgentius's *Mitologiae* shaped and influenced his later works, each
representative of at least one (and frequently more) of the strains in
medieval mythographic literary commentary, that is, Martianus, Boethius,
Ovid, Virgil, and Statius. Perhaps because of Fulgentius's attention to
other classical authors and because of his familiarity with grammar in
particular his allegorization of the *Aeneid* as the three stages of human life
may have been heavily influenced by Virgil commentaries, especially those
of Servius and Donatus. And finally, out of this view of the *Aeneid* as a

framed structure for these stages of life, Fulgentius probably glossed Statius, in the commentary on the *Thebaid* attributed to pseudo-Fulgentius, which again traces the allegorized life of its hero Theseus as a type of intellection. Fulgentius's interest in the Roman authors is of course obvious, but his respect for his North African predecessors—chiefly, Martianus and Macrobius—has been less studied.

Fulgentius, much admired in the Middle Ages, exists in numerous medieval manuscripts, although not all of his works were equally popular. Of the works attributed to him—the *Mitologiarum libri tres,* the *Expositio continentiae Virgilianae,* the *Expositio sermonum antiquorum,* the *De aetatibus mundi et hominis,*[2] and the *Super Thebaiden*[3]—the *Expositio sermonum antiquorum (Sermones)* is found most frequently in medieval manuscripts, although the *Mitologiae* was by far the most influential in the Middle Ages.[4] For these works and their author, the Belgian chronicler Sigebert of Gembloux (d. 1112) professes his esteem; the second and third Vatican mythographers used him, "facts of no small importance when it is remembered that Hyginus and some of the Vatican mythographers (principally the first) were certainly used as school-books," although Fulgentius was not a mere school author.[5]

Fulgentius was almost certainly a grammarian as well as a Christian and an African, aspects of his life reflected in his works. Fulgentius (actually Fabius Planciades Fulgentius *vir Clarissimus*)[6] flourished during the ascendancy of the Vandal kings, that is, between 439, a date after the composition of Martianus Capella's *De nuptiis,* mentioned in the *Sermones,* and before 533, the date of the collapse of the Vandal empire, because the Vandals were clearly still in power at the time of his *Mitologiae.*[7] Often confused with Fulgentius Bishop of Ruspe,[8] our Fulgentius was also a Christian who reveals, in another of his works, *De aetatibus mundi et hominis,* a familiarity with the Old and New Testament; in the exposition on Virgil, makes the Roman poet acceptable to Christians; and in *Mitologiae,* praises groups like bishops and priests—all of which suggests that he may have been at least a lay member of the Church.[9] Most likely he lived in Africa: he intended to use the twenty-three letters of the Libyan alphabet for the twenty-three books of *De aetatibus mundi* and mentions the alphabet in the prologue; in one manuscript he is identified as "Carthaginiensis."[10] In addition, all of his works are marked by an African style labeled *tumor Africanus* for its "pompous elegance"; the style resembles that of the African mythmakers Martianus Capella and Apuleius.[11] Finally, he was probably a grammarian, which we suspect because the *Sermones* was dedicated to the grammarian Calcidius and because its emphasis falls upon education.[12]

Fulgentius's inter- and intratextuality is a reminder that the teaching of grammar permits making strong connections between unlikely subjects. All of his works bear the distinctive mark of the grammarian. The first of his mythographic works, the *Mitologiae,* compiles various myths from Martianus, Boethius, the *Aeneid,* Ovid, and Hyginus in its three books. The *Continentia Virgiliana,* "directly connected with the Mythologicon, to which it is subsequent in date, and to which it forms as it were an appendix,"[13] allegorizes the *Aeneid* as the stages of life and in particular the education of the wise man. The other, minor, works equally reveal the grammarian's hand, often straddling several disciplines: the *Sermones* is a dictionary of sixty-six Latin words covering categories of religion, navigation, funeral rites, etc.; *De aetatibus mundi et hominis* traces the moral history of the world from Adam and Eve to the rule of Valentinian (364–75) by using the Bible as a chief source, through the rhetorical device of leipogrammata[14] in the planned twenty-three books to represent the twenty-three letters of the Libyan alphabet. This work reminds us of the *Continentia Virgiliana* because Fulgentius tries to parallel human development with "res gestae," a scheme he abandons after book 7: Cain and Abel, in book 1, represent natural jealousy; Noah and his children, in book 2, represent pride; and so forth with the remaining sins. The *Super Thebaiden,* which may not have been written by Fulgentius, was certainly a less popular work in the Middle Ages; it merely allegorizes the *Thebaid.* There apparently existed other works not surviving today—works on physiology and numbers mentioned in the *Expositio* on Virgil (*Cont. Virg.* 13); a *Liber differentiarum Fulgentii* recorded in the ninth-century catalog of St. Gall;[15] and a spurious work, the *Super Bucolica et Georgica Virgilii,* possibly a forgery.[16]

Within these works the extent and importance of Fulgentius's debt to the earlier Neoplatonic and North African scholars such as Martianus, Servius, and Macrobius has not been sufficiently realized, although the Greek and Neoplatonic sources used by Fulgentius in the commentary on the *Aeneid* have recently been analyzed.[17] The North African Lactantius Placidus's *Narrationes* and his commentary on Statius's *Thebaid* are simply grammatical rather than Neoplatonic in cast. Servius found that grammatical comments could supply the hidden allegorical meaning behind Virgil's text, especially the sixth book with its descent into the underworld. Macrobius (who interspersed glosses on Virgil throughout his books) codified a similar grammarian's intent in the early chapters of his commentary on Cicero's *Somnium Scipionis,* before examining the Ciceronian fragment as an insight into the other world. And Martianus, in *De nuptiis Philologiae et Mercurii,* imaginatively reconstructed a world of his own, an overworld, peopled by gods a late classical audience would have viewed as an old-fashioned literary convention, whom they might properly meet and understand with assistance from those divine handmaids, the liberal arts.

That Martianus may have influenced Fulgentius has been suggested: Fulgentius is acknowledged to be the "earliest writer to cite Martianus, and perhaps the first to compose a commentary on *The Marriage,*" notes the translator of Martianus, the eminent William Stahl. The commentary he means is Fulgentius's *Expositio sermonum antiquorum* (The explanation of obsolete words), in which Fulgentius acknowledges, in definition 45, "unde et Felix Capella in libro de nuptiis Mercurii et Philologiae ait," most probably an indebtedness to specific denotations.[18] This short work explains obscure Latin words often having to do with religious customs or practices and thought necessary for reading the ancient authors, so that it belongs to the same tradition as Varro's *De lingua Latina,* Pliny's *Natural History,* Pompeius Festus's epitome of the *De verborum significatu* by the Augustan scholar Verrius Flaccus, as amplified by Paul the Deacon, and the early fourth-century Nonius Marcellus's *De compendiosa doctrina.* Not only was Fulgentius indebted to Martianus in the *Sermones* but also, as Stahl has suggested, "The allegorical setting of Fulgentius's *Mitologiae* was inspired by Martianus, and his style shows definite traces of Martianus' influence."[19]

I would argue that to both Macrobius and Martianus Fulgentius pays his respects by means of imitation and borrowing. For the narrative frame in *Mitologiae* emphasizing the lies of pagan poetry sheltering hidden truth he owes fealty to Macrobius in the commentary on the *Somnium Scipionis* and his theory of fabulous narrative; for the Muse Calliope who dominates the frame-dialogue with him he owes fealty to Martianus's invocation of her at the opening of *De nuptiis,* as he does for much of the material and ordering of myths in his first book. (The second book is more closely tied, in fact, to the myths found in the more or less contemporary *Consolatio Philosophiae* of Boethius [d. 524], a scholar better known in medieval schools for his translations of Aristotle into Latin and the texts that would dominate the trivium and quadrivium. The third book is inspired by Ovidian and Apuleian myths, in particular.)

Macrobius, Martianus, and Fulgentius were all committed to the concept of knowledge embodied in the seven liberal arts; all three had compiled mythographic encyclopedias—Martianus in the mythological frame of the first two books of De nuptiis, Macrobius in the Saturnalia, Fulgentius in the Mitologiae. In imitation of Martianus, the Mitologiae depicts an encyclopedic cosmos of the gods embodying Virgilian knowledge, as we shall see, and accessed by means of the Neoplatonic theories of fabulous narrative articulated by Macrobius.

Fulgentius's synthesis of the major mythic structures of these works, framed by his interpretative dialogues, either with Calliope the Muse of epic poetry or Virgil the epic poet himself, would powerfully sway both commentators and poets in the Middle Ages. For in these frames he both rationalizes the lies of pagan poetry as sheltering truth and also defends the deployment of grammatical exegesis to discern their truths. The rationalization, coupled with the exemplary text, propelled the methods and substance of classical mythography into the Christian Middle Ages. In addition, by epitomizing the major myths of what would become the major mythographic commentary authors, he provided an efficient compendium for use by later grammarians, philosophers, preachers, and poets.

The net effect of Fulgentius's work on mythography was to invite overall allegorical interpretations of Virgil's works. In the eight and ninth centuries Fulgentius's allegorical interpretation of the order of the composition of Virgil's works as reflective of the stages in the life of man extended into the Berne scholia's interpretation of all the Eclogues as having allegorical levels. And this allegorization of Virgil's life led eventually to the educational, natural, and moral allegorization of the Aeneid by Bernard Silvestris in the twelfth century. Bernard's Neoplatonic moralizations of this life as an underworld also derived in part from the glosses on book 6 of the Aeneid by the tenth-century writer Remigius of Auxerre. The tradition of Neoplatonic-Neopythagorean glosses on Virgil's underworld fed into Fulgentius's method of allegorizing the stages of a human life, Aeneas's and Virgil's.[20] By the twelfth century, literary theory could draw on a complex, fourfold system of descents into the underworld in the Virgil commentaries of William of Conches and Bernard Silvestris.

Fulgentius's use of and support for the writings of Virgil sanctioned the later reading of him, particularly in the sixth to the twelfth centuries. It was not a sure thing that Virgil would be admired; Gregory of Tours transmitted incidents and legends of the Aeneid only while condemning them. But Lupus of Ferrières advised Regimbert to study Virgil; and Anselm in the eleventh century also recommended reading him.[21] After the twelfth century, perhaps because of the translation of Aristotle by Averroes and the interest in scholastic logic which displaced grammar in general, interest in Virgil suffered a slight decline, if the number of school commentaries represents a valid index; he only recovered his stature in the *Rinascimento*.

To trace Fulgentius's mythographic development, in the *Mitologiae* we will examine the sources of the frame, consider the nature of the myths collected, and then reveal how each of his other two major mythographic works, on the *Aeneid* and the *Thebaid*, grew out of the last. The allegories in each Fulgentian mythography reflect his preoccupation with the seven liberal arts, with wisdom as the highest virtue, with classical poetry as a means to an end of understanding Latin and therefore with language as a reflection of the human process of thought and thinking—the primacy of words as symbols of ratiocination.

I. CALLIOPE, MAGISTERIAL MUSE OF EPIC POETRY, IN THE *MITOLOGIAE*

Fulgentius's meeting with Calliope, the Muse of epic poetry, in the frame dialogue of the *Mitologiae* is important because she explains the rationale for such myths—the particular connection between mythology and heroic poetry. And yet, about this frame narrative Leslie George Whitbread has remarked that it is "a highly personal, whimsical, digressive, and distended affair, which only gradually achieves its introductory function," with the Muse Calliope singled out as inappropriate and ironic; she is "treated as impersonally as the rest when she appears among the Muses in 1.15, and she is not mentioned in connection with her son Orpheus when he is dealt with in 3.10; it is natural for his age that Fulgentius seems quite unaware of the irony involved in having Calliope, a creature of myth, guide him in explaining myth away." Whitbread does not restrict his criticism to the frame narrative, but also attends to the collection's Greek myths (used with Roman names) as being listed in "a loosely planned order."[22]

An understanding of how Fulgentius is using his models—Macrobius, Martianus, Boethius, and Ovid—will explain what is actually brilliant mythographic synthesizing in these perceived flaws:—for the whimsical dialogue, Fulgentius looked to Macrobius; for the Muse Calliope, and why she is first singled out from the Muses, then ignored in discussions of the Muses and of her son Orpheus, to Martianus; and for the order of the myths, to a synthesis of his sources—Martianus, Boethius, and Ovid.

In fact, Fulgentius does not so much explain away myth as instead reveal its masked secrets in the best Macrobian sense: "Mutatas itaque uanitates manifestare cupimus, non manifesta mutando fuscamus . . . certos itaque nos rerum praestolamur effectus, quo sepulto mendacis Greciae fabuloso commento quid misticum in his sapere debeat cerebrum agnoscamus" ["What I wish to do is expose alterations away from the truth, not obscure what is clear by altering it myself. . . . I look for the true effects of things, whereby, once the fictional invention of lying Greeks has been disposed of, I may infer what allegorical significance one should understand in such matters"] (*Mit.* 1. prol.; Helm, p. 11). The grammarian declares that he will provide "ita somniali figmento delusam" ["dreamlike nonsense expounding trifles suited to sleep"] but trifles like "quae nostrum achademicum rethorem ita usque ad uitalem circulum tulit, quo pene dormientem Scipionem caeli civem effecerit. Uerum res publica uideat quid Cicero egerit" ["those of which our Academic orator Cicero has given a lively account, almost making the sleeping Scipio into a citizen of heaven—but what Cicero achieved his own *Republic* may show"] (Helm, pp. 3–4). The reference to dreamlike nonsense invokes Macrobius's section on dreams (*Somn. Scip.* 1.3), during which is outlined the danger of stripping away the false, outer covering supplied to protect naked Nature from base men.

Fulgentius, who appears to echo these pronouncements, casts Calliope in the role of Macrobius addressing philosophers: having advised Fulgentius to receive the teachings of the Muses in his home (she has heard that barbarians ban literature in their houses), she also warns him that "Tam secretis misticisque rebus uiuaciter pertractandis ampliora sunt auctoritatum quaerenda suffragia; neque enim quippiam ludicrum quaeritur, quo ludibundo pede metrica uerborum commoda sarciamus" ["If such recondite and mystical matters are to be vigorously studied, the full approval of the authorities must be sought; for no trifling must be pursued, whereby we find ourselves patching up correct styles of verse with some frivolous lines"] (*Mit.* 1. prol.; Helm, p. 12). She imitates Macrobius in his cautioning that these secrets must not be revealed foolishly or indiscriminately to those who cannot understand or appreciate them: Macrobius has noted that when a philosopher is not prudent and openly reveals these holy truths, or secrets of Nature, as did Numenius when he interpreted the Eleusinian mysteries, not only does he debase and offend the gods, but also he allows base men to see Nature openly naked (*Somn. Scip.* 1.2.17–19). As if conscious of Macrobius's insistence on prudence for the philosopher, Calliope endows herself with *philosophia,* the culmination of the liberal arts and personified in Boethius's *Consolatio,* and perhaps to suggest the celestial origins of the truths about the gods and the World Soul treated in fabulous narrative, associates with Urania, the Muse of astronomy whom Martianus linked with the outermost of all the heavenly spheres (*De nupt.* 1.27). But she then addresses Fulgentius as *homunculus,* little man, perhaps because of his own arrogant and unlikeable persona, but perhaps also a play on Macrobius's "base man" unable to perceive the reason for such naked truths being shrouded in fiction. Calliope then offers the persona "Fulgentius" an appropriately vulgar girlfriend for consolation, Satyra (satire, comedy, but probably meant to denote that baser stew of prose and verse often found in prosimetra like those of Martianus or Boethius, and termed "Menippean satire"), which the homunculus declares that he will spurn because of his wife (although, ironically, the *Mitologiae* also mixes verse and prose in what might be termed a *satura*).

The work begins with Calliope's lecture on the *idos,* "idol," which she identifies as a "species," literally something seen, a shape or figure, but also an idea, an appearance, an ornament, a vision or apparition, a likeness or image, connoting the deceptive and demonic quality of the imaginary experience it projects. As a word *species* offers the concept of appearing to be rather than being, and also the concept of the god, an externalization not only of human suffering but also of human ignorance. In the story of Syrophanes of Egypt who lost his son and made an idol to replace him we have an etiological story of the development of the gods, a condemnation of them, and as well the reiteration of the thesis that human ignorance leads to the belief in gods of self-devising. The dreamlike figure the bereaved seems to see after such a loss appears real; the desire to create renewed life for the deceased enhances the credibility of the vision. Calliope cites Petronius and Mintanor, both of whom suggest that fear first prompted the invention of the gods, or more specifically, that human suffering made a god of grief.

Most important for the Neoplatonic concept of the heroic descent, Calliope notes that to invent out of ignorance and suffering initiates a fall into an underworld (*baratrum*) of continuing irrationality and even immorality, an experience truly infernal: "Exhinc ergo inueteratus error humanis pedetemtim consertus discipulis baratro quodam sceuae credulitatis prolabitur" ["Thence, therefore, a deep-rooted error, gradually taken up by human devotees, edged forward into what is a pit of perverse credulity"] (*Mit.* 11.1; Helm, p. 17).

Fulgentius specifically uses the figure Calliope, the Muse of epic poetry said by Martianus, at the beginning of his own satura, to be "conubium diuum componens Calliopea / carminis auspicio te probat annuere" ["happy to have Hymen bless the opening of her poem about a wedding"] (*De nuptiis* 1, my translation). Martianus clearly expects that this mixture of prose and verse in *De nuptiis*, in particular rendered through the dactylic hexameter of epic, will be perceived as a work overseen and inspired by this Muse. In Fulgentius, Calliope and the Muses have appeared because the birds have summoned them—in verses which refer to the "Ascrean shepherd" (Hesiod), Virgil the Mantuan, and Homer the Maeonian, all commentators on or writers of mythological or epic (heroic) poems; Martianus is not mentioned. But Calliope as the Muse of epic poetry is the only Muse to converse with Fulgentius, declaring him to be "Anacreonticis iamdudum nouus mistes initiatus es sacris" ["a new recruit to the sacred rites of Anacreon"] (*Mit.* 1 prol.; Helm, p. 10). The metaphor draws attention to his extravagant Anacreontic allegories, expressed in an equally extravagant style that duplicates the prose of Martianus, as suggestive of sacred religious rituals. And the goddesslike Calliope herself—associated by Martianus with the "sphere of the Cyllenian," that is, of the planet Mercury, also god of eloquence (*De nuptiis* 27)—is later singled out in the Martianus commentaries for extensive glossing. Most important, Calliope appears to be the source for this allegorical material about the gods and heroes provided to Fulgentius and through him to his master.

The movement of the *Mitologiae*, at least as reflected in the frame links, proceeds from wise god (Calliope) and ignorant human (Fulgentius the reader) in book 1, to the relationship reversed in book 2, with Fulgentius as learned, culminating in another reversal in book 3, with Fulgentius as ignorant and his master as wise—perhaps because Fulgentius hopes to win his favor. But the reductive and ironic movement seems to undercut the efficacy of the mythography—perhaps deliberately, to portray yet another idolatry, that of the human master transformed into a godlike being because of his power over Fulgentius.

But Calliope continues in this book with other lectures on the gods, and soon Fulgentius drops the pretense that she is lecturing. The speaker in the prologue to the second book becomes the homunculus Fulgentius addressing his master once again (as he did at the beginning of the first prologue), with Calliope absent. The emphasis falls on the relationship between writer and reader (particularly Fulgentius's master), with the stress positive, on the learning and knowledge available here and on the wisdom and goodness of God. Fulgentius calls this work "meam stultitiam" ["foolishness of mine"], hoping that the reader may either improve his knowledge (but if he does so, the reader should attribute this improvement to God and not Fulgentius), or else blame Fulgentius for his folly. His view of his scholastic effort is moral: "sicut enim liuoris nota est silere quod noueram, ita non crimen est enarrare quod senseram. Ergo si his amplius sapis, lauda mentem purissimam quae quod habuit non negauit, si haec ante nescieras, habes arenam nostri studii ubi tui exerceas palestram ingenii" ["Just as it is a sign of malice to keep silent on what I know, so it is not a fault to explain what I have understood. Therefore, if you do learn more about these matters, praise the sincerity of a mind which has not held back what it possessed; and if you were ignorant of these matters before, you at least have from my efforts an arena in which you can exercise your own talents"] (*Mit.* 2. prol.; Helm, p. 35).

In the third book, in contrast, the emphasis falls on the ignorance of Fulgentius and the wisdom, not of God, but of Fulgentius's master. The most self-deprecating of the three prologues, and the briefest, it reiterates the ignorance and stupidity of the narrator and underscores the fallen, irrational inclination of the self-deceived. Fulgentius merely asks the wise master "ut doctissimus corrigis" [to "set right with your great learning"] (*Mit.* 3. prol.; Helm, p. 58) whatever he has found to be absurd. Fulgentius has begun, rather pompously, almost by personifying that fault within him as sin, in religious terms, in his comment that "Inscientiae formidolosa suspecto semper excusandi quaerit suffragia, quo quidquid ignorantia incursionum mater peccauerit, id ueniae absoluat petitio quae culpas uestire consueuit" ["The shy glance of ignorance is always begging leave to make excuses for itself so that, whatever mistakes are made through lack of knowledge, one who deserves critical attacks may be absolved by a plea for indulgence which has always covered over errors"] (*Mit.* 3. prol.; Helm, p. 58). With this odd reversal, and the use of the Macrobian metaphor of covering or cloaking the shameful (*vestire*) to shield the secrets of Nature from the eyes of base men, the tract returns to the prologue's (and Calliope's) warning about the ignorance of the barbarians who threaten with inquisition and torture the literate few able to write their own names. Is his master, if displeased, likely to do the same to Fulgentius? (Is patronage a matter of survival for him?)

Although the first book deals with the macrocosmos, the return to the microcosmos in books 2 and 3, and therefore to the human propensity for idolatry motivated by the irrational, illustrates the need for education, for literacy. The selection of tales in all three parts seems to underscore this frame progression, despite the suggestion that the three parts are unified but differentiated: the first, on the gods of the pantheon; the second, on the three lives, active, contemplative, and voluptuous; and the third, a continuation of the first two.[23] This polemical theme of the need for education, one popular in the period, may explain Fulgentius's careful indebtedness to Martianus's De nuptiis, which in its last seven books (of nine) allegorizes the seven liberal arts.

Much of the first book of the Mitologiae—not just the particular gods glossed but also the ordering and the emphasis on at least two of them, Apollo and Mercury—is modeled upon hierarchies and narrative emphases contained in De nuptiis. The order of the gods basically reflects that of Martianus as the major gods enter into the Assembly of the Gods to discuss Mercury's quest for a proper bride: first Jupiter and Juno, rulers of the world, are followed by his father Saturn, Sol and Luna, and Jupiter's brothers Neptune and Pluto; then the children of Jupiter enter, including Mars, Castor and Pollux, Hercules, Venus and Diana, Ceres, and Vulcan (De nuptiis 66–87). The order in Fulgentius, based similarly on the Stoic physical allegorization of the genealogy of the gods, begins with the principle of finite time, Saturn (from sacrun nun, perhaps "sacred intelligence"), followed by his children, linked with the four elements and the four cosmic regions, Jove (fire, aether) and Juno (air), Neptune (water), Pluto (earth). The external created world which the gods represent is described, appropriately, by the Muse of epic poetry. After this, Fulgentius adds a long section on the underworld (earth) dominated by Pluto and his associates, that is, his three-headed guard dog Cerberus, the Furies, Fates, and Harpies, the bride he abducted, Proserpina, and her mother Ceres. This section recalls Martianus's description of the inhabitants of the sublunary region below the moon and in the air governed by Pluto, god of the underworld, and Proserpina as Luna (De nuptiis 160–68).

The gods thereafter in Fulgentius include the sons of Jupiter who are also planets or stars—Apollo and Mercury—both of whom play central roles in the drama of De nuptiis. Mercury in Martianus's first two books searches for a bride with the help of Apollo the sun, truth itself (in book 1), and then marries her (book 2). Apollo, son of Jupiter and Latona and also the sun, dominates chapters 12 through 17 of Fulgentius's first book, devoted to his attributes, appearance, and related symbols and figures, such as the crow and the laurel, both under his protection, the nine Muses, linked traditionally with him as the tenth Muse, his son Phaethon, and then iconographical details about his symbols—the tripod, arrows, and python associated with him, and the fact that he is a father but also beardless. As the sun Apollo stands for the midheavens, the sky above the underworld ruled by Pluto; much of his presence in Fulgentius seems to be at least generally influenced by Philology's prayer to the sun in Martianus (*De nuptiis* 185–93)—itself derived from the long sections on the sun in Macrobius's *Saturnalia.*

As conduit for the speech of Jove in Martianus (*De nuptiis* 92) and the divine messenger who will marry an earthly Philology, Mercury reappears in Fulgentius without the more positive Stoic qualities attributed to him but with the same emphasis. Fulgentius assigns a long chapter to Apollo's half-brother, Mercury, son of Jupiter and Maia and the fastest-moving planet: his attributes, appearance, and related symbols and figures, such as wings, feathered heels, caduceus, cap and cock, his Greek name Hermes, his role as god of thieves, his swiftness, and his defeat of Argus. Mercury is unlike Apollo, ruler of the upper heavens, in that he is not fixed and moves now up, now down: "Utraque etiam regna permeare dicitur, superna atque inferna, quod modo uentis in altum nauigans currat, modo dimersus inferna tempestatibus appetat" ["He is said to pass through both realms, the upper and the lower, because now he rushes aloft through the winds, now plunging down he seeks out the lower world through storms"] (*Mit.* 1.18; Helm, p. 30).

The myths introduced at the end of the first book—Danaë, Ganymede, Perseus and the Gorgons, and Admetus and Alcestis—do not come from Martianus originally but from Ovid's *Metamorphoses,* as is apparent in the opening lines of the Perseus fable: the Gorgons' story, he reminds us, "poetae grammaticorum scolaribus rudimentis admodum celeberrimi" ["has been written by Lucan and Ovid, poets perfectly well known in the first teaching stages taken with schoolmasters"] (*Mit.* 1.21; Helm, p. 32). These Ovidian fables, however, are introduced, at the end of the Mercury section, as examples of the "underworld" of "poetica garrulitas" ("poetic garrulity," my translation) of the lying Greeks ("mendax Grecia," *Mit.* 1.18; Helm, p. 31)—and therefore of mendacious Mercury.

Such Greek lies are being exposed, laid bare, because Mercury slew Argus, who in Greek means *uacuos,* "idle"—the construction (or deconstruction) of eloquence demands exercise, discipline. As lies, these fables exemplify the impossibility of seduction of Danaë by a golden shower of coins and of the seizure of Ganymede by an eagle (or the spoils of war). Ganymede, like Danaë (*Mit.* 1.19) and, implicitly, Latona (1.12) and Maia (1.18), was a victim of Jove's amorous intentions—his abduction a scandalous secret typical of the concealing "garrulitas" of the Greeks. Fulgentius, apparently anxious to make clear the thematic link between these impossible (and scandalous) fables and the Mercury section, literally adjoins one fable to another by means of continuing dependent clauses. Mercury's chapter (*Mit.* 1.18) ends with an incomplete sentence that slides into the dependent clause which forms the whole of chapter 19 ("Of Danaë"), and is only completed with the first line of chapter 20 ("Of Ganymede"):

> Solet igitur adludere his speciebus et honeste mendax Grecia et poetica garrulitas semper de falsitate ornata [19 begins] dum et Danaë imbre aurato corrupta est non pluuia, sed pecunia [20 begins] et raptum . . . Ganimedem aquila non uere uolucris, sed bellica praeda.

> [This is the usual fashion in which Greece and its poetic gossiping, always decked in falsehood and yet lying with good intent, refers to such fabrications, {chapter 19 begins} as when Danaë was seduced by a golden shower, not rain but coins {chapter 20 begins}, and Ganymede was seized by an eagle, not a real bird but the spoils of war.]

The remaining myths of book 1, also examples of Greek fabrication, similarly bear ties to earlier myths, particularly through genealogy, but also through the Neoplatonic tension between flesh and spirit. Perseus (*Mit.* 1.21) is the son of Danaë (1.19), and, like Apollo and Mercury, he is also the son of Jove (1.3). In the Perseus fable, the three Gorgons represent the three kinds of terror, that which weakens the mind, that which fills the mind with terror, and that which puts gloom on the face; Perseus, aided by Minerva, "uirtus adiuuante sapientia" ["manliness aided by wisdom"] (*Mit.* 1.21; Helm, p. 33), defeats them, as represented by the beheaded Medusa (see fig. 6, of the constellation figuring forth this idea). Manliness is not afraid, in short, especially when bolstered by such wise help.

And in the next fable, Admetus and Alcestis, a thematic gloss provides a link to the Perseus fable, and returns us to the introductory fable on the idols of Syrophanes and the *barathrum* of irrational credulity, that underworld in which emotion masters intellection. In this fable, Alcestis takes the place in hell of her sick and dying husband Admetus; the latter is understood, "in modum mentis" ["in an allegory of the mind"], as the one whom fear (*metus*) seizes, and Alcestis as the boldness (*praesumptio*) which a fearful one desires. "Ergo mens praesumptionem sperans sibi coniungi duas

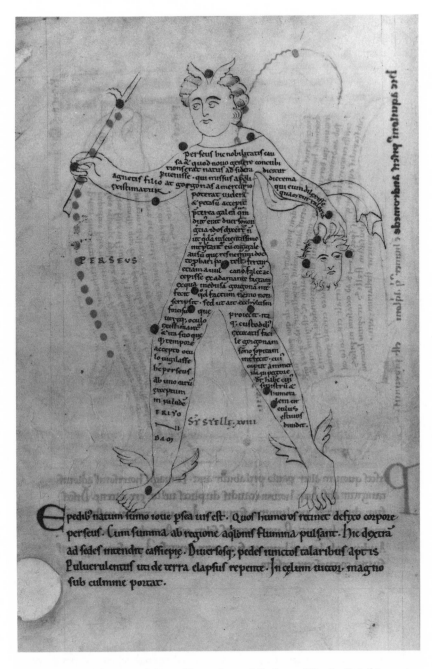

6. Perseus and Medusa's head. From Cicero, *Aratea*. MS. Cotton Tiberius C. I, fol. 22v (ca. 1122, English—Peterborough). By permission of the British Library, London.

feras [dispares] suo currui subiungat, id est suae uitae duas uirtutes asciscat, animi et corporis, leonem ut uirtutem animi, aprum ut uirtutem corporis" ["Thus the mind hoping for succour harnessed two opposed wild beasts to its chariot—that is, adopted two strengths, of mind and body—the lion for strength of mind and the wild boar for strength of body"] (*Mit.* 1.22; Helm, pp. 34–35). Boldness, in place of fearfulness, is exposed to death (Alcestis in place of Admetus), and strength (Hercules, who dragged away from hell both Cerberus and Alcestis) rescues this *praesumptio* from hell. The fable, like that of Perseus, reveals the Neoplatonic theme, once again, of the conflict between wisdom and irrationality within the microcosm. This Neoplatonic conflict is reflected in the cosmic structure (the increasing materiality of regions ranging from Jove, fire, to air, water, earth, or Juno, Neptune, to Pluto), the two concepts, microcosmic and macrocosmic, tied together by the fable of Syrophanes and the *idos* created by the microcosm in grief.

In book 2 the same Neoplatonic theme appears, but for the most part reflected in relationships, often couplings, between humans and gods, or in the adventures of heroes, half-god, half-man, rather than in the stories of gods per se. Frequently humans must battle their vices through strength of mind and wisdom; because these vices are often mythographically represented as female, love relationships therefore abound here (but not to be taken literally). The human figures who interact with the gods include Paris, who must choose among Minerva, Juno, and Venus; Prometheus, who steals fire from the gods; Ulysses; King Midas, who avariciously begs Apollo for a wish; and Endymion, with whom the moon falls in love. The demigods, or products of unions between humans and gods, engage in various unusual adventures, sexual or adversarial, such as adultery and onanism, child sacrifice, transsexuality, and rape. They begin with Hercules, Dionysius, and Helen, Castor, and Pollux (Clytemnestra is omitted). The monsters—those unnatural creatures who represent unions between a human and a thing, or a god and a thing, or even, in a sense, themselves— include Tiresias, who changes gender unnaturally; the son of Juno, Vulcan, cuckolded by Venus, but conceiving a son unnaturally, Erichthonius; the Centaurs (product of Ixion and a cloud); and the Giant Tantalus, who tests the gods by offering them Pelops, his son.

These tales of unnatural acts and unusual sexual relationships seem to defy Macrobius's strictures against the use of fabulous narrative for the delineation of scandalous acts by the gods (as well as for discourses on God, the Good, the First Cause, the Mind, Intellect, or Nous, *Somn. Scip.* 1.2.14).

Fulgentius was not alone in justifying the inclusion of such stories; his contemporary, Boethius, in his own prosimetrum, refers to the same set of demigods—Hercules and Omphale, and Cacus, and Antaeus (*Consolatio* 4 m7); Tiresias (5 p2); Ulysses and the Sirens (1 p1), and Ulysses and Circe (4 m3); and Ixion and Tantalus (3 m12). Because Boethius wrote *De consolatione Philosophiae* in prison before he was executed in A.D. 524, however, it seems difficult to posit absolutely and definitely influence on Fulgentius before A.D. 533, the last likely date for the completion of the *Mitologiae*. Even less likely, for the same reason, is the influence of Fulgentius on Boethius;[24] the strongest possibility is that the two scholars drew from a common Neoplatonic source, or from the Servian Virgil (but not Martianus, whose influence is felt only in Fulgentius).[25] Nevertheless, the parallels between Boethius and Fulgentius, especially in relation to Fulgentius's second book, deserve another look.

The first of Boethius's mythological poems (*Consolatio* 3 m12) begins with a description of Orpheus's woe over the loss of his wife, continues with his descent into the underworld and a description of its inhabitants, and concludes with a moral. This moral explains that he who looks back at Eurydice in the underworld because he has been overcome or conquered by her or it (that is, the inferior and infernal, the irrational), loses whatever excellence he has gained (specifically, the privilege to descend into the underworld conferred by the Judge of Souls upon the superior poet who excels by revealing his grief in song).

The second mythological poem (*Consolatio* 4 m3) begins with a description of Circe's magical transformation of the men of Ulysses into beasts, continues with the reason why Mercury favored Ulysses as an exception to Circe's transforming power, and concludes, again, with a moral. This moral explains that Circe had power over the human body (Ulysses's sailors) but not over the human mind (Ulysses).

For the third poem (*Consolatio* 4 m7), its three separate parts seem to form a series in themselves connected by the idea of the quest or adventure, at different stages. Agamemnon is described killing his daughter at the *beginning* of the Trojan War to help impel the ships on to war and the avenging of his brother. Ulysses is described when in the *middle* of his odyssey he confronts and triumphs over Polyphemus. Hercules is seen in the full course of his twelve Labors, which in a sense encompass beginning, middle, and *end* of the hero's career, or human life. Ulysses and Hercules, but not Agamemnon, are understood as examples of wisdom battling ignorance and irrationality.

In Fulgentius's second book, Homeric, Virgilian, and what I will call Boethian heroes, humans who consort with the gods, and underworld criminals engage in relationships which either reflect this psychomachia between reason and passion or explain the physical workings of the cosmos. Among the sixteen fables delineated in this book is the Virgilian story of one cause of the Trojan War, the enmity of Juno resulting from the Judgment of the Trojan Paris. He chose disastrously from the three goddesses representing the contemplative life (Minerva), the active life (Juno), and the sensual life (Venus); choosing the last, Venus, he initiated the Trojan War when he fell in love with Helen. Another cause for Juno's enmity was the rape of the woman Leda by Jupiter in the form of a swan, which reveals the union in love between lust and pride. Because Jove took on the appearance of a swan to couple with Leda, destruction ensued, in terms of the egg from which were born Castor, Pollux (both symbols of destruction) and Helen (cause of the Trojan War), for the swan is a reviler of other birds. Hence Jove, symbol of power, when coupled with Leda, results in insult or reviling: "Thus all power getting involved with insults changes the appearance of its magnanimity" (*Mit.* 2.13).

The enmity of Juno toward the wise Theban hero and demigod Hercules occurs because Jove spends a very long night with his mother, Alcmene, during which the hero is conceived. In chapters 2 through 4 of the second book of the *Mitologiae,* Hercules falls in love with the spinner Omphale (lust), battles the cattle stealer Cacus (evil), and wrestles with and triumphs over the giant Antaeus (lust). Other enemies of Juno in book 2 include criminals mentioned in Boethius's fable of Orpheus (*Consolatio* 3 m12), for example, Ixion, who attempted intercourse with a Juno-shaped cloud; thereafter, the cloud gave birth to the Centaurs, and because Juno represents dominion, striving for dominion results merely in a cloud, "the mere simulation of worth" (*Mit.* 2.14; see fig. 7, the Centaur as a constellation). But Ixion eventually fell, so those who strive for dominion through arms are at one time up and the next down, like a wheel. Tantalus, also punished in hell, offered his son Pelops to the gods as a supper dish (*Mit.* 2.15) in a gesture of pride.

The crafty Greek hero Ulysses confronts the deceitful Sirens, which means that wisdom, which "ab omnibus mundi rebus peregrina est" ["is a stranger to all things of this world"] (*Mit.* 2.8; Helm, p. 48), passes by the "delectationum inlecebras" ["allures of pleasure"] or love, signified by the Sirens. He also (as in *Consolatio* 4 m3) resists the lustful Circe, in Fulgentius because he is married to Penelope, chastity (*Mit.* 2.10).

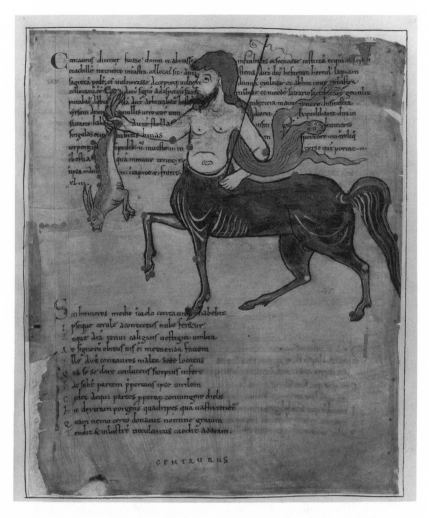

7. Centaur. From Cicero's *Aratea*, 11. 207–13. MS. Cotton Tiberius B V, part 1, fol. 43 (ca. 991–1016). By permission of the British Library, London.

Ovidian fables in book 2 of the *Mitologiae* demonstrating either Juno's enmity or the gods' include the stories of Tiresias, turned into a woman by Juno for the wrong answer, who represents the masculine-feminine seasons and therefore time; and of Prometheus, who stole fire from the gods as a gift of courage to the human race. The adultery of Venus and Mars behind the back of Juno's son Vulcan represents valor corrupted by lust. As a gloss on such love, Glaucus's feeling for Scylla is blind lust, for Glaucus is one-eyed and in Scylla's loins nestle wolves and sea dogs (signifying bestiality). Minerva, wisdom, resists Juno's son Vulcan, the heat of desire and the fire of rage; appropriately, her foolish opponent Midas, avarice, means "nihil sciens" ["knowing nothing"], for a miser is stupid (Mit. 2.10). As a result of Vulcan's desire occurs the nonfemale birth of Erichthonius, envy: "Et quidnam aliut subripiens furor sapientiae generare poterat nisi certamen inuidiae" ["And what else but the strife of envy could the rage of wisdom slipping away produce?"] (Mit. 2.11). Another product of Jupiter's adultery, this time with Semele (or lust, in Fulgentius), Dionysius (or Bacchus, drunkenness, Mit. 2.12) is discussed in the light of the Bacchae, the four stages of intoxication, or wine, forgetting, lust, and madness. A fable symbolizing the conjoining of upper (aerial, Juno-controlled) and lower worlds details the love between the moon (or Diana) and Endymion (Mit. 2.16), naturally explained as his discovery of the track of the moon or because night dew (coming from the stars and moon) enhances the success of shepherding sheep.

In the last, third, book most of the tales deal with the relationship between pairs or doubles, divided selves—two men or a man and a woman, often in their opposition signaling the Prudentian tension between vice and virtue—but on a more strictly human level. The fables of pairs often reflect as well the theme of transformation of which Ovid (43 B.C.–A.D. 17) was so fond in the Metamorphoses and which contributes to the unity and therefore narrative continuity of what Brooks Otis terms Ovid's "epic" as a "carmen perpetuum," continuous song.[26] From Ovid's roughly chronological Metamorphoses, beginning with the origin of the world and ending with the entrance of contemporary Caesar Augustus as a near-divine or epic hero, in four main sections,[27] Fulgentius approximates the structure of his own work, if one understands the first book in terms of the creation of the regional and planetary gods, followed in book 2 by the sons of the son Jove and related demigods and monsters, and concluding, in this third book, with the more consistently human figures. While Fulgentius moves as Ovid does from the creation of the universe to the microcosmos, the human race is not historically chronicled here. At any rate, the third book in particular seems to be indebted for its emphasis on transformation to Ovid—in the Heroides or Metamorphoses, or perhaps Lactantius Placidus's epitome of the latter in the Narrationes—or to Apuleius's Metamorphoses (although Fulgentius has picked tales from Ovid to insert in all three books).[28] The metamorphic tales, or tales at least of change and wondrous transformation, in this third book in particular include the stories of Bellerophon, who battles the Chimaera by riding Pegasus, born from the blood of transformed Medusa; Perdix, who becomes a partridge in Ovid but not in Fulgentius; Actaeon, the stag; Berecynthia and Attis, the hyacinth; Psyche and Cupid (from Apuleius's *Metamorphoses,* as Fulgentius declares), the god who changes form for his wife; Peleus and Thetis, water and mud whose marriage for fire (Jove) produces the perfect man Achilles; Myrrha, changed into a myrrh tree by her incestuous love for her father; Marsyas, whose skin was flayed off because of his temerity in challenging Apollo to a music contest; Orpheus, who twice loses Eurydice; Phineus, blinded and plagued by the Harpies; and Arethusa, who turned into a fountain to avoid the love of Alpheus. The only nonmetamorphic tale in book 3 is that of Hero and Leander, which, however, is about the changes wrought by love, old age, and death.

But in addition in the third and last book, thematically and symbolically the most reduced and diminished of the three, those who may not be heroes are engaged in the heroic (and epic) Neoplatonic (and Prudentian) battle of the soul against vice. As in previous books, such vices are often equated with women deities or the earth, *material/mater.* The battle as depicted in this book, however, does not always result in victory for the protagonist of the fable, and his (or her) metamorphosis signals this defeat of will. Bellerophon's relationship with Anteia represents the struggle between good counsel and lust. Perdix loves his mother, the earth, or Polycastes, too much, and so he puts away hunting for agriculture. Actaeon turned to a stag by Diana represents fear in that he had the heart of a stag and thus took a "nudam artis suae rationem" ["naked reckoning of his skill"] (*Mit.* 3.3; Helm, p. 62). Hero and Leander represent love, but because they die in the sea this means that desire dies with youth's end. Berecynthia, supposedly mother of the gods and queen of the mountains, as power contaminated by raging passion was too unstable to love; as a result Attis was castrated (love was cut off by that excess) and died:

> Ergo potentiae gloria semper et amore torretur et liuore torquetur citoque abscidit quod diligit, dum tamen amputet illud quod odit. Denique omnis nunc usque potentia nescit circa suos diuturnum seruare affectum, et quod amauerit cito aut zelando amputat aut fastidendo horrescit.
>
> [Thus the renown of power is always both aflame with love and devoured by envy, and speedily cuts off what it delights in, while it

also severs what it hates. Finally all power, now and always, cannot preserve affection among its followers from day to day, and what it loved it soon cuts off through passion or fears through revulsion.] (*Mit.* 3.5; Helm, p. 66)

Psyche and Cupid exemplify the spirit captured by greed, "Cupid" from *cupiditas.* Peleus and Thetis produce Achilles, or water and mud produce an almost perfect man, except for his heel; it is the heel his mother gripped as she dipped him that leads to his downfall, that is, his lustful desire for Polyxena. Myrrha, who fell in love with her father and turned into a myrrh tree that produced Adonis (loved by Venus) suggests that a father "omnium rerum solem esse dicebant, cuius opitulatu cuncta germinum adolescit maturitas" ["is the sun of all things, by whose aid the growth of plant life develops"] (*Mit.* 3.8; Helm, p. 72).

The note sounded in the final four tales demonstrates Fulgentius's literal concern with music and art, his figurative concern with the Neoplatonic light of truth contrasted with the darkness of this evil earthly life. Marsyas, the Satyr who attempted to compete with Apollo and lost (and was judged by the ignorant Midas), represents the solitary fool. Orpheus who lost Eurydice because he looked behind him as he was leading her out of Hell represents matchless sound losing the theory of the subject when an explanation is sought (both of these fables are replete with mystical theory and terms and allegorize the art of music). Phineus typifies the Macrobian fool Numenius who revealed a secret of the gods and had his food snatched away by the Harpies because "rapina ei aliquid de suo comedere non permittit" ["pillaging refuses to share anything of itself"] (*Mit.* 3.11; Helm, p. 79), which verges into the wonderful fable of Alpheus and Arethusa that concludes that the light of truth means evil must be forgotten. Both these final tales remind the reader, in different ways, of the point of the *Mitologiae* (and much else that Fulgentius wrote). Ending with the human choices we must all make, we return to our beginning point: Aeneas's descent into the underworld, emphasized in Fulgentius's *Expositio continentiae Virgilianae.*

II. THE VIRGILIAN HERO IN NORTH AFRICA

The *Continentia Virgiliana* in its thirty chapters contains a dialogue between the "homunculus" of the *Mitologiae,* Fulgentius the grammarian cast in the role of pupil, and a "magister," although not the Philosophy-like Calliope, or even the silent "master" addressed later in the satura, but the shade of Virgil,[29] who will plumb the literal and figurative content of the *Aeneid*. The form of this dialogue reaches beyond that between Fulgentius and Calliope in the *Mitologiae* to the debates in Cicero's *De natura deorum* and Macrobius's *Saturnalia,* but it also differs from them: instead of debating varying philosophical points of view concerning the existence of the gods (*De natura deorum*), or the merits of the various *artes* revealed in Virgil (*Saturnalia*), it contrasts sets of pairs—the literal versus the allegorical interpretation of a literary text, *scientia* versus *sapientia,* paganism versus Christianity, and two very opposed rhetorical styles. The homunculus, in a florid rhetorical style, sides with literalism, *scientia,* Christianity, all of which except the religion mark him as a "little man" in more than one sense. Virgil, however, stands for allegorism, *sapientia,* paganism, expressed in a lean virile clear and simple style—he represents a classical "giant." In a sense, Fulgentius continues the interests expressed by Cicero and Macrobius: he is once again debating the "existence" of the gods and he is certainly demonstrating Virgil's superiority.

The reasons for the mythographer's contrasts are both literary and defensive, in the manner of the early Greek apologists for Homer's myths. Fulgentius attempts to justify Virgil to the Christian world by showing that a wise and humble pagan may outshine a pedantic and proud Christian, a "little man" in reality. There seems to be no other explanation for the Christian but very unattractive character of the homunculus, who responds to the clear and moral adages of the philosopher (whom he addresses as "tu") with clerical, moralistic, and pompous pronouncements. To Virgil's explanation of Misenus's battle against Triton as the battle between the vainglorious man and contrition, "omnis ergo contritio omnem uanam laudem extinguit" ["for contrition destroys all vain praise"] (*Cont. Virg.* 8; Helm, p. 96), Fulgentius replies showing clearly that *his* "vainglory" has not yet been destroyed by his contrition: "I fully approve, Doctor, of your explanation, for the wholesome and God-given precept of us Christians charges that a 'broken and a contrite heart, O God, thou wilt not despise.'" The pagan Virgil, like his protagonist Aeneas, seems heroic and worthy of emulation.

I would argue, however, an even more interesting innovation: Fulgentius as author manipulates and reverses the grammatical roles of the classroom drama to depict the schoolmaster–alter ego "Fulgentius" as literal-minded inquisitor of the figure posturing as "student," the literary giant Virgil. The homunculus Fulgentius ironically questions his own teacher Virgil on the literal level of the narrative, and Virgil responds in a most unpuerile way by explaining its figurative meaning. For example, Fulgentius describes the contents of the first book of the *Aeneid*, after which Virgil expounds upon its moral significance, as indeed the teacher should in his lectures: the shipwreck of the Trojans can be read "in modum periculosae natiuitatis" ["as an allegory of the dangers of birth"] (*Cont. Virg.* 11; Helm, p. 91). The homunculus rarely strays from his pedagogic interest in the trivium and quadrivium, often boasting of his accomplishments in these fields: "In the book on physiology I recently brought out, dealing with medical matters, I discussed fully the whole art of arithmetic concerning the numbers seven and nine, and it will be a sign of discursiveness if I insert in one book what I have already discussed in others" (*Cont. Virg.* 13). The character Virgil's disquisitions, in contrast, touch frequently upon philosophy, etymologies, and moral matters of the mind and soul: for example, the Cyclops has a single eye "quia nec plenum nec rationalem uisum puerilis uagina portat et omnis aetas puerilis in superbia erigatur ut Ciclops" ["because this wildness of youth takes neither a full nor a rational view of things, and the whole period of youth is roused to a pride like that of the Cyclops"] (*Cont. Virg.* 15; Helm, p. 94).

Finally, the form of expression of the two characters differs: Fulgentius's manner of speaking communicates the flowery and bombastic, the rhetorical adornment for its own sake, whereas Virgil's is lean and spare, its strength the clarity, and truthfulness, of grammar. Fulgentius floridly begs the poet for a favor in an elaborate *occupatio* that details his awareness of the philosophical secrets veiled by Macrobian *fabula*:

> Cui ego: Seponas quaeso caperatos optutus, Ausonum uatum clarissime, rancidamque, altioris salsuram ingenii iocundioris quolibet mellis sapore dulciscas: nam non illa in tuis operibus quaerimus, in quibus aut Pitagoris modulos aut Eraclitus ignes aut Plato ideas aut Ermes astra aut Crisippus numeros aut endelecias Aristoteles inuersat, nec illa quae aut Dardanus in dinameris aut Battiades in paredris aut Campester in catabolicis infernalibusque cecinerunt, sed tantum illa quaerimus leuia, quae mensualibus stipendiis grammatici distrahunt puerilibus auscultatibus.

> [Most famed of Italian bards, I beg you cast off your wrinkled frowns and soften the sharp acidity of your lofty mind with a flavor of sweet honey. For I do not seek in your writings what Pythagoras busies

himself with in his harmonic numbers, or Heraclitus with his fires, or
Plato with his essence, or Hermes with his stars, or Chrysippus with
his numbers, or Aristotle with his perfect forms; nor am I concerned
with what Dardanus sang of powers, or Battiades of demons, or
Campester of ghosts and spirits of the lower world. I want only the
slight things that schoolmasters expound, for monthly fees, to boyish
ears.] (*Cont. Virg.* 3; Helm, pp. 85–86)

Virgil's blunt, dense reply relies on earthy, physical, corporeal imagery
without direction from the scholarly and literate tradition of the schools—
it derives from the natural world of experience. " 'Putabam,' inquit, 'uel te
homuncule creperum aliquid desipere, in cuius cordis uecturam meas
onerosiores exposuissem sarcinulas; at tu telleris glabro solidior adipatum
quidpiam ruptuas' " [" 'I thought, little man, that you would make
nonsense of anything abstruse had I opened up my weightier bundles to
convey its essentials; but, more dense than a clod of earth as you are, you
may snore over anything heavy' "] (*Cont. Virg.* 4; Helm, p. 86).

This idea of worthy pagan heroism is of course echoed in the thesis of the
Aeneid as the tale of "arms and the man," here signifying *uirtus,* "manliness," and *sapientia,* "wisdom," a human perfection in body and soul
contrary to the effeminate literalism and science of the imperfect homunculus. For this classical topos of *sapientia et fortitudo,* applicable to the
education of princes, applies to all, as evidenced by the first line of the
Aeneid, in which Virgil proclaims he will *first* sing of *arms* and the *man.*
Those three words, "arma, uirum, primus," sum up the three stages of "uita
humana," to possess, control, and ornament.

> "Arms," that is, manliness, belongs to the corporeal substance;
> "man," that is, wisdom, belongs to the intellectual substance; and
> "the first," that is, a ruler ["*princeps*"] belongs to the power of
> judgment; whence this order, to possess, to control, to ornament.
> Thus in the guise of a story [*historia*] I have shown the complete state
> of man: first, his nature; second, what he learns; third, his attaining to
> prosperity. (*Cont. Virg.* 10; bracketed Latin in Whitbread)

The process of human life depends upon educational and experiential
self-actualization. Virgil further explains that the first stage is natural, for
each creature capable of being taught is born with "virtus animi,"
"strength of soul," to allow it to be taught. In the second stage, learning
artificially adorns nature, like gold, for its improvement: "Ita et ingenium

natum est prouectible; proficit quia natum fuit; accedit felicitas ut prode sit quod proficit" ["So the mind is born to be developed; it develops because it was born; excellence works towards its own advancement"] (*Cont. Virg.* 10; Helm, p. 90). Finally, in the third stage of human life, experience hammers out the gold like a workman beating out the metal with his hammer—through discipline.

As in the *Mitologiae,* the dramatic conflict between flesh and spirit in the *Continentia* expressed through the heroic metaphor involves a Neoplatonic privileging of spirit. Fulgentius organizes his interpretation of the *Aeneid* (expressed rather humorously through the voice of Virgil, as we have just seen) by means of these three chronological stages of human life—nature, learning, and experience—with learning occupying the privileged place. Thus Aeneas becomes a type of the heroic man who progresses morally through his various journeys, a secular parallel to Christ. Fulgentius follows Servius and Macrobius in emphasizing the sixth book of the *Aeneid* as the most important, the middle stage of learning that outweighs the first stage, of nature, reflected in books 1 to 5, and the third stage, of experience, reflected in books 7 to 12. His mythological glosses on Virgil also follow Servius and Macrobius, with the greatest number, some twenty, deriving from book 6, followed by seven from book 1; from five books come three or fewer—books 3, 4, 8, 9, and 12; the other five have none at all. His method in glossing mythological figures can be safely described as Stoic in its use of outlandish etymologies and in the explanation of the gods as moral faculties.[30]

Fulgentius's dominating allegory of the lower world also derives from the Neoplatonic views of Servius and Macrobius and the understanding of life on earth as an *inferno,* views stressed especially (as we have seen previously) because of the commentators' focused attention on the sixth book and the descent into the underworld as truth's forgetting of evil memory as it conjoins with knowledge of that lower world.

His interpretation differs from theirs in its setting up an opposition between nature, associated with birth and the power of Juno (or goddess of birth), and perfection, associated with human development and wisdom and the power of Jupiter as manifested through Apollo, Mercury, Minerva, and so forth. Natural human gifts, the acquired gifts of learning, and the gain of good through virtue sum up the three stages in human growth as represented by the journey of heroic Aeneas. The three divisions of the *Continentia* and the three stages of human life, or Aeneas's journey, engage human faculties—the emotions and senses in the first stage, the faculties of epistemology and education in the second, and in the third various moral qualities—which are symbolized by various gods in this elaborate allegorization. The second stage prepares the human race for the third: Aeneas sees in the lower world of the sixth book "illic et poenas malorum et bonorum retributiones et amantum considerans tristes errores oculatus inspicit testis" ["both the punishments for the evil, the rewards for the good, and the sad wanderings of those given over to passion"] (*Cont. Virg.* 22; Helm, p. 98). Education will help the hero choose the good in his experiences (the third stage) rather than the evil and passionate, that which is controlled by the body.

Juno and Aeolus, the god of winds functioning in the aerial region, control human birth and therefore, as the first stage of human life, or nature (*Aeneid* 1–5), control the primitive epistemological faculties of infancy that include grief, silence, desire, and covetousness (Venus, Achates, Iopas, Cupid in book 1). Then adolescence and youth are expressed through the wildness and irrationality of the Cyclops (against whom Ulysses also battled) in book 3. For the passion of adolescence, represented by Aeneas and Dido in Juno's Carthage in book 4 (see fig. 8), Mercury, god of intellect, is the only rescue. As a result ensue the youthful, and male, games of Aeneas in book 5 to represent "a more prudent maturity following the examples of his *father's memory,* exercising the body in deeds of valor" (*Cont. Virg.* 17, my emphasis), succeeded by flaming shipwrecks that signify that the storms and tempests representing the recklessness of youth are overcome by the fire of intellect lit by true order, or Beroe.

The Macrobian sun god Apollo, god of learning and light linked to the Muses as a tenth Muse, appropriately teaches Aeneas, the man who has given up his youth with its "wandering sight" (Palinurus, whose name comes from *planonorus* and means "errabunda visio," who has been lost at sea). Aeneas descends into the underworld only after finding the temple of Apollo in book 6 of the *Aeneid,* all of which represents the second stage of human life, that of learning. Now Aeneas must prepare for the future by penetrating obscure (dark?) and secret mysteries of wisdom, "sapientiae obscura secretaque misteria" (*Cont. Virg.* 18; Helm, p. 96). To do so— which is also to enter the underworld—he must pluck the golden bough, or the study of philosophy and letters, which Virgil compares to the golden apples of the Hesperides (Aegle, Hespera, Medusa, and Arethusa, or study, intellect, memory, and eloquence). In his journey through the underworld, Aeneas uses the golden bough (or apples) to combat infernal figures and monsters who represent vices in antithesis to learning and therefore also

8. Aeneas before Dido. MS. ex Vindobensis Lat. 58, fol. 55v (10th c.). Courtesy of Biblioteca Nazionale "Vittorio Emanuele III" di Napoli, Naples. Photograph by Gioielli.

reveal the nature of this earthly life as a dark underworld governed by sorrow, mutability, dissent, old age, and death. As agents of such discord, Charon the boatkeeper represents time; Cerberus with his three heads allegorizes brawling and legal contention; Deiphobus and Dido are fear and lust; the iron tower, which is guarded by the Fury Tisiphone of "raging voice," symbolizes pride and conceit (*superbia* and *tumor*). The Giants Ixion, Salmoneus, and Tantalus also exemplify pride.

As Apollonian aids to combat these monsters, Aeneas has various pagan figures and gods. Rhadamanthus is judge "who knows how to control the flow of words is also the one who condemns and denounces pride" (*Cont. Virg.* 22; Helm, p. 101). Proserpina, Queen of the underworld, is memory, queen of knowledge, "scientiae regina memoria est": after Aeneas hangs the golden bough on the gateposts and enters Elysium, learning is over and memory must be perfected, for memory, advancing (*proserpens*), "in elisis . . . dominatur perenniter mentibus" ["reigns forever supreme in liberated minds"] (*Cont. Virg.* 22; Helm, p. 102). Other aids are provided by Musaeus (gifts of the Muses), Aeneas's father Anchises (the One Father, for "Anchises" means "patrium habitans," living in one's own land, just as there is only one God on high ("unus Deus enim pater, rex omnium, solus habitans in excelsis," *Cont. Virg.* 22; Helm, p. 102), and the river Lethe, which signifies that he must pursue gravity and forgo youthful levity.

The stage most distantly removed from Juno's hegemony, nature and birth, is the last third of the hero's journey (*Aeneid*, books 7–12), when he must discipline his soul through the experience of good and evil by means of Prudentian, that is, allegorical and epic, battle and conflict. Again he is aided by appropriate gods and heroes, who align mostly with Jupiter (and Minerva as wisdom) and against Juno. Aeneas as founder of the Empire in book 7 reaches Ausonia or Italy (increase of good achieved through learning), where he wishes to marry Lavinia ("laborum uiam," the road of toil), "for at this stage of life Everyman [*unusquius*] learns the value of toil in furthering his worldly possessions" (*Cont. Virg.* 24; Helm, p. 104; Latin in Whitbread). Even the genealogy of Lavinia follows the Macrobian allegorization: she is daughter of Latinus, from *latitando,* "being concealed," and descendant of Caunus, from *laborans sensus,* "toiling mind," who is married to Marica, *merica, cognitatio,* "thought." Aeneas's aid in book 8 comes from heroic companions, including Evander, helped by Juno's adversary Hercules. "Evander," from *evandros* in Greek, means "bonus uir" and suggests "Ergo iam perfectio uirilis humanae bonitatis societatem inquirit, a qua bonitatis uirtutes, id est Herculis gloriam audit, quemadmodum Cacum occiderit, quod nos Latine malum dicimus" ["Manly perfection seeks the comradeship of human goodness, whence it learns the manly qualities of goodness, that is, the feat of Hercules when he slew Cacus, whom in Latin we call evil"] (*Cont. Virg.* 25; Helm, pp. 104–5). Vulcan, Juno's only real son, clothes Aeneas in his arms with the protection of "burning counsel," which protects an "ardens consilium" ["ardent mind"] against attack. Demonstrating his virility in book 9, Aeneas fights Turnus, or fury, from *furibundus,* a word meaning furious rage, "contra omnem enim furiam sapientiae atque ingenii arma reluptant" ["for the arms of knowledge and of the mind resist all fury"] (*Cont. Virg.* 26; Helm, p. 105). Other victories include Aeneas's slaying in book 10 of Mezentius, "the despiser of the gods," an example of the spirit in the body which condemns the good created by God. Turnus's friend Messapus (from *misonepos,* meaning "orrens sermonem" or "defying speech") is also overcome; in book 11, Aeneas displays his armor. The Prudentian battle is never-ending, as the conclusion forecasts: in book 12 Juturna, who represents lasting destruction, as sister of "the raging mind" must quit the war, which means that destruction prolongs rage so that it is unending. The conclusion shows Juturna wheeling Turnus's chariot: "rotae enim in modum temporis ponuntur; unde et Fortuna rotam ferre dicitur, id est temporis volubilitatem" ["for the wheel symbolizes time, whereby Fortune is said to have a wheel, that is, mutability"] (*Cont. Virg.* 29; Helm, p. 135).

Given this allegorized life of Aeneas and, by extension, of his own author and poet, Virgil, probably the mid-fourth-century *Vita of Virgil* of Aelius Donatus, with its tripartite division of Virgil's literary career, influenced Fulgentius's use of Virgil as a character in the frame dialogue of the commentary on the *Aeneid.* Certainly the tripartite stages in human heroic life appear to mirror the allegorization of Virgil's own life as reflecting the three stages in his three works, the *Eclogues,* the *Georgics,* and the *Aeneid*— the pastoral, agricultural, and heroic. Although most of Donatus's commentary has been lost, this *Vita* of Virgil remains, along with a dedicatory letter and his introductory comments on bucolic poetry; the general nature of his commentary is, however, known from comments in Servius and others. When the remainder of the commentary had been lost, the *Vita* was affixed as a preface to his commentary on the *Eclogues* and thereafter used regularly in the schools; it was also repeated by Servius in his preface to his own commentary on the *Eclogues* as an introduction to his Donatan allegorization of Virgil's life, "Et dicit Donatus, quod etiam in poetae memoravimus vita." The order of composition of Virgil's works in following the natural sequence of human life reflects also cultural life: "in scribendis carminibus naturalem ordinem secutum esse Vergilium: primo enim pastoralis fuit in montibus vita, post agriculturae amor, inde bellorum cura successit" (Servius, *In Buc.,* prooem.). Loosely paraphrased and related to the specific works of Virgil, these lines have been interpreted to mean, "Vergil, in composing his works, followed an order corresponding to the life of man. The first condition of man was pastoral, and so Vergil wrote first of all the *Eclogues;* afterwards it was agricultural, and so he wrote next the *Georgics.* Then, as the number of the race increased, there grew up therewith the love of war; hence his final work is the *Aeneid,* which is full of wars."[31] In addition, the *Eclogues* themselves have been construed as biographical, inviting similar transfers to other Virgilian works and to Virgil. In the *Vita* the *Eclogues* were said to have been written to celebrate Pollio, Varus, and Gallus, and to honor Augustus, making them both private and public poems. Certainly the fourth eclogue, addressed to Pollio, is public, but the first and ninth, about Virgil's farm and Gallus's love, and the fifth, about the death of Virgil's brother, are private. The application of such a biographical reading of Virgil's *Eclogues* may have begun with Asconius Pedianus or even Virgil himself.[32]

Fulgentius's reading may then also have been shaped by Servius's more topical allegorization of the stages and incidents in Virgil's own life in the commentaries on the *Eclogues* and *Georgics.* These topical glosses are in nature very like the euhemeristic glosses in Cicero's *De natura deorum,* Servius's commentary on the *Aeneid,* and Macrobius's *Saturnalia:* they likewise celebrate the special and "divine" in the noteworthy human, in this case, the apotheosized Virgil. Such topical or historical allegorism had been anticipated by similar if sporadic references in Servian commentary on the *Aeneid,* in fifty-three notes mostly describing Aeneas as a type of Augustus apparently provided by Servius because he had assumed that one of Virgil's purposes, in addition to imitating Homer, was to praise Augustus through his ancestors ("Intentio Virgilii haec est, Homerum imitari et Augustum laudare a parentibus").[33] But Servius applies what might be termed political or topical or personal allegory to the *Eclogues* especially, reading various literary characters and incidents as veiling actual persons and incidents important in Virgil's own life. In the first eclogue, "Tityrus" is Virgil and the god to whom he will sacrifice is Augustus. In the second eclogue, even with the opening lines missing, "Corydon" is probably Virgil and "Alexis" is Alexander, slave of Pollio given to Virgil at a banquet, while "Menalcas" and "Amaryllis" are more willing lovers than Cebes and Levia, whom Virgil actually loved. The eighth eclogue, which has no allegorical comment within, invokes "Pollio," a name which may refer actually to Augustus. The tenth eclogue is not entirely allegorical, for Gallus speaks in his own voice, even though mistress Cytheris is known as "Lycoris." In the first and the ninth eclogues, Virgil in reality refers to the confiscation of his farm.

All of these practices helped to shape the Fulgentius commentary on

Statius's *Thebaid.* It seems likely that Fulgentius and not some Carolingian imitator was the author of that commentary, given the many Fulgentian traits, including etymological allegories, evident therein. Fulgentius here grafts the idea of the journey of human life onto the structure of Statius's story. Statius unifies the *Thebaid* by means of Stoic typology, in that the Stoics believed that an individual guilty of one sin is guilty of them all. The use of balances and contrasts throughout the epic to bolster this Stoic typology not only helps to unify it but also to explain Fulgentius's later fantastic allegorization of the entire work (rather than individual lines, phrases, and words, as Lactantius's commentary does). Hence Oedipus exemplifies bitterness or hatred; Eteocles, tyranny; Polynices, vengeance or envy; Adrastus, tranquillity or wisdom; Tydeus, anger; Amphiaraus, priestly piety; Hippomedon, brute force; Parthenopaeus, innocence; Capaneus, blasphemy; and Theseus, mercy or justice. Fulgentius likewise conceives the narrative as the hero's own mythic story—perhaps because of the victory and homecoming of Theseus, who incarnates *sapientia et fortitudo.* As is the case with Hercules in book 2 of the *Mitologiae,* every crisis in the history of Thebes demonstrates the singular triumph of these qualities over adversaries which personify appropriately educational flaws.

By so adapting a familiar allegorical and Stoic schema to unfamiliar material—only Lactantius Placidus had completed a commentary on the *Thebaid,* and his was primarily devoted to grammatical and rhetorical information—Fulgentius evidences that ingenuity grounded in the strength of previous example which he learned from Macrobius. Fulgentius's application of the pattern of a Virgilian life-journey unifies an epic narrative criticized from its inception for its lack of unity and of hero,[34] although such a unification would not engender a strong or significant *Thebaid* commentary tradition.

Fulgentius unifies the epic story of Thebes by tracing the story of its conqueror Theseus as a triumph over a family divided and discordant. Employing an implicit Stoic analogy between the macrocosm ruled by the sun (Macrobius's Apollo, god of light and truth), and the microcosm ruled by the soul, Fulgentius interprets the city of Thebes as the soul of man, for in Greek it is pronounced *"theosbe,"* that is, "the goodness of God" (*Sup. Theb.,* trans., p. 240), governed by inappropriate rulers, and he interprets Theseus as God himself. The genealogy of Oedipus allegorizes this spiritual analogy. In the human soul sacred light rules, because of which, it becomes joyful: Laius, from *lux ayos,* "sacred light," is married to Jocasta, "pure joy." When Oedipus ("licentiousness," because derived from *edo,* "licentious beast"), is born, joy (Jocasta) is defiled. At maturity Oedipus therefore slays his father: licentiousness snuffs out the sacred light. From the incestuous union spring only female or feminine-souled children (feminine because immoral, evil). Oedipus's two sons especially represent greed and lust, which grow so well that he blinds himself in his grief over their growth. The argument between Polynices and Eteocles divides the soul until the root of all evils, Eteocles, holds sway—he rules the first year, and Polynices enters exile with the Greeks and marries Adrastus's daughter. This means that the lustful flee to worldly wisdom in an attempt to compensate for the abandonment of lust, marrying foreknowledge, or providence, daughter of philosophy.

In the remainder of the allegorization, the valorization of Christianized scholastic knowledge provides a means for philosophy and the seven liberal arts to battle ignorance and immorality paganized through a specific link with idolatry and the North African and Egyptian cult of Isis. When Polynices seeks to rule again, the greedy Eteocles refuses, forcing the seven kings of Greece (the seven liberal arts supporting philosophy, or Adrastus) to vow vengeance. On their way to battle because they excessively thirst for worldly knowledge, the kings (or seven liberal arts) drink at a stream which Hypsipyle (love of Isis, or idolatry) has found. To yield to this thirst is fatal, as it was for Archemorus, foster child of idolatry slain by a serpent (the Adversary). As the Seven battle Eteocles, or greed, each dies except Adrastus, "For philosophy, though it may perish for the greedy, is not in itself destroyed" (*Sup. Theb.*, Helm, p. 185; trans., p. 242). When the two brothers meet, they destroy each other, after which pride (Creon, who curbs all things) arises in the mind, prevents their burial (that is, keeps unconcealed the worldly branches of knowledge). After their wives, or feelings, ask Theseus (God) for help, he defeats Creon, as pride is overcome by humility, leaving "Thebe id est humana anima quassata est quidem, sed diuinae benignitatis clementia subueniente liberatur" ["Thebes, that is, the soul of man, left shattered; but it is freed when the grace of the goodness of God comes to its aid"] (*Sup. Theb.*, Helm, p. 186 ; trans., p. 243).

In addition to this history of the "soul of man," or the history of the city of Thebes, so clearly influenced by Fulgentius's interest in the Virgilian history of Trojan Aeneas, founder of the Empire, the *Super Thebaiden* also includes at the beginning, like the *Mitologiae* and *Continentia*, a debate or dialogue introducing the commentary. Herein appears a most familiar Fulgentian exposition on poetic fictions covering moral precepts. In a well-known passage the commentator compares the moral truths with the kernel of a nut hidden under a shell.

> in nuce enim duo sunt, testa et nucleus, sic in carminibus poeticis duo, sensus litteralis et misticus; latet nucleus sub testa: latet sub sensu litterali mistica intelligentia; ut habeas nucleum, frangenda est testa: ut figurae pateant, quatienda est littera; testa insipida est, nucleus saporem gustandi reddit: similiter non littera, sed figura palato intelligentiae sapit.

> [Just as there are two parts to a nut, the shell and the kernel, so there are two parts to poetic compositions, the literal {sensus litteralis} and the allegorical meaning {misticus}. As the kernel is hidden under the shell, so the allegorical interpretation {mistica intelligentia} is hidden under the literal meaning; as the shell must be cracked to get the kernel, so the literal must be broken for the allegories to be discovered; as the shell is without taste and it is the kernel which provides the tasty flavor, so it is not the literal but the allegorical which is savored on the palate of the understanding.] (Sup. Theb., Helm, p. 180; trans., p. 239)

With this metaphor we return to the notion that the lies of the Greeks mask truths, by which the *Mitologiae* demonstrated Fulgentius's adaptation of Macrobian allegories. The difference here is Fulgentius's dependence on the Augustinian image of the text as having a body and a soul, a literal or carnal meaning and a figurative or spiritual meaning. The image beautifully fits the Neoplatonic and Augustinian "city of man" which this commentary on the *Thebaid* reveals under the carnal or literal meaning of the text, a pagan and fallen city eventually redeemed by God in the figure of the hero Theseus. Like Christ, and like the other types of Virgilian hero, from Aeneas to Ulysses and Hercules, Theseus, too, descended into hell with his friend Pirithous, although the commentary does not mention this.

In its metaphor for the Neoplatonic view of the human soul in the body, the *Super Thebaiden* aptly sums up Fulgentius's contribution to mythography, conditioned by his regard for his North African predecessors and late antique prosimetra (a form whose combined poetry and prose represents a kind of nut with kernel). From its more Neoplatonic orientation the Servian descent into the underworld will take on new, moralistic and ecclesiastical significance in subsequent mythographies, applied to Ovid's Cupid by two great multicultural scholars, Isidore of Seville and Theodulf of Orleans.

Chapter Four

OVID'S CUPID AS
DEMON OF FORNICATION:
THE EPISCOPAL MYTHOGRAPHIES
OF ISIDORE OF SEVILLE AND
THEODULF OF ORLEANS

In a very important mythological poem, "De libris quos legere solebam" ("The Books I Used to Read"), Theodulf of Orleans pretends to imitate Ovid himself by reworking the *Fasti* and the *Metamorphoses*,[1] but actually he glosses classical myths by way of the grammarians and other scholars. This innovative mythographer applied what he knew from contemporary school commentaries to the new texts that he was reading. He tells the reader that his favorite authors include the classical poets Virgil, Ovid, Horace, Lucan, and Cicero; the way that he interprets them derives from the commentaries of Servius and Fulgentius on the descent of Aeneas into the underworld, and from Isidore's "De diis gentium" in book 8 of the *Etymologiae*.

Theodulf, in "De libris," uses Isidore to gloss the demonic figure of Cupid, although he also "Virgilizes" his Ovidian poem—that is, he adapts to Ovid old-fashioned Virgil commentary predominant in the schools. In particular, he uses the mythographic convention of moralization of the sixth book of the *Aeneid*—tracing the *descensus ad inferos* of Aeneas—as a model upon which to base his own interpretation of the underworld. His ingenuity in employing analogy anticipates a new mythographic commentary tradition on Ovid that will flourish much later. His reasons for applying such glossation to Ovid, however, derive in part from the emphasis on theory of *fabula* in Isidore's *Etymologiae* and the presentation of the origin of the gods in the chapter called "De diis gentium." Theodulf found Isidore particularly congenial, perhaps because he too was—almost certainly—Spanish, but also because of the succinctness of the Iberian's mythographies. For example, Theodulf used Isidore's imagery of earth-gods with drums (*Etym.* 8.11.61) for his own informing myth of Tellus: "Alia Pictura, in qua erat imago terrae in modum orbis comprehensa" ["Another Picture, in which there was an image of the earth comprehended in the mode of an orb"].[2]

Isidore of Seville (fl. 602–36) was enormously influential in the Middle Ages: there remain extant a thousand manuscripts of the *Etymologiae*,[3] and, "Save for the Scriptures, there was no other book which enjoyed such a wide circulation in the Middle Ages."[4] See, for example, the authority granted to him by means of the *accessus*-like portrait in a twelfth-century English manuscript (fig. 9). In addition to his excellence as a scholar, Isidore was also well known as a model of stylistic excellence in Spain and the Middle Ages in general.[5] In the tradition of the Roman encyclopedists of the Republic and Empire interested in preserving Hellenistic learning (Varro, Verrius Flaccus, Pliny, and especially Suetonius), Isidore gathered together and summed up in the *Etymologiae* the "dead remnants of secular learning."[6] Indeed, his work is an encyclopedia of all known subjects and arts—not only the seven liberal arts, themselves occupying three of the twenty books, but also other subjects, including law, medicine, history, holy writ, celestial and terrestrial hierarchy, geography, zoology, metallurgy, agriculture, crafts.[7]

Theodulfus, or Theodulf, of Orleans (ca. 760–821),[8] as a member of Charlemagne's cadre of scholars intent on preserving the classics in order to learn Latin well enough to read the Bible,[9] brought with him the values of old-fashioned Roman education. Theodolf was a Goth, whose native land was possibly Italian, Spanish, or even French, but most probably Spanish.[10] In Spain, the Romanized education that produced Isidore still flourished and Theodulf was able to encourage and foster the Carolingian renaissance of classical authors.[11] Theodulf was a Benedictine whom Charlemagne drew into the royal circle; he ruled as bishop from the abbey at Fleury for twenty years (from 801 to 821) until Charlemagne died, when he was sent into exile and thereafter soon himself died.[12] Best known for the Palm Sunday poem, "Gloria, laus et honor tibi, sit, rex Christe, redemptori," he was, however, not a particularly religious poet. He expressed his more obvious love of classical learning most clearly in *Carmina* 46, "De septem liberalibus artibus in quadam pictura depictis" ("On the Seven Liberal Arts Depicted in This *Pictura*"), in which the seven liberal arts are personified and appear with identifying symbols.[13]

Two influential scholars from different generations but probable Iberian ties thus expressed their admiration for books, and classical learning,

9. Isidore. MS. Bodley 602, fol.
36r (13th-c. English, school of
Matthew Paris). By permission
of the Bodleian Library,
University of Oxford.

similarly, while rationalizing study of the gods in slightly different ways.
The approach of the earlier scholar Isidore essentially fossilizes the Stoic
etymologizing allegories of the gods, both moral and physical, and also
voices and therefore preserves the late patristic euhemerism of Augustine
and Lactantius. By contrast, Theodulf, though strongly influenced by
Isidore, produced an innovative rationalization of the gods. Both of them
reveal an explicit polemical concern with the seven liberal arts, with
education, as the means to the literacy of clerics charged with the
conversion and salvation of others and hence with the growth of the
Church.

Why Isidore as a Christian scholar should write such an encyclopedia as the *Etymologiae* becomes clearer upon examination of the period during which he flourished. Spain in the sixth to seventh centuries was very Roman, very civilized, and the Visigothic conquest of the country had been gradual and well-assimilated. MacFarlane notes that "The country was being unified under the Visigothic kings of Toledo, and in 578 King Reccared would resolve the religious conflict between the Catholic Hispano-Romans and the Arian Visigoths by embracing the Catholic faith."[14] Probably Isidore was Hispano-Roman,[15] even though his family moved to Seville at the time of Isidore's birth, for his family originally belonged to Cartagena (his father Severianus was an important Hispano-Roman citizen there, his brother Leander was born and grew up there), was of orthodox religion, and bore Roman names. Perhaps because of the early death of his parents, all of the children in the family—two brothers, Leander and Fulgentius, and a sister, Florentina—entered the Church: Fulgentius was bishop of Astigi, Florentina was a nun; Leander, who raised Isidore, later became the bishop of Seville; Isidore, who in 589 entered a monastery as either clerk or monk, succeeded Leander after his death in 599 (Isidore died on April 4, in 636).[16]

Isidore's works express this conflation of cultures and interests. During his forty years as bishop of Seville he wrote many works with a scriptural, patristic, or ecclesiastical subject—*Prooemia*, on the contents of each book of Holy Scripture; *De ortu et obitu patrum*, on the deeds of the Fathers; the *Officia*, on why everything is done in the Church; *De nominibus legis et evangeliorum*, on the mystic names of persons in the Bible; on heresies, *De haeresibus;* the *Sententiae; Contra Judaeos*, which proves the Catholic faith by means of the Law and the Prophets; *De viris illustribus*, with a rule for monks. But he also wrote works not ostensibly biblical, although their secular subjects were explained or paralleled by his usual patristic concerns: the *Synonyma*, in two books, in which Reason comforts the Soul; *De natura rerum*, about the elements, explained by looking at the Church Fathers and philosophers; *De numeris*, on arithmetic, because of scriptural numbers. And many of his other encyclopedic works are more secular in nature, often centering on the etiology of things or concepts, including *Differentiae*, on the differences of words and things; *Chronica*, from the beginning of the world to his own time; another history, *De origine Gothorum et regno Suevorum et etiam Vandalorum historia;* the *Quaestiones;* and the unfinished *Etymologiae*, the work of most interest to us, and which, according to Ernest Brehaut, in condensed form contains everything he wrote elsewhere.[17]

Isidore the mythographer is represented by "De diis gentium," chapter

11 of book 8 of the *Etymologiae*. Theodulf was not the only Carolingian it touched. "De diis gentium" was copied almost verbatim by the Carolingian Hraban Maur (784–856)[18] and thereafter influenced many later generations: John of Damascus in the eighth century, Vincent of Beauvais in the mid-thirteenth century, Guido delle Colonne, Ralph Higden, and Trevisa, the author of *Gest hystoriale* in the fourteenth century, as well as John Gower and John Lydgate.

An examination of Theodulf's use of classical myth in "The Books I Used to Read," overlain as it is with patristic exegesis,[19] will reveal his conflicted personal situation as an ecclesiastic alien to the Carolingian court, a man even more firmly focused than Isidore on the conservative Roman education and mythography prevalent in the provinces. Theodulf's point is that we can read the pagan authors if we read with care, wisely, using the commentators to guide our way into the underworld of pagan mythology described by the mendacious poets. Theodulf has interpreted the underworld as figuratively inhabited by the pagan gods, an underworld dominated by vision and falsity, a Neoplatonic realm of moral death and wickedness. This interpretation set the pattern for the mythological dream vision poetry so popular in the late Middle Ages. Not only did he leave behind Ovidian *carmina* as models for later generations of poets, Theodulf also advanced the idea of Ovidian commentary, although such commentaries would not indeed burgeon until the twelfth century. And his understanding of Ovid had been filtered through his innovative[20] countryman Isidore.

Theodulf uses the tradition of Virgil commentary on book 6 of the *Aeneid* as a model for his conflation of two different mythographic traditions, one Ovidian and Isidorian, on Cupid, one Virgilian and Servian, on Aeneas. In this conflation of traditions he defines vice as an underworld, a wrong turn, to which we are led by our illicit sexual desires in particular, but also as the underworld of poetry, a place of falsity, lies, the deceits and manipulations of the tongue, of dreams—an underworld into which the seductive poetry of the classical poets draws us.

I. THEODULF'S ISIDORIAN CUPID IN "DE LIBRIS," CARMINA 45

In "De libris quos legere solebam" Theodulf invokes the malicious figure of Cupid that originates in Ovid's *Metamorphoses* in the fable of Daphne and Apollo.

> Primus amor Phoebi Daphne Peneia, quem non
> fors ignara dedit, sed saeva Cupidinis ira,
> Delius hunc nuper, victa serpente superbus,
> viderat adducto flectentem cornua nervo

[Now the first love of Phoebus was Daphne, daughter of Peneus, the river-god. It was no blind chance that gave this love, but the malicious wrath of Cupid. Delian Apollo, while still exulting over his conquest of the serpent, had seen him bending his bow with tight-drawn string.] (*Metamorphoses* 1.452–56)

Ovid's "wanton boy" Cupid (addressed as "lascive puer") is appropriately petty, both small and mean-spirited, in his angry response to Apollo's demeaning (if truthful) suggestion that Cupid should be lighting the fires of love instead of competing with the warrior Apollo and his bow:

> "quid" que "tibi, lascive puer, cum fortibus armis?"
> dixerat: "ista decent umeros gestamina nostros,
> qui dare certa ferae, dare vulnera possumus hosti,
> qui modo pestifero tot iugera ventre prementem
> stravimus innumeris tumidum Pythona sagittis.
> tu face nescio quos esto contentus amores
> inritare tua, nec laudes adsere nostras!"

["What hast thou to do with the arms of men, thou wanton boy? That weapon befits my shoulders; for I have strength to give unerring wounds to the wild beasts, my foes, and have but now laid low the Python swollen with countless darts, covering whole acres with plague-engendering form. Do thou be content to light the hidden fires of love, and lay not claim to my honours."] (*Metamorphoses* 1.456–62)

In response, "Venus's son" warns that,

> "figat tuus omnia, Phoebe,
> te meus arcus . . . quantoque animalia cedunt
> cuncta deo, tanto minor est tua gloria nostra"

["Thy dart may pierce all things else, Apollo, but mine shall pierce thee; and by as much as all living things are less than deity, by so much less is thy glory than mine"] (*Metamorphoses* 1.463–65)

This foil for the bow-bearing Apollo directs his malice (*ira*) to Apollo by means of a sharp gold-tipped arrow of love and to the god's first love, Daphne, by means of a blunt lead-tipped arrow causing flight from love. Flying to Parnassus,

> sagittifera prompsit duo tela pharetra
> diversorum operum: fugat hoc, facit illud amorem;
> quod facit, auratum est et cuspide fulget acuta,
> quod fugat, obtusum est et habet sub harundine plumbum.
> hoc deus in nympha Peneide fixit, at illo
> laesit Apollineas traiecta per ossa medullas;
> protinus alter amat, fugit altera nomen amantis
> silvarum latebris captivarumque ferarum
> exuviis gaudens innuptaeque aemula Phoebus.

[He took from his quiver two darts of opposite effect: one puts to flight, the other kindles the flame of love. The one which kindles love is of gold and has a sharp, gleaming point; the other is blunt and tipped with lead. This last the god fixed in the heart of Peneus' daughter, but with the other he smote Apollo, piercing even unto the bones and marrow. Straightway he burned with love; but she fled the very name of love, rejoicing in the deep fastnesses of the woods, and in the spoils of beasts which she had snared, vying with the virgin Phoebe.] (*Metamorphoses* 1.466–76)

Cupid as a subverter of reason also appears in the *Aeneid*, where he kindles madness in Queen Dido ("donisque furentem / incendat reginam," *Aeneid* 1.663) as a result of his deceptive substitution for Ascanius, at the instigation of his mother Venus, to protect his brother Aeneas. Again this pejorative role crops up in Servius's comment on the first line of book 4 of the *Aeneid*, where Dido is described as having long been "smitten" by a "love-pang" and feeding the "wound" with her life-blood, "wasted with fire unseen" ("At regina gravi iamdudum saucia cura / volnus alit venis et caeco carpitur igni," *Aeneid* 4.1–2). Servius glosses *saucia* ("smitten") by noting that it was Cupid indeed who has made this wound with his arrow ("SAUCIA hinc subiungit 'vulnus alit.' et bene adludit ad Cupidinis tela, ut paulo post ad faculam, *ut* 'et caeco carpitur igni': nam sagittarum vulnus est, facis incendium," *In Aen.* 4.1). No doubt Virgil is behind the fact that Cupid also figures in the "irrationabilis et instabilis amor" of Augustine's *Contra Faustum Manichaeum* (20.9).

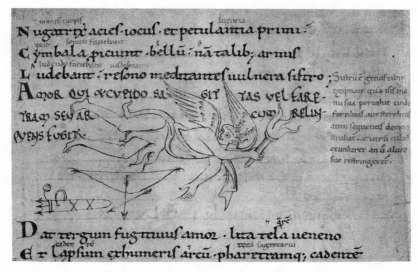

10. Cupid in Flight. MS. P. A. 22, fol. 17v (11th–12th c.). Courtesy of Bibliothèque Municipale de Lyon.

The boyish god will remind Theodulf of the youthful desires of amorous love that will ensure a quick and permanent descent to hell—and an apt warning to all schoolboys. In "De libris," Theodulf depicts Cupid as a winged nude boy ("Fingitur alatus, nudus, puer esse Cupido," "De libris" 33) carrying arrows and a bow, "deadly weapons and a torch" ("Ferre arcum et pharetram toxica, tela, facem," "De libris" 34). This description is then followed by a mythographic gloss which Theodulf found in the encyclopediast Isidore, for Theodulf makes no distinction here between what is appropriate for poetry and what for prose: Cupid is *alatus,* or winged, Theodulf explains, "fickle and naked because of his manifest crimes," and a boy, *puer,* because "he lacks skill and reason": "Quod levis, alatus, quod aperto est crimine, nudus, / Sollertique caret quod ratione, puer" ("De libris" 35–36). Isidore's own gloss in the *Etymologiae* similarly explains the reason for this boyish god's wings, in his instability: "Qui ideo alatus pingitur, quia nihil amantibus levius, nihil mutabilius invenitur. Puer pingitur, quia stultus et irrationabilis amor" ["He is depicted as winged, because there is nothing more flighty than lovers, nothing more fickle. He is depicted as a boy, because love is foolish and irrational"] (*Etym.* 8.11.80). For the currency of this concept of winged Cupid, consider the image of

Cupid in flight, from an eleventh- or twelfth-century Lyons manuscript (fig. 10). By means of the image of bow and arrow Theodulf describes the process of deceit, manipulation, and rationalization involved in illicit *amor:* "Mens prava in pharetra, insidiae signantur in arcu, / Tela, puer, virus, fax tuus ardor, Amor" ["His depraved mind is symbolised by the quiver, his trickery by the bow, / the boy's arrows are poison and his torch is the ardour of love"] ("De libris" 37–38). Isidore's Cupid holds a bow and arrow as a like sign of destructive emotional power: "Sagittam et facem tenere fingitur. Sagittam, quia amor cor vulnerat, facem, quia inflammat" ["He is depicted as holding an arrow and a torch, an arrow because love wounds the heart, a torch because he sets it afire"] (*Etym.* 8.11.80).

In the dramatic narrative of what seems to be a didactic poem, Theodulf takes the place of Ovid's obstreperous Apollo and attacks the boyish god. Using a series of rhetorical questions he echoes that initial denigration of the love-god in the *Metamorphoses* by the god of poetry and wisdom.

Mobilius, levius quid enim vel amantibus esse
    Quit, vaga mens quorum seu leve corpus inest?
Quis facinus celare potest quod Amor gerit acer,
    Cuius semper erunt gesta retecta mala?
Quis rationis eum spiris vincire valebit,
    Qui est puer effrenis et ratione carens?
Quis pharetrae latebras poterit penetrare malignas.
    Tela latent utero quot turculenta malo?
Quo face coniunctus virosus prosulit ictus.
    Qui volat, et perimens vulnerat, urit, agit?

[For what could be more changeable or fickle than lovers
    Whose minds wander and whose bodies are lascivious?
Who can conceal the crimes passionately committed by Love
    Whose evil deeds will always be exposed?
Who with the coils of reason could bind
    That boy who is uncontrollable and irrational?
Who could see into the wicked darkness of his quiver to count how
    Many cruel weapons lie in the evil womb
Whence shoots its blow, poisoned and mingled with fire,
    Which soars, deals a deadly wound, burns, and hounds us on?]
       ("De libris" 39–48)

Clearly, the scholar Theodulf wants his audience to understand the Ovidian battle in his poem as allegorical and Prudentian (Prudentius in line 16 is "noster et ipse parens"), between reason and desire.

> Est sceleratus enim *moechiae daemon* et atrox,
>> Ad luxus miseros saeva *barathra* trahens.
> Decipere est promptus, semperque nocere paratus,
>> Daemonis est quoniam *vis, opus, usus* ei.

> [The *demon of fornication* is terrible and wicked,
>> It drags wretches down to the brutal *purgatory* of loose living.
> It is prompt to deceive and always ready to do harm,
>> Since it has the Devil's *force, resources,* and *experience* at its
>> command.] ("De libris" 49–52; my emphasis)

Taking up Isidore's definition of Cupid as "daemon fornicationis," Theodulf transforms the personification of cupidity into "moechiae daemon," the *daemon* or demon as an inhabitant of the underworld associated with adultery. After using bow and arrows this Cupid draws the lecherous into an abyss, an underworld or "barathrum" (pit, dungeon, inferno) of "loose living," of vice, encouraged by the Devil.

The allusion to the descent into the underworld leads Theodulf to a fantastic interpretation of the two Virgilian gates of sleep—the false gate of ivory, the true gate of horn (*Aeneid* 6.893–96). These two gates also parallel the doors of Dis and in Macrobius's cosmology are identified as the portals of Cancer and Capricorn in the Milky Way from which souls descend at birth and to which they reascend after death. Theodulf tells us:

> Somnus habet geminas, referunt ut carmina, portas,
>> Altera vera gerit, altera falsa tamen,
> Cornea vera trahit, producit eburnea falsa.
>> Vera vident oculi, falsa per ora meant.
> Rasile nam cornu, tenere et translucet ocellus,
>> Obtunsumque vehit oris hiatus ebur.
> Non splendorem oculus, non sentit frigora cornu,
>> Par denti atque ebori visque colorque manet.
> Est portis istis virtus non una duabus,
>> Os fert falsa, oculus nil nisi vera videt.

> [Sleep has two doors, so poetry relates,
>> one bears the truth and the other falsehood.
> The gate of horn draws in truth, the ivory gate brings out falsehood.

>The eyes see the truth and falsehood passes through the lips.
>For horn is smooth, and the eye is also tender and translucent,
>>While the opening of the mouth bears a barrier of ivory.
>The eye experiences no light, and horn feels no cold,
>>the tooth and ivory alike have strength and colour.
>Those two gates do not have the same properties,
>>The mouth bears falsehoods, the eye sees nothing but the truth.]
>>>("De libris" 53–62)

Associated literally with Aeneas's choice of two doors from which to depart from hell in book 6 of the *Aeneid,* the gates are interpreted here as the entryway into the bodily underworld of the microcosm—the false gate of dreams and nightmares (the mouth) and the true gate of poetry (the eyes). Theodulf's specific equation of mouth and eye, most likely borrowed from Servius, resembles the first Vatican mythographer's gloss on the same Virgilian passage (Mythogr. I 223/228), in which the mythographer explains rather literally how ivory resembles the bone of teeth and horn the color of eyes.[21]

This idea of this world, and our bodies, as an inferno, or inferior place, would appeal to those Carolingian scholars concerned with education and conversion to Christianity. A whole series of school commentaries on the sixth book of the *Aeneid* increasingly emphasize Aeneas as the Everyman whose descent into the underworld is perceived as a model for the moral choices, virtuous or vicious, which the Christian makes on earth and which determine salvation or damnation after death. Cupid indeed rules the vicious path in the Servian gloss on the golden bough, the path which our hero Aeneas should avoid. This Christianized view of the *Aeneid* rationalizes study of this classical work and suggests that other, similar, classical works—even Ovid's *Metamorphoses*—may similarly veil truths important to the Christian beneath their mythological fable.

II. ISIDORE'S VIRGILIAN UNDERWORLD OF DEMONIC GODS

As we have seen previously, the most important aspect of the mythographic model provided for commentary in the early centuries A.D. by the sixth book of Virgil's *Aeneid* was the epic descent into the underworld. As a result of Servius's glosses, Hades was transformed into a moral space symbolic of human life where we make choices guided not by rationality but by concupiscence. A century or so later, Fulgentius's *Aeneid* commentary, in its similar focus on the sixth book, presented the successful descent as the mastery of education and learning. (Fulgentius was probably the more influential of the two for Theodulf's magisterial allegory in *Carmina* 45). Familiarity with the important sixth book of the *Aeneid* may have prompted Boethius's interest in the three central mythological heroes of the *Consolatio,* Orpheus, Ulysses, and Hercules. In each case, Boethius accordingly renders the fable as a Neoplatonic conflict, between the "underworld" of dark passion and the hero's attempt to control it by understanding it.

In the first of the three mythological poems, Boethius's manner of framing and moralizing the descent of wise Orpheus into an underworld of vice suggests an awareness of this early commentary on Virgil's sixth book. This poem, at the end of book 3, opens with an anticipation of the success of the hero Hercules:

> Felix qui potuit boni
> Fontem visere lucidum,
> Felix qui potuit gravis
> Terrae solvere vincula.

> [Happy was he who could look upon
> The clear fount of the good;
> Happy who could loose the bonds
> Of heavy earth.] (*Consolatio* 3 m12)

In contrast to Hercules is Orpheus, even though his harping for Pluto and Proserpina succeeded in returning Eurydice to him in hell. The meter elaborates on Orpheus's loss of his wife a second time because he looks back to see if she follows safely behind him. The meter concludes with:

> Vos haec fabula respicit
> Quicumque in superum diem
> Mentem ducere quaeritis.
> Nam qui Tartareum in specus
> Victus lumina flexerit,
> Quidquid praecipuum trahit
> Perdit, dum videt inferos.

> [To you this tale refers,
> Who seek to lead your mind
> Into the upper day;

For he who overcome should turn back his gaze
Towards the Tartarean cave,
Whatever excellence he takes with him
He loses when he looks on those below.] (*Consolatio* 3 m12)

The gloss, by asserting the Neoplatonic structure of hell as below, infernal, inferior, and earthly, and the heavens, "upper day," as above, superior, supernal, correlates the macrocosmic body and soul with that of the microcosm. In this sense, Orpheus's gaze backward upon this underworld, during his quest for excellence, expresses a lack of self-discipline or self-control.

More than human, the hero should dominate the underworld. Also clear is that the underworld that Augustine or Isidore imagines as adversarial for our hero is full of demons and devils—the classical gods rather than Tityus, Tantalus, and Cerberus. Like Theodulf's vision, Isidore's of the underworld depends upon a Fulgentian view of the *Aeneid* that will affect his conception of the classical gods he supposedly considers demonic.

The cosmic catalogue of the gods provided by Isidore in "De diis gentium," although a vibrant world full of gods that will be eventually recast as an "underworld," like the genealogy of the first Vatican mythographer, presents us with a World Soul that defines the separate regions of the world it helps to animate and structure. As a catalogue of the gods it is heavily etymological and allegorical, indeed, Neoplatonic and Stoic in its old-fashioned preservation of earlier Greek and Roman philosophical rationalizations of the gods, despite Isidore's euhemerism elsewhere in the encyclopedia. And although there are other mythological references outside of "De diis gentium," most of them are straightforward and literalistic, explaining the origin of a thing in conjunction with a god or goddess, often with etymologies.[22] This information (especially as understood by Servius, Macrobius in the *Saturnalia* and, behind him, Cicero in *De natura deorum*, Augustine, and Lactantius)[23] ultimately transcends the literal and euhemeristic: indeed, the ordering of the gods is roughly cosmological, and the roles played by most of the figures center on the natural world and its attributes.

Isidore follows the order of the catalogue of gods in Augustine's *De civitate Dei* (7.2; Augustine is discussing and borrowing from Varro)—that is, Janus, Jove, Saturn, Genius, Mercury, Apollo, Mars, Vulcan, Neptune, Sol, Orcus (Pluto), Liber Pater, Tellus, Ceres, Juno, Luna, Diana, Minerva, Venus, and Vesta.[24] The order of the hundred sections in Isidore begins with Saturn, followed by Jupiter, Janus, Neptune, Vulcan, Pluto, Liber, Mercury, Mars, Apollo, Diana, Ceres (Ops, Proserpina, Vesta, Tellus, and Magna Mater), Juno, Minerva, Venus and Cupid, Pan, and briefly, Isis, Serapis, the Fauns, Genius, Parcae, Fortune, Fate, Furies, Nymphs, Heroes, Penates, Manes, Larvae, Incubi.

This list differs from Augustine's in that Isidore has consciously re-arranged the order to reflect the celestial hierarchy: beginning with the door to the universe (Janus) and moving from the farthest heavens (Saturn, Jupiter, as planets but also as first principles, time, governor of all things); the four elements, of water (Neptune), fire (Vulcan), earth (Pluto and the underworld), and then the lower planets, Mercury, Mars, Apollo, Diana (the moon); and the gods of earth and air (Ceres, Juno) and the lesser inhabitants of these lower regions—Fauns, Genius, Parcae, Fortune, Fate, Furies, Nymphs, Heroes, Penates, Manes, Larvae, Incubi (see table 2).

Throughout "De diis gentium" Isidore takes care to articulate the etymological signification of each god's name. As first principle, of finitude, Saturn is first in the catalogue (*Etym.* 8.11.30); his name is related to time and means "sated with years": "Hunc Latini a satu appellatum ferunt, quasi ad ipsum satio omnium pertineat rerum, vel a temporis longitudine, quod saturetur annis." In Greek his name is Chronos, for time, because he devoured his own children, just as age eats up the passing years and is never sated as the years go by: "Hunc Caeli patris abscidisse genitalia dicunt, quia nihil in caelo de seminibus nascitur" ["This god they say cut off the genitalia of his father Caelus, because nothing is born in the heavens from seeds"] (*Etym.* 8.11.32). Hence Saturn is linked with agriculture, or the years and time, or wisdom, "quod intus acuta sit," because it is sharp on the inside.[25]

The regions of what will be understood as the "underworld" are governed by Saturn's three sons, Jupiter, Neptune, and Pluto; the gateway to the underworld, however, is ruled by Janus, cosmic god of doorways. Isidore draws on Cicero, Augustine, and Lactantius—among others—for details of his etymologies. "Jove" comes from "iuvando," and "Jupiter" from "iuvans pater," "helping father," presiding over all, "hoc est, omnibus praestans." His private title is Iovis Optimus, Jove Most High, and he assumes many bestial forms when engaging in his licentious acts in reflection of his vice—bull (Europa); shower of gold (Danaë); eagle (Ganymede); serpent; swan (Leda).[26] Janus (*Etym.* 8.11.37) comes directly from Macrobius's *Saturnalia* to represent the gate of the world or the heavens, or months, and like a gate has two faces, one to the east and one to the west, or sometimes four, making him a double Janus to stand for the

TABLE 2
ISIDORE'S GODS AND BEINGS

God or Being		*Physical Meaning*
Saturn	Time	
Jupiter	One God, World Soul	
Janus	Door to the Universe	
Neptune		Water
Vulcan	Fire	
Pluto	Earth/Underworld	
Liber		
Mercury		Planet
Mars	Planet	
Apollo	Sun	
Diana	Moon	

Sublunary	*Earthly* (region below the moon)
Ceres (Ops, Prosperpina, Vesta, Tellus, Magna Mater)	Earth
Juno	Air
Minerva	
Venus and Cupid	
Pan	
Isis	
Serapis	
Fauns	
Genius	
Parcae	
Fortune	
Fate	
Furies	
Nymphs	
Heroes	
Penates	
Manes	
Larvae	
Incubi	

four quarters of the world, the elements, or the seasons. Neptune governs the waters of the world, from "nube tonans." Lesser deities are related to these natural regions and their elements, Vulcan associated with fire, from "volans candor," original with Isidore, or "volicanus," because fire is born out of the clouds, "Ignis enim e nubibus nascitur." Specifically, he is said to be born from Juno's thigh because lightning bolts are born from air, "fulmina de imo aere nascantur" (*Etym.* 8.11.39–40). The lameness occurs because by nature fire is never upright, but always in motion. And Vulcan governs craftsmanship of the furnace because without fire no metals take form. Finally, Pluto in Greek, or Diespiter or Dis pater in Latin (usually the title of Jupiter), is Orcus because he receives the dead—*orca* is a large vessel that receives water, as Pluto receives the dead. Charon in Greek is the same. Liber comes from the freeing of semen; wine excites libido and hence wine is drunk during the Liberalia (Liber is effeminate to arouse lust in men, not in female warriors, 8.11.43–44).[27]

The other members of the "select gods"—and also, in other catalogues, planetary deities or rulers of other natural regions—include Mercury, Mars,[28] Apollo the sun,[29] Diana the moon,[30] Juno, the aerial region beneath the moon,[31] Minerva, anomalously placed,[32] Venus,[33] and Ceres, or earth.[34] The female deities are all sublunary and natural, or material. The other gods and beings in Isidore's catalogue bear some relation to earth or the region between earth and moon—Pan, Isis, and the minor figures like the Fates, Fortune, Furies, Nymphs, Heroes, Penates, Manes, Larvae, Lares, Incubi.

The other figures associated with earth reveal their real affiliation with the most inferior of the cosmic regions, often termed an underworld. Pan, his name Greek, bears the name Silvanus in Latin, a "deus rusticorum," or god of rustics, "quem in naturae similitudinem formaverunt; unde et Pan dictus est, id est omne. Fingunt enim eum ex universali elementorum specie" ["whom they have fashioned in the likeness of nature, and from whence he is called Pan, that is, everything {all}. They depict him, in fact, from the whole {total} substance of the elements"] (*Etym.* 8.11.81). This god of nature images forth all the species and elements in nature, that is, his horns suggest the rays of the sun; his spotted skin, the stars in the heavens; his red face, aether; his seven-reed pipe, the harmony of the heavens. The section concludes with minor deities of earth like the Egyptian Isis and Serapis (8.11.84–86); the Fauns, whose name is taken from their prophetic nature, "a fando" (8.11.87); and Genius, so called because he has the power of begetting all things or from begetting children (8.11.88).

At the end of this section Isidore concludes that these gods are "fabulous figments of the pagans," created things—"Haec et alia sunt gentilium fabulosa figmenta" (*Etym.* 8.11.89), perhaps another reason he uses the word "fingunt" so frequently, as in the portrait of Pan—to suggest the created, fabulous, imagined reality also linked with the rhetorical device of "pictura," the figure with no necessary basis in reality. The gods are images, "daemones" who people an underworld both pagan and unreal. With this transition he moves finally to Fate, past, present, and future; the Parcae, who order human life, keep it going, and end it; the blind and whimsical goddess Fortune; the three Furies who beget the perturbation of wrath, avarice, and lechery in human souls (8.11.92–95); and the Nymphs of the water. He finishes with the Heroes who inhabit the air, as well as the Penates, the household gods, the Manes as gods of the dead existing between moon and earth, the Larvae as the demons of evil men (8.11.99–101).

Isidore's approach, so he has declared at the opening of the chapter, is ostensibly euhemeristic: he is interested in discrediting paganism by exposing pagan gods as human. He argues that the gods were once mortal, died, and were subsequently worshiped as gods—Isis by the Egyptians, Jove on Crete, Juba by the Moors, Faunus by the Latins, Quirinus by the Romans, Minerva by the Athenians, Juno on Samos, Venus on Paphos, Vulcan at Lemnos, Liber on Naxos, and Apollo at Delos or Delphi. This origin of the gods was enhanced by the poets in their songs. The gods also were said to have invented various arts, an assertion that helps to enhance their stature: medicine, by Aesculapius; craftsmanship, by Vulcan; or else the arts took their names from the gods, for example, merchandise from Mercury, and so on.

We recall that the early Fathers used euhemerism as a tool against the pagans, for example, Justin Martyr (A.D. 103–67) in his *Oratio ad Graecos* and *Cohortatio ad Graecos,* in which he objects to the pagan gods because of their sinfulness. Others understood the demigods, such as Hercules, Castor and Pollux, and Aesculapius, as deified men, and therefore applied that theory to all the gods. Examples include Clement of Alexandria, Tertullian, Minucius Felix, and the Church Father Lactantius (A.D. 260–330), who quoted Euhemerus in his *Institutiones divinae,* as well as Augustine in his *Epistolae* and *De civitate Dei,* who cited Mercury and Aesculapius.[35]

Isidore as Christian and as bishop clearly wishes to debunk the pagan gods as potential icons and idols—as artificial figures, or demons, who will divert souls from the true faith. Indeed, he also links the gods with the underworld forces of the Devil in his explanation that, after the deaths of those who had founded cities, others made icons or images of them to soothe their grief—although Isidore interpolates into this passage an assertion that demons substituted for these images and led men into pride, defined as the worship of icons or images (for example, Prometheus, Minerva, Jove, to whom sacrifices were made). He concludes this section with a long description of demons, the devil, Satan, Antichrist, and Assyrian and Hebrew devils. Among them he sets Priapus as Moab or Baal: this god of gardens because of his gigantic member appropriately ensures the fecundity of any garden, in a definition drawn from Servius (*In Georg.* 4.109–11).

Most important for Theodulf and later mythographers, Isidore repeats material on the underworld drawn from Macrobius's commentary on the *Somnium Scipionis* (1.10.11) and Servius's commentary on the *Aeneid* (6.137 and elsewhere) to present it as inferior, below, and like the body of man, in which the spirit becomes sad when incarcerated. About the rivers of the underworld Isidore declares that the Styx represents "tristitia" either "quod tristes faciat vel quod tristitiam gignat" ["because it makes sad people or because it begets sadness"]. He also defines it as below:

> Inferus appellatur eo quod infra sit. Sicut autem secundum corpus, si ponderis sui ordinem teneant, inferiora sunt omnia graviora, ita secundum spiritum inferiora sunt omnia tristiora; unde et in Graeca lingua origo nominis, quo appellatur inferus, ex eo quod nihil suave habeat resonare perhibetur. Sicut autem cor animalis in medio est, ita et inferus in medio terrae esse perhibetur. Vnde et in Evangelio legimus (Matthew 12:40): "In corde terrae." Philosophi autem dicunt quod inferi pro eo dicantur quod animae hinc ibi ferantur.

> [It is called *inferus* because it is below. For as in respect to the body the lower parts are all heavier {if they keep to an orderly arrangement of their weight}, just so in respect to the spirit the lower parts are all sadder; hence also in the Greek language the origin of the name by which the underworld is called is said to be derived from the fact that it has nothing sweet. Moreover, just as the heart of a living creature is in its middle, so also the underworld is considered to be in the middle of the earth. Whence we read in the Gospel {Matthew 12.40}: "In the heart of the earth." However, the philosophers say that the under-world {*inferi*} is so-called because souls are brought there {*ibi ferantur*} from here.] (*Etym.* 14.9.10–11)

The underworld region associated with the demonic gods, and the human body as an underworld, as inferior and below, require the valor and understanding of a strong mind for mastery.

III. THE DEMONIC HERO OF THE UNDERWORLD, *VIS MENTIS*

The interpretation of the gods of the heavenly regions as *daemones* also inhabiting an underworld like that of false and lying classical poetry will appeal to Theodulf, who as we know refers to the rhetorical device of "pictura" in several poems. His source will be yet another aspect of Isidore's rationalization of the pagan gods—Isidore's euhemeristic interpretation of them, coupled with the *Aeneid* book-6 glosses on the underworld as the planetary circles of the cosmos (which also seems to have affected Isidore's etymological catalogue of the gods, as we have seen). But in Theodulf the irrationality and madness of the underworld are concealed by the falsity of lies and vice, depicted by a deceptive and Neoplatonic cover of smoke: "Gressibus it furum fallentum insania versis, / Ore vomunt fumum probra negando tetrum" ["Madness walks backwards, stepping like cunning thieves, / from its mouth belching foul smoke and denying what is right"] ("De libris" 29–30). It is up to the mind, then, functioning like the hero Aeneas who descends into the underworld to consult the Sibyl—or like the hero Hercules battling against Cacus in his cave—to perform heroically (that is, rationally) in understanding these underworld figures: "*Vis* sed eos *mentis* retegit, perimitque, quatitque, / Nequitia illorum sic manifesta patet" ["But *forceful resolve* exposes, destroys and crushes them / and so their wickedness is starkly revealed"] ("De libris" 31–32; my emphasis).

The heroic *vis mentis* may have been inspired by Isidore's definition of heroes as "venerable men of the air," as well as by the poetic underworld inhabited by mythological figures viewed as *daemones*. That a poetic construct might be used to house a certain subject is clarified by Isidore in the first book of his *Etymologiae* when he defines the heroic type of poetic work (as contrasted with the elegiac and bucolic): "Heroicum, enim carmen dictum," as said of song in which "the matters and deeds are narrated of strong men," "virorum fortium res et facta narrantur." Isidore defines heroes specifically as "viros aerios," men situated in the sky and worthy of heaven, venerable because of their wisdom and fortitude: "Nam heroes appellantur viri quasi aerii et caelo digni propter sapientiam et fortitudinem" (*Etym.* 1.39.9). Clearly Isidore has in mind Aeneas as a type of hero who descends into hell, signifying the same epic wisdom and fortitude as Fulgentius's hero in his *Continentia Virgiliana.*

Isidore derives his definition from Augustine's ancient classical definition of the *heros*, that invisible soul who occupies that aerial region between the moon and the highest region of clouds and winds (compare *De civitate Dei* 7.6: "heroas et lares et genios"). Isidore's passage attributes the *heros* to the realm of Juno:

> Heroas dicunt a Iunone traxisse nomen. Graece enim Iuno *Hera* appellatur. Et ideo nescio quis filius eius secundum Graecorum fabulam *Heros* fuit nuncupatus; hoc videlicet velut mysticum significante fabula, quod aer Iunoni deputetur, ubi volunt heroas habitare. Quo nomine appellant alicuius meriti animas defunctorum, quasi *aeroas,* id est viros aerios et caelo dignos propter sapientiam et fortitudinem.

> [They say that "heroes" derived their name from Juno, for in Greek Juno is called *Hera.* And therefore a son of hers was named *"Heros"* according to a fable of the Greeks. By this the fable expresses an allegory because air is assigned to Juno, where it is said that heroes live. The souls of the dead which have some merit are called by this name, *aeroas,* that is, men of the air and worthy {deserving} of heaven because of their wisdom and fortitude.] (*Etym.* 8.11.98; emphasis in original)

Isidore's source may well have been *De civitate Dei,* wherein Augustine explains that the hero derives his name from the Greek name of Juno, Hera, because she is mistress of the celestial region beneath the aether (Jupiter):

> Hoc enim nomen a Iunone dicitur tractum, quod Graece Iuno *Hera* appellatur, et ideo nescio quis filius eius secundum Graecorum fabulas Heros fuerit nuncupatus, hoc videlicet veluti mysticum significante fabula, quod aer Iunoni deputetur, ubi volunt cum daemonibus heroas habitare, quo nomine appellant alicuius meriti animas defunctorum.

> [For this name is said to be derived from Juno, who in Greek is called Hêrê, and hence, according to the Greek myths, one of her sons was called Heros. And these fables mystically signified that Juno was the mistress of the air, which they suppose to be inhabited by the demons and the heroes, understanding by heroes the souls of the well-deserving dead.] (*Civ. Dei* 10.21)[36]

But Augustine sandwiches this passage on heroes between an ecclesiastical introduction and a classical ending, in his attempt to incorporate pagan literary meaning into ecclesiastical practice. "Si ecclesiastica loquendi consuetudo pateretur, nostros heroas vocaremus" ["If the ordinary language of the Church allowed it, we might more elegantly call these men our heroes"]. Augustine means by these heroes "tanto clariores et honoratiores cives" who have "quanto fortius adversus impietatis peccatum et usque ad sanguinem certant" ["bravely fought and shed their blood against the impiety of sins"]. He begins almost wistfully, and he ends with two references to the *Aeneid,* to Juno's words "vincor ab Aenea" ["I am worsted by Aeneas"] (*Aeneid* 7.310), and to Helenus's religious advice to Aeneas, "Iunoni cane vota libens dominamque potentem / supplicibus supera donis" ["to Juno joyfully chant vows, and win over the mighty mistress with suppliant gifts"] (*Aeneid* 3.438–39).

Augustine suggests that the ecclesiastical "heroes" should overcome Hera by divine virtues rather than gifts—the ecclesiastical heroes should be called "heroes" not because they inhabit the air along with the demons but because they have conquered the demons, including Juno.

> Sed a contrario martyres nostri heroes nuncuparentur, si, ut dixi, usus ecclesiastici sermonis admitteret, non quo eis esset cum daemonibus in aere societas, sed quod eosdem daemones, id est aerias vincerent potestates et in eis ipsam, quidquid putatur significare, Iunonem, quae non usquequaque inconvenienter a poetis inducitur inimica virtutibus et caelum petentibus viris fortibus invida. Sed rursus ei succumbit infeliciter ceditque Vergilius, ut, cum apud eum illa dicat: "Vincor ab Aenea," ipsum Aenean admoneat Helenus quasi consilio religioso et dicat: "Iunoni cane vota libens, dominamque potentem / Supplicibus supera donis. . . ." Non omnino, si dici usitate posset, heroes nostri supplicibus donis, sed virtutibus divinis Heran superant.

> [But for a quite opposite reason would we call our martyrs heroes— supposing, as I said, that the usage of ecclesiastical language would admit of it—not because they lived along with the demons in the air, but because they conquered these demons or powers of the air, and among them Juno herself, be she what she may, not unsuitably represented, as she commonly is by the poets, as hostile to virtue, and jealous of men of mark aspiring to the heavens. Virgil, however, unhappily gives way, and yields to her; for, though he represents her as saying, "I am conquered by Aeneas," Helenus gives Aeneas himself

this religious advice: "Pray vows to Juno: overbear / Her queenly soul with gift and prayer."... Our heroes, if we could so call them, overcome Hêrê, not by suppliant gifts, but by divine virtues.] (*Civ. Dei* 10.21)

If the Christian martyr is a hero because he has conquered the demons of air, including Juno so hostile to virtue, then the problem in Augustine's eyes is twofold: the good Christian battles his own vices and, when he reads, the creations of the hostile pagan text, often doubly seductive because it is poetry.

The seductions of (classical) poetry also introduce the first prose section of Boethius's *Consolatio Philosophiae,* when Philosophy upbraids the Muses of poetry who linger by the bed of the depressed Boethius as Sirens, "usque in exitium dulces" ["beguiling men straight to their destruction!"] (*Consolatio* 1 p1). The idea of the sweetness of poetry as whorish—seducing man's reason so that he succumbs to passion—provides a novel twist to the story of Ulysses successfully bypassing the Sirens, but it also introduces a rationale for Boethius's placement of moralized mythological fables in select meters and directs the methodology of the moralization. Philosophia explains that these "scenas meretriculas" ["theatrical tarts"] interfere with the rational process; they "infructuosis affectuum spinis uberem fructibus rationis segetem necant hominumque mentes assuefaciunt morbo, non liberant" ["choke the rich harvest of the fruits of reason with the barren thorns of passion. They accustom a man to his ills, not rid him of them"] (*Consolatio* 1 p1).

When Boethius comes, then, to the fable of his pagan hero Ulysses confronting Circe, who poisons his men so that they are transformed into beasts, the encounter is moralized elegiacally as the dragging down of man from himself, not harming the body but wounding the mind, against which Ulysses is impervious because of Mercury's aid:

Haec venena potentius
Detrahunt hominem sibi
Dira quae penitus meant
Nec nocentia corpori
Mentis vulnere saeviunt.

[Those poisons do more powerfully
Drag down man from himself—
Dire they are!—that deep within do move,

And leaving the body unharmed
Cruelly wound the mind.] (*Consolatio* 4 m3; my emphasis)

Again in a poem in book 4, on the protagonists Agamemnon, Ulysses (and Polyphemus), and Hercules (and his Twelve Labors), Boethius contrasts the pain and suffering of this earthly underworld—the discord of the Trojan War, the cuckolding of Menelaus, the unhappy sacrifice of Iphigenia, coupled with the bitter loss of Ulysses's men to the Cyclops and the harshness of Hercules's labors—with the celestial journey to the stars guaranteed by bravery and virtue: "Superata tellus / Sidera donat" ["Earth overcome / Grants you the stars"] (*Consolatio* 4 m7). Boethius, like Augustine and Theodulf, equates the pagan hero's descent into the underworld with that of the reader who must, finally, emerge from darkness and turn to the light.

IV. THE POEM AS AN UNDERWORLD, THE READER AS HERO

For Theodulf as Bishop, the struggle with the pagan text and his own love for its underworld of mythological "demons" may be paramount. Most of Theodulf's poem is concerned with justifying a love of the classics. At the beginning of *Carmina* 45, whose full title is "De libris quos legere solebam et qualiter fabulae poetarum a philosophis mystice pertractentur" ["Concerning the Books which I Used to Read and the Manner in which Philosophers Can Find a Mystical Meaning in the Fables of the Poets"],[37] Theodulf mentions that "Namque ego suetus eram hos libros legisse frequenter, / Extitit ille mihi nocte dieque labor" ["These were the books which I was accustomed to read frequently and this was the work before me night and day"] ("De libris" 1–2). Here he lists hierarchically three groups of authors he most often reads—first, the Church Fathers and standard patristic writers like Gregory, Augustine, Hilary, Pope Leo, Jerome, Ambrose, Isidore, John, Cyprian; second, late classical writers who were also Christian poets, men like Sedulius, Paulinus, Arator, Avitus, Fortunatus, Juvencus, and his countryman Prudentius; and third, classical grammarians like Pompeius and Donatus and classical poets like "talkative Ovid," Virgil, Horace, Lucan, and Cicero. Despite this emphasis on Church authority, most of the poem is riddled with allusions to mythological gods and heroes and to the works of Ovid, Virgil, and Isidore.

The full subtitle of Theodulf's poem is thus explained: Theodulf notes that "In quorum dictis quamquam sint frivola multa" ["Although there

are many frivolities in their words"], "Plurima sub falso tegmine vera
latent" ["much truth lies hidden under a deceptive surface"] ("De libris"
19, 20). The idea of truth hidden beneath a false outer layer or cloak
(*tegumen*) is Macrobian and Augustinian, the traditional justification for
reading classical poetry that reappears at every medieval renaissance (in
twelfth-century France in Hugh of St. Victor's *Didascalicon* and Alan of
Lille's *Anticlaudianus;* in fourteenth-century Italy in Dante, Petrarch,
Boccaccio, and Salutati; and in fourteenth-century England in Chaucer,
Gower, and others). In fact, Theodulf suggests this is the nature of poetry
rather than, say, philosophy: "Falsa poetarum stilus affert, vera sophorum,
/ Falsa horum in verum vertere saepe solent" ["Poets' writing is a vehicle
for falsehood, philosophers' brings truth; / They transform the lies of poets
into veracity"] ("De libris" 21–22).

Indeed, Theodulf may be drawing, once again, on Isidore; early in the
Etymologiae, the Bishop of Seville reveals his interest in rhetoric and "other
speaking"—that which transcends the thing itself, the literal, or envelops
and includes it. Isidore distinguishes catachresis from metaphor by noting
that "haec et a metaphora differt, quod illa vocabulum habenti largitur,
haec, quia non habet proprium, alieno utitur" ["the former gives a name to
something which has one, while the latter {metaphor} uses another's name
because it doesn't have one of its own"] (*Etym.* 1.37.6), as, for example, in
Virgil's Centaur (*Aeneid* 5.157). Isidore defines various rhetorical terms in
this section of book 1—*antiphrasis,* as illustrated by the names "Parcae"
and "Eumenides," for the Fates and the Furies, and then, more important,
enigma and *allegory,* terms that will themselves enlarge on Macrobian dicta
and poetic practice in the Middle Ages:

> Aenigma est quaestio obscura quae difficile intellegitur, nisi aperia-
> tur, ut est illud (Iudic. 14:14): "De comedente exivit cibus, et de forte
> egressa est dulcedo," significans ex ore leonis favum extractum. Inter
> allegoriam autem et aenigma hoc interest, quod allegoriae vis gemina
> est et sub res alias aliud figuraliter indicat; aenigma vero sensus
> tantum obscurus est, et per quasdam imagines adumbratus.

> [Aenigma is an obscure question which is difficult to understand
> unless it is interpreted, like this quotation (Judges 14.14): "Out of
> the eater came forth meat, and out of the strong came forth sweet-
> ness," meaning that from the mouth of a lion a honeycomb was drawn
> out. But there is this difference between allegory and aenigma:
> allegory has a double force and indicates one thing figuratively lying

under another; whereas aenigma is only an obscured perception, hinted at by means of certain comparisons.] (*Etym.* 1.37.24)

Isidore has defined allegory already as "other speaking": "Allegoria est alieniloquium. Aliud enim sonat, et aliud intellegitur" ["Allegory is speaking in another way. For it says one thing, and something else is understood"] (*Etym.* 1.37.22). Of the other kinds of figures of speech Isidore defines, he includes *charientismos* ("a trope by which harsh things are said more pleasingly; for instance, when we inquire, 'Has anyone asked for us?' The reply is given, 'Good luck.' That means that no one has asked for us"); *paroemia*, a proverb; *sarcasmos;* its antithesis, *astysmos; homoeosis (similitudo* in Latin). In this last figure there are three kinds, the icon, parabola, and paradigm (*imago, conparatio, exemplum*). These are defined as follows: "Icon est imago, cum figuram rei ex simili genere conamur exprimere" ["Icon is an image, figure, when we attempt to describe the appearance of a thing from a similar kind of thing"]; "Parabola conparatio ex dissimilibus rebus" ["A parable is a comparison of unlike things"]; and "Paradigma vero est exemplum dicti vel facti alicuius aut ex simili aut ex dissimili genere conveniens eius" ["But a paradigm is an example of someone's word or deed being compared with a class {of things} either similar or dissimilar to the matter which we are describing"] (*Etym.* 1.37.32, 33, 34).

But these figures express connections between real things, relationships which have nothing to do with falsity or truth. Isidore distinguishes *fabula* from *historia,* "Fabulas poetae a fando nominaverunt, quia non sunt res factae, sed tantum loquendo fictae" ["The poets named fables from 'fando,' 'speaking,' because they are not things done, but only fashioned with words"] (*Etym.* 1.40.1). Such fictions include the use of animals as an image of the mores of human life, as in Aesop's *Fables;* the use of gods to represent natural phenomena, or causes, as in "Vulcanus claudus," Vulcan lame,

quia per naturam numquam rectus est ignis, ut illa triformis bestia (Lucret. 5.903): "Prima leo, postrema draco, media ipsa Chimaera": id est caprea, aetates hominum per eam volentes distinguere; quarum ferox et horrens prima adolescentia, ut leo; dimidium vitae tempus lucidissimum, ut caprea, eo quod acutissime videat; tunc fit senectus casibus inflexis, draco.

["Lame Vulcan" because by its nature fire is never upright; {and another reference to the natural order is} that three-form beast (Lucretius 5.903): "In front a lion, after a snake, in the middle a chimera"—that is, a she-goat, meaning by this {creature} to distinguish the ages of man. The first is fierce and bristly adolescence, that is, the lion; the mid-point of life is the brightest time, that is, the she-goat, because she has very sharp eye-sight; and then comes old age, bent and twisted like the snake, by misfortunes."] (*Etym.* 1.40.4)

In seeming echo of the Fulgentian diagram of Aeneas's three-stage journey, the lion, the wild she-goat or roe (*capraea*), and the snake represent the three stages of human life, adolescence, prime, old age. *Fabula* usually involves animals reflecting the human on the tropological level; *historia,* in contrast, is "narratio rei gestae, per quam ea, quae in praeterito facta sunt, dinoscuntur" ["a narration of deeds, and by means of it things which happened in the past are learned"] (1.41.1).

Upon this concept and practice Theodulf depends in creating allegorical and mythographic personifications, and their glosses, in "De libris quos legere solebam." Theodulf's poem celebrates the truth of the virtues veiled by heroic mythological figures—Proteus as truth, Virgo or Erigone as justice (in that she killed herself for her father), Hercules as virtue, opposing Cacus, theft: "Sic Proteus verum, sic iustum Virgo repingit, / Virtutem Alcides, furtaque Cacus inops" ("De libris" 23–24).

Thus Theodulf can conclude that (poetic, pagan) vice and deception can only be overcome by (philosophic) openness, unmasking:

Verum ut fallatur, mendacia mille patescunt,
    Firmiter hoc stricto pristina forma redit.
Virginis in morem vis iusti inlaesa renidet,
    Quam nequit iniusti conmaculare lues.

[A thousand lies blatantly attempt to pervert the truth;
    when it is plainly revealed, it returns in its previous beauty.
The untainted power of justice shines like a virgin,
    the foulness of injustice cannot corrupt it.] ("De libris" 25–28)

Although Theodulf's figures of Proteus, Erigone, and Hercules do not derive specifically from Isidore, and indeed would have been known to Theodulf from Servius or perhaps the Berne scholia on Virgil,[38] the practice of using mythological figures as signs of particular virtues or other abstractions is modeled on and theorized by Isidore. This idea that names reflect physical reality mirrors Isidore's belief in words: he argues that if one understands the original meaning of a word (and the alternate name of the *Etymologiae* is *Origines*), then one can understand the reality represented by that word; different functions are described by different derivations (*Etym.* 1.29.1–2). This concept is expressed in relation to the multiple significations of the gods in his "De diis gentium," as we can see in Isidore's long portrait of Mercury (perhaps influenced by Martianus's allegorical frame involving Mercury in *De nuptiis Philologiae et Mercurii*). Mercury, as winged god, resembles the unstable, armed Cupid in some ways.

Mercury has three different names expressive of different cultures and functions (*Etym.* 8.11.45–49). As the Roman "Mercury," he represents conversation, or eloquence, *sermo* (in a definition taken from Augustine's *De civitate Dei*):[39] "Nam ideo Mercurius quasi medius currens dicitur appellatus, quod sermo currat inter homines medius" ["Mercury is called so, as if running between, or in the middle, because conversation runs in the middle between men"]. And "Ideo et mercibus praeesse, quia inter vendentes et ementes sermo fit medius" ["because conversation takes place between sellers and buyers, he governs commerce"]. Hence, "Qui ideo fingitur habere pinnas, quia citius verba discurrant" [he also has "wings, because words run about quickly"].

His Greek second name, "Hermes," means "messenger," from Greek *ermeneuse,* which in Latin means "intermediary." He is said to be a messenger "Nuntium dictum," "quoniam per sermonem omnia cogitata enuntiantur" ["because through speech all thought is announced"]. He is the teacher or master of thieves or robberies, "Ideo autem furti magistrum dicunt, quia sermo animos audientium fallit," that is, "because eloquence deceives the minds of the listeners." He holds a caduceus, on which snakes wriggle, or with which he forces apart snakes, that is, poison ("Virgam tenet, qua serpentes dividit, id est venena"). From Servius (*In Aen.* 4.242) comes the notion that those who are at war or at variance with each other are appeased by the speeches of ambassadors (go-betweens), as snakes are separated by a rod.[40] "Nam bellantes ac dissidentes interpretum oratione sedantur" ["For armies and dissidents are calmed by the speech of intermediaries"], and Isidore adds that, according to Livy, envoys for peace are called *caduceatores,* bearers of Hermes's caduceus, that is, the flag of truce; "ita pax per caduceatores fiebat" ["peace was made by the *caduceatores*"].

"On account of his excellence and knowledge of many arts," Mercury bears yet a third name, again Greek, "Trismegistus," which is, however, associated with North African culture and means "thrice-greatest."[41] As the Egyptian god of wisdom, ibis-headed Thoth (in Greek; originally Djeheuty) served as divine scribe at the judgment of the dead and, like

Mercury (Hermes), was linked with writing and therefore knowledge: he transmitted to Isidore ancient Egyptian knowledge of hieroglyphs. Isidore, however, provides him with the wisdom of a dog: "qui ob virtutem multarumque artium scientiam Trimegistus, id est ter maximus nominatus est. Cur autem eum capite canino fingunt, haec ratio dicitur, quod inter omnia animalia canis sagacissimum genus et perspicax habeatur" ["For this reason he is depicted with a dog's head because among all animals the dog is considered to be the wisest and cleverest species"]. Animal-headed beings were often perceived as Egyptian, as was the case with the animal-headed Egyptian forces which backed Cleopatra confronting the anthropomorphized Roman gods on Aeneas's shield piece.

Borrowing from Isidore, Theodulf's tour-de-force in "De libris" relies on the *descensus ad inferos* from the *Aeneid*'s sixth book to refocus attention on the dangers of the underworld and the means by which an educated hero can resist them: his poem is about how to read texts whose immorality or paganism can subvert the unaware reader. This monitory theme is dear to Theodulf, as other poems testify. *Contra iudices* (*Against Judges*, ca. 799), a poem dedicated to Charlemagne, in its description of an imagined Hercules vase is critical not only of the dangers of anger and lust but also of the limitations of pagan justice and pagan gods.[42] By using these mythological figures in "De libris" and elsewhere, Theodulf asks us also as readers to delve, Aeneaslike, beneath the surface even of his poem to its truthful underworld. If we recall that Aeneas leaves Virgil's underworld through the false gate, the gate of ivory, because this is the gate through which the *manes* or spirits of the dead pass after death, we might then see Theodulf's point about mythological exegesis, about reading the classics. If we peer beneath the "veil" of the figure Cupid—who is after all naked already—this "uncovering" of the god reveals his evil, as in fact the poem shows. We as readers can then return to the "upper air," after delving into this "underworld" of a visionary poem, full of lying figures such as Cupid, himself a type of shade.

The visualization of the arts in Theodulf's "pictura" contributes to what might be termed that same *artes* topos shared by Martianus Capella and Isidore, and even to a lesser extent, Boethius, in that Philosophy represents the culmination of study of the seven liberal arts; the use of the Isidorian rhetorical term "pictura" reminds us that the image is fictitious or literary, without basis in reality. But even Isidore depended upon the seven liberal arts in part as structure for his encyclopedic *Etymologiae*. He did not choose exclusively one of the two conventional methods of unifying the encyclopedia, either the seven liberal arts (as in Martianus and Cassiodorus) or the digest of all knowledge (as in Varro, Pliny, and Suetonius); Isidore includes both. The first three books center on the arts (grammar in the first, rhetoric and dialect in the second, arithmetic, geometry, music, and astronomy in the third) and the last twelve books, on an epitome of all knowledge. In a sense, Isidore throughout follows Cassiodorus, who describes a preparatory study of the seven liberal arts but who adds to it in *De institutione divinarum litterarum,* the religious education of the monk.[43] Interested in training the priest, Isidore describes in the first three books the education of the secular clergy in the liberal arts, followed by medicine, laws and times, books on services of the Church, God, angels, and orders of the faithful, and book 8, on the Church and its sects. In miniature Isidore rehearses a plan for the medieval university.[44] His encyclopedia was used by Vincent of Beauvais in his widely read thirteenth-century compendium, including the citation of whole passages.

If the mythographic tradition can be said to evolve and develop in the Middle Ages, it does so essentially parallel to the evolution and development of humanistic education—the preservation of classical learning, especially during periods of renaissance. Because study of the pagan gods by necessity accompanied study of pagan texts, the rationalization for reading the classics became especially strong during periods of tentative and tenuous Christianity, when conversion was of paramount importance and Latin literacy was tied to building the Church in provincial empires. This was all true of Isidore's and Theodulf's seventh- and eighth-century Spain, when Visigoth bumped elbows with Hispano-Roman, and even more so in the next century, in Carolingian France and Alfredian England. In France Charlemagne's scholars imported from various regions in Europe were brought together to enhance a literary education, the arts, and classical humanism. In England Alfred also brought together scholars to implement his program of clerical education through vernacular translation. Out of these two courts came a strong desire to preserve classical learning, and literacy, and therefore also to advance Christianity, but accompanied by a rationalization of the pagan gods found in classical poetry. It is not unlikely, then, to find the two motives entwined: an education in the seven liberal arts, and a classical education, may involve as well explaining a classical poet's use of the gods. The next stage in mythographic history would be to collect those explanations of the gods.

Chapter Five

THE "UNIVERSAL GENEALOGY" OF GODS AND HEROES IN THE FIRST VATICAN MYTHOGRAPHER

Between the late antique and late medieval periods three greatly influential mythographic collections appeared, known today only as the three Vatican mythographies and numbered to reflect different dates of composition, in no case earlier than the fifth century or later than the twelfth. Each borrows from the earlier versions as well as interweaves source material from the other extant mythographic traditions. Despite their importance for the Middle Ages—for other mythographers and commentators who relied on them, in particular the author of the *Ecloga Theoduli*,[1] and for poets writing in the vernacular in France, Italy, and England—only in 1987 did a critical edition of the first two mythographies appear;[2] in relation to the later, third, mythography, Charles S. F. Burnett has promised a critical edition of one of its major sources and pointed to the need for an edition of this handbook.[3] The purpose for which they were compiled and the nature of their specific contribution to the development of the mythographic tradition will help us understand their importance for the Middle Ages. In this chapter the first Vatican mythography, earliest in date, and its place within the history of the myth collection will be analyzed—as an example of annotated "universal genealogy."

The myth collection may have originated as a genealogical epic or genealogical history intended to place the origin of the gods within the larger creation of the cosmos, although in the Middle Ages its existence may be attributed more to the needs of the grammarian than to the needs of the philosopher or theologian. As what we might call a literary form the myth collection even in antiquity was relatively rare. Most important in Greek were Hesiod's epical *Theogony* and Apollodorus's library of myth, the *Biblioteca*. In Latin most important was Ovid's mythological epic, the *Metamorphoses*, which was followed, in the first century A.D., by Hyginus's stories in the *Fabulae* and his astrological series in the *Astronomica*. In the

Middle Ages the mythological handbook (that is, with explanations added for the myths) appeared in the sixth century with Fulgentius's *Mitologiae* and the seventh century with Isidore's "De diis gentium," although as a form it would not in fact dominate until late in the Middle Ages. In the thirteenth and fourteenth centuries the form was incorporated (like Isidore's "De diis gentium") into the larger encyclopedia, as happened with Ovid commentaries such as the *Ovide moralisé* and *Ovidius moralizatus*. Finally, the amalgamation of encyclopedia and myth collection—an encyclopedia of myth—can be found in the late medieval collections of allegorized classical myths such as Boccaccio's *Genealogia gentilium deorum* and Christine de Pizan's epistolary miniature, *Epistre Othea.*

Not all myth collections depend upon a genealogical history for their purpose or means of organization; nor do all genealogical lists appear necessarily within a myth collection. Most anciently used by Hesiod as a structural principle in his *Theogony,* the genealogy of the gods did reappear in the Middle Ages. Among the extant but rare post-antique genealogies we can number the first-century genealogy included at the beginning of Hyginus's *Fabulae,* which is not at all like the first Vatican mythographer's genealogy; the genealogy at the beginning of the twelfth-century Florentine commentary on Martianus Capella; the recently discovered genealogy based on that of Paolo of Perugia in the fourteenth century, according to Vittore Branca (there is another by Franceschino degli Albizzi and Forese da Donati, in the appendix to Hortis);[4] and the comprehensive *Genealogia gentilium deorum* of Boccaccio (also fourteenth-century).

Up to this point this study has revealed little mythographic interest in history or genealogical history precisely because mythology, rather than mythography, exists more as a form of legendary stories of the gods and heroes than what might be termed human history. One major exception exists, as discussed in chapter 1, in the methods of the Greek Euhemerus and his follower, the Roman Ennius, which were specifically centered on the human origins of the "gods." It is true that euhemeristic analysis for the most part played a minimal role in the subsequent history of mythographic literary analysis in the Middle Ages. And yet aside from the euhemerist's polemical desire to demythologize the gods, there is another, historicizing, tendency in classical epic that contributes to the mythographic tradition indirectly. The development of classical epic and non-epic bears out a repeated literary interest in national history as well as in mythological history, as we can see when we examine Euhemerus's place in the history of epic.

Classical epic frequently involves the appearance of the gods, even though the mythological epic constituted only one form of post-Homeric epic and at that not always the predominant form. Even post-Homeric epic, aside from the Greek cyclic epics completing the *Iliad* and the *Odyssey* such as the *Thebais, Cypria, Aithiopis, Iliuoersis, Telegonia, Nostoi*, and others, did not always include myth.[5] Of the three basic types of post-Homeric Greek epic beginning from the late fifth century B.C., most examples of which have been lost, only one type was the mythological epic, called the Apollonian or Antimachean (presumably because of Apollonius's *Argonautica* and the now-fragmentary *Thebais* by Antimachus of Colophon). A new form of Roman mythological epic developed in the second quarter of the first century, the short or Callimachean (Hesiodic) epic introduced by the Greek émigré Parthenius and his disciple the Roman aristocrat C. Helvius Cinna; this mythological epic influenced a host of others, now lost, and was transformed into other genres. For example, in another descendant of the short epic—the elegiac *Fasti*—Ovid, who believed that elegies were Callimachean and not Homeric, romanized the lost *Aitia* ("Causes") of the learned Alexandrian poet Callimachus.[6] Finally, the older form of Greek Homeric mythological epic was revived under Maecenas's patronage by a group of poets, including Horace and Virgil, committed to Alexandrian ideals of polish and workmanship.[7]

Of these post-Homeric epics there also existed two nonmythological, historical, types—the panegyric-historical, on Alexander's campaigns, and the regional-historical, on the history of various cities. As an heir to Greek epic, the Roman epic began succeeding when it started probing Roman and not Greek history, as in the national epic of Ennius's *Annales* (a Homeric treatment of the early legends of Rome which included the stories of Aeneas, Mars, Illia, and so on, in chronological order but with more attention given to recent than to ancient history), although it still needed to distinguish between the recent and the heroic past, because the recent had *"not yet been mythologized."*[8] Most of these epics were literary failures,[9] either because history cannot be forced into the heroic mode of poetry, or because the mythological epic, in time, became anachronistic.

Euhemerism—and the equivalent of the national epic, or the epic of cities—does survive in the Middle Ages, adapted to the Christian need for rationalization of pagan history. The problem of genealogies of the gods, in the Middle Ages, is to fit them into the larger biblical and Christian understanding of human history. The fall of Adam and Eve after the eating of the fruit of the tree of knowledge of good and evil and their expulsion from paradise catalyzed human history and the birth of the human redeemer, Christ, at least for the Christian Middle Ages. But in pagan terms, human history begins with the adulteries of Jupiter and culminates in the birth of Augustus Caesar, as in Ovid's *Metamorphoses*. Even if the gods are euhemerized—imagined as important men and women whose "temples" are in fact actual burial places—then contemporary poets would have to be descended literally and metaphorically from the heroes and poets of a bygone era, figuratively, the writers of the word descended from the Word.

In medieval terms, however, the adulteries of Jupiter can be used to explain national differences. The point is that "genealogy" conveys both "generation" and "history" of the human race, and is modeled most profoundly on the story of the Creation in the book of Genesis. For example, for Boccaccio, "The *Genealogy* owes its structure ultimately to the Bible. Its mythical generations, as recorded in the chapter headings and table of rubrics, echo, and allude to, genealogical passages in the vulgate of both testaments. . . . In the ancient Hebrew, the same word, *tōedot,* means both generation and history, so that the Bible passes on to Eusebius, Jerome, and their medieval followers an essentially genealogical mode of universal history."[10]

By this term of "universal genealogy" may be understood patriarchal authority—the authority of the male line of inheritance, the passing of power from father to son, and more metaphorically, in pagan myth, the transmission of the *logos spermatikos,* as the Stoics termed it, from generation to generation. Such genealogical mythologies in the hands of medieval mythographers reveal a kind of chauvinism that, beginning in the twelfth century, accompanied the birth of nations and the rise of the vernacular. For this reason the genealogy of the gods and of the nations from which countries in Western Europe derived eventually conferred political legitimization upon royal leaders in difficult times. Such was the goal of Geoffrey of Monmouth in his linking of the legends of King Arthur with the history of Troy in his twelfth-century "chronicle." One of the major implications of the genealogical structure, whether in the first Vatican mythographer or in Boccaccio, is its similar constitution of authority through history.

In the early Middle Ages, the genealogy of the gods, serving as a mnemonic device and given its additionally chronological nature, in a very practical way allowed students of Latin reading the ancient epics to remember the sexual and familial relationships of the gods. Even in the later Middle Ages, in vernacular mythographic collections, there exist visual examples of such genealogies, for example (fig. 11), an illustration of Celius's genealogy, in founding the kingdom of Crete, in an early four-teenth-century Provençal mythographic collection in London. Such was probably the case with the genealogical myth collection of the first Vatican mythographer, although little is certainly known about his country of origin, his date, his identity; we know little about his purpose in compil-ing the mythography; and little or no scholarly interest has been evinced concerning his contribution to mythography or early medieval letters. But his probable dates, his use of sources, and his historical and scholastic context argue for this grammatical purpose.

The most likely date for the first Vatican mythographer is the late eighth, or more probably the ninth century, despite the wide range of dates offered by previous scholars. Possible dates have ranged from a terminus postquem of A.D. 415—because of the first Vatican mythographer's refer-ence to Orosius (Mythogr. I 215/219)[11]—to an antequem based on the twelfth-century date of one manuscript.[12] A pre-Carolingian date was presented as most likely by Elliott and Elder, although Elliott separately has noted that, "It is interesting to consider the possibility that the work may have been written in England or Ireland during the so-called 'dark period' on the continent,"[13] that is, the sixth and seventh centuries. They argue for this earlier date in part because the many errors in the manuscript imply frequent copying and therefore an earlier date; its lack of allegory and its directness suggest a pre-Carolingian approach. However, because the first Vatican mythographer cites both Fulgentius and Isidore (d. 636) he must have written no earlier than the late seventh century.[14] More recently, Winfried Bühler argues for a ninth-century date because of similarities between the first Vatican mythographer and the Horace scholia (sixth to ninth centuries), although she also has insisted on a late date because of parallels with the *Ecloga Theoduli* (now believed to be ninth-century or later).[15] The latest editor looks to Bernhard Bischoff's assign-ment of the mythography (as well as the manuscript) to the twelfth century as a major guideline in determining date, without fully considering the dependence of the tenth-century Remigius of Auxerre (in his commentary on Martianus Capella, especially) on the first Vatican mythographer.[16] Such dependence would certainly place our mythography earlier than the tenth century—and as we have noted, after the eighth century.

Not only are the mythographer's dates uncertain, his identity remains a mystery, with "Adanan the Scot" (St. Adamnan of Iona?) providing perhaps the most sensible attribution. Among the suggestions have been

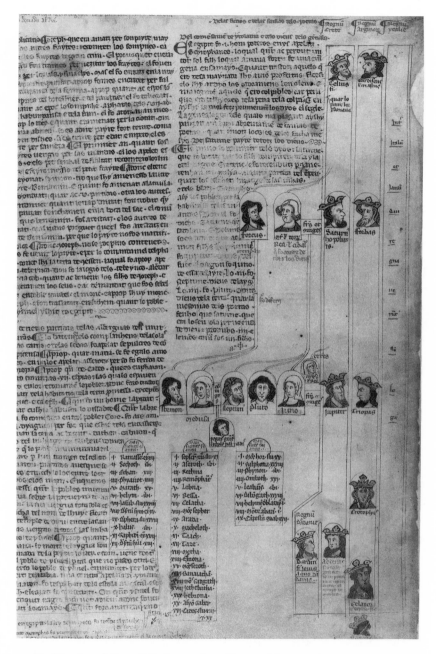

11. The kingdom of Crete: Celius's genealogy. Phorcys, Rhea or Cybele, Saturn; from Phorcys: Sthenno, Medusa; "brothers" of Rhea: Neptune, Pluto, Juno, etc. From "De las ficcios ede las fabulas dels poetas," epitome of third Vatican mythography. Egerton MS. 1500, fol. 6r (ca. 1313, Provençal). By permission of the British Library, London.

the very old one of Hyginus, offered by Mai (but an Hyginus of the fifth century), as based on the Explicit of the second book;[17] of Lactantius Placidus, offered by Bode;[18] and of a "learned Irish scholar of the eighth or ninth century," which fits Adanan the Scot, because of the similarity between the text and that of the Berne scholia on Virgil (which have been attributed to Adanan), offered by Schulz and Elliott and Elder.[19] Although none of these has been definitively proven, the last has merit for a number of reasons, not least of which is the supposed purpose of the first Vatican mythographer in writing the collection, in reaction to the temper of the times.

If we assume, as did Elliott and Elder, a decreased interest in education in the late antique period and therefore infer this mythographer's reformative grammatical interest either from his collecting of scattered scholia from Servian and Lactantian commentaries, or from his presenting a package of myths convenient for grammatical purposes,[20] then we might also, mistakenly, assume that the collection is uninteresting, as Elliott and Elder did in their later article: "The stories are presented in a starkly business-like style, with so little attention given to their poetic or imaginative qualities that one can safely conclude that the author of this treatise had no time for matters of the spirit. His task, one feels, was to provide 'mythological facts,' and in as straightforward and concise a fashion as possible."[21] But is it a coherent collection—is the collection indeed a collection, or merely a catalog of assorted and unrelated fables?

Its three books do seem to lack any order in their seemingly random presentation of heroes and gods in what may be a magisterial annotation of classical figures from school texts such as Virgil's *Aeneid.* The stories (229 of them in Kulcsár's edition, 234 in Bode's) are allocated unequally, with about a hundred stories each in books 1 and 2, and about thirty in book 3, the book divisions clearly designated in the manuscript. But "this division appears to mean little, whether one looks at it from the point of view of the subjects of the myths or from that of sources. . . . No definite rationale in the order of the myths in Book I is observable."[22] Although there is sometimes a sequence of stories from Servius or Fulgentius dealing with a particular god—there is an Apollo series (Mythogr. I 112/113–116/118), a Hercules series (49–68/69), and a Liber Pater series (118/120–121/ 123)—with the exception of the Hercules series these all appear in book 2, the only one of the three that has been described as manifesting a unity of sorts. This book, for Elliott and Elder, reflects "what we may perhaps rightly call the traditional order in mythographical literature, as seen in

Fulgentius, *Myth. Vat.* 2, and the like . . . , i.e. Saturn, Jupiter, Neptune, Pluto, the Furies, the Fates, the Harpies, Proserpina, Apollo, the nine Muses, Apollo and the 'corvus' and 'laurus,' Mercury, and Liber."[23] With the abbreviated fables of the third book, we are mostly given Roman stories (Regulus, Torquatus, Camillus, the seven civil wars of Rome, Atilius Serranus, Fabius Maximus, and Claudius Marcellus), but even this is a series of only seven stories (Mythogr. I 215/219–222/226).

In a hint that shall be taken up in this chapter, Elliott and Elder suggest a loose order based on the first Vatican mythographers's sources, as if the compiler had moved first to one text, then another, to create a series, if one can be said to exist, because of the relevance of the source, and revealing originality, if such is the appropriate term, in the way he adds, excises, arranges, or changes the order of his material.[24] This method, *conflatio,* which is apparent in the hands of a compiler such as Isidore, derives from *adnotatio,* note-taking while reading, and is defined as the often mixed-up but occasionally logical assembly of extracts on a particular topic.[25]

In support of this uneasy structure to the mythography, what has been determined, with some degree of certainty, is the use of sources by the first Vatican mythographer, primarily Virgil, Statius, Ovid, their commentaries by his near-contemporaries, and Fulgentius's *Mitologiae.* While there may be a problem in reconstructing some of the mythographer's sources, if only because some may have been lost, even these lost works were probably commentaries on Virgil or excerpts from a mythological handbook, and it is possible some have been preserved in the Berne scholia on Virgil.[26] The first Vatican mythographer took most of the mythological material that can be traced from the extant commentaries—primarily from Virgil's *Aeneid* as interpreted by Servius (ninety references), from the scholia on the *Thebaid* by Lactantius Placidus (thirty-three references), from Fulgentius's *Mitologiae* (twenty or twenty-one references), from Ovid, as summarized, once again, by Lactantius Placidus in the epitome called *Narrationes fabularum* (twenty-one references), and then from Servius on the *Georgics* (twenty-three references) and *Eclogues* (ten references), with a handful of glosses from Hyginus's *Fabulae,* Isidore's *Etymologiae,* the Berne scholia on the *Eclogues* and *Georgics,* the scholia on the *Achilleid* and on Lucan, the Servius *Scholia Danielis,* and Solinus;[27] a recently discovered major source is the ninth-century Horace scholia.[28] Often in these references the mythographer will borrow word for word, especially from Servius and the Statius scholia, which means he had direct access to the texts;[29] Zink believes that he borrowed directly from Fulgentius, but Schulz argues instead that he used a common source, for otherwise he would have included more of Fulgentius's moralizations.[30] There is also some direct (word-for-word) quotation from Hyginus, Servius, the Servius *Scholia Danielis,* Lactantius Placidus (besides the scholia on the *Thebaid* and *Achilleid,* also from the *Narrationes*), and Isidore.[31]

What has the first Vatican mythographer found most attractive in these sources? Certainly he uses these sources and material derived from other classical epics and their commentaries in the manner of many early grammarians, literally and historically, to emphasize certain figures more than others. Accordingly, most of the fables in his collection involve straightforward narrative summaries designed to disseminate factual information about the hero or god concerned, with no discernible pattern imposed overall, and very little interpretative commentary. In reflection of Servius's chief interests, the sixth book of the *Aeneid* provides the most grist for his mill, with the first, third, and eighth books following in popularity.[32] The first Vatican mythographer does not seem to use the Servian glosses on the sixth book polemically, unlike other early medieval commentators who also depended heavily on glosses on the sixth book of the *Aeneid* to rationalize interest in the demonic (mythological) inhabitants of the underworld—commentators like Theodulf of Orleans, for example—or to rationalize glossation of Boethius—commentators like Remigius of Auxerre, for example. The compiler is truly a compiler and not a mythographer per se, as Schulz has indicated in his very full analysis of direct and indirect sources used by the first Vatican mythographer. Occasionally the first Vatican mythographer will include an interpretative comment, either natural allegory or etymologies which suggest a moral signification, and more rarely, a moral allegory in itself. Where these occur, they are almost always drawn from Servius on the *Aeneid,* though the first sixteen myths in book 2 are based on Fulgentius's *Mitologiae.*

Given this literalistic and historical emphasis, when the first Vatican mythographer came to write his collection he must have been conveniently struck by what might be termed the "universal genealogy" of history as evidenced in his sources. Within these commentary sources the first Vatican mythographer finds most interesting the concept of the "Mycaenan" classical epic (that is, the post-Homeric mythological epic promoted by several Augustan poets patronized by Maecenas), especially the *Aeneid,* which can be read as Trojan history. But the mythographer also turns to the later Roman versions of essentially nonmythological epic, what might be termed versions of ancient history and legend, whether Greek, Theban, or

Trojan (Roman), such as Statius's *Thebaid* and *Achilleid,* and Lucan's *Pharsalia,* as well as commentaries on non-epic works, especially the Servian commentaries on the *Eclogues* and *Georgics,* and possibly even the similar but later Berne scholia on the same Virgilian works. Statius's *Thebaid* can be read as Theban history, with Greek history summarized in portions of Virgil and Ovid in the commentaries on the *Eclogues* and *Georgics.*

In his interest in history he may also have been responding to the strong literary and scholastic valorization of history in this time period. In addition to the classical epics (and their commentaries) used by the first Vatican mythographer which disseminated historical and legendary information about heroes and cities, history and historical cycles were also popular in the developing vernacular heroic epic and patristic materials of the time during which the Berne scholia and the first Vatican mythography were written (whether we assume a date as early as the seventh century, or as late as the ninth), at least in Anglo-Saxon England. To this geographical area the mythographer has been previously linked because of his tie with the Berne scholiast (probably Adanan the Scot).

Many works of this period reveal a keen interest in time and the human workings against mutability, loss, death. Among them can be found the historical sagas recreated in the epic of *Beowulf* and the chronicles of nations, as well as translations of Orosius's *Universal History,* the hexameral books of the Bible, with their sense of creational history, the histories of saints (*Guthlac A* and *B*) and apostles (*Andreas*), Old Testament Apocryphal history (*Judith,* for example) and the history of the finding of the True Cross (*Elene*). Unlike later periods, in this period there is more of a sense that the king's history is the nation's history, that fall and decrepitude stymie even the greatest heroic and human effort, as in *Beowulf.* Set against this gloomy backdrop is the jeweled vision of the Cross as timeless, heroic, eternal, and full of the life and light excluded from the finite and limited span of the human. God's history—from the beginning, with the fall of Lucifer—cyclically repeats itself in human history as warrior enmity visited upon tribal chief, national division resulting from that envy of power. But God's history, and its battles, mirror the chroniclers' history, the rise and fall of kings.

If the first Vatican mythographer *was* the Berne scholiast, Adanan the Scot, whose moralizations he frequently echoes, then the mythographer and the scholiast share an interest in history as a reflection of human frailty that can be traced back to the Romans and Greeks and ultimately to the ancestral gods themselves. No doubt the mythographer's interests in the monumental poet Virgil, and, as we shall see, in the imperial and apotheosized Caesar Augustus, and in the heroes Prometheus, Aeneas, Perseus, and Hercules reflected some need for the valorization of wisdom and strong role-models current in the times. Indeed, Charlemagne, Holy Roman Emperor and instigator of some of the most significant educational and cultural reforms of the entire Middle Ages, was believed to have descended from Priam, through his son Hector's own nephew Francio (in the late thirteenth century this was changed to Hector's "son"),[33] as was Henry Plantagenet, through Arthur, from Brutus, eponymic founder of Britain and great-grandson of Aeneas, according to Geoffrey of Monmouth writing in the twelfth century.

The purpose of the following sections of this chapter will be to suggest ways in which important sources and analogues may have influenced the thematic layers of this seemingly chaotic collection in its understanding of the past and future of the gods and mankind. Glossing in the manner of his predecessor Lactantius Placidus in the *Narrationes,* that is, as a summarizer or epitomizer, or in the scholia on Statius, as an "annotator" (and both groups of commentaries are important sources for the first Vatican mythographer), our mythographer historicizes—makes literal—the mythographic tradition. But it is especially the concept of genealogical history in the Berne scholia that bears some resemblance to that of the mythographer. We will first examine the methods of glossation used by Lactantius Placidus, then the historical and cyclical glosses of the Berne scholiast, before turning to the specific genealogical mythography of the first Vatican mythographer.

I. THE LITERAL GLOSSES ON STATIUS AND OVID IN LACTANTIUS PLACIDUS

Lactantius's three commentaries have much in common beyond the citation of the name "Lactantius Placidus" in various manuscripts.[34] There are few known manuscripts of Lactantius Placidus; of the commentary on Statius's *Thebaid* Paul van de Woestijne acknowledges four—and there are fewer still of the sketchier, unfinished commentary on the *Achilleid.*[35] The poem *Narrationes fabularum,* or *Argumenta,* attributed to Lactantius exists in only seven manuscripts.[36] Nevertheless, parallels among these works exist, primarily in their use of sources, their methodologies, and their interest in glossing a certain kind of fable.[37]

The sources of the works attributed to Lactantius belong to a relatively early period of medieval commentary, and one scholar believes the *Narrationes* was written much before the time of Lactantius Placidus.[38] The sources of Lactantius on Statius's *Thebaid* include Virgil and Servius, Statius, and Lucan. The sources of Lactantius's epitome of Ovid, the *Narrationes,* include Lactantius's own scholia on Statius, the *Scholia Danielis,* and Hyginus. Many of the sources parallel those previously discussed for the first Vatican mythographer; if the mythographer was Adanan the Scot, or else taught in northern England, then it is interesting to note that there was a copy of Statius at York in the eighth century.[39] Most important, there is genealogical information from Hyginus that resurfaces in the *Narrationes*[40] and which may have therefore affected the reading of these epic cycles in the first Vatican mythographer. The emphasis on metamorphosis and generation in Lactantius's epitomizing of the Ovidian *Metamorphoses*[41] may very well have also influenced the first Vatican mythographer in terms of the latter's attention to begetting and genealogy as a cosmic principle.

For the most part, Lactantius's glossation consists of very literal explanatory phrases for names, or their variants, for heroes, gods, places, unusual things, curious rhetorical expressions or figures (e.g., periphrasis, oxymoron).[42] In the commentary on the *Thebaid,* some of which involves marginal or interlinear scholia rather than continuous commentary,[43] most of the remarks merely clarify Statius's references in the first seven of the twelve books. As in the *Narrationes,* at the beginning of each book (except one) Lactantius summarizes its contents in a paragraph. His commentary is more extensive for the earlier books than the later, with two-thirds on the first six books, perhaps because these earlier books are larded with bombastic speeches, rhetorical devices, and very little action. For example, note the plethora of names—many puzzling or obscure, most unidentified by Statius, who assumes a learned and pagan audience, but demanding literal explanation by Lactantius:

And now he [Tydeus] had accomplished the full measure of a journey made rough by *forests and seashore:* where lay the marsh of Lerna and the *burnt Hydra's heat makes warm the depths of those unrighteous* waters, and where through the length of Nemea scarce is heard the scanty song of the yet timid shepherds: where Ephyre's *eastern side* slopes to the winds of Orient and the *Sisyphian havens* lie, and the wave that vents its *wrath upon the land* lies in the curved retreat of Lechaeum sacred to Palaemon. Thence passes he by *Nisus,* leaving thee, *kindly Eleusis,* on his left hand, and at last treads the *Teumesian fields* and enters the Agenorean towers. There he beholds the cruel Eteocles high upon a throne and girt round with bristling spears. (*Thebaid* 2.375– 85; emphases indicate passages Lactantius glossed)

Lactantius's originality primarily lies in the selection of source or sources from which he quotes to clarify Statius's terms; he most frequently cites Virgil, but quotations from Lucan, Juvenal, and others occasionally appear, to amplify or support a difficult notion. For example, the difficult rhetorical figure *hypallage,* in which the relationships among or between things are interchanged, is involved in Statius's description of Cerberus: "iam sparsa solo turbaverat ossa" (*Thebaid* 2.29). Lactantius explains that Statius does not mean that "he disordered the (already) scattered bones" but that "he disturbed (gnawed) and fragmented (shattered) the bones." "Turbauerat et sparsa fecerat," he declares, citing Virgil on Cerberus (*Aeneid* 6.417–25) to indicate that the canine porter was positioned on top of the bones, "ossa super recubans," as he gnawed and devoured them. The Virgil citation helps to define the rhetorical figure and thereby also to interpret the text.

But occasionally a more allegorical interpretation will surface, often of a natural or physical or moral etymological (Stoic) nature. Statius alludes to Apollo's eternally blooming cheeks (*Thebaid* 1.704); Lactantius Placidus explains that they bloom eternally because Apollo is the sun and the sun is fire, and therefore the god never grows old. In another natural interpretation the sign of union between Jove and Juno is said to be lightning— a mixture of fire (Jove) and air (Juno). Psychology and religion are intermingled in a projection of microcosmic trauma into the cosmos through Lactantius's gloss on the word "conubium" in Statius's explanation of Oedipus's relationship with his mother (*Thebaid* 1.69). The physical union of son with mother might indeed be said to be "sweet ecstasy and fatal union," "dulces furias" in the words of Statius's Oedipus, according to Lactantius; he "bene totum, etiam quod ignarus admisit, imputat Furiae, ut beneficiorum assiduitate suffulta tamquam suum sibi uindicet parricidam" ["well imputes the whole thing, even what he did in ignorance, to the Fury"]. These interpretations are, however, relatively few in number, at least in comparison with the large number of truly allegorical expositions in Fulgentius, the Berne scholiast, or the third Vatican mythographer.

II. HISTORICAL AND NATURAL ALLEGORY IN THE BERNE SCHOLIAST ON VIRGIL'S *ECLOGUES* AND *GEORGICS*

The importance of the Berne scholia in the transmission of the mythographic tradition has been underestimated, not only for their influence on the first Vatican mythographer but also for later mythographers. In addition to the influence of the Berne scholia (and Paulus Festus's epitome) on glossaries of ancient lore,[44] their comments on various earthly gods—Ceres, Proserpina, Bacchus—may have influenced the twelfth-century William of Conches in some of his Neoplatonic and Chartrian glosses on Macrobius's commentary on the *Somnium Scipionis* and also, later, Christine de Pizan's *Epistre Othea*, a work that feminizes many of the basically male mythographies.

In contrast to the generally literal or rhetorical glossation method of Lactantius, the Berne scholiast, probably "Adanan the Scot," approaches the *Eclogues* and *Georgics* allegorically, as did Servius earlier, but within a biographical-historical mode possibly prompted by an awareness of Donatus's *Vita* of Virgil. Donatus had interpreted the order in which Virgil had written his three great works—the *Eclogues, Georgics,* and *Aeneid*—as exemplary of the three stages of human life, pastoral, agricultural, and heroic. Donatus had also internally and specifically applied this autobiographical-historical figuring to the first work, the *Eclogues*, understood as a personal and public record of Virgil's own life, first, in his relationships with Pollio, Varus, and Gallus, and second, in his relationship with Caesar Augustus, whom these poems were intended to honor. The reason for Donatus to interpret these texts so may have been Virgil's own open address to Pollio in the fourth eclogue, although the subjects of the first and ninth, concerning Virgil's farm and Gallus's love, and the fifth, concerning the death of his brother, must be construed as, in fact, they are, private.

In the *Eclogues* the subject matter may be pastoral but because they also touch on the story of Virgil's life and his farm, the Berne scholiast heavily glosses them as topical and historical. This means that he may interpret characters and events not only in the light of Virgil's life but also in the light of the fortunes of the Roman Empire. Thus, of the second eclogue, for example, he declares that it can be interpreted on three levels, one literal (*historaliter*) and two allegorical (*allegorice*): literally, it tells the tale of an old shepherd; allegorically, it relates the story of Virgil and Alexis, Pollio's boy-servant, and also the story of Virgil and Augustus. This method is used

consistently throughout: the expression or line of Virgil is cited from once
to three times, and each time it is mentioned a different level of understanding is intended, usually beginning with a literal or factual recitation
of explanatory detail, followed by a natural (physical) or moral explanation,
and culminating in political allegorism.

Thus, the Berne scholia on the *Eclogues* and *Georgics* provide complemen-
tary mythological glosses that elaborate the allegorization of Virgil's life
outlined in the *Vita Donatiana*. For the pastoral phase of human life,
represented by the *Eclogues*, Adanan chiefly reveals, underlying the mythological allusions, the autobiographical and political allegory concerning
Virgil's farm. For the agricultural phase of human life, represented by the
Georgics, Adanan chiefly reveals the natural and physical allegory: underlying the mythological allusion is the science of tillage, planting, rearing of
cattle, and bee-keeping. Moralizations occur primarily in the *Eclogues* and
not the *Georgics*, perhaps because the gods mentioned in the former are not
always sufficiently explained by political references.

Of the two Virgilian works the Berne scholiast writes more mythological or mythographic glosses to the *Eclogues* than to the *Georgics*—of the
Ovidian allusions, fourteen comment on the *Eclogues* but only six on the
Georgics[45] (while the first Vatican mythographer seems to find more
mythological material in the *Georgics* than in the *Eclogues*).[46] Within the
Eclogues itself, most can be found in the sixth eclogue,[47] perhaps because
this philosophical and mythological poem (called an *agrestis*) lends itself
most readily to Adanan's favorite kind of interpretation—the figurative.
By far the largest number of mythological and allegorical references can be
classified as topical, whether concerning Virgil himself or the Roman
Empire. These are frequent in the *Eclogues*, but much less so in the *Georgics*
(perhaps because it is an agricultural poem). Physical and moral allegoristic
readings of myth in both works reveal an underlying "history of the gods"
by means of a Stoic genealogy.

Topical allegorical mythological glosses on the *Eclogues* frequently
unveil the figure of Caesar in their gods and heroes, no doubt in reflection
of imperial worship of the head of state as incarnating the analogue to the
genius Iovis, the national *genius* (and perhaps derived from mentions in
Horace or Horace scholia).[48] Apollo is "allegorice Caesar filius Iovis," who
also controls the sun (Schol., *Ad Buc.* 3.62, 4.10). But Jove and Caesar are
also linked genealogically: on "Ab Ioue principium" the gloss reads "Iouis,
Caesaris," meaning, "adolatur Agusto quia ab Ioue duxit originem" ["Augustus is worshiped because from Jove he derives his origins"] (Schol., *Ad*

Buc. 3.60). Because Jove is also glossed here as the cosmic seed-fire that initiates heat in the human soul, Virgil's Damoetas is also declaring, the scholiast says, "With love [cosmic, caloric, sexual] I begin." In another gloss, the offspring of the gods, the seed of a Jupiter-to-be, or "lord of the world," which shall grow, is applied to Octavius (Schol., *Ad Buc.* 4.49).

In glosses on the fourth eclogue, the age of Augustus is viewed as a reinactment of the heroic age of Troy with Antony seen as a second Achilles. In the new circuit of ages to begin after the Hesiodic Age of Iron (allied with Apollo, "ad Apollinem pertinere ait," as previous ages have been allied, the gold first with Saturn, then the silver with Jupiter, and then the bronze with Neptune), Caesar will be honored in special, "in honorem Caesaris," because Augustus wishes to be accepted as Apollo, "quia Apollinem se Augustus uult accipi" (Schol., *Ad Buc.* 4.49). There will appear a second Tiphys, a second ship named Argo, a second Trojan War, and a second Achilles (Antony) sent to Troy (Italia) (Schol., *Ad Buc.* 4.36).

Antony's succession to Julius is explained in eclogue 5 when Julius Caesar is identified allegorically with Daphnis, who was cut off by a cruel death (Schol., *Ad Buc.* 5.20–21), lamented by the Nymphs and then deified as king of shepherds, son of Mercury and Hersa. Also Julius Caesar is the Daphnis who led on, "adduxit," "reliquias Liberi patris et sacra Romae," the "dances of Bacchus" (Schol., *Ad Buc.* 5.30).

Perhaps the most incongruous of all the political allegorizations occurs in eclogue 7 when Priapus is revealed to be Antony. Literally Thyrsis has suggested to Priapus that the offerings of a bowl of milk and cakes are all he can expect from year to year; figuratively, Thyrsis is Aemilius Macer and Priapus is Antony, or here the keeper of a poor man's garden, and the matter under consideration involves the confiscation of Virgil's farm (Schol., *Ad Buc.* 7.33). Of course Priapus more traditionally had ruled gardens and, as Adanan points out, is celebrated in the month of March, but elsewhere (Schol., *Ad Georg.* 4.109–11) Priapus embodies in addition a spirit of fertility not totally in keeping with imperial dignity (but certainly with cosmic generation).

Some mythological glosses not explained through political allegory present their material directly and prosaically without much allegorical elaboration, often by drawing upon material found in Ovid's *Metamorphoses,* Hyginus, or Isidore, and stated very much in the manner of the first Vatican mythographer. Amphion is the son of Jove and Antiopa and the singer who moved mountains (Schol., *Ad Buc.* 2.24); Daphnis, the son of

Apollo and Psamathes, is king of beautiful shepherds and a noble poet (also identified with Pollio, 2.26); the Dardan Paris is identified as Alexander, son of Priam and a shepherd of Dardania (2.61); Narcissus is a flower who was once a boy, interpreted as the son of Apollo (2.48).

Some of the straightforward glosses provide interesting explanations for puzzling references. When Menalcas asks Damoetas, "Was it not you, Master Dunce, who at the cross-roads used to murder a sorry tune on a scrannel straw?" Adanan reminds us that the cross-roads were associated with "sorry" songs because of shepherds singing there and because there Ceres searched for her daughter Proserpina (Schol., *Ad Buc.* 3.27). Similarly, when Damoetas asks this riddle, "Tell me in what land—and you shall be my great Apollo—Heaven's space is but three ells broad," Adanan replies literally that this may actually refer to a place in Sicily of high altitude (probably Mount Etna) where Proserpina was raped, "rapta est," by Dis Pater (Schol., *Ad Buc.* 3.104–5).

The eight histories from Ovid's *Metamorphoses* in eclogue 6 receive much attention from Adanan, although little moralization, perhaps because his explanations seek to refresh the memories of schoolboys reading Virgil's *Eclogues,* or merely to elucidate puzzling mythological references for readers to come. Thus his explanations remain mostly prosaic for the stones that Pyrrha threw, Saturn's reign, the birds of the Caucasus, Prometheus's theft, and others.[49]

The allegorical mythological glosses on the *Eclogues* are conveyed through moral interpretations, some etymological, and natural (physical) interpretations derived from the Stoics. While the glosses do not appear in a sequence that conveniently adds up to a genealogy, they do reflect the usual Stoic history of the gods beginning with the sons of Saturn and mostly concerned with earthly processes and the origins of civilization. For example, in the Virgilian text, Pallas or Minerva, who inhabits cities that she builds, entices those of us who live in the woods (that is, the shepherds). Adanan notes that "Allegorice 'silvae' carmen," meaning that the woods which the shepherds inhabit are poems and that Minerva (wisdom) lures them into places where she lives (philosophy, Schol., *Ad Buc.* 2.61). The Parcae who govern human fate are defined respectively through a citation from Lucan, "alia nendo, alia texendo, alia rumpendo" ["one spinning, one weaving, one breaking {the thread}"] (Schol., *Ad Buc.* 4.47). Two figures, a god and a demigod, are used by Adanan to gloss the lines "Him on whom his parents have not smiled, no god honors with his table, no goddess with her bed" (Virgil, *Eclogues* 4.62–63): first, Vulcan, rejected by the goddess

Minerva when he desired to sleep with her, and then Hercules, who received his parents' benediction and thereafter won rewards. Implicit in this contrast of the two figures is a moral typology; the later figure— Hercules—would receive a highly elaborate moralization of his labors in the later Middle Ages and Renaissance.

Adanan also deploys fanciful etymological moralizations to explain disparate concepts and terms in the *Eclogues.* There were three kinds of faun (or shepherd) in antiquity, fauns deriving from *fando* (report or hearsay, in the sense of oracular utterance, given their prophetic gifts) and including fauns, Sileni, and satyrs. Believed to be a species of demon ("sed genera daemoniorum a quibusdam creduntur"), they were all modeled on Faunus, father of Latinus and protective deity of shepherds because he initiated grazing (Schol., *Ad Buc.* 6. intro.). Faunus's horns and goat's feet were attributed to him as a result of his identification with Pan.[50] Adanan also defines the Pierian Maids as the Muses, "Pierides" a corrupted form of "piae heredes," meaning heiresses of Pieros, their father (Schol., *Ad Buc.* 6.13).

The natural (physical) allegorizations included in Adanan's comments on the *Eclogues* involve very few myths, mostly isolated major gods understood as part of the World Soul, such as Diana (the moon), Ceres (connected with the earth), and Jupiter himself. Lucina is Diana in Latin or Ilithyra in Greek, "quae parturientibus lucem praebere dicitur quae duas lampades duasque pupillas habere dicitur, quod nascentibus pueris lucem perennem det, vel quod luci praesit" [the goddess of birth "offers light to women in labor and has two lamps or two eyes because she gives lasting light to newborns or because she controls light"] (Schol., *Ad Buc.* 4.10). The three mortal needs, to eat, drink, and be clothed, are intimated by the reference to the annual obligation for sacrifices to Ceres, Bacchus, and Daphnis, explained implicitly as grain, wine, and wool or mutton: " 'Cereri' autem propter aridos, 'libero' propter humidos fructus, Daphnidi propter pecudum prouentus" [" 'to Ceres,' moreover, on account of dry produce {crops}, 'to Liber' on account of moist fruit, to Daphnis on account of increase in sheep"], with Daphnis once more representing the king of shepherds (Schol., *Ad Buc.* 5.79). The Stoic natural interpretation of Jupiter is again invoked, that is, Jupiter as generative fire or the World Soul, as a gloss on the line "Iuppiter et laeto descendet plurimus imbri" ["Jupiter, in his fullness, shall descend in gladsome showers"] (Virgil, *Eclogues* 7.60). Adanan explains that "Iuppiter, aer, imber, . . . idest mixti multa cum pluuia fulgurum ignes cadent, quos putabant Iouem significare, nam Iuppiter pro igne solet poni" ["Jupiter, air, heavy rain, . . . that is, fires of lightning will fall mixed with much rain, which they believed signified Jove, for Jupiter is accustomed to be regarded as fire"].

In general, although the mythological glosses in the commentary on the *Eclogues* are more interesting and more extensive than those in the commentary on the *Georgics,* in the latter commentary, when allegorizations do occur, they extend the Stoic natural and physical explanations of the gods as representations of parts of the universe or natural forces. These non-political glosses are related especially to the agricultural science of each of the four books of the *Georgics,* with their respective agrarian subjects of tillage, planting, the rearing of cattle, and the keeping of bees. From this rich material derive many of the later medieval glosses on gods connected with earthly processes, especially attractive to Chartrian philosophers— Apollo and Diana (sun and moon), Bacchus and Ceres (earthly gods of vine and grain), Neptune (water), Pan (nature, woodlands), Priapus (gardens). Most of these mythological references can be found in the first book, perhaps because of its long invocation of the gods, with the fewest in the second, and a roughly equal number in the third and fourth books.

Virgil's invocation of the gods in the first book of the *Georgics* actually, notes Adanan, catalogues powers needed in tillage, beginning with the sun and the moon and ending with Caesar Augustus, who has not yet chosen his divine sphere, but powers reflective of the Stoic belief that all the gods represented the varied powers of one god, "Stoici dicunt unum deum, sed pro uario officio uaria nomina dicuntur" (Schol., *Ad Georg.* 1.7). Thus Liber Pater and Ceres are identified as Sol, Apollo, and Luna, Proserpina. As sun and moon Liber and Ceres are called upon "Chaoniam pingui glandem mutavit arista" ["to change Chaonia's seed or acorn for the rich ear of corn"], meaning to bring a good harvest of corn, but Adanan glosses *arista* (ear of corn) not only as a crop but also as Aristaeus, son of Apollo and Cyrene, and probably invoked separately a few lines later as "spirit of the groves" (*Georgics* 1.14). Aristaeus, according to Adanan, prevented pestilence in Greek cities by using the whitest cattle for ploughing the island Cea; Adanan says he is invoked here because he first discovered the use of the plough, and he also loved Eurydice, wife of Orpheus.[51]

Neptune, another great power, as water is associated with the horse in five glosses on this god "for whom," says Virgil, "Earth smitten by thy mighty trident, first sent forth the neighing steed" ["fudit equum magno tellus percussa tridenti"] (*Georgics* 1.13). In the first, euhemerist, explanation of the Berne scholiast, the horse produced by the smiting of earth by the trident of Neptune in Thessaly is identified as the speedy Arion, sent by Neptune to Adrastus, from which action Neptune is said to be an equestrian ("unde Neptunus equester dictus est"). In a second, natural, explanation in this same gloss, the horse is identified as water, *aqua*, specifically "ubi cum aliquando flumen esset statiuum et quondam diruptum inundasset, dictum est Neptunum percussisse tridenti, quia non credebant, tantam uim aquae humano motu excitatam, sed diuino" ["the flood or tempest, said to be caused by the striking of Neptune's trident because such powerful agitation of water must come from a divine and not a human motion"]. The historical meaning of the horse is as Hippocentaurus: "Neptunus tridenti percussit scopulum in Thessalia, in qua primum equi domari coeperunt a Thessalis. QUI adsidentes equis cum tauros sequerentur. . . . Illi dicti sunt NepheloCENTAURI UEL Hippocentauri" ["in Thessaly Neptune smote a rock with his trident, and there horses first began to be tamed and used by men for riding; because men riding horses pursued and wounded bulls they were called Nephelcentaurs or Hippocentaurs"]. One special horse in a fourth definition becomes Pegasus "quia Neptunus in principio terram percussit tridenti et inde equus Pegasus prosiliuit" ["because Neptune in the beginning smote earth with his trident, the source from which Pegasus sprang"], and in the fifth the horse becomes Neptune himself, because Ops, his mother, "*EQUUM,* quoniam ab Ope pro Neptuno sit equus subpositus Saturno, pro Ioue lapis, hic conuenit Neptunum inuocare de equis dicturum" ["substituted a horse for him to protect him from his father Saturn when he tried to devour his sons, just as she substituted a stone for Jove"].

Minerva, whom Virgil invokes as inventor of the olive in the *Georgics,* according to Adanan is invoked by some because she is like oil, that is, "quod nulli possit misceri incorruptus et integer, comparabilis uirgini deae, quae ex uno parente progenita est, quam sapientiam interpretantur, uirtutem inuiolabilem" [because it is "incorruptible, whole, and cannot be mixed, and Minerva as a virgin goddess was begotten by only one parent and thus interpreted as wisdom, or inviolable virtue"] (Schol., *Ad Georg.* 1.18–20). The "boy of the crooked plow" in the same passage is revealed by Adanan to be either Triptolemus or Osiris, and as Triptolemus or the favorite of Demeter his myth is related to that of Ceres and Proserpina, itself interpreted elsewhere as a vegetation myth. Silvanus with the cypress in his hand concludes the catalogue of gods and rural powers, his myth recited by Adanan in a straightforward fashion and apparently derived not only from Ovid's *Metamorphoses* but also Servius's commentaries (*In Georg.* 1.19, *In Buc.* 10.26, and *In Aen.* 3.680).

References to the gods in the remainder of this first book of the *Georgics* are glossed in Adanan's scholia without much allegorization.[52] Ceres dominates. She appears in glosses on Lethe and on the reason that oblivion is induced by poppies, in Virgil, "Letharo perfusa . . . somno" ["steeped in Lethe's slumber"]: Ceres asked Jove, "nam Ceres Ioue admonente dicitur cibo papaueris orbitatis oblita, et reuera papauer gignit soporem; nam ad dolorem obliuiscendum in potionibus datur" ["for Ceres, at Jove's urging, is said to have forgotten her bereavement by means of the food of the poppy, and in reality the poppy begets sleep; for it is given in potions for forgetting pain"] Schol., *Ad Georg.* 1.78); and in glosses on Osiris or Triptolemus (Ceres was not the first to teach men to use iron in turning the earth, Schol., *Ad Georg.* 1.147); she is also glossed as the mother of Eleusis and Vesta (Schol., *Ad Georg.* 1.163) and her name can be used as a metonymy (*metonymice*) for fruits and grains, because one cuts down grains, "quod subiungit 'succiditur' " Schol., *Ad Georg.* 1.278).

The second book of the *Georgics,* on planting, includes few mythological references, mostly Stoic and natural as in the first book, and many involving Bacchus or Liber Pater, perhaps because of the emphasis on horticulture. Interpretations of Bacchus would re-emerge with greater philosophical structure in the twelfth century through the Neo-Stoic and Neoplatonic moralizations of William of Conches. This god figures prominently in Adanan's glosses on the first book, as a god of the vine, and in one "mystical" interpretation as identical with Iacchus and his mystic fan or basket. This latter confusion of Bacchus with Iacchus would permit later commentators to interpret Bacchus as a type of Christ (chiefly William of Conches in glossing Macrobius's commentary on the *Somnium Scipionis*). Among the implements of planting and harvest listed by Virgil in book 1 appear "the common wicker ware of Celeus, arbute hurdles and the mystic fan of Iacchus" (*Georgics* 1.166). On the *vannus* or winnowing basket Adanan reveals that Iacchus is actually Bacchus ("IACCHI, id est Bacchi"), the basket necessary for harvesting grains and fruits, and called so because it is large enough to hold what has been produced in a year: "alueus ex uiminibus factus, corio desuper tectus, quo in areis rustici utuntur, discernens fruges et paleas. Vannus dictus quasi annus quod patens sit" ["a hollow vessel made out of switches, covered additionally with hide, which the rustics use on threshing floors, separating grain from chaff. This winnowing basket {'vannus'} said meaning 'annus,' the produce of the year, because it is open"], but "MYSTICA, quia mysteriis Liberi patris adhibetur, et MYSTICA, quia instrumentum purgationis est" ["understood mystically, the basket is used in the mysteries of Liber Pater as an instrument of purgation"]. In the second book, Virgil sings of Bacchus as well as of forest saplings and the "offspring" of the olive because Bacchus is a god of the vine and also Liber Pater, said to rule over bushes ("uirgultorum Liberum praesidem dicit," Schol., *Ad Georg.* 2.2). Adanan finally identifies Pater as not only Liber Pater but also as a general name for all the gods, with the invocation of "pater o Lenaee" (Virgil, *Georgics* 2.4), who makes the field teem with the harvest of the vine. In addition to a minor reference to the dragon's teeth sown by Jason (Schol., *Ad Georg.* 2.141), the second book contains only one other interesting mythological allusion. This Stoic natural explanation rationalizes Virgil's use of Venus in speaking of the springtime renewal of the herds, "et Venerem certis repetunt armenta diebus" ["and in their settled time the herds renew their loves"] (Virgil, *Georgics* 2.329). Adanan cleverly defines Venus here as the generative principle: "Vere enim incipiunt omnia generari, per Veneris concubitum coeuntibus IV elementis, igni humore terra aere" ["everything comes from the congress of Venus, in the binding together of the elements, fire, water, earth, air"].

The third book of the *Georgics* scholia, on the raising of cattle, begins as usual with a list of the gods and goddesses associated with beasts, that is, with Magna Pales, identified as Ceres, or Vesta, mother of the gods; Apollo as the shepherd of Amphrysus; and then various other figures such as Eurystheus, Busiris, Hylas, Latona, Hippodame, and Pelops, recited without moralization in the glosses on the first six lines of book 3. In addition to similarly brief and prosaic references to Ixion, Pollux, Saturn and Ops, and Pelethronion (inhabited by the Centaurs), Adanan provides one interesting moralization of Bacchus in glossing the spotted lynxes that drove Bacchus's car from India. They resemble panthers but their spots, because of their variety, link them to Liber Pater to indicate that the use of wine makes men's minds wavering and unstable ("Lynces' ferae, consimiles pantheris, Libero patri adsignatae propter uarietatem macularum, quibus indicatur uini usum uarias et lubricas hominum mentes efficere," Schol., *Ad Georg.* 3.264). Putting on white fleece in the guise of a ram, Pan beguiles Luna by giving her a gift of wool (Schol., *Ad Georg.* 3.392); Chiron is glossed as "inventor medicinae" (Schol., *Ad Georg.* 3.550); and

Melampus, son of Amythaon, who tried to purify or cleanse both his mother and the Proetides, could not accomplish this either through medicine or religion (Schol., *Ad Georg.* 3.550).

The fourth book of the *Georgics* is on beekeeping and the few "mystical" or moral allegorizations of mythological references relate to beekeeping, bees, and honey. One predatory bird for the bees is identified as Procne (Schol., *Ad Georg.* 4.15). The scarecrow in a fragrant flowery garden who guards against thieves and birds by holding a willow-hook is revealed to be none other than Priapus, god of gardens, in Virgil's classical version of the rustic figure:

> invitent croceis halantes floribus horti
> et custos furum atque avium cum falce saligna
> Hellespontiaci servet tutela Priapi.
>
> [Let there be gardens fragrant with saffron flowers to invite them, and let the watchman against thieves and birds, guardian Priapus, lord of the Hellespont, protect them with his willowhook.] (Virgil, *Georgics* 4.109–11)

He is "lord of the Hellespont," says Adanan, because of a town on the Hellespont in which he was born, and also because he is believed to control all magic arts ("Creditur enim omnibus magicis artibus officere"). Priapus is defined also as the tutelary god of gardens, "qui apud ciuitatem Hellesponti colitur, de qua pulsus est propter uirilis membri magnitudinem; postea in numerum deorum receptus est" ["worshipped in a town on the Hellespont from which he was driven because of the size of his virile member; afterwards he was received into the number of the gods"]. How the bees discovered Jove hidden by his mother in a cave after they had followed the music of the Curetes' cymbals (made to drown out Jove's cries) and then fed the baby honey leads to a discussion of the Curetes, the inhabitants of Crete, later, the priests of Jupiter, identified as Corybantes, usually the priests of Cybele. Their names are interpreted etymologically by Adanan: the Curetes are called Corybantes either because they were the nurses of Jove, or because they belonged to the first age, or because they were created out of the tears of Jove (Schol., *Ad Georg.* 4.151).[53] Finally, the book concludes with a long section devoted to Aristaeus, who, despairing when he lost his bees, questioned his Nymph mother about his fate on earth; of course Orpheus blamed him for Eurydice's death, as she had been fleeing his amorous advances when the snake bit her (Schol., *Ad Georg.*

4.317ff). He is called "cupidus pastor," perhaps for this reason (Schol., *Ad Georg.* 4.493). There follow several minor references—to Philomela as a nightingale, the symbol of mourning (Schol., *Ad Georg.* 4.511), and to the Ciconian dames who tore apart Orpheus in their Bacchic frenzy (Schol., *Ad Georg.* 4.520).

The Berne scholiast's emphasis throughout the *Eclogues* on topical history and, in the *Georgics,* on cyclical change, or cosmic and earthly generation and regeneration, together add up to a strong bias toward a "universal genealogy," which will blossom in the hands of the first Vatican mythographer.

III. THE GENEALOGY OF THE GODS AND THE FIRST VATICAN MYTHOGRAPHY, BOOKS 1 AND 2

The first Vatican mythographer's focus on the fable of the individual figure and on the primacy of the individual throughout deconstructs his text into a motley assembly of fables. Nevertheless, structural patterns and motifs are eventually revealed by work's end. Book 1's unpatterned emphasis on heroes and demigods yields in book 2 to a Fulgentian sequence of eighteen myths based primarily on the four chief gods and Apollo and Mercury. The rest of book 2 (eighty or so myths) describes in order the adulteries of Jupiter and other gods and kings, the founding of Troy, and the children of these kings, until we arrive at the rivers of hell and Aeneas's descent (Mythogr. I 199/202–200/203). And in book 3, after the first myth defines the divine and human genealogical principle, the rest of the fables focuses on peripheral figures involved in the Troy story or Roman history.

These patterns can be discerned through what might be termed the accessus to the first Vatican mythography, to draw on Alastair Minnis's term, in the first fable, on Prometheus, through its end fable, on the Pleiades, and through its unifying "summary of contents," in what might be termed the accessus to the third book (Mythogr. I 201/204), a genealogy of the gods. This detailed study of the first Vatican mythographer will examine the parameters of this genealogy in beginning and end myths, which provide closure, and the correlation of this genealogy with the other myths actually included in the collection.

Just as Ovid alludes to Prometheus briefly in the *Metamorphoses* to suggest one version of part of the creation story, the first Vatican mythographer, like later commentators on Ovid, for example, Pierre Bersuire, begins with Prometheus, bringer of fire and exemplar of *prudentia*—and therefore antithesis of much of what the mythography describes as typical human behavior. In the very first myth, on the idea of Prometheus as a thief of fire (from Servius, *In Buc.* 6.42), Prometheus's crime and punishment are rationalized allegorically. Prometheus typifies the prudent and rational man, his heart eaten by the eagle as a sign of that excessive care demanded in knowledge of the stars:

> Hec autem omnia non sine ratione finguntur, nam Prometheus uir prudentissimus fuit, unde et primus astrologiam Assyriis indicauit quam residens in Caucaso monte nimia cura comprehenderat. Dicitur autem aquila cor eius edere, quod est nimia sollicitudo qua ille assecutus syderum omnes motus deprehenderat. Et hoc quia per prudentiam fecit, duce Mercurio, qui prudentie et rationis deus est, ad saxum dicitur religatus. Deprehendit preterea rationem fulminum et hominibus indicauit, unde celestem ignem dicitur esse furatus, nam quadam arte ab eodem monstrata supernus ignis olim eliciebatur qui mortalibus profuit donec bene eo usi sunt. Nam postea malo hominum usu in perniciem uersus est.

> [Moreover, not without reason are all these stories told, for Prometheus was a very wise man. He was the first to teach the Assyrians knowledge of the stars, which he had learned with great carefulness while living in the Caucasian Mountains. Moreover, it is said that an eagle eats his heart, as this represents the great diligence with which he followed and learned all the motions of the stars. And because he did this through foresightedness, under the guidance of Mercury, who is the god of foresight and reason, it is said that he was bound to a rock. Furthermore, he learned the cause of thunderbolts and taught it to men; hence he is said to have stolen the heavenly fire. For by a trick shown him by Mercury he once extracted from heaven fire, which was profitable to mortals as long as they used it well. For afterwards, by men's abuse of it, it was turned to destructiveness.] (Mythogr. I 1/1)

As an antitype of another first man who is not mentioned—the foolish Adam—Prometheus the star-gazer functions very much like Remigius's Hercules who for apotheosis looks to the stars at the end of his life. A very intelligent *accessus* to this motley collection of disordered fables, it suggests a touchstone for interpretation, to which the end fable adds. In this last myth, the stars—the Pleiades—again play a key role. The introductory and frame fable of Prometheus as a type of Adam, the summary genealogy of the gods two-thirds of the way through (in the "accessus" to book 3 of the collection), and this last myth provide a very rough kind of theme and organization: the seven Pleiades, or constellations fixed in the heavens, point to the celestial as a sign of the ultimate human and Christian destination.

In the first Vatican mythographer, the two most prevalent patterns are linked by an emphasis on history, that is, on origins and endings, the cyclical repetitions of time and the consequences of history: from birth to death, one might argue, or the descent from heaven to earth, and the return to the heavens after death. This pattern, of tracing the creation of the world, or of man's ingenuity in remaking his universe, is an ancient one common to many mythologies from around the world, modeled on the book of Genesis in the Old Testament, and continuing down, in genealogical lists, to Boccaccio in his *Genealogia gentilium deorum* in the fourteenth century. But the form of this "universal mythological history" is less easy to detect here than in Boccaccio: in fact, although the work includes a genealogy (as the first myth of the third book), it comes closer to the end than to the beginning of the mythography. And yet, this genealogy deserves a closer look because of its function as an epitome of the diffused and scattered myths in the first Vatican mythographer.

The genealogy (Mythogr. I 201/204; see table 3),[54] is more or less structured according to begetter ("Item genuit"): Oceanus, Celius, Phorcys, Saturn, Atlas, Jupiter (and his Trojan progeny resulting from the union with Electra), nearly sixteen lines, followed by the mating of Jupiter with an unnamed daughter of Atlas, leading to the Greek House of Atreus. A different Greek house, that of Theseus, is also traced: Thetis Major *genuit* Thetis, mother of Achilles, and Clymene, mother of Feton (Phaeton) and Aethra, mother of Theseus, who marries Aegeus, son of Neptune. Jupiter also fathers Hercules. In the Theban line, Agenor begets Cadmus and Europa; Cadmus marries Hermione or Harmonia, daughter of Mars and Venus; Laius fathers Oedipus (compare Mythogr. I 148/151), who himself fathers four children; there are other Theban begetters, Adrastus as father of Argia and Deiphyle, Cestius (Thestius) as father of Althea and her brothers, with Althea and Oeneus (son of Parthaon, himself son of Mars), as parents of Meleager and Tydeus, Gorge and Deianira.

In this medieval genealogy, then, the metaphor for cosmic creation is sexual intercourse, chiefly by the head god Jupiter or Jove. The joining of two different things—heaven and earth, male and female, soul and body—

TABLE 3
GENEALOGY OF THE GODS
(FROM THE FIRST VATICAN MYTHOGRAPHER, MYTH 201/204)

I. The Major Gods and the Royal Hero of Troy: Aeneas

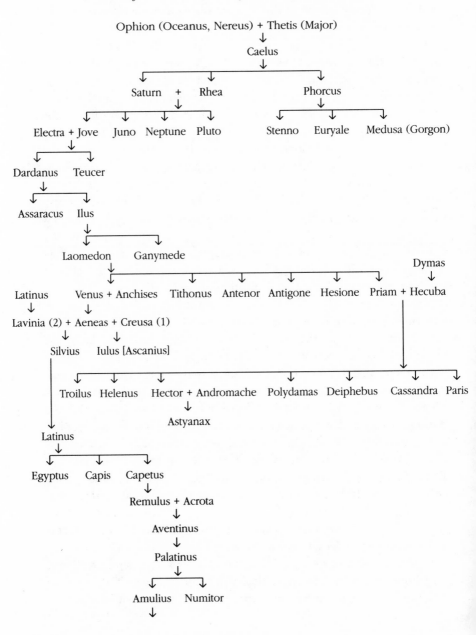

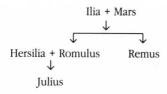

Ilia + Mars
↓

Hersilia + Romulus   Remus
↓

Julius

II. The Royal Kings of Greece

A. The House of Atreus

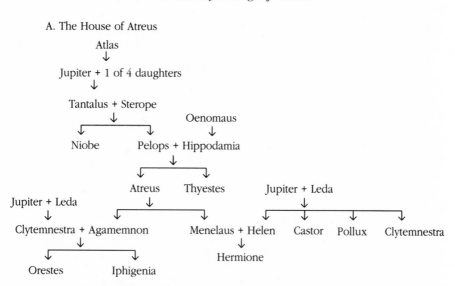

Atlas
↓

Jupiter + 1 of 4 daughters
↓

Tantalus + Sterope
↓   Oenomaus
↓

Niobe   Pelops + Hippodamia
↓

Atreus   Thyestes   Jupiter + Leda

Jupiter + Leda   ↓   ↓
↓

Clytemnestra + Agamemnon   Menelaus + Helen   Castor   Pollux   Clytemnestra
↓   ↓

Orestes   Iphigenia   Hermione

B. Theseus, Hero and Leader of Athens (Two Versions)

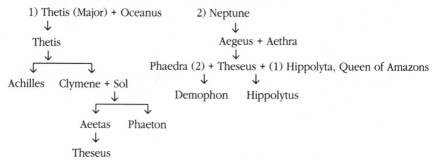

1) Thetis (Major) + Oceanus   2) Neptune
↓   ↓

Thetis   Aegeus + Aethra
↓   ↓

Achilles   Clymene + Sol   Phaedra (2) + Theseus + (1) Hippolyta, Queen of Amazons
↓   ↓   ↓

Aeetas   Phaeton   Demophon   Hippolytus
↓

Theseus

III. Theban Kings and Heroes

A. Cadmus, Founder of Thebes, and Brother of Europa

Agenor
↓

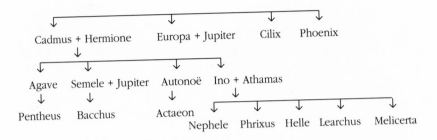

Cadmus + Hermione   Europa + Jupiter   Cilix   Phoenix

Agave   Semele + Jupiter   Autonoë   Ino + Athamas

Pentheus   Bacchus   Actaeon   Nephele   Phrixus   Helle   Learchus   Melicerta

B. Amphion, Theban Hero and King (after Cadmus and brother Zethus)

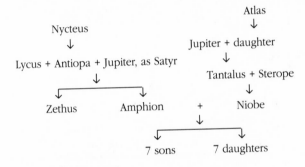

Atlas

Nycteus

Jupiter + daughter

Lycus + Antiopa + Jupiter, as Satyr

Tantalus + Sterope

Zethus   Amphion   +   Niobe

7 sons   7 daughters

C. King Oedipus and his Sons and Daughters-in-Law

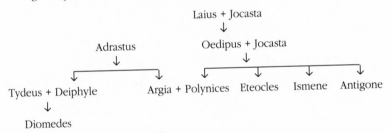

Laius + Jocasta

Adrastus   Oedipus + Jocasta

Tydeus + Deiphyle   Argia + Polynices   Eteocles   Ismene   Antigone

Diomedes

D. Meleager and his sister Deianira (wife of hero Hercules)

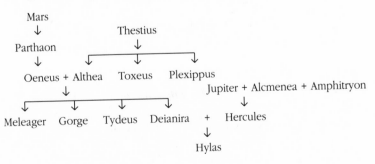

Mars

Thestius

Parthaon

Oeneus + Althea   Toxeus   Plexippus

Jupiter + Alcmenea + Amphitryon

Meleager   Gorge   Tydeus   Deianira   +   Hercules

Hylas

IV. The Genealogy of the Secondary Gods

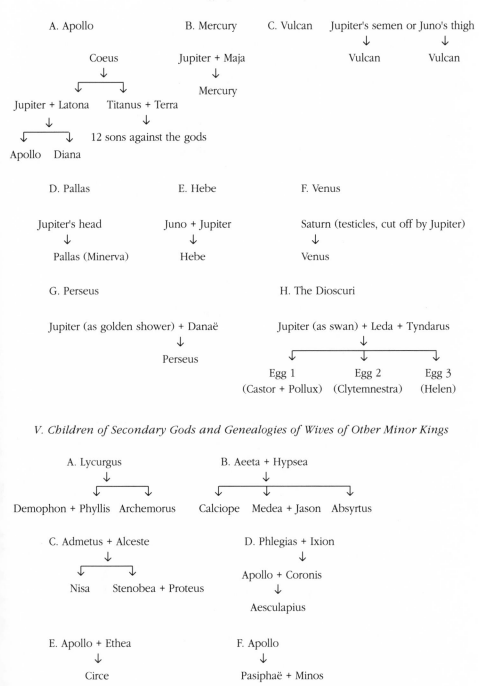

A. Apollo

Coeus
↓
Jupiter + Latona Titanus + Terra
↓   ↓
Apollo Diana   12 sons against the gods

B. Mercury

Jupiter + Maja
↓
Mercury

C. Vulcan   Jupiter's semen or Juno's thigh
↓   ↓
Vulcan   Vulcan

D. Pallas

Jupiter's head
↓
Pallas (Minerva)

E. Hebe

Juno + Jupiter
↓
Hebe

F. Venus

Saturn (testicles, cut off by Jupiter)
↓
Venus

G. Perseus

Jupiter (as golden shower) + Danaë
↓
Perseus

H. The Dioscuri

Jupiter (as swan) + Leda + Tyndarus
↓
Egg 1   Egg 2   Egg 3
(Castor + Pollux) (Clytemnestra) (Helen)

V. Children of Secondary Gods and Genealogies of Wives of Other Minor Kings

A. Lycurgus
↓
Demophon + Phyllis Archemorus

B. Aeeta + Hypsea
↓
Calciope Medea + Jason Absyrtus

C. Admetus + Alceste
↓
Nisa   Stenobea + Proteus

D. Phlegias + Ixion
↓
Apollo + Coronis
↓
Aesculapius

E. Apollo + Ethea
↓
Circe

F. Apollo
↓
Pasiphaë + Minos

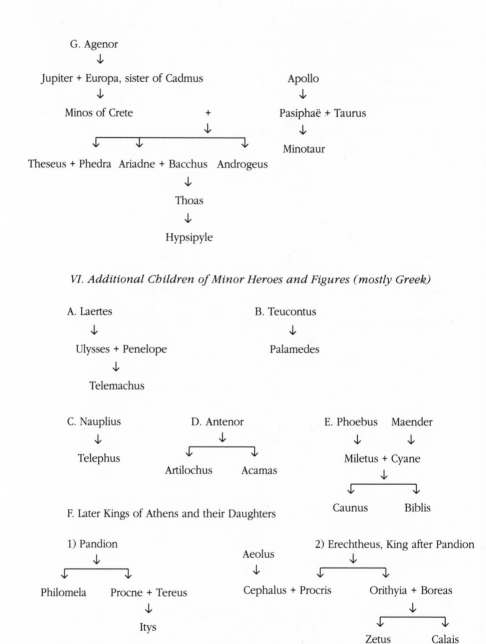

G. Agenor
↓
Jupiter + Europa, sister of Cadmus   Apollo
↓   ↓
Minos of Crete   +   Pasiphaë + Taurus
↓   ↓
Theseus + Phedra   Ariadne + Bacchus   Androgeus   Minotaur
↓
Thoas
↓
Hypsipyle

VI. Additional Children of Minor Heroes and Figures (mostly Greek)

A. Laertes   B. Teucontus
↓   ↓
Ulysses + Penelope   Palamedes
↓
Telemachus

C. Nauplius   D. Antenor   E. Phoebus   Maender
↓   ↓   ↓   ↓
Telephus   Miletus + Cyane
Artilochus   Acamas   ↓
                                      Caunus   Biblis

F. Later Kings of Athens and their Daughters

1) Pandion   2) Erechtheus, King after Pandion
↓   Aeolus   ↓
↓   Cephalus + Procris   Orithyia + Boreas
Philomela   Procne + Tereus   ↓
↓
Itys   Zetus   Calais

was necessary for the generation of new life, a tertium quid with its own identity, qualities, name, and potency. Hence the family tree represented a genetic history, a metaphor for the cosmic chronology known as the history of the world—and human history. And the way in which Jupiter managed his sexual unions provided a moral base for the various nations (continents) such couplings engendered. A rape, an abduction, an incest, might result in progeny condemned to repeat the sins of the fathers, in this case, Jupiter, the father of us all and equivalent to Adam.

Because of the anticipation by the first Vatican mythographer of the important symbol of the genealogy as a procreative historical principle— the ordering and temporally hierarchical list that would have unified the chaotic spewing forth of fable and story in the first book—the mythographer can denigrate from the beginning sexual congress that involves rape, adultery, fornication, illicit love affairs. The Athenians, in fable 2, seem to be associated with the qualities of Minerva, who gave them her name (in Greek "Attis," or "Athena" for the city). But then in fable 3 we learn there were two Scyllas, one who loved Glaucus the marine god, the other the daughter of Nisus who loved Minos too much and too intimately. The mythographer is swept up already in his pageant of sexuality and betrayal, of frustrated, impossible, and violent passion, moving to Tereus and Procne in fable 4, who "eam uiciauit in itinere et ei linguam . . . abscidit" ["rapes her on the journey and cuts off her tongue"]. Acis and Galatea love miserably in fable 5, or rather Acis loves her miserably; Silvanus, god of trees, loves a boy, Cyparissus, in fable 6, mother Ceres searches for and finally obtains her raped daughter Proserpina in fable 7. These are for the most part unsuccessful, and immoral, love relationships—delineated in a book of secrets (Celeus and Triptolemus, in fable 8, do not seem to fit). In fables 12 through 18 fathers sacrifice sons to test the gods (Tantalus and Pelops, in a Ceres series), Tityus longs for Latona; Ixion mistakenly sleeps with clouds in the shape of Juno; frustrated Circe does not sleep with Ulysses; Tiresias, seeing two snakes copulate, beats them apart with a rod and is changed into a female. Io is loved by Jove but transformed into a heifer.

More important than this historical rationalization of the sexual congresses of the gods was the second role of the genealogy in the Middle Ages: the begetting of the gods becomes a metaphor for natural processes. In its rough structure the genealogy was adapted to the moral and ethical purposes of the mythographers and their handbooks. First and foremost, as a metaphor for the creation of the world the genealogy (or in particular this genealogy), functioned as medieval cosmology or physics, indicating how the world evolved out of separation of the waters above (Oceanus) and below (Thetis) from the heavens (their son Celius). This process resulted in progeny, represented by time (Saturn) and space, or nature (his sister Rhea), rulers of the first age, and their dark brother Phorcys. The first Vatican mythographer describes this process as "begetting." From these elemental parents was born the created universe as we know it. The marriage of time and space (nature) engendered the four elements, represented by the four rulers of the regions of the world, Jupiter (fire), Juno (air), water (Neptune), and earth (Pluto), all seen as kin ("Saturnus de Rea genuit Iouem et Iunonem et Neptunum et Plutonem," Mythogr. I 201/204).

The order of the introductory myths in the second book of the mythography depends especially on a "Universal Genealogy"—a sort of begetting spirit that begins with Saturn as son of Pollux and Ops who mates with Rhea to have three sons (but no Juno): Jove, Neptune, and Pluto, who govern heavens, waters, and the earthly underworld (Mythogr. I 101/102). The Fulgentian order of gods is revised to reflect this cosmic sexual principle of Stoic generation (101/102–116/118) and the four hierarchical regions of the universe. The first Vatican mythographer, however, avoids Fulgentius's extensive moralizing and allegorizing in his comments; he does say, for example, in a passage on Jove taken from Fulgentius (*Mit.* 1.3), that "Mystically they put Jove first as fire, hence also he is called Zeus in Greek, that is, life or heat; Juno is put second as air" (Mythogr. I 104/105). That is, Jupiter is fire because all receive life through fire (the Stoic concept of the World Soul consists of fiery seeds) and hence Juno, both sister and wife, is air. "Neptunus" (Mythogr. I 106/107) comes from "nube tonans" in Latin (and from the Greek Possidonius, Poseidon) and governs the element of water; in a Fulgentian addition (*Mit.* 1.4), he carries a trident because water has a triple virtue, that is, it is "liquida, fecunda, potabilis," "fluid, productive, and drinkable." His wife Amphitrite bears a Greek name from *amphi,* or in Latin *circumcirca,* "around," because water is enclosed by all three elements, the fire and air of sky and the earth. The fable of Pluto (Mythogr. I 107/108) comes from Fulgentius (*Mit.* 1.5–6), where he is said to govern earth because *plutos* in Greek means riches, *diuicie,* no doubt found in the earth. In an Isidorian aside (compare *Etym.* 8.11.42) the first Vatican mythographer notes that Pluto is also called Orcus because he receives the dead, "quia tenebris abdicatum inferis praeesse tradunt" ("because they say that, cast into darkness, he rules over the underworld"). The three-headed dog

Cerberus at his feet represents the *invidia* of human quarrels brought about by nature, cause, and accident.

The familiars of the earthly underworld ruled by Jupiter's brother Pluto are recognized in the next few myths. The three Furies are named so through Fulgentian etymologies (from *Mit.* 1.7), "Allecto," meaning *impausabilis,* unstoppable, "Thesiphone," *istarum vox,* or their voice, and "Megaera," for *magna contentio,* great contention (Mythogr. I 108/109). The three Fates are called Parcae by antiphrasis "quod nulli *parcant,*" "because they spare no one." Their names come from Greek etymologies known to us from Fulgentius (*Mit.* 1.8)—Clotho, *evocatio,* summons; Lachesis, *sors,* destiny; and Atropos, *sine ordine,* without order (Mythogr. I 109/110). The three Harpies (from *Mit.* 1.9) describe the process of plundering—Aello, *alienum tollens,* carrying off what is another's; Occipito, *cicius auferens,* quickly escaping with; Celeno, *nigra,* black (Mythogr. I 110/111). Pluto's wife Proserpina (Mythogr. I 111/112) is the daughter of Ceres, the goddess of corn, because Ceres is *gaudium,* joy, which attends the increase of crops (from Fulgentius, *Mit.* 1.10, and Isidore, *Etym.* 8.11.61, 56–58). Proserpina comes from *proserpant* (*fruges;* creeping forward, or crops). The first Vatican mythographer then says (in a definition not found in Fulgentius) she is also known as Vesta, from *vestita,* because she is dressed in grasses; and as Diana, as if *duana,* apparently two because the moon Luna appears both during the day and at night; and as Lucina, because *luciat,* she gives light; and as Trivia, three-figured because of the three regions she governs. Luna, Diana, and Proserpina (also called "Latonia" from her mother Latona, and in Greek Hecate) are, then, all one god. Previously, the first Vatican mythographer has explained that Diana is known as well by the names of Juno and Proserpina, for, although Diana is a virgin, nevertheless she is invoked by those who are giving birth and for this reason has several names, Juno, Diana, Proserpina: "unde, cum Diana sit uirgo, tamen a parturientibus inuocatur. Hec nanque est Iuno, Diana, Proserpina" (Mythogr. I 37/37). As the moon Diana also figures in the myth of Endymion, who loved her (Mythogr. I 224/229).

In the genealogy at the beginning of book 3, the planets, or the other major gods, were defined by, and derived from, the relationships of the major gods: Saturn, father of Jupiter, was the oldest (farthest away from the earth), and was castrated by Jupiter (as he himself was said to have castrated his father Celius). Venus sprang from the severed testicles of Saturn hurled into the ocean by Jupiter ("Item Venus de spuma testiculorum Saturni a Ioue de regno expulsi"). From Jupiter and Latona came Apollo (sun) and

Diana (moon) ("Item Iuppiter de Latona filia Cei genuit Apollinem et Dianam"). Jupiter's union with Maia produced Mercury, the messenger of the gods and the closest to earth after the moon ("Item Iuppiter concubuit cum Maia et genuit Mercurium"). Only Mars lacks a genealogy in this list.

The first Vatican mythographer's long Apollo sequence (Mythogr. I 112/113–116/118) is partly dependent on Fulgentius (*Mit.* 1.12–16) but expressive of the by now conventional image drawn from Macrobius and Martianus—Apollo as revealer, source of knowledge. Apollo's genealogy is given in the first book's myth of the sisters Latona and Asterie (Astarie, Mythogr. I 37/37): Asterie rejected Jove and was turned into a bird, from whom an island sprang that was the same place to which Latona was taken on the order of Jove when Python pursued her. Because Jupiter consorted with her, Latona gave birth to Apollo and Diana on this island, later called Delos. The mythographer explains that "Delos" comes from a Greek word meaning *manifesta,* "uel, quod uerius fuit, quia cum ubique Apollinis responsa obscura sint, manifesta illic responsa dantur" ["or, what was more true, because in that place Apollo's responses are given clearly, although everywhere else they are obscure"] (Servius, *In Aen.* 3.73). Apollo is called the sun (Mythogr. I 112/113), "Hunc et diuinationis deum ponunt eo quod Sol omnia obscura manifestat in lucem" ["he is god of omens because the sun reveals in the light all that is obscure"]. He is also called *solus* (the sun is unique), from *solum,* "alone," and called "Phoebus," from *ephebus,* "adolescent," hence depicted as a boy because the sun rises daily and in new light is born ("quasi effebum, hoc est adolescentem; unde et Sol puer pingitur eo quod cottidie oriatur et noua luce nascatur"). The four horses of the sun have names whose meaning expresses their significance: Eritreus (Erythaeus) in Greek *rubeus,* "blushing," "eo quod sol matutino lumine rubicundus exsurgat" ["because the sun rises red in the morning light"]; Acteus (Actaeon), *splendens,* "resplendent"; Lampus, *ardens,* "burning"; and Filogeus (Philogeus), *terram amans,* "loving the earth," "eo quod uespere occasibus Sol protinus incumbat" ["because in his evening setting the sun descends straight down"]. Apollo is associated with the nine Muses as a tenth Muse in a very Fulgentian description (*Mit.* 1.15), largely "because there are ten modulations of the human voice" (Mythogr. I 113/114). Other Apollo myths in this sequence (Mythogr. I 114/115–116/118) include the story of the crow and Coronis (similar to *Mit.* 1.13); Apollo and Daphne (like *Mit.* 1.14); Apollo and Iacinthus (from Servius, *In Buc.* 3.63); Apollo and Eridanus (or Phaeton, like *Mit.* 1.16 and Servius, *In Aen.* 6.659).

The first Vatican mythographer then moves to the couplings of Jupiter and Maia (producing Mercury, Mythogr. I 117/119), followed by Jupiter and Semele (producing Liber Pater, Bacchus, 118/120, and his adventures, Mythogr. I 119/121–121/123), Jupiter as sole begetter of Minerva (Mythogr. I 122/124), and Jupiter and Juno (producing Vulcan, 125/128). As the mythographer arrives at those gods associated with the earth, he rehearses the conflict between prudence and sexuality witnessed above, presenting Jupiter's children as various intellectual faculties or qualities humans would do well to inculcate or exercise. The favorable fable on Mercury, resembling material from Isidore (*Etym.* 8.11.45–49), etymologizes his name from *medius currens,* running between, because conversation (*sermo*) runs in the midst of all, and delineates his role as an announcer and messenger, epitomizing oratorical ability. He is called Trismegistus because he has knowledge of many arts, that is, *ter maximus,* and depicted with a dog's head "because the dog is considered to be the wisest and cleverest species among all animals."

When Jupiter slept with Semele, the child that resulted after she burned to death from the force of his real nature as lightning was nourished in Jupiter's thigh—in a sense, like Minerva, born of him alone. In a shorthand (and negative) transmission of Fulgentius (*Mit.* 2.12), this fable portrays Semele as one of four sisters, together called Bacchae, "et mistice per has [quattuor] ebrietatis genera signantur, id est uinolentia, obliuio, libido, insania" ["and mystically by these are signified the four stages of drunkenness, that is, intoxication, forgetfulness, lust, madness"] (Mythogr. I 118/120). The remainder of the myth differs from Fulgentius, for it is taken from Lactantius's *Narrationes*[55] and is a straightforward recitation of Juno's suspicion and the consequence of the adultery, although it introduces at the end Fulgentian Liber Pater, or Dionysus, son of Semele, "tigribus sedere dicitur, quod omnis vinolentia feritati semper insistat, et Lieus dicitur quasi lenitatem prestans" ["said to ride on tigers because intoxication goes with savageness; and he is called Lieus as if governing softness, that is, of minds"]. He is depicted as a young man, "quia ebrietas nunquam matura est" ["because drunkenness is never mature"]. Liber's activities occupy four fables in all (Mythogr. I 118/120–121/123).

The daughter of Jove alone, springing from his head (Mythogr. I 201/204), Minerva (from Isidore, *Etym.* 8.11.71–5) as the goddess of wisdom was the inventor "multorum ingeniorum," "of many ingenious things" (Mythogr. I 122/124). In Greek she is called Athena but Minerva in Latin, from "munus artium uariarum," the gift of various arts. She was born from the head of Jove because the judgment of a wise man, who discovers (*inuenit*) all things, is in the head. Her other names, based on geographical associations, include Tritonia and Pallas, the latter also possibly deriving from the name of a giant she killed. The mythographer links her with the contest between Marsyas and Apollo, because Marsyas found the flute she had invented and discarded (Mythogr. I 122/125), and follows this with three other fables linked with earth and earthly love: Priapus, called so from his gigantic male member, and the Nymph Lothos (taken from Servius, *In Georg.* 2.84, 4.3); the rustic god of nature Pan, called so from "omne," "everything" and depicted as being defeated by the god Amor because "Amor omnia uincit," "love conquers all" (taken from Isidore, *Etym.* 8.11.81); and Vulcan who, himself the child of Jupiter and Juno, nevertheless desired Minerva, in the spilling of his seed on earth producing the appropriately named Erichthonius, from *heris,* or "lis" (dispute) and *chthon,* or "terra" (earth) (from Hyginus, *Fabulae*).[56]

In addition to these gods who were clearly themselves divine progeny of Jupiter and others, other figures signifying various nations and continents sprang up: Troy or Europe, Athens or Greece, and Thebes. Europe evolves from the union of Jove with Electra, herself the daughter of Atlas and Pleione, from which Aeneas derives his lineage. Greece is the result of the union of Jove and another one of Atlas's daughters: "The same Jupiter slept with one of the four daughters of Atlas. . . , and begot from her Tantalus; Tantalus from Stirope begot Niobe and Pelops" (Mythogr. I 201/204). Thebes was founded by Cadmus, son of Agenor, in following his sister Europa, although he married Hermione or Harmonia, the daughter of Venus and Mars. And from these nations sprang leaders and kings whose exploits fill up the myths with which we are concerned.

IV. NATIONAL HISTORIES IN THE FIRST VATICAN
MYTHOGRAPHY, BOOK 3: THE HEROES PROMETHEUS,
AENEAS, PERSEUS, AND HERCULES

The national genealogies, the heroic cycles, transmit from father to son the seeds of their own destruction, passing on to future generations the consequences of the mistakes of their ancestral gods, chiefly Jupiter. If we examine more particularly the different cycles of myth conveniently summed up in the genealogical preface to the third book, we will discover the flawed ancestry of the Trojans, the Greeks, the Thebans, so condemned to repeat their errors in their begetting of sons and daughters. Their flaws are flaws in leadership as well as morals. For this reason their nations are doomed—the sons and daughters for the most part eventually die out.

"For the most part," because certain sons exist as exceptions to this general and widespread failure. The product of human and divine parents, they attempt to lead their nations wisely or to act heroically and virtuously in the face of adversity. Indeed, much of the redemptive action evident from the genealogy as well as the mythography itself springs from these heroes and demigods. If Prometheus (Mythogr. I 1/1) is interpreted as a man of prudence and wisdom, he serves as an appropriate model for all the heroes and as an antithesis to both human and god engaged in illicit sexual activity in this mythography. Hercules, associated with the region around Thebes, and his deeds occupy some twenty-five fables in book 1; his great-grandfather Perseus (on his mother's side) appears in six fables (Mythogr. I 72/73, 127/130–131/134). And the most important hero, Trojan Aeneas, whose journey is recited near the end of book 2 (Mythogr. I 199/202), links many of the fables scattered throughout the three books, although his failed relatives occupy much of the mythographer's attention. The first thirty-three fables of book 3 emphasize the wedding at which Paris made his disastrous judgment, the Troy legends, and related Roman history, perhaps to indicate the mythographer's awareness that a Trojan founded Italy and initiated its chronicles, leading almost inexorably into nearly contemporary history. But to understand all the heroes and their cycles we must explore their origins, which is to say, their genealogies and what they tell us about the nation and its best members.

Troy is doomed because its male ancestry is tainted by betrayal and deception. Jupiter treacherously overthrew his own father Saturn, a deceit that will echo in his own great-grandson Laomedon's treacherous refusal first to pay Jupiter's brother Neptune, who had helped him build Troy's walls, and later to pay Hercules, another son of Jupiter and great-grandson of Perseus (Mythogr. I 133/136, 134/137). Laomedon is the father of Antenor, who betrayed his country by allowing in the Trojan horse, and grandfather of Aeneas. (The entire genealogy begins with the coupling of Electra, daughter of Atlas and Pleione, with Jupiter: "Atlas from Pleione begot Sterope, Maia, Electra, and four others. Jupiter from Electra begot Dardanus and Teucer, Dardanus begot Ylus and Asaracus, Ylus [begot] Laomedon and Ganymede. Laomedon begot Anchises, Tythonus, Antenor, Antigone who was changed into a stork, Hesione, and Priam" (Mythogr. I 201/204). Laomedon is also grandfather of Paris, who abducted Helen and initiated the Trojan War: "Priam from Hecuba, daughter of Dimas, king of the Thebans, begot Troylus and Helenus, Polydamas, Deiphebus, Cassandra, Paris, [and] Hector who from Andromache begot Astyanax." Unfortunately, it is the grandson of Oceanus, Achilles, who will kill Hector: "Thetis the elder, wife of Oceanus, bore Thetis, mother of Achilles and Clymene; Clymene was the wife of Sol and bore Phaethon." Because Achilles is the son also of mortal Peleus, his mother Thetis, in fear for his death, in vain was consoled by Neptune (Mythogr. I 204/207).

The Trojan national problem is a flawed judgment in the face of prophecy and fate—in short, of reality. From the beginning Troy suffered from this failure: when the fates prevented Jupiter from marrying Thetis, daughter of the elder Thetis and Oceanus, because the offspring who would be born would drive Jupiter from the kingdom as he himself had driven out Saturn (Mythogr. I 204/207), she then married Peleus (205/208), although this marriage did not prevent the fulfilment of the prophecy. Such flawed judgment is also reflected in Paris's decision, at the wedding of Peleus and Thetis, to choose Venus as the most beautiful of the three goddesses Juno, Venus, and Pallas in the competition designed by Discord. In addition, discord appropriately marks the completion of the story of Troy when the nation falls to the Greeks during the Trojan War, just as the concept of discord has marked Saturn's fall from power at the hands of his own son Jupiter (Laomedon's own great-grandfather). Further, just as Rhea attempted to hide Jupiter from Saturn, who devoured all his sons except Jupiter (Mythogr. I 103/104), so also Hecuba, in response to a prophecy that will doom her son (and her nation), repeats the mistake of her husband's ancestor when she attempts to hide her son Paris from her husband Priam. The fall of Troy includes these sign-posts (Mythogr. I 206/209–210/213)—Achilles kills Hector; Troilus, son of Hecuba and Paris, fights the Greeks; Achilles wishes to marry Troilus's sister Polyxena; Priam kills a son; and the versions of Priam's death are listed.

Only one line is preserved, holy, sanctioned, if we tease out the one hero who escapes his cousins' destiny and whose progeny are believed in the Middle Ages to have founded present-day Italy, France, and England— Aeneas's line. Virgil's hero, as son of Venus and Anchises and nephew of Priam, escapes Troy to marry Lavinia, daughter of the king of Italy. Aeneas's sons and grandsons will thus bear children who will found Rome, Britain, Cornwall, and other countries, as his ancestor Dardanus founded what was to become Florence and as his uncle Antenor (at least according to the first Vatican mythographer, 201/204), traitor though he was, founded

Padua (or Venice, depending upon the version). Although there are other adventures of Aeneas delineated in the mythography after the fall of Troy—Dido flees her brother and appears in Carthage and through her cunning wins a greater than cowhide-sized patch of Carthage (she had cut it into little strips so the cowhide could surround a large area), which explains her rise to power as queen (Mythogr. I 211/214–212/216); Anchises and Venus consort (Mythogr. I 213/217), giving birth to Aeneas; Dionysius is the tyrant of Sicily (Mythogr. I 214/218); Aeneas descends into the underworld and encounters Lethe and the two doors into Elysium (Mythogr. I 223/227, 228)—nevertheless, it is Aeneas's role as founder of Italy that is stressed by the genealogy and by the sequence of fables chronicling his line. The genealogy at the opening of book 3 states that

> Anchises from Venus begot Aeneas, Aeneas from Creusa begot Iulus, also named Ascanius. After the latter's [Creusa's] death, Aeneas, arriving in Italy, from Lavinia, daughter of Latinus and betrothed to Turnus, begot Silvius, Silvius begot Latinus, Latinus begot Epitus, Capis, and Capetus, Capetus begot Romulus and Acrota, Acrota begot Aventinus, Aventinus begot Palatinus, Palatinus begot Amulius and Numitor, Amulius begot the priestess Ilia, with whom Mars lay and begot Romulus and Remus. The wife of Romulus was Ersilia, from whose stock sprang Julius Caesar.

While the mythographer does not detail all of these in separate myths, still, in the myth of Amulius and Numitor, Romulus and Remus are mentioned (in a gloss derived from Servius, *In Aen.* 1.273), to focus attention on the origins of the Roman state and the brothers' wolfish and martial nature:

> Vt autem pro Romo Romu<lu>s diceretur, blandimenti genere factum est, quod gaudet diminutione. Quod a lupa dicunt<ur> al<i>ti, fabulosum figmentum est ad celandam auctorum Romani generis turpitudinem. Nec in<con>grue fictum est, nam et mer-etrices lupas uocamus unde et lupanaria, et constat hoc animal esse in tutela Martis.

> [Moreover, that he was called Romulus instead of Romus came about from a sort of flattery which delights in the diminutive. That they are said to have been nursed by a wolf is a fiction created to conceal the baseness of the founders of the Roman race. And not unfittingly was

this story told, for we call harlots "lupae"{she-wolves}, and from this comes the name for brothels, "lupinaria." It is known that this animal is under the protection of Mars.] (Mythogr. I 30/30)

Regulus as the Consul of the Romans appears, as do other leaders and events: Torquatus, Camillus, the seven civil wars of Rome, Atilius, Fabius Maximus, Marcellus, another Marcellus (Mythogr. I 215/219–222/226).

The Greeks suffer similarly, disastrously, but from the unnatural (miscegenous, incestuous) sexual foibles of Jupiter, who, in the guise of various beasts, sleeps with women and whose wife Juno is his own sister. Jupiter was the great-grandfather of Atreus, father of Agamemnon and Menelaus—

Likewise Jupiter slept with one of the four daughters of Atlas [those whose names are not recorded], and begot out of her Tantalus, Tantalus from Sterope begot Niobe and Pelops. Pelops from Ippodamia, daughter of Oenomaus, who beat him in the chariot-race with the aid of Myrtilus, begot Atreus and Thyestes, Atreus begot Agamemnon and Menelaus, Menelaus from Helena begot Hermione, Agamemnon from Clytemnestra begot Orestes and Iphigenia. (Mythogr. I 201/204)

—he was also the father of Helen and Clytemnestra, sisters born from one of the two eggs produced from the rape of Leda by Jupiter in swan-form ("Item concubuit cum Leda uxore Tindari in specie cigni, inde duo oua nata sunt ex quorum altero Castor et Pollux, ex alio Clitimestra et Helena nate sunt"). The two sisters Helen and Clytemnestra married the two brothers Agamemnon and Menelaus, in a sense in their repetitions of their mother's rape attaining a kind of angry vengeance on the rapist—their own father Jupiter as the principle of seminality. Helen, who cuckolds Menelaus when she is raped (*rapta,* abducted) by Paris, thereby triggers the Trojan War. Clytemnestra (Mythogr. I 144/147), who consorts with Aegisthus in Agamemnon's absence and who murders her husband on his return from the war with Troy, is the mother of doomed and crazy children, including the distraught Orestes, Iphigenia, victim of her father's lust for battle and sacrificed by him to Diana to gain sailing winds, and father-loving Electra. Indeed, the original incest between Jupiter and Juno produces as a consequence unnatural relationships between parent and child. Clytemnestra's own father-in-law, Atreus himself, descended from a grandfather who sacrificed his child out of pride: Tantalus, to test the divinity of the gods, offered up his son Pelops as dinner to the visiting deities. Only Ceres bit into a shoulder, and for this error brought Pelops back to life with an ivory replacement; but Tantalus was sent to hell.

From a different Greek house, Ulysses in Ithaca nevertheless is a hero who also cunningly overcomes a tricky enemy, again revealing the association of subterfuge with Greece. In the genealogy (Mythogr. I 201/204), Laertes begot Ulysses, Ulysses from Penelope begot Telemachus; the mythographer then adds immediately that Nauplius begot Palamedes. In the mythography, the reason for this coupling of two brief genealogies becomes clear. In book 1, Palamedes, who tricked Ulysses into going to war, thereafter was himself tricked by means of a letter written by the vengeful Ulysses; the letter implied that he had betrayed the Greeks for that gold which Ulysses himself had buried in the ground and as a consequence he was killed.[57] The fable here stresses the cleverness of Palamedes, in a conclusion drawn from Servius (*In Aen.* 2.81): "Hunc autem constat fuisse prudentem, nam et tabulam ipse inuenit ad comprimendas ociosi sediciones exercitus" ["It is well-known, moreover, that he was clever, for he himself invented a board-game {draughts} to suppress rebelliousness in the troops when they had time on their hands"] (Mythogr. I 35).

Much later in the history of the Greek kings we find parents sacrificing their children, out of ignorance, out of pride, out of wrath. Therefore, even though Agamemnon, Ulysses, and the other Greeks triumph over the Trojans by means of their cunning ruse of the Trojan horse—cunning also because of the Trojan predilection for and skill with horses—their cunning is worthless, a cold and heartless intellectual ability that, in its most degenerate form, will permit even the sacrifice of progeny to advance an end. Pandion, father of the sisters Philomela and Procne, allows Philomela to leave with Tereus in order to join her married sister, but of course Tereus rapes and mutes her. When Procne discovers this incestuous and awful act, she serves up his son Itys to him at dinner. It is *his* son—the genealogies are traced patrilineally; the punishment fits the crime. So also Erechtheus, king of Athens after Pandion, produces two daughters, Procris and Orithyia, with similar fates. Boreas rapes Orithyia, jealous Theban Cephalus mistakenly kills his wife Procris (Mythogr. I 228/233). The genealogy reads, "Erechtheus, king of Athens, who succeeded Pandion, father of Philomena and Procne, wife of Tereus and mother of Atis, begot Procris and Orithyia; Procris had Cephalus who was from the stock of Aeolus. Boreas raped Orithyia and begot from her Zetus and Calais" (Mythogr. I 201/204).

The Greeks will nevertheless also triumph over the Thebans, a nation more than any other suffering from division and self-destruction and therefore like the Trojans unable to master themselves. Unlike the Trojans, however, the Thebans do not rape women, or deceive and betray their own kind. Their national sin, if one can term it so, is fratricide, self-destruction, disorder itself—the cosmic and familial equivalent of irrationality. The very site of Thebes and its origin signals its nature (Mythogr. I 145/148–148/151). The son of the Greek king Agenor, Cadmus, following his sister Europa when she is abducted by Jove in the form of a bull, founds Boeotia by following a cow (*bos*) until she lies down. After fighting a terrible battle with a serpent he is advised by Minerva to sow the teeth of the serpent; he finds that they leap up as armed soldiers and destroy each other until only a handful survive, who become the kings of Thebes feuding discordantly among themselves. Even after he marries Hermione and has children, his daughters self-destruct or kill their sons: Agave during the Bacchanalia rips apart Pentheus; Semele demands that Jove make love to her in his own shape, after which she is burned to a cinder (Mythogr. I 118/120); Autonoe's son Actaeon, after seeing Diana naked, is transformed into a stag and dismembered by his own dogs; Ino marries Athamas and watches her mad husband kill their children. "Cadmus accepted Hermione daughter of Venus, wife of Vulcan and Mars, from whom he begot Agave, Semele, Autonoe, and Ino. Agave bore Pentheus; Semele bore Bacchus; Autonoe bore Acteon; Ino, wife of Athamas after Nephile—who had borne Frixus and Helles—bore Learcus and Melicerta" (Mythogr. I 201/204). Amphion, a later king, raises the walls of Thebes with his music but then marries Niobe, whose pride turns her to stone and kills her seven sons and seven daughters ("After Cadmus, Licus came to power, whose wife was Antiopa daughter of Nicteus, with whom he slept in prison in the form of a satyr and begot Cetus and Amphion, who succeeded Licus and accepted Niobe, from whom he begot seven sons and the same number of daughters," Mythogr. I 201/204).

Most of the Thebans seem to deny or ignore Pallas, literally as goddess or figuratively as wisdom: Oedipus sleeps with his own mother Jocasta, who produces two sons, Eteocles and Polynices, who kill each other during a civil war, and two daughters, Ismene and Antigone. At this point in the Theban history Theseus of Athens quells the nation; it is important to remember that he is Neptune's grandson (Pittheus "also begot Aethra, Aethra Theseus. Neptune begot Aegeus, Aegeus Theseus, Theseus from Hippolyta queen of the Amazons, whom he overcame, Hippolytus; he also begot Demophon," Mythogr. I 201/204). Even so, later on Meleager, brother to Deianira, kills his own uncles in a boar-hunt; in revenge his own mother ends his life (the genealogy reads, "Adrastus also begot Argia and Deiphyle. Mars also begot Partaon, Partaon begot Oeneus. Cestius begot Althea, Toxius and Phlexyppus. Oeneus from Althea begot Meleager and Tydeus, Gorge and Deianira. Meleager begot Partenopeus, Tydeus, Tytides," Mythogr. I 201/204). This material has appeared earlier (143/ 146), but with Oeneus as father of Tydeus, Meleager, and Partaon. And Meleager's sister Deianira inadvertently kills her husband Hercules by means of a poisoned cloak that she sends him as a gift.

In the area of Thebes the hero Hercules, like the heroes Aeneas and Perseus, from whom he is descended on his mother's side, serves as a type of Prometheus. A demigod, son of Jupiter and Alcmene, wife of Amphitrion, he marries "Deidamia" to beget Hylas (Mythogr. I 201/204). His role as a type of Prometheus is to overcome earth and reach for the stars, as we can see in the adversaries he defeats. In the myth of Hercules and Cerberus (Mythogr. I 57/57), which resembles a variety of Servian passages (*In Georg.* 2.152 and *In Aen.* 6.395), Cerberus is earth "quae omnium corporum consumtrix est" ["because he consumes the bodies of everything,"]. Cerberus's name is taken from the Greek and means "carnem vorans," a gloss also found in a scholium on the *Thebaid.*[58] In the story of Cacus and Hercules (Mythogr. I 66/66, from Servius, *In Aen.* 8.190), the name "Cacus" comes from the Greek for evil, and the giant is said to vomit fire from his mouth because he used to lay waste the fields with fire: "Ignem ore vomere dicitur, quia agros igne vastabat."

The connection between Hercules and Perseus is made when the first Vatican mythographer transits from the story of Bellerophon the son of Perseus to the Chimaera and Hercules, and on to Perseus himself (Mythogr. I 68/69–72/73). In the second book a Perseus series is initiated by a fable on the genealogy of Phorcys, father of the Gorgons taken from Fulgentius (*Mit.* 1.21) on the Gorgons, whose names mean "terror" in Greek (Mythogr. I 126/129–127/130). Perseus, like the other heroes in this mythography, and certainly like his descendant Hercules, demonstrates self-control and wisdom in the face of overwhelming terror—the Gorgons, the three stages of terror, with "Sthenno" signifying *debilitas,* "Euryale," *lata profunditas,* and "Medusa," *amentia* or *obliuio.* It is no accident that Perseus (manliness or strength) defeats Medusa with the aid of Minerva, "quia uirtus auxilio sapientie omnes uincit terrores" ["because strength with the aid of wisdom conquers all terrors"]. From Medusa's blood Pegasus or *fama* was born, "quia uirtus omnia superans bonam sibi adquirit famam" ["because strength overcoming all acquires for itself a good reputation"]. Given the alternate explanation of the Gorgons as cultivators of earth ("unde et Gorgones quasi ge orges, id est terre cultrices, ge enim Grece Latine terra, orgia dicitur cultura"), the heroism of Perseus reminds us of the general Promethean theme once again, sounded against the backdrop of earthly desires, fears, and the general emotional inferno with which life on this earth is associated.

The consistent emphasis throughout the mythography on earth as an underworld, both in cosmic, physical terms and in microcosmic, spiritual terms, and the inhabitants of earth as imprisoned, fallen, fleshly, prey to the appetites and emotions, is clarified by one of the final myths in book 2. Beginning as an Aeneas myth—it concerns his descent into the underworld in book 6 of the *Aeneid,* probably drawn from Servius (*In Aen.* 6.703, 705, 714)—it zeroes in on the river Lethe (*Aeneid* 6.749) as a source of oblivion and forgetfulness for souls before they return to flesh again, an explanation offered to Aeneas in his visit to the underworld by his father Anchises. The passage in the *Aeneid* immediately precedes the famous exposition on the Stoic concept of the World Soul and the fiery seed of Generative Reason which begets all that is created. For the first Vatican mythographer, the juxtaposition of the hero Aeneas, his descent into the underworld, and the general contextual passage in the *Aeneid* on the reproduction of the species is, I believe, intended as a reminder of the "Universal Genealogy," the theme of his entire collection. Indeed, after Anchises tells Aeneas that these souls are owed second bodies by Fate, the mythographer asks why they are "owed" bodies and answers his own question. According to the mythographer, Anchises notes that souls *must* return, because there is no other place for souls to come from; they *can* return, because they are immortal; and they *desire* to return, because of the river Lethe's purgative forgetfulness erasing bad memories of life on earth.

> Cuncta animalia a deo originem ducunt, que quia nasci cernimus, reuertuntur procul dubio; nam unde cuncta procreantur? Deinde posse sic probat: quia inmortales sunt anime, et sunt que possunt reuerti. Tercium est, utrum uelint, quod dicit fieri per Letheum fluuium. Et hoc est quod dicturus est. Sed incidentes questiones faciunt obscuritatem. Sane de hoc fluuio queritur a prudentioribus, utrum de illis viiii sit qui ambiunt infernum, an praeter viiii, et datur intelligi quod ab illis nouem separatus sit.

> [All living things derive their origin from God; and because we perceive that they are born, without doubt they return. For from

where are all things created? Secondly, the ability {to return} is proved thus: since souls are immortal, they are also able to return. And thirdly, whether they desire it, this he says is brought about by the river Lethe. And this is what he intends to say, but questions which present themselves reveal there is a lack of clarity. Indeed, concerning this river wise men ask whether it is one of those nine which encircle the underworld, or is it in addition to the nine; it is given to be understood that it is separate from the nine.] (Mythogr. I 198/201)

Wise men explain that we have a lot of memories by the time of old age; they use Lethe as a symbol of old age, in that, after death, and after Lethe cleanses our memories, we return to flesh. This gloss leads the mythographer to the following philosophical position on the body as a vicious underworld:

Ergo Letheus est obliuio morti semper uicina. Si anima est eterna et summi spiritus pars, qua ratione in corpore non totum uidet? Nec est tantae prudentie tantaeque uiuacitatis ut omnia possit agnoscere? Immo quia cepit in corpus descendere, potat stulticiam et obliuionem, unde non potest implere uim numinis sui post nature sue obliuionem.

[Therefore Lethe is oblivion, which is a near-neighbor to death. If the soul is eternal and a part of the Highest Spirit, why does it not see the whole when it is in the body? And does it not have such great wisdom and such great vitality that it can know everything? On the contrary: when it begins to descend into the body, it imbibes folly and oblivion, and hence cannot attain the power of its divinity after forgetting its own nature.]

Another reason that Aeneas is, like Hercules, Perseus, and Prometheus, a hero for the mythographer is the fact that he, like the soul that descends into the body, returns from the underworld to its source, just as he prudently fled from Troy and all that the Trojans represented to the medieval mind, including poor judgment, excessive cupidity, betrayal.

At the end of the mythography, the author returns to the theme of cupidinous love in conflict with the prudent desire to understand the stars (Mythogr. I 224/229–227/231). Here the heavens mate with the earth—a god is involved with a human, usually in a love relationship which ends disastrously for the human; the problem is that humans do not know how to handle divine power. Such instances occur in the myths of divine Luna and human Endymion, of divine Berecynthia (Cybele, Ceres, Ops, Rhea) and human Attis, of divine Cupid and human Psyche, of Perdix's excessive love for his god-like mother, followed by the concluding fables, from Hyginus's *Astronomica,* on the dog-star of the suspicious Cephalus and Procris (228/233) and the Pleiades (229/234). Look, for example, at Berecynthia and Attis, taken from Fulgentius (*Mit.* 3.5): she wanted to be in a position of power, so she is called Cybele as well, from the Greek for *gloriae firmitas,* firmness of glory. The myth of Attis, whom Berecynthia as an old woman loved passionately and jealously, and because of whose jealousy he castrated himself and died from the hemorrhaging, is explained in a Fulgentian line, "Ergo potentie gloria semper et amore torretur et liuore torquetur, citoque abscidit quod diligit, dum tamen amputet illud quod odit" ["Thus she is always both aflame with love and the glory of power and devoured by envy, and quickly cuts off what she loves, provided only she severs what she hates"] (Mythogr. I 225/230). The first Vatican mythographer's point is that whatever regeneration occurs, occurs as stellification, or apotheosis, that is, occurs physically, not spiritually, in his final repudiation of the earthly and subsequent incarnation into part of the heavens.

To ascend to the heavens by means of the ladder of wisdom will become a popular Carolingian theme in the commentaries on Boethius and Martianus Capella penned by Remigius of Auxerre and others, as we shall see in the next two chapters. Whether the first Vatican mythographer merely anticipates this desire, or whether he, too, belonged to and participated in that rebirth of letters associated with the Carolingian and Alfredian periods will probably remain unknown. This need for monumental heroes, especially given the recapture of the great literary and mythological heroes of Greece and Rome, seems to dominate the late ninth and tenth centuries.

Chapter Six

ORPHEUS, ULYSSES, HERCULES: SCHOLASTIC VIRGILIZING OF THE BOETHIAN HERO BY KING ALFRED, THE ST. GALL COMMENTATORS, AND REMIGIUS OF AUXERRE

The impact of the Boethius commentaries on medieval mythography, like that of the Martianus commentaries, has only begun to be assessed. Sandwiched chronologically in between the early Virgil commentaries and the later Ovid and Fulgentius commentaries and handbooks, the Boethius commentaries assimilate epic mythological materials, particularly the Virgilian and (surprisingly) Homeric, in their attempt to explain Boethius's mythological references. Most of the mythological glosses in the Boethius commentaries, like the other mythological glosses of the early Middle Ages (on the *Aeneid, Thebaid, Pharsalia*), concern stories from classical epics—especially, and in the greatest number, from the *Aeneid,*[1] but also from Homer's *Iliad* and *Odyssey,*[2] Ovid's *Metamorphoses,*[3] and even allegorical epics like Martianus Capella's *De nuptiis Philologiae et Mercurii.* It is no accident that the twelfth-century Erfurt commentator on Boethius regarded the *Consolatio Philosophiae* as an imitation of Martianus's first books, inferior only to Virgil in poetry and Cicero in prose.[4]

Athough there are eleven passages in the *Consolatio* with mythological resonance sufficient for glossing, only three of these receive extended attention (that is, beyond a sentence or two) in the medieval commentaries; each focuses on an epic hero, or a type of an epic hero. These long passages come from core poems in two of the five books—book 3, poem 12, and book 4, poems 3 and 7. In the book 3 poem, Orpheus descends into a Virgilian underworld similar to that of Aeneas—but an underworld of vice, this fallen earth itself. In poem 3 of book 4, Ulysses confronts Circe and his men are transformed into swine. In the last poem of book 4,

Boethius describes three classical heroes—Agamemnon and Ulysses from the *Iliad* and *Odyssey,* and Hercules, as a type of Aeneas.

The mythographic signification of the sixth book of the *Aeneid,* and Aeneas's descent into the underworld, charges Boethius's mythological meters with an infernal moral flavor. Of the three central passages involving mythological figures, each presents an epic hero who descends or has descended into the underworld, although not necessarily engaged in the descent at the moment described in the text. Just as Aeneas encounters his dead father, offering him prophecies concerning his son's future, so also Orpheus wishes to retrieve his wife and restore her to life; Ulysses, before leaving Circe, must seek out Tiresias (and others) in the lower world for information about his future; Hercules descends into the underworld to retrieve Cerberus or to rescue Theseus in his attempted rape of Proserpina.

The mythological glosses on those three poems present a unified whole through the hero, who remains constant in his journeying despite his change of name and identity, from Orpheus to Ulysses to Hercules. At the end of book 4 of the *Consolatio,* the ascent to the stars by Hercules contrasts with the descent of Orpheus into the underworld; as an exemplum of endings and beginnings together, the homecoming odyssey of Ulysses after the Trojan War in the Ulysses poem is consciously coupled with the beginnings of the Trojan War in the Hercules poem, where Ulysses, Agamemnon, and the bow and arrows of Hercules played a role in the gathering of the army. To moralize on all of these journeys, but most appropriately in relation to the Hercules story, to which it is appended, Remigius of Auxerre and several of the other commentators gloss Boethius's "Ite nunc fortes" ["Go then, you brave ones"] (*Consolatio* 4 m7.32) as showing that heroes who perform brave deeds like Hercules may thereafter attain immortality. The last gloss in the Remigius group, this moral is a more fitting end to the heroic mythological glosses in the *Consolatio* than that provided by the later tenth-century K Reviser of Remigius for Boethius's fifth-book recitation of the Ovidian story of Tiresias's blindness as a result of the wrong answer given to Juno about who enjoys lovemaking more, man or woman (*Consolatio* 5 p3).[5]

The power of Aeneas as a model and of the interpretations of his descent into the underworld by Servius, Macrobius, and Fulgentius help to unify the similar moralizations of these Boethian heroes and their descents and also to comment on, gloss, the "descent" of the protagonist Boethius into his own "underworld" of despair. The process of transfer from Virgil to Boethius can be summed up by interpreting the *Consolatio* as the epic quest of a fragmented hero, represented by the narrator Boethius through his irrationally overwhelmed persona and that lapsed and weakened rational faculty which must be instructed by Philosophy. Because he has fallen—that is, descended into an emotional underworld marked by depression and paralysis—the hero, to pick himself up, to return to the upper air, must understand the nature of the hell he inhabits, must explore its parameters, but guided by rationality and intelligence.

Together Boethius and Philosophy, occupying the roles of Aeneas and the Sibyl, must journey into wholeness, a quest whose center is marked by the profound fables of the mythological poems in the third and fourth books. Of course the reference to classical images in Boethius occurs more often in his poems than in the prose passages, perhaps because the *prosa* are more frequently devoted to straightforward philosophical discourses (often by Philosophy), while the *metra* are devoted to fabulous and "poetic" renditions of the same point along the theoretical lines enunciated in Macrobius's commentary on the *Somnium Scipionis* (see fig. 12, Boethius and the Muses, which appears to illustrate the seductions of poetry that Philosophy must battle in the *Consolatio*). The medium of the narrative seems to mirror the dramatic interplay between characters, and of ideas.

The psychological narrative of the exiled and depressed Boethius provides a frame for the major epic heroes mentioned in the prosimetrum. If we recognize these heroes as typical of Everyman in the course of their lives, it may well be that the Donatan interpretation of Virgil's life in three stages, exploited by the Berne scholia, has influenced this particular unifying frame. All three heroes mirror the progress of the narrator from failure and despair (the looking back of Orpheus) to the final achievement of perfection (in *Consolatio* 4 m7, with Hercules). All three of these commentary passages, with their tripartite structure of problem, solution, and moral, also illuminate the thematic conflict between the body and the soul, the irrational and the rational, beginnings and endings, whether of life or of quests.

The focus falls ultimately on the epic figure of Hercules as an exemplar of *sapientia et fortitudo,* in a translation of the early medieval interest in education and wisdom. But this merely shifts interest—even from its earliest use in medieval schools the classical epic and similarly heroic figures were interpreted in terms of the glorification of wisdom. The sources for some of the moralizations of these stories in these glosses on Boethius (as is true also for the Martianus Capella and *Ecloga Theoduli* glosses and commentaries) explicitly laud the allegorical virtues of educa-

12. Boethius and Muses. From
De consolatione Philosophiae. MS.
Auctarium F. 6.5, fol. 1v (12th
c., English). By permission of
the Bodleian Library,
University of Oxford.

tion or wisdom. The weapons of the hero in his epic battle are those of
Philosophia—specifically, her handmaidens, the arts. The glosses on
Boethius's heroes mostly derive from the commentaries on the *Aeneid* by
Servius and Fulgentius and from compilations like Fulgentius's *Mitologiae*
or the first Vatican mythographer.[6] That is, these glossators perceive the
classical hero (specifically, Ulysses, Aeneas, Orpheus, Hercules) as an
Everyman who descends into the underworld (this life) to battle the vices,
as in Prudentius's psychomachia—but here exemplified by various classical monsters or adversaries (Sirens, Circe, Polyphemus, Busiris, Hydra).

The early glosses on Boethius glorified wisdom as represented by the
means of obtaining it, an education in the seven liberal arts. The earliest
mention of a commentary occurs in Gottschalk's reference to "exponentes"

on the *Consolatio;*[7] Servatus Lupus of Ferrières (d. 862) wrote the first extant commentary on the meters;[8] and the earliest commentary extant on the whole of the *Consolatio* is that of the Welsh Asser.[9] Early English commentators, that is, Asser, King Alfred, and even John Scot Eriugena (who taught on the continent but who was probably Irish), in glossing the *Consolatio* all stress the importance of education. Asser and King Alfred, of course, were instrumental in propagating the educational reforms of the ninth century in England, as attested by Alfred's various Old English prefaces to the *Cura pastoralis,* Orosius's *History,* and Augustine's *Soliloquies.* John Scot may have been familiar with teaching methods in England that promoted the vernacular. Additional support for the link between Alfredian reforms and the growth of interest in the *Consolatio* can be found in the use of the vernacular in many of the glosses not only in Old English but in Old High German (particularly in the Anonymous of St. Gall and Notker Labeo's later translations).

Reflective of the early desire to educate by translating from Latin to the vernacular, the glosses of King Alfred, Asser, and the Anonymous of St. Gall Minor and Major contain vernacular glosses—in Old English and Old High German—as well as Latin glosses, although these vernacular glosses are often very slight. The most significant of these is King Alfred's translation of Boethius into Old English, which amplifies the narrative without adding extensive moralization, although the changes he makes in translating Boethius often suggest interpretations of the myths involved. In comparison with the much more fanciful and moralized glosses of Remigius of Auxerre, these interpretations may seem insignificant, but the fact of their existence argues for the importance of the commentaries in which they appear in relation to the emphasis on education in England and on the continent and for the growth of the vernacular in these early periods. Both trends contributed to the desire to interpret Boethius as allegory of a Christian education—a paean to the seven liberal arts and the schools.

The development of a commentary tradition on Boethius thus begins in England, propelled by the educational reforms of King Alfred and his scholars in the ninth and tenth centuries. Interested in the idea of wisdom for pedagogical reasons, these powerful figures—chiefly Alfred as translator, his own scholar and biographer Asser, and the Anonymous of St. Gall (perhaps an Irish scholar summoned from the St. Gall monastery)—influence a similar Carolingian development on the continent, especially in the moralized Boethius of Remigius of Auxerre (either Irish or Frankish/

Burgundian) and his most important reviser, the K Reviser (probably a tenth-century Englishman).[10] (John Scot's ninth-century commentary on Boethius remains lost, despite recent attempts at identification.)[11] Remigius's interpretation of Boethius predominates until the twelfth century and the advent of Chartrian Neoplatonism, in particular the important Boethius glosses of William of Conches. But even after the twelfth century the Remigius Boethius continues through Remigian copiers like the Erfurt Commentator (pseudo-John Scot) and the Vatican Commentators.

By examining the development of Alfredian and Carolingian glossation on the Boethian hero we can trace the process by which Orpheus, Ulysses, and Hercules came to be explicitly linked with Aeneas (or Virgil) and the descent into the underworld. Although they are not so identified in King Alfred's translation, by the time of Remigius's very full commentary, they are. Each of these commentators contributed to the Virgilizing of Boethius, which is to say, the moralizing of Boethius in the manner of Fulgentius on the sixth book of the *Aeneid*. King Alfred, bent on educational reform, slightly endears Orpheus to us, making him familiar and somewhat heroic; he portrays the other mythological moral heroes educationally. Writing probably after Alfred and Asser, the Anonymous of St. Gall Major, who explicitly Virgilizes this mythological material, will thus remind Remigius, who also wrote a brief commentary on book 6 of the *Aeneid*, of the Aeneas-like nature of Orpheus, Ulysses, and Hercules, their common experience of descent, and the quality of the underworld as a moral fleshpot. Perceiving the analogy between the descent of the hero Aeneas in the sixth book of the *Aeneid* as an education in the branches of knowledge associated with the earthly underworld, Remigius, who wrote a brief commentary on the *Aeneid*, uses him as a model for the heroes Orpheus, Ulysses, and Hercules. Remigius may have been influenced in his interpretation of the *Aeneid* by Servius and Fulgentius, but was no doubt directed to the Virgilizing of Boethius in particular by means of the Anonymous of St. Gall Major. In the latter's *Consolatio* commentary is found a moralization of Orpheus's search for Eurydice that will inspire Remigius and his revisers to apply the same method to the other two significant mythological meters in the commentary, both of which involve an epic hero who descends into the underworld, like Orpheus. Finally, Remigius's revisers, especially the one known as K, will even add Fulgentian moralizations to the Remigian glosses. Let us look more carefully at the links in this Virgilizing chain.

I. THE TRANSLATION AND CONVERSION OF ORPHEUS IN THE WEST SAXON KING ALFRED'S BOETHIUS

With a single exception, the changes made by King Alfred in Boethius's mythological passages (*Consolatio* 2 p6, 3 m12, 4 m3, 4 m7) embellish the narrative without moralization; the most important, because the most moralized and the most changed, is the Orpheus poem. The first reference is insignificant, and concerns Busiris;[12] the second concerns Orpheus, whom Alfred rationalizes into a more positive figure by domesticating the terrors of hell and by transforming his mistake of "looking back" into Christian conversion and education.

Instead of condemning Orpheus for his failure, as Boethius has implied in his moral to the poem, "Quidquid praecipuum trahit / Perdit, dum videt inferos" ["Whatever excellence he takes with him / He loses when he looks on those below"], Alfred explicitly acknowledges Orpheus's skill as a musician by explaining that "se hearpere wæs swiðe ungefræglice good" ("that harper was extraordinarily good") with a "swiðe ænlic wif" ("exceedingly beautiful wife").[13] By making Orpheus a hero, Alfred reduces the possibility of the condemnation of Orpheus for allegorical reasons— that is, for looking back at Eurydice and thereby losing her forever— especially damning if Eurydice represents concupiscence and the underworld represents terrestrial pleasures, as in later commentaries. And Alfred enhances the possibility of equating Orpheus with wisdom—which later commentators will indeed take up.

Consistent with this glorification of Orpheus's harping—and a whitewashing of the hero—is Alfred's concomitant lessening, by domestication, of the terrors of hell, in contrast to the treatments by Asser and the continental glossators. The "beasts" of hell are calmed by Orpheus in the same way the beasts of earth have been calmed by his superior music, according to the Ovidian description in the *Metamorphoses*: Cerberus the three-headed dog welcomes him by wagging his tail and playing with him as would any dog welcoming his master: "þa he ða ðider com, ða sceolde cuman ðaere helle hund ongean hine, æs nama wæs Ceruerus, se sceolde habban þrio heafdu; 7 [ongan] onfægnian mid his steorte, 7 plegian wið hine for his hearpunga" ["When he then thither had come, then the dog of hell, whose name was Cerberus {and} who had three heads, came to meet him, and showed his gladness by wagging his tail, and played with him during his harping"]. The horror of other infernal monsters is similarly diminished by means of familiarization, especially after Orpheus begins playing his music. Charon (clearly confused with Cerberus) like the hell-hound also has three heads and is depicted as aged. Ixion's wheel stops moving; Tantalus, who later in the Middle Ages represents the sin of greed, is here only "ungemetlice gifre," "immoderately greedy," and when the music begins he becomes silent, "he gestilde." In contrast to this dramatic and narrative depiction, Asser, like the continental commentators, stresses the vices of the three: Ixion tried to sleep with Juno but instead slept with her substitute, a cloud, for which he was condemned to be bound by serpents to an eternally turning wheel. Tityus is glossed as "son of the earth" who made love to the mother of Apollo (Latona) and was punished by a vulture who eternally eats his liver; Tantalus is described briefly.[14]

Of all the Boethius commentaries, the West Saxon King Alfred's translation (written sometime between 887 and 899) is the most original;[15] that is, the least indebted to previous commentary, with one exception—the source of Alfred's information on mythology added to the translation. For this reason, perhaps, as Sedgefield says, "Alfred's version was probably too individual to have much influence."[16] Earlier scholars believed, because of similarities in their glosses,[17] that Alfred was indebted to Remigius or his revisers. Later scholars discarded this view as anachronistic—Remigius wrote his commentary in 901–2, whereas Alfred translated the *Consolatio* earlier, in 887–99. Scholars then explored the relationship between Alfred, Asser, and the Anonymous of St. Gall Minor and Major.[18] Of these three, the relationship between West Saxon Alfred and the Welsh Asser has not been carefully studied, primarily because only recently has a single manuscript been identified as the work of Asser or someone of his school.[19] But Alfred does not seem familiar with many of Asser's identifications, additional evidence that his translation preceded Asser's commentary, or perhaps he chooses not to use them.[20] And Alfred's mythological treatment of his heroes differs from that of Asser, whose brief scholia would not have helped Remigius much.

Because of recent evidence offered by Professor Wittig that the extant Boethius commentaries available to Alfred do not explain the changes in Boethius made by the West Saxon king,[21] I believe that Alfred's translation probably preceded the Asser commentary and that the St. Gall Minor and Major followed both. Given the insularity of the translation and the Asser commentary, we might also assume that the British versions preceded the continental ones, particularly as there were insular scholars sent to the St. Gall monastery primarily for the purposes of education[22] precisely along the lines suggested by Alfred in his reforms. (Of course, it is entirely possible that a monk returning from St. Gall brought back with him to England a copy of the St. Gall commentary, which Asser then used in composing his commentary.) Even though there seems very little correspondence between Alfred and the so-called Asser, there exist glosses in Alfred and Asser similar to St. Gall Minor.

Given the originality of Alfred's translation and lacking any commentary on Boethius that might have contributed to Alfred's understanding in a provable way, it seems clear that Alfred's educational moralizations reflect the kind of reforms expressed in his preface to the *Cura pastoralis* rather than a scholar's readings of florilegia and mythographic handbooks. In contrast, the commentary we call Asser's (Vat. lat. 3363) must have served as a kind of school epitome of Boethius.[23] Alfred's interests in general reflect the scriptural, patristic approach of the Anglo-Saxons— Alfred especially likes Augustine and Gregory—and accordingly the translator has been generally regarded as more severe with the pagan tales, many of which Alfred views as false and wishes to exchange for biblical stories.[24]

Yet Alfred vindicates the use of pagan myth as illustration—and therefore also vindicates the errant hero—by explaining Orpheus's looking back at the underworld as a positive step in the process of spiritual education, the examination of conscience. Each man who looks back on what he has lost looks back on the hell of his former sins—but he looks back *in this life,* at sins for which he will be later punished. Alfred counsels his reader that these "spells," *Ꝺas leasan,* teach (*lærað*) man (and we know Alfred was interested in education) to flee the darkness of hell and come to the light of true goodness, *godes liohte.*[25] The Christian image of God's light to which man should turn underscores the idea of religious conversion with which Alfred himself was concerned; the pagan hero Orpheus becomes a type of the potential convert to Christianity.

This highly original interpretation of Boethius was itself based on Alfred's confusion of the Furies or Eumenides—those avengers—with the Parcae or Fates—those who determine the length of human life. This confusion may have guided Alfred's interpretation of the moral and therefore the subsequent glossators' analogous interpretation of all three epic heroes. If the Furies punish man by pursuing him only when he is guilty of a misdeed, but are equated with the Fates who govern the beginning, span, and end of each man's life, then the whole of man's life is gloomy and punishing, a view characteristic of the Anglo-Saxon homilist. From this dark life the Christian convert would gladly escape into the paradisal light of the afterlife. Alfred defines "ultrices deae," the vengeful goddesses, as the Parcae who know no respect for any man, punish him for his deeds, and rule man's fate: "Parcas, ða hi secgað ðæt on namum men nyt[on na]ne are, ac ælcu men wrecen [be his] gewyrhtu; þa hi secgað ðæt walden ælces mannes wyrde."[26] He may have made this mistake through a hasty reading of the first Vatican mythographer who juxtaposes the Furies (Mythogr. I 108/109) with the Parcae (109/110). Only Alfred and the Anonymous of St. Gall Minor make this mistake; Asser correctly identifies the goddesses as the Furies Alecto, Tisiphone, and Megaera, always full of wrath and furor, who punish guilty souls.[27]

The other two mythological exempla in Alfred are also less moralized, although both are at least tenuously linked with education or the Church. In *Consolatio* 4 m3, to Circe's transformation of Ulysses's men into beasts, Alfred adds a genealogy for Circe (or Kirke) as the daughter of Apollo, the latter the son of Job or Jove, himself son of Saturnus; here Alfred emphasizes her skill in witchcraft. Asser's treatment differs: in his most interesting gloss, Boethius's "daughter of the sun" is known by the Marsi as Angitia, called so from snakes (perhaps an indirect reference to her witchcraft).[28] Alfred's moral emphasizes Boethius's point that she transforms bodies but not minds, for "The sins of the mind draw unto themselves the whole body, but the infirmity of the body cannot altogether draw in the mind."[29] It is interesting to note that "Kirke" in Old English also means "Church," Ecclesia, which Alfred may have intended as an implicit contrast with the witch Circe in the same way he identifies Jove with Job, Old Testament and ecclesiastical parallels analogous to the typological methods of the ninth-century "Theodulus."

The son of Job or Jove, Hercules, according to Alfred's Philosophy defeats the nine-headed serpent Hydra (in *Consolatio* 4 p6) as one who arrives at a conclusion, or understanding, by means of the pedagogical tool of dialogue, which is heroic. The narrator who wants to know about Providence and Fate is like Hercules grappling with the Hydra: "Swa is ðisse spræce þe þu me æft acsast; uneaðe hire cymð ænig mon of, gif he ærest on cemð; he cymð he næfre to openum ende, buton he hæbbe swa scearp andgit swaaðær fyr" ("So it is with this subject thou art asking me about; a man can hardly get quit of it once he enters upon it; and he never reaches a clear conclusion, save he have an understanding keen as fire").[30] The monster—a water-serpent in Asser,[31] "un nædre" in Alfred—is only defeated by the hero when, "mid aenige craefte," "with some skill," he piles up firewood around it and burns it, another homely image similar to the domestication of the infernal "beasts." The translation of Orpheus and Hercules into wise, Christian schoolmasters anticipates other transformations, specifically the more philosophical, Virgilian, interpretation of the Boethian heroes as types of Aeneas.

II. ORPHEUS, ULYSSES, AND HERCULES AS TYPES OF AENEAS IN THE ANONYMOUS OF ST. GALL

The Anonymous of St. Gall Major explicitly Virgilizes the Boethian mythological meters by linking them with the sixth book of the *Aeneid*, dealing with the underworld. The best example is the Orpheus poem's description of the inhabitants of the underworld as a psychological allegory of the effects of sin and evil (*Consolatio* 3 m12). This religious elaboration binds the meter with book 6 of the *Aeneid* more carefully and shows how the pagan gods came to be associated with hell at the beginning of the vernacular tradition. Thus St. Gall sums up these "tres fabulas.i.ixionis. tantali. tityi" as coming from the fifth book (in reality the sixth book) of the *Aeneid*. They are, however, presented here in philosophical and Christian terms.

The Anonymous of St. Gall contributes chiefly to the mythographic tradition as a Neoplatonic and Christian repository for mythological materials. The second earliest commentary on the whole *Consolatio* (only Asser would be earlier), St. Gall was probably written by a monk at St. Gall, perhaps Iso (d. 871),[32] or one of the Irish or Scots monks frequenting St. Gall in the ninth and tenth centuries.[33] St. Gall apparently was a grand center of the study of Boethius; at present we know of three Boethius manuscripts from St. Gall and four from the nearby Abbey of Einsiedeln, and in the year 872 the library contained two exemplary copies of the *Consolatio*.[34] It is thus possible that the Anonymous of St. Gall was composed there and that Notker (also a monk of St. Gall) in his glosses and translation used a compilation of St. Gall and Remigius's glosses on Prudentius, in that both have been found in a manuscript of St. Gall attributed to Iso.[35]

The Anonymous of St. Gall exists in two versions, a shorter (Minor) and a longer (Major).[36] In addition to a manuscript from St. Gall, 845, the longer is in part contained in a manuscript from Einsiedeln, 179, originally from St. Gall; in addition to a manuscript from St. Gall, 844, the shorter is contained in part in a Naples manuscript associated initially with St. Gall.

But it is unclear whether the longer version is an extension of the shorter, or the shorter an abbreviation of the longer.[37] Without attempting to decide the vexed question of which version preceded the other, in our discussion we shall assume that two versions exist of the Anonymous of St. Gall, one shorter, which we will call Minor (derived from Tax's collation of St. Gall MS. 844 and Naples MS. IV.G.68),[38] and one longer, which we will call Major (derived from Tax's collation of Einsiedeln 179 in particular with St. Gall MS. 845).

The differences between St. Gall Minor and Major are really ones of degree. St. Gall Minor stresses, in its brief and relatively few mythological glosses,[39] grammatical and rhetorical items and brings to its work a much stronger moralizing tendency than either Alfred or Asser. St. Gall Major expands some of these glosses, includes some Old High German glosses (according to Petrus Tax), and strengthens what might be termed a Christianizing, more sophisticated tendency overall. That is, St. Gall Minor's Oedipal reading of Orpheus interprets the hero's weakness in part as uxoriousness (linked to Ixion's desire for Juno) and his strength—his songs—as originating in the fountains (or doctrines) of his mother Calliope.[40] In this reading, then, the underworld into which Orpheus descends in Boethius's poem is identified with *carnalia,* for the inhabitants described represent primarily the vice of concupiscence.

In the more Christian interpretation of St. Gall Major (as found in St. Gall MS. 845), Philosophy is both the wisdom of God and also Christ himself;[41] the World Soul (*Consolatio* 3 m9) is the sun, analogous to the soul in man in that it is located in the middle of the world, as the soul is located in man's heart in mid-body, and in that it too has three faculties like those of man (also like an egg, with three parts, of sky, earth, and sea).[42] And the Titans are interpreted in the light of the tower of Babel and the confusion of tongues,[43] as they are in the *Ecloga Theoduli.* In explanation Pierre Courcelle declares that the glossator seems embarrassed by Boethius and wishes to assure us that his author is Christian—"catholicum Boetium."[44] The specific glosses in St. Gall Major all relate the fables to the *Aeneid* and reflect the Christian rationalizations of these poems.

The underworld, then, is earthly, and the infernal is perceived as the chains of earth, in contrast to true happiness, identified as wisdom and goodness; therefore the man is happy who looks into the fountain of shining good and "qui potuit boni," who can do good, with the fountain—"doctrines" in Asser—here wisdom, and the highest good, or God, "fontem.i.sapientiam. summum verumque bonum.i.deum." He also is happy who breaks the chains of earth, or who is not entangled in earthly things, with the "vincla" or heavy chain of earth becoming thoughts of the body, "carnis cogitationem.sarcinam carnis," and who prefers the celestial to the earthly, "qui potuit praefente [or: *praeferre*] terrenis celestis. uel qui terrenis rebus non est implicitus." Initially, the poet Orpheus is "fatidicus," prophetic, and he thinks "profound thoughts."[45]

St. Gall Major's underworld is both external, that is, the earth understood morally, and also internal, a place of vice and despair: "Qui tartarem in specus: in uoraginem uiciorum. uel ignorantie uel ad terrena quae deducunt in tartarum." With the loss of Eurydice the mind is alarmed when it is thrust into the underworld (and the inferior realm—"mente consternatus est. qui alterum in infernum detrudet"). In contrast to this darkness, like St. Gall Minor, St. Gall Major finds upper day to be God. Further, one loses his excellence when he turns to vice, ignorance, or the earthly. He is overcome (*victus*) by earthly cupidity ("Victus s. terrena cupiditate") and thus he looks back into the underworld, the inferior ("Dum uidet inferos.i.dum sequitur carnalia").

The underworld inhabitants differ from those glossed by St. Gall Minor: here they are interpreted with explicitly philosophical and Christian moralizations. And St. Gall Major also corrects the shorter version's mistakes: instead of the Parcae the "Ultrices" are the three Furies; instead of merely desiring ("cupiens") Juno (as in Asser), Ixion wants to rape her, "uoluit violare." Ixion's wheel, which functions to torment him, is Fortune's wheel whose caprices educate: "Uelox praecipitat rota: significat illos radiis rotarum pendere districtos. qui nihil consilio prouidentes. nihil ratione moderantes. nihil uirtutibus explicantes. seque et omnes actus suos fortune permittentes, casibus et fortuitis eventibus semper rotantur" ["The swift Wheel turns them headlong: the meaning is that those {men} hang bound to the spokes of the wheels who, taking planned forethought for nothing, directing nothing by reason, solving nothing by virtues, and entrusting themselves and all their deeds to fortune, are always spun around by chance and casual events"]. Orpheus's woe (or else his singing) so touches the punished in hell that they are not bothered any longer by their punishments, that is, Tantalus, though thirsty, "ignores the waters he now might drink." Tantalus in an extraordinary *Ecloga Theoduli*-like comparison with biblical figures is then compared with the rich man whose crumbs fed Lazarus, but who went to hell when the beggar Lazarus went to heaven. The rich man of course wanted his thirst to be cooled but it was impossible.[46] Tantalus ignores the waters he now might drink because of an error of the soul, "error animae," obliterating the majesty of his prior life. The vulture, representing the torments of conscience by evil-doing, "tormenta male conscientiae obnoxia," stops eating the liver of Tityus, who rebelled against Jove, because of the songs—and because such interior considerations flagellate the feelings.

St. Gall Major also relates the fable of Ulysses and Circe (*Consolatio* 4 m3) to Virgil (*Aeneid* 3.386)—"unde uirgilius"—in glossing "Vela neritii ducis," "The ship of Ulysses," although the comment is mostly a paraphrase. Like St. Gall Minor he declares Circe is daughter of the sun because of her beauty. In addition he says that the island is called Circe from her name and that Ulysses grew a horn in his right part, a novel gloss on the Boethian fable. The glossator expands St. Gall Minor's identification of the "poisons" that make man forget that he is human, poisons more powerful than those of Circe which affect only the body, as the *vicia* of *ira, avaricia, rapacitas,* and *fraus.* They horribly wound the mind "per odium. per auariciam," and according to the glossator transform it; "haec comparatio fit a contrario quam tamen ideo infert. ut ostendat maius esse mentem mutari in beluas quam corpora" ["this comparison is made from the contrary which nevertheless concludes for the reason that it reveals it is better to be changed into monsters in mind than in body"].

The glosses on the poem about the three great heroes who have "overcome the earth" (according to its moral, *Consolatio* 4 m7) all spring from the *Aeneid,* or perhaps the commentaries on Virgil (Agamemnon who sacrifices his daughter does so as a priest, a "sacerdos" like Calcas). "Unde virgilius": this phrase for St. Gall Major almost comes to express in moralized shorthand a tropological and even etymological (Stoic-like) interpretation. "Itachus" is identified with Ulysses, the one from Ithaca who mourned his lost companions, as coming from "Odysseus" or "omnium peregrinus," the eternal wanderer, that is, he who has wandered far from the island of Ithaca. His adversary Polyphemus is a Cyclops and a giant, but also "nouus iuuenis," a modern (or inexperienced) young man. Hercules, the third hero, in his Labors receives the greatest attention, with the monsters or adversaries he confronts moralized either naturally (physically) or morally (theologically).

The monsters generally represent earthly attachments or inducements, as St. Gall Major's gloss on the Boethian moral makes plain: "When you overcome the earth," *superata tellus,* or as he says *terrena,* the earthly, the stars will be yours, "sidera donat," just as Hercules became a star, "vt hercules per uim celum penetrauit. sic et vos. Regnum enim celorum vim patitur" ["when Hercules penetrates the heavens through strength. So also you {will do}. Truly the kingdom of the heavens submits to strength"], presumably because we all want to reign in heaven. Hercules first encountered the Centaurs, a monstrous race from Africa, born from the union of Ixion and the cloud (referring back to *Consolatio* 3 m12), mixed with horse because of their agility, as if they were one with their horses, the result of which is that they fight well (St. Gall Major seems to take pains to demythologize—euhemerize—the Centaurs). The golden apples of the Hesperides consecrated to Minerva in the region of Thessalica are guarded in the garden of Venus against the daughters of Atlas by a watchful dragon, whom Hercules kills; thereafter he takes away the golden apples. Cerberus, the "infernal dog" caught by Hercules, in a moralization extremely important in later glosses is explained as three-headed because he represents cupidity, the earthly, or vice. Hercules in contrast represents reason, hence Cerberus is the earth which consumes all bodies (as in death), as the etymology makes clear, from *creoborus* as if to say, "carnem uorans," "devouring flesh." The Hydra is a serpent with heads, "serpens cum capitibus," similar to St. Gall Minor's water serpent, from the Greek called "excedra," that which exceeds or surpasses (perhaps because of its everincreasing heads). Achelous is confused with Acheron, the infernal river, so that when Hercules breaks his horns and makes him bury his face in his banks the St. Gall Major glossator explains this as dividing the river into rivulets. Antaeus is "filium terre," who becomes stronger when in contact with the earth; Cacus is merely "monster."

The Christian allegorization and moralization of the St. Gall Major will prove as important to Remigius of Auxerre as his rather consistent Virgilization of Boethius's mythological meters. Indeed, the major influence on Remigius would have been the Anonymous of St. Gall rather than Alfred: according to Kurt Otten, because Alfred's translation lacks true commentary, Remigius may have used the Anonymous of St. Gall for rhetoric and metrics and for scholia on Neoplatonism and the Bible and Church Fathers (especially Augustine).[47] Otten does add that there are glosses in Alfred not from the Anonymous of St. Gall but like those in Remigius. Granted the apparently frequent contacts between England and France, it is possible that a copy of Alfred or Asser may have been given to Remigius[48] by Grimbald, a colleague of Asser, a French monk, and, like Remigius, a protegé of Archbishop Fulco of Rheims.

III. THE BOETHIAN HERO'S DESCENT INTO THE
NEOPLATONIC VIRGILIAN WORLD IN REMIGIUS OF AUXERRE

Remigius extends the moralistic glosses we have seen in insular and early continental commentaries to combine a Christianizing influence with a Neoplatonic bias. In the Virgil commentary attributed to him, Remigius was the first mythographer to link the Neoplatonic allegorizations of the sixth book of the *Aeneid* with the similarly Neoplatonic Christian view of this world as the underworld. His commentary on the sixth book of the *Aeneid* expresses his interest in the descent into the underworld and in earthly life as a moral hell, no doubt influenced by the Servian gloss on the golden bough (*Aeneid* 6.136) and the Anonymous of St. Gall's Christianized moral glosses. This work must have led to his own Virgilized moralization of Boethius. In applying the fruits of his *Aeneid* commentary to his mythological glosses in the Boethius commentary, Remigius connects pagan and mythological figures with the epic hero's descent into a moralized underworld that plays a prominent role in Neoplatonic philosophy.

For the first time all the mythological references are unified by what seems to be the theme of epic psychomachia.[49] The epic hero as an Everyman engages in a philosophically epic conflict between his wisdom or virtue and the temptations of the flesh exemplified by classical figures and monsters. The hero's tropological battle pits concupiscence and reason against the will, or concupiscent desire, in terms of the microcosm; in terms of the macrocosm, the allegorical battle is between the material or "inferior" (under-) world and a higher spiritual reality.

The importance of these innovations for the history of mythography needs to be emphasized. Remigius's linkings would lead to William of Conches's Neoplatonic glosses on the myth of Orpheus's descent into the underworld in his Boethius commentary defining the four types of descent open to man (natural, vicious, virtuous, and artificial), and also to Bernard Silvestris's system of the four descents applied in particular to the sixth book of the *Aeneid*. But Remigius was doubly important for the history of mythography: in addition to his influential commentary on Boethius, Remigius also wrote one of the most important commentaries on Martianus Capella and has been identified as the second Vatican mythographer.[50] Finally, he had a very strong influence on Bernard's commentary on the *Aeneid*, particularly in Bernard's glosses on the underworld and the heroes Orpheus, Hercules, Theseus, and Ulysses.

This Burgundian (possibly Frankish or Irish) teacher and scholar was especially important to medieval Boethius studies: his commentary provoked philosophical disputes on the continent in the tenth and eleventh centuries to such an extent that commentaries like that of Bovo II of Corvey or the Anonymous of Einsiedeln were thereafter written to attack him. Among the later English revisers of his Boethius commentary, known as T, B.N., and K, the K Reviser of Remigius defended Remigius against such attacks.)[51] Remigius's interest in Boethius and the moralizing of the *Consolatio* reflected his larger interest in education and in philosophy—or we might turn this around, noting Remigius's interest in education as a reflection of Boethius's influence. Better still, one might say that Remigius both reflected the views of contemporary education and was himself responsible for advancing them.

Throughout his life his approach in teaching and in his scholarship broadcast a humanistic bias. Born about 841, he succeeded his master Heiric as head of the school in the Benedictine house of St. Germain at Auxerre,[52] then went to Rheims at the behest of Archbishop Fulco, after the Norman "devastation." When Fulco was assassinated by Baldwin, the Count of Flanders, in 900, Remigius went to Paris where he opened a school connected with the Monastery of St. Germain des Prés (the first Public School of Paris and the germ of the University). As the "first master of note in the city which came to be known as the nurse of letters,"[53] he expressed his interest in the schools and education by means of the style and format of his commentary on Boethius, which resembles an annotated edition for use in classes whose purpose is to instruct and moralize. (The K Reviser of Remigius may very well have been one of Remigius's students.)[54] He was the first teacher of dialectic at Paris, a Realist (like John Scot) rather than a Nominalist (like Heiric of Auxerre). At this school he became especially interested in theology and secular authors like Boethius. The works he expounded included Genesis, Psalms, and the Song of Songs, and, from secular authors, Boethius, Martianus Capella, possibly Virgil in the *Aeneid,* Donatus, Priscian, Phocas, Eutyches, Cato Minor, Juvenal, Persius, Terence, and Bede's *Ars metrica* (most of these commentaries have been attributed to Remigius but not all have been printed in full).[55]

At the school in Paris Boethius was apparently regarded as a Christian and a martyr; for this reason Remigius may have been predisposed toward Boethius. But in addition Remigius may have regarded Boethius highly because Remigius was a relative of Lupus of Ferrières, who also wrote a comment on Boethius's meters, and also a pupil of Heiric, who had similarly expounded on Boethius. (Remigius apparently used the notes of Heiric as Heiric had used those of John Scot; it has even been suggested that the annotated copies of Boethius may be based on Heiric—a common link between Asser and Remigius.)[56] Possibly he wrote his commentary on the *Consolatio* toward the end of his life, in Paris, after John Scot's philosophy had become a main interest, likely finishing it after 900, perhaps 902–8.[57] (he died in the first decade of the tenth century in Lorraine). And he may even have written the commentary on Boethius's *Consolatio,* the *Opuscules,* and the handbook of mythology identified as the second Vatican mythography—if Remigius's, then written *after* the commentaries on dialectic and on Martianus Capella.[58] Evidence exists, however, that he held these same humanist and philological interests in earlier days under Heiric,[59] for the broad subjects Remigius chose to cover in his Boethius commentary[60] and the sources he actually used, especially in the mythological glosses, however different from the names cited in the text,[61] reveal a wide range of authors.[62]

In the *Aeneid* commentary Remigius uncovers a unifying link between the underworlds of Boethius and Virgil, in the Servian notes on the golden bough (*In Aen.* 6.136), which in Servius reflected moral choices at adolescence leading to two different paths or journeys in human life, those of virtue and vice (as we have seen in chapter 2, in a Macrobian/Neoplatonic context). For Servius, in another *Aeneid* passage, the letter Y mixes virtues and vices, or that which leads to merits and penalties: for the inferior things restrain or imprison human life, defined as the soul while it exists in the body (*In Aen.* 6.477). This image, ultimately deriving from Plato's "Vision of Er," eventually detaches itself from Virgil's commentaries, as we will see in Remigius's own Martianus glosses discussed in chapter 7. But in Remigius's *Aeneid* commentary, the image links the nine "islands" of the underworld.

That is, the Y with its two allegorical paths houses the nine circles of the underworld here in Remigius. Remigius glosses the sixth book of the *Aeneid* in a manuscript (B.N. MS. Parisinus 7930) that may be tenth-century and that includes the *Eclogues, Georgics,* and *Aeneid,* with annotations both marginal and interlinear.[63] Many of the notes concerning lines in the sixth book (specifically *Aeneid* 6.264, 6.282, 6.298–99, 6.638–724, and 6.743) derive from Servius and are not original, although comments regarding the nine circles of hell (6.426, 6.430, 6.434, 6.440, 6.477, 6.548, 6.638, 6.656, and 6.679) are apparently by Remigius. Servius's gloss on the Y was also cited by Remigius in his commentary on Martianus

Capella (Remi., *In Mart.* 43.18), which supports the attribution of the Virgil commentary to this important scholar. It is more likely that Bernard Silvestris, in multiplying Aeneas's descents into the underworld into fourfold allegorical significance in his own commentary, was familiar with one or the other of the two Remigian commentaries, though he could have known the Servian passage directly.

Remigius focuses on Virgil's line "Hic locus est partes ubi se via findit in ambas" ["Here is the place where the road divides in two directions"] (*Aeneid* 6.540), as if to dramatize the Pythagorean concept of the split ways, the Y as symbol of human life, and then he actually acknowledges Pythagoras and the Servian passage: "Iam ventum est ad bivium. loquitur secundum phitagoram propter supra dictam rationem" ["Now one comes to the fork. It is said according to Pythagoras on account of the reason said above"]. Then, after some comments on the significance of the nine Muses' names, appears this graphic note explaining that "Novem insule inferorum dicuntur esse ad modum Y littere facte in pedibus V in brachiis IIIIor" ["Nine islands of the underworld are said to have been made like the letter Y, five in the feet, four in the arms"]. To understand the arithmetic of the drawing (fig. 13), the editor, Savage, notes:

> A large drawing of the letter Y then follows with one circle attached to the lowest part. There are two circles drawn on each side of the lower limb; these circles are joined together in groups of two by a cross bar which intersects horizontally this lower part. Similarly in the upper part there are two circles on the right and left respectively of the two upper limbs. It will be observed that there are nine circles in all.[64]

Remigius also provides annotations on the significance of the four upper circles (that is, two for each arm of the Y) which illustrate the moral difference of the two paths. In the top circle on the left exist those to be incarnated but not saved, "In hac que debent corporari nec salvari," and in the bottom circle on the left those not to be incarnated but destined for damnation, "In hac que debent non corporari et penitus sunt dampnandi." For the two circles on the right, in the top circle are placed those both to be incarnated and saved, "In hac que debent corporari et salvari," and in the bottom, those not to be incarnated but saved, "In hac que debent non corporari et salvari." These circles of the underworld in conjunction with the two paths represented by the Y very likely influenced the moral cosmology not only of Dante in the *Commedia* but also of Bernard Silvestris in his commentary on the *Aeneid.*

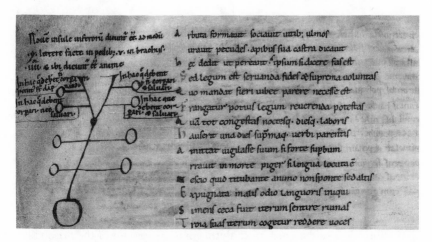

13. Drawing of Pythagorean Y of human life with nine circles of hell. Glosses on *Aeneid* 6. MS. Parisinus 7930, fol. 204v (possibly by Remigius of Auxerre; before the end of the 10th c.). Courtesy of Bibliothèque Nationale, Paris.

This Virgilian schema of the underworld provides a Remigian touchstone for use in examining the forays of the Boethian heroes into the cupidinous underworlds they should reject in favor of education, wisdom, virtue. Because of the fullness of elaboration of these heroes their mythological resemblance to each other is heightened; their scholastic rejection of all that is philosophically female (that is, the world, the flesh, the devil) becomes heroic when set against the threat of damnation in the Other World. Remigius neither condemns these figures as pagan and immoral deities (like the early Boethius commentators and early Christians) nor does he provide long, allegorical elaborations (like the later Boethius commentators). Further, most of the sources for these mythological references are the standard commentators: Fulgentius in the *Mitologiae* and the *Continentia,* the first Vatican mythographer, Servius's commentary on the *Aeneid* and *Georgics,* and Remigius's own commentary on Martianus Capella, at least for the moralizations. Conventional even in his more straightforward descriptions, as editor Bolton indicates, Remigius used Hyginus, Orosius, Ovid, and Isidore for these.[65] As in the earlier glossators, most of the glosses in Remigius and his revisers are concentrated in the three main story cycles of Orpheus and the underworld (*Consolatio* 3 m12), Ulysses and Circe (4 m3), and Agamemnon and the Trojan War, Ulysses, and Hercules (4 m7). But in addition there are sketchy passages elsewhere, represented by the Muses as Sirens (1 p1); Lethe (1 p2); Busiris (2 p6); Alcibiades (3 p8); Otus and Ephialtes (3 p12); the Labyrinth of Daedalus (3 p12); Phaethon (4 m7; only in K); and Tiresias (5 p3). Of all of these, in relation to the full cycle of mythological glosses, the shortest of the three major glosses is the passage on Ulysses and Circe, the longest (by far) is the last (on 4 m7). Remigius's most extensive change occurs in lengthening the glosses on the Labors of Hercules, which are now discussed in great detail (4 m7, 4 p6, 2 m2, 2 p6). And in Remigius it is once again Orpheus who, identified with Aeneas in his descent in the sixth book, portrays choices the other heroes will explore in their own journeys.

The long poem on Orpheus's descent in book 3 is the point toward which the introductory mythological poems move as they gloss the dramatic narrative interplay between Boethius and Philosophy. Remigius generally interprets the whole Orpheus myth as a moral comment on the afterlife of the damned soul, a kind of Carolingian *Inferno,* here made representative of the wrong earthly choice of the hero Orpheus. The myth is divided into two major parts, the first part of the myth concerning the mourning of Orpheus after Eurydice's death and the second, his descent into hell to retrieve her where he encounters various pagan monsters. Remigius's opening gloss, on Boethius's moral "Felix qui potuit," identifies Orpheus's journey as a learning process: "Hoc carmen fabulosum est illos respicit qui postquam viam veritatis agnoscunt et in ea proficiunt, rursus ad seculi desideria revertuntur sicque opus inceptum miserabiliter perdunt" ["This is a mythological poem referring to those who, after they learn the way of truth and progress in it, return again to worldly desires and so lose miserably the work begun"].[66]

The descent, so clearly intended to echo Aeneas's descent in the sixth book of the epic, becomes a paradigm for all moral choice and the "fall" experienced by Orpheus when he looks back. The infernal is associated with the inferior *in this life,* and the superior, with the supernal: the revising glossator continues, on the same three words, "Felix qui potuit," with "Figmento poetico ortatur nequaquam mentes hominum ad inferiora detrudere sed semper superiora, hoc est vera requirere. *Qui potuit* respicere mentis intuitu ad bonum verum debet erigere" ["In this poetic fiction he urges the minds of men not to turn to lower things but always to higher things, that is, to seek out the truth. *He who has been able* to look back by his mind's contemplation ought to raise it to the true good"] (in B.N., K, and T). The gloss proper begins with line 3 of Boethius's poem: "terrenas cupiditates" are interpreted by the revisers as earthly desires ["the bonds of heavy earth"] (B.N., T), or by Remigius as "divitias" (earthly riches, an idea in line with Remigius's interpretation of Pluto in his commentary on Martianus Capella), as in the early insular commentaries and the St. Gall commentary.

Remigius also glosses the hell to which Orpheus looks back in the concluding Boethian moralization of the fable, as earthly vice: the lemma "Tartareum" (*Consolatio* 3 m12, line 55) signifies the whirlpool of earthly vice "in lacunam vitiorum" (B.N. and K), or "In voraginem et profunditatem vitiorum, res terrenas quas debet calcare animus et subicere sibi" ["in a deep abyss of vices, earthly things which the mind ought to spurn and keep under subjection to itself"] (B.N., K, T). This hell is opposed to the "upper day" toward which Orpheus should turn, glossed as truth or God: the lemma "superum diem" means "in Deum" (Remigius) or "in verum vel in celestem lucem" (B.N., K, and T). On "upper day," the revisers (B.N., K, and T) continue the gloss by quoting Luke 9:62 about the man who looks back after putting his hand on the plow, for which he loses the kingdom of God as, anagogically speaking, does Orpheus: "Ut non respiciatis ea quae sprevistis, videlicet ne aliquis ad lucem perennem tendens respiciat retro. Unde legitur: nemo mittens manum suam super aratrum respiciens retro aptus esse potest regno Dei" ["That you may not look again on the things which you have spurned, that is, that no one who is heading for eternal light may look back. Hence it is written: no one putting his hand to the plow and looking back is fit for the kingdom of God"]. That is, whoever lusts after the things of this world after looking for the highest good loses all. Thus in Boethius's phrase, "he loses when he looks on those below," and for Remigius what he "loses" ("perdit") is the things of this world, *temporalia.*[67]

Remigius keys his interpretation—one similar to many of his later moralizations in the commentary—to the theme of lamentation in a tripartite gloss on "Trenara," Taenara (*Consolatio* 3 m12). The interpretation anticipates his later moralizations in that, throughout, to be vicious is to be unhappy. The hero inhabits a psychological hell of his own making when he descends into vice. That the inferno itself is identified with life on earth can be seen from Remigius's Servian and Neoplatonic division of the world into three parts, heaven, sea, and underworld, governed by the three brothers, Jupiter, Neptune, and Pluto; the last in effect governs earth as an underworld. Literally "the gates of hell, a promontory in Laconia, and songs of lamentation" (according to the K Reviser), in clever Remigius "Taenara" signifies lamentation in all three denotations through the "Tre,"

for "three," substituted as a prefix common to all three terms: "TRENARA
dicuntur LAMENTABILIA carmina. Trene dicuntur *lamentationes,* hinc et
Trene Hieremie. Quidam TRENARA dicunt quod est promuntorium Laco-
nie ubi dicitur descensus esse ad inferos. Unde Virgilius: Tenareas etiam
fauces alta hostia Ditis" [" 'Trenara' means mourning songs. 'Trene' means
lamentations, hence also the lamentations of Jeremiah. Whence some say
'Trenara' refers to a promontory of Laconia where is said to be the descent to
the underworld. Hence Virgil: 'Even the jaws of Taenarus, the lofty portals
of Dis' "].[68] Piling Pelion on Ossa, Remigius adds that Trenara is a place
where lamenting souls descend into hell. He may have derived the linking
idea of lamentation from the Anonymous of St. Gall Major, who defines
"Trenara" as "infernalia.i.lamentabilia," but who stresses only the promontory rather than the sad songs.

Remigius has earlier taken care to establish a lack of internal self-
examination and consciousness as infernal, morally reprehensible, non-
rational. His gloss on Lethe as an infernal river whose powers bring
oblivion to the soul: "Lethus fluvius inferni, ex quo potantes anime
obliviscuntur preteritorum laborum" ["Lethe is a river of the underworld;
drinking from it, souls forget their past labors"] derives from a passage in
the *Consolatio* in which Philosophy offers to bring Boethius to his senses
from a lethargic swoon by wiping from his eyes the "dark cloud of mortal
things" (1 p2). The gesture of Philosophy is reminiscent of the powers of
Lethe in the underworld. It is interesting to note the correspondence with
Remigius's gloss on Martianus Capella (*In Mart.* 49.5), "Loethos Grece
sopor vel oblivio, hinc Loetheus fluvius de quo feruntur animae potare
oblivionem transeuntes in corpora," in which "Loethos" is Greek for
"stupor" or oblivion; hence, the river Lethe from which souls are said to
drink oblivion as they pass into bodies. But in the other reviser versions
lethargy involves pain in the head, called so from Lethe, the infernal river:
"Loethargus . . . dolor quoque capitis dictus est a Loetheo infernali
fluvio."[69] In short, the "lethargy" felt by the narrator Boethius represents a
pain or condition of forgetfulness of self which is reminiscent symbolically
of Lethe, in the reviser versions, or, in Remigius, needs to be erased by the
understanding of Philosophy. The danger creates a model against which all
of the other mythological heroes in Boethius must be tested.

Further, Remigius innovatively infuses his Eurydice-figure, understood
in malo, with the associated significations of the Cupid-figure in the glosses
of Servius, Isidore, and Theodulf. Cupid, cupidity, was tied to Dido's mad
love for Aeneas in *Aeneid* book 4, at least in Servius (as discussed in chapter

4). Similarly, Eurydice, or rather, Orpheus's longing for her, leads Orpheus to descend, Aeneas-like, into the underworld of *temporalia*. As I have noted, "the bonds of heavy earth" (*Consolatio* 3 m12, line 3) which will bind Orpheus are interpreted as earthly cupidity, or as earthly riches, in a sense equivalent to the personification of *cupiditas,* both desire, concupiscence, in the general sense, and avarice specifically. A projection of Orpheus's desire, Eurydice in the final, summarizing, portion (belonging only to the English reviser K), is identified *in malo* as *carnalis concupiscentia,* carnal concupiscence. This theme recurs in Boethius's concluding moralization of the fable to explain the hell to which Orpheus looks back—away from the "upper day" glossed as truth or God—as earthly vice. Orpheus loses Eurydice as the man who cares about them loses the things of this world, "temporalia."

In the first part of the myth, involving Orpheus's mourning, the point of the mythological gloss is to define the relationship between Orpheus and his wife as representative of soul and body, on the tropological level, or of skill and understanding, on the allegorical level of the *artes.* In Boethius, Orpheus retreats to the wilderness where his song of mourning makes the woodlands dance, the rivers stand still, and all the animals make peace with one another. In Remigius, Orpheus's action is likened to that of the *theologus,* or the "one who discourses about the gods" who leads man from wild ways to a civilized life ["quoniam homines ab agresti conversatione ad civilem perduxit vitam"] (in Remigius, B.N. and K). Because this wilderness mourning does not calm Orpheus, even though it calms nature, of which he is *dominus,* he descends into hell to retrieve Eurydice. The K Reviser's very long gloss on Boethius's word *dominum* recites the story of Orpheus and Eurydice as found in the first Vatican mythographer (Mythogr. I 75/76),[70] followed by an allegorization of the *artes* from Fulgentius (*Mit.* 3.10), and ending with a short comment by K himself. In the Fulgentian passage, Orpheus means "best voice," "matchless sound," from "optima vox," and Eurydice is "profound" or "deep judgment," "profunda deiudicatio." Aristaeus, the shepherd who desired and pursued her, is "best," "optimum," and the serpent who kills her is "cleverness," "astutia." Remigius's use of Fulgentius in presenting his allegory of the relationship between Orpheus and Eurydice varies the old freshman argument against studying literature, specifically that art must not be openly analyzed, for when art is studied, that is, "raised up," toward the light (as if from an underworld), then the melody's voice sinks down (as if in an underworld), dies, because art contributes to the appealing sound only through secret (and not public) powers.[71]

In the K Reviser's summarizing portion of the first part of the Orpheus poem, Orpheus, instead of fixing his mind on God, looks back at Eurydice, who represents "terrenam dignitatem," earthly importance (esteem), and "carnales concupiscentias," carnal concupiscence. The K Reviser's one original contribution is to attribute this Neoplatonic analysis to Boethius.[72] Hence Orpheus descends to hell, where in Boethius he sings songs drawn "from the foremost springs / of his goddess mother," this last identified by the commentators as Berecynthia or as the Muse Calliope.[73] The "springs" or "fountains" are explained literalistically as the domicile of Muses and Nymphs, consecrated to the mother of the gods, Berecynthia, and mentioned here because they are nurses to poems, especially those of Orpheus to his sweet wife.[74]

In the second part of the Orpheus story, Remigius describes various inhabitants (both persecutors and victims) of hell, moralizing the monsters from sources beyond the insular and continental Boethius commentaries that he does not always fully understand. For Remigius, Hades ("inferus") represents the world's cupidity and its inhabitants—Cerberus, the Furies, Ixion, Tantalus, Tityus, Pluto, Tartarus—as they listen to the sad songs of Orpheus record specific vices—the whirlpool of Tartarus as "earthly vice in the soul," Tantalus as greed, Ixion as the avaricious businessman, and Tityus as the lecherous (because his liver—the seat of lust—is gnawed by vultures).

The hellish persecutors of man who represent spiritual or psychological adversaries begin with the doorkeeper: "Stupet tergeminus novo / Captus carmine" ["Taken by his strange song . . . / Three-headed Cerberus stands benumbed"]. Human mortality or Cerberus is *tergeminus* in that his name comes from *creosboros,* flesh-eater or "carnem vorans," because there are three ages, infancy, youth, and old age through which death enters on earth.[75] Other hellish persecutors are introduced—the Furies, or the "ULTRICES SCELERUM DEAE" in line 32, explained either as "daughters of the night" or as the three parts of discord.[76]

Remigius then turns to the punished inhabitants of hell to reveal the cupidity of man. Again Remigius (R and T) derives his gloss from the first Vatican mythographer (Mythogr. I 14/14) in explaining Ixion, whose "attempted violence" on Juno resulted in his being bound to a whirling wheel and who represents the cupidinous and greedy businessman whirled about by worldly cares ("Per Ixionem autem cupidi figurantur et avari quia labentis mundi desideria sectantes semper repulsa patiuntur"). Tantalus, who in Boethius now might drink that water of which he has been deprived but who instead pauses to listen to Orpheus's new song, is glossed as "avaritia" in a straightforward passage (by K and T) because he served his dismembered son Pelops to the gods to test their divinity, with Ceres (the only god who failed to discern the hoax and ate Pelops's shoulder) signifying the earth that attempts to eat up the body ("terra quae corpus resolvint").[77] Tityus (lust) is explained by the two revisers (B.N., T) as a giant whose liver feeds a vulture eternally because he attempted to rape Latona, the mother of Apollo and Diana whose arrows downed him initially.[78] A Servian gloss (*In Aen.* 6.596) adds to Remigius's moralization that the liver is the seat of lechery ("luxuriosi") as the spleen is the seat of laughter ("risus") and the gall is the seat of anger ("ira").

The tension between the denizens of the earth, or the underworld, who feel imprisoned by its limitations, and Olympus is heightened by a very literal mythological reference, just before this gloss to the Giants Otus and Ephialtes (*Consolatio* 3 p12) who made war on the heavens, and after this gloss, to the labyrinth of Philosophy's arguments likened to Daedalus's underworld labyrinth. Philosophy refers to the fable of the Giants who were subsequently and deservedly overthrown in trying to prove there is a supreme good that rules wisely. All four of the Remigian revisers describe the Giants: Otus and Ephialtes grew nine inches in a month ("crescebant singulis mensibus novem digitus") and tried to overcome Jove by piling one mountain atop another.[79] This gloss is followed in the commentary by a gloss on "labyrinthum," which Boethius accuses Philosophy of constructing in her arguments. " 'Ludisne,' inquam, 'me inextricabilem labyrinthum rationibus texens, quae nunc quidem qua egrediaris introeas, nunc vero quo introieris egrediare, an mirabilem quendam divinae simplicitatis orbem complicas?' " [" 'Are you playing a game with me,' I said, 'weaving an inextricable labyrinth with your arguments, since at one time you go in where you are going to come out again, and at another come out where you went in?' "] (*Consolatio* 3 p12). Hinting at the underworld nature of the labyrinth, Remigius's gloss on the labyrinth defines it as an "inexplicabilis domus" built by Daedalus.[80]

The commentary's narrative sequence of stages in epic moralization of the hero's descent into the underworld should continue with the short medial gloss on Ulysses and Circe in book 4 of the *Consolatio.* In fact, however, in commenting on the first prose of book 1, Remigius has begun his glosses with a heroic and Homeric metaphor involving Ulysses as a type of the philosopher (Boethius) and lover (Orpheus). The book 4 gloss depends implicitly upon the lover as a Ulysses who must guard against the

14. Sirens, ibis, coot. Bestiary. MS. 22, fol. 167v (ca. 1175). Courtesy of the Masters and Fellows of Corpus Christi College, Cambridge.

Sirens—inducements to a lower and more carnal kind of love. Philosophy has described the Muses of Poetry as "whores from the theatre" (presumably a kind of obscene theatrical poetry)[81] whose sweetness leads to death; in this gloss, Remigius tries to explain their deceptions as those similar to perfumes which stir the passions of lovers. The actual word used by Philosophy of the Muses of poetry is "Camenas," which is glossed as the "Sirens." Remigius sees them (very literalistically)[82] as maritime monsters—three beautiful sisters—whose songs deceive many (see fig. 14). They have wings and claws because love passes on and wounds, "quia amor transit et uulnerat."[83]

The gloss on the Ulysses poem in book 4, although very short in comparison with the Orpheus and Ulysses-Hercules glosses, presents Ulysses as a scholastic epic hero signifying a wisdom that resists love and aided by the god Mercury who signifies eloquence. One can see in this gloss an epitome of *De nuptiis,* in that Ulysses's prudence seems to complement Mercury's eloquence, together the two qualities exemplifying the best of man. Remigius's characteristic interests—not only in Martianus Capella and mythology but also in education, in the two branches of the trivium and quadrivium—shine through. Ulysses, or Narcicius,[84] after the Trojan War "sicut et reges Romanorum"—"just like also the kings of the Romans," wishes to return to the fatherland—perhaps like Aeneas traveling to Italy and Rome, the "true home," after the Trojan War. He resists Circe, "solis filiae," because of his prudence, but his "imprudent" men succumb to her songs. That is, poison is more effective when mixed with songs "of various types," "in varias formas seu species"—the songs linking her with the Siren-like Muses of poetry seducing the philosopher Boethius. As daughter of the sun, Circe turns the men into beasts through love of her because there is nothing more beautiful and sweet in this world than the sun and thus she is a noble and sweet poison.[85] Ulysses's men are saved by Mercury, glossed as "deus eloquentie" as he is in the Martianus commentaries: because of his speed (from the wings with which he is always depicted), or because he is a messenger for the gods ("cursor deum"); appropriately, he bears a caduceus (a rod entwined with serpents) for breaking up quarrels ("ad lites dirimendas").[86]

The longest gloss, on Agamemnon, Ulysses, and most especially, the involved Labors of Hercules, as in the other two major glosses is concerned with defining spiritual heroism within a scholastic context, but here more explicitly. Its length can be explained primarily as the allegorical excesses of the K Reviser, who is responsible for most of it (Bolton is careful to indicate the extant Remigian alternate glosses).[87] Boethius's moral rouses his heroes to right action instead of sloth or cowardice, "Ite nunc fortes ubi celsa magni / Ducit exempli via! Cur inertes / Terga nudatis?" ["Go then, you brave, where leads the lofty path / Of this great example. Why in indolence / Do you turn your backs in flight?"] (*Consolatio* 4 m7, lines 32–34). One of the first of the Remigian glosses (on line 1, "Bella bis quinis operatus annis" ["Having worried a decade"]) defines for students of the poem the "heroism" of these epic figures: this song is addressed "ad eos qui per virtutem aeternum nomen volunt sibi adquirere" ["to those who wish to acquire a virtuous name forever"], a gloss that borrows from Boethius, "Superata tellus / Sidera donat" ["Earth overcome / Grants you the stars"] (line 35). Agamemnon and Ulysses, the first two of the three heroes studied in this long gloss, receive little attention in comparison to the hero Hercules, although Ulysses especially is regarded in the usual

Remigian fashion as an exemplar of wisdom and cunning. Agamemnon's reasons for avenging his brother's dishonor by waging war on the Trojans and sacrificing his daughter Iphigenia (to appease Diana, who had stilled the winds needed by the ships at Aulis for sailing to war) are listed briefly by Remigius, drawing mostly on the first Vatican mythographer (Mythogr. I 20/20).[88]

In contrast, Ulysses's enemy Polyphemus the Cyclops is moralized in two opposing ways, *in bono* by Remigius and some revisers (K and T) and *in malo* by the K Reviser alone. *In bono,* Polyphemus signifies the "most prudent" because he has in his head only one eye and the philosophers say that the head is the seat of wisdom; he is defeated by Ulysses, who signifies "astutia."[89] The less attractive and more common interpretation of Polyphemus[90] is Fulgentian, a kind of "wild child," or "wild childhood." Basically, the word *Cyclops* can be explained by three Greek components: "achus," "tristitia" (sadness) in Latin, "ciclops," "circulus" (circle) in Latin, and "pes," "puer" (boy, boyhood) in Latin. In K's words, which are Fulgentius's, "Iam pueritia nutritorum timore minus feriata tristitiam cogitandi nescit et puerilem etatem exercet" ["childhood, enjoying idleness without fear of those who nurture it, does not know the grief of reflection and indulges its youthfulness"] (*Cont. Virg.* 15). Thus the Cyclops represents boyhood because his chief motivation, like that of a boy, is pride; he is one-eyed because understanding is neither complete nor rational in boyhood; his pride is quelled by the "ignis ingenii," the fire of intellect, of the "most wise" Ulysses; his name is Polyphemus, which means "loss of fame," because the "blindness of adolescence follows youth's pride and indifference to reputation."[91]

In the long gloss on Hercules and his many adversaries, we see again the Remigian conflict of the wise hero, which we saw in Orpheus and again in Ulysses, with the monster or adversary he battles, an exemplar of vice or ignorance, which we saw in the many underworld monsters and inhabitants of the underworld and again in the Cyclops Polyphemus. The identity of Hercules as a wise hero able to resist worldly or carnal inducements or stresses has been foreshadowed by a gloss from book 3 on Alcibiades. An important gloss for the commentary because it unifies the Hercules references (in *Consolatio* 2 p6 and 4 m7) and extends the importance of this hero for the Middle Ages in general, it refers to a passage in which Philosophy has reminded Boethius to fix his gaze on the stability of the heavens and stop admiring base things, because the beauty of a person passes away. "Quod si, ut Aristoteles ait, Lynceis oculis homines uterentur, ut eorum visus obstantia penetraret, nonne introspectis visceribus illud Alcibiadis superficie pulcherrimum corpus turpissimum videretur?" [" 'And if,' she asks him, 'as Aristotle says, men enjoyed the use of Lynceus's eyes so that their sight penetrated obstacles, would not the superficially very beautiful body of Alcibiades seem most vile when his inwards could be seen?' "] (*Consolatio* 3 p8). This leads to the comment by Remigius in B.N. and also in the K Reviser that Alcibiades may be explained in five ways—first, as a leader of the Greeks with a beautiful body; second, as a beautiful woman; third, as a poet; fourth, as Hercules, who in his youth was sparkling ("vel Herculis qui in iuventute glaucitatem adeptus est"); or fifth, also as Hercules, called by that patronymic because of his father or his mother.[92] The confusion here between Alcibiades and Hercules fills in the blanks in the book 4 glosses; the hints about Hercules's youth and beauty as clearly insufficient to guarantee heroism or wisdom, and unreliable as a means of resisting the forces of mutability and concupiscence, anticipate his later growth as a strong and wise hero. Hercules as Alcibiades also types Boethius in his initial despair as erroneous and provides hope for change in the future with an alteration of choices.

The gloss on Alcibiades also sets up the genealogy of Hercules as a predisposition toward self-actualization—as son of Jupiter and Alcmene, he is a demigod, or hero, whose very existence as the product of adultery would invite Juno's jealous wrath and subsequent testing but simultaneously guarantee his success during that testing and during his Labors. In this long passage the English K Reviser once again embellishes upon the already extravagant allegorizations provided by Fulgentius in the *Continentia Virgiliana* and also the *Mitologiae* (probably known to K through the second Vatican mythographer, who may have been Remigius himself; thus K would be collating two of his master's works here). The many adventures of Hercules glossed by Remigius and the revisers include the Labors plus incidental adventures. The Labors (those commanded by King Eurystheus of Mycenae, for which Hercules was granted divinity) are glossed primarily in the Remigian commentaries on the book 4 poem (but also mentioned in *Consolatio* 4 p6, 2 m2, and 2 p6).[93] Other adventures found in the glosses which do not concern the Labors of Hercules include the rescue of Hesione and anger at Laomedan's treachery, the death of Busiris (in *Consolatio* 2 p6), and, in one gloss, his marriage with Deianira, the shooting of Nessus, and his own death (in K, the story of Philoctetes is a postscript to the Hercules story).[94]

All of the commentators comment on line thirteen, "Herculem duri celebrant labores" ["Harsh labors make the fame of Hercules"], but they say there are ten[95] instead of the usual twelve. Only the K Reviser devotes a whole page of gloss on line thirteen and Hercules's Labors (mostly from Fulgentius's *Mit.* 2.2, on Hercules) to define by means of etymology and moralize the heroism of Hercules in particular (the passages taken directly from Fulgentius have been italicized to show K's indebtedness to the mythographer) as the powers of the mind.

Hercules quasi Heracles id est heroncleos dicitur, hoc est virorum fortium fama. Arx mentis esse intelligitur que omnes equanimiter adversitates sustinet et temporalium erumnarum molestia sunt victrici curam. Depugnat ut invisibili creatoris contemplatione quoniam creature possibile est in celestibus delectetur. *Hercoles qui et Alchei nepos dicitur, alce enim presumptio interpretatur. Nam et Almenam matrem habet, hoc est quasi almeram quod Latine salsum dicitur. Nam ex igne ingenii ut ex Iove et ex presumptione ut ex Alce et ex salsedine sapientie ut ex Almena quid nascitur nisi fortitudinis gloria.*

[*Hercules is called Heracles, that is,* heroncleos, *the fame of strong men.* He is understood to be the citadel of the mind which endures with equanimity all adversities and the troubles of temporal afflictions are a concern to it as it overcomes {them}. He fights so that, by invisible contemplation of the Creator—since it is possible to the created—he may delight in celestial things. *And Hercules is said to be the grandson of Alcaeus, for* alce *in Greek is translated as the assumption of power; and he has as mother Alcmene, for* almera, *which in Greek means salty. So from the fire of the mind, from Jove, the assumption of power, from his grandfather Alcaeus, and the saltiness of wisdom, from Alcmene, what else but the renown of valor is produced?*][96]

In the same gloss on this line, the K Reviser delineates the epic heroism of the wise Hercules in his conflict with Juno, who represents "carnalis concupiscentia et inanis gloriae cupiditas" ["carnal concupiscence and the desire for empty glory"], and who sends to the baby Hercules two serpents, which he kills. The serpents signify mortal anxieties, "mortales curas," quelled by the strength of Hercules's mind, "adversitatis mentis virtute." For the K Reviser, Hercules in killing the snakes emblemizes the soul in exile, condemned to wander in this unstable world with a mind fortified with right—presumably belief in God as epitome of wisdom—to withstand adversity.[97]

The K Reviser's misogynistic "explanation" of the reason for the
Labors—Juno's jealousy of Alcmene, Hercules's mother, and the human
woman's relationship with Jove—is followed by a description of the Labors
in the manner of the first Vatican mythographer (or his sources, Hyginus
and Servius); they help define the attributes of the masculine heroism of
mind incarnated in Hercules and part of the (generally equally misogynistic) educational process which the Labors represent. Of the Labors, the one
to which the K Reviser gives the longest gloss concerns Cerberus, Phaethon
(an interpolated myth not found in Boethius), and Cacus and Antaeus (all
taken from Fulgentius). Most of the descriptions are as cursory as that of
the first Labor, wherein the Centaurs, half horse and half man, are overcome
by arrows while playing in water. The gloss on the second Labor, the
Nemean lion, indicates that Hercules was sent by King "Aristeus" (Eurystheus) to overcome the lion; the skin was later worn by the hero as a sign
of strength (the last point only in K). The third gloss identifies the
Stymphalian birds which troubled Alcinous, King of Pheacus, as "Arpies,"
etymologically the dogs of Jove, called "arpies" from "rapiendo," because
arpo is Greek for *rapio*.[98] The fourth Labor, the golden apples stolen from
the dragon, is mentioned in the reference to the garden of the Hesperides
where the dragon watched over the apples. The K Reviser here supplies a
moralized, explicitly Fulgentian gloss on the three daughters of "Athlan-
tis," probably taken from the first Vatican mythographer (Mythogr. I 38):

> Tres Hesperides dictę sunt id est Eglespeer, Medusa et Erethusa quas
> nos studium, intellectum, memoriam et facundiam dicimus id est
> quod primum sit studere, secundum intellegere, tertium memorare
> quod intelligis. inde ornare dicendo quod terminas. Huic ornato *aureo*
> studii virtus rapitur per mentis excellentiam.[99]

A translation of Fulgentius's version is nearly identical:

> [There are said to be three Hesperides, namely, Eglespeer, Medusa,
> and Erethusa, who we say are study, comprehension, memory and
> eloquence; that is, the first thing is to study, the second to compre-
> hend, the third to utter what you comprehend, and then to adorn with
> eloquence what you determine. From this golden eloquence the virtue
> of learning is stolen through excellence of mind.] (*Cont. Virg.* 20,
> trans., p. 129)

Note that the K Reviser runs together the names of two of the Hesperides,
Egle and Esper, into one, "Egleesper." The result is to minimize the role

played by eloquence (probably viewed as rhetoric here); strength or manliness ("virtus," Hercules) merely steals "ornato *aureo,*" "golden eloquence" (the golden apples), which ensues from study, understanding, and memory, with ornamentation ("facundia") finishing one's work.

The fifth Labor, Cerberus, is followed, after a brief description of what should have been the sixth (on Glaucus and the flesh-eating mares), by the interpolation on Phaethon by the K Reviser; the Cerberus and Phaethon glosses include the most heavily moralized passages among those on the Labors, perhaps because both of them detail "descents" into the underworld. In Boethius's poem Hercules shackles the monster Cerberus with a triple chain, which leads the glossators (Remigius and B.N.) to comment on the etymology of the name, from *creos boros* or *carnem vorans,* "devouring flesh." Then Remigius and his revisers explain literally the myth of Hercules's descent into the underworld to rescue Theseus and apprehend Cerberus, by drawing upon the first Vatican mythographer (Mythogr. I 57). Hercules's success in bringing the monster into the "superior light" stems from his absorption, from the moment of his birth, of the poisonous herb aconita. Only the K Reviser adds a long, allegorical passage from Fulgentius (*Mit.* 1.5–6) in which Pluto, the master of the dog Cerberus, is described as "wealth," *divitiae,* from the Greek, because riches are associated with the earth and because Pluto was banished to the underworld where "sola terra e materia sit cunctis obscurior elementis" ["this sole product of the earth is more hidden than the other elements"]. Cerberus the three-headed dog is placed at Pluto's feet because he represents the three kinds of human envy, natural, fortuitous, and accidental; he is in fact named from *creoboros,* flesh-eater, because human envy or hate is always insatiable.[100] The K Reviser (and Fulgentius) differentiate among the three types by declaring that hate is "natural" in that it is found in opposing (bestial) pairs, dogs and rabbits, wolves and sheep, snakes and men; it is "fortuitous," or by cause, as in the passions and envies of love; it is "accidental," that is, what is reinforced casually in words between men.

After a brief recital of Labor six, the K Reviser interpolates the myth of Phaethon and the four horses of the sun into his discussion, perhaps stirred by the mention of the flesh-eating mares against whom Hercules was victorious in his encounter with "Glaucus" (a mistake; the adversary should be Diomedes, in this gloss derived from the first Vatican mythographer, Mythogr. I 61). Here Phaethon as man can choose to act wisely or let the four horses pull him toward death. What is most interesting about the gloss is that the commentator once again interprets mythological gods (here Apollo) pejoratively, as representing loss contrasted with supernal gain, and the only defense against loss and death in human life as wisdom itself. This exegetical concept is consonant with interpretations of other mythological heroes like Aeneas, Orpheus, Ulysses, and Hercules, who similarly represent wise action, or strength that comes from wisdom. By stressing the value of wisdom, the K Reviser has dovetailed his original interpolation with the other mythological and mythographic glosses. Specifically, the four horses of the sun, or the four ages of man, Eritheus [Erythaeus], "red," for birth and infancy; Acteus [Actaeon], "beautiful," the beauty of boyhood; Lampus, "shining," man in his prime; Filogeus [Philogeus], "loving earth," old age, hence bent toward the earth), representing ignorance, belong to Apollo, "perditio," in contrast to the true sun, Christ, whose light signifies truth. The true sun Christ gave his son, the human race (Phaethon), the four virtues of temperance, prudence, fortitude, and justice plus four ages to rule earthly life, but Phaethon, "quasi fanon dicitur, id est apparens" ("as if to say *fanon,* that is, appearing") every day moves toward death. The gloss ends with a Boethian moral stressing the value, once again, of wisdom.[101]

Despite the mostly literal recitation of the remaining Labors,[102] those treating of the Hydra, Antaeus, and Cacus receive allegorical (and Fulgentian) treatment in the hands of the K Reviser to reveal Hercules's allegorical nature as an exemplar of virtue as well as wisdom in a psychomachia with the vices. Labor seven, the quelling of the many-headed Hydra, reflects the characteristic Remigian theme of wisdom conquering concupiscence, primarily because of the aid granted to Hercules by Minerva. The gloss on Labor nine, Antaeus or Antheus, begins literalistically but ends, in the K Reviser at least, allegorically. The literal portion stems from Lucan,[103] who explains that because the giant Antaeus was the son of earth he could only be overcome by being elevated above the earth, which renewed his power (although an alternate gloss, in Remigius and T, explains he was king of Libya). The allegorical conclusion in the K Reviser has been taken, once again, from Fulgentius (*Mit.* 2.4): Antaeus represents a form of lust, "in modum libidinis ponitur," hence called in Greek *antion,* or in Latin "contrarium," "contrary"; he was born from earth because libido alone is born from the flesh ("ideo et de terra natus, quia sola libido de carne nascitur"). Touching the earth made Antaeus stronger because when lust comes into contact with flesh it becomes more wicked ("Libido enim quanto carni consenserit, tunc iniquior surgit"). It is accordingly overcome by the glory of virtue ("Denique a virtutis gloria superatur"). The K

Reviser (actually Fulgentius, cited word for word) explains that "Omnem enim mentem dum virtus sustulerit et carnalibus denegaverat aspectibus, victrix statim extingit" ["when virtue lifts aloft the whole mind without permitting it to consider the desires of the flesh, it wins the battle"].[104]

Labor ten, when Hercules slew Cacus to pacify Evander, once again demonstrates the triumph of virtuous Hercules as hero of the monastic schools in an extended allegorical (Fulgentian) treatment from the K Reviser. The more literal portion in the gloss comes from Servius's commentary on the *Aeneid* (*In Aen.* 8.190) and especially the first Vatican mythographer (Mythogr. I 67/68). Here Geryon, called Geriontiaforus, was king of Erithie and triple-bodied (*tergeminus*), either because he ruled over three islands or because he had three heads when he was born. He was sent by Eurystheus at Juno's urging to fight Hercules: before he battled him, Hercules slew the dog Othrus, Ithmus, and the shepherd Erithones. Once victorious, he took Geryon back to Greece. Cacus, a son of Vulcan (and thus grandson of Juno) who belches smoke, stole the cattle from Hercules that came from the spoils of victory and dragged them by their tails to a cave, where he hid them. It is this portion of the myth that leads to the allegorization, drawn directly from Fulgentius's *Mitologiae* (2.3). Cacus's name comes from "kakos" in Greek, which means "evil," as evidenced from the dark smoke he belches, opposite of the light and hence the truth.[105] Cacus's particular form of evil is deceitful and two-faced, "dupplex": in leading away the cattle he drags them so that he reverses their tracks; later he hides them in his cave so no one will see them.[106] In addition, Cacus particularly wants what belongs to Hercules because not only does Cacus represent evil but also Hercules represents virtue; of course Virtue here overcomes this deceitful evil and recovers his property ("Ideo et bona Hercolis concupiscit id est quia omnis malignitas est virtuti contrarium . . . sed virtus et malos interficit et sua vincat"). The K Reviser adds, as if pedantically, "Noli emulari in malignantibus nec tibi plus deterius eveniat" ["Do not vie with evil-doers, lest it turn out worse for you"].

The brief gloss on Labor eleven, the killing of the boar, is followed by a very long gloss on the "final" Labor, what the commentators conclude is Hercules's last act—his marriage to Deianira, his shooting of Nessus, and his apotheosis into a star, followed, in the English K Reviser only, by the story of the loyalty of his friend Philoctetes.[107] In B.N. and K, the literal narrative is restated, to which is added, in an Ovidian citation, that the "Omnipotent Father" sped him through the heavens on his chariot and set him among the stars, where "Atlas felt his weight, for after Hercules he himself [Atlas] is said to sustain the heavens."[108] This "sustaining of the heavens" in aid of Atlas apparently constitutes Hercules's very last Labor. In the K Reviser only, a postscript is included which narrates the birth, life, and death of Hercules and the story of Philoctetes, who set fire to the hero's pyre on Mount Etna and thereby received the hero's famous bow and arrows.[109]

The last Labor, which results in Hercules's death and subsequent apotheosis as a star, is caused by Nessus the Centaur's vengeful animosity toward him and frustrated desire for Deianira, and correspondingly by Hercules's uxorious regard for his wife Deianira (a strangely similar echo of Orpheus's excessive love for Eurydice). There is also a genealogical and chronological correspondence between the two myths of the brave and wise heroes. The Centaurs were begotten as a result of Ixion's frustrated desire for Juno (*Consolatio* 3 m12), a criminal act punished by torments in the hell into which Orpheus must descend to retrieve his wife. The Centaur Nessus also, Ixion-like, desires to rape Hercules's own wife, in the Remigian gloss but not in Boethius. In both myths Juno is a significant and powerful force whose very singular femaleness, celibacy, rivets attention on the chief monastic and scholastic danger, that of the desires of the flesh. Orpheus, born in the Egypt founded as a result of the initial adulteries of Jupiter so loathsome to Juno, betrays his own wisdom by his own anxiety about the seductions of eloquence, the power of the wife—he looks backward, at this life, not forward, toward the stars. Juno also figures in the life of her disliked stepson Hercules, in that she is responsible for the first Labor he undertakes and, indirectly, for the last Labor, since she caused the very life of the Centaur who cunningly deprives him of life through his weakness— his love for and trust in Deianira, which will encourage his donning of the poisonous and burning cloak. But Hercules's great strength and wisdom earlier in his adventures earn him immortality as a constellation. His second Labor, involving the defeat of the lion, is written into the text of the heavens as a sign of heroic victory and a promise, on a Christian level, of eternal life (see fig. 15, for the constellation illustrating the victory of Hercules over the Nemean lion).

Remigius is not explicitly misogynistic in his commentator's allegoresis, nor on the other hand does he elaborate on the myths of female deities and humans Juno, Eurydice, Helen and Clytemnestra (implicitly), Circe and Penelope (implicitly), Alcmene and Deianira. Yet his interest in female deities and uxorious gods, particularly from North African and

15. Hercules and the Nemean lion (constellation). MS. Phillip. 1832, fol. 82r (ca. 820–873, English). Courtesy of Staatsbibliothek zu Berlin, Preussicher Kulturbesitz.

Middle Eastern cultures, will develop into a full-blown exegesis in his commentary on Martianus Capella and (possibly) the second Vatican mythography (if indeed he was its author, as I believe he must have been). From the Virgilian and masculine Neoplatonic heroism he charts in his Boethius glosses, within a monastic and scholastic context, he will move to a Martianan and feminine Neo-Stoic cosmography in his later glosses, within what must have been a wider political and intellectual context in the Carolingian court.

Chapter Seven

THE UXORIOUS GODS IN REMIGIUS OF AUXERRE'S NEO-STOIC COMMENTARY ON MARTIANUS CAPELLA

The gods entered the mainstream of medieval thought, as we have seen, through Virgil's sixth book of the *Aeneid* (the idea of the underworld connecting both the shades and the artificial "undertext" of poetic *figurae*) and through astrology. Part of the problem of assimilating the classical gods into medieval thought derived from their messy sexual escapades. Largely because of Macrobius's influence in establishing fable as a cloaked truth, the gods in general then came to be seen as planets in the heavens or the signified truths of morality and theology. But Macrobius's vexed problem of the gods' sexuality—their castrations, adulteries, incests, rapes, and the like—continued to concern the commentators, even if they came to react in a Neo-Stoic manner to those sexual couplings by the gods, as did the first Vatican mythographer.

From the idea that the act of creation viewed in anthropomorphic terms is analogous to sexual congress and that the fiery seed of the Stoic World Soul continues to reproduce and regenerate the created world it is a short step to the Neoplatonic idea that the congress is sanctified by marriage. And, although it has not previously been demonstrated that Stoic thought was present in medieval thought much earlier than the twelfth century,[1] major works with some Stoic residue were transmitted to the twelfth century through copies made in the ninth (the earliest date of many extant manuscripts). In relation to Stoic physics these major works would include the second book of Cicero's *De natura deorum* and Calcidius's commentary on the *Timaeus* of Plato, along with portions of the fourth book of Boethius's *Consolatio* (on fate and Providence, 4 p4–6) and, of course, the famous passage in the *Aeneid* when Anchises in the underworld describes the cosmic order to Aeneas (*Aeneid* 6.724–31). Even recently, however, the

Martianus commentaries have not been perceived as a vehicle for Stoic ideas, though indeed they are.

For the most part commentators in the Middle Ages turned to Martianus and his *De nuptiis Philologiae et Mercurii* only after the Carolingian Renaissance was well under way, during the reign of Charlemagne's grandson, Charles the Bald (840–77); these commentators, mostly Irish scholars, created a new commentary tradition that lasted through the twelfth century.[2] Among them are numbered the minor or fragmentary ninth-century glosses of the English, Welsh, and Irish—the anonymous Cambridge commentator, Martin of Laon, John Scot—and the long and very important commentary by the Burgundian (or possibly Frankish or Irish) Remigius of Auxerre, who, if not himself Irish, then definitely studied under Irish (or Irish-influenced) teachers. These were followed by minor tenth- and eleventh-century glosses by the Italian Rather of Verona and the German Notker Labeo and the heavily Remigian commentary of the Anonymous Barberinus. The tradition, dominated as it was by Remigius of Auxerre writing around the year 900, culminated in the fantastic and confused twelfth-century Florentine Commentary, reputedly based on the lectures of William of Conches, and the expansive twelfth-century commentaries by Bernard Silvestris and Alexander Neckam.

For the Martianus commentators of the ninth century, the Carolingian period dominated by new political and social interests in education and the seven liberal arts, the mythographic material offered another opportunity to celebrate their schools and the subject matter of the schools, especially grammar, in which discipline much of the first two books of Martianus would serve nicely to educate pupils. The joining of eloquence and wisdom in the wedding of Mercury and Philology symbolized the goal of education in the arts leading to the study of philosophy and then of scripture.[3] This celebration of education can be said to permeate all three major Carolingian commentaries, those of Dunchad, John Scot, and Remigius. Among these commentaries, the most significant—that is, most used and copied, most persuasive and pervasive in interpreting Martianus Capella and therefore in bringing into the Middle Ages a view which would have its own life—belonged to Remigius of Auxerre, copied in sixty-four to seventy manuscripts,[4] to be rivalled only by Bernard Silvestris in the twelfth century. Despite the heavy dependence of Remigius's commentary on the glosses of Dunchad and John Scot and his borrowing from the lectures of his two masters, Servatus Lupus of Ferrières and Heiric of Auxerre, "Usually, in accordance with Gresham's law of scholarship,

Remigius' commentaries ultimately drove from the field those from which he had so generously borrowed."[5] All of the others, for one reason or another, were lost or remained uncopied, perhaps because of the geographical isolation of an author or changes in literary fashion, as was the case in the twelfth century with Alexander Neckam, whose unfinished commentary came into being after interest in Martianus had declined and when new pedagogic interests—chiefly in Aristotle, but also in Ovid's *Metamorphoses*—had replaced that in Martianus.

In general, in the Martianus commentaries the knots of mythographic analysis cluster at the central places in Martianus's narrative wherein the gods are introduced—primarily in the first book, and very early in the first book, on Hymen and his family (Bernard Silvestris on Martianus stops less than halfway through the first book), although there is also much mythological material in the second. Remigius's commentary, the only full commentary on all nine books, centers on books 1 and 2, with the minor mythographic references in books 3 to 9 altogether occupying about a third of the total material. Thus, most—at least half—of the mythological references come from the first book, a fact unsurprising if one recalls that the first book concerns the betrothal of Mercury (male, eloquence) and Philology (female, wisdom); the second, which follows in first in the number of mythographic glosses, concerns their marriage; and the last seven of the nine books are devoted to the "seven liberal arts" who serve as handmaidens of Philology when she marries Mercury. Because the first book introduces the major gods, there exists far more description and elaboration than in later books. And in that first book, the opening passage on Hymen and the concept of the wedding will focus attention on the god of weddings.

From a mythographic point of view, there are two places in book 1 where a panoply of gods can be observed. First, Mercury journeys through the heavens as he searches for an appropriate bride, where of course he encounters inhabitants of the various spheres on the way until he reaches Jove's habitation. Second, all of the deities are summoned to an assembly where they agree that Mercury should marry Philology. In the second book, after a similar assembly of Muses and Phronesis (Wisdom, Philology's mother), the bride, Philology, must also ascend through the heavens, of which in particular the lower spheres closest to earth are described, to marry the Cyllenian and embrace the god's way of life. Given earlier mythographic patterns—what might be termed the Chain of Being pattern, which appears in Fulgentius and in the first Vatican mythographer—

and the pattern of the *descensus ad inferos* in the commentaries on book 6 of the *Aeneid*—the descent, assembly, and ascent of the various characters would therefore fit into a familiar mythographic context.

In terms of his contribution to the mythographic tradition, the space Martianus devotes to some of the gods—Apollo and Mercury, most obviously, as we have already noted in discussing his influence on the Fulgentian *Mitologiae*—would also affect the approach of commentators and therefore the way in which the gods and their train of mythographic accretions would develop in the Middle Ages. In addition to those two, who were also planets, commentators singled out especially female figures—which included Hymen, Calliope and the Muses, Venus, Cupid, Diana, Juno, Pallas Athena, and Pluto, as well as the seven liberal arts (which had developed their own iconographic tradition by the ninth century). Indeed, Martianus was important in disseminating the iconography of the seven liberal arts as female figures in tapestries, reliefs, stained glass, and illuminations in manuscripts, from the Middle Ages to the Renaissance. "They range from a group of carved statues of the arts adorning the bed of Countess Adèle, daughter of William the Conqueror, to a series of sculptured figures on the west facade of the cathedral of Chartres."[6] What these figures add to the persuasive power of the mythographic tradition is the female deity, who had been skirted by the earlier grammarians and even, as we shall see, by the early Martianus commentators.

How did this feminization of mythology occur in Martianus? When *De nuptiis* was written, in the early fifth century, the mythological context had changed since the days of Virgil and Ovid. If no one truly believed in the "select gods," still, astrology and the Magna Mater cult flourished, along with Eastern cults and Mithraic mysticism, especially in North Africa. Hymen, the god of marriage invoked by Martianus at the beginning of *De nuptiis,* was understood by both of the first two Vatican mythographers as an Athenian youth who participated, along with the virgins, in the sacred rites of Ceres known as the Eleusinian mysteries. Much of this ambience colors the satura of Martianus and will be responsible for the direction taken by the late Carolingian mythographic tradition, which is toward the feminization of mythography after a period of late antique grammatical misogyny. In Fulgentius, especially, nearly all of the central fables refer to masculine gods, with wives—Ops, Juno, Proserpina—introduced as afterthoughts in the sections on the male gods. Because of Fulgentius's profound influence in the Middle Ages the commentators pick up his emphasis, for the most part, and the first Vatican mythographer stresses the male heroes, the male gods, by stressing genealogy. Boethius also centers especially on male heroes in his mythological meters, which are glossed so fully by the Carolingians. These authors' misogyny, however, is balanced by Martianus's interest in the female deity, which creates new directions for mythography in his commentaries through his allegorical and philosophical concept of marriage. This concept of marriage carried with it a Stoic rationale which the Carolingian Martianus commentators would extend in their mythographic glosses.

According to Michael Lapidge[7] the two basic principles of ancient Stoic thought were monistic and materialistic: first, the entire universe was one substance, but with two principles, god and matter, which interpenetrate. God (Jove) as fiery aether, or the substance of the sun and stars, was also generative and vital, in contrast to the destructive terrestrial fire. Thus this generative reason could also be identified with universal mind, reason, Providence—for the twelfth century, the World Soul viewed as Natura subordinated to God.

In keeping with the Stoic concept, Martianus refines his definition of the World Soul so as to incorporate the *dii penates,* or the household gods of the universe (*De nuptiis* 41), each of whom represents some aspect of Jove himself in his capacity as Generative Reason, the *animus mundi.* These aspects are reflected in their names and genders. In his comment on the *penates* Remigius cites the verses from the lost work of the Stoic Valerius Soranus on Jupiter *omnipotens,* both *progenitor* and *genetrix,* along with similar concepts from the Stoic Varro.

Sciendum autem quia philosophi unum dicunt esse Deum caeli et terrae et rerum ommium creatorem, qui pro multiplici dispositione qua mundum variis modis regit diversis appellatur vocabulis. Dicitur enim Vitomnus quod vitam praestet, Sentinus quod sensum; vocatur Iovis in aethere, Iuno in aere, Diana in terra. Plerumque etiam unus idemque non solum diversis nominibus sed et vario sexu appellatur. Iuxta illum versum Valerii Sorani:

Iupiter omnipotens rerum regumque repertor
progenitor genetrixque deum deus unus et idem.

In magnis ergo dispositionibus quasi masculino genere effertur, in minoribus femininum quodam modo nomen accipit. Nam et Varro dicit quia cum unus idemque sit homo, a corpore dicitur homo, ab anima sapiens. Ita etiam Deus cum unus idemque sit, multis tamen pro dispensationis suae diversitate censetur vocabulis.

[It must be known, moreover, that the philosophers say there is one God, creator of heaven and earth and all things, who, in accordance with the manifold arrangements by which he rules the world in various ways, is called by diverse names. He is called Vitumnus because he gives life, Sentinus because he gives sensation; he is called Jove in the aether, Juno in the air, Diana on earth. Usually also the one and the same is called not only by diverse names but by both sexes. According to a verse of Valerius Soranus:

Omnipotent Jupiter, author of things and kings,
Father and mother of the gods, one and the same god.

Therefore in great arrangements he is described by the masculine gender, while in lesser ones he receives a feminine name. For Varro says that, although a person is one and the same, he is called human because of his body and wise because of his soul. So too, although God is one and the same, nevertheless in accordance with the diversity of his accomplishments he is described by many names.] (Remi., *In Mart.* 26.4)

If Jupiter as the One God contains diversity and both male and female, then the universe in fact allows for and depends upon sexual difference. The doctrine of corporal seminal particles of reason, which explains human reason as a spark of the divine in the human body, was assimilated into Christian theology by concealing the issue of corporality.

Universal creation and sexuality, or cosmic "copulation," was veiled by the Neoplatonic image of marriage in the commentaries. The commentaries, particularly of Remigius, would thus flesh out the extant corpus of mythographic material with previously marginal glosses from the Virgil's *Eclogues* and *Georgics,* for example, on earthly processes and gods, and from Isidore, who also includes much from Martianus in his *Etymologiae,* with the feminine gods and personifications Fulgentius had ignored. Remigius's teacher Heiric of Auxerre had studied under Hraban Maur, who had copied verbatim much of "De diis gentium" from Isidore in his *De universo* and who himself had studied under Alcuin.

Martianus explains his subject by declaring the importance of marriage to the ancient gods and peoples:

Cum inter deos fierent sacra coniugia procreationis undique numero-
sae, liberique praeclues ac nepotum dulcium aetheria multitudo et
inter se quodam caelicolarum complexu ac foedere potirentur, prae-
sertimque potissimos conubialis bearet adiectio, idque deditum
mundo loquax triviatim dissultaret humanitas, poetaeque praecipue
Oeagrium citharistam secuti caecutientisque Maeonii suaviloquam
senectutem epica uulgo lyricaque pagina consonarent nec aliquid
dulcius Ioui inter aetherias uoluptates una coniuge loquerentur.

[There was a time when on all sides amongst the gods the sacred
weddings of a numerous generation were being celebrated; the noble
children of the gods and the celestial multitude of their beloved
descendants were also for their part winning the embraces and
pledges of the dwellers in heaven. The fruit of marriage especially
delighted the great gods, and the human race in its chatter spread the
news through the streets of the gift that had been given to the world.
The poets, who were disciples of the Thracian lyre player [Orpheus]
and the blind Maeonian [Homer], old and eloquent, published epic
poems and lyrics about the marriages; they sang that amongst the
delights of heaven nothing pleased Jove more than his wife alone.]
(De nuptiis 3)

The uxorious Jove introduces the major subject matter of the early
portion of De nuptiis that will catalyze John Scot's Neo-Stoicism and
Remigius's clearer, more humanistic balancing of gender. John explains
the relationship of Jupiter and Juno through physical or natural allegory,
with Jupiter as the power of fire and Juno as the moist cool air beneath, the
intersection of which provides generative seed creating and nourishing all
mutable things on earth,[8] and which is aided by the fiery spark of natural
desire ("eiusque seminibus ipsa nimia siccitate non solum marcescentibus
verum etiam morientibus, naturali appetitu auxilium postulat ab ignea
qualitate, ex qua omnia quae de terra et aqua nascuntur, ut nascuntur
moventur" ["and its seeds, through excessive dryness not only withering
but even dying, it demands aid by its natural appetite from the fiery
quality, from which all things which are born from earth and water are set
in motion as they are born"] (John Scot, In Mart. 5.14). John relates to this
Stoic concept of the fiery World Soul, originally called Logos spermatikos,
Generative Reason, the three Parcae as arbiters of fate, or "the indissoluble
exigency of diverse qualities." More specifically, the physicists say that
nothing can be born out of the heat of fire or the aridity of earth without

the intermediary of humid air and cool water, or, more poetically, "Let Vesta be understood as nothing other than living flame, / And you see no bodies born from flame" (John Scot, *In Mart.* 5.15).[9]

Although Remigius does not incorporate this Neo-Stoic belief here, he is familiar with the concept of the World Soul as Generative Reason, as evidenced in his own discussion of the gifts of Jupiter and Juno on the day Psyche, the *anima,* daughter of Entelechia and the sun, is born. According to Martianus (*De nuptiis* 7) Jove gives her a diadem taken from his daughter Eternity; Remigius explains that by Jove philosophers understand the world, *mundus,* and of Jove, as if *Iavis,* "id est universalis vis" (Remi., *In Mart.* 7.11). Juno adds a golden band for her hair, interpreted physically by John as the *rationis connexio* (connection of reason) with eternity (John Scot, *In Mart.* 7.10). Within the context of this birthday Remigius presents the familiar natural-physical explanation of Jove and Juno, aether and air, the latter interceding and mediating between heaven and earth in order to enhance fecundity on earth (Remi., *In Mart.* 7.16).[10] In book 7, on arithmetic (*De nuptiis* 732), Remigius notes that Jupiter represents the One, the monad, as Juno signifies the Two, the many, in response to Martianus's concept that the monad, which is unity, extends itself in any direction and forms the dyad, or Juno, wife of the monad (Remi., *In Mart.* 368.9). (Remigius will also explain the changing physical forms assumed by lecherous Jupiter intent on seduction—as bull, golden shower, swan (*De nuptiis* 589)—as "multiformis" rather than "transformis," "ideoque versiformis Iuppiter vocatur," Remi., *In Mart.* 292.11).

Juno in many ways dominates the satura, as we shall see—as wife of Jove, as air, as goddess of childbirth, as synonym for Diana, Proserpina, Lucina, the moon, especially in the second book balancing out this first book. One might agree with Remigius that this is a work concerned not only with Jupiter, the source of all creation and the patriarchal creational principle, but also with Juno, the matriarchal generational and rational principle. Whereas John Scot launches into a Neo-Stoic differentiation of the two early in his commentary, thereafter remaining for the most part more intrigued by the conventional glosses on the male deities and heroes, Remigius omits this philosophical rationalization and instead concentrates carefully on adding to John's glosses on the deities more elaborate explanations of the female gods. An interest in the female is also reflected in the mythographic glosses on Terence (*Ad Andriam, Eunuchus,* especially, but also one gloss in the *Heautontimorumenos*) attributed to Heiric of Auxerre, Remigius's teacher, or to Remigius himself, with the mythographic glosses extant primarily concerning only female deities such as Venus, Juno, Danaë, Ceres, Omphale, and Minerva.[11]

And why did these Carolingian commentators, especially Remigius, perceive as important the role of the female deity and her uxorious mate in their text? Although there is no way of proving any one theory, the most compelling has to do with Celtic paganism. The earliest glosses and commentaries betray a Celtic (Welsh or Irish) connection, John Scot and Heiric of Auxerre were both Irish, and the role of the mother goddess in native Celtic religion may have attuned these scholars to the signs of the distantly related Magna Mater cult in Martianus. Of the four insular or continental commentaries on Martianus—the anonymous Cambridge glosses with Old Welsh marginalia, "Dunchad" (Martin of Laon), John Scot (Johannes Scottus Eriugena), and Remigius of Auxerre—Remigius is the most distantly removed from Ireland (although he may have been Irish), but the most influential in spreading this feminized mythography. But all of them, even the earliest Welsh glosses, manifest a similar mythological interest in female deity unusual within what is explicitly a male-dominated tradition.

I. THE HIBERNIAN CONNECTION, THE VERNACULAR, AND THE FEMININE

The very earliest glosses on *De nuptiis* are Welsh; the next generation of commentators, Irish, some of whom taught in France. These Old Welsh glosses suggest an insular interest in communicating through the vernacular similar to the ninth-century Boethius glosses in Old English and the eleventh-century Boethius and Martianus glosses in Old High German. Mythologically, the earliest, literalistic glosses in Welsh on the Latin text (eighth- or more likely ninth-century), in Cambridge University Corpus Christi Library MS. 153,[12] refer euphemistically to Jove's intercourse with mortal women in the fable of Dionysius's birth—choices of lemma which privilege the female, pagan, and sexual[13]—and residually Stoic. The Old Welsh gloss identifies in a clumsy philological way the diverse Latin names of Apollo and Genius, in each case noting "another name," just as another Old Welsh gloss explains that the Latin names Fluonia, Februalis, Februa, Interduca, Domiduca, Unxia Cinctia, and others are all "enuein di iunoni," names of Juno. Most striking is the resemblance of the Old Welsh glosses with those of manuscript 330 of the same Cambridge library, evidence of insularity shared with the Martianus glosses of Martin of Laon

(Dunchad).[14] These slightly later Martianus glosses in Latin exhibit an Irish script rather than Old Welsh glossation, but were responsible for transmitting to later glossators on the continent, as we shall see, the allegorical interpretation of Martianus.

The ninth-century commentary of "Dunchad" is now accepted as that of Martin of Laon,[15] an Irish bishop who taught at the monastery of St. Remi in Rheims and in Laon, who lived 819–75, and who died in Laon.[16] While the "Dunchad" commentary on Martianus differs from those of John Scot and Remigius of Auxerre, it does resemble Martin of Laon's notes for lectures on Greek, the *Scholica Graecarum glossarum*.[17] This *Scholica*, partly written by Martin himself, explains Greek words, although in a faulty way.[18] The few mythographic references in the *Scholica* are sufficient to establish a knowledge of Fulgentius's *Mitologiae*—itself filled with fanciful etymologies from the Greek—and of Martianus's text.[19]

In addition to Celticism, the background common to the early Martianus glossators also included similar educational values and experiences. Gautbert, writing at the end of the tenth century, notes that a genealogy of teachers from diverse, often multicultural, backgrounds offered to their students the focused and accessible world of classical learning—teachers such as Aldhelm, Bede, Hraban Maur, Alcuin, Smaragdus, Theodulf, John Scot, Helias, Heiric, Hucbald, and Remigius.[20] Such multiculturalism mixed with classical humanism is typical of both John Scot and Remigius of Auxerre, in their roles as students, as teachers, and as commentators.

John Scot (Johannes Scottus Erigena or Eriugena), according to Prudentius, Bishop of Troyes and a good friend, was Hibernian: "Te solum acutissimum Galliae transmisit Hibernia," he writes; in addition, of course, John also knew Greek—and only in Ireland was it cultivated and studied at this time. John, apparently born around 800–815, went abroad before 847 to find security at the court of Charles the Bald, where he was made head of the palace school to teach the young princes in the Emperor's entourage.[21] For Charles the Bald John Scot translated into Latin the works of the pseudo-Dionysius (*The Divine Names, The Heavenly Hierarchy,* and some *Epistles,* certainly), as well as the *Ambigua* of Maximus the Confessor, and provided commentaries on the pseudo-Dionysius, Martianus Capella, Priscian, and Boethius (this one has not in fact been found);[22] he is also believed to have written a commentary or lectured on Servius on Virgil.[23] He was involved in two theological controversies, one about predestination (arising from his response to the writings of Gottschalk that evil has no real being, contained in his thesis *De praedestinatione,* written 851) and one about the Eucharist (*De eucharistia,* not extant; the controversy was started by Paschasius Radbertus in 831).[24] Although he was still in France in the year 877, by 878, according to William of Malmesbury, he had emigrated to England, upon the invitation of King Alfred, to teach at the Abbey of Malmesbury; he was reputed, also according to William, to have been stabbed to death by his students.

For our purposes the most important pupils of Martin (and later John Scot) were the Irish Heiric or Eric of Auxerre and Heiric's own (possibly Irish) pupil and protegé, Remigius of Auxerre.[25] Remigius, if not Irish himself, was at least taught by Irish scholars, or by scholars who had been taught by the Irish. Thus he also inherited this monolithic educational learning at the palace school: from Heiric of Auxerre, who had also taught the son of Charles the Bald, Remigius inherited techniques for expounding classical texts, and through Heiric, the textual critical methods of Heiric's teacher Servatus Lupus of Ferrières (who had received knowledge of the liberal arts from Hraban Maur), the system of biblical exegesis of Heiric's teacher Haimo of Auxerre, and the philosophical speculation of Heiric's teacher Helias of Laon (John Scot's student).[26] Remigius spent his own life as a teacher, so well known that he earned the title of "egregius doctor" and was termed "in divinis et humanis scripturis eruditissimus."[27] In 883 he and another student, Hucbald of St. Amand, were called to Rheims because Archbishop Fulco had restored schools previously destroyed by the Normans and sought the two best teachers to guide young clerics (even Fulco became a student). After Fulco's death, in 900, Remigius left Rheims to teach the liberal arts, especially music and dialectic, in Paris at a monastery school, possibly St. Germain des Prés, drawing students such as Odo of Cluny, possibly Abbo of Fleury, and Hucbald of Liège. Although it is not known when Remigius died, it was probably not after 908.

That he may have been politically sensitive to the need for greater attention to female figures in the text is plausible if we recall that the mother of his sovereign Charles the Bald was the powerful—and literate— empress Judith.

The *Annales Mettenses* say that she was "well instructed in all the flowers of wisdom." Her praises are sung by Walafrid Strabo, and by Ermoldus Nigellus. Rhabanus Maurus dedicated to her his commentaries on the books of Judith and Esther; and Freyculf dedicated to her the second part of his *Chronicle* that she might use it for the instruction of her son, Charles the Bald. In the Bibliothèque d'Avranches there is still preserved (MS no. 2428) a *Universal History* extending from the creation to the end of the fourth century, written probably by Florus, the antagonist of John the Scot, which is dedicated to the empress Judith.[28]

Remigius's uxorious gods, understood by means of Stoic allegorization, may indeed have been intended similarly in Judith's honor.

Finally, the knowledge of and interest in Greek of the Irish scholars may also have primed their Stoic philosophizing in the glosses on Martianus, for they are all highly interested in grammar, classical intertextuality, and annotation of the text. Martin of Laon's glosses on Martianus, like the Welsh glossiasts', are preoccupied with synonyms, etymologies, identifications, and similarly grammatical operations; unlike them he is anxious to note symbolical or allegorical interpretations. In a philological or grammatical approach consonant with the "literary" methods pursued in the monastic schools of this period, he identifies alternate or obscure names and titles of some of the gods. Possibly marginalia from a heavily glossed manuscript, but full of wrong explanations, elementary allusions, guesses from contexts made out of ignorance, what has been edited of Martin of Laon (by Cora Lutz) of course is yet very minimal given the loss of much of Martin's work.[29]

John Scot's approach in the commentary, which can be dated between August 21, 859, and February 25, 860,[30] is, in the view of his modern editor Cora Lutz, to emend Martianus's text with variant readings and to comment on possible rearrangements of words to simplify the text; to provide transitions and thus strengthen continuity; to explain the meaning of the allegory; to uncover misleading rhetorical devices; to identify and analyze meters, and to comment, incompletely and sporadically, on philosophy in glosses that corroborate those from his other works; indeed, his approach is primarily philosophical rather than cosmological (like Martin's) or literary (like Remigius's).[31] Further, despite his knowledge of Greek and certain defects in the commentary's subject and style, John was eager to find mistakes in Martianus—his paganism and errors in logic, for example.[32] Although much of the commentary on books 1 and 2 is devoted to John's own ideas, John's sources probably included either Martin of Laon's glosses or some other prototype and Martianus Capella himself, as cited in other scholia or commentaries; the Neoplatonic metaphysics of Calcidius's commentary on the *Timaeus,* Macrobius's commentary on the *Somnium Scipionis,* and Pliny's *Historia naturalis,* on cosmology and the soul;[33] the dialectical works of Augustine on Aristotle's *Categories* and *On Interpretation,* and Boethius on Porphyry and those same two works of Aristotle, as well as Isidore and Cassiodorus on the same subject, a few rhetorical gleanings from Cicero's *De inventione* and minor references to Theophrastus and others. His mythological sources included Fulgentius, Hyginus, Servius's commentaries on Virgil, Macrobius's *Saturnalia,* the first Vatican mythographer, Augustine's *De civitate Dei,* Isidore (and the works of Solinus, Juvencus, Virgil, and Ovid are mentioned as sources only in a few glosses).[34]

Remigius's commentary on Martianus reflects his vocational dedication. Because he treats a long sentence or short paragraph as a unit, "The total effect of the commentary is that of the oral presentation of a professor's class notes on a text which presents difficulties of content and interpretaton."[35] Although Remigius uses both John and Martin of Laon, he names John only seven times and never mentions Martin; yet when the two earlier commentaries disagree, he prefers Dunchad. His borrowing is by no means slavish and his interest, unlike that philosophical and theological bent of John, remains with grammar and mythography.[36] Perhaps because of both his early schooling and his later professional acumen he relies on many sources, both glosses and glossaries, citing directly these poets: Simonides, Valerius Soranus, Terence, Horace, Virgil, Persius, Lucan, Juvenal, Statius, Prudentius—as well as the prose writers Varro, Cicero, Pliny, Priscian, Solinus, Macrobius, Servius, Fulgentius, Calcidius, and John Scot; he refers to material in Homer, Plato, Aristotle, and Orosius, some used directly, some from an intermediate source.[37] In addition, he has borrowed without acknowledgement, possibly through an intermediary, from Pliny, Augustine, Servius, Festus, Isidore, Macrobius, Fulgentius, Hyginus, Solinus, the first Vatican mythographer. And of course he often coincides with the second Vatican mythographer.

Remigius's commentary on Martianus and the mythography some scholars believe he compiled, the second Vatican mythography, were written late in his career (some scholars believe at the very end), but he indeed lectured on many of these source authors and others even as early as Auxerre, including Horace, Persius, Juvenal, Prudentius, Martianus, and perhaps Boethius.[38] While he has been described as using his master's lecture notes on Persius for his own purpose, and possibly also Heiric's notes on Juvenal, themselves possibly drawn from lectures of Servatus Lupus of Ferrières plus marginalia accompanying Persius from antiquity,[39] the range of Remigius's writings is so extensive that he cannot be described as a mere pedagogue. Cora Lutz has divided his extant and attributed writings into seven groups: first, theological treatises, including works of biblical exegesis on Genesis, the twelve minor prophets, the Song of Songs, Psalms, the letters of St. Paul, Matthew, and the Apocalypse, as well as works of dogma on the celebration of the Mass, the Twelve Homilies, and a commentary on Boethius's *Opuscula sacra;* second, philosophical treatises like the commentary on the *Consolatio Philosophiae* of Boethius; third, works on grammar, including commentaries or scholia on Donatus's works—the *Ars minor, Ars maior, Barbarismus*—and on the works of Priscian, including *Partitiones XII versum Aeneidos,* Phocas, Eutyches, and two works of Bede; fourth, commentaries or scholia on literary works, such as the *Disticha Catonis,* Sedulius, Prudentius, Martianus Capella, Juvenal, Horace, Terence, Avianus Arator, and also the two accessus, to Persius and Virgil (Lutz omits the Terence scholia because at the time they had not been printed and existed only in a thirteenth-century manuscript owned by Yale); fifth, excerpts from Valerius Maximus; sixth, letters; and seventh, a textbook, *Fundamentum scolarium.*[40]

The three major Martianus glosses all treat female deities as they follow the chronology of Martianus's text. Martin of Laon, in the fragments we have from the last third of book 2, focuses on the earth; from the early references to the Sibyl come minor cults, many associated with the moon (Diana); then he glosses Mercury and the sun or Apollo—all of them figures clustered conveniently in Martianus's first two books and many of them very similar to material contained in Macrobius's *Saturnalia.* This emphasis and focus in this commentary and others illustrates how Martianus and his account of the heavens—the hierarchy of planets, or the astrological conception of the gods—was so important in the Middle Ages. The ascent of Mercury and Apollo through the spheres to gain Jove's advice is based on Neoplatonist concepts of astrology and cosmology. In the later books, on the seven liberal arts, there are very few references of significance. Martin's sources, which he usually paraphrases, include Servius, Isidore, the Macrobius commentaries, Virgil; on myths he finds useful Servius, Fulgentius, Augustine, and an unidentified source common to the second Vatican mythographer (who was probably Remigius of Auxerre himself).

John Scot's longer analyses demonstrate an understanding of physical (natural) or moral levels of allegory—what I have termed "Neo-Stoic" interpretations of the gods—in addition to identifications of the names and functions of the minor gods—for example, "Portunus" as the god of boats being navigated into ports (John Scot, *In Mart.* 5.19), or Aesculapius as the son of Apollo and inventor of the art of medicine (John Scot, *In Mart.* 5.19).

In Remigius, the mythography shifts far more to the moral undermeanings of the gods. While he tries to relate the mythographic figures to each one of the seven liberal arts, in general he seems much less interested than John in an elaborate philosophical mythography; instead he is briefer, matter-of-fact and more or less grammatical in his discussion, with twice as many glosses on the various gods in book 1 as in book 2. In Remigius, a certain pattern is followed: at the beginning of each book there is some myth or mythographic commentary, then toward the end strictly specialized, highly technical material.

For all of these commentators, however, the marriage of Mercury and Philology celebrates the philosophic concept of cosmic and microcosmic union, with the concept of balance—of earth and the heavens, female and male—as the corollary to that hypothesis. If book 1 introduces the masculine, the divine bridegroom Mercury, coming from the heavens, then book 2 introduces the feminine, the human bride Philology, coming from earth, the underworld: divine and human, male and female (see the illustration of their marriage in figure 16). How the feminization of Martianus is continued in the commentary tradition reflects primarily the commentators' pedagogic allegiance to their written text particularly during a period when the wedding of human wisdom (to which Benedictine learning aspired) and divine eloquence (the Word as Christ) became the goal of education within the monastic school. We shall begin with the mythographic figures in the first book, proceed with those in the second book, and conclude with those in the third to the ninth books.

Marriage itself as a Neoplatonic moral, cosmogonic, and pedagogical emblem feminizes the mythographic tradition in the specific Martianus commentary group just as Hymen, god of weddings, feminizes an essentially masculine (aetherial, Jovian) cosmos. Especially in Remigius's commentary Hymen manifests a divine genealogy yet is predominantly earthly, feminine, human in function and role, perhaps because the human soul longs to be reunited with its heavenly origins. Invoked at the opening of the satura, Hymen has, as father, Bacchus (god of the vine), and as mother, Venus (goddess of love); he is related to the Muses and the Graces. His father Bacchus was son of Semele, Cadmus's doomed Theban daughter, and Jupiter; this god of wine and the vine was nurtured in Jupiter's thigh after Semele burned to a cinder, his gestation implying the conundrum of

16. Marriage of Mercury and Philology. Incipit to an edition with glosses of Martianus Capella's *De nuptiis*. MS. Canonici Miscellaneous 110, fol. 123r. By permission of the Bodleian Library, University of Oxford.

heavenly and masculine pregnancy and birth, or the spiritualizing of flesh. Thus, Hymen and his ancestors and kin can be said to embody the concept of marriage as that which exists between couples, between body and soul, and between the shimmering elements of the universe married harmoniously with Idea to produce the created structure and inhabitants of the world. Altogether they suggest that marriage is in some way harmony (and Harmonia, daughter of Venus and Mars, otherwise known as music, will be the last handmaiden introduced, at the end of book 9).

In the remainder of the first book, Martianus takes different opportunities to dramatize various lists or catalogs of the deities, planets, and inhabitants of the (primarily masculine) cosmic spheres. Because the narrative has arranged for such a possibility so skillfully, the entry or introduction of these "characters" allows Martianus to map the heavens. This mapping typifies the predominant conceptual mode of book 1 which is celestial rather than earthly, divine rather than human, male rather than female. The emphasis in this book sharply contrasts with that in the second, as we move to the polar opposite—earthly, human, female, or Philology rather than Mercury. But in anticipation of this imminent feminizing context we have the introduction of the more normal "select" gods, more than half of which are female—especially in the guests invited to the assembly of the gods from all the sixteen regions of the heavens (*De nuptiis* 41, 45–61), and then their entrance into the assembly (70–88). Martianus's tableau of the regions provides an encyclopedia of grotesqueries for his medieval readers. Most interesting, toward the end of this section (and the end of this first book), is the similarity to the glosses on the gods found in the Terence scholia of the same period or earlier, possibly written by Remigius or his teacher Heiric of Auxerre.

The second book of *De nuptiis* receives less attention from the commentators John Scot and Remigius than the monumental first book. Nevertheless, it is vital to the mythographic focus: the bride Philology manifests links with the earthly realm governed by Juno, ruler of air between moon and earth. The wife of Jupiter appears in all of her roles, including goddess of childbirth (*De nuptiis* 149–167). If "feminine"—marginalized, invisible—is the appropriate adjective to describe the inhabitants of the air and earth not normally stressed in such works, then here flourishes the feminine as a metaphor for the human (in counter to the masculine and divine). It is no accident that Pallas Athena, the female goddess born from Jove's head in a male usurpation of birthing, along with the inhabitants of earth and air reappears in the allegory most prominently in book 2 (*De nuptiis* 149–67).

Philology experiences trepidation in book 2, as Martianus's reminder that mythology, ravaged as it often is by the scandalous and reprehensible, will here be made respectable by the allegorical act of marriage: the earthly is always salvaged by the celestial. After one night, Philology must enter the assembly, where she will be examined by Jove, apotheosized, and then married to Mercury. In a brilliant humanizing touch Martianus allows his bride to experience sudden trepidation: she fears that if she ascends to the heavens she will forget or forego "the myths and legends of mankind, those charming poetic diversities of the Milesian tales" (*De nuptiis* 100). Remigius glosses "mythos" as "fabulae," and as a book of mythologies, "mythologiarum liber appellatur"; Martianus's "charming poetic diversities" are glossed as "carminum voluptates," Miletus as a city or island on which Thales was one of seven sages, whence he is called Milesius (Remi., *In Mart.* 43.1). The Carolingian commentary, intent on preserving and rationalizing antiquity, thus as a text itself celebrates the act of allegorical interpretation of a carnal, pagan, literary text. Indeed, this book, in celebrating Philology, celebrates all acts of interpretation, beginning with the word, the name, even the letter.

The last book of *De nuptiis,* also glossed by Remigius, book 9, contains the greatest number of mythographic references of the last seven books, on the arts of the *trivium* and *quadrivium* who serve Philology as handmaidens.[41] It cites as its major myth the uxorious uncoupling of Orpheus from Eurydice as a coda to the earlier glosses on marriage as a cosmic and generative act. The most important myth in books 3 to 9, this myth is also linked in book 9 with Harmonia, or music. Books 3 through 8 generally duplicate material related to the seven liberal arts from books 1 and 2. In these later books Minerva appears as *sapientia;* the arts are *feminine* servants related to Minerva and are the goal to which all education in the arts aspires. If there is a mythographic paradigm that dominates this entire satura and its commentary tradition, it is that found in book 7 (Arithmetic), in which Venus and Hymen oppose Pallas (essentially the mythographic dilemma of the later *De planctu Naturae* of Alan of Lille). Venus, associated with *operae nuptiarum,* and Hymen, *deus nuptiarum,* are linked through the rules of Hymen, the Hymeneia or marriage rites, and opposed (according to a handmaiden of Venus whispering to Mercury) to Pallas and her works and laws (*De nuptiis* 725; Remi., *In Mart.* 363.17). Perhaps because Remigius does not wholly accept this opposition he elects a god to govern the more physical aspects of the marriage rite: Priapus is "deum nuptiarum quem nuptae colunt" (Remi., *In Mart.* 363.22).

The most important figures in the Martianus commentaries are, first, Hymen and his parents Bacchus and Venus and their related kin, as well as those couples Martianus describes as "dominated by the female" (*De nuptiis* 4), including Jupiter and Juno, Dis and Portunus, Gradivus or Mars and Nereia, Aesculapius and some unnamed other, Saturn and Ops (Cybele), Janus and the Argive goddess, Osiris and Isis. The commentary proceeds with long glosses on Mercury and Apollo (attention to them has already been preserved in Fulgentius from Martianus), and their kin, the World Soul (Remi., *In Mart.* 13.1), the select gods as well as those minor and obscurely grotesque figures drawn from the sixteen regions of the heavens, and the gods who enter into the assembly, chiefly Saturn, Ops, and their progeny. In book 2 the deities are more earthy and earthly, more female— Juno, or Diana, and Athena, the inhabitants of the underworld dominated by the Great Mother. In books 3 to 9, most significant among the liberal arts is Harmonia, Music, and in particular her proponent the uxorious poet Orpheus, who demonstrated the power of the poet in establishing the principles of Pallas Athena on earth to fight the inexorable steps of Mars, god of warfare but also Mors, Death.

II. HYMEN AND HIS KIN:
FEMALE DOMINATION IN MARRIAGE

By presenting Hymen, god of weddings, as the god of cosmic marriage linking diverse elements in the universe, Martianus and his commentators attempt both to articulate and resolve, at least in part, the Platonic problem of sexual difference—why there exist two sexes, how this corporal difference marks the larger body of the universe, and, most important, the universal significance of male and female joining together, harmonizing, dissolving difference. For his depiction of Hymen Martianus drew upon Claudian's *Epithalamion of Palladius and Celerina*[42] and gave him Bacchus for a father and Venus for a mother to illustrate the ritual pageantry of weddings as well as the physiological stages leading to sexual consummation. Invoked to bless the beginning of the Muse Calliope's poem, Hymen has been chosen, according to Martianus, because dancing pleases him (Bacchus is his father), or he sings at weddings (and weddings are the province of his mother), or he is supposed to garland thresholds blooming with flowers (supplied by the three Graces). In his commentary, however, John Scot incorporates the Stoic explanation of Hymen as the universal principle of harmony. For John, Hymen is celebrated and invoked in

Martianus's frame because so much depends on a wedding—that of Mercury and Philology—and because Hymen is depicted as presiding over conception, embodying the cosmic principle of unity that binds together the four elements in the microcosm and in the great world, the four universal regions. In contrast, Remigius simply defines him as "god of weddings," "natural conception," "deus . . . nuptiarum, id est naturalium conceptionum" (Remi., *In Mart.* 3.5), followed by a focus on physiology and faculty psychology, perhaps in part to underscore and rationalize Remigius's general attention to divine gender.

The hymen, of course, refers most literally to a mark of female difference. According to John, only women have a third *membranula* (in addition to those two governing intelligence and the heart, shared with men), called a "hymen," for which reason the god is said to preside over conception. In relation to the two common membranes, in Remigius one, called *menica* in Greek, is found in the brain, from which the fistulae of the five senses proceed, and the other, called *fren* in Greek, divides the lower parts of the belly from the higher parts of the breast, whence is derived the term *frenesis passio*, the "frenetic passion," because it can lead to madness if it is injured.[43] The hymen is a little membrane found in young girls, for which reason Hymen is called god of weddings ("Hymen Grece dicitur membranula, et est proprie muliebris sexus in qua fiunt puerperia, inde dictus est Hymeneus nuptiarum deus," Remi., *In Mart.* 3.5). But he also explains the hymen (as John Scot does, *In Mart.* 208.11) as a bond between lower and higher, an entry-way from outer to inner—that which "marries" the body to the rational soul. Hymen in Remigius has the duty of garlanding thresholds—the mark at which "outer" and "inner" converge—because Bacchus is his father and Venus is his mother and "because after excessive agitation [nimiam petulantiam] comes the excitement of desire [excitaria libidio]" (Remi., *In Mart.* 4.1).

For Remigius this genealogy is apt because of Hymen's function in binding together the disparate parts and beings of the universe, a power that derives from his mother, or universal love ("Hymeneum enim hoc loco nihil aliud accipimus nisi amorem illum et concordiam qua elementa omnia et universitas subsistit creaturarum," Remi., *In Mart.* 3.14). Venus's role demands a Manichaean view of love; accordingly, Remigius offers two Venuses, the universal Venus, *casta* or chaste, and earthly Venus, *turpis* or filthy, along with two Cupids, *cupiditas honesta et turpis* (Remi., *In Mart.* 3.14). In Martianus, when "Desire, inflamed by Venus, glows on your face" (*De nuptiis* 1), "cupiditas" is translated as the god Cupid who represents both fleshly and chaste desire, although later in the text Martianus and the commentators will explain "Cupid" as a half-brother to Hymen, having a different father, with the second, chaste, Venus married to Vulcan instead of Bacchus.

Poetry, beauty, and creativity are all related to the power of universal love and harmony—the ability to resolve difference. In relation to the first Venus, "Camena" is the name Martianus uses for Hymen's mother Venus and it comes from *canendo*, or like *canens melos*, used for the Muses singing well. Then the Muses are the *copula*, the holy bonds; Hymen, as *copula sacra deum*, forms the sacred bond among the gods, but the plural form also suggests the *proles deorum*, offspring of the gods, or the nine Muses born from Jove and Juno (Remi., *In Mart.* 3.6). The beauty associated with the chaste Venus emerges also in her specific relationship with Calliope, the Muse to whom this poem belongs, as bearing a name derived from "callion phone, id est pulchra vox," "beautiful voice," or, alternatively, from *callos*, "beautiful," and *poio*, "I make," the word from which *poeta* is derived (Remi., *In Mart.* 4.3). Similarly, the Graces are explained by Remigius as the daughters of Jove and Juno, related to Hymen because he is the grandson of Jupiter; they convey in the commentary aspects of Venus's nature as concordant love and of Hymen's role as *copula*. Although the Graces are three, they have one name, "Carite," and one beauty ("unius pulchritudinis") and are depicted nude because it is not possible for grace to be fictitious or insincere, and as one turning away from us ("una nobis aversa") and two toward us ("duae nos respicientes") because "gratia simpla a nobis profecta dupla solet reverti" {"a single kindness {or favor} coming from us usually returns two-fold"}. Remigius understands the three as three gifts, beauty, voice, and gesture or physical agility, and he quotes John Scot's statement that the three gifts are given to those who sing and declaim well, by which things also all love is won over ("Haec enim tria dantur bene canentibus et rhetorizantibus quibus etiam conciliatur omnis amor," Remi., *In Mart.* 4.2).

Within marriage, female dominance leads Martianus to feminize mythology: it is Juno who has the power to alter Jupiter's decree because he is uxorious and delights in her embraces:

> nec solum supernum regem attestabatur uxorium, idque etiam Diti propositum, idque Portuno, certumque esse Gradivum Nerienis Neriae coniugis amore torreri.

[Not only the king of the gods was thought to be under feminine domination; this was also said of Dis and Portunus {Neptune}, while it was regarded as beyond question that Gradivus {Mars} was aflame with love for his wife Nereia, the daughter of Nereus.] (*De nuptiis* 4)

And Martianus adds others—Aesculapius, who experiences the same passion, uxorious Saturn and Ops, Janus and the Argive goddess, with Isis having felt the same way toward her husband Osiris. The couplings introduce into Western European culture through the commentators North African and Middle Eastern myths of the gods current in late antiquity, such as those of Isis and Osiris. John Scot will for the most part avoid glossing the feminine counterparts; Remigius will not.

For the uxorious husbands Dis, Portunus, and Gradivus, John Scot and Remigius provide conventional mythographic readings, with Dis as Pluto, god of the lower regions, Portunus as Neptune, Gradivus as Mars marching off to war.[44] But Remigius's glossation is markedly more gender-conscious than John's in the next pairs, associating the lesser Junos in a descending hierarchy with emotion, sadness, and the underworld, just as the lesser Jupiters are associated with knowledge, power or strength, and death. For John, Aesculapius was merely the inventor of medicine, whereas Remigius adds that "Esculapius" is called Asclepios in Greek, the son of Apollo and Coronis torn from the uterus of his mother, "de secto matris utero eductus" (Remi., *In Mart.* 5.20). Saturn's wife Ops (Berecynthia, Rhea, or Cybele) in Remigius is connected with the Magna Mater cult in a gloss that transcends John's very brief physical interpretation (see figure 17, of Saturn, Cybele, the Corybantes, Jupiter, Apollo, Mars, and Mercury). For John, she signifies earth that is fertile and solid, hence her names "Ops," wealth, and "Cybebe" (*sic*), cube (John Scot, *In Mart.* 5.21).[45] Compare the fuller, richer detail in Remigius: Rhea is called Ops because of the *opulentia* she grants to mortals ("Cuius uxor Rea Ops dicta est ab opulentia quam mortalibus tribuit"), and equated with Cybele, ". . . cubele a soliditate. Ipsa est enim terra qua nihil solidius est in elementis" ["cube-like, from her solidity, for she is the earth itself, than which there is nothing more solid in the elements"]. Remigius declares in explanation that, in Greek, *cubus* means "solid," hence we call three-dimensional numbers (or figures) "cubes" ("Cubum enim Greci solidum dicunt, hinc et solidos numeros cubos vocamus"). Alternatively, "Cybele" is derived from the Greek for the rotation of heads which her priests, called *galli*, exercise in sacred rites: "Vel CYBELE dicitur apo tu kybiste tin cephale, id est a rotatione capitis quam exercebant in eius sacris galli, id est sacerdotes illius" (Remi., *In*

17. Saturn, Cybele, Corybantes, Jupiter, Apollo, Mars, Mercury. From Remigius of Auxerre on Martianus. MS. Latinus 14271, fol. 11v (ca. 1100). Courtesy of Bayerische Staatsbibliothek, Munich.

Mart. 5.22). Later, Remigius will identify Ops as the Great Mother, recording accurately the Magna Mater cult of late antiquity with which Martianus was no doubt familiar (*De nuptiis* 687; Remi., *In Mart.* 341.15).

Both John Scot and Remigius elaborate the theme of excessive love between wife and husband, expressed in glosses on Janus's wife and Isis. Drawing on the *Saturnalia* of Macrobius, both commentators urge a conventional reading of Janus,[46] but only Remigius offers an innovative reading of Janus's fascination with his "Argive" wife ("Argionam . . . miratur"; oddly, the appellation is usually Juno's). Remigius cites the proverbial expression, "Where love, there is the eye; where pain, there the hand" (presumably to comfort, but possibly also the cause of the pain, just as gazing at the beloved may also result in *amor*: "Quid si miratur? 'Ubi amor, ibi oculus; ubi dolor, ibi manus' "). The Egyptian Isis, Queen of Memphis and daughter of Inachus, king of the Argives, was beset by never-ending grief when her husband Osiris was killed by his brother; John Scot, tells how she had to collect the various pieces for burial from the swamps of Memphis and Styx—John glosses the names as "complaint" or *querela* and "sadness" or *tristitia*, respectively (John Scot, *In Mart.* 6.2). In elaboration of the sadness of the weeping Argive, Remigius describes the swamps of the Styx as infernal. Isis's search for her husband in a sense leads into the next search in *De nuptiis*, that of Mercury for a bride.

Inappropriate Virgins: Pallas Athena, Urania, Psyche

In the section of Martianus's *De nuptiis* devoted to Mercury's search for a bride (par. 7), the narrative material balances genders of the protagonist gods. John Scot in this early section prefers to concentrate on the conventional male deities, and Remigius, ever sensitive here to the gender issue, on the female. Remigius especially again finds of interest female figures such as Maia, Mercury's mother and Atlas's daughter, as well as possible (but ultimately inappropriate) brides such as Psyche, the human soul, for whose birth various gifts are offered (John Scot does however include a long gloss on Maia as mother that Remigius omits). At the end of Martianus's thematic introduction to what follows, Mercury, the protagonist, is impressed by the emphasis upon marriage among the gods and wishes to marry, a desire applauded by his anxious mother Maia who sees him in his youthful prime garbed in an embarrassingly short cape—a sight that amuses Venus. In a psychological interpretation totally ignored by Remigius, the anxious mother of Mercury is glossed as "mater tristis" by John, sad because her only son has not yet begun the search for a wife (John Scot, *In*

Mart. 6.8). She is the *nutrix,* nurse and nourisher (from Isidore, *Etym.* 14.8.17), daughter of Atlas, from "sustinens," holding up or sustaining, and hence mother of the Athlantiades (John Scot, *In Mart.* 24.9). Instead of exploring this psychological gloss in full, Remigius admits Maia's anxiety briefly but chiefly defines her only as one of the seven Pleiades (stars), daughters of Atlas (*De nuptiis* 5; Remi., *In Mart.* 6.9), an astrological background he introduces to explain the interesting narrative situation involving Mercury (a planet) greeting his mother (a constellation).

Early definitions of Pallas Athena in glosses on book 1 are embellished later in the commentaries, especially her strength as goddess of wisdom and her identity as daughter of Jove, Stoic World Soul.[47] In book 1, Martianus says that Mercury fears offending Pallas Athena because, however much he desired her foster-sister Sophia (or Wisdom) as a bride, he must reject her because of her commitment to virginity (*De nuptiis* 6). John Scot prefers to single out Mercury's nature as eloquence, the sign of intelligence in human kind (John Scot, *In Mart.* 6.20),[48] whereas Remigius instead engages in a long gloss on Pallas Athena, in many ways the most important deity in his commentary, in a discussion of the birth gifts of various gods to Psyche. Although John will in fact take up this deity epitomizing the Carolingian ideal of wisdom (John Scot, *In Mart.* 7.10, and continuing in 7.16), Pallas Athena reappears at different, crucial moments throughout the entire satura, especially in book 6 (geometry) and book 9 (music).

A goddess whose three names of Tritonia, Minerva, and Athena express different attributes or faculties, the Greek Pallas—from the name of the giant whom she killed in the Tritonian swamps—represents wisdom because it destroys the stupidity lying in the mud of miserable ignorance: "sapientia interficit stultitiam iacentem in luto miserabilis ignorantiae" (Remi., *In Mart.* 7.3). Remigius here incorporates John's gloss on Pallas: when John declares that Pallas represents the always new, "Pallas nova interpretatur" (John Scot, *In Mart.* 7.16), Remigius moralizes, explaining that wisdom suffers no old age, "sapientia enim nullam admittit vetustatem, nullumque senium" (Remi., *In Mart.* 7.3). Remigius's other glosses on Pallas's names are more or less the same as John's. Tritonia comes from the Greek *trito noia,* or in Latin *tertia notitia;* for Remigius this "tripartite knowledge" is of God, the soul, and the creature ("Deum, animam, et creaturam"), but for the more theologically oriented John, the term recalls three faculties of the rational soul ("sensus ratio animus") and its association with virtue.[49] The human soul Psyche, like Minerva, participates in the eternal, that without corruption, as symbolized in *De nuptiis* by the gift that Pallas offers to Psyche—a red veil and breastband from her own bosom. So also Remigius, drawing on John, explains "Tritonia" as wisdom and eternity, who is said to be a virgin because she never receives corruption, but always enjoys wholeness—literally, integrity: "sed perpetua gaudet integritate" (Remi., *In Mart.* 7.16). In a definition that will pass down to the fourteenth-century Robert Holkot, the Latin "Minerva" indeed means "not mortal," from the Greek (*mi,* or *non,* and *erva,* or *mortalis*). Both commentators add a Fulgentian etymology (*Mit.* 2.1) of Athena as *immortalis,* from the Greek "athanate" (John Scot, *In Mart.* 7.16; Remi., *In Mart.* 7.3).

The wisdom Pallas Athena represents is situated within an earthly and heavenly context related through the plane of correspondence between microcosm and macrocosm. In the invocation to book 6 of *De nuptiis,* the "armed virgin" Pallas as wisdom (see figure 18, in illustration of the text, "Virgo armata decens, rerum sapientia, Pallas," *De nuptiis* 567), appropriately governs on earth as goddess of the arts, *dea artium.* She is described by Remigius as three-fold, in that all discourse consists of the arts of the trivium used to describe the other four arts, the quadrivium, which depend upon the faculty of understanding; "mathematics, that is, theoretical knowledge, is composed of these."[50] In the heavens her ontological nature as ardent flame reveals her kinship to Stoic concepts of celestial fire. As daughter of Jove, said to have been born from Jove's head, she signifies the highest and simplest fire; Jove is aether and "ingenium iqneum est, quod fovetur Pallade, id est sapientia" ["all memory, wit, is fire kindled by wisdom"]. This sexless engendering will perhaps catalyze the later androgyny of her numerical association with "seven": in book 7 (arithmetic) this is her number according to Remigius because, like the prime number seven, wisdom springs from no number and because seven results from the combination of male three with female four, and Pallas, the mannish goddess, is described as a strong virgin who overcame the giant of the same name (*De nuptiis* 738, Remi., *In Mart.* 372.17).

The idea that wisdom is powerful, emblematized by Minerva as an *armed virgin,* suggests the usefulness of knowledge as means of self-defense that leads to peace. For this reason, the Gorgon Medusa glares from Minerva's breast: to suggest the stunning paralysis caused by the power of knowledge (Remi., *In Mart.* 286.10, on *De nuptiis* 572). In addition, the competition between Minerva and Neptune over the naming of Athens argues for her peaceful role. Said by Martianus to have as a sign the olive because through

18. Pallas Athena. "Virgo armata decens, rerum sapientia, Pallas." From Remigius of Auxerre on Martianus. MS. 177, fol. 14r (10th–12th c.). By permission of Österreichische Nationalbibliothek, Heldenplatz, Austria.

her the disciplines of learning are acquired by vigils at oil lamps whose oil is fueled by the olive, Minerva in Remigius comes to supervise nocturnal labor because of her connection with the olive tree as a symbol of peace. Awarded the naming of the city she and Neptune had jointly built after a dispute settled by the gods (Remi., *In Mart.* 286.5, on *De nuptiis* 570), she was deemed by the gods to have offered the better gift to the human race: when Neptune produced the horse for war, Minerva, throwing down the lance, created the olive to be used as a sign of peace.

Psyche, the human soul, like Pallas Athena is an inappropriate virgin (*De nuptiis* 7). Her attractions as a potential bride for Mercury include her celestial endowments relating to wisdom, foresight, and imagination (the gifts of Juno and Minerva, Apollo, and Vulcan); an important drawback is the mixed blessing of desire for good that can be subverted by the influence of the body (Venus and Cupid). Martianus's allegorization of human psychology centers on the event of Psyche's birth, for which the gods' gifts include Juno's golden hair-band (reason), Minerva's gift of the red mantle (the three parts of the soul), Apollo's laurel branch or "wand of foresight" that reveals birds, lightning, the motion of heavens and stars. (For John, and later Remigius, the laurel represents the virtue or power of divination and conjecture, "divinationis et coniecturae virtutem," thus indicating divine instinct [Apollo] uses natural power in divining; John Scot, *In Mart.* 7.19). Because the soul was thought to originate from the heavens, Urania gives Psyche a mirror in which she can see herself and understand her origins; this has been hung in her room by Sophia, or Wisdom, and offered by Urania, Muse of Astronomy. "Urania," according to John, comes either from the Greek word for "recognitio," (recognition or recollection, as in self-examination) or from the Greek word for "libertas" (in that the power to recognize one's origins in the image and likeness of the creator occurs through *free* will; John Scot, *In Mart.* 8.1). Vulcan, the craftsman of Lemnos and brother of Jove, gives Psyche little flames that always burn, to light up shadows and the night; for both John and Remigius, who draw on Augustine's *De civitate Dei* (7.16), Vulcan represents another aspect of the World Soul: destructive earthly fire, related to aether, or Jove, the equivalent on earth of Jove in the heavens (Remi. and John Scot, *In Mart.* 8.4).

A Neo-Stoic version of Original Sin, the myth of Vulcan married to Venus who bears as her son Cupid reveals the ambiguous blessing to humankind of imagination and desire. Vulcan is not only brother to Jupiter (aether) but also son of Juno (air) (Remi., *In Mart.* 37.6, on *De nuptiis* 87), a combination of the celestial and earthly whose birth distorted his form and nature (that is, he is depicted as limping because fire is never upright; he was injured as he was hurled from the aether to earth at birth). John and Remigius offer the Neo-Stoic and *in bono* view of Vulcan's gift to Psyche of earthly fire: the *terrenus ignis* "expels the shadows of human ignorance" and represents *ingenium,* the memory, wit, or imagination born with every man ("sub figura generalis ingenii ponitur, ex quo veluti quidam igniculi ad expellendas ignorantie nebulas rationabili incenduntur naturae," John Scot, *In Mart.* 8.4).[51]

But the Neoplatonic, *in malo,* view of Vulcan as husband of Venus is expressed by John as the heat of pleasure, from whence "the Lemnian" Vulcan may be understood "quasi limnium, id est stagnosum" ["as a stagnant swamp"], "ut per hoc intelligas non alibi ardorem libidinis habitare, nisi in paludosis {locis} carnalis concupiscentiae ubi veluti quidam venere miscetur" ["so that through this it is understood that the ardor of desire dwells nowhere else but in the swampy places of carnal lust where it is mixed with sexual desire"] (John Scot, *In Mart.* 8.4). For Remigius, because as earthly fire Vulcan represents obscene desire, he is depicted as the husband of Venus ("Ponitur etiam Vulcanus pro igne obscenae cupiditatis, unde et Veneris fingitur maritus"). He is dirty, "lutosus" or full of mud (earthy), hence well called Lemnius, because obscene pleasure exists in muddy and unclean minds ("Et bene LEMNIUS lutosus vocatur quia obscena voluptas in lutosis et in immundis mentibus versatur" (Remi., *In Mart.* 8.4).

The gifts to the human soul of Vulcan's wife Venus, or Aphrodite—all the pleasures available to the senses, ointment, garlands, an appreciation for perfume and honey, desire for gold and jewelry, rattles and bells to lull a baby to sleep, and especially Pleasure, to provide desire through titillation—similarly offer a mixed blessing because of the ambiguity of pleasure as a good. Her origin explains this mixed blessing: Aphrodite's name is derived by John from the Greek for *spumea* or foam, in that she was born "de spumis castrati Saturni," that is, from the "foam" of castrated Saturn.[52] The Cyprian is glossed by John as "mixtura," or intercourse, in that "Phisici enim miscendorum seminum potentiam ipsi stelle quae Venus dicitur attribuunt" ["Physicians attribute to the star Venus the power of mixing seeds"] (John Scot, *In Mart.* 6.16). Following the Neo-Stoic view, John explains the foam, "spumas ferventium, as "seminum sive animalium sive aliarum rerum quibus nascuntur omnia quae in hoc mundo oriri videntur significat, ubi intelligendum quod praefata dona superiorum numinum bonas ac naturales humanae animae virtutes insinuant, que non aliunde nisi ex bonorum hominum causa et principio procedunt" ["seeds or spirits or other things of which are born everything that can be seen in this world"], in short, a kind of generative fiery seed, so that the gifts of Venus, *in bono,* can also be "understood as the natural good powers of the human soul that come only from the good deeds of men" (John Scot, *In Mart.* 8.8). Perceived *in malo,* such natural powers are often tainted by a Neoplatonic form of Original Sin and thus such gifts can reflect "general and specific desire" (John Scot, *In Mart.* 8.8). The desires which she governs and which she stimulates in Psyche prompt John to think of the seeds of Venus as those associated with Original (and mortal) sin, such as concupiscence, lasciviousness, and avarice. John's more moralistic and theological emphasis on Venus is softened by Remigius in a gloss otherwise basically the same.[53]

The dangers of pleasure culminate in the subversion of the soul by Cupid, Venus's son; in Martianus's allegory, Cupid takes Psyche from Virtue and shackles her in adamantine chains (*De nuptiis* 7). In a paraphrase of the Ovidian description of Cupid adopted by both Isidore and Theodulf, John Scot explains that the virtues of the soul are ambushed by the arrows of vice, "Faretratus deus CUPIDO dicitur quia virtutibus animae quatinus eas sagittis vitiorum interimat insidiatur" (John Scot, *In Mart.* 9.1).[54] Remigius follows Theodulf even more closely, echoing "De libris": the son of Venus "Fingitur alatus, nudus, puer esse Cupido / Ferre arcum et pharetram" ["is depicted as a nude, winged boy, bearing a quiver"] ("De libris" 33–34). He is nude, "quia turpitudo a nudis peragitur, vel quia nihil secretum est in turpitudine" ["because for shameful deeds one must be naked, or because nothing is secret in turpitude"] (Remi., *In Mart.* 8.22). He is winged with a quiver, "quia turpis amor et velociter pertransit et mentem stimulat conscientia perpetrati criminis" ["because immoral love passes quickly, and the guilty knowledge of a crime committed pricks the mind"]. He appears boyish, "quia turpis amor puerilis est et sic in amantibus sermo deficit sicut in pueris" ["because immoral love is childish and speech {conversation} is wanting in lovers, as in children"].

At this point Remigius invokes the Virgilian context of the fourth book of the *Aeneid*, when Dido starts to speak to Aeneas but falls mute in mid-word ("Incipit effari, mediaque in voce resistit," *Aeneid* 4.76). This mute state is reminiscent of Theodulf's use of Dido's cupidinous silence. Such an association helps to explain a later gloss on Cupid, in book 7 of *De nuptiis* (arithmetic): in the text various whispering muttering deities are enjoined to silence by a black boy, identified by the modern translator as Harpocrates, the Egyptian sun god Horus who as a youth was regarded by the Greeks and Romans as the god of silence (*De nuptiis* 729; tr. Stahl p. 275n19), but by Remigius as Cupid, who is black "because he renders love foul, or because the practitioners of such voluptuous practices seek after the shadows and obscure places" (Remi., *In Mart.* 366.8).

The Escape to the Masculine:
Mercury and Apollo's Ascent to
Father Jupiter and the Assembly of Gods

The problematic of the search for the female and of the feminine domination implied by the existence of Hymen as a necessary cosmological principle leads to a reaction—flight toward, or escape to, the masculine, as incarnated in the aetherial paterfamilias Jupiter and his phallogocentric judiciary powers. The assembly of gods gathered to debate the choice of a bride—the validation of the female by the male—in its very assembly reduplicates the patriarchal cosmic hierarchy (that is, reduplicates and reinforces the masculine). Within this mutually reinforced masculine ascent the mapping of the heavens reinforces as well the principle of genealogy associated with creational history and the hegemony of patriarchy within the universe.

That Mercury and Apollo are *fleeing* what might be termed their impotence in the face of the necessity of the female and *returning* to a masculine empowerment is imaged in Martianus by an emphasis upon (phallic) rods, the failure of (masculine) ratiocination, and the omnipresence of a (female, mutable) cave and its Sibyl. These sons of Jupiter, Mercury as messenger of the gods, or eloquence, and Apollo as divination and truth, conjoin because Mercury needs advice from Apollo about a bride, and Mercury therefore gives his caduceus to Virtue (*De nuptiis* 9), after which he and Virtue inquire about Apollo's whereabouts in the cave of the Sibyl ("divinum consilium," according to John Scot, *In Mart.* 9.22). Of Mercury's serpent–entwined caduceus Remigius says that it is the staff of heralds, signifying a peaceful embassy; Mercury is said to have a wand "because the speech of eloquence ought to proceed by the straight path of reason and its very manifest duty of speaking forth; or because the star of Mercury does not, like certain planets, go through the curving movements of an arc when it is with the sun, but is borne on a straight path crossing only eight parts of the latitude of the zodiac" (Remi., *In Mart.* 9.11).

In Martianus, Apollo's failure and impotence are greater than those of Mercury, although Remigius and John reinforce a more positive reading of Mercury's willingness to accept and incorporate the feminine, rather than to retreat from it, by means of the conventional allegorizations by Macrobius and Fulgentius of the Pythian and the places with which he is associated (Delos, Licia, Helicon, Parnassus).[55] When Mercury finally finds Apollo near Delphi and thus close to the symbolic and regenerative peak of

Parnassus, the Pythian, "distressed by contact with those who sought his advice, had long ago given up his reputation as a prophet" (*De nuptiis* 10).

Both Remigius and John gloss the cave of Apollo, but Remigius develops its feminine aspect more strongly; he describes this temple of Apollo as part of the country of Cumae in which the powerful Sibyl ("Iovis consilium," plan of Jove) practiced her oracular craft ("vaticinabatur," Remi., *In Mart.* 9.22). Even Apollo's original triumph in mastering the phallic Python is subverted by Remigius, who glosses "the Pythian" in terms of the serpent he has killed but also because of the Greek for "to question," *pytho,* or *interrogo* (Remi., *In Mart.* 10.6), "because men asked questions of, consulted, Apollo"—as did Nero, once, disastrously for Apollo. "Apollo had given the response that Nero would be killed by the Roman people. Therefore Nero, fearing lest the divinity's authority would make the people more bold to accomplish this, ordered the god's temples to be closed. Being thus offended, Apollo scorned to be called 'augur.' "[56] In the cave, in line with Apollo's demoralized departure, they also find the discarded accoutrements of his profession—old laurel and ivy, a rotting tripod, mildewed sandals and an account of prophecies. Even Apollo's sturdy tripod sends feminized visions, of a prophetic nature, to the dreamer (*De nuptiis* 10; Remi., *In Mart.* 10.6; compare John Scot, *In Mart.* 10.8).[57]

In an ever-increasing, desperate attempt to escape his own impotence in the face of female necessity, Apollo later moves to "an Indian mountain's secret crag" (*De nuptiis* 11), which Remigius identifies as Nisa; "the Cirrhaean retreat," for Remigius the recesses of a mountain of "Archadia" in whose cave cluster the vicissitudes of the ages, is visited by Mercury and Virtue. Martianus's curious imaginative allegory of the prophetic hollows of the (female and womblike) cave grants a vision of both time and eternity in the ages and the music of the gods (or the harmony of the spheres)—he captures the Macrobian descent of the soul through the spheres along with the afterlife return. Seven rivers of different colors flowing from heaven nearby this cave represent the Neoplatonic system of planetary influences on character and destiny, according to John Scot, who uses as sources Isidore (*Etym.* 3.4) and Macrobius (*Somn. Scip.* 1.12)—slowness, Saturn; sanity, Jove; furor, Mars; vital motion, the sun; beauty, Venus; agility, Mercury; and bodily humors, or growth, the moon.[58] In a gloss added by Remigius, souls, after leaving the body, depending on their merit during life, travel either to be punished, "puniri," or cleansed, "purgari," within the seven spheres: below the circle of the moon is the underworld, the "infernum" (Remi., *In Mart.* 13.6), with its fiery river Phlegethon (used by

Dante in the *Inferno*) that originates from the sphere of Mars ("in Martis circulo dicunt oriri"). "The Elysian fields, where cleansed souls rest, is located below the circle of Jove. The Platonic sect says that the cleansed souls again return to bodies, there to be re-polluted by the substance of the body and begin to need cleansing again."[59] The message to Apollo and Mercury is to reiterate the cosmic context of the Eternal Mother.

The triumph of the celestial female is Neo-Stoic: the rejuvenation of nature through the "seeds of creation" is facilitated by the sun, or Apollo, whose movements control and guide the four seasons (*De nuptiis* 16–19). Apollo sits high above on the other side of the rivers, holding four closed jars (iron, silver, lead, and glass) containing the four elements—the "seeds of creation," according to Martianus—of fire, air, water, and earth. Each jar has a mythic name and is tied to one of the four seasons. According to the commentators, the iron jar of summer is called Mulcifer's (or Vulcan's) Whirlwind, etymologically as if "mulcens" or "mollificans ferrum," from melting or softening iron; fire indeed can soften the hardest iron, which in Remigius links the earthly fire of Vulcan causing storms to Jove's aetherial fire of creation (Remi. and John Scot, *In Mart.* 14.11). The silver jar of spring in the commentators is called Jove's Smile because all the world (that is, Jove) laughs in springtime, which is when his serenity is first manifested in its annual course (John Scot, *In Mart.* 14.14; Remi., *In Mart.* 14.13); for Remigius, this is a serene time of temperate air when "the earth regenerates itself, the sky is bright, the sea is calm." The lead jar of winter is called Saturn's Ruin and in John is used as a pretext for introducing the Venus and Adonis myth understood (from Macrobius's *Sat.* 1.21.1–4), as a sun or vegetation myth which ends in tears (John Scot, *In Mart.* 14.16). Adonis represents the sun, the boar represents the defilement (*spurcitia*) of winter, and Venus mourning when the sun recedes (or is obscured) in winter is a pathetic fallacy for wintry bluster, or crying rivers of tears; Remigius repeats the myth and adds that Venus complains tearfully for the missing Adonis, or the sun, because she signifies the beauty of earth which produces, as we know, the tears of rain and rivers.[60] The glass jar of autumn, containing seeds of air, is called Juno's Bosom because, according to John, in this season all seeds of fruit mature ("autumn" from "autumnando," or maturing, "maturando fruges," John and also Remi., *In Mart.* 14.16). Because Apollo has the power to send either healthy breezes from these jars or dread pestilence, when humans want to avert a plague they can recite this Greek verse, "Long-haired Phoebus dispels the cloud of Pestilence," first addressing Mercury but also submitting to the Clarian Apollo (*De nuptiis* 19; commentary 15.7).

Rejuvenated by this reaffirmation of his role as cosmic moderator (a more feminized function than that of tyrannical rule but one without which the universe could not continue), Apollo recommends Philology as a bride, upon which Virtue convinces Mercury and Apollo that they should ascend to Jove to ask his permission for Mercury to marry Philology. Indeed, as they ascend, they are escorted by the nine (female) Muses, each of whom is associated with one of the nine planetary spheres (Martianus begins from the outermost sphere of the fixed stars and Urania, representing astronomy, and ends with the earth and Thalia, as Muse of comedy, *De nuptiis* 27). The reason for this association is that these are "the nine sounds made by the lyre of Jove, or the world" ("hoc est novem sonorum liram Iovis, id est mundus, dicitur habere," John Scot, *In Mart.* 19.17). The detailed Greek etymological definitions of the Muses derive primarily from Fulgentius (*Mit.* 1.15); they explain more about the planetary spheres involved than about the Muses themselves.[61]

Mercury's flight from the feminine is also accompanied by a warning of the danger in feminizing (read: perverting, diverting) his function as god of eloquence. This danger is epitomized in Hermaphroditus, Mercury's bastard son from a liaison with Venus, identified by the commentators as the monster of lascivious speech. This bastard son is introduced in the narrative when Apollo and Mercury reach Jove's palace, notice that Juno keeps close to Jove, and ask her for her opinion; among other reasons she accedes because she fears Mercury may succumb to Venus's wiles and sire a brother for Hermaphroditus (*De nuptiis* 34). This name (declare the commentators) combines his parents' Greek names, Hermes and Aphrodite (Remi and John Scot, *In Mart.* 22.16; probably from Isidore, *Etym.* 11.3.11). Remigius adds a long gloss on Hermaphroditus as an androgynous figure who signifies eloquence bent to lascivious ends, largely because of the influence of his maternal origin.

> Venus autem Afrodite dicitur, hoc est spumea, quia peracta voluptas instar spumae deletur et citissime praeterit nihilque suum nisi poenitudinis stimulum in conscientia derelinquit. Ermafroditos autem dicimus homines utriusque sexus quos et androgios vocamus; aner enim vel ander Grece vir, ginex mulier. Ermafroditus autem significat quandam sermonis lascivitatem, qua plerumque neglecta veritatis ratione superfluous sermonis ornatus requiritur.

[Moreover Venus is called Aphrodite, that is foam, because when passion is sated, like foam it is destroyed and passes quickly away, leaving nothing of itself except the prick of repentance in the conscience. We give the name Hermaphrodite to persons having both sexes, and call them androgynous; for *aner* or *ander* in Greek means "man," and *ginex,* "woman." Moreover Hermaphrodite signifies a certain wantonness of speech, where generally, disregarding the reason of truth, a superfluous ornamentation of speech is sought.] (Remi., *In Mart.* 22.16)

Juno approves of their request for many other reasons, one of which is that Mercury had once nursed at her breast, receiving a "draught of immortality" there (*De nuptiis* 34). The latter event is explained by Remigius: "Et bene Iunonis uberibus Mercurius dicitur educatus quia sermo, voce ex aere percusso formata, quodam modo perficitur atque nutritur" [that is, as "education, in that speech {Mercury} formed by percussion in air [Juno] is therefore in some mode perfected and nourished by her"] Remi., *In Mart.* 22.12). Astrologically, Remigius notes that Mercury was apparently sent to her by Maia in May when the sun was in Taurus and the air was warm. Another reason to agree that she is pleased is because Phoebus, "who usually brought her calmness," has asked her and he has also brought her daughters the Muses hither; she generally likes marriages and is ruler of marriages (*De nuptiis* 34; Remi., *In Mart.* 20.18); Apollo has addressed Juno as "Pronuba," "supporter" (*De nuptiis* 31), which epithet is explained by John because she is the tutelary of marriage ("nuptiarum ministra," John Scot, *In Mart.* 21.5; in Remigius, she is "paranimpha et ministra nuptiarum," Remi., *In Mart.* 21.4).

While Juno then uses her influence to deliberate the matter with Jupiter, Pallas drifts down (*De nuptiis* 39);[62] she demurs from advising her father because she is herself a virgin and suggests that the decision to approve the marriage will need to be made by the inhabitants of the heavens—essentially the faculties of Jupiter, both male and female, as World Soul. These *penates* or "senators," the companions of Jove ("intimi et secretales ipsius Iovis," *De nuptiis* 41), are summoned by Jove's scribe, rather logically, to an assembly to discuss the marriage. According to Remigius, "penates" comes from the word *panates,* or "omnia consentientes," "agreeing in all things," their names kept secret because they all agree with Jove, or bind themselves to Jove (Remi., *In Mart.* 26.4); the commentator is glossing Martianus's explanation that, "because they were bound by mutual promises in every respect, [Jove] gave the group a name derived from their union [consentes]" (*De nuptiis* 41).

The Stoic World Soul explained by means of this "consensus" of Jovian faculties, Remigius turns next to the twelve "select gods," the Greek and Roman Olympians also invited to the assembly, who balance female and male in their numbers.[63] Listed in Martianus within a couplet from Ennius which is repeated by John (*In Mart.* 26.11) and by Remigius (*In Mart.* 26.13), the gods include all but Saturn and the moon, John notes (26.12). Both commentators acknowledge St. Augustine's *De civitate Dei* (7.2–3) as a source for the powerful seven (Juno, Vesta, Minerva, Ceres, Diana, Venus, Mars in the first line of Ennius's couplet) and five (Mercury, Jupiter, Neptune, Vulcan, Apollo, in the second). Originally, in Augustine's source Varro, the select gods numbered twenty—twelve male gods, Janus, Jove, Saturn, Genius, Mercury, Apollo, Mars, Vulcan, Neptune, Sol, Orcus, and Liber Pater, and the eight female gods, Tellus, Juno, Luna, Diana, Minerva, Venus, Vesta, and Ceres (Remi., *In Mart.* 26.15; Augustine (but not Remigius, or at least not in this book) goes on to discuss Varro's presentation of the role of male and female gods in engendering all life in the universe. Because the invited deities are described by Martianus as occupying sixteen regions of the heavens (*De nuptiis* 45–56), the guest-list thus provides ample opportunity for Remigius to comment on each at length, but he does not take advantage of it. Martianus includes some very obscure gods and some Etruscan gods[64] which failed to interest the later Middle Ages, while the select gods have already been fully glossed, either in Martianus's own text or in Macrobius and Isidore.[65] Both obscure and well-known gods jostle with personifications (Fortune, Health, Goodwill, Swiftness) and with the old Italian households gods refurbished by the Stoics and the emperors (Vesta, Genius, the Manes, various Lares).

Martianus then relists the gods by means of their narrative entry into the assembly according to the Stoic concept of elemental matter (aether, air, water, earth) with a genealogical order more closely tied to the Isidorian classification in the *Etymologiae*. Because of this more deliberately focused Stoic emphasis the female deities—chiefly, the wives, Ops, Jove's nurse Vesta, Neptune's wife (Thetis, according to John; Styx, according to Remigius), Proserpina—are allowed a more prominent role than in the other late antique narratives and mythographies. The chief gods, led by Saturn and Ops, appear according to their genealogical place within the royal cosmic family, with the brothers of Jove and Saturn's sons, Neptune and Pluto, and their wives, the progeny of Jove, and so forth.

The iconography of Saturn and his wife Ops (*De nuptiis* 70–71) is astrological, Stoic elemental, and religious, as his commentators explain, and sums up the process of cosmic mutability and regeneration. Slowly entering, the white-haired Saturn (though believed to be capable of appearing young again) wears a grey cloak over his head and holds a dragon eating its own tail. For Remigius (Remi., *In Mart.* 33.6–11), he walks slowly "because his star is the slowest, taking thirty years to round its course"; his head covered with a grey cloak signifies his old age and the frigidity of the planet. Representing Time, he carries a dragon in his right hand eating its tail to signify the passing of the year, the beginning of a new year immediately following the end of the preceding, and fire-breathing because it consumes all with flames, as the year does everything which it produces. He has white hair, though Saturn is believed to be capable of being young, because of the frigidity of winter, and because the year grows old in winter but comes young in spring.

Ops, "a full-bodied old mother" ("grandaeva corpulentaque mater," *De nupt.* 71, my translation), might very well be for Martianus the Magna Mater herself. John explains that she is "Terra autem semper fecunda est diversis rerum nascentium generibus ac veluti palla quadam herbarum diversitatibus vestitur" that is, Terra, from whose coupling with Saturn the other gods were born; her flowery dress covered with a green mantle inscribed with the crops from the fields signifies the diverse classes for things born and the veil for the diversity of plants (John Scot, *In Mart.* 33.12). Remigius finds her "full-bodied" because "terrae elementum crassius et corpulentius est caeteris," ["the elements of earth are heavy and full-bodied"] (Remi., *In Mart.* 33.12); she is called "mother" because "earth is the mother of all" ("est terra mater omnium"). In Martianus "ever so prolific and surrounded by her offspring" (*De nuptiis* 71), Ops in Remigius expresses her fecundity by means of her many children.

Vesta, as old as Ops, accompanies her (*De nuptiis* 72) and is the granddaughter of Rhea, daughter of Saturn, who functions as goddess of flocks and of the household. Also a goddess of fire in Remigius, she is said to be Jove's nurse "quia ferunt philosophi terreno igni caelestem nutriri" ["because philosophers believe earthly fire nurtured the heavenly"] (Remi., *In Mart.* 33.18). But hers differs from the aethereal and celestial fire of Jove, or the destructive earthly fire of Vulcan: John declares that hers is the fire which aids human civilization, so that she clings to Ops (Earth)

because fire is always nourished by earthly matter ("Veteres siquidem
Vestam dicebant flammam humanis usibus necessarium quae Opi, id est
Terre, adherebat quia terrena materia semper nutritur," John Scot, *In Mart.*
33.14); in Remigius, the stories relate that she is the nourisher (nurse) of
the gods, because the vigor of earthly fire raises "vapors" up from the earth
and the water; and by these vapors the stars are nourished, according to the
scientists ("fisici"; from *Etym.* 3.49). Later on, Isidore will be used by
Remigius and John to differentiate the functions of each god in a comment on
Martianus's Vulcan (*De nuptiis* 87: "Jove is aether pure and simple; Vulcan is
destructive or noxious earthly fire, whence he is called 'volicanus,' or volcano,
from 'volans candor'; Vesta is fire used and adapted for mortal use").[66]

After Sol and Luna enter, in come the two brothers of Jove, Neptune and
Pluto, one greener than the sea, the other pale from the dark (*De nuptiis* 78):
their appearance mirrors their conventional physical mythographies as the
regions and elements of water and earth.[67] The wives of each, however,
receive more than the usual mythographic attention from Remigius and
John Scot, as seems to be typical in the commentaries on Martianus, in
their roles as the lower part of water and earth. Neptune brings with him
"the nurse of all things, the hostess of the gods" (*De nuptiis* 81). In John,
Neptune's wife is Thetis (the lower part of the ocean, the earth subject to
the sea, but he adds the possibility that her name may be Styx, the infernal
marsh, because the gods exist or were born and reigned on islands:

> Thethis siquidem inferior pars oceani dicitur vel potius solum maris,
> hoc est terra mari subiecta, unde et nomen accepit Tethis et enim positio
> interpretatur. Alii dicunt Neptuni uxorem Stigem esse, hoc est infer-
> nalem paludem quam et nutricem deorum fabule fingunt, ea opinione
> ducti quia existimant deos in insulis habitasse et regnasse natosque
> fuisse ut Saturnum Iovemque in Creta, Apollinem in Delo et Licia,
> Neptunus quoque in maritimis Grecie partibus regnasse traditur.

> [Thetis is called the lower part of the ocean, or rather, the bed of the
> sea, that is, the earth lying under the sea. This is why she received the
> name Thetis, also interpreted as "position." Others say the wife of
> Neptune is Styx, that is, the underworld swamp which the fables
> describe as the nurse of the gods. They are of this opinion because they
> think that the gods lived and reigned and were born on islands, as it
> is traditionally said that Saturn and Jove reigned on Crete, Apollo in
> Delos and Licia, and Neptune in the maritime regions of Greece.]
> (John Scot, *In Mart.* 36.2).

Remigius agrees with this interpretation of Styx as the wife of Neptune, nurse ("nutrix") and hostess ("hospita") of the gods, "quia omnes dii de terris per purgationem, quam Stix significat, caeleste meruerunt consortium" ["because all the gods received their share of heaven from earth by means of purification, which Styx signifies"] (Remi., *In Mart.* 36.2).

The wife of Pluto, Hecate or Proserpina, is likewise interpreted as an earthly Stoic agent of generation. In Martianus, the wife of Pluto was "overjoyed at the accessions that came to them; she so readily gave the fruits of the earth to those who asked her that mankind swore by a great deity to pay her back one per cent" (*De nuptiis* 81). John identifies her as Echate (Hecate), a girl, that is, a seed-plot or garden, "seminariam" (John Scot, *In Mart.* 36.4). In his Fulgentian explanation, basically repeated by Remigius, she is the fertile earth and mother of plenty ("fertilis terra est copiosissimaque mater frugum") who gives back a hundred times whatever seed is sown, so men dedicate one percent of their crops as a sacrifice, to enhance her good will. She governs the life of herbs and grasses, the seeds of earth, and the forests and pastures that regenerate so fully and generously.[68]

Following their entry come the sons and daughters of Jupiter (but also Saturn's daughter Venus): Mars, Bacchus, the twins Castor and Pollux, and Hercules, then Venus and Diana, Ceres, and Vulcan (*De nuptiis* 82–87). Many of these, especially the female deities at the end, along with Juno, Danaë, Minerva, and the symbol of the Pythagorean Y in book 2, are also glossed in the Terence scholia of the ninth century. In the gloss on Liber-Bacchus as the urbane and seemly companion said to liberate or free (hence "Liber") because wine stimulates the heart (Remi., *In Mart.* 36.9), Remigius then quotes Terence, suggesting that our monk knew or indeed may even have authored the Terence commentary: "Sine Cerere et Libero friget Venus" ("Without bread and wine Venus grows cold," from Terence, *Eunuchus* 732).[69] But the figures most extensively glossed by the Martianus commentators within the group are the female deities Venus, Diana, and Ceres, followed by Vulcan, the son of Juno, whose fiery powers are linked with those of his father as the World Soul; the others (some of which receive greater attention elsewhere in the commentary, for example, Mars) are identified by their conventional astrological and moral functions.[70] Remigius provides glosses at the conclusion of this section especially on Venus and Ceres, barely mentioning Diana, who enters the assembly together with Venus. One the mother of all conception, the other a virgin, the former in Martianus wears a garland of roses and is also the patroness of modesty; the latter carries a bow and quiver (*De nuptiis* 85).

This description, rather strangely, triggers a misogynistic diatribe in John that projects corporality, the problem of the body, onto the female as the object of masculine desire, although it begins conventionally enough: "Venus vero admodum pulcra humanisque generationibus veluti omnium mater delectata fingitur" ["Venus is depicted as beautiful and as taking pleasure in human procreation, being the mother of all"] (John Scot, *In Mart.* 36.17). But then he adds that she is the girl one would like to fondle, and not the wife who injured Vulcan: "Hoc dicit quod poete libidinis et pudicitiae simul principatum mendacissime Veneri adtribuunt. Pudicam quidem eam dicunt ne Vulcano iniuriam facere videantur eius uxorem blasphemantes, libidinosam vero quia meretricum dominam" ["The poets falsely attribute to Venus preeminence in lust and chastity at the same time. Indeed, they call her chaste lest they seem to wrong Vulcan by blaspheming his wife, but lustful because she is the ruler of harlots"] (John Scot, *In Mart.* 37.3). Remigius elaborates on the girl and the wife by presenting two different Venuses, or rather, two attitudes toward desire distinguished by Venus's liaisons with two different gods and her resulting sons, Hermaphroditus and Cupid; the first is illicit, voluptuous desire, the second, legitimate, and honest or chaste love: "Duae namque sunt Veneres, una voluptuaria et libidinum mater quae fertur Ermafroditum genuisse, altera casta quae praeest honestis et licitis amoribus. Duo enim sunt amores; est enim amor castus, est et incestus, quem ad differentiam illius casti pluraliter semper amores dicimus" (Remi., *In Mart.* 37.1). The mother of Hermaphroditus is associated with illicit desire, a role with which Venus is also linked in the Terence scholia;[71] the other Venus governs honest and legitimate love. In his comments on Martianus's second book (*De nuptiis* 144) Remigius will define Venus herself as double:

Duae sunt Veneres, una casta et pudica quae praeest honestis amoribus, quae etiam fertur uxor Vulcani, altera voluptuaria libidinum dea, cuius filius est Ermafroditus. Sic etiam sunt duo amores, alter bonus et pudicus quo virtutes et sapientia amantur, alter impudicus et malus, quem ad distinctionem boni amoris pluraliter amores dicimus.

[There are two Venuses, one pure and chaste, who governs honorable love and is also called the wife of Vulcan; the other, the pleasure-loving goddess of desire, whose son is Hermaphroditus. So also there are two loves, one good and chaste, which loves virtue and wisdom, the other unchaste and evil. To distinguish the latter from the good love, we call it *loves* {*amores*} in the plural.] (Remi., *In Mart.* 62.11)

Two succeeding glosses, on Ceres and Genius, support the commentators' borrowing from (or possible authorship of) the Terence scholia. Remigius accepts John's explanation of Ceres (*De nuptiis* 86) as a mother searching for her abducted daughter Proserpina in the underworld as the mythological basis for his more elaborate definitions of her as the goddess of grain and agriculture, the growth of fruits (John Scot, *In Mart.* 37.4). Ceres as nurse of earth and of men accompanies Venus and Diana "kindly" ("grata"), or as Remigius glosses it, "gratiosa," graciously, in that "through her grace she gives the fruits (of earth) to mortals; a most 'venerable' (*grava*) woman because the earth itself is the heaviest of all elements (*gravissima omnium elementorum*), 'nurse of earth' because she nourishes and is nourished, and also a nurse of men because she grants produce, crops (*fruges*). She is called 'Ceres' as if from *creres*, from creating, whence the ancients called her Bona Dea, the Good Goddess"; Remigius, still thinking of Terence's striking line about love, bread, and wine, adds a quotation from Juvenal, "And they appease the good [goddess] with the fat belly of a tender pig" (Remi., *In Mart.* 37.3).

In John, but not in Remigius, one of the last mythographic references in book 1 seizes upon yet another of those few also found in the Terence scholia—the Genius figure[72]—although the glosses are not at all the same in the two commentaries. In Martianus, Mercury is called "my true genius" by Jupiter (*De nuptiis* 92), a "nomen naturale," for John (John Scot, *In Mart.* 39.14). Because Mercury is the son of Maia and Jupiter, when his father mentions him as "devoted to the honors of his uncles" (*De nuptiis* 92), John explains he means by "uncles" the other planets, since Mercury is messenger of the gods and as a planet moves up and down. He is Jove's *genius,* meaning the active agent of the World Soul charged with the responsibility of regenerating the world,[73] for his uncles' "honors," to which he is devoted, would apparently be distributed to the soul descending through the planetary spheres at birth—beauty from Venus, slowness from Saturn, fervor from Mars, temperance from Jove, motion from Mercury, humors from the moon, and all this from the sun moving through the signs of the zodiac (John Scot, *In Mart.* 40.3).

At the end of book 1, the assembly affirms Jupiter's decision to approve the marriage of these two diverse beings, Mercury and Philology; in addition, Philology is to be offered immortality as a result of her union with a god, which reminds the Carolingian reader that wisdom indeed offers immortality. The heroic apotheosis of wisdom, also found in the

Carolingian Boethius glosses, humanizes Martianus's allegory for its ninth-century readers: the assembly also decides other heroes deserve immortality, specifically, the Trojan or Roman heroes Aeneas and Romulus, "amongst others whom the Nile or Thebes proffered" (*De nuptiis* 95)—Remigius, like John, selects from Egypt Osiris and Isis, and from Thebes, Cadmus (Remi., *In Mart.* 41.1). In the commentators, as they proceed patiently onward with their interpretation of the second book—that which is human rather than divine, full of knowledge rather than eloquent inspiration—the mythography focuses even more intensely on the female deities conventionally relegated in the earlier commentaries to a marginal or secondary position.

III. JUNO'S FEMALE, EARTHLY UNDERWORLD

In the second book of Remigius's commentary appears a reworking of the well-known Servian passage on the Pythagorean Y of the underworld (Servius, *In Aen.* 6.136), although Remigius does not here mention the Virgilian context of the passage. In chapter 6, above, I have discussed the use of this passage in a commentary on the sixth book of the *Aeneid* attributed to Remigius himself (Paris Bibliothèque Nationale, Parisinus 7930). There, the "Y" is linked to nine "islands" of the underworld (see figure 13). Here, in a context of life choices and marriage, paraphrasing Servius Remigius declares,

> Pythagoras namque y litteram ad similitudinem humanae vitae invenit, unde Persius: "Diduxit trepidas ramosa ad compita mentes." Nam y littera ab una virgula incipit et in quoddam bivium finditur. Sic et natura humana in pueritia simplex est nec facile apparet bonum an malum iter apprehendat; in adolescentia vero iam aut virtutes eligit, quae per dexteram virgulam breviorem et angustiorem significantur, aut ad vitia deflectit, quae notantur per sinistram subaudis virgulam latiorem.

> [For Pythagoras {the Samian} found that the letter Y was like human life, hence Persius says {*Satire* 5.35}: "It {error} led my fearful mind astray on branching paths." For the letter Y begins with a stem and is split into a fork. So too, human nature in childhood is simple, and it is not readily apparent whether it will take a good or bad path; but in adolescence now it either chooses virtues, which are indicated by the

shorter and narrower right-hand branch, or turns to vices, which are
denoted by the wider left-hand branch.] (Remi., *In Mart.* 43.18, on
De nuptiis 102)

Because the cosmic underworld is the landscape to be explored in this
book of Martianus, as traveled by his protagonist Philology, the passage is
connected in the commentators with bridegroom Mercury as messenger of
the gods and as psychopomp. One of Philology's rationalizations for the
marriage involves numerology, when she counts the letters in her name and
his, using his Egyptian name Thoth or Thouth (*De nuptiis* 102; see Stahl's
note). This unusual name was picked because it was given to him by Jove
and is known to humankind only through the Egyptians (whose founding
queen Io was responsible for inventing the alphabet while she was incarcerated in the form of a heifer able to communicate only by striking her hoof
against a stone). The third letter of Thouth in Greek (θωύθ) is the upsilon,
or Y, regarded by "the Samian sage" as "representing the dual ambiguity of
human fate," says Martianus. In Remigius, this sage is rightly identified as
Pythagoras, who, tradition says, taught that the letter through its bifur-
cated upper part symbolized the choice between good and evil in human
life. The word Thoth, in short, by means of its upsilon or Y is used to
emblematize the moral hinge of human life: the god Mercury accompanies
the soul after death, and its path at that point is determined by its merit
during its earthly life, leading either to the left or the right.

In Martianus, the god's marriage to Philology, or knowledge, may well
help to inform and guide this journey through the underworld. Drawing
on the Egyptian belief in Thoth as god of wisdom and divine scribe at the
judgment of the dead, Martianus here reasserts a Near Eastern myth that
will, in the glosses of the Carolingians, confirm the Neo-Stoic association
of the underworld with Juno's aerial region. In addition, Remigius's
insertion of the Servian passage on the cosmic spheres as infernal purgatory,
at which dense Neoplatonic center nestles the earth, underscores the moral
nature of human life as vicious and corporally dominated. The medieval
reaction to this Servian idea has resurfaced in various texts, including the
Carolingian scholia on Terence.[74] This concept will be used to structure
the twelfth-century system of descents into an underworld, made by
Orpheus and Aeneas in the glosses on Boethius by William of Conches and
on Virgil by Bernard Silvestris, and also the fifteenth-century journey of
Aeneas in the work of Cristoforo Landino.

Philology's journey is described in Martianus by means of the Neoplatonic image of the soul's purgation or punishment in the afterlife—in effect, the journey to the other world after death—that here begins with the underworld. Thus, Philology, after realizing the numerical concord between her name and Mercury's, anoints herself with an ointment given her by "the old man of Abdera" (Saturn, according to the commentators, *In Mart.* 46.15) to protect her mortal limbs from the fires of the stars as she ascends through the spheres (*De nuptiis* 110; in John, the spheres represent the virtues by which the soul is liberated to love of the eternal, John Scot, *In Mart.* 46.16). But in fact, after she dresses, Aurora appears, and "sleep flees to Lethean shores" (*De nuptiis* 116), that is, to the river of the underworld: "Lethe" from Greek means "sleepiness or oblivion," the river from which they say souls drink forgetfulness as they pass on into bodies (Remi., *In Mart.* 49.5).

And other references to the underworld surface, if indirectly. One convoluted reference (*De nuptiis* 119) turns on the image of the psychological hell of earthly irrationality and vice (an idea explored in the commentaries on Boethius discussed in chapter 6) which wisdom can set right. When the Muses sing for her, Calliope refers to the "the fountain of the Gorgonian horse," Pegasus, who struck the ground with his hoof and created Helicon, the fountain that inspires the Muses; Pegasus is "Gorgonian," in the commentary of Remigius, because he was born from the blood of the Gorgon, or "terror." The three Gorgons represent the three kinds of terror—weakness, madness, oblivion (*debilitas, stupor* or *amentia, oblivio*)—overcome by Perseus and his crystalline shield and sickle-shaped sword with the aid of Pallas Athena, wisdom (from Fulgentius, *Mit.* 1.21, cited by name in Remi., *In Mart.* 50.16).[75] Tartarus (*De nuptiis* 126) is glossed by Remigius as a "lower circle" to which the planet Mercury descends when he is retrograde, almost to the border of the lunar circle ("ad confinium lunaris circuli descendit," Remi., *In Mart.* 55.15); Mercury returns there at the moment when the Muse Thalia, as the Muses address Philology, praises Philology's bridegroom. Apparently as the guide for the soul in the afterlife Mercury functions as the shade Virgil to the Dante-like soul. The underworld now has come to denote that area beneath the moon where earth and sea are found; for Mercury "has power over those areas," for which reason he returns to them: "quia ipse habet virtutem in terra et in mari" (Remi., *In Mart.* 55.15).

Because of such life-and-death power Mercury, as he moves in his life-journey, also restores, or can restore, the fortunes of Osiris glossed as the king of Egypt, husband of Isis, "qui apud Aegyptios cultum vinearum repperit" ["who among the Egyptians invented the cultivation of vine-yards"] (Remi., *In Mart.* 55.21; see, however, *De nuptiis* 158), as did Liber among the Indians. Martianus declares that Jove knows Osiris is weighted down by "sationibus genitalibus" ["the life-giving seed"] (*De nuptiis* 126) which Mercury has discovered. Remigius, rewording John, explains that "[Mercury] ipse praeest seminibus, et per ipsum discernitur quo tempore debeant gravari vineae foetibus vel quo tempore putari vel coli" ["Mercury rules over the seeds, and through him it is decided at what time the vines ought to be heavy with fruit and at what time they should be pruned or cultivated"] (Remi., *In Mart.* 55.21).

Because of Philology's drink from the cup of immortality, she will never "behold Vedius and his wife" (*De nuptiis* 142), that is, she will no longer be human, or bound by the condition of her body. Vedius controls that corporal underworld and its flux. Vedius, correctly glossed by Remigius (*In Mart.* 61.20), is Pluto or Orcus and his wife is Proserpina or Allecto; Philology is now free from the mortal condition and will not see Pluto and his wife, and her soul will not leave her body (and she will not therefore have to fret over her earthly sins as she would if she were to be judged in the afterlife by Pluto as Orcus).[76] Accordingly, the Eumenides, the Chaldean manifestations Philology will no longer fear, are glossed as "Furiae infer-nales," "the infernal furies" who "meet the souls and torture them. Moreover they are called Eumenides by antiphrasis, that is, good goddesses instead of bad ones" (Remi., *In Mart.* 61.24).

Philology must no longer worry about the femaleness of her body, an idea signaled by the approach of Juno, goddess of wives and mothers. Philology addresses her as "*Juno* because of your help" ("a juvando," *De nuptiis* 149); indeed, in Remigius, she is called the helper because "no animal can live without the air" she represents (Remi., *In Mart.* 63.10). But virgin Philology adds that those who have suffered physical pollution also call Juno other names, such as Lucina, or Lucetia, Fluvonia, Februalis, and Februa—that is, women who have participated in earthly and cyclical processes of renewal, including mothers and brides (*De nuptiis* 149; see Stahl's note). So in his comment on these names Remigius explains Fluvonia from the contraceptive use of the discharges of seeds to free women from childbirth ("a fluoribus seminum quia liberat feminas a partu"), a concept (according to Martianus's translator Stahl) connected with the menstrual flow (*fluere,* to flow) and with Juno Fluvonia as patron of pregnancy because it was believed the menstrual flow nourished the fetus. Juno Februalis or Februa purifies women when the after-birth emerges ("FEBRUALEM vel FEBRUAM quia purgat eas post partum secundis egredientibus"), "Februo" being a Greek word meaning "I purge" and "Februus" referring to Pluto "because he governs purgations" ("Februo Grecum verbum est, Latine purgo, hinc et Februus dicitur Pluto quia praeest purgationibus," Remi., *In Mart.* 63.12)

Brides summon Juno, Philology continues, as Iterduca or Domiduca, for she protects their journeys and brings them to the houses of husbands; as Unxia because she puts a favorable sign on anointed doorposts; as Cinctia when brides remove their girdles, or *cingulus* (*De nuptiis* 149). Remigius offers obvious and less-obvious etymologies (Remi., *In Mart.* 63.16). In addition, those whom Juno protects during the crisis ("in bello") of childbirth call her Opigena (*De nuptiis* 149; but the name is Saticena or Soticena in John and Remigius). The commentators cite the *Aeneid* ("At non in Venerem segnes nocturnaque bella") to explain the "nightly battle of the bed" that results in the work of birth (*Aeneid* 11.736). The feminine counterpart of Saturn, Saticena is so called from *satio*, "planting," and as Saturn frees the men from marriage, Juno frees the women ("dictam quia Saturnus liberat mares de nuptiis, Iuno vero feminas," Remi., *In Mart.* 64.1); Soticena is so called from *sociando*, that is, because she joins man and woman (John Scot, *In Mart.* 64.2).

Juno rules the air, the region by some scholars defined as the sublunary region beneath the moon into which individuals are born; when Philology calls her Hera, "named from your kingdom of the air," the words "Hera" and "air" are spelled with the same Greek letters (*De nuptiis* 149). This ancient definition of the goddess has previously prompted ingenious etymological connections, in mythological discussions by Augustine and Isidore, between Hera and the *hero,* the shade of the worthy mortal who inhabits her region, although only Martin of Laon relates the goddess to the spirit: the "Heroes" are called so because of their association with earth, whose master is Hera ("HERAM id est terram dominam antiquam," Dunchad, *In Mart.* 67.20, on *De nuptiis* 160). The Martianus commentators who understand this background seem to enjoy their elaborations on the kin of the *hero*. Indeed, one of Juno's other names is Curitis, from *curis,* strength, meaning "powerful" (a spear, according to Martianus's translator Stahl; John Scot understands her as a protector of spearmen). She is evoked in battle according to Remigius because the name means "royal or strong or potent" ("id est regalem vel fortem sive potentem. Curis Grece virtus, inde Curitis, id est potens"); "Servius, however, says Juno is called *Curitis* from *currus,* 'a chariot,' because fighting men use chariots" (Remi., *In Mart.*

64.4). The inhabitants of the aerial region ruled by Juno (*De nuptiis* 150–167) include according to a hierarchy of importance the *daemones*, demigods, oracles, *heroes*, Manes, and then Fauns, Satyrs, Nymphs and the other creatures of the more earthly region.

Juno's "heroes" are identified through a hierarchy of classical figures, shades and beings, known from the Homeric stories and their Roman equivalents—"living souls glowing with conflicting atoms." At the highest level of air (above Mt. Olympus) exists a region to be understood only by reading, Philology concludes, *peri eudaimonias*, "about blessedness" (*De nuptiis* 149). Remigius glosses this as "de bona daemonitate": he calls the *daemones* good because there are also bad ones, just as we speak of good and bad angels (Remi., *In Mart.* 64.12). Through similar messengers located between the sun and the moon, dreams and oracles are transmitted as celestial signs, thunderbolts, and so on (*De nuptiis* 151). These messengers include such portents as came to the heroes Anchises, Diomedes, and Ulysses (Remi., *In Mart.* 65.6). In this same group of beings is the *genius* who serves superior gods and is served by lower; he has two natures:

> a universal guardian is assigned to all men, a particular Genius to each individual, whom they have called the Supervisor because he is to supervise all that is to be done; prayers are made to the Genius of a people when the universal guardian is invoked, and each individual owes obedience to his own supervisor. The spirit is called a genius because he is immediately assigned to a person at the moment when the person is generated. As a guardian and most loyal kinsman, he protects the minds and spirits of all men; and because he announces to a higher power the secrets of their thoughts, he can also be called an angel. The Greeks called them all *daemones,* from the Greek word for "distributing," and in Latin they call them *medioximi.* (*De nuptiis* 152–54)

Remigius adds that the *genius* is a "natural god" or angel who is attributed to each one born (Remi., *In Mart.* 65.8); Martianus calls him a "guardian" and "most faithful kinsman" because he is attributed to those born and flowing out from seeds. But there are in fact two types of *genius,* one good who impels the soul toward virtue, one evil who stimulates it to vice (Remi., *In Mart.* 65.15). Related to the *genius* is the *daemon,* called so from the Greek for "omnia scientes," knowing all, so that they serve as the messengers of God, "utpote nuntii Dei," also called *medioximi* because they are in a middle position, between men and God (Remi., *In Mart.* 65.19);

and also the Lares (*De nuptiis* 155), spirits of mortals who leave the body after death.

In the upper section of the space between earth and moon live the demigods known as Semones or Semidei (*De nuptiis* 156). The examples given include Hercules, son of Jupiter and Alcmene, conceived during a night of double length and odious to Jupiter's wife Juno (according to Remigius, *In Mart.* 66.14, she sent two serpents to kill him while he slept in his crib, but instead baby Hercules destroyed them both). Other demigods are Tages and Hammon; the former Remigius links with the river Tagus in Spain (but see Stahl's note to *De nuptiis* 157; Tages was an Etruscan divinity, or rather a grandson of Jove who taught the Etruscans the art of divination), his name meaning "powerful," and he began to speak the moment he was born (Remi., *In Mart.* 66.17). Hammon appeared with ram-horns and wool clothing to reveal "to a thirsty people the water of a fountain" (*De nuptiis* 157); Remigius terms him the Libyan Jove, "id est Iovis Lybicus" (Remi., *In Mart.* 67.1). Martianus mentions other half-gods, such as Dionysus (who discovered the vine in Thebes), Osiris and Isis (who discovered wine and grain-cultivation, respectively, in Egypt), Triptolemus (also grain-cultivating, following Ceres, in Attica), Pilumnus (milling grains, in Italy), Aesculapius (inventing medicine, in Greece; *De nuptiis* 158, glossed *In Mart.* 67.4–9). These "half-men, half-gods" have celestial souls and human form (Semones being "semihomines," and Hemitheos or Semidei "dicuntur non quod dimidii homines vel dimidii dii sint, sed quia non perfecti dii," "are called so not because they are half men or half gods but because they are not perfect gods," Remi., *In Mart.* 66.9).

From the middle of the aerial region to the mountains and earth are these demigods and the *heroes,* called so because the ancients named the earth Hera (*De nuptiis* 160) and they are her sons (Remi., *In Mart.* 67.18); in the commentaries, like mortals they are strongly pulled by ties to earth and its corruption. These beings include the Manes, guardians of the human body "who have flowed from the seeds of parents," according to Martianus. For Martin of Laon, Manes belong to the aerial region under the moon as infernal gods under the power of Pluto or Orcus (Dunchad, *In Mart.* 68.2). And for Remigius, the Manes are called good, "from what is by hand (*manu*), that is, the good;" or from flowing (*manando*), "quia de SEMINIBUS PARENTUM MANAVERUNT quamquam sola corpora per generationis traducem nascantur" ["because they have 'flowed from the seeds of parents,' although only bodies are born through the action of generation"]; "sed a coniunctione corporis ipsae quoque animae MANES appellantur"

["but from their connection with the body, souls too are called Manes"]
(Remi., *In Mart.* 67.21). All the air beneath the moon is governed by
Summanus (*De nuptiis* 161), also called Pluto, as if "summus Manium," the
chief of the Manes. Remigius explains (*In Mart.* 68.2) that he is the
principal infernal power of the area called by poets the underworld. Of the
different types of beings in this region, the Manes assigned to bodies at the
moment of conception also remain with bodies after death, says Martianus,
and are then called Lemures (ghosts) (*De nuptiis* 162), as if "LEMURES quasi
Lares morantes, subaudis cum corporibus" ["Lares lingering with the
bodies"], Remi., *In Mart.* 68.7). If the Manes have been good in their
previous life, they are called Lares of homes and cities, according to
Martianus; if evil, and corrupted by the body, they are Larvae and Maniae
(*De nuptiis* 162–163). The Larvae, according to Remigius, are "evil Lares,"
or "noxious shades," as the Lemures are not, and the Maniae are the insane,
for "mania" is Greek for "insane" (Remi., *In Mart.* 68.8). The Manes are
also known as *daemones,* either *agathos,* good, or *kakos,* evil (*De nuptiis* 163).

Close to earth, air in its turbulence hinders the movement of the souls
escaping bodies in a region called Pyriphlegethon, where wicked souls
condemned by Vedius (Pluto) are hurled (*De nuptiis* 166). In Remigius the
infernal river of fiery Phlegethon extends downward "from the circle of
Mars to the circle of the moon, by this image signifying the turbid and
heavy nature of this lower air, which is composed of fire brought down
from the higher regions and water drawn from the lower ones; as a result
the air becomes dense and thick, in which it is thought sinful souls are
cleansed" (Remi., *In Mart.* 69.1). Finally, that part of the earth inaccessible
to humankind is populated in its woods, lakes, rivers, etc., by beings—
Pans, disciples of the god of the woods, Fauns or Fones (from *fando*), Satyrs,
Silvani of the forest, Nymphs of the water, Fatui and Fatuae or Fantuae or
Fanae (those who infatuate; Fanes after these because they prophesy, *De
nuptiis* 167). These beings die but have a long lifespan and great powers of
foreknowledge. Now that Martianus has mapped out the underworld
adumbrated in book 1, he returns to his allegory, specifically Philology's
ascent through the spheres.

Philology's apotheosis begins at the circle of the moon, which allows for
glosses on its phases and the goddesses associated with them, and then
passes through the spheres of bridegroom Mercury and his friend and
brother Apollo the sun, with its panoply of Macrobian-Fulgentian
mythographies in the commentators. In all of these cases the strong
influence of the dominant feminine affects the selection of myths glossed.

As Philology moves from moon and Mercury to the sun, the female deities in the text shift subtly from virgin to fecund and sexual maternal figures—from Diana to Berecynthia.

At the moon's sphere Philology sees a spherical body, like a mirror, made up of the smoothness of heavenly dew (this certainly resembles Dante's description of the moon's sphere in the *Paradiso*), wherein appears the sistra of Egypt (associated with the worship of Isis), the lamp of Eleusis (associated with Ceres), Diana's bow, and Cybele's tambours—in short, the moon as crescent, half, gibbous, and full (*De nuptiis* 169–170).[77] The number three elsewhere in Martianus (in the seventh book, on arithmetic; *De nuptiis* 738) refers to a virgin, the "threefold goddess" who, in Virgil's phrase (*Aeneid* 6.247), is the ruler of heaven and hell; Remigius, using John directly, notes that this ruler is threefold, Lucina in the heavens, Diana on earth, and Proserpina in the underworld (*In Mart.* 369.2).

In Mercury's sphere Martianus does not violate both aesthetic and social considerations by illustrating the meeting of Philology and her bride-groom; instead, in line with his feminizing direction, he provides a female guardian of the god's home, a maiden named Themis, Astraea, or Erigone, who bears an ebony tablet with the image of an Egyptian bird called the ibis, connected with Thoth or Mercury (*De nuptiis* 174–75). Erigone, daughter of Icarius, hung herself in grief after her father's death and as a reward was transformed—apotheosized, like Philology, for whom she acts as foil—into the constellation of Virgo, the Virgin. In Remigius, Erigone has custody of Mercury's house because she signifies skill at trading: she is Themis, obscurity or darkness; or Astraea, that is, "starry"; or Erigone, "quae contentiosa vel litigiosa interpretatur," "interpreted as contentious or litigious" (John insists on "contentiosa femina" ["contentious *woman*"] John Scot, *In Mart.* 71.17). All these terms describe rhetoric because "the eloquence of the rhetor is sometimes obscure and involuted, sometimes clear, sometimes even provokes quarrels and disputes" (Remi., *In Mart.* 71.16). Martianus has dissociated the pejorative and ruthless image of Mercury's sphere from the god himself, who represents not business in the allegory so much as the praiseworthy goal of eloquence.

Of the tablet Martin of Laon comments that it describes under *figura* the art of the negotiator (Dunchad, *In Mart.* 71.19); the art of trade has long been associated with the archtrader Mercury (for example, in Fulgentius, *Mit.* 1.18). Martin misogynistically declares that Mercury's name comes from "mercatorum kirios," "lord of merchants," that is, "dominus," with Erigone in charge of the art of business in this sphere of Mercury because, like a virgin, the art of business at first seems sweet but afterwards, in the process, becomes vile. On the tablet a pair of intertwined serpents caresses the head of the ibis, clearly a reference to the caduceus of snakes associated also with Mercury, in that a gold-headed rod is depicted under them. Under the right foot of the ibis is a tortoise and scorpion, and under the left foot a goat. For Martin the image of a bird signifies the velocity with which all business, impelled by the love of money, is conducted throughout all regions of earth; the black tablet signifies a color that leads to death. In Fulgentius, the caduceus of snakes signifies the idea that commerce sometimes gives control and the scepter, that it sometimes hides a snakelike wound; in Martin, the serpents intertwine to suggest that in business the tongue is poisonous at deceiving (Dunchad, *In Mart.* 71.19).

In the next sphere, that of the sun (*De nuptiis* 182–93), the commentators invoke in a long, conventional section the order and description of the equivocal names for the sun and their linked functions drawn from Macrobius's *Saturnalia* (1.17.7 and 1.21.3–6), with many significations from Fulgentius's *Mitologiae* (1.12), itself, we recall, a possible reinterpretation of Macrobius.[78] Near-Eastern myths also surface for Apollo as Lyceus, Serapis, Osiris, Mithras, Dis, Horus, Typhon, Attis, Hammon, and Adonis (191-2). These names depend mostly upon the sun's different functions, place-names, or related figures. Lyceus[79] is identified by Martin as Seraphis, king of the Egyptians, who was translated into a god after death and for whom his queen Isis constructed a sepulchre. Remigius, using John Scot, glosses Serapis as the greatest idol of Egyptians, venerated as Isaeus on the Nile because he was the husband of Isis, who made for him a very noble sepulchre; *Isos* comes from the Greek for fair or just, "aequus vel iustus," hence Isaeus means the same (Remi., *In Mart.* 74.10). In Martin, Apollo or Sol is also called "Memphis" because Martianus had said in Memphis Phoebus is known as Osiris. For a similar reason he is apparently called Mithras because "Mitra" is the queen of Egypt. As "Attis," explained in a Fulgentian vegetation allegory by Martin, he is a flower deity, for Attis means "flower" in Greek, loved by earth, or the goddess Berecynthia "altitudo terrarum" ["the height of the earth"] (the queen of mountains in Fulgentius, *Mit.* 3.5), mother of the gods who flourished on the mountains like spring flowers. Attis is adored through the figure of the sun, because the sun is the ruler and creator of all the flowers ("quia omnium florum princeps est sol et quodam modo creator," Dunchad, *In Mart.* 74.12).[80]

Other names for the sun are also linked with vegetation myth. The figure Martianus terms "the bountiful youth with the curved plough" may be Osiris (according to Martianus's translator Stahl, note to *De nuptiis* 192), but is identified by Martin as "Triptolemus" (Dunchad, *In Mart.* 74.12), as he is by Remigius, "a boy who, following Ceres, taught agriculture to the whole globe" (Remi., *In Mart* 74.12). "Byblius Adon" (*De nuptiis* 192) is glossed by Remigius as "Egyptian," since some say that "Biblos" is a city of Egypt (Remi., *In Mart.* 74.13), rather than of Phoenicia, as the modern translator of Martianus indicates; Remigius repeats John Scot on Adonis and reminds us that this was covered in the first book (i.e., Remi., *In Mart.* 14.16). Adonis in Martin, however, like the sun who "disappears" in winter, was slain in the winter and mourned by Venus (Dunchad, *In Mart.* 74.13), a very important mythological description of the natural cycle of the passage of seasons probably taken from Macrobius's *Saturnalia* (1.21.3–6), except that Macrobius's description of Proserpina as ruler of the lower hemisphere (or the six lower zodiacal signs) is not mentioned in Martin. Martin merely establishes that the loss of Adonis signifies the sinking of the sun into the lower part of the heavens so that nothing grows, as in winter, and Venus (the spirit of generation rather than the upper heavens, or upper six zodiacal signs, as in Macrobius) laments.[81]

At the very end, Philology reaches the Galaxy where the divine senate is resident in the abode of Jove. In addition to the gods there appear other immortalized figures, among them poets and philosophers like Orpheus and Aristoxenus (*De nuptiis* 212), the former of whom will play an important mythographic role in the last book of *De nuptiis*. Like the other semi-divine beings—*heroes*, among them—who inhabit the underworld, these poets exhibit the feminized traits of imagination, creativity, and most important, eloquence informed by wisdom.

IV. ORPHEUS, THE UXORIOUS THRACIAN POET, AND THE POWER OF MUSIC (HARMONIA)

Orpheus, who has also appeared in Boethius (*Consolatio* 3 m12 and its glosses), exemplifies the liberal art of music (or Harmonia) celebrated in the ninth and final book of *De nuptiis*. His uxorious relationship with Eurydice, a foil for the wedding of Mercury and Philology, recapitulates and symbolizes both macrocosmic and microcosmic marriage and harmonizes several of the themes, including that of female domination, present throughout the satura (and the commentaries, e.g., Remi., *In Mart.* 480.15, 480.19). Orpheus (from *orea phonu;* "sweet voice"), a Thracian bard, traversed Erebus (the underworld) to retrieve Eurydice, "profunda inventio." Allegorized in terms of the arts, Remingius's myth of the couple is the only one of the many medieval mythographic interpretations of Orpheus and Eurydice to do so so explicitly.[82]

Ipsa ars musica in suis profundissimis rationibus Euridice dicitur, cuius quasi maritus Orpheus dicitur, id est *orios phone* id est pulchra vox. Qui maritus si aliqua neglegentia artis virtutem perdiderit velut in quendam infernum profundae disciplinae descendit, de qua iterum artis regulas iuxta quas musicae voces disponuntur reducit. Sed dum voces corporeas et transitorias profundae artis inventioni comparat, fugit iterum in profunditatem disciplinae ipsa inventio quoniam in vocibus apparere non potest, ac per hoc tristis remanet Orpheus, vocem musicam absque ratione retinens.

[The art of music itself in its most profound principles is called Eurydice, whose husband is called Orpheus, that is, *orios phone,* "beautiful voice." If this husband by some negligence loses the power of his art, he descends into a certain underworld of profound learning, from which he brings back a second time the rules of his art according to which musical sounds are arranged. But when he compares the corporeal and transitory sounds to the creation {*inventio*} of profound art, creation {*inventio*} itself flees again to the profundity of learning, since it cannot appear in sounds; and for this reason Orpheus remains sad, retaining the sound of music without its principles.] (Remi., *In Mart.* 480.19)

This marriage and relationship of Orpheus and Eurydice both mirrors and acts as a foil for the relationship of Mercury and Philology that will culminate in marriage, that is, harmonious union, and in its failure serves as a warning: if Orpheus is the poet, "sweet voice," then Eurydice is the deepest or most profound understanding of the art of music whose loss triggers his descent into the lower world—the abyss—of instruction, knowledge. This fable traces the stages of writer's block in the Carolingian age. Its successful resolution, allegorically speaking, occurs in Orpheus's subsequent taming of wild beasts: he plays the same song that made the tiger less wrathful, the Thracian mountain Ismaros see the foliage on trees grow stiff, the Thracian river Strymon check the flow of her waters, the Scythian river Tanais that divides Asia from Europe reverse, the lamb lie down with the wolf, the hare and the dog together (*De nuptiis* 197).

Another poet, the Theban Amphion, *optimus cytharista* for Remigius and similarly regenerative in his harmonious music, brings life to bodies stiff with cold, animates mountains, and makes sensible the rocks (*De nuptiis* 908); when he persuaded the destroyer Alexander to rebuild the many-doored wall of Thebes it was both with his music and his staunch patriotism (Remi., *In Mart.* 481.14). And when Arion sang while he was drowning in the middle of a storm in Scylla's straits, dolphins (Remigius glosses, "bull-calves of the sea") came to save him (*De nuptiis* 908), a rescue that implies the self-regenerative properties of music (Remi., *In Mart.* 481.16). Other figures who used instruments or made music, finally, include the Amazons who "brandished their weapons to the tune of reed pipes" (*De nuptiis* 925), glossed etymologically by Remigius as "without a (right) breast," so that they could properly use bow and arrow, or as "living without men" (from *ama zoin*; Remi., *In Mart.* 491.20). One Amazon—according to Remigius, the queen (Remi., *In Mart.* 492.1)—came to Alexander in the hopes of bearing his child, but he gave her a flute instead and she was happy. All of these figures in their eloquence combined with wisdom actualize the wedding of Mercury and Philology, or the implementation of the goals symbolized by Jove's daughter Pallas Athena.

An icon for and offspring of Jupiter Genetrix and Progenitor, Pallas Athena in the more humanized environment in the later books offers a goal for mortal aspirants to wisdom. Throughout this last book and indeed all the last seven books, the figure of Pallas Athena or Minerva, whom we have already discussed (as did the commentators on book 1 and 2), dominates and recurs, along with the myths associated with her, for example, Perseus's conquest with her aid of the Gorgon Medusa—perhaps to illustrate the end result of all the liberal arts as *sapientia*. Indeed, in book 6, on geometry, and 7, on arithmetic, the number seven (the number of planets, chords, ages of man, vital organs or members, months of gestation—according to John Scot, *In Mart.* 285.14) is associated with, given by, Pallas. She is addressed as the Heptad (*De nuptiis* 567, 738), perhaps because, as Stahl indicates in his note on this passage of Martianus, seven is the only number that is both prime and has no factor in common with others within the decad and is thus linked with Athena who sprang fully armed from Jupiter's brow, self-begotten and permanently virgin (non-begetting)—an emblem of the seven months of human gestation as understood at that time. Martianus has declared, after all, "because the heptad begets no number it is called virgin. Because it springs from no number, it is called Minerva, and because it is the sum of masculine and feminine numbers, it is named for the mannish goddess Pallas; for seven consists of three and four" (*De nuptiis* 738; see Stahl's note). The head of Medusa "glares" from Athena's breast (*De nuptiis* 572) because the foolish, hearing the prudence of the wise, become stupefied, as if turned into stone: the wisdom which Minerva represents overcomes stupidity ("Medusa ponitur in figura stultitiae, ideo Minerva dicitur eam interfecisse quoniam vero stulti prudentiam sapientum audientes stupefacti fiunt, ideo finguntur veluti in saxa moveri," John Scot, *In Mart.* 286.10).

The allegorical landscape throughout the commentary reveals an underworld foolish, uneducated, stupefied, whose iconography clatters with the armaments of war and death, the realm of Mars (or Mors, death); in a sense, wisdom (Pallas Athena) is the only resource to use against death. The last reference in book 7 is to Mars, identified with the number nine, the appropriate end of the first numerical series according to Martianus because it is he "by whom all things are brought to an end" (*De nuptiis* 741). Mars is often understood as being like death, *mors,* which derives from "Mars," or "separatio corporis et animae" (John Scot, *In Mart.* 211.6). "Mars" comes from *megalos Ares* (in Greek), or "magna virtus" (in Latin); because the last is the end of all numbers, Mars is called so from "mors," death, and associated with nine, "quia mors finit omnia," "because death ends everything," or called so from "mactus virtute," that is, full of virtue, "plenus virtutis" (Remi., *In Mart.* 375.12). That this death marking the underworld signifies both physical and spiritual loss is bolstered by Silvanus (the character in Martianus) wanting Saturn's scythe (the one Jove used to castrate his father) and not Mars's spear (*De nuptiis* 425) because Saturn signifies the year of Jove, or of increasing life: life castrates time with the scythe because whatever grows in a year (Saturn) is cut down by Jove, or the life of the human body ("Vita ergo castrat tempus cum falce quia quicquid in anno, id est in Saturno, crescit, castratur ab Iove, id est vita humani corporis," John Scot, *In Mart.* 211.6).

The *figurae* of the arts are forced to adopt deceptive practices in order to deal with the warmongering that goes on continually. For example, in book 3, grammar, the liberal art, personified as an old woman, enters the senate of the gods "in a Roman cloak" "according to the (Roman) custom of Romulus" and "because of . . . the race of Mars" (*De nuptiis* 223); this occurs, says Remigius, among other reasons because of the bellicose nature of Mars and his Roman sons ("propter Romulum et Remum qui se ferebant filios Martis et Reae; sive MARTIAM GENETEM id est bellicosam. Romani enim praecipue bellorum studio calluerunt," Remi., *In Mart.* 82.16). Honesty and integrity of wisdom oppose the deceptive practices necessitated by warfare: in the fifth book, on dialectic, Athena's Gorgon hisses at Dialectic because she, too, is snake-like or deceptive (*De nuptiis* 331)—and Remigius explains this as the serpentine hair of Medusa (Remi., *In Mart.* 153.9).

In the ninth book, not only is music the last of the arts to appear but also her appearance brings to a close the debate of the senate of gods and the wedding celebration: she harmoniously concludes the narrative and the allegory simultaneously. After Apollo finishes his speech, Jupiter orders Harmony, the last maiden of the arts and of Apollo, to come forward. Venus is startled by the warm reception given her daughter (*De nuptiis* 901); apparently (says Remigius) she is called a daughter both of Juno and of Venus, and Jove's daughter because of celestial harmony ("propter armoniam caelestem"), but Venus's because of the delectation of all the senses ("Veneris propter delectationem, quia delectatio omnium sensuum ad Venerem pertinet," Remi., *In Mart.* 477.10). For Martianus, Harmony, or the seventh art, of music, is the art most conducive to poetry. When Hymen sings a hymn and others bustle around waiting for Harmony to arrive, minor figures enter (*De nuptiis* 905), including the musicans Orpheus, Amphion, and Arion. They (eventually) master nature or the underworld by means of the harmony of their music: at the end of the poem describing their feats, Martianus apostrophizes, "O Harmony, verily surpassing the great divinities whose praises you have sounded; you have been able with your song to subdue Erebus, the seas, the stones, the wild beasts, and to bring sensation to rocks" (*De nuptiis* 908).

The prosimetrum appropriately ends, then, with the introduction of the musicians Orpheus, Amphion, and the others and the harmony for which they strive, in what may be termed a self-conscious and self-reflexive return to the opening of the work, in which Martianus as writer addresses his posterity, his son. In the closing lines Martianus admits to his son that he has written a "melange," termed a *fabula, miscellum, famen* (*De nuptiis* 997; I follow Dick, but Willis alters the word to "flamen"). Remigius glosses this *miscellum* as "vario, mixto," and *famen* as "fabulis, carmine, historia. Miscillum famen, mixta fabula, ex vero et falso" (*De nuptiis* 533.12). This *miscellum* in its thousand paragraphs has mixed story, song, history, "mixed fable, out of true and false." In a sense much of Martianus (and the commentary on Martianus) has attempted to define the nature of "mixed writing," whether poetry and prose, old and new, pagan and Christian. To mix ancient texts with modern enthusiasm is to echo the practice of fabulous narrative. The use of the myth, the *mitologos,* is the same as speaking in defense, the apology or *apologos* ("from" plus "speech"), Martianus notes in book 5 (Rhetoric, *De nuptiis* 558), but as corrected by Remigius, "Mitologos autem et APOLOGOS idem est, id est sermo de fabulis," "mythology is the same as apology, that is, discourse or words from fables" (Remi., *In Mart.* 279.3). Perhaps the connection between explanation and fable also illuminates John's synonym for *commenta* in book 3 (grammar; John Scot, *In Mart.* 81.2)—"fabulas": these glosses are for the most part fables, stories. There are, however, for Remigius differences between the fable, the image, and the apology: "Differt inter fabulam imaginem, et apologon. FABULA nec vera est nec veri similis; IMAGO et veri similis est et vera esse potest; APOLOGOS veri similis est, sed fieri non potest" ["The fable is neither true nor the likeness of truth; the image is the likeness of truth and is able to be true; the apology is the likeness of truth but is not able to exist"] (Remi., *In Mart.* 279.3). Again Martianus (and his interpreters) return to the idea of the word as a complex and varied reflection of truth.

So the penultimate voice belongs to Satire, who confesses, in a marvelous switching of artistic reality with natural meaning, that, although she playfully composed this mixture of learned and unlearned, gods and Muses, nevertheless she was inspired by the aged Martianus. Described as "a bee separated from his blossoms by the sickle" (*De nuptiis* 999), the persona "Martianus" is glossed by Remigius in a passage beginning with the word "scythe": the scythe borne by Old Man Saturn has cut down the time of Old Man Martianus ("FALCE scilicet cum falce pro tempore dixit quia Saturnus falcem gestat. . . . Saturnus quippe deus temporum senex depingitur, sic et iste senex erat quando hos scripsit libros et ideo dicit," Remi., *In Mart.* 534.12). For this reason Martianus writes this prosimetrum to his son, both these posterities, work and son, also "mixtures" that attempt to ward off time and death.

Perhaps because of this humanization—and feminization—of mythology Martianus and his commentaries attracted the interest, first, of Carolingian thinkers, and then of scholastic and Chartrian/Parisian thinkers like William of Conches (who borrowed from them) and Bernard Silvestris (who added his own commentary to them). Their own Chartrian Neoplatonism in effect extended the blend of late antique Stoicism and North African and Middle Eastern mythology and religion in Martianus, colored of course by an elaboration quite different from that of the Carthaginian Martianus. That the commentary tradition on Martianus came to an abrupt end in the twelfth century was caused in part by the arrival of Aristotle and all the excitement that new ways of thinking can produce. Before that happened, however, the second Vatican mythographer—perhaps Remigius himself—would incorporate Stoic mythographies into his compilation of myths. And Martianus, like Boethius, would be translated into the vernacular and transmitted to German schools, where the Old High German of Notker Labeo would stimulate its own new thinking.

Chapter Eight

OEDIPUS AND THE DAUGHTERS OF SATURN: GENDER AND GENEALOGY IN THE SECOND VATICAN MYTHOGRAPHER

Two anonymous works carry one step farther Remigian transmogrification of classical myth with its privileging of female deity: the second Vatican mythography and the near-contemporary epitome known as the *Ecloga Theoduli,* the latter more poetic and mythological than mythographic. The second Vatican mythography, not much later in date than the first Vatican mythography, was written probably during the Carolingian period (but in any case no earlier than Isidore and no later than the tenth century),[1] possibly by Remigius of Auxerre or someone of his school,[2] or perhaps, I would suggest on the gendered basis of some of the unusual interpretations, by an anonymous woman ecclesiastic familiar with Remigius's mythographic commentaries. As successor to the first Vatican mythography the second Vatican mythography shows marked improvement in three ways—the length of its stories, given its multiple and varied sources; its improved style; and the design of its series[3]—although like the first it rarely depends upon allegorical moralization and, "as in the case of the first mythographer, the originality seems to consist almost wholly of the selection of material."[4]

The second Vatican mythography creates a suitable context for its transmittal of Remigian mythography by appropriating the first Vatican mythography's genealogy (Mythogr. I 201/204) as a structural principle (perhaps encouraged by the Martianus commentaries). Just as the first mythography's organization of its myths, especially in the second book, by a genealogical principle reflected a sense of early medieval history, so also the genealogies of the second Vatican mythography transcend a mere chain of divine being through which generative authority descends. Within this recently re-edited mythography[5] consisting of a proem and 230 fables (in Bode; 275 in Kulcsár) presented without book divisions, what order it has, in the view of Elliott and Elder, comes from the emphasis on cosmic hierarchy: "We begin with Saturn, pass on to his children, then to the other chief gods and goddesses, then to minor divinities, then to the giants and Titans, the prophets and seers, outstanding mortals, and so on."[6]

Generally, medieval mythographies prefer this genealogical and hierarchical organization, as evidenced in the second book of the first Vatican mythography, Fulgentius's *Mitologiae,* and Isidore. That the second mythographer knew the first, was guided by the first in selecting myths, even if the first was not used as a direct source, and likely used the same sources as the first mythographer, has been argued by Keseling; the second mythography does not name its sources.[7] Elliott agrees, noting that their similarity of sources would be highly coincidental if the second mythographer did not know the first and they were several centuries apart.[8] In addition to the second Vatican mythography's probable awareness and use of the first Vatican mythography, the other genealogically-organized myth collections of Fulgentius, Hyginus, and Isidore are favored as sources much more than in the first mythographer: Fulgentius, with forty-six fables rather than twenty or twenty-one; Hyginus, twenty rather than one or two; and most importantly, Isidore, with ten rather than one or two.

Granted the similarity of sources in the two mythographies—primarily Servius, Statius scholia, Horace, Fulgentius, Hyginus, Isidore,[9] and, I would add, the Carolingian commentaries on Boethius and Martianus, neither of which have been included as sources by Keseling or Kulcsár— most notable is the reliance on mythographers like Fulgentius and Isidore with their Stoic cosmographic organizations. To this end the second Vatican mythography takes from both the Boethius and Martianus commentaries the Stoic cosmic idea of the four elemental regions of earth, each governed by a different child of Saturn (time) and Rhea (matter, space). Thus the mythography begins with Jupiter (aether, fire), Juno (air), Neptune (water), and Pluto (earth).

Just as the Carolingian Boethius glosses emphasize the heroes of Orpheus, Ulysses, and Hercules, so also much of this second mythography is organized by means of a series of fables centering on national heroes—in particular, through the sagas of Argos, Thebes, and Troy. The heroes of Argos and Thebes, rather curiously, have been traditionally linked not so much with Jupiter and his infidelities as with Juno and are stressed here perhaps as a result of the influence of the Carolingian uxorious Stoic gods. At the same time, the author is interested in the apportioning of events over time and space—how national founders propagate, what happens to their heirs.

For this good reason the "chronicle" of the second Vatican mythography ends—not by accident—as it has begun, with a fabulous figure: the first fable tells of the Chimaera, the last is the story of Oedipus and the Sphinx. Both end and beginning fables tally the demarcations of mortal life.[10] In Oedipus's riddle, posed by the Sphinx, man the monster first crawls on four feet, then, clutching onto tables, walks upright on three and afterwards two, and finally hobbles along on three—including his cane—until he is once again reduced to four at life's end.

As wise as Oedipus was in solving this riddle, he did not apply to his own life his understanding of the implications of the natural progression and limitations of mortal life. Blind, he slept with his own mother, destroyed his family, destroyed his nation, and only then made literal what was already figurative, by blinding himself (see figure 19, of Oedipus, Jocasta, Eteocles, and Polynices). This awful truth is scandalous, and more than scandalous, is monstrous, even if necessary to know in order to avoid reenacting the same sequence of events. The begetting of children who are also the brothers of their father is unnatural, illogical, unnecessary, immoral. Knowing the truth means seeing not just the future clearly, but, as these fables indicate, also the past. Understanding substantially who our parents were and who their ancestors were also helps us better understand ourselves.

The second Vatican mythography, by giving the myths a structure that is roughly chronological and based on a Stoic understanding of cosmic genealogy and gender, intends to help others (royal princes) understand the past through this literate education in myth. The Carolingians, as we have thus far observed, because of their interest in education, valorized wisdom by displaying it within an heroic mythological context. The larger interest in classical wise heroes—in Prometheus as prudent and in the cycle of creation in which such classical figures appear as if impelled by a knowing Shaper—was similarly displayed in the first Vatican mythography. Orpheus, Ulysses, and Hercules, in the Boethius glosses, all try to master the dark Neoplatonic underworld of the flesh in order to reach the light of "sovereign day"—and of God. Finally, Pallas Athena, the armed virgin of wisdom, portrays a monastic ideal in the Martianus glosses, an androgynous figure who in her ontology transcends the singular issue of gender.

Cy lenluit liltoire de y calte
royne des thebains
O calte royne des
thebains fu noble
et repute entre lez

19. Oedipus, Jocasta, Eteocles, Polynices. MS. Royal 16 G V, fol. 27r (14th c.). By permission of the British Library, London.

A pendant to Oedipus's monstrous blindness and Sphinx-truth, the first fable of the second Vatican mythography's collection (for Kulcsár; omitted in Bode) introduces the similarly fabulous myth of the Chimaera as sign of the chronologies of life. Its three anatomical components of lion, wild she-goat or roe (*capraea*), and dragon illustrate the stages of life through which humans pass, from adolescence to the most perceptive period, which we might identify as perfect or middle age,[11] and finally, old age. Because fables most frequently utilize such animals anthropomorphically but also morally, tropologically— figuratively—the second Vatican mythography may be anticipating his/her own moralization of the gods in these fables, in the sense that these fables may likewise illuminate the phases (and problems) of human life. The mythographer actually adds a verbatim Isidorian passage on *fabula* (discussed previously in Chapter 4, pp. 241–2); just as the gods can represent natural phenomena or causes, as "Vulcanus claudus," Vulcan limping, represents flickering fire, so too the Chimaera is a figure for the stages and mores of human life:

> ut illa triformis bestia [Lucret. 5, 903]: "Prima leo, postrema draco, media ipsa Chimera": id est caprea, etates hominum per eam volentes distinguere, quarum ferox est et horrens prima adolescentia, ut leo; dimidium vite tempus lucidissimum, ut caprea, eo quod acutissime videat, tunc fit senectus casibus inflexis ut draco.

> [so also that triform beast {Lucretius 5.903}: "In front a lion, in the rear a dragon, in the middle a chimera"—that is, a she-goat, by which (the poets) mean to indicate the ages of man. The first of these is adolescence, fierce and terrifying like a lion; the middle part of life is the most lucid, like the she-goat, because she sees very acutely; then comes old age, subject to twisted circumstances, like a dragon.} . . .
> (Mythogr. II, Kulcsár, 1 ; Isidore, *Etym.* 1.40.4)

The introduction assumes Martianan proportions in its treatment of fable and gender in the first two fables. The second Vatican mythography's substitution of the Isidorian passage on fabula for the first Vatican mythography's provocative thematic and unifying introductory fable on Prometheus provides a theoretical rationalization of the gods by means of icon, fable. Moreover, its resultant careful connection of deity with place in the list of gods that follows (Kulcsár 2, Bode Prooem., derived from Isidore 8.11.1–5) reveals gendered North African and Middle Eastern associations of myths found in the Martianus commentaries.

By beginning the collection with this passage, the second mythographer establishes the handbook as more fabulous, more fashioned and imaginary than historical. This distinction in Isidore established artificial reality as textual, poetic, in contrast to physical or natural reality. Quoting Isidore verbatim (*Etym.* 1.40.1), the mythography declares in its opening sentence, "Fabulas poete a fando nominauerunt, quia non sunt res facte sed tantummodo loquendo ficte" ["The poets named fables from speaking {*fando*}, because they are not deeds {actually} done, but only imagined in the telling"] (Mythogr. II Kulcsár 1; not in Bode).

Isidore distinguished the concept of fable from history in the same passage used by the second Vatican mythography as the Prooemium, an important explanation for the stories of troubled men like Oedipus of Thebes. In the *Etymologiae,* Isidore explains that "Historia est narratio rei gestae, per quam ea, quae in praeterito facta sunt, dinoscuntur" ["history is the narration of deeds through which the facts of the past are learned"] (*Etym.* 1.41.1). Although he does not quote this definition, that the second Vatican mythographer bears this in mind is clear because he passes, in the second part of the Prooemium (Kulcsár 2), to a euhemeristic discussion of the various gods as actual individuals worshipped as divine after death, whose images (as we shall see) he eventually links with the false, demonic idols and, in effect, with the iconographic portraits of the gods in this collection. The second Vatican mythographer explains, quoting Isidore again (*Etym.* 8.11.1) and Augustine (*Civ. Dei.* 6.8), "Hii quos pagani deos asserendo uenerantur, homines olim fuisse produntur et pro uniuscuiusque uita uel meritis colere eos sui post mortem ceperunt ut apud Egyptum Ysis, apud Cretam Iuppiter, etc." ["Those whom the pagans venerate, claiming they are gods, are said to have once been human beings, and in accordance with the life and merits of each their own people began to worship them after death, as Isis in Egypt, Juppiter in Crete, etc."] (Mythogr. II 2/Prooem.).

The problem in organizing such a collection is acknowledged by the second Vatican mythographer: the pagan honoring of images of brave men after their death is an error suggested to those coming after by evil spirits or demons who take advantage of some occasion or other ("Sed paulatim hic error posteris demonum persuasu irrepsit ut, quos illi pro sola nominis memoria honorauerunt, successores ut posteri deos estimarent et colarent," Mythogr II 2/Prooem., from Augustine, *Civ. Dei* 6.8). It is no accident that for the mythographer as for Isidore the word "fingunt" implies the fashioned, fabulous, artificial "reality" of the Theodulfian *pictura,* of which the Chimaera (*Etym.* 19.16.1) serves as one example.

This problem is in part ameliorated by the second Vatican mythography's second Isidorian, and Neo-Stoic, explanation of the gods, also serving as an apt introduction to the collection. By showing an etymological similarity between the god and its cosmic function, the second Vatican mythography justifies the use of figure and imagery for reasons of interest to the schoolmaster who teaches the classics. The second Vatican mythography expresses the bond here in terms of poetics: "in quorum etiam laudibus accesserunt poete et compositis carminibus in celos sustulerunt. Ab actibus autem uocantur ut Mercurius quia mercibus preest, Liber a libertate" ["the poets joined in praising them and extolled them to the skies by composing poems. Moreover, they are named from their activities, as 'Mercury,' because he is in charge of trade, 'Liber' from liberty,"] etc. (Mythogr. II 2/Prooem.).

Finally, the second Vatican mythography's third and most philosophical explanation in this "introduction" to the mythography offers the idea of divine gender as Stoic, implicitly a reflection of the balancing of natural (or elemental—earth, air, fire, water) forces:

> Stoici dicunt non esse nisi unum deum et unam deam eademque esse potestate que pro ratione officiorum et actuum uariis nominibus appellantur. Deum eundem Solem, eundem Liberum, eundem Apollinem uocant, item deam eandem Lunam, eandem Dianam, eandem Cererem, eandem Iunonem, eandem Proserpinam dicunt. Numina autem utriusque sexus esse uidentur, ideo quia incorporea sunt et quod uolunt, corpus assumunt.

> [The Stoics say there is only one god and one goddess, and they have the same power; they are called by various names in accordance with their duties and activities. The same god is called Sol, Liber, Apollo; and the same goddess, Luna, Diana, Ceres, Juno, Proserpina. Moreover, divinities are seen to be of either sex, because they are incorporeal and assume whatever body they wish.] (Mythogr. II, 2/Prooem.)

This important Stoic passage, from Servius on the *Georgics* (1.5) and in its last sentence resembling Servius on the *Aeneid* (7.416), fixes upon the sexuality of the god as a philosophical and natural issue. It is also one of the first in mythographic tracts to discuss gender consciously. As suggested above, it may here have been influenced—directly or indirectly—by the Neo-Stoicism of Remigius's commentary on Martianus.

The concept of gender, which surfaced explicitly in mythography for the first time in the Martianus commentaries, elevated to greater prominence Stoic physical rationalization of the gods; it also fleshed out the female deities previously depicted in somewhat marginal roles and thereby supplemented the Carolingian program. Given the second Vatican mythography's explicit reliance on Isidore in the prologue, also important to the collection will be the Iberian bishop Isidore's injection into the continental mainsteam tradition of figures marginal to the authority of the Graeco-Roman mythography. North African and Middle Eastern figures, many of them female, no doubt inspired by the Magna Mater cult, entered into received school authority through this back door (Remigius borrowed heavily from Isidore, too, for his project of feminization in his Martianus Capella commentaries, a bolster for the attribution of authorship of the second Vatican mythography to him). In Isidore as in Martianus female deities Diana, Ceres, Juno, Minerva, Venus, and others are all associated with the sublunary, aerial, or earthly realm identified as "matter," "underworld," *inferus.*

Given such gendered intertextuality, it is important to note that there occurs a healthy influx of and balancing by female deities (Isis, Minerva, Venus, Juno) in the second part of the Prooemium (Kulcsár 2) in a discussion of euhemeristic relationships of pagan god or hero to place of origin, most of which are Greek or Roman, but including other countries, chiefly Africa and Asia Minor. Specifically, Isis is worshipped in Egypt; Minerva, in Athens; Juno, on Samos, an island off of the coast of Asia Minor, across from Ephesus; Venus, in Paphos, a city on the island of Cyprus. In addition to Isis and Juno, in Africa and near Asia Minor, the Prooemium adds Juba, king of Numidia, part of Mauretania, also in Africa. Of course the usual male Greek and Roman deities are there, Jupiter on the island of Crete; Faunus in Latium, or the Latin territories of the Roman people (he is the mythical son of Picus and grandson of Saturn; and he is the father of Latinus, king of Latium); Quirinus in Rome; Vulcan on Lemnos, an island in the Aegean sea; Liber on Naxos, the largest island of the Cyclades in the Aegean; Apollo on the island of Delos. Through this conduit glosses on female deities arrived in the hands of the fifteenth-century mythographer Christine de Pizan which she would appropriate for her *Epistre Othea à Hector* and *Livre de la Cité des Dames.*

TABLE 4
MYTHS (GODS, HEROES, CITIES)
IN THE SECOND VATICAN MYTHOGRAPHY

The Gods and Their Attendants

Chimaera

Saturn	
Jupiter, son of Saturn; eagle	Fire
Juno, daughter of Saturn; peacock	Air
Iris	
Jupiter's sister-wife; her temple in Argos	
Neptune, son of Saturn	Water
Pluto, son of Saturn	Earth/Hades
Tricerberus	
Furies	
Harpies	
Parcae	
Proserpina	
Apollo, son of Jupiter	Sun
Diana, daughter of Jupiter	Moon
Mars, son of Jupiter	Mars
Venus, daughter of Saturn	Venus
Three Graces	
Minerva, daughter of Jupiter	
Priapus	
Vulcan, son of Juno	
Mercury, son of Jupiter	Mercury
Orpheus	
Cybele, daughter of Saturn	Earth
Atalanta	
Pan	
Faunus	
Nymphs	

Heroes and Cities

Prometheus and the First Man
Epaphus, founder of Memphis in Egypt
Cadmus, founder of Thebes
Proserpina, daughter of Ceres, in Sicily
Perseus of Mycenae (Argos)
Minos of Crete, Theseus of Athens
Jason and the Argonauts
Oedipus of Thebes
Hercules of Tiryns (Argos)

Greek sea-myths
Trojan series
Series on descendants of first Athenian kings
Mixed series

Oedipus and the Sphinx

If one traces through the second Vatican mythography the genealogies of the heroes celebrated in various series, it will be evident that Juno and the Argives dominate. Unlike some of the other mythographies in which the children of Jupiter, or in particular Pluto and his denizens, seem to overwhelm all others (Neptune's line never seems to receive much attention), nearly all of these genealogies[12] in this mythography relate back to the power of Juno.

One might well conclude that heroes, especially Argive heroes linked with Juno, solve riddles and overcome monsters. Perseus will overcome Medusa; Oedipus, the Sphinx; and Bellerophon, the Chimaera. Later on, Hercules, descendant of Perseus (and of the initial father of the first worshipper of Juno), will overcome not only Geryon, but also Cerberus, Hydra, and the Nemean lion. It is another late Carolingian paradigm to adapt these classical heroes to the medieval educational use of fabula and riddle.

Even the first and the last of the fables are connected through Juno if one correctly perceives both their moralizations and also their linked geneal-

TABLE 5

NEPTUNE'S LINE

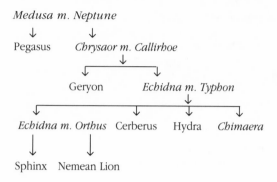

ogy, with Juno and Oedipus winning over Neptune and the Chimaera/ Sphinx. We recall that this mythography ends with Theban Oedipus's resolution of the riddle of the Sphinx—Juno (air) overcoming Neptune (water), in effect, although Oedipus fails to learn from the riddle sufficiently to take control of his own life and destiny. The Chimaera (Mythogr. II 1/Prooem.) and the Sphinx (Supplement V/230) are kin, and both are descended from Neptune through Medusa, one of the Gorgons (and therefore normally included under the rubric or realm of "Pluto," earth). From Medusa's blood (after Perseus severed her head) Pegasus was born. But before that Neptune raped her and she gave birth to Chrysaor, who married Callirhoe in Greek mythology. From them Geryon and Echidna were born, and when Echidna married Typhon, four monstrous children appeared, Echidna, Cerberus, Hydra—and the Chimaera, with whom the mythography begins. It may seem no accident, then, that the Chimaera would have been the aunt to sister Echidna's children, that is, the Nemean lion (conquered by Hercules), and the Theban Sphinx (conquered, in a sense, by Oedipus; see table 5).

Throughout this mythography, it is important to understand the genealogies in order to make sense of the fables. Using the theoretical accessus (as I prefer to see it) as a touchstone for the later myths, this chapter will focus in particular on the relationship between gender and genealogy, paying especial attention to innovation and assuming convention wherever it appears. One important difference between the first and the second mythography is that the second overlays some of what it garners from its sources— Hyginus, the Statius scholia, the first mythography, etc.—with Fulgentian moralization and allegorization, as if to highlight some fables. In addition, the second Vatican mythography will add, often at appropriate series demarcation points in the usually literalistic recitation (especially true of the second half), an "Explanation of these Fables." A way of drawing attention to the existence of a coherent series, this technique will also help to focus subsequent mythographic attempts—in particular the twelfth-century third Vatican mythography. After a closer examination of the second Vatican mythography, we shall pass in the next chapter to what might be termed the distillation of its history, in the *Ecloga Theoduli*.

I. THE GENDER OF GENEALOGY: JUNO AND THE ARGIVES

To see how Juno is particularly emphasized in this mythography it is necessary to pay close attention to her place within the original family of the gods and its privileged spot in the conventional cosmography. As noted above, the mythography is roughly (and conventionally) organized by the Chain of Being—gods; heroes (Hercules, Oedipus, Ulysses); men changed into rivers, birds, trees, flowers; and then men in time. In the first section, although the mythographer lists Saturn's children Jupiter, Juno, Neptune, and Pluto, s/he has omitted from the list, as do most medieval mythographies, his other daughters Vesta the virgin and Ceres, perhaps because they disrupt the neat Stoic parallels of the four children of Saturn with the four elemental cosmic regions of fire, air, water, and earth. In the series selected by the second Vatican mythography, one reflective of the ordering in Martianus commentaries, the gods and heroes fabulized begin with the father and son Saturn and Jupiter, followed by Jupiter's signs and symbols, his eagle, his wife Juno, Juno's peacock, Iris, Juno as sister and wife of Jupiter, and her first temple. The mythographer then turns to Jupiter's two brothers Neptune and Pluto, along with a long section on Pluto's signs and symbols—Tricerberus, the Furies, the Harpies, the Parcae, the wife of Pluto.

There exists an alternate, genealogical, interpretation possible for the cosmic regional organization of planetary deities which, in its emphasis on the descendents of Saturn, would give greater prominence to the usually omitted female deities Juno, Venus, and Minerva. Following Saturn each of his children is treated—Jupiter, Juno, Neptune, Pluto; then Apollo and Diana (sun and moon, children of upper and lower air, or fire and air, water and earth), Mars, Venus and the three Graces, Minerva and Priapus, Vulcan, Mercury, and various earthly heroes and beings, Orpheus, Cybele, Atalanta, Pan, Faunus, Nymphs, etc. The children of Jupiter include Apollo and Diana, Mars, Venus, Minerva, Vulcan, and Mercury; of these only Mars and Vulcan can be considered children of Juno, a deity both child of Saturn in her own right and wife of Jupiter.

This genealogical method seems truer to the text, but all the same, initially at least, the second Vatican mythography pays little attention to female deities. Isidorian terms like *pingitur* and *fingitur* are the verbs used to characterize the patriarchal Saturn and others, in line with the description of fabulous purpose in the accessus. The mythography begins with Saturn (Mythogr. II 3/1), but mostly ignores Rhea, unlike Remigius on Martianus but like Fulgentius in the *Mitologiae,* and with careful historical and genealogical detail bolstered by iconography. Saturn is son of Caelus, husband of Ops, and he reigned first in Latium, which explains his veiled head, "latens," and the reason for his name "Saturn," that is, his role as agricultural guide ("quia per annone prerogationem populos ad se traxit"). He is called Saturn from "saturando," "annis saturetur," "full of years" ("quidam Saturnum a saturando dictum uolunt, alii Saturnum quasi annis saturetur dicunt"). Next, his role as planet is clarified: he is portrayed ("fingitur") as slow, old, and cold, astronomical qualities appropriate to the outermost planet. But his iconography also has a Stoic (natural or physical) resonance: he bears a sickle because he is god of years ("deus temporum") and one year follows after another, or else because of his wisdom (from Servius, *In. Georg.* 1.336).

Interest quickly collects around daughter Juno although the second Vatican mythography begins with the myth of the four children. The myth of the four children has been disseminated by the influential Fulgentius; the Stoic elaboration of the four regions is in part reinforced by Boethian glosses which invest them with an even more philosophical and moral character, perhaps because of the Carolingian Martianus commentaries. Jupiter and Juno represent the higher regions, Neptune and Pluto the lower, but it is into three regions the brothers have divided the world for ruling: "unde et iii fratres orbis imperium dicuntur inter se diuisisse," an idea incorporated into the Boethius commentaries (on *Consolatio* 2 m12; "Tria autem hec numina, licet diuisa imperia teneant, uidentur tamen inuicem regni totius habere potestatem," Mythogr. II 3/1). Jupiter has the heavens, Neptune, the water, because it is closer to heaven than to earth, "quia aqua uicinior est celo quam terra," and Pluto, earth. The passage then concludes with signs of the three brothers as represented in Remigian commentaries on Boethius and Martianus—the three-pronged lightning bolt for Jupiter, the trident for Neptune, and (three-headed) Cerberus for Pluto. Specifically, Jupiter, from *iuuando*, "helping" (Mythogr. II 4/2), is understood as fire, for nothing may exist without heat, "nulla enim res sic fouet omnia quemadmodum calor"; the eagle is Jove's guardian, called his armsbearer (*armiger*) because so full of heat that the coldest giant stone rattles, when warmed under a breeding eagle, as if an egg, according to Lucan ("Aquila autem in tutelam Iouis ponitur eiusque armiger dicitur quia nimii caloris est adeo ut etiam oua, quibus supersidet, coqueret nisi admoueat gigantem lapidem frigidissimum, ut testatur Lucanus," Mythogr. II 5/3, from Lucan, *De bello civile* 6.676).

Why Juno is left out of the ruling divisions is made clearer by the mythographer's Stoic and markedly gendered interpretation. Juno is defined as air (Mythogr. II 6/4), also called "Juno" from *iuvando;* she mates with Jupiter but not with the lower, watery Neptune or earthy Pluto: "Dicitur autem Iuppiter catenis eam ligasse, quod aer igni celesti coniunctior duobus deorsum elementis misceatur, id est aque et terre, que elementa duobus superioribus grauiora sunt" ["Jupiter is said to have bound her in chains, because air closer to celestial fire is united with the two lower elements, that is, water and earth, which are heavier than the two elements above"] (Mythogr. II 9/7, probably from Fulgentius, *Mit.* 1.3). This Stoic concept of gender is reflected in a highly original, gendered gloss on Juno as "Deam etiam partus et preesse nuptiis uolunt quod diuitie semper pregnantes sunt et nunquam aborciant" ["goddess of birth and ruler of marriages because riches are always pregnant and never abort"] (Mythogr. II 6/4). She is also identified as the queen of the gods, called "Curitis" in her role as protector of spearmen. The signification of Juno as air, sister and wife of fiery Jupiter, explains her handmaiden Iris, the rainbow (8/6). The bird of Juno, the peacock (7/5), matches Jove's eagle (for a visual depiction of her iconography, see figure 20).

Juno's connection with the Argives is made explicit in the second Vatican mythography's first linking with the historical from this physical interpretation: "Who made the first temple for her" (Mythogr. II, 10/8). In a scholium from Lactantius on the *Thebaid* 1.252, the first temple-maker is identified as Phoroneus, son of Inachus king of the Argives; his daughter Niobe was the first mortal he copulated with. We recall Juno is normally termed "the Argive," as we saw in the Carolingian commentaries on Martianus—always associated with the more marginal Eastern religions;

20. Juno crowned, in crimson robe with ermine. From Seneca, *Tragedies*. MS. Canonici Latin classical 90, fol. 1r (1399–1400, Italian). By permission of the Bodleian Library, University of Oxford.

here at the beginning of the mythography she is revealed to be first worshipped in Argos, an area with contacts with Egypt and the Levant in the Mediterranean. Three cities were linked with Argos—each with its own hero in the Argive sagas of the Bronze age. Tiryns boasted Hercules; Argos, Diomedes; and Mycenae, Perseus. And the saga begins with Inachus, father of Io and Phoroneus, of whom the latter fathered Niobe; from Io will come the founder of Thebes, Cadmus, and eventually the hero Perseus and thereafter the hero Hercules (see table 6).

Obliged to continue the Stoic natural/physical interpretations of the elemental regions, neverthless, after covering Jupiter and Juno the mythographer offers little attention to Jupiter's brother Neptune and instead offers a long series on the signs and creatures of Pluto (Mythogr. II 12/10). Neptune and his wife Amphitrite (from the Greek for "around," *amphiena,* "eo quia tribus elementis aqua conclusa sit," Mythogr. II 11/9) are ignored perhaps because he represents an element bounded by the other three ("eumque secunde sortis regnatorem perhibent," from Fulgentius, *Mit.* 1.4). Pluto, ruler of earth, is called so from the Greek for "riches" because it was believed that riches were accorded to earth only, and, like his creatures, he is described in Fulgentian terms (from *Mit.* 1.5). With this definition, as is usual in medieval mythography, there is a further Neoplatonic interpretation of the classical god of the underworld, associated with the Stoic region of earth, so that earth is hell and the dense moral bottom of the universe.

An underworld that is, for the most part, populated by female inhabitants emerges in the moral interpretation of the ruler's subjects, which appears to have been bolstered perhaps by the Boethius glosses on the earthly underworld into which various heroes must descend. The one exception is the three-headed and contentious dog Tricerberus, morally understood as "flesh-eater" (Mythogr. II 13/11, descended from Neptune but part of Pluto's realm, and taken from Fulgentius, *Mit.* 1.6). The female series begins with the Furies, "not at all good" (Mythogr. II 14/12; they are daughters of Night and Acheron, in a genealogy from Isidore, *Etym.* 8.11.95, but as the stages of contention, from Fulgentius, *Mit.* 1.7); and the pillaging Harpies (Mythogr. II 21/13, the "dogs of Jove," daughters of Thaumas and Electra, but because identified as the same Furies just discussed, clearly to the second Vatican mythography part of Pluto's realm; and from Fulgentius, *Mit.* 1.9). In addition, the dispensers of human life on earth are understood as death, or the Parcae (Mythogr. II 22/14; *evocatio, sors, sine ordine* are the stages they represent, from Fulgentius *Mit.* 1.8). The

TABLE 6
THE ARGIVE LINE

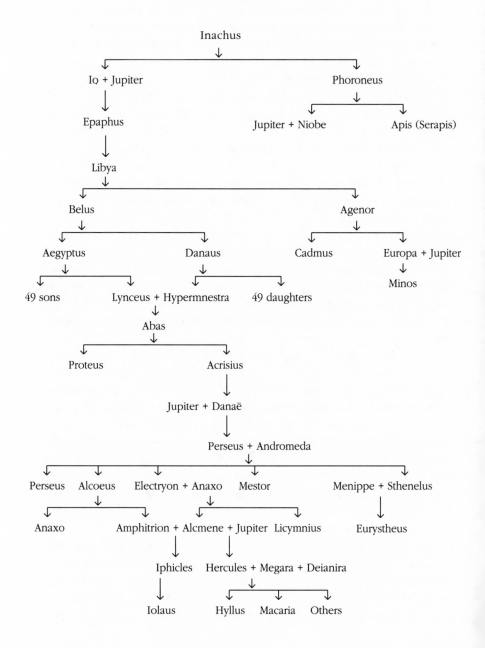

wife of Pluto, Proserpina, signifies earthly crops because she is the daughter of Ceres, goddess of corn (Mythogr. II 23/15, from Fulgentius, *Mit.* 1.10), but she is also a triple goddess, Luna in the heavens, Diana on earth, Proserpina in hell. In Kulcsár's edition of the second mythography, in only two of the eleven manuscripts, "On the Wife of Pluto" is followed by "On the Elysian Fields" (fable 24) and "On the Nine Circles [of Hell]" (25), detailing the location of the Elysian Fields in the purer air near the lunar sphere (from Servius, *In Aen.* 5.735) and its relation to the other eight planetary spheres of the "underworld" (from Servius, *In Aen.* 6.426), which structure, as we have seen, has carried with it a Neo-Stoic resonance congenial to the second Vatican mythography.

At this point, having itemized the elemental children of Saturn, the mythographer has at least two options: either turning to the children of the children of Saturn, especially Jupiter (whose many adulteries seem to have populated the world) or, seeing the four elemental divisions of the cosmos as fire, air, water, and earth, returning to fire and air to list the planets of the heavens. In a sense, aware of both traditions, she tries to follow both ordering principles.

First, the mythographer re-emphasizes the genealogical principle in Jupiter's family line to assert an interest in female otherness and resistance. The overcoming of father by son and the aid of the son and resistance to the father by the Great Mother both enter into this mythography, as we can see in these fables. In "De vita Iovis" (Mythogr. II 26/16), Ops or Rhea conceals Jupiter from Saturn with the help of her "demonic and knowing ministers," the Curetes and Corybantes ("demones ministri Matris Deum, quasi demones qui totum sciunt"), because she knows that he wishes to devour all of his sons, given the prophecy that Saturn's son would drive him from the kingdom (from Servius, *In Aen.* 3.104, and Lactantius on Statius's *Achilleid* 387 and *Thebaid* 4.784). The mythographer discusses Jupiter's desire for the daughter of Titan, Asterie, who resisted and fled from him and was turned into a quail; after he had thrown her into the sea there sprang from her a floating island named Ortygia (or Delos, to which her sister Latona, also pursued by and resisting Jupiter, fled. Latona, raped by Jove, becomes mother of Apollo the sun and Diana the moon. Diana is a virgin, invoked by women in childbirth because her mother gave birth without obstetric aid; she was also born before Apollo because the night (when the moon predominates) precedes the day.

Second, once this genealogical structure has introduced Apollo the sun and Diana the moon as part of Jupiter's family line, the mythography doubles back to the planetary order of the gods: the sun (Mythogr. II 28/18–34/24) and moon (35/25–38/28) create their own series greatly indebted in detail both to Martianus and to Fulgentius (*Mit.*, book 1), and related to the Carolingian commentaries on Martianus, followed by the remaining planets, Mars (39/29), Venus (40/30–47/36), and Mercury (53/41–56/44)—who are also, of course, with the exception of Venus, the children of Jupiter. (The fables in between Venus and Mercury have a special reason for their being, which is more genealogical than planetary and which will be discussed in detail when we come to them).

The second Vatican mythography's themes—of the dominance of the mother deity and the succession of sons after father—continue to crop up in each of the conventional series relating to Apollo,[13] Diana, who resists being loved,[14] Mars, and Venus. Mars (Mythogr. II 39/29) is Jupiter and Juno's son as well as a planet, identified as Death, god of war (from Isidore, an etymology also favored by the Carolingian commentaries on Martianus).[15] His paramour planet Venus (Mythogr. II 40/30) is Aphrodite here, daughter of Saturn rather than of Dione and Jupiter as she is in the Martianus commentaries, and of the two significations of Venus, *in bono* and *in malo,* only her *in malo* meaning is present, and indeed, provided in this mythographer's usual open manner: "Fingitur autem Venus nata per damnum quia omnes uires usu uenerio debilitantur qui sine corporis damno non geritur" ("Venus is depicted as born through loss because all physical strength is weakened by sexual intercourse, which is not per-formed without loss to the body"). Her lecherous insignia include the rose, the conch, and the dove (Mythogr. 42/31–44/33, taken from Fulgentius *Mit.* 2.1); also emphasized are her somewhat incestuous relationships and kinships, with Adonis, son of Myrrha, her son Cupid, and the three Graces (Mythogr. II 45/34–47/36, taken from Fulgentius, *Mit.* 3.8; see also the Martianus commentaries, 8.22 and 4.2). Her naked son Cupid, armed with bow and quiver, comes directly from Isidore, recalling Theodulf and Remigius on Martianus;[16] the description of the three Graces is very close to Remigius on Martianus.[17]

Because so much of this collection involves Juno's direct or indirect influence—and her "genealogy"—it is important to allow the mythogra-pher to pick up a loose thread at this point, to weave together the coherent unity it is in fact. This loose thread is that of the four regions, in that fire (Jupiter), water (Neptune), and earth (Pluto) have been mostly covered (only Mercury, the last of the translunary planets and the last important son of Jupiter and Juno, has not). But air (Juno) has not been fully examined.

The aerial region between the moon and earth (sometimes termed the underworld) allows for fables to be inserted concerning Erichthonius, Priapus, Minerva, Vulcan, Mercury, the reasons for Mercury's name, the lyre, Orpheus, Jupiter and the Etna Nymph, Cybele, Atalanta, Pan, Faunus, the Nymphs, Astraeus, Aeolus, the Titans, the Statute of Jove, and Otus and Ephialtes.

Some of this aerial section is given over, first, to Minerva (Mythogr. II 48/37, 50/39), whom, we recall, plays an enormously important role in Martianus's *De nuptiis* and who looms over much of the Carolingian commentary of Remigius of Auxerre. Second, attention is also paid to Vulcan (48/37, 51/40), who recurs as a figure in the same text and in the commentaries on Martianus. What both share is their role as progeny of a unique parent, respectively of Jupiter or of Juno. As the daughter in Greek myth of Zeus and Metis, in a contrasting Roman myth (filtered through a medieval lens), Minerva springs motherless out of Jove's head, or more precisely, his "beard": she is born "ex barba" of Jupiter, "et quia ex capite eius est orta et in capite quinque partiti sensus pollent, dea dicitur esse sapientie" ["and because she was born from his head, where the five senses are controlled, she is said to be goddess of wisdom"] (48/37).

In a bold and unusually open sexual reading, the second mythographer alters the fable of Juno's son Vulcan, in this case, as a warning against female masturbation. Like Minerva, Vulcan was engendered without intercourse and carried by Juno in a strange place, according to the first Vatican mythography within Juno's thigh (Mythogr. I 173/176, which focuses on both Minerva and Vulcan). In fact this unusual, unnatural place of pregnancy explains Vulcan's deformation, according to the second Vatican mythography: "Iuno autem tactis suis genitalibus locis protulit Vulcanum, et quia loca genitalia inmunda sunt et deformia, deformi figura apparuit fuscus et claudus" ["Juno produced Vulcan from touching of her genitals; because they are unclean and deformed, he appeared dark and lame, with a misshapen figure"] (Mythogr. II 48/37). Then follows a description of his consequent isolation, "Qui cum deformis esset et Iuno ei minime arrisisset, ab Ioue precipitatus est in insulam Lemnum" [when "Jupiter sent him to the island Lemnus because of his deformity and because Juno did not smile on him"].

In a later fable, the Stoic (natural) explanation of Vulcan's nature as fire rationalizes the earlier description of his unnatural birth, his deformity, and his mother's repugnance toward him: as lightning he is the appropriate (but indeed disfigured) product of fire and air, deformed because he falls through the air. In a passage drawn from Servius on Lemnos (*In Aen.* 8.454), and Isidore on fire as distorted (*Etym.* 8.11.41), the mythographer declares:

> Vulcanus autem ignis est, et dictus est Vulcanus quasi uolicanus quod per aerem uolet. Dicitur autem Vulcanus a Iunone propter deformitatem deiectus, quam aerem esse constat ex quo fulmina procreantur. Ideo autem Vulcanus de femore Iunonis fingitur natus quia fulmina de imo aere nascuntur, unde et Homerus dicit eum de aere precipitatum in terras quod omne fulmen de aere cadat. Quod quia crebro in Lemnum insulam iacitur, ideo in eam dicitur cecidisse Vulcanus. Claudus autem dicitur quia per naturam numquam rectus est ignis.

> [Vulcan is fire and is called Vulcan from *Volicanus* because he flies through the air. Also, Vulcan is said to have been cast out by Juno because of his deformity, as she is known to be air, from which thunder-bolts are created. Moreover, Vulcan is depicted as having been born from Juno's thigh because lightning bolts are born from the lowest air. Hence Homer says that he was hurled from the air onto the earth, because every thunderbolt falls from the air. Because thunderbolts frequently strike upon the island of Lemnos, for this reason it is said that Vulcan fell upon it {that is, the island}. Moreover he is called lame because fire by its nature is never upright.] (Mythogr. II 51/40)

The near-coupling of Minerva and Vulcan, when Vulcan's seed spills to earth and itself engenders a deformed son, Erichthonius (half-man, half-serpent), will also result in Erichthonius's founding of one of the Royal Families of Athens. Because Vulcan created the thunderbolt for Jove, his father promised him whatever he desired—in this case, his half-sister Minerva, who nevertheless refused him. Accordingly, this royal family will include other unusual or deformed kings, Pandion (father of Procne and Philomela), Erechtheus (father of Cecrops, the third king, and Metion), Aegeus, grandson of Cecrops, and the last, the hero Theseus (none of these Athenian kings much interests the mythographer, however). The description of the near-coupling and its result appears in the fable "On Erichthonius" (Mythogr. II 48/37) and is based on Fulgentius (*Mit.* 2.11) and Servius (*In Buc.* 4.62): Erichthonius is born as a product of both earth (*chthon* in Greek) and the strife (*eris* in Greek) of his parents, or, morally, envy. Just as his grandmother Juno smiled rarely on her deformed son

Vulcan, so also his mother Minerva gives the child with a snake or dragon form in his lower body, hidden in a basket, to the two sisters Aglaurus and Pandora, daughters of Erythia (and not of Cecrops, as in Hyginus, *Fab.* 166). After the virgins are piqued by curiosity and open the container, Minerva drives them mad; her son Erichthonius invented the racecourse when he grew up, the first to join four horses to the chariot.

Both virginal children, Minerva and Vulcan, alone and together, bear some mythological relation to the air, the region dominated by Juno; and both suggest singular virtues. Minerva is given moral, Fulgentian attention in her fable, as the intellectual and chaste paradigm for monastic education (Mythogr. II 50/39). The armed virgin appealed to the ninth century (as she would to Christine de Pizan in the fifteenth), interpreted in this fable as she was in the Carolingian commentaries on Martianus (which themselves drew on Fulgentius, *Mit.* 2.1), that is, as wisdom able to overcome fear (that is, the Gorgon).[18] But also the natural (Stoic) reading of Vulcan (Mythogr. II 51/40) is taken from Martianus and Servius (*In Aen.* 8.414), and Vulcan's struggle with Minerva interpreted as psychological allegory (nearly verbatim from Fulgentius, *Mit.* 2.11). The second mythographer says Vulcan was united with Minerva "quia etiam aliquando sapientibus furores surrepant" ["because sometimes madness creeps upon even the wise"] and she defends her virginity with arms "quia omnis sapientia integritatem morum suorum contra furiam uirtute animi uindicat" ["because all wisdom by strength of mind protects the integrity of its own character against fury"], whence Erichthonius is born, for *eris* is Greek for strife, for what could creeping madness generate upon wisdom except the strife of hatred? Minerva conceals her rage in her heart, for every wise man conceals his madness in his heart. She appoints a dragon as guardian, which is destruction, and gives her son to the two virgins, "Pandora" meaning the universal gift and "Aglaurus" the forgetting of sadness; "Sapiens enim dolorem suum aut benignitati commendat, que omnium munus est, aut obliuioni" ["the wise man entrusts his grief either to that kindheartedness which is the gift of all or to forgetting"].

Unlike the chaste Minerva and the frustrated Vulcan, Priapus signifies earthly fertility and therefore does not seem at first to fit into this series of aerial denizens associated with Juno or her "children," especially as he is identified as Adonis, the *son* of Venus (Mythogr. II, 49/38). However, the second Vatican mythography does stress his connection with the earth, the last of the four regions to have inhabitants glossed, and because Priapus is also equated with Liber Pater (Bacchus), the son of Jupiter and Theban

Semele (daughter of Cadmus), it may be that the mythographer is assuming he is yet another son of Jupiter. In a rarely cited passage from Servius (*In Georg.* 4.111), Priapus is revealed as a god of gardens known for the large size of his virile member, "propter uirilis membri magnitudinem post in numerum deorum receptus meruit esse numen hortorum"; because of his fertile role he is misread (perhaps because of the Martianus glosses on Adonis) as Sol or Adonis, who affects Venus as the seasonal changes of earth and is therefore identified with Liber Pater (Bacchus, or wine) as instrumental in keeping Venus (love) warm, along with Ceres (bread).[19]

The last of the planets to be introduced, Mercury (Mythogr. II 53/41–56/44), also having strong earthly ties, is introduced as a son of Jove and of Maia (also of Celum and Dies, of Liber and Proserpina "qui animas evocat," who summons souls, and of Jove and Cyllenes, by whom Argus was killed, 53/41). The four genealogies, reminiscent of Cicero's *De natura deorum,* convey four related but different significations, primarily centering on the Fulgentian-Remigian god of eloquence associated with the lyre and the musician Orpheus. Here he is son of Maia and grandson of Atlas, that is, the god "qui *litteras monstravit,* menses instituit, sidera expertus est, lyram invenit, quam etiam septem chordis propter numerum Atlantidum (eo quod mater ejus una earum esset) instruxit" ["who revealed letters {of the alphabet}, instituted the months, is expert in stars, invented the lyre which has seven chords because of the number of the Pleiades of which his mother had been one"] (55/43). But his other parentings explain his other roles—as god of merchants and of thieves, as Anubis the wise dog-headed god—despite his major role as eloquence and communication which is in line with the Carolingian commentaries on Martianus.[20]

The figure of Cybele (Ceres), the ignored daughter of Saturn, helps to unify another series of myths relating to earth beginning with the story of Jupiter and the Etna Nymph, who in evading him asks for help from Terra (Mythogr. II 57/45). This series mostly involves Nymphs, Pan the god of nature (Mythogr. II 60/48, from Isidore, *Etym.* 8.11.81), the infernal god Faunus of earth (Mythogr. II 63/49, from Isidore, *Etym.* 8.11.103), Cybele, and other chthonic creatures. Cybele (Ceres, Demeter in Greek), one of the original children of Saturn and Ops, is rarely identified as such in the medieval mythographies (because there are only four cosmic regions and therefore only four rulers necessary). Further, as the mother of Proserpina, Cybele is often lumped together with earth (Pluto), which would explain her presence among these earthly inhabitants—inhabitants not of hell at all. In addition, Atalanta the daughter of Schoeneus (59/47) does not seem to fit here among the dryads, naiads, etc., although she may have been included because of the origin of the three golden apples in the Garden of the Hesperides (or because the mythographer knows she is pursued by Meleager, a descendant of Aeolus). Even the Titans (Mythogr. II 65/51, 67/53, 68/54, 73/55) are gods of earth, Giants, who piled mountain atop mountain to reach Jupiter and battle with him.

At this point, the second Vatican mythography changes direction dramatically. Just as the first Vatican mythography began with heroes and only in the second book turned to the gods, so also the second Vatican mythography shifts from the gods to the heroes as the mythography centers on the dense earthly center of the universe and the beginning of human time. Put another way, if much of the first part of this mythography traces the genealogy of the progeny of Jupiter and the planetary gods from a variety of different sources (Martianus, Fulgentius, Isidore, and perhaps the Carolingian commentaries on Martianus), then what ensues might be termed a combination of the history found in the first Vatican mythography with the moralization of heroes in the Carolingian Boethius glosses. Both, of course, reflect Stoic principles. Thus we now turn to figures belonging to the very first earthly families.

II. THE GENEALOGIES OF HEROES:
FROM PROMETHEUS TO OEDIPUS AND HERCULES

Hereafter, and until the end of the second Vatican mythography, follow series on specific heroes associated with their nations, presented in a mostly literalistic, historical, fashion, and whose attraction for the compiler appears to be solely genealogical, once we perceive the connecting interstices. The mythographer offers first an early series of figures, including the hero Prometheus, father of Deucalion; next, Epaphus in Egypt and the founding of Thebes by his great-grandson Cadmus; then a series on Proserpina, daughter of Ceres, granddaughter of Saturn, and originally from Sicily; a Perseus or Argos cycle; a Cretan Minos-Theseus cycle; Jason and the Argonauts and Thebes; followed by Oedipus of Thebes; and Hercules; concluding with Greek sea-myths; a Trojan series; a series on the descendants of the first Athenian kings; and in the last few fables a mixed series (Bode's fables 227 and 230 are included in Supplement V by Kulcsár).

Although we do not need to examine all these fables, the genealogical web might be clearer if we show the national and familial lines in these series—as well as the unconventional interest of the second Vatican mythography in matters of gender and sexuality spelled out in much more explicit form than is usual even in mythographies.

Prometheus. By stressing the creation by Prometheus, the first figure discussed in the first Vatican mythography, of an Adam-like figure and the creator's own "fall" (Mythogr. II 81/63–91/73), the second Vatican mythography places this whole genealogical mythography at the beginning of earthly history. Prometheus is important here because he creates the first man in a miniature Stoic allegory. This fable follows an important regenerative and typological myth on the birth, to Saturn and Philyra, of the Centaur Chiron (80/62), a Chimaera-like being who raised both the hero Achilles (actually the son of Thetis and Peleus) and the demigod Aesculapius (son of Apollo and Coronis). The fable of Chiron can, for some medieval writers,[21] foreshadow the coming of Christ, for Chiron sacrifices his immortality to save Prometheus from eternal torment in Tartarus. Though the Vatican mythographer does not include this detail, he does look back to the story of Chiron as he tells Prometheus's story (80/62). Prometheus makes man not from clay, as in one source (Fulgentius, *Mit.,* 2.6), but by using a little from all animals—that is, putting the energy or life of the lion in his stomach, along with the fear of the rabbit, the cunning of the fox, the prudence of the serpent, the simplicity of the dove. Because, however, "Fecit autem hominem inanimatum et insensibilem" ["he made man inanimate and insensible"], Minerva agreed to help Prometheus with a soul by supplying heavenly gifts, and took him to the sky, where he stole fire by applying a torch to the wheels, and then used this fire to give man a soul. Because "Prometheus" in Greek means the same as *providentia dei,* and Minerva, *caelestis sapientia,* man was therefore made through "divine foresight" and "heavenly wisdom" (Mythogr. II 81/63)

The charity and wisdom of this *exemplar* are revealed in the next two fables. In "The Sacrifices of Prometheus," we read that when Prometheus wanted to help poor men who had to sacrifice entire victims, he sacrificed two bulls, leaving one hide with meat, one hide only with bones. Jove, picking the one with bones, took fire away from mortals so that they could no longer cook meat. Jove's anger at Prometheus was caused by his having stolen the heavenly fire to give some back to men, for which he had Prometheus bound in iron on Mount Scythia in the Caucasus for 30,000 years and set an eagle the task of plucking out his liver. Fortunately, because Hercules was told the way to the Hesperides when he returned, he killed the eagle for Prometheus, which freed him: Hercules, rather than

TABLE 7
FAMILY OF PROMETHEUS

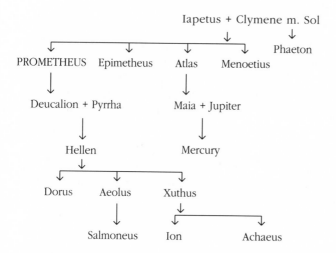

Chiron, occupies the role of Savior to the mythological Adam (Mythogr. II 82/64). In "Jupiter and Thetis" Prometheus is a "vir prudentissimus," or *prudentia* incarnate, because he warns Jupiter not to marry Thetis, having learned from the Fates that the one born from Jupiter and Thetis will drive Jupiter from his kingdom, a knowledge that results in his freeing (83/65). The remainder of the fable duplicates the first story told in the first Vatican mythography, on the man to first teach astrology to the Assyrians.

In the first group, of Prometheus and the earliest families, the second Vatican mythography stretches wide a genealogical net to show the origins of human ties with the families of the gods and along the way unusual sexual, or dominant female (Magna Mater-influenced) readings of some fables. Among the distant connections can be found the great-grandson of Prometheus, Salmoneus, son of Aeolus (Mythogr. II 74/56). This Aeolus was son of Hellen, grandson of Deucalion and Pyrrha, and thus great-grandson of Prometheus, which will place Salmoneus still very early in human history. The mother of Prometheus was Clymene (75/57), elsewhere perceived to be the wife of Iapetus and therefore mother of Prometheus and Atlas and great-grandmother of Mercury—also identified as the mother of Phaeton, son of Sol.

Of the blood of the Giants rebellious against Jupiter, Callisto (Mythogr. II 76/58) was daughter of Lycaon and a Nymph; her father Lycaon (78/60) was changed into a wolf for serving human flesh—Arcas, his daughter's son by Jupiter—to Jupiter as a test of godhead. The wife of Oceanus, Thetis (77/59) gave birth to the Oceanids; she is also nurse of Juno.

Within this Prometheus series, Icarus is a companion of Liber (son of Jupiter and Theban Semele, herself a descendant of Inachus's daughter Io) and father of the virgin Erigone, whose fable reveals an uncharacteristic sexual gloss (Mythogr. II 79/61). In this fable Icarus, to whom Liber (Bacchus) has given wine (or the vine) to teach men how to grow the grape, is slain by shepherds who have become drunk from the wine and who believe they have been poisoned; Icarus's daughter, led to his body by his dog, then hangs herself out of grief, to be apotheosized thereafter into the constellation Virgo along with the dog Sirius.[22] Because of the mistake, afterwards Apollo tells the Athenians that they could check the pestilence that had befallen them—which caused girls to hang themselves—by finding the bodies of Erigone and Icarus. They are unable to do so, but to show their devotion and to seem to be searching in another element, they hang a rope in the trees for men to swing on and thus appear to be searching in the air.

Such "swinging" lends to the establishment of symbolic rites (which seem to have been either obscene or sacred, possibly related to the Orphic mysteries). Because so many "swingers" fall, they create effigies to swing in place of themselves; for this reason they are called "oscilla," because in these their faces (os, face or mouth) were moved. And yet, "Alii dicunt oscilla esse membra uirilia de floribus facta que suspendebantur inter columnia inter duas columnas ita ut in ea homines acceptis clausis personis inpingerent et ea ore cillerent, id est mouerent, ad risum populo com- mouendum, et hoc in Orpheo lectum est" ["Others say the 'oscilla' were male members made of flowers suspended in the space between two columns, so that men, after receiving enclosed masks, could strike them and swing them by their mouths, to make people laugh; and this is read about in the case of Orpheus"]; this gloss is not contained in the first Vatican mythography's fable on Icarus and Erigone (Mythogr. I 19). To this is added a gloss that will appeal, according to the second Vatican mythography, to wise men, that is, that the sacred rites of father Liber/ Bacchus pertain to the purgation of the soul ("Prudentioribus tamen aliud placet qui dicunt sacra Liberi patris ad purgationem anime pertinere").

Within this same "Prometheus" series there is a series of eight fables

(Mythogr. II 84/66–91/73) that do not seem to relate very well to the hero or to early families and in fact mostly concern children, especially proud or errant daughters: Juno plays a role in the fables of the sons Cleobis and Bito, rewarded with death, and of sharp-tongued Chelone. Pretus, king of the Argives, has three proud daughters punished with insanity; proud Antigone, daughter of the Trojan king Laomedon, is transformed into a stork by Juno; proud Arachne is transformed into a spider by Minerva; proud Niobe, wife of Amphion and daughter of Tantalus, from whom the Greek house of Atreus descends, loses all seven daughters and sons to Latona. In addition, Glaucus spurned Venus's rites, so she caused his horses to go mad and kill him; and the son of Prometheus, Deucalion, along with what the second Vatican mythography terms his sister Pyrrha, is saved, Noah-like, by Jupiter after a Deluge intended to cleanse the world of its sinful human race, after which they regenerate men and women by throwing stones over their shoulders to the "mother" earth, "quippe omnium rerum genetricem" (91/73).

The rest of the mythography is organized according to the genealogy of early families, mostly from the East and North Africa, with Junoesque (female) ties. In the next series, Egyptian ruler Epaphus and the founding of the city of Thebes by his great-grandson Cadmus (Mythogr. II 92/74–114/92) introduce an Argive-Theban cycle, part one, in its brief compass, largely (and appropriately) indebted to the scholia on the *Thebaid*. If we recall the genealogy, Inachus begets Io and Phoroneus; Io, mating with Jove, conceives Epaphus, founder of Memphis and father of Libya (a name given to the African country); from Libya come Belus and Agenor. Belus has two sons, Aegyptus and Danaus, and Agenor fathers Cadmus, founder of Thebes, and Europa, who is the mother of Minos of Crete. From the Io-Belus-Aegyptus side of the family comes Perseus, and eventually Hercules. From the Io-Agenor-Cadmus side of the family comes Oedipus and a host of other doomed Thebans. This cycle, interrupted by a series of seventeen fables on Proserpina, resumes thereafter and contines for what can be construed as the remainder of the mythography. Among the cycles of mostly flawed national heroes appear series on Perseus (132/110–142/119); Cretan Minos-Theseus (143/120–151/128); Jason and the Argonauts and Thebes (157/134–165/142); Oedipus of Thebes (166/143–170/147); and Hercules (171/148–193/166). From this point onward, the mythography is preoccupied with Homeric material, including Greek sea-myths (194/167–221/194); a Trojan series (222/195–258/215); the descendants of the five Athenian kings (259/216–263/219); it finishes with a minor series of more historical figures and oracles that continues until the end fable of the riddle of the Sphinx (230).

Cadmus, Founder of Thebes. In the Epaphus-Cadmus cycle (Mythogr. II 92/74–114/92), perhaps it is the lack of a female generator for the Thebans that led to the destruction of their women. The first fable shows us Lycus's wife Antiopa rejected by her husband for sleeping with Epaphus, after which Jupiter in the form of a Satyr sleeps with her; then Dirce, the new wife of Lycus, becomes angry because she thinks Lycus is responsible for Antiopa's pregnancy, and she binds Antiopa in chains (Antiopa escapes and bears two sons, Zethus and Amphion, at the crossroads; later these sons kill Dirce by tying her to a bull). Other fables in this series (93/75–105/83) trace the lives and adventures of Epaphus; Jupiter and Europa, Epaphus's great-granddaughter; his grandson Agenor and Agenor's sons, primarily Cadmus; and then the fates of Cadmus's daughters in the fables following—the eldest Semele and the second daughter Ino; Semele's son with Jupiter, Liber; the third daughter Autonoë and her doomed son Actaeon; Autonoë's husband Aristaeus, the fourth daughter Agave, mother of doomed Pentheus torn apart in the frenzies of the Bacchae, that is, in celebration of the god who was his cousin (see table 8).

The founding of Thebes, and Cadmus's family, is doomed in part because Cadmus initially kills a snake sacred to Mars and then later marries Hermione, product of the adulterous union of Mars and Venus; martial discord will disrupt, divide, and kill all the line down to Megara, whose wedding to Hercules injects a new semi-divine blood line (that of Jupiter) into the family. Of Cadmus's daughters, Semele will be burned up because she longs to feel Jupiter's divine power in its natural form of thunderbolt; however, Jupiter will save (and nurture in his thigh) her son Bacchus (Liber). Ino and one son are chased and killed by her husband Athamas, who, maddened by Juno, has already killed the other son; Autonoë's son Actaeon is torn apart by his own dogs because he sees Diana bathing; Agave, driven mad by Liber, kills her own son Pentheus. The mythographer explains (drawing on Fulgentius, *Mit.* 2.12) that the four daughters represent the four stages of inebriation—excess wine, the forgetting of things, desire, and madness ("Quatuor autem sorores . . . filie Cadmi esse dicuntur quia iiii sunt ebrietatis genera: uinolentia, rerum obliuio, libido, insania, unde et nomina hec iiii Bache acceperunt"). Pentheus's granddaughter Jocasta inadvertently marries her own son Oedipus, and her sons/grandsons Eteocles and Polynices will war against each other for control of Thebes.

TABLE 8
FAMILY OF CADMUS, FOUNDER OF THEBES

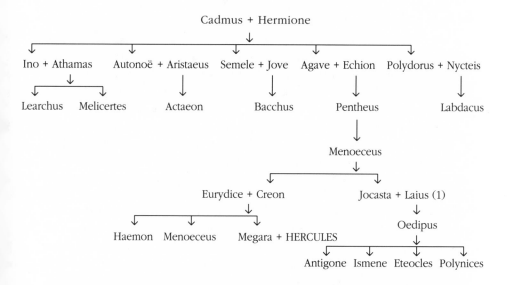

There are other Theban fables remaining in this series, mostly connected with Juno, some concerning prophecy and foreknowledge, others concerning pre-Theban Egyptian ancestors—for example, Tiresias the Theban sage (Mythogr. II 106/84) who changes sexes and is blinded by Juno for confessing that women enjoy sex more than men; about his sex-change the second Vatican mythography offers a Stoic interpretation centering on vegetation myth and elemental conflict between Jupiter and Juno.[23] This fable is followed by several others on prophets or oracles (107/85–110/88)—Branchus, in the Temple of Apollo; Mopsus, son of Apollo and Mantus; the Cumaean Sibyl loved by Apollo and her nine books. The Argive-Theban cycle resumes with fables in many cases identical to glosses in Carolingian commentaries on Martianus (111/89–114/92)—on the daughter of Inachus, Io, who is worshipped in Egypt as Isis; on her role as *genius* of Egypt who controls the rise and fall of Nile waters; on Osiris killed by Typhon; and on the mystical winnowing fan of the Theban deity Liber Pater used to purge the soul.[24]

Proserpina. In the next series Saturn's granddaughter Proserpina is granted unusual mythographic power. The second Vatican mythography not only rehearses the way in which she came to rule the underworld, but also explores figures with ties to her—her kin, companions, and the inhabitants of her realm, including the origin of the Eleusinian mysteries—drawn mostly from scholia on the *Thebaid* and Servius on the *Aeneid* and *Georgics* (Mythogr. II 115/93–132/109). In the first fable, Venus becomes angry because Proserpina spurned Pluto as a husband out of fear of Typhoeus (originally probably Tartarus),[25] and counsels Pluto to seize her when she gathers flowers on Mount Etna, which he does in the next fable. Ceres searches for her daughter (116/94), eventually in the city of Eleusis (118/96), where she becomes the wet nurse of Eleusius's son Triptolemus, and she makes him immortal by covering the boy with fire, so that he will grow faster (119/97). In anger she kills Eleusius and confers upon her foster son, Triptolemus, an eternal gift, so that he rides her chariot of serpents to spread grain. Triptolemus came to Lycus, king of Scythia, where he was deceived (120/98). In the next fable, on King Cepheus, the instituting of the sacred rites is presented. Finally, Ceres found her daughter, and it was determined that, like the moon, Proserpina would spend six months above, that is, growing, and six months below, that is, diminishing; or in relation to the single month, on average of fifteen days in each cycle waxing and waning (122/100). Now the Sirens are introduced as companions of Proserpina who became part bird to help look for her when she was lost (123/101); the primarily Fulgentian gloss seems to echo the Boethian glosses on the Sirens, as Philosophy calls poetry in the *Consolatio* (1 p1).[26]

Male challenges to the power of female deity are introduced for the remainder of the Proserpina series by the cunning Ulysses, who evades Proserpina's Sirens in that Boethian gloss. The criminals of the underworld—Tantalus, Danaus and Egestus (related to the Cadmus series), Tityus, Sisyphus, Ixion (Mythogr. II 124/102/–129/107)—can also be found in the Boethius poem on Orpheus and its glosses (*Consolatio* 3 m12) and in Servius's comments on *Aeneid* book 6. Tantalus, who tested Ceres (mother of Proserpina) by offering her his own son Pelops as dinner, also includes a definition of Mercury, god of prudence because he calls the goddess back to heaven and away from earth; Tantalus is by contrast damned to the underworld (from Servius, *In Aen.* 6.603).

Damnation to the underworld for abrogation of female generation and matriarchy through incest also links the fable of Danaus and Egestus (Aegyptus),[27] both sons of Belus, brother of Agenor (the father of Cadmus). Each brother has fifty children by fifty wives, Danaus, daughters, Egestus, sons; the latter sons wish to marry the daughters but are thereafter killed by their protesting wives (except for Hypermnestra and Lynceus), who for their excessive filial concern are damned to carry water from a leaky jar for eternity (Mythogr. 125/103).

Tityus (Mythogr. II 126/104) is damned to an eternity of pain from a vulture's incessant eating of his liver, prescribed because of his love for Latona; the next fable (127/105) first describes Sisyphus's punishment, that is, pushing a stone up a mountain and letting it roll down (apparently meted out because he confessed Jove's rape of Aegina, the daughter of the river Asopus), and then, citing Lucretius and drawing on the Boethius glosses for the idea of our life as an underworld, follows with an out-of-place example of moralization on Tityus's lechery nearly identical to the Remigian gloss on Boethius's Tityus.[28] The mythographer does return to both Lucretius and Sisyphus's stone thereafter, identifying those who will be crushed by the rock as superstitious because they always have useless fears and think badly about the gods and heaven, and those who push the rock as those involved in a life of ambition, petition, negotiation (a gloss taken from Lucretius's *De rerum natura* 3.995).

Ixion is condemned to hell where he is bound to a turning wheel because of his desire for Juno, although in fact he slept not with her but instead with her cloudy shape, which begot for him the Centaurs. The mythographer's explanation, drawn nearly verbatim from Fulgentius, justifies the son of Phlegyas and ruler of the Lapiths as "dignitas," "worth," which unfortunately strives for dominion, Juno, and instead receives a cloud, that is, an imitation of the kingdom.[29]

> Democritus therefore writes that in Greece Ixion first strove for the glory of a kingdom, and first of all acquired for himself one hundred horsemen; hence these were called Centaurs, that is, one hundred armed men, and finally came to be called *centippi,* as they are depicted as combined with horses. But a short time after acquiring the kingdom Ixion was defeated and lost it; hence he is said to have been condemned to a wheel, because the spinning of the wheel turns always unceasingly. Therefore it is clear that all who strive for rule with arms and violence suddenly sustain forcible losses and injuries. (Mythogr. II 129/107)

The matter of truth versus falsehood that this fable calls up is asserted by means of a prefatory Fulgentian epigram about the difference between Latin and Greek speech: "Just as in Latin speech nothing is more pleasing than truth, so in Greek nothing is more elaborate than falsehood." The related Centaur myth, on the marriage of Pirithous and Hippodamia to which many Centaurs were invited, concerns a battle that occurred between the Centaurs and Lapiths when one Centaur attempted to rape the bride; present also at this battle was Ceneus, formerly a maiden, who as a reward for intercourse with Neptune received a change of sex and invulnerability as a reward (Mythogr. II 130/108). Through the god Neptune, a one-line fable is related to the preceding one when he is angered by the sacrilege to the gods on the part of the Phlegian people (Mythogr. II 132/109; from Mythogr. I 202/205).

Perseus. The story of Danaus and Egestus (Aegyptus) anticipates the next series (132/109–138/115) which at first glance appears unconnected even within itself but which is linked by the hero Perseus. As great-grandsons of Epaphus and cousins of Cadmus, the brothers are ancestors of the hero Perseus who dominates the Argive fables (Mythogr. II 132/109–142/119). Acrisius was the father of Danaë, the mother of Perseus (Jove, in the form of a golden shower, was his father); Perseus defeated the Gorgons; Atlas refused hospitality to Perseus and was hence changed into a mountain by the Gorgon's head; Minerva, who helped Perseus defeat Medusa, also invented the double flute.

The most interesting portions reflect a feminizing turn in Medusa's role and in fables related to her in the psychological allegorization of the Gorgons and Minerva (drawn from Fulgentius, *Mit.* 1.21, and from Mythogr. I 127/130). The three Gorgons, Sthenno, Euryale, and Medusa, were daughters of Phorcys and the Nymphs of Cretus, and therefore related to Neptune; Perseus as son of Jupiter perhaps appropriately tricks and overcomes them, including the most beautiful, Medusa, whose snaky hair indicates that she is more shrewd (*astutior*) than her sisters (Mythogr. II 135/112). The Fulgentian interpretation of the Gorgon as "terror" defines each of the three as different—mental debilitation (Sthenno, *debilitas*), great despair (Euryale, *lata profunditas*), and oblivion (Medusa, *obliuio,* Mythogr. II 136/113). Because the Gorgons are defeated by Perseus indicates that "uirtus auxiliatrice sapientia omnes terrores uincit" ["virtue {his name in Greek} with the aid of wisdom {Minerva} kills all terrors"]. The Gorgon's head is said to appear on Minerva on her breast because in that place is all wisdom, which confounds others and tests the stony (unfeeling) and unskilled; from the blood of her severed head comes Pegasus, or fame, "quia omnia uirtus superans famam sibi querit" ["because when virtue triumphs over all, fame seeks it out"]. Fables linked with

Minerva assert her wisdom or, better, the stupidity of others. Minerva's inventing of the flute (138/115) segues into a brief series on stupidity in judging musical competitions: Midas, as judge of the competition between Marsyas and Apollo, called Marsyas the winner in an act of stupidity that so angered the god that he bestowed upon Midas asses' ears (139/116); Midas who turned everything he touched to gold signifies the miser who knows nothing (140/117). Minerva and Neptune return to compete over the founding and naming of the city of Athens (Mythogr. II 142/119; from Servius, *In Georg.* 1.12, but like Mythogr. I 12/12). Neptune offered war horses, but Minerva offered the olive tree associated with peace; because she won, the name of the city of Athens comes from the Greek for *immortalis*—Minerva as Athena.

Theseus. At this point begins a conjoined Cretan Minos-Athenian The-

TABLE 9

FAMILY OF THESEUS

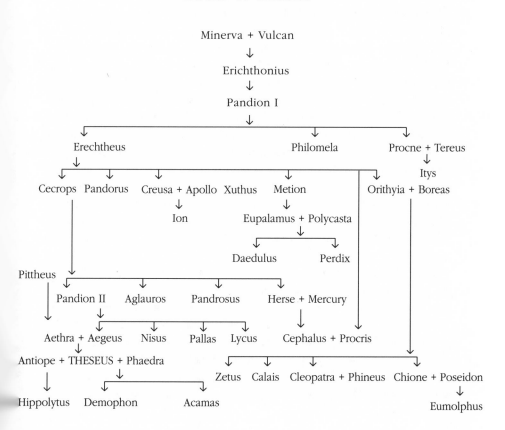

seus cycle (Mythogr. II 143/120–156/133) connected historically by family ties and morally by family sins, again a series not at first glance clearly cohesive because of the squeezing of apparently unrelated material into one fable after another. Minos, son of Europa and grandson of Agenor, counts Epaphus, Io and Jupiter, and Inachus as ancestors; Minos is connected mythologically with Theseus, who will overcome Minos's stepson, the Minotaur, and with Ariadne's help depart from the Labyrinth. Theseus, however, comes from a very different family: his father was Aegeus, his grandfather, Pandion II, son of Cecrops; Cecrops sprang from Erechtheus and Erechtheus, through Pandion I, from Erichthonius— the marginal child of Minerva through Vulcan, Juno's son (see table 9).

The conflict between the two heroes Minos and Theseus expresses the moral enmity between adultery, fornication (Jupiter's tendency), and abstinence, or at least unusual, often parent-child, especially mother-son relationships (Minerva's tendency), although even here the tension is not pure and uncontaminated. The initial myth (Mythogr. II 143/120) of Pasiphaë's passion for the bull (very like Mythogr. I 47/47) is followed by a fable (Mythogr. II 144/121, like Mythogr. 43/43), which seems to describe the adultery of Mars and Venus but which in fact describes Venus's inspiration of Pasiphaë with a mad passion for the bull, and the art of Daedalus, who makes for her a wooden cow covered with the skin of a beautiful heifer to use in consummating her passion, after which she gives birth to the Minotaur, then imprisoned in the Labyrinth (also created by Daedalus). The second Vatican mythography presents a series of myths about Minos and Scylla's love for him, even to the point of betrayal of her own father Nisus: Minos's son Androgeus is killed at Athens after winning over everyone in wrestling (Mythogr. II 145/122); Scylla, who loves Minos, nevertheless occupied in besieging her country, then severs her father Nisus's purple lock, on which his safety depends, in order to win Minos's love (which of course he denies to her, and she eventually turns into a bird 146/123).

At this point Theseus, distantly related to Daedalus, as we can see from the above genealogical tables, enters the narrative series, and thus this fable that conjoins their fates shows a thematic and narrative interwining as well. In the third year of the Minotaur's terrorism, Theseus kills the monster by means of Ariadne's revelation of her father Daedalus's trick of the thread, afterwards carrying off (*rapta*) Ariadne and abandoning her on the island of Naxos (where she is then loved by Liber and apotheosized as a star; Mythogr. II 147/124, from Mythogr. I 43/43). Aegeus, father of

Theseus, kills himself because he thinks his son has been eaten by the Minotaur, whereas in truth Theseus has forgotten to change the color of his sails to signal his success (Mythogr. II 148/125). Back on Crete, to escape from prison Daedalus and his son Icarus fashion wings but the inexperienced Icarus unfortunately falls into the sea. The second Vatican mythography returns to Pasiphaë almost as if the other fables have not intervened: she gives birth to twins after sleeping with Taurus (a male secretary to Minos), with one twin the son of Minos and one of Taurus (Mythogr. II 149/126).

Although the next two fables pick up sequential loose threads—Theseus and Scyron, who used to kill his guests; and Theseus, Phaedra, and Hippolytus—the latter fable launches into the theme of sexual relationships between mothers or stepmothers, and sons. The interest apparently centers on the renewal of life achieved through the agency of a maternal figure—even if, in the case of Hippolytus, "mortis conditionem euadere non potuit" ("he could not evade the condition of death"). The mythographer links the anger of Theseus toward Hippolytus, who allegedly raped his spurned stepmother Phaedra, to the anger of Apollo against the supposedly adulterous Coronis and the god's penitent rescue of baby Aesculapius after he kills her. Interestingly, in a passage in Virgil's *Aeneid,* after Hippolytus dies, Aesculapius, at Diana's request, restores him to the heavens from the underworld, which incurs Jove's wrath, so that Aesculapius takes his place in hell and Hippolytus, disguised as Virbius (as if *bis virum,* twice a man), is concealed in Trivia's groves (*Aeneid* 7.761–82). The second Vatican mythographer excludes some of this, but does note other mother-son (or quasi-son) myths—the mother of the gods and Attis, Minerva and Erichthonius, Venus and Adonis.

The final sons of sons occupy the last few fables in stories of monstrous generation, maternal domination, rape, or near-rape. Orion, son of Neptune by Euryale, daughter of Minos (Mythogr. II 152/129), is explained as the son of Oenopion, but springs in fact from the union of an ox-hide and urine, buried in the ground. Perdix, son of Eupalamus (and of Polycasta, in Mythogr. II 153/130) and therefore part of Theseus's family (Eupalamus was son of Melion, who was son of Erechtheus), is like Orion a hunter, chaste, and mother-dominated; both Perdix and Orion either love Terra too much or are killed by her. The story of Bellerophon (accused of rape by Proteus's wife Stenoboea) seems to repeat the Theseus-Phaedra-Hippolytus story (154/131). Finally, in the fable of Jupiter and Leda, the child of that union, Helen, is abducted by Theseus when a young girl; Theseus and

TABLE 10
FAMILY OF JASON

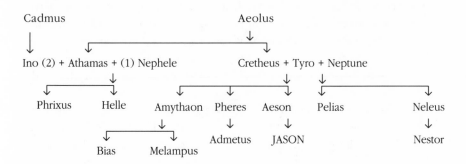

Pirithous take her to Egypt and then Pirithous is directed to ask for Proserpina's hand in marriage, although once in the underworld they are held captive, to be rescued by Hercules (155/132–156/133).

Jason and the Argonauts. A series on Jason and the Argonauts, thematically unified in part by tension between parents, or parental authority, and children (Mythogr. II 157/134–165/142), is followed by Oedipus of Thebes (166/143–170/147), again, a clearly-focused series only if the reader is already aware of the connecting narrative and genealogical glue. Jason is descended from Aeolus, a great-grandson of Prometheus. Aeolus had two sons, Athamas and Cretheus; it is from Cretheus that Jason springs (see table 10).

The series begins with the birth of Phrixus and Helle to Athamas and Nephele, children who are nearly sacrificed by their stepmother Ino maddened by Liber Pater at the request of Juno. Although they escape by mounting a golden ram, one child falls into the sea (the Hellespont), the other sacrifices the ram at Colchos in Mars's temple, where it is guarded by a dragon. In the next fable the father of Jason, Aeson, appears: he is driven away by his half-brother Pelias, who takes the throne of Iolcus and sends Jason on a quest for the golden fleece, on the Argonauts' ship Argo. Jason depends upon the help of Juno and the art of Medea to remove the fleece; Medea restores Jason's father to youth with magic herbs and she aids the nurse of Liber at his request (Mythogr. II 159/136–161/138; the last two in part very much like Mythogr. I 185/188). Also of the Argonauts, Pollux boxes with the contentious Amycus, king of Bebrycia (Mythogr. II 163/140), and wins, which according to Amycus's terms means the king must

die. Jason's second bedding, with Hypsipyle, occupies a fable that begins
with the foil for that adultery, the affair of Venus and Mars behind the back
of Vulcan of Lemnos—and it is on Lemnos where Hypsipyle lives and bears
Jason's two sons. Later, when the other Lemnian women discover Hypsipyle has not killed her father (their husbands married Thracian women
because they made no offerings to Venus, which impelled them to kill all
the men on the island), Hypsipyle is forced to escape and is captured by
pirates, to be ultimately reconciled with her own sons at the funeral games
of her captor's son (Mythogr. II 164/141, like Mythogr. I 130/133). Jason
and the Argonauts are given directions by Phineus, king of the Arcadians,
who revealed the deliberation of the gods and was blinded, after which
Harpies snatched food from his lips as punishment (Mythogr. II 165/142;
he is glossed morally, with the Fulgentian etymologies of *Mit.* 2.11, as
blind avarice). Interestingly, Phineus marries Cleopatra, who is herself tied
by marriage to Minerva's line (her mother was Orithyia, daughter of
Erechtheus; her sister Procris marries Cephalus).

Oedipus of Thebes. Through the monstrous Harpies a brief Oedipus
(Theban) series (Mythogr. II 166/143–170/147) is appended to Jason and
the Argonauts by means of the Sphinx whose riddle Oedipus must solve.[30]
From Oedipus of Thebes the second Vatican mythography turns to other
geographically related figures, although somewhat randomly presented:
Oeneus, descendant of Aeolus, king of Calydon (Aetolia), and father of
Meleager; Meleager himself, who kills the boar ravaging the countryside
for Atalanta and because he also kills his uncles has his life ended by his
mother; Arpalice, a warrior daughter of a father (Pelops?) captured by the
Greeks; Oenomaus, who gives his daughter in marriage to Pelops, son of
Tantalus, because he bribed the charioteer of her father to leave out a pin in
a wheel of a rival's chariot and therefore won the requisite four-horsed race;
the sons of Pelops, Atreus and Thyestes, who clash because Thyestes sleeps
with Atreus's wife Aëropa; Thyestes's grandson and son (by means of his
daughter, Pelopia) Aegisthus, prophesied to avenge him. (Aegisthus does
so by taking Clytemnestra, wife of Agamemnon, in adultery, after which
her son Orestes kills Aegisthus; see table 11.)

Hercules. A long Hercules series, connected to the mixed fables above
because he married Meleager's sister Deianira, mostly relays the Labors
(Mythogr. II 171/148–193/166) but also other adventures, in which
Hercules figures as a wise hero, as in the Boethius glosses of Remigius and
his advisers (from which the second Vatican mythography derives some of
his or her source material, as well as from both works of Hyginus,

TABLE 11
HOUSE OF ATREUS

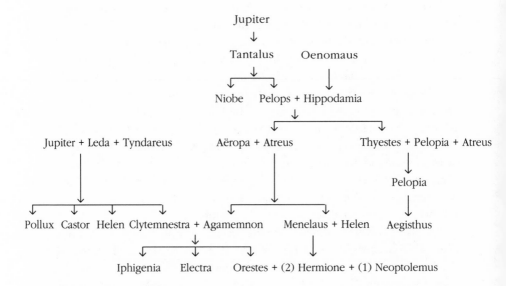

Lactantius on the *Thebaid,* and Servius on Virgil, especially the *Aeneid).* Hercules is identified by his alternate name, Alcides, or *virtus,* strength, virtue, which is taken from Alceus (Alcoeus), the father of the cuckolded husband of Alcmene, Amphitrion; Alceus was also one of the sons of Perseus and Andromeda. Hercules's strength stemmed more from his mind than his body, and thus the twelve Labors he performed correlate with the twelve signs of the zodiac: "Sed Hercules a prudentioribus magis mente quam corpore fortis inducitur adeo ut xii eius labores referri possint ad aliquid, nam cum plura fecerit, xii tantum ei assignantur propter agnita xii signa" ["But Hercules is considered by wiser men as strong more in mind than in body; hence his twelve Labors can be referred to something, for although he performed more, only twelve are assigned to him on account of the known twelve signs"] (Mythogr. II 173/149).

But the mythographer tones down the Boethian interpretation of the monsters as vices which Hercules prudently overcomes: they are mostly adversaries he literally defeats by means of his strength and wisdom. Exceptions include Cerberus, as earth the flesh-eater, or the cupidity of earthly life (Mythogr. II 173/149), and Cacus, or evil (176/153), both found in Remigius on Boethius, the first from Servius *(In Aen.* 6.395) and the second from Fulgentius *(Mit.* 2.75). There are also allegorical, Fulgentian, interpretations which focus on Hercules in relation to various women, especially as a rescuer, one of whom, Alcestis (Mythogr. II 177/154), was herself viewed by Fulgentius as a foil for the wise hero, and the other of whom, Omphale (178/155), more misogynistically repesents lust because of her name, meaning "navel," the seat of lust (the first from *Mit.* 1.22 and the second from 2.2).

In this series the organizational pattern and connectives are much easier to detect than in the preceding series on various heroes and their individual genealogies and adventures, largely because Hercules appears in nearly every fable and because the mythographer follows a roughly chronological pattern in tracing his life. From his conception by Jupiter during the triple-length night of lovemaking with Alcmene (Mythogr. II 171/148) and baby Hercules's killing of the two snakes sent by Juno (172/148), the mythographer moves to his encounters, mostly with adversaries that seem to reflect the occasions of the twelve (rather than ten) Labors.[31]

The sea-myths related to Neptune as progenitor (Mythogr. II 194/167–218/191) boast only the loosest unity, and most are not very interesting,[32] with the exception of the myths influenced by glosses on Boethius, such as that of Polyphemus (201/174). In this fable the mythographer repeats the identification of the one-eyed Polyphemus as blind, overcome by the *prudentia* of the hero Ulysses, also found in Remigian glosses on Boethius (*Consolatio* 4 m6; however, here the second Vatican mythography adds that some commentators note Polyphemus had one, two, or three eyes, "quod totum fabulosum est," for this "uir prudentissimus" is said to have had an eye in his head next to his brain, "quia perspicatius prudentia quam corporeo intuitu cernere uidebatur" ["because he seemed to have clearer understanding through his wisdom than through his physical sight"].

A series of transformations into trees, flowers, unguents, and birds, perhaps linked by the Ovidian idea of transformation, but perhaps also linked by a chain-of-being motif, interrupts the watery series;[33] the remainder of the fables in this series are linked, if at all, only tenuously.

The Trojan Royal Family. In the Trojan series (Mythogr. II 219/192–254/210), the last discernibly coherent series in the mythography, the second Vatican mythography again patiently reconstructs by means of individual fables on the principal characters the sequence of events leading up to the fall of Troy. Most interesting, given the preoccupation of this mythographer with genealogy, is the first fable, which details the origins of the

Trojans in the conception of Dardanus upon the mating of Jupiter and Electra (in a manner similar to Mythogr. I 132/135; see table 12). Subsequent fables in this series will further elucidate familial relationships.

The Troy story is built upon betrayal and deceit, upon things taken, or unwisely kept. Laomedon, father of Priam, asks Apollo and Neptune to help him build Troy's walls, but reneges on payment, after which Neptune in anger sends a sea-monster to Troy which can be placated, according to Apollo, only by virgin sacrifices. This initial angering of Neptune is the foundation upon which the city rises and will ultimately lead to its destruction (Mythogr. II 220/193). In the meantime Laomedon's brother Tithonus is loved by Aurora; their son Memnon will aid Troy during the war (221/194). And also Anchises, the grandson of Laomedon's uncle Assarcus, will consort with Venus to produce Aeneas, the founder of Italy (222/195); Anchises is crippled by lightning after he boasts over wine of his relationship with her. Foreshadowings of the ultimate fall of Troy appear in the prophecies of Cassandra, daughter of Priam and grand-daughter of Laomedon (223/196), whom no one believes, and in the dream of Hecuba, wife of Priam pregnant with Paris (225/197), of a city burning which will be caused by her son Paris; although Priam demands his death, his mother sends him to a shepherd to be raised. The deceit and theft associated with Troy is anticipated also in Jupiter's rape of Laomedon's brother Ganymede during the war with the Titans (226/198). At this point the mythographer returns us to the problem of Laomedon with the sea-monster by interjecting the fable of Hercules and Hylas, his companion (227/199), who accompany the Argonautic expedition until Hylas falls in the river and is taken by Nymphs. Even Hercules is deceived by the Trojans: when he arrives at Troy he delivers Laomedon's daughter Hesione from the monster but is himself not recompensed as promised, so he overcomes Laomedon and gives his daughter to Telamon (from which union issues Teucer). After this, Paris eventually steals Helen and initiates the Trojan War.

Ulysses and the Greeks. The second Vatican mythography then briefly[34] turns to the Greek side of the story and in particular the national theme of unforgiveable sacrifice of offspring, with the Greek foreshadowings of doom that are given to Ulysses very early in the saga (Mythogr. II 228/200). Wily Ulysses, who had apparently been told by an oracle that he would return home alone after twenty years if he went to the wars, pretends to be mad by plowing with two different beasts and sowing salt in the fields, but Palamedes, the envoy of Menelaus, places Ulysses's son Telema-

TABLE 12
TROJAN ROYAL FAMILY

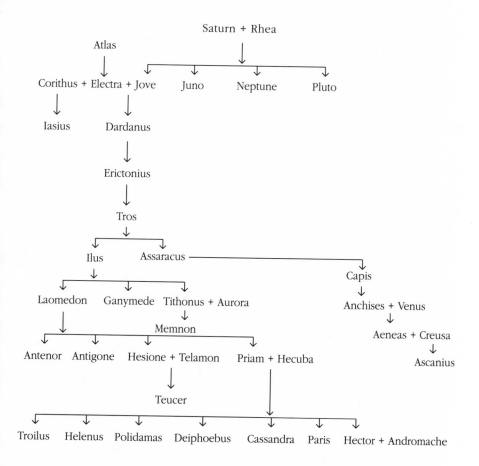

chus before the plow and Ulysses swerves to avoid him. From that point Palamedes, son of Nauplius and grandson of Neptune and Aminoe, daughter of Danaus, becomes Ulysses's enemy. Ulysses's revenge is to trick Agamemnon by means of a letter into thinking Palamedes is a traitor and thereafter kill him. The cunning of Ulysses is matched by that of Nauplius after his son's death: after the fall of Troy Nauplius deceives the returning Greeks into thinking that dangerous rocks are in fact safe, after which most of them perish (229/201).

The whole Oresteia, beginning with Agamemnon's mistake in sacrificing his daughter Iphigenia to Diana in order to move the Greek ships to war with the appropriate winds, is summarized in the next fable; this actual sacrifice contrasts with Ulysses's refusal to sacrifice his son to the plow in order to remain at home instead of going to war. Because of this sacrifice, Agamemnon's wife Clytemnestra sleeps with Aegisthus; Orestes her son then kills both of them and is pursued by the Furies. He escapes from Tauris with his sister, and she marries Pylades. Neither child of Agamemnon will produce offspring.

The Judgment of Paris. The interpretation of the Judgment in effect rounds out the whole of the second Vatican mythography by focusing on the conjunction of elements in the Stoic cosmic marriage—perhaps chosen because of the Carolingian interest in Martianus Capella's Marriage—and the role of will in the individual's life. After two fables (Mythogr. II 247/203–248/204) which explain the etiology of the Myrmidons who fought with Ajax at the request of Eacus for extra men for defense, the second Vatican mythography offers a very long double fable (248/205–249/206) on the Judgment of Paris and thus the second cause of the Trojan War (also found in part in the first Vatican mythography 204/207–205/208)—identified as cupiditas. The first part presents the literal version, the second, the Fulgentian moralization of the fable. Because Jupiter feared sleeping with Thetis, mother of the nymphs, thinking she would bear a son prophesied to be greater than his father, the mortal Peleus marries her. At their wedding all of the gods are invited except Discordia, who comes anyway to disrupt the festivities by throwing a golden fruit (apple) through the door, inscribed with the message that the fairest should take it. The three goddesses Juno, Venus, and Minerva all vie for the apple, until Jove decrees Paris should decide; tempted by Venus's promise of the beautiful Helen, he rejects Juno and Minerva, whose subsequent enmity towards Troy ensures its fall. Thereafter Thetis and Peleus do produce a son greater than his father—Achilles, whose mother, fearing his death, dips him into the river Styx, making all of him but his heel immortal. Later, because Agamemnon took from Achilles the captive maid Briseis, Achilles refuses to fight the Trojans; his friend Patroclus uses his armor to kill Sarpedon, son of Jove and Europa, and is later killed by Hector. After Achilles obtains new armor from Vulcan and kills Hector, because he desires Polyxena she is left before his tomb, where Achilles is killed by Apollo in the form of Paris by means of an arrow through his heel.

The Stoic natural moralization of this material comes from Fulgentius (Mit. 3.7), used nearly verbatim: Thetis as a nymph signifies water;

therefore, Jove cannot sleep with her because he is fire and water extinguishes fire. The marriage of Thetis and Peleus symbolizes the concord necessary to bind diverse elements in such a creation and therefore Jove invites all the gods to the wedding, for in a human different gods rule different parts (Jove, the head; Minerva, the eyes; Juno, the arms; Neptune, the breast; Mars, the heart; Venus, the kidneys and sex organs; Mercury, the feet). Peleus, from "Pelops" in Greek, means "earth" or flesh, and together he and Thetis produce the body of man, their union blessed by Jove (fire, the soul): "Peleus nanque ut terra, id est caro, Thetidi ut aque, id est humori, coniungitur, Iuppiter ut ignis, id est anima, utrumque iungere dicitur." Discord is not invited to the wedding because of the concord between the two elements necessary for a human to be produced; when she arrives, the apple she is said to have thrown in to the wedding feast signifies *cupiditas,* desire, "nam in aureo malo est quod uideas, non inest quod comedas" ["for in a golden apple there is something to see, not to eat"] (Mythogr. II 249/206).

The three goddesses, according to the mythographer (but not to Fulgentius), represent tripartite life for humanity, that is, the theoretical, the practical, and the voluptuary (the latter related to the golden apple and literally love of money, related to desire through "lust of the eyes"). The second Vatican mythography (and Fulgentius before him or her) relates the three goddesses to the three lives: Minerva as *theorica,* or the contemplative life, involves the search for knowledge and truth; Juno as *practica,* or the active life, seeks adornment and possessions; and Venus as *philargica* or *voluptaria,* the voluptuary life, is devoted to lust and is sinful. Jove could not judge between these, Fulgentius (*Mit.* 2.1) and the second Vatican mythographer agree, because humans have free will (*liberum arbitrium*) and thus should not be constrained by Jove's choice.

Morally, Paris, because he was neither beautiful, wise, nor talented, chose as an animal rather than as a human. Ironically, he will be responsible for ending the life of desiring Achilles, a foil for Paris, even though this fable does not say so. The mythographer returns from this digression to a moralization (from Fulgentius, *Mit.* 3.7) of Thetis's dipping of her son Achilles into the Styx, which signifies her desire to make him perfect. Because she held him by the heel, only that spot made him vulnerable—an appropriate place because of the vein running from the kidneys to the toe, the seat of lust. Achilles's desire for Polyxena ends his life, her name in Greek meaning "to be a foreigner to many," because "love causes minds to travel"—or become distracted ("quia amor peregrinari facit mentes"). The remainder of the Trojan fables continue the narrative aftermath of the fall of Troy, with fables either about Trojans or Greeks.[35]

Of this last group, the three fables on Circe may derive from the Carolingian glosses on Boethius as well as from fables in the first Vatican mythography (especially Mythogr. I 15/15), but all colored by the Fulgentian interpretation of Circe as lust (*Mit.* 2.9), with Ulysses, as wisdom, married to Penelope the chaste. In this fable Ulysses can sail past Circe because all wisdom condemns lust and is married to chastity; lustful Circe signifies "manus operatio," manual labor, because her name comes from "cironore," "judgment of the hand" or "working skill" (a Fulgentian etymology) and "labores enim manuum libidinosa mulier non diligit" ["the lustful woman does not respect manual labor"] (Mythogr. II 256/212). Circe is depicted as a daughter of the sun because nothing is brighter than the sun (an interpretation found both in the glosses on Boethius's *Consolatio* 4 m6 and on *De nuptiis*). That she loves Picus (Mythogr. II 257/213), who also spurns her and is therefore transformed into a wood-pecker, appears also in the first Vatican mythographer (Mythogr. I 179/182).

As if reminded of the unfinished Greek family line beginning with Minerva's near-son Erichthonius, the second Vatican mythography turns to descendants of the earliest kings, all of whom suffer unfortunate endings to their love relationships. Cephalus, husband of Procris, is the son of Herse, the Athenian king Cecrops's daughter, and Mercury (although the mythographer does not reveal this lineage in 260/216) and beloved by Aurora (mother of Memnon, who died at Troy); Cephalus accidentally kills his suspicious wife Procris when she follows him to spy on his hunting (Mythogr. II 260/216). The horrible story of the second Athenian king Pandion's two daughters, Procne and Philomela, and the rape and tongue-cutting of the second by the husband of the first, Tereus, is told next (261/217). Leander drowns while attempting to swim the Hellespont for love of Hero (262/218). The Athenian youth Hymeneus is revealed as the god of marriage, in a fable influenced by the Martianus glosses on Hymen, as we can see if we compare it with the version of the first mythographer. The first Vatican mythography tells the euhemeristic story of the beautiful Athenian boy Hymen who despaired of marriage because he himself sprang from middle-class parents; he participated, along with the virgins, in the sacred Eleusinian mysteries of Ceres, was abducted by pirates, escaped, and married (Mythogr. I 74/75). In contrast to this historical fable, the second Vatican mythography offers from the beginning Hymen's alternate role as "deus nuptiarum," which explains the assertion of both texts that brides still invoke his name as the liberator of their virginity (that is, one who sets them free from virginity; Mythogr. II 263/219). At the very end of the mythography, the second Vatican mythographer (in Bode's version of the fable ordering) seems spurred by the euhemerism of the Hymen fable to offer similarly historical figures, or else obscure figures taken from the *Pseudacronis scholia in Horatium uetustiora,* especially on the *Epodes.*[36]

Oedipus Revisited. The second Vatican mythography finishes in Bode, as we noted previously, with the riddle of the Sphinx solved by Oedipus of Thebes, the answer an appropriate conclusion to this series of fables of heroic and flawed human life constituting the destiny of nations. Given the emphasis on historical families and on the oracles of the gods with which the collection ends, perhaps this Oedipal solution to the human riddle can be termed oracular. It is man who first crawls on all fours as a child, next walks upright (with help) on three and then on two legs, thereafter using a crutch to move about on three supports before he returns to all fours at life's end—man is a monster whose transformations puzzle and deform even him. Such a riddle provides an apt segue to the riddling debate of the *Ecloga Theoduli.*

A similar "History of the World"—the "Universal Genealogy" of the first Vatican mythography—will be epitomized, and repeated, by the anonymous author of the *Ecloga Theoduli,* written perhaps a little later but nearly contemporary. The chief difference—among several—is an innovative addition of Old Testament legends, whose superiority to classical fables of gods and heroes is debated behind the poetic masks of two shepherds. Such an innovation is the next logical step in the development of mythography: it should have been clear by now, to the medieval monks if not to us, that the parable of the Creation is similar in both the biblical and mythological accounts; that Saturn as Time might be analogous to the serpent who tempts Eve; that Deucalion and Pyrrha parallel Noah and his wife; that the Titans who attempt to overthrow Jove resemble Nimrod who builds his tower. The 230 myths of the second Vatican mythography (in Bode; Kulcsár lists 275) are pared and polished in the forty classical myths of the *Ecloga,* almost a mnemonic table of the longer work; this abbreviated form implies that the details of the specific fable, and its moralization, must be assumed as familiar to the listener. Despite these differences, another bond between the two might be termed their common "matter of gender," possibly as a result of the Carolingian commentaries on Martianus and possibly also because, as anonymous works, both may have been written by women. In the *Ecloga* this "matter" appears in the names of the debaters and, in the course of the debate, a set piece on the sexes, which we shall discuss in more depth in the next chapter, on the Germanic mythographies.

Chapter Nine

ATLAS AS NIMROD, HYDRA AS VUÚRM: GENDER AND MULTICULTURALISM IN THE *ECLOGA THEODULI*, NOTKER LABEO, AND BERNARD OF UTRECHT

Virgil had used the eclogue as a vehicle for hidden truths about Roman political history, which interested scholars in the Middle Ages less than his so-called Messianic, or fourth, eclogue, with its veiled prophecy of the coming of a divine child, especially popular in the ninth century.[1] Generally, though, as we have previously seen, Virgil's *Eclogues* were not much read in the Middle Ages and mythography in general was not much advanced through any commentary tradition related to them. Some time after 850 (probably in the tenth century), an unknown poet using the name "Theodulus" adopted the eclogue form once again, but to *unveil,* or reveal, a multicultural religious history. The *Ecloga Theoduli,* a 352-line debate poem, conjoins a roughly chronological series of figures from Graeco-Roman mythology to a series from the Hebraic Old Testament to ask a difficult question: how does pagan myth compare as a moral lesson in relation to the legends of the Old Testament? It is the very question of which the Alexandrians had been so fond centuries past.

Drawing its style from Virgil's third and seventh eclogues,[2] this amoebaean pastoral consists of a dialogue or debate in thirty-seven pairs of dactylic hexameter quatrains (with single internal, not strictly leonine, rhyme) between two shepherds following an introduction that explains how the two met and how their altercation led to a competition in song. "Pseustis," a transliteration of the Greek for "(female) liar" but according to the *accessus* meaning "stans in falsitate," is a goatherd from Athens; he sums up forty myths.[3] Alithia ("veritas Dei," from *ali,* taken from the Hebrew word for truth, and *thia,* or God, and in fact King David's descendant) is a female virgin shepherd who argues for the subjects of Old

Testament biblical legend—although scripture, as the Word of God, is privileged throughout as the superior text. While the pagan myth of Pseustis precedes the biblical legend of Alithia in each pair of quatrains, the whole is structured by Bible chronology: verses 37–180 on the Patriarchs, Exodus, occupation of Canaan, and Judges; verses 189–244 on the Kings and Prophets; verses 253–84 on the Exile (285–344 represent the conclusion).[4] At the end when the pagan begins to weaken and Pseustis admits his inferiority, a judge, Alithia's sister Fronesis (or Wisdom), intercedes and Alithia receives a concluding hymn of triumph and praise (in eight lines, attributed by scholars to a later reviser and omitted from some manuscripts).

In the light of the Christian primacy of the New Testament and the Word, both pagan fable and Old Testament story lay outside, anterior. But of the two, Old Testament story prefigured New Testament truth and thus could be understood as superior in its veracity to classical fable, no matter how apparently clever the pagan fable appeared to be. One immediate consequence of this debate between the pastoral representative of each point of view was the enhancement of non-mythographic, euhemeristic (historical) typology used to characterize the individual gods. But by coupling the traditions of classical mythology and biblical typology, the anonymous author of the *Ecloga Theoduli* would affect the way later generations of mythographers would interpret classical fable, *as if* conjoined with biblical story (although these later scholars would rely more and more on the New rather than the Old Testament).

Because "Theodulus" is probably a symbolic name reflective of the work's meaning ("Servant of God") rather than the Italian scholar imagined by later commentator Bernard of Utrecht in his *accessus*, it is possible that the debate poem was penned by a woman ecclesiast. Recent studies of medieval women religious writers have explored their reluctance to assume an authoritative and authorial position, partly because of their lack of education and their sense of inadequacy, so that many of their works may be listed as "anonymous." When educated women mystics such as Julian of Norwich or Margaret of Oingt do write, they often confess their female ignorance and frailty in what has been identified as a modesty topos.[5] Although we have no concrete evidence about the identity of "Theodulus" as male or female, evidence in the text suggests at least a feminizing trend: the female shepherd Alithia ("truth of God") who promotes scripture has the edge over the male goatherd Pseustis ("[female] liar") who promotes classical mythology. And in the course of the literal debate there occur, according to Betty Nye Quinn, mini-quarrels about the sexes (*Ecl. Theod.* 4–5 with 8–9, 269–76, 296 and 312 with 300 and 316).

For the debate is one between representatives of each sex, a *pastor* (*Ecl. Theod.* 4) and a *virgo* (9). The use of the word *pastor* is somewhat ironic if the work has been written by a woman: surely it points to the priest, the "good shepherd" of parishioners (including women), in a use current in, for example, Gregory's *Cura pastoralis;* the *virgo* also reminds us of the Virgin, a type of the female ecclesiastic destined to win by virtue of that same spiritual typology dramatized in the *Ecloga* (see figure 21, a pictorial accessus to a thirteenth-century copy of the *Ecloga*). Further, and perhaps ironically, the chronology of Old Testament history, divisible into three epochs, concludes with an account of the Exile—but one in which only females figure (with the exception of Daniel).

The domination of one sex—the male—at beginning and the other at end mirrors both the order in which the sexes debate throughout and also the appearance and reality of victory. Fronesis asks that Pseustis begin first because he is male, the female Other to follow: "Perge prior, Pseusti, quia masculus; illa sequaci / Aequabit studio" ("Being the man, you go first, Pseustis. She'll follow and keep up with you," *Ecl. Theod.* 34–35). Further, the misogyny of Pseustis rests upon the old female intellectual deficiency argument: "Mens robusta viri levitate cadit muliebri" ["The strong mind of the man is ruined by female frivolity"], he declares, citing women's use of the herb hippomanes (an abortifacient?) to "make their limbs bloody," and the example of Medea (*Ecl. Theod.* 269, 270–72). Alithia counters with the telling example of strong-minded Judith and Holofernes, "crazed with passion":

Femineas vires expavit dux Olofernes
Insignis viduae vesano captus amore:
Deflent Assirii, quod crediderit mulieri.

[The general Holofernes, crazed with passion for the famous widow, was in complete awe of woman's strength. The Assyrians weep, because he trusted a woman.] (*Ecl. Theod.* 273–76)

The virgin is virtuous, faithful—and militant. When Pseustis remarks, "Cede, dies, caelo, quia nescit cedere virgo" ["Give in, day, to the sky, because the virgin does not know how to yield"] (296, repeated in 312), Alithia counters, "Fige, dies, cursum, ne perdat virgo triumphum" ["Keep to your course, day, lest the virgin lose her triumph"] (300 and 316).

21. Pseustis (Liar), Fronesis (Judgment), Alithia (Truth). Frontispiece to *Ecloga Theoduli*. MS. Latinus 15158, fol. 13v (13th c.). Courtesy of Bibliothèque Nationale, Paris.

The advent of this innovative work, so little known today but so important as a school-text in the later Middle Ages, would radically change the mythographic tradition. With its memorable quatrains the *Ecloga Theoduli* preserved classical mythology and its coupling with biblical figures throughout the Middle Ages. Extant in over two hundred manuscripts, it was part of the school curriculum by the end of the eleventh century and, by the fourteenth century, comprised part of the *Auctores octo,* a canon of eight authors used for elementary Latin instruction.[6] It accrued its own commentary tradition lasting into the fifteenth century: variations on the dominant Bernard of Utrecht commentary were offered by the twelfth-century English scholar Alexander Neckam, the fourteenth-century French scholar Odo (Eudes) of Picardy and the English scholar "Stephen Patrington" (which essentially duplicated Neckam), and the fifteenth-century Anonymous Teutonicus.[7]

Such currency argues that the poem had greater power in the development of the mythographic tradition and its vernacularization than has been credited in the past; true, as a literary work, however much imitated in the eleventh century,[8] the *Ecloga* generally appeared to have little influence on medieval literature and was not translated. Most influential in England, as a handbook of classical mythology it was helpful to Geoffrey Chaucer, as evidenced by his allusions to it in *House of Fame* and *Legend of Good Women* (the legend of Demophon and Phyllis), and also to a Boethius commentator, probably Nicholas Trivet, of the fourteenth century.[9] Apparently in general the *Ecloga* was not acknowledged or cited explicitly as a mythographic source in the Middle Ages.[10] Because of its probable Germanic origins and influence on Notker Labeo's glosses on Boethius and Martianus it may have transmitted its mythography directly or indirectly to the English Boethius commentator and to Chaucer (who also translated Boethius into Middle English). It also includes mythological references found later only in Boccaccio and Dante. As a storehouse of mythological reference the *Ecloga* has never been fully analyzed for influence on later vernacular poetry.

Its unusual mythographic features include, first, of course, its conjunction of the mythological with biblical typology in a Virgilian pastoral debate; then, its relatively brief mythographic exposition in extension of the Carolingian interest in mythological genealogy as history found in the second Vatican mythography—even though the *Ecloga* is also imbued with a feminizing Stoicism familiar from the Carolingian commentators on Martianus. These changes would most directly influence other Germanic commentators of this transitional period, and indirectly, after the French philosophers of the twelfth century, the Ovidian mythographers of the thirteenth and fourteenth centuries.

The two most important commentators directly affected by the *Ecloga* were Notker Labeo (d. ca. 1022), who in his glosses translated into Old High German portions of Boethius and Martianus Capella by using as a base the Remigius glosses on both, and Bernard of Utrecht, who wrote the primary commentary on the poem (ca. 1091) dedicated to the Swabian, Conrad of Utrecht (the commentary was also very popular in Swabia and

Bavaria). If the *Ecloga* conjoins the Latin mythological tradition with the Hebrew typological tradition, then Notker, through his mythological glosses in the vernacular, couples the Latin mythological tradition with the epic heroism and literalism of the native Germanic tradition, leaving intact the Latin for untranslatable (and immoral, sexually explicit) words and concepts. Bernard of Utrecht, in his late eleventh-century commentary, influenced by the Carolingian Boethius and Martianus commentaries and the Vatican mythographies, and the mounting literalism of all, in commenting on the *Ecloga* interweaves all of this.

The late extension of the Alfredian and Carolingian educational reform and emphasis on the vernacular into Switzerland and Southeastern Germany would generally facilitate the transmission of the mythographic tradition. That Remigius had taught at Auxerre and Rheims before moving to Paris may explain the migration of materials from Northeastern France to Southwestern Germany and even to the Netherlands, at St. Gall and apparently Utrecht. In 998 Notker's bishop Hugo commanded him to direct his attention in teaching to the seven liberal arts, a goal which no doubt influenced Notker's decision to translate both Boethius and Martianus Capella, relying heavily for both on Remigius's commentaries. The Carolingian interest in education had long been shared by the abbey at St. Gall where Notker taught, and copies of previous commentaries were available at the monastery. The *Ecloga* commentary by Bernard of Utrecht, dedicated to Conrad of Utrecht (bishop from 1075–99), was probably written in 1091 because the dedicatory epistle imitates the end of the third letter of Yves de Chartres, written in that year.[11]

The more conservative temper of the times would, however, result in the omission or suppression of material considered offensive to the Church. The rationalization of the gods as planets, or assimilation of the Latin and learned culture into what might be understood as more native and heroic in the vernacular, concerned with warfare and victory, had led, in the *Ecloga Theoduli,* to the comparison of pagan mythology with Old Testament history. Notker's use of sources in both commentaries included the *Ecloga Theoduli,* the first Vatican mythography, and other Boethius materials (the Anonymous of St. Gall, for example), all available at St. Gall. When Notker translated into Old High German works by Boethius and Martianus, he added native heroic and mythological significations to the accumulated glosses on the gods and subtly changed the shape of both prosimetra by making the metrical mythological heroes more Germanic and by suppressing the Stoic references to gender.

In Notker's glosses we find an interrelationship with the *Ecloga*. In the Boethius glosses, the gods are euhemerized into historical figures and the heroes' battles with adversaries loom as Germanic epic confrontations with a hostile and threatening nature. There is accordingly an elegiac wistfulness in much of Notker very like that of other heroic vernacular poems in both Anglo-Saxon and Old High German which attempt to recuperate early national history. There is little effort to moralize and mythographize the gods figuratively; we are back in the more literalistic, historical waters of the first Vatican mythography. And yet, in relation to Boethius, Notker's greatest originality is to parallel Boethius explicitly with biblical material, centuries ahead of the *Ovide moralisé* and Pierre Bersuire. Thus he relates the giants Otus and Ephialtes (*Consolatio* 3 p12), to the war on heaven and the tower of Babel, the moral of the Orpheus poem to Luke 9:62 on entering the kingdom of God (as did Remigius), and Phoebus (4 m1) to Christ, although even this may not be original but in fact drawn from the revisions of Remigius and from earlier sources like Theodulf of Orleans and Fulgentius.[12]

In his translation of Martianus, Notker avoids the femininizing emphasis found in Remigius on Martianus, and once again generally prefers the masculine gods. But unlike the Neo-Stoic glosses of the Carolingians, Notker's Martianus glosses emphasize the gods as literal planets or as aspects of the earthly agricultural processes with a definite contemporary cast. When he does not borrow directly from Remigius or John Scot on Martianus, his translations into Old High German nevertheless avoid translation of terms relating to concupiscence, moral and theological abstractions, or the underworld. His literalism in the vernacular reduces and simplifies the gods to animistic forces of the earth or of the body.

The commentary of Bernard of Utrecht, influenced by the continuing dominance of the philosophical Martianus commentaries so important in the post-Carolingian period, nevertheless also reflects the trend toward literalization of myth found in the Vatican mythographers, the *Ecloga,* and Notker Labeo while it anticipates the kind of scholasticism of which the University of Paris would become so fond. Bernard is aware of Stoic philosophy, decisively ignores whatever references to gender may have been prevalent in the earlier mythographies, and transfers the Germanic interest in pagan heroism to his Old Testament heroes in particular, despite the occasional mythological hero like Hercules. Bernard's chief sources in his glosses, as we might expect, are Servius, Martianus and his commentaries, Boethius commentaries, Isidore, and the Vatican mythographies.

Bernard pulls together diverse strands of mythographic commentary—the historical or literal (from the first Vatican mythography and the Berne scholiast), which often becomes euhemeristic, the Stoic natural or physical, as well as the etymological, moral, or tropological (from Remigius on Martianus and Boethius, echoed by the second Vatican mythographer), and which Bernard calls "Misterium" or "Physice." Bernard also isolates the allegorical (the specific Christological interpretation), which was just beginning to be applied to classical heroes like Hercules in the Boethius glosses, and applies it only to Old Testament heroes like Samson and David in an updating of scriptural typology; he calls these "Allegoria." By layering all of these, he achieves a new form of mythographization that will powerfully influence later scholars.

Its method, more than its content, is important for mythographic reasons: Bernard expresses his awareness of the Stoic interpretations of myth transmitted via the Carolingian commentators on Martianus and the Vatican mythographers by a restrictive equation. Bernard's method with the fable and the history is to comment on the same quatrain three times under different headings, first the literal levels (getting the sense right) under "hoc fabulose" (for Pseustis's "inferior" pagan readings) and "hoc historaliter" (for Alithia's "superior" biblical quatrains). But the higher levels involve *misterium* (for Pseustis) and *allegoria* (for Alithia), the former representing classical fabula euhemeristically, and the latter essentially interpreting the Old Testament typologically, that is, as a prefiguration of the New Testament. In addition the pagan myths are interpreted *per phisicem,* that is, naturalistically, in the Stoic manner, and the scriptural legends, morally or tropologically, that is, with the individual representing moral abstractions. His association of the classical tradition with Stoic physical allegory omits much of the mythographic tradition, which is accordingly transferred to the Hebraic tradition.

Because Bernard's commentary couples the biblical and the classical, along with the *Ecloga* itself and Notker's glosses it no doubt helped to influence later medieval (thirteenth and fourteenth century) juxtapositions, chiefly in relation to Ovid, for example, by Robert Holkot and Pierre Bersuire, who link the ecclesiastical or scriptural with undermeanings of the classical text. Christine de Pizan will also use this latter method in her early fifteenth-century allegorized Ovid, *L'Epistre Othea.* Let us turn now to an analysis of the mythographic methods of the *Ecloga.*

I. GENDER AND MYTHOGRAPHY IN THE *ECLOGA THEODULI:* (FEMALE) OLD TESTAMENT VERSUS (MALE) PAGAN FABLE

Although the date and authorship of the *Ecloga* have been debated, consensus is for the tenth century[13] and for an author living in northern Europe, given the reference in the third verse indicating that south of the Alps there were no more linden trees, from which Manitius has argued that he was a Saxon.[14] Given what we know from internal evidence regarding its mythography, a later rather than an earlier date is likely, probably around the year 1000. Because Martianus Capella is cited in the *Ecloga* and Martianus was not really popular in the Middle Ages until the third decade of the Carolingian period, the *Ecloga* was clearly not written before that decade and was—contrary to some scholarly opinions—possibly written after, perhaps in the tenth century. And of the possibilities for author-ship—Gennadius Theodulus,[15] "Godescalc," possibly Gottschalk of Or-bais (ca. 805–ca. 867) or an author from Rheims[16]—one possibility I would like to take up here is that of the earliest known poet in Germany, from the Ottonian period, the female canon Hrosvitha of Gaudersheim, or Hrotsvit (ca. 932–ca. 1000).[17]

Perhaps the most telling sign of common interests in both the Saxon Hrotsvit and the *Ecloga* author is the focus upon the feminine as heroic and ideal, expressed by means of triumphant female characters in the drama of human salvation.[18] In addition, that Hrotsvit authored the *Ecloga Theoduli* is plausible given her dates; her use of rhyme, not only in her dramas but also in her legends and epics; her demonstrated continuing interest in the clash between pagan and Christian; her many innovative works in genres that borrow from classical authors (she apparently knew Horace, Ovid, Statius, Lucan, Boethius, Terence, Virgil); and finally, her knowledge of Christian writers like Prudentius and of medieval grammatical commen-taries like that of Isidore.[19] I would add Fulgentius to the list: the Prooemium to her works presents a dialogue between Terence and "Per-sona" most reminiscent of the exchange between Virgil and Fulgentius in the *Continentia Virgiliana.* The dialogue or debate is a form also used in the *Ecloga.* Finally, her etymological explanation of her name "Hrotsvit" in its symbolism resembles that of the name "Theodulus": referring to herself as "clamor validis Gandeshemensis," or "the strong voice of Gandersheim," in the introduction to her dramas, she translates into Latin the Old Saxon for "Strong Voice," that is, "suid" plus "hruot"—or Hrotsvit.

In Hrotsvit's other works mythological references, while not plentiful, do illustrate a thematic pattern of conflict between pagan and biblical, although Hrotsvit firmly identifies Christ or the Christian and not merely the Old Testament as the truth against which the pagan god introduced must be measured. For example, in the play *Sapientia* the characters Hadrian, Antiochus, and Spes (Hope) joke about the natural versus spiritual change suggested by the fire of Vulcanus and the calming power of Christ:

> ADRIANUS. Aeneum vas, plenum oleo et adipe, cera atque pice,
> ignibus superponatur, in quod ligata proiciatur.
> ANTIOCHUS. Si in ius Vulcani tradetur,
> forsitan evadendi aditum non nanciscetur.
> SPES. Haec virtus Christo non est insolita,
> ut ignem faciat mitescere, mutata natura.

> [HADRIAN: Place a bronze pot full of oil, wax, fat, and pitch over the flames, and tie her up and throw her in.
> ANTIOCHUS: Perhaps when she is given over to Vulcan's force, there'll be no way to escape the fire.
> SPES: Christ's mighty power has been known to change the nature of fire, to make its rage harmlessly expire.][20]

The Christianized Terentian comedy apparent from this brief snippet argues convincingly for likeness with the *Ecloga*, also in its dialogue humorous.

If one considers the origins of Pseustis in Athens, home of Greek *philosophy*, meaning Stoicism and Platonism as well as mythology and pagan religion, then the scholastic distinctions of the *Ecloga* become more clearly parallel to those in Hrotsvit's other works. All the gods mentioned by Hrotsvit in her works are connected with the natural world, especially the sun, but also grain, the heavens, fire, and they would be familiar (to us and perhaps to Hrotsvit) from the predominant Neo-Stoic glosses in the Carolingian commentaries on Martianus and in the second Vatican mythography. Phoebus appears in the legends *Maria* (lines 360, 364) and *Theophilus* (424) and the epic *Primordia coenobii Gandeshemensis* (210); Ceres appears in the epic *Gesta Ottonis* (554 and 575); Oceanus appears in the legend *Pelagius* (106) and also *Gesta Ottonis* (135); Vulcanus appears in the play *Sapientia* (5.24). Further, Stoicism explicitly surfaces in Hrotsvit's reference to Phoebus in *Primordia* because of the reference to aether ("Ut Phoebus radios spargebat ab aethere primos, / Fit notum, fama cunctis prodente iocunda," "As Phoebus spreads the first rays from the aether, / Let it be noted, fame for all together producing delight"),[21] lines according to von Winterfeld similar in language to Boethius (*Consolatio* 2 m3.1: "Cum polo Phoebus roseis quadrigis / Lucem spargere coeperit," "When Phoebus from his roseate car / Begins to spread his light across the sky").[21]

If Stoicized mythography offered to medieval schoolmasters a figurative paraphrase of the origins of Original Sin and the fall of humankind, then knowledge of that veiling history would be valuable for Christians familiar with the story of creation and fall outlined in the Old Testament. The scholastic catechism in the *Ecloga* begins then with the analogous story of Saturn of Crete (*Ecl. Theod.* 37–40, castrated *genitor*, Dante's Old Man of Crete in *Inferno*, canto 14, lines 94–111), paralleled with Adam (41–44, for whom the punishment of death guarantees the necessity of offspring). This fable is followed by Jupiter's expulsion of Saturn from Italy (45–48, the Silver Age succeeding the Golden Age), paralleled by Alithia with Adam and Eve leaving Eden (49–52). Pallas Athena's "grandson" Cecrops and the sacrifice of bulls to Jove (53–56) are paralleled with Cain and Abel and their very different sacrifices to God (57–60). Lycaon of Arcadia transformed into wolf as he opposes Jove (61–64) is equated with Enoch and his *raptus* into heaven (65–68). The regenerative floods experienced by the new Adam and Eve, Deucalion and Pyrrha (69–72), are like those of Noah and his wife (73–76); although the succeeding and related pair, Ganymede abducted into the heavens by Jove's eagle (77–80) and the raven and dove sent out for signs of life after the deluge (81–84), seem tenuously matched. The analogous pairs continue with:

85–88	The Gigantomachia
89–92	The Tower of Babylon
93–96	The Death of Peonus
97–100	Abraham
101–4	Daedalus and Icarus
105–8	Abraham and Isaac
109–12	Phyllis and Demophon
113–16	Sodom and Lot
177–20	Diomedes
121–24	Jacob

In addition, there is at least one Stoicized cosmological passage in the *Ecloga*, curiously like some of the passages in the works of Hrotsvit, though it also recalls the Martianus commentaries and the second Vatican mythography. This passage concerns the "nomina mille deum" of paganism in contrast to the Trinity of Christianity, paradoxically three-in-one. In attacking the many names of the gods of Dis, Pseustis cries,

> Nomina mille deum vatem defendite vestrum
> Qui colitis Ditem, qui stelliferam regionem,
> Qui partes mundi, qui stagna sonantis abissi:
> Nomina mille deum vatem defendite vestrum.

> [Defend your bard, o gods with a thousand names, who dwell in the land of Dis, in the region of the stars, in the different parts of the universe, in the pools of the sounding abyss, defend your poet, o gods with a thousand names!] (*Ecl. Theod.* 181–84)

The Oneness of the three-personed God signals, in contrast, majesty, glory, virtue, without beginning and end. The point of similarity between Hrotsvit and "Theodulus" resides in their explicit mythological contrast between figures ruling cosmic regions and the true God. The idea may very well have derived from the other sources used by "Theodulus" (and Hrotsvit).

Even though the *Ecloga* culminates in Fronesis granting victory to Dominus, the One God, it actually ends with references to classical deities as metaphors for natural forces. By means of this balance the original ending seems to stress an equality between classical fable and Old Testament legend. At the end of the *Ecloga* the pairs of quatrains might be said to conclude (we will examine them in greater detail in discussion of Bernard of Utrecht's commentary) with Mopsus and Calchas, two pagan priests who understand veiled truths (*Ecl. Theod.* 325–38), contrasted with the Evangelists and the Virgin (329–32). The ambiguity of the ending warranted a seven-line and more explicitly Christianized *coda* to the debate by a later poet, at least in some manuscripts. In the original ending, Fronesis begins with:

Mortales cuncti quod contendunt adipisci
Nec, si perficiant, vitae discrimina curant,
Ex insperato Dominus tibi contulit ultro:
Ut cessare velis, devictus supplicat hostis.

[Spontaneously and unexpectedly, the Lord has conferred upon you
that which all mortals strive to obtain, and for which they make light
of life's dangers, if only they can achieve it: a beaten foe is begging
you to lay off!] (*Ecl. Theod.* 337–40)

In line with the notion of balance and symmetry found throughout
Hrotsvit, Fronesis then adds at the very end of the original conclusion a
focus upon mythological figures such as the Thracian bard, the Manes,
Phoebe, Oceanus:

Treïcius vates commovit pectine *Manes,*
Te moveant lacrimae; iam tollit cornua *Phoebe;*
Sol petit *Oceanum,* frigus succedit opacum:
Desine quod restat, ne desperatio laedat.

[The *Thracian bard* moved the *spirits of the dead* with his plectrum; let
tears move you. *Phoebe* is already rearing her horns; the sun is making
for the *ocean,* a cold night is coming on; stop now, lest despair lead to
harm.] (*Ecl. Theod.* 341–44; my emphasis)

The interpolated seven lines (*Ecl. Theod.* 345–51) refer explicitly to the
triune God as omnipotent and eternal ruler, leaving no doubt as to the
outcome of the debate.

   The major sources for the *Ecloga*—in form and in mythological reference—are mostly either classical or late classical, or Carolingian and
mythographic. Its combination of frame debate and epitome of various
mythological tracts also echoes Fulgentius's *Mitologiae,* which sets the
grammarian against Calliope, and whose three books of fable (as I have
argued earlier) reveal mythographical miniatures of Martianus, Boethius,
and Ovid. In its form a debate between truth and error, the *Ecloga* may be
indebted to Prudentius's *Psychomachia;*[22] another dialogue model, in some
ways a fantasy itself drawn from the schools using the works of Virgil as
grammatical texts, is Fulgentius's *Continentia Virgiliana,* which also provides a kind of debate (or at least interlocution) between a pagan and a
Christian, in the figures of Fulgentius the "homunculus" (or pupil) and

Virgil the "magister." Certainly the variety of mythological sources for the *Ecloga* supports such an interpretation of mythographic debate, in addition to the model of Virgil's *Eclogues* and the commentary of Servius, Ovid's *Metamorphoses,* Prudentius, Sedulius, and Martianus Capella. And yet another source for one passage is Isidore and (as source or parallel) for three passages, the first Vatican mythographer.[23]

The use the *Ecloga* makes of the *Metamorphoses,* particularly in its genealogical and historical form, shows Ovid was receiving more attention than in the past, perhaps because of the influence of Theodulf of Orleans. The Ovidian passages are legion, beginning with Saturn's castration by Jupiter (*Ecl. Theod.* 37–40; *Metamorphoses* 1.114ff).[24] And there are references to Ovid's *Heroides,* 2 for Phyllis and 6 and 12 for Medea.

What has not been much noticed are the parallels between the remaining mythological passages in the *Ecloga* and both of the Vatican mythographies, as well as Carolingian commentaries on Boethius and Martianus Capella, illustrating the transmission of glosses from mythography to mythography, in particular, from the north of France to Germany. For the sacrifice of bulls to Jove in the myth of Cecrops (*Ecl. Theod.* 53–56), the author drew on Isidore (*Etymologiae* 8.11.9–10), a favorite source also for the Martianus commentators of the period. For the parallel between the Giants' assault on Jupiter and Nimrod's tower of Babylon (*Ecl. Theod.* 85–92), the *Ecloga* may have had access to the unknown source used by Notker in glossing Boethius (*Consolatio* 3 p12), possibly a St. Gall source (unless it is original with the *Ecloga* and Notker borrowed from this work). Because it is so unusual a juxtaposition, it should be cited in full, especially as it also mentions Vulcan in the mythological quatrain, the son of Jove who helped him defeat the Giants by creating thunderbolts, but omits explicit mention of Nimrod in the scriptural quatrain, leaving the creation of the tower to the "posterity of Adam."

PSEUSTIS: Surrexere viri terra genitrice creati:
Pellere caelicolas fuit omnibus una voluntas;
Mons cumulat montem, sed totum *Mulciber* hostem
Fulmine deiectum Vulcani trusit in antrum.

ALITHIA: Posteritas Adae summa Babilonis in arce
Turrim construxit, quae caelum tangere possit.
Excitat ira Deum: confusio fit labiorum;
Disperguntur ibi; nomen non excidit urbi.

[PSEUSTIS: Men arose, the progeny of Mother Earth, united in their desire to drive out the inhabitants of heaven. Mountain is piled on mountain, but Mulciber cast down their whole opposing army with a thunderbolt and thrust them into Vulcan's cave.

ALITHIA: On the highest point in Babylon the descendants of Adam built a tower to touch the sky. God is moved to anger: there is a confusion of tongues; they are dispersed on the spot; the name of the city is not lost.] (*Ecl. Theod.* 85–92)

In relation to other Boethius and Martianus references, the fable on Orpheus (*Ecl. Theod.* 189–92) may also have derived from the Boethius glosses on *Consolatio* 3 m12 so popular at this time, as very likely did the fable on Phaethon's four horses (245–48), or at least from the K Reviser's interpolation into the Remigian glosses on the Herculean Labors (*Consolatio* 4 m7). The fable of Hercules's conception and struggle with the snakes as a baby (165–68) and of some of his Labors (173–76) seem to epitomize glosses on Martianus for the former and on Boethius (4 m7 again) for the latter. The reference to the twelve select gods mentioned in Ennius's couplet (288f) echoes Martianus (*De nuptiis* 42) but does not necessarily prove correspondence with the commentaries, although it does reflect interest in Martianus. The various fables on Mercury (especially in lines 197–200) and on Proserpina (317–20) may also have been drawn from Martianus commentaries, filled as they are with references to these figures.

References in the *Ecloga* to the Vatican mythographers include the unusual description of Juno suckling Mercury (*Ecl. Theod.* 197–200), which corresponds to the first Vatican mythography, fable 117/119, as does the passage on Ganymede and Jupiter (77–80) with fable 181/184.[25] Others from the second Vatican mythography not previously identified focus on Jove and Europa (141–44), "Europa" a name given to the third part of the world ("Nomen donat ei, quod habet pars tertia mundi"), as suggested by the early cosmic genealogy of second Vatican mythography. In addition, the *Ecloga's* mistake of Bellerophon (rather than Perseus) defeating the Gorgon with the help of Pallas Athena (213–16) recalls the second Vatican mythography (Mythogr. II, 154/131; the *Ecloga's* indebtedness to the first Vatican mythography 70/71 rather than to the second Vatican mythography for this mistake was first noted by T. W. Baldwin in 1941). The last fable, on Mopsus and Calchas (325–38), even if drawn from Servius (*In Buc.* 6.72), seems placed in line with its near-final position in the second Vatican mythography (268/224).

Because the *Ecloga Theoduli,* however important as an epitome of previous mythographic works and as an agent of their transmission in the Ottonian period following the Carolingian Renaissance, was not in fact truly influential as a schoolbook until the late eleventh century (an influence thus concurrent with Bernard of Utrecht's commentary), we shall first discuss the glossed paraphrases of Notker Labeo on Boethius and Martianus before examining the mythographic interpretation of the *Ecloga.* These glosses, like the *Ecloga,* are important for paralleling mythographic insights used in the Vatican mythographies and in the Carolingian commentaries on Boethius and Martianus, mostly by Remigius. But in addition the innovations in their mythography—their re-interpretation— would influence the mythographers of the twelfth century and later on both Boethius and Martianus—and other authors. At least these glosses helped to transmit to Bernard of Utrecht interpretations of Boethius and Martianus that he would find helpful in glossing those passages in the *Ecloga* especially close to those sources.

II. NOTKER LABEO'S ANTI-CAROLINGIAN MULTICULTURALISM

Notker's Germanic Reading of the Boethius Glosses

At St. Gall, available for Notker's use, were the Anonymous of St. Gall glosses on Boethius and continental or Anglo-Saxon manuscripts of the revisions of Remigius on Martianus. In addition, certainly an interest in the seven liberal arts similar to that of King Alfred, and before him, Alcuin and Cassiodorus, is clear from the history of the Abbey of St. Gall itself and also from the life of Notker. The school had been founded in the days of Othmar and consisted of an outer school for laymen and secular clergy-to-be, and an inner school for oblates. Latin grammar was taught to German-speaking Swabian (Swiss) youths by means of Virgil, Ovid, and Christian poets.[27]

While the Abbey at St. Gall was known for its school and for its scholarship, particularly commentaries and translations, nevertheless Notker represented through his own scholarship in the macaronic transla-tion-glosses the tip of an iceberg.[28] In his own writings and in teaching Notker revealed an especial interest in the arts, which he used (in accord with his bishop's instructions to him in 998) as a means to an end, that is, especially for the study of ecclesiastical works.[29] Other Latin works (besides the *Consolatio* and *De nuptiis*) that he translated into German with this end in mind and with the help of classical writers like Aristotle and Cicero to elucidate difficult phrases included Boethius's *De sancta Trinitate,* the *Disticha Catonis,* Virgil's *Eclogues,* Terence's *Andria,* Aristotle's *Categories, Hermeneutics,* and *Elements of Arithmetic,* the Psalter, and a third of the Book of Job; he also wrote a volume on rhetoric. Of these works the Psalter was the most popular, although his greatest contribution to scholarship was his system of orthography, devised so that he could spell with accents in his vernacular passages.

In his Boethius glosses Notker preserves the basically Remigian moralizations on mythological glosses while adding original comments that reflect his cultural or religious biases primarily through parallels flavored by the Bible or Germanic heroic literature. This structure itself recalls the *Ecloga Theoduli,* with its alternations of pagan and biblical materials. Indeed, Notker in his Boethius glosses on 3 p12, on Otus and Ephialtes, apparently either used the *Ecloga Theoduli,* 85–92 (possible if the eclogue was written no later than 1000, the date of its earliest manuscript, as Bühler has argued), or, less probably, influenced the *Ecloga Theoduli,* for that reference appears nowhere else.

The history of Boethius commentary grows complex after Remigius and his revisers; copies of his Boethius commentary were read in England in Anglo-Saxon monasteries and widely recopied in the tenth and eleventh centuries[30] because Remigius had Christianized Boethius. Thus Boethius studies were especially concentrated in monasteries associated with the reforms of Dunstan, Ethelwold, and Oswald—that is, the tenth-century reformation resulted in patristic and homiletic writings by the Anglo-Saxon Ethelwold and Wulfstan, vernacular history, drawings of the Winchester school, and the spiritual regeneration of monastic rule, and also literary, humanistic, and Neoplatonic outlooks that grew out of the study of the classics.[31]

On the continent, Boethius studies continued in the writing of commentaries and also of translations in the tenth and eleventh centuries, with commentaries either embellishing the Remigian model or focusing solely on the poem entitled "O qui perpetua" (*Consolatio* 3 m9). Such (generally minor and unimportant) commentaries and glosses included that of Adalbold of Utrecht (970–1026), who, like Remigius, wished to harmonize Christianity and Platonism.[32] Poppo of Fulda, in the early eleventh century, wrote a commentary now lost. The translations of the *Consolatio* included the Old High German translation-glosses by Notker (supplemented by Latin glosses drawn from the commentary of Remigius plus an anonymous commentary on Boethius, possibly St. Gall Major, perhaps one of the two manuscripts entered at St. Gall in 872 but subsequently lost),[33] and the Provençal translation with its lesser attention to the Latin sources.[34] After the commentary of Adalbold of Utrecht, the ardor for Boethius study cooled in the eleventh century—no new work was accomplished. Exemplifying this new trend, Master Otloh of St. Emmeram denigrated the simplicity of dialecticians who trusted in the philosophical study of Boethius more than in study of sacred writers.[35]

This stasis in the evolution of the interpretation of Boethius stemmed from a desire to shun anything that smacked of the explicitly pagan, or at least non-Christian. Even the translations of Boethius into the vernaculars, while an innovation in Boethius studies and in mythography, are primarily conservative, intended to preserve the vitality of the original text and help the new vernacular languages to proliferate. Notker Labeo, for example, deliberately and firmly deemphasizes classical myths by euhemerizing or naturalizing them, or by making them typological.

Thus the attractively ambiguous "O qui perpetua" (*Consolatio* 3 m9), which reveals Stoic cosmogony as reflected in God's universe through the "Spiritus Sanctus," received the only new and unusual philosophical attention. Its survival attests to the power of the Boethian text and epitomizes the new anti-Carolingian (that is, anti-pagan, anti-mythological) reading common also to Notker. Four different, but related, individual comments on Boethius's poem exist, beginning with the early tenth-century Anonymous Bruxellensis, written before the comment of Bovo II of Corvey (d. 916). Initially some scholars believed the Bruxellensis was originally written by John Scot, or at the least combined material from John Scot and Remigius; now it is accepted as a graft of material on to Remigius in an intelligent, skillfully crafted compilation.[36] This gloss was succeeded, in the transitional period ranging from the tenth to the early twelfth centuries, by glosses that depended heavily upon it and on each other—by the tenth-century Bovo II of Corvey, the eleventh-century Adalbold of Utrecht (bishop 1010–26), and the twelfth-century *Explanatiuncula* in the Anonymous Monacensis. The French Bovo II of Corvey combined Remigius and the Anonymous Bruxellensis in his gloss on "O qui perpetua."[37] Bovo merely identified the qualities of the temperament granted to the soul as it descends from the heavens to earth at birth, that is, the quality of ratiocination from Saturn, the ability to lead from Jupiter, and so on, with a different quality provided by each sphere; the schema was taken from Macrobius's commentary on the *Somnium Scipionis,* and, on the World Soul itself, from Servius at the beginning of the sixth book of the *Aeneid.*[38] The passage is heavily Christian Neoplatonist. Adalbold of Utrecht's twelfth-century commentary on "O qui perpetua," itself influenced by Bovo, was used, along with the Remigius commentary on all of the *Consolatio,* by the Anonymous Erfurt Commentator in his glosses on Boethius.[39] Finally, the twelfth-century *Explanatiuncula* of the Anonymous Monacensis (Munich, Bayerische Staatsbibliothek MS. Clm. 14689, fols. 88–94) "modestly" fulfils two purposes in its comments on Boethius's poem: first, it describes the knowledge required to understand Boethius's verse well; second, it directly explicates the text in the manner of Bovo II of Corvey.[40]

Most of Notker's glosses are actually translations either of Boethius's Latin or Remigius's or St. Gall's—brief but informative identifications in Old High German[41]—yet his glosses also reveal an originality not found in other commentators. In part his exegetical contributions evince greater humanism and learning than others', often in harmony with Notker's other works[42]—an intertextuality in which can be discerned the specifically Germanic reception of the Latin mythographic tradition. His native culture and Old High German language themselves color the familiar mythological subject matter.

Notker's Boethius translation and glosses exist in twenty-one manuscripts, mostly treating the first four books, and are both interlinear and contextual.[43] The Latin alternates with Old High German, a few lines or even words at a time, with compressions of and additions to Remigius's Latin in both Latin and Old German. In his glossing Notker minimizes allegory, preferring to use his Latin authority for especially moral interpretations or to pinpoint the fabulous in his sources. His changes can be mistakes (for example, when he confuses the "Arbiter Umbrarum"—Pluto—with Vulcan), additions (for example, in the quotations from Virgil and Ovid added at the end of Boethius's Orpheus poem, or material from Remigius on Martianus on Saturn and Mercury added to *Consolatio* 4 m1 and 4 m3, or the apparently original geographical material in the Labors of Hercules in 4 m7), or interpretations affected by the heroic nature of Old High German (for example, Hercules's battle with the "vuúrm," serpent or dragon, Hydra).

As in other Boethius commentaries, the most extensive mythographic passages in this line-by-line gloss concern the heroes Orpheus, Ulysses, and Hercules (*Consolatio* in 3 m12, Orpheus's descent into hell, and, in an even longer gloss, 4 m7, with brief mention of Agamemnon's sacrifice of Iphigenia, Ulysses and Polyphemus,[44] and a lengthy exposition on Hercules's Labors), but also, in Notker, on Hercules and Hydra (4 p6). Other mythographic passages document equally heroic occasions: Hercules and Achelous (2 m2), Otus and Ephialtes (3 p12), and Ulysses and Circe (4 m3).

An influence reflective of Germanic heroic epic poems appears in the gloss on the monstrous Hydra, in Boethius a situation explained figuratively as "a kind of matter that, when one doubt is cut away, innumerable others grow in its place, like the heads of the Hydra; nor would there be any limit to them, if one did not repress them with the most lively fire of one's mind" (*Consolatio* 4 p6). Notker understands "Hydra" as Greek for the Latin *excedra* and thus translates the word into Old High German as "vuúrm" to evoke images of Germanic dragons like Beowulf's *wyrm* or Sigurd Fafnisbane's *orm* although the remainder of his gloss derives primarily from the commentaries. Further, the battle between Hercules and Hydra in the Lernian swamps has been characterized by Boethius himself as a fabulous battle, between the "fire of the mind" and doubts; in the translation Notker uses the Latin word "fabula," ever conscious of the distinction between the literal and moral levels of understanding of the text.[45]

Notker had earlier adapted the Latin term "fabula" to express Macrobian understanding of how fables can be appropriately used to conceal natural or cosmic truths. In a mythological explanation of how Ops (Saturn's wife, or Terra), meaning Plenty, came to be associated with the cornucopia, Notker says at this point in Boethius (*Consolatio* 2 m2) that there occurs a "suspensio uocis," which "Fabulę ságent," "fables tell."[46] He recites the fable plainly with the principal figures identified—the horn was taken in battle from Achelous (a river in Greece) by Hercules, who then gave it to Plenty: "únde ér iz kâbe gnúhte. díu ministra íst fortunę" {"and he gave it to Plenty, who is the handmaiden of Fortune"}. In Boethius "Ops," or "Plenty," is merely personified, pouring from a cornucopia of riches apparently identical to Achelous's horn, although Notker does not say so—he construes "Plenty" as a goddess, perhaps familiar in concept from popular Germanic culture as much as classical mythology. What he does mention is how Plenty received her horn of riches, using portions of Remigius to do so.

Notker legitimates some of the pagan references by scripturalizing, or Christianizing, them, very much like the Germanic commentators on

Boethius's "O qui perpetua", the Anonymous of St. Gall, and the author of the *Ecloga Theoduli*. The gloss on Otus and Ephialtes (*Consolatio* 3 p12) complements the Christianized glosses on the Orpheus poem immediately following it, although much of the information related is factual and literalistic, and derives in part from the first Vatican mythography, fable 82/83. The battle between these Giants, sons of Neptune, and heaven is interpreted dramatically by Notker as the Old Testament battle between the Giants who created the tower of Babel and the Christian God, in echo of the *Ecloga* parallel between the mythological Giants and Nimrod, in building the "Tower of Babylon" (*Ecl. Theod.* 85–92).[47]

Where he can use a mythological or rhetorical image to strengthen what he sees as Boethius's underlying Christianity he will, often by means of Old High German instead of Latin. The gloss to the moral of the Orpheus story in Boethius,[48] which applies to those "Who seek to lead your mind / Into the upper day," in the Latin of Notker is phrased so that "upper day" is identified as God ("in superum diem.i.deum) but in the Old High German remains "day," "án den ûf-uuértigen tág," eternal and unchanging day, a clear metaphor for paradise. This image appears in the same passage as that of the image of the man plowing, from Luke 9:62. Comparing Orpheus who looks back at his wife and loses everything, Notker invokes the man who looks back after putting his hand on the plow and thereby loses the kingdom of God because of his unfitness.[49] The two figures are alike because they have been overcome, conquered: Notker first explains the reason for such vanquishment in the Boethian text, "Nam qui uictus," "For whoever is conquered," as by "carnis desideriis," "carnal desires," and the significance of the loss of "all the excellence he has gained," as "spiritualia bona," "spiritual good," thereafter adding the striking revision of Remigius found in B.N., K, and T (that is, primarily tenth-century continental manuscripts but not in Remigius himself) utilizing Luke 9:62. And the gods whom Orpheus found unmoved by his mourning of the loss of his wife are specified as "hîmel-góta," supernal gods or "gods of the heavens," to distinguish them from the infernal gods to whom Orpheus then turns for relief, "hélle-góten" (S/St p. 240, Tax p. 180).

Notker resorts to Latin from the commentaries to emphasize, authorize, or dissociate himself from a reading, in the last instance from that which is morally repugnant, infernal, or sexual. For example, the Furies of Orpheus's hell in Old High German are "dîe drî réche-gérnun suésterâ," "the three vengeful sisters," but in Latin, "conscientia sceleratorum," representing guilty consciences; Notker tailors the gloss from the Anonymous of St.

Gall on Tityus and the vulture who gnaws at his liver[50] for his Macrobian purpose here. In his Old High German gloss on Tantalus, Notker mirrors Tantalus's presumption in testing the divinity of the gods (or else Notker's own interest in and reference for divinity) by leaving in Latin the words for "divinity" and "gods and goddesses."[51] In the Old High German recitation of the myth of Tityus, Notker uses Remigius's Latin for Latona's "conjugal" relationship with Jove ("iouis uxore") and Apollo and Diana ("dáz ráh apollo. únde diana filia latonę" ["That was avenged by Apollo and Diana, the daughter of Latona"] and, after identifying the story as a "fabula" in line with earlier rhetorical definitions, masks the horribleness of the Remigian comment on the sin of lechery by leaving the phrase in Latin.[52]

Notker's borrowing even from his main source in his own glosses on Martianus is evidenced in his gloss on Ulysses and Circe (*Consolatio* 4 m3) which, while not very moralized, nevertheless reveals Notker's use of the Remigian commentary on Martianus Capella[53] in his elaboration on the figure of Mercury who plays such an important role—as bridegroom and exemplar of eloquence. Notker does follow Remigius in identifying the poisons used by Circe as vices, "Hęc uenena.i.uitia" (S/St, p. 273, Tax, p. 200), thus moralizing a relatively literalistic gloss. Through Mercury's pity Ulysses is saved from Circe's poisons, that "Arcadian flyer," as Boethius terms him, and Notker provides an extensive gloss on his accoutrements—winged sandals, rod, caduceus—and his home, Mount Cyllenius in Arcadia, in information in part derived directly from Fulgentius, Remigius and the Boethius revisers, but also from Remigius on Martianus (Remi., *In Mart.* 6.6), that is, from his gloss on "Cyllenius" and on his caduceus, rod, and winged sandals—information that carefully deletes Remigius's moralization of the gods.[54]

The no-doubt landlocked Notker is fascinated by estuaries and the access to the sea suggested by his mention in the gloss of such Latin words (not found in Remigius) as "in occidentali oceano," "insularum," "ęstuarium maris," "Aestuarium," "ab ęstuando," "accessus maris," "recessus," "Estus," "inquietudo," "accedendo et rececendo." Or perhaps his own inability to comprehend these nautical terms, because of his landlocked situation, makes him anxious to translate and explain them in Old High German.[55] Even in the Herculean Labors, to which Notker applies the most original interpretations in all of his glosses, his glosses often treat myths mapping Mediterranean islands and rivers. Aeneas finds Hercules at the islands of the Strophades after he has downed the *volucres* (Stymphalian birds), which Notker identifies as "Arpie" and with whom King Alcinous contended in Achaia.[56] Ovid calls them "Stymphalides," from the lake, Stymphalus; Notker adds a gloss taken from Remigius and his revisers (and earlier from the first Vatican mythography and then Fulgentius) but not in St. Gall: the Harpies are dogs of Jove called so from "plundering" because "arpo" in Greek means "plunder." The second long and original gloss is geographical rather than mythological in its emphasis on the location of the garden on an island near Mount Atlas known as the Hesperides, from which Hercules steals from the dragon golden apples.

Notker, who also was responsible for transmitting Remigian moralizations on Martianus Capella to later commentators, did not essentially affect the twelfth-century moralizations on Boethius. Despite his anti-mythological Germanic alterations to the Remigian paradigm, his glosses were probably not very influential in determining the course of the mythographic tradition in the Middle Ages largely because of their use of a decentralizing vernacular; the next truly influential commentary would be that of William of Conches, in the twelfth century. Yet these glosses are important because they did transmit mythographic material to the great twelfth century, some later glossators did build on Notker's mistakes, and they illustrate (in a very postmodern sense) the historical presence of a new multicultural reading of mythography also evident in Notker's Martianus glosses.

Notker's Germanic Reading of the Martianus Glosses

In general, Notker's mythography in the Martianus commentary is less innovative than that of Remigius or even the Anonymous Barberinus, a Remigian reviser prior to Notker whose commentary Notker's glossation in part resembles. Notker's "paraphrase" abbreviates Remigius's commentary, adding in Old High German even briefer glosses which seem to translate what Notker sees as the most important mythological definitions and concepts, leaving in Latin single words or phrases untranslatable or unseemly. Notker declares in Old High German his principle of translation to be one of revealing meaning where possible, but, partly in Latin, he adds that he will supply a clarification in a gloss above.[57]

The pattern Notker establishes resembles that in his Boethius glosses, one of vernacular materialism and literalism in that he retains in Latin moral, philosophical and theological abstractions and sexual and infernal references. His omission of Carolingian mythography for the most part is extensive; what he translates into Old High German reduces the deities in general through simple physical allegorization to natural processes very like the approach of the Anonymous Barberinus. Familial relationships among the gods are stressed, as well as places and geographical regions around the world. There is much less than normal concern with the Stoic and Neoplatonic moral interpretations, chiefly used for etymologies of names or glosses on the deities as planets. Notker's native Germanic lens for reading the mythographic tradition subtly appropriates and changes Graeco-Roman culture.

His Latin rubrics for the commentary reveal, however, a degendering and literalistic mythology centered primarily on the names of deities, especially in the first book (satire—in honor of Hymen, the seven planets, the signs of Jove and Juno, the intellectuality of the world, Pluto and Neptune, Mars and Liber, Castor and Pollux, Hercules, and Vulcan), and on abstractions, such as the seven liberal arts, in the second (praise of philology and astronomy, music, geometry, *ars poetica,* philology and physics, rhetoric, divination, foretelling, and augury, conjecture, praise of Mercury, a series of goddesses including wisdom—"Fronesis. Dikia. Sofrosine. Andreia. uel Yskis"—philosophy, and the three Graces). These rubrics also provide an original means of organizing his material, for the first book involves fifty-six sections, the second, forty-eight. It is possible that his rubrical approach influenced the so-called twelfth-century Florentine Commentary on Martianus reputed to have had its origins in the lectures of William of Conches, just as it is possible that many of William's glosses on natural gods (Bacchus, Ceres, Proserpina, and others) in the Macrobius commentary may have been drawn from the post-Remigian glosses on Martianus. If so, the Neoplatonic character of Chartrian philosophy may in fact reflect the simplification of Carolingian Stoic mythography found in the Anonymous Barberinus and Notker and, in relation to Notker especially, a reaction to his vernacular materialism and literalism.

Post-Remigian Glosses on Martianus like the Anonymous Barberinus have been generally regarded as significant historically simply because of their scholastic interest in the Carthaginian and not for any instrinsic originality. Used as a text in the schools from the Carolingian period into the eleventh century, Martianus's *De nuptiis* functioned, according to Claudio Leonardi, "come modello a sviluppi mitografici e mitologici," as a model for the developing of mythography and mythology.[58] In the tenth century some of the figures more representative of the culture in Italy knew and echoed Martianus, even if they did not gloss him—the glossator of the *Gesta Berengarii,* Rather of Verona, Stefano and Gunzo of Novara, Eugenio Vulgario, and Liutprand of Cremona.[59] In the eleventh century at St. Gall in Switzerland Notker Labeo went one step further by presenting the commentary of Remigius on Martianus in German, noting especially the rhetorical features.

One reason for the extension of Martianus from France to Germany, Switzerland, and Italy was the political situation in Germany, which favored the enhancement of learning in general, and in particular a new intellectual commerce between St. Gall and other centers, including Italian ones. The kingdom of Otto attracted Italian scholars knowledgeable in the ancient authors, such as Rather of Verona and Liutprand of Cremona.[60] Rather, a Bishop of Verona for three periods (931–34, 946–48, 961–68), hailed from the monastery school at Lobbes; during his long life and career (890–974),[61] he glossed Martianus briefly, in 954, drawing from Martin of Laon, although there are no mythological references.[62] Luitprand of Cremona was a Langobard, born in 920 in Pavia from a highstanding family.[63] But even earlier, the glossator of the *Gesta Berengarii,* perhaps a teacher in Verona between 915 and 924, understood Greek and used as models and sources Virgil and Servius on Virgil, Statius's *Thebaid* and Lactantius on Statius, the Latin *Iliad,* Martianus, Fulgentius, and Isidore, among others.[64] In addition, Gunzo of Novara was at St. Gall in January of 965, a scholar with so much faith in the study of literature that he owned over a hundred books, including Martianus Capella, Calcidius's Latin translation of Plato's Timaeus, a work by Aristotle translated into Latin by Boethius, and Cicero's *Topics.*[65]

Of the Latin commentaries dating from the same transitional period as Notker, the Anonymous Barberinus is the most important. The Anonymous Barberinus (Vat. Barb. Lat. 10) is found in a late twelfth-century manuscript with an accessus written in a late Carolingian hand.[66] Although not original—it basically supplies marginal and interlinear glosses on the first two books by using Remigius verbatim, transposing, paraphrasing, condensing, or expanding him, and where changing him using some unidentified source (not Martin of Laon or John the Scot)[67]—the Anonymous Barberinus does offer basically new philological glosses consisting of etymologies, explications of texts, allegorical interpretations, reading aids, and lexicography.[68] These suggest the role of the glossator as a schoolmaster.[69] Many glosses also perpetuate the Remigian interest in female deities and their Neo-Stoic role in cosmography and cosmology. Of the expanded borrowings and original mythographic contributions in the Barberinus commentary (and its editor, Raia, has made identification of Barberinus interpolations into the Remigius base easy to discern by italicization),[70] those of interest in the transmission of both Martianus and the mythographic tradition through the Middle Ages mostly concern figures in book 1 of *De nuptiis,* most of them feminine, either associated with human sexuality, or with natural or cosmic reproduction—Venus, Hymen, Venus's sons Cupid and Mercury (*sic*); Ops, Ceres, and the Magna Mater cult; Mercury's mother Maia; Phoebus and Bacchus; some of the Muses; Juno and her son Vulcan; Genius.

Such contributions signal an interest in gender and genealogy—lifted from the same Stoic context as in the Carolingian mythographers of Martianus, but without the sophistication and extensive philosophical context found there, and with the ecclesiastical moralist's (or the school-master's pedagogical and disciplinary) motives in mind in warning against the dangers of uncontrolled human sexuality. The very existence of such gendered glosses, in contrast to Notker's later suppression or omission of such readings and his transmogrification of them into something more practical, earthy, and Germanic, through their highlighting explains Notker's backlash—what might be construed as his reactionary degendering.

In the Barberinus's first book, the genealogy of Hymen (from *De nuptiis* 1) and his allegorical role as corrective for his mother Venus's lovemaking and his father Bacchus's drinking extend Remigius and may have influenced Alan of Lille's allegorization of this family in the twelfth-century *De planctu Naturae.* Here, after the Remigian explanation of Hymen as "membranula" and as the god who rules that membrane, the commentator defines Hymen as son of Venus and Bacchus (as in Remi., *In Mart.* 4.1) because Hymen is born after the wantonness of Venus and Bacchus, "quia post natiuam petulantiam que datur ex Venere et Bacho." Hymen's *remedium* is, for Barberinus, marriage, the urge to legitimize love within a natural union ("*hoc est amor naturalium coniunctionum*"), as a means of correcting and reforming physical desire (Venus) ("*Corrigitur Venus illaque correctio superfluae Veneris est Himeneus,*" Barb. Raia 207; italics indicate a non-Remigius gloss). Unchecked, Martianus's Venus gives his Psyche for "all her senses every kind of pleasure" (*De nuptiis* 7), interpreted in the Barberinus as vicious pleasures that appeal to the five senses and thereby compel the rational soul to confront original sin: "*Sed Venus contulit omnia uicia sensibus animae qui exercentur per corporea instrumenta. Quod ostendit per gustum, odoratum, tactum, uisum, auditvm*" ["But Venus gives all vices to the senses of the soul which can be exercised through the corporeal instruments. Which she manifests through taste, smell, touch, sight, hearing"] (Barb. Raia 218–19; cf. Remi., *In Mart.* 8.7).

The explicitness of this gloss—the use of *corrigitur* suggesting the need for erasure, reform—may very well have influenced Alan of Lille's allegorization of Venus's two relationships (Venus-Hymen-Cupid and Venus-Anti-genius–Jocus) in the twelfth-century *De planctu Naturae*. In that Latin prosimetrum the correct union is also the one sanctified by marriage, Venus-Hymen-Cupid. The difference among them is that Vulcan is the husband of chaste Venus in Remigius, Bacchus, in the Barberinus, but in Alan, Hymen is.

The Barberinus elaborates on the dangers of uncontrolled sexual desire by shifting Remigius's focus on a double Venus to her other two sons Cupid and, oddly, Mercury and her two husbands Bacchus and Vulcan. The double-aspected Venus in Remigius led to two antithetical roles for the goddess, immoral and chaste. The gloss on Venus's sons—deriving from the Remigian interpretation of the Muse, or Camena (Calliope), Hymen's mother, as equivalent to Venus herself ("his pro Venere ponitur," Remi., *In Mart.* 3.5)—explains that, "*Cum Venus sit dea luxuriae, tamen Mercurius fingitur eius filius, quia* Venus alia turpis alia honesta" ["Although Venus is the goddess of lechery, nevertheless Mercury is depicted as her son, because Venus is sometimes immoral, sometimes chaste"]; the last part derives from a discussion of Cupid and the Cyprian (in Remi., *In Mart.* 3.14). Son Hymen's singing at weddings is a skill attributed to, and a province of, his mother Venus, who joins partners in marriage "because you love" ("*Hoc habes ex genitrice, quae coniungit quod tu amas,*" Barb. Raia 208). Son Cupid is depicted as naked "quia maxime agitur Venus inter nudos" ["because Venus is aroused most greatly among the naked"] (Barb. Raia 220; the gloss on Cupid is taken from Remi., *In Mart.* 8.22, and Theodulf of Orleans). Venus's bond with husband Vulcan is explained morally, without Stoic residue, as voluptuous, earthly: "Et bene dicitur Lempnius quasi Limnius, quia lemnius dicitur ignis obscene Veneris, quod nichil aliud est nisi quod Venus semper habitat in lutosis mentibus. Sed hic dicitur Lemnius ignis naturalis ingenii" ["Vulcan is well called Lemnius as if Limnius, because *lemnius* is the name for the obscene fire of Venus, which means nothing but that Venus always dwells in dirty minds"] (Barb. Raia 218, from Remi., *In Mart* 8.4).

Astrologically, Venus as a planet marks the beginning of the under-world in Barberinus's unusual reading of the Servian paradigm of the Neoplatonic universe used later by Dante in his cosmological construction in the *Paradiso* of the lower half of Paradise as morally tainted (Barb. Raia 228). Seven planetary streams contribute the usual aspects to human temperament as the soul descends through the spheres: from Jove the desire to reign, from Mars wrath, and so on (*De nuptiis* 15; Remi., *In Mart.* 13.1). But the planetary streams below Venus, as if identical to the various infernal rivers, also punish and purge souls in the afterlife: "notat hic animas purgatione, et penam recipere in circulis planetarum" ["this notes that the souls by purgation also receive punishment in the planetary circles"] (in echo of Remi., *In Mart.* 13.6). In Remigius the association of the spheres with the infernal was triggered by mention of Mars's circle as a parameter, "et infernum quidem dicunt esse infra circulum lunae, cuius fluvium Pyrflegetonta, id est igneum Flegetontem, in Martis circulo dicunt oriri" ["and they say that the underworld is below the orbit of the moon, whose river Pyrflegethon, that is the fiery Phlegethon, they say originates in the orbit of Mars"] (13.6); further, Elysium is said to be located above the circle of Jupiter, where purged souls go. Therefore the Barberinus links the other planets with infernal rivers: "The philosophers indeed say that the underworld [infernum] exists in the circle of the moon [in circulo lune], and they say in the circle of the moon whatever exists from earth up to the moon. And Phlegethon they say exists in the circle of Mars—*in Venus, Lethe, in Saturn, Styx. Styx and Saturn signify sadness.*"

The nine Muses, the daughters of aerial Juno, are also linked with the planetary spheres (ending with Clio, the moon, and Thalia, the earth; Barb. Raia 240–41). Erato especially relates to Juno (Hera in Greek) and the *heroes* of the air (from Augustine and Isidore) because of an unusual etymology of her name: " 'Erato' is fortitude, teaching the discovery of likeness. 'Erato' is said from heroes; *heroas* in Greek is *fortis* in Latin, hence heroes, that is, brave" ("*ab heroas; heroas, Graece, fortis Latine, et inde heroes, quasi fortes*"; compare Remi., *In Mart.* 19.20).

As mother of the Muses Juno explains their creativity (Juno reappears in Barberinus, *In Mart.* 20.14, when Mercury and Apollo approach her for her help). Her children, as also with Venus in this commentary, reflect her specialized functions. The goddess of brides (lit. "veiled"), *dea nubentium*, Juno supports marriage; two of her roles (and names) are connected in that she is also called Lucina, because she gives light to children at birth ("et *dicitur Lucina quia pueris nascentibus dat lucem,*" Barb. Raia 242, drawn from the Berne scholiast). In another extravagant Fulgentian allegorization, her own offspring, the Muses, and her nursling Mercury are connected through the Remigian Stoic identification of Juno as "aer inferior" (Barb. Raia 244). Her "filias" are the nine instruments (four teeth, two lips, and so forth), called "filias" "quia formatione aeris, uox existit," "because by the formation of air, sound exists." Further, Juno is fond of Mercury, the messenger of the gods whom she has nourished at her breast, or, as the Barberinus explains, *"Hoc est ex habundantia aeris. Vel aliter, mediante aere, deificatur sermo, cum de diuinis se intromittit"* ["From an abundance of air. Or otherwise, with air as an intermediary, discourse is deified, when it is busy with divine matters"] (Barb. Raia 244). This nursling Mercury is glossed later when Jupiter acknowledges that Mercury is his trust, speech, benefi-cence, true genius, and messenger of his mind, the sacred Nous, as the "genius," the god of generation (*De nuptiis* 92): *"Scilicet naturalis deus, qui praeest cunctis. Naturale est cunctis loqui"* ["That is, a natural god [god of nature?], who presides over all. It is natural for all {men} to speak"] (Barb. Raia 267). Finally, Juno's other son, Vulcan, reflects creative intelligence, *"Acumen ingenii"* (Barb. Raia 251), and later still, as the son of Juno, is the greatest at the art of making things, *"Quia ipso maxime ars fabricia"* (Barb. Raia. 264).

Of Barberinus's original interpolations on deities, especially female deities, many relate goddesses to the Magna Mater cult or to Stoic elemental matter as the female cosmic procreative principle (*materia: mater*), but with the Stoic elaboration found in Remigius excised. Ops, or Cybele, is called Ops on account of her fertility (Remi., *In Mart.* 5.22) but Cybele, or Cubele, from *cubos,* or solidity, that is, from the rotation of the head as insane persons do during the blood-letting of her festivals, *"Quia qui colebant festum eius sanguinolenti rotabant capita sua ut insani,"* followed by an original insertion of the Greek for *rotatio* and *caput* (Barb. Raia 213). In a similarly original etymology for the name of the daughters of Atlas, of which Mercury's mother Maia was one, the Pleiades are called so "from their mother, because she was called Pleias. Or the Pleiades are called *etotos,* which is *pluralitas,* because in them is plurality" (Barb. Raia 214). Finally, Barberinus promotes Pallas Athena, goddess of wisdom, to divine rather than mortal status by interpreting her as *eternitas,* an expression of both human and divine wisdom: "Est enim utramque scientiam continens, *id est eam quae habetur de diuinis rebus et eam quae habetur de humanis rebus"* ["For she contains both (kinds of) knowledge, that is, the one which concerns divine matters and the one which concerns human affairs"] the italicized remark from Remi., *In Mart.* 7.1 and 7.3; Barb. Raia 215–16). Saturn's wife Ops is old, *"Scilicet terra ipsa erat talis"* ("Certainly earth was of such a kind as her," Barb. Raia 259), especially because Ops is prolific—she contains within her all seeds (*"Quia omnia semina in se continet,"* Barb. Raia 259). Barberinus adds the Remigian identification of Neptune's wife as

Styx, "the nurse of all things" (Barb. Raia 263, from Remi., *In Mart.* 36.3) and the Fulgentian-Remigian identification of Pluto's wife as "Proserpina," "*Bonis prouentibus*," "with good crops," named from "creeping forward" (Barb. Raia 263), a gloss which will be picked up in the twelfth century by William of Conches in his own glosses on Macrobius. Her mother Ceres is glossed, originally, as "*Dea res creans, quae interpretatur femina*" ["goddess creating things, who is interpreted as female"] (Barb. Raia 264).

In degendering Martianus and his commentators, including, possibly, the Anonymous Barberinus, Notker Labeo resorts to vernacular literalism and Germanic heroism as tools. The literalism of Notker's mythography is rendered, for example, by the definition of old Saturnus as "altcot," "old god," "oldest of the gods" (Notker, p. 117), or Janus, usually bearing two faces or heads (from Remi., *In Mart.* 6.1), as "ter zuihóubito," "the two-headed" (Notker, p. 7). The selection of place-names and geographical explanations, or the association of deities' names with places, from the many in Remigius, rounds out Notker's literalism, as when he defines Venus as "the Cyprian" (p. 7), or when he explains Licium as a temple on the island of Delos (Notker, pp. 7, 11).

Equally literal and practical is the system of earth deities Notker creates by means of his translation into Old High German, a system which accentuates mutability, change, and natural process. Saturn or Chronos, as time, epitomizes Notker's interest in mutability, for the god chiefly abstracts the sequence of the seasons in one year. Entering the assembly of the gods with a dragon in his hand (*De nuptiis* 70) to signify the yearly cycle (Notker, p. 33), Saturn reflects the changes we associate not only with mutability but with aging and the agricultural season: "Únde ímo gefállet táz er héize comedens. uuánda tempus frízet ál dáztir íst," "And it is fitting to him that he should be called *comedens*, for *tempus* devours all that exists" (Notker, p. 34). Thereafter, Notker adds the notion that Time in a single year grows old in winter and becomes young in spring (from Remi., *In Mart.* 33.11). Earthy in nature like her husband, Ops is "corpulent" "quia terrae elementum crassius et corpulentius est ceteris" (Remi., *In Mart.* 33.12): "Uuánda diu érda íst tícchesta dero elementorum," "For the earth is the fattest of the *elementorum*," the elements (Notker, p. 34). Her daughter Vesta—although her relationship is not mentioned—signifies according to the philosophers earthly fire which nourished the aether, Jove ("Nutrix autem . . . , quia ferunt philosophi terreno igni caelestem nutriri," Remi., *In Mart.* 33.18), or "Uuánda celestis ignis (ist óbe ethere. únde úmbe etherem.) únde dáz chédent philosophi mít temo érdfiure gezúgedôt uuérden," "For *celestis ignis* (is above *ethere* and around *etherem*), and the *philosophi* designate that as being nourished with the earth-fire" (Notker, p. 34).

Vulcan, who gave Jove lightning and thunder, becomes in Notker a type of his Germanic equivalent, maybe Wotan, because of his destructive power as fire. As the fire that never walks upright, crippled Vulcan (*De nuptiis* 87) is defined by Notker's recitation of the fable of his deformation—when Juno hurled him from the heavens to Lemnos (Notker, p. 43). A maker and "fabricator" in the Barberinus, Vulcan is merely one of the three kinds of fire here, the destructive kind, in contrast to Jove's aetherial fire and Vesta's usable form that warms: "Uuélih téil dero uuérlte. ist àne fíur? Aber dóh sínt tríu fíur zeuuizenne. Ein fíur íst iouis. únscadeháftiz. ánderiz íst uulcanus scádonde án dien blícchen. daz trítta íst uesta. dâr uuír ínsíh pi uuármen" ["What part of the world is without fire? But there are three kinds of fire to be distinguished. One fire is Jove, harmless. The second is Vulcan, destructive with lightning. The third is Vesta, by which we warm ourselves," Notker, p. 43, from Remi., *In Mart.* 37.6]. More figuratively, this "Lemnius faber" or "fiúr dáz nio erlósken nemág ('insopibiles eternitatis igniculos')" ["fire that can never be extinguished"] also represents natural imagination: "Uuánda dero sèlo liehtet naturale ingenium . dáz nû hier lemnius bezéichenet" ["For the soul is illuminated by *naturale ingenium,* which is what Lemnius designates here"] (Notker, p. 9).

Of the more earthly and earthy figures associated with the underworld, including the four inhabitants of the fifth region of the sixteen regions of the heavens (*De nuptiis* 49), Notker glosses two: "Ceres frugum dea," "chórngéba," "Grain-Giver," and the Genius who is attributed to each one born, "ánaburto," "the Innate," but not Tellus or Vulcan, father of earth (Notker, p. 28). The "Grain-Giver" is, simply, she who gives the gift of crops to mortals, "quae gratiam frugum mortalibus tribuit" (Notker, p. 42). Typical of Notker's agriculturization of what had been constructed as cosmic and cosmographic processes is his treatment of Ceres's daughter Proserpina. The life of everything growing, the girl signifies the growing things newly shooting from earth every year: "Proserpina dáz íst álles érdrâtes tiehsamo. díu íst puella. uuánda érdsamo iârogelîches níuuer chúmet" ["Proserpina is the flourishing of all the fruits of the earth. She is *puella,* for every year new seed comes forth"] (Notker, p. 41). In contrast is the more specialized function of Proserpina in Remigius's Fulgentian gloss on "puella" as the vigor of grasses and of all things which grow from the earth by means of seed; she is rightly called a (young) girl because the seeds of the earth are renewed every year (Remi., *In Mart.* 36.4).

Also connected with earthly processes as simplified metonymies are Tellus, a numen of earth in Remigius, who becomes "érdcot," "earth-god" (Notker, p. 97). Pluto is not an "inferorum deus" but a "héllegóte" (hell-god); Portunus is not a "deus portuum" (Neptune is supposedly "deus portuum," Notker says, from Remi., *In Mart.* 5.18–5.19), but a "méregóte" (sea-god); and Gradivus, or "Mars," "uu͜gcot" (war-god). Mercury, who rules seed (in Remi., *In Mart.* 55.21), can restore the fortunes of Osiris, who falls because heavy with the corn seed he has made in Egypt: "dér in egypto den chórnsâmen fánt. Uuánda sin gérta tôdet únde chícchet. str͜t zérendo. únde sûona máchondo. quia praeest frugibus" ["who found {introduced} the corn seed in Egypt. For his staff kills and brings to life, ending strife and causing reconciliation. *quia praeest frugibus*"] (Notker, p. 66, on *De nuptiis* 126; Osiris is connected with a wine cult and responsible for the sowing of "corn-seed," "chornsamen," in Notker, p. 66).

Notker portrays even the sun, regulator and modulator of the world, as an agricultural catalyst and excises many of his Remigian names (Remi., *In Mart.* 73.10), along with his Neoplatonic associations. The names (and myths) that remain focus on the sun as a boy named Attis, Triptolemus, and Adonis (Notker, p. 84, from Remi., *In Mart.* 74.12–13). As in the Carolingian (and Fulgentian) glosses, for Notker the boy Attis represents flowers loved by Berecynthia, earth, their story indicative of how Earth is constricted by the cold but relaxed by the heat: "Dû bíst ter scôno blûomo. dér íu chínt uuás. tén berezinthia mínnôt. táz chit terra. uuánda si íst in uuíntere betàn. únde lángêt sia des lénzen. sô blûomen sínt" ["You are the beautiful flower, which previously was a youth, {a flower} which Berecynthia loves, that is to say, Earth, for she is constricted in winter, and she longs for spring, when there are flowers"]. Triptolemus was a boy who, because of Ceres, brought the use of the plow to the world, "dû bíst ter fúorogébo *triptolemus*" ["you are the food-giver Triptolemus"]. Most elliptically and literally, Adonis was a boy loved by Venus, "dáz uenus uuéinota. erslágenez fóne demo ébere" ["for whom Venus wept, slain by a boar"]. Ignoring the abstract Remigian gloss on Apollo as the principle of celestial music who educated the nine Muses (Remi., *In Mart.* 22.8), Notker admits only that they are daughters of Juno and Jove, or of inferior air and superior fire, and that they were taught by Apollo who more literally represents music, or the musician: "Íhméino musas. tíe iouis únde iunonis tóhterun gehéizen sínt. uuánda uox i͜o uuírdet fóne ethere únde aere. Tíe lèret apollo uuánda ér gât míttêr dero planetarum. únde métemêt íro musicam" ["I mean the *musas,* who are called the daughters of Jove and Juno, for a *vox* always comes from *ethere* and *aere.* Apollo teaches them, for he goes in the middle of the *planetarum* and directs their *musicam*"] (Notker, p. 23).

Notker's Old High German glosses frequently single out only simple family relationships—an emphasis possibly indicative of the fierce native interest from the earliest of times in Germanic clan-structure, but also, as we have seen, attractive to the Barberinus and in general expressive of the genealogical structure principle in the genre of the mythography collection. In comments on *De nuptiis* 4, Saturn is defined as castrated by his son, "saturnum (trûregen) s. fóne des súnes âhtungo" ["Saturn {the sad}, that is, from his son's persecution"]; Isis looked for Osiris ("marito") after his "brûoder [brother] tiphone" killed him, and she found him in a swamp near Memphis; Maia is "mûoter" of Mercury (Notker, p. 7, from Remi., *In Mart.* 5.22; 6.2; 6.9). "Latoius" (Apollo) is glossed as son of Latona in Latin (Notker, p. 15). Vulcan "Iovialis" is glossed as the "brother" rather than the son of Jove, or aetherial fire, "sînen brûoder uulcanum" (Notker, p. 26), but the Latin qualifies "quasi," "as if Jove's brother," obviously to show the closeness to Jove's of Vulcan's destructive earthly fire. The entry of the gods into the assembly (*De nuptiis* 62), as glossed by Notker (using Remi., *In Mart.* 31.6) depends upon familial relationships: Saturn is "their father" (from *sator,* "Saturnus íro fáter," Notker, p. 33), Castor and Pollux are the twins whose mother was Leda, "but not of one father," "náls éines fáter" (Notker, p. 41; "quamquam non ambo de iove," Remi., *In Mart.* 36.12), and so forth.

In his translations of classical mythological battles and deaths Notker frequently appropriates the literal and corporal for the Old High German and leaves in the Remigian Latin the more figurative and rhetorical. For example, in describing Pegasus, born from the blood of the severed head of Medusa, Notker uses the vernacular to emphasize the literal blood: "dés rósses pegasi. dáz ûzer démo blûote uuárd gorgone" ["from the horse Pegasus, which was formed out of the blood of Gorgon"]; this fountain allows poets to drink of fame—the blood of the dead Medusa stressed as much as the fountain liquid of fame: "sáment tien poetis. Pegasus chît fáma. uuánda poetę, sínt famosi. be díu chît man sîe getrúnchen hában dés prúnnen. dén pegasus ûzer dero érdo slûog. mít sînemo fûoze" ["with the *poetis;* Pegasus means *fama,* for the *poetę* are *famosi.* For that reason it is said that they have drunk of the fountain which Pegasus struck out of the earth with his hoof"] (Notker, p. 60). What is missing is the long myth of the female Gorgons as told by Remigius. Like Notker Remigius identifies Pegasus as fame, a figure who with his hoof stamped into being the fountain from which poets drink ("Pegasus, qui fama interpretatur, et pede suo fontem castalium sive pegaseum produxit. finguntur autem poetae de illo fonte potare, quia figmentis poeticis maxime fama iuvatur," Remi., *In Mart.* 50.16).

Martianus's heroic mythological battles, though reduced to a dramatic tension between adversaries, take on an epic cast. In book two of *De nuptiis* (157), in a description of baby Hercules's struggle with the two serpents sent by maddened Juno to kill him, Notker portrays a battle with "worms" more akin to Beowulf's battle with the Grendel family monsters and the dragon, or to Sigmund's use of a snake to try the courage and skill of three ten-year old boys in the *Volsunga Saga,* than to a hero's battle with a mythological adversary: "Tíe (sc. vuúrme) uuárf ín iuno ána. dò éines náhtes sîn mûoter alcmene in guán be ioue. únde yfidum be íro chárle amphitrione. Sî uuárf sie béide ána vuúrme. áber hercules eruuérita síh. yfidus nemáhta," "Juno threw him to them (sc. the serpents), when one night his mother Alcmene had [conceived, bore] him with Jove, and [had] Yfidus [=Iphicles] with her husband Amphitrion. She threw them both to the serpents, but Hercules defended himself, [while] Yfidus could not" (Notker, p. 75; compare Remi., *In Mart.* 66.14). It is the *failure* of Yfidus, and Notker's contempt for him, that highlights the success of Hercules.

As in his Boethius glosses Notker depends upon Latin more than Old High German to conceal, rephrase, or rationalize sexual behavior, gynecological details and reproductive acts, immorality, and other aspects of the underworld. He also uses Latin in mythological passages for the more obvious reason that there is no corresponding Old High German word, for example, with abstractions, whether rhetorical, moral, psychological, philosophical, or theological.[71] Thus Remigius's long gloss on Hymen as nuptial god is exchanged only for the brief translation of the Latin definition ("qui fertur deus esse nuptiarum id est naturalium conceptionum," Remi., *In Mart.* 3.5) which neutralizes his role into a nature force: "himeneum dén álte líute hábeton fúre hîgot. únde fúre máchare állero natûrlichero miteuuist," "Hymen, whom the ancients held to be a marriage-god, and to be the originator of all natural intercourse" (Notker, p. 4).

Because of the role of Venus as the desire which enters through "her five physical senses" ("íro ûzeren fínf sínnen," Notker, p. 9, from Remi., *In Mart.* 8.8), the Macrobian and Neoplatonic idea of the soul descending through

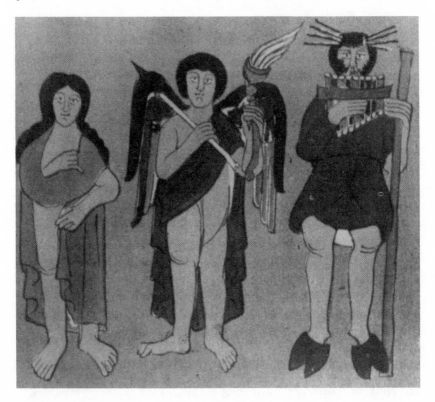

22. Venus, Cupid, and Pan. From Hraban Maur, "De universo." MS. 132 (ca. 1022–35).
From Abbazia di Montecassino, Italy.

the planetary spheres and receiving some imprint from them is rehearsed
again in Notker in Old High German, which renders the planetary
qualities more corporal and earthy than in Latin. In Remigius, according to
philosophers, what the descending soul receives from each planet is life
from the sun (because it is in the middle of planets and gives life to all the
world); body from the moon, because it is wet; from Saturn slowness and
cold, given its distance from the other spheres; temperance from Jove; *fervòr*
and *iracundia* from Mars; *voluptas* from Venus; *prudentia* from Mercury,
"quia cum sole gradiens quodam modo inexhausta luce sapientiae radiatur," "because moving with the sun, it shines with the inexhaustible light
of wisdom" (Remi., *In Mart.* 13.1). Notker, very much in the manner of
the Anonymous Barberinus, changes the order of the planets and to a
degree their attributes in the Old High German, drawing in part on a

passage from John Scot on Martianus (19.36–20.5).[72] Note that he retains in Latin only the concept of desire, associated with Venus—which is listed first, moving outward eventually to Saturn (see the pictorial association of Venus, Cupid, and Pan in figure 22).

> Táz uuás ál fóne díu. dáz sie síh uuàndon fóne stella ueneris háben uoluptatem. álso síe óuh uuândon dia sêla síh háben fóne dero súnnun. únde den lîchamen fóne demo mânen. únde blûot fóne marte gesprâchi fóne mercurio. héili fóne ioue. lâzi fóne saturno. blûot fóne marte.

> [That was all from the fact that they thought themselves to have *voluptatem* from *stella veneris,* as they also thought they had their soul from the sun and their body from the moon, and blood from Mars, eloquence from Mercury, health {prosperity} from Jove, tardiness from Saturn, blood from Mars.] (Notker, pp. 13, 14)

Notker's Old High German alters the Remigian (Latin) paradigm: from Mars comes blood, *blûot,* repeated twice, rather than wrath (perhaps, as the editor suggests, from his rosy color, the Latin gloss *sanguineus,* written above "Martis" on Notker, p. 15, and meaning "warlike"); and eloquence ("gesprâchi") rather than prudence from Mercury (perhaps as a result of other Carolingian glosses on Martianus); health, prosperity, *héili,* from Jove; tardiness, *lâzi,* from Saturn. Notker even links the two planets of the life-giving sun and the eloquent Mercury elsewhere in glossing Virtue's statement that Mercury and Apollo should never be separated (*De nuptiis* 25) through the idea of running—for Mercury always runs with the sun ("Mercurius lóufet io mit sóle," Notker, p. 19). (However, later Mercury is regarded as the "Deo rationis," "démo góte dero rédo," "the god of reason," p. 52, a gloss not found in Remigius.)

Other feminine reproductive acts or unusual sexual practices are explained in Latin in terms of astrology or rhetoric. For Maia's son Mercury permitted to nurse at Juno's breast Notker draws on Remigius (*In Mart.* 22.13) to explain the astrology of the moment: because the sun and Mars were in Taurus, the air (Juno) was warm, "Sîd alle iouis chébesa iuno házzeta. ziu mínnota si dánne maiam? Âne daz iuno íh méino diu lúft. tánne uuármên gestât. sô díu súnna in taurum gât. târ maia inter pliadas lósket" ["Since Juno hated all of Jove's concubines, why did she then love Maia? Because Juno, I mean the air, begins to grow warm when the sun goes into Taurus, where Maia lies *inter pliadas*"] (Notker, p. 23). For this past reason and also for a present one, which is that Juno wants Mercury to marry because she wants to avoid another affair with Venus like the one that produced Ermafroditos (*De nuptiis* 34), Mercury seeks out Juno's help. Notker glosses the fornication as Remigius has (*In Mart.* 22.16) except that he ignores all the revealing bits about Venus deriving from the foam and indeed signifying desire: he prefers to fornication the idea of the wife and the man and therefore lifts only those passages dealing with the literal affair, the definition of Hermaphroditus as two-sexed, and the moralization of Hermaphroditus as lascivious words.

> Petrógen gechôse dáz uuârheite gelìh ést. táz ánterot ten uuídellen. uuánda er hábet uuîbes líde dóh er man sî. . . Sô man uuállicho chósot. táz man lóterlicho méinet. sô chíndot mercurius pe uenere. únde sô geuúnnet er be íro ermafroditum.

> [Deceptive talk that looks like truth, that is what the hermaphrodite is, for he has a woman's members even though he is a man . . . The way one speaks euphemistically what one means as lascivious. Thus *Mercurius* begets a child with *Venere,* and thus he has *Ermafroditum* with her.] (Notker, p. 24).

Notker's view of Venus is as we have already observed generally not as generous or tolerant as that of Remigius, who envisions two Venuses. While Notker in his gloss on that very passage dutifully follows Remigius (*In Mart.* 37.1) by acknowledging the two—"Uuánda zuô ueneres sínt. éiniu pudica ánderiu inpudica," "For there are two *Veneres,* one *pudica,* the other *inpudica*" (Notker, p. 42)—his conservative Latin gloss in explanation reflects his moral repugnance for her "únde turpis," as his gloss on the chaste Venus reflects his respect—"sô castus amor íst" (Notker, p. 81, from Remi., *In Mart.* 72.16). Notker does, however, logically assign two Cupids to the two Venuses, one naked, one dressed (the latter from Remi., *In Mart.* 38.9, the unnamed boy with a wreath who holds a finger to his lips when Jupiter calls for silence of *De nuptiis* 90): "Táz kezîerta chínt íst cupido. démo cupidini úngelîchiz. tén man nácheten mâlet. uuánda er deus turpidinis íst" ["The adorned child is Cupid, unlike the Cupid that is depicted naked, for he is *deus turpidinis*"] (Notker, p. 44).

Juno as Pronuba and as ruler of the aerial region known as the underworld (mostly appearing in book 2) is associated with two forbidden topics—gynecology and the shades. Notker preserves much of the Latin from Remigius because of the difficulty of explaining her names and because of the topic itself. As Pronuba she governs marriages, "hoc est que preest nuptiis" (Notker, p. 72, from Remi., *In Mart.* 63.4), but is also known as Lucina, or Lucetia, Fluvonia and Februa (*De nuptiis* 149). As Fluvonia she is responsible for the feminine flow, "fluorem feminis prestantem" and is called so, as in the Remigian source, from the discharge of seeds, because she frees females from bearing, "Fluvonam a fluoribus seminum, quia liberat feminas a partu" (Remi., *In Mart.* 63.12), translated by Notker as "flôzkë bun án dero hîtate," "flow-giver during the marital act" (Notker, p. 72). She is called Februa because of her governance of the post-partum expulsion of the placenta, "quia purgat eas post partum secundis egredientibus" (Remi., *In Mart.* 63.12); Notker rephrases the Latin here, "februuam i. purgatricem egredientium secundarum" (Notker, p. 73). Her last name in Notker is Soticena or Saticena, glossed by Remigius (*In Mart.* 64.1), but Notker ignores everything except a translation of these names, "Sâmogébun álde hîfûogun," "Seed-giver or marriage-maker" (Notker, p. 73).

Notker is conscious of the way that rhetoric can be used to cloud obscurely what is immoral or fearful or infernal. For example, Erigone, the virgin guardian of the home of Mercury (speech, eloquence), as Themis signifies "obscuritas"; as Astraea, a star; and as Erigone, "contentiosa." Notker observes, "Dáz ímo obscuritas únde contentiosa dîenoên. dáz keuállet ad rhetoricam" ["That *obscuritas* and *contentiosa* serve him, that is appropriate *ad rhetoricam*"] (Notker, p. 79, from Remi., *In Mart.* 71.16). Accordingly, Notker uses Latin to dissociate from the terrors of the infernal, specifically for glosses on Pluto, the Styx, Lethe, Vedius, Charon, the demons, Manes, and other inhabitants of the aerial region.[73]

What, then, are we left with of the Carolingian commentators after the Anonymous Barberinus, after Notker? The renaissance of classical philosophy and methodology in that period allowed mythography to reveal the subtext of gender and genealogy, of education as heroic process. Whereas the Barberinus on Martianus continues the transmission of gender while suppressing and simplifying the philosophical elaboration, Notker suppresses much of the gender and genealogy while translating, or interpreting, what is left in Germanic heroic terms. Both of these may have influenced the next generation of commentators at Paris. What influence, if any, did they have on the major *Ecloga* commentator, Bernard of Utrecht, in his comments on a work notable for its iconoclasm, its consciousness of gender, its Stoic flavor, its lack of mythography and general literalism?

III. THE SCHOLASTIC *ECLOGA*:
BERNARD OF UTRECHT AS LITERARY CRITIC

Bernard of Utrecht both looks back to the past and ahead to the future in writing his commentary. In general, like the author of the *Ecloga* and Notker he reverts back to the literalism of the genealogical history in the Vatican mythographies to which so much of his exposition is indebted for its elaboration on narrative and its expunging of gender. But he also looks forward to the theorizing and scholasticism of the University of Paris in crafting his literary criticism—looks forward, that is, to the Neoplatonic theory of fabulous narrative in William of Conches and the Neo-Stoic scholasticism of Bernard Silvestris. He foregrounds the mythological and mythographic methods of the *Ecloga* in an explicit theoretical presentation.

Very little is known about Bernard of Utrecht, a commentator who has often been confused with Bernard Silvestris because he too was supposed to have written a commentary on the *Ecloga*.[74] It is, at any rate, impossible for the commentary by Bernard of Utrecht to be the actual commentary by Bernard Silvestris because Conrad of Utrecht, the bishop to whom it was dedicated, died before Bernard Silvestris was born; also, much of it was used verbatim by Conrad of Hirsau in the early twelfth-century *Dialogus super auctores,* before Bernard Silvestris flourished. Although the date for the commentary is not known precisely, because of the dedicatory epistle to Conrad of Utrecht it must have been written during his tenure as bishop, that is, between 1075 and 1099, the date this Swabian died at the hands of a Frisian assassin; as mentioned above, Huygens believes it was written in 1091, the same year as a letter to Yves de Chartres on which this letter is modeled.[75] Further, according to Jacobs, after Bernard wrote the commentary, manuscripts were dispersed in central and southern Germany—Bavaria and Swabia (all manuscripts of Bernard with one exception come from this area, the exception being MS. Burney 251)—and it was plagiarized and copied by others, after which it was used as a school text or as lecture notes for the *Ecloga Theoduli.* However, perhaps because of the commentary's later date, Bernard's commentary, "first and fullest" in Jacob's words, was never incorporated into the *Liber Catonianus,* which included the *Ecloga* by the end of the tenth century, like other commentaries.[76]

In mythographic method applied to individual fables, Bernard's commentary differs little from previous commentaries except that it makes explicit its approach—it is conscious of its theoretical bias—in the accessus and it organizes and distinguishes between different kinds of interpretations much more systematically than any earlier mythography in the text itself. Sigebert of Gembloux, who used passages from Bernard's *Vita Theoduli* and another part of the prologue, said that Bernard, in commenting on the *Ecloga*, "divinas historias et saeculares fabulas allegorica expositione dilucidavit"[77] ["elucidated divine history and secular fables through allegorical exposition"]. This echoes the *Intentio* of Bernard as outlined in the accessus in which he carefully rationalizes his attempt to demonstrate the excellence of the "entire Catholic tradition" over pagan rites, truth over falsity: "Intentio Theodoli esse videtur quasdam de ecclesiasticis et paganis scriptis conferre sententias, ut tantum Catholicam tradicionem excellere ostendat ritum gentilem, quantum excellit veritas falsitatem."[78] Other signs of Bernard's awareness of his role as "literary critic" come in the accessus, in the patient explanation of the work's genre, title, meaning, style, and so forth, and in his etymological analysis of the characters in the *Ecloga*: Pseustis, from the "falsitas" that he extols; Alithia, from the "veritas" she defends; and Fronesis, or Prudence, as she who reconciles the debate.

Of course, in the Dedicatory Epistle to Conrad, Bernard notes that his interpretation of the *Ecloga* is always qualified by the nature of his audience and the necessary stages through which that audience—schoolboys—must progress to understand: he begins first with what the ancients and moderns require in exposition at the beginnings of books, then he explains the *Ecloga* both *ad literam* and *allegorice,* and in certain places *moraliter,* using the meanings of words for boys in a manner suitable for children.[79] This means that he starts from the beginning by answering puerile questions, for example, what is a book, an author, an eclogue, and so forth, reaching eventually the more complex questions of order, explanation, characterization, mode, and so forth.

Unusual also in the history of mythographic commentary is Bernard's clarification of mythographic method. In line with the kind of distinctions the *Ecloga* has made between pagan and scriptural, mythological and typological, Bernard classifies allegorical interpretation explicitly for the two kinds of narratives, Fabula or Historia, as Misterium or Allegoria, Phisice or Moralitas, respectively. "Fabula" is said neither of deeds nor of things: "Fabula igitur est quod neque gestum est, neque geri potuit, dicta a fando, quod in dictis tantum non in factis constet" ["because a fable is what has not been done and could not have been done, derived from *fando* {speaking} because it consists of words only, not deeds"]. "Historia," on the other hand, "est res gesta, sed a memoria hominum remota, tracta a potoystorin, id est videre; solos enim fieri rem videntes olim scribere licebat" ["refers to a real deed, but one remote from the memory of men, derived from *potoystorin,* that is, 'to see,' for formerly only those seeing the actual happening were permitted to write about it"].[80]

Of the two kinds of fable—and here Bernard appears familiar with Macrobius on the *Somnium Scipionis*—there is the beast fable, or Aesopian fable, about transformations, or beasts talking with others, and there is fable that is "mixta," mixed, "que dicitur mixtologica, id est humane similitudinem vite retinens" ["which is called mythological, that is, retaining the likeness of human life"]. These images either entertain or instruct in morality "sub quibus plerunque veritas occulitur," "concealing truth underneath." But the species of history differs: it can be daily, calendrical (based on the calendar), annual (based on the year), or chronological (based on many periods of time).

Finally, in the text itself, Bernard divides his commentary on the *Ecloga* into three books, such a division emphasizing the thematic and formal principles of symmetry and balance implicit in the *Ecloga.* The first contains his long literary prologue; the second, roughly the first half of the *Ecloga* (up to Hercules and his Labors as compared with Samson); the third, containing the second half.

The literary nature of this commentary even allows for Bernard's consciousness of his own role vis-à-vis that of "Theodulus," in a long tradition of similar medieval commentators on ancient poems. Bernard of Utrecht echoes Servius's use of the Donatan *Vita Virgiliana* included at the opening of the commentaries in describing the various styles of oration used in accord with various subject matter. Although he does not (like Donatus) link them with three phases of life, nevertheless Bernard notes that the poet depends upon three styles of oration: the low, *humilis,* as in Virgil's *Bucolics;* the middle, *mediocris,* as in the *Georgics;* and the high, *grandiloquus,* as in the *Aeneid.* He also notes that his poet, by imitating Virgil's *Eclogues,* follows the usual model of Roman imitation of Greek or other Latin authors, as in Horace of Lucilius, Terence of Menander, Sallust of Livy, Boethius of Martianus, Virgil of Homer, and Statius of Virgil's *Aeneid.* Clearly he sees the *Ecloga* as a text to be expounded and not as an exposition. Note that he also compares the order of narrative (*ordo*) used in the *Ecloga* with the artificial order of the *Aeneid,* in which Aeneas first describes the shipwreck, then the fall of Troy, even though the natural order was reversed[81]—in a passage later borrowed by Bernard Silvestris in his commentary on the *Aeneid.* While Bernard draws on the usual Carolingian sources for the details of many of his specific interpretations, he is unique in his use of this scholastic method of balance and antithesis, one which Pierre Bersuire would later use so effectively in his *Ovidius morali-zatus,* a mythography that similarly contrasts the pagan with the scriptural and ecclesiastical, and Robert Holkot in his mythographic commentaries on the scriptures.[82]

And yet he seems most conservative, most the pedagogue, in his repression of the feminism of the *Ecloga*—like Notker. Given Notker's rigorous repression of sexual information through his preservation of the safe and distant Latin, it is perhaps no accident that Bernard ignores the battle of the sexes and moralizes it—he refuses to understand the battle literally, and instead explains it figuratively, as a battle between good and evil. Let us compare the passages on the sexes in the *Ecloga* with Bernard's commentary.

In the first conflict (*Ecl. Theod* 4–5 and 8–9), according to Bernard, the male speaks first because "Mas enim dignior est femina," the male is more worthy than the female (Bernard, *In Theod.* 1.105). In the debate over the evil of women (*Ecl. Theod.* 269–72)—one of which Bernard is conscious because he introduces it so, "Hic quarundam feminarum scelera Pseustis Alithiae probitati opponit" ["Pseustis compares the wickedness of certain women to the goodness of Alithia"] (*In Theod.* 3.870)—Bernard chastizes Alithia for her response to Pseustis's statement that "Mens robusta viri levitate cadit muliebri" ["The strong mind of the man is ruined by female frivolity"]. He says, "Hoc ad improprium Alithiae inducit probatque per maleficia" ["This leads to the impropriety of Alithia and demonstrates through wrongdoings"] (*In Theod.* 3.874–75). Of his glosses on the three fables of evil women subverting various men—Phaedra subverting Hippolytus, Philomena the sister-in-law subverting Tereus, and Medea subverting Jason—only two of the cases, Tereus and Jason, supply a Misterium, and the latter is very literal. In relation to Tereus, the change of the three principals into kinds of birds to Bernard suggests alienation from humanity: "Thereus upupa factus dicitur, quia a conspectu hominum remotus est et in desertis ut illa avis vixit, Progne hirundo, quia in alienis pauper vivens edibus, de sua semper conquesta est miseria, soror autem facta est philomena quia de eius erumna facta est cantilena, Ytis vero fasianus quia patri factus est cibus: fasianus siquidem comestibile sonat" ["Tereus is said to have become a hoopoe, because he was removed from the sight of men and lived in the desert like that bird; Procne, a swallow, because poor, and living in others' homes, always complained of her misery; her sister, moreover, became a nightingale, because from her distress there came a song; Ytis become a pheasant, because he was food for his father: since the pheasant is said to be edible"] (*In Theod.* 3.895–904). But in commenting on Alithia's defense, which focuses on Judith and Holofernes, Bernard's allegorization foreshadows Holofernes as the devil while Judith, "mulier vero qua deceptus est humanitas Christi est" ["the woman who deceives him is the humanity of Christ"] (3.953–956). Morally she represents the human mind confronting Satan, Holofernes, who attacks our city, or our body (3.974–75, 986).

In the next instance of a sexual battle, when Pseustis scoffs twice that the day must yield to the sky because the virgin does not know how to yield (*Ecl. Theod.* 296, 312), Bernard ignores the battle to define the virgin who does not know how to yield as truth, *veritas* (*In Theod.* 3.1164: "omnis enim qui male agit odit lucem," "everyone who acts badly hates the light"). Alithia's double invocation of the day to remain so the virgin will not lose (*Ecl. Theod.* 300, 316) is a reminder for Bernard that the light of the sun is equated with the truth of Christianity, although he changes the daughters to sons (or more neutrally to children: he adds that, "Ipsi enim filii lucis sunt et lucis opera facere debent hortante domino" ["They themselves are truly the sons of daylight and have to do the works of light at the master's urging"], followed by Matthew 5:16, on the relationship between seeing good works and the light illuminating the hearts of men.

It may very well be that Bernard's sources, especially the often literalistic genealogies of the Vatican mythographies on which he drew so frequently, were largely responsible for dictating the old-fashioned fables he repeats. Through many of these sources philosophical interpretations of myth trickle into his commentary, whether Pythagorean, Stoic, or Neoplatonic. In addition to Servius, especially the proem to his commentary on the *Ecloga*, Martianus Capella, and also Isidore,[83] Bernard's sources include the commentaries on Martianus Capella, especially by Remigius, the Boethius commentaries—as well as Fulgentius, through the Vatican mythographies of which Bernard seems so fond. Many of the fables in the Vatican mythographies share with these Carolingian commentaries similar readings of the gods.

That Bernard was familiar with the organization of both the first Vatican mythography and the second is clear from an interesting interpolation in a gloss based initially on a passage from Martianus listing Ennius's twelve select gods (*De nuptiis* 42). Here he identifies "Protheus" (*Ecl. Theod.* 286) not as Prometheus but Proteus, "pastor omnium aquaticorum animalium," in a passage drawn from Virgil's *Georgics* 4.387 and Servius on *Georgics* 4.399 (Bernard, *In Theod.* 3.1086–90, 1096–99). But he does list from the second Vatican mythography's opening, in the corresponding Alithia quatrain (*Ecl. Theod.* 289–292), the passage on Syrophanes of Egypt and the worship of idols, as if reminded of the connection between the opening of the first mythography (where Prometheus plays an important role as first man) and the opening of the second mythography (which borrows from Fulgentius in discussing Syrophanes's idols). According to Huygens's notes, the Vatican mythographies (or Fulgentius preserved within them) suggest lines for Bernard's comments on a very large number of fables from the *Ecloga.*[84]

Rather than examine these individually I would like to focus briefly on Bernard's treatment of Athenian king Cecrops (*Ecl. Theod.* 53–56) for his skillful amalgamation of different sources into one relatively literal but philosophically resonant fable, in this case, Pythagorean. In this particular instance, Bernard's sum is more than the total of its parts. Here he draws on the second Vatican mythography fable 39 and Fulgentius (*Mit.* 2.1) for the etymology of "Pallas" (and "Athens"), and on Isidore (*Etym.* 8.11.9–10) for Cecrops's animal sacrifice to Jupiter. Bernard describes the competition between Neptune and Pallas over the name of Athens— reciting the literal fable of the gifts offered by each; the horses by Neptune, to be used in war, the olive by Pallas, signifying peace and light. Because Pallas won, the city is called Athens, from " 'athanate parthene,' that is, immortal virgin" (*In Theod.* 2.150–5). In the Misterium by means of an implicit Christian rationalization Bernard defends the first Athenian king, who sacrificed cattle, from a criticism based on the Pythagorean belief in transmigration of souls into different bodies (presumably including those of the cattle),[85] but his physical interpretation refers back to the conflict between Neptune and Pallas over the name of the city, to add an acerbic note that the men of this city did not make use of either sailing or philosophy, the benefits (respectively) of sea and land, for which reason they say that the conflict between Neptune and Pallas is only about the *name* of the city and not its character ("Ex urbis autem nomine inter Neptunum et Palladem ideo certamen esse aiunt, quia dubium est utrum magis homines huius civitatis maris aut terrae commodo vel navigatione aut philosophia utantur," *In Theod.* 2.169–72).

Several of the glosses in the *Ecloga* indebted to the Vatican mythographers deserve closer attention for Bernard's literalization of their meaning. Juno as the wet-nurse of Mercury (*Ecl. Theod.* 197–200, from Mythogr. I

117/119) actually is dismissed with a rationalization of her nursing as representing her esteem for the god: "Ac si diceret: tam valens fuit Mercurius, ut omnes credant eum a Iunone lactatum, quamvis natus fuerit de Maia pelice" ["As if to say: Mercury was so strong that all believe he was nursed by Juno, although he was born from her rival, Maia"] (*In Theod.* 3. 183–85). The description of Ganymede's abduction by the eagle (*Ecl. Theod.* 77–80, from Mythogr. I 181/184) is explained in the Misterium as the noble youth captured and made a friend, in the process replacing another: "quo in bello Ganimedem honestissimum iuvenem equo deiecit captumque in amicorum numero ascivit et reiecta qua prius utebantur Hebe, hunc catamitum sibi fecit" ["In this war he threw the noble youth Ganymede from his horse, seized him, and admitted him into the number of his friends; and after rejecting Hebe, whom they formerly employed, he made Ganymede his catamite"] (according to Huygens, taken from Servius on *Aeneid* 1.28, about the honors paid to the ravished Ganymede and Juno's hostility toward the Trojans as a result; Bernard, *In Theod.* 2.357–60). The focus of the fable on Tithonus and Aurora (*Ecl. Theod.* 221–24, from Mythogr. I 136/139) falls upon Memnon's loss and the inconsolate mother (3.493–502), with a brief description of the reason for Tithonus's transformation into a cricket (3.471–77).

Much of Bernard's fabulizing echoes the Carolingian Boethius glosses, filtered through the typological lens of the *Ecloga*. Bernard's gloss on Nimrod's tower and the Giants battling Jove (*Ecl. Theod.* 85–92) derives from commentary on a line of Boethius (*Consolatio* 3 p12)—indeed, Bernard names Boethius (and Cicero) in the Misterium: "Tullius autem Gigantes contra deos belligerantes quosvis naturae repugnantes intelligit, Boetius vero eos, qui dum sunt impliciti terrenis, celestia discutere aut consequi nituntur" ["Although Tullius {Cicero} understands the Giants in their warring against the gods as some men or other fighting against nature, Boethius, on the other hand, understands them, while they are involved in earthly matters, to be shaking up heavenly matters; or they are striving to pursue them"] (*In Theod.* 2.409–11; see figure 23, with "Atlas" representative of the Giants). The Boethius glosses of Remigius on this passage defined "earthly" as exactly the label applied to the Giants. (Bernard's physical explanation is not interesting, as we might expect—it defines the Giants as mountains colliding with the clouds above them, and so on.) In the construction of the tower (*Ecl. Theod.* 89–92) the poet's vague "posteritas Adae" is revealed by Bernard as "Nembroth" (*In Theod.* 2.419– 50). In the Allegoria, Nembroth is *diabolus* and *tyrannus*, his tower a sign of

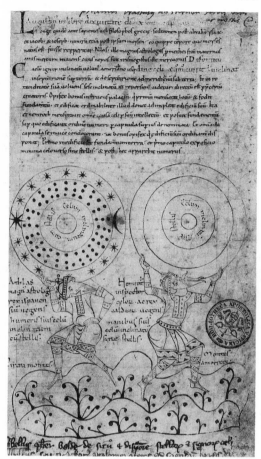

23. Atlas and Nimrod, each holding a globe. From *Dialogus inter magistrum Nemroth et discipulum Joathon de astronomia, de computo, de temporibus.* MS. Palatinus Latinus 1417, fol. 1r (11th–12th c.). By permission of Biblioteca Apostolica Vaticana, Rome.

superbia in that he wishes to compare himself to God. An alternative explanation reveals Nembroth's companions as heretics who question Christ's divinity, their tongues divided because their discordant dogma is divisive. The image anticipates that of Dante in the canto on the heretics, in *Inferno* 8–9.

Also from the Remigian Boethius glosses come Orpheus and Eurydice (*Ecl. Theod.* 189–92), interpreted first morally, then as educational allegory, and finally as an allegory of music technology. Eurydice first leaves Orpheus when she is pursued by Aristaeus, so that she is killed by a serpent (a Virgilian interpolation commonly credited by modern scholars to Bernard Silvestris). In the Misterium, Orpheus represents "optima vox," as he does in Remigius, and Eurydice is "profunda iudicatio, quia facundiae comes esse debet discretio." Aristaeus is "best," "quod optimum sonat," with Orpheus returning to the superior regions from the underworld because the soul must seek the good, and Eurydice is retained by Proserpina in the underworld because she signifies *avaritia* and Proserpina is named from "creeping forward," "porro serpens" (Bernard, *In Theod.* 3.95–109). Bernard cleverly glosses his own gloss by drawing on Juvenal (*Sati.* 14.139): "Crescit amor nummi, quantum ipsa pecunia crescit," "the love of money increases as money itself increases." The physical interpretation centers on the art of music and picks up the alternate interpretation of Orpheus associated with the first Vatican mythography. Orpheus again is "best voice" and Eurydice is "best judgment," "optima iudicatio." Thereafter the gloss becomes original, supposedly Pythagorean, and based on the artistic process in music or science: "In omnibus autem artibus sunt primae artae, sunt secundae. Verbi gratia: in medicina prima est gnostica, secunda dinamica, in musicis musica prima, secunda apotolesmatica" ["In all the arts, however, there are first arts and second ones {i.e., Orpheus and Eurydice, or the application}. For example: in medicine, diagnosis is first, treatment, second; in the musical arts, music is first, the effect, second"}. What follows is a complex musical allegorization having to do with the relationship between musical composition (Eurydice) and performance (Orpheus) and the work necessary to achieve both.[86]

The fable on Phaethon's horses (*Ecl. Theod.* 245–48) distantly echoes the K Reviser's gloss (on *Consolatio* 3 m12), but also construes Phaethon as an astrologer. Bernard repeats the standard Fulgentian etymological gloss on the four names of Ericteus (Erythaeus), from "rubens," or "blushing"; Acteon, from "splendens," "resplendent"; Lampos (Lampus), from "ardens," or "burning"; and Philogeos (Philogeus), from "amans terram," or "loving the earth" (also found in the first Vatican mythographer, 113/114). These etymological glosses are followed by the four names as given by Ovid (*Metamorphoses* 2.153–54), Eoüs, "oriens," or "rising," "surgens," "ascending"; Aethon, from "elatus," or "raised high"; Pyroïs, from "igneus," "fiery"; and Phlegon, from "acclinis," "inclined toward" (Bernard, *In Theod.* 3.675–84; see chapter 5, p. 192, and chapter 6, p. 237). The Misterium presents Phaethon as an astrologer: "astrologus in cursu solis describendo studuit, quare solis dictus est filius et eius rexisse currum" ["the astrologer was diligent in charting the path of the sun; therefore he was called the son of the sun and was said to have driven his chariot"] (*In Theod.* 3.712–14).

The double set of fables summing up Hercules's life and death also organize carefully the long Remigian glosses on Boethius on Hercules (from *Consolatio* 4 m7)—but also several from Remigius on Martianus. In relation to Hercules's conception and battle with the snakes (*Ecl. Theod.* 165–68), from Remigius on Martianus, the Misterium suggests that the doubled night during which Jove lecherously slept with Alcmene was accomplished by magic (*In Theod.* 2.1040–50). The physical interpretation from Fulgentius also interprets Hercules morally and etymologically as "Heracleos," "fame credited to strong men," depicted as being born out of Alcmene, "a false humor," and Jove, "ardor," because he acquires good, fame, and wisdom by means of labor; Juno, "dignity," from the Greek *axiona,* sends snakes at his birth because of envy over the fame of his strength (*In Theod.* 2.1052–59).

In the second part, on Hercules's Labors and death (*Ecl. Theod.* 173–76), it is clear there is a long tradition of commentary on the Labors epitomized from the *Consolatio* (4 m7). Physically, Bernard supplies a variant set of his earlier etymologies, glossing Alcides as "virtus" (from the Boethius glosses), and Hercules as "Heracleos," that is, "famosus," "quia virtus bonam famam consequitur" ["because good fame follows on virtue"]. Alcmene is interpreted "falsum," and Jove, "fire," from which Hercules is produced because "virtus" is born out of wisdom and love (*In Theod.* 2.2.1141–45). The adversaries he confronts—the dragon, Geryon, the Hydra, Cacus, Cerberus, and so on—are morally presented but differently from the Boethius glosses. Geryon is tri-form because of the three "diversities" in life, without which the human cannot obtain self-esteem (*dignitas*), and Cacus "etiam sibi secreto nocebit, quia secretum aliquod malum semper obesse solet dignitati; per Cacum etiam quidam intelligi volunt detractionem, quae plerumque obstat dignitati" ["will harm even himself by a secret, because some secret evil is always accustomed to hinder worth: by Cacus, besides, some mean slander, which generally stands in the way of worth"] (*In Theod.* 2.1154–56). A much-traveled definition of the hero's adversary Cerberus as earth is drawn from Servius (named by Bernard) but also from the Boethius glosses (on *Consolatio* 3 m12): "Quod autem Cerberum ab inferis traxisse dicitur, sic accipit Servius, quod omnes cupiditates et vicia terrena contempsit et domuit. Nam Cerberus terra est, omnium consumptrix corporum" ["Because he is said to have dragged Cerberus from the underworld, so Servius understands that he despised and vanquished all earthly desires and vices. For Cerberus is earth, the destroyer of all bodies"] (*In Theod.* 2.1132–34).

Bernard's use of Martianus and the Carolingian commentaries on him reveals his interest in the twelve select gods, especially Mercury, Proserpina and Pluto, and even Fronesis, who also figures in *De nuptiis*. The twelve select gods (*De nuptiis* 42, *Ecl. Theod.* 288f, from Ennius's *Annales* 1.62–63) come directly from Martianus, but Bernard merely lists the twelve. The epitome of Mercury's various roles (*Ecl. Theod.* 197–200) may very well draw upon Remigius on Martianus: he is first defined as ruling the art of incantation or medicine, particularly because he has access to the underworld and can summon souls back to life, a skill symbolized by his caduceus or wand. But of course his role is also moral, guide of sinners who must be punished after death.[87] In the Misterium, Bernard appends the Fulgentian etymology to the definition, "Fulgentius tamen Mercurium quasi mercicurium, id est mercatorem," but this definition of the trader is applied differently: "vult accipi, qui utraque regna permeare dicitur, quia mari et terra discurrit hoc hominum genus" {"Fulgentius claims Mercury is understood as *mercicurium,* that is, a trader; Mercury is said to traverse both kingdoms, because this class of man {traders} goes out on sea and land"} (3.191–94). No doubt influenced by the Martianus commentaries and their portrayal of Mercury as god of eloquence, Bernard here describes the raising and lowering of his *virga,* rod, as rhetorical praise and blame (3.194–197). But as *sermo,* speech, Mercury, because of his mobility and speed, is also defined as if it were the Latin name for the Greek *hymen,* "to discourse," in a passage that must have been influenced by Martianus commentaries or at the least the Martianus text itself, and his relation to the underworld is also traced through his role as messenger.[88]

Bernard discards the allegorical glosses on Martianus in glossing Proserpina (*Ecl. Theod.* 317–19) for a straightforward summary of her abduction by Pluto and her eating of the three "mali grana." And yet what might be termed his response to the Pluto of the Carolingian Martianus commentators gives rise to a rather brilliant synthesis of glosses on the whole of the second book of *De nuptiis* and what turns out to be two different interpretations of the underworld—as pagan afterlife and as Neoplatonic earth.

At the beginning of the third book (in fact on the second half of the *Ecloga*), Bernard digresses briefly on the prevarications of the gentile books—in effect, why should Christians study pagan works? It is at this point that he returns to the "moderns" and their use of "ancients" as authorities—but pointing out that the moderns prefer the more modern to the more ancient, that is, Terence to Menander, Horace to Lucilius, and even Priscian to Donatus. This provides an important introduction to his opening glosses on the *Ecloga* dialogue (181–184) contrasting Dis and the thousand names of the pagan gods with the triune Oneness of God. Dis is Pluto "regi inferorum," king of the shades, just as Jupiter rules the heavens (*In Theod.* 3.32–33). Bernard divides the regions of the underworld in a wholly innovative manner: Pluto reigns over the region above, that is, what might be termed the earthly underworld of woods, mountains, and fields (3.34–35), but Demorigon reigns over the inferior beings of the underworld, those who require punishment: "Tradunt enim duos esse inferos, unum in quo regnat Pluto, quem supra tetigit, alium de quo psalmista ait: 'ex inferno inferiori,' ubi Demorigon regnat, qui periuria deorum punire credebatur" ["They say there are two underworlds, one in which Pluto rules, and the other about which the Psalmist says: 'from the lower hell,' where Demorigon rules, who was believed to punish the false oaths of the gods"] (*In Theod.* 3.35–38). Then follows a long discourse on the philosophers' interpretations—Platonic, Hesiodic-genealogical, Epicurean, and Stoic—culminating in a discussion of the three rulers of the cosmic regions and what had been a clearly Stoic discursion even in the *Ecloga*.

> De diis enim inter philosophos, immo philosopholos litigium fuit "et adhuc sub iudice lis est." Alii namque ut Plato volebant unum deum et secundum quod diversis preerat diversa sortiri vocabula, scilicet dum celum regeret Iupiter, id est iuvans pater, dum plueret tempestatesque faceret Neptunus, id est nube tonans, Pluto vel Februus dum in inferno animas puniret vocaretur; alii tres, ut Apuleius et Porphirius, deorum esse ordines dixerunt: deos in celo quid in terris agatur ignorantes, demones in aëre, qui aliquibus sacrificiis placati preces hominum diis offerrent, manes animas ubique vagantes. Alii, ut Esiodus in Teugonia, primo deos genitos, inde semideos, post heroas, inde innocentes homines, ultimos sceleratos, alii nullum, ut Epicuri, dicentes cuncta casu regi, alii unum, ut Stoici, et ubique, cuius providentia regantur cuncta, alii, ut Varro, rei cuique deum preesse suum et partem horum esse in celo, partem in aëre, partem in terra, partem in aquis et partem in inferno, secundum quem haec est invocatio.

> [For concerning the gods, among the philosophers, rather the "little philosophers," there has been a dispute, and "the case is still in court" {not yet decided}. For some, like Plato, claimed there was one god, and according as he was in charge of different things, he acquired different names: for instance, when he ruled the sky, he was called

Jupiter, that is, *iuvans pater,* "helping father"; when he rained and caused storms, Neptune, that is, *nube tonans,* "thundering from a cloud"; Pluto or Februus when he punished souls in the underworld. Others, like Apuleius and Porphyrius, said there were three ranks (orders) of gods: gods in the sky, not knowing what was done upon earth; demons in the air, who when appeased by some sacrifices offered the prayers of man to the gods; and the Manes, souls wandering everywhere. Others, like Hesiod in the *Theogony,* believed that first the gods were born, then the demigods, afterwards heroes, then innocent men, and last, wicked men. Some, like the Epicureans, claimed there was no god, saying that all things are ruled by chance; others, like the Stoics, believed there was one god by whose providence all things are ruled; others, like Varro, said that each thing has its own god in charge and that some of these {gods} are in the sky, some in the air, some on earth, some in the waters, and some in the underworld; according to him, this is the invocation.] (Bernard, *In Theod.* 3.45–60)

Most innovative in this disquisition is Demiorgon, the chief principle of the underworld conceived as moral and therefore merely analogous to the cosmic ruler of the literal underworld, Pluto, who reigns over earth; this name constitutes the source for Boccaccio's Demigorgon as original principle (Boccaccio even mentions a "Theodontius"—clearly intended to be Theodulus—and the source of his reference is not lost, as scholars of Boccaccio had feared). This may very well suggest the two-fold nature of many of the Martianus commentaries, split between the upper world and lower (that is, the underworld, earth) and the gods populating each.

Also influenced by Martianus is Bernard's use of Fronesis at the very end when the debate becomes strangely abstract, with Pseustis discussing the zodiac while Alithia discusses the conversion of St. Augustine. At this point both the *Ecloga* and the commentary end with an explicit mention of Martianus Capella, and "Stillbon" or Mercury being married to Philology, daughter of Fronesis or Phronesis.[89] But in the Misterium, the glosses are much indebted to the Carolingian commentaries: Mercury is speech, *sermo;* Philology is love of reason, *amor rationis;* their union is achieved through the seven liberal arts in a very neat listing of the process of knowledge (*In Theod.* 3.1478–82).

Even the ending of the commentary is pervaded by the harmonizing influence of the Martianus commentaries, in which "wedding" suggests bonding of equals rather than subordination of one to the other. Bernard introduces Fronesis as mediator by saying, "Hic introducitur Fronesis, reconcilians Alithiae Pseustim" (*In Theod.* 3.1494), not at all a denigration of Pseustis but a reconciliation. Fronesis, "Prudence," was mother of Philologia in *De nuptiis;* here, she is sister of Alithia. She represents not only prudence but justice balanced with mercy, as Bernard reminds us in the stages of the judicial process, beginning with inquiry, in the cause of truth, followed by equity, and ending with pity.[90]

Other commentators later in the twelfth century, such as Alexander Neckam, will attempt to redo Bernard's glossing; there will follow no new commentaries until the fourteenth and fifteenth centuries, when Stephen Patrington and Odo of Picardy emerge. But Bernard's will remain dominant despite these other attempts in the next few centuries. And it is especially in the twelfth century that the incipient literary criticism and deductive reasoning and scholasticism of Bernard of Utrecht will bloom in the Chartrian (or Parisian) philosophy of William of Conches and Bernard Silvestris.

Chapter Ten

THE VIRGILIAN JUDGMENT OF PARIS AND THE PROBLEM OF THE BODY: FROM NEOPLATONIC TO NEO-STOIC IN THE GLOSSES OF WILLIAM OF CONCHES

The development of twelfth-century Platonism and Neo-Platonism has been well-documented,[1] particularly as it flourished in the writings of the Norman philosopher and scholar William of Conches,[2] who was aware of Platonic ideas not only from Plato's *Timaeus* (on which he commented), but also from Macrobius's commentary on Cicero's *Somnium Scipionis* which in turn derived from Plato's *Republic.* In addition, his major work, the *Philosophia mundi,* is full of Platonist ideas—in particular, the view of Nature as God's handmaiden, called goddess, in whom we can see God's grandeur reflected as in a mirror and who is frequently identified with the third Person of the Trinity, the *anima mundi.*[3] Accordingly, if the universe reflects God, so the "little universe," the microcosm, mirrors him back in miniature, the human soul a spark of divine wisdom, flesh composed of the elements and guided by the physical laws of the external universe. This correspondence is encouraged in William's reading of the *Timaeus,* although in all of his glosses he was fascinated by the faculties of the human soul incarnated in the body, that is, intelligence, memory, reason, and free will.[4]

In the Middle Ages the planes of correspondence between microcosmos and cosmos had been best visualized through the imagery of celestial wedding in the writings of that other Neoplatonist, Martianus Capella, on whom William also lectured; the concept of microcosmos as *artifex,* or *auctor,* like God—and the process of artificial creation, like that of natural creation—had been fired by the idea of imaginative vitality, essentially Stoic in nature.[5] Most important, William's interpretation of the poetic text as an underworld, of textuality as carnal, set against the spirituality of its incarnated truth, resurrects the Augustinian (and Neoplatonic) understanding of text in *De doctrina Christiana*. William appears to echo Plato's original debate in the *Republic* on the value of poetry—even though this debate was not fossilized in the extent version of Cicero's *Somnium Scipionis,* the fragment often appended to manuscripts of Macrobius's commentary (and excerpts of that same fragment are cited along the way in Macrobius's commentary). For William uses the mythological fables of the ancient poets to clarify philosophic (Neoplatonic) ideas about nature and human nature, the macrocosm and the microcosm, and the "little world" of the text.

What has not been recognized so clearly is that William in various works also synthesized Stoic concepts from Cicero's *De officiis,* Seneca's *Epistolae,* and *De beneficiis* in the *Moralium dogma philosophorum,* which he wrote for the benefit of the young Prince Henry Plantagenet (in 1154 Henry II of England), as attested by his goal, "ad normam rationis vitam reducere" ["to conform life to the norm of reason"].[6] Such interest in Stoicism also developed during his prolific career through a wide range of mythographic commentaries. William's contribution to the mythographic tradition emerged from the heavily sexual glossation associated with the gods previously in the feminizing Neo-Stoic Carolingian Martianus and his Neoplatonic rationalization of them.

William contributed to mythography generally and Boethius studies specifically, in his earliest glosses, through the systematic Neoplatonization of mythological glosses. He was the first commentator to approach the gods and the problem of human sexuality consistently and holistically, attempting to fit both into a coherent philosophical context that accounted for the problem of the feminized body. William used the grammarian's techniques of etymologization to assimilate into a single, cohesive, Neoplatonic system previously existing strands of commentary on Virgil, Boethius, Martianus Capella, and the genealogy of the gods. Once the importance of his early commentary on Boethius is understood, the interrelationship of glosses in his later commentaries on Macrobius, Martianus, Juvenal, and the *Timaeus* will become clearer. These glosses provide a Neoplatonic rationale for what Theodore Silverstein has termed, in the cosmographic works of Bernard Silvestris, a "fabulous cosmogony,"[7] but what had become, in the hands of the Carolingians, part of a Neo-Stoic mythography.

In the rich period of the twelfth century, which owes so much to the earlier Carolingian renaissance of classical humanism, William, one of its most influential thinkers—and mythographers—emerged early, in the 'thirties. In the twelfth-century schools of northern France, particularly at Chartres and Paris, but also at Laon and Orleans, classical humanism resurged, overspilling the narrow confines of any one school and extending eventually into England.[8] The classics became intrinsically interesting to scholars while they also continued to provide a means of learning the liberal arts of grammar, rhetoric, and dialectic. The presence of Platonism in the thought of the period invigorated the arts and therefore commentaries on the classics—as would the later advent of Aristotle revolutionize both the direction of the universities and the nature of philosophic inquiry.

William was both influenced by, and himself influenced, great men, although little is known about his life and not much more about his professional accomplishments.[9] He studied under the man John of Salisbury termed the "most perfect of the Platonists of our time" (*Metalogicon* 4.35), Bernard of Chartres, and perhaps also Abelard; between 1137 and 1140 or 1141 he taught the prince who would be Henry II, John of Salisbury, and Petrus Helias, among others, most probably at Paris, possibly at Chartres, or after retirement, in Normandy; and in his earlier works he heavily influenced Bernard Silvestris.[10] Although William in his Priscian glosses regarded himself as a *physicus,* or "natural philosopher," a term echoed in a recent designation of the group to which he belonged as "cosmologists,"[11] he was in fact a grammarian and inherited the old-fashioned technique of etymologizing from earlier grammarians like Isidore, Fulgentius, and Remigius of Auxerre.[12]

In that same grammatical tradition—which evolved in the Middle Ages parallel to the mythographic tradition—he wrote a number of glosses on classical authors. According to his *Dragmaticon,* the following works belonged to his youth: the glosses on Boethius's *Consolatio,* Macrobius's commentary on the *Somnium Scipionis,* and the first version of Priscian's *Institutes,* plus the *Philosophia mundi;* the middle works included glosses on the *Timaeus* and the *Dragmaticon;* in his old age he revised his glosses on Priscian's *Institutes.* In addition, he is also believed to have lectured and/or commented on Martianus Capella's *De nuptiis,* in a form now perhaps partially preserved in the so-called Florentine Commentary,[13] and also on Juvenal in glosses written probably in the 1130s, when William was teaching at Chartres, that is, after the earliest commentaries but before that on the *Timaeus.*[14] Probably William's Martianus commentary—if it is indeed preserved in the Florentine Commentary, or mythography—was thought out at the same time as the Boethius and Macrobius commentaries, if not actually written down then, if we accept William's promise in the Boethius glosses to complete such an exposition: he does not deal with the branches of divination "quia super Martianum hoc exponemus," "because we explain this in the commentary on Martianus."[15] Further support for the dating of this commentary appears in the Macrobius commentary, in the section on sounds caused by firmament and planets, where William interjects, "quid Marcianus intellexerit loco suo dicemus" ["what Martianus understood we shall say in its place"]. I would agree with Dronke, who concludes that "The commentaries on Boethius and Macrobius would seem to belong to the earliest part of William's career. It seems likely enough that in the years that followed William carried out his intention of expounding Martianus."[16]

The key to his philosophic interpretation of the classical fables can be found in his Virgilian interpolation into the Boethius glosses, the earliest of all his commentaries, which recurs in different forms elsewhere in his glosses. William borrows the Judgment of Paris story from Virgil commentary for use in the Boethius glosses, in relation to the fable of Ixion in the Orpheus poem, because of the connection with Juno (who was opposed to both Paris and Ixion); again in the Martianus glosses, in which Hercules is substituted for Paris (Juno, stepmother to Hercules, is hostile to both heroes); and finally, as an analogue for Vulcan (another son of Jupiter and Juno) in the Pallas/Minerva fable in the *Timaeus* glosses.

William's concern is with the problem of the body, in particular the problem of semen, within a life devoted to contemplation. Justifying human (in particular male) sexuality by means of denial, abstinence, or mythographic rationalization is his constant theme. Of the three goddesses to whom Paris might have offered the golden apple of Discord, the focus of William's mythological insertion, his subversive innovation, in almost all of his glosses is either Juno or Minerva, in their frustration of male desire. Both are virgins, both either sister/wife or daughter to Jupiter, and in any case not-Venus. The gendered body as a cultural sign reflects the problem of its assimilation into Christian monosexual institutions, like the monastery and in William's time the university. In exploring how William fantasized the body we will discover how he appropriated and cannibalized features of the corporal from various commentary traditions.

In the Boethius glosses William's innovative interpolation of the Virgilian myth of the Judgment of Paris into the fable of Ixion serves as a key to and sign of his Neoplatonic approach to the individual and to the World Soul in other glosses. His Neoplatonic moralization of both Ixion and Paris finds a place in mythography for the vexed hero as an Anyman, "quilibet homo." Anyman must choose between diverse roles and moral avenues; the problem of his own male sexuality interferes, whether expressed as frustrated desire for Juno or unbridled passion for Venus. The unbridling of virility causes psychological problems for William's heroes—irrationality, or in cosmic terms, hell, in fact (see figure 24, an illustration of the respective punishments of Ixion and Tantalus). His mythography attempts to cope with this mythological version of Original Sin by means of philosophical rationalizations in all of his glosses.

In the Boethius glosses the link between the two myths occurs through Juno, the object of Ixion's desire and at the same time one of the three goddesses whose beauty or value Paris was supposed to judge. For William the goddess comes to represent the active life, chiefly through Fulgentius's allegorization of the three goddesses in the Judgment of Paris in terms of the three lives, Pallas Athena as *vita theorica,* the contemplative life, Juno as *vita practica,* the active life or riches, and Venus as *vita philargiria,* the voluptuous life. Paris himself symbolizes the human will, in that the choice of Paris belongs to each man, and like him most men fail by giving the apple of victory to Venus, voluptuousness. William declares:[17]

INTEGUMENTUM DE IXIONE: Fabula Ixionis talis est quod voluit concumbere cum Iunone violenter, sed interposuit Iuno nubem et cedidit semen in terram et nati sunt inde gigantes. Vnde in inferis rote subditus volvitur. Cuius veritas talis est. Iuno ponitur pro activa vita. Vnde in fabulis invenitur quod tres dee Iuno, Pallas, Venus iudicio Paridis que dignior esset aureo pomo quesierunt, quia Iupiter diffinire noluit. Quod non fuit aliud quod tres vite sunt, scilicet teorica id est contemplativa, practica id est activa, philargiria id est voluptaria. Et ponitur Pallas pro contemplativa, Iuno pro activa, Venus pro voluptaria. Quod potest probari per premia que promittuntur Paridi. Pallas namque promittit sapientiam quia contemplatione fit aliquis sapiens. Iuno divicias quia per activam vitam acquiruntur divicie. Venus promittit feminam quia in ea est maxima voluptas. Iste tres dee pro pomo certant, id est pro beatitudine, quia unaqueque videtur facere beatum. Sed Iupiter hoc noluit diffinire ne libertatem arbitrii videretur auferre. Vnde querunt iudicium Paridis, scilicet cuiuslibet hominis. Sed Paris adquiescit Veneri quia maxima pars sceptrum dicitur portare, quia per talem vitam sceptrum acquiritur.

[INTEGUMENTUM ON IXION: The fable of Ixion is that he wished to rape Juno, but Juno interposed a cloud between them and his semen

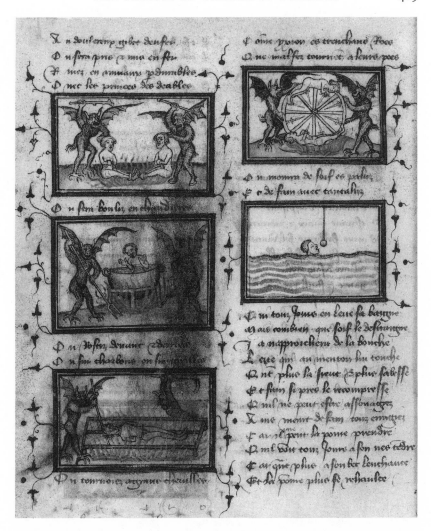

24. Ixion and Tantalus. From Guillaume de Lorris and Jean de Meun, *Roman de la Rose*. MS. Douce 332, fol. 178v (15th c., French). By permission of the Bodleian Library, University of Oxford.

fell to earth; from this were born the Giants. Hence in the underworld he revolves bound to a wheel. The truth of this is as follows. Juno signifies the active life. Hence in the fables it is found that three goddesses, Juno, Pallas, and Venus, asked Paris to decide which was worthier of the golden apple, because Jupiter was unwilling to settle the matter. This means that there are three lives: the theoretical, that is, contemplative; the practical, that is, active; and the philargical, that is, sensual. Pallas signifies the contemplative, Juno the active, Venus the sensual. This can be proved by the rewards each promised to Paris. For Pallas promised wisdom, because a man becomes wise through contemplation. Juno promised riches, because wealth is acquired through an active life. Venus promised a woman, because she is the greatest source of pleasure. The three goddesses contended for the apple, that is, for happiness, because each one seems to make a man happy. But Jupiter was not willing to make the decision lest he seem to take away free will. Therefore they sought the judgment of Paris, that is, of Anyman. But Paris yielded to Venus, because most people are said to be under a scepter, as through such a life a scepter is acquired.]

William may be using the Judgment of Paris to gloss the myth of Ixion's desire for Juno. In resorting to the metaphor of a scepter for power or domination, William seems to confuse the rule of Venus with the goddess of rule, Juno, whose peacock and scepter he recalls, along with her animosity toward the hero Hercules, emblem of wisdom and eloquence, as belonging to Venus in the lines that follow the above passage on Venus: "Item dicitur in tutela pavonem habere propter varietatem vestium que talem vitam comitantur. Dicitur noverca Herculis quia talis vita inimica et noverca est sapientis" ["Likewise she is said to have the peacock under her protection on account of the varied dresses that accompany such a life. She is called the stepmother of Hercules because such a life is hostile and a stepmother to the wise"]. This ambiguity may be deliberate on William's part as a means of glossing the attractions of the active life *as if* voluptuous and therefore concerned with the feminizing pursuit of the beauty, adorn-ments, and falsity of the material world.

Therefore, explains William, implying connections between the volup-tuousness of Venus and the Juno desired by Ixion, Juno is a symbol of the active life that the king of the Lapiths wants to embrace, but the cloud which he finds himself embracing instead represents the obscuring of reason caused by preoccupations inherent in the active life. From this event the Centaurs were born; the sperm which flow to earth signify the human will oriented toward the things of this world, and the Giants or Centaurs born from the union of Ixion and the earth represent the cares of earthly things, a monstrous or split self torn between the rational and the irrational. The punishment of Ixion, bound to his wheel, symbolizes the mutability of the active life which menaces all men attached to perishable things.

> Huic Iunoni aliquis violenter vult coincombere ut Ixion quando laborando tali vita vult beatitudinem acquirere. Sed Iuno interponit nubem et *semen cadit in terram,* de quo nascuntur gigantes, quia talis vita obscuritatem rationis homini confert et totam intentionem in temporalibus facit ponere. Inde nascuntur gigantes vel centauri id est cure terrenorum: ge enim terra est. Que cure in parte sunt rationales in parte irrationales ut centauri qui in parte sunt homines in parte boves. Vnde dicitur Ixion in inferis rota volvi quia qui tali vite est subditus modo extollitur prosperitate modo deprimitur adversitate. Sed Orpheo audito velox rota non precipitat ixionium caput quia sapiens et eloquens docet qua ratione mutabilis vita vitari possit, vel quia sapiens et eloquens docet quare rote et mutabilitati talis vite nullus submitti debeat. Et hec est *velox rota,* scilicet divitiarum mutabilitas, *velox,* quia cito transit.

[A man wishes to rape this Juno, like Ixion, when, struggling under such a life, he wishes to attain happiness. But Juno interposes a cloud and *the semen falls to the ground,* from which are born the Giants; because such a life confers obscurity of the reason upon man and makes him turn his whole intention to temporal things. Hence are born the Giants or Centaurs, that is, concern for earthly things: for "ge" is "earth." These concerns are in part rational, in part irrational, like the Centaurs, who are part men, part oxen. Hence it is said that Ixion revolves on a wheel in the underworld, because one who is subject to such a life is at one time lifted high by prosperity, at another pressed down by adversity. But when Orpheus is heard the swift wheel does not turn downward Ixion's head, because a wise and eloquent man teaches how an uncertain life can be avoided; or because a wise and eloquent man teaches how no one ought to be subjected to the wheel and the mutability of such a life. And this is the *swift wheel,* namely, the mutability of riches, *swift* because it quickly passes away (my emphasis.)]

This innovative gloss teaches that the "swift wheel" (symbol of fortune and the active life of Juno) should be avoided by the wise individual (unlike Ixion). In effect, William's Judgment of Paris asserts as a moral corrective for the evils of concupiscence (Juno or Venus) the Judgment of Eurydice—whose name, etymologically, means "judgment of good"—natural desire.[18] William's positive interpretation of Orpheus's wife (in contradistinction to the earlier Remigian tradition) reflects the feminizing (Neo-Stoic) influence of the Martianus glosses.

The remaining, briefer, glosses in the Boethius commentary extend the moralizations of heroes as exemplars of wisdom who frequently must choose between the active and contemplative lives. In his gloss, on Agamemnon, Ulysses, and Hercules (*Consolatio* 4 m7), William again uses Fulgentius (probably through the Vatican mythographers) to cast his heroes as exemplars of wisdom. Agamemnon sacrifices his daughter vainly, in the pursuit of "inanis gloria";[19] Ulysses in his conflict with Polyphemus represents wisdom confronting the sophomoric youth whose pride destroys fame: "Poliphemus interpretatur 'perdens famam' et ponitur pro puerili superbia quia nichil de fama sed de voluptate est curiosa" ["Polyphemus is interpreted as 'destroying fame' and is regarded as youthful pride, because he is diligent about nothing of fame but about pleasure"].[20] Hercules's apotheosis signifies the transition from the active to the contemplative life, achieved through the performance of Labors mostly consisting of conflicts with vicious monsters until he reaches, through the contemplative life, that heaven which his shoulders support at the very end of his adventures.[21] As wisdom he must battle *luxuria,* or Antaeus (son of earth whose power remains strong as long as he is in contact with earth): "Antaeus ponitur pro luxuria; qui bene dicitur Anteus, id est contrarietas,—anti enim contra,—quia nocet anime et corpori luxuria" ["Antaeus means lechery; he is well-named 'Antaeus,' that is, opposition—*anti* means *contra*—because lechery injures the soul and the body"].[22] Hercules as exemplar of wisdom similarly triumphs over the Centaurs, who mix *rationabilia* and *irrationabilia,* "quia omnia irrationabilia in se et in aliis sapiens domat." The Nemean lion that Hercules overcomes symbolizes anger ("quia sapiens omnem frendentiam superfluae irae a corde suo removet"), the Harpies symbolize avarice. For his efforts Hercules finds pure contemplation and the joys of eternity, "requies et respiratio," symbolized by the golden apples of the Hesperides, the daughters of Atlas ("ingenium, ratio, memoria") who are gardeners of the treasure of perfect wisdom. Here William intermingles two traditions, as in the *Ecloga Theoduli,* by adding a biblical gloss on the two wives of Jacob, Leah and Rachel, who represent respectively the contemplative and active lives.[23]

In reading the myths in Boethius, William philosophically systematizes the conflicts between matter and spirit in mythologizing the little world of the human soul, but he also shows awareness of the Platonic denigration of poetry as opposed to philosophy. The Boethius glosses[24] center on the same mythological passages which were the focus of earlier commentaries, although this is difficult to see, given the fact that the glosses have not yet been published in full in any edition. William's original contribution here is to unify the mythological interpretations by means of a Neoplatonic system of descents into the underworld in the Orpheus poem, descents derived originally from Aeneas's descent into the underworld in book 6 of the *Aeneid,* but associated in Boethius with Orpheus's descent to retrieve his wife Eurydice. In William's gloss, as we have just seen, his interest in the underworld explored by Orpheus allows him to expand greatly the treatment of the figure Ixion, whose lust for Juno sent him there. In this expansion William finds room to equate Ixion with the Trojan Paris, and thereby use the lustful Lapith as a hinge to join several Neoplatonic interpretation of myths.

I. ORPHEUS AND THE WORLD SOUL: WILLIAM AND THE ERFURT BOETHIUS COMMENTARY

William, sensitive to changes in Boethius commentary after Notker Labeo, interprets the mythological poems in Boethius according to a system of descents into an underworld inspired perhaps by the commentary of Remigius on book 6 of the *Aeneid.* In developing these glosses William may have been familiar with the Boethius commentary tradition after Notker Labeo, which demonstrated a Neoplatonic shift in interest to "O qui perpetua" (*Consolatio* 3 m9), on the World Soul. The most important of these intermediate commentators was the Erfurt commentator, in whose glosses on Boethius material from both Boethius and Martianus commentaries was organized by contemporary Neoplatonic glosses on "O qui perpetua" and the World Soul. This commentator thus offered William material for new glosses and new interpretations, particularly relating to *Consolatio* 4 m3 and 5 p2 (the latter on Tiresias. As a result of these interpretations William focuses on the individual will in the mythological heroes Orpheus, Ulysses, Hercules, but makes more explicit the relationship among the heroes and their infernal descents into an underworld by philosophizing on the nature of different kinds of descents and different kinds of underworlds, macrocosmic, microcosmic, integumental.

In his gloss on Orpheus (in *Consolatio* 3 m12), William provides the

25. Orpheus and Mercury. From Martial, *Epigrams*. MS. Canonici Latin classical 85, fol. 2v (15th c., Italian). By permission of the Bodleian Library, University of Oxford.

justification for many of his other Neoplatonized mythological glosses through a system of multiple allegorical descents relating the microcosm to the macrocosm. This most original gloss replaces with an extended and unified allegorization the traditional moralization of the inhabitants of hell as vices, and interpolates the story of the Judgment of Paris in the gloss on Ixion.[25] Moreover, it elaborates on the hero Orpheus through glosses taken from Fulgentius and others so that he becomes, truly, a Boethian exemplar of the virtuous combination of wisdom and eloquence (see figure 25, for Orpheus with Mercury, god of eloquence) akin to the hero Hercules, just as his wife Eurydice represents concupiscence as natural desire, "boni iudicatio," or judgment of good.[26] The underworld is allegorized by using the familiar Macrobian system of descents—the underworld is viewed as a metaphor for the inferior, either the body, this world, or hell, so that

Orpheus may be said to descend into hell first when he is born, second when he succumbs to the temptations of the body and acts viciously, third when, armed with wisdom, he exposes himself to this world and its temptations, and fourth, through magic arts, when he consults the demons. The descents are outlined in William's gloss on a line in Boethius, "Quid sit infernus et quot modis ad illum descendatur":

Infernum vocaverunt philosophi hanc sublunarem regionem quia inferior pars mundi est et plena miserie et doloris. Sunt diversi descensus: naturalis scilicet cum anima alicuius corpori coniungitur, non quod de celestibus ubi ante esset descendat sed quia sunt causa [cause] quare corpori coniungatur. Vel descensus anime dicatur [dicitur] coniunctio eiusdem cum corpore, quia scilicet tunc a propria dignitate descendit cum est subiecta passionibus corporis. Alius descensus est ut viciosus qui bipertitus est: alter enim per magicam artem, alter per alia vicia. Per magicam artem, cum aliquis demonibus loquitur ut Eneas antequam ad inferos descendit Misenum sepelivit quia ut magica arte ventura cognosceret eum [sic] demonibus sacrificavit. Per alia fit dum aliquis in temporalibus totam intentionem ponit. Est alius descensus non vitiosus cum scilicet aliquis sapiens ad cognitionem temporalium descendit ut, cum parum boni in eis vidit, ab eorum amore concupiscentiam extrahat. Hoc modo ad inferos descendere virtus est, sed duobus predictis modis vicium.

[The philosophers called this sublunar region the underworld because it is the lower part of the world and full of misery and pain. There are various descents: namely, the natural, when the soul of someone is joined to a body, not because it descends from the heavenly {regions} where it was before, but because there are reasons why it is joined to the body. Or the union of the soul with the body is called a descent of the soul because then it descends from its own high station when it is subjected to the passions of the body. Another descent is one of depravity, which is bipartite: for one is by means of the art of magic, the second by other vices. It is magic art when someone speaks to demons; as for instance Aeneas, before descending to the underworld, buried Misenus because in order to learn the future through magic, he sacrificed {him} (sic) to demons. It is an instance of other vices when a man gives all his attention to temporal matters. There is another descent which is not depraved, when a wise man descends in pursuit of knowledge of temporal matters so that, when he finds little good in them, he may withdraw his desires from the love of them. To descend to the underworld in this way is a virtue, but in the two aforesaid ways, a vice.][27]

The point is that only education prepares microcosmos for a virtuous descent into this world—as represented by the wise Orpheus who nevertheless looks back at his wife Eurydice, concupiscence that has "died" as a result of having been bit by the snake of temporal good. What is interesting is William's use of the word "integumentum" (literally "covering" or "protection") to describe the myth, as if it were a cloak or cover concealing something hidden. The concept derives from his belief in Boethius's perfection, which therefore makes William look for some underlying reason for his use of what seems to be a less than attractive story: "Qui apologus primum videndus est, deinde quid sapientes tali integumento voluerunt intelligere; nec credendum est a tam perfecto philosopho, scilicet Boecio, aliquid superfluum vel pro nichilo posuisse in tam perfecto opere" ["It must first be seen as a story, then what the wise {philosophers} meant to be understood by such an *integumentum*. It must not be believed that anything superfluous or worthless was contained in such a perfect work by such a perfect philosopher, namely Boethius"].[28])

The myth of Orpheus and Eurydice thus unifies and exemplifies the four descents: together husband and wife symbolize the natural descent, or the soul (Orpheus) wedded to natural concupiscence (Eurydice); Eurydice's fall into temporal pleasure signifies the vicious descent; Orpheus's wise descent into the underworld to rescue his judgment from its bad choice represents the virtuous descent; and Orpheus's own consultation with demons of the underworld, his descent to discover the whereabouts of his wife, in itself involves the magic arts.[29]

William does gloss some of the underworld inhabitants encountered by Orpheus in his descent innovatively and not merely as representation of human vice. As in earlier commentaries, Tantalus still represents avarice,[30] Cerberus signifies "carnes vorans," or *invidia,* with his three heads representing three different kinds of envy, or *ira naturalis, ira causalis,* and *ira invererata,* in a transformation of Remigius's three (natural, causal, and accidental); the three Furies signify bad words, thoughts, and actions (taken from Remigius and before him, Fulgentius). But other figures present unusual pedagogical challenges no doubt linked to glosses on their appearance in the sixth book of the *Aeneid*: Tantalus comes from *teantelon,* "volens visionem";[31] Tityus suggests the philosopher's perpetual but vain efforts to master the mystery and practice of divination.

This descent into hell in William's key passage in his mythological glosses on Boethius—also his longest and probably most discussed and cited gloss—is linked to several other unusual glosses through its Neoplatonism, in some cases as filtered through Macrobius. In the "Expliciunt glosulae Vuillelmi de Conchis super Boetium de consolatione Philosophiae" on the Muses as Sirens (*Consolatio* 1 m1), William involves Boethius's text in the Platonic debate about the value of poetry, showing his early interest in the *Republic* debate that will surface more explicitly in the Macrobius commentary. Here he first platonizes the distinction between poetry and philosophy as he would later in the glosses on the distinction between body and soul. He explains that the Muses are "Camenae" etymologically from "singing sweetly," "canentes amene," or "quelibet scientie," "knowledge of any kind." He then divides them into two classes: first, the Muses affiliated with philosophy are sound because they "preserve man by the soundness and constancy of reason" through the declarations of philosophy, and second, the Muses affiliated with poetry are "wounded" because they "tear apart men's hearts, and make them unstable" in that they recall pleasure or sorrow—the emotions—to the memory "rather than guiding or consoling."[32]

In addition to this strikingly Platonic issue, William from the beginning unifies his glosses by means of the tension between body and spirit, the corruptible and the ideal. A book 2 gloss (on the cornucopia, *Consolatio* 2 m2) identifies Hercules as a combination of wisdom and eloquence, the ideal microcosm vaunted by Martianus Capella's *De nuptiis,* in short: "Hercules pro sapiente et pro eloquente ponitur; unde dicitur monstra terre domare quia sapiens et eloquens omnia vicia domat" [" 'Hercules' means wise and eloquent; whence he is said to tame the monsters of earth because the wise and eloquent man tames all vices"].[33] William cites an etymology for the name of Hercules as a combination of "wrangling" and "glory" that underscores this signification in that wisdom's fight against vice appears glorious: "Qui bene Hercules dicitur, id est lite gloriosus,—her enim lis, cleos gloria,—quia sapiens lite et pugna contra vicia gloriosus apparet" ["He is well called 'Hercules,' that is, 'glorious in strife'—'her' means 'dispute,' 'cleos,' 'glory'—because the wise {man} appears glorious in strife and in the battle against vices"].[34]

In contrast to this ideal, the gloss on the Giants Otus and Ephialtes (*Consolatio* 3 p12) allegorizes them as representing the human body, in that the word "Giants" etymologically means "born from earth": "Gigantes dicuntur quasi gegantes, id est geniti a terra—ge enim est terra—et hec sunt corpora humana que ex terra genita sunt quia plus terre habent quam aliorum elementorum" ["They are called Giants, as 'gegantes,' that is, born from earth—'ge' is earth—and these are human bodies which have been begotten from earth because they have more of earth than of other elements"]. Thus the Giants' battle with the gods can be understood as a conflict between the flesh and the spirit. They pile mountain atop mountain to reach Heaven because of pride in their desire to expel the gods, that is, immortal souls that are like gods; but they are themselves subdued by the gods because pride cannot triumph over reason and intellect.[35] The Giants' revolt suggests the pretention of the sons of earth who accumulate too many temporal goods—as if piling Pelion on Ossa.

The origins of William's Neoplatonism in his first commentary most likely derive from the developing tradition of Boethius commentary following the Carolingians and the Old High German glosses of Notker Labeo. In the twelfth century the *Consolatio* regained much of the favor it had lost in the eleventh century, primarily through the support of Conrad de Hirsau's *Dialogus super auctores,* in which a master explains to a student how it is possible that Boethius may be a Christian even though he never cites Scripture.[36] This revival of interest was facilitated within the School of Chartres (and in Paris) by means of the privileging of all Boethius's works, including treatises on the arts of music, arithmetic, and logic, as well as his theological writings, and of the *Consolatio* itself as the blend of eloquence and wisdom.[37] During this *aetas Boethiana* (I would adapt the tripartite schema of Ludwig Traube to rename the medial *aetas Horatiana* he inserted after Virgil and before Ovid),[38] commentaries based on earlier commentaries flourished. These included the Vatican Reginenses manuscripts 72 and 244, probably derived from much earlier versions of the Anonymous of St. Gall; the Anonymous of Erfurt (or the pseudo–John Scot, called so because of the belief held previously that this commentary did indeed belong to the ninth-century scholar John Scot), which combines Adalbold of Utrecht on "O qui perpetua" and Remigius and his revisers with original glosses; the Anonymous Vaticanus latinus 919 (fols. 198r–205r), which exists only in a truncated and mutilated form containing the end of the third book and the beginning of the fourth on the *Consolatio;* and finally, the most original commentary since that of Remigius, by William himself, written about 1125.[39]

The trend in the developing Boethius tradition is away from Neo-Stoic moralization and Christianization of the text and toward Neoplatonic allegorization. Vaticanus latinus 919, even in its truncated form, conflicts with William over Plato. And Vatican Reginenses 72 and 244, two supposedly twelfth-century manuscripts, constitute a paraphrase and epitome of the earliest commentaries, the Asser (Vat. lat. 3363) and the Anonymous of St. Gall;[40] neither commentary is in itself important, except in recognition of the preservation of early Boethius studies in the twelfth century, specifically of the St. Gall glosses. While it is true both these are commentaries and not glosses, that is, not marginalia or interlinear glosses in a text of Boethius's, nevertheless, they remain very simple and straightforward, in their brevity rather like those of Asser and the St. Gall comments. One, according to Pierre Courcelle, is a long paraphrase of the Boethian text and without originality, given its concord with earlier commentaries.[41] Vatican manuscript Reginensis 72 in at least two glosses is indebted to the Anonymous of St. Gall Minor (e.g. on "volucres" as the Harpies).[42] Vatican manuscript Reginensis 244 in several of its glosses mirrors the St. Gall commentaries, especially the Minor, not only in details but by moralizing Orpheus and Circe.[43]

The transmission of the Anonymous of St. Gall moralizing culminates in the Anonymous Erfurt Commentator, a source for William on Boethius in several respects: because Erfurt uses glosses on both Boethius and Martianus in his commentary, unifying them in particular by returning to the original text of Boethius, he truly functions as a literary critic. Although the Anonymous Erfurt text was originally thought to be a ninth-century commentary on the *Consolatio* by John Scot,[44] it is now accepted as a twelfth-century commentary, probably prior to William's rather than indebted to him. Erfurt also points William to the tradition of Martianus commentary established by Remigius and Notker Labeo, which would prompt William's own commentary. Finally, by incorporating the recent interest in the "O qui perpetua" glosses by Adalbold of Utrecht and Remigius, on the World Soul, Erfurt will offer ideas about the correspondences between microcosm and macrocosm so evident throughout William's glosses.[45] If William's Boethius as a whole reveals indebtedness in particular to Remigius and Notker Labeo, nevertheless clearly Erfurt supplied new and original glosses (for *Consolatio* 4 m3 and 5 p2) that entered the tradition.

The originality of Erfurt as a literary critic is evidenced specifically in the ways he tries to unify each gloss and to interpret the context in which it appears, despite his use without acknowledgment of great hunks of

Remigius and Notker Labeo on Boethius.[46] In addition, in the earlier portions of the commentary Erfurt adds new glosses on the Lares (*Consolatio* I p3), the Bacchae (3 m3),[47] Cybele (3 m9), and Aristaeus (3 m12)[48] and elsewhere embellishes most of the other (conventionally glossed) Boethius passages. Even in his use of Remigius on Boethius, Erfurt changes Remigian glosses by filling them out with additional citations from other classical authors or contemporary commentators, or by compressing them.[49] His gloss on the Lares is drawn without acknowledgment from Remigius's commentary on Martianus Capella; within the mythographic references in the Boethius commentary is interpolated this one from Remigius (*In Mart.* 27.10) involving Roman religion rather than classical mythology (and it later appears in Nicholas Trivet's fourteenth-century commentary on Boethius). The reference to the Lares (in Roman religion a guardian spirit of the house or family, whose totem was the dog, very rarely mentioned in medieval commentaries) occurs when Boethius identifies Philosophy as the "nutricem meam cuius ab adulescentia *laribus* obversatus fueram" ["the nurse who brought me up, whose *house* I had frequented from my youth," my emphasis]. Erfurt glosses the Lares as meaning both household and society, that is, warmed and lit by the governing spirit, the Lars Domus, whose presence is signaled by fire on the literal or metaphorical levels: "In LARIBUS eius O<BVERSATVS> E<RAM> <id est> intra eius domum, id est conuersationem. Lar domus dicitur uel ignis" (Silk, p. 26). Apparently Boethius has become familiar with society, intercourse, in the household of nurse Philosophy, signified by metonymy through her Lares.

Another Martianus gloss that reappears in Erfurt's comments on "O qui perpetua," supposedly indebted to the Boethian comment of Adalbold of Utrecht,[50] is interpolated into what appears to be an anticipation of the Chartrian/Parisian interest in the goddess Nature. This gloss in Erfurt's Boethius involves a learned discussion of cubes and solids, longitudes and latitudes, a solipsistic identification of Cubeles as Cybeles: Cybele is the earth, mother of the gods, because she remains solid and immobile ("Vnde etiam Cubeles uel Cybeles terra quae dicitur mater deorum, quia stat solida et immobilis fixa suis radicibus," Silk, pp. 168–69). The definition combines two glosses in Remigius's commentary on Martianus Capella, the first linking her with the solidity of earth, the second linking her with Ops, Earth, as mother of the gods: "CYBELE dicta est quasi cubele a soliditate. Ipsa est enim terra qua nihil solidius est in elementis. Cubum enim Greci solidum dicunt, hinc et solidos numeros cubos vocamus" (Remi., *In Mart.* 5.22; cf. also 70.8).

As a commentary Erfurt's Boethius hangs together much more so than other commentaries, unified especially by heavy moralization based especially on the idea of the underworld and of the monsters as vices. Erfurt also attempts to organize the material by the introduction of the gloss on the "arbiter umbrarum" (Pluto) that epitomizes the world as divided into three parts, heaven (Jupiter), water (Neptune), and earth (Pluto). This tripartite mythological division of the World Soul appeals to Erfurt partly, no doubt, because of the long emphasis on comments on "O qui perpetua" (*Consolatio* 3 m9) by Adalbold of Utrecht and others and because of the Chartrian/ Parisian interest in the *anima mundi*. Certainly by introducing the gloss at the beginning Erfurt also rationalizes and explains the discussion of the underworld as earth and of the inhabitants of said underworld as various vices.[51] The Boethian glosses on the World Soul probably affected Erfurt's gloss on the Orpheus poem (which, like the normally extensive glosses on 4 m3, 4 p6, 4 m7, and 5 p3 is shorter than in other, earlier commentators). Unlike earlier glossators, Erfurt omits much of the literal recitation of the myth and zeroes in on its literary or moral signification, much of which appears personalized or Christianized.[52] In his gloss on Orpheus's descent, Erfurt unifies his comment much more clearly than had earlier commentators by introducing his discussion with the moral that usually occurs at the end; this practice is usual for him.[53] Erfurt's moral is that no one should look back after he finds both the place of true good, and the highest good, and that he who lays aside carnal desire to understand the light of true blessedness is to be praised. Appropriately, then, this song is about those who ruin their work because they return to human desires—Orpheus who looked back at Eurydice.[54]

Erfurt's most important new gloss—because it arises out of his interpretation of the whole text—is a Tiresias gloss (*Consolatio* 5 p3). The last gloss, as it was in Remigius, is framed by Erfurt in its literary context; its use of Tiresias as an example of a self divided is a Neoplatonic idea accounting for the problem of human sexuality that might very well have appealed to William of Conches. The persona Boethius is having trouble understanding the idea of divine foreknowledge and free will—he argues that even if God knows that one of two things may happen, what is such knowledge worth unless He knows which? "Aut quid hoc refert vaticinio illo ridiculo Tiresiae? 'Quidquid dicam, aut erit aut non?' " ["Or what does it have to do with that ridiculous prophecy of Tiresias?—'Whatever I say will either happen or not?' "] (5 p3.74).[55] Erfurt glosses this passage by narrating how Tiresias, after dividing two copulating serpents with a rod, was changed into a woman; when Juno asked him who enjoyed making love more, man or woman, Tiresias replied "woman," and was struck blind by Juno, but granted divinity by Jupiter. While this part of the gloss is derived from the first Vatican mythography (Mythogr. I 16/16), the remainder is Erfurt's: he relates the Tiresias quotation back to the text, apparently in an attempt to explain how Tiresias's double answer reflects his two natures and thus also the uncertainty of human knowing about fate: "Quod etiam dixi, quoniam nihil differret Dei prouidentia a uaticinio Tiresiae si incerta prouideret, nec differret etiam ab humana opinione si diceret incerta sicut homines quorum est incertus euentus" ["Which also I have said, because the Providence of God would not differ from the prophecy of Tiresias, if he foresaw doubtful things, nor would it be different from human opinion if he said doubtful things, just as men whose fate is uncertain"].[56]

An example of Erfurt's interest in the vexing problem of divine sexuality as rehearsed so fully in the Carolingian commentaries on Martianus, the Tiresias gloss also perhaps pointed to what William of Conches saw as a solution to the problem—Neoplatonic philosophical explanations of classical myths about the gods' sexuality and apparent immorality. To continue his work as an exegete William found justification for his philosophic task in Macrobius and his underlying Neoplatonic theory of fiction.

II. THE NEO-STOIC GODS IN WILLIAM'S NEOPLATONIC THEORY OF FICTION: THE MACROBIUS GLOSSES

William's approach to classical fable in Macrobius provided the theoretical foundation for nearly all of his mythological glosses in the remaining commentaries. In Macrobius's commentary on the *Somnium Scipionis*, to which he turned after glossing Boethius but before glossing Martianus (although he may have been reading these authors concurrently), William uncovered a literary theory that would support the use of mythological fables inherited from previous mythographers—and thus he alters Macrobius in accord with the authority of that tradition he inherited, which existed in quite different form in Macrobius's own day. Concurrent reading of the authors would explain the reasons for similarities in so many of the mythological glosses found in both (assuming the Florentine Commentary on Martianus reflects his lectures, if not his actual writings), which deal almost exclusively with the Neoplatonic concept of Nature veiling Idea.

Rather appropriately, William's Neoplatonic approach grows out of the early Boethius glosses and the concept of the descent into the underworld used to justify both the use of myth and to bolster a theory of fiction.

The corrupting "underworld" (or flesh) of the text is host for the meaning, the truth so dear to the philosopher, except when the truths it veils involve immoral behavior (adultery, castration) by the gods. Despite Macrobius's specific prohibition against this type of immoral mythological fable, excluded from fabulous narrative, William himself endorses the use of it most enthusiastically. In his gloss on book 1, chapter 2 of Macrobius's commentary on the *Somnium Scipionis,* William rationalizes the philosophic use of such immoral fable specifically by means of the Neoplatonic concept of Idea immanent within Nature, used analogously of the meaning hidden within the literal text. Where Macrobius has castigated stories about the "dii adulteri," "gods who are adulterers" (*Somn. Scip.* 1.2.11), William explains, "hec *verba* sunt turpia, sed tamen *per illud adulterium* aliquod honestum et pulcrum revera habet significari, utpote de adulterio Iovis legitur cum Cybele, Semele, et huiusmodi alliis [*sic*] que in loco suo exponentur" ["the *words* are base, and yet *by that adultery* something honorable and beautiful must indeed be meant: as can be read in the case of Jupiter's adulteries with Cybele, and Semele, and other things of this kind which will be expounded in due course"] (my emphasis).[57]

The "verba" are immoral, "turpia," but the signification, the meaning, of those words is worthy and beautiful. William seems to argue that such myths can be used if they are not improperly revealed. His guide here might very well be Plato's discussion of myth-interpretation in *Timaeus* 41de, for in his gloss on that passage in the *Timaeus* William scoffs at those "nescientes modum Platonis loquendi de philosophia per integumenta" ["not knowing about the mode of Plato speaking of philosophy through the {purely grammatical} notion of *integumentum*"].[58] That is, they do not understand the way *integumentum* cloaks philosophy; they understand it literally. For this reason the Eleusinian mystery was inappropriately revealed by the philosopher Numenius (mentioned in Macrobius, *Somn. Scip.* 1.2.19).

The two-fold meaning of the words echoes St. Augustine's theory of multiple senses used to justify seemingly immoral passages in the New Testament, in a passage from his *De doctrina Christiana* familiar throughout the Middle Ages. The Church Father had warned the student against reading a text "carnally," that is, by the letter only, and instead encouraged reading spiritually, that is, according to its figurative meaning. This approach implies that a text, particularly a biblical text, like a human has a body and soul.

Sed uerborum translatorum ambiguitates, de quibus deinceps loquendum est, non mediocrem curam industriamque desiderant. Nam in principio cauendum est, ne figuratam locutionem ad litteram accipias. Et ad hoc enim pertinet, quod ait apostolus: *Littera occidit, spiritus autem uiuificat.* Cum enim figurate dictum sic accipitur, tamquam proprie dictum sit, carnaliter sapitur. Neque illa mors animae congruentius appellatur, quam cum id etiam, quod in ea bestiis antecellit, hoc est, intellegentia carni subicitur sequendo litteram. Qui enim sequitur litteram, translata uerba sicut propria tenet neque illud, quod proprio uerbo significatur, refert ad aliam significationem. . . . Ea demum est miserabilis animi seruitus, signa pro rebus accipere; et supra creaturam corpoream, oculum mentis ad hauriendum aeternum lumen leuare non posse.

But the ambiguities of figurative words, which are now to be treated, require no little care and industry. For at the outset you must be very careful lest you take figurative expressions {*figuratam locutionem*} literally. What the Apostle says pertains to this problem: "For the letter killeth, but the spirit quickeneth [*Littera occidit, spiritus autem uiuificat*]." That is, when that which is said figuratively {*figurate*} is taken as though it were literal, it is understood carnally {*carnaliter*}. Nor can anything more appropriately be called the death of the soul than that condition in which the thing which distinguishes us from beasts, which is the understanding, is subjected to the flesh in the pursuit of the letter. He who follows the letter takes figurative expressions as though they were literal and does not refer the things signified to anything else. . . . There is a miserable servitude of the spirit in this habit of taking signs for things, so that one is not able to raise the eye of the mind above things that are corporal and created, to drink in eternal light.][59] (3.5.9)

This concept of the carnality of text and the immanence of spiritual meaning within it is similar to the Neoplatonic concept of the underworld as earth or flesh into which the soul may descend in four ways, virtuously or viciously, in William's Boethius glosses on *Consolatio* 3 m12. If the letter is married to signification, then any "adultery" of meaning must be put right—in William's anticipation of the realist/nominalist controversy later in the Middle Ages.

William's concept of *integumentum* greatly influenced twelfth-century scholars to discuss classical fable, in particular from a Neoplatonic moral perspective. Bernard Silvestris declares that for myth the integument cloaks truth just as the body does the soul and hence should be understood by means of the intellect. He defines *integumentum* as a "type of exposition which wraps the apprehension of truth in a fictional narrative, and thus it is also called an *involucrum*, a cover."[60] John of Salisbury in the same century described "involucrum" as the fictitious cover concealing divine prudence and, like Bernard, also cited the *Aeneid* as an example.[61] Synonyms for these Neoplatonic textual relationships multiplied: the letter (*littera*) is the surface meaning of a poem, also known as history (*historia*)—defined in a very specialized sense as "the grammatical construction of the text"; a synonym for this "outer covering" of the poem is the *cortex* or husk (also known as *sensus, pallium, tectorium, tegmen, paille* in Old French, *chaf* in Middle English). This literal meaning must be distinguished from the doctrinal or moral theme or thesis, the truth hidden under the *cortex,* which was also called the *nucleus* or *sententia,* and the *fruyt* (fruit or grain) later in Middle English.[62]

For William all the myths mentioned specifically by Macrobius (*Somn. Scip.* 1.2.11) are rationalized (made "honorable and beautiful") specifically through the philosophical truths of Nature. Those Macrobian myths include Saturn castrating Caelus and being himself castrated, Bacchus conceived as a result of Semele's adultery with Jupiter, Venus committing adultery with Mars, Ceres hunting for her raped daughter Proserpina. The rationalizations for these fables come from the Stoicized Martianus glosses and assume two forms: the macrocosm as a reflection of the immanence of God, or the microcosm as a mirror of the macrocosm (an artistic working-out of the relationship between dreamer and dream vision in Cicero's *De re publica*—see the visual epitome of this concept in figure 26). What becomes, then, a Neoplatonized network of Neo-Stoic Macrobian glosses will reappear in large part in William's later mythological glosses in the Juvenal and *Timaeus* commentaries.

The "honorable and beautiful" truths William discovers behind Jupiter's adulteries with Semele allow him to create a mythological version of a Neoplatonic natural genealogy through the interrelationship of Jupiter, Juno, his mortal concubine Semele, her son Bacchus, Jupiter's father Saturn, and the gods Mars and Venus, Ceres, Proserpina, and Pluto. After reciting the literal myth of the destructive results of Semele's sleeping with Jupiter in his fiery, natural form as lightning, William explains that Jupiter represents the aether, his wife and sister Juno the lower air, and

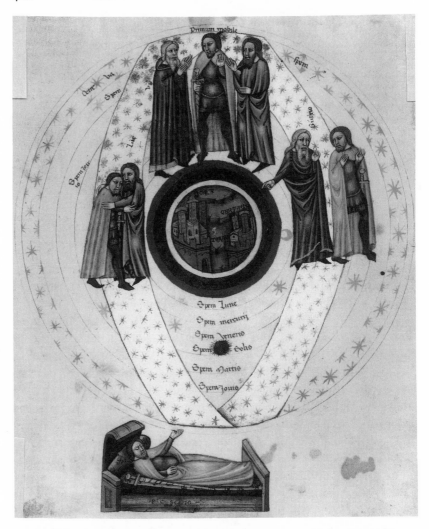

26. Scipio, sleeping in bed, with diagram of planetary spheres. From Macrobius's *Somnium Scipionis*. MS. Canonici Latin classical 257, fol. 1v (1383, Italian). By permission of the Bodleian Library, University of Oxford.

Semele the earth. Specifically, Juno is termed Jupiter's "wife" "quia inferior aer subditus est superiori, et coniunctus" {"because the inferior air is set below the superior aether , and joined to it"]; she is his "sister" "quia inter quatuor elementa nullum est simile ei ita ut aer" ["because among the four elements none is like the aether except air"]. Their fabulous relationship signifies a Stoic version of vegetation myth, for superior aether (Jupiter) impregnates the earth in winter, and thus Bacchus is born, in that from this union comes the vines—"Sed superior eter concubuit cum Semele, id est cum terra, quia superior inde nascuntur; sed mediante Iunone, quia per calorem celestium arbores et fructus generantur" ["but through Juno's mediation, for through the heavenly heat trees and fruit are generated"]. As the vines bearing grapes Bacchus is called "bis natus," "twice-born," first prematurely to Semele, afterwards at full gestation from the thigh of Jove ("ad tempus nativitatis a femore Iovis"), in that the vines turn green in the spring when "inpregnate per calorem solis" ["impregnated by the sun's heat"] and then bear ("emittunt") grapes in the summer. From his role as the "vines," Bacchus in this gloss is transformed into the World Soul.[63]

William also cosmologizes the other taboo Macrobian myths from book 1, chapter 2—of the castration of Saturn, the adultery of Mars and Venus, and the rites of Ceres and Bacchus—Neo-Stoically. The castration of Saturn by his son Jupiter, from which act Venus was born, is explained in the Macrobius commentary as, first, the ripening of fruits by the warmth of the upper element, which makes them ready for harvesting, and second, the casting of the fruits into the sea, that is, the human belly, from which Venus or *luxuria* (sensual delight) is born.[64] William in addition explains the adultery of Mars and Venus as the conjunction of Venus as benevolent star and Mars as malevolent star, with him corrupting her through his "malice."[65] Finally, the true role of Ceres involves "earth's natural power of growing into crops and multiplying them," just as Bacchus is "earth's natural power of growing into vines."[66] The rape of Proserpina is rationalized differently, by explaining that Ceres is the earth, Proserpina the moon, and Pluto the shadow that obstructs it. Proserpina, daughter of Ceres, was seized by Pluto while playing; her mother searched for her with lighted torches. Later Jupiter decreed the mother should have her for fifteen days and Pluto the other fifteen days of the month. William's Neo-Stoic explanation is that:

> This is nothing but that the name Ceres is used to mean the earth, called Ceres on analogy with "crees" (you may create), for all things are created from her. By Proserpina is meant the moon, and her name is on analogy with "prope serpens" (creeping near), for she is moved nearer to the earth than the other planets. She is called earth's daughter, because her substance has more of earth in it than of the other elements. By Pluto is meant the shadow that sometimes obstructs the moon.[67]

William also identifies the search of Ceres as the heat of summer which longs most for the moon's moisture to help the fruits increase, especially at night when the moon is near; the results of Jupiter's decision mean that half the month Proserpina remains in the upper hemisphere, half in the lower, beneath the earth.

In the Juvenal glosses, William also uses the term *integumentum,* but to indicate a way of disguising immoral or embarrassing vices or character traits—of royalty, heroes, or gods—by means of *satura,* satire. The concept of integumentum also explains why Juvenal chose satire to cloak the gluttony of the emperor—because such an activity was dangerous. The philosopher's integument differs in that it covers up, conceals, the immorality of gods.[68]

But there William also discusses idolatry as the opposite from *integumentum:* making divine what is in fact temporal and earthly. By employing St. Augustine's distinction between two kinds of love, one that enjoys things for their own sakes (*cupiditas*), another that uses things for the sake of love of God (*caritas*), he explains that the pagans worshipped the earthly (bread and wine) as if it were divine (Ceres and Bacchus). The products of life obtained from crops were honored by the uncultivated pagans through feasts devoted to Ceres and Bacchus: "Deinde sibi indulgendo, commedendo, et bibendo magnam partem diei consumebant" ["through indulging themselves, through eating and drinking, they consumed a great part of the day"] (*In Iuvenalem,* p. 91). The phrase "et fruitur dis," "and enjoy the gods," used by classical poets (Horace and Juvenal especially) almost as metonymies for bread and wine, leads later on, in a second manuscript's gloss on *Satire* 1.47–49, to the explanation of the gods specifically as Ceres and Bacchus.

William explains by drawing on St. Augustine in *De doctrina Christiana,*[69] as if to say, the pagans enjoyed bread and wine (or any temporal thing) for themselves instead of for the love of God—in effect, they enjoyed them too much, making gods—Ceres and Bacchus—out of bread and wine. Then, in a more explicit contrast between pagan and Christian belief, William declares "quia inter frui et uti dicimur quibus non propter se sed propter aliud utimur, ut temporalibus si bene his utamur non propter se sed ut vivamus utimur et ut celestia promereamur" ["that we are said to exist between things to be enjoyed and things to be used, which we use not for themselves but for another purpose, just as *temporalia* should be used not for their own sakes but so that we may be sustained and merit the heavens"] (*In Iuvenalem,* p. 109). The pagan's error is the opposite of the Neoplatonist

Christian's truth: this world, and all of its earthy and earthly processes and products, is not in fact divine, but a sign of the divine, immanent in this world.

The gods Ceres and Bacchus (among others) are personified as aspects of the natural process of harvesting because the literary form in which they are used, satire, is according to William used by or intended for the rustic or uncultivated (even barbarian), whether pertaining to land or to farmers (in the Accessus: "id est ab agrestibus dicta est," *In Iuvenalem,* p. 91); it is associated with pagans because of the rustic associations of the word "paganus" (meaning "country-dweller"). Thus, for William, *satura* is the tool of the pagan poet as *integumentum* is the tool of the Christian philosopher; the idolatry of the former contrasts with the Christianity of the latter.

William makes explicit comparisons between Christian and pagan integuments, although Bernard Silvestris later in the century will differentiate the methods of treating mythology and Scripture. For William *integumentum* or *involucrum* is a Macrobian literary term that refers to classical myth containing philosophical ideas about the World Soul, the mind, and other kinds of moral truth, including Christian truth.[70] For Bernard and others, *allegoria* is a literary term that refers to scriptural story containing the Word of God.[71]

As we have argued here, William used Neo-Stoic explanations of the gods from his Martianus, Juvenal, and Plato glosses in a continuing meditation on Macrobian literary theory—in response to the problem of the impropriety of such immoral fables. In the Martianus glosses, William will innovate by presenting Juno's adversary Hercules as a hero who plays a role in the Judgment of Paris; William will thereby again link two different myths (Hercules and Paris) and again two different traditions (there, genealogical historical and Boethian), but within the context of a third tradition (Neo-Stoic and Martianan).

III. JUNO'S ENEMY HERCULES AS NEO-STOIC CROSSOVER HERO IN THE "MARTIANUS GLOSSES"

Juno's antipathy to Paris and thus to his cousin Aeneas, and later to Hercules (product of Jove's liaison with Alcmene), and William's interpolation of the Paris myth in the gloss on Ixion and Juno in the Boethius commentary (*Consolatio* 3 m12), culminate in what is a quite extragavant house of myths in William's so-called Martianus commentary. Juno's association with three major myths unifies this portion of the Florentine "Commentary"—through her Stoic role as *aer* conjoined with *aether* in cosmic creation she is linked with the important myth of Hymen as god of weddings both cosmic and human, or the incarnation of the World Soul; as "mother" of Vulcan, Jupiter's son, she is linked with the myth of Jupiter-Juno-Vulcan as active agent of the World Soul; and as cosmic ruler of air, or the active life, she is therefore involved, as one of the three goddesses, in the Judgment of Paris. Because of her dual role, as cosmic force and as moral equivalent of the life of riches and ambition, the Judgment of Paris comes to be interpreted as a fable with Neo-Stoic coloration. Its point is, as always in relation to the monastic and scholastic ideal of human perfection in the Middle Ages (a rarer humanist ideal in the secular Renaissance), that the wise individual should shun the deceptive allure of the active life.

Key to an understanding of the later mythographic glosses in the Juvenal and *Timaeus,* the so-called "commentary on Martianus" also provides glosses parallel to those found in the Boethius and Macrobius commentaries. Too, William's rationalizing and assimilative method reappears to a certain extent in the "commentary on Martianus" (attributed to William or one of his students, but which we shall call William's for convenience). In this "Martianus commentary," an understanding of the microcosm similar to that in the Boethius glosses is invoked through the symbol of the marriage of Mercury, or eloquence, and Philology, or wisdom. In addition to the glosses on gods as representations of various psychological faculties, the "Martianus commentary" celebrates cosmic and microcosmic marriage, presided over by Hymen, god of weddings. It thus shares the Carolingian genealogy of the gods found in the Vatican mythographies and their Martianus commentaries. That is, the gods are part of the *anima mundi,* the Stoic generative reason that regenerates and repopulates the world, and the "little soul" of humankind shares that spark of universal reason.

I identify the work as a so-called "Martianus commentary" because in its organization this work reveals one Polaroid snapshot of a moment in the transmutation of Martianus commentary to genealogical mythography handbook like that of the Vatican mythographers, particularly one we have not yet examined—the third Vatican mythography. The commentary is part of a tripartite work of mythology in a fifteenth-century manuscript in Florence. The mythology sequence opens with a *Genealogia deorum et heroum,* and there follows an *Allegoria et expositio quarumdam fabularum poeticarum,* with a third rubric, *Expositio super librum Martiani Capelle De nuptiis Philologie,* which would seem to mark the beginning of the Martianus commentary proper.[72] In fact, however, the rubric *Expositio* introduces merely a brief digression in the continuous mythological handbook that begins with the title *Allegoria*—a digression in the form of an accessus to Martianus. The *Allegoria,* then, *is* the myth handbook that its title (and some aspects of its form) imply, rather than a set of glosses covering *De nuptiis* paragraphs 1 through 5 (before the *Expositio* digression) and 6 through 102, up through the beginning of book 2 (after the digression).[73] While there are differences in style and treatment between the two parts (before and after the accessus), they do form a continuous set of myths; the prefatory *Genealogia* is also certainly, I would argue, intended as part of a single mythological handbook.

Further, the recomposed fables in the Martianus commentary portion of the Florentine manuscript do derive from Carolingian commentaries on Martianus[74] and are synthesized by William, who is intelligent enough to recognize the gods when they appear in other commentaries and thereby assimilate their functions, whatever the lack of intelligence evidenced in this particular draft (or student version of lecture notes).[75] The explicit references to many classical authors in what is more accurately termed the "Florentine mythography" often mask actual use of the Carolingian commentators on those authors; therefore, William's indebtedness to the Carolingians in this work has not previously been revealed very explicitly, though Dronke finds plenty of evidence of his Neoplatonism and parallels in William's other works (chiefly the *Philosophia mundi*) and in the subsequent commentaries of Bernard Silvestris.[76] References are made to "Boethius," meaning the Boethius commentaries, or William's own glosses on Boethius (50v, 64r),[77] more proof that the Florentine work may be by William; to "Remigius," presumably denoting the Carolingian's commentary on Martianus,[78] as well as to "Rabanus" (Maurus?);[79] in addition there are explicit references to "Virgil,"[80] "Plato,"[81] "Macrobius,"[82] "Pythagoras,"[83] and so forth. There is also material in the text from familiar early and Carolingian sources the commentator has not identified—again, ultimately taken from Fulgentius, perhaps through Remigius on Martianus or on Boethius, or the Vatican mythographers.[84] Most likely William's assimilation of the mythography in his sources can be reconstructed from an analysis of his method in a portion of the work.

In order to follow the steps in that working method, let us first reconsider the relationship of the three parts of William's draft mythography. In its emphasis on begetting and procreation, the brief *Genealogia deorum et heroum* resembles the genealogy at the beginning of the third book of the first Vatican mythography more than the preface to Hyginus's *Fabulae:* the first Vatican mythography begins with Ophion, Oceanus, who begets Caelum, who begets Saturn, Phorcys and Rhea, and concludes with the human figures Procris and Cephalus, Orithyia and Boreas; Hyginus depends on an initial Ovidian schema (Mist, Chaos, Night, Day, Erebus, Ether) that ends with the horse Pegasus from Neptune and Medusa and the three-formed Geryon from Chrysaor and Callirhoe. William emphasizes this inheritance in the *Genealogia* basically by stringing together a series of chronological "begets" from the begetting of Saturn by Caelum down to Hercules and Theseus. The Florentine text includes a few glosses and identifications in this genealogy—for example, Aeolus, king of the winds, dwells in the regions of Aeolia ("in qua Eolus rex ventose dicitur habitare," 50r). The text also stresses marriages (for example, "Phorcys king of Libya had three daughters, Sthenno, Medusa, Euryale, who had only one eye, were called Gorgons," 50r) and adulteries (for example, Jupiter lay with Alcmene wife of Amphytrion and begat Hercules "nocte gemmata," in a double-lengthened night).

Continuing the idea of generation and regeneration, the *Allegoria* portion of the mythography begins with Hymen, *deus nuptiarum,* as a kind of cosmic principle of love, related to a discussion of birth, semen, and the seven cells of gestation, and then repeats the above genealogical sequence in its notes on Saturn and his children (interrupted by two short digressions on Orpheus and the Fates), and their mates, Jupiter-Juno, Pluto-Proserpina, and so forth.

The *Allegoria* with its full notes also does follow the signposts provided by Martianus in paragraphs 5 and 6 of *De nuptiis.* After the *Expositio* rubric, the commentary is less full, offering slightly briefer coverage of gods from the rest of *De nuptiis* book 1, especially toward the end where there are seven or eight glosses per page (and only up to *De nuptiis* 102, early in book 2, the first note or two in Martianus). One possible reason for combining the two parts of Martianus, book 1, in the *Allegoria* may have stemmed from the repetitive catalogues of gods and planets in the text and in earlier commentaries, the first catalogue describing the origin of the cosmos (Saturn, his sons, the uxorious gods); the second catalogue, reflected in Mercury's journey to find Apollo and then their mutual ascent to reach Jove; the third catalogue, the list of gods invited to the Assembly of the Gods from the sixteen regions of the cosmos, followed by the entry of the gods into the palatial assembly hall to decide whether Mercury should marry Philology.

The yoking of the two seemingly incongruous methods in this mythography—genealogy and commentary—can be explained. Hymen, as wedding god, is also a force of life and hence an appropriate force to invoke as the creative and generative cosmic principle, given its antithesis of limitation, finitude, destruction, as epitomized by the action that follows creation, in Saturn's (Time's) brutal severing of his father's genitals. From such a cycle humankind can rescue itself only through its attempt to regenerate the species; so Venus was born from Saturn's dismembered parts. In this manner, however, humankind rescues itself only for one moment, condemned to repeat the process of physical renewal eternally. A loftier way of ensuring individual immortality is suggested by Martianus's allegory: the apotheosis of Philology (Wisdom) in order to marry Mercury (Eloquence), or the opportunity afforded by an education in the seven liberal arts. Appropriately, given its beginning, the entire mythography ends, if abruptly, but nevertheless with a sense of closure, on the famous Servian (pseudo-Pythagorean) passage on the letter Y as a symbol of human life (possibly the earlier catalytic inspiration for the notion of the descent into the underworld with which the passage is linked as early as Remigius's supposed commentary on the sixth book of the *Aeneid*). Birth is one kind of fall, even if natural, as life involves choices which can separate us from ultimate good and lead to everlasting fall.

William's understanding of Martianus can be visualized in a diagram of this textual moment in which two forms or genres, merge into one. This "Table of Contents," or outline of the Florentine mythography, includes the appropriate folio number in the manuscripts, the contents of its eleven major sections (Hymen, Saturn, Uxorious Gods, Mercury, Philology, World Soul, Apollo, List of Gods Invited to Assembly, the Gods' Entry into the Assembly Hall, the Cosmos, and the Pythagorean Y as Human Life), and its relationship, if any, with the text of Martianus. Certainly in the *Allegoria* the ordering sequence of gods is taken from Martianus and will be indicated by Roman numeral and within each such section by alphabetical letter. Citations of Martianus text (using Dick's page and line numbers) behind each entry denote my identification of the sign-post in the sequence of book 1 where the god or figure appears; parentheses indicate the source of interpolated glosses from other portions of Martianus which I have identified, and brackets denote Dronke's identification. Asterisks indicate passages edited by Dronke (see table 13).

The major myths in the Martianus commentary linked by the antipathy of Stoicized Juno involve three significant Stoic gods or demi-gods,

TABLE 13
TABLE OF CONTENTS OF THE FLORENTINE COMMENTARY

	Folio	Topic	De nuptiis
	49r–50r	*Genealogia deorum et heroum*	
	50r	*Allegoria et expositio quarumdam fabularum poeticarum*	
		Book 1 of *De nuptiis*	
I.	50r–v	Hymen (Cosmic Love)	3.5, 3.13
II.	50v	Saturn, his sons, and wife (Cosmos)	5.1–2
		Orpheus	5.7
		Parcae	5.16
III.	51r	Uxorious Gods	
		Jupiter and Juno	5.12–15
	51v–52r	Pluto and Proserpina	5.18, 36.4
		Portunus and Neptune	5.19
		Neptune's wives (Oceanus, Thetis, Leucothea, Amphytrite)	47.15
	52r–52v	Nereus (and Pythius)	5.19, 10.6 19.11
		Sapientia, Vates, Gradivus (Mars)	5.19, 65.2
	52v	Apollo, Coronis, and Aesculapius	5.20
	53r	Saturn, Ops, and Cybele	5.21–22
	53v	Janus and Argione	6.1
		Isis and Osiris	6.2
IV.	54v	Mercury (Eloquence)	6.6 (see 72.4)
		Pleiades and Maia	6.9
		Zodiac	6.9
		deus palestre	6.11
	55r	*Expositio super librum Martiani Capelle de Philologie*	
	54v	Mercury	6.11–12
	55v	Thorus	6.11
		Mercury and Philology	
	56r	Mercury and Venus: Hermaphroditus	6.13 (see 22.16)
V.	56r–58r	Philology (Wisdom)	
		Sophia	6.20
		Pallas Athena	7.3
		Fronesis	7.5
		Entelechia	7.10
	57r–58r	The Descent of the Soul through the Planetary Spheres (Macrobian schema)	

heroes—Hymen, Vulcan, and Hercules—who in a sense take the place of importance previously accorded the older Neoplatonic heroes Aeneas, Orpheus, and Ulysses. William's awareness of Stoicized Juno appears in a discussion of the old elemental and cosmic (natural) interpretation of the four "sons" (sic; Juno is included) whom Saturn (Chronos) intended to devour—Jove (aether, "Iovis omnis plena aethereus," fol. 51r), Juno (air, "ut mens divina," fol. 50v; also 55r), Neptune (water), and Pluto (earth). Saturn's savagery toward the human body and the created world (both of which recombine these four elements) is attested by his interpretation as "Chronos," time. Against such destruction William sets a passage on the Stoic idea of begetting seed based on the well-known *Aeneid* World Soul passage (6.724–32). He also defines Jupiter as the Stoic concept of Universal Life, the superior fire, beginning and end, that propels the generative energy of the cosmos: "Jupiter ut ait Rabanus superioris ignis . . . principio et fine" (58r–v). And he makes much of Juno as *practica,* that is, *activa vita* (51r), an idea taken from Fulgentius (*Mit.* 2.1) via the second Vatican mythography (fable 249/206) on the Judgment of Paris ("Juno practicam, id est activam . . . designat")—an idea that fascinates William throughout the commentary.

The first hero, or demi-god, Hymen, is interpreted in three different ways drawn from different traditions, in which commentators stress the theme of sexual differentiation and difference that will appeal to Platonizing William. These three approaches are termed historical (euhemeristic, genealogical) or else fabulous (mythological), physical (Neo-Stoic), and philosophical (Neoplatonic): "De Hymeneo triplex est lectio: historica sive fabulosa, physica et phylosophica." All three derive (despite recent assertions that the myth is Chartrian and therefore indebted only slightly to earlier sources[85]) from Carolingian materials. While the Hymen myth is not a word-for-word tracing of one earlier source, nevertheless it recombines three different sources—for the historical portion, dealing with the Athenian youth known for his beauty, from the second Vatican mythography; for the more physical and physiological details concerning the hymen as *membranula,* from Remigius on Martianus; and for the Neoplatonic view of the cosmic god, from the application of Neoplatonic Boethius glosses to Neo-Stoic Martianus glosses.

William's euhemeristic (historical) version, drawn from the second Vatican mythography, describes Hymen as a beautiful, effeminate (or androgynous?) young Athenian whose social inequality to the girl he loves leads to cross-dressing, capture by pirates, and, his true sex discovered, return to his family. After he convinces others he will free the girls if allowed to marry his beloved, he is subsequently invoked at weddings.

> Secundum historiam Hymeneus Atheniensis iuvenis virginem equabat pulchritudine, et amore cuiusdam forma parem, sed nobilitate superiorem inarserat. Sed quamvis imparitate repulsam passus, virginali habitu inter virgines conversatus est, et a pyratis inter eas captivatus, vir esse deprehensus, ad suos remissus est. Promisit se virgines redemptione d<on>aturum si quam petierit eius uti coniugio concedatur. Conceditur et redimitur, et similiter amore suo usus est. Unde inolevit aliorum consuetudo, propter nuptialem illum in nuptiis tanquam deum invocare.

> [According to the {realistic} story Hymenaeus, a young Athenian, rivalled a girl in beauty, and burned with love for a girl who was his equal in looks but of higher birth. Though rejected because of the social inequality, he put on a girl's dress and kept company with the girls; along with them he was captured by pirates but, being seen to be a man, was sent back to his people. He promised he would get the girls freed if he were allowed to marry the one he desired. This was granted and she was freed, and he likewise enjoyed his love. Thus among others a custom arose of invoking him at weddings for the marriage's sake {*on account of that marriage,* meaning Hymenaeus's own}, as if he were a god. (Fol. 50r–v.)[86]

Although William excises this material from his rendition, his source, the second Vatican mythography, introduces the Eleusinian mysteries of the Magna Mater cult by associating the virgins with the practice of their religious rites; when they are abducted by pirates, they are removed from this feminine context. The second Vatican mythography also distinguishes between two rather than three readings of Hymen—the first, a fabulous account of the "deus nuptiarum" (god of weddings), as some call him; the second, an historical account of a young man who prevents calamity on the wedding day, as others say, for which he is invoked in weddings; he notes that the first is false, because of magic, and the second, true:

> Hymenaeus was a boy of Athenian race. When he had passed the years of childhood, but was not yet a man, he was said to have such great beauty that he could pass as a woman. When one of his fellow citizens, a girl of noble birth, fell in love with him, since he himself was of modest parentage, he despaired of marriage. However, since he

loved the girl with the utmost degree of love, as far as possible he satisfied his heart with the sight of her. *When the noble women and maidens were celebrating the sacred rites of Ceres of Eleusis, pirates, arriving suddenly, carried them off.* In their midst was Hymenaeus, who had followed his sweetheart there (and who was believed to be a girl). When therefore the pirates had carried their prey over far-away seas, finally in their travels they arrived at a certain region, where, overcome by sleep, they were put to death by pursuers. Leaving the maidens there, Hymenaeus returned to Athens and secured from the citizens an agreement to his marriage with his beloved, if he should return their daughters to them. When he returned them as promised, he received the wife he had longed for. Because this marriage was a happy one, the Athenians resolved to combine the name of Hymenaeus with marriages.] (Mythogr. II 263/219; my emphasis.)

William also provides a fabulous (mythological) account of Hymen as god very like the second Vatican mythography's "false" magical account. A likely source for this reading would be any of the major Carolingian commentaries on Martianus's opening, although his editor has suggested that William is borrowing directly from the opening of *De nuptiis,* that is, for Hymen, child of Cypris and Bacchus, as *copula sacra deum,* the holy bond of the gods who binds together the elements, souls to bodies, the two sexes in physical love. The opening passage in William reads, "Secundum fabulam vero filius est Bachi et Cypridis seu Camene, id est Veneris, et <est> deus nuptiarum, cuius officium est psalle<re> in nuptiis, cantare ad talamos, et coronare limina sertis" ["According to the fabled account, however, he is the son of Bacchus and of Cypris or Camena, that is, of Venus, and he is the god of weddings, whose function it is to play the cithara at weddings, to sing at the bridal chamber, and to deck the doors with garlands"].[87] In relation to possible Stoic connections with this reading of Hymen, William, as we have seen, provides lengthy natural (Stoicized) expositions for Hymen's father Bacchus, especially in his Macrobius commentary, as he will again in the Juvenal and *Timaeus* glosses.

William's second, Neo-Stoic, portion of the long myth, on Hymen as *membranula,* the caul or amnion, that is, the amniotic sac in which children are conceived, comes from Remigius on Martianus (and therefore only indirectly and distantly from Servius, *In Aen.* 4.99). In this bifold account, William first identifies Hymen as *membranula* and details his genealogy, then glosses both pieces of the account in a Neo-Stoic manner reminiscent of his Macrobius glosses.

> Hymeneus est membranula, in qua concipiuntur puerperia, matrix videlicet, que septem continet cellulas impressione humane forme signatas, in quibus semen retentum quasi sigillo vero impressum in hominis formam transsumitur, unde Hymeneus vis illa seminis retentiva dicitur. Deos enim appellaverunt antiqui quasdam nativas rerum potentias, ut potentiam producendi segetem Cererem dicebant, et potentiam creandi uvas Bachum.

> [Hymenaeus is the little membrane in which children are conceived, {in} the womb, that is, which contains seven little cells marked with the impress of the human form in which the semen that is retained is, as if impressed by a seal, is transmuted into the human form. So Hymenaeus is the name for the retentive power of the semen, for the ancients called certain innate powers of things gods, as they called the power of producing the harvest Ceres, and the power of bringing forth grapes Bacchus.][88]

Within this passage the first portion is nearly identical to Remigius on Martianus, who declares that Martianus introduces these verses in honor of Hymen, "deus . . . nuptiarum, id est naturalium conceptionum. Hymen Grece dicitur membranula, et est proprie muliebris sexus in qua fiunt puerperia, inde dictus est Hymeneus nuptiarum deus" ["god . . . of weddings, that is, of natural conception. In Greek Hymen means the amniotic membrane {caul}, and it is specifically characteristic of the female sex; in it childbirth takes place. Hence Hymenaeus is called the god of weddings"] (Remi., *In Mart.* 3.5). Then follows in Remigius a long discussion of the two membranes men and women have in common, with a third found only in women (William exchanges this for seven cells in the womb that receive the sperm—a passage found also in Bernard Silvestris); Remigius continues with his gloss on "Camena," Hymen's mother Venus, deriving the name etymologically from singing, "canendo," to refer generally to all the Muses "singing well."

In the Neo-Stoic glosses which William provides for this information, Hymen, the god of weddings, functions as a joiner of the four (cosmic) elements and of the human (microcosmic) sexual "seeds" reflective (in their difference) of those of the larger macrocosm.

Bene ergo Hymeneus, quia preest puerperiis, deus nuptiarum dicitur, quoniam legitima maris et femine copula hunc semper finem expectat, quod in procreanda prole appetitur. *Psallit ergo talamis,* postes coronat, quoniam hec officia actum coniugatorum precedentia gaudium prolis auspicantur. Huius autem bene pater dicitur Bachus, nam cum Cerere et Bacho calet Venus: excitatur motus, quo maxime gaudet Hymeneus. Unde et Camena, hoc est voluptas sive delectatio, eius mater est, vel Cypris, id est mixtura, nam et seminis particulis proportionaliter sibi conmixtis hominis corpus producitur, et quatuor elementa sicut in mundi constitutione—quoniam microcosmus est—proportionaliter aptantur.

[Hymenaeus, therefore, because he is in charge of childbirths, is aptly called god of weddings, for the lawful sexual union of man and woman always looks forward to this goal, inasmuch as it is desired for the procreation of children. That is why he plays in the bridal chamber and garlands the door, for these tasks, which precede the sexual union of the couple, augur the joy of progeny. His father is aptly called Bacchus, for with Ceres and Bacchus Venus grows hot: the motion Hymenaeus most delights in is aroused. So too Camena, that is voluptuousness or delectation, is his mother, or Cypris, that is commingling, for the human body is produced from the particles of seed proportionately commingled, and the four elements are adjusted proportionately, as in the ordering of the world—for the human body is a microcosm.][89]

But the key Neoplatonic portion of the myth applies part of the commentaries on Boethius's "O qui perpetua" on the World Soul to Neo-Stoic Remigius on Martianus. Martianus, we recall, had invoked Hymen as a *copula sacra deum* or "sacred principle of unity amongst the gods" that binds together the four elements, the four regions of the universe:

atque auram mentis corporibus socias,
foedere complacito sub quo natura iugatur,
sexus concilians et sub amore fidem.

[Through you, Mind is breathed into bodies by a union of concord which rules over Nature, as you bring harmony between the sexes and foster loyalty by love]. (*De nuptiis* 1)

William trades on this Neoplatonist reading of Hymen in the final glorious ballooning of the god's significance as a force of cosmic love, the Anima Mundi transformed from generative to unifying force (although it is possible William is also locating that force within a specific figure, Hymenaeus):

Secundum phylosophiam vero sic expone. Per Hymeneum accipe vim propagationis naturalem, videlicet amores, quos in gloria invicem diligunt, et inter se considerantur, quo Philosophia:

hanc rerum seriem ligat
terras ac pelagus regens
et celo imperitans amor.
Hic si frena remiserit,
quicquid nunc amat invicem
bellum continuo geret.

Hic est spiritus sanctus, qui quendam caritatis ardorem omnibus rebus infundit. Hic deus nuptiarum dicitur, id est sacre coniunctionis elementorum compositor. Filius Camene est—id est iugabilis elementorum concordie, sive etiam celestis armonie. Unde Camena dicitur quasi canens amena, delectatione musicarum consonantiarum. Quemadmodum enim novem sunt Muse, Camena est una ex octo earum facta, ita est in mundi compositione: novem sunt soni, unus in spera, septem in planetis, nonus autem in terra. Horum octo—scilicet spere et septem planetarum—celestem composuerunt continentiam, ex cuius beneficio omnia mundi corpora proportionaliter conservantur. Cypridis quoque, id est mixture, est filius, quoniam spiritus in diversorum coniunctione consideratur. Eius quoque pater est Bacchus, quoniam per hunc anima mundi intelligitur, que est spiritus domini, qui replevit orbem terrarum et amorem divinum singulis generavit.

[But the philosophical interpretation is as follows. Take Hymenaeus as the natural power of propagation, that is to say the loves which they who love cherish mutually in glory; and these loves are regarded as reciprocal where Philosophia says:

This order of things is bound
by the love ruling earth and sea
and dominating heaven.

If this love relaxed its reins,
all things that now love each other
would at once wage war.

He {Hymenaeus} is a holy spirit, who infuses an ardent love in all
things. He is called god of weddings, that is, he composes the holy
conjunction of elements. He is the son of Camena—that is joined
together to the concord of elements, or the same celestial harmony. So
the name Camena is said as if it were "canens amena" {singing lovely
things}, in the delight of musical harmonies. For even as there are
nine Muses, and Camena is considered, or became, one of eight of
these, so it is in the composition of the world: there are nine sounds,
one in the firmament, seven in the planets, but the ninth on earth.
Eight of them—the sounds of the firmament and the planets—have
harmonized all that heaven contains, and thereby all the world's
bodies are maintained in due proportion. So too he is the son of
Cypris, or commingling, for the Spirit can be perceived in the
conjunction of diverse things. And his father is Bacchus, for by
Bacchus the world-soul is meant, which is the Spirit of the Lord that
filled the universe and generated divine love in each thing.][90]

Thereafter William's commentary refines the concept of the World Soul to
utilize both Neoplatonic and Neo-Stoic ideas.[91]

Among these ideas can be found Jove as superior fire, cosmic Generative
Reason, in whose two sons, Vulcan and Hercules, William takes a related
philosophical (Neo-Stoic and Neoplatonic) respective interest in part
because of Juno's animus toward them. From the Remigian glosses (*In
Mart.* 37.6) comes the fourfold Neo-Stoic definition of Vulcan, a lesser
kind of fire, who represents both cosmic and microcosmic psychological
and corporal regenerative energy—a projection of the force incarnate in
Jove as Anima Mundi. As Mulciber Vulcan signifies a superior fire related
to Jove (as long as he remains with him in the heavens). Second, as Lemnius
he signifies a destructive fire, "noxius ignis," lightning, deformed by air as
it descends, hence his name, from *volicanus*, or *voluens canis*, which explains
Vulcan as "claudus," lame, unable to walk upright once he completes his
fall to earth (from Martianus, *De nuptiis* 7). Thirdly, he signifies an evil fire,
"ignis libidinis," because he is married to Venus, "voluptas"—yet because
he is "claudus" (crippled, lame), he is "impotens." Fourthly, he signifies a
creative fire, the fire of *ingenium* linked to memory and used by poets.

Finally, William substitutes Hercules for Paris here, as if he recalled his interpolation of the Judgment of Paris into the Ixion-Juno gloss on Boethius, *Consolatio* 3 m12, in which Hercules also played an exemplary role. The interpolation would appear to be an intentional association of two mythological figures, one a flawed son of Priam, the other a heroic son of Jove, and both linked by Juno's antipathy. William declares, "Et nota quid fuit tres deae que *herculem* admiratur: Juno, Pallas et Venus." Hercules, whose conception resulted from a double-length night of lovemaking between Jupiter and mortal Alcmene, is heroic in nature, as we know already from the Carolingian Boethius glosses (on *Consolatio* 4 m7) and William on Boethius (3 m12). As in the latter commentary by William, Hercules is here also opposed by Juno, the goddess William identifies throughout this commentary as the active life. The opportunity for this unusual association comes in response to the mention of Hercules in Martianus (*De nuptiis* 84). The three goddesses in William's Boethian Judgment of Paris represent the three Fulgentian lives, active, contemplative, and voluptuary, or "mixed"—Pythagorean. But here William does support the latter attribution by noting that, "Incerta vita pictagorae est que Venus" ["the uncertain life of Pythagoras is of Venus"], especially as it is clear that Juno is the active life and Pallas the contemplative, but finally he says: "Venus ut impediat. Juno ut pulveat. Pallas ut retineat" ["Venus that she might entangle. Juno that would contest. Pallas that would hold back"], with Venus understood as "mater omnium generationium." As Cypris she represents "mixtura" and is responsible for "mixing" or uniting the human sexual seeds about which William has written in the long gloss on her son—Hymen.

This cross-fertilization of commentaries (Boethius and Martianus) and of philosophical interpretations (Neoplatonic and Neo-Stoic) is characteristic of William throughout his glosses, including those believed to follow the Martianus commentary. Many of the glosses in the Juvenal and *Timaeus* commentaries reflect these earlier glosses on Boethius, Macrobius, and Martianus, their mythographic interpretations of gods and heroes definitely Neo-Stoic, whatever the ostensible Platonic or euhemeristic context.

IV. NEO-STOIC HERCULES AND VULCAN
IN THE JUVENAL AND *TIMAEUS* GLOSSES

The myths in both William's Juvenal and *Timaeus* commentaries can be divided into two groups, allegorizing the microcosm or the macrocosm. Generally, for the first group William uses faculty psychology in a

Neoplatonic way to allegorize human duality. For the second group he uses
Neo-Stoic concepts of cosmology to allegorize the parts of Nature. In the
Juvenal glosses reappear heroes who are troubled by their body and human
sexuality, those wise Homeric or Statian heroes who Aeneas-like descend
into the underworld in Boethius, that is, Ulysses and Hercules, along with
Theseus. In addition to glosses on heroes who descend into the underworld,
William's Juvenal glosses express that early Macrobian-Martianan interest
in cosmic (earthly, natural) fertility—what the twelfth century incorporated into Natura, the new World Soul, as the heir of the Stoic *anima
mundi*. His myths in Juvenal, nearly identical to those in his own
Macrobius and Martianus commentaries, include Mercury and Vulcan,
Ceres and Bacchus as natural principles of fertility (grain and wine), and
Cybele as the earth; another sexual myth, concerning a human rather than
a divine figure, focuses on Pasiphaë in her adultery with Taurus. The
mythological glosses on the *Timaeus*—and there are relatively few, as one
might expect—are prefaced by the glosses on Plato's discussion of interpreting myths, in *Timaeus* 41de. In the *Timaeus* commentary William
again expresses this interest in earthly and human sexual myths associated
with Martianus or the commentaries on Martianus—those of Pan, Semele,
Pallas/Minerva, Vulcan, Ceres and Bacchus, Venus and Priapus, and the
genealogy of the gods.

William's glosses on Juvenal are purported to have been written during
the decade of the 1130s, when he was teaching at Chartres (or Paris), that
is, after the Boethius glosses but before the *Timaeus* glosses;[92] they may in
fact have been copied down from William's lectures by one of his students
because they do not seem very mature and consist mostly of plot summaries
of the sort typical of the glosses of the first two Vatican mythographers, or
Hyginus. Yet contemporary sources for the mythographies in the Juvenal
glosses reveal William's mark, for they include the Remigian glosses (or
William's own glosses) on Martianus Capella[93] and the *Ecloga Theoduli;*[94]
other sources of, and parallels for, the Juvenal glosses have been identified
by William's editor as Isidore, Servius on the *Aeneid,* Ovid, Macrobius's
Saturnalia, Fulgentius, the three Vatican mythographers, and William's
own glosses on Boethius.

The early Neoplatonic Virgilian-Boethian interest in the problem of the
body within the heroic (ideal human) life reappears in the Juvenal glosses
as expressed by the hero Ulysses battling against Youth as an adversary, in
Polyphemus, or by Hercules battling against the hell-hound Cerberus in an
attempt to rescue Theseus and his companion Pirithous. Ulysses and

Polyphemus come from William's glosses on Boethius (*Consolatio* 4 m3), as this scholastic allegorization found only in the second manuscript might suggest by its very nature (*In Iuvenalem* 1.10–12, p. 100). The fable is an allegory of human life, particularly of the life of the mind that transcends corporal change and flux. Ulysses represents wisdom, his name stemming from "olonxeon," Greek for "always traveling" (because this life is a journey, *peregrinatio*); the cyclops Polyphemus represents the pride (*superbia*) of youth that he encounters on that journey. To avoid the single vision of Polyphemus one must, like Ulysses, see everything and desire nothing. Ulysses's men are changed into beasts because of their (youthful) desire for *temporalia*, which Ulysses shuns.

> For Polyphemus, that is, childish vision, is pride, because it seems to a child that he knows and sees many things. He has only one eye, that is, only contemplation of temporal things, and this he has in his forehead, that is, an ostentatious display, because children turn their attention to ostentation and boasting. Ulysses plucks out the eye of childish pride, because the wise man is Ulysses is called *olonxeon*, that is, the far-ranging wanderer (a traveler through all lands), since here is (his?) pilgrimage. But our life is in heaven; he scorns the contemplation and desire for temporal things. (*In Iuvenalem*, p. 101)

Hercules's rescue of Theseus and Pirithous from the underworld reflects William's habitual interest in rationalizing male sexuality, here focused on raping Proserpina. Theseus, a type of Orpheus, and his friend Pirithous, as his companion in need of rescue a type of Eurydice, although here intent on carrying off Proserpina, descend into the underworld. The shades detain Pirithous but release the demigod Theseus: "Cum eodem, ut Proserpinam raperet, ad inferos descendit quo agnito inferi Piritoum quia tantum erat homo retinuerunt, sed Theseo quia erat semideus licentiam redeundi concesserunt; quia nolens sine socio reverti ibi remansit" ["With him, in order to carry off Proserpina, he descended to the underworld. When he was recognized, the shades kept Pirithous because he was only a man, but because Theseus was a demigod, they granted him permission to return; Theseus, being unwilling to return without his companion, stayed there"] (*In Iuvenalem* 1.4, p. 95).

Similarly, the bestial desire of Pasiphaë for "Taurus" is euhemerized to reveal, in the gloss on *mugitum labyrinthi*, that "Taurus" was the *cancellarius*, or secretary, of Minos—that is, not a bull inhabited by Neptune, but a real person (*In Iuvenalem* 1.50–55, pp. 110–11). The rationalization echoes that of the second Vatican mythography on the same fable, where he is a *notarius* (notary; Bode 126).

Also in the Juvenal glosses, the etymological definition of "Vulcan," ostensibly from Isidore (*Etym.* 8.11.39), echoes the Florentine mythography: Vulcan is associated with Mount Etna in Sicily, where there is perpetual fire, because "Vulcanus enim quasi volitans candor ignis dicitur, vel quasi volicanus quia ad alta volat et canus est in favillis" ["For Vulcan, that is, flying is called 'brightness of fire,' or, meaning volcano {'volicanus'} because he flies {'volat'} to the heights and is white {'canus'} in glowing ashes"] (*In Iuvenalem* 1.8–9, p. 98). Juno's son Vulcan must deal with the problem of the body inherited from his mother Juno, which is expressed mythologically as a desire for wisdom, Pallas Athena. According to William's Plato glosses, before the Deluge, in what is now Athens, Pallas Athena was the presiding goddess, allegorized as wisdom.[95] Pallas refused to couple with Vulcan, fire or "fervor ingenii" ["heat of ability"], or what we would call talent, and his seed fell to the earth to produce Erichthonius. He is regarded as human in his upper part and as dragon in his lower, quia ex sapientia predicta nascitur et cura celestium que rationalis est et cura temporalium que utilis est et astuta ut draco" ["because from the aforesaid wisdom is born both concern for heavenly things, which is rational, and concern for temporal things, which is useful and clever like the dragon {or snake}"].[96] Erichthonius becomes a symbol of the microcosm, his serpent part suggestive of an excessive concern with earthly matters and tending to vice, his human part in its rational and virtuous functions suggestive of celestial concerns: "Sed illa superior, hec inferior, quia illa cura, scilicet celestis, dignior est ista. Sed quia cura temporalium sine aliqua turpitudine vix aut nunquam haberi potest, ad hanc celandum currus parat, id est rationem et intellectum et virtutes" ["But the former is superior, the latter inferior, because one concern, namely the heavenly, is worthier than the other. But because concern for temporal things can seldom or never be considered to be without some baseness, to conceal this it prepares chariots, namely, reason and intellect and virtues"].

Finally, in the second book of the Juvenal commentary reappear glosses on Bacchus and Ceres recognizable from the Macrobius glosses. William mentions, in a gloss on the Sarmatians as people who imitate the Curii and live like Bacchanals, that the Bacchanalia was a festivity of insanity called so in honor of Bacchus, "id est bacanaliter; id est insane baccare, enim insanire est et dicitur a Baco qui quamdam insaniam ultra modum

<sumpsit>" ["that is, as at the Bacchanalia, that is, to rave madly, for it is madness and so called from Bacchus, who took on madness beyond measure"} (*In Iuvenalem* 2.4, p. 141). And Cybele also still represents the earth, "Cibeles quasi Cubeles, mater deorum, terra dicitur et pingitur turrita propter turres et alia edificia que in terra sunt" ["as if Cubeles, mother of the Gods, said to be earth and depicted as turreted on account of the towers and other edifices which exist on earth"] (*In Iuvenalem* 2.103–11, p. 155).[97]

In the *Timaeus* glosses, William finds philosophical and cosmological explanations for the immorality of the gods denigrated by Macrobius, but in addition the focus in this commentary is more etiological than that of his other commentaries. While there exists no commentary by William on the *Saturnalia,* that he may have read the work is possible to surmise because of his interest in Macrobius's commentary on the *Somnium Scipionis;* he may also have been drawn to its Neoplatonism because of his similar interest in the *Timaeus.* In the *Timaeus* glosses, the myths most relevant to the Macrobius commentary occur in the second book, on Ceres in *Timaeus* 40c and on Jupiter-Semele, Oceanus-Thetis, and Rhea-Cronos, in 40e,[98] because in the first book William is generally interested in faculty psychology—free will, the soul, intelligence, memory and reason[99]—but with little attention to myths of the gods.

Ostensibly following Plato, William in fact explores the origins of various gods in an elaborate Neo-Stoic genealogy in which all the gods represent names for ancient processes of cosmic generation, beginning with the union of time and matter (Saturn and Ops), in a conjunction drawn straight from Macrobius's *Saturnalia* rather than the commentary on Cicero, or else from William's own Martianus commentary. William then allegorizes the family history of the gods, beginning with Earth and Heaven from whom were born Oceanus and Thetis, and from them Phorcys, Cronus and Rhea. Earth, the most ancient and first-born of the gods, is made a guardian and artificer of night and day out of Ceres or Cybele, explained in a myth also found in the Juvenal commentary: Cybele is called a goddess because of "Cibeles," food or sustenance, whence "Cubeles" because the body is three-dimensional, literally, composed of cubes, or "Ceres" as if "Crees," "you may create," because out of herself she creates seeds ("DEAM quia Cibeles vocatur a quibusdam quasi 'Cubeles' quia est cubicum corpus, vel Ceres quasi 'Crees' quia ex se creat germina").[100] Finally, both Thetis and Oceanus are children of the heaven and earth just as Jupiter and Juno are the children of Saturn (Cronos) and Rhea (Ops). That is, fire (Jupiter) and air (Juno) are children of time (Saturn) and primordial matter (Rhea), because *temporalia* is made from matter; the brothers of Jupiter and Juno, Neptune and Pluto, are the other two elements, water and earth.[101] William also explains Semele as earth, as he has previously in the Macrobius commentary.[102]

William uses the etymologizing principles of Neo-Stoicism to rationalize this history, as he has in his commentaries on Macrobius and Martianus. For example, Thetis is mud, *limus,* whence she is said to be wife of Oceanus because mud binds with water and is concealed under it; she is called "Thetis" from "thesis"—the falling of the voice in prosody—because it is a sinking down ("unde coniux Occeani dicitur quia limus coniunctus est acque et suppositus, dictus a 'thesi' quod est depressio").[103]

The consistency of William's mythographic glosses—from the earliest Boethius to the latest *Timaeus*—depends, then, upon a synthesis of Neoplatonism and Neo-Stoicism, in commentaries which would greatly influence others in later generations. After William, Boethian studies changed, shifted more to translations into other vernaculars, as in the thirteenth and fourteenth-century French translations of Jean de Meun, Renaud de Louhans, and Charles d'Orleans, and translations into Middle English (by Chaucer), Spanish, "Flamand," and Greek.[104] Certainly Boethius commentaries continued to flourish in the fourteenth and fifteenth centuries: the fourteenth-century commentary of Nicholas Trivet attempted a new nominalistic approach, but was followed by a prolusion of lesser commentaries derivative of the earlier, Carolingian and twelfth-century paradigms.[105] In the Neoplatonic descents of William's Boethius and the Platonized Neo-Stoicism of his Martianus commentary, reflected in the Juvenal and *Timaeus* glosses, and in his Neoplatonic theory of *integumentum,* studding the glosses on Macrobius, Juvenal, and the *Timaeus,* he would greatly influence one other innovative, synthesizing twelfth-century commentator—Bernard Silvestris.

Chapter Eleven

THE VIRGILIAN HERO'S VIRTUOUS DESCENT IN MARTIANUS CAPELLA: THE NEO-STOIC INTERTEXTUALITY OF BERNARD SILVESTRIS

The mythographic tradition culminates in the twelfth century in the system of descents schematized by William of Conches and reinterpreted by Bernard Silvestris. In this system many of the singular emphases of various commentary traditions are collected into a coherent frame. First, the gods of the underworld are interpreted Stoically, that is, as diverse names for natural things. Second, the focus on the sixth book of the *Aeneid* and its *descensus ad inferos* continues to reveal human life as a Neoplatonic underworld. Third, the Carolingian hero, classically educated, wise and powerful, masters the infernal and vicious underworld(s). Fourth, the Stoic World Soul is assimilated into the Neoplatonic view of the gods as aspects of Nature, regenerating the macrocosm and pricking the microcosm to regenerate both naturally and spiritually. Fifth and finally, Virgil and Martianus are accorded a "Boethian" re-reading to single out the virtuous descent as their common denominator—a signal that literary criticism has become inbred and incestuous. Clearly the times are ready for a new approach to letters and to the classical text—the same classical text, in this case, Martianus, has been read and re-read to exhaustion (perhaps one explanation for the incompletion of both the commentaries on Martianus by Bernard and Alexander Neckam). Thereafter, *De nuptiis* would cease to appeal to commentators, at least for glossation in the usual commentary-like form.

Many of the classical gods involved in the integuments of Bernard are associated with either the *descensus ad inferos* or with a cosmic journey; the denotations and connotations of their names form part of Bernard's elaborate and logical deconstruction of their meaning. One god or figure may occasionally convey more than one signification. Explicitly invoking the ancient grammatical practice of the Stoics, in the commentary on the *Aeneid* Bernard discusses the multiple levels of allegoresis, specifically the natural, or physical, and the moral or tropological (often etymological).

> Hic autem diversus integumentorum respectus et multiplex designatio in omnibus misticis observari debet si in una vero veritas stare non poterit. Ergo in hoc opere hoc idem reperitur quod idem nomen diversas designat naturas et contra diversa nomina eandem: idem diversas ut Appollo aliquando solem, aliquando, divinam sapientiam, aliquando humanam sapientiam designat.

> [Hence, one must pay attention to the diverse aspects of the poetic fictions and the multiple interpretations in all allegorical matters if in fact the truth cannot be established by a single interpretation. This principle holds, therefore, in this work because the same name designates different natures, and conversely, different names designate the same nature, so that Apollo sometimes designates the sun, sometimes divine wisdom, and sometimes human wisdom.] (Bern. Sil., *Sup. En.* 1.72, p. 9; trans., p. 11)

In the accessus to his commentary on Martianus, Bernard similarly echoes and embellishes this Neo-Stoic pronouncement on the multiple names of the gods, although here, he takes care to differentiate the *equivocationes* (different names for the same thing) from the *multivocationes* (the same name for different things). An example of the first is Juno, another name for the air, also known as the practical life. An example of the second is Mercury, meaning the planet, but "Mercury" also signifies the god of eloquence.

> Notandum est integumenta equivocationes et multivocationes habere. Verbi gratia: apud Virgilium nomen Iunonis ad aerem et ad practicam vitam equivocatur. Quod enim ibi legitur Iunonem venire ad Eolum, significat aerem nativitatem hominis iuvare. Quod vero dicitur venisse cum Pallade et Venere ad iudicium Paridis, figurat vitam practicam et theorica necnon etiam voluptatem, ut de his iudicet, sensui se proponentes. Set hec melius super Virgilium enodata repperies. Ibidem etiam multivocatio est quia Iupiter et Anchises eiusdem sunt nomina. Hic vero, quia communis philosophorum est sententia hominem ab elementis vel stellaribus spiritibus beneficia contrahere, eodem nomine vocantur cause et effectus. Verbi gratia: nomen Mercurii ad stellam et ad eloquentiam equivocatur,

quia a stella habetur vis interpretandi. Ab aere quoque per contemperationem habetur opulentia. Ideo Iunonis nomine utrumque nuncupat figurate. Ideoque distinguendum erit ad quot res subiectas integumentorum nomina equivocentur.

[It should be noted that *integumenta* have double and even multiple meanings. For example: in Vergil the name Juno is an equivocation for the lower air and the practical life. When you read that Juno came to Aeolus, this signifies that the lower air aids the birth of man. But when you read that she came to the judgment of Paris together with Pallas and Venus, she stands for the practical life, submitting herself to the judgment of sense (i.e. the affective quality) together with the theoretical and the voluptuous life. But you will find these matters explained in more detail in my commentary on Vergil. In Vergil there are multivocations as well, because Jupiter and Anchises are names for one and the same (i.e. God). In this work {*De nuptiis*} cause and effect are called by the same name, on the basis of the commonly accepted philosophical notion that man derives benefits from the elements or the stellar spirits. For example: the name of Mercury is equated with the planet as well as eloquence, because the ability to interpret is derived from the planet. In addition, wealth is obtained by mixture from the lower air. Therefore the author uses the name of Juno to signify both (i.e. lower air and practical life) in a figurative manner. And therefore one will have to distinguish how many subjects the names used in *integumenta* can refer to.] (Bern. Sil. *In Mart.*, 2.93–109, pp. 46–47; trans. Westra, "Introduction," p. 25.)

There exists, in short, a close connection between macrocosm and microcosm through what appear to be astrological influences (and Bernard was identified at least in one manuscript as the author of an astrological treatise, the *Liber fortunae*; see figure 27, with its significant portrait of Bernard).

Just as William Neoplatonizes Stoic material in Martianus, using as a frame the philosophic descent into the underworld borrowed, in the Boethius commentaries, from *Aeneid* book 6, so also his follower Bernard returns to Virgil's *Aeneid*[1] with a Neoplatonic Boethian reading of the descents to reclassify and recharacterize the myths. That Bernard read the *Aeneid* in a "Boethianized" way has been acknowledged by contemporary scholars.[2] But in addition Bernard himself explicitly compares the descent of Mercury in Martianus to the descent of Aeneas in Virgil in the accessus to his commentary on Martianus:

27. Bernard Silvestris. From *Liber fortunae*. MS. Digby 46, fol. 25v (ca. 1375). By permission of the Bodleian Library, University of Oxford.

In truth it [*De nuptiis*] is an imitation of an *auctor,* because he [Martianus] emulates Virgil. Indeed, just as in that poet's work Aeneas is led through the underworld to Anchises accompanied by the Sibyl, so also here Mercury is led through the regions of the world to Jove accompanied by Virtue. And so in the book *De consolatione* Boethius ascends through false good to the highest good led by Philosophy. Thus these three figures represent for the most part the same thing. Therefore, Martianus imitates Virgil; Boethius, Martianus. (Bern. Sil. *In Mart.* 2.114–24, p. 47, my trans.)[3]

What Bernard did not know about this process and what has not yet been noted by scholars, largely because their interests are not exclusively mythographic, is that this borrowing, in the course of the tradition's evolution, has involved a double process. After the Virgilian descent into the underworld (itself allegorized at length by Servius, Fulgentius, and Remigius of Auxerre) was used implicitly as a model by Boethius in the *Consolatio* meters, thereafter it was used both implicitly and explicitly by the Carolingian Boethius commentators, including William, who schematized the descent so scholastically. That is, Bernard borrows a *Neoplatonized* Virgilian descent into the underworld from the Boethius commentaries and then *reapplies* it, appropriately "Boethiusized," to his reading of the first six books of the *Aeneid.*

Most important, Bernard also borrows William's Neoplatonic system of descents (from his Boethius glosses), in particular, the virtuous descent—in order to characterize Aeneas's philosophical (or metaphorical) descent in book 6, which is usually (and especially in works written in later periods) adapted to the third part of Aeneas's journey, to Italy (the domain of Pallas Athena, and reflective of the contemplative life). And when Bernard then turns to Martianus for commenting, his ultimate interest is in Philology, her ascent to the heavens and, presumably after the work is finished, her return to earth as Mercury's bride. His interest here can be linked with his interest in the Boethian virtuous descent witnessed in his commentary on the *Aeneid.* In both commentaries his concern (as has been observed)[4] remains in the allegorical journey, as it does also in the *Cosmographia* (a prosimetrum like the *De planctu Naturae* of Alan of Lille and not a commentary at all), especially the journey from earthly to divine knowledge, an interest that will most influence Dante in the *Commedia.*[5]

Bernard is chiefly interested in book 6 of the *Aeneid* in his commentary, which emphasizes the afterlife (literally the descent into the underworld).

The hero must choose between vicious and virtuous descents, that is, the soul must descend into the underworld of temporal pleasure either for vicious gratification or for virtuous education to protect itself against vice. In Bernard's comments on book 6 occur ninety-eight mythological references, although there are only twelve in book 1, none in 2, four in 3, one in 4, and two in 5. The reason for the greater numbers in book one is simple: because he has amplified the Fulgentian notion of the *Aeneid* as a metaphor for the stages of human life, book one represents birth, that is, an allegorization of the natural descent in the underworld or of the soul into the underworld of the body at birth. The other books, because they do not specifically involve descents into an underworld, receive less attention: from infancy in book 1, Bernard turns to boyhood in 2, adolescence in 3, youth in 4, manly age in 5, and then knowledge of the future life in 6.

The hero who pursues virtue through wisdom (eloquence and philosophy) is Aeneas, like Ulysses in making this journey (as Virgil is like Homer in writing this epic, according to Bernard at the beginning of the commentary) and also, in the descent into the underworld, like Hercules and Orpheus, and also Theseus and Pirithous, all of these mythological heroes representative of the human spirit that descends into the underworld of flesh, of virtue, and of Hades. Hercules, or Alcides, as one of his Labors bravely and skillfully descended into the underworld to fetch the three-headed dog Cerberus. Orpheus, a wise and eloquent man, descended into hell to rescue his wife Eurydice, concupiscence. Theseus, a rational and virtuous man, descended into the *inferno* along with the eloquent man Pirithous to rescue Proserpina (see figure 28). These types of Aeneas all share the qualities of wisdom and eloquence supported by Bernard and associated with the trivium and quadrivium. They are implicitly modeled upon the perfect man, Christ, who also descended into the underworld to harrow hell, although this relationship remains unarticulated in the commentary. Finally, the heroes help to unify not only this long sixth book with its discussion of the four descents but in effect all of the commentary.

In the Martianus commentary, Bernard also organizes and makes coherent rather inchoate materials, this time of the Martianus commentary tradition begun in the Carolingian period. Perhaps for the reason of coherence most of the mythographic references cluster at the beginning of the commentary, in the accessus, in the section on Hymen, and in the section on the wives of the gods. Bernard's means here, as in the *Aeneid* commentary, is borrowed from William's system of Boethian descents into

C este
It auec nous te conuient force
Se tu de grant wertu fais force
Vers heruiles te fault vurer
E t ses wullances remirer
E n qui il ot trop de bernage
E t pourtant se a ton lignage
F ut contraire et ot attame
N auics me pourtant suprne

28. Hercules and Cerberus, Theseus and Pirithous. From Christine de Pizan, *Epistre d'Othea a Hector*. MS. Laud Miscellaneous 30r (ca. 1454, French). By permission of the Bodleian Library, University of Oxford.

the underworld. And as in the *Aeneid* commentary, his primary interest concerns the virtuous descent, or what William has termed the wise man's descent into the underworld armed with a knowledge of its ways, in order to protect himself from the allure of temporal good. That this is a divine attribute has been signaled in previous commentaries, whether by William or Bernard, by the nature of the wise hero as a demigod. Orpheus is son of the Muse Calliope; Hercules of Jupiter; Theseus is his own god, to use Fulgentius's etymology in the *Super Thebaiden*—from *theos suus* (Helm, p. 186).

In the accessus Bernard selects Theseus, companion of Pirithous, to gloss as an embodiment of the ideals of *De nuptiis:* a paradigm for wise and virtuous behavior, in addition, because of his association with the mortal Pirithous, the demigod makes clear that the return from the descent into the underworld can only be performed successfully by those with a divine heritage. Citing Boethius (or more probably the commentaries on Boethius, perhaps William himself, on wisdom, the "mistress of virtues," *Consolatio* I p3.3, repeated by Bernard, *Sup. En.* 6.333–34, trans. p. 78), Bernard also utilizes the Fulgentian etymologies of Theseus and Pirithous in discussing, in a section devoted to the "utilitas," or purpose, of the commentary, the necessary yoking of *sapientia* and *eloquentia* both in forms of discourse and in leading the good life.

> Quia vero eas nescit inanes et contemptibiles, his caducis hominem inherere facit. Quod, ut arbitror, illa de Theseo et Pirithoo fabella videtur apte figurare. Dicitur enim Theseus quasi "theos eus" (id est bonitas, deus) sapientia, quam Boetius virtutum magistram dicit. Pirithous vero quasi "perhite," id est circumlocutionis vel circuitionis deus, est eloquentia. Qui quidem ad inferos descendunt dum ad temporalia sapientes et eloquentes animadvertunt. Sed alter semideus, alter vero ex toto mortalis invenitur, quia sapientia in theorica interminabilis, in practica vero transitoria. Eloquentia vero tota cum animalis interitu dissolvitur. Ideoque, revertente ad superos altero, alter in inferis detinetur, quia sapientia a temporalibus ad eterna resurgente, eloquentia caducis immoratur.

> [But because he does not know that they {political preferments} are vain and contemptible, he {Cicero} makes man cling to these perishable {transitory} things. Thus, I think, that fable about Theseus and Pirithous seems to portray aptly. For Theseus, named from "theos eus" (that is, goodness, god) is wisdom, which Boethius calls the

teacher of virtue. But Pirithous, derived from "perhite," that is, god of circumlocution or periphrasis, is eloquence. When they descend to the underworld, it means that wise and eloquent men are turning their attention to temporal matters. But one is found to be a demigod, the other wholly mortal; because wisdom in theory is endless, in practice, transitory; but the whole of eloquence perishes with the death of the living being. And so, while one returns to the upper world {*ad superos*}, the other is kept in the underworld {*in inferis*}; because, though wisdom rises from the temporal to the eternal, eloquence remains among things which are transitory]. (Bern. Sil., *In. Mart.* 2.134–46, pp. 47–48.)

Like the other masters of the Platonizing twelfth century who depend so heavily on Carolingian glosses for their mythography, Bernard recombines existing material innovatively to cross-fertilize the different mythographic and commentary traditions. As a grammarian Bernard was graced with the talents of an assimilator. A friend and disciple of Thierry of Chartres, he was associated with Tours and Orleans as centers of grammatical and rhetorical study and consequently was responsible for various rhetorical texts (including a treatise on the *ars dictaminis*), grammatical commentaries on the *auctores* Virgil and Martianus, Chartrian cosmological and astronomical works like the *Mathematicus, Experimentarius,* and his most famous work, the *Cosmographia* (finished by 1147).[6] In all these works he depends heavily on his sources and on others' ideas: in the commentary on the *Aeneid,* for example, he actually cites by name Horace (*Epistles* and *Satires*), Lucan's *Pharsalia,* Ovid's *Metamorphoses, De arte amandi,* and *Fasti,* Statius's *Thebaid,* Persius, Juvenal, Pliny, Cicero's *De inventione,* Sallust's *Bellum Catilinae,* and Terence's *Eunuchio.*[7] In fact, however, he actually uses as sources Servius, the Vatican mythographers, William of Conches on Boethius, Calcidius's *Timaeus,* Macrobius, Martianus Capella, Isidore, Fulgentius, Cicero's *De natura deorum,* Varro's *De lingua Latina,* and Apuleius's *Metamorphoses.*[8]

One way in which he was most original, however, derived from his treatment of *fabula,* which made him considerably different from contemporaries like William who shared his interest in classical mythology. For William, Christian *integumentum* was no different from pagan *integumentum,* but according to Bernard, the method of treating Scripture and of treating mythology should differ. In the commentary on Martianus 2.70–92, the term *allegoria* refers to historical narrative, that which has actually occurred, linked with Scripture; the term *integumentum* refers to fabulous narrative, linked with the philosophical. Jacob is an example of the one, Orpheus, an example of the other.

> Figura autem est oratio quam involucrum dicere solent. Hec autem bipertita est: partimur namque eam in allegoriam et integumentum. Est autem allegoria oratio sub historica narratione verum et ab exteriori diversum involvens intellectum, ut de lucta Iacob. Integumentum vero est oratio sub fabulosa narratione verum claudens intellectum, ut de Orpheo. Nam et ibi historia et hic fabula misterium habent occultum, quod alias discutiendum erit. Allegoria quidem divine pagine, integumentum vero philosophice competit.[9]

> [Figurative discourse is a mode of discourse which is called a "veil." Figurative discourse is twofold, for we divide it into allegory and *integumentum*. Allegory is a mode of discourse which covers under an historical narrative a true meaning which is different from its surface meaning, as in the case of Jacob wrestling with the angel. An *integumentum,* however, is a mode of discourse which covers a true meaning under a fictitious narrative, as in the case of Orpheus. For in the case of the former history, and in the latter fiction, contains a profound hidden truth, which will be explained elsewhere. Allegory pertains to Holy Scripture, but *integumentum* to philosophical scripture.] (Bern. Sil. *In Mart.* 2.70–78, p. 45.)

Note that Bernard also uses the term *oratio* (mode of discourse) generally for both types, although *figura* and *involucrum* are equivocal. His theory is derived from Macrobius (or inspired by William on Macrobius): he is aware of the Macrobian distinction between philosophy and fiction, and the subjects permitted the user of fabulous narrative—the soul, the spirits of upper or lower air, and the gods, but not God and Mind, except when the philosophers need to attribute qualities to them that transcend human comprehension and can only be understood by analogy and simile (*Somn. Scip.* 1.2.13–14).

> Non tamen ubique, teste Macrobio, involucrum tractatus admittit philosophicus. Cum enim ad summum, inquit, deum stilus se audet attollere, nefas est fabulosa vel licita admittere. Ceterum cum de anima vel de ethereis aeriisve potestatibus agitur, locum habent integumenta.

[However, a philosophical treatise does not allow the use of a "veil" everywhere, as Macrobius bears witness. For he states that, when the pen dares to approach the highest divinity, it is wrong to admit even the permissible kind of fiction. But when the souls or the powers of the upper or lower air are discussed, *integumenta* have their place.] (Bern. Sil. *In Mart.* 2.78–82, p. 24).

For the latter use of the integument, he cites as a model the obscuring of divine truth that requires the agency of the sibyl, or the philosopher, to clarify, as in the soul's descent into the earthly underworld from the aether (the natural descent), in Aeneas's descent into the underworld (the artificial descent literally, the virtuous descent figuratively), or, more Neoplatonically, in the soul's perception of truth while incarcerated in blind flesh (the virtuous or vicious descents, depending on the choice made).

Unde Virgilius humani spiritus temporalem cum corpore vitam describens, integumentis usus est. Qui idem introducens Sibillam de deis agentem inquid: "Obscuris vera involvens," id est divina integumentis claudens. Plato quoque, de mundano corpore aperte locutus, cum ad animam ventum est, dicit figuraliter eius materiam numerum esse. De stellis quoque evidenter pronuntians, mistice de spiritibus dicturus ad involucrum se convertit, dicens quia celi et terre filii sunt Oceanus et Thetis. Ergo et iste, humane nature deificationem pandens, nichil absque misterio efferens, ut prudens theologus fatur.

[Hence Vergil, when describing the temporal life of the human spirit within the body, used *integumenta*. The same author, when introducing the Sybil speaking about the gods, says: "Wrapping truth in obscurity" {*Aeneid,* Bk. 6, line 100}, that is, hiding the divine through *integumenta*. Plato too, after he had spoken in a literal fashion about the worldly body, when he came to speak of the soul, said figuratively that its matter is number. Also speaking plainly about the stars, he had recourse to "a veil" when he wanted to speak mystically about the spirits, saying that Oceanus and Tethys are the children of heaven and earth. Therefore this author {i.e. Martianus}, unveiling the deification of human nature, speaks like a prudent theologian, because all his utterances contain a hidden truth.] (Bern. Sil. *In Mart.* 2.82–92, pp. 24–25.)

In his construction of the virtuous descent of Aeneas in his commentary on the *Aeneid,* Bernard would create a paradigm of mythographic heroism useful to subsequent commentators, namely, his contemporaries John of Salisbury and Alexander Neckam, who turned it to their own mythographic purposes. It would also prove useful to him in constructing the descent of Mercury in the Martianus commentary.

I. THE VIRTUOUS DESCENT OF AENEAS
IN THE VIRGIL COMMENTARY

Bernard's full-length allegorization of the first six books of the *Aeneid* is innovative while it sums up many earlier treatments of the *Aeneid:* in its very long allegorization of the sixth book, that concerning the descent into the underworld, it applies the system of the four descents conceived by William of Conches in his glosses on Boethius (in particular, the myth of Orpheus's descent into the underworld in *Consolatio* 3, m12) to Aeneas (and other heroes like him).[10] As a consequence, John of Salisbury (d. 1180) will interpret Aeneas's stay with Dido tropologically as a vicious excursion, and Alexander Neckam (1157–1217) will interpret mythological figures from various works, including the *Aeneid,* tropologically as the vices themselves (for example, rivers of hell), with emphasis in most of the glosses on the sixth book of the *Aeneid.*

Whereas Bernard's contemporaries utilized the implications of the vicious descent in their incidental *Aeneid* glosses, Bernard preferred the virtuous "descent"—or perhaps what might be termed the virtuous "reascent," if one looks at Aeneas's return to "sovereign day" after his initial descent into the underworld. Bernard's Aeneas descends into the underworld virtuously to learn more about creation through the trivium, quadrivium, and philosophy (taking a cue from Fulgentian educational allegory) which will enable him to withstand the temptations of temporal good and thereby become more virtuous. But John's Aeneas descends almost viciously, or perhaps psychoanalytically, in that he reviews his past life by looking at his mistakes (and vices) to prepare himself for an undoubtedly Christian future in the Other World.

Aeneas, Bernard's hero of the virtuous descent, represents Everyman and therefore typifies the means of mastering the underworld of the sixth book. His name means "the human spirit" and derives from the Greek *ennos demas,* "habitator corporis" or "inhabitant of the body," with *demas,* the body, described as a "vinculum" or bond because it incarcerates the soul. Aeneas is the son of Anchises and Venus because "Eneas vero et Anchise et

Veneris filius est quia spiritus humanus a deo per concordiam in corpore incipit vivere" ["the human spirit comes from God through concord to live in the body"] (Bern. Sil. *Sup. En.*, 1.72; trans. p. 12). That the human body is in Neoplatonic terms the underworld, its rivers, vices, is expounded at the beginning of the sixth book (6.1). Because there is nothing lower than the human body, it is an *infernus* ("Cum itaque nihil sit inferius humano corpore, infernum id appellaverunt"), and souls suffering from imprisonment in the underworld are actually suffering from corporal vices ("Quod autem legimus in inferis animas coactione teneri quadam a spiritibus carcerariis, hoc idem docebant pati anime in corporibus a viciis"). The four rivers of the underworld therefore can be identified as vices—Phlegethon, wrath; Lethe, oblivion; Styx, hatred; and Acheron, sadness ("Quattuor etiam fluvios in eis assignabant: Flegetontem ardores irarum, Leten oblivionem mentis maiestatem sue divinitatis obliviscentis, stigem autem odium, Acherontem tristiciam," 6.1; trans. p. 32).

Aeneas as the human soul plunges into the underworld in four ways during his narrative journey, all appropriated from the four descents of Orpheus in William on Boethius, with Aeneas's virtuous descent occupying the privileged place. In this uncommon virtuous descent a wise person (such as Orpheus and Hercules) descends by contemplation of worldly things in order to protect himself from their temptation and understand the Creator through creation; but in the natural descent common to everyone, the soul enters the mutable regions at birth and gradually accepts viciousness. In the vicious descent an individual is overwhelmed by worldly things, as was Eurydice, but in the artificial descent a magician uses artifice to converse with demons about the afterlife.[11]

In the sixth book the descents of vice and virtue receive the most attention, just as the first book covers the first descent, of nature at birth; the virtuous and vicious descents resemble the two paths (or branches, or forks), virtuous and vicious, of the Servian golden bough, the Pythagorean Y (in both authors, a gloss on *Aeneid* 6.136). According to Bernard, only through the golden bough of philosophy can Aeneas find and open the passage to the underworld; the raised right branch signifies the path to life, and the lowered left branch the path to death or "entrance into substance from non-being." This tree is like humanity, which is divided into the two branches of virtue and vice, and also like the letter Y.[12] The choice of the right-hand path of Virtue, the one to Elysium, implies for Bernard the speculative life; it is also attained when Paris (or sense) gives the golden apple to one of the three goddesses, here Pallas (the speculative life) rather

than Venus (pleasurable life) or Juno (active life). Therefore, the specific
route to virtue winds through wisdom—the beginning of poetic studies
(the Hesperian shore) and the philosophical arts (the Camenae), accompanied by study or joyless habit (Achates) and fostered by teaching
(Latona, from whom wisdom or Apollo proceeds) to obtain a glimpse of
Aurora (the first glow of knowledge illuminating the eyes of the human
mind). Aeneas's journey to acquire wisdom, virtue, and eloquence involves
a reliance upon the wisdom and virtue of others, most of whom appear in
the sixth book[13] and range from the Sibyl, as intelligence or divine counsel,
to Minerva, as cognition, and Agamemnon, as reason.[14]

Bernard's commentary was the most important and influential medieval
commentary on Virgil's work, although its approach and specific glosses
can be traced to earlier treatments by Servius, Macrobius, Fulgentius,
Remigius, and William of Conches which it might be helpful, at this
point, to recapitulate. From Servius Bernard takes the very concept of
line-by-line commentary and applies it in particular to the sixth book,
(Bernard's commentary covers only six books and only the sixth is a
line-by-line commentary, by far the longest of the six). From Servius (or
Servius as copied by Remigius on the *Aeneid* or on Martianus Capella), he
also takes the symbolism of the Pythagorean Y with its two paths, vicious
and virtuous, supplemented by the Neoplatonic concept of human life as
an underworld and the circles of hell associated with the vicious fork of the
Y. From Macrobius's commentary on the *Somnium Scipionis* he takes the
Neoplatonic idea of the soul's descent into the underworld of the body (or
of earth) as a natural descent into the underworld. From Fulgentius he
takes the descent into the underworld in the sixth book as a positive, or
virtuous, descent into hell—essentially the pursuit of wisdom through
learning. And from the glosses of William of Conches on Boethius he takes
the frame of the four descents into the underworld—natural, at birth;
vicious and virtuous, at adolescence; and artifical, through demonic sacrifice and petition—inspired by Orpheus's descent into the underworld in
Consolatio 3 m12.

In Bernard, Orpheus, Theseus, and Hercules as types of Aeneas descending virtuously also master the underworld (*Aeneid* 6.119–123 and
392–93). Orpheus descends into hell to rescue Eurydice (natural concupiscence or appetite), who trod upon a serpent (temporal good), was poisoned
(with pleasure through the senses), and died (or descended into the
underworld of temporal things). Orpheus's virtuous descent is achieved

through cognition and the pacification of the rulers of the underworld with wisdom and eloquence:

> Uxore sua permotus Orpheus ad inferos descendit, id est ad temporalia per cognitionem, ut visa eorum fragilitate concupiscentiam inde extrahat. Umbrarum dominos demulcet, id est temporalium possessores. Tandem postquam diu cantavit, id est sapientiam et eloquentiam diu ibi exercuit, uxorem recipit, id est concupiscentiam a terrenis extrahit, hac lege quod eam perdat si retro respiciat, id est si iterum ad temporalia se reflectat.

> [Moved by desire for his wife, Orpheus goes to the underworld: he descends by investigation to temporal matters so that, once he has seen their fragile nature, he may withdraw his appetite from them. He charms the lords of the shades, that is, the possessors of temporal good. After he has sung for a while (after he has there exercised wisdom and eloquence), he regains his wife (he removes appetite from earthly matters) with the stipulation that he will lose her if he looks back (if he thinks again about the temporal).] (Bern. Sil. *Sup. En.* 6.119; trans. p. 55.)

Theseus in this same section is described as having made a virtuous descent into the underworld ("Hic ad inferos descendit secundum descensum virtutis") and as typifying the rational and virtuous man ("Per hunc intelligimus rationalem et virtuosum") because of the etymology of his name from "divine" (*theos*) and "good" (*eu*; *Sup. En.* 6.122, repeated on p. 88; cf. trans. pp. 55, 84). Later he represents the wise man as Pirithous represents the eloquent man; they descend into the underworld in order to rape Proserpina. That is, "Dum enim cursus solis et lune et similes aliorum astrorum naturas cognoscunt, philosophari circa mundana amant, sed sapientia sua sapientem educit. Solum vero eloquentem garrulitas sua magis vincit" ["they learn the course of the sun and moon and the natures of the stars {and} they love to philosophize about mundane matters, but their 'wisdom' drives out true wisdom. Indeed, their garrulity greatly defeats true eloquence"] (*Sup. En* 6.393 trans., p. 84). The wise man here occupies a more enviable position than the merely eloquent man.

Hercules also descends virtuously: "Hic quoque eodem descensu descendit" (*Sup. En.* 6.123). This descent is more fully glossed later as "the contemplation of temporal things," but because he is "a demigod, rational and immortal in spirit, irrational and mortal in body, he returned from these things when he rose again" to the celestial ("sed quia est semideus, id est rationalis et immortalis in anima, irrationabilis et in corpore mortalis, redit dum ab eis ad celestia resurgit," *Sup. En.* 6.392; trans. p. 83). His specific descent involves a labor to retrieve the doorkeeper Cerberus, which for Bernard symbolizes the victory of virtue over vice ("Hercules virtuosum significat") as does the etymology of his name: "Alcides" means "brave" (*fortis*) and "beautiful" (*pulcher*); he is called Hercules from *her* (strife) and *cleos* (glory) because he is admired for his exploits. "Cerberus" epitomizes a two-fold but related meaning—first, as earth, "as if *caerberos,* that is, *carnem vorans,* 'devouring the flesh.' " He consumes the flesh and leaves the bones. He has three heads: Europe, Asia, and Africa," or three qualities (most hot, most cold, and medium).[15] Second, as the "janitor" of Orcus he represents the *corpus humanum:* "Cerberus ergo ianuam Orci custodit quia eloquentia oris instrumentum et claudit et aperit. Hercules hunc vinctum extrahit dum in preceptionibus et regulis ceteris comprehendit" ["Therefore Cerberus keeps the door because eloquence opens and closes the instrument of the mouth. Hercules drags out the chained Cerberus when he comprehends eloquence through precepts and other rules"] (*Sup. En.* 6.392; trans. p. 83).

Other Herculean Labors mentioned by Bernard reveal his similar role as the wise man. As *sapientia* he battles the Hydra, *ignorantia,* cutting off heads when he devises questions which lessen ambiguity, only to find other heads springing up ("Hic autem capud ydre amputat, dum unam questionis ambiguitatem certificat et tunc plures subcrescunt," *Sup. En.* 6.287; trans. p. 69). Finally, "Videns vero Hercules laborem suum cassum, ydram comburit, id est videns sapiens studium suum parum utile, vivacissimo igne mentis ignorantiam dissolvit cum fervore inquirendi eam investigat et splendore cognoscendi illustrat" ["Hercules, seeing his labor is in vain, burns up the Hydra, that is, a wise man, seeing his study insufficiently useful, burns up ignorance with the most vigorous fire of the mind when he investigates ignorance with the fervor of inquiry and illuminates it with the splendor of knowledge"] (trans. p. 69; see figure 29).[16] Hercules also appears in the role of the wise man when he visits the avaricious man, Phineas (from *Aeneid* 6.289). Phineas binds his sons (a metaphor for the reduction of intellect and discretion caused by a sordid way of life), after which he is blinded by the gods and the Harpies snatch away his food, until the wise Hercules can shoot them (with sharp rebukes). As both a wise and virtuous hero Hercules appropriately conquers his adversaries ignorance

29. Hercules and Hydra. MS. Additional 22325, fol. 1v (1472). By permission of the British Library, London.

(Hydra) and vice, specifically avarice (Phineas), both together representing the great adversary of the human body or life on earth itself (Cerberus, the doorkeeper for Hades).

The emphasis on both Hercules and Orpheus as types of the wise and virtuous man probably derives specifically from the Boethius commentaries (the glosses on *Consolatio* 4 m7 and 3 m12), because neither Servius nor Fulgentius stresses the importance of these heroes as comparable to Aeneas. Bernard's commentary ends just as Aeneas and the Sibyl prepare to enter the gates of Elysium and the golden bough is placed on the threshold of the Cyclops' wall (the firmament) to suggest that greater or renewed mental energy is required for the contemplation of more heavenly matters.

Most of the figures, gods, and mythological personifications in Bernard represent one or more Neo-Stoic facets of the descents, primarily the virtuous or vicious, and with emphasis on the sixth book, although in that book there exist other figures with natural or physical significance (unrelated however to the natural descent).[17] The physical references occur mainly in the first and sixth books because of the natural and virtuous descents, except for one isolated literalistic reference to the Strophades as whirlpools in book 3 and to Mercury as a star in book 4. In the first book, after a Neo-Stoic analysis of Jupiter, the chief god, as fire and Juno as air or earth, with Neptune as god of the waters, Pluto as god of Erebus, Saturn as time and Ops as matter, Bernard thereafter uses Fulgentian etymologies to describe the physical regions through which the soul must pass as it descends, rather Neoplatonically, at birth into the underworld of its earthly home. In the last aerial region, its ruler Juno is also goddess of child-bearing; Aeolus, god of winds, means "world-destruction," and actually represents the child's birth; Juno's attendants are atmospheric effects or storms; Iris is the rainbow; Deiopea is atmospheric splendor; Venus is universal harmony; Mercury is a star and Apollo the sun; and then the soul reaches the sea, with Triton the sea-god and Cymothoë the sea-goddess.

Afterwards, in the sixth book, the earthly powers of generation are listed: the Fates represent generation (Clotho), variation (Lachesis), and corruption or death (Atropos); Cybele is the solid earth and Dis is the earth, while Ceres, Bacchus, and Pales all embody the earthly powers for producing grain, wine, and pastures. This hierarchy of the forces of air, sea, and earth mirrors that hierarchy found in the first book of Bernard's *Cosmographia*, entitled *Megacosmus*.[18] In addition, some figures in this book may also represent a more fallen version of those figures from the second book of the

Cosmographia, entitled *Microcosmus,* engaged in creating the body and soul of the First Man—the equivalents of Natura, Physis, Imarmene, and their helpers[19]—in Eurydice as natural concupiscence; Genius as the god of human nature; Triton as the annoyance of flesh; Cerberus the earth by which we enter the sublunary realm; and Caeneus or Caenis, son or daughter of birth.

Very few of the gods interpreted in conjunction with the vicious or virtuous descents appear prior to the sixth book, and those that do reflect some aspect of fallen human emotional growth without moral stigma or sanction.[20] Many allegorizations of vicious descents appear in the third book because adolescence marks a period of moral choice in its transition from infancy to maturity, even though the majority are included in that sixth book which explores Avernus ("without pleasure") and its jaw ("vanities"). With the "wandering sight" (Palinurus) of book 5, we descend into the underworld where we encounter "universal dread" (Deiphobe), "sadness" (Achilles), and "temporal glory" (Misenus). Numerous monsters mirror vice in the sixth book,[21] as various human characters from the *Aeneid* embody perversity.[22]

Bernard's interest in the systematization of education—the kind of description found in Hugh of St. Victor's *Didascalicon*—is certainly also reflected in his choice of Martianus's *De nuptiis* as a commentary text. Although the descents are not mentioned per se in his unfinished commentary, the glosses on individual gods and figures reveal his scholastic vision of the opportunities available to humankind desirous of emulating Philology's apotheosis.

II. THE VIRTUOUS DESCENT OF MERCURY
IN THE MARTIANUS COMMENTARY

Like Aeneas, Orpheus, and Theseus, among other heroes, in Bernard's interpretation of Martianus Capella's *De nuptiis,* Mercury, god of eloquence, performs the equivalent of a "virtuous descent," but instead of learning about the underworld, retrieving a lost wife, or abducting Pluto's wife, Mercury marries the mortal Philology. Once married, Mercury and Philology activate the heroic (demigod) ideal to which the individual should aspire in any "virtuous descent" that the educated man or woman might make. This idea of Mercury as hero of the virtuous descent underlies the actual ascents of Mercury (and others) both in the nine finished sections (in addition to preface and *accessus*) of Bernard's unfinished commentary on books 1 and 2 of Martianus (ca. 1130–50), which ends at *De nuptiis* paragraph 37,[23] that is, during the ascent of Mercury and Apollo to Jove, and also in the proposed but unfinished eight additional sections.[24] The ascents in the first two books, when compared with Bernard's sections, include, first, the initial ascent of Mercury through the heavens with Virtue to meet Apollo (section 6), the further ascent of both Mercury and Apollo to meet with Jupiter (section 8), the ascent of various gods summoned for the assembly of gods (unfinished section 11), and the ascent from earth for the marriage and subsequent apotheosis (a permanent "ascent") of Philology (unfinished sections 16 and 17). At the same time, the apotheosized Philology, immortalized, deified, by the end of the allegory, comes the closest to being "her own god," successor to the demigod Theseus, often interpreted as "wisdom"—and the immortal Pallas Athena, goddess of wisdom.

In this marriage of descents/ascents the very concept of a wedding also links the figurative virtuous "descent" with the literal natural descent. Assuming even greater importance than it has in William's draft mythography-commentary on Martianus, "marriage" primarily signifies *coniunctura,* the joining of wisdom and eloquence, but also of male and female, matter and spirit. "Marriage" as *coniunctura* provides a legitimate means of dealing with Original Sin—the urges of the flesh with which we are all born and which spark reproduction (and hence survival) of the species, but which simultaneously prick us toward those pleasures that lead to sin and the vicious descent.

In a brilliant (and rather original, at least for Bernard) interpretation of this symbolic concept of marriage, speech, "sermo," is construed as masculine, like Mercury, and explanation, reason, "ratio," as feminine, like Philology. When Mercury's semen inseminates Philology, then speech that contains scientific doctrine fertilizes understanding ("Filios quidem infuso semine gingnit Mercurius in Philologia, dum scientias doctrina collata format sermo in ratione nostra, unde ille masculino, hec feminino effertur vocabulo," Bern. Sil. *In Mart.* 2.42–46). Therefore the god of weddings, Hymen (chapter 3), catalyzes this joining of two disparate and different things, both things related to the microcosm's regeneration of the species. First, the god directs the sperm to the mother-to-be and thereafter guides the development of the child through the "seven cells" (equivalent, no doubt, to what was thought to be seven months of gestation). This represents what Bernard elsewhere (in the *Aeneid* commentary discussed in the previous section) terms the natural descent, or the fall of the soul into the flesh. For this reason, Hymen, as the World Soul, also governs the harmony, or music, of the spheres: we recall that in the Macrobian schema, the descending soul collects temperamental attributes from the various planetary spheres through which it passes on its way to the body and the moment of birth. Thus the regeneration of the microcosm intersects with the regenerating power of the macrocosm, or the World Soul. Bernard in fact invokes the passage on the World Soul from Boethius (*Consolatio* 2 m8), followed shortly by the famous Stoic discussion of God as having many dispositions, recited by Augustine in *De civitate Dei* (7.9.56–60). Jupiter, *Juris pater,* is the name of the one God; the names of the other gods reflect his individual and respective powers, that is, Apollo for wisdom, Bacchus for wine-producing, Ceres for seeds.

The genealogy of Hymen reflects what might be termed the integumental origin of the virtuous and natural descents in a cosmological equivalent of the Fall and introduction of Original Sin into the universe. That is, if the marriage of Mercury and Philology elevates the individual in a restoration equivalent to Christian conversion and the Resurrection of Christ on which it is based, then the flaw or crime it restores can be traced back mythologically to Hymen's origins, as can Christ to Adam and Eve and their Fall, or descent from grace—"vicious descent." Earlier, in the Vatican mythographers, the desire of Saturn (Chronos, Time) to murder his children, including Jupiter, has suggested the power of indefatigable mutability in the world; the castration of Saturn by Jupiter (Prime Mover, Aether, etc.) resulted in one means of defeating the inexorability of time, that is, sexual desire leading to reproduction (Venus). But this mythological cycle of destruction/reconstruction lacks any moral equivalent of Christian redemption. Hymen, as god of marriage, in Bernard's commentary on Martianus provides this equivalent: he is in one version of the myth the son of Venus and Bacchus.

Bacchus is understood in Bernard anagogically as divine love, "divinus amor," and Hymen, god of marriage, as "concordia" that is produced when plurality marries divine love "Bacus vero in Venere Himeneum gingnit, dum divinus amor in rerum pluralitate concordiam facit. Concordia enim est actus divini spiritus, quem suscipit rerum pluralitas, neque aliter esset concordia nisi et Cipris dissona misceret et Bacus ea uniret" ["Bacchus begets Hymen with Venus, when divine love creates concord in a plurality of things. Concord indeed is an act of the divine spirit, which the plurality of things receives and concord is nothing else than that Cypris commingles dissonant things and Bacchus unites them"] (Bern. Sil. *In Mart.* 3.251–

60). Thus harmony, or concord, replaces difference with consensus because of divine will—Hymen comes from Venus (difference) and Bacchus (divine will, love)—"Unde diffinitur concordia dissentientium consensus. Dissensus ergo a Cipride, consensus a Baco" ["Whence concord is defined as the agreement of those who disagree. Disagreement therefore from Cypris, agreement from Bacchus"] (3.259–60).

Drawing most likely on William's Macrobius glosses, Bernard adds to this anagogical interpretation of Bacchus an allegorical interpretation, as World Soul, and a tropological interpretation, as the individual soul. That is, in relation to the anagogical interpretation, Bacchus (divine spirit, will) is the brother of Apollo, and both are sons of Jupiter and human mothers: Apollo (wisdom), as Latona's son represents what might be termed the more rationally directed son of the two ("duos filios maiores Iovis, Apollinem et Bacum, id est divinam sapientiam et voluntatem," Bern. Sil. *In Mart.* 3.221–4). In relation to the allegorical interpretation, Bacchus, "insania," is the son of Semele and signifies the World Soul as the wine-producing (and terrestrial) natural power: "Bacus autem insania interpretatur, quod nomen in omnibus figuris secundum sensuales congruit, quia ipsi vino et opulentia insaniunt" ["Bacchus, moreoever, is interpreted as madness, for the name corresponds in all figures in accordance with the sensual people, because they are maddened by wine and opulence"]. In relation to the tropological interpetation, Bacchus, the individual soul, is first torn apart by Giants, our bodies ("gegantes," begotten on earth, specifically, the Giant Briseus who fought the gods) and then lifted up to heaven by the winnowing fan—the tripartite soul, or imagination, reason, and memory—understood as earthly wealth (3.175–225).

On the anagogical level, Venus or Cypris, mother of Hymen, as the plurality of things ("ad pluralitatem rerum"), represents material and natural plenitude, or difference, whether "the qualities of the seasons, the humors of the body, or the faculties of the soul," and is called "Cypris," "because she is interpreted as a mixture" (In mundo enim est pluralitas elementorum, in temporibus qualitatum, in corporibus humorum, in animis potentiarum. Huic figure convenit nomen Cipridis, quod mixture interpretatio est," Bern. Sil. *In Mart.* 3.251–5). In other words, she is nature's plenitude, organized into the hierarchy of the "fair chain of love," or the Great Chain of Being, familiar to us from Lucretius's *De rerum naturae*, Macrobius's commentary on the *Somnium Scipionis,* and Boethius's *De consolatione Philosophiae.*

But Bernard connects Venus, cosmic plurality and mother of the god of marriage, with the heroic journey or descent of Aeneas on which the interpretations of other "descents" and journeys is based. In a long peroration on the goddess, Bernard actually begins with her role in the *Aeneid* as goddess-mother of Hymen's half-brother, the mortal hero Aeneas. As a star ("ad stellam"), Anchises's lover lights the way for her son journeying from Troy to Italy, "Matre dea monstrante viam," "My mother goddess pointing me the way" (*Aeneid* 1.382); "Ad stellam, ut in Virgilio habes Venerem presentem Enee semper dum exulat quia, ut ait Varro, ex quo recessit Eneas a Troia, donec ad Laurentem agrum veniret, stellam Veneriam semper videri. Unde in discessu legitur: 'Iamque iugis summe surgebat Lucifer Ide.' Et alibi: 'Matre dea monstrante viam' " ["To a star, as in Virgil you have Venus always appearing to Aeneas when he is in exile because, so says Varro, from that time when Aeneas retreated from Troy until he arrived at the Laurentine fields, the star of Venus is always to be seen. Whence in the departure is read, 'and now above Ida's topmost ridges the day-star was rising.' And elsewhere: 'My mother goddess pointing me the way"] (Bern. Sil. *In Mart.* 3.226–60—the second Virgil line, from *Aeneid* 2.801).

Allegorically Venus as the daughter of Saturn who sprang from the sea, or rather from the severed testicles of Saturn, also functions as earthly beauty and natural fertility ("ad pulcritudinem terre"), in other words the product of Jupiter's castration of the earth's heat and moisture, or Saturn's virility, because both are subject to time: "Ad secundam figuram respicit quod Venus nata est de testiculis Saturni, quia terre pulcritudo habet esse ex calore et humore, que sunt Saturni virilia, quia his agit tempus. Set melius ad tertiam. Iupiter enim pudenda Saturni abscindit, dum mundus calorem et humorem a tempore rapit. Hoc autem est in autumpno, quia hoc tempus nec calidum <nec humidum>, cum contrarias habeat naturas" ["As to the second figure, it means that Venus was born from the testicles of Saturn, because the beauty of earth is considered to be from heat and moisture, which are the manly organ of Saturn, because with these he governs time. But better to the third {figure}. Jupiter indeed cuts off the genitals of Saturn, when the world seizes the heat and moisture from time. This moreover exists in autumn, because this period of time is neither warm nor moist, when it has contrary natures"] (Bern. Sil. *In Mart.* 3.235–41).

Tropologically, if the castration of Saturn resulted in earthly division, limitation, finitude and mutability, then Venus "ad voluptatem carnis," also represents that spark of desire that will promote reproduction of the species, the renaturing of human nature. But to love, one's stomach must be full—survival precedes reproduction, and the restocking of natural goods, for purposes of life, is a necessity prior to creation of progeny. Linked with Ceres and Bacchus (Liber) in the citation of Terence's *Eunuchus* 732, "Without Ceres [bread] and Liber [wine], Venus [lovemaking, love] grows cold," "Ex his Venus nascitur dum voluptas carnis inde concitatur: 'Sine Cerere,' enim 'et Libero friget Venus.' Exigit enim natura ut stomacus per membrum proximum et subditum purgetur" ["From these Venus is born, when the pleasure of the flesh is then aroused: 'Without Ceres and Liber Venus grows cold.' For Nature demands that the stomach be purged by the member which is nearest and under it"] (Bern. Sil. *In Mart.* 3.245–247),[25] she is "Nuda pingitur vel quia crimen libidinis minime celatur vel quia consilium nudat libido" ["depicted as nude either because the crime of lust is not concealed or because lust lays bare its intent"] (3.248–50).

A more fully developed conception appears in the *De planctu Naturae* of Alan of Lille, where Venus figures as the handmaiden of Nature responsible for the regeneration of the created world and of humankind in particular, the relationship between them enhanced by that familiar twelfth-century plane of correspondence between macrocosm and microcosm. In the *De planctu*, Venus is Nature's sub-vicar who, along with her husband Hymen and son Cupid (desire), figuratively uses her anvil to hammer out new living things and her writing pen to trace properly the classes of things according to the rules of Nature's "orthography." Nature is "vicar of God" who is depicted as a coiner stamping out copies of all things from the original; her priest Genius as god of human nature is depicted as a scribe who with his pen and parchment maintains human reproduction and also the idea of humankind as a rational animal.[26]

Note that Bernard in his allegory of the figure of Hymen extends and embroiders his genealogy and his posterity: Venus, daughter of Saturn, joins with Bacchus, son of Jupiter and Semele, to produce Hymen, one of six children (along with the three Graces, Jocus, and Cupid). Bernard later allegorizes these children as representing the five grades of love:

Quos arbitror esse illos quinque gradus amoris, quod comprehendit versus iste:
    Visus et alloquium, contactus et oscular, factum.

Ultimi mares leguntur, eo quod plus vigoris habeant. . . . Causa ergo est voluptas Ioci, id est delectationis que est in osculis, et Cupidinis, id est coitus, et Himenei, id est nuptiarum. Magna autem cure est Iocus voluptati nostre, major coitus, maxime nuptie.

[Those are believed to be the five stages of love, which this verse sums up: "Sight and speech, touch and kiss, act." The last are considered male, because they have more vigor. . . The cause is the pleasure of Sport, that is, of the pleasure which exists in the kiss, and of Cupid, that is, in sexual intercourse, and of Hymen, that is, in weddings. Of great concern, however, our desire is Jocus {Play}, greater still, coitus, the greatest, marriage.] (Bern. Sil. *In. Mart.* 3.813–40, my trans.)

The latter two, Jocus and Hymen, had appeared previously in the *De planctu* of Alan, sons respectively of Antigamus (Antigenius) and Hymen. In that prosimetrum, Venus, already mother of Cupid by Hymen (her husband, not her son as in Martianus and his commentators), commits adultery with Antigamus ("anti-marriage," denoting "unnatural," non-propagative, sexual relationships such as homosexuality or courtly love), also called Antigenius ("anti-Genius," denoting the antithesis of Genius, the priest of Nature and god of human Nature, or agent of sexual reproduction, in the mythographies).[27] Alan's allegory suggests that Venus, human sexuality, when coupled with the intention not to reproduce, engenders the bastard "Sport," meaning "Game," "Play."

Dyone igitur duo dati sunt filii, discrepantia generis disparati, nascendi lege dissimiles, morum titulis discrepantes, artificii disparitate difformes. Ymeneus namque uterine fraternitatis michi affinis confinio, quem excellentioris dignitatis extollit prosapia, ex Venere sibi Cupidinem propagauit in filium. Antigenius uero, scurrilis ignobilitatis genere deriuatus, adulterando adulterinum filium Iocum sibi ioculatorie parentauit. . . . Ille albis inargentatos nitoribus argenteos fontes inhabitat. Iste loca perhenni ariditate dampnata indefesse concelebrat. Iste in deserta planicie figit tentoria. Illi uallis complacet nemorosa.

[Two sons were given, then, to Dione's daughter, different by discrepancy of origin, dissimilar by law of birth, unlike in their moral reputation, different by diversity of skill. Hymenaeus is closely related to me by the bond of brotherhood from the same mother and a lineage of outstanding merit gives him an exalted position. He

begat from Venus a son, Desire. On the other hand the buffoonish
Antigenius, sprung from an ignoble line, in rakish fashion fathered,
in adultery with Venus, a bastard son, Sport. . . . The former dwells by
the silvery fountains, bright with their besilvered sheens; the latter
tirelessly haunts places cursed with unending drought. The latter
pitches his tent in flat wastelands; the former finds his happiness in
sylvan glades.][28]

We can in effect use Bernard's allegory of marriage in the commentary
to gloss Alan's *integumentum,* or we can use Alan's allegory to refract back on
Bernard. Basically for both writers marriage casts a sanctifying and
sacramental grace on sexual unions, demonstrated by the yoking of Venus
and Hymen (Alan), or by the child of Venus and Bacchus, Hymen
(Bernard). Its absence confers a damning sterility on sexual play and union,
demonstrated by Venus and Antigenius (Alan), or the other child of Venus
and Bacchus, Jocus, or Sport, and to a certain extent Cupid (Bernard). Alan
contrasts the seriousness of the coupling of Venus and Hymen with that
frivolous coupling of Venus and Antigenius, "Illius natiuitatem matrimo-
nii excusat sollempnitas. Istius propaginem diuulgati concubinatus accusat
uulgaritus" ["The former's birth finds its defence in a solemnised marriage,
the commonness of a commonly-known concubinage arraigns the latter's
descent"] (trans. Sheridan, p. 165; ed. Häring, pp. 155–156). Clearly the
tone of the union, as in animal pedigrees, is determined by the father and
reflected by the moral character of the son. The ignoble union of Venus and
Antigenius results in an illegitimate son who "loca perhenni ariditate
dampnata indefesse concelebrat" ["tirelessly haunts places cursed with
unending drought"].[29]

Bernard's (and Alan's) family of classical gods headed by Venus and
Bacchus (or Venus and Hymen) seems to allegorize the workings of the
Stoic cosmic generative seed, also known as the *anima mundi.* It is no
accident that Bernard inserts a discussion of these seed shortly following
his long gloss on Venus. Bernard invokes Plato's *Timaeus* (through Calcidius's commentary) to define *semina* as the beginnings of all things, the four
elements, the seasons, the humors of the body, and the body and the soul of
men: "Anima enim terre, carni scilicet, ad tempus committitur et cum
augmento virtutis et meriti recipitur. Unde in *Thimeo:* 'Huius universi
generis sementem faciam animam' " ["The soul, indeed, is entrusted to
earth, that is, the flesh, for a time, and is received with an increase of virtue

and merit. Whereas in the *Timaeus:* 'Of this universal race I shall make the soul the crop' "] (Bern. Sil. *In Mart.* 3.303–7).

Perhaps because of this natural and physical allegory witnessed in the fabulous theogony of the commentary on *De nuptiis,* Bernard also comments on Tiresias, whom we have seen previously in the Erfurt commentary on Boethius (*Consolatio* 5 p3). Here Tiresias signifies what might be considered a type of Saturn on earth, or *mundana perhennitas*—literally, worldly perpetuity, but more likely the enduring perennial cycle that governs and regulates the seasons. Specifically, for Bernard as for the Erfurt Commentator and Fulgentius before him, Tiresias's drama of changed sexes comes to represent an allegory of the changing seasons. Because Tiresias has been blinded by Juno for his revelation that women enjoy sex more than men (although granted divinity for his answer by Jupiter), his "ridiculous prophecy," as Boethius terms it, the ambivalent "Whatever I say will either happen or not" is linked to his ambivalent sexuality, both male and female. Even in Fulgentius, for this reason Tiresias is associated with the double-faced month of January, which, looking backward to the past and forward to the future, sums up the year's changes (Fulgentius may have derived this connection from Macrobius's *Saturnalia* 1.9.4, in which, we recall, Janus was a four-fold god whose control over celestial portals amounts to the changing of the seasons). For Fulgentius Tiresias signifies the Stoic "allegory of time," "in modum temporis,"

> quasi teroseon id est aestiua perennitas. Ergo ex uerno tempore, quod masculinum est quia eodem tempore clusura soliditasque est germinum, dum coeuntia sibi adfectu animalia uiderit eaque uirga id est feruoris aestu percusserit, in femineum sexum conuertitur, id est in aestatis feruorem. Ideo uero aestatem in modum posuerunt feminae, quod omnia patefacta eodem tempore suis emergant folliculis. Et quia duo concipiendi sunt tempora, ueris et autumni, iterum conceptu prohibito ad pristinam redit imaginem. . . . Denique duobus diis id est duobus elementis arbiter quaeritur, igni atque aeri, de genuina amoris ratione certantibus. Denique iustum proferat iudicium; in fructificandis enim germinibus dupla aeri quam igni materia suppetit; aer enim et maritat in glebis et producit in foliis et grauidat in folliculis, sol uero maturare tantum nouit in granis. Nam, ut hoc certum sit, cecatur etiam a Iunone, illa uidelicet causa, quod hiemis tempus aeris nubilo caligante nigrescat, Iuppiter uero occultis uapor-

ibus conceptionalem factum ei futuri germinis subministrat, id est quasi praescientiam.

[an allegory of time, as for *teroseon,* that is perpetual summer. Thus in springtime, which is masculine because at that season there is a closing and immovability of plants, when he saw the creatures coupling with passion and struck at them with his staff—that is, with the heat of ardor, he is turned into the feminine gender, that is, into the heat of summer. They took summer to be in the form of a woman because at that season all things blossom forth with their leaves. And because there are two seasons for mating, spring and autumn, having stopped their conceiving he returned again to his former appearance. ... Then he is sought as a judge between the two divinities—that is, the two elements, fire and air—as they argue on the true meaning of love. He gives an honest judgment, for in the blossoming of plants twice the amount of air as of fire is required; for air combines with the soil and helps produce the leaves and impregnate the shoots, but the sun serves only to ripen the grain. In proof of this, he is blinded by Juno, for the reason that wintertime grows black with dark clouds in the air, but Jove assists with the conceiving of future growth by hidden vapors, that is foresight; for this reason January is depicted with two faces, so that it can see both what is past and what is to come.] (*Mit.* 2.5)

Bernard's more closely Stoicized version deletes the month of January (he discusses Janus in this Macrobian way later, however, in 5.840–73) and the whole issue of foreknowledge so important to the Erfurt commentator, and instead focuses on the cosmic conflict between Jupiter and Juno, or the two sexes, as a battle between the elements (or regions) of fire and air. The seventh year of Tiresias's changed sexuality becomes equivalent, for Bernard, to the seventh month of gestation, or the seventh month of the year (September), the month of Mars, or the beginning of autumn. The separation of the two serpents by means of Tiresias's rod signifies the coming of winter and the cold that will induce sterility. Bernard's idea became very influential: his interpretation, according to Westra's notes, is also found in Arnulf of Orleans on the *Metamorphoses* 3.4; the third Vatican mythographer 169; and Neckam's commentary on Martianus (Digby manuscript 221, fols. 39vb–40va; Bern. Sil. *In Mart.*, p. 67n). The twinning of Tiresias is followed, appropriately, by the next mythographic gloss, on the twins Pollux and Castor, again an incarnation of the human spirit incarcerated in flesh.

Bernard takes care to explain the matings of the other cosmic gods as Stoic (and thereafter physical) allegory (5.7–18). In his second important section of the commentary devoted to mythographic exegesis, "On the Wives of the Gods," Bernard interprets the union of Jupiter and Juno as the joining of fire and air, Oceanus and Thetis as water and earth, Apollo and Clymene as heat and wetness, and Pluto and Persephone as earth and moon. This proper and natural joining of elements, "elementorum iunctura," is distinguished from the adultery of other figures, which is punished by damnation in the underworld, or else monstrous and unnatural progeny such as Hermaphroditus and the Centaurs. Here Bernard points to Tityus and Latona, Tantalus and Juno, Aleus and Terra, Mercury and Venus, Ixion and Juno.

With one stroke of the pen, Bernard successfully relates two different mythographic traditions: the Stoic concept of mythographic genealogy (or theogony), in the natural mating of the gods, and the Neo-Platonic descent into the underworld, in which the classical damned represent the vices which the armed soul should learn from and avoid. Indeed, in conjoining to this the unnatural and monstrous couplings of the gods, such as Mercury and Venus, or Ixion and Juno, which result in strange progeny, he ties together much of the mythological genealogy found in the first two Vatican mythographers.

His ingenuity as an assimilator and synthesizer also operates on the system of Boethian descents into the underworld, which, in this later commentary, he combines with what appears to be Aristotelian science (via Boethius's *Liber de persona et duabus naturis contra Eutychen et Nestorium* 6), to amplify (not surprisingly) the natural descent into the body experienced by different classes of being. He begins from a theological stance: "Inferos primi theologi humana corpora dixerunt quia in ordine nature nil inferius invenerunt" ["The first theologians called the human body an underworld because in the order of nature they found nothing lower"] (Bern. Sil., *In Mart.* 5.633–4, p. 115). Because the rational soul is immortal but the body subject to mutability, the way the two converge at birth and separate at death is complex and interesting, largely because of the celestial origin of the soul and the earthly origin of the body. By necessity the arrival of spirit in the human body involves a "fall," or descent to the earthly. But there are four kinds of bodies:

Caducorum autem alia animata, alia inanimata. Animatorum alia animata et sensibilia, alia autem animata et insensibilia. Sensibilium alia vegetata anima rationali, alia non. Habes ergo hec quatuor genera caducorum corporum: inanimata ut lapis, animata tantum ut arbor; animata et sensibilia tantum ut aliquod brutum animal; animalia et sensibilia et vegetata anima rationali sunt humana.

[Of the perishable {bodies}, some are animate, some inanimate. . . Of the animate, some are animate and capable of sensation, others animate and without sensation. Of those with sensation, some are livened by a rational soul, others not. You have, then, four kinds of perishable bodies: inanimate, like a stone; merely animate, like a tree; animate and sensate only, like a brute animal; animate and sensate and livened by a rational soul, human beings.] (Bern. Sil., *In Mart.* 5.643–49, p. 115).

Most interesting, having categorized the natural descent in terms of the Great Chain of Being, Bernard then relates the Great Chain of Being (stones, plants, animals, humans) to the second part of the world, the realm of the sublunary underworld ruled by Pluto and Proserpina (earth and moon, we recall) in which all embodied beings, such as birds, fish, animals, trees, and plants, are believed to live because of the requisite air, water, and sustenance ("quia ibi corporibus exute vivere creduntur; sublunarem vero regionem, cuius omnia animantia caduca sunt, inferos dixerunt. Huius reges sunt Pluto et Proserpina quia eius termini sunt terra et luna, quarum efficatia in hac mundi parte maior est," Bern. Sil., *In Mart.* 5.660–7, p. 116). Bernard then bolsters this unusual convergence of glosses from different traditions by the now conventional interpretation of Pluto, earth, as riches (found in Boethius in 3 m10.13–14); Proserpina, the moon, as "iuxta serpentem," her abduction by Pluto explained as the effect on her of the earth's gravitational pull; and her mother Ceres, as if "res creantem," "creating things," as the humors, the earth mother, *materia.* The explanation derives in part from William's glosses on Macrobius.[30]

Nor does he slight either the other regions, or the other paired cosmic gods—Neptune and Amphitrite, or Thetis in a definition borrowed from William's glosses on the *Timaeus;* Saturn and Ops; Cybele; Janus and the Argive; Isis and Osiris; and of course Mercury and his own search for a wife. In most of these cases Bernard painstakingly interweaves the glosses collected from a variety of contemporary and by now familiar sources to present a convincingly coherent web of natural allegorization.

He also provides, in section 6, a long Neo-Stoic and Neoplatonic fourfold gloss on Vulcan as cosmic fire, the human soul, wrath, and *ingenium*, followed by a long gloss on his wife Venus as that desire of the flesh with which we are born, Original Sin (Bern. Sil., *In Mart.* 6.810–81, 6.888–955, pp. 156–60; see figure 30, of Venus, Vulcan, Graces, Cupid, and others). It is perhaps limiting to argue that Vulcan "is imagination, or *concupiscentia* in a complex sense, at once *ingenium* and *vis ignita,* a link between the physical and mental levels of *conceptus rerum*" or related in particular to the classical concept of "genius,"[31] which came from a different philosophical and religious tradition altogether. As usual, Bernard relates the four different significations to the different myths in which Vulcan figures. Vulcan represents cosmic fire because he is son of Jupiter (aether) and Juno (air). In another sense he is "our soul" ("Animus autem noster dicitur Vulcanus") as son of Jupiter and Juno "quia opus Dei est," "because it is the work of God" (6.824–26, p. 156). As the human soul he sums up the faculties of "innate *ingenium*" (instinct? memory?), or "vis naturalis omnia concipiendi; rationem que naturalis est potentia omnia discernendi; memoriam que est vis nature omnia retinendi" ["the natural ability for apprehending everything; reason, or the natural power for discerning everything; and memory, or the power of nature for retaining everything"] (Bern. Sil., *In Mart.*, 6.830–2, p. 156). When he attempts to copulate with Minerva and his falling seed engenders Erichthonius, he signifies "voluntatis calorem" ("the heat of will," hence, wrath, Bern. Sil., *In Mart.* 6.850, p. 157). Finally, he represents *ingenium* from the etymology of his name, "quasi volicanum, quia semper esse in discursu dicunt," as if "volicanus," because "always said to exist in running about" (Bern. Sil., *In Mart.* 6.869–70, p. 157).

Elsewhere in the commentary Bernard will Boethianize his Martianus commentary—that is, draw on glosses from William's Boethius, often repeated in his own *Aeneid* commentary, then reintroduced into the glosses on Martianus's text. The originally Fulgentian Stoic interpretation of Peleus and Thetis as the union of earth and water, with their son Achilles as a type of first man (Bern. Sil., *In Mart.* 6.660–73, p. 151), is especially appealing to this cosmographer who would allegorize the creation of the first man in part 2, "Microcosmus," of his *Cosmographia.* This allegorization is quickly followed by the interpretation of the three goddesses judged by Paris (or *sensus*) as the theoretical, practical, and voluptuous lives. Of course William of Conches, in the Boethius glosses, inserted this within the passage on *Consolatio* 3 m12 (Orpheus's descent into the underworld and

30. Venus, Vulcan, Graces, Cupid; Mercury, Argus. Preceding *Exposicio fabularum 15 librorum Ovidii Metamorphoseos*. MS. Rawlinson B. 214, fol. 198v (ca. 1450, English). By permission of the Bodleian Library, University of Oxford.

the description of its inhabitants, chiefly Ixion, who desired Juno), and in the Florentine Commentary on Martianus, in what he understood as the "Judgment of Hercules." Rather interestingly, Bernard here relates these three lives to the active and contemplative lives as represented by Lia and Rachel (Bern. Sil., *In Mart.* 6.699–702, p. 152)—in a passage that will be reinserted, in the fifteenth century, in a commentary on the *Aeneid* by Cristoforo Landino.

The interweaving of one commentary tradition with another, the flux of

Neoplatonic and Neo-Stoic glosses even within one commentary, should convince us that medieval mythography was not in fact static, but fluid, animate, having its own existence separate from the commentaries in which it (for the most part) lived and breathed. Even within the same commentary, once the commentator understands this separate existence of the tradition, he will re-introduce the same interpretations whenever an opportunity arises (Rachel and Lia reappear in Bernard's Martianus commentary, 10.310–24, p. 234, and so do Pollux and Castor, themselves related to the contemplative and active lives, in 10.478–90, p. 240).

Indeed, Bernard introduces what might be understood as Ovidian mythography in a section on metamorphosis that zeroes in on the twins Pollux and Castor (born from one of the three eggs produced by the union of Jupiter and Leda, immortal and mortal). The twins are normally glossed in commentaries on Virgil (as in fact Bernard acknowledges about his own, *In Mart.* 3.624, p. 69, and *Sup. En.* 6.121, pp. 55–56) as figures for the human soul and body. Although Ovid received the greatest attention from other twelfth, thirteenth, and fourteenth-century mythographers and commentators, the later passage is important for what it tells us about seepage from yet another tradition, one we have barely discussed in this volume because so incipient. Nevertheless, it fits into this commentary on Martianus, laden as it is with glosses from other commentary traditions, because it hinges on the concept of *descensus* and *ascensus* so important in structuring passage between the mortal or earthly and the infernal or otherworldly, or, conversely, the divine or supernal and the mortal or earthly.

Bernard, interested in the way humans becomes beasts, or gods, draws on the idea of metamorphosis to distinguish descent into bestiality from ascent to divinity: "Set quia duas esse metamorphoses monstravimus, unam de homine in bestiam, alteram de homine in deum, et prima pulchriorem non efficit, ut excludatur prima et intelligatur altera, additur: *sive per Geminos*" ["But because we have shown that there are two metamorphoses, one from human into beast, the other from human into god, and the first does not make him more beautiful, so that the first is excluded and the second understood, is added: 'or if through twins' "] (Bern. Sil., *In Mart.* 10.470–3, p. 240). These of course are the twins Pollux and Castor, one mortal, one a god; as sons of Leda, or "the zeal for knowing," or *invidia,* they also represent respectively "perditio," or "loss," and extreme evil. Because their mother Leda signifies the human mind desiring happiness in the zeal for good, then Jupiter has begotten, by means of the love of God, Pollux, the contemplative life, and by means of carnal love, Castor, the active life. Most significantly, because of the foreshadowing of Philology's ultimate apotheosis, Bernard notes that, "Castori Pollux confert deitatem, quia accio ad contemplationem transiens assequitur immortalitatem" ["On Castor Pollux confers deity, because action passing over to contemplation acquires immortality"] (Bern. Sil., *In Mart.* 10.488–90, p. 240).

CONCLUSION: VIRGIL AND MARTIANUS
IN THE *AETAS OVIDIANA*

Although commentaries on Virgil and Martianus after the twelfth century would not enjoy the considerable influence of past centuries, the influence of the system of descents on later allegorical treatments of Aeneas and the epic journeys of the hero would continue. Aeneas came to be moralized as a type either of the passionate and self-indulgent youth or of a wise and rational man capable of controlling his excesses, the view depending on whether the hero was seen as a Trojan (and therefore self-indulgent, according to John of Salisbury) or as an Italian (and therefore wise and rational, according to Dante and Petrarch). By the fourteenth and fifteenth centuries, however, both views of Aeneas would be incorporated into an extensive allegorization of his life as expressed through his journeys. Cristoforo Landino would see the tripartite journeys as representative of three phases of Aeneas's life, each controlled by a different goddess (Venus, Juno, Minerva) and each reflective of one of the three lives (Troy, voluptuous life; Carthage, active life; and Italy, contemplative life). It is possible to see Landino's three lives as a reworking of the vicious and virtuous descents.

Even in the twelfth century the ages of man associated with Virgil's journey would reappear in new contexts—Virgilized readings of Martianus, for example, as in Alexander Neckam's commentary. The long history of Virgil commentary up to the fourteenth century reveals a major contribution to the evolution of medieval mythography in its use of the simile of the life journey and the descent into the underworld. Because of the medieval emphasis on the fourth and sixth books of the *Aeneid,* the one book, with the liaison between Aeneas and Dido, and the other book, with the descent into the underworld, figures from the *Aeneid* (and indeed the whole of the epic) were interpreted tropologically (the Neo-Stoic natural or physical allegories of Bernard not making much headway), and classical mythology in general was rationalized because of its particular association with that sixth book involving the underworld. Too, in the examples of

John of Salisbury and Alexander Neckam we can see the major mythographic influence of the *Ecloga Theoduli* making an impression: beginning with this work, it became imperative for mythographers to juxtapose the classical with the biblical, which led ultimately to the fourteenth-century allegories of Pierre Bersuire and Robert Holkot in a similar mode, the classical myth viewed as fable covering Christian and biblical truth. More important, classical fable and epic became worthy of Christian (rather than Neoplatonic) attention.

Preferring the vicious descent to Bernard's emphasis on the virtuous descent, his followers John of Salisbury and Alexander Neckam condense and use the commentary on the *Aeneid* for their own mythographic purposes. Indebted to Bernard particularly for the use of etymologies and the concept of philosophy and truth hidden by arcana,[32] John of Salisbury contrasts classical exemplars of the vices with biblical exemplars of the virtues in the manner of the *Ecloga Theoduli* but with a more directly moralistic and polemical purpose, and he emphasizes Original Sin and the necessity for the exercise of individual will throughout. His moralized glosses on Virgil appear throughout the *Policraticus,* with his most important and influential moralization centered on the structure of the *Aeneid.*[33] In accord with his highly moralistic purpose in seeking to reprove paganism and enhance Christianity, John denigrates judgmentally the Romans, Trojans, pagan gods, and even Aeneas. Perhaps also for this reason he rarely allegorizes his various myths overall, as if to diminish their importance.

John's interest in classical mythology was probably prompted by study of the arts for three years, until the end of 1141, under William of Conches (himself a pupil of Bernard of Chartres and with whose writings Bernard Silvestris was familiar).[34] John's fondness for referring to classical poets was probably produced by his excellent memory of school training in Virgil, Lucan, Statius, Ovid, the satirists, and Boethius's *Consolatio.*[35] But his background also included theological and administrative preparation: he later began study in Paris with Gilbert de la Porrée, and, after working some years as a papal clerk and in the papal chancery (1147–53), he then became secretary to Theobald of Canterbury, the Archbishop, in 1153.

Given this grammatical and administrative background, John's writings rather appropriately embrace the defense of the trivium in the *Metalogicon* and statesmanship and philosophy in the *Policraticus,* both finished in 1160 after he had been accused of slander.[36] The latter work, which was dedicated to Thomas à Becket, sprang from Becket's advice to write down a complaint about the unrelability of fortune and therefore John addresses the Muses à la Boethius. In his *Policraticus* John also includes glosses on Virgil which no doubt reflect the current scholastic practice of rationalization of mendacious classical fable by means of analysis of underlying poetic truth. John refers to this double level, psychological and spiritual meaning covered up by the literal, when he adds to a gloss on book 6 of the *Aeneid* the explanation, "Constat enim apud eos qui mentem diligentius perscrutantur auctorum Maronem geminae doctrinae uires declarasse, dum uanitate figmenti poetici philosophicae uirtutis inuoluit archana" ["it is agreed by those who devote their activities to the investigation of the meaning of authors that Virgil has evinced his power in a double field by arraying the mysteries of philosophic moral perfection in the gossamer of poetic fancy," translated more literally, "by enveloping the secrets of philosophic virtue with the vanity of poetic figment"] (*Policraticus* 8.24, ed. Webb, 2:817–818, trans. Pike, p. 404).

The key to his allegorization of the *Aeneid* is the fourth book, evidence of his clear dissimilarity from Bernard. The book does not parallel youth, as in Bernard, but the crucial advent of manhood itself, to show that relinquishing Dido means attaining reason and hence manhood, just as it also means giving up youth and its childish or vicious practices: "Ergo et uirilis etas puerilia et iuuenilia erubescit et, si a peruersa uoluptate et immundo amore nauigii sui soluere non potest anchoram, praecidit et funem" ["Therefore mature manhood blushes at childish things, and if one has not power to weigh anchor and flee from perverted pleasure and impure love, he will sever the cable"] (*Policraticus* 8.24, ed. Webb 2:817c–d, trans Pike, p. 404). Here Aeneas's liaison with Dido represents for John a lapse from reason and hence a wallowing in the pleasures of hunting, lechery, and gluttony.

Other references to the fourth book and Dido's affair with Aeneas support John's tropological interpretation of it as symbolic of the pastimes of non-rational—one might say even effeminate—youth, in its manifestation of venery and gluttony. As an example of the evils of hunting John cites the passage from the *Aeneid* when Aeneas and Dido consummate their union while the others hunt (4.160ff). Symbolically, this suggests for John the correspondence between the "soft" and the "hard" hunt (the former especially pejorative because of the lovers' hidden and dark arbor away from the "light"). This secrecy "possibly happened because such a pursuit, owing to its consciousness of guilt, [*conscientia turpitudinis*], shuns the light, while the joy of lawful wedding is illumined by the fire of hymeneal torches" (*Policraticus* 1.4, trans. Pike p. 14). Earlier in this discussion of hunting John has characterized the sport as self-indulgent and vicious, presided over by a goddess (Artemis) instead of a god because such a role might degrade him ("Et forte deam uenatoribus praeferunt, quia mollitie hac uel malitia deos suos noluerint infamare," 1.4, ed. Webb, 1:391). Artemis transformed Actaeon into a stag after he had seen her naked, which resulted in his being chased and killed by his own dogs; Artemis reminds John of Venus, the huntress who mourned Adonis's death by a boar. Clearly hunting leads to death and bestiality, whether viewed literally or figuratively. In contrast to the hunter using the sport for his own ends is the heroic hunter who uses it to aid others—Hercules, who captured the Arcadian deer (in *Aeneid* 6.802–4). This act seems justified to John because Hercules sought "non uoluptati suae, sed publicae prospexit utilitati" (1.4, ed. Webb, 1:391), that is, sought not his own pleasure but public good, just as Aeneas killed seven stags not to boost his own vanity but to keep his followers (and his race) alive. Most hunters share the character of the Centaur Chiron, who taught both Achilles and Bacchus to hunt: by hunting man loses his "desirable" humanity and in his conduct takes on bestial characteristics to become a monster: "A leuitate siquidem ad lasciuiam, a lasciuia ad uoluptatem, et cum induruerint, ad flagitia et quaeuis illicita pertrahuntur" ["From levity to lewdness, from lewdness to lust, and finally, when hardened, they are drawn into every type of infamy and lawlessness"] (1.4, ed. Webb, 1:393d, trans. Pike, p. 18). The soft and hard hunts, witnessed in the fourth book of the *Aeneid,* demonstrate the loss of reason in all its manifestations—whether levity, lust, lewdness or infamy and lawlessness—discussed by John.

John adds to the crimes of the soft hunt lechery and intemperance, drawn from his contrast of Dido's extravagant feast for Aeneas (in the fourth book of the *Aeneid*) with that frugal dinner set by king Evander for him (in the eighth book of the *Aeneid*), in a section devoted to feasting and drinking (*Policraticus* 8.6). In general all the references to the fourth book and specifically to Dido, whether in regard to her actual love for Aeneas, her feast for him, or their affair, are characterized by a stress on immoderation, vice, and Aeneas's loss of reason. John may have been influenced here by Macrobius's *Saturnalia* rather than Servius.[37] That is, John applauds Iopas's learned and philosophic songs at Dido's feast (*Aeneid* 1.723–49), because song edifies and instructs the reason, whereas he damns Dido's behavior, because—to continue the feasting metaphor—"the infatuated queen's soul drank in long draughts of inevitable and fatal love, which the philosopher [Aristotle] defines as passionate desire for union" (*Policraticus* 8.6, trans. Pike, p. 323). Evander's feast, frugal and sedate, seems the

opposite: appetite remains only frugally satisfied rather than sated because
there is serious business to conduct: "Plausum conuiuii uarius sermo
prosequitur, eoque Veneris munia procurante mens ebria longum insolu-
bilem et pestiferum bibit amorem, quem diffinit philosophus esse concupiscentiam coeundi" ["Desultory conversation followed the applause at
Dido's banquet; this paved the way and the infatuated queen's soul drank
in long draughts of inevitable and fatal love, which the philosopher defines
as a passionate desire for union"] (8.6; ed. Webb, 2:729 c, trans. Pike, p.
323). John makes explicit his condemnation of Dido as an example of
effeminate rule lacking in prudence (in that she was too quick to admit
Aeneas; *Policraticus* 6.22); he apparently regards prudence as a quality
necessary in a magistrate and a head of a commonwealth and also in the
individual.

Viewing the six books as does Bernard, as a metaphor for the six ages of
humankind, John regards the fourth book as a time when corruption rather
easily begins to incline the individual toward evil and then punishment
("quia natura hominis ab adolescentia sua prona est ad malum," *Policraticus*
8.24, ed. Webb, 2:818)—that time when, according to the Pythagorean Y
of human life, moral choice begins. That is, John reads the *Aeneid* as a
somewhat simplistic psychomachia between the vices and virtues for the
individual soul—Aeneas. Throughout, he consistently centers on the
tropological level of allegorical interpretation, particularly in relation to
individual free will. John elaborates Bernard's idea that Aeneas represents
the soul, etymologically signifying "body-dweller," from *ennos* and *demas*
in Greek, and accordingly, as in Bernard, the six books (he also ignores the
last six of the twelve total books) correlate with the six ages of man—
childhood, boyhood, youth, manhood, civic maturity and near old-age,
and, in the sixth book, old age and the descent into the underworld. (He
rationalizes the sixth book as a metaphor for the descent into one's self.)
Throughout these ages John stresses the human freedom to choose: "Prima
ergo etas nutricem, secunda custodem habet, tertia quo liberior, eo facilius
errat, nondum tamen procedit ad crimina" ["The first period, then, has its
nurse; the second its guardian; the third, the freer it is the more easily it is
led astray but not yet so far as to commit crime"] (8.24, ed. Webb, 2:817,
trans. Pike, p. 403). John believes that free will, bolstered by grace, is the
means of raising oneself up from the troublesome prison of Original Sin:
"ut ex quo libero licet depresso coeperit uti arbitrio, per se cadat sponte in
culpam et inde merito suo praeceps prolabatur in penam; erigi tamen
nequaquam potest ad bonum, nisi gratia Dei supponat manum suam" ["so

that from the moment he began to enjoy free will, though under limitation, he of his own accord fell into sin and then, as he deserved, plunged headlong into punishment. In no way can he be raised to goodness unless God in his grace places a supporting hand beneath him"] (8.24, ed. Webb, 2:818, trans. Pike, p. 404).

For John, the *Aeneid* with its paganism, Aeneas as a fallen and depraved Everyman, the hedonistic Trojans and lascivious Dido, exemplify the "Epicureorum uia"—a way leading to death: "Lata est ergo Epicureorum uia et haud dubiam, ducit ad mortem" ["Broad therefore is the way of the Epicureans, and it leadeth indubitably to death"] (*Policraticus* 8.24, ed. Webb, 2:818, trans. Pike, p. 404). In this book the illicit affair with Dido conveys the childish loss of reason; then Mercury (the personification of reason) teaches Aeneas that forbidden love is not destined to be happy. Mercury's rational counsel about a child speaking as a child and a grown man speaking as a grown man ("docetque illum qui, dum fuerat paruulus, sapiebat ut paruulus, loquebatur ut paruulus, agebat ut paruulus, fuga irrefragabiliter apprehensa, euacuare quae erant paruuli," 8.24, ed. Webb, 2:817) echoes 1 Corinthians 13:11, a method of linking *integumentum* and biblical passage he will use again here. In the manner of the *Ecloga Theoduli*, John parallels this incident from the *Aeneid* with the biblical example of Joseph from Genesis 39:12, a model of chastity and reason in manhood who has relinquished his vicious youth, "sic et patriarchiae pudicus filius pallium reliquit adulterae, ne adulterii crimine in uolueretur," because he leaves his "garment in the hand of the adulteress that he might not be implicated in the crime of adultery" (*Policraticus* 8.24, ed. Webb, 2:817).

What is unusual in this rather conventional mythography is John's explicit coupling of classical and Christian—one step beyond the coupling of classical and Old Testament found in the *Ecloga Theoduli*. His use of the classical hero Aeneas as a pagan example of excess and self-indulgence in contrast to the good life of the Christian witnessed in the Bible derives from his view of the purpose of mythological stories as moralistic and reveals his dislike of the Romans. Mythology functions to warn against vices and flaws and to give pleasure through poetic expression, although such tales can also cloak historical facts, the mysteries of nature, and the origin of customs, at least according to the Athenians and the Spartans, Greeks highly respected by John.[38] His "historical facts" resemble the Greek practice of euhemerism, the "mysteries of nature" resemble the natural (or physical) allegory of the Stoics, and the origin of customs, that which has been termed allegorism *ex ritu* in the Servian *Scholia Danielis*.

John's general view of the Roman nation (and the description of its origins in the *Aeneid*) was negative because of its descent from the Trojans, a superficial nation whose delight in flattery the Romans inherited (*Policraticus* 3.10). Too, the founding of Rome was shrouded in sin and paganism: Romulus as founder of Rome murdered his brother and engaged in parricide, and the Roman emperors were worshipped as divinities. In establishing the promised land of the Roman race, which goal had been prompted by dreams directed from Anchises, Jupiter, and Apollo, Aeneas was guided by oracles who were themselves aided by demons and not by divinity. These pagans John regarded as a "tainted race," "impious toward God" and "eager to persecute our saints" (2.15, trans. Pike, p. 78.)

The other books of the *Aeneid* do not hold much fascination for John except the fifth and especially the sixth books. Here again John changes Bernard's catalogue of the ages of man reflected in the six books: book 5 is not just Bernard's stage of manhood but specifically civic maturity in near old age and book 6 is not just old age but a descent into the underworld via a metaphorical descent into one's self. The fifth book thus provides a prolegomenon for this self-examination: in this age man begins taking stock of himself, "The protagonist reviews the honors held by his sires, venerates his ancestors, and, as if he were solemnizing games at the tomb of an Anchises, in them he recalls the misery of his exile" (*Policraticus* 8.24, trans. Pike, p. 404).

And in the sixth age of man, and the sixth book, Aeneas as a decrepit Everyman looks at the errors of his past now that his emotions are "numbed" and his powers "waning," in a spiritual experiencing of loss and decay: "cum iam frigescat affectus uiresque deficiant, non tam senectutem sentit quam senium et uelut quendam descensum ad inferos, ubi quasi rebus inutiliter gestis totius anteactae uitae recognoscat errores" ["Since by now his emotions are numbed and his powers are waning, he experiences not so much old age itself as its decay and, as it were, a descent to the lower world, to review there the errors of his past life, as though all his achievements had come to naught"] (*Policraticus* 8.24, ed. Webb, 2:817, trans. Pike, p. 409). The sixth age is the most frustrating to the hero, "as though all his accomplishments had come to naught." Aeneas reviews his past by reviewing the *errors* of his past life, seen as a descent into the inferior and the infernal, a *descensus ad inferos*. This is expressed in the *Aeneid* by the loss of Palinurus and Misenus, "the pilot who fell asleep and who incited to rash battle." Thus the descent into the underworld—the exploration of one's past—begins ("Dum uero hinc egregitur, transit ad sextum et amissis

Palinuro et Miseno, duce scilicet nauigii dormitante et temerarii praelii incentore"). A more positive note is offered in the signification of the embraces of Lavinia and the kingdom of Italy, which John renders implictly as a kind of union with God in the Heavenly City: "et discat alia uia incedendum esse his qui uolunt ad dulces Lauiniae complexus et fatale regnum Italiae quasi ad quandam arcem beatitudinis pervenire" ["He learns there that another way must be traveled by those who wish to attain the fond embraces of Lavinia and the destined kingdom of Italy as a sort of citadel of beatitude"] (8.24, ed. Webb, 2:818, trans. Pike, p. 404).

In the *Aeneid* as a whole John sees life on earth as the infernal and inferior underworld itself. His specific association of Aeneas's dreams with the underworld of the sixth book of the *Aeneid* may have caused John to identify the Trojans with immoral forces, given the appearance of the above denigration in a chapter on dreams in which the scholar specifically explains meaningless or troubled *insomnia*. He draws upon Servius's comments on *Aeneid* 6.282–84 to show the connection between such dreams, the fall season, and the underworld's demons: "in libro in quo totius philosophiae rimatur archana, sensisse uisus est, dum labentia folia apud inferos uariis somniis onerauit" ["Virgil apparently noted this in that he burdens the falling leaves with various kinds of dreams in the book in which he investigates all the mysteries of philosophy"] (*Policraticus* 2.15, ed. Webb, 1:430, trans. Pike, p. 78).

Alexander Neckam (1157–1217) in his glosses on the *Aeneid* emphasizes primarily the sixth book of the *Aeneid* and the vicious descent and reveals the influence of Bernard Silvestris and John of Salisbury in individual moralizations. These mythological glosses appear primarily in the second book of his long work, *De naturis rerum,* a manual of scientific knowledge which catalogues the entire universe according to the four elements and their properties. Despite the apparent scientific emphasis, the treatise abounds in grammatical derivations and moralization, and most of his mythological glosses can be traced back either to Virgil, to a Virgil commentary, or to Ovid; his interest in mythology and moralization equals his interest in science and natural phenomena, if not exceeds it. Although much confusion surrounds the Neckam canon—fewer than half of forty titles attributed to him can be identified positively, and twenty-four items in his bibliography remain listed as "dubious, unidentified, or lost"[39]— nevertheless he is believed to have written two very important mythographic commentaries, one on Martianus Capella[40] and one on the *Ecloga Theoduli.*[41] He has also written other theological and exegetical works, principally *De laudibus sapientiae divinae* (1211) and *Expositio in Canticum Canticorum.*

Possibly his contacts with the University of Paris and its writings influenced his selection of classical texts to be glossed; such contacts undoubtedly affected his view of classical fable. An Englishman born in 1157 in St. Albans, Alexander was educated at the abbey school of Dunstable, near St. Albans (outside present London), and, beginning in 1180, taught at the University of Paris as a "distinguished professor"; returning to England and the school at Dunstable in 1186, where he became master until 1187, he then entered the Augustinian order at Circencester, was elected abbot in 1212, and died at Kempsey, near Worcester, in 1217.[42] His association with the University of Paris was responsible also for bringing to England especially continental modes of exegesis, given the earlier French commentaries on Virgil, Martianus Capella, Ovid, and Fulgentius. These are strong arguments for attributing the authorship of the mythographic work of the third Vatican mythographer to Alexander Neckam rather than to Alberic of London,[43] although his late dates perhaps eliminate him as possible author of that seminal work cited in so many earlier Chartrian commentaries. Despite this major obstacle to the attribution, one of the most cogent arguments in support of the attribution is Alexander's view of classical fable: in *De naturis rerum,* when he alludes to Cadmus sowing dragon's teeth, he reveals that moral truths underlie the fables of poets in that their metamorphosis into armed men who kill each other teaches that litigation, and spiritual death, result from poisonous detraction (*Nat. rerum,* p. 189). Such an interest would later make him a prime authority for the fourteenth-century mythographer Robert Holkot in his commentary *In proverbia Salomonis,* where the name "Alexander" appears more than that of any other ancient or modern writer in the second half of the book.[44]

Most of his mythological allusions in *De naturis rerum,* imbedded in what is really a scientific encyclopedia, concern either the infernal, the sixth book of the *Aeneid,* or the inferior and pagan. Chiefly he discusses the rivers of the underworld, the three Furies, and Achates, companion of Aeneas. Most of the figures veil human vice—the rivers represent chagrin, wrath, sadness, the Furies represent disorganized thinking, speech, acting, and only Anchises represents a positive quality—worthiness of loving and doing.

The identification of the rivers of the underworld with excessive emotion is not new. Avernus is described as a deep lake in Italy, "nebularum

procreator multaeque parens caliginis. Et dicitur Avernus quasi sine vere"
["the procreator of mists and parent of much fog. And it is called Avernus,
that is, 'without spring' "] (*Nat. rerum*, p. 133). For this reason it is called
an *under*world ("Hinc est quod transumitur vocabulum ad designationem
inferni"). In addition, Cocytus and Phlegethon are rivers, and Styx is a
horrid swamp in Egypt; because they are horrid places they are described as
infernal rivers ("fluvii infernales") by the poets. The three represent
"luctus, ardor, et tristicia," that which moves us to "tears, ardor, and
sadness," all excessive (and therefore infernal) emotions.

Alexander's interpretation of the rivers of the underworld as symbols of
human vice derives ultimately from Macrobius's commentary on the
Somnium Scipionis (1.10.10), Isidore's *Etymologiae* (14.9.6), Servius's commentary on the *Aeneid* (6.265), Fulgentius's *Continentia Virgiliana* 22 (p.
102), Bernard's commentary on the *Aeneid* (*Sup. En.* 6.107 and 6.438–9,
pp. 51 and 93), and the various Boethius commentaries on *Consolatio* 3
m12. Macrobius in his commentary on the *Somnium Scipionis* defined
Acheron (not mentioned by Alexander) as chagrin over doing something,
Phlegethon as the fires of wrath, Cocytus as that which moves us to tears,
and the Styx as that which plunges human minds into hatred, and Servius
and Bernard amplify these definitions. Further, very like Isidore who also
comments on Cocytus and the Styx (*Etym.* 14.9.6–7), and in approach very
like the author of the *Ecloga Theoduli* who juxtaposes classical fables with
appropriate biblical legends, Alexander mentions Job in the context of this
discussion. Once again he resembles John of Salisbury.

Alexander introduces a by now familiar Neoplatonic rationalization of
poetry as a kind of fictional underworld when admitting that, just as much
has been said about the infernal rivers without cause, so also without cause
much concerning the three Furies has been fabricated. Alexander rationalizes his discourse on the infernal and mythological by declaring that there
exists much utility under the figments of the poets which can be ferreted
out through diligent investigation ("In figmentis quidem poetarum a
diligenti investigatore multa reperietur utilitas," *Nat. rerum*, p. 134). His
interpretation of the Furies, following the exposition on the infernal rivers,
derives from Bernard's commentary on *Aeneid* 6.280 (*Sup. En.* 2.11, p. 69).
Delivering a Fulgentian interpretation of the Furies, he etymologizes
Allecto as the restless mind, "inquietudo mentis, proveniens ex variis
cogitationibus": "Et dicitur Allecto, ab alliciendo, quia voluptas in cogitatione consistens, mentem allicit ad consensum. Putaverunt quidam Alecto
dici, quasi sine lecto, eo quod vanitas cogitationum quiete carere videatur"

["And Allecto is so-called from *alliciendo,* 'enticing,' because the pleasure existing in thought entices the mind to agreement. Some have thought Allecto means *sine lecto,* 'without a bed,' because vain thoughts seem to be without rest"] (*Nat. rerum,* p. 134). Tisiphone, similarly, represents "mala locutio" ["evil speech"] from *thesis* or "theme," and *phonos* or "sound," and Megaera represents "malus actus" ["evil act"] from *mene geros,* or "deficiens actus" in Latin—"deficient act." The three together, Alexander concludes, describe the process through which we incline to evil, beginning with the thought, the words, and then the act, or, changing the order, the thought followed by the act and then the habit ("Sic igitur tres furiae sunt mala cogitatio, mala locutio, malus actus, aut secundum aliam intelligentiam mala cogitatio, malus actus, perversa consuetudo," p. 134).

Alexander includes one positive—and Neoplatonic—reference to Achates, Aeneas's close companion, whom he compares with an agate because he signifies the worthiness of loving and doing and is thus worth "carrying": "Unde Aeneas Achatem socium habuisse dicitur familiarem, eo quod virtute illius lapidis gratiam multorum adquisivit, et a multis ereptus est periculis. Portatus namque lapis achates portantem amabilem et facundum et potentem facit" ["Hence Aeneas is said to have had Achates as his close companion because by virtue of that stone {achates, "agate"} he acquired the favor of many and was rescued from many dangers. For when the agate is carried, it makes its bearer likeable and eloquent and power-ful"] (*Nat. rerum,* pp. 177–78). Similarly, a stone used by Medea is said to be medicinal, because she used it in her incantations: in words, herbs, and stones there exist many virtues accessible with diligent investigation ("In verbis et herbis et lapidibus multam esse virtutem compertum est a diligentibus naturarum investigatoribus").

Alexander also treats Actaeon (from John of Salisbury's discussion of the *Aeneid*) as a symbol of levity and inconstancy, or *voluptas,* and Midas (from Ovid's *Metamorphoses* or some later commentary thereon) as *avaritia.* While the passage on Actaeon may have been drawn from *Metamorphoses* 3.230, it was inspired by John of Salisbury's treatment of the myth in the *Policraticus,* even though in the *De naturis rerum* Actaeon is discussed in a section on animals rather than the evils of hunting, as in the *Policraticus.* Still, he is developed as a type of young man who consumes all of his patrimony in order to give himself to the voluptuous symbol of hunting— in short, a man who has already given himself to the flesh ("Mutantur in cervos hi quorum amor totus et intentio tota in venationibus detinentur," *Nat. rerum,* p. 218). Thus his transformation into a stag after beholding the naked Diana becomes appropriate punishment for the excessive desire to hunt: "In hoc voluptuosa venatio repraehenditur." Such an excessive desire reflects a psychological imbalance; thereafter, Actaeon's dogs do not know him because their master has not adequately "mastered" them—"Minime videntur dominum cognoscere, qui eum verbis turpibus dehonestant" ["Those who dishonor their master with base words seem not to know him"].

Alexander thus transforms the myth (as Actaeon was transformed into a stag) into a Macrobian discourse on fable and how it should be perceived by others, particularly the philosopher. Actaeon's major problem has been that he has attempted to learn the secrets of prudence violently and inappropriately and he is thus changed into a stag, which suggests that he must then appropriately take flight from thought: "Iste est Actaeon qui importune secretis colloquiis prudentium se ingerit. Sed in cervum mutandus est, ut scilicet fugam cogatur arripere" ["That man is Actaeon who inappropriately thrusts himself into the private conversations of the wise. But he must be changed into a stag so that he is compelled to take flight"]. For Alexander the fable clearly reveals the reasons why Actaeon becomes a stag—because the stag reflects Actaeon's levity and inconstancy, just as Diana signifies *sapientia* (from the Greek *dios neos,* or the Latin "per dies innovata," or "innovans"), or the wisdom Actaeon desires to see (like many philosophers) naked and unadorned ("Voluptatibus enim dedito et curiositatibus videtur quod sapientia nuda sit et ornatu decenti careat," *Nat. rerum,* p. 218). When Diana washes herself, it means she wishes to admit no one who rudely offers himself ("nullum admittere vult qui se ingerat importune"); her nymphs embody those "qui sapientiae diligentem dant operam" ["who give careful attention to wisdom"]. At the end Alexander relates the myth of Actaeon and Diana to the secrets of Solomon, just as he has previously related the rivers of hell to the travels of Job, and as does the *Ecloga Theoduli* (and John of Salisbury).

In addition to this interesting and rather original interpretation of an Ovidian fable, there exists one other tropological interpretation of an Ovidian reference in *De naturis rerum,* to Midas, from *Metamorphoses* 11.104. The mythological fable is praised for having illustrated *avaritia* in Midas's turning to gold everything that he touches. "O quam competenter avaritiae vota damnat illud antiquorum figmentum, fingentium Midam optasse ut quicquid tangeret fulvum verteretur in aurum" ["Oh how properly that story of the ancients damns the desires of avarice when they depict Midas as having desired that whatever he might touch be turned into reddish-yellow gold"] (*Nat. rerum,* p. 322).

If we compare Alexander Neckam's later commentary on Martianus with Bernard's, we discover that there are differences which can be in part explained by the fad of Ovidian scholasticism that coincided with the translation of Aristotle into Latin and his adoption as part of the arts curriculum. Jupiter, as "universalis vis," couples with various mortals to engender demigods not usually glossed in Martianus commentaries, such as Danaë, wife of Acrisus and mother of Perseus, or Leda and the swan and her sons Pollux and Castor. Further Ovidian parallels are found in the myth of the competition between Apollo and Midas adjudicated by Pallas Athena, in which Midas means either avarice or "knowing nothing," and in the myth of Prometheus, the first man, created out of mud by Minerva.[45]

Other differences appear to be ingenious transfers from the old paradigms by Alexander, such as the conjunction of the concept of the nine circles of the underworld (adapted from Servius on *Aeneid* 6, in particular) with Bernard's *Aeneid* commentary adaptation of the Fulgentian ages of man. This transfer appears to be triggered by glosses on the rivers of hell, beginning with Lethe: some say that the river Lethe flows around the nine circles of hell, so that they argue for the river Lethe as an image of old age ("Alii tamen magne auctoritatis viri qui de Lethee fluvio utrum de illis novem circulis inferos circu[m]euntibus esse disputaverunt et ab illis eum seperaverunt. Letheum fluvium ymaginem senectutis esse volverunt"). For they say that our soul is vigorous and quick and full of memory from boyhood to mature old age, but afterwards all memory slips away in extreme old age; and after it has passed away, death occurs ("Nam anime inquiunt nostre vigent et alacres sunt et plene memoria a pueritia usque ad virentem senectutem, postea vero omnis memoria labitur in nimia senectute, qua lapsa[m], mors intervenit"). Therefore the river Lethe represents the forgetfulness of old age ("Ergo fluvius letheus oblivio senilis, est morti semper vicina").[46]

Alexander then explicitly relates the nine circles of the underworld to the individual earthly human ages, acknowledging the Virgilian context (or rather, the Silvestran commentary on Virgil ("describit virgilius") for this schema. Throughout the nine circles of the underworld Virgil describes the souls, beginning with the most juvenile: the first holds the souls of infants ("primum tenere animas infantium"); the second, those who through guilelessness are not able to aid themselves ("secundum eorum qui per simplicitatem sibi adesse nequiverunt"); the third, those who, to escape their troubles, kill themselves ("Tertium qui vitantes erumpnas se occiderunt"). Then come the circles of maturity: the fourth includes those who loved ("Quartum eorum qui amarunt"); the fifth, those who are brave ("Quintum virorum fortium"); the sixth, the guilty who are punished by judges ("Sextum nocentium qui a iudicibus puniuntur"). Thereafter come the more otherworldly circles—the seventh is where souls are purified ("Septimum in quo anime purgantur"); the eighth, of souls already purified ("Octavum animarum iam purgatarum"); the ninth, the Elysian Field glossed by Servius—the Other World itself, "wholly imaginary, most subtly invented" ("Novum campum heliseum, vel totum fabulosum est, subtillissime ut ait servius adinventum").

Alexander then attempts to relate the nine circles to the demons and "cupiditates de quibus tristitia nescitur id est stix," the desires from which sadness is not known, that is, the Styx, with the identification of prelapsarian desire-Cupid / *cupiditas*-demon perhaps drawn from Theodulf's Isidorian portrait in "Books I Used to Read." And he concludes—perhaps rather predictably, given the Neoplatonic ambience of so many of the twelfth-century glosses—"Unde dicunt novem esse circulos stigis, que inferos cingit, id est terram" ("Whence they say there are nine circles in the Styx, which bind the underworld, that is, earth").

The ingenious interrelating of a gloss from one tradition to a similiar but different gloss in another tradition, and the use of new glosses to revitalize old ones is stunning. Let us look once again at Alexander's patterns: he takes the Servian gloss on the circles of hell in book 6 of the *Aeneid*, using Theodulf's "Virgilized" Ovid gloss, that is, the Virgilized figure of demonic Cupid, to amplify what he means, and then uses the entire schema as a gloss on Bernard's own Fulgentian allegory of the ages of man—which appears in *his* commentary on the *Aeneid*. What is most revealing is the appearance of this palimpsest of glosses within Alexander's *Martianus* commentary—a much-glossed mythographic tradition which does not require extra glossation, but which provides a loose frame for *adnotationes* on the myths of the gods. And it is this loose mythographic frame—witnessed earlier more dramatically in its draft-mythography form in William of Conches's Florentine Commentary on Martianus—which may very well have inspired the frame for the mythographies in the handbook of the third Vatican mythographer, possibly Alexander Neckam himself.

This blending of Boethian-Virgilian and Ovidian glosses in Alexander once again demonstrates the intertextuality of the twelfth century—its cross-glossation of classical texts which resulted in the fusion of various commentary traditions. What William of Conches initiated, Bernard

Silvestris and his successors, John of Salisbury and Alexander Neckam, continue. Most interesting in the creeping in of Ovid glosses is a new trend—the advent of commentary on Ovid, which, as Ludwig Traube early on acknowledged, was a late medieval phenomenon in comparison to the other commentary traditions of Virgil, Lucan, Statius, and Boethius. The power of this new commentary tradition, propelled as it was by the advent of Aristotle into the university curriculum in the twelfth century, would revolutionize letters and deserves a volume all of its own.

In the later twelfth and thirteenth centuries the Ovid commentary and the revitalized mythographic handbook come into their own, eclipsing the Martianus commentary and altering the Boethius and Virgil commentaries. Commentaries on new texts borrowed from the extant mythographic tradition for explanations and methodology. Such a revolution in what had been a scholastic phenomenon would reach outside the classroom controlled by the cleric and schoolmaster and into the court and the dramatically changing world of the brilliant fourteenth and fifteenth centuries in Western Europe.

NOTES

INTRODUCTION

1. See, for example, *Iliad* 9.443, 19.443; *Odyssey* 11.561, 3.94.

2. Northrop Frye, "New Directions from Old," in *Myth and Mythmaking,* ed. Henry A. Murray (New York: Braziller, 1960), p. 11n.7.

3. Roger Hinks, *Myth and Allegory in Ancient Art* (London: Warburg Institute, 1939), p. 4.

4. William Harris Stahl, *The Quadrivium of Martianus Capella: Latin Traditions in the Mathematical Sciences,* vol. 1 of *Martianus Capella and the Seven Liberal Arts* (New York and London: Columbia University Press, 1971), p. 56.

5. *Inferno* 9, *Purgatorio* 25, 32. See *Petri Allegherii super Dantis ipsius genitoris Comoediam commentarium,* ed. Vincentio Nannucci (Florence, 1845), pp. 124, 471, 523, 526.

6. See "Medieval Misogyny," *Representations* 20 (1987): 1–24, esp. p. 1: "Like allegory itself, to which (for reasons we do not have time to explore) it is peculiarly attracted, antifeminism is both a genre and a topos, or, as Paul Zumthor might suggest, a 'register'—a discourse visible across a broad spectrum of poetic types." See also p. 24: "The danger of woman, according to this reading of the phenomenon of misogyny, is that of literature itself."

7. Dante Alighieri, *Epistolae,* letter 10.7.

8. See Jacques Derrida, *Of Grammatology,* trans. Gayatri Spivack (Baltimore: Johns Hopkins University Press, 1976).

9. Ulmer, "The Object of Post-Criticism," in *The Anti-Aesthetic,* ed. Hal Foster (Seattle: Bay Press, 1983; rpt. 1991), pp. 83–110, esp. pp. 87 and 88–89.

10. Ulmer, pp. 90–95. "Grammatology has emerged on the far side of the formalist crisis and developed a discourse which is fully referential, but referential in the manner of 'narrative allegory' rather than of 'allegoresis.' 'Allegoresis,' the mode of commentary long practiced by traditional critics, 'suspends' the surface of the text, applying a terminology of 'verticalness, levels, hidden meaning, the hieratic difficulty of interpretation,' whereas 'narrative allegory' (practiced by post-critics) explores the literal—*letteral*—level of the language itself, in a horizontal investigation of the polysemous meanings simultaneously available in the words themselves—in etymologies and puns—and in the things the words name. The allegorical narrative unfolds as a dramatization or reenactment (personification) of the 'literal truth inherent in the words themselves.'" Ulmer, p. 95, citing Maureen Quilligan, *The Language of Allegory* (Ithaca, N.Y.: Cornell University Press, 1979), pp. 30–33.

11. Hyginus, *Astronomica* 2.32, ed. Bernard Bunte (Leipzig, 1875).

12. See Verbeke, *The Presence of Stoicism in Medieval Thought* (Washington, D.C.: Catholic University of America Press, 1983), esp. chap. 1, pp. 1–19. Quotations are from pp. 3–4.

13. See M. Spanneut, *Le Stoïcisme des pères de l'Église de Clément de Rome à Clément d'Alexandrie* (Paris: Seuil, 1969). See also the monumental study by Marcia L. Colish, *The Stoic Tradition from Antiquity to the Early Middle Ages,* vol. 2: *Stoicism in Christian Latin Thought through the Sixth Century* (Leiden: E. J. Brill, 1985).

14. The "middle ages" during which classicism lay dormant span a period of time defined in different and rather arbitrary ways, from as early as A.D.. 46 to as late as A.D.. 1453, as Charles Homer Haskins notes in *The Renaissance of the Twelfth Century* (Cambridge, Mass.: Harvard University Press, 1927), p. 4.

15. Seznec, *The Survival of the Pagan Gods: The Mythological Tradition and its Place in Renaissance Humanism and Art,* trans. Barbara F. Sessions from the 1940 edition (New York: Harper and Row, 1953), pp. 6, 21, 28.

16. Panofsky, *Studies in Iconology: Humanistic Themes in the Art of the Renaissance* (1939; rpt. New York: Harper and Row, 1967), p. 27.

17. See Nees, *A Tainted Mantle: Hercules and the Classical Tradition at the Carolingian Court* (Philadelphia: University of Pennsylvania Press, 1991), esp. pp. 3–17.

18. Bernal, *Black Athena: The Afroasiatic Roots of Classical Civilization,* vol. 1: *The Fabrication of Ancient Greece, 1785–1985* (New Brunswick, N.J.: Rutgers University Press, 1987).

19. Finke, *Feminist Theory, Women's Writing* (Ithaca, N.Y., and London: Cornell University Press, 1992), p. 25, substitutes "noise" for "alterity" in quoting Alice Jardine, *Gynesis: Configurations of Women and Modernity* (Ithaca, N.Y.: Cornell University Press, 1985), pp. 114–15. Finke uses as examples of cultural noise in the Middle Ages the Trobairitz and female mystics.

20. Desmond, *Reading Dido: Gender, Textuality, the Medieval Aeneid* (Minneapolis: University of Minnesota Press, forthcoming, 1994). Desmond examines the allegory of Dido as *libido* in Augustine, Fulgentius, and Bernard Silvestris, the courtly Dido in romance, and Dido in Chaucer, Christine de Pizan, Gavin Douglas, and William Caxton.

21. Huguccio of Pisa, *Derivationes magnae,* Cambridge, MS. Gonville and Caius 459/718, fol. 97: "Commentum vero est expositio verborum iuncturam non considerans sed sensum. Deservit enim expositioni sententiae alicuius libri et non coniunctioni litterae. Accipitur etiam quandoque largius, scilicet pro quolibet libro. Sed tunc sic definitur: commentum est plurimorum studio vel doctrina in mente habitorum in unum collectio. Glosa est expositio sententiae et illius litterae quae non solum sententiam sed etiam verba attendit quia glossa est expositio sententiae litteram continens vel exponens." See the partial transcription by G. Paré, *La Renaissance du XIIe siècle: Les Écoles et l'enseignement* (Paris: J. Vrin; Ottawa: Institut d'Études Médiévales, 1933), p. 118; my translation.

22. See Bradford Wilson, ed., *Glosae in Iuvenalem,* Textes philosophiques du Moyen Âge, 18 (Paris: J. Vrin, 1980), p. 80. The text, as cited in William of Conches, *Glosae super Platonem,* p. 57, reads, "Etsi multos super Platonem commentatos esse, multos glosasse non dubitemus, tamen quia commentatores, literam nec continuantes nec exponentes, soli sententie serviunt, glosatores vero in levibus superflui, in gravibus vero obscurissimi vel nonnulli reperiuntur, rogatu sociorum quibus omnia honesta debemus excitati, super predictum aliquid dicere proposuimus, aliorum superflua recidentes, pretermissa addentes, obscura elucidantes, male dicta removentes, bene dicta imitantes."

23. Thomas Kuhn, *The Structure of Scientific Revolutions* (Chicago: University of Chicago Press, 1962), p. 90.

CHAPTER 1: THE ALLEGORIZATION OF CLASSICAL MYTH IN THE LITERARY SCHOOL COMMENTARY

1. Critical surveys of the early allegorists include especially Ann Bates Hersman, *Studies in Greek Allegorical Interpretation* (Chicago: Blue Sky Press, 1906), pp. 7–23 on the Greeks; Stanley Tate Collins, *The Interpretation of Vergil, with Special Reference to Macrobius* (Oxford: Blackwell; London: Simpkin, Marshall, 1909), pp. 11–12; three articles by J. Tate, "The Beginnings of Greek Allegory," *CR* 41 (1927): 214–15; "Plato and Allegorical Interpretation," *CQ* 23 (1929): 142–54; and "On the History of Allegorism," *CQ* 28 (1934): 105–14; and, especially, Jean Pépin, *Mythe et allégorie: Les Origines grecques et les contestations judéo-chrétiennes* (Paris: Aubier, 1958), and the excellent and thorough Félix Buffière, *Les Mythes d'Homère et la pensée grecque* (Paris: Les Belles Lettres, 1956). More recent, and emphasizing Homer but tracing both the Greek and Latin traditions into late antiquity and, more briefly, the Latin Middle Ages, is Robert Lambertin, *Homer the Theologian: Neoplatonist Allegorical Reading and the Growth of the Epic Tradition* (Berkeley, Los Angeles, and London: University of California Press, 1986).

2. The best—clearest and most concise—outline of the four senses of allegory and the varying definitions of each in the Middle Ages can be found in Harry Caplan, who relates them to the *ars praedicandi* in "The Four Senses of Scriptural Interpretation and the Mediaeval Theory of Preaching," *Speculum* 4 (1929): 282–90. See also the fine discussion of the early history of the four senses in "The Bible and Allegory," chapter 9 of Robert E. McNally, S.J., *The Bible in the Early Middle Ages* (Westminster, Md.: Newman Press, 1959), pp. 53–61, and also Charles Donahue, "[Patristic Exegesis in the Criticism of Medieval Literature:] Summation," in *Critical Approaches to Medieval Literature: Selected Papers from the English Institute, 1958–59,* ed. Dorothy Bethurum (New York and London: Columbia University Press, 1960), pp. 61–82. See also E. C. Knowlton, "Notes on Early Allegory," *JEGP* 29 (1930): 159–81; Stephen Manning, "The Nun's Priest's Morality and the Medieval Attitude toward Fables," *JEGP* 59 (1960): 403–16;

and D. W. Robertson, Jr., *A Preface to Chaucer: Studies in Medieval Perspective* (1962; rpt. Princeton: Princeton University Press, 1969). The fullest, most monumental study of allegory in the Middle Ages is Henri de Lubac, *Exégèse médiévale. Les quatre sens de l'écriture,* Théologie, vols. 41–42, 59; two vols. in 4 (Lyon: Aubier, 1959–64). See also the very recent discussion of the "Doctrine of the Four Meanings" in the chapter on patristic exegesis in Tzvetan Todorov, *Symbolism and Interpretation,* trans. Catherine Porter (Ithaca, N.Y.: Cornell University Press, 1982), esp. pp. 112–30.

3. I am grateful to Paul Oskar Kristeller for this information, conveyed to me in a letter of August 30, 1985.

4. J. Reginald O'Donnell, "The Sources and Meaning of Bernard Silvester's Commentary on the *Aeneid*," *MS* 24 (1962): 233–36.

5. Diogenes Laertius, 8.21 of *Lives of the Eminent Philosophers,* trans. R. D. Hicks, 2 vols. (London: Heinemann; New York: Putnam's, 1925). This volume contains information about many philosophers whose writings are no longer extant.

6. Xenophanes, frag. 11, in Hermann Diels, *Die Fragmente der Vorsokratiker,* 3 vols. (Berlin: Weidmannsche, 1952; rpt. 1960), trans. Kathleen Freeman in *Ancilla to the Pre-Socratic Philosophers: A Complete Translation of the Fragments in Diels, Fragmente der Vorsokratiker* (Oxford: Blackwell, 1952), p. 22. The Homeric use of scandalous stories about the gods, it has been suggested by Eric A. Havelock, functions as a disguise for something else, specifically instruction about Greece. See "Prologue to Greek Literacy," in *Lectures in Memory of Louise Taft Semple (Second Series)* (Cincinnati: University of Cincinnati, 1971), pp. 34ff.

7. Heraclitus, in Diels, frags. 42, 57; Freeman, pp. 27–28. Basically Heraclitus did not believe in the gods and discounted the poets who used them: "What intelligence or understanding have they? They believe the people's bards, and use as their teacher the populace, not knowing that 'the majority are bad, and the good are few,' " Diels, frag. 104; Freeman, p. 31.

8. Pherecydes of Syros, in Diels, frag. 5; Freeman, p. 14.

9. Cited in Origen, *Contra Celsum* 6.43, trans. Henry Chadwick (Cambridge: Cambridge University Press, 1965), p. 359. See also J. Tate, "On the History of Allegorism," p. 107, on the role of Pherecydes.

10. For the Porphyry scholium citing Theagenes, see the *Scholium Venetum B on the Iliad* 20.67, in William Dindorf, ed., *Scholia Graeca in Homeri Iliadem,* vol. 4 (Oxford: Clarendon Press, 1877; rpt. Amsterdam: Hakkert, 1969), p. 231.

11. Mentioned by Diogenes Laertius, *Lives* 2.11.

12. Anaxagoras is cited by the Byzantine Syncellus, *Chronika* 140C.I, in Diels, frag. 61, no. 6.

13. This detail from Anaxagoras is according to John Edwin Sandys, *A History of Classical Scholarship,* vol. 1: *From the Sixth Century B.C. to the End of the Middle Ages,* 2d edition (Cambridge: Cambridge University Press, 1906), p. 30; see also the

twelfth-century scholia of John Tzetzes on the *Iliad, Exegesis in Iliadem,* ed. Gottfried Hermann, appendix to Jakob Diassorinos, *Draconis Stratonicensis Liber de metris poeticis* [forgery], ed. Franciscus de Furia (Leipzig, 1814), p. 94.

14. Anaxagoras, in Diels, frag. 19; Freeman, p. 86.

15. See Tatian's comments on the lost *De Homero* of Metrodorus in *Oratio adversus Graecos, PG* 6:854. He regards Metrodorus as childish in his treatment of the Homeric gods.

16. These identifications are attributed to Metrodorus by a variety of sources. Hesychius (prob. 5th c. B.C.) equated Agamemnon with aether. The Herculaneum Rolls (ca. 110–ca. 40–35 B.C.), authored supposedly by Philodemus (according to Th. Gomperz in his article on Metrodorus in *Sitzungsberichte der Wiener Akademie,* Phil. hist. classe, 116 [1873]: 12–14) equated the other gods and heroes with the appropriate natural forces; cited in Diels, frag. 61, no. 4. See also the discussion in Buffière, p. 127.

17. Epicharmus, in Diels, frags. 52a, 53; Freeman, p. 39.

18. Prodicus is cited by Sextus Empiricus, *Adversus mathematicos* 9.18, in *Opera,* vol. 3, ed. Hermann Mutschmann, rev. J. Mau (Leipzig: B. G. Teubner, 1961).

19. Democritus, in Diels, frag. 30; Freeman, p. 8: "Of the reasoning men, a few, raising their hands thither to what we Greeks call the Air nowadays, said: Zeus considers all things and he knows all and gives and takes away all and is King of all." For the "Tritogeneia" passage, see Diels, frags. 1b, 2; Freeman, p. 91.

20. Plato, *Cratylus* 395A. See also 391d-e on "Xanthus" and 394c on Agis, Polemarchus, and Acesimbrotus. For Plato's discussion of names and their relation to reality, see *Charmides* 163d in *Plato,* vol. 8, trans. W. R. M. Lamb (London: Heinemann; New York: Putnam's, 1927), and in *Cratylus* 391d–397e in *Plato,* vol. 6, trans. H. N. Fowler (London: Heinemann; New York: Putnam's, 1926). See also Cicero, *Nat. deorum* 1.118. For Plato and the importance of literacy, as opposed to the oral tradition associated at the time with poetry, see Eric A. Havelock, *Preface to Plato* (Cambridge, Mass., and London: Belknap Press of Harvard University Press, 1963), esp. chap. 1, pp. 3–19, but also the entire first part.

21. Hersman, pp. 17–18.

22. According to a list of his works supplied by Diogenes Laertius, *Lives* 7.4, and Cicero, *Nat. deorum* 1.36, Zeno of Citium wrote five books entitled *On Homeric Problems* and also the scholia on verses 134 and 139 of Hesiod's *Theogony.* All of the Stoics, according to Cicero, wrote to show "physica ratio non inelegans inclusa est in inpias fabulas." See Cicero, *Nat. deorum* 2.24. Zeno of Citium rationalized the gods, especially Juno and Jupiter, by "arguing that these were merely names given symbolically to mute and inanimate forces," according to Cicero, *Nat. deorum* 1.36. For studies of classical Stoicism see Brad Inwood, *Ethics and Human Action in Early Stoicism* (Oxford: Clarendon Press, 1985), and Marcia L. Colish, *The Stoic Tradition from Antiquity to the Early Middle Ages,* vol. 1: *Stoicism in Classical Latin Literature* (Leiden: E. J. Brill, 1985).

23. According to Minucius Felix, *Octavius* 19.10, in *Tertullian: Minucius Felix,* trans. Gerald H. Rendall, based on the unfinished version by W. C. A. Kerr (London: Heinemann; New York: Putnam's, 1931).

24. Cicero, *Nat. deorum* 2.15, and Diogenes Laertius, *Lives* 7.135.

25. Cicero, *Nat. deorum* 3.24.

26. Collins, *Interpretation of Vergil,* p. 12. A list of Cleanthes's works appears in Diogenes Laertius, *Lives* 7.175. See also the discussion of the followers of Zeno in Cicero, *Nat. deorum* 1.37, 39–41.

27. Euhemerus's work and Ennius's translation survive only in quotations. See Euhemerus, *Reliquiae,* ed. Geyza Némethy (Budapest, 1889), and Ennius, *Annales,* in *Carminum reliquaiae,* ed. Lucian Müller (St. Petersburg, 1884). For Persaeus, see Cicero, *Nat. deorum* 1.38.

28. In Ennius's lines, quoted in Cicero, *Nat. deorum* 2.4.

29. Hersman, p. 15.

30. Hecataeus, frags. 346, 349, in *Fragmenta historicorum Graecorum,* ed. Karl Müller and Theodore Müller (Paris, 1841).

31. Strabo, *Geography* 9.422, in *The Geography of Strabo,* ed. and trans. Horace Leonard Jones, vol. 4 of 8 (London: Heinemann; New York: Putnam's, 1917).

32. John Daniel Cooke, "Euhemerism: A Medieval Interpretation of Classical Paganism," *Speculum* 2 (1927): 397. For the history of euhemerism see also Paul Alphandery, "L'euhémérisme et les débuts de l'histoire des religions au moyen âge," *Revue de l'histoire des religions* 109 (1934): 25–27. On p. 12 Alphandery notes the similarity between the apotheosis of men into gods in paganism and of men into saints in Christianity.

33. See J. M. Ross, introduction to Cicero, *The Nature of the Gods,* trans. Horace C. P. McGregor (Middlesex: Penguin Books, 1972), p. 18.

34. See Cornutus, *Theologiae Graecae compendium,* ed. C. Lang (Leipzig, 1881), and Heraclitus of Pontus, *Allégories d'Homère,* ed. and trans. Félix Buffière (Paris: Les Belles Lettres, 1962). In his texts Heraclitus of Pontus opposes the vices to the virtues, as in the struggle of Athena with Ares and Aphrodite, or wisdom with folly and incontinence, or in Odysseus's wanderings, which represent vices and temptations the sage must reject. Other examples oppose Hermes to Leto, logical speech to forgetfulness, and Apollo to Poseidon, the sun to water.

35. Ross, introduction, p. 54.

36. Hersman, p. 21 (or else they all, pseudo-Heraclitus included, had a common source).

37. See Don Cameron Allen's interesting first chapter in *Mysteriously Meant: The Rediscovery of Pagan Symbolism and Allegorical Interpretation in the Renaissance* (Baltimore and London: Johns Hopkins University Press, 1970), esp. pp. 3–18. Among the pagans attacking Christianity whom he mentions are Valerius Maximus, Horace, the younger Pliny, Tacitus, Suetonius, and then, later, Lucian or

Philostratus, Fronto (in a book now lost), Celsus in his *Book of Truth,* and Porphyry in his lost *Against the Christians.*

38. J. W. H. Atkins, *English Literary Criticism: The Medieval Phase* (Cambridge: Cambridge University Press, 1943), p. 12.

39. Henry Osborn Taylor, *The Emergence of Christian Culture in the West: The Classical Heritage of the Middle Ages,* 3d ed. (1911; rpt. New York: Harper, 1958), pp. 12, 14.

40. Hersman, p. 22.

41. Caplan, "Four Senses," p. 285.

42. Clement of Alexandria, *Stromateis* 5.12.78, 5.8.44–55, in *Opera,* ed. Wilhelm Dindorf (Oxford, 1869), vol. 3 of 4.

43. For example, Origen, *Contra Celsum* 6.22 (Mithraic mysteries), 6.23 (mysteries of Cabeiri), 6.71 (Stoicism), 7.58 (Platonism), and 2.55, 7.53–54 (Christ's life).

44. *De principiis* 4.11–16 (4.2.4–9), in *Origène: Traité 24s principes,* trans. into French and Latin by Henri Couzel and Manlio Simonetti, vol. 3 (books 3–4), no. 268 of Sources Chrétiennes (Paris: Éditions du Cerf, 1980), pp. 310–41. Caplan, "Four Senses," p. 285, notes that Origen classified Philo with the Christian Fathers, perhaps because he applied Greek allegoresis to Hebrew Scriptures and thus justified the reading of the Old Testament.

45. Tertullian, *De resurrectione carnis, PL* 2:821–22, 811; *Adversus Marcionem, PL* 2:316, 345–46, 356, 387, 469–70, 478, 499–500.

46. Jerome, *Commentarii in Ezechielem prophetam* 4.16 (*PL* 25:125); also in *Epistola 120 ad Hedibiam, PL* 22: quaest. 12; as well as the comments in Ezekiel 16 and Amos 4.

47. Jerome, *Epistola 22 ad Eustochium* 29.6–7, *PL* 22:394.

48. For Jerome's *Libri nominum Hebraicorum,* see *PL* 23:1199ff. See also O'Donnell, p. 236.

49. Augustine, *De utilitate credendi,* ed. Joseph Zycha, CSEL, no. 25 (Prague, Vienna, and Leipzig, 1891), pp. 7ff.

50. Augustine, *De doctrina Christiana* 3.5. The passage from Second Corinthians is also mentioned in Augustine's *De spiritu et littera* 4, *PL* 44:203.

51. See the preface to Eucherius, *Formulae spiritualis intellegentiae,* ed. Karl Wotke, CSEL, no. 31 (Prague, Vienna, and Leipzig, 1894), pp. 3–6.

52. See Gregory, *Moralium libri, sive expositio in librum b. Job, PL* 75:513.

53. Both of Isidore's works on allegory can be found in *PL* 83 (97–130, 207–424). See also McNally, pp. 55–56.

54. Don Cameron Allen surveys these Greek Christian apologists—Justin, Athenagoras, Theophilus, Tatian, Clement, and Celsus. In addition see Henry Chadwick, *Early Christian Thought and the Classical Tradition: Studies in Justin, Clement, and Origen* (Oxford: Clarendon Press, 1966). Typology is really a form of symbolism dealing with *historia* on the literal level, rather than a form of allegory.

On typology see Erich Auerbach, "Figura als Realprophetie bei den Kirch-envätern," *AR* 22 (1938): 436–89; "Typological Symbolism in Medieval Litera-ture," *Yale French Studies* 9 (1952): 3–10; and *Typologische Motive in der mittelalterli-chen Literatur,* Schriften und Vorträge des Petrarca-Institute Köln, no. 2 (Krefeld: Scherpe, 1953); Johan Chydenius, *The Theory of Medieval Symbolism,* Commenta-tiones Humanarum Litterarum, 27.2 (Helsinki: Societas Scientarum Fennica, 1960); and Hugh T. Keenan, "A Check-List on Typology and English Medieval Literature," *Studies in the Literary Imagination* 8 (1975): 1–166.

55. Justin, *Apologia pro Christianis, PG* 6:410–11, 426. For example, he notes, "In imitation therefore of that Spirit of God which [i.e. spirit] is said to be carried above the waters, they call Prosperina daughter of Jove," with Minerva paralleling the Verbum (6:426).

56. Theophilus, *Ad Autolycum, PG* 6:1146–47.

57. Tatian, *Oratio adversus Graecos, PG* 6:854.

58. See also Augustine's discussions of allegory's three levels, in *De vera religione, PL* 34:165–66, and in relation to the Bible in *De civitate Dei* 13.21. Don Cameron Allen, p. 16, remarks that St. Augustine is "clearly discoursing on distinctions in the literal or historical reading."

59. Augustine, *De Genesi ad litteram* 1.1, ed. Joseph Zycha, CSEL 28, 3 (Prague, Vienna, and Leipzig, 1984), p. 3.

60. For a discussion of the impact of Hebraic exegesis, see Donahue, "Patristic Exegesis in the Criticism of Medieval Literature: Summation," in Bethurum, pp. 61–82. I disagree that typology can be seen as anything but a form of the historical or literal (rather than allegorical) level: typology works by correspondence of two literal or historical figures. Donahue argues that typology mixes Hebraic and Hellenic: Hebraic came first, but both affected Christian exegesis. An example of an early Hebraic interpreter is Melito of Sardis (fl. 161–80), whose Abraham offers Isaac as a prefiguration of the death of Christ: "The method is historical, concrete, Hebraic. The word 'allegory' as that word is commonly understood does not describe it. To distinguish it from allegorical interpretation, the earlier and Hebraic method is now sometimes called 'typological' " (Donahue, pp. 64–66). The difference between Greek allegorizing and Hebraic typology, according to Donahue, is that typology compares two concretes, whether persons, events, or utterances, but finds an unsuspected layer of meaning in the original record even though concrete remains concrete (Moses is still Moses). In Greek method, the original literal meaning is no longer alive: Athena (prudence) pulled Achilles by the hair (wrath).

61. *Venerabilis Baedae opera,* ed. Giles, 7:246–47, cited in the introduction to *Venerabilis Baedae opera historica,* ed. Charles Plummer, 2 vols. (Oxford, 1896), 1:lxii; and St. Thomas Aquinas, *Summa theologica* 1, art. 10, reply obj. 3, ed. Thomas Gilby (Cambridge: Blackfriars, 1964), vol. 1: *Christian Theology,* p. 38 (trans. p. 39).

62. Of the demigods, Hercules, Castor and Pollux, and Aesculapius were

viewed as deified men; see Cooke, pp. 396–402. There was apparently no uniform attitude toward the classics among the Christian Latin writers; attitudes ranged from approval to condemnation. But a knowledge of pagan literature and learning was favored as a means to bolster arguments and advance understanding of Holy Scripture. The study of pagan literature and learning was not only permitted but necessary, as there were only pagan schools in the Empire. These are the conclusions of Gerard L. Ellspermann, *The Attitude of the Early Christian Latin Writers toward Pagan Literature and Learning,* Catholic University of America Patristic Studies, vol. 82 (Washington, D.C.: Catholic University of America Press, 1969). See also Roy J. Deferrari, "Early Ecclesiastical Literature and Its Relation to the Literature of Classical and Medieval Times," *PQ* 6 (1927): 102–10, and Edward Kennard Rand, *Founders of the Middle Ages* (Cambridge, Mass.: Harvard University Press, 1928; London: Humphrey Milford/ Oxford University Press, 1928).

63. Tertullian, *Adversus Marcionem, PL* 2:260–61; on the father-gods, *Apologeticus,* trans. T. R. Glover, 8.4–5, 16, 14.2–4; on Moses, 19.1, 19.3; on poets, *Ad nationes* 2.7, *PL* 1:594–95.

64. Euhemerus is actually mentioned (through Ennius's Latin translation) in 4.29 of Arnobius's *Adversus nationes,* ed. August Reifferscheid, vol. 4, CSEL (1875; rpt. New York: Johnson Reprint Co., 1968).

65. Lactantius, *Divinae institutiones* 1.9.1–7, 1.13.8. See also Ellsperman, p. 67. See the translation of books 1–7 by Sister Mary Francis McDonald (Washington, D.C.: Catholic University of America Press, 1964).

66. For Augustine's objections to the pantheon (its variety, licentiousness, and demonic possession) see *Civ. Dei* 2.29, 3.5, 4.10–11, 9.9. See also Don Cameron Allen, pp. 15–16; and for discussions of Jupiter, Juno, Hercules, Neptune, Liber, and Flora, see Sister Mary Daniel Madden, *The Pagan Divinities and their Worship as Depicted in the Works of Saint Augustine exclusive of The City of God,* Patristic Studies, vol. 24 (Washington, D.C.: Catholic University of America Press, 1930), pp. 8–27, 127.

67. *Civ. Dei* 1.3 (Virgil); 18.14, 7.18. Augustine refers to Euhemerus's doctrine specifically in *De consensu evangelistarum.* See Madden, pp. 15–17, 8.

68. Merovingian and Carolingian commentators used multiple-sense allegorical exegesis: see Aldhelm in *De virginitate,* 4, in *Opera,* ed. Rudolf Ehwald, MGH 15:232; Hrabanus Maur, in *Expositio in epistolam ad Galatas* 4.24, *PL* 112:330; Bede, who uses both a threefold (*Opera* 7:317, 196–97; 8:22–23) and a fourfold (*Opera* 6:96–97; 7:246–47; 8:100) system of classification, in "Introduction," *Opera historica,* ed. Plummer, 1:lvi ff.

69. See John of Salisbury, *Policraticus* 7:12, ed. Clement C. J. Webb, vol. 2 (Oxford, 1909), pp. 143, 144.

70. See Bonaventure, *De reductione artium ad theologiam,* in *Works of St. Bonaventure,* ed. and trans. Sister Emma Thérèse Healy, 2d ed. (St. Bonaventure, N.Y.: Franciscan Institute, 1955), pp. 27, 29.

71. See Hugh of St. Victor, *Didascalicon de studio legendi* 6.3, ed. Charles Henry Buttimer (Washington, D.C.: Catholic University of America Press, 1939), p. 116. The definition of *allegoria* cited in the text comes from *De scripturis et scriptoribus sacris* 3, in *PL* 175:12.

72. St. Thomas Aquinas defines the meanings of scripture as literal or historical, allegorical, tropological, or moral. These are divided into two classes, the historical and the spiritual or mystical, in *Summa theologica* Ia, I, art. 10, reply obj., ed. Gilby, 1:36, 38, 40. In a work acknowledging St. Thomas's influence entitled "Tractatulus," it is declared that senses can be multiplied in four ways; see "Tractatulus," trans. H. Caplan, "A Late Mediaeval Tractate on Preaching," in *Studies in Rhetoric and Public Speaking in Honor of James Albert Winans* (1925; rpt. New York: Russell and Russell, 1962), pp. 7off. The first is according to the *sensus historicus* or *literalis* (by simple explanation of words); the second is according to the *sensus tropologicus,* "instruction or the correction of morals," to be used mystically or openly—openly, as in "Just as David conquered Goliath, so ought humility to conquer pride," or mystically, as in "Let thy garments be always white," Ecclesiastes 9:8 ("At all times let thy deeds be clean"). The third, *sensus allegoricus,* explicates by a "sense other than the literal": "David rules in Jerusalem" allegorically signifies that Christ reigns in the Church Militant. Exemplification by simile is used, as in lives of the saints or Christ, so the hearer will follow in his footsteps. The fourth is the *sensus anagogicus,* mystically or openly used, whereby "the minds of the listeners are to be stirred and exhorted to the contemplation of heavenly things." "Blessed are they that wash their gowns in the blood of the Lamb that they may have right to the tree of life," Revelations 22:14 (Vulgate), mystically means "Blessed are they who purify their thoughts that they may see Jesus Christ, who says: 'I am the way, the truth, and the life' " (John 14:6); openly, "Blessed are they of clean heart, for they see God." The allegorical sense the "Tractatulus" conflates with the typological (Augustine's analogical): "When the things of the Old Law signify the New, there is an allegorical meaning; when things done by Christ or the *figurae* of Christ [the just who preceded Christ] are signs of what we ought to do, there is a moral [or tropological] meaning; finally, if one regards these things as pointing to eternal glory, there is an anagogical meaning."

73. Hugh of St. Cher is cited in E. V. Dobschütz, "Vom vierfachen Schriftsinn," in *Harnack-Ehrung: Beiträg zur Kirchengeschichte ihrem Lehrer Adolf von Harnack zu seinem siebzigsten Geburtstage dargebracht von einer Reihe seiner Schüler* (Leipzig: Heinrichs, 1921), p. 12n. See also Frederick William Farrar, *History of Interpretation* (London, 1886), p. 295.

74. See Bonaventure, *De reductione artium* 5–7, ed. Healy, pp. 26–29 (Bonaventure's emphasis).

75. *Summa theologica* 1, art. 10, reply obj. 3, ed. Gilby, 1:38 (trans. p. 39).

76. Dante, "Epistola 10," "To Can Grande della Scala," in *Epistolae (The Letters of Dante),* emended and trans. Paget Toynbee, 2d ed. (Oxford: Clarendon Press,

1966), pp. 173–74, Latin, p. 198, English. All references to the letter derive from this edition. The *Convivio* (*The Banquet*), 2.1.2–15, also defines the four senses: see *The Literary Criticism of Dante Alighieri,* ed. and trans. Robert S. Haller (Lincoln: University of Nebraska Press, 1973), pp. 112–14.

77. See Cassian, *Collatio* 14.8, *De spirituali scientia, PL* 49:962ff.

78. Eucherius, *Formulae,* ed. Wothke, pp. 3–6.

79. McNally, p. 55.

80. Angelom of Luxeuil, *Enarrationes in libros regum, Praefatio apologetica, PL* 115:243ff; cited by Caplan, "Four Senses," p. 287f.

81. Bonaventure, *De reductione artium* 5–7, trans. Healy, pp. 27, 29.

82. Robert of Basevorn, *The Form of Preaching (Forma praedicandi),* trans. Leopold Krul, in *Three Medieval Rhetorical Arts,* ed. James J. Murphy (Berkeley, Los Angeles, and London: University of California Press, 1971), p. 183 (the entire tractate runs from p. 109 to p. 215).

83. Guibert of Nogent, *Liber quo ordine sermo fieri debeat,* in *PL* 156:25–26; also Caplan, "Four Senses," p. 282. Guibert has been translated by Joseph M. Miller, "Guibert de Nogent's *Liber quo ordine sermo fieri debeat:* A Translation of the Earliest Modern Speech Textbook," *Today's Speech* 17 (1969): 46.

84. Murphy, *Rhetoric in the Middle Ages: A History of Rhetorical Theory from Saint Augustine to the Renaissance* (Berkeley, Los Angeles, and London: University of California Press, 1974), p. 275. For the history of the art of preaching, see esp. chap. 6.

85. Robert of Basevorn, *Form of Preaching (Forma praedicandi),* in Murphy, ed., *Three Medieval Rhetorical Arts,* pp. 126–27. See also Murphy, *Rhetoric in the Middle Ages,* p. 270, which notes that "to the medieval mind, even Christ in his preaching was merely following a Creation-old pattern set by God the Father. Preaching was the second act of God following the creation of Man himself, and preaching formed for many ages the primary means of communication between God and man."

86. Such usage of the four senses by preachers was intended to help in the attack on Lollard and Mendicant heresies, as evidenced in a sermon of ca. 1400 by Master Robert Rypon, sub-prior of Durham, to which we shall later return. G. R. Owst has concluded that "biblical literalism, therefore, was clearly the mother of heresy. The Letter killed. It was only the Spirit that made alive" (*Literature and Pulpit in Medieval England: A Neglected Chapter in the History of English Letters and of the English People,* 2d ed. [1961; rpt. Oxford: Blackwell, 1966] p. 61). For a discussion of the homilists' use of allegory and the four senses, see Owst's chapter 2, "Scripture and Allegory." Indeed, Owst states, "The homilist may prefer on other occasions to mingle natural and Biblical *figures* together to illustrate his point. We have now to examine the influence of current modes of expounding Scripture in a more formal and systematic fashion. For it is here that we find a source, not merely of the naturalistic type of *example,* but also of the animal satire

and similitude, of marvellous narrations and devil stories, and certain lively allegoric features common alike to the later religious drama and to such famous allegories as *The Vision of Piers Plowman* and *The Pilgrim's Progress*" (pp. 56–57). For the history of allegorical exposition and the commentators thereupon, as well as the use of exposition in popular sermons, see Beryl Smalley, *The Study of the Bible in the Middle Ages* (1952; rpt. Notre Dame: University of Notre Dame Press, 1964), esp. chapter 5, "Masters of the Sacred Page."

87. "Tractatulus," in Caplan, "A Late Mediaeval Tractate," pp. 70ff. The related principle of employing kinds of explication is a type of rhetorical *inventio.*

88. Murphy, *Rhetoric in the Middle Ages,* p. 327. Richard of Thetford's *Ars dilatandi sermones* survives in twenty-seven manuscripts and is echoed by Robert of Basevorn (see, for example, Oxford Magdalen College MS. 168); it has been published (incompletely) as the third part of a work by St. Bonaventure, *Ars concionandi,* in *Opera omnia* (Quarrachi: Ad claras aquas, 1901), 9:16–21. Another translation appears in Harry C. Hazel, "A Translation, with Commentary, of the Bonaventuran 'Ars Concionandi' " (diss., Washington State University, 1972). Murphy, *Rhetoric,* p. 328, declares that "Richard's listings are remarkable only in that they demonstrate the continuing popularity of the 'four senses of interpretation,' the identification of metaphor as a separate form of support, and the relegation of reasoning to a place as merely one method among many."

89. In Murphy, *Three Medieval Rhetorical Arts,* p. 183.

90. The passage has been translated by Murphy, *Rhetoric in the Middle Ages,* p. 302.

91. Dante, "Epistola 10," par. 7, ed. (pp. 173–74) and trans. (p. 199) Toynbee.

92. Ibid., par. 8, ed. p. 174, trans. p. 200.

93. See the summary of the controversy in L. Jenaro-MacLennan, *The Trecento Commentaries on the Divina Commedia and the Epistle to Cangrande* (Oxford: Clarendon Press, 1974), pp. 1–3. MacLennan regards the epistle as a commentary itself of unknown authorship and studies its textual relation to the other commentaries. For a very different view, assuming Dante's authorship of the letter and using it (along with the definition of fourfold allegory in the *Convivio*) to interpret the *Commedia,* see Robert Hollander, *Allegory in Dante's Commedia* (Princeton: Princeton University Press, 1969). For Dante's distinction between the allegories of the poets and of the theologians, see also Hollander, "Dante *Theologus-Poeta,*" *Dante Studies* 94 (1976): 91–136; and the fourth chapter of Marcia L. Colish, *The Mirror of Language: A Study in the Medieval Theory of Knowledge,* rev. ed. (1968; rpt. Lincoln: University of Nebraska Press, 1983).

94. Robert W. Ackerman, "The Pearl-Maiden and the Penny," in *The Middle English Pearl: Critical Essays,* ed. John Conley (Notre Dame and London: University of Notre Dame Press, 1970), p. 162, but see also pp. 149–62. Related and similarly ignored interpretations include the Pearl-Maiden as an allegorical teacher, like Boethius's Philosophy, or Grace Dieu in *Le Pèlerinage de la vie humaine.*

95. Owst, pp. 61ff.

96. See William Vantuono's preface to vol. 2, *Patience and Sir Gawain and the Green Knight,* in *The Pearl Poems: An Omnibus Edition* (New York and London: Garland, 1984), in which he claims that *"Patience* reveals the poet's knowledge of the *artes praedicandi"* (p. ii) in that it has a prologue (lines 1–60) as a statement of theme, a body (61–257) in which the theme is dilated, and an epilogue (528–31) in which occurs the peroration of the medieval sermon accompanied by a restatement of the theme. See also Vantuono, "The Structure and Sources of *Patience,"* MS 34 (1972): 401–21; for comparable studies of *Cleanness,* see Michael H. Means, "The Homiletic Structure of *Cleanness,"* *Studies in Medieval Culture* 5 (1975): 165–72; and Doris E. Kittendorf, "Cleanness and the Fourteenth Century *Artes Praedicandi,"* *Michigan Academician* 11 (1979): 319–30.

97. See William Donald Reynolds, "The *Ovidius moralizatus* of Petrus Berchorius: An Introduction and Translation" (Diss., University of Illinois, 1971), p. 46.

98. See Eva Matthews Sanford, "Lucan and the Civil War," *CP* 28 (1933): 121–27; and also her "Lucan and his Roman Critics," *CP* 26 (1931): 233–47; George Meredith Logan, "Lucan in England: The Influence of the *Pharsalia* on English Letters from the Beginnings through the Sixteenth Century" (Diss., Harvard University, 1967); David Vessey, *Statius and the Thebaid* (Cambridge: Cambridge University Press, 1973), esp. chapter 2.

99. The argument for the *Metamorphoses* as an epic work comes from Brooks Otis, *Ovid as an Epic Poet* (Cambridge: Cambridge University Press, 1966), 2d ed., esp. chapter 1.

100. Chaucer, *Troilus and Criseyde* 5.1791–92, quoted from *The Riverside Chaucer,* ed. Larry D. Benson, 3d. ed., rev. from Fred C. Robinson (Boston: Houghton Mifflin, 1987).

101. On the popularity of Virgil in the Middle Ages, see Georg Zappert, "Virgils Fortleben im Mittelalter: Ein Beitrag zur Geschichte der classischen Literatur in seinem Zeitraume," *Denkschriften der kaiserlichen Akademie der Wissenschaften* 2.1 (1851): 17–70; Terence Anthony McVeigh, "The Allegory of the Poets: A Study of Classical Tradition in Medieval Interpretation of Virgil," *DAI* 25 (1964): 1894 (Fordham); and Paul F. Distler, *Vergil and Vergiliana* (Chicago: Loyola University Press, 1966), esp. chapter 8, pp. 135–92.

102. *Confessions* 1.13. See also Collins, pp. 11ff. In relation to the commentators' Homeric treatment of Virgil, see also Domenico Comparetti, *Vergil in the Middle Ages,* trans. E. F. M. Benecke, 2d ed. (1895; rpt. New York, Leipzig, Paris, and London: G. E. Stechert [Alfred Hafner], 1929), pp. 57–58, who finds that Alexandrian fondness for allegorizing evident in Servius.

103. On legends concerning Virgil himself in the Middle Ages, see J. S. Tunison, *Master Virgil: The Author of the Aeneid as He Seemed in the Middle Ages* (Cincinnati, 1888); Vincenzo Ussani, "In margine al Comparetti," in "Virgilio nel

Medio Evo," *SM* n.s. 5 (1932): 1-42; F. J. E. Raby, "Some Notes on Virgil, Mainly in English Authors, in the Middle Ages," *SM* n.s. 5 (1932): 59-371; John Webster Spargo, *Virgil the Necromancer: Studies in Virgilian Legends,* Harvard Studies in Comparative Literature, no. 10 (Cambridge, Mass.: Harvard University Press, 1934); and John J. H. Savage, "Some Possible Sources of Mediaeval Conceptions of Virgil," *Speculum* 19 (1944): 336-43.

104. Comparetti, pp. 34-36. See also Collins, pp. 9-10, on the study of Virgil around 400 A.D.: "The grammarians had obscured him by conjectures in hard places, by wanton interpretation, and by far-fetched explanations: the rhetoricians had turned him into an authority for 'figures' and a storehouse for 'themes' for declamation; the pedants prized him only as a *'doctus poeta,'* possessing that learning and 'correctness' which secured the popularity of Statius; while only a few here and there had any idea of Vergil's real merit, or the aim of the *Aeneid."*

105. For the use and importance of Virgil in the schools of this period, especially in the fourth century, see Comparetti, p. 64n.50, who cites as authorities Ausonius, Sidonius Apollinaris, Orosius, and of course Fulgentius; also Comparetti, pp. 76-77, 119.

106. Gregory of Tours, *Historia Francorum* 4.47, *PL* 71:308.

107. Comparetti, pp. 125-26.

108. T. W. Valentine, "The Medieval Church and Vergil," *Classical Weekly* 25 (1931): 65-67. This led to such veneration of Virgil that an unknown medieval hymn writer in a mass of St. Paul describes St. Paul as stopping at Virgil's tomb in Naples on his way to Rome, says Valentine. In addition, the practice of composing a Virgilian *cento,* or lines taken from Virgil and composed into a poem, often on Christian subjects, implied a conviction that Virgil professed Christian ideas and beliefs: see Lynn Carroll Stokes, "Fulgentius and the *Expositio Virgilianae Continentiae"* (diss., Tufts University, 1969), p. 5.

109. Valerie J. Edden, "Vergil and his Eclogues in Late Antiquity and the Early Middle Ages" (diss., University of Birmingham, 1971), preface.

110. See especially H. C. Coffin, "The Influence of Vergil on St. Jerome and on St. Augustine," *Classical Weekly* 17 (1923-24): 170-75; Courcelle, "Les Pères de l'Église devant les enfers Virgiliens," *AHDLMA* 30 (1955): 5-74; and for the influence of Virgil on Arnobius, Tertullian, Martianus, Nonius Marcellus, Augustine, Lactantius, Apuleius, Minucius Felix, Dracontius, and Fulgentius, see Stephane Gsell, "Virgile et les Africains," in *Cinquantenaire de la Faculté des Lettres d'Alger (1881-1931)* (Algiers: Société Historique Algérienne, 1932), pp. 5-42.

111. Jerome, *Epistola ad Eustochium* 1.12, *PL* 22:394; see also especially *Epistles* 35 and 49. Of the Roman authors, according to Coffin, "The Influence," p. 171, Jerome knew not only Virgil but also Sallust, Suetonius, Cicero, Quintilian, Terence, Lucan, Persius, and Valerius Maximus, and among the Greeks, Aristotle, Homer, Hesiod, Plutarch, and Plato.

112. Jerome uses Virgil in a discussion of the rhetorical figure *aposiopesis;* as an

authority for the fact that incense came from Sheba; and on the subject of placating the gods so that they do not injure men. He will often use a Virgilian phrase without acknowledgment. Jerome was apparently angry at writers who cited pagans in support of Christian doctrine, thereby linking the classical and the Christian. See Coffin, "The Influence," p. 172.

113. See *Civ. Dei* 1.8 especially; Augustine apparently believed in Virgil as the Messianic prophet and also believed that he had imitated passages of the Bible. Virgilian references or imitations occur in discussions of mythology, natural phenomena, scientific subjects; the gods mentioned include Jupiter and his place in the pantheon; Juno as sister and wife of Jove; Neptune, ruler of the sea and builder of the walls of Troy; Pluto, king of the underworld, and his queen Proserpina; then Mars, Rhea Silvia, Venus and Adonis, Mercury, Minerva, Cybele, the Fates, Janus, Proteus, Hercules, and Rhadamanthus (even using some of Virgil's phrases).

114. "Et plorare Didonem mortuam quia se occidit ob amorem, cum interea me ipsum in his a te morientem, Deus vita mea, siccis oculis ferrem miserrimus," *Confessions* 1.13.

115. See Henry Nettleship, "The Ancient Commentators on Virgil," in *The Works of Virgil*, ed. John Conington and Henry Nettleship, vol. 1: *Eclogues and Georgics*, 5th ed., rev. F. Haverfield (London, 1898). See also Collins, chapter 2.

116. Nettleship, p. lix, declares, "I have little doubt that much more of Asper's work is embodied in the commentary of Servius than its author chooses to acknowledge," an opinion supported by a comparison of the Verona scholia with Servius.

117. Nettleship, p. lxii. For Probus see the Georg Thilo and Hermann Hagen edition of Servius, which includes *Probi qui dicitur in Vergilii Bucolica et Georgica commentarius* 3:323–90.

118. These minor glossators either survive in notes or are mentioned in Servius and other commentators. In addition, Pollio is mentioned in Servius and Iulius Haterianus is mentioned in Macrobius and the Verona scholia (wherein many of these names appear). For the Verona scholia, see the Thilo and Hagen Servius, 3:393–450 (*Scholiarum Veronensium in Vergilii Bucolica Georgica Aeneidem fragmenta*). These names appear in the Verona scholia more frequently than in the commentaries of Philargyrius or Servius; probably these authors were used either directly by Philargyrius and Servius, or indirectly, through handbooks.

119. See Thilo and Hagen's edition of Servius 3:3, for the Donatus *Vita*.

120. See Servius 3:1–189, for *Iunii Philargyrii Grammatici explanatio in Bucolica;* see also Edden, pp. 157–59.

121. For the long and complicated controversy concerning the relationship between the Servius "vulgate" and the *Scholia Danielis,* concluding with the consensus that the "vulgate" is Servius, *Danielis* is later, see first Émile Thomas, *Essai sur Servius et son commentaire sur Virgile* (Paris, 1880), which in its first part

details the pseudo-Servius (additions to Italian manuscripts in the fifteenth century, the additions of Pierre Daniel in 1600, and additions after the sixteenth century) and in its second, the true Servius, his life and commentary, and the rapport between this and other commentaries. Thilo and Hagen print the "vulgate" Servius in ordinary characters and the *Scholia Danielis* in italics; Thilo believes the *Danielis* was compiled by an English or Irish scholar of the eighth or ninth century from the same sources Servius used. More recent buttressing of this position concerning the "vulgate" as Servian can be found in G. P. Gould, "Servius and the Helen Episode," *SCP* 74 (1969): 101–68, esp. 102–22; and C. E. Murgia, *Prolegomena to Servius 5: The Manuscripts,* University of California Publications, Classical Studies, no. 11 (1975), pp. 3–6.

For the view that the fuller 1600 Servius *Danielis* is the lost commentary by Aelius Donatus (fl. A.D. 350 as "grammaticus urbis Romae") which preceded Servius, see Rand, "Is Donatus's Commentary on Virgil lost?" *CQ* 10 (1916): 158–64. For the view that Servius's commentary on Virgil and additions to it printed by Daniel are indebted to Donatus, see H. J. Thomson, "Seruius Auctus and Donatus," *CQ* 21 (1927): 205–6. For the Servius *Danielis* as a compilation of both Donatus and Servius, because it is fuller and the author of the Terence commentary was familiar with the Virgil commentaries, see George Byron Waldrop, "Donatus, the Interpreter of Vergil and Terence," *HSCP* 38 (1927): 75–142; see also Savage, "More on Donatus' Commentary on Virgil," *CQ* 23 (1929): 56–59. Also, for evidence that Donatus's commentary was accessible in the ninth century at Liége, see Savage, "Was the Commentary on Virgil by Aelius Donatus Extant in the Ninth Century?" *CP* 26 (1931): 405–11. For the view that Daniel is two commentaries, Servius plus Donatus, and the Thilo edition therefore only one commentary, to which medieval additions were made, see Savage, "The Manuscripts of the Commentary of Servius Danielis on Virgil," *HSCP* 43 (1932): 77–121. For a discussion of the history of scholarship on the question, with plans for a new edition, and with the conclusion that Thilo includes Servius printed in roman type and *Servius auctus* (or *Danielis*) in italics to indicate additions; that the Servius *Danielis* additions came from the ninth-century manuscript from Fleury (now B.N. lat. 1750, and see University of Leiden Voss. 79); that possibly the Servius *Danielis* then is the lost Donatus commentary, see Rand, "Une nouvelle édition de Servius," *Académie des Inscriptions et Belles-Lettres* (Comptes Rendus des Séances de l'Année 1938), 4th series (Paris: Auguste Picard, 1938), pp. 311–24. However, for the view that Servius *Danielis* is not Donatus (otherwise material from it would have been included in Macrobius's *Saturnalia*), and that the *Scholia Danielis* therefore mixes medieval additions with Donatus and Servius scholia, see Nino Marinone, *Elio Donato, Macrobio, et Servio, commentatori di Vergilio* (Vercelli: Presso l'autore, 1946).

122. According to Comparetti, rhetoric was a neglected art, the few rhetorical

texts which have survived having been mostly ignored (p. 60). This includes the rhetorical commentary on Virgil by Tiberius Claudius Donatus, which has not been reprinted since the sixteenth century, and treatises attached to the Virgil manuscripts which cite examples from the poet to illustrate rhetorical figures, such as Iulius Rufinianus's treatise (in *Rhetores Latini minores,* ed. Helm, pp. 38ff); and the *Exempla locutionem* of the late-fourth-century Arusianus, used in the rhetorical schools (pp. 62ff).

123. In *Partitiones duodecim versum Aeneidos principalium,* vol 2 of *Institutionum grammaticarum libri,* in Heinrich Keil, ed. *Grammatici Latini,* 7 vols. (Leipzig: B. G. Teubner, 1855–1923), 3:459–515, Priscian takes the first line of each book of the *Aeneid* and asks a pupil to analyze each word grammatically and metrically so that in twelve lines the pupil uses all the chief rules of grammar and prosody.

124. Servius's sources are discussed by E. G. Sihler, "Serviana," *AJP* 31 (1910): 5, 7; Nettleship, p. xcvii; and Thomas, *Essai sur Servius,* pp. 187, 195ff.

125. See above, note 98; see also H. J. Thomson, "Lucan, Statius, and Juvenal in the Early Centuries," *CQ* 22 (1928): 24–27, who reveals that not only Statius but also Lucan and Juvenal were out of favor from the second to part of the fourth centuries.

126. Statius, while much read in the Middle Ages, was not so attractive to mythographic commentators: see Carlo Landi, "Intorno a Stazio nel Medio Evo e nel Purgatorio Dantesco," *Atti e Memorie della Real Accademia di Scienze, Lettere, ed Arti in Padova* n.s. 37 (1920–21): 201–37, esp. pp. 201–32. There are few commentaries on him listed, for example, in the *Summary Catalogues of the Bodleian Library Manuscripts Holdings.* Most of the manuscripts involved are editions; only two provide extensive scholia or glosses, both on the *Thebaid* (although there are more editions here of the *Achilleid*): the thirteenth-century MS. Rawl. G.114 and the fifteenth-century Auct. X, 1.1.25 (*Summary Catalogue* 14839; 16903).

127. See Brian Stock, "A Note on *Thebaid* Commentaries: Paris, B.N., lat. 3012," *Traditio* 27 (1971): 468–71, here, p. 468. These three autonomous commentaries, in addition to the one by Fulgentius, have been variously attributed: one, to Remigius of Auxerre, according to Courcelle, "Étude critique sur les commentaires de la *Consolation* de Boéce (IXe-XVe siècles)," *AHDMLA* 14 (1939): 18–19; the second, from the thirteenth century, is by Martianus de S. Benedicto, and the third is by Lactantius Placidus. Stock does not believe that the commentary by "Fulgentius" is from the fifth- and sixth-century period but instead from 1120–80, which to him explains why commentaries on the *Thebaid* are so rare, though widely read in the Middle Ages.

128. Henry Osborn Taylor, *The Emergence of Christian Culture in the West: The Classical Heritage of the Middle Ages,* 3d ed. (1911; rpt. New York: Harper, 1958), p. 50.

129. William Harris Stahl, *Martianus Capella and the Seven Liberal Arts,* vol. 1:

The Quadrivium of Martianus Capella: Latin Traditions in the Mathematical Sciences, With a Study of the Allegory and the Verbal Disciplines (New York and London: Columbia University Press, 1971), p. 40.

130. The Anonymous Erfurt Commentator declares: "Sed iste longe nobiliore materia et facundia praecellit, quippe qui nec Tullio in prosa nec Virgilio in metro inferior floruit": Cited in Edmund Taite Silk, ed., *Saeculi noni auctoris in Boetii consolationem Philosophiae commentarius,* Papers and Monographs of the American Academy in Rome, vol. 9 (Rome: American Academy, 1935), p. 4.

131. Stahl, *Quadrivium,* p. 56.

132. The most recent edition is in *Martianus Capella* by James A. Willis (1983). Eyssenhardt edited an early edition of the work, but its mistakes were noted in 1896 by John E. B. Mayor, "Martianus Capella," *CR* 10 (1896): 368; and Claudio Leonardi, "I codici di Marziano Capella," *Aevum* 33 (1959): 443–89; 34 (1960): 1–99; 411–524; the latter volume includes full lists of the 241 Martianus manuscripts. Martianus was not translated into English until the work of Stahl and Johnson (1977).

133. There does exist an overview by Paul Wessner in "Martianus Capella," in *Paulys-Wissowa* 14:2003–16, and an excellent, concise overview of Martianus's influence in Stahl, *Quadrivium,* pp. 55–72. But the handful of special interest studies either look back to antiquity, as in Stefan Weinstock, "Martianus Capella and the Cosmic System of the Etruscans," *JRS* 36 (1946): 101–29; or else single out some aspect of its treatment of the *artes,* as in Florentine Mütherich, " 'De Rhetorica.' Eine Illustration zu Martianus Capella," in *Festschrift Bernard Bischoff zu seinem 65. Geburtstag dargebracht von Freunden, Kollegen, und Schülern,* ed. Johanne Autenrieth and Franz Brunhölze (Stuttgart: Anton Hiersemann, 1971), pp. 198–206; or look at the work as a literary artifact, as in Fanny Lemoine, *Martianus Capella: A Literary Re-Evaluation,* Münchener Beiträge zur Mediävistik und Renaissance-Forschung, no. 10 (Munich: Arbeo-Gesellschaft, 1972). A single study has examined the source and influence of the *sapientia-eloquentia* concept— Gabriel Nuchelmans, "Philologia et son mariage avec Mercure jusqu'à la fin du XIIe siècle," *Latomus* 16 (1957): 84–107.

134. Stahl, p. 55; Stahl also notes, on p. 30, that "it is becoming apparent that Martianus, more than any other writer, was responsible for the fondness for unusual vocabulary evident in the writings of the Carolingian masters, and that he was one of the most pillaged of late Latin authors in the Middle Ages." According to Cora E. Lutz, "Remigius' Ideas on the Origin of the Seven Liberal Arts," *M&H* 10 (1956): 32–49, Martianus was an enormously popular author in the Middle Ages: his *satura* "was responsible for determining the pattern of education in the mould of the seven liberal arts for eight centuries" (p. 33). The chief source for studying the influence of the classics in the early Middle Ages is Manitius, *Geschichte* 9.2.1:504–19 on Martianus.

135. Leonardi, "I codici," 33:443–89; 34:1–99, 411–524. Stahl indicates,

however, that we have little knowledge of a manuscript tradition before the third generation in the Carolingian age (p. 31).

136. For a survey of Martianus Capella's influence, see Stahl, pp. 55–67; also Willis, "Martianus Capella and his Early Commentators" (diss., University of London, University College 1952), pp. 16, 24, on Boethius, Fulgentius, and Martianus in Great Britain (he notes slight use by Bede and parallels between the Latin of *Hisperica famina* and Martianus). See also Lutz's excellent survey in her edition of Remigius of Auxerre's *Commentum in Martianum Capellam*, 1:40–49, which acknowledges the influence of Martianus on writers of mythology (especially the third Vatican mythographer, Konrad of Mure's thirteenth-century mythological dictionary *Fabularius,* and, in the fourteenth century, John Ridewall [Ridevall] in his *Fulgentius metaforalis,* Boccaccio in his *Genealogia,* and Coluccio Salutati in his *De laboribus Herculis* and on the glossaries and other treatises (including the fourteenth-century commentary on Dante by Benvenuto Rambaldi).

137. Stahl, p. 70.

138. The commentary tradition has been examined, if at all, only briefly. For a brief and general survey of the commentary controversy and recent scholarship, see Stahl, "To a Better Understanding of Martianus Capella," *Speculum* 40 (1965): 102–15, though his longer study is contained in volume 1 of *Martianus Capella and the Seven Liberal Arts.* However, the best overview of the extant commentaries belongs to Lutz, in "Martianus Capella," found in *Catalogus Translationum et Commentariorum: Medieval and Renaissance Latin Translations and Commentaries,* vol. 2 of 3, ed. Paul Oskar Kristeller (Washington, D.C.: Catholic University of America Press, 1971), pp. 367–68, and, with John J. Contreni, in her "Addenda et Corrigenda," in vol. 3 (1976), pp. 449–52.

139. The eclipse lasted from the sixth to the ninth centuries; only Cassiodorus, Virgilius of Toulouse in the sixth century, and Julian of Toledo in the seventh century seem to have read the *Consolatio,* the Teutonic sackings of libraries having affected its very survival. Where it continued to exist, mostly in Italy, its classical and mythological bias made it too pagan for those secluded in monasteries whose study focused mostly on the Bible and Church Fathers. See Bolton, "The Study of the *Consolation of Philosophy* in Anglo-Saxon England," pp. 33–34.

140. Courcelle, "La Culture antique de Remi d'Auxerre," *Latomus* 7 (1948): 247. On Boethius's existence and survival in the Middle Ages, see also Courcelle's "La Survie comparée des *Confessions* augustiniennes et de la *Consolation* boécienne," in *Classical Influences on European Culture A.D.. 500–1500,* ed. R. R. Bolgar (Cambridge: Cambridge University Press, 1971), pp. 131–42; on Boethius's influence on the Middle Ages, see Howard Rollin Patch, *The Tradition of Boethius: A Study of His Importance in Medieval Culture* (1935; rpt. New York: Russell and Russell, 1970); in chapter 2 he provides a brief overview of Boethius commentaries, and in chapter 3 he discusses translations.

141. For a discussion of Boethius's genre, see Luigi Alfonsi, "Storia interiore e storia cosmica nella 'Consolatio' boeziana," *Convivium* 23 (1955): 513–21. He also discusses the correspondences between microcosm and macrocosm in the work. But in addition, according to Courcelle, the work can be seen as Menippean satire (in its alternation of prose and poetry), consolation, protreptic (in its turning of the narrator toward God), and apocalypse (in its similarity of apocalyptic setting to Hermes Trismegistus's *Poimandres* or Hermas's *Shepherd*), in *Late Latin Writers and their Greek Sources*, trans. Harry E. Wedeck from the 2d edition, *Les Lettres grecques en Occident de Macrobe à Cassiodorus* (Cambridge: Cambridge University Press, 1969), p. 296.

142. Courcelle carefully surveys the manuscripts for each Boethius commentary in "Étude critique," pp. 5–140; this earlier study, along with an analysis of central figures and concepts in Boethius, was published in *La Consolation de Philosophie dans la tradition littéraire: Antécédents et postérité de Boèce* (Paris: Études Augustiniennes, 1967). According to L. Biehler's edition of Boethius (vol. 194 of CC [Turnholt: Brepols, 1957]), of the eighty-four extant early manuscripts, eight come from the ninth century, five from the late ninth or early tenth centuries, and seventy-one from the tenth or eleventh centuries. The commentaries were probably more important than Boethius himself in the period of the ninth to the fifteenth centuries, according to Silk in a paper on "The Study of Boethius' *Consolatio Philosophiae* in the Middle Ages," whose abstract was published in *TAPA* 62 (1931): xxxvii–xxxviii. An overview of published and promised editions of, and articles on, the commentaries, with special emphasis on the pseudo-John Scot, was provided by Hubert Silvestre, "A propos de nouvelles éditions de commentaires à la 'Consolatio' de Boèce," *Scriptorium* 9 (1955): 278–81.

143. See Fabio Troncarelli, *Tradizioni perdute: L'antica "fortuna" della "Consolatio Philosophiae"* (Padua: Antenore, 1980), esp. chapter 3.

144. Bolton, "The Study," p. 37.

145. Alcuin lists Boethius as one of the books in the York library as of 790, although this may have been a translation of Aristotle. Yet he may have brought back to England a copy of the *Consolatio* after one of his visits to Italy, possibly even the copy Rudolph Peiper, the 1871 Teubner editor of Boethius, thinks is the one from which all extant manuscripts derived (on p. xvii); he discusses the commentaries on pp. xli–xlvi. See Bolton, "The Study," p. 34.

146. Manitius, *Geschichte* 9.2.1:33.

147. C. S. Baldwin, *Medieval Rhetoric and Poetic to 1400: Interpreted from Representative Works* (New York: Macmillan, 1928), p. 151: "At the fall of Rome the Trivium was dominated by *rhetorica;* in the Carolingian period by *grammatica;* in the high middle age, by *dialectica.*"

148. Gilbert A. A. Grindle, *The Destruction of Paganism in the Roman Empire from Constantine to Justinian* (Oxford and London, 1892), pp. 1–2, 10; and Walter Woodburn Hyde, *Paganism to Christianity in the Roman Empire* (Philadelphia:

University of Pennsylvania Press; London: George Cumberlege/Oxford University Press, 1946), p. 19.

149. H.-I. Marrou, *A History of Education in Antiquity,* trans. from the 3d French edition by George Lamb (New York: Sheed and Ward, 1956), pp. 322–33, but see also chapter 9 on Christianity and classical education.

150. Grindle, p. 30.

151. See the *Codex Theodosianus,* in *Codices Gregorianus, Hermogenianus, Theodosianus,* ed. Gustav Haenal, Corpus Iuris Romani Anteiustiniani, fasc. 2–6 (Leipzig and Bonn, 1837–42).

152. Taylor, *The Emergence of Christian Culture in the West,* p. 49.

153. Raby, *Secular Latin Poetry* 1:42.

154. Ibid. 1:99.

155. Marrou, pp. 345–46.

156. Ibid., p. 347; such dualisms are witnessed in the careers of Ennodius, Cassiodorus, and St. Gregory the Great.

157. Marrou, p. 347, indicates that the humanistic literary tradition continued in Byzantine strongholds like Ravenna (until 751), and in Rome and Naples, which were never conquered by the Lombards; on secular education and for the Felix of Padua story, see p. 349.

158. According to Bede, *Historia abbatum auctore Baeda,* chapters 1–7 in *Opera historia,* ed. Plummer, 1:364–70; see also "Introduction," pp. xviii–xx.

159. Greek had not been much known from the fourth century in Italy, less so in the sixth and seventh centuries, so that by the seventh century "wellnigh" the only knowledge of Greek was that of the Irish, according to Taylor, *Emergence,* p. 44. For the origin of the Irish priests, see Marrou, p. 349.

160. Ludwig Biehler, *Ireland: Harbinger of the Middle Ages,* trans. from the 1961 German ed. (London, New York, and Toronto: Oxford University Press, 1963), p. 1. This synthesis was not influenced by that of the Italian scholar Cassiodorus—the Irish monastery had always concentrated on the things of the mind (p. 2).

161. Kathleen O. Elliott and J. P. Elder, "A Critical Edition of the *Vatican Mythographers,*" *TAPA* 78 (1947): 198–99.

162. Marrou, p. 350. Accompanying Alcuin were the *Scoti,* Clement, Joseph, Dungal; accompanying Paul were Peter of Pisa and Paulinus of Aquileia.

163. When the Scots came to be called Scots (*Scoti*), after the Irish emigrants (*Scotti*) had colonized the western coast of Caledonia in the fifth and sixth centuries, then the Irish were called *Hiberni, Hibernienses, Hibernici.* John Scotus, properly Scottus Eriugena (John Scot) was an Irishman, one of the ninth-century *Scotti;* the thirteenth-century philosopher John Duns Scotus was Scottish, one of the *Scoti* (Biehler, pp. 2, 4).

164. For example, John Scot "Eriugena," "scion of Eire," was a theologian and philosopher (Biehler, pp. 10, 4c). For other reasons for the emigration of the Irish cleric, see Marrou, pp. 349–50, and also J. M. Clark, *The Abbey of St. Gall as a*

Centre of Literature and Art (Cambridge: Cambridge University Press, 1926). On the copying of classics, see Sanford, "The Use of Classical Latin Authors in the *Libri manuales*," *TAPA* 55 (1924): 190. Only one *liber manualis* has been found earlier than the ninth century; most of them began to be collected at St. Gall upon Charlemagne's orders, although there were probably earlier collections that linked late classical works with these collections.

165. Biehler, p. 2. The Irish established *Schottenmönche*, or monastic houses, in Ratisbon, Vienna, Erfurt, Würzburg, Nuremberg (p. 4).

166. Irish glosses appeared in early manuscripts in Würzburg, St. Gall, Karlsruhe, and Milan. Apparently it was Irish scholarship and not their traditions of art (except for fine manuscript illuminations) that was preserved on the continent (Biehler, p. 4).

167. W. P. Ker, *The Dark Ages* (Edinburgh and London: Blackwood, 1911), p. 20.

168. For this attribution to Asser see Troncarelli's controversial argument in *Tradizioni perdute* (cf. n142).

169. According to information supplied to me by Petrus Tax. See chapter 6, nn 34, 36, 37.

170. C. S. Baldwin, p. 151.

171. Raby, *Secular Latin Poetry*, 1:307.

172. Raymond Klibansky, "The School of Chartres," in *Twelfth-Century Europe and the Foundations of Modern Society,* ed. Marshall Clagett, Gaines Post, Robert Reynolds (Madison, Milwaukee, and London: University of Wisconsin Press, 1966), p. 5. An example is Bernard of Chartres, with whom this change of organization is associated. He read both pagan and late-antique works.

173. Charles Homer Haskins, *The Renaissance of the Twelfth Century* (Cambridge, Mass.: Harvard University Press, 1927), p. 7. On libraries see James Stuart Beddie, "Libraries in the Twelfth Century: Their Catalogues and Contents," in *Anniversary Essays in Mediaeval History by Students of Charles Homer Haskins* (Boston and New York: Houghton Mifflin, 1929), p. 21. On the popularity of classical texts, see Beddie's "Ancient Classics in the Mediaeval Libraries," *Speculum* 5 (1930): 3–20. However, the most popular and common book was the Bible (especially Genesis, Kings, Job, the Psalms, Song of Songs, and the Old Testament Apocrypha—Tobit, Judith, Maccabees—Apocalypse, and Paul's Epistles), followed by the Church Fathers, especially Augustine, Ambrose, Jerome, and Gregory (there was neither much Greek nor many Antenicene Fathers like Tertullian). Augustine's *De civitate Dei* was his best known work (Beddie, pp. 9–10).

174. For lists of known catalogues compiled to the year 1500, see Beddie, "Libraries," p. 1. The largest libraries in this century, with 342 to 546 volumes, were those of Corbie, Durham, and Cluny (Beddie, "Libraries," p. 2).

175. Beddie, "Ancient Classics," pp. 5, 6, 10. For a list and history of pagan

works employed as texts for instruction in the ninth through the thirteenth centuries, see M. Boas, "De librorum Catonianorum historia atque compositio," *Mnemosyne*, n.s. 42 (1914): 17–46; and for the twelfth century, see Haskins, "A List of Textbooks from the Close of the Twelfth Century," *HSCP* 20 (1909): 75–94.

176. See R. W. Hunt, "The Deposit of Latin Classics in the Twelfth-Century Renaissance," in *Classical Influences on European Cultures AD* 500–1500, ed. R. R. Bolgar (Cambridge: Cambridge University Press, 1971), pp. 51–56; and B. L. Ullman, "Classical Authors in Certain Mediaeval *Florilegia*," *CP* 27 (1932): 1–42.

177. Haskins, *Renaissance*, p. 6.

178. Rand, "The Classics in the Thirteenth Century," *Speculum* 4 (1929): 260.

179. Haskins, *Renaissance*, p. 93.

180. Rand, "Classics," p. 260.

181. See Sanford, "The Use of Classical Latin Authors," pp. 190–248; Rand, "Classics," p. 264n; and Ullman, "Classical Authors," pp. 1–42.

182. See Beryl Smalley, *English Friars and Antiquity in the Early Fourteenth Century* (Oxford: Blackwell; New York: Barnes and Noble, 1960), and Judson Boyce Allen, "Mythology and the Bible Commentaries and *Moralitates* of Robert Holkot" (Diss., Johns Hopkins University, 1963), p. 114.

CHAPTER 2: THE HELIOCENTRIC COSMOGONY
AND THE TEXTUAL UNDERWORLD

1. For Macrobius's view of Virgil, see the commentary on the *Somnium Scipionis* 2.8.1. For Macrobius as a Virgil critic, see especially Stanley Tate Collins, *The Interpretation of Vergil, with Special Reference to Macrobius* (Oxford: Blackwell; London: Simpkin, Marshall, 1909), pp. 15–20.

2. The dates of 395 and 410 were offered by H. Georgius in "Zur Bestimmung der Zeit des Servius," *Philologus* 71 (1912): 518–26, but Georg Wissowa, who has compared passages on items in both works, believed that the commentary was written earlier than the *Saturnalia*, in *De Macrobii Saturnaliorum fontibus capita tria, dissertatio inauguralis philologica* (Warsaw, 1880), p. 12. More recently, Alan Cameron has revived the argument and redated Macrobius's career to the early fifth century, with both the *Saturnalia* and the commentary written *after* 430. He does so by identifying Macrobius as "Theodosius," praetorian prefect of Italy in 430, in "The Date and Identity of Macrobius," *JRS* 56 (1966): 25–38. The supposed date on which the debate takes place in the *Saturnalia* could then be 384, a year before Praetextatus actually died. This would eliminate many conceivable embarrassments, including those relating to the paganism of some of the guests.

3. Nino Marinone, *Elio Donato, Macrobio, et Servio, commentatori di Vergilio* (Vercelli: Presso l'autore, 1946), in his appendix (p. 85) has noted 627 comments on the *Aeneid* in the *Saturnalia*: 58 references in *Sat.* 3.1–9, 136 in 4, 256 in 5.1–17, 89 in 6.1–5, and 45 in 6.6. There are scattered references in other books:

2 in 1.3–5, 7 in 3.10–12, 13 in 5.18–22, and 5 in 7. The average number of references to each book of the *Aeneid* is 52 (ranging from a low of 41 to book 5 to a high of 69 to book 10).

4. For a modern discussion of the genre of the symposium, see Jacques Flamant, *Macrobe et le néo-Platonisme latin, à la fin du IVe siècle* (Leiden: E. J. Brill, 1977), esp. pp. 172–232.

5. Most recently the Neoplatonism of Macrobius has been explored by Flamant, passim.

6. On the Neoplatonic and Greek sources of Macrobius, see especially Pierre Courcelle, *Late Latin Writers and their Greek Sources,* trans. Harry E. Wedeck (Cambridge, Mass.: Harvard University Press, 1969), pp. 13–47, mostly on Porphyry.

7. See Porphyry, *Philosophus Platonicus opuscula,* pp. 59ff. But see also these works on the sources of the commentary, in particular: Karl Mraz, "Macrobius' Kommentar zu Ciceros Somnium: Ein Beitrag zur Geistergeschichte des 5. Jahrhunderts n. Chr," *Sitzungsberichte der preussischen Akademie der Wissenschaften, Philosophischen-historische Klasse* (Berlin: Preussischen Akademie der Wissenschaften, 1933), pp. 232–86; on the importance of the *Dream of Scipio* in the fourth century (through the commentaries of Macrobius and Favonius Eulogius—and the work of Firmicus Maternus) and influence of the Platonic-Pythagorean use of the *Dream of Scipio,* see Courcelle, "La Postérité chrétienne du *Songe de Scipion,*" REL 36 (1958): 205–34. On ideas about myth, the world, the soul, immortality, glory, the great year, and their sources in the *Dream of Scipio* of Cicero, see Pierre Boyancé, *Études sur le Songe de Scipion: Essais d'histoire et de psychologie religieuses,* Bibliothèque des Universités du Midi, fasc. 20 (Bordeaux: Feret and Sons; Paris: E. de Boccard and C. Klincksieck, 1936).

8. For a discussion of Macrobius's *Somnium* commentary and a French translation of a brief adaptation of the commentary in a tenth- or eleventh-century hand, in MS. 10066–77 of the Bibliothèque Royale of Brussels, fol. 88r, see Hubert Silvestre, "Une adaptation du commentaire de Macrobe," *AHDLMA* 29 (1962): 93–101; for its literary influence see, for example, Kathryn L. Lynch, *The High Medieval Dream Vision: Poetry, Philosophy, and Literary Form* (Stanford: Stanford University Press, 1988).

9. See Valerie J. Edden, "Vergil and his Eclogues in Late Antiquity and the Early Middle Ages" (Diss., University of Birmingham, 1971), pp. 155ff.

10. On the manuscript tradition of the *Saturnalia,* see Antonio La Penna, "Studi sulla tradizione dei *Saturnali* di Macrobio," *Annali della Scuola Normale Superiore di Pisa,* Lettere, storia, e filosofia, series 2, no. 12 (1953): 225–52. On its influence see Edden, pp. 155ff; Davies, trans., *Saturnalia,* pp. 23–25; and Melchior Schedler, *Die Philosophie des Macrobius und ihr Einfluss auf die Wissenschaft des christlichen Mittelalters,* Beiträge zur Geschichte der Philosophie des Mittelalters, Texte und Untersuchungen, vol. 13 (Münster: Aschendorffsche, 1916), part 1.

11. For further notes on the use and adaptation of Macrobius in medieval authors like John Scot, the Anonymous of Brussels (MS. 10066–77), Rupert of Deutz, Arnulf of Orleans, Geoffrey of Breteuil, and the author of the *Florilegium morale Oxoniense,* see Hubert Silvestre, "Note sur la survie de Macrobe au Moyen Âge," *C&M* 24 (1963): 170–80. For the literary model of the *Saturnalia,* see T. R. Glover, *Life and Letters in the Fourth Century* (Cambridge: Cambridge University Press, 1901), pp. 173ff; see also Collins, p. 15.

12. According to Collins, p. 20, Macrobius's originality in the *Saturnalia* consists of using not only historical persons but actual speeches, as is the case with his character Servius. On the relationship between Servius, the *Scholia Danielis,* and the *Saturnalia,* see Marinone, *Elio Donato, Macrobio, et Servio.* Some scholars believe that Macrobius did not use Servius directly, but instead earlier commentaries also used by a grammarian. The character Servius, however, reveals his model's expertise in etymologies, dialects, and stylistic devices. For recent literary analysis of the characterization of Servius as modest, and for a fine close reading of the dramatic interplay among the characters, see Robert A. Kaster, "Macrobius and Servius: *Verecundia* and the Grammarian's Function," *HSCP* 84 (1980): 219–62; for an analysis of Servius's role as grammarian in his own commentary, in contrast to Macrobius's fictional and dramatic use of his statements, see also, by the same author, "The Grammarian's Authority," *CP* 75 (1980): 216–41.

13. Servius cites Plotinus, for example, in his *Aeneid* commentary 4.653–54 and 6.136. See also E. G. Sihler, "Serviana," *AJP* 31 (1910): 11–14.

14. See J. W. Jones, Jr., for his excellent classifications of the allegorical glosses in Servius, in "Allegorical Interpretation in Servius," *CJ* 56 (1960): 217–26, which he summarizes in his more recent "The Allegorical Traditions of the *Aeneid,*" in *Vergil at 2000: Commemorative Essays on the Poet and his Influence,* 107–32, ed. John D. Bernard (New York: AMS Press, 1986). For a summary of some of Servius's myths, see John Prentice Taylor, "The Mythology of Vergil's *Aeneid* according to Servius" (diss., New York University, 1917); on Servius's use of Ovid's *Metamorphoses,* see Alfredus Leuschke, *"De Metamorphoseon" in scholiis Vergilianis fabulis* (diss., University of Marburg, 1895; Marburg: Typis Friederici Typhographi Academici, 1895); for an index of names and things in Servius (and Donatus), see J. F. Mountford and J. T. Schultz, *Index rerum et nominum in scholiis Servii et A. Donati tractatorum* (Ithaca, N.Y.: Cornell University Press, 1930); finally, for a discussion of Servian philosophy, see Edith Owen Wallace, *The Notes on Philosophy in the Commentary of Servius on the Eclogues, the Georgics, and the Aeneid of Vergil* (New York: Columbia University Press, 1938).

15. Gods are in fact discussed in the later books of the *Saturnalia,* as in the first, mostly in conjunction with religious practices. For example, the Penates or household gods are mentioned in *Sat.* 3.4 in relation to the *delubrum* or shrine and identified as originally Apollo and Neptune who supposedly built the walls of Troy, a belief attributed to Virgil (see *Aeneid* 3.118). Macrobius extends this

definition to encompass the Stoic belief that the Penates represent those to whom we owe our breath, or *penitus,* hence Jupiter of the mid-aether, Juno of the lower air and earth, and Minerva of the highest part of aether. He cites Virgil, who seems to include Juno and Vesta in this group (Juno in *Aeneid* 1.734 and 3.437–8; and Vesta in 2.293). Macrobius also mentions Hercules as Mars in *Sat.* 3.12, in describing the kinds of leaves worn or used in sacrifices to Hercules, and Achelous and Ceres as water and corn in 4.18, changed to grape and corn to represent Liber and Ceres when they changed eating practices (here from the *Georgics* 1.7).

16. In fact Macrobius begins his explanation of the *Saturnalia*'s origin with two euhemeristic interpretations of Saturn. Called "chief of the gods," Saturn first arrived in Italy when it was ruled jointly by Janus and Cameses (this is derived from Hyginus; *Sat.* 1.7.19–25). Later Janus ruled alone, but because Saturn had taught Janus the laws of husbandry in using the fruits of the earth, Janus allowed him to share the kingdom, for which reason December as a month celebrates the Saturnalia and January as a name contains that of Janus. Saturn is regarded as the inventor of grafting, cultivating fruit trees, and the science of fertilization, for which reason "His reign is said to have been a time of great happiness, both on account of the universal plenty that then prevailed and because as yet there was no division into bond and free—as one may gather from the complete license enjoyed by slaves at the Saturnalia" (1.7.26: "regni eius tempora felicissima feruntur, cum propter rerum copiam, tum et quod nondum quisquam servitio vel libertate discriminabatur, quae res intelligi potest, quod Saturnalibus tota servis licentia permittitur"). The second euhemeristic explanation of the Saturnalia focuses on Hercules (*Sat.* 1.7.27), who left men behind him in Italy because he wanted them to protect his altar, or because he was angry with their negligence in protecting his herds. When attacked, these men found a high hill and became Saturnians because of the name of Saturn, their protector, and in return they created the Saturnalia in his honor.

17. An idea taken from the Greek *Antiquitates Romanae* (1.15, 1.19) of Dionysus of Halicarnassus (Davies, trans., *Sat.,* p. 60).

18. An idea taken from Hesiod's *Theogony,* lines 173–200, the source as well for the idea that Saturn's eating of his children represents another function of time, that which creates and destroys and then recreates all things (line 459).

19. According to Willis's note, this idea derives from Aristophanes's *Lysistrata,* line 1119, and Hesychius of Alexandria, *Lexicon,* s.v. *sathun.*

20. See Jones, "Allegorical Interpretation," p. 220n19: cf. Servius, *In Aen.* 1.47 and pseudo-Heraclitus, 151, Cornutus, 3.19, and Cicero 2.26.66; Servius, *In Aen.* 1.388 and Cornutus 2; Servius, *In Aen.* 1.71 and Cornutus 22; Servius, *In Aen.* 1.142 and Cornutus 4, pseudo-Heraclitus 7; Servius, *In Aen.* 1.292 and Cornutus 28; Servius, *In Aen.* 3.104 and Cornutus 6, Cicero 2.25.64.

21. In book 1 of Servius's commentary on the *Aeneid,* there are six physical interpretations of the gods: on Juno and Jupiter (1.47); Aeolus and Juno; Aeolus

alone; Neptune (1.142); Jupiter, Venus, and Mercury; Vesta and Fides (1.292). In book 8 there are nine: on Juno (twice); Cerberus (8.297); Vulcan (three times, e.g. 8.414); Aeolus; Iris (8.623); and Isis. In the books with fewer physical references we find three in book 2 (Minerva; Vesta [twice]); five in book 3 (Dardanus; Proserpina; the Harpies; Minerva; *genius*); three in book 4 (Juno; Tellus-Juno; Jove and Minerva); four in book 6 (Helena, Castor, and Pollux; Phlegethon; Tityus and Tantalus; and Ceres, 6.603); and four in book 7 (Neptune; Juno [twice]; Neptune and Messapus). There are only one each in books 5 (the birth of Venus, 580), 10 (Hercules), and 12 (Orcus). Line references are to the interpretations mentioned in my text.

22. For example, in his commentary on *Aeneid* 6.893, on the two gates, of horn and ivory, Servius declares that the gate of horn into sleep provides true dreams; the gate signifies the eyes, because they have the color of horn and do not feel the cold; the gate of ivory signifies the mouth, by means of the teeth, and provides false dreams, because we know what we speak can be false, but what we see is without doubt true.

23. From Atum came Shu and Tefnut, and from them, Geb and Nut, whose progeny included Osiris, Isis, Seth, and Nephthys. See the clear discussion of George Hart, *Egyptian Myths* (Avon: British Museum Press, 1990; rpt. 1991), esp. pp. 9–28.

24. There is an alternate explanation provided here by Macrobius that points to the serpentine movement of the sun in its course through the sky which in effect "puts an end" to the serpent when it finishes. Etymologically, too, when the sun ends his course by bringing the summer solstice marked by the longest day of the year, he is termed "Pythius," "as if hastening to the end," because his journey seems serpentine.

25. From Virgil's *Georgics* 1.5 and Servius's comment.

26. Cicero gives, in *De natura deorum,* six different genealogies of Hercules (3.42), three of Jupiter (3.53), four of Vulcan (3.55), six of Mercury (3.56), three of Aesculapius (3.56), four of Apollo and three of Diana (3.57), five of Dionysus (3.58), four of Venus (3.59), five of Minerva (3.59), and three of Cupid (3.59).

27. The *Aeneid* books goven the most euhemeristic glosses by Servius are: book 1 (6), book 3 (8), and book 6 (7); only three or four such references are found in the commentary on books 2 (3), 7 (4), 8 (4), and 10 (3). Only one or two are found in books 4 (2), and 9 (1), with none at all in books 11 and 12.

28. For Palaephatus and euhemerism, see the proem to *De incredibilibus,* ed. N. Festa, in *Mythographi Graeci,* vol. 3.2 (Leipzig: B. G. Teubner, 1902).

29. See Wilfred Pirt Mustard, "The Etymologies in the Servian Commentary to Virgil," *Colorado College Studies* 3 (1892): 1–37, esp. p. 32. He cites Sayce, *Science of Language,* 2.259. Most of Servius's rationalizations involve either heroes or monsters and not the gods, although he does mention the originally human nature of figures like Jupiter (*In Aen.* 3.359), Phorcys (5.824), Saturn (8.319), and Faunus (10.551, 10.558). Of the heroes and monsters he lists as having once lived, we find

Aeolus, Romulus, Thyestes, Hercules, Hymenaeus, and Atlas (book 1); the Myrmidons (book 2); Antandros, the Penates, Thracus, Scylla and Charybdis, Typhoeus, and Polyphemus (book 3); Ammon and the Hesperides (book 4); the Minotaur, Orpheus, Briareus, Typhon, the Gorgons, and Phaeton (book 6); Circe, Geryon, and Hippolytus (book 7); and Casus (book 8).

30. Reginald O'Donnell, "The Sources and Meaning of Bernard Silvester's Commentary on the *Aeneid*," *MS* 24 (1962): 235. For the view that Porphyry was the real master of Macrobius's thought, and a detailed examination of that idea, see Courcelle, *Late Latin Writers*, chapter 1. In Porphyry's commentary on *Odyssey* 13.102–12 there is a mystical description of the universe much like that of Fulgentius in the *Mitologiae*.

31. Nonmythological references to Virgil are few: on three and four as blessed numbers (*Aeneid* 1.94), see *Somn. Scip.* 1.6.44; on the Dardanians as Italians (*Aeneid* 3.94), see *Somn. Scip.* 1.7.8; on the value of political virtues (*Aeneid* 6.664), see *Somn. Scip.* 1.8.6; on the four kinds of passion, fear, desire, grief, and joy (*Aeneid* 6.733), see *Somn. Scip.* 1.8.11; on the passivity of the verb "to stand" (*Aeneid* 6.652), see *Somn. Scip.* 2.15.15.

32. Macrobius may be drawing here on Servius on *Aeneid* 6. Certainly the passage is repeated in the Middle Ages, most notably in 6.107 of the commentary on the *Aeneid* attributed to Bernard Silvestris.

33. In commenting on *Aeneid* 6.545, "I shall fulfill the number and rejoin the shades," Macrobius explains that the soul does not fail but merely leaves the body when its duties are done (*Somn. Scip.* 1.13.12); on *Aeneid* 6.724, 6.726–32, and 8.403 he uses the Virgilian lines to describe the World Soul animating the universe and engendering souls and all of creation (*Somn. Scip.* 1.14.14); see also *Somn. Scip.* 2.3.11 for mention of the World Soul, based on *Aeneid* 6.728–29. The universe is regarded as having a body, in *Somn. Scip.* 1.17.5 (from *Aeneid* 6.727), and the outermost sphere of the universe is regarded as a "supreme god," called "Jove" in Virgil (*Eclogues* 3.60), who is responsible for the fiery seeds that engender life on earth (Virgil's line reads, "With Jove I begin, ye Muses; of Jove all things are full," "ab Iove principium, Musae, Iovis omnia plena," glossed in *Somn. Scip.* 1.17.14). Note that this last idea is Stoic rather than Neoplatonic.

34. Macrobius scatters nonmythological, mostly cosmological and astronomical, references to Virgil (usually the *Georgics*) throughout the *Somnium* commentary—on eclipses of the sun (from *Georgics* 2.478 in *Somn. Scip.* 1.15.12); the poles of the earth, one above us, one below, "seen of black Styx and the shades infernal" (from *Georgics* 1.241–42 in *Somn. Scip.* 1.16.5); the Dog Star (from *Georgics* 1.217–18 in *Somn. Scip.* 1.18.15); the temperate zones given to the mortals by the gods (from *Georgics* 1.237–38 in *Somn. Scip.* 2.5.16); the Zodiac (from *Georgics* 1.237–39 in *Somn. Scip.* 2.8); the sun's course as a great year (from *Aeneid* 3.284 in *Somn. Scip.* 2.11.6); and on the unperishability of the living universe (from *Georgics* 4.226 in *Somn. Scip.* 2.12.13).

35. I exclude the *Scholia Danielis*. Mythological references in Servius's commentary on book 6 of the *Aeneid* include: Mars, Venus, and Vulcan (14); Pasiphaë and the Minotaur (14); Orpheus and Pluto (119); Helena, Pollux, Jove, and Castor (121); Proserpina (136); Phlegethon (265); Briareus, Hercules, and the Hydra (287); Typhon and the Echidnae, the Chimera and Bellerophon (288); the Gorgons and Harpies (289); Tartarus and Acheron (295); Hercules and Cerberus (395); Styx (439); Tityus (596); Tantalus, Ceres, Pelops, and Mercury (603); Orpheus and Calliope, and the seven chords (645 and 917); Eridanus, Acheloia, Phaeton, Aristaeus-Sun (659); Elysium-Lethe (705); *manes* and *genii* (743).

The *Scholia Danielis*, whatever their origin, offer heavily allegorical glosses for book 4, unlike the Servian glosses, and they also provide a new kind of allegorism, that which Jones, "Allegorical Interpretation," p. 224, terms *ex ritu Romano* because it interprets the text in the light of Roman religion—for example, with Aeneas as *flamen* and Dido as *flamenica*. Most of the twenty examples of such allegorical interpretation in the *Scholia Danielis* also derive from the fourth book.

Books of Servius's commentary on the *Aeneid* (again excluding the *Danielis*) with the next-highest numbers of mythological if not allegorical references are as follows. Book 1 has thirteen: Juno and Jupiter (line 47); Aeolus, or Juno and Aeolus (52, 71, 78); Neptune (142); Jupiter, Venus and Mercury (223); Amulius and Numitor, Vesta and Mars, Romulus (272); Vesta, Fides, and Janus (292); Achates (312); Thyestes and Atreus (568); Hercules, Hyla Aolchos, Priam and Teucer (619); Hymenaeus (651); and Hercules, Atlas, and Nilus (741). Book 8 has thirteen: Liber (43); Juno, Lucina, Matrona (84); Cacus, Arcades, Vesta (190); Hercules and Mars (275); Cerberus and Amphiaraus (297); Saturn (Janus, Jupiter) (319); Vulcan, Venus (389); Vulcan (414); Minerva (438); Vulcan, Juno, Jupiter, Aeolus (454); Hercules, Geryon, Evander (564); Iris (623); and Isis, Nile as *genius* of Egypt (696). Book 3 has twelve: Antandros and Hecuba (6); Penates, Jupiter, Juno, and Minerva (12); Lycurgus (14); Neptune and the Nereids; Jove and Latona; Python, Diana, Apollo, Proserpina, Vulcan (73); Dardanus and the raising of Jove by the Corybantes (104); Proserpina, Atalanta, Hippomenes, and the Corybantes (113); daughters of Pontus and Earth, Ocean, Harpies, daughters of Thaumantis and Electra (241); Minerva (281); Scylla and Charybdis, Phorcys, Glaucus and Circe, Jove and Hercules (420); Typhoeus-Jove (578); *genius* (607); and Polyphemus and Ulysses (636).

The remaining books boast relatively few. There are only eight in book 7: Circe and the Sun (19); Neptune (23); Venus and Adonis, Juno, Mephitis-Leucothea (84); Circe, Pomona, Mars (190); Juno (311); Geryon and Hercules (662); Neptune and Messapus (691); and Hippolytus, Minos and Pasiphaë, Apollo and Cyclops (761). There are six in book 2: Myrmidons (7); Minerva and the Trojans (16); Vesta (296–97); Neptune and Minerva (610); and Limbo (615). There are six in book 4: Juno, Lucifer, and Jove (130); Tellus and Juno (166); Ammon (196); Jove and Minerva (201); and Hesperides, Atlantis, and Hercules (484). There are four in book 10: Hercules, Juno, and Venus; Liber (18); Hercules (91); and Faunus (551, 558). There are three in book 5: the birth of Venus (801); Phorcys, son of Neptune and the Nymphs (824); and Ulysses and the Sirens (864); and one each in books 9, to Jupiter, Saturn, and the Giants (561), and 12, to Orcus (139).

36. Although many of Servius's etymologies come from the Greek without additional glossing—as in the names Arcturus (*In Aen.* 1.744 and *In Georg.* 1.67), Charon (*In Aen.* 6.299), Cumae (*In Aen.* 3.441, 6.2), Iris (*In Aen.* 5.606, 9.2); Kronos (*In Aen.* 3.104); and Prometheus (*In Buc.* 6.42)—many of them are in fact false, and probably responsible for later, more elaborate mythographic glosses. See Mustard, *Etymologies* pp. 32–37, esp. p. 32. For example, in book 1, Achates's name is derived from the Greek for *sollicitudo;* for this reason he is Aeneas's companion, because anxiety or solicitude is always a king's companion (*In Aen.* 1.312). In another place (1.174), because *achates* is said to be a type of stone (agate) used to spark fire, Achates is well said to be his companion ("nam achates lapidis species est: bene ergo ipsum dicit ignem excussisse. unde etiam Achatem eius comitem dixit"). Vesta is apparently called so "quod variis vestita sit rebus" (*In Aen.* 1.292), because she is dressed in various things. Domenico Comparetti, *Vergil in the Middle Ages,* trans. E. F. M. Benecke, 2d ed. (1895; rpt. New York, Leipzig, Paris, and London: G. E. Stechert [Alfred Hafner], 1929), points out that the appearance of the most obvious Greek words (those used most frequently by the Church and the schools) in glossaries and encyclopedias is misleading, because medieval authors did not generally know Greek (p. 167).

37. Servius continues, "quod autem dicit 'patet atri ianua Ditis sed revocare gradum superasque evadere ad auras hoc opus hic labor est' aut poetice dictum est aut secundum philosophorum altam scientiam, qui deprehenderunt bene viventium animas ad superiores circulos, id est ad originem suam redire: quod dat Lucanus Pompeio [9.13] ut 'vidit quanta sub nocte iaceret nostra dies': male viventium vero diutius in his permorari corporibus permutatione diversa et esse apud inferos semper" ["Because {Virgil} says, 'the door of gloomy Dis stands open; / but to recall thy steps and pass out to the upper air / this the task, this the toil,' either it is said poetically or according to the ancient knowledge of philosophers, who discovered that the souls of those who have lived their lives among the inhabitants of the underworld always rightly return to the upper regions, that is, to their origin: therefore Lucanus {*De bello civile* 9.13} notes to Pompey that 'he saw the thick darkness that veils our day': those {souls} who have lived their lives wrongly, however, tarry longer still in these bodies by means of various inimical permutations, change and remain"] (*In Aen.* 6.127; my translation of Servius, with translations of Virgil and Lucan from H. R. Fairclough and J.D. Duff).

38. *Somn. Scip.* 1.12.12: "Ipsum autem Liberum patrem Orphaici *noun ulikhon* suspicantur intellegi, qui ab illo individuo natus in singulos ipse dividitur. ideo in illorum sacris traditur Titanio furore in membra discerptus et frustis sepultis, rursus unus et integer emersisse, quia vos, quem diximus mentem vocari, ex

individuo praebendo se dividendum, et rursus ex diviso ad individuum revertendo et mundi implet officia et naturae suae arcana non deserit."

39. By Peter Dronke, *Fabula: Explorations into the Uses of Myth in Medieval Platonism,* Mittellateinische Studien und Texte, vol. 9 (Leiden and Cologne: E. J. Brill, 1974), p. 176n2; Cicero's preference is strong especially in the second book centering on Stoic philosophy (p. 22n).

40. William of Conches, cited in Dronke, ibid., p. 70, on *Somn. Scip.* 1.2.10.

CHAPTER 3: THE VIRGILIAN HERO IN NORTH AFRICA

1. Noted by Leslie George Whitbread, *Fulgentius the Mythographer* (Columbus: Ohio State University Press, 1971), p. 99.

2. The author's name given in *De aetatibus mundi et hominis* is "Fabio Claudius Gordianus Fulgentius," but according to M. L. W. Laistner, *De aetatibus mundi* was written by Fabius Planciades because of the similar style and fantastic etymologies. See "Fulgentius in the Carolingian Age," in *Mélanges Hrouchevsky* (Kiev: Ukrainian Academy of Sciences, 1928), pp. 445–56, rpt. in the more accessible *Intellectual Heritage of the Early Middle Ages,* sel. Laistner, ed. Chester G. Starr (Ithaca: Cornell University Press, 1957), pp. 202–15, here, p. 204. All references to Laistner come from the 1957 reprinting.

3. Laistner notes, on p. 203, that *Super Thebaiden* is attributed to another Fulgentius, the Bishop of Ruspe, in the unique manuscript, Paris, B.N. lat. 3012, which dates from the thirteenth century. This attribution may well predate the writing of the manuscript, given the familiarity of ninth-century scholars with the writings of both figures. Laister concludes, on p. 206, that the work is by Fulgentius the mythographer, contrary to modern scholars' belief that it is a post-Fulgentian compilation (because the Greek etymologies are far-fetched—according to Rudolf Helm—and because "Surculus" was not used as a nickname for Statius before the tenth century). In support of his argument Laistner declares that parts of the work have been found in the ninth-century *Scholica* of Martin of Laon and therefore it could not have been written as late as the tenth century; further, the Greek is no worse than that which occurs elsewhere in Fulgentius. According to Laistner it was only a less popular work than the other Fulgentian pieces. In contrast, Brian Stock argues that the *Super Thebaiden* now extant was actually written 1120–1180 and not in the sixth century, in "A Note on *Thebaid* Commentaries: Paris, B.N., lat. 3012," *Traditio* 27 (1971): 468–71. If Stock is right, the lack of a precedent could explain why commentaries on the *Thebaid* are rare, even though it was a widely-read text in the Middle Ages. Until more definite proof has been adduced for such a late date, *Super Thebaiden* will be regarded in this study as a Fulgentian (and sixth-century) work.

4. Laistner, p. 210.

5. Domenico Comparetti, *Vergil in the Middle Ages,* trans. E. F. M. Benecke, 2d

ed. (1895; rpt. New York, Leipzig, Paris, and London: G. E. Stechert and Co. [Alfred Hafner], 1929), p. 119. For the identification of Fulgentius's name and Sigebert's profession of admiration, see Sigebertus Gemblacensis (Sigebert of Gembloux), "De scriptoribus ecclesiasticis," *PL* 150:28.

6. See Lynn Carroll Stokes, "Fulgentius and the *Expositio Virgilianae Continentiae*" (diss., Tufts University, 1969), pp. 56–63. "Fabius Planciades" were his father's and grandfather's names. Calliope calls him "Fabi" and then "Fulgentius" in the *Mitologiae,* and "Planciades" is a third name, unusual because it is a patronym of Plancius by Greek analogy and should be "Plancianus," suggesting perhaps an adoption. See also Michael Zink, *Der Mytholog Fulgentius. Ein Beitrag römischen Litteraturgeschichte und zur Grammatik des afrikanischen Lateins* (Würzburg, 1867), p. 8: "vir Clarissimus," which appeared in the title of a manuscript of Fulgentius, referred to the class of *Clarissimi* and included famous or renowned civil servants. The lowest rank consisted of nobles from wealthy families, and the ranks ascended from *Linie Illustres* to *Spectabiles, Clarissimi, Perfectissimi,* and *Egregii,* making the *Clarissimi* very definitely a middle rank.

7. According to Stokes, pp. 46–47.

8. Much of the early scholarship on Fulgentius attempted to pinpoint his identity, primarily because for so long he was confused with Fulgentius Bishop of Ruspe. For this erroneous identification, see Otto Friebel, *Fulgentius, der Mythograph und Bischof,* Studien zur Geschichte und Kultur des Altertums, vol. 5, nos. 1 and 2 (Paderborn: Schöning, 1911). But based on stylistic differences in the writing of the two men, Rudolf Helm concludes they are not the same, in "Der Bischof Fulgentius und der Mythograph," *RMP* 54 (1899): 111–34. See also, for this conclusion, F. Skutsch, "Fulgentius," in Paulys-Wissowa 7: 215–27. Pierre Langlois, "Les Oeuvres de Fulgence le mythographe et le problem des deux Fulgence," *Jahrbuch für Antike und Christentum* 7 (1964): 94–105, sees no substantial barrier to identifying the two Fulgentiuses. Laistner doubts that their works—theological works by the Bishop of Ruspe and profane and mythological works by Fabius Planciades—could have been written by the same person, and he argues that the ninth-century scholars never identified the mythographer as the bishop. See Laistner, p. 203.

9. Stokes, p. 45; Zink also believes he was Catholic, p. 11.

10. Stokes, p. 45; Zink, p. 4; Comparetti, p. 116.

11. Stokes, p. 45; and Stéphane Gsell, "Virgile et les Africains," in *Cinquantenaire de la Faculté des lettres d'Alger* (1881–1931) (Algiers: Société Historiques Algérienne, 1932), pp. 5–42.

12. Stokes, p. 45. According to Zink, as one of the *Clarissimi* he was a truly distinguished *grammaticus,* well-known in Carthage, because professors normally filled the lesser ranks of the *Spectabiles,* in Theodosius and Valentian II (p. 9).

13. Comparetti, p. 114. For the order of composition of these works, see Whitbread, *Fulgentius,* pp. 8–9: he began with the *Mythologies* and continued with

the *Content of Virgil, Explanation of Obsolete Words, On the Ages of the World,* and *On the Thebaid.*

14. Stokes, pp. 40–42. "Leipogrammata," or lipogrammatic writings, intentionally omit one or more letters (or words containing those letters) as a poetic or formal device. So Fulgentius in the fourteen completed sections (ending in O) omits the names of Adam and Eve in the first section, on A. Sometimes a related letter will be substituted for the omitted letter.

15. Mentioned by Paul Lehmann, *Mittelalterliche Bibliothekskataloge Deutschlands und der Schweiz; herausgegeben von der Bayerischen Akademie der Wissenschaften, München* (Munich: Oscar Beck, 1918), 1:89, who is then cited by Laistner, p. 206.

16. Comparetti, p. 108.

17. Gabriele Rauner-Hafner, "Die Vergilinterpretation des Fulgentius Bemerkungen zu Gliederung und Absicht der *Expositio Virgilianae continentiae,*" *MJ* 13 (1978): 7–49, points to Neoplatonic underpinnings of the Virgil commentary and similar glosses in the pseudo-Heraclitus, especially in regard to etymologizing tendencies.

18. Cited in 123.4–6, Helm's edition, and on p. 172 of Whitbread's *Fulgentius.* Stahl notes the existence of a commentary on Martianus's first two books catalogued, "Item commentum solempne Fulgencii insignis viri super duobus libris Marcialis (sic) de nupciis Mercurii et philologie," cited from *Mittelalterliche Bibliothekskatalogue,* 2:16.3, in William Harris Stahl, vol. 1 of *Martianus Capella and the Seven Liberal Arts: The Quadrivium of Martianus Capella, Latin Traditions in the Mathematical Sciences 50 B.C.–A.D. 1250* (New York and London: Columbia University Press, 1971), p. 56n3.

19. Stahl, *Quadrivium,* pp. 56–57.

20. Stanley Tate Collins, *The Interpretation of Vergil, with Special Reference to Macrobius* (Oxford: Blackwell; London: Simpkin, Marshall, and Co., 1909), pp. 9–10.

21. Comparetti, p. 77; St. Gregory of Tours, in "Prooemium" to *Libri miraculorum* 714, *PL* 71:706, declares, "Non enim oportet fallaces commemorare fabulas, neque philosophorum inimicam Deo sapientiam sequi, ne in judicium aeternae mortis Domino discernente cadamus. . . . Non ego Saturni fugam, non Junonis iram, non Jovis stupra, non Neptuni injuriam, non Aeoli sceptra; non Aeneadum bella, naufragia, vel regna commemoro: taceo Cupidinis emissionem; non Ascanii dilectionem hymenaeosque, lacrymas, vel exitia saeva Didonis: non Plutonis triste vestibulum, non Proserpinae stuprosum raptum non Cerberi triforme caput; non revolvam Anchisae colloquia, non Ithaci ingenia, non Achillis argutia, non Sinonis fallacias; non ego Laocoontis consilia, non Amphitrionidis robora, non Jani conflictus, fugas, vel obitum exitialem proferam," etc.

22. Whitbread, *Fulgentius,* pp. 15, 16.

23. Stokes, pp. 37ff, has described the three-part structure by noting in particular that the first part focuses on the contemplative life, as exemplified by Minerva and

witnessed in priests, etc.; the second, on the active life, exemplified by Juno's avarice, and witnessed in Fulgentius's contemporaries; and also in the second, on the voluptuous life, exemplified by Venus's pleasure-seeking and his contemporaries' murders, pillage, malice, related to Hercules versus Antaeus, Ulysses versus the Sirens, or wisdom battling lust; the third part continues this, with the emphasis falling more on the denigration of lust. He argues that the progression is Ovidian in its movement from the gods to the heroes and human history.

24. In his forthcoming Cambridge University Press book on Virgil commentary in the Middle Ages, Chris Baswell in his chapter on Virgilized Boethius argues that the process worked conversely to the way I suggest, that is, that Boethius was himself deliberately Virgilizing his own poem. He agrees that it is unlikely, if possible, for Fulgentius to have influenced Boethius.

25. No one has yet argued that Martianus affected Boethius: there is little evidence of Martianus's influence in the quadrivium books of Boethius, where it might be expected, declares Stahl, *Quadrivium*, p. 57. Martianus probably did not know Greek, at least not enough to use Greek sources; Boethius translated and used Greek technical manuals, whereas Martianus depended upon Latin manuals primarily, according to Stahl, 1:58.

26. The *Metamorphoses* exhibits an epic style in its meter, diction, narrative, solemn tone, long speeches, and the concealment of the personality of the epic writer, according to Brooks Otis, *Ovid as an Epic Poet* (Cambridge: Cambridge University Press, 1966), chap. 1, pp. 23–24, 49.

27. The first section of Ovid's *Metamorphoses,* consisting of the first two books, deals with the divine love of the gods or a "divine comedy"; the second, from books 3 to 6, line 400, with the avenging gods; the third, from the sixth book, line 400, to book 11, with human lovers; and the fourth, from the twelfth book to the end of the fifteenth, with Rome and its deified ruler (Otis, pp. 47ff).

28. Ovid and Fulgentius both discuss the Creation, Phaethon, and the Raven in their first books, but then Actaeon, from an early book of Ovid (*Metamorphoses* 3), is found in the third and last book of the *Mitologiae;* Tiresias, from *Metamorphoses* 3, appears in *Mit.* 2; Mars and Venus, from *Metamorphoses* 4, in *Mit.* 2; Perseus, from *Metamorphoses* 4 and 5, in *Mit.* 1; Hercules, from *Metamorphoses* 9, in *Mit.* 2; Orpheus and Eurydice, from *Metamorphoses* 10, in *Mit.* 3; Adonis, the same; Midas, from *Metamorphoses* 11, in *Mit.* 2, and so forth.

29. See J. W. Jones, Jr., "Vergil as *Magister* in Fulgentius," *Classical, Mediaeval, and Renaissance Studies in Honor of Berthold Louis Ullman,* ed. Charles Henderson, Jr. (Rome: Edizioni di Storia e Letteratura, 1964), 1:273–75. Jones argues that Virgil here functions like a schoolmaster to suggest the ubiquity of allegorizing interpretation in the schools of Fulgentius's day, and that possibly Fulgentius was either a pupil or teacher in the grammar schools. See also Seth Lerer's interesting discussion in *Boethius and Dialogue: Literary Method in The Consolation of Philosophy* (Princeton: Princeton University Press, 1985), pp. 56–69, in which he analyzes Fulgentius's

"comic restructuring of the patterns of student/teacher colloquy fashioned by the earlier authors," p. 57, with the dialogue functioning as a foil for that of the *Consolatio.* He also notes, in Fulgentius's reading of Aeneas's allegorical journey in the twelve books, Aeneas's similar confrontations with authoritative figures like Virgil/ Philosophy. Lerer's work on Fulgentius's frame was apparently written concurrently with, or even after, my own, although his book appeared before this one.

30. Zink, pp. 28–32; for Fulgentius's other allusions to and citations from classical authors, see Armand Gasquy, *De Fabio Planciade Fulgentio, Virgilii interprete,* Berliner Studien für Classische Philologie und Archaelogie, part 6, vol. 1 (Berlin, 1887). Servius's etymologies and allegories in all three commentaries influenced Fulgentian practice, although the words *allegoria, allegoricis,* and *allegorice* do not appear in Servius's commentary on the *Aeneid,* but only in his later commentaries on the *Eclogues* and *Georgics;* and technically these terms there referred to a specific rhetorical figure and not to the late medieval (Dantesque) concept of polysemous levels. See E. G. Sihler, "Serviana," *AJP* 31 (1910): 4. See also Harrison Cadwallader Coffin, "Allegorical Interpretation of Vergil with Special Reference to Fulgentius," *Classical Weekly* 15 (1921): 33–5, on the Virgil commentary. For Tertullian's influence on Fulgentius, see Whitbread, "Fulgentius and Dangerous Doctrine," *Latomus* 30 (1971): 1157–61.

31. Servius, ed. Thilo and Hagen, 3:3. The loose paraphrase appears in Comparetti, p. 56.

32. Comparetti, p. 59.

33. Thilo and Hagen, 3:4 (*In Buc.,* proem). For these citations see Jones, "Allegorical Interpretation in Servius," *CJ* 56 (1960): 217–26.

34. The episodic and disjointed *Thebaid* can be seen as unified if one regards the epic hero as multiple—the Seven (including the sons of Oedipus) trying to regain Thebes—or as single, the city of Thebes itself. See David Vessey, *Statius and the Thebaid* (Cambridge: Cambridge University Press, 1973), especially chap. 2. For discussions of the literary tradition and merit of the Statius commentary of Fulgentius, see Carlo Landi, "Intorno a Stazio nel Medio Evo e nel Purgatorio Dantesco," *Atti e Memorie della Real Accademia di Scienze, Lettere, ed Arti in Padova,* n.s. 37 (1920–21): 201–37, esp. pp. 220–26; also Margaret Ruth Reynolds, "Statius and his Influence from the First Century to the Fifteenth Century," (diss., University of Birmingham, 1971), pp. 211–14, which is mostly a summary of the Statius *Thebaid.*

CHAPTER 4: OVID'S CUPID
AS THE DEMON OF FORNICATION

1. For Theodulf's contribution to Ovidian poems, see generally Salvatore Battaglia, "La tradizione di Ovidio nel medioevo," *Filologia romanza* 6 (1959): 185–224, esp. pp. 209ff. Of his 426 verses in hexameters he imitated Ovid twice (Cuissard, *Théodulfe, évêque d'Orléans, sa vie et ses oeuvres* [Orleans, 1892], p. 51). His

imitations differed from those of his contemporaries in that his Romanized and Christian education is reflected therein, as in "De libris." For an annotated text of "De libris," see *Carmina* no. 45, pp. 545–44, in Ernest Duemmler, ed., *Poetae Latini aevi Carolini*, in *Poetarum historica, Latinorum medii aevi*, vol. 1, MGH (Berlin, 1881).

2. See Duemmler, p. 547n. The particular section on Tellus in Isidore describes the goddess of fields (also known as Ceres, Ops, Proserpina, Vesta, and Magna Mater) as possessing a drum to signify the orb of the earth: "Quod tympannum habet, significare volunt orbem terrae" (*Etym.* 8.11.62); the idea is drawn from Augustine, *Civ. Dei* 7.24 on Varro. Katherine Nell MacFarlane notes that Vesta's round temple, with fire inside (Vesta herself), resembles the round earth, in "Isidore of Seville on the Pagan Gods (*Origines* VIII.11)," *Transactions of the American Philosophical Society*, vol. 70 (Philadelphia: American Philosophical Society, 1980), p. 25. If Theodulf's "pictura" here is based upon a written source, that is, from Isidore, there is no need to look elsewhere (for example, various art objects) for corroboration.

3. William G. Rusch, *The Later Latin Fathers* (London: Gerald Duckworth, 1977), p. 199.

4. Maurice Hélin, *A History of Medieval Latin Literature*, rev. ed., trans. Jean Chapman Snow (New York: William Salloch, 1949), p. 12.

5. See Jacques Fontaine, "Isidore de Séville auteur 'ascétique': Les Énigmes des *Synonyma*," *SM* series 3, 6.1 (1965): 163; the style was even termed *stilus isidorianus*. John of Garland in the thirteenth century defines this as "clausule similem habentes finem secundum leonitatem et assonantiam."

6. According to Ernest Brehaut, "An Encyclopedist of the Dark Ages: Isidore of Seville," *Studies in History, Economics, and Public Law* 48 (1912): 1–275, here, p. 16. Brehaut also describes the *Etymologiae* as a "cross-section of the debris of scientific thought at the point where it is most artificial and unreal." Among the earlier encyclopedists, Marcus Terentius Varro (A.D. 116–27) compiled his *Disciplinae* on the liberal arts and medicine and architecture (he also wrote encyclopedias on Roman antiquities and Latin language, of which only a partial *De lingua latina* has survived); Verrius Flaccus wrote the first Latin lexicon at about the same time; Celsus wrote his *Artes* and the elder Pliny, *Naturalis historia*, in the next century; and Suetonius, in the reign of Hadrian, his *Prata*. Fontaine comments on the curious hybrid of classical and medieval in Isidore, in *Isidore de Séville et la culture classique dans l'Espagne wisigothique*, 2 vols. in 1 (Paris: Études Augustiniennes, 1959), p. 826.

7. In the twenty books of the *Etymologiae* Isidore ranges from *grammatica* in the first to rhetoric and dialectic in the second, mathematics (a combination of arithmetic, geometry, music and astronomy) in the third, medicine in the fourth, law and the division of time—chronology—in the fifth, theology in books 6 to 8 (ecclesiastical books and offices in 6; God, angels, and the saints in 7; the Church and its sects in 8, as well as a section on the universe and the gods);

a potpourri in the ninth (language, reigns, militia, citizens, in relation to the histories of various peoples); "vocum certarum alphabetum" (words and alphabets) in the tenth; men and monsters ("de homine et portentis") in the eleventh; zoology in the twelfth; cosmography and geography in the thirteenth and fourteenth; architecture and building and field surveying in the fifteenth and part of the nineteenth; jewels and metals, or mineralogy, in the sixteenth; "de rebus rusticis," including agriculture, in the seventeenth; military science (war, circus, theatre) in the eighteenth; ships, buildings, and clothing in the nineteenth and twentieth; unfinished, the twentieth book focuses on food and domestic and agricultural matters.

8. Theodulf's dates have not been completely verified; we know that he flourished around 786 and died in 821. He was apparently born around 750, according to "Théodulfe, évêque d'Orléans," *Histoire littéraire de la France par les religieux bénédictins de la congrégation de Saint Maur* (Paris, Palmé, 1866), 4:459–74; or 760, according to his editor Duemmler; he became Bishop of Orleans in 783, was Abbé of Saint-Benoît in 801, Ambassador to the Pope in 816, imprisoned and exiled in 817, and died in 821. For material relating to his life and works, see also Charles Cuissard, *Théodulfe, évêque d'Orléans, sa vie et se oeuvres, avec une carte du Pagus Aurelianensis au IXe siècle* (Orleans, 1892), esp. chaps. 2 through 5, pp. 41–103 (the rest concerns the ninth-century religious background); and Hans Liebeschütz, "Theodulf of Orleans and the Problem of the Carolingian Renaissance," in *Fritz Saxl 1890–1948: A Volume of Memorial Essays from His Friends in England,* ed. Donald J. Gordon (London, Edinburgh, Paris, Melbourne, Toronto, and New York: Thomas Nelson and Sons, 1957), pp. 77–92.

9. Charlemagne, in his own biography viewed as a type of Roman Augustus, wanted to help the Frankish Church and preserve society's strength by restoring various literary activities in the monastic and clerical corps and encouraging the study of Latin. See Liebeschütz, pp. 77, 79. Largely as a result of the Emperor's initiatives, the Carolingian period—according to the prologue to the *History* of Gregory of Tours—renewed the classical tradition of learning, that is, the appreciation of poetry and literary composition. For an overview of Theodulf's historical and literary influence within this period and thereafter, see Raby, *Secular Latin Poetry* 1:187–97; and Manitius, *Geschichte* 9.2.1:536–43. Note that Theodulf is believed to be the author of the *Libri Carolini,* according to Ann Freeman, "Theodulf of Orleans and the *Libri Carolini,*" *Speculum* 32 (1957): 663–705. And his use of classical authors influenced other scholars, for example, Alberic of Monte Cassino, whose citation of eleven classical authors (Virgil, Lucan, Terence, Persius or Horace, Ennius, Boethius, Sallust, Cicero, and Augustine) may have come from Isidore's *Etymologiae:* see H. M. Willard, "The Use of the Classics in the *Flores Rhetorici* of Alberic of Monte Cassino," *Anniversary Essays in Mediaeval History by Students of Charles Homer Haskins,* ed. C. H. Taylor (Boston and New York: Houghtin Mifflin, 1929), esp. pp. 362–63.

10. Theodulf's name appears in manuscript in diverse forms (Theodulfus, Theudulfus, Teudulfus, Theotolfus, all variants originating in the Gothic language, according to Cuissard, p. 42). Cuissard notes, however, that scholars are divided over his nationality and birthplace: he is believed Italian because of an epitaph (from *Gallia Christiana,* vol. 8, col. 1422, about manuscript 9621 of King's Library), which speaks of "Hesperia," supposedly Italy, as in the Garden of the Hesperides: "Né dans l'Hespérie, j'ai été en seveli dans cette terre, climats bien éloignés et séparés par de grands espaces. Séduit par la douceur de Charlemagne, j'ai abandonné patrie, nation, demeure foyer, pour venir couler en ce pays d'heureuses annés." In Theodulf's works, however, "Hesperia" always means Spain (Cuissard, p. 45); Theodulf thinks of Saragossa as his "Father City," according to *Carmina* 45, line 16 (Manitius, *Geschichte* 9.2.1:543); Smaragdus or Maragdus was his "Master"; and he refers to himself as Geta or Getulus in his *Carmine* and elsewhere refers to himself as "Hesperia genitus" (born in Spain). See Manitius, *Geschichte* 9.2.1:538; Raby, *Secular Latin Poetry* 1:187–97.

11. See Raby, 1:180. Theodulf likes to think of Prudentius as "a poet of his own country," and refers to and quotes him frequently. Theodulf probably brought to the Carolingian court from Spain the poems of Martial and Cyprian (see Manitius, *Geschichte* 9.2.1:541n2). Of course the Fathers and Christian poets were more important to him than the classical poets. But "Theodulf came to the Franks as the countryman of Martial and Prudentius" (Raby, *Secular Latin Poetry* 1:197). From Spanish culture in addition to Martial also came the two Senecas, Lucan, Quintillian, Hyginus, Columella, Orosius, and the Emperors Trajan and Hadrian.

12. On Theodulf's closeness to Charlemagne, see Cuissard, pp. 43–44. Some historians think Theodulf married, because of his epistle to "Gisla" (possibly either a sister of Charlemagne who became in 757 a religious or a first spouse of Charlemagne born in 781). Note also that in 797 Theodulf and Leidrad, Bishop-Designate of Lyons, were each appointed Missus Dominicus (King's representative) in Southwest Gaul, with the designated function of inspecting king's officials in the administration of justice (Liebeschütz, p. 83).

13. This early mention of "pictura," a rhetorical term that would be used in the fourteenth century by classicizing friars intent on "picturing" the gods iconologically, is not as unusual as it might seem: note that Isidore defines the term (*Etym.* 19.16.1) as the physical, concrete, visible picture, painted by a real painter, of a thing that does not exist, for example, the Chimaera or Scylla: "sicut qui Chimaeram tricipitem pingunt, vel Scyllam hominem sursum, caninis autem capitibus cinctam deorsum" ["like those who depict the Chimaera as three-headed, or Scylla as human in her upper part but girded below with dogs' heads"]. Isidore's equation of *pictura* and *mendacium* should counter the asseverations of art historians that Theodulf must necessarily have been describing art objects he had himself observed. For example, I doubt that the figure of Cupid in "De libris quos legere solebam" could have been found in Carolingian sculpture or painting; it

anticipates what in fact would become a rather late Gothic convention. For a discussion of *Carmina* 46, "On the Seven Liberal Arts," see Raby, 1:187–97.

14. MacFarlane, p. 3.

15. Brehaut, p. 20; Fontaine, *Isidore*, pp. 5–9.

16. A somewhat fabulous thirteenth-century version of Isidore's life by Lucas Tudensis appears in *Acta sanctorum* for April 4 (*Aprilis I*); in addition, there is a life by Rodericus Cerratensis from the fourteenth century; most important, his friend Braulio, Bishop of Saragossa, summarized his life and described the impression made by Isidore on men of his own time, in *Sancti Braulionis, Caesaraugust. episcopi praenotatio librorum Isidori, PL* 82:65. Modern accounts can be found in Fontaine, *Isidore*, pp. 5–9; Brehaut, pp. 20–24; and MacFarlane, pp. 3–4.

17. Brehaut, p. 26.

18. In 15.6 of Hraban Maur's *De universo libri XXII*, in *Opera omnia, PL* 111:426–36; on Hraban's sources see Joh. Bapt. Hablitzel, *Hrabanus Maurus. Ein Beitrag zur Geschichte der mittelalterlichen Exegese*, in Biblische Studien, vol. 11, pt. 3 (Freiburg: Herdersche, 1906); and Elisabeth Heyse, *Hrabanus Maurus' Enzyklopädie "De rerum naturis": Untersuchungen zu den Quellen und zur Methode der Kompilation*, Münchener Beiträge zur Mediävistik und Renaissance-Forschung, no. 4 (Munich: Arbeo-Gesellschaft, 1969), esp. pp. 65–155. See also Cooke, p. 403.

19. Liebeschütz declares, p. 91, that, "His poems show that what the Carolingian restoration had brought about was a revival of patristic synthesis, and not the renaissance of a pre-Christian classical spirit." Noted also is the autobiographical cast to his poems (Liebeschütz, p. 86).

20. See, for example, R. P. M. Hubert, "Isidore de Séville novateur? (*Origines*, I, xviii-xix)," *REL* 49 (1971): 290–313.

21. The first Vatican mythographer's passage reads, "Physiologia uero hoc habet quod per portam corneam oculi significantur, qui et cornei sunt coloris et duriores ceteris membris, nam frigus non sentiunt. Per eburneam uero portam os designatur a dentibus, unde et Eneas per eburneam emittitur portam. Vel dicitur eburnea quasi ornatior porta, n<empe> ea que supra Fortunam sunt."

22. In his discussion of music (*Etym.* 3.21.5–8) Isidore attributes the invention of the reed-pipe to Mercury or Faunus (Pan to the Greeks). Elsewhere he provides a Macrobian correlation between the stars and faculties of the soul (in Macrobius acquired when the soul descends from the Milky Way to earth)—spirit from the sun, the body from the moon, ingenuity and language from Mercury, *voluptas* from Venus, blood from Mars, temperance from Jove, moisture from Saturn (5.30.8). In addition to this cosmological equation, he links gods with the months of the Roman calendar (5.33). Often he is interested in explaining the nature of a race, people, place, etc., by means of etymology: thus in "De gentium vocabulis" he relates the one-breasted nature of the Amazons to their Greek name, "sine mamma" (9.2.62–64). In books 13 and 14, on cosmography and geography, the

Peloponnese as the second part of Greece comes out the reign of Pelops (13.4.12). In book 15, on architecture and surveying, various gods have established cities: Ilus, son of Apollo, founded Ilium in Phyrgia (15.1.39); Cecrops founded the citadel of Athens; Amphictyon sacrificed to Minerva and gave the name Athens to the city, because Minerva in Greek is Athena (15.1.44); the city of Janiculum comes from Janus, Saturnia from Saturn (15.1.50), and so forth. As an example of architecture Isidore discusses the labyrinth built by Daedalus on Crete (15.2.36). On the invention of rustic things Osiris and Triptolemus are said to have invented plowing with oxen (17.1; Ceres in Greece used some sort of iron implement to turn the earth; she is also mentioned in 17.3 as governor of grains or seeds).

But there are Ovidian metamorphoses included also—Hyacinthus is a purple flower whose name was borrowed from the boy of the same name (17.9.15–16). In book 18, on military science, Isidore mentions, among other things, in a chapter entitled, "De quadrigis," that the four-horsed chariot (*quadriga*) was first used by Erichthonius, ruler of Athens, in an elaborate etiology most likely derived from Servius on *Georgics* 3.113: this son of Vulcan was engendered when Vulcan's seed spilled to the ground as Minerva resisted him, and hence he is a demonic portent, a devil, who dedicated his chariot to Juno and who was therefore the inventor of the *quadriga*: "Fuit autem Minervae et Vulcani filius de caduca in terram libidine, ut fabulae ferunt, procreatus, portentum daemonicum, immo diabolus, qui primus Iunoni currum dedicavit. Tali auctore quadrigae productae sunt" (18.34.2; elsewhere Erichthonius is described as being a snake, or having snake-legs, which allies him with the diabolic and which explains his need for a chariot).

23. Isidore's principal sources for "De diis gentium" include Augustine, *Civ. Dei,* Lactantius, *Institutiones divinae,* Servius on Virgil, and, I would argue, the *Sat.* of Macrobius: Saturn (*Etym.* 8.11.30–32) from the *Sat.* 1.10.20; Janus (*Etym.* 8.11.37) from *Sat.* 1.7.20; Mercury (*Etym.* 8.11.45) from *Sat.* 1.17.5; Apollo (*Etym.* 8.11.53) from *Sat.* 1.17. There are other sources, chiefly the Church Fathers: Augustine again, *Contra Faustum Manichaeum; De baptismo contra Donatistas; De Genesi ad litterum; De Trinitate;* then Eusebius, Gregory the Great, Jerome (for biblical references), plus Junius Philargyrius, Lactantius again, for *De ira Dei;* Prudentius, *Contra orationem Symmachi;* Solinus, *Collectanea rerum commentarii,* Tertullian, *Ad nationes, De idolatria, De praescriptione haereticorum.* On this subject in general see MacFarlane, p. 7, and the detailed specific notes on pp. 11–12 and 17–36.

24. *Civ. Dei* 7.2; Augustine borrows from Varro. See MacFarlane, p. 17.

25. The Saturn material comes from Varro, *De lingua Latina,* 5.64, Augustine, *Civ. Dei* 4.10, Servius, *In Aen.* 3.104, Cicero, *Nat. deorum,* 2.63–64 and 3.62, and Lactantius, *Institutiones divinae* 1.12.2–3 (MacFarlane, pp. 17–18).

26. For Jove, see Cicero, *Nat. deorum* 2.64; Lactantius, *Institutiones* 1.11.18–19; and Augustine, *Civ. Dei* 18.13 (MacFarlane, p. 17).

27. Isidore's gloss on Vulcan derives from Servius, *In Aen.* 7.454; *Institutiones*

1.14.5; on Neptune and Liber, from Augustine, *Civ. Dei* 7.16 and 6.9, respectively.

28. Mercury will be discussed below. Mars as the god of war is called so because he fights through men in essentially three kinds of fighting: in the case of the Scythians, both men and women fight; in the case of the Amazons, women only; and in the case of the Romans and other races, males only. Thus Mars is associated with death: "Item Martem quasi effectorem mortium. Nam a Marte mors nuncupatur" (*Etym.* 8.11.51: "death is named from Mars"). Because he committed adultery with Venus, war's outcome is uncertain.

29. Apollo (*Etym.* 8.11.53–55), associated with the sun ("Ipsum Titan, quasi unum ex Titanis, qui adversus Iovem non fecit"), governs medicine and divination. He is also called "Phoebus," "quasi ephebum, hoc est adolescentem" (from Lactantius, *Institutiones* 2.9), an "ephebus," a male Greek youth eighteen to twenty years old linked with the sun because each day it is reborn as new light; he is termed the Pythian because he conquered the serpent Python.

30. Diana (*Etym.* 8.11.56–58), the moon and sister of the sun, Apollo, like him is depicted with bow and arrows because both shoot rays to earth; she is the divinity of roads and hence, according to Isidore, depicted as a virgin because a road gives birth to nothing. Her name, so Isidore suggests in an etymology original with him, comes from "Duana," perhaps from *duo,* because the moon is seen both day and night, "quod luna et die et nocte appareat." But she has other names and functions: she is called Lucina because she gives light, and Trivia, because she represents three figures in one (Luna, Proserpina, Diana), probably an idea drawn not as Isidore declares from the *Aeneid* itself but from Servius's gloss on the passage (*In Aen.* 4.511). Note that the three goddesses are identified as Diana, Juno, and Proserpina in the *Aeneid* (3.73), with Juno probably intended in her role as Juno Lucina; see MacFarlane's discussion on pp. 23–24. As Trivia, according to MacFarlane, she is the counterpart of the Greek Hecate Triodotis, called so because she oversaw the Italian three-way crossroads, a situation regarded as "uncanny." See Varro, *De lingua Latina* 7.16, in MacFarlane, p. 23.

31. With Ceres, or earth (*Etym.* 8.11.59–64), Isidore arrives at that demarcation between the moon and the earth that offers a plenitude of beings—a region often identified as the underworld. Ceres, identified with the earth from her function in the creating of fruits and growth of plants, has many names whose etymologies accurately describe her various functions—Ops (a personification of material wealth, in antiquity indeed the "work" of earth, "because the earth becomes better through work," being worked, as in agriculture, "quod opere melior fiat terra"); Proserpina (Isidore offers an incorrect etymology for this goddess, actually a daughter of Ceres, from "the creeping forward of plants," "quod ex ea proserpiant fruges"); Vesta ("because she is clothed with grasses or various things, or from standing under her own power," "quod herbis vel variis vestita sit rebus, vel a vi sua stando"; see Augustine, *Civ. Dei* 7.24 and Servius, *In*

Aen. 1.292); Tellus (goddess of the fields, drawn from Ovid's *Fasti* 1.673–74 and used later by Theodulf), and the Magna Mater, complete with Corybantes, or priests, "Matrem vocatam, quod plurima pariat; magnam, quod cibum gignat; almam, quia universa animalia fructibus suis alit" ["called 'mother' from her fertility, 'great' because she produces food, 'bountiful' because she nourishes all living things with her fruits"]. She is depicted with a drum (to signify the orb of the earth), a key (because the earth is locked up in winter and opened in spring for the crops to come forth), a wheeled chariot (because the earth is suspended in air and the world rotates and spins) drawn by lions (because her cultivation of land stymies wildness), and a turreted crown and throne (to indicate that towered cities stand upon wealth).

32. Juno (*Etym.* 8.11.69–70), also associated with Jupiter as wife and sister (as air to fire), is provided an incorrect etymology, from *ianua,* which seems to link her with Janus (in her role as goddess of childbirth controlling the doors of birth: "Iunonem dicunt quasi ianonem, id est ianuam, pro purgationibus feminarum, eo quod quasi portas matrum natorum pandat, et nubentum maritis," 8.11.69). Note that Servius (*In Aen.* 2.610 and 7.610) also associates her with doors; see MacFarlane, p. 27. Isidore describes her relationship with Jove as the mixing of water and earth (for Juno, rather than air) and fire and air (for Jupiter, rather than aether) as responsible for universal begetting ("Poetae autem Iunonem Iovis adserunt sororem et coniugem: ignem enim et aerem Iovem, aquam et terram Iunonem interpretantur; quorum duorum permixtione universa gignuntur," 8.11.69). The connection with water and earth, of course, explains her presence in this more "earthly" section of the universe, although, MacFarlane notes, Varro also ties her to the earth (in *De lingua Latina* v.65, 67).

33. Minerva (Athena in Greek, *Etym.* 8.11.71–75) means *femina,* according to MacFarlane, a mistranslation of "Athena" meaning "without need of a nurse (*thēlē,* "breast," or *thēlus,* "female") because she comes out of Jove's head full-grown. Isidore derives her Latin name "Minerva" from "munus artium variarum," whence he interprets her as art and as reason, "quia sine ratione nihil potest contineri." "In cuius pectore ideo caput Gorgonis fingitur, quod illic est omnis prudentia, quae confundit alios, et inperitos ac saxeos conprobat" ["On her breast is depicted {*fingitur*} a Gorgon's head because in that place is the whole of prudence {wisdom}, which confounds others and proves them ignorant and obdurate"]. Also, ["quod et in antiquis Imperatorum statuis cernimus in medio pectore loricae, propter insinuandam sapientiam et virtutem" ["on antique statues of the emperors we see this in the middle of the breast-plates, to make known their wisdom and virtue"].

34. Venus (*Etym.* 8.11.76–80) derives her name from the fact that 'without her power a woman does not cease to be a virgin,' "Venerem exinde dicunt nuncupatam, quod sine vi femina virgo esse non desinat" (8.11.76, from Augustine, *Civ. Dei* 6.9, quoting Varro). Her name "Aphrodite" comes from her generation out of

bloody foam; sperm was also believed to be formed from blood ("Aphros" is Greek for foam: "illud aiunt quod per coitum salsi humoris substantia est; et inde *Aphroditen* Venerem dici, quod coitus spuma est sanguinis, quae ex suco viscerum liquido salsoque constat," 8.11.77). She is called Vulcan's wife because she cannot fill her office without heat; because she is born when Caelus's genitals, severed by Saturn, are flung into the sea, this means that "nothing is created unless moisture falls from the heavens to earth" ("nisi humor de caelo in terram descenderit, nihil creatur," 8.11.79). Her son Cupid, desire, is the demon of fornication, as we have already seen, depicted as a boy holding a bow and arrows for all the reasons listed above (*Etym.* 8.11.80).

35. Isidore's euhemeristic notes on Quirinus and on the gods as founders of the arts come from Lactantius, *Institutiones* 1.15.9, 1.18.21. See Cooke, "Euhemerism: A Mediaeval Interpretation of Classical Paganism," *Speculum* 2 (1927): 396–410, here, pp. 398ff.

36. MacFarlane notes, "The heroes were originally the spirits of dead leaders who were believed to watch over their people in death as in life, and to whom shrines were erected and offerings made" (p. 34). She cannot identify the source for the information concerning the fortitude of the hero, although she sees a link between "Hera" and "heros"—through the Indo-European root *sar,* "guarding," preserved in Latin *servare.*

37. For textual criticism and interpretation of the sixty-three poems in the Sirmonds Manuscript, see Dieter Schaller, "Philologische Untersuchungen zu den Gedichten Theodulfs von Orléans," *Deutsches Archiv für Erforschung des Mittelalters* 18 (1962): 13–91.

38. Theodulf's heroic figures derive mostly from Virgil, or Servius on Virgil, despite Battaglia's and other contemporary scholars' descriptions of "De libriis" as an "Ovidian" poem. Duemmler's annotations (*Poetae Latini* 1:543–44) link the references to Proteus and Hercules to Virgil's *Georgics* (4.387ff), *Bucolics* (4.6), and *Aeneid* (8.193). I would argue for Servius's commentary on all of these passages rather than the poem itself; and instead of *Bucolics* 4.6 for Virgo (Erigone) I would substitute *Georgics* 1.33. There is, according to editor Duemmler, an allusion to Ovid's *Fasti* 1.572 in "Ore vomunt fumum probra negando tetrum."

39. Augustine, *Civ. Dei* 7.14; MacFarlane, p. 21.

40. Servius, *In Aen.* 4.242; MacFarlane, p. 22.

41. Lactantius, *De ira Dei* 11.12, according to MacFarlane, ibid. The dog's head gloss comes from Servius, *In Aen.* 8.968.

42. See Lawrence Nees, "Theodulf's Mythical Silver Hercules Vase, *Poetica Vanitas,* and the Augustinian Critique of the Roman Heritage," *Dumbarton Oak Papers* 41 (1987): 443–51. This essay has been expanded and included in *A Tainted Mantle: Hercules and the Classical Tradition at the Carolingian Court* (Philadelphia: University of Pennsylvania Press, 1991), in a re-examination of the question of reception of classicism in the Carolingian court.

43. Brehaut, pp. 86–87; see also Fontaine, ". . . la formule de Cassiodore prend un relief nouveau et personnel dans le context des *Origines*. La grammaire est 'origine' des disciplines, comme l'étymologie est 'origine' des vocables: c'est dire d'un mot sa place privilégéie par rapport aux autres 'artes'" (*Isidore*, p. 53).

44. Brehaut declares, "It is evident, therefore, that we have here in embryo, as it were, the organization of the medieval university; law and medicine have only to be secularized and freed from their subordination to theology, and the medieval university in its complete form appears" (p. 88). For examination of Isidore's knowledge and sources, see Fontaine, *Isidore*, passim; but esp. 1:735–830 on his assimilation of classical material.

CHAPTER 5. THE "UNIVERSAL GENEALOGY" OF THE GODS AND HEROES IN THE FIRST VATICAN MYTHOGRAPHER

1. See Winfried Bühler, "Theodulus' *Ecloga* and Mythographus Vaticanus I," *California Studies in Classical Antiquity* 1 (1968): 65–71, esp. p. 70.

2. See the recent critical edition of the first two mythographers by Kulcsár. The history of the editing of the first Vatican mythographer has been traced by Kathleen O. Elliott, "Text, Authorship, and Use of the First Vatican Mythographer" (diss., Radcliffe College, 1942), who also therein provides an edition. She notes (p. 1) that Angelo Cardinal Mai in 1831 as *bibliothecarius* of the Vatican Library published the first edition of the three Vatican mythographers (based on three interrelated collections of myths in Vatican manuscripts). This edition, according to Kathleen O. Elliott and J. P. Elder's 1947 summary of her 1942 dissertation, "A Critical Edition of the *Vatican Mythographers*," *TAPA* 78 (1947): 189–207, was marred by Mai's omission of the titles of the manuscripts with which he had worked, "beyond mentioning laconically in his preface that the text of this or that one was preserved 'in uno tantum Svecorum olim Reginae, nunc vaticano, codice' or 'in palatino chartaceo' or in a book that once belonged to Fulvio Orsini" (p. 192). It was also marred by incorrect transcriptions and forced (euphemized) texts (pp. 189, 192). Elliott has determined that Vat. Reg. lat. 1401 (which also contains the second Vatican mythography) provided the text for Mai in his edition of the first Vatican mythography, and this is the manuscript upon which Elliott also based her edition. Elliott and Elder in their summary (and update) of the introductory comments in her dissertation include "views on the general characteristics, sources, dates, authorship, and manuscripts of each of the three collections of myths." Bode also published an edition of all three mythographies, in effect a second edition of Mai's for the first two mythographies but a revised edition for the third, in that he added three additional manuscripts (according to Elliott, "Text," p. 1). Unlike Mai's, Bode's edition includes critical notes on parallel passages, possible sources, *lectiones variae*, and index, and there exists at the end an *Observationes in mythographum primum* (164–76). For the first

Vatican mythographer Bode used Mai's often inaccurate text plus some emendations from possible sources like Servius and Fulgentius and some, in Elliott and Elder's words, added "by his own ingenuity" (see Bode, "Prooemium," p. xix). Because the handiest edition of all three Vatican mythographers, despite its flaws, is still Bode's, I will refer to the numbering of the myths in my text according to both editions, with Kulcsár's fable number in first place followed by Bode's. Where they agree I will include only one number. All references are to Kulcsár's text unless otherwise noted.

3. See Charles S. F. Burnett, "A Note on the Origins of the Third Vatican Mythographer," *JWCI* 44 (1981): 160–66, which indicates (p. 161n6) that he is working on an edition of one of the major sources of the mythography, the *De mundi coelestis terrestrisque constitutione* of pseudo-Bede; he also points out the need for a critical edition of the third Vatican mythographer.

4. See the Spring 1989 issue of *Studii sul Boccaccio,* edited by Vittore Branca, and also the study by Attilio Hortis, *Studji sulle opere latine del Boccaccio: Con particolare riguardo alla storia della erudizione nel medio evo e alle letterature straniere* (Trieste, 1879), appendix 2, pp. 537–42, for the genealogy according to Franceschino degli Albizzi and Forese dei Donati. For information concerning the genealogy in the Florentine Commentary, see chap. 10 of this study.

5. For the history of Greek and Roman epic, see the excellent summary by Brooks Otis, *Virgil: A Study in Civilized Poetry* (Oxford: Clarendon Press, 1963), chap. 1.

6. These Callimachean or Hesiodic Latin epics that have been lost include Cato's *Dictynna,* Caecilius's *Magnus Mater,* Cornificius's *Glaucus,* and Calvus's *Io.* See Otis, pp. 22–23. Only one Hesiodic epic is extant—Catullus's *Peleus and Thetis.* This type of epic differs markedly from these others, or from the works by Cicero or Ennius earlier, because "myth is no longer to him [Catullus] a mere convention, a required part of the epic style, but the index of a moral reality;" for him, Theseus's betrayal of Ariadne represents the betrayal of love and morality (Otis, ibid., p. 29). The form of the Callimachean epyllion transformed by Ovid in the *Fasti* was represented by Callimachus's *Aitia* (ibid., p. 33).

7. It was because Virgil did not believe that a Homeric epic had yet been written in Latin that he tried to write one by following the principles outlined in Horace's *Ars poetica:* "It was not simply by copying a Greek or Roman model that Virgil learned to write the *Aeneid.* His first problem was to appreciate the defects, the poetical unavailablity, of his Roman epic predecessors. This fact has as yet been quite insufficiently appreciated" (Otis, ibid., p. 20). And so he turned to a different model: "Homer was excellent because he showed consistency of plot and style. He did not, like the author of a *Cyclic Epic,* promise more than he could perform (e.g. a history of the *whole* Trojan war). . . . Homer actually promises something much more limited: to sing of *one* man and *one* phase of his adventures—not a mass of uncoordinated myths and miracles" (ibid., p. 36).

8. Ibid., p. 6.

9. Ibid., p. 18: such were the fourth-century B.C. Greek mythological epics by Menelaus of Augai on Theseus, Theolytos of Methymna on Bacchus or the Bacchae, Neoptolemos of Parium on Dionysius, and Theolytos and Cleon of Kurion on the Argonauts.

10. Thomas Hyde, "Boccaccio: The Genealogies of Myth," *PMLA* 100 (1985): 737-45, here, p. 742. See also R. Howard Bloch, *Etymologies and Genealogies: A Literary Anthropology of the French Middle Ages* (Chicago: University of Chicago Press, 1986), chap. 1, for a fine discussion of the idea of the genealogy and the naming principle.

11. Elliott and Elder, p. 198.

12. Vat. Reg. lat. 1401. Elliott and Elder, p. 192; Elliott, "Text," notes that Gruppe, in following Mai, incorrectly identified the ante quem as tenth to eleventh century because of the date of the manuscript.

13. Elliott, "Text," p. 193.

14. Whitbread, *Fulgentius,* p. 5, cites this argument of Otto Rossbach in "Ein falscher Hyginus," *JCP* 131 (1885): 408.

15. See Bühler, "Die Pariser Horazscholien: Eine neue Quelle der Mythographi Vaticani 1 und 2," *Philologus* 105 (1961): 123-35.

16. For Bernhard Bischoff's views on the twelfth-century date see the notes in Bühler, "Die Pariser Horazscholien," pp. 134-35. Kulcsár traces the additions of sources to various manuscripts of the second Vatican mythographer and settles for a span between the eighth and twelfth centuries for both of the mythographers as based on the twelfth-century date of the key first Vatican mythographer manuscript. See the introduction to Kulcsár, pp. vi-xvi, esp. vi and xvi. Note, however, that the latest date possible may be the ninth or tenth century because of Remigius's use of the first Vatican mythography in his commentary on Martianus Capella: see Bühler, "Theodulus' *Ecloga,*" p. 71.

17. Elliott, "Text," p. 179. The Explicit of book 2 reads "Explicit liber secundus Hygini fabularum," referring to the Hyginus of *Fabulae* (p. 180). But Mai argued that this Hyginus lived in the fifth century ("Praefatio," p. vii). Early on scholars proved that the first Vatican mythographer was not, as Mai had thought, Hyginus: see Rossbach, pp. 408-10.

18. Bode, "Prooemium," pp. xvi-xvii.

19. Richard Schulz, *De mythographi Vaticani primi fontibus* (Halle: C. A. Kaemmerer, 1905), p. 74; see also Eliott and Elder, pp. 198-99, who declare, "The suggestion has been advanced, owing to resemblances between Mythographus 1 and the Berne scholia, that the author of the former, too, was an Irishman of the eighth and ninth centuries."

20. Overmeyer [Elliott], "Text," p. 191.

21. Elliott and Elder, p. 195.

22. Ibid., p. 193; see also Overmeyer [Elliott], "Text," p. 188.

23. Elliott and Elder, p. 194. On p. 194n16 they point out exceptions to the "traditional order," probably deriving from an *Aeneid* commentary: fable 30 in book 1 deals with Amulius and Numitor, fable 74 in book 1 with Tarquin and Lucretia, fable 202 in book 2 with the flight of Aeneas and Cato cited as a source (Bode's numbering).

24. Ibid., p. 194. Note, for example, that fable 205 is taken from Servius, *In Aeneid* 6.618, except for its last line, which in fact is the lemma and comment of Servius on *Aeneid* 6.620: "Discite iustitiam vel nunc in poenis locati." On page 198 they indicate that "What element of originality there is would appear to be confined entirely to the realm of selection, rejection, and arrangement of stories." They argue that the mythographer will take several stories in succession from one source, then combine several sources in composing one fable (e.g., fable 23 is taken from scholia to the *Thebaid* 2.281 and the *Achilleid* 1.28, noted on page 198n28). These are marked by the expressions "alii dicunt" or "aliter."

25. For this definition see Isidore's dedication to King Sisebut in the *Epistolae* (*Etym.*, vol. 1).

26. See Elliott and Elder, p. 198.

27. For complete studies of the mythographer's sources, see Schulz, passim, and Elliott, notes, passim. The first Vatican mythographer in his first book has compiled a series of thirty-eight myths taken primarily from Servius's commentaries on Virgil, particularly the commentaries on the *Aeneid* up to book 8. Half as many come from the commentaries on the *Georgics,* and only a handful from the commentary on the *Eclogues.* The next highest proportion, but only thirteen to fourteen (not even as many as on the *Georgics*) come from the scholia on the *Thebaid.* Next in order, but only seven or eight, come from Lactantius in the *Narrationes.* Then there are a few taken from Fulgentius, Hyginus, the Berne scholia, Isidore, and the *Scholia Danielis.*

In the second book, almost the same number come from Servius on the *Aeneid* (although they go beyond book 8—some derive from book 11), that is, thirty-three, and then about nineteen from the scholia on the *Thebaid,* and fifteen from Fulgentius, followed by thirteen from the *Narrationes,* with only about seven from Servius on the *Eclogues* and three from Servius on the *Georgics,* one from Servius *Danielis,* one from Isidore, one from the commentary on Lucan. A higher portion come from Fulgentius and Lactantius Placidus than in the first book.

And in the third book, nineteen derive from Servius on the *Aeneid,* one from Servius on the *Georgics,* three from Fulgentius, one from the scholia on the *Achilleid,* and one from Hyginus.

28. See Bühler, "Die Pariser Horazscholien," pp. 123–35.

29. Elliott and Elder, p. 196; the mythographer tends to shorten Servius by omitting the grammatical notes, the Greek citations, and discursive quotation of other authors. From both Servius and the scholia on Statius, however, he cites a whole series of stories (pp. 194–95).

30. See Michael Zink, *Der Mytholog Fulgentius: Ein Beitrag römischen Littera-turgeschichte und zur Grammatik des afrikanischen Lateins* (Würzburg, 1867), p. 11; Schulz, p. 13. It is therefore an overstatement, perhaps, to argue as does D. E. H. Alton, "The Mediaeval Commentators on Ovid's *Fasti,*" *Hermathena* 20 (1926–30): 119–51, here, p. 149, that "it is manifest that Mythographus I depends wholly on Fulgentius, but that Mythographus II and G derive from Hyginus; finally, that G is closer than Mythographus II to Hyginus." Elliott and Elder note that the order of myths in the first Vatican mythographer is the same as that in Fulgentius book 2; often both will use the same phrasing, although first the one and then the other will lengthen the myth. And Fulgentius relies more heavily on mystical explanations excluded from the first Vatican mythographer.

31. See Overmeyer [Elliott], "Text," pp. 182–90. Of these direct citations, Elliott and Elder (pp. 196–97) note that the first Vatican mythographer agrees only once with Hyginus (fable 31 with Hyginus fable 259, attributed to Servius), and that fable 100/101 involves the only myth cited directly from the Servius *Scholia Danielis* (*Aeneid* 1.505). Did he use a shorter Servius with a gloss from the longer on this scholium? In addition, the first Vatican mythographer agrees once with Solinus (fable 78/79 with Solinus 32.17), but rarely agrees completely with Isidore, although fable 122/124 agrees except for the first sentence with *Etym.* 8.11.71–75; other agreements with this passage can be found in fable 106/107; fable 112/113 with *Etymologiae* 8.11.53; fable 117/119 with *Etymologiae* 8.11.45–49.

32. Most of the Servius or Servius *Danielis* references derive from the commentary on book 6 of the *Aeneid* (27 references), followed by book 1 (14) and 3 (12) and 8 (12). A handful of references concern books 2 (7), 4 (4), 5 (3), 7 (6), 9 (1), 10 (1), and 11 (3). This allocation reflects the amount of commentary on individual books of the *Aeneid* in Servius, with books 1 and 6 receiving the greatest attention.

33. See Sandra L. Hindman's *Christine de Pizan's "Epistre Othéa": Painting and Politics at the Court of Charles VI,* Pontifical Institute of Mediaeval Studies, Studies and Texts, no. 77 (Toronto: Pontifical Institute of Mediaeval Studies, 1986), pp. 35–37.

34. The Statius scholia are attributed to Lactantius Placidus in the gloss on *Thebaid* 6.342 (p. 317), although apparently the name was inserted subsequently (that is, not by Lactantius Placidus himself): in commenting on "mundo succinta latenti," whether the earth "be encompassed by yet another world we view not," Lactantius refers to the stability of the antipodes and says, "sed de his rebus, prout ingenio meo committere potui, ex libris ineffabilis doctrinae Persei praeceptoris seorsum libellum composui Caelius Firmianus Lactantius Placidus." In other manuscripts is inserted the name "Caelius Firmianus Lactantius" (the name of the patristic author of the *Institutionum divinarum* in the early fourth century): see, for example, Philipp Kohlmann, "Beiträge zur kritik des Statius-scholiasten," *Philologus* 33 (1874): 130.

There is some confusion regarding the authorship of several works usually attributed to a Lactantius Placidus. A glossary of Latin, especially ancient Latin, by Lactantius Placidus entitled *Glossae Luctatii Placidi grammatici,* including Latin commentaries, is discussed in Wilhelm Siegmund Teuffel, *History of Roman Literature,* rev. Ludwig Schwabe, translated from the fifth edition by George C. W. Wahr, 2 vols. (London and Cambridge, 1892), 2:472. For the attribution of the scholia on the *Thebaid,* see Teuffel, 2:321.10, and Teuffel's belief that "Luctatius" and "Lactantius Placidus" are the same. An anonymous work entitled "Narrationes fabularum quae in Ov. Metam. occurrunt" in fifteen books is identified in various early editions (but without explanation) as by Lactantius Placidus, for example, in the 1591 edition and in Muncker's edition (Teuffel 1:249.2). "Lactantius" as a name appears only in a fifteenth-century manuscript of the *Narrationes* without the *Metamorphoses* (Laurentianus XC, 99) and in early fifteenth- and sixteenth-century editions, according to Otis, "De Lactantii qui dicitur Narrationibus Ovidianis," *HSCP* 46 (1935): 209–11.

For arguments on the common authorship of the Lactantius commentary on Statius and the *Narrationes,* see Otis, "The *Argumenta* of the So-Called Lactantius," *HSCP* 47 (1936): 131–63; and also the detailed study by Franz Bretzigheimer, "Studien zu Lactantius Placidus und dem Verfasser der Narrationes fabularum Ovidianarum" (diss., Bayerischen Julius-Maximilians-Universität; Würzburg: Richard Mayr, 1937), who, in contrast, argues that the two authors were not the same: the author of the *Narrationes* reveals a Christian side lacking in the author of the *Thebaid* scholia. For more general information on Lactantius, see Paulys-Wissowa, 23:356–361; and Teuffel, 2:116–21.

35. Paul van de Woestijne's four manuscripts of the Lactantius *Thebaid* commentary begin with the oldest, Valentinianus 394, followed by Monacensis 19482 and Parisinus 8063 and 8064; see "Le Codex Valentinianus 394 de Lactantius Placidus," *Revue belge de philologie et d'histoire* 19 (1940): 37–63, here, pp. 37–38nn. For an edition of Lactantius's *Thebaid* scholia, see Richard Jahnke, ed., vol. 3 of *P. Papinius Statius,* or *Lactantii Placidi qui dicitur commentarios in Statii Thebaida et commentarium in Achilleida* (Leipzig, 1898), although for scholia on Statius from a fifth manuscript, Parisinus 10317 (only partly used by Kohlmann, Wotke, Lindenbrog, and Jahnke), see John M. Burnam, *The Placidus Commentary on Statius,* University of Cincinnati Bulletin, no. 3 (Cincinnati: University of Cincinnati Press, 1901). For a discussion of Lactantius's scholia on Statius not included in Jahnke and found in MS. Monac. membran. lat. 19482, MS. Monac. 6396, and MS. Bamberg M.IV.11, see Eduard Wölfflin, "Zu den Statiusscholien," *Philologus* 24 (1866): 156–58; for various Statius manuscripts, see Philipp Kohlmann, "Beiträge zur kritik des Statius-scholiasten," *Philologus* 33 (1874): 128–38; on an incomplete presentation of Lactantius's commentary see Manitius, "Aus Dresdener Handschriften. II: Scholien zu Statius' *Thebais,*" *RMP* 57 (1902): 397–421; for variants in the manuscripts including scholia, others' as well as Lactantius's,

plus a criticism of the Jahnke edition, see Alfred Klotz, "Die Statius-scholien," *Archiv für lateinische Lexicographie und Grammatik* 15 (1908): 485–525; on Statius glosses in MS. 41 in Biblioteca Seminario Patavino, see Carlo Landi, "Di'un commento medievale inedito della 'Tebaide' di Stazio," *Atti e memorie della Accademia di Scienze Lettere ed Arti in Padova*, n.s. 28 (1911–12): 315–44; for another Lactantius manuscript see van de Woestijne, "Le Codex Valentinianus 394," pp. 37–63; on the Statius manuscripts only see D. E. Hill, "The Manuscript Tradition of the *Thebaid*," *CQ* n.s. 16 (1966): 333–46.

For editions of Statius (beside Mozley's Loeb Classics, cited in my text) see H. W. Garrod, ed., *P. Papini Stati Thebais et Achilleis*, Scriptorum Classicorum Bibliotheca Oxonienses (Oxford: Clarendon Press, 1906); Alfred Klotz, ed., *P. Papini Stati Thebais*, vol. 2, fasc. 2 of *P. Papini Stati operum* (Leipzig: B. G. Teubner, 1908); and P. Kohlmann, ed., *Achilleis et Thebais* (Leipzig, 1884). See also O. A. W. Dilkie, ed., *Statius: Achilleid* (Cambridge: Cambridge University Press, 1954); a new edition has been promised by Sweeney for Teubner. For more general commentaries on Statius see David Vessey, *Statius and the Thebaid* (Cambridge: Cambridge University Press, 1973).

The total number of surviving manuscript copies of the *Thebaid*, with comments, amounts to 112; there were 95 of the *Achilleid*, according to Paul M. Clogan, "A Preliminary List of Manuscripts of Statius' *Achilleid*," *Manuscripta* 8 (1964): 175–78. The scholia on the latter work, by Lactantius and others, are very skimpy; further, the non-Lactantius scholia and glosses on the *Achilleid* and the *Thebaid* are much less full than those attributed to Lactantius himself: they often merely identify by epithet or short tag a geographic or mythological allusion or a grammatical or rhetorical construction, without transmitting any more of the myth, as does the Lactantius *Achilleid*. According to Clogan in his edition of *The Medieval Achilleid of Statius* (Leiden: E. J. Brill, 1968), p. 7n: "Scholars have conjectured that the original scholia of Lactantius Placidus were fuller than the extant versions and that another group of Statius scholia may have been combined with extracts from Lactantius Placidus." On the incomplete preservation of his commentary and medieval scholia on the *Achilleid*, see Max Manitius, "Dresdener Scholien zu Statius *Achilleis*," *RMP* 59 (1904): 597–602. On the manuscripts of Lactantius on the *Thebaid*, see Clogan, "The Manuscripts of Lactantius Placidus' Commentary on the *Thebaid*," *Scriptorium* 22 (1968): 87–91; and on medieval glossed manuscripts on the same poem, Clogan, "Medieval Glossed Manuscripts of the *Thebaid*," *Manuscripta* 11 (1967): 102–112. See also Robert Dale Sweeney, *Prolegomena to an Edition of the Scholia to Statius*, Mnemosyne Bibliotheca Classica Bateva, supp. 8 (Leiden: E. J. Brill, 1969).

36. Manuscripts of Lactantius's *Narrationes* are seven in number, according to Otis, "The *Argumenta* of the So-Called Lactantius," *HSCP* 47 (1936): 131–63, here, p. 131n1. Otis believes that the scholiastic passages in the *Narrationes* were not part of the summary, but instead crept into the text at an early date to make

this a kind of annotated edition of the *Metamorphoses,* with a common ancestor of two distinct families of manuscripts no later than the ninth century (pp. 139–40). Probably the *Argumenta* and the scholia, both marginal to begin with, existed as early as the fifth or sixth century (p. 140).

37. See Bretzigheimer, pp. 23–52, for a comparison of Hyginus, Servius, and Lactantius Placidus on Statius with the passages in the *Narrationes.*

38. For the sources of the anonymous (non-Lactantius) Statius scholia, see Clogan, "Medieval Glossed Manuscripts," p. 103; for the sources of Lactantius's *Thebaid* commentary see Paul van de Woestijne, "Marginaliën bij Lactantius Placidus," *L'antiquité classique,* n.s. 17 (1948): 573–84; Einar Heikel, "Lactantii Placidi de dei nomine narratio," *Suomalaisen Tiedeakatemian Toimituksia* 12.3 (1913): 1–9; on Lactantius's borrowings from Servius, see van der Woestijne, "Les Scolies à la *Thébaïde* de Stace: Remarques et suggestions," *Antiquité Classique,* n.s. 19 (1950): 149–163. For the sources of the *Narrationes*—for the citations of Hyginus, the commentary on the *Thebaid* by Lactantius, and Servius *Danielis*—see Otis, "De Lactantii," pp. 209–11; also Otis, "The *Argumenta,*" pp. 134ff. In the commentary on the *Thebaid,* Lactantius's favorite authorities, often cited indirectly, are Virgil and Statius, of course, followed by Lucan. Other authorities, cited many times but less than the above, include, first, Horace (51 references), followed in order by Ovid (31), Homer (24), Sallust (21), Terence (20), Cicero (17), Juvenal (14), Pythagoras (7), and Lucretius (6). With five or fewer references (often only one or two) are such writers as Seneca (1), Martianus (1), Persius (5), Petronius (1), Pindarus (1), Thucydides (1), Varro (3), Hesiod (2), Boethius (1), Sedulius (1), Euripides (3), Ennius (4). Judging from the Greek names and simple etymologies occasionally included, as with Orion (on *Thebaid* 7.256), Lactantius knows some Greek, especially given his citations of writers like Pindar, Hesiod, and Homer. His dates must be later than those of Martianus (and Boethius), who is cited by name in the gloss on *Thebaid* 1.265 (4.106, for Boethius). But Hyginus, from whom he plagiarizes frequently, is not cited by name.

39. Manitius, *Geschichte* 9.2.1:634.

40. The Hyginus genealogy that reappears in the *Narrationes* has been analyzed by Bretzigheimer, p. 51; see also C. Lange, *De nexu inter opera mythologica Hygini* (Bonn, 1865). Bretzigheimer also acknowledges these myths in the *Narrationes* as deriving from Hyginus: Cadmus, Perseus, Ascoaphus, Callisto, Meleager, Nessus, Glaucus, Scylla, Tiresias (pp. 23ff).

41. I would argue that Lactantius's selection of epitomes hinges on "metamorphosis," in fact, the epitome *is* his interpretation, as in the case of Phaethon, whose tale delineates four changes: his sisters turning into trees, their tears into amber and then jewels, and Cygnus into a swan (book 2), in Hugo Magnus, ed., *P. Ovidi Nasonis Metamorphoseon libri XV et Lactantii Placidi qui dicitur Narrationes fabularum Ovidianarum* (Berlin: Weidmann's, 1914), p. 691. This will be discussed at greater length in the chapter on Arnulf of Orleans and John of Garland in volume 2 of this

study. Lactantius's glosses generally take the form of annotations on the text. An example from the *Narrationes* scholia might be a brief explanatory phrase, for example "Tmolum, montem Lydiae" (*Narrationes* book 1, line 3), or an interpretative scholium, such as "plura vero opera Arachnes poeta rettulit fuisse quam Minervae, ut hanc scientia artis, quae potentior est, illam labore contendisse demonstraret" (*Narrationes* 1.7, ed. Magnus, p. 662). See Otis, "The *Argumenta,*" p. 138. For divergences from Ovid, see Bretzigheimer, pp. 52ff; and Otis, "The *Argumenta,*" pp. 135–36; in his edition Magnus provides notes indicating sources for some of these divergences from Ovid. See also Friedrich Walter Lenz, *Ovid's Metamorphoses: Prolegomena to a Revision of Hugo Magnus' Edition* (Dublin and Zurich: Weidmann's, 1967), who repeats the arguments concerning the two possible explanations for the form in which the *Narrationes* may have survived: either as marginal or interlinear glosses, combined in the fifteenth century (p. 76), or as the remnants of an extensive commentary or an epitome (the latter improbable because "the unidentifiable author reports something that either is not in Ovid or appears in him differently," p. 82).

42. Some of the comments explain rhetorical terms and devices—for example, on line 58 of book 1 of Statius's *Thebaid,* when Oedipus cries "tuque umbrifero Styx livida fundo, quam video" (trans. Mozley: "and thou O Styx, whom I behold, ghastly in thy shadowy depths"), Lactantius Placidus comments "paene oxymoron. quid enim caecus uidet?" (Jahnke, p. 7). Indeed, what *does* a blind man see? Some of the comments, as literary criticism, are exceedingly superficial and literalistic. But they do serve to identify puzzling mythological references and figures in a straightforward, nonallegorical manner. Etymology is occasionally used to bolster a literary (and moralistic) interpretation (for example, of the name Oedipus, in *Thebaid* 1.69, Jahnke, p. 9).

43. The scholia (marginal and interlinear annotations) mostly fall into one of three groups: very short notes on grammatical constructions, longer notes on short explanations of various mythological allusions, and literary criticism on the meaning of the poem (see Clogan, "Medieval Glossed Manuscripts," p. 103). Most of the Lactantius references involve straightforward, literalistic transmissions of myth, taken directly from Apollodorus, Servius, Ovid, Hyginus, et al., that is, a recitation of mythological or geographical details, taken from the legend or myth, and often an etymological description, occasionally citing the Greek, as in this definition of the Amazons from Lactantius on *Achilleid* 1.353: "Amazones dictae sunt, uel quod simul uiuant sine uiris quasi 'ama zobau,' uel quod unam mammam exustam habent quasi 'anev mazov,'" their name explained in terms of their life without men ("ama zobau") or in terms of their burned-off breast ("anev mazov," Jahnke, p. 498).

44. See Wallace M. Lindsay and H. J. Thomson, *Ancient Lore in Medieval Latin Glossaries,* St. Andrews University Publications, no. 13 (London, Edinburgh, Glasgow, etc.: Humphrey Milford/Oxford University Press, 1921).

45. For a discussion of the interrelationship of the Virgil commentaries and Ovid's *Metamorphoses,* see Alfredus Leuschke, ' *"De Metamorphoseon" in scholiis Vergilianis fabulis'* (Diss., University of Marburg, 1895; Marburg, 1895). In the Berne scholia Leuschke finds these Ovidian myths: Callisto (*Georgics* 1.245, also Servius, *In Georg.* 1.246); Daphnis (*Eclogues* 3.12); Hyacinthus (*Eclogues* 3.107, also in Servius, *In Buc.* 3.63); Erysichthona (*Eclogues* 10.62, also in Servius here and *In Aen.* 3.34); Cyparissus (*Georgics* 1.20, also Servius *In Aen.* 3.680 and *In Buc.* 10.26); Atalanta (*Eclogues* 6.61, also in Servius); Glaucus and Scylla (*Eclogues* 6.74 and 77, and also in Servius, *In Buc.* 6.74 and *In Aen.* 3.420); Glaucus alone (*Georgics* 1.437, also in Servius here and *In Aen.* 5.823); Scylla and Nisus (*Eclogues* 6.74 and also in Servius); Phaethon (*Eclogues* 6.62, and in Servius here, plus *In Aen.* 10.189 and 6.659); Phyllis and Demophoon (*Eclogues* 5.10 and in Servius); Deucalion (*Eclogues* 6.41); Procne and Philomela (*Eclogues* 6.78 and 79, and in Servius for 6.78); Latona (*Georgics* 1.378, also in Servius here); Ceyx and Alcyone (*Georgics* 1.399, also in Servius); Philyra and Saturn (*Georgics* 3.93, and in Servius); Narcissus (*Eclogues* 2.47 and in Servius).

46. In the first Vatican mythographer, according to Elliott and Elder, most of the citations from the Servian commentary on the *Georgics* come from book 1 (19) and 3 (10), with just a few from 2 and 4 (3). On the *Bucolics* (or *Eclogues*) there are just a few, most from 6 (5), 5 (3), 3 and 9 (2), and 2 and 8 (1).

47. There are thirteen Berne scholiast mythological glosses on eclogue 6, followed by eclogue 3 (10), 8 (8), 4 (7), with only a few comments in 2, 5, 7, one reference in 1, and none in 9.

48. See Jane Chance Nitzsche, *The Genius Figure in Antiquity and the Middle Ages* (New York and London: Columbia University Press, 1975), pp. 14–15.

49. The first Vatican mythographer reacts like the Berne scholiast to Virgil's allusions to Hylas's tale and Pasiphaë (Berne Scholiast, *Ad Buc.* 6.43–46), the daughters of Proetus (6.48), Atalanta and Hippomenes (6.61), Phaethon's sisters (6.62), Gallus (6.65), and Scylla and Nisus (6.74), although Scylla, daughter of Nisus, reminds the Berne scholiast of the Scylla loved by Glaucus, this the daughter of Phorcys and the Crataeid Nymphs, and he cites Virgil's *Aeneid* 1.200 to bolster the myth. (A very similar version appears in fable 3 of the first Vatican mythographer.) The Tereus and Procne myth is recited in *Ad Buc.* 6.78–79, and mentioned in 8.47; Tityrus, Orpheus, and Arion are linked in 8.55–56. The Berne scholiast defines Circe in *Ad Buc.* 8.70 as the evil transformer of the companions of Ulysses into beasts and the Hamadryades in *Ad Buc.* 10.62 (containing the reference to the Ovidian myth of Erysichthon in *Metamorphoses* 8.738) as those who live in the woods.

50. See Charlton T. Lewis and Charles Short, *A Latin Dictionary* (1879; rpt. Oxford: Clarendon Press, 1969), s.v. "Faunus."

51. "Cum aliquando in quasdam Graeciae ciuitates grauis pestilentia ueniret, responsum dedit, aliter pestilentiam non posse sedari, nisi suo filio Aristaeo

uouissent candidissima armenta; illae electos iuuencos candidos in Ceam insulam duxerunt et ibi reliquerunt. Hic Aristaeus, qui Eurydicen, uxorem Orphei in prato flores legentem, intermixtam Nymphis, adamauerit. Inuocat eum, quia hic primus aratri usum inuenit" (Berne Scholiast, *Ad Georg.* 1.8). According to Lewis and Short (s.v. "Aristaeus"), Aristaeus first planted olive trees and taught men to keep bees and treat milk.

52. Tethys is mentioned briefly by the Berne scholiast in *Ad Georg.* 1.31, and Erigone at length in 1.33, first as the zodiacal sign of the Virgin (in a passage like Hyginus's *Astronomica* 2.4), and then (in a passage very like that of Hyginus in *Fab.* 130) as the daughter who hung herself from grief over her father's death and thus represents Justice (a reference also used by Theodulf of Orleans). There follow references to Tartarus and Proserpina (Berne Scholiast, *Ad Georg.* 1.36–39), Deucalion and Pyrrha (1.62), Arcturus (1.68). Also mentioned are Maia, as representative of all of the Atlantides (1.225), the sterile Eumenides, Ceyx and Alcyone (1.399), Nisus and Scylla (1.404), and Glaucus, Panopea, and Melicerta (1.437).

53. The name of the Curetes, or Corybantes, can be explained, "quod galeas primi sicut 'conos' habuerint militares, quae adhuc *khosumboi* uocentur" ["because he first had military helmets like cones, which {helmets} are still called *khosumboi*"], or because they were created from Jove's tears, which we call the pupils in the eyes, *khoren* in Greek "quas nos pupillas in oculis dicimus, *khoren* Graeci appellant." He continues, "Alii Corytas dictos eo quod armis fuerint tecti; alii Corybantes et Corytas dictos putant, quod fuerint *khoreioi* idest primae aetatis; quos alii nutritores alii ministros Ious appellant" ["others say 'Corytas' because they were protected by arms. Others suppose they are called Corybantes and Corytes, because they were *khoreioi*, that is, in the first age"] (Berne Scholiast, *Ad Georg.* 4.151).

54. Table 3 was originally published as the appendix to Chance, *Christine de Pizan's Letter of Othea to Hector, Translated, with Introduction, Notes, and Interpretative Essay* (Newburyport, Mass.: Focus Press, 1990), pp. 135–38. The rubrics are mine and not those of the first Vatican mythographer.

55. See *Narrationes fabularum Ovidianarum*, 3.3.

56. Hyginus, *Fab.* 166.

57. Ibid., 95 and 105.

58. See Lactantius Placidus's gloss on *Thebaid* 2.29.

CHAPTER 6: ORPHEUS, ULYSSES, HERCULES

1. Boethius refers to a Virgilian underworld, to Lethe, in *Consolatio* 1 p2. In addition much of Boethius's material concerning Hercules derives from the *Aeneid.* Minor references to Hercules can be found in 2 m2 (Achenous and Hercules), 2 p6 (Busiris and Hercules), 3 p8 (Hercules as Alcibiades), and 4 p6 (Hercules and the Hydra).

2. From the *Odyssey* and the tales of Ulysses comes the first mythological

reference to appear in the *Consolatio*—the Muses treated as Sirens (in 1 p1), from the twelfth book. From this epic also come the story of Circe and Ulysses (in 4 m3), in the tenth-twelfth books; the allusions to Agamemnon and the Trojan War (4 m7), passim; and Hercules (4 m7), in the seventh and eighth books (only the Cacus and destruction of Troy episodes). Boethius's commentators were not directly familiar with Homer and cited Homeric material—specifically on Ulysses and Circe and Polyphemus—from references in Servius or Fulgentius.

3. Other images refer to Ovid's *Metamorphoses*—the labyrinth (in *Consolatio* 3 p12), from *Metamorphoses* 8.155; Orpheus (in *Consolatio* 3 m12), from *Metamorphoses* 10.3ff; and Tiresias (in *Consolatio* 5 p3), from *Metamorphoses* 3.324ff.

4. One Boethius gloss even seems to derive from a general understanding of the first two books of Martianus Capella's prosimetrum—in *Consolatio* 4 m3 the aid granted by Mercury, god of eloquence, to the stymied Ulysses in the cave of the Cyclops Polyphemus echoes the kind of marriage of eloquence and philology in *De nuptiis Philologiae et Mercurii.* For the Anonymous Erfurt Commentator's interesting observation on Boethius's imitation, see the edition by Edmund T. Silk, *Saeculi noni auctoris in Boetii consolationem Philosophiae commentarius,* Papers and Monographs of the American Academy in Rome, vol. 9 (Rome: American Academy, 1935), p. 4.

5. Diane K. Bolton, "The Study of the Consolation of Philosophy in Anglo-Saxon England," *AHDLMA* 44 (1977): 43n8.

6. The early Boethius glossators' moralizations may have been drawn from a variety of sources. In *Consolatio* 3 m12, sources for the moralizations of Orpheus, Ixion, Tantalus, and Tityus include Servius's commentary on the *Aeneid.* Orpheus singing to animals at peace with one another (in 3 m12) comes from Servius (*In Aen.* 6.645); underworld inhabitants from 3 m12, like Ixion, Tantalus, and Tityus, come from Servius (*In Aen.* 6.596, 6.603). Glosses on Orpheus and Tantalus—beginning with Remigius or K, his reviser—derive from the Carolingians' chief source, Fulgentius's *Mitologiae,* via the Carolingian transmitter, the first Vatican mythographer. Portions of the Orpheus myth in *Consolatio* 3 m12 come from *Mit.* 3.5 and 3.10. Some of the glosses on Tantalus, in *Consolatio* 3 m12, can also be traced to *Mit.* 2.15. In *Consolatio* 4 m3 the Ulysses and Circe gloss derives from Servius's commentary on the *Aeneid* (7.517) and the Ulysses and Polyphemus gloss derives from Servius (*In Aen.* 3.636) as well as Fulgentius (*Cont. Virg.* 15). Much of the moralized material concerning Hercules in *Consolatio* 4 m7 derives from Servius or Fulgentius on the *Aeneid* or the latter's *Mitologiae.* A confusion between Alcides (Hercules) and Alcibiades, who appears in *Consolatio* 3 p8, depends on Servius (*In Aen.* 6.392). Other references, including Hercules and Cerberus, the golden apples of the Hesperides, Cacus, and Antaeus, come from Fulgentius (*Mit.* 1.6, 2.2; *Cont. Virg.* 20; *Mit.* 2.3; 2.4).

7. In Gottschalk, *Oeuvres théologiques et grammaticales de Godescalc d'Orbais: Textes en majeure partie inédits,* ed. Cyrille Lambot (Louvain: Spicilegium Sacrum Lovaniense Études et Documents, 1945), p. 474.

8. Boethius, *Philosophiae consolationis libri quinque,* ed. Rudolfus Peiper (Leipzig, 1871), pp. xxiii-xxviii.

9. Asser's commentary is contained in MS. Vat. lat. 3363, according to Fabio Troncarelli, "Per una ricerca sui commenti altomedievali al *De consolatione* di Boezio," in *Miscellanea in memoria di Giorgio Cencetti* (Turin: Bottega d'Erasmo, 1973), pp. 363–80.

10. No critical edition of Remigius on Boethius or the tenth- and eleventh-century revisions of Remigius's Boethius yet exists, although snippets have been published by Stewart, Silk, and Bolton. See H. F. Stewart, "A Commentary by Remigius Autissiodorensis on the *De consolatione Philosophiae* of Boethius," *Journal of Theological Studies* 17 (1915): 22–42; in the appendix to Silk's edition of the pseudo-John Scot on Boethius (the Anonymous Erfurt Commentator) appear glosses on *Consolatio* 1 m1, 1 p1, 1 p6, 1 m7, 2 p1, 2 m6, 2 p7, 3 p1, 3 m8, 3 m9, 4 m1, 5 p1. Of course not all of these have mythographic import. Most of the other major cycle glosses have been included in Bolton, "The Study of the *Consolation of Philosophy* in Anglo-Saxon England," pp. 3–78, in a long appendix, pp. 60–78, with many of the minor, noncycle glosses found in footnotes (pp. 33–78). Bolton's edition includes glosses from four manuscript categories which she identifies as Remigius (R) and two other versions (B.N. and T), along with the famous K revision of Remigius (K). R represents those snippets included in Stewart and Silk plus the Paris manuscripts B.N. nouv. acq. 1478, B.N. lat. 15090 (continental), as well as Oxford, Corpus Christi MS. 59, and Cambridge, Gonville and Caius College MS. 309/707, both twelfth century. T represents the type exemplified by Cambridge Trinity College MS. 0.3.7—the closest to Remigius but belonging to the reviser group). B.N. represents the type exemplified by Paris, B.N. MS. lat. 6401A—the closest to the continental reviser. K represents the type exemplified by Cambridge, University Library MS. Kk.III 21—similar to B.N., but the fullest of all. Of these manuscripts, all except the last probably came from the continent; K is regarded as English, formed from glosses taken from manuscripts represented by R, B.N., and perhaps MS. Vat. lat. 3363 (the supposed Welsh Asser), along with glosses taken from Fulgentius and others and added by the glossator himself ("Study," pp. 49–50). There are few major differences between the original and the revisions of the mythological glosses (Bolton, "Remigian Commentaries on the 'Consolation of Philosophy' and their Sources," *Traditio* 33 [1977]: 393). Some of the revisions may have been written by Remigius's students hearing the same lectures and others, like the English K, may have been composed from written sources. Bolton also notes that "it is possible that all the reviser versions originated on the continent. . . . In none of them is there any internal evidence of authorship or nationality" ("Study," p. 49). The major general difference between Remigius and his K reviser, according to Bolton, is that Remigius recalled the sense of his source but not the exact words, whereas the English reviser copied every relevant source without providing any synthesis. I would add, in relation to the mythologi-

cal glosses, that the English K reviser in his fondness for Fulgentius supplied even more elaborate moralizations than had Remigius himself. The K reviser also exposes an interest in male bonding in some of his glosses. I will treat all four manuscript types as "Remigius," unless there are significant differences in a particular gloss. For an excellent overview of the provenance of Boethius commentaries in the early Middle Ages, especially in England, see Bolton, "Manuscripts and Commentaries on Boethius, *De consolatione Philosophiae* in England in the Middle Ages" (B. Litt., Oxford University, 1965), p. 191.

11. That the commentary existed is evidenced by a *Vita Boetii* with the name of John Scot (Johannes Scottus) in MS. Laurentianus 78.19, written in an Irish hand of the twelfth century and bearing insular orthography and abbreviations, and two substantial notes written by an Irishman in his own language. See Silk, "Notes on Two Neglected Manuscripts of Boethius' *Consolatio Philosophiae*," *TAPA* 70 (1939): 352–56. The most recent candidate probably is not in fact the lost commentary of John Scot, even though it is likely that John Scot did indeed write one: a part of John Scot's commentary was said to have been included in the twelfth-century MS. Heiligenkreuz 130. See Nicholas M. Häring, "Four Commentaries on the 'De Consolatione Philosophiae' in MS. Heiligenkreuz 130," *MS* 31 (1969): 287–316, with a description of the manuscript on pages 288–95. This twelfth-century manuscript, from a Cistercian community of French origin in Heiligenkreuz near Vienna in Austria, has four Boethius commentaries buried within what appear to be only three, the first of which has been attributed to John Scot. The first commentary is an interlinear and marginal glossing of the text of Boethius with interspersed Greek words that mark the possible hand of the adept Greek scholar John Scot. A second commentary, probably early twelfth century, begins on folio 77; a third, a continuous text belonging to the Anonymous Erfurt commentators Q 5 group of commentaries (to which Silk's pseudo-John Scot or Anonymous Erfurt is closely related but which is nevertheless heavily Remigian), breaks off in the second book at prose 7, line 31, on folio 92; Häring believes that this missing part was used to provide glosses for the first commentary, which, beginning as it does in the third book, actually therefore conflates two works. The fourth (fols. 93–121) is substantially the same as that of William of Conches in the twelfth century.

That the first commentary probably was not written by John Scot can be attested by a gloss on Alcibiadis on folio 34 which seems post-Remigian, even as late as the twelfth century, because this particular moralization on *Consolatio* 3 p8, based on a fanciful (and not very Scotian) etymology of Hercules's name Alcides, is repeated verbatim only in post-Remigian, generally eleventh- or twelfth-century, commentaries. The gloss tells us that some say Alcibiades was the name of a famous and beautiful woman who was the mother of Hercules, who is for that reason called Alcides; but that this is false. Hercules is called Alcides from the Greek "Alceidos" as if to say "strong" and "beautiful," in that "Alce" means "power" and "idea" "form." The gloss reads: "Alcibiadis est nomen mulieris famose pulchritudinis quam dicunt matrem fuisse Herculis. Unde Alcideneum uocatum. Sed hoc falsum est. Nam Alcides dictus est quasi Alceidos quoniam fortis et pulcher fuit. Alce enim uirtus, idea forma uocatur" (Häring, p. 300). This first commentary much resembles what has been proven to be a twelfth-century commentary, the pseudo-John Scot or the Anonymous Erfurt, itself deriving from Remigius and Adalbold of Utrecht, which will be discussed at greater length in chapter 9. See the text of Anonymous Erfurt in Silk, *Saeculi*, p. 144.

12. Busiris, according to Alfred, is the name of a tyrant who used to kill his guests but was himself killed by Hercules, son of Job or Jove, by drowning in the Nile—"with God's right" ("swið rihte be Godes dome," 2 p6). The idea of the tyrant is taken from Orosius, *Historiarum adversus paganos libri vii* 1.11.2 and cited by Karl Heinz Schmidt, *König Alfreds Boethius-Bearbeitung* (Göttingen: Georg-August-Universität, 1934), pp. 25–26. Schmidt thinks that Alfred found the Orosius gloss on Busirus in the first Vatican mythographer, myth 65, possibly also a source for Remigius (the second Vatican mythographer, according to some scholars) (p. 26).

13. Walter John Sedgefield, ed. *King Alfred's Old English Version of Boethius: De consolatione Philosophiae* (Oxford, 1899), p. 101. For a translation, see Sedgefield's *King Alfred's Version of the Consolation of Boethius* (Oxford: Clarendon Press, 1900), p. 116; for translations of only the poems see Samuel Fox, *King Alfred's Anglo-Saxon Version of the Metres of Boethius, with an English Translation and Notes* (Oxford and Leicester, 1835). The edition and translation by Sedgefield make it easy to discern which passages have been changed extensively because additions and elaborations are cast in italics. I cite the Orpheus material (*Consolatio* 3 m12) from Sedgefield's edition, pp. 101–2.

14. For an edition of the work I will assume to be Asser's commentary, see the appendix to Troncarelli, *Tradizione perdute: L'antica "fortuna" della "Consolatio Philosophiae"* (Padua: Edifrice Antenore, 1980), pp. 141–201. Asser's affinities with the continental commentaries may be seen in the story of Ixion (compare Mythogr. I 14/14 and Mythogr. II 128/106 and 92/74); in the story of Tityus (compare Mythogr. I 13/13 and Mythogr. II 126/104); and Tantalus (compare Mythogr. I 12/12 and Mythogr. II 124/102). Troncarelli also sees a parallel between Asser's Tantalus story and the third Vatican mythographer's version.

15. See Bolton, "Study," p. 37.

16. Ed. Sedgefield, pp. xxxii–xxxiii.

17. Originally Georg Schepfs found affinities between notes in the vernacular of Alfred and the Latin commentaries, specifically one written by Froumond, bound with a tenth-century manuscript of the *Consolatio*, in the Öttingen-Wallerstein Library at Maihingen (known as the K reviser type of Remigian revision) and the annotations in Munich MS. no. 19452, of the tenth or eleventh century (known as Y). But Bolton has shown that the K reviser of Remigius

obviously came after Remigius and was English. For a study of the manuscripts of commentaries on the *Consolatio* Alfred might have used—although some were lost in World War II—and a presentation of variants in the manuscripts for various commentators, see Schepfs, "Zu König Alfreds 'Boethius,'" *ASNSL* 94 (1895): 149–60.

18. I am using here the designations devised by Petrus Tax, who has been studying the St. Gall commentaries extensively. See notes 37 and 38 to this chapter. On other Latin Boethius commentaries: Brian S. Donaghey, "The Sources of King Alfred's Translation of Boethius' *De consolatione Philosophiae*," *Anglia* 82 (1964): 32, thinks that Alfred and Remigius both used the Anonymous of St. Gall Minor, with Alfred perhaps going through the Asser adaptation. This would make the Anonymous of St. Gall first, followed by Asser, Alfred, and Remigius. See also Kurt Otten, *König Alfreds Boethius,* Studien zur Englischen Philologie: Neue Folge, vol. 3 (Tübingen: Max Niemeyer, 1964), who compares Alfred with Remigius, Einsiedeln 155, and the Anonymous of St. Gall (pp. 120, 129–133).

19. Courcelle suggested in "Étude critique sur les commentaires de la Consolation de Boèce (IXe–XVe siècles)," *AHDLMA* 14 (1939): 5–140, that MS. Vat. lat. 3363 (pp. 45–46) might be the lost commentary of Asser (possibly the most ancient of all the Boethius commentaries) because of its great rapport with the Anonymous of St. Gall. For Courcelle, the dates supported this idea: Asser's commentary would have been written in 895 and Alfred's translation in 897–901, with Remigius's commentary (in 901–2) deriving both from the Anonymous of St. Gall on the one hand and Asser on the other. I disagree with Courcelle, who believes that the Anonymous of St. Gall was an exemplar for both Alfred (through Asser) and for Remigius (directly). More recently, Troncarelli attributes MS. Vat. lat. 3363 to the Welsh monk Asser or someone of his school, in "Per una ricerca sui commenti altomedievali" (pp. 363–80), and he edits it in the appendix to his book, *Tradizioni perdute,* pp. 141–201. Because MS. Vat. lat. 3363 shows unequivocal "Welsh symptoms," Troncarelli (pp. 146, 150) links the manuscript with Glastonbury, suggesting that Asser (ca. 909) who lived in Sherbourne, only 25 km from Glastonbury, may have been the author.

20. According to F. Anne Payne, *King Alfred and Boethius: An Analysis of the Old English Version of the Consolation of Philosophy* (Madison, Milwaukee, and London: University of Wisconsin Press, 1968), most of Alfred's changes occur in the fifth book—the least interesting, for mythological purposes. See also, in a book-by-book paraphrase, Schmidt's study of how Alfred changed the Latin Boethius, cited above.

21. See the study of Alfred and Asser by Joseph S. Wittig, "King Alfred's *Boethius* and Its Latin Sources: A Reconsideration," in *Anglo-Saxon England,* vol. 11, ed. Peter Clemoes (Cambridge: Cambridge University Press, 1983), pp. 157–98. The "commentary" Alfred was said to have used might very well have been not a commentary on Boethius at all, but a copy of the first Vatican

mythography. Certainly Alfred's Old English translation (or at least the fact of its translation) influenced other vernacular translations such as the Old High German translation of Notker Labeo, which primarily uses Remigius (see the chapter on Notker which follows) and the anonymous tenth-century Provençal translation. This Provençal translation is available in an old edition edited by Franz Hündgen, *Das altprovenzalische Boethiuslied unter beifügung einer Übersetzung, eines Glossars, erklärender Anmerkungen, sowie grammatischer und metrischer Untersuchungen* (Oppeln, 1884), with a modern German translation; but this was a popular and not a learned work, and there is no accord between the Provençal Boethius and the Latin sources. See Courcelle, "Étude," p. 47.

22. For information on the history of St. Gall, see James Midgley Clark, *The Abbey of St. Gall as a Centre of Literature and Art* (Cambridge: Cambridge University Press, 1926).

23. The mythological and mythographic glosses in MS. Vat. lat. 3363 (Asser) are very slight in comparison to those of later Boethius commentaries, including the St. Gall commentary. It is clear that Asser's glosses help a reader to identify puzzling references without providing moralization of the myths; the simplicity and brevity of these references suggest only fossilization of mythography. The longest and most involved passages concern *Consolatio* 3 m12 (Orpheus), 4 m3 (Ulysses), and 4 p6 and 4 m7 (Hercules), as in later commentaries, although there also exist minor references to myths. Most of them briefly identify names: for example, in 2 p6, the allusion to the myth of Busiris who killed his guests and was himself killed by Hercules comes from Orosius, according to Asser (ed. Troncarelli, *Tradizione perdute,* p. 175, 17r). Other identifications occur in glosses on *Consolatio* 3 m12, where Dominus is Pluto, "deus infernalis," Tergeminus is Cerberus the three-headed dog, *ianitor inferni* or doorkeeper of the underworld (cf. Mythogr. II, Bode's fable 11, from which derives Mythogr. III 6.22). On *Consolatio* 4 m7, "Ithacus" is Ulixis, from the fatherland of Ulysses, and Polyphemus is a Giant; the Centaurs that Hercules tamed are "sons of earth," the "Volucres" or Birds are the Stymphalides, Antaeus is an African giant, and so forth. The longer identifications, according to Troncarelli, are similar to passages in the first and second Vatican mythographers: if the first mythographer can be identified as Adanan the Scot and second as Remigius of Auxerre, then probably Asser copied from the first but was copied by the second. In their literalism, the Asser glosses resemble those in Hyginus's *Fabulae,* the source of most of the first mythographer's mythological paraphrases. Most of the mythographic glosses explain the underworld inhabitants of Boethius's Orpheus poem, but without the originality of Alfred. Indeed, the only figurative interpretation supplied appears within the epithets.

24. Bolton, "Study," p. 37.

25. Sedgefield, ed., p. 103.

26. Ibid., p. 102.

27. Troncarelli, *Tradizioni perdute,* pp. 190–91, 36v right and left margins: "et

ips[ae] dicuntur Furie, quia o[m]ni tempore plene sun[t] ira et furore; et ip[sae] puniunt animas in e. . ." with this gloss, says Troncarelli, echoing Mythogr. I 14/14, Mythogr. II 14/12, and the rest from Mythogr. III 6.23. Like Alfred and unlike Asser, the writer of the Anonymous St. Gall Minor identifies "ultrices deae" with "furie.parce" and the names of the three Furies listed in a frame— Allecto, Megaera, and Thesiphone in *Consolatio* 3 m12. That such an identification is found both in the insular Alfred translation and the continental St. Gall Minor glosses establishes a connection between the two. This particular gloss is found in only one of the many Remigian and continental manuscripts—MS. Paris B.N. 1478—and may have originated from the first mythographer's juxtaposition of the myth of the Furies (Mythogr. I 108/109) with that of the Parcae (Mythogr. I 109/110). St. Gall MS. 845 (p. 182) is cited in Courcelle, "Étude critique," p. 55. It is possible that Alfred used the first Vatican mythographer for this gloss, especially likely if the latter author was indeed Adanan the Scot, as has been speculated.

28. For Alfred, see Sedgefield's edition, p. 116. Asser is cited in Troncarelli, *Tradizioni perdute,* p. 193, 41r, right margin.

29. Trans. Sedgefield, p. 127; trans., p. 127; trans. p. 135.

30. Ed. Sedgefield, p. 127; trans., p. 148.

31. Cited in Troncarelli, *Tradizioni perdute,* p. 195, 45r right margin; Troncarelli sees this as similar to Mythogr. III 13.20–28.

32. Courcelle, *La Consolation de Philosophie dans la tradition littéraire: Antécédents et postérité de Boèce* (Paris: Études Augustiniennes, 1967), pp. 260, 267.

33. For a history of this German-Swiss (Swabian) community, see Clark, *The Abbey of St. Gall.* The monastery had been founded by St. Columban and St. Gall in 610, and from 613–720 was an Irish hermitage obeying the Rule of St. Columban; it was a Benedictine abbey from 720–759, dominated by the Swabians, with the Irish then in a minority.

34. Ed. Peiper, pp. xi, lxi; Courcelle, "Étude critique," p. 39. According to Courcelle, there are four manuscripts of the Anonymous of St. Gall (p. 120): Einsiedeln MS. 179, pp. 95–185, tenth century; St. Gall MS. 845, pp. 3–240, tenth century; Paris B.N. MS. 13953, fols. 25v–41v, tenth century; and Naples, Biblioteca Nazionale MS. IV.G.68, fols. 1v–92v, ninth century (pp. 52–56; described, pp. 119–20). (There also exist nine fragmentary manuscripts, most of them from the tenth century, he says, among them St. Gall MS. 844, and two with *Consolatio* 3 m9 in isolation.) Einsiedeln MS. 179 includes Old High German glosses here and there, and St. Gall MS. 845 is a copy of this. Paris B.N. MS. 13953 is an abridgment, but independent and without contamination (there are no words in OHG cryptography such as FLKZZF for "flizze"). Of Naples MS. IV.G.68 he says only that it issued from the monastery at St. Gall.

35. Paris, B.N. MS. Paris. 13953; see Courcelle, "Étude critique," p. 39.

36. Petrus W. Tax refines Courcelle's work in a letter to the author on May, 27, 1980.

37. Tax declares that "St. Gall 845 is only a primitive and partly awkward and even faulty copy of this [i.e., Einsiedeln MS. 179]; it doesn't have textual value, and it is also not complete. The other MSS I have seen (and which I am going to study and collate) seem to be closer to *An. minor* or even less complete." That is, St. Gall MS. 845 is a bad copy of the St. Gall Major. But then, St. Gall MS. 844 is a badly used copy of St. Gall minor: Tax has collated the base manuscript (Naples MS. IV.G.68) with St. Gall MS. 844, and "The gloss is a copy of the one in the Naples MS., but because 844 was used extensively already in early times, many glosses have been rubbed off and can be recognized only with special lighting, if at all." These comments were made in a second letter to the author, on July 7, 1980. Tax has in part collated St. Gall MS. 844 with the Naples manuscript of the shorter version, Anonymous St. Gall Minor; he is also editing St. Gall Major from Einsiedeln 179. All references to St. Gall Major or Minor in this text are to Tax's transcriptions.

38. The Anonymous of St. Gall Minor is represented by MS. Naples IV.G.68 (whose commentary on Boethius is also found in St. Gall MS. 844). The Naples manuscript is owned by the Biblioteca Nazionale of Naples; it contains a fragment of a commentary on the first book of the *Consolatio,* Lupus of Ferrières's analysis of Boethius's poems, the *Vita* of *Tempore Theodorici Regis,* the *Consolatio* with scholia and glosses, Boethius's *Arithmetic,* Prudentius's *Psychomachia,* most of book 4 of Martianus Capella (on rhetoric), miscellaneous liturgical fragments with neums and *probationes pennae.* See Silk, "Notes," p. 352; Silk talks about Naples MS. IV.G.68 and another neglected Boethius manuscript, Laurentianus 78.19 at the Biblioteca Laurenziana in Florence (pp. 352–55). Written in a late-ninth-century hand, the Naples manuscript manifests in three different places pressmarks of St. Gall, with scattered German glosses. Silk says, "It is quite probable that the book was not only studied at St. Gall but written there as well." Petrus Tax has generously shared his editing of glosses for the Naples IV.G.68—the St. Gall Minor—on *Consolatio* 4 m3 (Circe), 4 m7 (three heroes), and 4 p6 (Hydra) in the letter of July 7, 1980. From the St. Gall Major (Eins. 179), Professor Tax also transcribed for me glosses on 2 p2 (Croesus) and 2 p6 (Busiris). (Note there is no long gloss on 3 m12, as there are in Asser and Alfred.)

39. The mythological glosses in the St. Gall Minor (Naples MS. IV.G.68) begin with *Consolation* 3 m12 (fols. 56v–57r). Most of it is very simple, with comments occurring in the form of paraphrases and occasional moralizations of the tropological or moral variety, that is, centering on the virtues and vices of the individual man. For example, this myth or *fabula* of Orpheus shows that no one should turn back, "Haec fabula monet ut nemo aspiciat retro." "Turning back" to the underworld here involves, as it does in later commentaries, the suggestion that the underworld represents the lower pleasures of man. Other minor moralized references include the identification of Pluto as "arbiter" of the underworld, the judge of souls. Of interest, too, in this regard is the moral, which allegorizes the

entire myth of Orpheus: those who wish to look to "sovereign day should read this fable," and the phrase "sovereign day," "in superum diem," is glossed as "deum. in supernum," "God in the heavens." He who is "conquered by looking into the inferno," *victus,* as Boethius's text makes clear, is according to St. Gall "superatur," overcome by desire ("hic concupiscit," says St. Gall), which returns him to *carnalia.* The moralization provided for the second major mythological passage is also markedly tropological. On *Consolation* 4 m3 (Naples MS. 64r): Circe as "daughter of the sun" is called so because of her beauty, "a pulchritudine." Boethius reminds us in this fable that poisons which allow man to forget himself are deadlier than Circe's because they corrupt the inner man; the glossator here identifies these corruptions as "auaritia" and "ira." Anonymous St. Gall Minor does go beyond Alfred or Asser in some of his grammatical identifications, although many are the same. In the third and last major mythological passage, we hear echoes of Asser's literalism in the description of Polyphemus, in *Consolation* 4 m7, as not only a Giant (Naples MS. 77r) but also as a "Cyclops having one eye in the front." The Centaurs are only men mixed with horses, the Birds, Stymphalides, the Hydra, "aquaticus serpens," Antaeus, "filius terre," with Cacus, a "monster." Because of the brevity and literalism of these glosses, the Minor must be regarded as a very early commentary, but whether it came before or after Asser is unclear.

40. In St. Gall Minor man (Orpheus) is helped by his songs, which are drawn from the fountains of his mother, the Muse Calliope, and the fountains are identified as "doctrines" ("fontibus: doctrinibus"). Orpheus's chief sin is indulging his wife ("Ueniam: indulgentiam uxori"), which is made to resemble, for the St. Gall glossator, the sin of Ixion "cupiens iunonem."

41. This St. Gall Major gloss can also be found in Paris, B.N. MS. Paris. 13953, fol. 26r, cited in Courcelle, "Étude critique," pp. 52–53.

42. MS. Einsiedeln 179, fol. 186, cited in Courcelle, "Étude critique," p. 54.

43. St. Gall MS. 845, fol. 182, cited in Courcelle, "Étude critique," p. 55.

44. "Étude critique," p. 52; the phrase "catholicum Boetium," cited p. 52n4.

45. The Lazarus passage reads "Site. pro siti. Significat epulas ante ora positas. his qui cottidie in hac vita epulis inseruiunt. vt tantalus ille diues. de quo in euangelio. erat homo dives. q. i 1. p. e. b; 7 [=et] . e. c. [cf. Luke. 16:19] illi uero sicut iste tantalus fame et siti cruciantur in inferno. significat autem ille.s. tantalus. omnes auaros et diuites. qui inexplicabilis carybdi mala ubertate contabescunt."

46. Otten, pp. 120–21.

47. Courcelle, *Consolation,* pp. 241–69.

48. Bolton, "Study," p. 45, sees the theme of the entire work in a related but different way, as the conflict between world and spirit, "light and dark, higher and lower, flesh and spirit," the carnal and vicious set against the spiritual and contemplative.

49. Ed. Stewart, p. 22n2.

50. Bolton, "Study," p. 38. Bolton classifies three types of later English groups of Remigian manuscripts, in addition to R (for "Remigius," by which she means the Remigian excerpts printed in Stewart and Silk, *Saeculi*).

51. All information concerning the life of Remigius is derived from Stewart, pp. 22–25; "Remi, Moine de S. Germain d'Auxerre," *Histoire littéraire de la France par les religieux bénédictins de la congrégation de Saint Maur*, new ed., vol. 6 (tenth century) (Paris, 1857), pp. 99–122; Hauréau, *Histoire de la philosophie scholastique* (1872; rpt. Minerva, 1966), 1:199ff; and Manitius, "Zür karolingischen Literatur," *NA* 36 (1910): 43–75, esp. pp. 43–56. That Remigius may have been Irish was posited by William Stahl and Richard Johnson, with E. L. Burge, in *Martianus Capella and the Seven Liberal Arts*, vol. 1: *The Quadrivium of Martianus Capella: Latin Traditions in the Mathematical Sciences*, 50 B.C.–A.D.. 1250 (New York and London: Columbia University Press, 1971), p. 63. Remigius, like John Scot and Martin of Laon, is described as immigrating to the Frankish lands in the ninth century.

52. Stewart, p. 24.

53. Courcelle, "Étude critique," pp. 56, 72.

54. Manitius, *Geschichte* 9.2.1:516ff.

55. Bolton, "Study," p. 37.

56. For the dating of the *Consolatio* commentary, see Courcelle, "La Culture antique de Remi d'Auxerre," *Latomus* 7 (1948): 247; and Bolton, "Remigian Commentaries," pp. 381–94.

57. Courcelle, "Étude critique," p. 31.

58. Courcelle, *Consolation*, p. 255.

59. They included grammar, linguistics, rhetoric, dialectic, philosophy, history, geography, archeology, science, and mythology. See Courcelle, "La Culture," p. 249.

60. Named as sources throughout Remigius's commentary are Virgil, Ovid, Persius, Juvenal, Avianus, Sedulius, Cato, Cicero, Lucan, Suetonius, Pliny the Elder, Solinus, Hyginus, Pacuvius, Plautus, Servius, the Bible, St. Jerome, St. Augustine, Claudianus Mamertus, *De statu animae*, and Ptolemy, Gregory the Nazanian, John Chrysostom, Plato, Aristotle, Alexander (the so-called "Letters"), the Greek works, if indeed read, undoubtedly read in translation rather than in the original, for Remigius did not know Greek. See Courcelle, "La Culture," pp. 250–33; Bolton, "Remigian Commentaries," pp. 382–94.

61. The authors Remigius actually used include Virgil, Ovid, Isidore, Servius, the first Vatican mythographer, Lactantius Placidus's *Narrationes*, and the commentaries on Statius's *Thebaid*, among others; and he used some of the works on which he had written commentaries: Persius, Juvenal, Avianus, Sedulius, and the *Disticha Catonis*—but not Martianus Capella, "although many of the Boethius glosses recall similar glosses in Remigius's commentary on the *De nuptiis Philologiae et Mercurii*" (Bolton, "Remigian commentaries," p. 383).

62. Paris, B.N. MS. Paris. 7930 has been partly edited by J. J. Savage, "Medieval Notes on the Sixth *Aeneid* in Parisinus 7930," *Speculum* 9 (1934): 204–12. The manuscript may be tenth century because "Gerbertus" is mentioned on folio 200; if this refers to Gerbert who became Pope in 999, then, Savage hypothesizes, this manuscript must be late tenth century, possibly donated by Gerbert (as Pope Silvester II) to a monastery either at Aurillac or at Rheims. That the commentary on the sixth book was written by Remigius has been argued from the existence of two hands, the first (inscribing notes chiefly from Servius and Servius *Danielis*) before the end of the tenth century, the second (whose notes are from an unidentified, probably nonantique source) from the end of the eleventh century, but primarily concerned with book 6, and hence possibly derived from the lost commentary on the *Aeneid* by Remigius. See Savage, p. 212n1.

63. The quotations from Remigius on the *Aeneid* (Paris, B.N. MS. 7930) are taken from Savage, "Medieval Notes," pp. 211–12. The translations are mine.

64. Ed. Savage, p. 211.

65. Bolton, "Study," p. 47.

66. Quotations of Remigius's commentary on *Consolatio* 3 m12 are from Bolton, ibid., pp. 61–66. The translations are mine.

67. That is, "illa scilicet temporalia dum ad inferni claustra dilabitur [B.N., K, R] vel ab hac vita transit [K]."

"Qui ad mundi cupiditatem respexerit post summum bonum inventum quicquid fecit Deo perdit dum ad terrena dilabitur. Potest etiam aliter iuxta litteram intellegi. Omnis enim iniquus inferis perpetuo cruciandus traditur. Quicquid boni putabat se possidere in mundo penitus perdit" [That is, "those temporal things, when he slips down to the doors of the underworld, pass away from this life.

"He who has looked back at the desires of the world after the discovery of the highest good, whatsoever he has done for God, perishes when he slips away to the earthly. This can also be understood in another way, according to the letter. Namely, everyone unjust is brought to the underworld for perpetual tormenting.

Whatsoever good he reckoned to possess in the world wholly perishes"] [B.N., K, R] (Bolton, ibid., p. 66; my translations).

68. Bolton, ibid., p. 44, my emphasis; cf. pp. 64–65. The reference to Virgil is from *Georgics* 4.467, but the reference to the promontory in Laconia actually comes from Servius's commentary (*In Georg.* 4.466).

69. Bolton, ibid., p. 43.

70. In the first part, from the first Vatican mythographer, the K reviser recites the story of Orpheus, son of "Oagrus" and the Muse "Caliope," the Thracian poet married to Eurydice. When the shepherd Aristaeus (son of Cineris, or Cyrene) pursues Eurydice with desire, a serpent bites her and she dies. Orpheus then

descends to retrieve his wife, does not succeed, returns to this world where he refuses to live with any other woman and is stoned by the Thracian women. See Bolton, "Study," pp. 62–63.

71. "Serpentem in quem incedit et moritur Euridice astutiam id est quasi hoc apertissime prenuntiasset. Omnis ars communionem hominum vitat quae serpentis ictu moritur quasi astutie intercoeptu, secretis velut inferis transmigratur, sed post hanc exquirendam atque elevandam sapientie divine canora vox descendit et ad studium bene vivendi invitat. . . ." ["The serpent on which Eurydice steps— and then dies—{he calls} cunning, that is, as if he has clearly foretold this. Every art {skill} avoids communion with men, which {art} dies from the bite of the serpent, that is, by the intervention of cunning, migrates as it were to the hiddem underworld, but after she has been sought for and lifted up, and having elevated her, the singing voice of divine wosdom descends and summons her to the pursuit of the living well"] (Bolton, "Study," p. 63; my translations).

72. Ibid., p. 46.

73. "Berocinthie" is found in B.N. and K and the Muse Calliope in R (Remigius), B.N., and K. Berocinthie, Berecynthia, comes from Berecynthus, a mountain in Phrygia sacred to Cybele, according to Bolton, "Study," p. 63n. She refers readers to Fulgentius, *Mit.* 3.5 and Remi., *In Mart.* 74.12, 286.17.

74. An explanation of this puzzling idea is provided by Remigius's commentary on Martianus Capella 286.17: the lemma is "fontingenarum," "fountain-born," in explanation of the Muses, because "moyca" in Greek means water, and also the Castalian Fountain was produced when Pegasus touched earth, and is thus called Yppocrene, or Fontingenae.

75. B.N., K, T, R (Remigius): "TERGEMINUS propter tria capita. De Cerbero dicit qui ideo *tergeminus* id est tria capita fingitur habere. Cerberus vero dicitur quasi creosboros id est carnem vorans qui propterea fingitur habere tria capita propter tres aetates id est infantiam, iuventutem et senectutem per quas introivit mors in orbem terrarum" (Bolton, "Study," p. 64), with the etymology, according to Bolton, coming from Fulgentius, *Mit.* 1.6, although he lacks the signification of the three heads.

76. The Remigius revisers generally do not confuse the Furies with the Parcae as does St. Gall Minor—only in one reviser manuscript (B.N. 1478) are the "three" identified as the Fates. Remigius just identifies the Furies as daughters of the night who punish the guilty, although the variant for Remigius, from Oxford, Corpus Christi College MS. 59 and Cambridge, Gonville and Caius College MS. 309/307, designates them as the three parts of discord through etymologies provided by Fulgentius (*Mit.* 1.7), perhaps as transmitted through the first Vatican mythographer (Mythogr. I 110/109): "Nota quod Greci finxerunt tres esse furias ad designandas tres partes discordie, scilicet Allecto quae impausabilis interpretatur et Tesiphonam quae vox eorum dicitur et Megeram quae magna contentio nuncupatur. Prius enim in corde, postea in voce, tandem in opere sic

discordia" ["Note that the Greeks have imagined three Furies to exist to designate the three parts of discord, namely Allecto, who is interpreted as unceasing, and Thesiphone, who is said to be their words, and Maegera, who is named great contention. First indeed in the heart, afterwards in the words, finally, in actions, as it were, discord exists"] (Bolton, "Study," p. 64).

77. The gloss is taken mainly from Fulgentius, *Mit.* 2.15, and first Vatican mythographer, fable 12 (for T and R). Note the similarity to Servius (*In Aen.* 6.596), on the "king of the Lapiths." In K only, Tantalus is punished by a black flint that hangs above him menacingly; this comes from Servius (*In Aen.* 6.603), which contains a lacuna.

78. The first part of this (exclusive of the identification of Latona) derives from Mythogr. I 13.

79. Bolton, "Study," p. 43n59, in all four, R, T, B.N., and K. This is very like Hyginus's *Fab.* 28.

80. Ibid.; this gloss is in R (Remigius) only.

81. Richard Hamilton Green, introduction to his translation of *The Consolation of Philosophy,* Library of Liberal Arts (Indianapolis and New York: Bobbs-Merrill, 1962), p. 4.

82. In the appendix of Silk, "Notes," p. 317.

83. Ibid., pp. 317–18. Bolton, "Remigian Commentaries," p. 32, says that Isidore 11.3.30–31 is a source for the Remigius revisers on the Sirens; in addition, see Remi., *In Mart.* 3.5 for the mother of the Muses.

84. The names begin with that of Ulysses, who is named Narcicius from the region of Naritia (actually Neritius from Neritos, a mountain in Ithaca and a small island in the vicinity); although the name is glossed in Ovid (*Metamorphoses* 13.712) as the False Ulysses, Remigius and his K reviser declare that it is the region in Greece from which he comes, "according to Virgil" (*Georgics* 2.438—but in actuality as glossed by Servius).

85. "Accedentes ad se dicitur vertisse in beluas quia illius amore homines in amentiam vertebantur et pro eo multa iurgia et prelia gesta sunt et multi perierunt," Bolton, "Study," p. 67.

86. The Remigius glosses on *Consolatio* 4 m3 (Ulysses and Circe) are edited in Bolton, ibid., pp. 66–68.

87. Ibid. The K glosses on *Consolatio* 4 m7 are edited by Bolton, ibid., pp. 69–76.

88. Ibid., pp. 68–69. But the Greek Agamemnon who waged war for ten years is an ambiguous choice for epic hero. The commentator B.N. regards Agamemnon as a hero who wages war with Troy because of Paris's dishonor to his brother Menelaus in the rape of Helen, although Remigius and his other revisers implicitly criticize Agamemnon by declaring that those who wage war fight more valiantly only when they know the outcome.

89. From Servius, *In Aen.* 3.636, notes Bolton.

90. According to Ovid, *Metamorphoses* 14.167ff. The K reviser glosses line eight to reveal the nature of Polyphemus as supposedly witnessed by Achiminides, who was afterward saved.

91. Bolton, "Study," p. 70. "Ergo iuventutis elationem et famem perditionem etatis cecitas sequitur quasi aperte dixisset noli puerili lascivia terrena dignitates affectare ne sapentiae famam perdas." The passage is drawn almost directly from Fulgentius, *Cont. Virg.* 15, though the last comment belongs to the K reviser: "The blindness of age follows the arrogance of youth, as if he had said clearly, do not pursue earthly honors with childish frivolity lest you destroy the reputation for wisdom."

92. Bolton, "Study," p.39n43; the Servian etymology makes Alcibiades a woman (*In Aen.* 6.392), but Remigius says this is false, Bolton, p. 48n96. This fifth idea refers to the name Alcides for Hercules, which, according to Servius (*In Aen.* 6.392), comes from *alce* (*virtus*) and *idea* (*forma*), p. 48n96.

93. These Labors of Hercules include: (1) the wounding of the Centaurs; (2) the winning of the spoils of the Nemean lion; (3) the shooting down with arrows of the Stymphalian birds; (4) the stealing of the golden apples from the dragon; (5) the return of Cerberus to the underworld with a gold chain (and the rescue of Theseus); (6) the conquering of Diomede (Glaucus) and feeding his savage mares his own flesh; (7) the burning of Hydra's heads; (8) overcoming the river Achelous by making him "bury his face in its banks"; (9) the killing of Antaeus on the Libyan beach; (10) the slaying of Cacus; (11) the killing of the Erymanthian boar; and (12) helping Atlas by bearing heaven on his neck.

94. On *Consolatio* 2 p6 the reference to Busiris is established as coming from Orosius, *Historiarum adversus paganos libri vii* 1.11 (Bolton, "Study," p. 47n86). It thus resembles the early Asser commentary.

95. As mentioned by Ovid, *Metamorphoses* 9.182–99. Indeed, the sixth Labor in the commentators, involving Diomede—whom the Remigian commentators call Glaucus—and his savage mares, is hardly glossed at all, and the twelfth Labor, involving Atlas, is buried in the adventure of the wounding of Nessus and marriage of Deianira, which itself is discussed in a gloss on the Boethian line "ultimus caelum labor in reflexo." The "problem" of the number of the Labors, whether ten or twelve, and how that problem is handled in the Carolingian period by Theodulf of Orleans, is discussed by Lawrence Nees, *A Tainted Mantle: Hercules and the Classical Tradition at the Carolingian Court* (Philadelphia: University of Pennsylvania Press, 1991), pp. 26–27ff.

96. Bolton, "Study," p. 71; my translation, adapted in the italicized portions from Whitbread's *Fulgentius* (*Mit.* 2.2, trans., p. 68).

97. "In carne quamdiu fidelis vivit equanimiter sustinet atque superat dilectione Dei et proximi roboratus, quasi apertissime haec verba sapientia pronuntiasset: Noli confidere in divitiis secularibus o Boetii quia tam cito transeunt et in terrena felicitate quia instabilis est sed equanimiter prosperitas ista visibilis et

momentanea adversitas recta mentis intentione in loco exilii et peregrinationis tuę contempnende sunt" ["While the faithful man lives in the flesh he is patiently sustained and survives strengthened by love for God and his neighbor, as if most clearly he had proclaimed these wise words: do not trust in secular riches, oh Boethius, because so very quickly they pass away, or in earthly happiness, because it is unstable, but with equanimity visible good fortune and transitory adversity should be despised with upright application of mind in the place of exile and of pilgrimage"] (Bolton, "Study," p. 71).

98. See Mythogr. I 56; according to Remigius and the revisers B.N. and K, these "rapatrices" were named "Stymphalidian" from the river Stymphalus, mentioned in Ovid (*Metamorphoses* 9.187).

99. Bolton, "Study," pp. 72–73.

100. Ibid.; "*Cerberum* vero canem pedibus eius subiciunt, id est quod mortalium iurgiorum invidie ternario complentur statu, hoc est naturali, casuali, accedente. . . . Cerberus autem carnem vorans interpretatur, ideo quia semper invidia humano odio insatiabilis est." The translation of the gloss on Pluto is Whitbread's (*Mit.* 1.6).

101. The moral on wisdom reads, "Sapiente recta mentis intentione providentie quod in hac presenti momentanea vita nondiu omnes homines victuros esse, quasi his verbis sapientia Boetium alloqueretur: Attende hos equos te usque ad mortem vehentes" ["By wise uprightness of mind and the application of foresight because in this present epheremal life men are not long to live, as if wisdom were speaking these words to Boethius: Pay attention to these horses bearing you all the way to death"]. Earlier, the K reviser has asked, "Quid sibi sapientia intelligere vult per dominos et equos, nisi hic quod isti ad moralem intellectum respiciunt?" ["What does wisdom mean by masters and horses, unless this, because they {the former} have regard for the moral intellect"]. This fable is derived from Mythogr. I 112/113, and Fulgentius, *Mit.* 1.12, 1.16. (Bolton, "Study," p. 74). The gloss on the four horses is also found in Remigius's commentary on Martianus Capella (*In Mart.* 20.10) where they represent the four seasons, and more distantly in Fulgentius (*Mit.* 1.12); but in K the gloss also adds an allegorical comment on Phaethon taken from Fulgentius, *Mit.* 1.16.

102. These literally recited Labors are seven, eight, and eleven. Labor seven involves the Hydra: Hercules kills the monster by means of fire with the help of Minerva (who we know signifies wisdom, once again) and Iolaus (in the text, "Eulus"); another source (perhaps the Anonymous of St. Gall glosses) provides K with the idea that the Hydra was a serpent with fifty heads. Labor seven derives from Hyginus, *Fab.* 30.3, and parallels Remigius, *In Mart.* 366.5. Labor eight, the division of the river Achelous into many smaller tributaries, derives straightforwardly from Hyginus (*Fab.* 31.7): when the shapechanging river Achelous fought with Hercules to win Deianira in marriage, he changed himself into a bull, but Hercules pulled off his horn and gave it to the Hesperides, and those goddesses

filled it with fruit and called it Cornucopia. In Labor eleven Hercules kills the boar, called "Meleagrum" instead of "Eurymanthian" by the commentators (perhaps because, as Bolton, "Study," p. 47n93, suggests, of a misreading of Ovid, *Metamorphoses* 8.281–424; she points to parallels in Servius, *In Aen.* 1.741 and Remi., *In Mart.* 428.19).

103. Lucan, *De bello civile* 4.593–653.

104. Bolton, "Study," p. 75. My translations.

105. "Kakon enim Grece malum dicimus, ergo omnis malitia fumum eructat id est aut contra sit veritati hoc est luci aut quod accervum sit videntibus ut fumum oculis, aut quod semper occultas obscurasque cavillationes obiciat" ["For in Greek Cacus means evil, therefore every malice belches smoke, that is, it is the opposite to truth, namely, the light, either because it is a {dark} mass, like smoke before the seeing eyes, or because it always tosses about hidden and dark quibblings"] (ibid., p. 76).

106. "Ideo et dupplex quod malitia multiformis sit, non simplex triplici etiam. Nocet malitia aut in evidenti potentior aut subtiliter falsus amicus aut occulte ut impossibilis latro. Ideo etiam subtractos boves transversis ducit vestigiis quod omnis malignus ut aliena invadat, transversa defensionis nititur via . . . . Denique in spelunca absconditur quod numquam malignitas aperta fronte liberior sit" ["And for that reason it is twofold because malice is multiform, not single, but threefold. Malice injures either being obviously more powerful, or subtly, as a false friend, or secretly, as a powerless thief. For that reason, moreover, he drags away cattle with their footprints sideways, because every evil man, in order to seize what belongs to another, relies on a sideways pass of defense. Finally he hides in a cave because malignity is never free when its face is revealed"].

107. In R (Remigius) and T, Nessus, a Centaur who is son of Ixion, is slain by Hercules when he attempts to carry across a stream—and then rape—Deianira; the dying Centaur gives to her some of his blood (poisoned by Hercules's arrow) as a charm to recall wandering love. Deianira of course uses it in a tunic which Lichas, Hercules's servant, brings to him and which kills Hercules, who nevertheless hurls his servant over a cliff before his anguish ends. After that, Hercules is apotheosized as a constellation.

108. "Quem pater omnipotens inter cava nubila raptum quadrigiiugo curru radiantibus intulit astris, sensitque Athlas pondum, nam post Herculem ipse dicitur caelum sustinere," Bolton, "Study," p. 78; see Ovid, *Metamorphoses* 9.271–3.

109. After being bitten by a snake at Lemnos on his way to Troy, Philoctetes was abandoned there by the Greeks for ten years on the advice of Ulysses, at which time an oracle declared that Troy could not be taken without the bow and arrows of Hercules. This declaration then necessitated Ulysses's return in order that he might be persuaded to rejoin the Greeks. (Much of this comes from Mythogr. I 59).

CHAPTER 7: THE UXORIOUS GODS IN REMIGIUS OF
AUXERRE'S NEO-STOIC COMMENTARY ON MARTIANUS
CAPELLA

1. See especially Michael Lapidge, "The Stoic Inheritance," in *A History of Twelfth-Century Western Philosophy,* ed. Peter Dronke (Cambridge, New York, and New Rochelle: Cambridge University Press, 1988), pp. 81–112, but particularly pp. 99–112, on physics. For the ancient and early medieval transmission of Stoicism (up to the sixth century), see the impressive two-volume study by Marcia L. Colish, *The Stoic Tradition from Antiquity to the Early Middle Ages* (Leiden: E. J. Brill, 1985).

2. Cora E. Lutz, "Remigius' Ideas on the Origin of the Seven Liberal Arts," *M&H* 10 (1956): 38. For the relationship between Charles the Bald, the Church, and the development of learning, see especially J. M. Wallace-Hadrill, *The Frankish Church* (Oxford: Clarendon Press, 1983), esp. pp. 241–57.

3. The ultimate educational goal for Remigius, as for John Scot, is not just mastery of the arts, but philosophy as their culmination (see Remi., *In Mart.* 287.23): "Philosophia significat omnes artes," with Philology called *amor sapientiae* and *veritatis intelligentia,* 57.14 and 287.23). Lutz, "Remigius' Ideas on the Classification of the Seven Liberal Arts," *Traditio* 12 (1956): 65–86, notes that Remigius explains the arts philosophically not as a creation of the human mind but as "part of the very structure of reality" (p. 78). Thus, morally the marriage of Mercury and Philology symbolizes a defense against evil, or the Furies, as vices; Remigius declares, "Now to have a clear understanding and to express oneself well is a virtue, but to take away understanding and clarity of expression is a vice" (Lutz, "Remigius' Ideas on the Classification," p. 79, quoting Remi., *In Mart.* 364.14).

4. Lutz declares there are sixty-four manuscripts, in "Remigius' Ideas on the Origin," p. 39, but in her introduction to her edition, she says that there are over seventy, mostly from the tenth to the twelfth centuries, and some very late, from the fifteenth to the sixteenth centuries, 1:40. See also her article, "Martianus Capella," in Kristeller and Cranz, eds., *Catalogus* 2:367–68.

5. J. P. Elder, "A Mediaeval Cornutus on Persius," *Speculum* 22 (1947): 240–48, here, pp. 243–44.

6. Lutz, "Remigius' Ideas on the Origin," p. 34.

7. Lapidge, "The Stoic Tradition."

8. The passage reads, "Sed si humiditate aeris, in cuius significatione Iuno interponitur, non fuerit posita, nequaquam caliditas ignis ariditati terrae potest succurrere, nam ignea potestas per humiditatem aeris et frigiditatem aquae omnia quae nascuntur de terra et auget et nutrit" (John Scot, *In Marc.* 5.14, p. 7).

9. The passage reads, "PARCAS autem intellige insolubiles diversarm qualitatum necessitates. Aiunt quippe phisici nihil ex caliditate ignis et ariditate terrae

quamvis unam immediatam syzygiam effecerint, nisi interiecta aeris humiditate frigiditateque aquae adiuncta, nasci posse. Hinc est quod quidam poetarum alludit, dicens, 'Nil aliud Vestam quam vivam intellige flammam, / Nataque de flamma corpora nulla vides' " (John Scot, *In Marc.* 5.15, p. 7).

10. The passage reads, "Sive etiam per SOCIALE VINCLUM coniunctionem superiorum et inferiorum elementorum debemus accipere quae utique per aerem fit qui medietatis obtinens locum coniungit superiora, id est ignem, et inferiora id est terram et aquam. Hoc est enim quod supra legimus poetice fictum quod Iuno iratum Iovem placaret mortalibus eumque a sua sententia revocaret, nam Iovis ipse est aether, Iuno aer. Cum ergo terra marcescentibus hieme seminibus suis solitum exposcat a Iove, id est ab aetherio igni, fomentum, non aliter tamen hoc fieri potest nisi intercedente et quasi mediante Iunone, id est aere, qui calorem aetherei ignis suscipiens terrae solitam affert fecunditatem" (Remi., *In Mart.* 7.16).

11. In the ninth-century scholia, mythographic references to the *Eunuchus* appear for Danaë, Ceres, Liber, and Venus (together), and Omphale. Those in *Andria,* or the *Ad Andriam,* both concern female goddesses. In addition, one reference to Dionysia and to Minerva exists in *Heautontimorumenos,* and one in *Phormio,* on *genius.* The ninth-century Terence scholia have been edited by Friederich Schlee, in *Scholia Terentiana* (Leipzig, 1893). Schlee groups them into three categories—grammatical Servius and Priscian scholia (on *Andria, Eunuchus, Heautontimorumenos, Phormio, Hecyra, Adelphos*), an absurd *Commentarii Oopeiis,* and a very brief commentary written after the eleventh century (p. 49). After the Servius and Priscian scholia, Donatus and Eugraphius commentaries appeared, apparently following their grammatical predecessors, for Donatus, on the *Andria, Eunuchus,* and *Phormio,* and for Eugraphius, on the *Andria.* Brief citations from the plays or references to them occur in Festus, Porphyry, Isidore, and various uncertain authors. Edward Kennard Rand, "Early Mediaeval Commentaries on Terence," *CP* 4 (1909): 359–89, discusses the four Carolingian commentaries, the *Commentarius antiquior, Commentum Brunsianum* (in a late-ninth-century manuscript, attributed to a member of the circle of Heiric or Eric of Auxerre, teacher of Remigius, or possibly by Heiric himself), *Expositio* (possibly by Remigius), and the *Commentum Monacensis.* Rand acknowledges that the early Carolingians did not know Terence—he was not in Alcuin's York Library; Rand speculates that he was among the manuscripts brought to Charlemagne from Italy or Ireland (pp. 387–88). "Later, after the new humanism fostered by Lupus of Ferrières had made headway, and a certain acquaintance with Greek had been disseminated by the Irish scholars, *Com Mon* was written by some associate of Eric, and the *Expositio* by Remigius or one of his circle. Meanwhile Donatus and Eugraphius had come in, and still a fourth commentary, devoted to philosophical and rhetorical analyses, had made its appearance, and is preserved in part in the revision of Eugraphius, with whose commentary it was conflated" (p. 388). Of the four, the *Expositio* had the greatest influence; it uses few sources, however, only Orosius, and, for the grammar,

commentaries on Virgil and Horace; parallels exist between the Terence scholia and the ninth-century Horace scholia, according to Remigio Sabbadini, *Il commento di Donato a Terenzio, Studi italiani di filologia classica,* vol. 2 (Florence and Rome, 1893), p. 37n2.

12. The Old Welsh glosses in Cambridge Corpus Christi MS. 153 have been edited by Whitley Stokes, in "The Old-Welsh Glosses on Martianus Capella," *Archaeologia Cambrensis,* 4th series 13 (1873): 1–22. Although he has identified this manuscript as eighth century, with the Welsh glosses found among the copious Latin glosses as bearing an eighth-century hand (p. 1), they are probably closer to ninth century. According to his description, the manuscript contains 86 leaves (with leaf 68 missing); the Welsh glosses begin in the second column of folio 1r with others to be found in the first fifteen folios, after which they reappear in fol. 38r to fol. 51v, and 57b, a, to fol. 66v.

13. Stokes, p. 12n56 and p. 13; Stokes uses the ancient Eyssenhardt text of Martianus Capella rather than the Dick or the more recent Willis: see the 1866 Teubner edition of F. Eyssenhardt, *Martiani Capellae De nuptiis Philologiae et Mercurii* (Leipzig, 1866), p. 42, paragraph 49. The Welsh for "another name for" also occurs in a gloss relating to Juno (Stokes, p. 2n2), and Genius, Stokes, p. 13n59 (from Eyssenhardt, p. 43; *De nuptiis* 152); equivocal names of the Sibyl are linked, Stokes, p. 13n60; finally, there also exists a reference to the mythical feminine birth of Dionysus from the thigh of Jupiter, "unde fabula est eum Iouis femine procreatum," p. 18n109 (Eyssenhardt, p. 241; *De nuptiis* 695).

14. According to William H. Stahl, Cambridge Corpus Christi MSS. 153 and 330 are fairly similar, and will appear, along with the glosses of Martin of Laon, in a commentary to accompany the forthcoming edition of the first two books of Martianus Capella by Jean Préaux: see Stahl's *Martianus Capella and the Seven Liberal Arts: The Quadrivium of Martianus Capella, Latin Traditions in the Mathematical Sciences, With a Study of the Allegory and the Verbal Disciplines* (New York and London: Columbia University Press, 1971), pp. 64, 79.

15. Originally Ludwig Traube, in "Computus Helperici," *NA* 18 (1893): 104, attributed this commentary's authorship to Dunchad or Dunchat. The reason for this identification stemmed from a superscription of a folio incorrectly inserted in British Library Royal MS. 15A.xxxiii with the words, "Commentum Duncaht [*sic*] Pontificis Hiberniensis quod contulit suis discipulis Monasterii Sancti Remigii docens super astrologia Capellae Varronis Martiani." See the edition of "Dunchad" (Martin of Laon) by Lutz, *Glossae in Martianum,* American Philological Monographs, no. 12 (Lancaster, Penn.: American Philological Association, 1944), p. 229. Robin Flower had argued earlier against the attribution of authorship of the Royal manuscript to Dunchad, because his name appeared on the title on folio 3, it covered only the note on the Comptus on that leaf, and it was an inserted leaf with different handwriting. He believed that the Royal manuscript contains the commentary of Remigius of Auxerre. See "Irish Commentaries on Martianus

Capella," *Zeitschrift für celtische Philologie* 8 (1912): 566–67. With the discovery and editing of Remigius's commentary on Martianus, a full and very complete text, Flower's theory was useless. Most recently Jean G. Préaux has suggested that Dunchad may be Martin of Laon; he has also discovered additional glosses in another anonymous manuscript (Leiden B.P.L. 88)—full glosses on books 1, 2, and 4 but very few on 3, 6, 7, and 8. See "Le Commentaire de Martin de Laon sur l'oeuvre de Martianus Capella," *Latomus* 12 (1953): 437–59.

16. See the *Annales Laudunenses* (the Annals of Laon), in *Reliquiae manuscriptorum omnis aevi diplomatum ac monumentorum, ineditorum,* ed. Johann Peter von Ludewig, 3 vols., vols. 10–12, Halae Salicae (Frankfurt and Leipzig, 1720–41), 3:443.

17. Martin of Laon's *Scholica* are contained in Laon MS. 444 and edited by M. L. W. Laistner, "Notes on Greek from the Lectures of a Ninth Century Monastery Teacher," *Bulletin of the John Rylands Library* 7 (1923): 421–56, here, pp. 426–47.

18. The Greek sources of Martin of Laon's *Scholica* include glossary material (parallels to the Philoxenus and Cyrillus collections), the Abstrusa and Abolita glossaries, the two oldest Latin collections. There are also some medical glosses (from Hermeneumata). Authors Martin used directly or second hand include Isidore, Fulgentius, Martianus, Sozomenus, John Scot, and two references to Juvenal and one to Virgil outside passages traceable to Virgil. See Laistner, "Notes," p. 424.

19. In Martin's *Scholica* the name of Aello, one of the three Harpies, is explained as deriving from "edin allom" (*sic;* should be *allon*), "id est alienum tollens," which means "carrying off another's" (Laistner, "Notes," p. 427); it is taken from Fulgentius, *Mit.* 1.9. Further, "Avernus" comes from a Greek word meaning "sine verno" (Laistner, "Notes," p. 427); this, too, derives from Fulgentius, probably the *Continentia Virgiliana.* "Agamemnon" means "fortis" (Laistner, "Notes," p. 430), and Calliope[a] or Calliphone, listed under the H's, means "bona vox," from the Greek word "Calli[op]oio" because "bene facio vel compono" (Laistner, "Notes," p. 438). The most interesting, and most confused, in that it identifies Hymen with Venus, occurs on "Hymen" (Laistner, "Notes," p. 446), identified not only as the place of conception but also, in the phrase "hymeneal," referring to the act of pleasure whence the "god [*sic*] of pleasure—or Venus—is said to derive": "id est locus conceptionum quem vulgo dicunt matricem. Est autem [H]ymenaeus actus voluptatis, inde deus voluptatis dicitur, quod est Venus."

20. See the edition of Gautbert's statement by L. Delisle, *Notices et extraits des manuscrits* 35 (1896): 311–12, cited in Lutz's introduction to Remi., *In Mart.* 1:1–2.

21. Henry Bett, *Johannes Scotus Erigena: A Study in Medieval Philosophy* (Cambridge: Cambridge University Press, 1925), p. 4. For John Scot's Greek, see *De praedestinatione contra Joannem Scotum,* from a fourteenth-century manuscript (*PL* 115:1194A), quoted in Bett, p. 2. Bett's study, esp. 1–18, examines his life and writings; see also Dom Maïeul Cappuyns, *Jean Scot Érigène, sa vie, son oeuvre, sa*

pensée, Catholic University of Louvain, Dissertationes ad gradum magistri in Facultate Theologica consequendum conscriptae, series 2, vol. 26 (Louvain: Abbaye du Mont César; Paris: Desclée de Brouwer, 1933), esp. chaps. 1 and 2 of part 1. But see also Lutz's introduction to *Iohannis Scotti Annotationes in Marcianum* (Cambridge, Mass.: Medieval Academy of America, 1939; rpt. New York: Kraus Reprints, 1970).

22. What was believed by Hubert Silvestre to be part of John's Boethius commentary—only on *Consolatio* 3 m9—was subsequently identified as part of a much later commentary by the twelfth-century Erfurt Commentator. See Silvestre's "Le Commentaire inédit de Jean Scot Érigène au mètre IX du livre III du 'De consolatione philosophiae' de Boèce," *Revue d'histoire ecclésiastique* 47 (1952): 44–122.

23. See John J. Savage, "Two Notes on Johannes Scotus," *Scriptorium* 12 (1958): 228–37.

24. Bett, p. 12.

25. See Préaux, pp. 437–59.

26. Introduction to Remi., *In Mart.;* Lutz, 1:5.

27. See J. Trithemius, *De scriptoribus ecclesiasticis,* chap. 28, cited in J. A. Fabricius, *Bibliotheca ecclesiastica* (Hamburg, 1718), p. 76.

28. See James Westfall Thompkins, *The Literacy of the Laity in the Middle Ages,* University of California Publications in Education, vol. 9 (Berkeley: University of California Press, 1939), p. 30, but see also pp. 32–33 on Charles the Bald as a patron of learning and scholarship and on the literacy of his wife Irmintrude. That Remigius's commentary on Martianus was considered important enough to be politically sensitive is indicated by the rare manuscript illumination devoted to it beginning in the early twelfth century—and illumination which directly linked the text to current political and ecclesiastical events. Erwin Panofsky, *Renaissance and Renascences in Western Art,* Figura, no. 10 (Stockholm: Almqvist and Wiksell, 1960), notes on page 85 that, "In the pictures accompanying Remigius of Auxerre's *Commentary on Martianus Capella*—which, though composed in the ninth century, did not begin to be illustrated until about 1100—Jupiter is represented in the guise of a ruler enthroned, and the raven which, according to the text, belongs to him as his sacred bird of augury is surrounded by a neat little halo because the illustrator involuntarily assimilated the image of a ruler enthroned and accompanied by a sacred bird to that of Pope Gregory visited by the dove of the Holy Spirit."

29. James A. Willis, "Martianus Capella and his Early Commentators" (diss., University of London, University College, 1952), pp. 37–38; and see Lutz, ed., Martin of Laon, *Glossae in Martianum,* pp. xi–xxx.

30. According to Cornelia C. Coulter, in "The Date of John the Scot's *Annotationes in Marcianum,*" *Speculum* 16 (1941): 487–88. His Martianus commentary, in what was thought to be a unique manuscript, was edited by Lutz as

Iohannis Scotti Annotationes in Marcianum. It was first identified as the work of John Scot by B. Hauréau, "Commentaire de Jean Scot Érigène sur Martianus Capella," *Notices et extraits des manuscrits de la Bibliothèque Impériale et autres bibliothèques* 20.2 (1862): 1–39. However, another copy of the commentary has been discovered by Lotte Labowsky, in Bodleian Auct. T. II 19, in which the commentary, beginning with book 2, is the same as Hauréau's manuscript and Lutz's edition; only the first book is different—shorter and less elaborate; see "A New Version of Scotus Eriugena's Commentary on Martianus Capella," *MRS* 1 (1941–43): 187–93. The manuscript thought to be the unique one (B.N. Lat. MS. 12960) also contains other Martianus commentaries as well as a Boethius commentary on Aristotle, an incomplete version of John Scot's *De divisione naturae* (31r–38v), and a fragment of a grammatical treatise of Priscian (116r–125v)—the Dunchad glosses on Martianus (25r–30v) and an incomplete Remigian commentary on Martianus (39r–46v). See Lutz, John Scot's *Annotationes,* p. xii. The best study of John Scot's commentary is that of E. K. Rand, "How Much of the *Annotationes in Marcianum* Is the Work of John the Scot?" *TAPA* 71 (1940): 501–23. See also Laistner, "Martianus Capella and his Ninth Century Commentators," *Bulletin of the John Rylands Library* 9 (1925): 130–38, and Willis, "Martianus Capella," pp. 42–104.

31. See Lutz, introduction to John Scot's *Annotationes,* pp. xiv-xx; Willis, "Martianus Capella," p. 80.

32. Willis, "Martianus Capella," pp. 82, 81.

33. See the discussion of Martianus's cosmology, with an elucidation provided by John Scot in *De divisione naturae,* in Hans Liebeschütz, "Zur Geschichte der Erklarung des Martianus Capella bei Eriugena," *Philologus* 104 (1960): 127–37.

34. See Lutz, John Scot's *Annotationes,* pp. xx-xxv on sources; Willis, "Martianus Capella," adds Dionysius Exiguus and the second Vatican mythographer, as well as individual sources for specific glosses (passim, pp. 84–103); however, if the second Vatican mythographer *is* Remigius it is not likely that John used the work. Finally, for a brief note indicating a comparison of the glosses of John with those of Remigius, see Rand, *Joannes Scotus,* in *Quellen und Untersuchungen zur lateinischen Philologie des Mittelalters,* ed. Ludwig Traube, vol. 1, part 2 (Munich: Oscar Beck, 1906), pp. 81–82. He finds that Remigius seems a fuller edition, but with little new material. "In a word, Remigius's 'improvements' of John's introduction are conflation, inflation, excision and transposition," p. 516. He also concludes that Remigius's fuller notes on books 1 (introduction), 4 (dialectic), and 8 (astronomy) suggest that John's much shorter books are only excerpts from the original work, given John's interest in all the seven liberal arts as preparation for the study of philosophy. However, Rand adds that he thinks that Remigius's text itself is only an excerpt from John's original work.

35. Lutz, introduction to Remi., *In Mart.* 1:24; for the commentary as a whole, see 1:17–39.

36. See Lutz, introduction to Remi., *In Mart.* 1:17, on his use of both Dunchad

and John. She notes that he borrows synonyms, sentences, or paragraphs, but usually assimilates the borrowings in his own words. Because there are places in the text which he glosses and John does not (and vice versa), she concludes that Remigius had other manuscripts with anonymous Martianus glosses. For a comparison of the three commentators, see also Willis, "Martianus Capella," pp. 125ff, who notices differences between John and Remigius in relation to approach and style.

37. There exist eight quotations from the Vulgate and one from each of these Christian writers—Claudius Mamertinus, St. Gregory, St. Augustine—along with popular proverbs. See Lutz, introduction to Remi., *In Mart.* 1:22–23. There also exist references to Isidore, *Etymologiae* and *De rerum natura* (53 in book 1) Servius (30 in book 1), Macrobius (25 in book 1), Pliny the Elder (at least 10), Solinus (1), with most of the mythographic items coming from Fulgentius (12 in book 1) and the first two Vatican mythographers (see Willis, "Martianus," pp. 172–78). Willis also acknowledges the influence of grammarians and commentators, specifically, Donatus's Terence commentary, Lactantius Placidus on the *Thebaid,* Nonius Marcellus, and Virgil (p. 178), with particular fondness for the classical poets Virgil, Horace, Ovid, Lucan, Juvenal, Persius, and Statius.

38. Elder, p. 246.

39. See Manitius, *Geschichte* 9.2.1:512.

40. Lutz, introduction to Remi., *In Mart.* 1:11–16. For a discussion of authorship of Remigius's commentary on Martianus, see Lutz, "The Commentary of Remigius of Auxerre on Martianus Capella," *MS.* 19 (1957): 137–56; for the accessus to Remigius's Martianus commentary in B.L. MS. Reg. 15A3 and for his Virgil commentary in Monacensis [Munich] 18059 and his Sedulius commentary in Paris B.N. MS. Lat. 13029, see also, by Lutz, "One Formula of Accessus in Remigius' Works," *Latomus* 19 (1960): 774–80. Maria de Marco in *"Remigii inedita,"* *Aevum* 26 (1952): 495–517, includes a bibliography of his works, among which are fifteen commentaries. More specifically, on Remigius's Persius scholia, see Elder, "A Medieval Cornutus," pp. 240–48; for *Remigii expositio super Priscianum,* see de Marco, pp. 503–17; and for Remigius on Priscian's *De nomine,* a longer version of the commentary in de Marco, see R. B. C. Huygens, "Remigiana," *Aevum* 28 (1954): 330–44, esp. pp. 330–42. On the Martianus and Sedulius commentaries, see Manitius, "Zwei Remigius-kommentare," *NA* 49 (1932): 173–83, 205. On his commentary on the *Ars de nomine et verbo* of the grammarian Phocas, see Mario Espositio, "Miscellaneous Notes on Mediaeval Latin Literature," *Hermathena* 38 (1912): 104–14, esp. note 2, pp. 107–9.

41. Few mythological references to the trivium exist in Remigius's glosses on books 3 to 5 of *De nuptiis;* more exist on the quadrivium in books 6 to 9, with the fewest in book 8 (astronomy) and the most in book 9 (music). The references are usually either to characters, figures, and events included in the allegorical frame, or else to figures reflective of the specific *ars*—for example, in book 3 (grammar)

the figure of *ypographia* (*De nuptiis* 223; Remi., *In Mart.* 82.10). In all of the books dealing with specific arts, the references are similarly direct and prosaic: in book 4 (dialectic), "Delian" is glossed as "Apollonia," from the name of the island where Apollo was born, and the name interpreted as *clara*, "et sole nihil clarius in corporalibus," "nothing is brighter than the sun in the material world" (*De nuptiis* 328; Remi., *In Mart.* 151.15).

42. See Claudian, *Carmina* 31 (lines 31–55), ed. Theodor Birt, MGH, vol. 10 (Berlin, 1892), noted by Stahl, *Quadrivium,* p. 85n4.

43. The passage reads, "Praeter hanc sunt duae aliae viris et mulieribus communes, quarum una est in cerebro, de qua fistulae quinquepertiti sensus profluunt, et Grece menica dicitur, inde menica dicitur passio. Est et alia quae dividit inferiora ventris et superiora pectoris, quam Greci fren dicunt, unde et frenesis passio vocata est, et freneticus homo quia, si quis hanc laesam habuerit, in amentiam vertitur" (Remi., *In Mart.* 3.5).

44. Dis is the Latin equivalent for the Greek "Pluto," the god of the lower regions, *inferorum deus,* and brother of Jove, son of Saturn and Rhea, his name "Dis" deriving from *dives* (Remi., *In Mart.* 1.4 or 5.18): "Et recte, nihil enim inferno ditius quod omnia recipit, licet exsaturari nequeat. Est enim unum de insaturabilibus, unde Horatius: 'Debemur morti nos nostraque' " ["Rightly called; nothing is more rich indeed than the depths of the earth because it receives everything, is insatiable. It is indeed one of the insatiable, as Horace says, 'We owe to death us and ours' "]. Portunus (*De nuptiis* 4) is god of ports (Remi., *In Mart.* 5.19), also called Neptunus or Melicerta. Gradivus is Mars, called so in Remigius for the same reason (and in the same words, more or less), used by John Scot: because he is seen marching (*gradiens*) off to war, "dicitur quasi gradiens divus ad bellum videlicet, vel quasi . . . potens divus," or because he is a powerful god (John Scot, *In Mart.* 5.19). In Remigius, he is called Gradivus because he engages in battle in steps, or marches out to battle, or from the vibration of the lance, or because he is the deity of force or power: Remigius declares, "Dicitur autem GRADIVUS vel quod gradatim eat in proelium, vel apo tu gradein, id est a vibratione hastae, sive GRADIVUS quasi kratos divus, id est potens deus, *gamma* in *kappa* mutata" (Remi., *In Mart.* 5.19).

45. Sources for John Scot's etymology of "Ops" include Servius, *In Aen.* 6.325, Augustine, *Civ. Dei* 7.24, and Macrobius, *Sat.* 1.10.19, according to John's editor Lutz, as well as Willis, "Martianus," p. 86. Ops is essentially antithetical to her husband; Remigius (but not John) depicts Saturn as an old man because his planet is of a very cold nature, being most remote from the sun and near the supercelestial waters; for old men are cold since they have very little blood ("Senex vero fingitur quia sidus eius frigidissimae naturae est utpote a sole remotissimum et aquis supercaelestibus vicinum, nam senes frigent in quibus est minimus sanguis," Remi., *In Mart.* 5.22).

46. Janus follows after Saturn in Martianus and in Macrobius because of his

historical connection with Saturn as first founder of Italy. He is depicted as two-faced because of his connection with the month of January that looks back into the past and forward into the new year, or four-faced, to represent the four climates of the world—hot, cold, wet, dry—or the four seasons (Remi., *In Mart.* 6.1).

47. In book 6 (geometry) of *De nuptiis* there are as many as sixteen references to Pallas Athena, related to the allegorical frame and the introduction of the personification of Geometry. Remigius's long passage on Pallas in book 6 (Remi., *In Mart.* 285.6ff) essentially resembles his book 1 glosses (7.3 and 7.16). However, in the second part of the passage, Remigius provides a new explanation of the origins of Pallas's names: "Sive PALLAS dicta a palla, id est muliebri vestimento cum quo ei sacrificabatur. Ipsa autem vestis palla dicta apo tu pallein, id est a rugis. Tritonia vel a palude Africae, vel apo tu tritin, id est a terrore, quia sapientia terribilis est stultis et vulgaribus, unde et arma dicitur habere, id est virtutes, ad expugnanda vitia et stultitiam" ["Or 'Pallas' is said from *palla,* that is, from the garment of a woman {a long, wide garment worn by Roman ladies} whenever a sacrifice is made to her. Moreover, the garment itself is named from *apo tu pallein,* that is, from its wrinkles. Tritonia, or from the African swamp, or *apo tu tritin,* that is, from terror, because wisdom is frightful to the foolish and common and wherefore she is said to have arms, that is, the virtues, for attacking vices and folly"] (Remi., *In Mart.* 285.6). Minerva, of course, is one of the handful of the gods also glossed in the ninth-century Terence scholia, in particular through her role as goddess of wisdom born from Jove's head: from *Heautontimorumenos* 5.5, line 13, Schlee, *Scholia Terentiana,* p. 126, comes her identification as goddess of memory, which is known to be in the brain ("Minerva dicunt esse natam ex Iove, videlicet de cerebro, et ideo dicitur dea memoriae, quam in cerebro esse constat").

48. In John Scot's commentary, the longest passage about Mercury (from *De nuptiis* 6) explains his name in Greek as Hermes, or *sermo,* and "Sermo siquidem eloquens et copiosus rationabilis naturae qui in homine spetialiter intelligitur subsistere maximum indicium est et speciale ornamentum" (John Scot, *In Mart.* 6.20). That is, Mercury represents eloquence in referring to the rational nature of man—in that men's speech sets them off from the animals and characterizes them as human—but his name also derives from "medius currens," running in the middle, to show that the eloquence of speech exists only as it is articulated (from Isidore, *Etym.* 8.11.45). Mercury is also called "the Arcadian" simply because he was born on an Arcadian mountain, a region in Greece where eloquence is fertile and poets flourish. But see also Remigius, who explains before the commentary proper begins that Mercury derives from *medius currens* "quia sermo inter duos seritur" ["because conversation is woven between two persons"] and from *mercator* and *kyrios,* because conversation most appropriately is associated with merchants, "mercatorum kyrios, id est dominus, quia sermo maxime inter mercatores viget," Remi., *In Mart.* 1:66.

49. "Non inmerito itaque Tritonia interulam, hoc est intimam suaeque nature proximam virtutem, rationabili animae largitur. Virtus quippe habitus animae est qui in quatuor partes dividitur, prudentiam temperantiam fortitudinem iustitiam" ["It is not without merit that the same Tritonia is associated with the soul, because the soul's nature is to be intimately associated with virtue, the pursuit of the rational soul. Virtue, as the habit of the soul, is divided into four, prudence, temperance, fortitude, and justice"] (John Scot, *In Mart.* 7.16).

50. This is so for Remigius, "quia, descriptis tribus, Grammatica videlicet, Dialectica, atque Rhetorica, quae tantum in sermone sunt, ingressurus est ad describendum artium quattuor reliquarum quadrivium quae in intellectu consistunt. In his quippe mathematica constat, id est doctrinalis scientia" (Remi., *In Mart.* 285.6).

51. For Remigius as for John Scot, "Sed hoc loco Vulcanus pro igne naturalis ingenii accipitur. . . . Ex quo naturali ingenio igniculi quidam INSOPIBILIS id est indeficientis et inextinguibilis, PERENNITATIS accenduntur quibus illuminetur anima ne opprimatur tenebris et caligine ignorantiae" ["In this place Vulcan represents the fire of natural wit. . . . From which small fires of *insopibilis,* that is, unfailing and inextinguishable permanence, are kindled, by which the soul is illuminated lest it be suppressed by the shadows and darkness of ignorance"] (Remi., *In Mart.* 8.4).

52. This derives from Isidore (*Etym.* 8.11.76); see also, for Venus as foam, Fulgentius (*Mit.* 2.1) and Macrobius (*Sat.* 1.8.6).

53. John Scot declares, "Omne vero quod merito originalis peccati ex corruptibili et mortali creatura naturalibus animae virtutibus et miscetur et inseritur per illecebrosa Veneris donaria significat." He continues, "Hinc est generalis et specialis libido, hinc avaricia, hinc insatiabilis connubendi pruritus ceteraqJe illicia quae dinumerare longum est, florum pulchritudine praetiosorumquae unguentorum alatibus nec non supervacuis tinnitibus, infructuosa quoque quietis corporibus veluti quadam somnolentia non inconvenienter significata" ["Hence is a general and special lust, hence avarice, hence an insatiable itch for marriage, and other inticements too many to count, not unfittingly signified by the beauty of flowers and jars of costly ointments and empty tinklings, also unprofitable drowsiness for sleeping bodies"] (John Scot, *In Mart.* 8.8). Compare Remigius's rewording of John on Venus's pleasures: "Per illecebrosa Veneris donaria significantur omnia vitia quae merito originalis peccati rationali animae ingeruntur. Distincte vero commemorat singulorum quinque sensuum voluptates per quas mortifera delectatio penetral animae irrumpit et eius castitatem incestat" ["By the enticing gifts of Venus are signified all the vices which thanks to Original Sin are put into the rational soul. He mentions distinctly the pleasures of the individual five senses, through which death-bringing pleasure breaks into the innermost part of the soul and defiles its purity"] (Remi., *In Mart.* 8.7). Remigius also glosses Aphrodite as John has, that is, as spume: "AFRODITE spumea interpretatur, afro

enim Grece spuma dicitur. Vocatur Venus AFRODITE quia de spuma maris et amputatis Caelii patris virilibus secundum fabulam nata est, sed et ipsa voluptas Veneria veluti spuma cito deletur" ["*Afrodite* is interpreted as foamy, for *afro* in Greek means foam. Venus is called Afrodite because, according to fable, she was born from sea-foam and the amputated genitals of her father Caelius, but also the pleasures of Venus vanish swiftly like foam"] (Remi., *In Mart.* 8.8).

54. This may also be a Christianized version of Servius (*In Aen.* 1.663), who explains Cupid's arrows as seizing or ambushing, "Sagittas vero ideo gestare dicitur, [vel quia amorem et libidinem sequitur punctura poenitentiae et dolor, vel] quia, ut ipse, incertae velocesque sunt" ["because love and desire are followed by penitence and pain, or because, like Cupid, they are uncertain and swift"] (the words in brackets are expelled by Thilo and Hagen from the Servian text but included by Remigius, who, however, may have added them himself rather than borrowing them directly from an expanded Servius). See also Willis, "Martianus Capella," p. 87.

55. The Apollo episode begins in *De nuptiis* 10 and in both commentators with section 10.6. John Scot says that Apollo is termed "the Pythian" because he defeated the Python, who was also used to provide auguries for the Sybil (John borrows here from Macrobius, *Sat.* 1.17.51–52). John explains that "AUGUR PITHIUS—Apollo est vocatus, quia fanum illius in Delo insula in quo auguria manifestabat Pithium est nominatum sive a pithone serpente cuius corium fuerat illic extensum ut fabule fingunt, sive, ut verior dicit ratio, a verbo *peythomai*, hoc est consulo vel interrogo" ["Apollo is called Augur Pithius, because his shrine on the island of Delos where he gave his auguries was called Pithian, either from the Python whose body had been stretched out there, as the fables relate, or, as truer reason says, from the word *peythomai*, that is, 'I consult or inquire' "] (John Scot, *In Mart.* 10.6).

The momentary equation between "Apollo" and the sun—the sun "modulates," "movetur," the heavenly spheres (John Scot, *In Mart.* 11.14) because Apollo, musician and poet (10.22) is full of harmony—leads to a series of Stoic and Macrobian synonyms in both John and Remigius expressing diverse functions. He is Phoebus, which means "new," because he is always discovered rising in a new place (from Isidore, *Etym.* 8.11.54); Auricomus (the golden-haired, like the sun); Sagittarius (the Archer, shooting rays); Vulnificus (the wounder, because, as Martianus admits, "he can penetrate what he strikes with the darts of his rays," *De nuptiis* 12). Remigius notes (*In Mart.* 11.14) of Phoebus as "new" that he is like a beardless boy and of Phoebus as Auricomus that the sun's splendid rays are like golden hair: "et re vera sol in ortu suo novus cernitur, unde et puer imberbis depingitur quia cotidie iuvenescit. AURICOMUS dicitur a splendore radiorum quasi aureas comas habens." He is also called Latoius, as the son of Latona (*De nuptiis* 16; John Scot, *In Mart.* 13.23; Remi., *In Mart.* 13.22). Other names by which he is known appear later in the narrative (*De nuptiis* 27) and are glossed therefore more fully by Remigius: he is called "Sun" because he provides the most light in comparison with the other stars; called Delius, "declaratio," because he illuminates all; called Apollo, the "destroyer," because by his heat he seems to drive all the fluids (that is, the sap) from the trees ("Dicitur Apollo, id est exterminans, eo quod suo calore omnes humores arborum pellere videatur"), and called Pithius, because "fidem auferens," taking away trust (Remi., *In Mart.* 19.11).

Appropriately, then, three places are associated with Apollo: Delos, the place where Apollo was born, is named from the Greek word *delos,* meaning "clarity," because on it Apollo gives clear responses, "quod in ea clara responsa reddebat Apollo" (John Scot, *In Mart.* 10.7; Willis suggests the source for this gloss is Servius, *In Aen.* 3.73, in "Martianus," p. 88); Helicon, a mountain peak in Parnassus sacred to Apollo; and Lycia, "an island in which Apollo was born and herded sheep, giving the sanctuary of Apollo a name deriving from 'Lycius' or 'Lupinus,' because he not only defended the sheep from wolves but also expelled them from the island." He declares, "LYCIA autem insula est propria Apollinis patria in qua natus et pastor fuit, et quoniam non solum pecora a lupis defendebat, verum etiam de tota insula expulerat, et ipse Lycius, id est Lupinus, et fanum eius in eadam insula Lycium est nominatum. Nam a Grecis dicitur lupus *lupos; lupos* autem vocatus quasi *luchnos* quia instar lucernae oculi eius noctis tenebras expellunt." John Scot adds a Greek etymology for "lupus," relating it to "lychnos," because his eyes, like the oil-lamp, *lucerna,* expel the shadows of night (John Scot, *In Mart.* 10.7).

Apollo's most likely habitats, John reiterates, would be Parnassus or Helicon (*In Mart.* 10.12). Helicon is sacred to Apollo and the Muses and is a mountain in Boeotia, not Phocis; Parnassus is a two-peaked mountain sacred to Apollo and the Muses at whose foot is located Delphi and its oracle. Where Mercury actually finds him is near Delphi, at "the Cirrhaean retreat," although he is said to have moved, not to Greece, but to an "Indian mountain's secret crag." Cirrha, near Delphi, and serving as a port for Delphi, is wonderfully explained by John as a mountain in India, "Cyrra mons est in India" (*In Mart.* 10.13).

56. "Pythius," for Remigius, "dictus est Apollo a pythone serpente quem secundum fabulam mox natus interfecit; vel quod melius est a verbo Greco quod est pytho, id est interrogo. Ipsum enim interrogabant et consulebant." Remigius's strange anecdote concerning Nero and Apollo appears in a gloss on the idea that the Pythian is "distressed by contact with those who sought his advice:" "Nam Apollo responsum dederat quod Nero interficiendus esset a populo Romàno. Timens ergo Nero ne auctoritate numinis audacior redderetur populus ad id peragendum iussit claudi templa illius. Ita quodam modo offensus Apollo DEDIGNABATUR 'AUGUR' APPELLARI" (Remi., *In Mart.* 10.6).

57. Remigius glosses "tripos" as "species est lauri tres habens radices Apollini consecrata, abundans iuxta templum Apollinis quod est in Claro insulam cui fertur inesse vis divinandi. Significat autem triplicem speciem divinationis quae

est in praesenti, praeterito, et futuro. Tripos etiam vocatur mensa Apollini corio pythii serpentis tecta" ["a species of laurel having three roots, sacred to Apollo, abundant near the temple of Apollo on the island of Claros, in which is said to be the power of divining; it signifies three types of divination, about the present, past, and future. Yet 'tripos' is also the name of the table covered with the skin of Apollo's Python snake"] (Remi., *In Mart.* 10.8).

58. John Scot, *In Mart.* 11.20; cf. Remigius, whose attribution of the spheres' influence on the corporeal and material differs from John's in its more astrological emphasis: "a sole quidem vitam, quia ille medius planetarum quasi quidam spiritus fertur vivificare mundum; a luna corpus, quia illa est humida; a Saturno tarditatem et frigiditatem, quanto enim extimae spherae vicinior, tanto tardior, et quanto a sole remotior, tanto frigidior est; a Iove temperantiam; a Marte fervorem vel iracundiam; a Venere voluptatem; a Mercurio prudentiam, quia cum sole gradiens quodam modo inexhausta luce sapientiae radiatur" ["from the sun, life, because it is in the middle of the planets, and is the spirit which vivifies the world; from the moon, the body, because it is moist; from Saturn, slowness and cold, for the closer it is to the outermost edge, the slower it is, and when it is most remote from the sun is the most entirely cold; from Jove, temperance; from Mars, fervor or ire; from Venus, desire; from Mercury, prudence"] (Remi., *In Mart.* 13.1).

59. "Elicios autem campos ubi purgatae animae requiescunt confingunt esse infra Iovialem circulum. Secta autem Platonica dicit animas purgatas iterum redire ad corpora ut ibi denuo polluantur ex concretione corporis et incipiant rursus egere purgatione, quod hic tangere videtur Martianus dicens ET QUAM ILLE subaudis fluvius Martis" (Remi., *In Mart.* 13.6).

60. John declares: "SATURNI EXITIUM hoc est geliditatis interitum. In hieme quippe omnium pene rerum interit honestas florum videlicet ac fructuum, hinc fingitur fabula Veneris atque Adonidis. Venus siquidem luget fusis lacrimis interemptum in quadam palude ab ipsa fera quae singularis dicitur, Adonidem. Est autem Venus iuxta cerebrum fabule in aestivo tempore honesta telluris superficies que recedentem Adonidem, id est solem, ad austrina et infima signiferi signa, ibidemque veluti a porco quodam, hoc est ab hiemis spurcitia, occisum, hoc est occultatem, fusis crescentium fluminum lacrimis luget, ita ut telluris honestas aestiva penitus videatur perire in hieme" (John Scot, *In Mart.* 14.16). Cf. Remigius, "EXITIUM SATURNI dicit non quod patitur Saturnus, sed quod infert. Hiemale enim tempore omnium rerum pulchritudo quodam exitio deperit, unde est ficta illa fabula Adonis et Veneris. Venus plangit Adonem fusis lacrimis ab apro interfectum quia terrae pulchritudo, quae significatur per Venerem, plangit solem, qui significatur per Adonem, ad australes circulos descendentem spurcitia hiemali quasi dentibus apri interfectum; tuncque lacrimas imbrium et fluentorum terra producit" (Remi., *In Mart.* 14.16). Cf. Martin of Laon's version in note 81 of this chapter.

61. John's definition of the Muses differs from Remigius's. In John, "Urania"

is "heavenly," from the Greek word for sky, "quae propter vocis acumen acutis-
simo spere sono coniungitur" ["which an account of the sharpness of the name is
connected to the sharpest sound of the sphere"] (John Scot, *In Mart.* 19.17).
"Polymnia," the Muse of sublime hymns, comes from the Greek for many
memories; she is linked with Saturn because of the slowness with which he moves
and for which one needs much memory, "quae Saturnie tarditati coaptatur; multe
quippe memorie commendata vix in oblivionem labuntur." "Euterpe," "well-
pleasing," is joined with tempering Jove, because she is the Muse of lyric poetry.
Eratho, love poetry, is joined with Mars because her name means "worthy of love";
she can be interpreted as "strong," possibly also because her name in Greek is
related to "warlike strength," which is attributed to Mars. Melpomene, tragedy,
comes from the Greek word for song and means "singing": "Hoc autem dicitur
quia sol ipse et canit ceterasque planetas in cantum suscitat" ["She is called so
indeed because the sun itself sings and raises up the other planets in song"].
Terpsichore, the Muse of choral dance and song, means "dilecta visu seu dilecta
pupilla" ["pleasing to the sight or pleasing to the eye"] "propter nimiam Veneris
claritatem" ["on account of the excessive clarity of Venus"]. Calliope is the
beautifier, linked with Mercury because she is Muse of epic poetry, and Mercury,
says John, controls poetic effects and the beauty of *sermones.* "Clio," the Muse of
history, means *gloriosa,* "quasi dea propter lunaris corporis pompam" ["as if a
goddess on account of the procession of the lunar body"]; she can also be
interpreted as "calling," "quoniam luna menstruum revocat lumen" ["since the
moon calls back her monthly light"]. Thalia, the Muse of comedy linked with the
earth, is not able to ascend from earth because the earth is always fixed and still,
whereas the world remains always in motion (ibid. 20.5). Remigius defines each
Muse briefly, not always identically to John's etymological discussion (Remi., *In
Mart.* 19.19–20.5); see also the earlier passage (ibid. 19.11), where Remigius
concludes, "Et physica ratione Apollini Musae applicantur" ["And the Muses are
joined to Apollo by scientific reasoning"]. Here, Urania represents the sublimity
of human intelligence, "humanae intelligentiae sublimitas"; Polymnia is the
capacity of memory, "capacitas memoriae." Third is Euterpe, "delectatio voluntatis, quia intelligentia memoriae iungitur et voluntati" ["delight of the will, for
intelligence is joined to memory and will"]; Eratho is "inveniens simile, nulla
enim re plus voluntas delectatur quam similium collatione" ["finding likenesses,
for the will enjoys nothing so much as comparing like things"]. Terpsicore is
called so "quasi artium delectatio sociatur, cogitationum enim perfectio sine
disciplinarum exercitatione fieri non potest" ["as if joined to the pleasure of
accomplishments, for the completion of a plan without exercising knowledge
cannot be accomplished"]. Calliope, Clio, and Thalia are related: "His omnibus
omnis humanae locutionis honestas gignitur quae Calliope signatur; inde Clio,
hoc est bona fama, nascitur; sub qua Thalia quasi in ultimo loco, hoc est positio vel
germinatio virtutum" ["The honor of all human speech, which is the meaning of

Calliope, is begotten in all of these; next Clio, who is good fame, is born; under whom Thalia in last place, that is the position or the sprouting of virtue"].

62. Remigius (*In Mart.* 24.14) explains that Pallas descends from a more sublime and splendid place, first, because "sapientia in excelsis habitat et omnem terrenae faecis supergreditur vilitatem" ["wisdom lives in lofty places and walks over the baseness of earthly impurities"]; and second, because according to the fable she was born from Jove's head. She was born without a mother: "non ex aliis exstantibus sed ex substantia Dei principium habuisse" ["she had her beginning not out of other substances but out of the substance of God"].

63. See the detailed description of the origins and artistic representations of the select gods in Charlotte R. Long, *The Twelve Gods of Greece and Rome* (Leiden: E. J. Brill, 1987), who argues that they ensured the well-being of the city state and later became patrons of the months and, in Egypt, were associated with the zodiac.

64. From the first region, the home of Jupiter, come the obscure "gods of the council, the god of welfare, the household gods, Janus, the secret gods of goodwill, and the god of night" (*De nuptiis* 45). See Stefan Weinstock, "Martianus Capella and the Cosmic System of the Etruscans," *JRS* 36 (1946): 101–29.

65. Of the already heavily glossed gods, included are Minerva, Pluto, Ceres, Tellus, Vulcan, among others. For the most part these gods receive little extensive mythography in the commentators (Pluto, in Remi., *In Mart.* 28.7, and Ceres, ibid. 28.12, are among the exceptions).

66. "Inter Iovem, Vulcanum, et Vestam hoc distat quia Iovis est aethereus ignis simplex et innocuus, nihilque perurens; Vulcanus vero intelligitur noxius ignis et perurens qualis est fulminum, unde et Vulcanus quasi volicanus, id est volans candor, interpretatur; Vesta vero est ignis usibus et utilitatibus mortalium accomodatus" (Remi., *In Mart.* 37.6; see also John Scot, *In Mart.* 37.6).

67. Neptune has a garland whiter than surf, Hades, black as night, says Martianus, and each is suited to his kingdom (*De nuptiis* 79–80). The commentators explain the text: Neptune is very green, says Remigius, "the color when the sea changes by the quality of the air" (John acknowledges his garland is foam; both authors, *In Mart.* 35.15). Pluto is that color because he is god of the underworld and shadows (Remi., *In Mart.* 35.15). Pluto (*De nuptiis* 81) is said to be richer than his brother through "the constant acquisition of whatever things come into being," and Neptune is despoiled and poor (because, says Remigius, like the ocean he is too large) and spits back (in the form of waves, says Remi., *In Mart.* 35.22) all the wealth that he engulfs. Remigius explains that Pluto is richer "quia infernus omnia recipit" ["because the underworld receives everything"], whence it is called in Greek Plutos, in Latin, Dis, interpreted as Dives (riches); Pluto is wealthy through whatever things are begotten out of earth (Remi., *In Mart.* 35.20).

68. Remigius identifies her not as Hecate but as Proserpina, called so from *proserpendo*: "Vis herbarum et omnium quae semine de terra surgunt Proserpina accipitur, unde et Proserpina vocata a proserpendo, id est porro et multum

crescendo" ["The vigor of the grasses and all things which grow from seed out of the earth is known as Proserpina, hence the name Proserpina is derived from *proserpando,* 'creeping forth,' that is, growing forth"] (Remi., *In Mart.* 36.4). This wife "Quae bene puella vocatur quia terrarum semina singulis annis innovantur" ["is appropriately called a girl because the seeds of earth are made new every year"] (ibid.). Man gives back to her one percent because she so readily gives the fruits of the earth to him: "per quod innuitur quod dictum est quia vis terrae centuplicatum restituit quod acceperit. Hinc et ipsa silvarum vel venatorum dea fertur quia silvas vis naturae de terra producit et venatio silvis et pascuis nutritur" ["the earth duplicates and multiplies by a hundred all the seeds that it accepts; whence in Greek Proserpina is called Echate. For 'Ekaton' in Greek means one hundred, and she is called Echate because the earth a hundred-fold duplicates what it receives in the way of seed. Hence she is also called goddess of forests and hunters because the vigor of nature produces forests from the earth and hunting is supported by forests and pastures"] (ibid.).

69. There are brief references to Ceres, Liber, and Venus in the glosses on *Eunuchus* 4.5, line 6 (Schlee, p. 107), as grains or bread, wine, and lechery. In *Heautontimorumenos* 1.1., line 110 (Schlee, p. 115), the gloss on *Dionysia* extends the association of Liber and wine, or the vine: the festival of Dionysus, Liber Pater, is also called the Saturnalia, Vulcania, Neptunalia. The Terence quotation turns up in the second Vatican mythographer, too (Mythogr. II 49/38; see chapter 8).

70. Mars, god of war, has a red complexion (*De nuptiis* 82), a color explained by Remigius (who basically agrees with John Scot here) "because this star is fiery, or because of the likeness of blood which flows in wars [activities governed by Mars], whence Mars is called so as if *mors,* Death" (Remi., *In Mart.* 36.7; Martianus also says he comes to eat everything and to drink even blood). Liber, or Bacchus, is described by Martianus as agreeable, drunk, and holding a sickle in his right hand and a "soporific bowl" (*De nuptiis* 82); his sickle, says Remigius, is intended for cutting grapevines and the bowl full of wine signifies drunkards' wantonness, that is, lascivious desires, "Lascivia enim libido vel instabilitas ebriosorum est" (Remi, *In Mart.* 36.10). Castor and Pollux (*De nuptiis* 83) are brothers born "of the same mother, Leda, though not both by Jove" (Remi., *In Mart.* 36.12). One shines like the morning star, and one like the evening star, says Martianus, but Remigius discusses the rising and setting of the constellation Gemini (ibid., 36.13). Hercules, the "god of incredible strength," follows, exhibiting his "Cleonaean lion skin" and "amazing muscles" (*De nuptiis* 84), his strength explained by means of his twelve Labors and his Cleonaean lion skin as glorious, from the Greek word for glory, *cleos* (Remi., *In Mart.* 36.14–16).

71. On Venus as goddess of desire, cf. the Terence scholia in *Commentarius antiquior,* beginning with *Andria* 1.1, line 93 (Schlee, p. 81), on *venusto:* "venustas dicitur a Venere, dea libidinis; inde quoque venustus pulcher sive formosus, qui pulchritudine Veneris delectatur" [" 'venustas' {charm} is named from Venus, the

goddess of desire; hence also the one who delights in the beauty of Venus is called charming, beautiful, or handsome"].

72. The final gloss, on Genius, is also linked with the Terence scholia. Rand, p. 385, argues that Heiric of Auxerre possibly uses the Brunsian scholiast's explication of *genius* as *voluptas* in the gloss on *Phorm.* 1.1.10, in Bruns 2:177 in poem St. Germanus 4.510. The phrase "genium curare memento" (its first two words taken from Horace, *Odes* 3.17) is coupled with "Quieti et voluptati operam dare. Contra Terentius: suum defraudare genium." See also the discussion of the individual Genius, in book 2, in Jane Chance Nitzsche, *The Genius Figure in Antiquity and the Middle Ages* (New York and London: Columbia University Press, 1975).

73. For the history of Genius's mythography (and in particular his role as a god of generation), see Nitzsche, esp. chap. 2.

74. The symbol of the Pythagorean Y is also found—like so many of the references at the end of the first book—in the ninth-century Terence scholia. See Rand, "Early Medieval Commentaries on Terence," p. 371; *Andria* 1.1.27, p. 17. Passages on the Y had appeared previously in Isidore, *Etym.* 1.3.7 and Servius, *In Aen.* 6.136, cited on pages 90–91 and 222.

75. According to Remigius's gloss, King Phorcys had three daughters, Stenno, Euryale, and Medusa, who had one eye and turned to stone whatever they saw, "unde et Gorgonae a terrore dictae sunt, Gorgo namque terror dicitur" (Remi., *In Mart.* 50.16). Against these Perseus was sent with "cristallino clipeo et arpen, quod est genus teli falcati, et adiutiorio Minervae eas interfecit." The gloss ends on the Fulgentian euhemeristic note: "Fuerunt autem locupletissimae, unde et Gorgones dictae quasi georges, id est terrae cultrices, enim [GE] Grece terra, orgia cultura dicitur. Mortuo patre, Medusa maior filia ei in regnum successit, quam Perseus rex Asiae interfecit et eius regnum abstulit" ["They were also very rich, whence they are called Gorgons, meaning *georges,* that is, farmers, for *Ge* in Greek means earth, and *origia* means cultivation. At their father's death, Medusa the oldest daughter succeeded him as ruler, whom Perseus king of Asia slew and took over her kingdom"] (ibid.). Perseus represents strength or "in figura virtutis ponitur, qui Gorgonam cum adiutorio Minervae occidit quia virtus auxilio sapientiae omnes terrores vincit" ["virtue, who with the help of Minerva killed the Gorgon because strength with the aid of wisdom conquers all terrors"] (ibid.).

76. "Vedius" is a form of Vedivus, Remigius declares (*In Mart.* 61.23), or "malus divus, quia terrorem incutit animabus" ["the evil deity, who incites terror in souls"]; this same is Orcus, "Orco Grece iuro, inde Orcus dictus quia quodam modo iurat quod nullam animam sine poena dimittat" ["Orco in Greek means *iuro,* 'I swear,' hence he is called Orcus because he swears that he will let no soul depart without punishment"].

77. The four symbols (*De nuptiis* 170) are linked with four different but related lunar and female deities in the commentaries—Isis, Ceres, Diana, and Cybele.

Together they represent variations on what Robert Graves identified as the three-fold goddess associated with the waning, full, and waxing phases of the moon. Martin of Laon and Remigius, using a passage from Servius (*In Aen.* 6.585), and possibly Isidore (*Etym.* 4.13), tie in the *sistrum* (sistra or rattle), of Egyptian origin, to Isis (Dunchad and Remi., *In Mart.* 70.7). Remigius associates the Eleusinian lamp with the torch which the moon takes from the sun, "Ergo lampadam Eleusinam ibi dicit fuisse propter facem quam ex sole suscipit luna, sive etiam facem dicit ibi fuisse quia luna praeest seminibus quae in terra ex rore proveniunt qui de corpore lunae cadit. Apud enim hanc civitatem primum Ceres Celeo regi usum serendarum frugum ostendit, et ideo per lampadem Eleusinam fertilitatem vult ostendere frugum cuius causa in luna est" ["or with light because the moon rules over the seeds which come forth on earth from the dew which falls from the body of the moon. For in this city {Eleusis} Ceres first showed King Celeus the art of planting grain, therefore by the lamp of Eleusis he means to indicate the fertility of fruits of the earth, whose origin is in the moon"] (Remi., *In Mart.* 70.7). As well they link the *timpanum* or kettledrum with Cybele (or Venus), through the moon's influence on the body: "CYBELEA id est Veneris quia corpora a luna sumuntur per Venerem" (Dunchad, *In Mart.* 70.8); Martin adds that "CYBELEA TIMPANA lunae deputantur quod cum omnia dicit corpora, maxime dum in motu sunt, musicam de se mittunt, sola vero terra, quae in statu est, nullum sonum de se reddit vel promit, proximo tamen sono, id est lunari, utitur" (ibid.), this latter about earth from Macrobius (*Somn. Scip.* 2.4), according to Willis ("Martianus," p. 40). In Remigius, the tambours belong to Cybele, the *mater deum,* or Ops, earth, because the drum-like earth is surrounded by the two hemispheres of heaven: "cui dantur tympana quia terra duobus caeli hemispheriis vallatur" (Remi., *In Mart.* 70.8). The bow, in the same passage, is associated with Diana the moon because she is a hunter and hunters use bows. The moon in another tradition is linked instead with Juno as goddess of childbirth: in the Terence scholia (*Andria* 3.1, line 15; Schlee, p. 86), in reference to Glycerium, a female character, "Glycerium intus scilicet ex dolore clamabat. Iuno Lucina dicitur eo, quod in lucem praeest nascentibus ipsa et Luna" ["from within," the gloss reads, "that is, cries out because of pain, for which Juno is called Lucina, because she is in charge of those being born into the light and so also called Luna"].

78. In the text of Martianus, the passage begins with Philology's address to the sun: "You are called in Latin *Sol* because you are the point of light *solus* [alone] in honor after the Father; they say that your sacred head bears twelve beams of golden light, because you make the twelve months and the twelve hours of daylight" (*De nuptiis* 188). The glossator Martin of Laon (followed later by Remigius) identifies his position of honor "post patrem" ("after the father") as one after Jove, in that "the philosophers" (probably the Neoplatonists) declare that deliberation, or Apollo, is born next after the soul, and after him Mercury, or speech: "id est Iovem. Ferunt phylosophi de generali anima Iovis consilium nasci, id est Apollinem. Post

Apollinem natus est Mercurius, quia post consilium fit sermo" (Dunchad, *In Mart.* 74.2). Martianus, however, has designated his name as Phoebus because he reveals celestial light, hence foretells secrets of the future (*De nuptiis* 190); Martin adds, in a gloss derived from *Sat.* 1.17.7 almost word for word and also from Fulgentius's *Mit.* 1.12, that Plato named the sun Apollo from the Greek "a iactura radiorum," from the casting of rays, that Apollo rules the divination of the future, and that as Phoebus he reveals what is obscure, or what is lost by night ("dissolvens nocturna amissa"), hence he is termed "novus," new, "imberbis," beardless, terrible, "terribilis," or long-locked, "crinitus."

79. According to Stahl the title "Lyceus" for Apollo may derive from the Greek stem which in Latin means "light"; he suggests, on page 59n132, a comparison with Macrobius, *Sat.* 1.17.33, 36–37; 1.20.18; 1.21.1, 9, 11, 13, 19.

80. Remigius, who more or less ignores the synonyms here because of his extended glosses on Apollo in the first book, also provides a long Fulgentian (and Scottian) gloss on Attis, loved as a boy by Berecynthia, in that "by Atthis we understand flower, in which figure the sun is adored because it is the principle and cause of all flowers, who was loved by Berecynthia, or earth" (Remi., *In Mart.* 74.12).

81. "ADON solem significat. Venus quae illum dilexerat terrenam superficiem aestivo tempore omni genere florum pulchram atque honestam; aper qui Adonem interfecit hiemem significat. Adon igitur ab apro vulneratur, id est sole ab altissima parte signiferi descendente quasi in inferioribus signiferi partibus absorbetur; ibi celerrimum cursum super terras agit ut vix a nobis videatur. Sed dum sol hiemali tempore in austrinis partibus moratur, tunc tota terrae superficies pulchritudinem deponit et copiam flumimum gignit quasi Venere totam pulchritudinem et copiam lacrimarum fundente" (Dunchad, *In Mart.* 74.13). Cf. the passages from John Scot and Remigius, note 60 in this chapter.

82. John Block Friedman, *Orpheus in the Middle Ages* (Cambridge, Mass. Harvard University Press, 1970), pp. 101–2, acknowledges Remigius's curious variation of the educational topos of *sapienta et eloquentia* without explaining the change. Eurydice, "profound thought," wisdom, suspects Orpheus, "beautiful voice," eloquence, in an inversion of gender most unlike even Remigius's Boethius glosses on Eurydice as *temporalia* and more closely related to the interpretation of Fulgentius. This gender reversal accommodates Remigius's similar gender sensitivity in the commentary on Martianus and perhaps in the Terence commentaries. Orpheus thus fails in not keeping the two (the musical articulation and musical idea) together. Closer to the larger intention of the commentator (but again, without referring to the implications of the gender reversal) is Lutz, "Remigius' Ideas on the Classification," p. 78: "By a vivid illustration Remigius depicts the unhappy result of the separation of *ratio* from *sermo,* the dissolution of the union between Philology and Mercury, as it affects one of the arts, music, in his interpretation of the Orpheus and Eurydice story."

CHAPTER 8: OEDIPUS AND
THE DAUGHTERS OF SATURN

1. Ferdinand Keseling, *De mythographi Vaticani secundi fontibus* (Halle: Typus Wischani and Burkhardti, 1908), also examines the order of myths, compares the first Vatican mythographer to the second Vatican mythographer and decides that the second Vatican mythographer flourished between the seventh and the tenth centuries, in that s/he mentions Isidore (d. 636), probably the ninth to the tenth, in that the earliest manuscript of the second Vatican mythographer is tenth century (p. 146). The second Vatican mythographer is identified by Kathleen O. Elliott and J. P. Elder as a Christian living after Isidore—*if* the proem was taken directly from Isidore rather than from an earlier, common source ("A Critical Edition of the *Vatican Mythographers*," *TAPA* 78 (1947): 189–207, here, p. 202). The resemblances between first Vatican mythography and second Vatican mythography—the absence of allegory, selection of stories, and use of the same sources—"probably will tell us that neither lived after the tenth century, but nothing else." But there are other characteristics of the second Vatican mythography one might define as Carolingian: in the words of Elliott and Elder, "To anyone familiar with grammatical literature of the Carolingian age, *Mythographus* 2 could easily seem to have belonged to that period; syntax, vocabulary, and method of definition all point to this."

2. Manitus argues that the second Vatican mythographer may be Remigius of Auxerre because of the compiler's dependence on Servius and Fulgentius; see Manitius, *Geschichte* 9.2.2:659n1. For the moralizing tendency of the second Vatican mythographer, see esp. 9.2.2:656; but see also 9.2.2:656–60 on the second Vatican mythographer. Elliott and Elder agree with Manitius that the author may be Remigius, largely because of the concord between the style, attitude, and word choice, although, "After going through Remigius's profane and secular works—a neither particularly pleasing nor light task—we have noted no parallels striking enough to confirm Manitius's suggestion" (p. 202).

3. "But he [the second Vatican mythographer] differs from the first in three notable respects: his stories are usually a good deal longer, owing partly to his habit of using more sources for one tale than *Mythographus 1* did; his style is better than that of the first, though it would hardly win any prize for composition today; and, most important, there is a definite system and purpose in the order of his myths," Elliott and Elder, pp. 199–200. Nevertheless, in the second Vatican mythography, the literary flaws of the first Vatican mythography—its seeming lack of order and structure, its didacticism, its lack of imagination—recur.

4. Elliot and Elder, p. 199; the second Vatican mythography is discussed especially on pp. 199–203. Elliott and Elder add, "like 1 he is probably composing a handbook for schoolboys. Indeed, *Mythographus 2* seems even more didactic in purpose than *1*."

5. The handiest edition (because it contains all three mythographers and because extant scholarship refers to its pagination and fable numeration) is Bode, but see also Kulcsár, who alters punctuation and spelling (normalizing the use of u for v, i for j) and subdivides fables, adding new material in a few cases from additional manuscripts and in some cases changing Mai/Bode's expansions of words abbreviated in the manuscript; he also supplies within notes the source citations contained in Bode and Keseling. He uses Mai's ordering of fables throughout rather than Bode's, which differs especially at the end of the second Vatican mythography (after Bode/Mai 199, or Kulcsár 227). In all references within this text, the first is to the fable numeration of Kulcsár, and the second, to Bode; the text used for citations is that of Kulcsár. Elliott and Elder long ago pointed to the need for a new edition because of manuscripts of the second Vatican mythography discovered after the early editions of Mai and Bode (p. 192).

6. Elliott and Elder, p. 200.

7. See Keseling, pp. 116–30, who also includes full tables at the end which show the ratio of correspondence between the first Vatican mythographer and the second Vatican mythographer, included with their sources (word-for-word correspondence in the latter case).

8. Elliott and Elder, p. 200.

9. Specifically, the previously identified major sources of the second Vatican mythographer include Servius (110 of the 230 myths are in some way based on or derived from Servius); the Statius scholia (74, with 20 in some way based on the scholia on the *Achilleid*, 54 on the scholia on the *Thebaid*); Fulgentius (46); Isidore (10); the Horace scholia (7); with additional inexact likenesses between the second Vatican mythography and the Virgil commentaries (including Servius, 50); Lactantius's *Narrationes* (15); Hyginus (20), the *Astronomica* (13), and *Fabulae* (7); and the Juvenal scholia (1). This analysis is based on the material presented in Keseling's study.

10. The Chimaera story is omitted in Bode, Kulcsár's fable 1; the Sphinx's riddle is Bode's fable 230, Kulcsár's supplement V.

11. See Mary Dove, *The Perfect Age of Man's Life* (Cambridge: Cambridge University Press, 1986).

12. For a convenient summary of the myths and clear genealogical tables, see Mark P. O. Morford and Robert J. Lenardon, *Classical Mythology*, 3d ed. (New York and London: Longman, 1985). To fill in relationships (or names) omitted by the second Vatican mythographer in the genealogies developed in the fable-series, I have used the tables and text of Morford and Lenardon, where corroborated by other ancient and medieval mythographic texts.

13. The second mythographer begins with the three-fold power of Apollo and devotes a chapter each to his names, his tripod, his four horses, his raven, his laurel, and the nine Muses associated with him (Mythogr. I 28/18–34/24). In fable 29/19, the diverse names for Apollo—also found in Remigius on Martianus, but

more distantly related to Macrobius's *Saturnalia* (see the discussions in chapter 1, pp. 77–81, and chapter 7, pp. 272–74)—identify him as a Titan who bore arms against Jove among the Achaemenians, Osiris to the Egyptians, Mithra to the Persians. He is also called Sol because he is alone and Pythius because he defeated the Python. The varied names of Apollo form a myth with many sources, according to Keseling, namely Isidore (*Etym.* 3.57 and 8.11.54), various portions of Servius on the *Aeneid* and *Eclogues,* Fulgentius's *Mit.* 1.12, and the scholia on Statius's *Thebaid* 1.717; however, it is very likely that the second Vatican mythographer found all these names in Martianus Capella (*De nuptiis* 10, 12–13), as did Remigius (*In Mart.* 10.6, 11.14). As god of light who dispels credulity, Apollo is also god of divination. In addition, in the passages on his insignia, the second Vatican mythographer is very similar to the Carolingian commentaries on Martianus, and to Fulgentius, for physical readings of the powers of the god of divination originally found in Martianus—the tripod suggesting his knowledge of past, present, and future (cf. Remigius, *In Mart.* 10.8); the four-horse chariot, the cycle of the four seasons through which the sun passes, from Fulgentius, *Mit.* 1.12; the raven who tattles on Coronis pregnant with Aesculapius, from the first Vatican mythographer (Mythogr. I 114/115) and in part from the fable in Fulgentius, *Mit.* 1.13; the laurel as sign of Daphne, pursued by Apollo, from Fulgentius, *Mit.* 1.14; and the allegory of the Muses in terms of knowledge and wisdom, clearly indebted to Fulgentius, *Mit.* 1.15 and the first Vatican mythographer (Mythogr. I 113/114) and also close to Remigius, *In Mart.* 19.11 and 19.17–20.5.

14. The genealogical ties with other planets follow: Diana the moon as sister of Apollo, a virgin called Duana, Lucina, and Trivia (Mythogr. II 35/25 from Fulgentius, *Mit.* 2.16 and Isidore, *Etym.* 8.11.56–58), is called Dictynna, or Britomartis, who threw herself into the sea rather than suffer capture by Minos of Crete, her body brought in by the nets of fishermen (36/26, from the scholia on the *Thebaid* 9.632); the confusion of names is also found in John Scot's commentary on Martianus. The second Vatican mythographer adds as well the Temple of Carya in Laconia sacred to Diana (37/27, also from the scholia on *Thebaid* 4.225), and Endymion the shepherd who loved Diana as the first man to discover the moon's track (38/28, from Fulgentius, *Mit.* 2.16 and Servius, *In Georg.* 3.391).

15. Mars in fable 39/29 is named god of war from causing death, taken according to Keseling from Isidore, *Etym.* 8.11.50–52. The second Vatican mythographer states he is called Mars "quia per mares pugnatur, ut Mars quasi mas dicitur, item Mars quasi effector mortium uocatur nam a Marte mors appellatur. Hunc adulterum dicunt quia bella gerentibus euentus incertus est, nudo uero pectore stat ut in bello quisque se sine formidine cordis obiciat" ["because fighting is done by males, so that he is called Mars, that is, 'male,' also called Mars as 'producer of deaths,' for death is named from Mars. They call him unchaste because the outcome for those waging wars is uncertain; he stands with his breast naked so that each one may oppose him without a fearful heart"]. Cf.

Remi., *In Mart.* 36.7, who explains his redness "propter sanguinis similitudinem qui in bellis funditur quibus Mars praeest, unde et Mars quasi mors vocatur" ["on account of the similarity of blood, which is shed in wars, over which Mars rules, and whence he is called Mars meaning 'death' "].

16. The second Vatican mythographer on Cupid declares, "Qui pharetratus, nudus, cum face, pennatus puer depingitur. Pharetratus ideo quia sicut sagitte corpus ita mentem uulnerat amor; nudus quia amoris turpitudo semper manifesta est et nusquam occulta; cum face autem quia turpis amor cum calore et feruore quodam accenditur; pennatus quia amor cito pertransit et amantibus nec leuius aliquid nec mutabilius inuenitur. Puer etiam fingitur quia sicut pueris per inperitiam facundia sic quoque nimium amantibus per uoluptatem deficit" ["He is depicted as a winged boy, with a quiver, nude, with a torch. With a quiver because as arrows wound the body so love wounds the mind; nude because the baseness of love is always manifest and nowhere hidden; with a torch because base love is kindled with heat and burning; winged because love passed through quickly and there is nothing lighter or more changeable than lovers. He is depicted as a boy because, as eloquence is lacking to boys through their inexperience, so too it is lacking to lovers because of their passion"] (Mythogr. II 46/35). Cf. Remi., *In Mart.* 8.22, who describes Cupid as evil, depicted as a nude boy, winged, with quiver: "Cupidinis dicit ut malum demonstraretur esse Cupidinem Veneris filium qui depingitur puer nudus, alatus, et pharetratus. Puer depingitur quia turpis amor puerilis est et sic in amantibus sermo deficit sicut in pueris. . . . Nudus depingitur quia turpitudo a nudis peragitur, vel quia nihil secretum est in turpitudine. Alatus et pharetratus depingitur quia turpis amor et velociter pertransit et mentem stimulat conscientia perpetrati criminis." See chapters 4 and 7.

17. Keseling indicates that the second Vatican mythographer used as sources scholia on the *Thebaid* 2.286 and Servius, *In Aen.* 1.720 for fable 47/36 on the Graces. An analogue very close in both time and space may be Remigius on Martianus, at least for a portion of the gloss. The second Vatican mythographer notes that the Graces are called Pasithea, Eugiale, Eufrosine, depicted nude, one turning away, but the other two turning toward us, consecrated to Venus, "quia earum pulsu cuncta animalia ad coitum prona fiunt" ["because they make the living inclined to coitus by means of their influence"]. The second Vatican mythographer states, "Gracie enim per horum fere numinum munera concilian-tur. Ideo autem nude sunt quod gracie sine fuco esse debent, id est sine simulatione, ideo conexe quia insolubiles esse gracias decet. Quod uero una auersa pingitur, due nos respiciunt, hec est ratio quia profecta a nobis gracia duplex solet reuerti" ["For the Graces are obtained through the gifts of almost all the divinities. They are nude because graces ought to be without deceit, i.e., without pretext; joined together because favors ought to be indissoluble. That one is depicted turned away and two facing, is because a favor coming from us usually returns two-fold"]. Cf. Remi., *In Mart.* 4.2, who declares, after noting the Graces are

daughters of Jove and Juno, "cuius nepos est Hymeneus ex Venere filia eius natus" ["whose grandson is Hymen, born from his daughter, Venus"], that "Gratiae tres sunt, quae et Carite dicuntur, unius nominis et unius pulchritudinis" ["there are three Graces, who are also called Caritae, of one name and one beauty"].

18. Fable 50/39 reads: "Minerua sapientie, armorum et lanificii dea esse dicitur, que pingitur armata, triplici ueste induta, caput Gorgone gestans in pectore. Minerua ideo de uertice Iouis dicitur nata quia ingenium in cerebro positum sit; ideo fingitur armata quia sapientia sit munita" ["Minerva is called the goddess of wisdom, arms, and wood-working. She is depicted as armed, clothed in a triple garment, wearing a Gorgon's head on her breast. Minerva is said to have been born from Jove's head because wisdom is located in the brain; she is depicted as armed because wisdom is fortified"] . The mythographer uses this to transit to the myth of Nyctimene, changed into an owl by Minerva because she unknowingly had sexual relations with her father (from Ovid, *Metamorphoses* 2.590).

19. The passage in the second Vatican mythographer declares: "Dicitur autem preesse hortis propter fecunditatem" (Mythogr. II 49/38). Specifically, the garden multiplies over the course of a year, "nam cum alia terra semel in anno aliquid creet, orti nunquam sine fructu sunt, et cum alia terra semel in anno prouentum habeat, ortus uero multiplicem. Est autem minister Liberi patris, deus libidinis et coitus, unde sacris eius interesse dicitur, nam: *Sine Cerere et Libero friget Venus.* Priapum quidam dicunt esse Adonem filium Veneris qui a feminis colitur." The passage that follows resembles the Carolingian Martianus glosses on Venus and Adonis, in terms of vegetation myth: "Secundum aliquos iste Adon fuit amasius Veneris quem aper interfecit unde nimium fleuit Venus. Quod ideo fingitur quia Adon est Sol, aper hyems, aper uero interfecit Adonem quia ueniente hyeme sol a calore deficit et moritur, Venus flet, id est terra, quia terra nihil parit cum sol hyeme obnubilatur." Cf. the passages from Dunchad, John Scot, and Remi., *In Mart.,* cited in notes 60 and 81 to chapter 7.

20. As god of merchants and of thieves Mercury appears in the second Vatican mythographer, "Preesse autem negotiis et furti rapinarumque deus esse dicitur" (Mythogr. II 53/41; from Isidore, *Etym.* 8.11.45–49, and Fulgentius, *Mit.* 1.18). He appears as Anubis the wise dog-headed god, "quia nihil cane sagacius esse dinoscitur" (Mythogr. II 54/42; from Servius, *In Aen.* 8.698). The etymologies of Mercury from "running between," signifying his nature as *sermo,* which runs between, or from his role as messenger of the gods, and related to the art of negotiation in trading or thievery, are found in Martianus, in Fulgentius, *Mit.* 1.18, and in the Martianus commentaries: "Mercurius igitur quasi mercium curius uel medius currens dicitur, quia sermo inter medios est, uel quia nuncius deorum est. Mercurius quasi medius inter deos et homines currens dicitur. Fingitur autem deus esse rapinarum et furti, quia negociatiores rapina et periurio semper sunt succincti" (Mythogr. II 54/42). All of his attributes are explained in terms of his role as eloquence—for example, his caduceus symbolizes the warring and dissi-

dence ended by oration; he invented the lyre (Mythogr. II 55/43). Because of this invention the fable of Orpheus and his lyre follows immediately.

21. The second Vatican mythographer follows Hyginus (*Astronomica* 2.15) for the stories of the sacrifices of Prometheus and Jupiter and Thetis (for this story see also Servius, *In Buc.* 6.42). Hyginus's depiction of a Christlike Chiron who is willing to die to save Prometheus (ibid. 2.38), is changed by the mythographer, who casts Hercules as the savior Prometheus.

22. The story of Virgo and Sirius is in Servius, *In Georg.* 2.380, and Hyginus, *Astronomica* 2.4; cf. also the first Vatican mythographer's fable of Icarus and Erigone (19/19).

23. Cf. Fulgentius's story of Tiresias (*Mit.* 2.5) and Hyginus's version (*Fab.* 75).

24. In Mythogr. II 112/90 Isis is "genius Egypti," who holds in her right hand a sistrum whose motion governs the Nile waters acceding or receding and in her left an urn signifying the flowing of all lakes (in Martianus Capella because Osiris was dismembered, *De nuptiis* 4): "Isis autem lingua Egyptiorum est terra quam Isin uolunt esse" ["Isis, moreover, in the tongue of the Egyptians is earth, which they supposed Isis to be"]. Also she is called Isis for having found the limbs of Osiris and placing them in a sieve, "Dicitur autem Isis inuenta Osyridis membra cribro superposuisse", Liber Pater (who is similarly torn into pieces) is identified with Osiris and in 114/92 the fan of Liber Pater therefore is said to pertain to mysteries involving the purgation of souls, since Liber is said to come from "freeing": "Nam idem est Liber pater, in cuius mysteriis uannus est quia Liberi patris sacra ad purgationem anime pertinent, et sic homines mysteriis eius purgabantur sicut uannus frumenta purgat. Vnde Liber ab eo, quod liberet, est dictus quem etiam Orpheus dicit discerptum esse a Gigantibus" ["For the same is Liber Pater, in whose mysteries is the *vannus* {fan, winnowing basket}, because the sacred rites of Liber Pater pertain to the purification of the soul, and so men were purified by his mysteries just as the *vannus* purifies grain. Liber is so called because he liberates—whom also Orpheus says was plucked from the Giants"]. Cf. Macrobius's treatment of Bacchus in chapter 2, pp. 75, 78, and the Berne scholiast's treatment of Liber Pater in the *Georgics* in chapter 5, pp. 175, 178–79.

25. In the story of Prosperina as told by Hyginus, *Fab.* 146–47, it is "Tartarus" the girl fears. Hyginus includes the story of Ceres at Eleusis.

26. The mythographer's Sirens come from Fulgentius, *Mit.* 2.8, and the same story is in Lactantius, *Narrationes* 5.9. The mythographer's treatment clearly recalls the *meretrices* of Boethius, *Consolatio* 1 p1. The passage on the Sirens (Mythogr. II 123/101) reads, "Secundum ueritatem autem meretrices fuerunt que quoniam transeuntes ducebant ad egestatem, his ficte sunt inferre naufragia. Sirene igitur Grece Latine trahitorie dicuntur, tribus enim modis illecebra trahitur aut cantu aut uisu aut consuetudine. Ideo igitur uolatiles dicuntur quia amantium mentes celeriter permaneant, inde gallinaceis pedibus finguntur quia libidinis affectu queque habita sparguntur. Per Vlixem autem, qui quasi olon xenos, id est

omnium peregrina, dicitur, ad mortem deducte dicuntur quia sapientia ab omnibus mundi illecebris peregrinatur" ["According to truth, they were harlots who, since they led by-passers to poverty, were imagined to cause them shipwrecks. Therefore they are called Sirens in Greek, and 'attractors' in Latin, for enticements attract in three ways: by song, by sight, by habit. They are called volatile because they swiftly pass over the minds of lovers. Then they are depicted with *gallinacei pedes* {chicken's feet, a kind of plant, a 'fumitory'}, because whatever they hold is sprinkled with the emotion of passion. Moreover, they are said to have been led down to death by Ulysses {i.e., *olon xenos,* "wanderer of all"}, because wisdom wanders away from the enticements of the world"].

27. The name Aegyptus for Danaus's brother is from Hyginus, *Fab.* 168.

28. The stories of Tityus and Sisyphus are in Servius, *In Aen.* 6.595–96; cf. for Sisyphus also Lactantius, the *Thebaid* gloss 2.389. The second Vatican mythographer's treatment is much longer than that of the first (Mythogr. I 162/165). Our life as an underworld is important to glosses on Boethius, *Consolatio* 3 m12 (e.g. Remigius, in Bolton, "A Study," p. 65; see above, p. 226). In the following passage, the mythographer cites Lucretius, *De rerum naturae* 3.978: "Sane de his omnibus mire reddit rationem Lucretius confirmans in nostra uita esse omnia que finguntur de inferis" ["Concerning all these Lucretius marvelously gives a reasonable account, confirming that in our life are all the things which are imagined about the underworld"]. Then: "Dicit namque Ticion amorem esse, hoc est libidinem que secundum phisicos et medicos in iecore est sicut risus in splene, iracundia in felle, unde etiam exesum a uulture dicitur in penam renasci, etenim libidini non sufficit res semel peracta sed recrudescit semper" ["For he says Tician is love, i.e., lust, which according to the physicians and doctors is in the liver, as laughter is in the spleen, and anger in the gall; whence, when what is eaten by the vulture is said to be reborn for punishment, since indeed, for passion the act committed once is not sufficient, but always happens again"] (Mythogr. II 127/105).

29. The mythographer's story of Ixion repeats material found in Lactantius, *Thebaid* 4.539; Fulgentius, *Mit.* 2.14; Servius, *In Georg.* 3.115; and the first Vatican mythographer (14/14).

30. The Oedipus story recalls Lactantius, *Thebaid* 1.66.

31. The first Labor of Hercules is with Cerberus (Mythogr. II 173/149); followed by Diomedes (174/151); Geryon (175/152); and Cacus (176/153); the rescue of Alcestis (177/154); the aid to Queen Omphale in killing a snake near a river in Lydia; and then more encounters, with Eryx, the son of Venus and Butes or instead Neptune (179/156); Busiris (180/157); a sexual encounter with Megara, daughter of Creon of Thebes (181/158); Euritus, who denied Hercules his daughter Ioles (182/159); the two lions, including the Nemean lion (183/160); Kulcsár follows with fable 184—Bode 227—on Avernus and Lucrinus, lakes full of fish related to Julius Caesar, and fable 185, on two mountains, Erimanthus and

Stymphalus. Next comes the dragon guarding the apples of the Hesperides (186/161); the rescue of Deianira from the Centaur (187/162); the battle with the Hydra (188/163); with Antaeus (189/164); with Achelous and Nessus, who tried to rape Deianira (190/165); and the death of Hercules and his pyre (191–92/165); with one last fable on the asylum given to the grandsons of Hercules after he had left earth (193/166). See chapter 6, especially notes 93 and 95, on the Labors in Boethius's commentaries.

32. In the second Vatican mythographer's fable 194/167, Phorcys, son of Neptune and the nymph Thoosa, is changed into a sea-god, as is Glaucus, son of Antedon, 195/168. Scylla, daughter of Phorcys and a nymph, was loved by Glaucus, who was himself loved by Circe, who, being angered, poisoned the spring in which Scylla was accustomed to bathe; when she went down into it, she was changed into various shapes up to her private parts (196/169). The whirlpool Charybdis follows (197/170); the pirate Tyrrhenians who were transformed into dolphins (198/171); Arion the poet-singer is saved from death by the dolphins (199/172); Arethusa the hunter is beloved by Alpheus but changed into a fountain because she spurned him (200/173); Polyphemus, son of Neptune, loves Galatea the nymph, herself loved by Acis the shepherd (201/174; after he is slain by the Cyclops he is transformed into a fountain today called Aci(da)lius). Ceyx's Alcyone so loves him that she kills herself after he dies at sea and thereafter both are transformed to halcyons, a type of kingfisher (202/175). Mergus (Hesurus), a son of Priam, is also changed into a diving bird when he jumps from the wall (203/176).

33. Cyparissus, beloved of Apollo, becomes a cypress after death (Mythogr. II 204/177); the succeeding fable offers a different interpretation, for he is beloved by Silvanus, god of the woods, who is responsible for his transformation into the cypress; Lothos, beloved of Priapus, is transformed into a tree (206/179); Narcissus, son of Alciope the nymph and Cephisus (a river-god in Ovid), is beloved by Echo, dies when he falls into the pool in pursuit of his own image, and is transformed into a flower of the same name (207/180); Hyacinthus, loved by Apollo, is accidentally slain during a game and is changed into a hyacinth (208/181); Amaracus is responsible for the origin of the best smelling unguent (209/182). The brief myths at the end of this series (210/183–212/185) seem to involve multiple brothers: Pilumnus and Pitumnus; two brothers called divine; the three Telchines brothers. Thereafter, I find no links between the fables other than their rule of Italian regions or islands (213/186–215/188): Tenes rules an isle of the same name; Ebalus, son of Telon, rules Capri; Maleus, king of Tuscany, invents the *tuba,* originally a war-trumpet. The last three (216/189–218/191) involve the dreams, oracles, or skill of warriors Codrus, leader of the Athenians, Cresus, king of Lydia, and Alcon of Crete.

34. In between Palamedes and Agamemnon (Mythogr. II 245/202), Kulcsár inserts fifteen fables not in Bode; they concern seemingly irrelevant Sicilian

geographical material on Dodona, Leucada, Pelorus, Eubea, Pachinus, and the Syracusans, as well as Roman historical material on Tullus Hostilius, his son Brutus, Tarquinius, Brenus, the civil war, Fabius Maximus, Marcellus, and the like.

35. There is a brief myth about Laocoon, the priest of Neptune at Troy, in Mythogr. II 251/207; Helenus, son of Priam who reigns in Greece by taking the throne from Pyrrhus, who is killed by Orestes (252/208); Hecuba, wife of Priam, who falls to the lot of Ulysses and, when she discovers Polymnestor has murdered her son Polydorus, blinds him and is herself changed into a dog (253/209). Indeed, many of these last fables concern the fate of the Greeks or their territories. Idomeneus of Crete lived in Italy after the fall of Troy (254/210); Circe transformed Ulysses's men into swine (255/211–257/213); Demophoon, son of Theseus, returning from Troy, loved Phyllis, queen of Thrace, but returning to Troy once again was delayed in coming back and she, dying from longing, became an almond tree (258/214); Laodamia, wife of the Greek Protesilaus, because he was killed at Troy killed herself (259/215).

36. From the *Pseudancronis scholia in Horatium* come Lycambes and his daughter Neobules (Mythogr. II 264/220), Bupalus (265/221), Tyrteus (266/222), Iarbita (267/223), Opimius (270/226). Other obscure figures, some oracular, some historical, include Mopsus (268/224), Apicius (269/225), the oracle at Dodona (Suppl. V 227/227), Julius Caesar (Suppl. V 228/228).

CHAPTER 9: ATLAS AS NIMROD, THE HYDRA AS *VUÚRM*

1. For a brief history of the eclogue in the Middle Ages, see George L. Hamilton, "Theodulus: A Mediaeval Textbook," *MP* 7 (1909–10): 169–85, here, p. 176 [p. 7 of the article, which appeared with two different sets of pagination]; and also, for the use of Virgil's *Eclogues* by "Theodulus," Shirley Law Guthrie, "The *Ecloga Theoduli* in the Middle Ages" (diss., Indiana University, 1973), chap. 1, pp. 1–20. She notes rather elegantly that, "For the audience of the *Ecloga,* necessarily an educated one, these conscious verbal references to the earlier pastorals both recall the Vergilian poems and contrast the limited, earthly setting and the transitory nature of property, life, and especially love in the earlier poems with the boundless, universal setting and everlasting life and love described by Alithia in the *Ecloga"* (p. 9).

2. For an excellent analysis of its Virgilian antecedents (the third and the seventh eclogues), see Morton Yale Jacobs, "Bernard's *Commentum in Theodulum:* Editio Princeps" (diss., University of North Carolina, 1963), pp. xlvi-vii; other scholars—Osternacher, Josef Frey, Walter W. Skeat, Manitius—have acknowledged as a model the third eclogue but not the seventh.

3. Betty Nye Quinn transliterated the Greek so in "ps. Theodolus," in Kristeller and Cranz, *Catalogus,* 386–87n3; for the accessus, published separately,

see R. B. C. Huygens, *Accessus ad Auctores: Bernard d'Utrecht, Conrad d'Hirsau, Dialogus super Auctores* (Leiden: E. J. Brill, 1970), pp. 26–27. For a critical edition of *Ecloga Theoduli*, see *Theoduli eclogam recensuit et prolegomenis instruxit Joannes Osternacher*, in Fünfter Jahresbericht des bischöflichen Privat-Gymnasiums am Kollegium Petrinum in Urfahr für das Schuljahr 1901/02 (Urfahr prope Lentiam: Programmate Collegii Petrini, 1902); this edition of the *Ecloga* is also appended to Jacobs, "Bernard's *Commentum.*" A translation of the *Ecloga* has recently appeared, by Ian Thomson in *Ten Latin Schooltexts of the Later Middle Ages,* trans. Thomson and Louis Perraud, Mediaeval Studies, vol. 6 (Lewiston, Queenston, Lampeter: Edward Mellen Press, 1990), pp. 110–157. All translations are from Thomson.

4. The structure of the biblical chronology of the *Ecloga* was first noted by Hans Vollmer, "*Theoduli Ecloga* und die *Catalogi* des Otto Brunfels," *Monatsschrift für die kirchliche Praxis,* n.f. 4 (1904): 321–33, here, p. 329.

5. See, for example, the discussion of this conflict in *The Writings of Margaret of Oingt, Medieval Prioress and Mystic (d. 1310),* trans. from the Latin and Franco-provençal by Renate Blumenfeld-Kosinski, Focus Library of Medieval Women (Newburyport, Mass.: Focus Information Group, 1990), pp. 73–76.

6. For the *Ecloga* manuscripts, see Joannes Osternacher in "Die Überlieferung der Ecloga Theoduli," *NA* 40 (1916): 329–76, here, p. 355, who notes that of 176 manuscripts known to him, 129 derive from the "Old Empire," with 30 of the remaining 47 English; he acknowledges 96 printed editions. More recently, Quinn has located 181 manuscripts; of these, 59 contain the poem, 47 contain glosses and/or the poem, and 76 contain a commentary and/or poem ("ps. Theodulus," pp. 383–408). It appears frequently in manuscripts containing grammatical treatises (for example, Cambridge, Trinity College MS. O.5.4, and Worcester Cathedral MS. F.147) or schoolbook authors (for example, Cambridge, Peterhouse MS. 207), or religious and moral tracts (included with the *Dittochaeum* of Prudentius, for example).

For its importance as a medieval school text throughout Europe, see especially Hamilton, "Theodulus: A Mediaeval Textbook," pp. 175–95, who explains that it was "recommended, prescribed, and used as a primary textbook of reading in medieval schools" (p. 176 [p. 7]); cited for its importance in reading by Conrad of Hirsau in *Dialogus super auctores sive didascalicon* in the first half of the twelfth century and in a sermon to scholars by Jacques de Vitry; regarded as a model of style, by the author of *Laborintus,* book 3; and used as a grammar text, in a decree allowing this one book to be used for primary instruction in a lower class of a grammar school in Breslau in 1267 by the papal legate Guido and also by Pierre Dubois in a plan for school missionaries (1292) later outlined in *De recuperatione Terre Sancte* (1305–7). It was also mentioned frequently in entries in the catalogues of medieval libraries (for example, the Library of Durham Cathedral, 6.9; the chronicle of the Monastery of Melsa, 3.140.96; the Library of Syon Monastery, 4.14). Included in what Boas calls the *Liber Catonianus,* a collection used as early as the end of the tenth century to instruct Latin pupils at the earlier stages, the *Ecloga* was the only Christian text among works that began with the *Disticha Catonis* and followed with the *Ecloga*, Avianus's *Fabulae*, Maximianus's *Elegiae*, the *Achilleid* of Statius, and Claudian's *De raptu Proserpinae*. See M. Boas, "De librorum Catonianorum historia atque compositione," *Mnemosyne* n.s. 42 (1914): 17–46. In addition, a later French collection in the fifteenth century entitled *Octo auctores* contains the *Ecloga* and was frequently used into the sixteenth century. See *Octo autores, Autores octo continentes libros: videlicet Catonem, Facetum, Theodulum, De contemptu mundi, Floretum, Alanum De parabolis, Fabulas Esopi, Thobiam, De modo punctuandi, Regimen mente honorabile* (Lyon, 1525). On the hegemony of the *Ecloga*, see also Manitius, *Geschichte* 9.2.1:573–74; and Quinn, "ps. Theodulus," p. 385; and also Guthrie's summary in chapter 3, pp. 46–79.

7. See Quinn, pp. 383–408, who lists all of the commentaries as well as their manuscripts; Jacobs establishes Bernard of Utrecht's dominance over later commentaries (p. v). For the commentary of Alexander Neckam (1157–1217), see Rome, Vatican Library MS. 1479, fols. 15v–25r, and possibly Paris, B.N. MS. 1862. Jacobs, p. xxi, on the basis of the Incipit and Explicit provided by Quinn in her *Catalogus* article, has decided that, "From these it is quite evident that the 'Neckam' does not constitute a maturer commentary than Bernard's. On the contrary, it is little more than a condensation of Bernard's material, resulting, in more than one place, in a garble of the original." "Stephen Patrington'"s fourteenth-century commentary is basically that of Neckam and is available only in early printed editions; an edition of Odo of Picardy's commentary (1406–7) appears in *Liber Theodoli cum commento noviter impressus* (London, 1508). Although Odo depends heavily on Neckam, he embellishes the commentary with advice on kingship and the responsibilities of government. For a five-part edition (apparently unfinished) of the Anonymous Teutonicus's commentary, see "Anonymi Teutonici commentum in Theodoli eclogam e codice Utrecht, U.B. 292 editum," ed. Arpád P. Orbán; (1) in *Vivarium* 11 (1973): 1–42; (2) 12 (1974): 133–45; (3) 13 (1975): 77–88; (4) 14 (1976): 50–61; (5) 15 (1977): 143–58. Guthrie, chapter 4, pp. 80–152, analyzes briefly many of these commentaries.

8. Imitations of the *Ecloga* appeared in Warnerius of Basel's *Synodicus,* in the second part of the eleventh century; and in *Pistilegus,* not extant but known and cited, at least the first lines, in the *Registrum multorum auctorum* of Hugh of Trimberg in 1280—and Hamilton notes that, in the first third of the thirteenth century, Henri d'Andeli, in *Bataille des sept arts,* makes "Theodulus" an important combatant within the forces of Grammar (see verses 332–44). For the French work, see *Oeuvres de Henri d'Andeli,* ed. A. Herón (1881; rpt., Geneva: Slatkine Rpts., 1979), p. 55. On its lack of influence on medieval literature (it was never translated into a vernacular), see Hamilton, "Theodulus: A Mediaeval Textbook," p. 174 [p. 5]. Hamilton, "Theodulus in France," *MP* 8 (1910–11): 611–12, notes imitations of the *Ecloga* in the Middle Ages and allusions to the work he missed in

the first article. See also Guthrie, chapter 5, pp. 169–229, on the *Ecloga*'s "Literary Fortune."

9. See Ferdinand Holthausen, "Chaucer und Theodulus," *Anglia* 16 (1893–94): 264–66; Hamilton, "Theodulus: A Mediaeval Textbook," p. 184, suggests the (probably English) Boethius commentator uses the *Ecloga* (lines 189–92, 341) to gloss Boethius's poem on Orpheus (*Consolatio* 3 m12). Jacobs, pp. lv-lvi, adds that there are echoes of the *Ecloga* in the *Maniciple's Tale,* the *Miller's Tale,* and possibly the *Nun's Priest's Tale.*

10. See Judson Boyce Allen, "An Anonymous Twelfth-Century 'De Natura Deorum,' " *Traditio* 26 (1970): 360.

11. See Huygens, "Notes sur le *Dialogus super auctores* de Conrad de Hirsau et le *Commentaire sur Théodule,*" *Latomus* 13 (1954): 420–28, here p. 420n1. See also the dedicatory epistle and introduction edited by Huygens in *Accessus ad Auctores,* pp. 55–57 (epistle), and 58–69 (introduction).

12. See Ingeborg Schroebler, *Notker III von St. Gallen als Übersetzer und Kommentator von Boethius "De Consolatione Philosophiae,"* Hermaea: Germanistische Forschungen, vol. 2 (Tübingen: Max Niemeyer, 1953), pp. 3, 10–11, 12–13; she summarizes his Christianizing by saying that "Notkers Erklärung wirkt zunächst wie ein wilder Synkretismus aus Altem Testament, Mythographen und allegorischer Auslegung—aber schlieβlich ist doch alles dem christlichen Gesichtspunkt untergeordnet: die Erzählung von Otus und Ephialtes est ein *spel,* ein Mythos, insofern nicht völlig ernst zu nehmen und nach Notkers Meinung eine Entstellung der Erzählung vom Turmbau zu Babel, anknüpfend an dessen archäologische Spuren," p. 13.

13. Although dates mentioned for the *Ecloga* range from the sixth to the eleventh century (a terminus ad quem), the most probable date is the tenth century. According to Skeat, cited in Hamilton, "Theodulus: A Mediaeval Textbook," p. 170, the author flourished between the sixth and tenth centuries; Winfried Bühler, "Theodulus' *Ecloga* and Mythographus Vaticanus I," *California Studies in Classical Antiquity* 1 (1968): 65–71, argues for the eleventh century as the latest possible date, based on the earliest manuscripts and on parallels between the first Vatican mythographer and the *Ecloga,* but indicates that it was probably not earlier than the ninth century "for general reasons" (p. 65), and indeed the ninth century may be the earliest possible date because of Remigius's dependence on the first Vatican mythographer in the commentary on Martianus (p. 71). Additional support for this date is offered by Manitius, who notes that the eclogue form and the Greek-based name were prevalent in the mid-ninth century in the Empire, *Geschichte* 9.2.1:570. See also, for the ninth-century date, Osternacher's edition, pp. 11ff, Paul von Winterfeld, "Der Mimus und die karolingische Ekloge," section 4 of "Hrotsvits literarische Stellung," *Herrigs Archiv für neuere Sprachen,* 114 (1905): 68–69; Hamilton, "Theodulus: A Mediaeval Textbook," p. 171. That the *Ecloga* was probably tenth century has been convincingly argued by

Karl Strecker, "Studien zu karolingischen Dichtern: VII. Ist Gottschalk der Dichter der *Ecloga Theoduli?*" *NA* 45 (1923–24): 18–20; Quinn, "ps. Theodulus," p. 384n5, does not resolve the debate beyond narrowing it to the ninth or tenth centuries, but Thomson, in his fine introduction to his translation, accepts Strecker's dating (p. 113).

14. Manitius, *Geschichte* 9.2.1:573.

15. The eighteenth-century editor Schwabe identified the author (on the basis of a well-known "biography" included in the accessus) as Gennadius Theodulus (ca. A.D. 529). See John Gottlob Samuel Schwabe, ed. *Theoduli Ecloga* (Altenburg, 1773), pp. 480–92. Skeat notes that "Theodulus" was also known as Theodosius and Theodore (in Hamilton, "Theodulus: A Mediaeval Textbook," p. 170). The Vita suggests "Theodulus" was a contemporary with the Fathers of the Church (perhaps a reason for his identification with John Chrysostom by "Patrington" and Odo of Picardy), Jacobs, p. liii.

16. After Schwabe's attribution was debunked, Manitius offered "Godescalc" because of the mention of indebtedness to him in the text (*Geschichte* 9.2.1:308, 572). Paul von Winterfeld had already noted that "Theodulus" is the Greek translation of the Germanic "Gotteschalk," meaning "slave of God," possibly referring to Gottschalk of Orbais (ca. 805–69) in his last years ("Der Mimus," pp. 68–69). Unfortunately, Gottschalk was interested in but knew little Greek, as illustrated by his query to Lupus of Ferrières about, and the latter's answer on, the meaning of certain Greek words (see *PL* 119:491). But he may have found this Christian Greek name "Theodulus" in a bilingual glossary.

Karl Strecker argued against Gottschalk of Orbais because of the general lack of rhyme in his verses and specifically of end-rhyme, which is peculiar to the *Ecloga* (a work that in genre and meter—leonine hexameters—is Carolingian) and is often associated with the diocese of Rheims (pp. 18–23). For the Carolingian metrical associations, see Ludwig Traube, ed. *Poetae Latini aevi Carolini*, MGH, vol. 3 (Berlin: Weidmann's, 1896; rpt. 1964), p. 711; for the diocese of Rheims and end-rhyme, see also von Winterfeld, "Der Mimus," pp. 68–69. But Manitius tells us that Gottschalk of Orbais, or "Godescalc," went to the cloister at Fulda after 822, where he developed a friendship with Walafrid and also perhaps Lupus and Hraban Maur. He then went to Corbie and Orbais, where he obtained a Rheims-style education by studying poetry and St. Augustine under Dunchad of Ireland (*Geschichte* 9.2.1:572). He could, then, have experimented with end-rhyme in the *Ecloga,* although he is not a likely candidate given Strecker's arguments.

17. I have derived this attribution from the context of von Winterfeld's article on "Hrotsvits literarische Stellung"—von Winterfeld does not in fact attribute the *Ecloga Theoduli* to Hrotsvit, but instead to Gottschalk.

18. Sandro Sticca notes that "in her six dramas, Hroswitha's fundamental purpose is to celebrate in dramatic form a symbolic representation of the spiritual wrestlings of her female *dramatis personae,* virgins, martyrs, and sinners, who find

moving dignity and religious fulfillment in the conflicting demands of sin and salvation, the dramatic context within which the drama of human salvation is articulated. . . . Hroswitha, transcending the narrow limits imposed by spiritual abstraction, utilized women as visible and vibrant figures to transmute, with unexampled immediacy, into drama the deep spiritual experience of the human drama of salvation." See "Sin and Salvation: The Dramatic Context of Hroswitha's Women," in *The Roles and Images of Women in the Middle Ages and Renaissance,* ed. Douglas Radcliff-Umstead, University of Pittsburgh Publications on the Middle Ages and Renaissance, vol. 3 (Pittsburgh: University of Pittsburgh Publications Center for Medieval and Renaissance Studies, Institute for the Human Sciences, 1978), pp. 3–22, here, pp. 8–9.

19. For a summary of Hrotsvit's learning, see the fine introduction by Katharina M. Wilson, "The Saxon Canoness: Hrotsvit of Gandersheim," in *Medieval Women Writers,* ed. Wilson (Athens: University of Georgia Press, 1984), pp. 31–32. Presumably Hrotsvit was familiar with these works from the Gandersheim library, as she reveals in the preface to book 1 of the three books of her chronologically generically arranged works, the first, containing the legends. See also, for Hrotsvit's classical learning, Helena Homeyer, ed., *Hrotsvithae opera* (Munich: Paderborn; Vienna: Schöningh, 1970), p. 8; Bert Nagel, *Hrotsvith von Gandersheim* (Stuttgart: Metzler, 1965), p. 43; Wilhelm Gundlach, ed., *Heldenlieder der deutschen Kaiserzeit,* 3 vols. (1896, rpt., Aalen: Scientia, 1970), 2:304.

20. *Sapientia* 5.24. I cite the edition by von Winterfeld, *Hrotsvithae opera,* Scriptores Rerum Germanicarum (MGH) (Berlin and Turin: Weidmann's, 1965), and for the translation of her six plays, *The Plays of Hrotsvit of Gandersheim,* trans. Katharina Wilson, vol. 62 of Series B: Garland Library of Medieval Literature (New York and London: Garland, 1989), p. 141. Translations of lines from her other works are my own.

21. *Primordia* line 210, ed. von Winterfield; my translations.

22. See James Holly Hanford, "Classical Eclogue and Mediaeval Debate," *Romanic Review* 2 (1911): 130.

23. For Servius as a major source of the *Ecloga,* see Josef Frey, "Über das Mittelalterliche Gedicht, 'Theoduli ecloga' und den Kommentar des Bernhardus Ultraiectensis," *Vierundachtzigster Jahresbericht über das königliche Paulinische Gymnasium zu Münster i.W. für das Schuljahr* 1903–1904 (Münster: Aschendorffschen, 1904), p. 13 (for Virgil, cf. *Ecl. Theod.* line 22 and *Aeneid* 2.709; line 29, *Eclogues* 7.17; line 37, *Aeneid* 3.117; lines 77ff, *Aeneid* 5.254ff; line 128, *Aeneid* 7.762). For the other *Ecloga* sources, see Manitius, *Geschichte* 9.2.1:573 (for Prudentius, Sedulius, and Servius, see also Frey, pp. 13 and 14–19). Isidore is added in the fullest listing of sources and parallels, Osternacher, *Quos auctores Latinos et Sacrorum Bibliorum locus Theodulus imitatus esse videatur* (Urfahr prope Lentiam: Programmate Collegii Petrini, 1907). The first Vatican mythographer is added, either as direct source or parallel text (that is, sharing the same source), by T. W. Baldwin, in

"Perseus Purloins Pegasus," *PQ* 20 (1941): 361–70. It was omitted from Bernard's commentary, but included in Odo of Picardy's, according to John M. Steadman, "The *Ecloga Theoduli,* the *General Estoria,* and the Perseus-Bellerophon Myth," *MS* 24 (1962): 384–87. See also Bühler, "Theodolus' *Ecloga,*" p. 70.

24. Other borrowings from Ovid include: Lycaon (*Metamorphoses* 1.165), Deucalion and Pyrrha (1.318ff), Ganymede (10.155, 11.756), Apollo and Aesculapius (2.629), Daedalus (8.155), Diomedes (12.622 and 13.88), Phaedra and Hippolytus (15.500ff), Europa and Jupiter (2.858), Amphiaraus (9.407), Io (1.588), Orpheus (10.3ff), Danaë and the golden shower (4.611, 6.113), Niobe (6.172ff), Medea, Hippomenes (7.394ff, 10.575), and Scylla and Minos (8.11).

25. Other correspondences with the first Vatican mythographer include the passage on Titan, Aurora, and Memnon (*Ecl. Theod.* 221–24) with fable 136/139 (Bode), according to Bühler, because it connects two stories, one found in Servius, *In Aen.* 4.585 (on Tithonus's transformation into a cicada) and 1.489 (on the Memnon myth).

26. The monastery had a history of Irish influence: it was founded by St. Columban and St. Gall in 610, with St. Columban leaving St. Gall behind when he went to Italy to found Bobbio; the first abbot was appointed in 720. See J. M. Clark, *The Abbey of St. Gall as a Centre of Literature and Art* (Cambridge: Cambridge University Press), 1926.

27. See Raby, *Secular Latin Poetry* 1:252–53.

28. See Hans Naumann, *Notkers Boethius. Untersuchungen über Quellen und Stil.* Quellen und Forschungen zur Sprach- und Kulturgeschichte der germanischen Völker, vol. 121 (Strassburg: Karl J. Trübner, 1913), pp. 1–69; see also Schroebler, *Die althochdeutschen Boethiusglossen und Notkers Übersetzung der Consolatio* (diss., Halle and Würzburg: Richard Mayr, 1934), p. 43.

29. See Naumann, p. 27, and Clark, pp. 248–54, for discussions of Notker's work and goals.

30. Pierre Courcelle, "Étude critique sur les commentaires de la Consolation de Boèce (IXe–XVe siècles)," *AHDLMA* 40 (1939): 78. For example, in Courcelle, *La Consolation de Philosophie dans la tradition littéraire: Antécédents et postérité de Boèce* (Paris: Études Augustiniennes, 1967), p. 290, describes MS. B.N. Parisinus lat. 10400, a tenth-century word-for-word reproduction of parts of Remigius (commentary on *Consolatio* 4 m6 to 5 p3) in confused order (on folios 90r–93v, but disjointed—90r, 90v, 93r, 93v, 92r, 92v, 91r, 91v).

31. Diane K. Bolton, "The Study of the Consolation of Philosophy in Anglo-Saxon England," *AHDLMA* 44 (1977): 33–78, here, p. 50. All translations of the excerpts from Remigius's *In Boeth.* are my own.

32. See Courcelle, "Étude critique," pp. 51, 73–76.

33. Courcelle, "Étude critique," p. 7, discusses diverse tenth- and eleventh-century German manuscripts of Boethius commentaries, distinguishing two main groups, one Remigian, one anonymous, which Notker either used directly or from

one of their compilations (pp. 46–47). Naumann, in his study of sources, agrees that Notker's commentary is a compilation of Remigius (R) and one other (X, p. 24), but see esp. pp. 1–23; on the actual Latin apparatus from Remigius also found in Notker, see pp. 34–59; see, for additional comparisons of Notker and other commentaries, especially the Remigian ones, Schroebler, *Die althochdeutschen Boethiusglossen* and also the fuller study by the same author, *Notker III.* The editors of the translation have indicated Notker's sources by following Naumann's practice of identifying Remigius as R and the anonymous commentator as X. That X is probably a version of the Anonymous of St. Gall Major is not only logical, given Notker's stay at St. Gall, but evidenced by recent scholarship, in that, for example, X on Tityus and the vulture (*Consolatio* 3 m12) identifies the vulture as the torments of a guilty conscience, "nihil aliud est intellegentis quam tormenta malae conscientiae," identical to the Anonymous of St. Gall Major—Einsiedeln 179 and St. Gall 845 ("Nihil aliud est intellegentis. quam tormenta male conscientiae obnoxia"). For the edition of Notker's Boethius used in this study, see *Boethius de consolatione Philosophiae*, in *Notkers des deutschen Werke*, ed. E. H. Sehrt and Taylor Starck, vol. 1, parts 1–3, Altdeutsche Textbibliothek, nos. 32–34 (Halle and Saale: Max Niemeyer, 1933–34); and also *Boethius, "De consolatione Philosophiae," Buch I/II-III-IV/V*, ed. Petrus W. Tax, vols. 1–3 of Die Werke Notkers des Deutschen (Tübingen: Max Niemeyer, 1986–90), with pages in the three volumes numbered consecutively as if part of one volume. Translations of many passages in Notker's OHG cited in my text have been provided by Joseph Wilson, who bases them on Sehrt's "Notker-Glossar," Sehrt and Legner's "Notker-Wortschatz," and comparison with the Latin texts. Apparently Notker also used the Remigian commentary on Martianus extensively in his glosses on that work, according to the editor of that work, Karl Schulte, *Das Verhältnis von Notkers Nuptiae Philologiae et Mercurii zum Kommentar des Remigius Antissiodorensis*, vol. 3, pt. 2 of *Forschungen und Funde*, ed. Franz Jostes (Münster i.W.: Aschendorffsche, 1911), p. 18, which includes parallel texts of Remigius and Notker on Martianus.

34. Courcelle, "Étude critique," p. 47. There is an old edition of the Provençal Boethius edited by Franz Hündgen, *Das altprovenzalische Boethiuslied unter Beifügung einer Übersetzung, eines Glossars, erklärender Anmerkungen, sowie grammatischer und metrischer Untersuchungen* (Oppeln, 1884), with a translation in German.

35. "Peritos autem dico magis illos, qui in sacra Scriptura quam qui in dialectica sunt instructi; nam dialecticos quosdam ita simplices inveni, ut omnia Sacrae Scripturae dicta iuxta dialecticae auctoritatem constringenda esse decernerent magisque Boetio quam sanctis scriptoribus in plurimis dictis crederent," cited by Martin Grabmann, *Die Geschichte der scholastischen Methode: Nach den gedruckten und ungedruckten Quellen*, 2 vols. (Freiburg im Breisgau and St. Louis: Herder, 1909–11, rpt. Graz: Akademische Druck- und Verlagsanstalt, 1957), 1:230, and discussed by Courcelle, "Étude critique," pp. 77–78.

36. For the Anonymous Bruxellensis—the gloss on *Consolatio* 3 m9 found in

Brussels, Bibliothèque Royale MS. 10066–77, fols. 157v–8r, believed at one time to be a portion of the missing ninth-century commentary by John Scot—see the edition by Hubert Silvestre, "Le Commentaire inédit de John Scot Érigène au mètre IX du livre III du 'De consolatione Philosophiae' de Boèce," *Revue d'histoire ecclésiastique* 47 (1952): 44–122. Silvestre, pp. 44–45, believes that this fragmentary commentary and not the Silk edition of the Anonymous Erfurt commentator represents the work of John Scot, largely because Courcelle, "Étude critique," convincingly placed the Anonymous Erfurt in the twelfth century and thus excluded a ninth-century attribution. Silvestre compares the Bruxellensis with Remigius's commentary to conclude it is distinct from Remigius's—more characteristic of John Scot's style in *De divisione naturae*—and possibly itself used by Remigius in his commentary (pp. 48ff). Courcelle, *La Consolation,* pp. 290–91, agrees with Silvestre that the Brussels commentary differs from that of Remigius, but he argues that it is not by John Scot, merely better put together and more intelligent.

37. See Bovo II of Corvey, "In Boetium de consolatione Philosophiae lib. III, metr. IX, commentarius," *PL* 64:1239–46; discussed by Manitius, "Beiträge zur Geschichte der römischen Prosaiker im Mittelalter" and "Beiträge zur Geschichte der römischen Dichter im Mittelalter," in *Philologus* 47–56 (1888–97) and supplement 7 (1899): 526–29; Huygens, "Mittelalterliche Kommentare zum 'O Qui Perpetua,' " *Sacris erudiri* 6 (1954): 373–427; and Édouard Jeauneau, "Un Commentaire inédit sur le chant 'O qui perpetua' de Boèce," *Rivista critica di storia della filosofia* 14 (1959): 62, who discusses it as a combination of Remigius and the Anonymous Bruxellensis.

38. Manitius, "Beiträge," p. 527.

39. Adalbold of Utrecht's commentary has been edited by Huygens, "Mittelalterliche Kommentare," pp. 404–27, and edited and discussed by Tullio Gregory, "Il commento a Boezio di Adalboldo di Utrecht," *Platonismo medievale, Studi e ricerche,* Istituto Storico Italiano per il Medio Evo. Storio Storici.—Fasc. 26/27 (Rome: Nella Sede dell'Istituto, 1958), pp. 1–16. Edmund Taite Silk describes it as indebted to Bovo II in "Pseudo-Johannes Scottus, Adalbold of Utrecht, and the Early Commentaries on Boethius," *MRS* 3 (1954): 1–40.

40. For the Anonymous Monacensis, see Courcelle, "La Consolation," p. 305; it appeared in Jeauneau, "Un Commentaire inédit," p. 62.

41. Because the editors of Notker have included the Latin from Remigius and the Anonymous of St. Gall, it is relatively easy to see the extent of Notker's originality or dependency on his Latin sources (most glosses suggest the latter). For example, Cerberus is identified as having three heads and being a door-guardian and an infernal dog, from the Remigian gloss "Stupet ter-geminus ianitor .i. cerberus . infernalis canis": "Erchám síh tô dér dríu hóubet hábento túro-uuárt," "Then the three-headed doorkeeper became frightened," Sehrt and Starck, p. 241; Tax, p. 180.

42. See Naumann, pp. 24–25, 60–70. Among these contributions Naumann lists a deeper religious Christian orientation and a more learned theological perspective; summaries of chapters; definitions (for example, of the *summum bonum*), and *sententia;* citations of classical authors not in R (Remigius) or X (probably Anonymous of St. Gall), such as Aristotle, Martianus, Terence, Pacuvius, Boethius's other works, Virgil, Servius, Isidore, Solinus, Cato, the *Ad Herennium,* Cicero, Priscian, Sallust, Livy, Suetonius, and Macrobius (commentary on the *Somnium Scipionis*); all of these, of course, might have been available together in *florilegia* or in other commentaries, as in Remigius's Sedulius commentary (Naumann, pp. 62–63); see also Schroebler, *Notker III,* p. 153, on the authors named by Notker; citations of Christian authors not in R or St. Gall, such as Augustine, Gregory's *Homilies,* the Rule of St. Benedict, Orosius, Bede, Ambrosius, Isidore (Naumann, pp. 62–63; Schroebler, *Notker III,* p. 156, suggests that Notker may have known Augustine through John Scot's *De divina predestinatione,* and such indirect contact possibly true of other sources as well); autobiographical or personal details; logical and rhetorical comments; and finally, alterations in the commentaries of R and St. Gall, whether expansions or omissions.

43. Schroebler, *Die althochdeutschen Boethiusglossen,* p. 43.

44. Notker merely explains why the Trojan War was initiated and why Agamemnon was a "sorrowing priest" (Notker glosses this as "Chalcas," Sehrt and Starck, p. 323; Tax, p. 228, as has Remigius, apparently thinking of the sacrifice of daughters common to the two "priests"), followed by a brief relation of Ulysses's adventure in Sicily with Polyphemus.

45. Notker on Boethius, Tax, p. 211.

46. The passage in Boethius begins, "Locus Communis si confundat copia" ["Should Plenty pour from cornucopia full / As much in riches as the sand / Stirred up by wind-whipped seas"], in *Consolatio* 2 m2.

47. Notker on Boethius, Sehrt and Starck, p. 233; Tax, pp. 175–76. That "Babel" and "Babylon" were regarded as identical, at least in the Middle Ages, "Nimrod" and "Nebuchadnezzar" the same, is attested by the recovery of the towering Gate of Ishtar (sixth century B.C.) and the Processional Way to the city of Babylon and its preservation in the Museum of Western Asiatic Antiquity in Berlin. See Joachim Marzahn, *The Ishtar Gate* (Mainz: Staatliche Museen zu Berlin Vorderasiatisches Museum, 1992) for a full description. Cf. chapter 10, pp. 616–17n46.

48. "For he who overcome should turn back his gaze / Towards the Tartarean cave, / Whatever excellence he takes with him / He loses when he looks on those below" (*Consolatio* 3 m12). See also chapter 4, pp. 140–41.

49. "Uuánda dér síh tára-nâh kelóubet . únde áber uuídere síhet zedero héllo . sînên gelüsten fólgendo . tér ferlíuset tára séhendo . táz er tíures keuuán" ["For whoever later rejects that and again looks back to hell, following his lusts, he will lose, while looking there, the precious thing he had gained"], that is, "spiritualia

bona . Iuxta illud in euangelio . Manum ponens in aratro . et respiciens retro . non est aptus regno dei" (Sehrt and Starck, p. 243; Tax, p. 181). In the Remigius Boethius revisers, "Ut non respiciatis ea quae sprevistis, videlicet ne aliquis ad lucem perennem tendens respiciat retro. Unde legitur: nemo mittens manum suam super aratrum respiciens retro aptus esse potest regno Dei," ed. Bolton, "Study," p. 66, on *Consolatio* 3 m12.

50. The whole *Consolatio* 3 m12 gloss is included in Sehrt and Starck, pp. 240–43; Tax, pp. 179–181; it has been discussed by John Block Friedman, *Orpheus in the Middle Ages* (Cambridge, Mass.: Harvard University Press, 1970), pp. 102–4, although Friedman's interesting discussion of the Orpheus gloss is partly invalidated by his assumption that Remigius on Boethius is the same text as that of the twelfth-century Anonymous Erfurt. And Notker's gloss on Ixion (father of the Centaurs, who slept with clouds in the shape of Juno) is virtually identical, in Old High German, to Remigius's Latin, with Ixion representing lust (because of his desire for Juno), except for Notker's labeling of the tale as an "exemplum" to demonstrate his interest in rhetoric rather than in morally distasteful matters (Sehrt and Starck, p. 241; Tax, p. 180); taken from the first Vatican mythographer, 14/14.

51. "Tér gáb sînen sún pelopem fúre frísking zeézenne diis et deabus. ze besûochenne íro diuinitatem" ["He gave his son Pelops as a sacrifice to the *diis* and *deabus* {for them} to eat, to test their *divinitatem*"], Sehrt and Starck, p. 242; Tax, p. 180; Remigius borrows from the first Vatican mythographer, 12/12.

52. "Díu fabula mánôt únsih tés ["The fable admonishes us of that"]. quia libido cuius sedes est in iecore. semel expleta non extinguitur ! sed recrudescit itervm," Sehrt and Starck, p. 242; Tax, p. 181, with the narration of the story in Remigius coming from the first Vatican mythographer, 13/13, and the moralization of Tityus as lechery from Servius, *In Aen.* 6.596.

53. From Remigius on Martianus come several Notker glosses on Boethius. Borrowing from Remigius on the Argive beloved of Janus, or Juno (*De nuptiis* 4) and then on Virgil, Notker uses citations to explain the Boethian concept of love as a law to itself when Orpheus fails. To underscore the instinctive response of love Notker begins with, "Quis enim modus assit amori," as a lead-in to Virgil, "Omnia uincit amor," coupled with the phrase from the Martianus commentary, "ubi amor. ibi oculus" ["where is love, there is the eye"], or "pedíu lóse dir. uuîo iz kefûor" ["therefore listen to how it happened"] (Sehrt and Starck, p. 243; Tax, p. 181). It is possible that a gloss on Boethius's Saturn was derived from Remigius's commentary on Martianus also, in that "cold, old Saturn" whom Boethius calls the "companion of that flashing sphere," Phoebus (*Consolatio* 4 m1), is described in detail not only as a *senex* and also a star whose coldness is explained by the length of his orbit (Sehrt and Starck, pp. 248–49). The sun, Phoebus, is identified as Christ, in a passage not drawn from Remigius. It is possible that the references to Mercury, Saturn, and the sun were influenced, at least in part, by

the plethora of ninth-century and later comments on Boethius's "O qui perpetua" (3 m9), given its list of planets and its Neoplatonic interpretation as the World Soul.

54. Notker does not allegorize the details as does Remigius: "Únde dóh tér infógeles uuîs flîegendo mercurius. tér in cillenio monte archadię, geûobet uuárd. ten nôtháften hérezógen úmbe irbármeda lôsti. fóne sînero uuírtenno gífte. îo dóh tie férien. dîe hábetôn úbel lîd getrúnchen. Mercurius tér alatis talariis kemâlêt uuírt. táz chît. mít kefídertên scúhen. dîe grece petasi héizent. tér máneta vlixem. dáz er fermíte circe. Tô iz áber sô geskáh. táz er úndánches tára chám. únde sî ánderên scancta. dáz ér trínchen neuuólta. tô téta ín is mercurius pûoz. mít sînero uirga. díu caduceus kenémmet uuás. tíu gágen állên díngen láchenháfte uuás" ["And yet Mercury, who flew like a bird, who was worshiped on *cillenio monte archadię,* liberated the distressed commander, out of pity, from the poison of his hostess; however, the sailors had drunk bad {poisoned} drink. Mercury is depicted *alatis talariis,* that is, with feathered shoes, which are called *grece petasi;* he admonished Ulysses to avoid Circe. However, when it happened that he was forced to go there, and she was giving drink to others, that he didn't want to drink; then Mercury freed them from that with his *virga,* which was called *caduceus,* which was a cure for anything"] (Sehrt and Starck, p. 273; Tax, p. 200. Cf. Remi., *In Mart.* 6.6, 9.11, 9.14).

55. Sehrt and Starck, p. 325; Tax, p. 229. A related fluvial emphasis appears in the third long gloss, on the battle between Hercules and the river Achelous who changes into a bull to fight (and be defeated by) Hercules, who takes away his horns: "Állíu uuázer sínt hórnahtíu. fóne dîen bóumen. dîe dâr úmbe stânt. Tér die bóuma dána tûot. tér hábet siu hórnlôs ketân. Uuánda óuh hercules ten stád errûmda des uuáldes. pedíu hábet er fluuio sîníu hóren genómen" ["All waters are 'horned' by the trees {lined with trees} that are around them. He who takes away the trees has made them hornless, for Hercules also cleared the riverbank of forest, and in that way he took away Fluvius's horns"] (Sehrt and Starck, p. 326; Tax, p. 229).

56. "Dánnân flúhen sie in strophades insulas. dâr sie ęneas fánt" ["From there they fled to the *strophades insulas,* where Aeneas found them"] (Sehrt and Starck, p. 324; Tax, p. 228).

57. Notker on Martianus has been edited by Schulte in *Das Verhältnis von Notkers Nuptiae,* with the text, Latin and Old High German, on pp. 1–89, and commentary on Notker on pp. 93–119. On Notker's method, see Schulte, p. 98: "Wenn 822,22 für summus die doppelte Wiedergabe méister . álde méisto ["master, or most {greatest, first}"] erscheint, so rührt dies daher, daß Notker aus summus manium hoc est princeps die Erklärung und das Erklärte übersetzt." The text is contained in MS. 872 of St. Gall Library, which, according to Schulte, "ist sicher nicht Notkers Exemplar, vielmehr liegen zwischen dem Original und Cod. 872 mehrere Glieder" (p. 103). He includes P. Piper's 1882 edition of Notker

here. All references to page numbers are to Schulte; translations from the Old High German are by Joseph Wilson.

58. In Claudio Leonardi, "I codici di Marziano Capella," *Aevum* 33 (1959): 469. Leonardi describes the extensive influence of Martianus after the Carolingian period and continuing into the eleventh century as a contribution to mythography, as a fundamental text of the schools, and as an example of the cultural legacy of the seven arts (pp. 469–71). On the commentaries in general see Robin Flower, "Irish Commentaries on Martianus Capella," *Zeitschrift für celtische Philologie* 8 (1912): 566–77.

59. See Leonardi, "I codici," p. 469. These minor tenth- and eleventh-century commentators (or glossators) will be discussed below; for Stefano di Novara, see Luigi Foscolo Benedetto, " 'Stephanus grammaticus' da Novara (sec. x)," *SM* 3 (1910): 499–500, which provides a summary of his life from lines of epitaphs.

60. Manitius, *Geschichte* 9.2.1:254.

61. For this Belgian Benedictine's Martianus glosses in Leiden Bibl. Voss. lat. 48, 2r–91v, see Leonardi, "Raterio e Marziano Capella," *Italia medioevale et umanistica* 2 (1959): 73–102, esp. tables 1–4, pp. 84, 88, 92, and 96, and more generally on his life and career, the article "Rathier, Evêque de Verone," in *HLF*. In addition, Leonardi, "I codici," discusses his life (pp. 339–47), the manuscripts, and glosses on his works (pp. 348–83). For an edition mostly of his late and patriotic works (written 961–968), see Petrus L. D. Reid, ed., *Ratherii Veronensis opera minora*, CCCM 46 (Turnhout: Brepols, 1976), but which does not include the Capella glosses; pp. xxii–xxxiii contains a good bibliography of his late works and works about him. One of the first editions of his works was that of the Ballerini brothers, *Ratherii . . . opera* (Verona, 1765), cols. 30–31, reprinted in *PL* 136:27–138.

62. See Leonardi, "Raterio e Marziano Capella," in which some of his interlinear and marginal glosses on Martianus are included, pp. 87–92. There are marginalia only on the first chapter of the first book (*De nuptiis* 1–22, 68–70), and on the books of the quadrivium (geometry, occasionally arithmetic, and with special insistence on the books of astronomy and music), according to Leonardi, p. 85. The *lettura* of Rather appears to be concentrated on the ninth book (music), part on the introduction, the final chiusura, and musical notions. The major source, according to Leonardi, "Raterio," p. 94, is Martin of Laon.

63. For Liutprand von Cremona, see Manitius, *Geschichte* 9.2.2:166–75.

64. See the *Gesta Berengarii imperatoris*, in *Poetae Latini aevi Carolini*, ed. Paul von Winterfeld, in *Poetarum Latinorum medii aevi*, vol. 4, fasc. 1, in *MGH* (Berlin, 1899), pp. 354, 361, 371, 392. For his sources, see Manitius, *Geschichte* 9.2.2:634–35, and G. Bernheim, "Der Glossator der *Gesta Berengarii imperatoris*," *Forschungen zur deutschen Geschichte* 14 (1874): 138–54.

65. For Gunzo (d. 967), see "Gunzon, Grammairien," *HLF* 6:386–93; also Manitius, *Geschichte* 9.2.2:532–33.

66. See Ann Rose Raia, "Barberini Manuscripts 57–66 and 121–130" (diss., Fordham University, 1965), esp. pp. 189–209, where she discusses the Anonymous Barberinus accessus written in a late Carolingian script and the anonymous marginal and interlinear glosses on the first two books of a manuscript from the late twelfth century, Barb. lat. 10. It is probable, then, that the original commentary was written during the late Carolingian period and recopied in the late twelfth century. The description of the thirty manuscripts in the Vatican containing the text of Martianus, four of these specifically in the Barberini collection, is found on pp. 167–88.

67. According to Raia, p. 195ff, only Remigius, of the three chief Carolingian commentaries, influenced this Barberinus commentary and, where Remigius is not used, it is original. The Barberinus cites Remigius by name only four times. See pp. 196–98 for examples of the four kinds of borrowing from Remigius. The text—keyed through notes to Lutz's edition—begins on p. 205 and concludes on p. 323.

68. Raia, p. 199, provides examples of the five types of original contribution to Martianus commentary by the Anonymous Barberinus: etymologies (see 14.14; 4.13; 4.16; 5.2; 5.11; 6.6; 9.9; 11.17; 14.10; 56.25); explications, that is, paraphrases or explanations of texts (see 8.7; 3.15; 4.20; 6.20; 10.22; 12.9; 14.19; 26.3, and passim); allegorical explanations (see 13.21; 10.14; 10.20; 11.21; 13.1; 13.2; 15.8; 15.17; and passim); reading aids, especially in book 2 (see 18.10; 18.2; 18.6; 32.15; 38.15; 38.17; 40.6; 46.16; and passim); and lexicography (see 6.15, 3.5; 4.13; 4.19; 5.7; 5.21; 6.21; 7.1; 8.2; passim).

69. Raia concludes, pp. 201–2, that the Anonymous Barberinus resembled Remigius in vocation, with these glosses probably lecture notes, given the manner in which Remigius is abstracted, the aspect of new contributions, the regularity of the shorthand notes, and the author's decision to write in the margins and not on a separate folio. Further, the additions made to Remigius are largely philological (definitions, etymologies), or else explicative of text or allegory, often made in an obvious or trivial way, especially toward the end.

70. Raia, p. 200, notes the following original Barberinus statements as having a mythological nature: see 3.5; 5.20; 5.22; 9.12; 24.14; 26.13–14; 33.14; 37.4; 37.6; 39.14; 42.6, and passim.

71. For example, the Muses, "sángcúttenna," "Song-goddesses," are glossed individually with Latin terms as in Remigius (*In Mart.* 19.17–20.5), that is, Urania "díu celestis héizet" ["who is called *celestis*], Polymnia "dáz chît plurima memoria" ["that is, *plurima memoria*"], Euterpe "tíu delectatio uoluntatis heîzet" ["who is called *delectatio uoluntatis*"] (Notker, pp. 20–21). And the Penates become merely "penates. sámoso panates. dáz chît omnia consentientes" (Notker, p. 26, from Remigius 26.4, "as if *panates,* that is, consenting to all"). The same is true of the Parcae (Notker, p. 29), glossed as they are in Fulgentius and in Remigius, and of the famous passage on the Pythagorean letter Y found in a variety of sources

including Remigius: Pythagoras of Samos declared that it symbolized the choice between good and evil in human life through its bifurcations (from Servius, *In Aen.* 6.136); after the straight path of childhood there is a fork, the path of virtue to the right, the path of vice to the left, with Notker duplicating the Remigian passage (*In Mart.* 43.18). Notker declares, "íh méino. y. dér fóne éinemo cínken ín zuêne síh spáltet. álso óuh ter ménnisco nâh tero chíndiscun eínfalti. éinuuéder gefáhet ze zéseuuun. álde ze uuínsterun. dáz chît ad uirtutes. álde ad uitia" ["I mean *y*, which divides itself from one staff into two, as the human after the simplicity of childhood turns either to the right or to the left, that is, *ad virtutes* or *ad vitia*"], Notker, p. 50.

72. For Notker's sources here, James C. King, *Notker latinus zum Martianus Capella,* vol. 4A of Die Werke Notkers des Deutschen (Tübingen: Max Niemeyer, 1986), p. 37.

73. Pluto, called "Dis" because the underworld receives all and is insatiable (Remi., *In Mart.* 35.20), is paraphrased in Old High German: "Uuánda diu hélla ferslindet ál dazter lébet. sî neuuírdet nîomer sât" ["For hell devours all that lives; it never gets enough {to devour}"] (Notker, p. 40). Neptune's wife, the "nurse of all things, the hostess of the gods" (*De nuptiis* 81), in Notker is "állero góto mágazohun" ["the nurse of all {the} gods"] (p. 40); Styx is the wife of Neptune, because all gods must be purged of earth ("omnes dii de terris per purgationem, quam styx significat, caeleste meruerunt consortium," Remi., *In Mart.* 36.2): "sîna chénun stigem. dáz chît purificationem . . . . Uuánda dii terrestres neuuúrtin nîomer cęlestes. úbe síe in stige [palude] neuuúrtin purificati. Díu tóufi gáb in cęleste consortium" ["his wife Styx, that is, *purificationem. . . .* For *dii terrestres* would never become *cęlestes* unless they were *purificati* in Stγx *{palude}*. Baptism gave them *cęleste consortium*"] (Notker, p. 40). Lethe, or rather Lethean shores (to which sleep flees when Aurora or Day appears, and which indeed in Remi., *In Mart.* 49.5 is the Latin for the Greek "sleep, or oblivion"), denotes in one gloss a river in which the souls forget everything of the body; the passage appears in Old High German heavily Latinized: "uuánda er obliuionem máchot. álso óuh tíu sélba áha tûot tien sêlon post mortem dâr trínchentên" ["For he causes *obliuionem,* as does the same river to the souls drinking there *post mortem*"] (Notker, p. 58). So also Vedius (Pluto) is identified in Remigius (*In Mart.* 61.23) as Vedivus, or "malus divus," because he inspires souls with terror, and as Orcus, the Greek word for "I swear," because he swears that he will let no soul go without punishment ("quia terrorem incutit animabus. Ipse est et Orcus. Orco Grece iuro, inde Orcus dictus quia quodam modo iurat quod nullam animam sine poena dimittat"). Notker again preserves much of the Latin denotation: "tîe ín héizent uedium. álso malum diuum. uuánda ér brúti tûot tien sêlon. Dér héizet óuh orcus. táz chît iurator. Uués íst er iurator? Áne dáz er ímo gelâzene animas. nelâze inpunitas" ["They {the Etruscan philosophers} call him Vedius, that is, Malus Divus, because he inspires souls with terror. He is also called Orcus which means

iurator {judge, one who is sworn}. For what reason is he *iurator,* except that he should not leave unpunished the souls committed to him?"] (Notker, pp. 71–72). Charon, the navigator for souls on the river Styx (Remi., *In Mart.* 62.2), performs his duty after death: "álle sêlâ charon dero héllo túrouuárt tâte des tôdes kechôron. fóre dero inmortalitate" ["Charon, the doorkeeper of hell, makes all souls taste death before *inmortalitate*"] (Notker, p. 72).

Notker also conserves Latin in the passages on aerial inhabitants such as the *daemones,* who are both good and bad, and are often understood as the angels: "(dero demonum gûoti). Also uuír angelos chédên bonos et malos. sô châden die álten. bonos demones et malos" [{"the goodness (virtue, quality) of the *demonum*}: as we say *angelos bonos et malos,* the ancients said *bonos demones et malos*"] (Notker, p. 73, from Remi., *In Mart.* 64.12). The *lemures* are the *lares* after death, "táz chît lares morantes," and the *larue* are evil *lares,* "dáz chît lares mali"; the *manie* are the insane, "dáz chît insanientes," and so forth in the other spheres (Notker, pp. 76–77; Remi., *In Mart.* 68.7–8).

74. Jacobs, p. xi. One example of this confusion can be found in the 1212 catalogue of books in the Amplonian Library in Erfurt: "Commentum Bernhardi Silvestris super Theodulum" runs the entry. Jacobs thinks it was a copy of the commentary by the Utrechtian Bernard, largely because in the same century Paris, B.N. MS. lat. 15, fol. 158, attributed to Bernard Silvestris a passage actually found in the Bernard of Utrecht commentary. In contrast, Hamilton argues for two commentaries, one by each of the Bernards; Quinn believes that Bernard Silvestris indeed wrote a different commentary, which is now lost.

75. Jacobs, p. viii. Huygens, "Notes sur le *Dialogus super auctores,*" indicates that Conrad of Hirsau in his introduction to *Dialogus super auctores* depends on the commentary on the *Ecloga Theoduli* by Bernard of Utrecht (p. 420). See also p. 420n1 on the dating.

76. Jacobs declares on p. xvin25 that some Neckam manuscripts show an association with the *Liber Catonianus,* for example, Munich MS. Clm. 391, which contains six of the school texts and the *Ethica Catonis* with commentary, and also other British manuscripts, Lincoln 132, Digby 100, Can. Lat. 72, and so forth.

77. See *Liber de scriptoribus ecclesiasticis,* cap. 169, *PL* 160:586. In addition to Sigebert of Gembloux and Conrad of Hirsau, Honorius of Autun (actually of Regensberg) used the *Vita Theoduli.*

78. Jacobs, pp. 9–10. All references to the commentary by Bernard derive from Huygens, ed. *Commentum in Theodolum,* Biblioteca degli "Studi medievali" (Spoleto: Centro Italiano di Studi sull'Alto Medioevo, 1977), which also prints a text of the *Ecloga.* But see also Jacobs, pp. 1–123, which includes Bernard's letter to Conrad and the accessus to the text; Huygens's does not. Of the eight manuscripts of Bernard's commentary (only one of which is unabridged and without gaps, Jacobs, p. xxx), Jacobs has used six, excluding the two from Einsiedeln and Salzburg. His main manuscript, one with "a careless and even

corrupt transcription," is M for Munich Staatsbibliothek, MS. Clm. 22293, fols. 1v–41r. In Jacobs's edition are two appendices, containing Osternacher's text of the original tenth-century *Ecloga Theoduli*, pp. 218–29, and a second containing the Epistola Bernardi "ex MS Hardenhousano," the text of Martene and Durand of Bernard's dedication to Conrad of Utrecht. To summarize the recent history of Bernard's *Ecloga* commentary, in 1904 Frey published part of Bernard's prologue and comments on two of Theodulus's quatrains; in 1954 Huygens published the critical text of the epistle and in 1977 the full text. For the idea of commentary, and this commentary, as literary criticism, see Guthrie, "The Ecloga," esp. p. 83 and pp. 230–40, and, on Bernard, pp. 86–101. The idea of commentary as criticism has been argued by Alastair Minnis and Judson Boyce Allen in a number of texts over the past twenty years; it is the foundation of this entire study.

79. "Primum itaque que et quot in librorum principiis antiqui et moderni requirenda censent proposui et exposui, deinde Theodoli eglogam ad literam, et allegorice, et plerisque in locis moraliter explanavi, novissime vero dictionum quoque naturas pueris pueriliter aperui" (Jacobs, p. 2).

80. Jacobs, p. 9.

81. Jacobs, pp. 10–11.

82. For the fable of Lycaon turned to wolf, in his commentary on Ecclesiastes, Holkot turned to Stephen Patrington's commentary on the *Ecloga,* according to Beryl Smalley, *English Friars and Antiquity in the Early Fourteenth Century* (Oxford: Blackwell, 1960), p. 157n1; see also Judson Boyce Allen, "The Library of a Classicizer: The Sources of Robert Holkot's Mythographic Learning," in *Arts libéraux et philosophie au Moyen Âge* (Montreal: Institut d'Études Médiévales, 1969), p. 729.

83. See Manitius, *Geschichte* 9.2.3:194–96, and Osternacher on Martianus.

84. Following Huygens's notes, and going through the *Ecloga*'s mythological material quatrain by quatrain in order where myths appear, we can detect Bernard's borrowings from the first two Vatican mythographers as follows (all fable numbers are from the Bode edition): for Saturn (*Ecl. Theod.* 37–40) as son of Pollux, Celius, or Demiorgon, from Mythogr. I 102, and as Cronos (Time), from Mythogr. II 1 or Fulgentius, *Mit.* 1.2; Hebe, son of Jove and Juno (45–48) from Mythogr. I 184; the battle between Minerva and Neptune over the naming of Athens (53–56) from Mythogr. II 39 or Fulgentius, *Mit.* 2.1; Lycaon transforming into wolf (61–64), from Mythogr. I 17 and II 60; Deucalion and Pyrrha (69–72) from Mythogr. I 189 and II 73; the abduction of Ganymede by Jove's eagle (77–80) from Mythogr. I 184 and II 198, 3; the Gigantomachia (85–88) from Mythogr. II 53 and I 204; the death of Peonis (93–96) from Mythogr. I 46 and II 128; Daedalus and Icarus, and Pasiphaë and Minos (101–4), from Mythogr. I 43 and II 126; Phyllis and Demophoon (109–12) from Mythogr. I 159 and II 214; Aeneas meeting Venus disguised as a cloud (117–20) from Mythogr. I 141 and II 229 and Diomedes as a bird from Mythogr. I 143; Hippolytus and Phaedra

(125–28) from Mythogr. I 46 and II 128; Europa and Jove (141–44) from Mythogr. I 148–49; Cadmus searching for Europa (141–44) from Mythogr. II 198; the avarice of Eriphile (149–52) from Mythogr. I 151–52 and II 78; Amphiaraus sent to the underworld (149–52) from Mythogr. I 43; Io's mutation (157–60) from Mythogr. I 18 and II 5 and 89; the conception of Hercules (166–69) from Mythogr. II 148 and I 50, Hercules as *heracleos* from Fulgentius, *Mit.* 2.2 and Mythogr. II 155, and Juno as Axiona from Mythogr. II 107; Tricerberus (170–73) from Mythogr. I 64, Deianira's cape from Mythogr. I 91 and II 70, Geryon from Mythogr. II 152 and I 68, Hydra from Mythogr. I 62, Cerberus as earth from Mythogr. II 149–50, and Alcides as virtue from Mythogr. II 149–50; for Orpheus as son of Apollo and Calliope (189–92) from Mythogr. II 44 and Fulgentius, *Mit.* 3.10; Mercury as Cyllenius (197–200) from Mythogr. I 18; Ceres (205–8) from Mythogr. II 227 and II 15, also Fulgentius, *Mit.* 1.10 and 11; the Gorgon and etymologies (213–16) from Fulgentius, *Mit.* 1.21 and Mythogr. I 130 and 131, Medusa's history from Mythogr. II 112 and 167, and for Bellerophon from Fulgentius, *Mit.* 3.1; the horses of the sun and their names (245–48) from Fulgentius, *Mit.* 1.12 and Mythogr. II 21, and for Phaeton's genealogy from Mythogr. I 118 and II 57; Danaë (253–56) from Mythogr. I 157, II 110, and Fulgentius, *Mit.* 1.19; Niobe (261–64) from Mythogr. II 71; Tereus (271) from Mythogr. I 4 and II 217; Scylla and her father (277–80) from Mythogr. I 3 and II 123; the Muses (285–88) from Fulgentius, *Mit.* 1.15, Mythogr. I 114, and Mythogr. II 24; Mopsus and Calchas (325–28), from Mythogr. I 194 and II 224; and finally, Ulysses's false eloquence (329–32) from Mythogr. I 35 and II 200.

85. "Aiunt enim Pythagoram et alios quosdam ex animalibus vesci prohibuisse, quem errorem Cicrops damnans pecora interfecit et comedit, affirmans haec creata in usum vescendi. Sanguinem autem non comedendum censuit, quem animam dixerunt esse antiqui. Unde sacra dicitur fecisse Iovi. Civitatem etiam condidit, quam a philosophorum multitudine inmortalem appellavit: sapientia enim semper viget" ["They say, truly, that Pythagoras and others prohibited the eating of any animal, which error Cecrops damning killed and ate flocks, affirming that those things were created to eat. Moreover he judged that blood was not to be eaten, which the ancients thought to be the soul. Whence he is said to have made offerings to Jove. Likewise he founded a city, which he called 'immortal' for its multitude of philosophers: wisdom indeed always flourishes"] (Bernard, *In Theod.* 2.158–64; Huygens, p. 37).

86. "Haec ab Aristeo tantum, id est ab optimo apprehendi laboratur. Ipsa enim ars ad paucos venit, quia ictu, id est astutia, serpentis intercepta, in secreta velut in infernum intrat. Sed ad hanc inquirendam Orpheus, id est cantorum vox, descendit inventamque elevat. Sed non est fas Orpheo eam aspicere nisi velit eam amittere, quia dum peritissimus Pytagoras numeros modis symphoniasque terminis et rithmos melis aptaret, horum non potuit reddere rationes, quas perquirere si insisteret, quod de arte tenebat elaberetur" ["This only by Aristaeus, that is,

{Eurydice} labors to be apprehended by the best {i.e., Aristaeus}. Art itself, moreover, comes to the few, because being intercepted by the strike, i.e., cunning of the serpent, she enters into secret places, that is, the underworld. But Orpheus, the voice of song, in searching for her, descends and once she is discovered raises her up. But it is not divine will for Orpheus to behold her unless he wishes to lose her because when the most learned Pythagoras fitted numbers to modes and symphonies to limits {ends, endings}, and rhythms to songs, he could not give reasons for these, and if he persisted in searching them {reasons} out, he would lose what he had of art"] (Bernard, *In Theod.* 3.110–130; Huygens, p. 80).

87. "Ipse enim internuncius est deorum, unde et medius fidius dicitur. Virgam, id est caduceum, ferre dicitur, cuius uno capite animas in morte sopit, alio vitae revocat. Dixerunt enim quidam animas privatas corpore in inferno puniri quae in corpore peccaverunt, denique punitas denuo intrare corpora, cui rei Mercurium dicebant preesse" ["He is moreover the messenger of the gods, whence he is called 'medius fidius' {so help me God}. He is said to carry a rod, that is, a caduceus, with one head of which lulls souls to sleep in death, with the other calls them back to life. Some have said that souls deprived of the body are punished in the underworld because they have sinned in the body, finally those punished again enter bodies, a matter which Mercury is said to be in charge of"] (Bernard, *In Theod.* 3.172–73; Huygens, p. 82).

88. "Alii Mercurium sermonem accipiunt, a Greco tractum *hymeneus,* quod est disserere; qui et Cillenius a mobilitate vel velocitate dicitur. Nichil enim sermone velocius, Oratio teste qui ait: *semel emissum volat irrevocabile verbum*" ["Others call Mercury discourse, from the Greek called *hymeneus,* which is to discuss, and who is called Cyllenius from his mobility or speed. Nothing indeed is faster than speech, according to Horace who says, 'once emitted the word flies, irrevocable' "]. Finally, his role as speech in relation to his role in the underworld is explored. "Hic sopire virga et excitare animas dicitur, quia sermone ad quod libet faciendum erigimur eodemque a qualibet re avertimur. Superum autem et inferorum dicitur internuncius, quia quod cogitatione concipitur, verbo ad noticiam dirigitur. Denique tantae est efficatiae, ut homo, cum sit moralis, in hoc similis deo videatur, quod quae intus concipit, quibuslibet sensualibus extra explicari possit. Nam cum animalia cetera quibuslibet sonis suos aperiant affectus, longe tamen sunt ab ista dignitate et amplitudine sermonis qui est hominis" ["This rod is said to lull to sleep and arouse souls, because by discourse we are aroused to doing something or other and we are in the same way turned away from something or other. He is called the messenger between the upper and lower worlds because what is conceived in thought is brought to knowledge by words {speech}. Finally he is of such effectiveness that man, since he is moral, in this respect is like a god, because what he conceives within can be explained by the senses without. For although animals reveal their feelings by certain sounds, nevertheless they are far

from that dignity and fullness of speech which is man's"] (Bernard, *In Theod.* 3.202–11; Huygens, p. 83).

89. Bernard's quotation of *Ecl. Theod.* 333–36 and his commentary reads: "EGREGIAM SOBOLEM CUI PER STILBONTIS AMOREM VI SUPERUM MAGNA SO-CIASTI TESTE CAPELLA, OBSECRO TE, FRONESI, IUBEAS RETICERE SORORI. Ordo est: OBSECRO TE, FRONESI, ut IUBEAS RETICERE SORORI id est Alithiae PER AMOREM STILBONTIS id est Mercurii CUI SOCIASTI EGREGIAM SOBOLEM id est Philologiam filiam tuam MAGNA VI id est multitudine SUPERUM TESTE CAPELLA Martiano, qui *De nuptiis Philologiae et Mercurii* componit librum, in quo Apollinis consilio et Iovis ceterumque deorum voluntate Philologiam Mercurio nupsisse et artes ei munera dedisse typica dicit ratione" [" 'Phronesis, for the love of Stilbon, to whom, as Capella testifies, you married your distinguished daughter, by the great power of the gods, please tell your sister to be quiet!' The order is, 'Phronesis, please,' 'tell your sister to be quiet,' that is, Alithia, 'for the love of Stilbon,' that is, Mercury, 'to whom you married your distinguished daughter,' that is, Philology, your daughter, 'by the great power,' that is, by a great number 'of the gods, as Capella testifies,' Martianus, who composed the book *The Marriage of Philology and Mercury,* in which by the plan of Apollo and by the will of Jove and all the gods he says in a symbolic way Philology married Mercury and gave the arts to him as gifts"] (Bernard, *In Theod.* 3.1463–71; Huygens, p. 133).

90. "Primum siquidem cuiusque iudicis est in causa veritatem inquirere, deinde equitatis lance inventam eosdem pensare decet, postea ipsi iudices fieri debent intercessores, illius eulogii memores quo dicitur: 'Iudicium sine misericordia illi qui non fecit misericordiam' " ["First indeed it is the duty of each judge to seek out the truth in a case; then it is proper, after it {truth} is discovered, for them to weigh it on the scales of justice; afterwards the judges themselves ought to become intercessors, being mindful of that passage where it is said: 'a judgment without mercy for the man who did not act in mercy' "] (Bernard, *In Theod.* 3.1531–35; Huygens, p. 136).

CHAPTER 10: THE VIRGILIAN JUDGMENT OF PARIS AND THE PROBLEM OF THE BODY

1. See Winthrop Wetherbee, *Platonism and Poetry in the Twelfth Century: The Literary Influence of the School of Chartres* (Princeton: Princeton University Press, 1972); and "Philosophy, Cosmology, and the Twelfth-Century Renaissance," in Peter Dronke, ed., *A History of Twelfth-Century Western Philosophy* (Cambridge, New York, and New Rochelle: Cambridge University Press, 1988), pp. 21–53; Édouard Jeauneau, "Notes sur l'école de Chartres," *SM* 3d series 5 (1964): 821–65; and "Macrobe, source du platonisme chartrain," *SM* 3d series 1 (1960): 3–24, rpt. in *"Lectio philosophorum": Recherches sur l'école de Chartres* (Amsterdam: A.

M. Hakkert, 1973), pp. 279–300; and Tullio Gregory, "The Platonic Inheritance," in Dronke, ed. *A History of Twelfth-Century Western Philosophy*, pp. 54–80.

2. See Dorothy Elford, "William of Conches," in Dronke, ed., *A History of Twelfth-Century Western Philosophy*, pp. 308–27; and, on the Platonic rationalism of William, see John Newell, "Rationalism at the School of Chartres," *Vivarium* 21 (1983): 108–26.

3. William, *Glosae super Platonem: Texte critique avec introduction, notes et tables*, ed. Jeauneau, Textes philosophiques du Moyen Âge, no. 13 (Paris: Librairie Philosophique J. Vrin, 1965), p. 60; Tullio Gregory, *Anima mundi: La filosofia in Guglielmo di Conches e la scuola di Chartres*, Medioevo e rinascimento, no. 3 (Florence: G. C. Sansoni, 1955), pp. 123–74; and also *Platonismo medievale: Studi e ricerche* (Rome: Pubblicazioni dell'Instituto di Filosofia dell'Università di Roma, 1958), pp. 122–38.

4. See Jacqueline Hatinguais, "Points de vue sur la volonté et le jugement dans l'oeuvre d'un humaniste chartrain (Guillaume de Conches, XIIe siècle)," *L'Homme et son destin d'après les penseurs du Moyen Âge. Actes du premier Congrès international de philosophie médiévale* (Louvain: Éditions Nawelaerts; Paris: Beatrice-Nawelaerts, 1960), pp. 417–29.

5. See Brian Stock, *Myth and Science in the Twelfth Century: A Study of Bernard Silvester* (Princeton: Princeton University Press, 1972); Gerard Verbeke, *The Presence of Stoicism in Medieval Thought* (Washington, D.C.: Catholic University Press of America, 1983), pp. 35–44; Michael Lapidge, "The Stoic Inheritance," in Dronke, ed., *A History of Twelfth-Century Western Philosophy*, pp. 81–112.

6. *Moralium dogma philosophorum de Guillaume de Conches*, ed. J. Holmberg (Uppsala: Almqvist and Wicksells, 1929), p. 72; see also Verbeke, p. 9.

7. Theodore Silverstein, "The Fabulous Cosmogony of Bernardus Silvestris," *MP* 46 (1948–49): 92–116; Peter Dronke, *Fabula: Explorations into the Uses of Myth in Medieval Platonism*, Mittellateinische Studien und Texte, vol. 9 (Leiden and Cologne: E. J. Brill, 1974), p. 176n2 and p. 22n, notes that William knew Cicero's *De natura rerum*, especially the second book, on Stoic philosophy.

8. For the argument that the movement was broader, spreading beyond the cathedral school of Chartres, see R. W. Southern, "Humanism and the School of Chartres," in *Medieval Humanism and Other Studies* (Oxford: Oxford University Press; New York and Evanston: Harper & Row, 1970), pp. 61–85; also "The Schools of Paris and the School of Chartres," in *Harvard 1982* (Cambridge, Mass.: Harvard University Press, 1982), pp. 113–37; *Platonism, Scholastic Method, and the School of Chartres* (Reading: University of Reading Press, 1979). These views have been qualified by Dronke, "New Approaches to the School of Chartres," *Annuario di estudios medievales* 6 (1969): 117–40; and by Nikolaus M. Häring, "Chartres and Paris Revisited," in *Essays in Honor of Anton Charles Pegis*, ed. J. R. O'Donnell (Toronto: Pontifical Institute of Mediaeval Studies, 1974), pp. 268–329. For the movement in England, which apparently cherished its own intellectual burgeon-

ing, see the revisionist arguments of Rodney M. Thomson, "England and the Twelfth-Century Renaissance," *Past and Present* 101 (1983): 3–21. A very sensible analysis of the philosophical contribution of all of the twelfth-century schools is contained in F. C. Copleston, *A History of Medieval Philosophy* (London: Methuen, 1972), chapter 7.

9. Jeauneau, "Note," p. 851; rpt. in Jeauneau's *"Lectio philosophorum,"* pp. 5–49.

10. See John of Salisbury, who supplies this biographical information on William in *Metalogicon*, 2.10, ed. Clemens C. J. Webb (Oxford: Clarendon Press, 1929), pp. 79–80: John says, "Deinde reversus in me et metiens vires meas, bona preceptorum meorum gratia, consulto me ad gramaticum [*sic*] de Conchis transtuli" ["However, I recovered my senses, and took stock of my powers. I then transferred, after deliberation and consultation, and with the approval of my instructors, to the grammarian of Conches"], from *The Metalogicon of John of Salisbury: A Twelfth-Century Defense of the Verbal and Logical Arts of the Trivium,* trans. Daniel D. McGarry (Berkeley and Los Angeles: University of California Press, 1962), p. 97. See also Jeauneau, who provides information about William's life in his introduction to the edition of William's *Glosae super Platonem*, pp. 9–10; for William's dates see also p. 14. For information about William's place in the School of Chartres, see Raymond Klibansky, "The School of Chartres," in *Twelfth-Century Europe and the Foundations of Modern Society,* eds. Marshall Clagett, Gaines Post, and Robert Reynolds (Madison, Milwaukee, and London: University of Wisconsin Press, 1966), pp. 3, 14. For Bernard Silvestris's use of William's Boethius commentary, as well as his concept of mythological fable (and his system of descents into the underworld), in his commentary on the *Aeneid* (with the great difference between the two commentators' definitions of "integument"; see below), see Jeauneau, "Note," p. 850, and Dronke, *Fabula,* p. 25.

11. The term *physicus* appears in Paris, B.N. MS. lat. 15130, fol. 125rb. Understanding the term as medical in nature, Jeauneau, "Note," p. 851, believes it was very possible that William "ait commenté l'un ou l'autre de ces traités de médecine qu'il cite sous les noms de Constantin l'Africain, de Johannitius, de Théophile, d'Isaac." For the term *cosmologist* see Wetherbee, "Philosophy, Cosmology, and the Twelfth-Century Renaissance," in Dronke, ed., *A History of Twelfth-Century Western Philosophy,* pp. 21–53: a "group of thinkers . . . united by their interest in the study of the natural universe as an avenue to philosophical and religious understanding," p. 21.

12. Diane K. Bolton, "Manuscripts and Commentaries on Boethius, *De consolatione Philosophiae* in England in the Middle Ages," (diss., Oxford University, 1965), p. 39.

13. For selections from the Florentine Commentary on Martianus (Florence, Biblioteca Nazionale MS. Conv. Soppr. I.1.28, fol. 50r–64v), see Dronke (he gives only fols. 50r–v, 56v–7v, and 57v–8r, on *De nuptiis* 1–3), in *Fabula,* pp. 167–83.

14. See *Glosae in Iuvenalem,* ed. Bradford Wilson, Textes philosophiques du Moyen Âge, no. 18 (Paris: J. Vrin, 1980), pp. 77–78, on the date of the Juvenal glosses. I would suspect the commentary to be pre-twelfth-century, not the work of William at all. Or perhaps it was written by a student of William, like the Florentine Commentary on Martianus Capella (according to Dronke's speculations). Wilson does admit, p. 63, that "W probably represents a version of the *reportatio* of William's lectures, while P more likely is a student's edition of William's own version which was published." According to Wilson, pp. 54–65, William uses *allegoria, translatio,* and *integumentum* to explicate the "ethical argument" of Juvenal.

15. See Jeauneau, "Note," p. 842, for this and the Macrobius passage; also Gregory, *Anima,* p. 27; mentioned in Dronke, *Fabula,* p. 167.

16. Dronke, *Fabula,* pp. 167–68; William's remark on Martianus is quoted on p. 167n2. See also Jeauneau, *Glosae super Platonem,* p. 14. According to Jeauneau, "Gloses de Guillaume de Conches sur Macrobe: Note sur les manuscrits," *AHDLMA* 35 (1960): 17–28, here, p. 26, William wrote the Boethius before the Macrobius and *Timaeus* commentaries.

17. The glosses of William on Boethius's Ixion are from MS. Troyes 1381, fol. 71, and are edited with others of William's Boethius comments by Édouard Jeauneau, "L'Usage de la notion d'*integumentum* à travers les gloses de Guillaume de Conches," *AHDLMA* 32 (1957): 51–52; my translations. The idea of three goddesses as reflective of the three lives is at least as old as Fulgentius (*Mit.* 2.1). Not all of the Boethius glosses appear in all manuscripts. Where a specific manuscript citation may be useful, until there is a critical edition of the glosses, I have so indicated.

18. See the glosses on Eurydice from B.L. MS. Egerton 628, translated by Wetherbee, *Platonism,* p. 97, and cited (from Jeauneau) in chapter 10, note 29 below.

19. B.L. Egerton MS. 628, fol. 191v, cited in Wetherbee, *Platonism,* p. 96n60.

20. MS. Troyes 1101, fol. 16ra, in Jeauneau, "L'Usage," p. 39. The source is Fulgentius, *Cont. Virg.* 15. In *Consolatio* 4 m3, on Ulysses, William reveals that the name "Ulysses" comes from the Greek for the "eternal pilgrim," "omnium peregrinus," seen earlier in the Remigian glosses on Boethius. See MS. Troyes 1381, fol. 75r, and MS. Troyes 1101, fol. 13vb, in Jeauneau, "L'Usage," p. 40: "Ulixes dicitur quasi Olonxenos, id est omnium peregrinus. Olon enim est inde holocaustum quasi totum incensum. Olon enim est omne, inde holocaustum quasi totum incensum. Xenos enim est peregrinus. Qui rediens de obsidione Troie diu per mare iactatur quia sapiens omnium temporalium est peregrinus secundum illud: 'conversatio nostra in celis est' " ["He is called 'Ulysses' as if Olonxenos, that is, the eternal traveler. Olon {Holon} means 'all,' and from it comes *holocaustum,* that is, wholly burned. Xenos, moreover, means 'foreign.' He, coming back from the siege of Troy, is tossed about by the sea for a long time, because the wise man

is a stranger to all temporal things, according to this saying: 'our way of life exists in heaven' "]. The latter citation comes from *Moralium dogma philosophorum* 3.20, according to Jeauneau. The etymology comes from Fulgentius, *Mit.* 2.8, probably through Mythogr. II 123/101.

21. B.L. MS. Egerton 628, fol. 194r, cited in Wetherbee, *Platonism,* p. 96.

22. MS. Troyes 1381, fol. 84r and MS. Troyes 1101, fol. 16rb, in Jeauneau, "L'Usage," p. 40. This comes from Fulgentius, *Mit.* 2.4.

23. William's glosses on Boethius's Hercules (Centaurs, lion, Harpies, Hesperides) are cited in Hatinguais, notes 12–13 on pp. 424–25.

24. William glosses the Muses as Sirens in *Consolatio* 1 m1, the battle between Hercules and Achelous in 2 m2, the Giants in the War with Heaven in 3 p12, the Orpheus myth of the descent into the underworld and the Judgment of Paris in 3 m12, Circe and Ulysses in 4 m3, and the three heroes Agamemnon, Ulysses, and Hercules in 4 m7. These have been edited in part by Charles Jourdain, "Des commentaires inédits de Guillaume de Conches et de Nicolas Triveth sur la consolation de la Philosophie de Boèce," *Notices et extraits des manuscrits de la Bibliothèque Impériale et autres bibliothèques* 20.2 (Paris, 1862): 40–82; and by J. M. Parent, *La Doctrine de la Création dans l'école de Chartres: Étude et textes,* Publications de l'Institut d'Études Médiévales d'Ottawa, vol. 8 (Paris: Librairie Philosophique J. Vrin; Ottawa: Inst. d'Études Médiévales, 1938), pp. 115–21. The full commentary is in London, B.L. MS. Egerton 628, fols. 165r–95r; B.L. MS. King's Library 15B III, fols. 1–143; MS. Troyes 1101, fol. 16ra. Selections from the Boethius have also been edited and discussed by Wetherbee, *Platonism,* pp. 92–104.

25. See Bolton, "Manuscripts," p. 215.

26. See Jeauneau, "L'Usage," pp. 41–53, for the entire glosses and discussion of *Consolatio* 3 m12; for the specific citations in the manuscripts, see MS. Troyes 1381, fols. 69v–70r, and MS. Troyes 1101, fols. 12va–vb.

27. This gloss occurs on fol. 70r of MS. Troyes 1381 and fol. 12vb of MS. Troyes 1101, plus Orleans 274, p. 26a. The passage is cited in Jeauneau, "L'Usage," p. 42.

28. From MS. Troyes 1331, fol. 69r, in Jeauneau, "L'Usage," p. 45.

29. The myth reads (Jeauneau, "L'Usage," p. 46): "Orpheus ponitur pro quolibet sapiente et eloquente, et inde Orpheus dicitur quasi Oreaphone, id est optima vox. Huius est coniunx Euridice, id est naturalis concupiscentia que unicuique coniuncta est: nullus enim sine ea nec etiam puer unius diei in hac vita esse potest. Vnde iterum finxerunt poete quemdam deum esse, scilicet genium, qui nascitur cum unoquoque et moritur. Vnde Horatius: 'deus alber et alter mortalis in unumquodque caput.' Genius est naturalis concupiscentia. Sed hec naturalis concupiscentia merito dicitur Euridice, id est boni iudicatio, quia quod quisque iudicat bonum, sive ita sit sive non, concupiscit. Concupiscentia hec ab Aristeo, dum vagatur per pratum, adamatur. Aristeus ponitur pro virtute: *ares* enim est virtus. Sed hec virtus hanc Euridicem, id est hanc naturalem concupiscen-

tiam, dum vagatur per pratum, id est per terrena que quemadmodum prata modo virent modo sunt arida, adamat id est sequitur quia semper virtus naturalem concupiscentiam a terrenis abstrahere nititur. Sed Euridice Aristeum fugit, quia naturalis concupiscentia contradicit virtuti quia appetit voluptatem propriam cui virtus contradicit. Sed tunc moritur et ad inferos descendit, id est terrenam delectationem. Sed, mortua uxore, Orpheus dolet quia cum sapiens videt intentionem suam et delectationem in temporalibus habitam displicet. Sed, cum cuncta modulationibus suis vincat, dolorem de amissa uxore non superet, suam concupiscentiam non potest a temporalibus auferre: inde maxime dolet. Sed tunc Orpheus ad inferos descendit ut uxorem extrahat cum sapiens ad cognitionem terrenorum descendit ut, viso quod nichil boni in eis est, concupiscentiam inde extrahat. Sed redditur ei hac lege ne respiciat quia 'nemo mittens manum suam ad aratrum et respiciens retro aptus est regno Dei' " (Luke 9:62). A partial translation of this passage can be found in Wetherbee, *Platonism*, p. 97. For the Orpheus background of this particular gloss, see the study by John Block Friedman, *Orpheus in the Middle Ages* (Cambridge, Mass.: Harvard University Press, 1970), esp. pp. 104–9; other sources here include Fulgentius, Remigius of Auxerre, and the third Vatican mythographer; and on the *genius* see Jane Chance Nitzsche, *The Genius Figure in Antiquity and the Middle Ages* (New York and London: Columbia University Press, 1975). Note the Remigian use of the passage from Luke concerning the man who puts his hand to the plow.

30. In MS. Troyes 1381, fol. 73, cited in Jourdain's edition, pp. 56–57n4: "Tantalus ponitur pro quolibet avaro qui plenus divitiis, mala egestatis in affluentia patitur, dum non vult in necessariis sua expendere, quia non sustinet acervum nummorum minuere."

31. Apparently from Macrobius's commentary on the *Somnium Scipionis* 1.10.10–13 and Fulgentius, *Mit.* 2.15, according to Hatinguais, "Points," p. 422.

32. The passage is cited and translated from B.L. MS. Egerton 628, fol. 165v in Wetherbee, *Platonism*, p. 93n51: "Sed sunt alie integre, alie lacere. Integre sunt philosophice sententie, quia integritate rationis conseruant hominem et constantia. Lacere dicuntur poetice sententie, id est, scientie fingendi et describendi metrice, quia lacerant corda hominum et inconstancia reddunt, reducendo ad memoriam uel uoluptatem uel dolorem, non instruendo uel consolando." I have altered his translations somewhat.

33. This passage is cited in Jourdain's edition, p. 55n3, from MS. Troyes 1381, fol. 38; the idea is very similar to Bernard's in his commentary on the *Aeneid,* and he probably borrowed it from William.

34. Jeauneau, "L'Usage," p. 40n5, cited from MS. Troyes 1381, fol. 83r, and MS. Orleans 274, p. 34b.

35. "Sed cumulant montem monti dum aliquis subditus carni unum temporale alii adjungit, et inde superbiam superbie, et hoc est, ut ascendant celum, id est, ut per ea fiant immortales et beati, et expellant deos, id est, animas subdant

que sunt immortales ut dii; sed ab ipsis diis dejiciuntur, dum ratione et intellectu superbie nichil valere ostenduntur" ["But they heap mountain atop mountain, when someone who is subject to the flesh yokes one temporal thing to another, and then pride atop pride, and that they may ascend to heaven, that is, so that through these things they may be made immortal and blessed, and expel the gods, that is, the souls which are immortal like gods, but they are evicted by these same gods, when they are shown by reason and intellect to have no control over pride"], from MS. Troyes 1381, fol. 68v, cited in Jeauneau, "L'Usage," p. 41n3; and, in the full form, in Jourdain, p. 56n1.

36. See Pierre Courcelle, "Étude critique sur les commentaires de la Consolation de Boèce (IXe–XVe siècles)," *AHDLMA* 14 (1939): 78.

37. See Wetherbee, *Platonism,* p. 74, but also passim; see also M.-D. Chenu, *Nature, Man, and Society in the Twelfth Century: Essays on New Theological Perspectives in the Latin West,* sel., ed., and trans. Jerome Taylor and Lester K. Little (Chicago and London: University of Chicago Press, 1968), pp. 142–58.

38. Traube defined three ages of commentary, the first, an *aetas Vergiliana,* of the eighth and ninth centuries; the second, an *aetas Horatiana,* of the tenth and eleventh centuries; and the third, an *aetas Ovidiana,* of the twelfth and thirteenth centuries. See *Lateinische Sprache und Literatur des Mittelalters* (Frankfurt: Peter Lang, 1974), p. 113.

39. See the discussion in Courcelle, "Étude critique," p. 133.

40. The Vatican Reginenses MSS. 72 and 244 are apparently similar to three other manuscripts, Arsenal 910, 1r–34v, twelfth century; Orleans 260, pp. 84–173, twelfth century; and Paris 15173, fols. 74v–75r, twelfth century; see Courcelle, "Étude critique," pp. 80, 131. Portions of Reginensis 72 have been edited by Dom André Wilmart: the vita and the first few glosses of Vat. Reg. 72 in "Reg. Lat. 72 (fol. 110–126): Commentaire de la 'Consolation' de Boèce," in *Analecta Reginensia: Extraits des manuscrits latins de la reine Christine conservés au Vatican,* in *Studi e testi* 59 (1933): 259–62. The two are also essentially the same, dated around the twelfth century (Wilmart, p. 259).

41. Courcelle, "Étude critique," p. 80.

42. Vatican MS. Reginensis 72, fols. 110–26, is written in a tiny script almost impossible to read. Its simplistic glosses include, for example, in a brief fifteen lines on *Consolatio* 3 m12, "Calliope" as a gloss on the lemma "matris" (apparently of Orpheus) (fol. 121r), and "summum bonum" as a gloss on "superum diem," "sovereign day," to show that good (God) and the light of truth are the same for those men who wish to raise their minds.

43. Vatican MS. Reginensis 244, fols. 43–65, is written in a much clearer, larger script, with the meter and prose divisions indicated in the margins, although its commentary, like that of Reginensis 72, is cursory. For example, like Reginensis 72, 244 provides simple glosses on *Consolatio* 4 m7, with "Atrides" a reference to Agamemnon and "volucres," to the Harpies. But in several of its more

complex glosses it also mirrors the St. Gall commentaries, especially the Minor. For *Consolatio* 3 m12 its gloss (a short one, fol. 58va to 58vb) indicates that that man is unhappy who is bound to this earth when he loves the things of this earth (fol. 58va)—in a striking parallel to the Anonymous of St. Gall Minor. In similar shorthand echoes of the earlier commentaries it also declares that Orpheus's mother is Calliope, that "Tenera" refers to the lower regions, that the Ianitor is "Cerberus," or guardian of the gate of hell, and in summary, that Orpheus is a type of man too bound to the earth (that is, to his wife). Another parallel with the Anonymous of St. Gall commentaries occurs in a gloss on *Consolatio* 4 m3. Circe's garden of herbs, termed (fol. 60ra) an "arborium herbarum" wherein men become monsters, is a place of natural things changed by magic. Like the St. Gall commentators, the Reginensis 244 commentator moralizes the fable, with Circe's poisons that transform the men into beasts as the vices, except that he adds to avarice and ire a new vice, *libido.*

44. See the arguments and edition of Edmund T. Silk, "Notes on Two Neglected Manuscripts of Boethius' *Consolatio Philosophiae,*" *TAPA* 70 (1939): 352–56; and also Silk, ed., *Saeculi noni auctoris in Boetii consolationem Philosophiae commentarius,* Papers and Monographs of the American Academy in Rome, vol. 9 (Rome: American Academy in Rome, 1935); references to Erfurt in the text will be noted by "Silk" and page number(s). Silk later retracted his attribution but insisted on the ninth-century date, in "Pseudo-Johannes Scottus, Adalbold of Utrecht, and the Early Commentaries on Boethius," *Medieval and Renaissance Studies* 3 (1954): 1–40. This date is disputed by G. Mathon, who argues it was not by John Scot and that it is more closely related to a disciple of William than to the gloss on *Consolatio* 3 m9 by Adalbold of Utrecht, in "Le Commentaire du pseudo-Érigène sur la *Consolatio Philosophiae* de Boèce," *Recherches de théologie ancienne et médiévale* 22 (1955): 213–57.

45. For a discussion of the sources of the Erfurt glosses on *Consolatio* 3 m9, see R. B. C. Huygens, "Mittelalterlicher Kommentare zum *O qui perpetua. . .,*" *Sacris Erudiri* 6 (1954): 373–427, here, pp. 404–27; for the previous (mistaken, I believe) dating of the commentary as post-William, see Mathon, 213–57.

46. On *Consolatio* 3 p12, on the Giants Otus and Ephialtes, Erfurt combines glosses found in Remigius and Notker (the latter of whom, like the *Ecloga Theoduli,* relates the war between the Giants and heaven to the tower of Babel built by Giants). Erfurt provides a literalistic recitation of the myth similar to, but more compressed than, Hyginus's *Fabulae* 28, indicating that the Giants grew nine digits every month and, at nine years, tried to overcome Jove by piling Pelion atop Ossa. Erfurt adds a line indicating his awareness of Notker's connecting of the Giants' war on heaven by piling mountain atop mountain with the biblical tower of Babel and its confusion of tongues: "Vel etiam ueritatem tangit, quia diuisione linguarum dispersit, quia diuisit eos in diuersas linguas. Ideo hoc dixit, quia nullus potest contra Deum nec Gigantes" ["Or also it touches truth, because it

dispersed {them} by means of the division of languages, because it divided them into different languages. For that reason he has said this, that no one there can {avail} against God, not even Giants"] (Silk, p. 213). He also adds his own moral gloss to suggest how the pursuit of individual will is counter to the search for the *summum bonum:* "Sic de Gigantibus patet uel aliter stultitiam quae in me erat pudet quae lacerabat summum bonum, dum illud in diuersa diuidere uolebat" ["Thus about the Giants it is clear, or otherwise shames the folly which was in me, which tore apart the highest good when it {folly} wished to divide it into different parts"] (Silk, p. 214—in anticipation, perhaps, of the long moral gloss on *Consolatio* 3 m12 with its discussion of the infernal inhabitants as vicious types of such Giants and Orpheus as a failed example of the pursuit of the *summum bonum*).

Erfurt's gloss on *Consolatio* 4 p6, on Hercules and the Hydra, reiterates that of Remigius and his revisers and Notker Labeo in the most literalistic way (Silk, p. 249); the normally long gloss on *Consolatio* 4 m7 is in Erfurt truncated because of a lacuna after the Agamemnon reference and prior to the apotheosis of Hercules. As in preceding glosses, Erfurt begins with the moral normally appended to the gloss, in this case taken directly from Remigius: this song pertains to those who wish to acquire an eternal name through virtue, particularly through fighting heroically against adversaries (Silk, p. 269). This moral is followed by a much fuller account of the causes of the Trojan War than is found in Remigius and earlier commentaries; most likely Erfurt depends on the first Vatican mythographer (fable 20) and the second (245/202). Mostly Erfurt adds a detailed description of how Iphigenia was summoned to be sacrificed for the winds to move the Greek navy, that is, through Ulysses's ruse that she was to be married at the port of Aulis; the powerlessness of Agamemnon's daughter invites the pity of Minerva, who saves her from being sacrificed: "Sed cum ante aram iam teneretur Mineruae iam inmolanda a Calc<h>ante sacerdote miserata Minerua circumstantium oculis nube opposita pro eadem Iphigenia ceruam supposuit illamque in regnum Tantali in Scyt<h>iam transtulit" ['But when she was already being held before the altar, soon to be sacrificed to Minerva by the priest Calchas, Minerva, taking pity on her, threw up a cloud before the eyes of the bystanders and put a doe in the place of Iphigenia, and transported her to Scythia to the kingdom of Tantalus"] (Silk, p. 269). The first Vatican mythographer, unlike Erfurt, stresses the cleverness of Ulysses. The end of the truncated gloss on 4 m7 echoes the Remigian gloss on "ite nunc fortes" ("Go now, strong men") that indicates Hercules was apotheosized for his brave deeds. The truncated gloss is followed by a clarification that these deeds should include good works: "Et dicit ut nudent terga <pr>o bono opere et <accingantur> armis uirtutum" ["And he says for them to bare their backs to good work and to gird themselves with the armor of virtues"] (Silk, p. 270).

47. Erfurt introduces a new gloss on the Bacchae in *Consolatio* 3 m3 in a discussion of the riches which do not accompany a man after death: in a confusion of Boethius's word "baccae" (gems which are like fruit) with the Bacchae,

"Bac<c>hae uero sunt mulieres quae in sacrificio Veneris bac<c>chantur" (Silk, p. 128), "The Bacchae are women who celebrate the festival of Bacchus in sacrifice to Venus."

48. Erfurt is the first to gloss *Consolatio* 3 m12 with the story of Aristaeus loving Eurydice, from Virgil, which sets a precedent for later commentaries, like those of William of Conches on the *Consolatio* and Bernard Silvestris on the *Aeneid:* "Secundum fabulam Orpheus cit<h>arista fuit cuius uxor Eurydice ab Aristaeo adamata, cum fugeret eum, in deserto latens interempta periit" ["According to the fable Orpheus was a cithra player whose wife Eurydice, desired by Aristaeus, when she fled him, perished, being killed as she hid in a desert place"] (Silk, p. 217).

49. In his edition of Erfurt, Silk notes embellishments of Remigius passim. On Remigian echoes: Erfurt's gloss on Lethe in *Consolatio* 1 p2.12 copies Remigius in suggesting it is a river of the underworld which obliterates the memory of earthly labors and in relating it to *Lethargum* (Silk, pp. 23–24), but Erfurt does add words acknowledging his citation of another's (Remigius's) work ("dicitur" and "Hinc . . . dicimus") and a citation from Virgil's *Georgics* 4.131 connecting Lethe with the poppy (Silk, p. 24). The gloss on Achelous in 2 m2 basically duplicates Remigius in its description of how Achelous the river transformed himself into a bull when fighting Hercules and how Atlas was subsequently overcome by the hero. Erfurt inserts within this passage a reminder of another Labor of Hercules, one that apparently will help his audience recall the hero—his retrieval of Cerberus from the underworld ("Qui descendens infernum Cerberum rapturus secum tulit," Silk, p. 25). The gloss on Alcibiades in 3 p8.25 simultaneously expands and reduces the original Remigius by confusing and inserting glosses found in the revisers. Erfurt, misunderstanding the five identifications provided by Remigius and the revisers for Alcibiades (as a leader of Greeks with a beautiful body, a beautiful woman, a poet, and Hercules in youth who was called by this name from his father or mother), explains that Alcibiades is a woman, the mother of Hercules from whom the hero takes his name "Alcides": "Alcibiades quaedam mulier fuit celebratissimae formae quam dicunt matrem Herculis fuisse et ideo eum Alciden nominatum" (Silk, p. 144). He also adds, from another place in one of the revisers, an etymology for the name Alcides ("Alce" in Greek but "strength" in Latin) derived from Fulgentius's *Mitologiae* 2.2 and Servius's commentary on the *Aeneid* 6.392: "Nam Alcides dictus est quasi alcedes, quoniam fortis et pulcher fuit. *Alce* enim Graece uirtus Latine dicitur. Alcos dicitur albus, idea forma" (Silk, p. 144).

Much of Erfurt's actual moralization of the Orpheus myth is indebted to Remigius. Orpheus's music makes the woods dance and the waters stand still because he is a theologian and leads men from wild ways to a civilized life, an idea restated from Remigius (Silk, p. 217). Erfurt also combines glosses from Remigius and the revisers on the songs of Orpheus as coming from the fountains of his goddess mother Calliope, who is also mother of the gods (but not labeled as Berecynthia, as in Remigius, a change consonant with Erfurt's general desire to euhemerize the myth): "FONTIBUS dicit MATRIS, id est Calliope, quia omnes fontes Musarum et Nympharum, in honore matris deorum dicuntur esse et poetae carmina a fontibus dicuntur accipere" ["FONTIBUS {'from the fountains'}, he says MATRIS {'of his mother'}, that is, Calliope, because all fountains of the Muses and Nymphs are said to exist in honor of the mother of the gods and the poets are said to receive songs from the fountains"] (Silk, pp. 217–18). Erfurt also adds a psychological comment on the grief of Orpheus as impotent, natural to those who are occupied with the trivial and who therefore exaggerate their pains: "Naturale est, ut cum dolentes in nulla re fuerint alia <occupati> toto se luctu<i> tradant et ideo ad exaggerandum dolorem addidit INPOTENS" (Silk, p. 218).

50. Huygens, "Mittelalterliche Kommentare," pp. 404–27.

51. The description of the inhabitants of hell who are soothed by Orpheus's song is preceded by a comment on "tergeminus," "triple" or "born in threes," a reference not to Cerberus with his three heads representing the three ages of man (infancy, youth, and old age), as it is in Remigius and his revisers, but instead to the three brothers under whose rule the world has been divided, in a gloss lifted from a passage in *Consolatio* 3 m12.40, on "arbiter umbrarum" (Pluto in B.N., K, and T). Erfurt has rearranged this, apparently in dislike or disbelief of the Cerberus reference: he restates the Remigian idea that there are three brothers who have among them divided up the world, Jupiter the sky, Neptune the sea, and Pluto the underworld: "TERGEMINUS dicit, quia tres dicuntur fuisse fratres qui inter se omnem mundum diuiserunt: Iupiter caelum Neptunus mare Pluto infernum" (Silk, p. 218). He does list each of the brothers as being characterized by something in threes—Jupiter, by the three-forked lightning, Neptune, by the trident, and Pluto, by Cerberus, who has three heads: "Et ut singuli in regno fratrem potentem habere uideantur aliquid tripliciter gerunt: Iupiter trifidum fulmen Neptunus tridentem Pluton Cerberum, qui tria capita habere dicuntur. Vnde et triplex dicitur" (Silk, p. 218).

52. Generally Erfurt slightly Christianizes his glosses, as in the standard catalogue of glosses on Trenara, Tantalus, Tityus, the Furies, and Ixion (Silk, pp. 218–19), a list which, after the gloss on Trenara, slightly reorders the list found in Boethius (and Remigius), which is Furies, Ixion, Tantalus, Tityus. The gloss on Trenara repeats the Remigian trifold definition: songs of lamentation, the lake near the underworld, and a promontory; Erfurt adds only a supposed etymology from the Greek: "nam trene Graece lamentatio Latine dicitur" (Silk, p. 218). He does leave out the quotation from Virgil's *Georgics* 4.467, found in Remigius. Each of the monsters or the damned inhabitants is glossed briefly through an explanation of his crime and punishment; occasionally additions are provided, mostly in Erfurt's role as literary critic, in an attempt to relate the myths more directly to members of Erfurt's audience. For example, after the reference to Tantalus (who served up his son Pelops as a dish for the gods), Erfurt adds an aside to the reader reminding him, "Quid rides? Mutato nomine, de te fabula narratur" ["whoever

laughs at this may find, with the name changed, that the fable actually has been told about him"] (Silk, p. 219, with the proverb taken from Horace, *Satires* 1.1.69–70). And in the gloss on Tityus, the Giant who longed for Latona, he adds the point that he who does not discover the light of the highest good, like Orpheus, returns to the orb of worthlessness; further, the souls are called "shadows" because they have no bodies: "Orpheus flendo indicat, ne aliquis inuenta luce summi boni redeat ad nequitias orbis. Vmbrae dicuntur animae, quia non habent corpora" (Silk, p. 219). Finally, he concludes this gloss on *Consolatio* 3 m12 by relating the Boethian adage that "love is a stronger law unto itself" back to the text, wherein this is said by the persona of Boethius with admiration, as if to say, "Quis talem legem dedit amantibus, saltem ut se mutuo non respiciant?" (Silk, p. 219).

53. Erfurt attempts to unify his glosses more than earlier commentators. The gloss on *Consolatio* 4 m3 actually begins with a comment about the end of 4 p6, in which Boethius has compared vices with various animals—avarice, wolf; angry man, dog; treacherous conspirator, fox; intemperate anger, lion; fearful and timid man, deer; lazy, stupid fellow, ass; volatile, inconstant man, bird; lust, sow—in order to show that anyone who ceases being virtuous ceases being a man and becomes a beast. Because Erfurt has concluded his gloss of *Consolatio* 4 p3 with the idea that these traits are irrational, that vices are full of poison which transform the soul but not the body, he has a perfect transition to 4 m3, in which the poisons of Circe transform the bodies but not the souls of Ulysses's men: "Quae uitia sunt satis dira uenena quae inuertunt animum. Si illa fuerunt dira uenena quae immutauere corpora non animos, tunc illa multo peiora sunt quae inuertunt animos. Sed illa satis fuerunt dira quae corpora mutauere et non animos, sicut ea quae uertere corpora sociorum Vlixis" ["Those vices are terrible poisons which alter the mind. If those were dire poisons which changed bodies, not minds, then those which alter minds are much worse. But those were very dire which changed bodies and not minds, just like the ones which altered the bodies of the companions of Ulysses"] (Silk, p. 236). While he has only followed his own practice of beginning rather than ending a gloss with a moralization, for this particular gloss he provides a stunning literary interpretation of Boethius's text and also an explanation for both earlier and later glossators' reasons for understanding the poisons of Circe as the individual vices (especially in the Vatican Reginenses 72 and 244). The actual gloss on 4 m3 is distinctly Remigian, though abbreviated, and consists especially of the reasons Ulysses's companions were transformed specifically into wild boars, lions, and tigers: "Secundam fabulam dicitur mutasse alios in aprum alios in leonem alium in tigridem. Et qui factus est tigris dicitur mitis tecta perambulare, quia licet mutatus esset corpore tamen id sibi manet animus quod erat prius" ["And he who was made a tiger is said to walk mildly around the house because, although he had been changed in body, nevertheless his mind remains what it was before"] (Silk, p. 237). Like Remigius

and his revisers, Erfurt comments on Ulysses's name as "Neritius," and like Remigius and Notker Labeo, who uses Remigius's commentary on Martianus Capella, he comments on Mercury (who saves Ulysses's men) by discussing in detail his birthplace, winged feet, caduceus, and rod. But Erfurt also, unlike Notker Labeo, preserves the Remigian moralizations on Mercury's nature as god of eloquence: that is, Mercury's winged feet depict the speed of speech, or his role as messenger of the gods; the caduceus is a rod entwined with serpents because of the rectitude of discourse or the breaking of disputation (Silk, p. 237). At the end of this meter, Erfurt once again attempts to unify the gloss. Boethius states, at the end of the Circe poem, that poisons which make man forget himself are more deadly than Circe's because they corrupt the inner man (a return to 4 p3); Erfurt converts this to a more Christian purpose, that is, to declare, "In hoc igitur apparet uitia acrioris esse uirtutis quam ipsa pocula herbarum, quae a contemplatione Dei mentem rationalem commouent et ad peiora deflectunt" ["vices are of a more acrid virtue than the poisonous herbs of Circe because they move the rational mind away from the contemplation of God and deflect it to worse things"] (Silk, p. 237).

54. "Hoc carmen est fabulosum; et ex toto beatificat illos qui exuti carnalibus desideriis erigunt se ad cernendam uerae beatitudinis claritatem. Et admonet haec fabula, ut nemo aspiciat retro postquam inuenit locum ueri boni ubi est situm et post inuentum summum bonum. Iam magnificat et felices praedicat illos qui ad eius claritatem peruenire poterunt. Quod carmen inde res<picit illos> qui postquam uiam ueritatis agnouerint et in ea profecerint rursus ad saeculi desideria reuertantur sicque opus inceptum perdant, sicut Orpheus perdidit uxorem retro aspiciens" ["This poem is fabulous; and wholly beatifies those who, stripped of carnal desires, raise themselves up to the clear perception of true beatitude. And this fable warns that no one should look behind after he discovers the place of true good where it is located, and after the discovery of the highest good. Now he esteems highly and calls happy those who have been able to arrive at its clarity. This poem then deals with those who after they have recognized the way of truth and have progressed in it again return to worldly desires and so they destroy the work that they have begun, exactly as Orpheus who, looking back, lost his wife"] (Silk, p. 217); Friedman, who imagines Erfurt as Remigius, includes a long discussion of this particular passage, p. 99.

55. The quotation is from Horace, *Satires* 2.5.59.

56. Silk, p. 290.

57. William, on Macrobius in Dronke, *Fabula* p. 71. Selections from William on Macrobius (*Somn. Scip.* 1.1–16) appear in Dronke, *Fabula,* pp. 68–78. For discussions of the Macrobius glosses, see Jeauneau, ed., *Glosae super Platonem,* and his "La Lecture des auteurs classiques à l'école de Chartres durant la première moitié du XIIe siècle. Un témoin privilégié: les 'Glosae super Macrobium' de Guillaume de Conches," *Classical Influences on European Culture A.D. 500–1500,* ed. R. R. Bolgar (Cambridge: Cambridge University Press, 1971), pp. 95–102. Some

of William's sources and parallels for the Macrobius glosses, according to his editor Dronke, who has not identified sources or parallels for all citations, include Servius, *In Georg.* (pp. 22n2, 54n1); Fulgentius, *Mit.* (but possibly transmitted through the Vatican mythographers); and Bernard Silvestris on the *Aeneid* (pp. 26n2, 29n3).

58. Edouard Jeauneau, "L'Usage de la notion d'*integumentum* à travers les gloses de Guillaume de Conches," *AHDMLA* 32 (1957): 53. For discussions of William's use of *integumentum*, and related excerpts from the glosses on Boethius, Juvenal, and the *Timaeus*, see Jeauneau, "L'Usage," pp. 35–100, and for discussion of his allegorical method in general, Hatinguais, pp. 417–29.

59. St. Augustine, *De doctrina christiana; De vera religione*, ed. Joseph Martin, CC 32 (Turnhout: Brepols, 1962), p. 83; trans. D. W. Robertson, Jr., *On Christian Doctrine* (New York: Liberal Arts Press, 1958), p. 75 (3.5.9).

60. "Integumentum est genus demonstrationis sub fabulosa narratione veritatis involvens intellectum, unde etiam dicitur involucrum" (Bern. Sil., *Sup. En.*, p. 3; trans., p. 5).

61. John of Salisbury, *Policraticus* 8.24, in Clemens C.J. Webb's edition, 2 vols. (1909; rpt., Frankfurt: Minerva, 1965).

62. Robertson, Jr., "Some Medieval Literary Terminology, with Special Reference to Chrétien de Troyes," *SP* 48 (1951): 669–92, esp. p. 692; see also his "Marie de France, *Lais, Prologue*, 13–16," *MLN* 64 (1949): 336–38, for discussions of *littera, sensus*, and *sententia*. Hennig Brinkmann, "Verhüllung ('Integumentum') als literarische Darstellungsform im Mittelalter," in *Der Begriff der Repraesentatio im Mittelalter: Stellvertretung, Symbol, Zeichen, Bild*, in *Miscellanea Mediaevalia*, vol. 8 (Berlin and New York: Walter de Gruyter, 1971), pp. 314–39, discusses the following terms—*integumentum, involucrum, aenigma, allegoria, ironia, antiphrasis, euphemismus, sarkasmus, icon, parabola, paradigma, metonymia, prosopopoeia, apostrophe, conformatio, mutatio, transmutatio*, and *symbolum*—many of which are rhetorical rather than grammatical terms.

63. William on Macrobius, in Dronke, *Fabula*, p. 71, on *Somn. Scip.* 1.2.9. "Because philosophers claim that the world-soul is shared out among all physical beings, though it does not exercise the same activity on them all . . . and because Bacchus is a name for the world-soul, that is why they invented a fable with hidden meaning about Bacchus" (William on Martianus, trans. Dronke, *Fabula*, p. 24).

64. William on Macrobius, in Dronke, *Fabula*, p. 70; trans. p. 26, on Macrobius 1.2.10. A rationalization for this cruel act can be found in part in the Juvenal glosses that identify Saturn with Wisdom because Chronos, or Time, is mistaken as Charon—a mistake that also explains William's earlier use of Saturn. The confusion of Charon, who transports the dead to the underworld, with Chronos, time, occurs when "the old man and son" (clearly meant to be Chronos and Saturn) is understood as *sapientia* or *prudentia*, because old men are wise. "Coron est tempus quasi cronorum quod interpretatur tempus, unde senex et filius p . . . lidemi [*sic*]

qui interpretatur multa sapientia. Dicitur quia in senibus auget sapientia et a antiquis prudentia" (*Glosae in Iuvenalem,* ed. Wilson, p. 162).

65. "Quia eius benivolentiam sua malitia corrumpit," William on Macrobius, in Dronke, *Fabula,* p. 72, taken in part from Fulgentius, *Mit.* 2.7.

66. William on Macrobius, in Dronke, *Fabula,* trans., p. 48; text, p. 75.

67. Ibid., trans., p. 54; text, pp. 75–76. Compare William's etymology of Ceres in *Glosae in Iuvenalem,* ed. Wilson, p. 197; see also Servius, *In Georg.* 1.39. Cf. this passage in Bern. Sil., *Sup. En.,* p. 161, on *Aeneid* 6.59.

68. "Alia causa quare scribit satiram, scilicet gulositas imperatoris. Sed quia non est ausus reprehendere illum notat per integumentum sic" (William, *Glosae in Iuvenalem,* ed. Wilson, p. 108). The actual myths of Juvenal glossed as integuments include those of Ceres and Bacchus, in the accessus (ed. Wilson, p. 91), and again in book 1 (pp. 109–11), along with Deucalion (pp. 118–21), and Hercules (p. 138); in book 2, Bacchus (pp. 141–42), Flora and Juno (pp. 149–52), Cybele (p. 155), Mars, Pan (pp. 158–60), and the rulers of the underworld (p. 162); in book 3, the Muses, Daedalus, and the Fates (pp. 168–69), and the Corybantes (p. 187); and in book 6, Saturn, Diana, and Genius (pp. 192–93).

69. St. Augustine, *On Christian Doctrine* (1.3): "Some things are to be enjoyed, others to be used, and there are others which are to be enjoyed and used. Those things which are to be enjoyed make us blessed. Those things which are to be used help and, as it were, sustain us as we move toward blessedness in order that we may gain and cling to those things which make us blessed. If we who enjoy and use things, being placed in the midst of things of both kinds, wish to enjoy those things which should be used, our course will be impeded and sometimes deflected, so that we are retarded in obtaining those things which are to be enjoyed, or even prevented altogether, shackled by an inferior love" (trans. Robertson, p. 8).

70. William on Macrobius, in Dronke, *Fabula,* p. 71. The idea that Bacchus is the soul or World Soul arises from the sacred rites of the Orphic sect, in which Bacchus is torn apart by the angry Titans, thereafter rising live with his limbs whole. The point for William is that Mind represents the indivisible. William refers elsewhere, in a gloss on *Somn. Scip.* 1.2.9 on the use of sacred rites as an example of truth in fiction, to the *vannus* or winnowing-fan used in the feast of Bacchus because of the god's role in the battle with the Giants. After Bacchus helped Jupiter fight the Giants with the jawbone of an ass, they tore him to pieces and put him into the winnowing-fan, but—here William adds a Christian interpretation—"on the third day he emerged whole and perfect" (trans. Dronke, *Fabula,* p. 22; text, p. 70). For the source of the *vannus,* see Servius, *In Georg.* 1.166 (Dronke, *Fabula,* p. 22n2).

71. For the use of allegory's four senses in scriptural exegesis and also in sermons, see Harry Caplan, "The Four Senses of Scriptural Interpretation and the Mediaeval Theory of Preaching," *Speculum* 4 (1929): 282–90. For the use of Neoplatonic cosmology or pagan myth in *involucrum,* see Chenu, "*Involucrum:* Le

mythe selon des theologiens médiévaux," *AHDLMA* 30 (1955): 75–9. For the distinction between the two, see Wetherbee, *Platonism,* pp. 36–48; and especially Brinkmann, pp. 314–339.

72. The "Florentine Commentary" in Bibl. Naz. Centr. MS. Conv. Soppr. J.1.29 (formerly at the monastery of San Marco), forms the last and longest part of the thirty-page tripartite mythology handbook: the *Genealogia deorum et heroum,* on fols. 49r–50r, the *Allegoria . . . fabularum poeticarum,* on fols. 50r–55r, and the *Exposito super librum Martiani,* fols. 55r–64r (but the digressive accessus is on 55r–v only). These three works are all copied in one hand. The manuscript as a whole was written by three different hands and also includes some letters of Petrarch (fols. 1r–8v, early letters; fols. 17r–45v, later letters including the *Itinerarium Syriacum*). In a context of letter writing, the mythographic material may have seemed relevant because of the emphasis on eloquence in Martianus's *De nuptiis Philologiae et Mercurii.* The manuscript has been identified as fifteenth-century by Cora Lutz, "Martianus Capella," *CTC* 2:379.

73. See Dronke, *Fabula,* pp. 167–72, although he has to stretch various portions of the *Allegoria* (i.e., fols. 50v–64v, including the *Expositio*) to make it seem a commentary on Martianus, especially between 3.13 and 6.11 (cf. Lutz's system using Dick's page numbers; *De nuptiis* 1–5), and he denies that the *Genealogia* is part of the whole text. For excerpts from the text, and his arguments, see especially his chapter 3 and appendix B. In opposition to this view, I would argue that the *Allegoria* as a whole is not so much commentary on Martianus as the first draft of a mythography loosely based on Martianus's work and possibly reflective of William's lectures. That is, in nature it is not a line-by-line commentary, like that of Remigius on Martianus, which has interests beyond the mythological, but a clearly focused description of various gods and personifications such as Sophia, Fronesis, Philology, Entelechia, and so forth. In the first *Allegoria* section (50r–55v), the long expositions on the gods do not contain lemmata from the Martianus text, but are introduced by "Nota quod" or "Nota quia," or separated by the sign for "paragraph"; the names of the gods and goddesses are also identified in the margins. In addition, the frame for the *Allegoria* may be said to expand and embellish *De nuptiis* 4 and 5 (covering two paragraphs in six folios, 50r–55v), whereas the section after the rubric *Expositio* much reduces *De nuptiis* 5–102 (nearly a hundred paragraphs in ten folios, in 55r–64v). Finally, the roughly-defined commentary portion covers only the first book of Martianus (even less than the commentary of the Anonymous Barberinus, on two books), although it epitomizes in its various notes and glosses on the gods in book 1 mythographic material from book 2 (as well as earlier commentaries on Martianus, including Remigius on book 2, or the second Vatican mythographer, Fulgentius, or the Boethius commentaries).

74. Dronke first argues that William's mythographic adaptation in the Martianus commentary consists of "fables built on fables," that is, "imaginative con-

structs which are developed from existing elements of fable in Martianus's work," with the author transforming matter freely, and "as it were" unifying three separate "fabulous moments" to make them aspects of a single fable, that is, his own (*Fabula,* p. 101). Dronke also declares, solely on the basis of three isolated "notes" (long, sustained glosses on Hymen, Sophia and Pallas, and Entelechia), that these excerpts based on William's teaching demonstrate the philosopher's Neoplatonic interest in the World Soul and the human soul, interrelated through the metaphor of the bond between children and parent, or *animae minores* as children of the *anima maxima:* Hymenaeus, child of Bacchus and Cypris; Sophia as child of Pallas-Pronoë; Psyche as child of Sol and Entelechia (*Fabula,* p. 113). Dronke distorts the "Platonistic" emphasis in the commentary partly because he focuses intensively only on the Hymen excerpt (50r–v) and the glosses on the two figures cited above (fols. 56v–58r), but in fact these are isolated, long, and exceptional. Dronke does not, however, apparently understand the conventional Neo-Stoic mythographic association between the World Soul and human begetting as reflected in the genealogy, specifically, the concept of the *anima mundi* as Generative Reason in the Vatican mythographies.

75. That this work may be a student version of William's lectures is supported by its haphazard organization, its deficiencies in identifying various gods and goddesses, and its heavy plagiarizing. Specifically, the Florentine work repeats material, stops for a digression, resumes, repeats itself again, the author's mind jumping from one subject to a related subject to another. He also inserts the accessus to the Martianus commentary *after* he has begun his *Allegoria.* Examples of his innovations in identifying and glossing the gods include that of Apollo married to many wives, among them the trivium arts and *medicina.* He confuses Hercules with Paris (fol. 63v), making the myth the "Judgment of Hercules," rather than of Paris; he sees Leucothoe (Aurora) as the wife of Neptune, and Venus as the wife of Mars, or Nerinea, because Venus was born from the foam of the sea, and "Nerinea" comes from Amaritudo and means "my love burns" (fols. 51v–52r).

76. There may be parallels between the Florentine Commentator and William (in passages in the *Philosophia mundi, Super Macrobium, Super Platonem, Super Boetium*), as evidenced in the Florentine by passages on Hymen (50r to 50v), Pluto and Proserpina (51v), and the Anima Mundi (57v) (Dronke, *Fabula,* pp. 172–79). Looking ahead, Dronke also perceives similiarities between Bernard's commentary on Martianus Capella and the Florentine Commentary in relation to the passages on Hymen and Pluto/Proserpina (pp. 180–83), although he acknowledges differences (p. 182). Dronke also tries to compare the Florentine Commentary with that of Bernard on Martianus, noting as an example in the Hymen passage Bernard's statement that there are seven cells in Hymen (p. 181)—but without realizing that that is the only original part of the Florentine gloss on Hymen.

77. William (in the Florentine mythography) cites by name Boethius (but

probably means the Boethius commentary he knew, or else his own commentary) in glosses on Orpheus (fol. 50v), the Parcae (fol. 51r), and the Pythagorean Y as a symbol of life (64r–v). Other glosses in the Martianus-dominant mythography are similar to the Boethius glosses, even if unacknowledged; for example, Hercules is "Alicides" (both *fortis* and *formosus,* since "Alcus i. fortis" and "idea, ida. i. forma," from Servius, *In Aen.* 6.392 and Boethius, *Consolatio* 3 p8. Knowledge of the Boethius glosses probably shaped the placement of some glosses within this different, Martianus, commentary tradition: for example, William's passage on Saturn is followed by two brief digressions, on Orpheus and on Pluto. The digression on Orpheus, about six lines, combines Boethius and Martianus—from Boethius, "Euagrius dicitur Orpheus a loco" (Dronke, *Fabula,* p. 170), plus 5.7 of Martianus, "Oeagrium Citharis tam" (Dronke, p. 179), to retrace the myths about Orpheus following his wife to the underworld and representing in his songs wisdom and eloquence to make the stones, etc., move. Perhaps because of the Boethian gloss on Orpheus in the underworld, *Consolatio* 3 m12, Pluto's role in the Florentine Commentary (50v) is triggered.

78. William (in the Florentine mythography) cites "Remigius" (that is, on Martianus) in a passage on the Styx in the underworld, on fol. 63v (from Remi., *In Mart.* 36.2). Other possibly Remigian (but unacknowledged) glosses include (among many) the Pluto-Proserpina myth (51r–v); Apollo and his wives, the trivium and *medicina,* 52v (after Orpheus); the Isis-Osiris myth (53v); Ops and Cybele (53r), all from Remi., *In Mart.* 5.22; Mercury/Hermes and Venus/Aphrodite, producing Hermaphroditus (56r), in part from Remi., *In Mart.* 72.4; the Venus-Adonis myth (60v); the two Cupids (63v), from Remi., *In Mart.* 8.22, 62.11. By far the greatest amount of material in William's Martianus derives from Remigius on Martianus.

79. William cites "Rabanus" (probably in mistake for Remigius on Martianus or the second Vatican mythographer, for I would doubt that William is referring here to Hraban Maur's *De universo* 15.6) in fol. 51r, on Pluto as *terre* (from Fulgentius, *Mit.* 1.5, cited by the K Reviser of Remigius on Boethius 3 m12, or Remi., *In Mart.* 35.20) and Jupiter as superior fire (fol. 58r). A common mistake throughout the Middle Ages (and today) is to think commentators use Isidore or Fulgentius directly instead of in *florilegia,* or in a commentary or mythographic handbook. Commentators are generally most aware of the very recent contemporary source.

80. William cites "Virgil" (perhaps referring to Servius on Virgil), on "Nerineia" as wife of Mars, "my love burns" (fols. 51v, 52v). See note 75.

81. William cites "Plato" (meaning the "Plato" of Calcidius's *Timaeus*) in a passage on faculty psychology, fol. 60v. From William's commentary on Plato's *Timaeus* (although unacknowledged), see also the glosses on Vulcan in 2.40c (p. 93); Ceres as Cybele (2.40c, pp. 93; 197); Saturn and his sons as the elements, and Oceanus and Thetis (2.40e, pp. 202–3).

82. William cites "Macrobius" on fol. 58r, on the planets and their attributes; this may in fact come from the twelfth-century Boethius glosses on the World Soul, in *Consolatio* 3m9. Another parallel between the Florentine Martianus commentary and William on Macrobius is the gloss on Pluto-Proserpina (see William on Macrobius, *Somn. Scip.* 1.2.19, Dronke, *Fabula*, trans. p. 54). Note also that Bacchus in fol. 63v is named from *bachor* and carries a winnowing fan or sickle in his hand, recalling William on Macrobius (trans. Dronke, pp. 22–23; but the details are in *De nuptiis* 82 as well).

83. William cites "Pythagoras" for the Y as human life, fols. 63r–64v, but this is really Servius on the *Aeneid* as filtered through the Martianus Capella commentaries (43.18), or Remigius on the *Aeneid*, or the Boethius commentaries on *Consolatio* 3 m12. William also attributes to Pythagoras a distinction between the active and contemplative lives (63v). William declares that the Y, or youth, is "uniformis et simplex," but referring explicitly to Boethius, adds "unde Boetius omnium hominem agenus surgit ab ortu," with a bifurcation, the right leading to the Good, the left to the underworld.

84. From unacknowledged sources—possibly one of the mythographers—comes a passage from Fulgentius, *Mit.* 1.15, on the nine Muses and Apollo representing the organs of the human voice (teeth, lungs, etc.), also found in Remigius on Martianus (here, fol. 60v). William also has a curious passage on the biblical Rachel and the Pharaoh relating to her as an example of the active life (61r). Hercules as Paris, and the Judgment he makes of Juno, Venus, and Minerva (as the three lives), comes essentially from Fulgentius, as filtered through William's own Boethius glosses on *Consolatio* 3 m12 (63v). And then there is much from the second Vatican mythographer, including a passage on Jove's eagle (63v–64r) possibly from fable 5/3: "Integumentum fabule est quid aquila dicitur suis Iovis gignem est."

85. Dronke quotes the "triplex lectio" passage in *Fabula*, p. 114; trans, p. 102. Dronke believes William has borrowed the fabulous portion, on Hymen as *copula sacra deum*, holy bond of the gods binding together elements, from Martianus's invocation, and the realistic and historical portion, on Hymenaeus as young Greek Ephebus, from Servius, *In Buc.* 8.30 and *In Aen.* 1.651, 4.99, 4.127; and Lactantius on the *Thebaid*, 3.283.

86. Dronke, *Fabula*, text, p. 114; trans., p. 102.

87. Ibid. The second Vatican mythographer prefers to this fabulous account of Hymen yet another euhemeristic one, this time of a Roman figure whose name is invoked to free virgins from virginity or to protect it: "ob quam adhuc causam nubentes eius quasi liberatoris uirginitatis, inuocant nomen. Vnde etiam apud Romanos Thalassio inuocatur. Cum enim in raptu Sabinarum plebeius quidam raptam pulcherrimam duceret, ne ei auferretur ab aliis, Thalassionis eam ducis nobilis esse simulauit cuius nomine remansit puelle tuta uirginitas" ["On account of this reason women {getting married} invoke his name as if the liberator of

virginity. Wherefore, moreover, among the Romans he is invoked as Thalassian {'Sea-Water'}. For when, in the rape of the Sabine women, a man seized and married {took off} a very beautiful woman, so that others could not take her away from him he pretended she was the wife of {belonged to} the noble leader Thalassio. By means of his name the virginity of the girl remained safe"] (Mythogr. II, 263/219).

88. William on Martianus, cited in Dronke, *Fabula,* p. 114; trans., p. 102. Italics indicate my own emendations of Dronke's translation.

89. Ibid., text, pp. 114–15; trans., pp. 102–3, emended.

90. Ibid., text, pp. 115 (from fol. 50v); trans., pp. 103–4; my emendations and additions are italicized. The verse is from *Consolatio* 2 m8. The comparable Boethian meter is 2 m8.13–18. The passage resembles Remi., *In Mart.* 2.3, 4, and William's commentary on Boethius, cited Wetherbee, *Platonism,* p. 95n51.

91. Dronke's edition stops at fol. 58r; the citations of William on Martianus that follow are based on my own transcriptions and translations.

92. Wilson, ed., *Glosae in Iuvenalem,* pp. 77–78. What moralization there is—*allegoria, translatio, integumentum*—appears to be employed to explicate the "ethical argument" of Juvenal (pp. 54–65).

93. A gloss based on Remi., *In Mart.* 5.19, identifies Mars as Gradivus, "quasi Cretus divus, id est potens deus, vel Gradivus quia gradatim inceditur ad bellum vel a gradin quod est vibrare" (*In Iuvenalem* 2.126–35, p. 158). Wilson cites also Isidore, *Etym.* 8.11.52, as well as Ovid's *Fasti* 5.251 and *Aeneid* 3.325. Flora, or Bona Dea, is a goddess, "pedissequa Veneris" and "dea meretricum" (*In Iuvenalem* 2.76–87, p. 149); this is supposedly taken from Macrobius's *Saturnalia* 1.12.21, Ovid's *Metamorphoses* 15.110–17, and Terence's *Eunuchus* 4.5.6, according to Wilson, but instead is very likely from Remigius on Martianus, as is Pan: "Lupercus dicitur Pan. Ille deus quasi arcens lupos et sic vocatur illius sacerdos, dicens 'agilis' quia saltando saciebat festa Panis" (*In Iuvenalem* 2.136–46, p. 160). In the later manuscript he is "deus pecudum." And the reason that Vulcan the smith limps, tied to the necessity of softening metal, is reflected in his name Mulciber, in a gloss also allied closely with Remigius on Martianus: "Hinc illud est quod 'claudus' legitur quia per anfractum incedit et quod baculo, ne cadat innititur, quia lignea materia ut non deficiat sustinetur. Huic etiam congruit, quod faber dicitur, quia in ea metalla liquefiunt vel emoliuntur, quod mulcifer dicitur quasi mulcens ferrum et mulciber quasi mulcens imbrem, quia eo [tepefi-ciunt] aquam. Dicit ergi auctor notum esse sibi antrum Vulcani" (*In Iuvenalem,* p. 98).

94. The gloss drawn from the *Ecloga Theoduli* relates the flood of Deucalion, intended to cleanse the vicious operations of man (*In Iuvenalem* 1.79–86, p. 118), to Noah's flood (*In Iuvenalem* 1.86–90, p. 120).

95. "Pallas in tipo sapientie ponitur," William, *Glosae super Platonem,* ed. Jeauneau, p. 92.

96. Ibid., pp. 93–94.

97. Supposedly this gloss resembles the third Vatican mythographer, ed. Bode, myth 2, chap. 3.

98. The myths glossed include Pallas Minerva (*Timaeus* 1.23d–e), Vulcan, and Erichthonius (William, *Glosae super Platonem,* ed. Jeauneau, pp. 92, 93–95), Ceres (2.40c, p. 197), Jupiter and Semele, Ocean and Thetis, and Rhea and Chronos (2.40e, pp. 202–3).

99. See Hatinguais, pp. 417–29.

100. The first part, up to *cubicum corpus,* comes from Remi., *In Mart.* 5.22. See also Mythogr. II 3 (Bode). The second comes from Isidore's *Etym.* 8.40.59–61 and Remi., *In Mart.* 28.12 and 37.3.

101. William, *Glosae super Platonem,* ed. Jeauneau, p. 203.

102. "'Jupiter, hortatu Iunonis, cum fulminibus et tonitrius accedens ad Semelem ut coiret, eam combussit et tamen filium non adussit,' tamen verum est et necessarium quod his verbis a prudente intelligitur. Intelligitur enim quod ab ethere vel ab igne, mediante aere, fulmina et tonitrua in terram descendunt: sed, quamvis illam desiccant in estate, tamen non omnino auferunt quin inde nascatur vinum" (ibid., p. 202).

103. Ibid., p. 203; cf. Mythogr. II 249/206; third Vatican mythographer, myth 11, chap. 210. The passage reads, "Qui sunt filii celi et terre: nisi enim esset celum, acqua, frigiditate sua et terre, in lapideam transiret substantiam ut cristallus. Iterum, si terra non esset, nec acqua, quia non esset quod eam sustineret nec limus qui ex mixtura terre et acque fit."

104. Jourdain, "Des commentaires," p. 41.

105. See Courcelle, "Étude critique," pp. 119–40, for a brief description of all the Boethius manuscripts, including those by Tholomaeus de Asinariis, Pierre de Paris, William of Aragon, the pseudo-Thomas Aquinas (William Whetley), Pierre d'Ailly, Regnier of St. Tron, Guillermus de Cortumelia, Denis (the Carthusian) de Leewis, Arnoul Greban, and Josse Bade d'Assche.

CHAPTER 11: THE VIRGILIAN HERO'S VIRTUOUS DESCENT IN MARTIANUS CAPELLA

1. Although there is some question as to the authorship of the *Aeneid* commentary, as witnessed in the title of the 1977 edition, *The Commentary on the First Six Books of the Aeneid Commonly Attributed to Bernardus Silvestris,* nevertheless Bernard Silvestris is affirmed as the author by Giorgio Padoan, "Tradizione e fortuna del commento all''Eneide' di Bernardo Silvestre," *Italia medioevale e umanistica* 3 (1960): 239; and Theodore Silverstein, "The Fabulous Cosmogony of Bernardus Silvestris," *MP* 46 (1948–49): 97n33; further, Winthrop Wetherbee argues that the commentary on Martianus was written by the author of the commentary on the

Aeneid, in *Platonism and Poetry in the Twelfth Century: The Literary Influence of the School of Chartres* (Princeton: Princeton University Press, 1972), p. 105n76. But see the recent speculative attribution of the *Aeneid* commentary to Bernard of Cerne, by Christopher Baswell, "The Medieval Allegorization of the *Aeneid:* MS Cambridge, Peterhouse 158," *Traditio* 41 (1985): 181–237.

2. I am grateful to Professor Baswell for sharing with me a portion of his unfinished book on *Aeneid* commentaries in the Middle Ages, entitled, "'Bernard' and Boethian Reading of the *Aeneid.*" See also his "Medieval Allegorization of the *Aeneid,*" pp. 181–237; and Wetherbee, *Platonism and Poetry,* pp. 124–25.

3. "Auctoris vero imitatio est, quia Maronem emulatur. Sicut enim apud illum ducitur Eneas per inferos comite Sibilla usque ad Anchisem, ita et hic Mercurius per mundi regiones Virtute comite ad Iovem. Ita quoque et in libro *De Consolatione* scandit Boetius per falsa bona ad summum bonum duce Philosophia. Que quidem tres figure fere idem exprimunt. Imitatur ergo Martianus Maronem, Boetius Martianum" (Bern. Sil., *In Mart.,* p. 67). For a list of slips and typographical errors in the 1986 (Westra) edition, see Baswell's review in *Speculum* 63 (1988): 733–36, here, p. 735. Modern discussions of the commentary can be found in Peter Dronke, *Fabula: Explorations into the Uses of Myth in Medieval Platonism,* Mittellateinische Studien und Texte, vol. 9 (Leiden and Cologne: E. J. Brill, 1974), chapter 4, "Fables of Destiny," pp. 119–43, and Wetherbee, *Platonism and Poetry,* pp. 104–25.

4. See Wetherbee, *Platonism and Poetry,* p. 124.

5. See David Thompson, "Dante and Bernard Silvester," *Viator* 1 (1970): 204; and Wetherbee, *Platonism and Poetry,* p. 105.

6. For information regarding Bernard's writings and Chartrian characteristics, see Wetherbee, *Platonism and Poetry,* pp. 104–5. In him we witness that Chartrian desire to bridge myth and science: see Brian Stock, *Myth and Science in the Twelfth Century: A Study of Bernard Silvester* (Princeton: Princeton University Press, 1972).

7. For sources see J. Reginald O'Donnell, "The Sources and Meaning of Bernard Silvester's Commentary on the *Aeneid,*" *MS* 24 (1962): 233–49; and Stanislaus Skimina, "De Bernardo Silvestri Vergilii interprete," in *Commentationes Vergilianae,* Academia Polona Litterarum et Scientiarum (Cracow: Polska Akademija Umiejéztnósci, 1930), p. 211.

8. Padoan, p. 237; Skimina, pp. 206–43.

9. For discussions of *integumentum* in Bernard, see Édouard Jeauneau, "Notes sur l'école de Chartres," *SM* 3d series 5.2 (1964): 850; and Dronke, *Fabula,* p. 25.

10. On the four descents in William, see pp. 409–12 and William on Boethius in Jeauneau, "L'Usage," p. 42. See Jane Chance Nitzsche's discussion of the four descents in William and in Bernard, in chapter 3 of *The Genius Figure in Antiquity and the Middle Ages* (New York and London: Columbia University Press, 1975).

11. "Descensus autem ad inferos quadrifarius est: est autem nature unus,

virtutis alius, vicii tercius, artificii quartus. Naturalis est nativitas hominis: ea enim incipit naturaliter anima esse in hac caduca regione atque ita in inferis descendere atque a divinitate sua recedere et paulatim in vitium declinare et carnis voluptatibus consentire; sed iste omnium communis est. Est autem alius virtutis qui fit dum sapiens aliquis ad mundana per considerationem descendit, non ut in eis intentionem ponat, sed ut eorum cognita fragilitate, eis abiectis, ad invisibilia penitus se convertat et per creaturarum cognitionem creatorem evidentius cognoscat. Sed hoc modo Orpheus et Hercules qui sapientes habiti sunt descenderunt. Est vero tercius vitii, qui vulgaris est, quo ad temporalia pervenitur atque in eis tota intentio ponitur eisque tota mente servitur nec ab eis amplius dimovetur. Taliter Euridicem legimus descendisse. Hic autem irrevocabilis est. Quartus vero artificialis est dum nigromanticus aliquis artificio nigromantico per aliquod execrabile sacrificium demonum petit colloquium eosque de futura consulit vita" (Bern. Sil., *Sup. En.* 6.1, p. 30; cf. trans., pp. 32–33).

12. "Hunc ramum intelligentia monet querere Eneam ut possit meatus ad inferos patere quia qui philosophia caret ei rerum agnitio non patet. Hic ramus est in ARBORE. Arborem Pitagoras appellavit humanitatem que in duos ramos, id est in virtutem et vitium se dividit. Cum enim in initio continuat, deinceps quidam in dextrum, quidam in sinistrum, id est quidam in vitium, quidam in virtutem se dividunt. Hec autem arbor gravedine carnis opacca est. Quia humanitas ad modum arboris dividitur, ideo hoc loco 'arbor' vocatur et a Pitagora per y caracterem furcate arboris formam habentem figuratur" (Bern. Sil., *Sup. En.* 6.136, p. 58; cf. trans., pp. 57–58). Cf. Servius and Remigius on *Aeneid* 6.136 and the discussions in chapter 2, pp. 90–91, and chapter 6, pp. 223–25.

13. The early books of the *Aeneid* provide a few examples of figures of virtue and vice: Mercury in the first book represents eloquence and Apollo represents divine or human wisdom; Cymothoe, delight; Creusa, concupiscence or the power of the search for the good; and Ascanius, the mean or "without degree." In the third book, Delos is glossed as the radiance or the honorable life; Anius as the wise man to whom nothing new happens; Italy as the nature of the soul, or growth; and Ulysses as "the sense of all things." The fourth book repeats Mercury as eloquence and the fifth introduces Iris as sense (or Beroes as reason).

14. Other figures from book 6 include the faculties or attributes of divine wisdom (Hecate), the Creator (Phoebus, or Jupiter as the World Soul), wisdom (Apollo, Minos, Minerva, Orontes), the qualities accompanying wisdom such as reflection, memory, pleasure, discovery of likenesses, etc. (the nine Muses), and the mind that rules the flesh (Phorcys). Virtue is another quality both sought by and necessary in the seeker—divine virtue (Aristaeus), virtue (Perseus, Aecus, and Menelaus), natural virtue (Leucaspis), ardent virtue (Phlegyas), goodness or righteous labor (Calais), those in whom virtue overcomes the debilities of age (Parthenopaeus), and glory (Boreas, Aeolus). For eloquence the exemplars include Trivia, Calliope, Mercury, Cerberus, Rhadamanthus, and Retheo.

15. In Bernard, Fulgentius is cited as defining the monster as eloquence and his three heads as the disciplines of the trivium—grammar, dialectic, and rhetoric. According to the *Continentia Virgiliana* of Fulgentius, Cerberus represents brawling and legal contention; according to *Mitologiae* 1.6, he represents the flesh eater *creoboros* with three heads for the three ages when death enters the world (or at infancy, youth, and old age). Possibly Bernard used the definitions supplied by the Boethian commentaries of Remigius and the K Reviser, particularly those which cite Fulgentius. Note that Bernard on *Aeneid* 6.392 cites Boethius: "Dicitur enim Hercules Grece, gloria litis Latine; labor enim eum celebrem reddit. Unde Boetius: 'Herculem duri celebrant labores.' Dicitur et Alcides quasi fortis et formosus. Fortis notat virtutem, formosus gloriam" (*Sup. En.,* p. 87).

16. The gloss on the Hydra may derive from the Boethius commentaries of Remigius and his K Reviser. Note that Bernard explicitly acknowledges Boethius in this passage (on *Aeneid* 6.287): "Quod autem hoc integumentum habeat intellectum hunc notat Boetius ubi dicit questionem 'vivacissimo igne mentis' comburendam esse" (*Sup. En.,* p. 71).

17. Physical glosses in Bernard's *Aeneid* 6 commentary include: Castor and Pollux as two stars; Proserpina as the moon and Pluto as the earth; Juno as the earth and Ixion as the sun; Hydra as a many-streamed water course; the Chimaera as a mountain topped with lions, with cattle at the middle and snakes at the foot; Phorcys as a god of the sea; Boreas as wind; Charon as time with his father Polydemon as the firmament; the Giants as creations of the earth and sun; Cerberus as the earth; and Teucer as god of time or the sun.

18. See *Bernardi Silvestris De mundi universitate libri duo megacosmus et microcosmus,* ed. Carl Sigmund Barach and Johann Wrobel (Innsbruck, 1876); it has been translated by Wetherbee in *The Cosmographia of Bernardus Silvestris* (New York and London: Columbia University Press, 1973), and reedited by Dronke (Leiden: E. J. Brill, 1978).

19. See chapter 4 of Nitzsche for an analysis of the allegorical figures who create the human being.

20. In the *Aeneid* commentary's first book, of infancy, appear Triton as wailing, or the annoyance of flesh, Iopas as childish silence, Venus as goddess of wantonness, and Dido as lust. In the third book, on adolescence, appear Crete as corporal nature and Italy as spiritual nature, or growth; the Cyclops as the many wanderings of adolescents; Drepanus as childish harshness; Antandros as inconstancy; Thrace as avarice; Ida the forest as beauty; Polynestor as the heaping up of money; Polydorus as much bitterness; the Strophades as revolutions of vices; Polyphemus as pride; Circe as the opulence of earthly things; Aetna as vainglory; and Achaemenides as sadness.

21. The Furies represent perverse thought (Allecto), evil speech (Tisiphone), and evil deeds (Megaera); the Centaurs embody terrestrial goods; in addition, Scylla stands for simulators concealing malicious detractions; the Hydra for

ignorance; the Chimaera for lust or self-indulgence; the Gorgons for attendants of the flesh and daughters of Phorcys, or ill-will (Stenno is weakness, Euryale is evil speech, and Medusa is evil activity); Pegasus for rumor; the Harpies for rapacity (Aello means "attack upon another," Ochiroe, "to steal quickly," and Celeno, "concealment"); and the three-headed Geryon for the man laden with three kinds of vice, concealed, revealed, and well known.

22. Phineus stands for the avaricious man and his companion Polydemon for the city of demons; Phaedra for the incestuous self-indulgent; Procris for a type of the suspicious; Evander for the passionate lover; Pasiphaë for unnatural loving; Laodamia for anxious loving; Sicheus for the vice of gluttony or drunkenness; Polybotes for those who do not attend to their sacred office's dignity; Ideus for those who care nothing for the loss of the fatherland through injuries to others; Agamemnon's phalanxes for the multitudes of vices; Helen for terrestrial opulence; Paris for sensuousness; Deiphobus for fear or public terror; Priamus for passion (from "superior pressure"); the Trojans for carnal men; the Trojan horse for self-indulgence; Bacchus for intoxication; Tartarus or the Inferno for the life of the evil in our dwelling place; Aloeus for the avaricious man; his sons for cupidity and wealth; Salmoneus for the tyrant; and Tityus for the inquisitive man spiritually consumed by study.

23. Bernard's commentary on *De nuptiis* contains, in addition to its preface and accessus, nine sections set by Bernard in the accessus—all comments on Martianus's first book up to chapter 37, and essentially Martianus's first ten chapters—a first "oration" (integument) on Hymen; a brief didactic oration on Martianus's son; the wives of the gods; the deliberation of Mercury about virgins; Virtue's plan; the ascent of Mercury with Virtue (to Apollo); the meeting of Mercury and Virtue with Apollo; the ascent of Mercury and Virtue with Apollo to Jove; and the deliberation of Jove, Juno, and Minerva on the marriage of Philology and Mercury.

24. According to the accessus Bernard also intended (but failed) to include eight additional sections, on the assent of Jove, Juno, and Pallas; the summoning of the gods; the meeting of the gods; the assent of the gods; the tokens of Philology and the *insignia* of her ornaments; the applause of the Muses; the ascent of Philology; and finally, and seventeenth, the apotheosis of Philology.

25. The *Eunuchus* line recurs in Mythogr. III, book 1, chap. 7, and in Bern. Sil., *Sup. En.* 10.21, pp. 10, 96, 102. Compare Remigius's use of the Terence tag as a gloss on Bacchus, *In Mart.* 36.10; see pp. 280-82.

26. Alan of Lille (Alanus ab Insulis), *De planctu Naturae*, prose 5, ed. Nikolaus M. Häring, *SM* 3d series 19.2 (1978): 845-46; trans. James J. Sheridan, *Plaint of Nature* (Toronto: Pontifical Institute of Mediaeval Studies, 1980), p. 156.

27. See Nitzsche, chapter 5.

28. Alan of Lille, *De planctu Naturae*, ed. Häring, pp. 849-50; trans. Sheridan, pp. 164-65.

29. Ibid., ed. Häring, p. 850; trans. Sheridan, pp. 59-60.

30. Cited in Dronke, *Fabula*, p. 182; the definitions of Ceres are nearly identical.

31. Wetherbee, *Platonism and Poetry*, pp. 121–22; see also pp. 118–122, and "The Theme of Imagination in Medieval Poetry and the Allegorical Figure Genius," *M&H* 7 (1976): 45–64.

32. For a comparison of Bernard and John of Salisbury, see Padoán, pp. 234–39. The etymology of Aeneas's name, used also by John of Salisbury, is apparently original with Bernard.

33. John of Salisbury's moralized comments on the *Aeneid* occur in *Policraticus* 1.4, on the self-indulgence of hunting; in 2.15, on prophetic dreams; in 3.10, on the frivolity of the Trojans; in 6.22, on the effeminancy and lack of prudence in feminine rule (by Dido); in 8.6, on the decorum of feasting, and in 8.9, on appetite; and, finally, in 8.24, on the framework of the *Aeneid*.

34. For information concerning John's life and writings, see Hans Liebeschütz, *Mediaeval Humanism in the Life and Writings of John of Salisbury*, Studies of the Warburg Institute, vol. 17 (London: Warburg Institute, 1950), pp. 8–19; see also the fine biography in Reginald Lane Poole, *Illustrations of the History of Mediaeval Thought*, 2d ed., rev. (London: Society for Promoting Christian Knowledge; New York: Macmillan, 1920), chapter 7, "John of Salisbury," pp. 176–97. On the biographical and cultural context, see, in addition, Poole, "The Masters of the Schools of Paris and Chartres in John of Salisbury's Time," *EHR* 35 (1920): 321–42, rpt. in *Studies in Chronology and History*, coll. and ed. Austin Lane Poole (Oxford: Clarendon Press, 1934), pp. 223–47. See also, in *Studies*, chapters 16 ("John Salisbury at the Papal Court," pp. 248–58) and 17 ("The Early Correspondence of John of Salisbury," pp. 259–86).

35. See Janet Martin, "John of Salisbury as Classical Scholar," in *The World of John Salisbury*, ed. Michael Wilks, Studies in Church History Subsidia, 3 (Oxford: Basil Blackwell, 1984), pp. 179–201, here, p. 196; also see pp. 196–201 on his use of classical poetry.

36. Both of John's works have been edited by C. C. J. Webb: *Policraticus*, 2 vols. (1909; rpt. Frankfurt am Main: Minerva G.M.B.H., 1965); and *Metalogicon* (Oxford: Clarendon Press, 1929). Three incomplete translations of the *Policraticus* exist, one by Joseph B. Pike, in *Frivolities of Courtiers and Footprints of Philosophers: Being a Translation of the First, Second, and Third Books and Selections from the Seventh and Eighth Books of the Policraticus of John of Salisbury* (Minneapolis: University of Minneapolis Press; London: Humphrey Milford, Oxford University Press, 1938); one by John Dickinson, in *The Statesman's Book of John of Salisbury, Being the Fourth, Fifth, and Sixth Books, and Selections from the Seventh and Eighth Books of the Policraticus* (New York: Russell and Russell, 1963); and one of excerpts from all but the second book, by Cary J. Nederman, that also contains an edition, *Policraticus: Of the Frivolities of Courtiers and the Footprints of Philosophers* (Cambridge and New York: Cambridge University Press, 1990). All of the quotations from the text and most

of the translations of the *Policraticus* in this study derive from the Webb edition and the Pike translation as follows: *Policraticus* 1.4, Webb 1:391–93, Pike 13–15; *Policraticus* 2.15, Webb 1:431, Pike 78; *Policraticus* 8.6, Webb 2:729, Pike 323; *Policraticus* 8.24, Webb 2:817–18, Pike 403–4. For a translation of the *Metalogicon*, see that of Daniel D. McGarry (Berkeley and Los Angeles: University of California Press, 1962).

37. Martin, p. 197.

38. On mythology, John claims that "The Thebans were held in little esteem by the Athenians and the Spartans (peoples of greater dignity, who clothed in the ornate veil of mythology historical facts, the secrets of nature, and the origin of customs [*historiarum gesta, naturae morumque mysteria uariis figmentorum inuolucris obtextentes*]). Their tales, however, served the useful purpose of admonition against defects of character and conduct, and the charm of their poetic form gave pleasure" (1.4; Webb, 1:390d; Pike, p. 14).

39. See Phillip W. Damon, "A Note on the Neckham Canon," *Speculum* 32 (1957): 99. For a bibliography of his works, see M. Espositio, "On Some Unpublished Poems Attributed to Alexander Neckaut," *EHR* 30 (1915): 450–71.

40. Alexander's commentary on the first two books of Martianus is contained in the Cambridge Trinity College MS. 884, fols. 38–63a (14th century) and in Bodleian MS. Digby 221, fols. 35b–88r (14th century), and is presently being edited by Catherine Emerson at the University of Toronto under the direction of Professor Virginia Brown. The late Judson B. Allen loaned me his unpublished transcription of Digby; all references to this mythography come from his transcription. Mythological glosses in it include, among others: *fabula,* 35r; Hymen, 36v; Calliope, 36v; Bacchus, 37v; Hercules, 39v; Jove and Juno, 39v; Pluto, 41r; Phlegethon, 42v.

41. Betty Nye Quinn lists a commentary on the *Ecloga* by Alexander in "ps. Theodolus," in *CTC* 2:383–408. She believes Alexander wrote one of the major commentaries, which remained in existence as late as the fourteenth century (circulated as the work of "Stephen Patrington") and which influenced the fifteenth-century commentary by Odo of Picardy. For the unedited text of Alexander Neckam (or "Stephen Patrington"), see Vatican MS. lat. 1479, fols. 15v–25r.

42. Information about Neckam's life and writings can be found in Manitius, *Geschichte* 9.2.3:784–94; and especially in Joseph de Ghellinck, *L'Essor de la littérature latine au XIIe siècle,* Museum Lessianum-Section historique, no. 4–5 (Brussels: L'Édition Universelle; Paris: Desclée de Brouwer, 1946), 1:150–54. See also the comments in the introduction to the edition of *De naturis rerum* by Thomas Wright, *De naturis rerum libri duo and De laudibus divinae sapientiae,* Rolls Series no. 34 (London: Longman, Roberts, and Green, 1863), pp. ix–xii. Subsequent references to *De naturis rerum* derive from this edition.

43. The identity of the third Vatican mythographer has not yet been definitely proven, although Alberic of London in recent years has enjoyed the staunchest support as a candidate among scholars. Yet even the scholar who first suggested Alberic as a leading candidate admits that the work is frequently attributed to Alexander Neckam in manuscripts and that Alexander's commentary on Martianus Capella depends heavily on the *Poetarius* (as the treatise on the pagan gods was frequently termed): see the article by Eleanor Rathbone, "Master Alberic of London, 'Mythographus Tertius Vaticanus,' " *MRS* 1 (1943): esp. pp. 35–37. The comments on Alexander Neckam belong to the late Richard Hunt, who apparently intended to complete a study of Neckam.

44. Damon, p. 99. In addition there are florilegia compiled from Alexander's works that exist elsewhere and hundreds of citations and allusions in writings of medieval and Renaissance writers.

45. I refer to J. B. Allen's transcription of Digby 221: the Jupiter gloss is on fol. 39rb; Danaë and Leda on fol. 38vb; Midas and Prometheus on 53rb.

46. Ibid., fol. 42ra, for the entire discussion of the underworld, its rivers, and its circles.

BIBLIOGRAPHY

PRIMARY SOURCES

Manuscripts

Ailly, Pierre d'. "Tractatus utilis supra Boetium." Paris. B.N. MS. 3122, fols. 110r–169v.

Anonymous Barberinus. Commentary on Martianus Capella, *De nuptiis* books 1–2 (12th c.). Rome. Vat. MS. Barb. lat. 10.

Anonymous Cambridge. Commentary on Martianus Capella (9th c.). Cambridge. Corpus Christi Library MSS. 153, 330.

Anonymous Galliensis [Anonymous of St. Gall]. Commentary on Boethius. Minor. Naples. Biblioteca Nazionale MS. IV.G.68, fols. 1v–92v. Major. Einsiedeln Stiftsbibliothek MS. 179, fols. 95–185.

Anonymous Reginensis. Commentary on Boethius. Rome. Vat. MS. Reg. 72, fols. 110–26; MS. Reg. 244, fols. 43–65.

Arnulf, of Orleans [Arnulfus Aurelianensis]. Commentary on Ovid's *Fasti*. Rome. Vat. MS. Reg. 1548.

Bernard, of Utrecht [Bernardus Traiectensis, Traiectensis, Ultrajectensis]. Commentary on the *Theoduli Ecloga*. Munich. Staatsbibliothek MS. Clm. 22293, fols. 1v–41r.

Cortumelia, Guillermus de. "Super libro Boetijde Consolatione Philosophiae." Rome. Vat. MS. Chigiani. E.VII. 229, fols. 1r–84v.

Florentine Commentary on Martianus Capella. Florence. Biblioteca Nazionale Centrale MS. Conventi Soppr. J.1.28, fols. 50r–64v.

Greban, Arnoul. "Commentum super Boetium." Paris. B.N. MS. 9323, fols. 1r–191. Rheims. MS. 896, fols. 1–355.

Guido, da Pisa, Fra'. "Expositiones et glose super Comediam Dantis." London. B. L. MS. Add. 31918.

Holkot [Holcot], Robert. "In librum duodecim prophetas." Oxford. Bodl. MS. 722.

Hopeman, Thomas. Commentary on Hebrews. London. B.L. MS. Royal 4.A.i.

Huguccio [Huguitio, Uguccio] of Pisa. "Liber derivationum," or "Magnae derivationes." Cambridge. MS. Gonville and Caius 459/718, fol. 97ff. Florence. Biblioteca Medicea Laurenziana MS. Pluteus XXVII Sinister. MS. 1, fols. 1r–453v. Oxford. Bodl. MS. 376 (14th c.).

Manegold, of Lautenbach [von Lutterbach]. "Explicationes Metamorphoseon Ovidii." Munich. Staatsbibliothek MS. Monacensis Latinus 4610, originally from Benediktbeuern, 144872, 14809.

Muglio [Moglio], Pietro da. Commentary on Dante. Poppi. Biblioteca Comunale MS. 45.

Neckam [Neckham, Nequam], Alexander. Commentary on the *Theodoli Ecloga*. Rome. Vat. MS. 1479, fols. 15v–25r.

———. "Super Marcianum De nupciis Mercurii et Philologie." Books 1 and 2. Oxford. Bodl. MS. Digby 211, fols. 34b–88.

Ralph, of Beauvais. "Liber Titani." London. B.L. MS. Add. 16380, fols. 111r–19v.

Rambaldi da Imola, Benvenuto. "Lucani Pharsalia cum Benvenuti enarrationibus." Ferrara. Biblioteca de' Padri Carmelitani di San Paolo MS.

Rather, of Verona. Martianus Capella with notes. Leiden. University Library MS. Voss. lat. F.48, fols. 2r–91v.

Regnier, of St. Tron. Commentary on Boethius. Paris. B.N. MS. 3122, fols. 110–169r.

Ridewall [Ridevall], John. Commentary on *De civitate Dei*, books 1–2, 6–7. Oxford. Corpus Christi Library MSS. 186–87.

Rossato, Alberto. "Liber poetarius de fabularum integumentis Ovidii Alberti Rossato." Stift Kremsmünster, Austria. MS. Cremifanensis 149 (3.vii.40), fols. 12a–61b.

Tholomaeus, de Asinariis. Commentary on Boethius. Paris. B.N. MS. 6410, fols. 1r–171v. Vienna. MS. 376.

Travesio, Giovanni. Commentary on Boethius. Turin. Biblioteca Nazionale MS. G.IV.2.

Trivet [Trevet], Nicholas. Commentary on Augustine's *De civitate Dei* (books 11–23) and on Seneca. Oxford. Bodl. MS. 292.

———. Commentary on Seneca's *Tragedies*. Oxford. Bodl. MS. Bodley 292.

———. "Exposicio super librum Boecii *De consolatione*." Oxford. Bodl. MS. Rawlinson G.187, fols. 46rff. Rome. Vat. MSS. 562, 563; Reg. lat. 1066; Rossian 358; Ottob. lat. 1671, 2026.

———. "Scriptum super sexto libro *Eneydos*." Venice. Biblioteca Nazionale Marciana MS. lat. xii, 42.

William, of Aragon. Commentary on Boethius. Erfurt. MS. 358, fols. 1r–25r.

William, of Conches. "Glosulae super Boethium." London. B.L., King's Library MS. Egerton 628, fols. 165r–95r. MS. 15B III, fols. 1–143. Paris. B.N. MS. lat. 14380.

———. "Super commentarius Macrobii in *Somnium Scipionis*." Rome. Vat. MS. Urb. lat. 1140.

Printed Materials

Acta sanctorum. Coll. Joannes Bollandus. Ed. Jean Baptiste Carnandet. 68 vols. 1643; rpt. Brussels: Culture et civilisation, 1965–70.

Adalbold, of Utrecht. "Il commento a Boezio di Adalboldo di Utrecht." Ed. Tullio

Gregory. In *Platonismo medievale, Studi e ricerche*, pp. 1–6. Istituto Storico Italiana per il Medio Evo Stori Storici, fasc. 26–27. Rome: Nella sede dell'Istituto, 1958.

Adanan, the Scot [Berne scholiast]. *Scholia Bernensia ad Vergilii Bucolica atque Georgica.* Ed. Hermann Hagen. Jahrbücher für classische Philologie, supp. 4, pt. 5. Leipzig, 1867.

Adnotationes super Lucanum. Ed. Johann Endt. Leipzig: B. G. Teubner, 1909.

Alan, of Lille [Alain de Lille, Alanus ab Insulis]. *De planctu Naturae.* Ed. Nikolaus M. Häring. *Studi mediaevali* 3d series 19 (1978): 797–879.

————. *The Plaint of Nature.* Trans. James J. Sheridan. Toronto: Pontifical Institute of Mediaeval Studies, 1980.

Alberic, of London [third Vatican mythographer?]. *Allegoriae poeticae, seu De veritate ac expositione poeticarum fabularum libri quatuor Alberico Londonensi authore.* Ed. J. C. Virense. [Paris], 1520.

————. *De diis gentium et illorum allegoriis.* In *Classicorum auctorum e Vaticanis codicibus.* Ed. Angelo Mai. Vol. 3. Rome, 1831.

————. *De diis gentium et illorum allegoriis.* In Mythographi Vaticani, *Scriptores rerum mythicarum Latini tres Romae nuper reperti.* Ed. Georgius Henricus Bode. 1834; rpt. Hildesheim: Georg Olms, 1968.

————. Prologue, *Poetria.* In *Beiträge zur altern Literatur oder Merkwürdigkeiten der Herzogl. öffentlichen Bibliothek zu Gotha.* Ed. Friedrich Jacobs and F. A. Ukert. Vol. 1, pt. 2. Leipzig, 1835.

Aldhelm. *De virginitate.* In *Aldhelmi opera.* Ed. Rudolf Ehwald. *MGH*, 15.

Alfred, King. *King Alfred's Anglo-Saxon Version of the Metres of Boethius, with an English Translation and Notes.* Trans. and ed. Samuel Fox. London, Oxford and Leicester, 1835.

————. *King Alfred's Old English Version of Boethius: De consolatione Philosophiae.* Ed. Walter John Sedgefield. Oxford, 1899.

————. *King Alfred's Version of the Consolation of Boethius.* Trans. Walter John Sedgefield. Oxford: Clarendon Press, 1900.

Alighieri, Dante. *Il convivio.* In *Opere minori: La vita nuova—Il convivio—Le rime.* Ed. Elisa Colesanti. I classici Azzuri, 30. Rome: Cremonese, 1956.

————. *Dante's Convivio.* Trans. William Walrond Jackson. Oxford: Clarendon Press, 1909.

————. *Dantis Alagherii Epistolae: The Letters of Dante.* Trans. and ed. Paget Toynbee. 2d edition. Oxford: Clarendon Press, 1966.

————. *La divina commedia.* Ed. C. H. Grandgent. Rev. Charles S. Singleton. Cambridge, Mass.: Harvard University Press, 1972.

————. *The Divine Comedy.* In *The Portable Dante.* Trans. Paolo Milano. 1947; rpt. New York: Viking, 1968.

————. *The Literary Criticism of Dante Alighieri.* Trans. and ed. Robert S. Haller. Lincoln: University of Nebraska Press, 1973.

Alighieri, Jacopo. *Chiose alla cantica dell'Inferno di Dante Allighieri atribuite a Iacopo suo figlio.* Florence, 1848.

———. *Chiose di Dante le quali fece el figiuolo co le sue mani: Messe in luce da F. D. Luiso.* Vol. 2: *Purgatorio.* Florence: G. Carnesecchi and Sons, 1904.

Alighieri, Pietro. *Petri Allegherii super Dantis ipsius genitoris Comoediam commentarium nunc primum in lucem editum.* Ed. Vincentio Nannucci. Florence, 1845.

Annales Laudunenses. In *Reliquiae manuscriptorum omnis aevi diplomatum ae monumentorum, ineditorum.* Ed. Johann Peter von Ludewig. Vol. 3 of 3. Halae Salicae, vols. 10–12. Frankfurt and Leipzig, 1720–41.

Andeli, Henri d'. *Oeuvres.* Ed. A. Heron. 1881; rpt. Geneva: Slatkine, 1974.

Anonymous Barberinus. "Barberini Manuscripts 57–66 and 121–130." Ed. Ann Rose Raia. Diss., Fordham University, 1965.

Anonymous of Erfurt. *Saeculi noni auctoris in Boetii Consolationem Philosophiae commentarius.* Ed. Edmund Taite Silk. Papers and Monographs of the American Academy in Rome, vol. 9. Rome: American Academy in Rome, 1935.

Anonymous Florentine. *Commento alla divina Commedia d'Anonimo Fiorentino del secolo XVI.* Ed. Pietro Fanfani. 3 vols. Bologna, 1866–74.

Anonymous Selmiano. *Chiose anonime alla prima cantica della divina Commedia di un contemporaneo del poeta pubblicate per la prima volta a celebrare il sesto anno secolare della nascita di Dante da Francesco Selmi con riscontri di altri antichi commenti editi ed inediti e note filoligiche.* Ed. Francesco Selmi. Turin, 1865.

Anonymous Teutonicus. "Anonymi Teutonici commentum in *Theodoli eclogam* e codice Utrecht, U.B. 292 editum." Ed. Árpad P. Orbán. *Vivarium* 11 (1973): 1–42; 12 (1974): 133–45; 13 (1975): 77–88; 14 (1976): 50–61; 15 (1977): 143–58.

Aquinas, pseudo-Thomas. Commentary on Boethius's *Consolation.* In *Sancti Thomae Aquinatis doctoris angelici ordinis praedicatorum opuscula alia dubia adjectis brevibus adnotationibus.* Vol. 3. In *Opera omnia,* 24: 1–147. Parma, 1869.

Aquinas, St. Thomas. *Summa theologica.* Vol. 1 of *Christian Theology.* Ed. Thomas Gilby. Cambridge: Blackfriars, 1964.

Arnobius. *Adversus nationes libres VII.* Ed. August Reifferscheid. CSEL, vol. 4. 1875; rpt. New York: Johnson Reprint Co., 1968.

Arnulf, of Orleans [Arnulfus Aurelianensis]. *Allegoriae super Ovidii Metamorphosin.* Ed. Fausto Ghisalberti. In "Arnolfo d'Orléans: Un cultore di Ovidio nel secolo XII." *Memorie del Reale Istituto Lombardo di Scienze e Lettere* 24 (1917–39): 155–234.

———. *Glosule super Lucanum.* Ed. Berthe M. Marti. Rome: American Academy in Rome, 1958.

Asser. Commentary on Boethius. Ed. Fabio Troncarelli. In the appendix to *Tradizioni perdute: L'antica 'fortuna' della 'Consolatio Philosophiae,'* pp. 141–201. Padua: Antenore, 1980.

Augustine, St. *De civitate Dei contra paganos libri (The City of God against the pagans).* Trans. George E. McCracken, William Chase Greene, David S. Wiesen, P. Levine, and E. M. Sanford. 7 vols. Loeb Classics. London: Heinemann/Cambridge, Mass.: Harvard University Press, 1957–72.

———. *Sancti Aurelii Augustini Episcopi De civitate Dei libri XXII.* Rev. Bernhard Dombart and Alfonsus Kalb. 5th ed. Bibliotheca scriptorum Graecorum et Romanorum Teubneriana. Stuttgart: B.G. Teubner, 1981. Vol. 1: i–xiii.

———. *The City of God.* Trans. Marcus Dods. New York: Modern Library, 1950.

———. *De doctrina Christiana; De vera religione.* Ed. Joseph Martin. CC 32. Turnhout: Brepols, 1962.

———. *De Genesi ad litteram.* Ed. Joseph Zycha. CSEL, vol. 28, no. 3. Prague, Vienna, and Leipzig, 1894.

———. *De utilitate credendi.* Ed. Joseph Zycha. CSEL, vol. 25. Prague, Vienna, and Leipzig, 1891.

———. *On Christian Doctrine.* Trans. D. W. Robertson, Jr. Indianapolis and New York: Bobbs-Merrill, 1958.

Bade d'Assche, Josse. *Duplex commentatio ex integro reposita atque recognita in Boetium: seu Boethum manis: De consolatione philosophica et De disciplina scholastica. Ea videlicetque divo Thome Aquinato ascribitur. Etque ab Ascensio recentius est emissa: una cum libello de moribus in mensa informádis omnibus inteneris annis constitutis per necessario a Sulpitio verulano edito.* 1506.

Balbi, Giovanni [Joannes Balbus]. *Catholicon Johannis Januensis.* Lyons, 1492.

———. *Catholicon.* Mainz, 1460. Rpt. facsimile, Westmead, Farnborough, Hants, England: Gregg International Publishers, 1971.

Bambaglioli, Graziolo. *Il commento dantesco di Graziolo de' Bambaglioli dal 'Colombino' di Siviglia con altri codici raffrontato.* Ed. Antonio Fiammazzo. Savona: D. Bertolotto, 1915.

Bargigi, Guiniforto delli. *Lo inferno della Commedia di Dante Alighieri col comento di Guiniforto delli Bargigi.* Ed. G. Zacheroni. Marseilles, 1838.

Baudri, of Bourgueil. Poem no. 216, "Fragment of a Moralized Mythology." In *Les Oeuvres póetiques de Baudri de Bourgueil (1046–1139)*, pp. 273–316. Ed. Phyllis Abrahams. Paris: Honoré Champion, 1926.

Bede, Venerable. *Historia ecclesiatica gentis Anglorum, Historia abbatum, Epistola ad Ecgberctum.* Ed. Charles Plummer. 2 vols. Oxford, 1896.

Berchorius, Petrus. *See* Bersuire, Pierre.

Bernard Silvestris. *The Commentary on the First Six Books of the Aeneid Commonly Attributed to Bernardus Silvestris.* Ed. Julian Ward Jones and Elizabeth Frances Jones. Lincoln and London: University of Nebraska Press, 1977.

———. *The Commentary on the First Six Books of the Aeneid.* Trans. Daniel Carl Meerson. In "The Ground and Nature of Literary Theory in Bernard Silvester's Twelfth-Century Commentary on the *Aeneid.*" Diss., University of Chicago, 1967.

————. *Commentary on the First Six Books of Virgil's Aeneid.* Trans. Earl G. Schreiber and Thomas E. Maresca. Lincoln and London: University of Nebraska Press, 1979.

————. Commentary on Martianus Capella. [Excerpts.] Ed. Édouard Jeauneau. In "Notes sur l'école de Chartres." *Studi medievali,* 3d series 5.2 (1964): 855–64.

————. *The Commentary on Martianus Capella's* De Nuptiis Philologiae et Mercurii *Attributed to Bernardus Silvestris.* Ed. Haijo Jan Westra. Studies and Texts, 80. Toronto: Pontifical Institute of Mediaeval Studies, 1986.

————. *Cosmographia.* Ed. Peter Dronke. Leiden: E. J. Brill, 1978.

Bernard, of Utrecht. *Commentum in Theodulum.* In "Bernard's *Commentum in Theodulum:* Editio Princeps." Ed. Morton Yale Jacobs. Diss., University of North Carolina, 1963.

————. *Commentum in Theodolum.* Ed. R. B. C. Huygens. Biblioteca degli "Studi medievali." Spoleto: Centro Italiano di Studi sull'Alto Medioevo, 1977.

Berne scholiast. *See* Adanan the Scot.

Bersuire, Pierre. "De formis figurisque deorum." Cap. 1 of *Reductorium morale, liber XV: Ovidius moralizatus.* Ed. Joseph Engels. Utrecht: Instituut voor Laat Latijn der Rijksuniversiteit, 1966.

————. "Petrus Berchorius, Reductorium morale, liber XV: *Ovidius moralizatus,* cap. ii." Ed. Maria S. van der Bijl. *Vivarium* 9 (1971): 25–48.

————. *Reductorium morale, liber XV, cap. ii–xv: Ovidius moralizatus.* Ed. Joseph Engels. Utrecht: Instituut voor Laat Latijn der Rijksuniversiteit, 1962.

————. Epilogue, *Reductorium morale.* Ed. Maria S. van der Bijl. In "Berchoriana: La collatio pro fine operis de Bersuire, édition critique." *Vivarium* 3 (1965): 149–70.

————. "The *Ovidius Moralizatus* of Petrus Berchorius: An Introduction and Translation." Trans. William D. Reynolds. Diss., University of Illinois, 1971.

————. "Selections from *De formis figurisque deorum.*" Trans. William D. Reynolds. *Allegorica* 2 (1977): 58–89.

Boccaccio, Giovanni. *Esposizioni sopra la Comedia di Dante.* Ed. Giorgio Padoan. Vol. 6 of *Opere.* Ed. Vittore Branca. I Classici Mondadori. Genoa: Arnoldo Mondadori, 1965.

————. *Genealogie deorum gentilium libri.* Ed. Vincenzo Romano. 2 vols. *Opere,* vols. 10–11. Scrittori d'Italia no. 200–201. Bari: Gius. Laterza & Sons, 1951.

————. *La Généalogie des dieux.* French trans. Laurent de Premierfait. Antoine Vérard, 1498; new edition, Paris, 1536.

————. *On Poetry: Being the Preface and the Fourteenth and Fifteenth Books of Boccaccio's Genealogia deorum gentilium in an English Version.* Trans. Charles G. Osgood. 1930; rpt. Indianapolis: Bobbs-Merrill, 1956.

Boccaccio (False), of Roveta. *Chiose sopra Dante testo inedito ora per la prima volta pubblicato.* Ed. William Warren Vernon. Florence, 1846.

Boethius, Anicius Manlius Severinus. *De consolatione Philosophiae.* Ed. L. Biehler. CCSL, vol. 94. Turnhout: Brepols, 1957.

———. *Philosophiae consolationis libri quinque.* Ed. Rudolfus Peiper. Leipzig, 1871.

———. *Boethius: De consolatione Philosophiae.* Trans. John Walton. Ed. Mark Science. EETS o.s. vol. 170. London: Humphrey Milford, Oxford University Press, 1927.

———. *The Consolation of Philosophy.* Trans. Richard H. Green. Library of Liberal Arts. Indianapolis and New York: Bobbs- Merrill, 1962.

———. *Tractates; De consolatione Philosophiae.* Trans. H. F. Stewart, E. K. Rand, S. J. Tester. Loeb Classics. London: Heinemann; Cambridge, Mass.: Harvard University Press, 1978.

———. *Das altprovenzalische Boethiuslied unter Beifügung einer Übersetzung, eines Glossars, erklärender Anmerkungen, sowie grammatischer und metrischer Untersungen.* Ed. and German trans. Franz Hündgen. Oppeln, 1884.

Bonaventure, St. *Ars concionandi.* In *Opera omnia.* Quarrachi: Ad claras aquas, 1901.

———. *Ars concionandi.* In "A Translation, with Commentary, of the Bonaventuran 'Ars Concionandi.' " Trans. Harry C. Hazel. Diss., Washington State University, 1972.

———. *De reductione artium ad theologiam.* Trans. and ed. Sister Emma Thérèse Healy. In *Works of St. Bonaventure.* St. Bonaventure, N.Y.: Franciscan Institute, 1955.

Bonsignore, Giovanni. *Ouidio methamorphoseos vulgare. Allegorie ed esposizioni delle Metamorfosis.* Venice, 1497; Milan, 1519.

Buti, Francesco di Bartolo, da. *Commento di Francesco da Buti sopra de divina Comedia di Dante Allighieri.* Ed. Crescentino. 3 vols. Pisa, 1858–62.

Chaucer, Geoffrey. *The Riverside Chaucer.* Ed. Larry D. Benson. 3d edition. Boston: Houghton Mifflin, 1987.

Christine, de Pizan. *L'Epistre Othea a Hector.* In Halina D. Loukopoulos, "Classical Mythology in the Works of Christine de Pisan, with an Edition of 'L'Epistre Othea' from the Manuscript Harley 4431." Diss., Wayne State University, 1977.

———. *The Epistle of Othea to Hector, or The Boke of Knyghthode.* Trans. Stephen Scrope. Ed. George Warner. London: J. B. Nichols and Sons, 1904.

———. *"The Epistle of Othea to Hector": Translated into Middle English by Stephen Scrope.* Ed. Curt F. Bühler. EETS, vol. 264. New York, Toronto, and London: Oxford University Press, 1970.

———. "The 'Livre de la Cité des Dames': A Critical Edition." Ed. Maureen Curnow. Diss., Vanderbilt University, 1975.

———. *The Book of the City of Ladies.* Trans. Earl Jeffrey Richards. New York: Persea, 1982.

Cicero. *De natura deorum; Academica.* Ed. and trans. H. Rackham. Loeb Classics. London: Heinemann; New York: Putnams, 1933.

———. *The Nature of the Gods.* Trans. Horace C. P. McGregor. Middlesex & New York: Penguin Books, 1972.

Clement, of Alexandria. *The Exhortation to the Greeks, the Rich Man's Salvation, and the Fragment of an Address Entitled to the Newly Baptized.* London: Heinemann; New York: Putnams, 1919.

―――. *Opera.* Ed. William Dindorf. 4 vols. Oxford, 1869.

Cornutus. *Theologiae Graecae compendium.* Ed. C. Lang. Leipzig, 1881.

Dante. *See* Alighieri, Dante.

De Foxton, John. *Liber cosmographiae: An Edition and Codicological Study.* Ed. John Block Friedman. Brill's Studies in Intellectual History, vol. 5. Leiden and New York: E. J. Brill, 1988.

Diels, Hermann, ed. *Die Fragmente der Vorsokratiker.* 3 vols. 1952; rpt. Berlin: Weidmannsche, 1960. *See* Freeman.

Digby Mythographer. "An Edition of an Anonymous Twelfth-Century *Liber de natura deorum.*" Ed. Virginia Brown. *MS.* 34 (1972): 1–70.

Dindorf, William, ed. *Scholia Graeca in Homeri Iliadem ex codicibus aucta et emendata.* Vol. 4. 1877; rpt. Amsterdam: A. M. Hakkert, 1969.

―――, ed. *Scholia Graeca in Homeri Odysseam.* 1875; rpt. Amsterdam: A. M. Hakkert, 1962. Vol. 1.

Diogenes Laertius. *Lives of the Eminent Philosophers.* Trans. R. D. Hicks. 2 vols. London: Heinemann; New York: Putnams, 1925.

Dionysius, the Carthusian [Dionysius Cartusianus, Denis de Lewis]. *D. Dionysii Cartusiani Enarrationes seu commentaria in V libros De consolatione Philosophiae B. Severini Boetii.* In *Opera omnia,* vol. 26. Tournai: S. M. de Pratis, 1906.

Donatus. *Vita Vergiliana. See* Servius, vol. 3.

Dunchad. *See* Martin of Laon.

Ecloga Theoduli. Ed. John Gottlob Samuel Schwabe. Altenburg, 1773.

―――. *Theoduli eclogam recensuit et prolegomenis instruxit Joannes Osternacher.* In *Fünfter Jahresbericht des bischöflichen Privat-Gymnasiums am Kollegium Petrinum in Urfahr für das Schuljahr 1901/02.* Urfahr prope Lentiam: Programmate Collegii Petrini, 1902.

―――. In *Octo autores. Autores octo continentes libros: videlicet cantonem. Facetum Theodulum. De contemptu mundi. Floretum. Alanum De parabolis. Fabulas Esopi. Thobiam. De modo punctuandi. Regimen mente honorabile.* Lyons, 1525.

―――. In *Ten Latin Schooltexts of the Later Middle Ages.* Trans. Ian Thomson and Louis Perraud. Mediaeval Studies, vol. 6. Lewiston, Queenston, and Lampeter: Edward Mellen, 1990.

―――. *See* Bernard of Utrecht.

Ennius, Quintus. *Annuales.* In *Carminum reliquae.* Ed. Lucian Mueller. St. Petersburg, 1884.

Erbse, Hartmut, ed. *Scholia Graeca in Homeri Iliadem (scholia vetera).* Vol. 4: *Scholia ad libros O-T continuens.* Berlin: Walter de Gruyter, 1975.

Erfurt Commentator [pseudo-John Scot]. *See* Anonymous of Erfurt.

Eucherius, of Lyons. *Formulae spiritualis intellegentiae.* Ed. Karl Wotke. CSEL, vol. 31. Prague, Vienna, and Leipzig, 1894.

Euhemerus. Excerpts. In *Reliquiae.* Ed. Geyza Némethy. Budapest, 1889.

Fabricius, J. A. *Bibliotheca ecclesiastica.* Hamburg, 1718.

Filelfo, Francesco. *Epistole Francisci Philelfi nuper lima acriori castigate cum quibusdam orationibus . . . superadditis.* Vol. iiii (r). Paris, 1507.

First Vatican mythographer. *See Mythographii Vaticani.*

Florentine Commentary on Martianus Capella. *See* William, of Conches.

Freeman, Kathleen, trans. *Ancilla to the Pre-Socratic Philosophers: A Complete Translation of the Fragments in Diels, Fragmente der Vorsokratiker.* Oxford: Basil Blackwell, 1952.

Fulgentius, Fabius Planciades. *Opera.* Ed. Rudolf Helm. 1898; rpt. Stuttgart: B. G. Teubner, 1970.

—————. *Expositio Virgilianae continentiae.* Trans. Lynn Carroll Stokes. In "Fulgentius and the *Expositio Virgilianae Continentiae.*" Diss., Tufts University, 1969.

—————. *Fulgentius the Mythographer.* Trans. Leslie George Whitbread. Columbus: Ohio State University Press, 1971.

Garin, Eugenio, ed. *Prosatori latini del quattrocento.* 1952; rpt. Turin: Giulio Einaudi, 1977. Vol 6.

Gesta Berengarii imperatoris. In *Poetae Latini aevi Carolini.* Ed. Paul von Winterfeld. *Poetarum Latinorum medii aevi.* In *MGH.* Berlin, 1899.

Gesta Romanorum: Entertaining Stories. Trans. Charles Swan. London: Routledge; New York: Dutton, 1924.

Glossaria Latina: Iussu academiae Britannicae edita. Nouvelle Collection de Textes et Documents. Paris: Les Belles Lettres, 1926 (vols. 2–3), 1930 (vols. 4–5).

Godman, Peter, ed. *Poetry of the Carolingian Renaissance.* Norman: University of Oklahoma Press, 1985.

Gottschalk [Godescalc], of Orbais. *Oeuvres théologiques et grammaticales de Godescalc d'Orbais: Textes en majeure partie inédits.* Ed. Cyrille Lambot. Louvain: Spicilesium Sacrum Lovaniense, 1945.

Guibert, of Nogent. "Guibert de Nogent's *Liber quo ordine sermo fieri debeat:* A Translation of the Earliest Modern Speech Textbook." Trans. Joseph M. Miller. *Today's Speech* 17 (1969): 46.

Guido, da Pisa, Fra'. "Dichiarazione poetica dell'Inferno dantesco di Frate Guido da Pisa." No. 59 in *Poesie di mille autori intorno a Dante Alighieri raccolte ed ordinate cronologicamente con note storiche, bibliografiche e biografiche.* Ed. Carlo del Balzo. Vol. 1. Rome, 1889.

—————. *Expositiones et glose super Comediam Dantis,* cantos 29, 34. Ed. Francesco Paolo Luiso. In "Di un'opera inedita di Frate Guido da Pisa." *Miscellanea di studi critici pubblicati in onore di Guido Mazzoni dai suoi discepoli.* Vol. 1, pp. 79–135. Florence: Tipografia Galileiana, 1907.

————. *Commentary on Dante's Inferno.* Ed. Vincenzo Cioffari. Albany: State University of New York Press, 1974.

Guillaume, de Conches. *See* William, of Conches.

Guillaume, de Lorris, and Jean de Meun. *Le Roman de la Rose par Guillaume de Lorris et Jean de Meun.* Ed. Ernest Langlois. 5 vols. Société des Anciens Textes Français, vols. 117–21. Paris: Honoré Champion, 1921.

————. *The Romance of the Rose.* Trans. Charles Dahlberg. Princeton: Princeton University Press, 1971.

Gunzo, of Novara. Glosses on Boethius. [Excerpts.] Ed. Édouard Jeauneau. In "L'Usage de la notion d'*integumentum* à travers les gloses de Guillaume de Conches." *AHDLMA* 32 (1957): 35–100.

Haenal, Gustav, ed. *Codices Gregorianus, Hermogenianus, Theodosianus.* Corpus Iuris Romani Anteiustiniani, fasc. 2–6. Leipzig and Bonn, 1837–42.

Henry of Aragón. *See* Villena, Enrique de.

Heraclitus, of Ephesus. *Allégories d'Homère.* Ed. and trans. Félix Buffière. Paris: Les Belles Lettres, 1962.

Hesiod. *Theogony.* Trans. Thomas Cooke. In *The Additional Lives* to *The Works of the English Poets.* Ed. Alexander Chalmers. Vol. 20, pp. 763–73. London, 1810.

Holkot [Holcot], Robert. *Liber moralizationum historiarum.* In *M. Roberti Holkoth . . . In librum Sapientiae Regis Salomonis praelectiones CCXIII,* pp. 705–50. Bale, 1586.

————. *Moralitates.* Venice, 1514; 1586.

————. *Super librum Ecclesiastici;* Venice, 1509.

Horace. *Ars poetica.* Ed. C. O. Brink. Cambridge and London: Cambridge University Press, 1971.

Hrotsvit. *Hrotsvithae opera.* Ed. Paul von Winterfeld. Scriptores Rerum Germanicarum (*MGH*). 1902; rpt. Berlin and Turin: Weidmann's, 1965.

————. *Hrotsvithae opera.* Ed. Helena Homeyer. Munich: Paderborn; Vienna: Schöningh, 1970.

————. *The Plays of Hrotsvit of Gandersheim.* Trans. Katharina Wilson. Garland Library of Medieval Literature, series B, vol. 62. New York and London: Garland, 1989.

Hugh, of St. Victor. *Didascalicon de studio legendi.* Ed. Charles Henry Buttimer. Washington, D.C.: Catholic University of America Press, 1939.

Huguccio [Huguitio, Uguccio] of Pisa. *Magnae derivationes* [extracts]. In *La Renaissance du XIIe siècle: Les Écoles et l'enseignement.* Ed. G. Paré. Ottawa: Institut d'Etudes Mèdièvales; Paris: J. Vrin, 1933.

Hyginus. *Astronomica.* Ed. Bernard Bunte. Leipzig, 1875.

————. *Fabulae.* Ed. H. J. Rose. Leiden: A. W. Sijthoff, 1934.

————. *The Myths.* Trans. and ed. Mary Grant. University of Kansas Publications Humanistic Studies, no. 34. Lawrence: University Press of Kansas, 1960.

Isidore, of Seville. *Etymologiarum libri XX.* Ed. W. M. Lindsay. 2 vols. Scriptorum Classicorum Bibliotheca Oxoniensis. Oxford: Clarendon Press, 1911.

John, of Garland. *Integumenta Ovidii: Poemetto inedito del secolo XIII.* Ed. Fausto Ghisalberti. Testi e documenti inediti o rari, no. 2. Messina and Milan: Giuseppe Principato, 1933.

―――. *Integumenta Ovidii.* Trans. Lester Kruger Born. In "The Integumenta on the Metamorphoses of Ovid by John of Garland—First Edited with Introduction and Translation." Diss., University of Chicago, 1929.

John, of Salisbury. *Metalogicon.* Ed. Clemens C. J. Webb. Oxford: Clarendon Press, 1929.

―――. *The Metalogicon: A Twelfth-Century Defense of the Verbal and Logical Arts of the Trivium.* Trans. Daniel D. McGarry. Berkeley and Los Angeles: University of California Press, 1962.

―――. *Policraticus.* Ed. Clemens C. J. Webb. 2 vols. 1909; rpt. Frankfurt: Minerva G.M.B.H., 1965.

―――. *Frivolities of Courtiers and Footprints of Philosophers: Being a Translation of the First, Second, and Third Books and Selections from the Seventh and Eighth Books of the Policraticus of John of Salisbury.* Trans. Joseph B. Pike. Minneapolis: University of Minnesota Press; London: Humphrey Milford, Oxford University Press, 1938.

―――. *The Statesman's Book of John of Salisbury, Being the Fourth, Fifth, and Sixth Books and Selections from the Seventh and Eighth Books of the Policraticus.* Trans. John Dickinson. New York: Russell and Russell, 1963.

―――. *Policraticus: Of the Frivolities of Courtiers and the Footprints of Philosophers.* Cambridge and New York: Cambridge University Press, 1990.

John Scot, of Ireland [Joannes Scottus Eriugena]. *Annotationes in Marcianum.* Ed. Cora E. Lutz. Cambridge, Mass: Mediaeval Academy of America, 1939; rpt. New York: Kraus, 1970.

―――. "Le Commentaire inédit de Jean Scot Érigène au mètre IX du livre III du 'De consolatione Philosophiae' de Boèce." Ed. Hubert Silvestre. *Revue d'histoire ecclésiastique* 47 (1952): 44–122.

Lactantius. *The Divine Institutes, Books 1–7.* Trans. Sister Mary Francis McDonald. Fathers of the Church, vol. 49. Washington, D.C.: Catholic University of America Press, 1964.

Lactantius Placidus. *Commentarii in Statii Thebaida et commentarius in Achilleida.* Ed. Richard Jahnke. *P. Papinius Statius,* vol. 3. Leipzig, 1898.

―――. *Narrationes fabularum Ovidianarum.* Ed. Hugo Magnus. In *P. Ovidii Nasonis Metamorphoseon libri XV et Lactantii Placidi qui dicitur Narrationes fabularum Ovidianarum.* Berlin: Weidmann's, 1914.

Lana Bolognese, Jacopo della. *Comedia de Dante degli Allagherii col commento di Jacopo della Lana Bolognese.* Ed. Luciano Scarabelli. 3 vols. Bologna, 1866–67.

Landino, Cristoforo. *Dante con l'espositione di Cristoforo Landino, e di Alessandro Vellutelli.* Venice, 1564.

―――. *De vera nobilitate.* Ed. Manfred Lentzen. Geneva: Librarie Droz, 1970.

―――. *De vera nobilitate.* In *Testi inediti e rari di Cristoforo Landino e Francesco*

Filelfo. Ed. Eugenio Garin. Testi e documenti a cura dell'Istituto di Studi Filosofia-Roma, no. 1. Florence: Fussi, 1949.

————. *Disputationes Camaldulenses.* Ed. Peter Lohe. Istituto Nazionale di Studi sul Rinascimento, Studi e Testi, no. 6. Florence: Sansoni, 1980.

————. *Disputationes Camaldulenses,* books 3–4. Trans. Thomas H. Stahel. In "Cristoforo Landino's Allegorization of the *Aeneid:* Books III and IV of the *Camaldolese Disputations.*" Diss., Johns Hopkins University, 1968.

————. *La critica del Landino.* Ed. Roberto Cardini. Florence: Sansoni, 1973.

————. *Reden Cristoforo Landinos.* Ed. Manfred Lentzen. Munich: Wilhelm Fink, 1974.

————. *Scritti critici e teorici.* Ed. Roberto Cardini. 3 vols. Rome: Bulzoni, 1974.

Libellus de deorum imaginibus (De deorum imaginibus libellus). In *Auctores mythographi Latini.* Ed. Augustino van Staveren. Leiden and Amsterdam, 1742.

————. In *Fulgentius metaforalis: Ein Beitrag zur Geschichte der antiken Mythologie im Mittelalter.* Ed. Hans Liebeschutz, pp. 117–28. Studien der Bibliothek Warburg. Leipzig and Berlin: B. G. Teubner, 1926.

Lucan. *Lucan: The Civil War.* Ed. and trans. J. D. Duff. Loeb Classics. London: Heinemann; New York: Putnams, 1928.

————. *Scholia in Lucani Bellum civile.* Pt. 1: *M. Annaei Lucani Commenta Bernensia.* Ed. Hermann Usener. Leipzig, 1869.

Lydgate, pseudo-John. *The Assembly of Gods.* Ed. O. L. Triggs. EETS, vol. 69. London, 1896.

Macrobius, Ambrosius Theodosius. *Conuiuiorvm primi diei Satvrnaliorvm.* Ed. Franciscus Eyssenhardt. Leipzig, 1868.

————. *Macrobius.* Ed. James Willis. 2 vols. Bibliotheca Scriptorum Graecorum et Romanorum Teubneriana. Leipzig: B. G. Teubner, 1963.

————. *Commentary on the Dream of Scipio.* Trans. William Harris Stahl. Records of Civilization: Sources and Studies, no. 48. 1952; rpt. New York and London: Columbia University Press, 1966.

————. *Saturnalia.* Trans. Percival Vaughn Davies. Records of Civilization: Sources and Studies, no. 79. New York and London: Columbia University Press, 1969.

Manegold, of Lautenbach [Lutterbach]. "Explicationes Metamorphosen Ovidii." Ed. Meiser. In "Über einen Commentar zu den Metamorphoseon des Ovid." *Sitzungsberichte der philosophisch-philologischen und historischen Classe der Königliche-Bayerische Akademie der Wissenschaften zu München,* pp. 47–89. Munich, 1885.

Martianus Capella. *De nuptiis Philologiae et Mercurii.* Ed. F. Eyssenhardt. Leipzig, 1866.

————. *Martianus Capella.* Ed. Adolf Dick. Corr. Jean Préaux. Bibliotheca Scriptorum Graecorum et Romanorum Teubneriana. Stuttgart: B. G. Teubner, 1969.

————. *Martianus Capella and the Seven Liberal Arts.* Vol. 2: *The Marriage of*

Philology and Mercury. Trans. William Harris Stahl and Richard Johnson, with E. L. Burge. New York: Columbia University Press, 1977.

Martin, of Laon [Dunchad]. *Glossae in Martianum.* Ed. Cora E. Lutz. Philological Monographs, no. 12. Lancaster, Pa.: American Philological Association, 1944.

―――. *Scholica.* Ed. M. L. W. Laistner. In "Notes on Greek from the Lectures of a Ninth Century Monastery Teacher." *Bulletin of the John Rylands Library* 7 (1923): 421–56.

Matranga, P., ed. *Anecdota Graeca e MSS. Bibliothecis Vaticana, Angelica, Barberiniana, Vallicelliana, Medicea, Vindobonensi, pars prima: Tzatzae et Heraclidis Allegorias Homericas comprehendens; pars secunda: Scholia vetera in Hom., Christophorus Contoleon, Nicephorus Gregoras, Leo Alliatius, Regulae Gramm. in Hom., Theodorus Prodromus, Constantinus Siculus, Leo Philosophus, Leo Magister, Acoluthus Grammaticus, Georgius Grammaticus, Iohannes Tzetzes, Constantinus Rhodius, Theodorus Paphlagon, Iohannes Gazaeus, Helias Syncellus, Ignatius Grammaticus, Christoph. I. A. Secretis, Arsenius Archiepiscopus, Manuel Palaeologus, Iohannes Catrares.* Rome, 1850.

Minucius Felix. *See* Tertullian.

Moglio [Muglio], Pietro da. Commentary on Boethius. [Excerpts.] In Lodovico Fratri, "Pietro da Moglio e il suo commento a Boezio." *Studi e memorie per la storia dell' Università di Bologna* 5 (1920): 239–76. Also in Graziella Federici Vescovini, "Due commenti inediti del XIV secolo al 'De consolatione Philosophiae' de Boezio." *Rivista critica di storia della filosofia* 13 (1958): 384–414.

Müller, Karl, and Theodore Müller, eds. *Fragmenta historicorum Graecorum.* Paris, 1841.

Mythographi Graeci. Ed. N. Festa. Vol. 3, no. 2. Leipzig: B. G. Teubner, 1902.

Mythographi Vaticani. *Mythographi Vaticani I et II.* Ed. Peter Kulcsàr. CCSL, no. 91c. Turnhout: Brepols, 1987.

―――. *Scriptores rerum mythicarum Latini tres Romae nuper reperti.* Ed. Georgius Henricus Bode. 2 vols. 1834; rpt. 1 vol. Hildesheim: Georg Olms, 1968.

―――. "Text, Authorship, and Use of the First Vatican Mythographer." Ed. Kathleen Overmeyer [Elliott]. Diss., Radcliffe College, 1942.

Neckam [Neckham, Nequm], Alexander. *De naturis rerum; De laudibus divinae sapientiae.* Ed. Thomas Wright. Rolls Series 34. London, 1863.

Notker, Labeo [Notker Teutonicus]. *Notkers des teutschen Werke.* Ed. Heinrich Hattemer. In *Denkmahle des Mittelalters. Saint Gallens altteutsche Sprachschätze.* Vol. 3. St. Gall, 1846.

―――. *Boethius, "De consolatione Philosophiae," Buch I/II–III.* Ed. Petrus W. Tax. Vols. 1–3, Die Werke Notkers des Deutschen. Tübingen: Max Niemeyer, 1986, 1988, 1990.

―――, trans. *Boethius de consolatione Philosophiae.* In *Notkers des deutschen Werke.* Ed. E. H. Sehrt and Taylor Starck. Vol. 1, pts. 1–3. Altdeutsche Textbibliothek, nos. 32–34. Halle and Saale: Max Niemeyer, 1933–34.

————, trans. *De nuptiis Philologiae et Mercurii.* In *Notkers des deutschen Werke.* Ed.
E. H. Sehrt and Taylor Starck. Vol. 2. Altdeutsche Textbibliothek, no. 37.
Halle and Saale: Max Niemeyer, 1935.

————. *Notker latinus zum Martianus Capella.* Ed. James C. King. Die Werke
Notkers des Deutschen, vol. 4A. Tübingen: Max Niemeyer, 1986.

Odo [Eudes], of Picardy. *Liber Theodoli cum commento noviter impressus.* London,
1508.

Origen. *Contra Celsum.* Trans. Henry Chadwick. Cambridge: Cambridge University Press, 1965.

————. *De principiis.* In *Origène: Traité 24s principes.* French and Latin trans. Henri
Couzel and Manlio Simonetti. Vol. 3, books 3–4, pp. 310–41. Sources
Chrétiennes, no. 268. Paris: Éditions du Cerf, 1980.

Osbern, of Gloucester. *[Glossarium Osberni.] Thesaurus novus Latinitatis, sive lexicon
vetus e membranis nunc primum erutum.* Ed. Angelo Mai. *Classicorum auctorum e
Vaticanis codicibus editorum,* vol. 8. Rome, 1836.

Ottimo Commentary on the *Divine Comedy. L'Ottimo commento della divina Commedia
testo inedito d'un contemporaneo di Dante citato dagli accademici della Crusca.* Ed.
Alessandro Torri. 3 vols. Pisa, 1827–29.

Ovid [Publius Ovidius Nasonis]. *Fastorum libri sex: The Fasti of Ovid.* Ed. and trans.
Sir James George Frazer. 5 vols. London: Heinemann; New York: Putnams,
1931.

————. *Metamorphoses.* Trans. Rolfe Humphries. 1955. Rpt. Bloomington and
London: Indiana University Press, 1972.

————. *Metamorphoses.* Ed. and trans. Frank Justus Miller. Rev. G. P. Goold. 3d
ed. 2 vols. In *Ovid in Six Volumes.* Loeb Classics. London: Heinemann; Cambridge, Mass: Harvard University Press, 1977.

————. *Ovid and the Art of Love: The Loves, The Art of Beauty, The Remedies for Love.*
Trans. Rolfe Humphries. Bloomington: Indiana University Press, 1957.

Ovide moralisé [French prose version]. Ed. Cornelius de Boer. In *Ovide moralisé en
prose (Texte du quinzième siècle). Verhandelingen der Koninklijke Nederlandse
Akademie van Wetenschappen te Amsterdam: Afdeeling Letterkunde* n.s. 61 (1954):
1–400.

———— [French verse version]. Ed. Cornelius de Boer. In *Ovide moralisé: Poème du
commencement du quatorzième siècle. Verhandelingen der Koninklijke Nederlandse
Akademie van Wetenschappen te Amsterdam* 15 (1915): 1–374; 21 (1920): 1–394;
30 (1931): 1–303; 37 (1936): 1–478; 43 (1938): 1–429. Rpt. 5 vols. Wi-
esbaden: Martin Sandig, 1966–68.

Papias, the Lombard. *Elementarium: Papiae elementarium littera A (A-Aequus).* Ed. V.
de Angelis. Testi e documenti per lo studio dell'antichità, vol. 58. Milan:
Cisalpino-Goliardica, 1977.

————. *Vocabulista.* Turin: Bottega d'Erasmo, 1966.

Pearl-Poet. *The Pearl Poems: An Omnibus Edition.* Ed. William Vantuono. 2 vols.

New York and London: Garland, 1984.

Petrarca, Francesco. *L'Africa.* Ed. Nicola Festa. Vol. 1 of *Edizione nazionale delle opere di Francesco Petrarca.* Florence: G. C. Sansoni, 1926.

———. *Africa.* Trans. Thomas G. Bergin and Alice S. Wilson. New Haven and London: Yale University Press, 1977.

———. "Ad Publium Virgilium Maronem." *Familiarum rerum libri* 24, 11. In *Le familiari,* vol. 4. Ed. Umberto Bosco, pp. 251–53. *Edizione nazionale delle opere di Francesco Petrarca,* vol. 13. Florence: G. C. Sansoni, 1942.

———. "Ad Publium Virgilium Maronem." Trans. Mario Emilio Cosenza. In *Petrarch's Letters to Classical Authors,* pp. 136–40. Chicago: University of Chicago Press, 1910.

———. "Coronation Oration." Trans. Ernest Hatch Wilkins. In *Studies in the Life and Works of Petrarch,* pp. 300–313. Mediaeval Academy of America Publications, no. 63. Cambridge, Mass.: Mediaeval Academy of America, 1955.

———. "De quibusdam fictionibus Virgilii." *Rerum senilium,* book 4, no. 4. In *Francesci Petrarchae opervm.* 3 vols. Basil, 1554. Rpt. Ridgewood, N.J.: Gregg Press, 1965. 2:867–74.

———. "De quibusdam fictionibus Virgilii." [Selections.] Trans. James Harvey Robinson and Henry Winchester Rolfe. In *Petrarch: The First Modern Scholar and Man of Letters.* 2d ed., pp. 234–36. London: Putnams; New York: Knickerbocker Press, 1914.

———. *Opere.* Ed. Giovanni Ponte. Milan: U. Mursia, 1968.

———. *Petrarch's Secret or the Soul's Conflict with Passion: Three Dialogues between Himself and S. Augustine.* Trans. William H. Draper. London: Chatto and Windus, 1951.

———. *Scritti inediti di Francesco Petrarca.* Ed. Attilio Hortis. Trieste, 1874.

Picardus, Odo. *See* Odo of Picardy.

Plato. *Charmides.* In *Plato,* vol. 8. Ed. and trans. W. R. M. Lamb. London: Heinemann; New York: Putnams, 1927.

———. *Cratylus.* In *Plato,* vol. 6. Ed. and trans. H. N. Fowler. London: Heinemann; New York: Putnams, 1926.

———. *The Republic.* Trans. Benjamin Jowett. 3d ed. Oxford: Clarendon Press, 1908. Vol. 1.

———. *Timaeus and Critias.* Trans. A. E. Taylor. London: Methuen, 1929.

Plutarch. *De Iside et Osiride.* Ed. and trans. J. Gwynn Griffiths. Cambridge: University of Wales Press, 1970.

Porphyry. *Philosophus platonicus opuscula selecta.* Ed. August Nauck. 1886; rpt. Hildesheim: Georg Olms, 1963.

Priscian. *Partitiones duodecim versum Aeneidos principalium.* In *Institutionum grammaticarum libri xvii,* vol. 2. Ed. Martin Hertz. In *Grammatici,* vol. 3 of 7. Ed. Heinrich Keil. Leipzig: B. G. Teubner, 1885–1923.

Rambaldi, of Imola, Benvenuto. *Commentum super Dantis Aldigherij Comoediam.* Ed.

William Warren Vernon. Rev. Jacopo Philippo Lacaita. 5 vols. Florence, 1887.

Rather of Verona. Martianus Capella with notes. In Claudio Leonardi. "Raterio e Marziano Capella." *Italia medioevale et humanistica* 2 (1959): 73–102.

———. *Opera minora.* Ed. Peter L. D. Reid. CCCM 46. Turnhout: Brepols, 1976.

———. *Ratherii . . . opera.* Ed. Ballerini brothers. Verona, 1765. Rpt. *PL* 136:27–138.

Regnier, of St. Tron. Commentary on Boethius. Anonymous edition by Colard Mansion. Bruges, 1477.

Remigius, of Auxerre [Antissiodorensis, Autissiodorensis]. "A Commentary by Remigius Autissiodorensis on the *De consolatione Philosophiae* of Boethius." [Excerpts only.] Ed. H. F. Stewart. *Journal of Theological Studies* 17 (1915): 22–42.

———. "The Study of the Consolation of Philosophy in Anglo-Saxon England." [Excerpts only.] Ed. Diane K. Bolton. *AHDLMA* 44 (1977): 61–78.

———. *Commentum in Martianum Capellam.* Ed. Cora E. Lutz. 2 vols. Leiden: E. J. Brill, 1962–65.

———. [Glosses on *Aeneid* 6 (attributed).] "Medieval Notes on the Sixth *Aeneid* in Parisinus 7930." Ed. J. J. Savage. *Speculum* 9 (1934): 204–12.

Ridewall [Ridevall], John. *Fulgentius metaforalis.* Ed. Hans Liebeschütz. In *Fulgentius metaforalis, ein Beiträg zur Geschichte der antiken Mythologie im Mittelater.* Studien der Bibliothek Warburg, no. 4. Leipzig and Berlin: B. G. Teubner, 1926.

Robert, of Basevorn. *The Form of Preaching (Forma praedicandi).* Trans. Leopold Krul. In *Three Medieval Rhetorical Arts.* Ed. James J. Murphy, pp. 109–215. Berkeley, Los Angeles, and London: University of California Press, 1971.

Salutati, Coluccio. *De laboribus Hercules.* Ed. Berthold L. Ullman. 2 vols. Bibliotheca Scriptorum Latinorum Mediae et Recentioris Aetatis. Zurich: Thesarus Mundi, 1951.

———. *Epistolario.* Ed. Francesco Novati. Vol. 2 of 5. Fonti per la storia d'Italia, nos. 15–19. Rome: Istituto Storico d'Italiano, 1891, 1905.

Schlee, Friederich. *Scholia Terentiana.* Leipzig, 1893.

Second Vatican mythographer. *See* Mythographi Vaticani.

Serravalle, Giovanni da. *Fratris Iohannis de Serravalle translatio et comentum totius libri Dantis Aldigherii cum textu italico.* Ed. Fratris Bartholomaei A. Colle. Prato, 1891.

Servius. *Servii Grammatici qui feruntur in Vergilii carmina comentarii.* Ed. Georg Thilo and Hermann Hagen. 3 vols. 1881–87; rpt. Hildesheim: Georg Olms, 1961.

Sextus Empiricus. *Adversus mathematicos.* Vol. 3. Ed. Hermann Mutschmann. Rev. J. Mau. Leipzig: B. G. Teubner, 1961.

Statius, P. Papinus. *Achilleis et Thebais.* Ed. P. Kohlmann. Leipzig, 1884.

———. *Statius: Achilleid.* Ed. O. A. W. Dilkie. Cambridge: Cambridge University Press, 1954.

———. *Thebais.* Ed. Alfred Klotz. Vol. 2, fasc. 2 of *Operum.* Leipzig: B. G. Teubner, 1908.

———. *Thebais et Achilleis.* Ed. H. W. Garrod. Scriptorum Classicorum Bibliotheca Oxoniensis. Oxford: Clarendon Press, 1906.

———. *The Medieval Achilleid of Statius.* Ed. Paul M. Clogan. Leiden: E. J. Brill, 1968.

Strabo. *The Geography.* Ed. and trans. Horace Leonard Jones. Loeb Classics. 8 vols. London: Heinemann; New York: Putnams, 1917.

Terence Scholia. *See* Schlee, Friedrich.

Tertullian. *Apologeticus; De spectaculis.* Trans. T. R. Glover. In *Minucius Felix.* Trans. Gerald H. Rendall. London: Heinemann; New York: Putnams, 1931.

Theodulf, of Orleans. "De libris quos legere solebam et qualiter fabulae poetarum a philosophis mystice pertractentur." *Carmina,* no. 45, in *Poetae latini aevi Carolini.* Ed. Ernest Duemmler. *Poetarum Latinorum medii aevi,* vol. 1. *MGH.* Berlin, 1881. Pp. 543–44.

———. "The Books I Used to Read" (*Carmina* 45). Ed. and trans. Peter Godman. *See* Godman, Peter.

Theoduli Ecloga. See Ecloga Theoduli.

Thierry, of Chartres. *The Commentaries on Boethius by Thierry of Chartres and His School.* Ed. Nikolaus M. Häring. Studies and Texts, no. 20. Toronto: Pontifical Institute of Mediaeval Studies, 1971.

———. "Two Commentaries on Boethius (*De Trinitate* et *De hebdomadibus*), by Thierry of Chartres." Ed. Nicholas M. Häring. *AHDLMA* 35 (1960): 65–136.

Third Vatican mythographer. *See* Alberic of London, Mythographi Vaticani.

Traube, Ludwig, ed. *Poetae latini aevi Carolini. MGH,* vol. 3. Berlin: Weidmann's, 1896; rpt. 1964.

Trivet [Trevet], Nicholas. Commentary on Boethius. [Excerpts.] In "Des Commentaires inédits de Guillaume de Conches et de Nicolas Triveth sur la Consolation de la philosophie de Bòece." Ed. Charles Jourdain. *Notices et extraits des manuscrits de la Bibliothéque Impériale et autres bibliothéques* 20.2 (1862): 40–82.

———. *Commento alle 'Troades' di Seneca.* Ed. Marco Palma. Temi e Testi, vol. 22. Rome: Edizioni di Storia e Letteratura, 1977.

Tzetzes, John. *Exegesis in Iliadem.* Ed. Gottfried Hermann. Appendix to Jakob Diassorinos. *Draconis Stratonicensis liber de metris poeticis* [forgery]. Ed. Franciscus de Furia. Leipzig, 1814.

Uguccio. *See* Huguccio, of Pisa.

Verona Scholia on Virgil. *See* Servius, vol. 3.

Virgil [Vergil]. *Aeneidos libri XII.* Ed. Remigius Sabbadini. Rev. Aloisius Castiglioni. Corpus Scriptorum Latinorum Paravianum. Turin, 1945.

———. *Virgil.* Ed. and trans. H. R. Fairclough. 2 vols. Loeb Classics. London: Heinemann; Cambridge, Mass.: Harvard University Press, 1974.

————. *The Aeneid.* Trans. Frank O. Copley. 2d edition. Indianapolis: Bobbs-Merrill, 1975.

————. *The Eclogues and the Georgics.* Trans. R. C. Trevelyan. Cambridge: Cambridge University Press, 1944.

Villena, Enrique de [Henry of Arágon]. *Los doze trabajos de Hércules.* Ed. Margherita Morreale. Biblioteca Selecta de Clásicos Españoles. Madrid: Real Academia Española, 1958.

Virgilio, Giovanni. *Allegorie librorum Ovidii Metamorphoseos a magistro Johanne de Virgilio prosaice ac metrice compilate.* Ed. Fausto Ghisalberti. In "Giovanni del Virgilio espositore delle 'Metamorfose.'" *Il giornale dantesco* n.s. 4, no. 34 (1933): 3–110.

————. Letters to Dante. Trans. Philip H. Wicksteed and Edmund G. Gardner. In *Dante and Giovanni del Virgilio.* Westminster: Archibald Constable, 1902.

————. Letters to Dante, Eclogues, Songs to Dante, and Epitaph. Ed. Carlo del Balzo. In *Poesie di mille autori intorno a Dante Alighieri raccolte ed ordinate cronologicamente con note storiche, bibliografiche e biografiche.* Vol. 1. Rome, 1889.

Walleys [Waleys; of Wales], Thomas. *Metamorphosis Ovidiana moraliter: A magistro Thoma Walleys . . . explanata.* [Revised version of book 15 of Bersuire's *Reductorium morale*—Avignon version—attributed to Walleys in the 1509–11 edition by Badius.] N.p.: Jacobus Parisius, 1509.

Walsingham, Thomas. *Archana deorum.* Ed. Robert A. Van Kluyve. Durham, N.C.: Duke University Press, 1968.

Wessner, Paul, ed. *Scholia in Iuvenalem vetustiora.* Stuttgart: B. G. Teubner, 1967.

William, of Conches. *Glosae in Iuvenalem.* Ed. Bradford Wilson. Textes philosophiques du Moyen Âge, 18. Paris: J. Vrin, 1980.

————. Glosses on Boethius. [Excerpts.] Ed. Charles Jourdain. In "Des commentaires inédits de Guillaume de Conches et de Nicolas Triveth sur la Consolation de la Philosophie de Boèce." pp. 40–82. *Notices et extraits des manuscrits de la Bibliothèque Impériale et autres bibliothèques* 20.2. Paris, 1862.

————. Glosses on Boethius. [excerpts.] Ed. J. M. Parent. In *La Doctrine de la Création dans l'école de Chartres: Étude et textes.* Publications de l'Institut d'Études Médiévales d'Ottawa. Vol. 8, pp. 115–21. Paris: J. Vrin; Ottawa: Inst. d'Études Médiévales, 1938.

————. Glosses on Boethius. [Excerpts.] Ed. Édouard Jeauneau. In "L'Usage de la notion d'*integumentum* à travers les gloses de Guillaume de Conches." *AHDLMA* 32 (1957): 35–100.

————. Glosses on Martianus Capella ["Florentine Commentary"] and on Macrobius. [Excerpts]. In *Fabula: Explorations into the Uses of Myth in Medieval Platonism.* Ed. and trans. Peter Dronke. Mittellateinische Studien und Texte, vol. 9. Leiden and Cologne: E. J. Brill, 1974.

————. *Glosae super Platonem: Texte critique avec introduction, notes et tables.* Ed.

Édouard Jeauneau. Textes philosophiques du Moyen Âge, no. 13. Paris: J. Vrin, 1965.

————. *Moralium dogma philosophorum.* Ed. J. Holmberg. Uppsala: Almqvist and Wicksells, 1929.

Wilson, Katharina M., ed. *Medieval Women Writers.* Athens: University of Georgia Press, 1984.

SECONDARY SOURCES

Alfonsi, Luigi. "Storia interiore e storia cosmica nella 'Consolatio' boeziana." *Convivium* 23 (1955): 513–21.

Allen, Don Cameron. *Mysteriously Meant: The Rediscovery of Pagan Symbolism and Allegorical Interpretation in the Renaissance.* Baltimore and London: Johns Hopkins University Press, 1970.

Allen, Judson Boyce. "An Anonymous Twelfth-Century 'De Natura Deorum.' " *Traditio* 26 (1970): 352–64.

————. *The Ethical Poetic of the Later Middle Ages: A Decorum of Convenient Distinction.* Toronto, Buffalo, and London: University of Toronto Press, 1982.

————. *The Friar as Critic: Literary Attitudes in the Later Middle Ages.* Nashville: Vanderbilt University Press, 1971.

————. "The Library of a Classicizer: The Sources of Robert Holkot's Mythographic Learning." In *Arts libéraux et philosophie au Moyen Âge,* pp. 721–29. Montreal: Institut d'Études Médiévales, 1969.

Alphandery, Paul. "L'Éuhemérisme et les débuts de l'histoire des religions au Moyen Âge." *Revue de l'histoire des religions* 109 (1934): 5–27.

Alton, D. E. H., and D. E. W. Wormell. "Ovid in the Mediaeval Schoolroom." *Hermathena* 94 (1960): 21–38; 95 (1961): 67–82.

Atkins, J. W. H. *English Literary Criticism: The Medieval Phase.* Cambridge: Cambridge University Press, 1943.

Auerbach, Erich. "Figura als Realprophetie bei den Kirchenvätern." *AR* 22 (1938): 436–89.

————. "Typological Symbolism in Medieval Literature." *Yale French Studies* 9 (1952): 3–10.

————. *Typologische Motive in der mittelalterlichen Literatur.* Schriften und Vorträge des Petrarca-Instituts Köln, no. 2. Krefeld: Scherpe, 1953.

Baldwin, Charles Sears. *Medieval Rhetoric and Poetic to 1400: Interpreted from Representative Works.* New York: Macmillan, 1928.

Baldwin, T. W. "Perseus Purloins Pegasus." *PQ* 20 (1941): 361–70.

Baswell, Christopher. "The Medieval Allegorization of the *Aeneid:* MS. Cambridge, Peterhouse 158." *Traditio* 41 (1985): 181–237.

Battaglia, Salvatore. "La tradizione di Ovidio nel medioevo." *Filologia romanza* 6 (1959): 185–224.

Beck, Roger. *Planetary Gods and Planetary Orders in the Mysteries of Mithras.* Leiden, New York, and Copenhagen: E. J. Brill, 1988.

Beddie, James Stuart. "The Ancient Classics in the Mediaeval Libraries." *Speculum* 5 (1930): 3–20.

————. "Libraries in the Twelfth Century: Their Catalogues and Contents." In *Anniversary Essays in Mediaeval History by Students of Charles Homer Haskins,* pp. 1–23. Boston and New York: Houghton Mifflin, 1929.

Benedetto, Luigi Foscolo. " 'Stephanus grammaticus' da Novara (sec. x)." *SM* 3 (1910): 499–508.

Bernal, Martin. *Black Athena: The Afroasiatic Roots of Classical Civilization.* Vol. 1: *The Fabrication of Ancient Greece, 1785–1985.* New Brunswick, N.J.: Rutgers University Press, 1987.

Bernheim, G. "Der Glossator der *Gesta Berengarii imperatoris.*" *Forschungen zur deutschen Geschichte* 14 (1874): 138–154.

Bethurum, Dorothy, ed. *Critical Approaches to Medieval Literature: Selected Papers from the English Institute, 1958–59.* New York & London: Columbia University Press, 1960.

Bett, Henry. *Johannes Scotus Erigena: A Study in Mediaeval Philosophy.* Cambridge: Cambridge University Press, 1925.

Biehler, Ludwig. *Ireland: Harbinger of the Middle Ages.* Trans. from the 1961 German edition. London, New York, and Toronto: Oxford University Press, 1963.

Bloch, R. Howard. *Etymologies and Genealogies: A Literary Anthropology of the French Middle Ages.* Chicago: University of Chicago Press, 1983.

————. "Medieval Misogyny." *Representations* 20 (1987): 1–24.

Blumenfeld-Kosinski, Renate, trans. *The Writings of Margaret of Oingt, Medieval Prioress and Mystic (d. 1310).* Focus Library of Medieval Women. Newburyport, Mass.: Focus Information Group, 1990.

Boas, M. "De librorum Catonianorum historia atque compositione." *Mnemosyne* n.s. 42 (1914): 17–46.

Boissier, [Marie Louis Antoine] Gaston. *La Fin du paganisme: Étude sur les dernières luttes religieuses en occident au quatrième siècle.* 2 vols. Paris, 1891.

Bolgar, Robert R. *The Classical Heritage and Its Beneficiaries.* Cambridge: Cambridge University Press, 1954.

————, ed. *Classical Influences on European Culture, A.D. 500–1500.* Cambridge: Cambridge University Press, 1971.

Bolton, Diane K. "Manuscripts and Commentaries on Boethius, *De consolatione Philosophiae,* in England in the Middle Ages." B.Litt. thesis, Oxford University, 1965.

————. "Remigian Commentaries on the 'Consolation of Philosophy' and their Sources." *Traditio* 33 (1977): 381–94.

————. "The Study of the Consolation of Philosophy in Anglo-Saxon England." *AHDLMA* 44 (1977): 33–78.

Boyancé, Pierre. *Études sur le Songe de Scipion: Essais d'histoire et de psychologie religieuses.* Bibliothèque des Universités du Midi, fasc. 20. Bordeaux: Feret and Sons; Paris: E. de Boccard and C. Klincksieck, 1936.

Branca, Vittore. *Studii sul Boccaccio.* Florence: Sansoni, 1989.

Brehaut, Ernest. "An Encyclopedist of the Dark Ages: Isidore of Seville." *Studies in History, Economics, and Public Law* 48 (1912): 1–275.

Bretzigheimer, Franz. *Studien zu Lactantius Placidus und dem Verfasser der Narrationes Fabularum Ovidianarum.* Diss., Bayerischen Julius-Maximilians-Universität, 1937. Würzburg: Richard Mayr, 1937.

Brinkmann, Hennig. "Verhüllung ('integumentum') als literarische Darstellungsform im Mittelalter." *Der Begriff der Repraesentatio im Mittelalter: Stellvertretung, Symbol, Zeichen, Bild. Miscellanea Mediaevalia,* vol. 8. Berlin and New York: Walter de Gruyter, 1971.

Buffière, Félix. *Les Mythes d'Homère et la pensée grecque.* Paris: Les Belles Lettres, 1956.

Bühler, Winfried. "Die Pariser Horazscholien: Eine neue Quelle der Mythographi Vaticani 1 und 2." *Philologus* 105 (1961): 123–35.

———. "Theodulus' *Ecloga* and Mythographus Vaticanus I." *California Studies in Classical Antiquity* 1 (1968): 65–71.

Burnam, John M. *The Placidus Commentary on Statius.* University of Cincinnati Bulletin, no. 3. Cincinnati: Cincinnati University Press, 1901.

Burnett, Charles S. F. "A Note on the Origins of the Third Vatican Mythographer." *JWCI* 44 (1981): 160–66.

Bush, Douglas. *Mythology and the Renaissance Tradition in English Poetry.* 1932; rev ed. New York: Norton, 1963.

———. *Pagan Myth and Christian Tradition in English Poetry: Jayne Lectures for 1967.* Philadelphia: American Philosophical Society, 1968.

Butler, Judith. *Gender Trouble: Feminism and the Subversion of Identity.* London and New York: Routledge, 1990.

Cameron, Alan. "The Date and Identity of Macrobius." *JRS* 56 (1966): 25–38.

Caplan, Harry. "The Four Senses of Scriptural Interpretation and the Mediaeval Theory of Preaching." *Speculum* 4 (1929): 282–90.

———. "A Late Mediaeval Tractate on Preaching." In *Studies in Rhetoric and Public Speaking in Honor of James Albert Winans,* pp. 70ff. 1925; rpt. New York: Russell and Russell, 1962.

Cappuyns, Dom Maïeul. *Jean Scot Érigène, sa vie, son oeuvre, sa pensée.* Universitas Catholica Lovaniensis. Dissertationes ad gradum magistri in Facultate Theologica consequendum conscriptae, series 2, vol. 26. Louvain: Abbaye du Mont César; Paris: Desclée de Brouwer, 1933.

Chadwick, Henry. *Early Christian Thought and the Classical Tradition: Studies in Justin, Clement, and Origen.* Oxford: Clarendon Press, 1966.

Chance [Nitzsche], Jane. *The Genius Figure in Antiquity and the Middle Ages.* New York and London: Columbia University Press, 1975.

―――. "The Origins and Development of Medieval Mythography: From Homer to Dante." In *Mapping the Cosmos.* Ed. Jane Chance and R. O. Wells, Jr, pp. 35–64. Houston: Rice University Press, 1985.

―――, ed. *The Mythographic Art: Classical Fable and the Rise of the Vernacular in Early France and England.* Gainesville: University of Florida Press, 1990.

Chenu, M.-D. *"Involucrum:* Le Mythe selon des théologiens médiévaux." *AHDLMA* 30 (1955): 75–79.

―――. *Nature, Man, and Society in the Twelfth Century: Essays on New Theological Perspectives in the Latin West.* Sel., ed., and trans. Jerome Taylor and Lester K. Little. Chicago and London: University of Chicago Press, 1968.

Chydenius, Johan. *The Theory of Medieval Symbolism.* Commentationes Humanarum Litterarum 27.2. Helsinki: Societas Scientarum Fennica, 1960.

Clark, J. M. *The Abbey of St. Gall as a Centre of Literature and Art.* Cambridge: Cambridge University Press, 1926.

Clogan, Paul M. "A Preliminary List of Manuscripts of Statius' *Achilleid." Manuscripta* 8 (1964): 175–78.

Coffin, Harrison Cadwallader. "Allegorical Interpretation of Vergil with Special Reference to Fulgentius." *Classical Weekly* 15 (1921): 33–55.

―――. "The Influence of Vergil on St. Jerome and on St. Augustine." *Classical Weekly* 17 (1923–24): 170–75.

Colish, Marcia L. *The Mirror of Language: A Study in the Medieval Theory of Knowledge.* Rev. ed. 1968; rpt. Lincoln: University of Nebraska Press, 1983.

―――. *The Stoic Tradition from Antiquity to the Early Middle Ages: Stoicism in Christian Latin Thought through the Sixth Century.* 2 vols. Leiden: E. J. Brill, 1985.

Collins, Stanley Tate. *The Interpretation of Vergil, with Special Reference to Macrobius.* Oxford: Blackwell; London: Simpkin, Marshall, 1909.

Comparetti, Domenico. *Vergil in the Middle Ages.* Trans. from the 2d. edition by E. F. M. Benecke. 1895; rpt. New York, Leipzig, Paris, and London: G. E. Stechert (Alfred Hafner), 1929.

Conley, John, ed. *The Middle English Pearl: Critical Essays.* Notre Dame and London: University of Notre Dame Press, 1970.

Cooke, John Daniel. "Euhemerism: A Mediaeval Interpretation of Classical Paganism." *Speculum* 2 (1927): 396–410.

Copleston, F. C. *A History of Medieval Philosophy.* London: Methuen, 1972.

Coulter, Cornelia Catlin. "Boccaccio's Acquaintance with Homer." *PQ* 5 (1926): 44–53.

―――. "The Date of John the Scot's *Annotationes in Marcianum." Speculum* 16 (1941): 487–88.

Courcelle, Pierre. *La Consolation de Philosophie dans la tradition littéraire: Antécédents et postérité de Boèce.* Paris: Études Augustiniennes, 1967.

―――. "La Culture antique de Remi d'Auxerre." *Latomus* 7 (1948): 247–54.

―――. "Étude critique sur les commentaires de la Consolation de Boèce (IXe–XVe siècles)." *AHDLMA* 14 (1939): 5–140.

―――. *Late Latin Writers and Their Greek Sources.* Trans. Harry E. Wedeck from the 2d ed. Cambridge, Mass: Harvard University Press, 1969.

―――. "Les Pères de l'Église devant les enfers Virgiliens." *AHDLMA* 30 (1955): 5–74.

―――. "La Postérité chrétienne du *Songe de Scipion.*" *REL* 36 (1958): 205–34.

―――. "La Survie comparée des *Confessions* augustiniennes et de la *Consolation* boécienne." In *Classical Influences on European Culture* A.D. *500–1500.* Ed. R. R. Bolgar, pp. 131–42. Cambridge: Cambridge University Press, 1971.

Cuissard, Ch[arles]. *Théodulfe, évêque d'Orléans, sa vie et ses oeuvres, avec une carte du Pagus Aurelianensis au IXe siècle.* Orleans, 1892.

Curtius, Ernst Robert. *European Literature and the Latin Middle Ages.* 1948, Trans. Willard Trask. 1953; rpt. New York and Evanston: Harper and Row, 1963.

Damon, Phillip W. "A Note on the Neckham Canon." *Speculum* 32 (1957): 99–102.

Deferrari, Roy J. "Early Ecclesiastical Literature and Its Relation to the Literature of Classical and Medieval Times." *PQ* 6 (1927): 102–10.

Derrida, Jacques. *Of Grammatology.* Trans. Gayatri Spivack. Baltimore: Johns Hopkins University Press, 1976.

Desmond, Marilynn. *Reading Dido: Gender, Textuality, and the Medieval* Aenid. Minneapolis: University of Minnesota Press, 1994.

Distler, Paul F. *Vergil and Vergiliana.* Chicago: Loyola University Press, 1966.

Dobschütz, E. v. "Vom vierfachen Schriftsinn." In *Harnack-Ehrung: Beiträg zur Kirchengeschichte ihrem Lehrer Adolf von Harnack zu seinem siebzigsten Geburtstage dargebracht von einer Reihe seiner Schüler.* Leipzig: Hinrichs, 1921.

Donaghey, Brian S. "The Sources of King Alfred's Translation of Boethius' *De consolatione Philosophiae.*" *Anglia* 82 (1964): 23–57.

Dove, Mary. *The Perfect Age of Man's Life.* Cambridge, London, and New York: Cambridge University Press, 1986.

Dronke, Peter. *Fabula: Explorations into the Uses of Myth in Medieval Platonism.* Mittellateinische Studien und Texte, vol. 9. Leiden and Cologne: E. J. Brill, 1974.

―――. "New Approaches to the School of Chartres." *Annuario di estudios medievales* 6 (1969): 117–40.

―――, ed. *A History of Twelfth-Century Western Philosophy.* Cambridge, New York, and New Rochelle: Cambridge University Press, 1988.

Duckett, Eleanor Shipley. *The Gateway to the Middle Ages.* New York: Macmillan, 1938.

―――. *Latin Writers of the Fifth Century.* New York: Holt, 1930.

Economou, George D. *The Goddess Natura in the Middle Ages.* Cambridge, Mass.: Harvard University Press, 1972.

Edden, Valerie J. "Vergil and his Eclogues in Late Antiquity and the Early Middle Ages." Diss., University of Birmingham, 1971.

Ehrhart, Margaret J. *The Judgment of the Trojan Prince Paris in Medieval Literature.* Philadelphia: University of Pennsylvania Press, 1988.

Elder, J. P. "A Mediaeval Cornutus on Persius." *Speculum* 22 (1947): 240–48.

Elliott, Kathleen O., and J. P. Elder. "A Critical Edition of the *Vatican Mythographers.*" *TAPA* 78 (1947): 189–207.

Ellspermann, Gerard L. *The Attitude of the Early Christian Latin Writers toward Pagan Literature and Learning.* Catholic University of American Patristic Studies, vol. 82. Washington, D.C. : Catholic University of America Press, 1949.

Espositio, Mario. "On Some Unpublished Poems Attributed to Alexander Neckam." *EHR* 30 (1915): 450–71.

Farrar, Frederick William. *History of Interpretation.* London, 1886.

Finke, Laurie A. *Feminist Theory, Women's Writing.* Ithaca, N.Y., and London: Cornell University Press, 1992.

Flamant, Jacques. *Macrobe et le néo-Platonisme latin, à la fin du IVe siècle.* Leiden: E. J. Brill, 1977.

Fletcher, Angus. *Allegory: The Theory of a Symbolic Mode.* Ithaca, N.Y.: Cornell University Press, 1964.

Flower, Robin. "Irish Commentaries on Martianus Capella." *Zeitschrift für celtische Philologie* 8 (1912): 566–77.

Fontaine, Jacques. "Isidore de Séville auteur 'ascétique': Les énigmes des *Synonyma.*" *SM* 3d series 6.1 (1965): 163–95.

———. *Isidore de Séville et la culture classique dans l'Espagne wisigothique.* 2 vols. Paris: Études Augustiniennes, 1959.

Foster, Hal. *The Anti-Aesthetic.* Seattle: Bay Press, 1983; rpt. 1991.

Freeman, Ann. "Theodulf of Orleans and the *Libri Carolini.*" *Speculum* 32 (1957): 663–705.

Frey, Josef. "Über das mittelalterliche Gedicht 'Theoduli ecloga' und den Kommentar des Bernhardus Ultraiectensis." *Vierundachtzigster Jahresbericht über das Königliche Paulinische Gymnasium zu Münster i.W. für das Schuljahr 1903–1904,* pp. 1–19. Münster: Aschendorffschen, 1904.

Friebel, Otto. *Fulgentius, der Mythograph und Bischof.* Studien zur Geschichte und Kultur des Altertums, vol. 5, nos. 1–2. Paderborn: Schöning, 1911.

Friedman, John Bloch. "The Cipher Alphabet of John de Foxton's *Liber cosmographiae.*" *Scriptorium* 36 (1982): 219–35.

———. *Orpheus in the Middle Ages.* Cambridge, Mass.: Harvard University Press, 1970.

Frye, Northrop. "New Directions from Old." In *Myth and Mythmaking.* Ed. Henry A. Murray, pp. 115–31. New York: Braziller, 1960.

Gasquy, Armand. *De Fabio Planciade Fulgentio, Virgilii interprete.* Berliner Studien für Classische Philologie und Archaelogie, no. 6, vol. 1. Berlin, 1887.

Georgius, H. "Zur Bestimmung der Zeit des Servius." *Philologus* 71 (1912): 518–26.

Ghellinck, Joseph de. *L'Essor de la littérature latine au XIIe siècle.* 2 vols. Museum Lessianum, Session historique, nos. 4–5. Brussels: L'Edition Universelle; Paris: Desclée de Brouwer, 1946.

Gibson, Margaret, ed. *Boethius: His Life, Thought, and Influence.* Oxford: Blackwell, 1981.

Glover, Terrot Reaveley. *Life and Letters in the Fourth Century.* Cambridge: Cambridge University Press, 1901.

Gould, G. P. "Servius and the Helen Episode." *HSCP* 74 (1969): 101–68.

Grabmann, Martin. *Die Geschichte der scholastischen Methode: Nach den gedruckten und ungedruckten Quellen.* 2 vols. Freiburg im Breisgau and St. Louis: Herder, 1909–11; rpt. Graz: Akademische Druck- und Verlagsanstalt, 1957.

Gregory, Tullio. *Anima mundi: La filosofia in Guglielmo di Conches e la scuola di Chartres.* Medioevo e rinascimento, no. 3. Florence: G. C. Sansoni, 1955.

Grindle, Gilbert E. A. *The Destruction of Paganism in the Roman Empire from Constantine to Justinian.* Oxford and London, 1892.

Gsell, Stéphane. "Virgile et les Africains." In *Cinquantenaire de la Faculté des Lettres d'Alger (1881–1931),* pp. 5–42. Algiers: Société historique Algérienne, 1932.

Gundlach, Wilhelm, ed. *Heldenlieder der deutschen Kaiserzeit.* 3 vols. 1894–99; rpt. Aalen: Scientia, 1970.

Guthrie, Shirley Law. "The *Ecloga Theoduli* in the Middle Ages." Diss., Indiana University, 1973.

Hablitzel, Joh. Bapt. *Hrabanus Maurus. Ein Beitrag zur Geschichte der mittelalterlichen Exegese.* Biblische Studien, vol. 11, no. 3. Freiburg: Herdersche, 1906.

Hamilton, George L. "Theodulus: A Mediaeval Textbook." *MP* 7 (1909–10): 169–85.

———. "Theodulus in France." *MP* 8 (1910–11): 611–12.

Hanford, James Holly. "Classical Eclogue and Mediaeval Debate." *Romanic Review* 2 (1911): 130.

Häring, Nikolaus M. "Chartres and Paris Revisited." In *Essays in Honor of Anton Charles Pegis.* Ed. J. R. O'Donnell, pp. 268–329. Toronto: Pontifical Institute of Mediaeval Studies, 1974.

———. "Four Commentaries on the 'De Consolatione Philosophiae' in MS Heiligenkreuz 130." *MS* 31 (1969): 287–316.

Harnach, Adolf. *The Expansion of Christianity in the First Three Centuries.* Trans. James Moffatt. 2 vols. Theological Translation Library, vols. 19–20. London: Williams and Norgate; New York: Putnams, 1904–5.

Hart, George. *Egyptian Myths.* Avon, England: British Museum Press, 1990; rpt. 1991.

Haskins, Charles Homer. "Albericus Casinensis." *Casinensia* 1 (1929): 115–24.

————. *The Renaissance of the Twelfth Century.* Cambridge, Mass.: Harvard University Press, 1927.

Hatinguais, Jacqueline. "Points de vue sur la volonté et le jugement dans l'oeuvre d'un humaniste chartrain (Guillaume de Conches, XIIe siècle)." In *L'Homme et son destin d'après les penseurs du Moyen Âge. Actes du premier Congrès International de Philosophie Médiévale,* pp. 417–29. Louvain: Éditions Nawelaerts; Paris: Beatrice-Nawelaerts, 1960.

Hauréau, M. B. "Commentaire de Jean Scot Érigène sur Martianus Capella." *Notices et extraits des manuscrits de la Bibliothèque Imperiale et autres bibliothèques* 20.2 (1862): 1–39.

————. *Histoire de la philosophie scholastique.* 2 vols. 1872, 1880; rpt. Minerva, 1966.

Havelock, Eric A. *Preface to Plato.* Cambridge, Mass., and London: Belknap Press of Harvard University Press, 1963.

————. "Prologue to Greek Literacy." *Lectures in Memory of Louise Taft Semple (Second Series).* Cincinnati: University of Cincinnati Press, 1971.

Heikel, Einar. "Lactantii Placidi de dei nomine narratio." *Suomalaisen Tiedeakatemian Toimituksia* 12.3 (1913): 1–9.

Hélin, Maurice. *A History of Medieval Latin Literature.* Rev. ed. Trans. Jean Chapman Snow. New York: William Salloch, 1949.

Helm, Rudolf. "Der Bischof Fulgentius und der Mythograph." *RMP* 54 (1899): 111–34.

Hersman, Anne Bates. *Studies in Greek Allegorical Interpretation.* Chicago: Blue Sky Press, 1906.

Hexter, Ralph J. *Ovid and Medieval Schooling: Studies in Medieval School Commentaries on Ovid's Ars amatoria, Epistulae ex Ponto, and Epistulae heroidum.* Münchener Beiträge zur Mediävistik und Renaissance-Forschung. Munich: Arbeo-Gesellschaft, 1986.

Heyse, Elisabeth. *Hrabanus Maurus' Enzyklopädie 'De rerum naturis:' Untersuchungen zu den Quellen und zur Methode der Kompilation.* Münchener Beiträge zur Mediävistik und Renaissance-Forschung, no. 4. Munich: Arbeo-Gesellschaft, 1969.

Highet, Gilbert. *The Classical Tradition: Greek and Roman Influences on Western Literature.* 1949; rpt. London, Oxford, and New York: Oxford University Press, 1967.

Hill, D. E. "The Manuscript Tradition of the *Thebaid.*" *CQ* n.s. 16 (1966): 333–46.

Hindman, Sandra L. *Christine de Pizan's "Epistre Othéa": Painting and Politics at the Court of Charles VI.* Toronto: Pontifical Institute of Mediaeval Studies, 1986.

Hinks, Roger P. *Myth and Allegory in Ancient Art.* London: Warburg Institute, 1939.

Histoire littéraire de la France; par les religieux bénédictins de la congrégation de Saint

Maur, et continue par des membres de l'Institut. Vols. 4–6 of 32. Paris, 1733–63.

Hollander, Robert. *Allegory in Dante's Commedia.* Princeton, N.J.: Princeton University Press, 1969.

——. "Dante *Theologus-Poeta.*" *Dante Studies* 94 (1976): 91–136.

Holthausen, Ferdinand. "Chaucer und Theodulus." *Anglia* 16 (1893–94): 264–66.

Hortis, Attilio. *Studji sulle opere latine del Boccaccio: Con particolare riguardo alla storia della erudizione nel medio evo e alle letterature straniere.* Trieste, 1879.

Hubert, R. P. M. "Isidore de Séville novateur? (*Origines,* I, xviii–xix)." *REL* 49 (1971): 290–313.

Huygens, R. B. C. "Accessus ad auctores." *Latomus* 12 (1953): 296–311; 460–84.

——. *Accessus ad auctores: Bernard d'Utrecht: Conrad d'Hirsau, Dialogus super auctores.* Leiden: E. J. Brill, 1970.

——. "Mittelalterliche Kommentare zum *O qui perpetua . . .*" *Sacris erudiri* 6 (1954): 373–427.

——. "Notes sur le *Dialogus super auctores* de Conrad de Hirsau et le *Commentaire sur Théodule.*" *Latomus* 13 (1954): 420–28.

——. "Remigiana." *Aevum* 28 (1954): 330–44.

Hyde, Thomas. "Boccaccio: The Genealogies of Myth." *PMLA* 100 (1985): 737–45.

Hyde, Walter W. *Paganism to Christianity in the Roman Empire.* Philadelphia: University of Pennsylvania Press; London: Geoffrey Cumberlege, Oxford University Press, 1946.

Inwood, Brad. *Ethics and Human Action in Early Stoicism.* Oxford: Clarendon Press, 1985.

Jardine, Alice. *Gynesis: Configurations of Women and Modernity.* Ithaca, N.Y.: Cornell University Press, 1985.

Jeauneau, Édouard. "Un Commentaire inédit sur le chant 'O qui perpetua' de Boèce." *Rivista critica di storia della filosofia* 14 (1959): 60–80.

——. "Deux rédactions des gloses de Guillaume de Conches sur Priscien." *Recherches de théologie ancienne et médiévale* 27 (1960): 212–47.

——. "Gloses de Guillaume de Conches sur Macrobe: Note sur les manuscrits." *AHDLMA* 35 (1960): 17–28.

——. "Gloses sur le Timée, du manuscrit Digby 217 de la Bodléienne, à Oxford." *Sacris erudiri* 17 (1966): 365–400.

——. "La Lecture des auteurs classiques à l'école de Chartres durant la première moitié du XIIe siècle. Un témoin privilégié: Les 'Glosae super Macrobium' de Guillaume de Conches." In *Classical Influences on European Culture A.D.. 500–1500.* Ed. R. R. Bolgar, pp. 95–102. Cambridge: Cambridge University Press, 1971.

————. "*Lectio philosophorum*": *Recherches sur l'école de Chartres*. Amsterdam: A. M. Hakkert, 1973.

————. "Note sur l'ecole de Chartres." *SM* 3d series 5.2 (1964): 839–52.

————. "L'Usage de la notion d'*integumentum* à travers les gloses de Guillaume de Conches." *AHDLMA* 32 (1957): 35–100.

Jenaro-MacLennan, L. *The Trecento Commentaries on the Divina Commedia and the Epistle to Cangrande*. Oxford: Clarendon Press, 1974.

Jones, J. W., Jr. "Allegorical Interpretation in Servius." *CJ* 56 (1960): 217–26.

————. "The Allegorical Traditions of the *Aeneid*." In *Vergil at 2000: Commemorative Essays on the Poet and His Influence*. Ed. John D. Bernard, pp. 107–132. New York: AMS Press, 1986.

————. "Vergil as *Magister* in Fulgentius." In *Classical, Mediaeval, and Renaissance Studies in Honor of Berthold Louis Ullman*. Vol. 1. Ed. Charles Henderson, Jr., pp. 273–75. Rome: Edizioni di Storia e Letteratura, 1964.

Kaster, Robert A. "Macrobius and Servius: *Verecundia* and the Grammarian's Function." *HSCP* 84 (1980): 219–62.

————. "The Grammarian's Authority." *CP* 75 (1980): 216–41.

————. *Guardians of Language: The Grammarian and Society in Late Antiquity*. Berkeley, Los Angeles, and London: University of California Press, 1988.

Keenan, Hugh T. "A Check-List on Typology and English Medieval Literature." *Studies in the Literary Imagination* 8 (Spring 1975): 1–166.

Ker, William P. "Boccaccio." In *Studies in European Literature, Being the Taylorian Lectures 1889–1899*, pp. 351–70. Oxford: Clarendon Press, 1900.

————. *The Dark Ages*. Edinburgh and London: Blackwood, 1911.

Keseling, Ferdinand. *De mythographi Vaticani secundi fontibus*. Halle: Typus Wischani and Burkhardti, 1908.

King, James C. *Notker latinus zum Martianus Capella*. Die Werke Notkers des Deutschen, vol 4A. Tübingen: Max Niemeyer, 1986.

Kirk, G. S. *Myth: Its Meaning and Functions in Ancient and Other Cultures*, pp. 3–14. Madison, Milwaukee, and London: University of Wisconsin Press, 1966.

Kittendorf, Doris E. "Cleanness and the Fourteenth Century *Artes Praedicandi*." *Michigan Academician* 11 (1979): 319–30.

Klibansky, Raymond. "The School of Chartres." In *Twelfth-Century Europe and the Foundations of Modern Society*. Ed. Marshall Clagett, Gaines Post, and Robert Reynolds, pp. 3–14. Madison, Milwaukee, and London: University of Wisconsin Press, 1966.

————, Erwin Panofsky, and Fritz Saxl. *Saturn and Melancholy: Studies in the History of Natural Philosophy, Religion, and Art*. London: Nelson, 1964.

Klotz, Alfred. "Die Statius-scholien." *Archiv für lateinische Lexicographie und Grammatik* 15 (1908): 485–525.

Knowles, David. *The Evolution of Medieval Thought*. Baltimore: Helicon Press, 1962.

Knowlton, E. C. "Notes on Early Allegory." *JEGP* 29 (1930): 159–81.

Kristeller, Paul Oskar. *Iter italicum.* Vol. 1: *Italy: Agrigento to Novara.* London: Warburg Institute; Leiden: E. J. Brill, 1963.

————, and F. Edward Cranz, eds. *CTC.* 2 vols. of 3. Washington, D.C.: Catholic University of America Press, 1971–76.

Kuhn, Thomas. *The Structure of Scientific Revolutions.* Chicago: University of Chicago Press, 1962.

Labowsky, Lotte. "A New Version of Scotus Eriugena's Commentary on Martianus Capella." *MRS* 1 (1941–43): 187–93.

Laistner, M. L. W. "Fulgentius in the Carolingian Age." In *Mélanges Hrouchevsky,* pp. 445–56. Kiev: Ukrainian Academy of Sciences, 1928. Rpt. in *The Intellectual Heritage of the Early Middle Ages.* Sel. M. L. W. Laistner. Ed. Chester G. Starr, pp. 202–15. Ithaca, N.Y.: Cornell University Press, 1957.

————. "Martianus Capella and His Ninth Century Commentators." *Bulletin of the John Rylands Library* 9 (1925): 130–38.

————. "Notes on Greek from the Lectures of a Ninth Century Monastery Teacher." *Bulletin of the John Rylands Library* 7 (1923): 421–56.

Lambertin, Robert. *Homer the Theologian: Neoplatonist Allegorical Reading and the Growth of the Epic Tradition.* Berkeley, Los Angeles, and London: University of California Press, 1986.

Landi, Carlo. "Di un commento medievale inedito della 'Tebaide' di Stazio." *Atti e memorie della Accademia de Scienze Lettere ed Arti in Padova* n.s. 28 (1911–12): 315–44.

————. "Intorno a Stazio nel medio evo e nel Purgatorio dantesco." *Atti e memorie della Reale Accademia di Scienze, Lettere, ed Arti in Padova* n.s. 37 (1920–21): 201–37.

Lange, C. *De nexu inter opera mythologica Hygini.* Bonn, 1865.

Langlois, Pierre. "Les Oeuvres de Fulgence le mythographe et le probleme des deux Fulgence." *Jahrbuch für Antike und Christentum* 7 (1964): 94–105.

La Penna, Antonio. "Studi sulla tradizione dei *Saturnali* di Macrobio." *Annali della Scuola Normale Superiore de Pisa* 2d series 12 (1953): 225–52.

Lapidge, Michael. "The Stoic Inheritance." *See* Peter Dronke, ed., *History of Twelfth-Century Western Philosophy,* pp. 81–112.

Lehmann, Paul. *Mittelalterliche Bibliothekskataloge Deutschlands und der Schweiz; herausgegeben von der Bayerischen Akademie der Wissenschaften.* Vols. 1–2 in 4. Munich: Beck, 1918. Vol. 1.

Le Moine, Fanny. *Martianus Capella: A Literary Re-evaluation.* Münchener Beiträge zur Mediävistik und Renaissance-Forschung, no. 10. Munich: Arbeo-Gesellschaft, 1972.

Lenz, Friedrich Walter. *Ovid's Metamorphoses: Prolegomena to a Revision of Hugo Magnus' Edition.* Dublin and Zurich: Weidmann, 1967.

Leonardi, Claudio. "I codici di Marziano Capella." *Aevum* 33 (1959): 443–89; 34 (1960): 1–99, 411–524.

————. "Raterio e Marziano Capella." *Italia medioevale et umanistica* 2 (1959): 73–102.

Lerer, Seth. *Boethius and Dialogue: Literary Method in the Consolation of Philosophy.* Princeton, N.J: Princeton University Press, 1985.

Leuschke, Alfredus. *"De Metamorphoseon" in scholiis Vergilianis fabulis.* Diss., University of Marburg, 1895. Marburg, 1895.

Lewis, Charlton T., and Charles Short. *A Latin Dictionary.* 1879; rpt. Oxford: Clarendon Press, 1969.

Lewis, C[live] S[taples]. *The Allegory of Love: A Study in Medieval Tradition* 1936; rpt. London, Oxford, and New York: Oxford University Press, 1968.

Liebeschütz, Hans. *Medieval Humanism in the Life and Writings of John of Salisbury* Studies of the Warburg Institute, vol. 17. London: Warburg Institute, 1950.

————. "Theodulf of Orleans and the Problem of the Carolingian Renaissance." In *Fritz Saxl 1908–1948: A Volume of Memorial Essays from His Friends in England.* Ed. Donald J. Gordon, pp. 77–92. London, Edinburgh, Paris, Melbourne, Toronto, and New York: Nelson, 1957.

————. "Zur Geschichte der Erklärung des Martianus Capella bei Eriugena." *Philologus* 104 (1960): 127–37.

Lindsay, Wallace M. "The Editing of Isidore's *Etymologiae.*" *CQ* 5 (1911): 42–53.

————. "Notes on Isidore's *Eytmologiae.*" *CQ* 6 (1912): 38–39.

————, and H. J. Thomson. *Ancient Lore in Medieval Latin Glossaries.* St. Andrews University Publications, no. 13. London, New York, and Toronto: Humphrey Milford, Oxford University Press, 1921.

Logan, George Meredith. "Lucan in England: The Influence of the *Pharsalia* on English Letters from the Beginnings through the Sixteenth Century." Diss., Harvard Univeristy, 1967.

Long, Charlotte R. *The Twelve Gods of Greece and Rome.* Leiden, New York, and Copenhagen: E. J. Brill, 1987.

Lot, Ferdinand. *The End of the Ancient World and the Beginnings of the Middle Ages.* 1931; rpt. New York: Harper and Row, 1961.

de Lubac, Henri. *Exégèse médiévale: Les Quatre sens de l'écriture.* 2 vols. in 4. Lyons: Aubier, 1959–64.

Lutz, Cora E. "The Commentary of Remigius of Auxerre on Martianus Capella." *MS* 19 (1957): 137–56.

————. "Martianus Capella." *CTC.* Ed. Paul Oskar Kristeller and F. Edward Kranz. Vol. 2 of 3, pp. 367–68. Washington, D.C.: Catholic University of America Press, 1971.

————, with John J. Contreni. "Martianus Capella. Addenda et Corrigenda." *CTC.* Ed. Paul Oskar Kristeller and F. Edward Cranz. Vol. 3 of 3, pp. 449–52. Washington, D. C.: Catholic University of America Press, 1976.

————. "One Formula of Accessus in Remigius' Works." *Latomus* 19 (1960): 774–80.

————. "Remigius' Ideas on the Classification of the Seven Liberal Arts." *Traditio* 12 (1956): 65–86.

————. "Remigius' Ideas on the Origin of the Seven Liberal Arts." *MandH* 10 (1956): 32–49.

Lynch, Kathryn. *The High Medieval Dream Vision: Poetry, Philosophy, and Literary Form.* Stanford: Stanford University Press, 1988.

MacFarlane, Katherine Nell. "Isidore of Seville on the Pagan Gods (*Origines* VIII.11)." *Transactions of the American Philosophical Society* 70.3 (1980): 3–40.

Madden, Sister Mary Daniel. *The Pagan Divinities and Their Worship as Depicted in the Works of Saint Augustine exclusive of the City of God.* Patristic Studies, vol. 24. Washington, D.C.: Catholic University of America Press, 1930.

Magnus, Hugo. *Studien zu Ovids Metamorphoseon.* Wissenschaftliche Beilage zum Programm des Sophien-Gymnasiums, Ostern 1887. Berlin, 1887.

Manitius, Max. "Aus Dresdener Handschriften. II: Scholien zu Statius' *Thebais.*" *RMP* 57 (1902): 397–421.

————. "Beiträge zur Geschichte der römischen Prosaiker im Mittelalter," and "Beiträge zur Geschichte der römischen Dichter im Mittelalter." *Philologus* 47–56 (1888–97), supp. 7 (1899).

————. "Dresdener Scholien zu Statius *Achilleis.*" *RMP* 59 (1904): 597–602.

————. "Philologisches aus alten Bibliotheks-katalogen." *RMP* 47 (1892): 1–152.

————. "Zur karolingischen Literatur." *NA* 36 (1910): 43–75.

————. "Zwei Remigius-kommentare." *NA* 49 (1932): 173–183, 205.

Manning, Stephen. "The Nun's Priest's Morality and the Medieval Attitude toward Fables." *JEGP* 59 (1960): 403–16.

Marco, Maria de. "Un nuovo codice del commento di Bernardo Silvestre all'*Eneide.*" *Aevum* 28 (1954): 178–83.

————. "*Remigii inedita.*" *Aevum* 26 (1952): 495–517.

Marinone, Nino. *Elio Donato, Macrobio, et Servio, commentatori di Vergilio.* Vercelli: Presso l'autore, 1946.

Marrou, Henri-Irénée. *A History of Education in Antiquity.* Trans. George Lamb from the 3d edition. New York: Sheed and Ward, 1956.

————. *Saint Augustin et la fin de la culture antique.* 4th edition. Paris: E. de Boccard, 1958.

Martin, Janet. "John of Salisbury as Classical Scholar." In *The World of John Salisbury.* Ed. Michael Wilks, pp. 179–201. Studies in Church History Subsidia, 3. Oxford: Blackwell, 1984.

Marzahn, Joachim. *The Ishtar Gate.* Mainz: Staatliche Museen zu Berlin Vorderasiatisches Museum, 1992.

Mathon, G. "Le Commentaire du Pseudo-Érigène sur la *Consolatio Philosophiae* de Boèce." *Recherches de théologie ancienne et médiévale* 22 (1955): 213–57.

Mayor, John E. B. "Martianus Capella." *CR* 10 (1896): 368.

McNally, Robert E., S.J. *The Bible in the Early Middle Ages.* Westminster, Md.: Newman Press, 1959.

McVeigh, Terrence Anthony. "The Allegory of the Poets: A Study of Classical Tradition in Medieval Interpretation of Virgil." *DA* 25 (1964): 1894 (Fordham).

Means, Michael H. "The Homiletic Structure of *Cleanness.*" *Studies in Medieval Culture* 5 (1975): 165–72.

Minnis, A. J. *Medieval Theory of Authorship: Scholastic Literary Attitudes in the Later Middle Ages.* London: Scolar Press, 1984.

Morford, Mark P. O., and Robert J. Lenardon. *Classical Mythology.* 3d ed. New York and London: Longman, 1985.

Mountford, James Frederick, and J. T. Schultz. *Index rerum et nominum in scholiis Servii et A. Donati tractatorum.* Ithaca, N.Y.: Cornell University Press, 1930.

Mozley, J. H. "Statius as an Imitator of Virgil and Ovid." *Classical Weekly* 27 (1933): 33–38.

Mras, Karl. "Macrobius' Kommentar zu Ciceros Somnium: Ein Beitrag zur Geistesgeschichte des 5. Jahrhunderts n. Chr." In *Sitzungsberichte der preussischen Akademie der Wissenschaften, philosophischen-historische Klasse,* pp. 232–86. Berlin: Preussischen Akademie der Wissenschaften, 1933.

Murgia, Charles E. *Prolegomena to Servius 5: The Manuscripts. University of California Publications, Classical Studies,* 11. Berkeley and Los Angeles: University of California Press, 1975.

Murphy, James J. *Rhetoric in the Middle Ages: A History of Rhetorical Theory from Saint Augustine to the Renaissance.* Berkeley, Los Angeles, and London: University of California Press, 1974.

Mustard, Wilfred P. "Dante and Statius." *MLN* 39 (1924): 120.

———. "The Etymologies in the Servian Commentary to Virgil." *Colorado College Studies* 3 (1892): 1–37.

———. "Petrarch's Africa." *AJP* 42 (1921): 97–121.

Mütherich, Florentine. " 'De Rhetorica.' Eine Illustration zu Martianus Capella." In *Festschrift Bernard Bischoff zu seinem 65. Geburtstag dargebracht von Freunden, Kollegen, und Schülern.* Ed. Johanne Autenrieth and Franz Brunhölze, pp. 198–206. Stuttgart: Anton Hiersemann, 1971.

Nagel, Bert. *Hrotsvith von Gandersheim.* Stuttgart: Metzler, 1965.

Naumann, Hans. *Notkers Boethius. Untersuchungen über Quellen und Stil.* Quellen und Forschungen zur Sprach- und Kultur- geschichte der germanischen Völker, vol. 121. Strassburg: Karl J. Trübner, 1913.

Nees, Lawrence. *A Tainted Mantle: Hercules and the Classical Tradition at the Carolingian Court.* Philadelphia: University of Pennsylvania Press, 1991.

———. "Theodulf's Mythical Silver Hercules Vase, *Poetica Vanitas,* and the Augustinian Critique of the Roman Heritage." *Dumbarton Oak Papers* 41 (1987): 443–51.

Nettleship, Henry. "The Ancient Commentators on Virgil." In the introduction to *The Works of Virgil*. Ed. John Conington and Henry Nettleship. 5th edition. Rev. F. Haverfield. Vol. 1: *Eclogues and Georgics*, pp. liv–xc. London, 1898.

Newell, John. "Rationalism at the School of Chartres." *Vivarium* 21.2 (1983): 108–26.

Nitzsche, Jane Chance. *See* Chance, Jane.

Nuchelmans, Gabriel. "Philologia et son mariage avec Mercure jusqu' à la fin du XIIe siècle." *Latomus* 16 (1957): 84–107.

O'Donnell, J. Reginald. "The Sources and Meaning of Bernard Silvester's Commentary on the *Aeneid*." *MS* 24 (1962): 233–49.

Osternacher, Joannes. *Quos auctores Latinos et Sacrorum Bibliorum locus Theodulus imitatus esse videatur*. Urfahr: Programmate collegii Petrini, 1907.

———. "Die Überlieferung der Ecloga Theoduli." *NA* 40 (1916): 329–76.

Otis, Brooks. "The *Argumenta* of the So-called Lactantius." *HSCP* 47 (1936): 131–63.

———. "De Lactantii qui dicitur Narrationibus Ovidianis." [Abstract of dissertation.] *HSCP* 46 (1935): 209–11.

———. *Ovid as an Epic Poet*. Cambridge: Cambridge University Press, 1966.

———. *Virgil: A Study in Civilized Poetry*. Oxford: Clarendon Press, 1963.

Otten, Kurt. *König Alfreds Boethius*. Studien zur englischen Philologie, n.s. 3. Tübingen: Max Niemeyer, 1964.

Owst, G. R. *Literature and Pulpit in Medieval England: A Neglected Chapter in the History of English Letters and of the English People*. 2d ed. 1961; rpt. Oxford: Blackwell, 1966.

Padoan, Giorgio. "Tradizione e fortuna del commento all' 'Eneide' di Bernardo Silvestre." *Italia medioevale e umanistica* 3 (1960): 227–40.

Panofsky, Dora, and Erwin Panofsky. *Pandora's Box: The Changing Aspects of a Mythical Symbol*. London: Routledge and Kegan Paul, 1956.

Panofsky, Erwin. *Hercules am Scheidewege und andere antike Bildstoffe in der neueren Kunst*. Studien der Bibliothek Warburg, 18. Leipzig and Berlin: B. G. Teubner, 1930.

———. *Renaissance and Renascences in Western Art*. Figura, no. 10. Stockholm: Almquist and Wiksell, 1960.

———. *Studies in Iconology: Humanistic Themes in the Art of the Renaissance*. 1939; rpt. New York: Harper and Row, 1967.

———, and Fritz Saxl. "Classical Mythology in Mediaeval Art." *Metropolitan Museum Studies* 4 (1932–33): 228–80.

Paré, G. *La Renaissance du XIIe siècle: Les Écoles et l'einseignement*. Paris: J. Vrin; Ottawa: Inst. d'Études Médiévales, 1933.

Patch, Howard Rollins. *The Goddess Fortuna in Mediaeval Literature*. 1927; rpt. New York: Octagon Books, 1967.

———. *The Tradition of Boethius: A Study of His Importance in Medieval Culture*. 1935; rpt. New York: Russell and Russell, 1970.

Pavlovskis, Zoja. "The Influence of Statius upon Latin Literature before the Tenth Century." *DA* 23 (1963): 3362 (Cornell).

Payne, F. Anne. *King Alfred and Boethius: An Analysis of the Old English Version of the Consolation of Philosophy.* Madison, Milwaukee, and London: University of Wisconsin Press, 1968.

Pépin, Jean. *Mythe et allégorie: Les Origines grecques et les contestations judéo-chrétiennes.* Paris: Aubier, 1958.

Pichon, René. *Lactance. Étude sur le mouvement philosophique et religieux sous le regne de Constantin.* Paris: Hachette, 1901.

Poole, Reginald Lane. *Illustrations of the History of Mediaeval Thought.* 2d. edition, rev. London: Society for Promoting Christian Knowledge; New York: Macmillan, 1920.

———. "The Masters of the Schools of Paris and Chartres in John of Salisbury's Time." *EHR* 35 (1920): 321–42. Rpt. in *Studies in Chronology and History.* Coll. and ed. Austin Lane Poole, pp. 223–47. Oxford: Clarendon Press, 1934.

Préaux, Jean G. "Le Commentaire de Martin de Laon sur l'oeuvre de Martianus Capella." *Latomus* 12 (1953): 437–59.

Priest, John F. "Myth and Dream in Hebrew Scripture." In *Myths, Dreams, and Religion.* Ed. Joseph Campbell, pp. 48–67. New York: Dutton, 1970.

Quilligan, Maureen. *The Language of Allegory.* Ithaca, N.Y.: Cornell University Press, 1979.

Quinn, Betty Nye. "ps. Theodolus." *CTC.* Ed. Paul Oskar Kristeller and F. Edward Cranz. Vol. 2, pp. 383–408. Washington, D.C.: Catholic University of America Press, 1971.

Raby, F. J. E. *A History of Secular Latin Poetry in the Middle Ages.* 2 vols. Oxford: Clarendon Press, 1934.

Raia, Ann Rose. "Barberini Manuscripts 57–66 and 121–130." Diss., Fordham University, 1965.

Rand, Edward Kennard. "The Classics in the Thirteenth Century." *Speculum* 4 (1929): 249–69.

———. "Dante and Servius." In *Thirty-third Annual Report of the Dante Society, Cambridge, Massachusetts, 1914,* pp. 1–11. Boston: Ginn, 1916.

———. "Early Mediaeval Commentaries on Terence," *CP* 4 (1909): 359–89.

———. *Founders of the Middle Ages.* Cambridge, Mass.: Harvard University Press; London: Humphrey Milford, Oxford University Press, 1928.

———. "How Much of the *Annotationes in Marcianum* is the Work of John the Scot?" *TAPA* 71 (1940): 501–23.

———. "Is Donatus's Commentary on Virgil Lost?" *CQ* 10 (1910): 158–64.

———. *Johannes Scotus.* In *Quellen und Untersuchungen zur lateinischen Philologie des Mittelalters.* Ed. Ludwig Traube. Vol. 1, pt. 2, pp. 87–106. Munich: Oskar Beck, 1906.

————. "The Mediaeval Virgil." In "Virgilio nel Medio Evo," *SM* n.s. 5 (1932): 418–42.

————. "Une Nouvelle édition de Servius." *Académie des inscriptions et belles-Lettres (comptes rendus des séances de l'année* 1938). 4th Series, pp. 311–24. Paris: Auguste Picard, 1938.

Rathbone, Eleanor. "Master Alberic of London, 'Mythographus Tertius Vaticanus.'" *MRS* 1 (1943): 35–38.

Rauner-Hafner, Gabriele. "Die Vergilinterpretation des Fulgentius Bemerkungen zu Gliederung und Absicht der *Expositio Virgilianae continentiae.*" *MJ* 13 (1978): 7–49.

Reynolds, Margaret Ruth. "Statius and his Influence from the First Century to the Fifteenth Century." Diss., University of Birmingham, 1971.

Robertson, Jr., D. W. "Marie de France, *Lais, Prologue,* 13–16." *MLN* 64 (1949): 336–38.

————. *A Preface to Chaucer: Studies in Medieval Perspectives.* Princeton, N.J.: Princeton University Press, 1962; rpt. 1969.

————. "Some Medieval Literary Terminology, with Special Reference to Chrétien de Troyes." *SP* 48 (1951): 669–92.

Rodnite [Lemay], Helen. "The Doctrine of the Trinity in Guillaume de Conches' Glosses in Macrobius: Texts and Studies." Diss., Columbia University, 1973.

Rose, H. J. "Mythographers." In *Oxford Classical Dictionary.* Ed. N. G. L. Hammond and H. H. Scullard. 2d ed. Oxford: Clarendon Press, 1970.

Rossbach, Otto. "Ein falscher Hyginus." *JCP* 131 (1885): 408–10.

Rusch, William G. *The Later Latin Fathers.* London: Duckworth, 1977.

Sabbadini, Remigio. *Il commento di Donato a Terenzio. Studi italiani di filologia classica,* vol. 2. Florence and Rome, 1893.

Sandys, John Edwin. *A History of Classical Scholarship.* Vol. 1: *From the Sixth Century B.C. to the End of the Middle Ages.* 2d ed. Cambridge: Cambridge University Press, 1906.

Sanford, Eva Matthews. "Lucan and Civil War." *CP* 28 (1933): 121–27.

————. "Lucan and his Roman Critics." *CP* 26 (1931): 233–57.

————. "Quotations from Lucan in Medieval Latin Authors." *AJP* 55 (1934): 1–19.

————. "The Use of Classical Latin Authors in *Libri manuales.*" *TAPA* 55 (1924): 190–248.

Savage, John Joseph H. "The Manuscripts of the Commentary of Servius Danielis on Virgil." *HSCP* 43 (1932): 77–121.

————. "Mediaeval Notes on the Sixth *Aeneid* in Parisinus 7930." *Speculum* 9 (1934): 204–12.

————. "The Medieval Tradition of Cerberus." *Traditio* 7 (1949–51): 405–10.

————. "More on Donatus' Commentary on Virgil." *CQ* 23 (1929): 56–59.

————. "The Scholia in the Virgil of Tours, Bernensis *165*." *HSCP* 36 (1925): 91–164.

————. "The Scholia on Vergil's *Eclogues* in Harleian 2782." *CP* 24 (1929): 274–78.

————. "Some Possible Sources of Mediaeval Conceptions of Virgil." *Speculum* 19 (1944): 336–43.

————. "Two Notes on Johannes Scotus." *Scriptorium* 12 (1958): 228–37.

————. "Was the Commentary on Virgil by Aelius Donatus Extant in the Ninth Century?" *CP* 26 (1931): 405–11.

Schaller, Dieter, "Philologische Untersuchungen zu den Gedichten Theodulfs von Orléans." *DAEM* 18 (1962): 13–91.

Schedler, Melchior. *Die Philosophie des Macrobius und ihr Einfluss auf die Wissenschaft des christlichen Mittelalters.* Beiträge zur Geschichte der Philosophie des Mittelalters. Texte und Untersuchungen, vol. 13, pt. 1. Münster: Aschendorffsche, 1916.

Schepfs, Georg. "Zu König Alfreds 'Boethius.' " *ASNSL* 94 (1895): 149–60.

Schmidt, Karl Heinz. *König Alfreds Boethius-Bearbeitung.* Göttingen: Georg-August-Universität, 1934.

Schreiber, Earl G., and Thomas Maresca, trans. *Commentary on the First Six Books of the Aeneid by Bernardus Silvestris.* Lincoln and London: University of Nebraska Press, 1980.

Schroebler, Ingeborg. "Die althochdeutschen Boethiusglossen und Notkers Übersetzung der Consolatio." Diss., Halle. Würzburg: Richard Mayr, 1934.

————. *Notker III von St. Gallen als Übersetzer und Kommentator von Boethius 'De Consolatione Philosophiae.'* Hermaea: Germanistische Forschungen, vol. 2. Tübingen: Max Niemeyer, 1953.

Schulte, Karl. *Das Verhältnis von Notkers Nuptiae Philologiae et Mercurii zum Kommentar des Remigius Antissiodorensis.* Forschungen und Funde, Vol. 3, pt. 2. Ed. Franz Jostes. Münster: Aschendorffsche, 1911.

Schulz, [Carl Robert] Richard. *De mythographi Vaticani primi fontibus.* Halle: C. A. Kaemmerer, 1905.

Seznec, Jean. *The Survival of the Pagan Gods: The Mythological Tradition and Its Place in Renaissance Humanism and Art.* Trans. Barbara F. Sessions from the 1940 edition. New York: Harper and Row, 1953.

Sihler, E. G. "Serviana." *AJP* 31 (1910): 1–24.

Silk, Edmund Taite. "Notes on Two Neglected Manuscripts of Boethius' *Consolatio Philosophiae.*" *TAPA* 70 (1939): 352–56.

————. "Pseudo-Johannes Scottus, Adalbold of Utrecht, and the Early Commentaries on Boethius." *MRS* 3 (1954): 1–40.

————. "The Study of Boethius' *Consolatio Philosophiae* in the Middle Ages." [Abstract of dissertation.] *TAPA* 62 (1931): xxxvii–viii.

Silverstein, H. Theodore. "The Fabulous Cosmogony of Bernardus Silvestris." *MP* 46 (1948–49): 92–116.

Silvestre, Hubert. "A propos de nouvelles éditions de commentaires à la 'Consolatio' de Boèce." *Scriptorium* 9 (1955): 278–81.

———. "Une Adaptation du commentaire de Macrobe." *AHDLMA* 29 (1962): 93–101.

———. "Note sur la survie de Macrobe au Moyen Âge," *C&M* 24 (1963): 170–80.

Skimina, Stanislaus. "De Bernado Silvestre Vergilii interprete." In *Commentationes Vergilianae*, pp. 206–43. Academia Polona Litterarum et Scientiarum. Cracow: Polska Akademija Umiejeztnósu, 1930.

Smalley, Beryl. *English Friars and Antiquity in the Early Fourteenth Century.* Oxford: Blackwell; New York: Barnes and Noble, 1960.

———. *The Study of the Bible in the Middle Ages.* 1952; rpt. Notre Dame: University of Notre Dame Press, 1964.

Southern, R. W. "Humanism and the School of Chartres." *Medieval Humanism and Other Studies*, pp. 61–85. New York and Evanston: Harper and Row, 1970.

———. *Platonism, Scholastic Method, and the School of Chartres.* Reading: University of Reading Press, 1979.

———. "The Schools of Paris and the School of Chartres." In *Harvard 1982*, pp. 113–37. Cambridge, Mass.: Harvard University Press, 1982.

Spanneut, M. *Le Stoïcisme des pères de l'Elige de Clément de Rome à Clément d'Alexandrie.* Paris: Seuil, 1969.

Spargo, John Webster. *Virgil the Necromancer: Studies in Virgilian Legends.* Harvard Studies in Comparative Literature, no. 10. Cambridge, Mass.: Harvard University Press, 1934.

Stahl, William Harris. "To a Better Understanding of Martianus Capella." *Speculum* 40 (1965): 102–15.

———, Richard Johnson, and E. L. Burge. *Martianus Capella and the Seven Liberal Arts.* Vol. 1: *The Quadrivium of Martianus Capella: Latin Traditions in the Mathematical Sciences, 50 B.C.–A.D. 1250.* New York and London: Columbia University Press, 1971.

Steadman, John M. "The *Ecloga Theoduli*, the *General Estoria*, and the Perseus-Bellerophon Myth." *MS* 24 (1962): 384–87.

Sticca, Sandro. "Sin and Salvation: The Dramatic Context of Hroswitha's Women." In *The Roles and Images of Women in the Middle Ages and Renaissance.* Ed. Douglas Radcliff-Umstead, pp. 3–22. University of Pittsburgh Publications on the Middle Ages and Renaissance, vol. 3. Pittsburgh: University of Pittsburgh Press, 1978.

Stock, Brian. *Myth and Science in the Twelfth Century: A Study of Bernard Silvester.* Princeton, N.J.: Princeton University Press, 1972.

———. "A Note on *Thebaid* Commentaries: Paris, B.N., lat. 3012." *Traditio* 27 (1971): 468–71.

Stokes, Lynn Carroll. "Fulgentius and the 'Expositio Virgilianae continentiae.'" Diss., Tufts University, 1969.

Stokes, Whitley. "The Old-Welsh Glosses on Martianus Capella." *Archaeologia Cambrensis* 4th series 13 (1873): 1–22.

Strecker, Karl. "Studien zu karolingischen Dichtern: VII. Ist Gottschalk der Dichter der *Ecolga Theoduli?*" *NA* 45 (1923–24): 18–20.

Sweeney, Robert Dale. *Prolegomena to an Edition of the Scholia to Statius.* Mnemosyne Bibliotheca Classica Bateva, supp. 8. Leiden: E. J. Brill, 1969.

Tate, J. "The Beginnings of Greek Allegory." *CR* 41 (1927): 214–15.

———. "On the History of Allegorism." *CQ* 28 (1934): 105–14.

———. "Plato and Allegorical Interpretation." *CQ* 23 (1929): 142–54; 24 (1930): 1–10.

Taylor, Henry Osbern. *The Emergence of Christian Culture in the West: The Classical Heritage of the Middle Ages.* 3d edition. 1911; rpt. New York: Harper, 1958.

———. *The Mediaeval Mind: A History of the Development of Thought and Emotion in the Middle Ages.* 4th edition. 2 vols. London: Macmillan, 1925.

Taylor, John Prentice. "The Mythology of Vergil's Aeneid according to Servius." Diss., New York University, 1917.

Teuffel, Wilhelm Siegmund. *History of Roman Literature.* Rev. Ludwig Schwabe. Trans. from the 5th edition by George C. W. Wahr. 2 vols. London, 1892.

Thomas, Emile. *Essai sur Servius et son commentaire sur Virgile d'après les manuscrits de Paris et les publications les plus récentes.* Pt. 1. Paris, 1880.

Thompkins, James Westfall. *The Literacy of the Laity in the Middle Ages.* University of California Publications in Education, vol. 9. Berkeley: University of California Press, 1939.

Thompson, David. "Dante and Bernard Silvestris." *Viator* 1 (1970): 201–6.

Thomson, H. J. "Lucan, Statius, and Juvenal in the Early Centuries." *CQ* 22 (1928): 24–27.

———. "Seruius Auctus and Donatus." *CQ* 21 (1927): 205–6.

Thomson, Rodney M. "England and the Twelfth-Century Renaissance." *Past and Present* 101 (1983): 3–21.

Todorov, Tzvetan. *Symbolism and Interpretation.* Trans. Catherine Porter. Ithaca, N.Y.: Cornell University Press, 1982.

Traube, Ludwig. "Computus Helperici." *NA* 18 (1893): 71–105.

———. *Lateinische Sprache und Literatur des Mittelalters.* Frankfurt: Lang, 1974.

Troncarelli, Fabio. "Per una ricerca sui commenti altomedievali al De consolatione di Boezio." In *Miscellanea in memoria di Giorgio Cencetti,* pp. 363–80. Turin: Bottega d'Erasmo, 1973.

———. *Tradizioni perdute: L'antica "fortuna" della "Consolatio Philosophiae."* Padua: Antenore, 1980.

Tunison, J. S. *Master Virgil: The Author of the Aeneid as He Seemed in the Middle Ages.* Cincinnati, 1888.

Tuve, Rosemond. *Allegorical Imagery: Some Medieval Books and their Posterity.* Princeton, N.J.: Princeton University Press, 1966.

Ulmer, Gregory L. "The Object of Post-Criticism." In *The Anti-Aesthetic.* Ed. Hal Foster, pp. 83–110. Seattle: Bay Press, 1983; rpt. 1991.

Ussani, Vincenzo. "In margine al Comparetti." In "Virgilio nel Medio Evo." *SM* n.s. 5 (1932): 1–42.

Valentine, T. W. "The Medieval Church and Vergil." *Classical Weekly* 25 (1931): 65–67.

Vantuono, William. "The Structure and Sources of *Patience.*" *MS* 34 (1972): 401–21.

Verbeke, Gerard. *The Presence of Stoicism in Medieval Thought.* Washington, D.C., Catholic University of America Press, 1983.

Vessey, David. *Statius and the Thebaid.* Cambridge: Cambridge University Press, 1973.

Vollmer, Hans. "*Theoduli Ecloga* und die *Catalogi* des Otto Brunfels." *Monatsschrift für die kirchliche Praxis* n.s. 4 (1904): 321–33.

Waldrop, George Byron. "Donatus, the Interpreter of Vergil and Terence." *HSCP* 38 (1927): 75–142.

Wallace, Edith Owen. *The Notes on Philosophy in the Commentary of Servius on the Eclogues, the Georgics, and the Aeneid of Vergil.* Diss., Columbia University, 1938. New York: Columbia University Press, 1938.

Wallace-Hadrill, J. M. *The Frankish Church.* Oxford: Clarendon Press, 1983.

Weinstock, Stefan. "Martianus Capella and the Cosmic System of the Etruscans." *JRS* 36 (1946): 101–29.

Westra, Haijo Jan. "The Commentary on Martianus Capella's *De nuptiis* Attributed to Bernardus Silvestris: A Critical Edition." Diss., University of Toronto, 1977.

———. "Martianus Capella." In *Addenda et Corrigenda to Volume 2. CTC.* Vol. 6: Ed. F. Edward Cranz. Washington, D.C.: Catholic University of America Press, 1986.

Wetherbee, Winthrop. *Platonism and Poetry in the Twelfth Century: The Literary Influence of the School of Chartres.* Princeton, N.J.: Princeton University Press, 1972.

———. "The Theme of Imagination in Medieval Poetry and the Allegorical Figure Genius." *M&H* 7 (1976): 45–64.

Whitbread, Leslie G. "Fulgentius and Dangerous Doctrine." *Latomus* 30 (1971): 1157–61.

Whittaker, Thomas. *Macrobius, or Philosophy, Science, and Letters in the Year 400.* Cambridge: Cambridge University Press, 1923.

Willard, H. M. "The Use of the Classics in the *Flores Rhetorici* of Alberic of Monte Cassino." In *Anniversary Essays in Mediaeval History by Students of Charles Homer Haskins.* Ed. C. H. Taylor. Boston and New York: Houghton Mifflin, 1929.

Willis, James A. "Martianus Capella and His Early Commentators." Diss., University of London, 1952.

Wilmart, Dom André. "Reg. Lat. 72 (fol. 110–126): Commentaire de la 'Consolation' de Boèce." In "Analecta Reginensia: Extraits des manuscrits latins de la reine Christine conservés au Vatican." *Studi e testi* 59 (1933): 259–62.

Wilson, Robert R. *Genealogy and History in the Biblical World.* New Haven, Conn.: Yale University Press, 1977.

Winterfeld, Paul von. "Der Mimus und die karolingische Ekloge." "Hrotsvits literarische Stellung," sec. 4. *Herrigs Archiv für neuere Sprachen* 114 (1905): 65–71.

Wissowa, Georg. *De Macrobi Saturnaliorum fontibus capita tria, dissertatio inauguralis philologica.* Diss., University of Warsaw. Warsaw, 1880.

Witt, Ronald G. *Hercules at the Crossroads: The Life, Works, and Thought of Coluccio Salutati.* Duke Monographs in Medieval and Renaissance Studies, no. 6. Durham, N.C.: Duke University Press, 1983.

Wittig, Joseph S. "King Alfred's *Boethius* and its Latin Sources: A Reconsideration." In *Anglo-Saxon England.* Vol. 11, pp. 157–98. Cambridge: Cambridge University Press, 1983.

Woestijne, Paul van de. "Le Codex Valentinianus 394 de Lactantius Placidus." *Revue belge de philologie et d'histoire* 19 (1940): 37–63.

———. "Marginaliën bij Lactantius Placidus." *L'Antiquité classique* n.s. 17 (1948): 573–84.

———. "Les Scolies à la *Thébaïde* de Stace. Remarques et suggestions." *L'Antiquité classique* n.s. 19 (1950): 149–63.

Wölfflin, Eduard. "Zu den Statiusscholien." *Philologus* 24 (1866): 156–58.

Zappert, Georg. "Virgils Fortleben im Mittelalter: Ein Beitrag zur Geschichte der classischen Literatur in seinem Zeitraume." *Denkschriften der kaiserlichen Akademie der Wissenschaften* 2.2 (1951): 17–70.

Zeller, E. *A History of Greek Philosophy from the Earliest Period to the Time of Socrates.* Trans. S. F. Alleyne. Vol. 1 of 2. London, 1881.

Zink, Michael. *Der Mytholog Fulgentius: Ein Beitrag römischen Litteraturgeschichte und zur Grammatik des afrikanischen Lateins.* Würzburg, 1867.

INDEX

Abbo of Fleury, 252

Abelard, 402; on Cicero, 28

Achates: in Bernard Silvestris, 458; etymology of, 522n36; in Neckam, 486

Achelous (river): in Anonymous Erfurt Commentator, 618n49; in Anonymous of St. Gall, 219; in Notker, 367, 601n55; in Remigius, 561n102; in William of Conches, 613n24

Acheron (river): in Bernard Silvestris, 457; in Macrobius, 487; in Neckam, 487; in second Vatican mythographer, 315

Achilles: as first man, 475; in first Vatican mythographer, 196; in second Vatican mythographer, 342, 343

Acis: in first Vatican mythographer, 189; in second Vatican mythographer, 589n32

Ackerman, Robert, 43

Acrisius, in second Vatican mythographer, 332

Actaeon: in first Vatican mythographer, 200; in Fulgentius, 115, 526n28; in John of Salisbury, 481; in Neckam, 488–89; in Ovid, 526n28; in second Vatican mythographer, 328

Adalbold of Utrecht, 364, 365, 550n11; on "O qui perpetua," 414, 415, 416, 598n39

Adam: in Bernard Silvestris, 465; and Eve, 160–61, 465; in first Vatican mythographer, 182; and Saturn, 357

Adanan the Scot, 17; as Berne scholiast, 171; as first Vatican mythographer,

162, 167–68, 169; as missionary, 57. *See also* Berne scholiast

Adelard of Bath, *De eodem et diverso,* 53

Admetus, in Fulgentius, 107, 108, 110

Adnotatio, definition of, 165

Adonis: in Dunchad, 293; in Fulgentius, 116, 526n28; in John Scot, 274, 575n60; in Martin of Laon, 581n81; in Notker, 379; in Ovid, 526n28; in second Vatican mythographer, 318, 321

Adrastus: in Berne scholiast, 177; in first Vatican mythographer, 201

Adultery: of Jupiter, 181, 198, 256, 301, 317, 421; liver as seat of, 229, 230; in William of Conches, 419. *See also* Gods, immorality of

Aegeus, in second Vatican mythographer, 320, 334–35

Aegina, in second Vatican mythographer, 331

Aegisthus, in second Vatican mythographer, 337

Aelius Donatus. *See* Donatus, Aelius

Aelous: in Florentine Commentary, 428; in second Vatican mythographer, 325

Aemilius Asper, 50, 507n116

Aeneas: allegorization of, 120–24; and Dido, 478, 480–83; etymology of, 456–57; as Everyman, 456, 483, 484; as fallen hero, 483; in first Vatican mythographer, 195; as *flamen,* 521n35; flight from Troy, 539n23; as founder of empire, 123–24, 197; in Fulgentius, 3; genealogy of, 184, 196–97; as human soul, 457; in

Caesellius Vindex, 50

Calchas (*Ecloga Theoduli*), 359, 362

Calcidius, 98; commentary on Plato, 242, 253, 470, 626n80

Callimachus, 83, 160

Calliope, 52, 96; in Anonymous Erfurt Commentator, 618n49; in Boethius commentators, 615n42; in Fulgentius, 101–5, 117, 360; in John Scot, 576n61; in Martianus Capella, 104; in Remigius, 262, 285, 374; in St. Gall Minor, 216, 555n40

Callirhoe, in second Vatican mythographer, 310

Callisto, in second Vatican mythographer, 326

Camenae (Muses): in Bernard Silvestris, 458; in Florentine Commentary, 436; in William of Conches, 437–38

Cameron, Alan, 515n2

Capella, Martianus. *See* Martianus Capella

Caplan, Harry, 495n1

Carnality: in K Reviser, 235, 239; in reading of texts, 419–20

Carolingian Renaissance, 16–17, 59, 157, 204, 401–2, 529n9; causes of, 58; educational reforms of, 54–55, 57, 139, 243, 302, 352; reception of classics, 535n42; Theodulf of Orleans in, 130, 530n11. *See also* Commentators, Carolingian; Renaissances, medieval

Cartusianus, Dionysius, 629n105

Cassandra, in second Vatican mythographer, 340

Cassian, John, 37

Cassiodorus, 513n156; *De institutione divinarum litterarum,* 157; service to Theodoric, 56; use of Boethius, 54, 511n139

Castor and Pollux: attributes of, 477–

78; in Bernard Silvestris, 473, 477–78, 632n17; in Neckam, 490; in Notker, 380; in Remigius, 578n70; in second Vatican mythographer, 336

Cathedral schools, French, 61

Catholic Church: patriarchy of, 6; use of myth, 1; use of mythography, 4–5. *See also* Apologists, Christian; Church Fathers

Catullus, 537n6

Cecrops, 607n85; in Bernard of Utrecht, 391; in *Ecloga Theoduli,* 357; in Isidore, 532n22; in second Vatican mythographer, 320, 334

Celsus, 528n6

Celts: influence on Dunchad, 250–51; pagan influence of, 250

Ceneus, in second Vatican mythographer, 332

Centaurs, 11; in Anonymous of St. Gall, 219; in Asser, 552n23; in Bernard Silvestris, 632n21; birth of, 406; in K Reviser, 236; in Remigius, 240, 562n107; in second Vatican mythographer, 331–32; in William of Conches, 407, 408

Centos, Virgilian, 506n108

Cephalus: in first Vatican mythographer, 204; in Florentine Commentary, 428; in second Vatican mythographer, 337, 344

Cepheus, King: in second Vatican mythographer, 330

Cephisus (river god), 589n33

Cerberus: as ages of man, 619n51; in Anonymous Erfurt Commentator, 618n49, 619n51; in Anonymous of St. Gall, 219; in Asser, 552n23; in Bernard Silvestris, 450, 460, 462; in Boethius commentaries, 547n6, 616n43; as earth, 395, 460, 463,

708

INDEX

Martianus Capella—*continued*
Neoplatonism of, 400; persona as old man, 298; and seven liberal arts, 54, 56, 99–100, 244, 255; Stoicism of, 243, 246; use of Cicero, 28; use of Macrobius, 68; use of satura, 245; on Virgil, 56
—*De nuptiis Philologiae et Mercurii*, 3–4, 99; Anonymous Barberinus on, 372–73; Apollo in, 272–75; battles in, 381; Bernard of Utrecht's use of, 353, 390, 395; Bernard Silvestris's use of, 353, 390, 395, 445–47, 449, 455; in Boethius commentaries, 205, 547n4; Carolingian commentaries on, 54, 243, 298, 342, 345, 351, 354, 356, 361, 363, 373, 383, 396, 427; commentaries after Remigius, 371; commentaries on, 44, 54, 57, 59, 60, 220, 250, 298, 408; dedication of, 297, 298; female figures in, 11; feminization of, 256, 258, 262, 351, 401, 408; Florentine Commentary on, 426; Genius figure in, 282; influence of, 52–54, 510n133–34, 511n136, 602n58; influence on Fulgentius, 99, 106–7, 245; John Scot on, 248–49, 253–56, 258, 260–63, 265–67, 269–82, 285, 287, 291, 293, 295–96, 298; Jupiter in, 248, 262–63; as literary artifact, 510n134; manuscripts of, 53, 510n135; Mercury in, 3–4, 106, 272–75; Neckam on, 485; Notker's translations of, 351, 352–53, 372, 601n57; pedagogical use of, 61, 371; Philology in, 284–93; prosimetrum of, 297, 547n4; Remigius on, 220–41, 244, 254–56, 258–63, 265–99; translations into German, 299, 372; translations of, 59; vocabulary of, 510n134; Welsh commen-

taries on, 250, 565n12–13; William of Conches on, 402–3, 425–39, 444, 626n77–78, 627n82
Martianus de S. Benedicto, 509n127
Martin of Laon, 372, 580n78; glosses on Martianus Capella, 253, 565n14; pupils of, 252; *Scholica graecarum glossarum*, 251, 523n3, 566n17–19; sources of, 566n18; use of Fulgentius, 566n19. *See also* Dunchad
Martyrs, as heroes, 149–50
Mathon, G., 616n44
Maur, Hraban. *See* Hraban Maur.
Maximianus, *Elegiae*, 592n6
Medea: in *Ecloga Theoduli*, 349; in second Vatican mythographer, 336
Medusa (Gorgon): allegorization of, 332; in Bernard Silvestris, 633n21; in first Vatican mythographer, 201; in Florentine Commentary, 428; in John Scot, 295; in Martianus Capella, 295; in Notker, 380; in Remigius, 297, 579n75; in second Vatican mythographer, 310, 332
Megaera (Fury), 214, 488, 559n76; in Bernard Silvestris, 632n21; in second Vatican mythographer, 588n31
Melampus, in Berne scholiast, 180
Meleager: in first Vatican mythographer, 200, 201; in second Vatican mythographer, 323, 337
Melion, in second Vatican mythographer, 335
Melito of Sardis, 500n60
Memnon, in second Vatican mythographer, 340
Memphis (sun god), 292
Mendicant heresies, 503n86
Menelaus, in first Vatican mythographer, 198
Menippean satire, 103
Mercury: and Aeneas, 447, 483,

728 INDEX

Venus—*continued*

179, 270–71, 293, 468, 475; iconography of, 318; in Isidore,
534n34; in John of Salisbury, 481;
in John Scot, 270–71, 281, 572n53,
575n60; in Macrobius, 81; in Martianus Capella, 260, 297; in Martin
of Laon, 566n19; as mother of
Aeneas, 467; in Notker, 381–82,
384; origin of, 275–76, 429, 467,
534n34, 572n52–53; in Ovid,
526n28; and Pasiphaë, 334; as
planet, 374–75, 382, 467; as plenitude, 466; in Remigius, 256, 259,
260, 261–62, 270–71, 280, 281,
572n53; in second Vatican
mythographer, 318, 330; in Terence
scholia, 578n69, 578n71; in Theodulf of Orleans, 374; as universal
harmony, 462; as voluptuous life,
343, 404, 406, 458, 526n23,
578n71, 632n20; and Vulcan,
535n34; in William of Conches,
421, 423, 440
Verbeke, Gerard, 9–10
Vernacular, translations into, 1, 5, 209,
365
Verona scholia, 50, 507n116, 507n118
Verrius Flaccus, 51; *De verborum significatu,* 50, 528n6
Vesta: etymology of, 522n36; as fire,
378; in Isidore, 528n2, 533n31; in
John Scot, 278–79, 564n9; in
Notker, 377–78; in Remigius, 278–
79
Vice: in Anonymous Erfurt Commentator, 620n53; in Bernard Silvestris, 463, 633n22; monsters
as, 338
Vincent of Beauvais, 157; use of
Isidore, 133

Virbius. *See* Hippolytus
Virgil: allegorization of life, 100, 124,
172; in Bernard Silvestris, 445; commentaries on, 44, 49–52, 60; in
Dante, 4, 47, 52; decline of interest
in, 101; as epic poet, 537n7; in first
Vatican mythographer, 167, 168;
gods in, 74; influence of, 9,
505n101, 506n110; justification by
Fulgentius, 117–20; knowledge of
liberal arts, 68, 69, 70–72; in Macrobius, 70–71; medieval conceptions
of, 505n103; moralization of, 129,
172–73; as necromancer, 48; pedagogical use of, 48, 49, 56, 360–61,
363, 506n104–5; popularity of,
505n101; prefiguration of Christ,
48, 49, 506n108; as prophet,
507n113; Renaissance commentaries on, 63; and St. Paul, 506n108;
Stoic readings of, 94; use by Lactantius Placidus, 543n38; use of *integumenta,* 455
—*Aeneid*; allegorization of, 49, 96–97,
98, 100, 220; and Anonymous of St.
Gall, 215, 218; Bernard of Utrecht
on, 388; Bernard Silvestris on, 456–
63; Christianized view of, 139; commentaries after twelfth century,
478–79; Cupid in, 135; Dido in,
271; Eridanus in, 6; in Fulgentius,
3, 96–97, 118–20; in John of Salisbury, 480–85; Macrobius on, 66; as
metaphor for stages of life, 450; moralization of, 129; Neckam on, 486;
Sybil in, 89; themes of, 119; underworld in, 2–3, 65, 84–85, 86, 88–
90, 139–40, 220, 242; virtue in,
631n13–14
—*Eclogues*; allegorization of, 100,
124, 172; Bernard of Utrecht on,